essentials of Economics

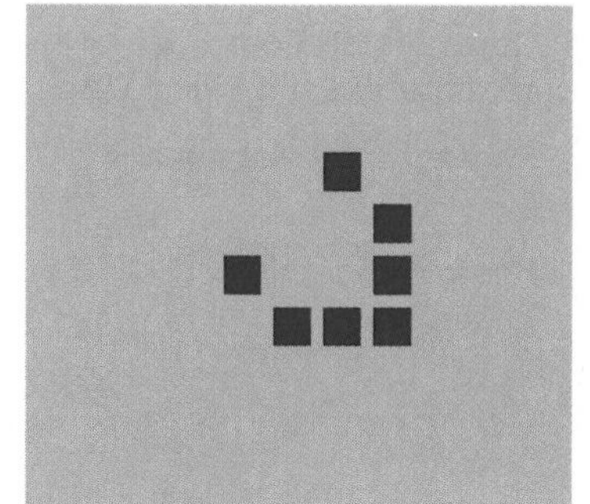

Robert L. Sexton
Pepperdine University

Australia · Canada · Mexico · Singapore · Spain · United Kingdom · United States

Essentials of Economics

Robert L. Sexton

Editor-in-Chief:
Jack W. Calhoun

Vice President/Team Director:
Michael P. Roche

Publisher of Economics:
Michael B. Mercier

Acquisitions Editor:
Michael Worls

Developmental Editor:
Andrew McGuire

Executive Marketing Manager:
Lisa Lysne

Senior Production Editor:
Kara ZumBahlen

Manufacturing Coordinator:
Sandee Milewski

Media Developmental Editor:
Peggy Buskey

Media Production Editor:
Pam Wallace

Compositor:
G&S Typesetters, Inc.

Printer:
QuebecorWorld, Versailles, KY

Design Project Manager:
Michelle Kunkler

Internal and Cover Designer:
Liz Harasymczuck Design

Cover Illustration:
© PhotoDisc and Digital Vision

Photography Manager:
John Hill

Photo Researcher:
Photopia

Printed in the United States of America
1 2 3 4 5 05 04 03 02

For more information contact South-Western
5191 Natorp Boulevard,
Mason, Ohio 45040.
Or you can visit our Internet site at:
http://www.swcollege.com

Library of Congress Control Number:
2002111497

ISBN: 0-324-17670-8

ABOUT THE AUTHOR

Robert L. Sexton is Distinguished Professor of Economics at Pepperdine University. Professor Sexton has also been a Visiting Professor at the University of California at Los Angeles in the Anderson Graduate School of Management and the Department of Economics.

Professor Sexton's research ranges across many fields of economics: economics education, labor economics, environmental economics, law and economics, and economic history. He has written several books and has published more than 40 research papers, many in top economic journals such as *The American Economic Review, Southern Economic Journal, Economics Letters, Journal of Urban Economics,* and *The Journal of Economic Education.* Professor Sexton has also written more than 100 other articles that have appeared in books, magazines, and newspapers.

Professor Sexton received the Pepperdine Professor of the Year Award in 1991 and 1997, and the Howard A. White Memorial Teaching Award in 1994; he was named a Harriet and Charles Luckman Teaching Fellow in 1994.

Professor Sexton resides in Agoura Hills, California, with his wife, Julie, and their three children, Elizabeth, Katherine, and Tommy.

To Julie, Elizabeth,
Katherine, and Tommy

Preface

Many years ago, I was walking across the campus of a small liberal arts college in Southern California and I asked a friend, "Who is that professor? I always see him holding class outside, underneath the orange trees across from the campus swimming pool." She said that was the new economics professor. Well, I wanted to be one of those students having class outside, so that summer I took my first econ class. Little did I know how much that seemingly whimsical decision would profoundly change my life. I soon discovered the depth and breadth of economics as we studied the economics of social, environmental, and political issues. I began to see the world from a whole new perspective, realizing that virtually everything we do has an economic dimension. In fact, I learned to see, experience, and understand the impact of economics on my life and those around me, which in turn has made me a lifelong student of the discipline.

When I decided to write *Essentials of Economics,* one of my primary goals was to bring to students that same feeling of excitement and relevance I experienced when I took my first economics class. In order to do this, I knew that I would have to write a book that was truly accessible and student friendly. I also knew that I would have to focus on those few principles and the wealth of applications that demonstrate the enormous scope of economics in our everyday life. These decisions were based on my experience of teaching thousands of students. I believe that if students experience a lively, brief, and relevant text that reinforces their mastery of economics, section by section, then they will better understand the economic concepts and issues that will shape their lives.

FEATURES OF THE BOOK

The Section-by-Section Approach

Essentials of Economics uses a section-by-section approach in which economic ideas and concepts are presented in short, self-contained units rather than in large blocks of text. Each chapter comprises approximately six to eight bite-sized sections, typically presented in two to eight pages, that include all of the relevant graphs, tables, applications, boxes, photos, definitions, and cartoons for the topic at hand. My enthusiasm for and dedication to this approach stems from studying research on *learning theory,* which indicates that students retain information much better when it is broken down into short, intense, and exciting bursts of "digestible" information. Students prefer information divided into smaller, self-contained sections that are less overwhelming, more manageable, and easier to review before going on to new material. In short, students will be more successful in mastering and retaining economic principles using this approach, which is distinctly more compatible with modern communication styles.

But students aren't the only ones to benefit from this approach. The self-contained sections allow instructors greater flexibility in planning their courses. They can simply select or delete sections of the text as it fits their syllabus.

Learning Tools

Key Questions Each section begins with key questions designed to preview ideas and to pique students' interest in the material to come. These questions also serve as landmarks for students: If they can answer these questions after reading the material, they may go forward with confidence.

Section Checks Section Checks appear at the end of each section and are designed to reinforce the key questions. Key points summarize major ideas and short questions (the answers to which can be found in the back of the book) give students an opportunity to check their mastery before proceeding. If students can answer these questions, they can feel confident about proceeding to the next topic.

Exhibits Graphs, tables, and charts are used throughout *Essentials of Economics* to illustrate, clarify, and reinforce economic principles. Text exhibits are designed to be as clear and simple as possible and are carefully coordinated with the text material.

Application Boxes Application boxes are scattered throughout the text as a way of reinforcing and checking student comprehension of important or more difficult concepts. Students can check their work against the answer given at the bottom of the box, providing them with immediate feedback and encouragement in the learning process.

In the News Boxes In the News boxes focus primarily on current events that are relevant and thought-provoking, such as classroom cheating, teen-age tobacco use, Napster and property rights, online shopping, and the safety of amusement park rides. These articles are placed strategically throughout the text to solidify particular concepts and to help students find the connection between economics and their lives.

Global Watch Boxes Whether we are concerned with understanding yesterday, today, or tomorrow, and whether we are looking at a small, far-away country or a large next-door neighbor, economic principles can strengthen our grasp on many global issues. Global Watch articles were chosen to help students understand the magnitude and character of the changes occurring around the world today and to introduce them to some of the economic causes and implications of this change. To gain a greater perspective on a particular economy or the planet as a whole, it is helpful to compare important economic indicators around the world. For this reason, Global Watch boxes will sometimes be used to present relevant comparative statistics.

Marginal Web Icons Throughout the book, students will see a Web icon that directs them to the Sexton Web site (**http://sexton.swcollege.com**). At that site, they can click on links to fun, interesting, and useful sites that will enhance chapter topics and help students make the connection between economics and everyday life. In addition, there are Web questions at the end of each chapter that send students to various Web sites in order to answer the questions.

Marginal Key Terms When key concepts are first introduced within the text, they are highlighted in boldface and the definitions appear in the margin for ease of student learning.

End-of-Chapter Summaries Each chapter ends with a brief summary that highlights the most important points of the chapter. This summary is useful for a quick review of the chapter.

End-of-Chapter Key Terms There is a list of the key terms at the end of each chapter that allows students to test their mastery of new concepts. Page references are included so students can easily find key terms within the chapter.

End-of-Chapter Questions Questions at the end of the chapter allow students to test their understanding of chapter concepts. Some of the questions are designed for review while others are designed to help students extend their thinking about core concepts. Each chapter features at least one Web question. The odd-numbered answers can be found on the student Web site and the even-numbered answers can be found in the Instructor's Manual or on the instructor's Web site.

Self-Contained Study Guide Providing added value for the student, each chapter concludes with a 6–10 page study guide that includes Fill in the Blank, True or False, and Multiple Choice questions as well as Problems.

Photos *Essentials of Economics* contains a large number of colorful pictures. They are not, however, mere decoration; rather, these photos are an integral part of the book, for both learning and motivation purposes. The photos are carefully placed where they reinforce important concepts, and they are accompanied by captions designed to encourage students to extend their understanding of particular ideas.

Biographical Sketches Six biographical sketches, on Adam Smith, Jeremy Bentham, David Ricardo, Alfred Marshall, John Maynard Keynes, and Milton Friedman, have been added on the inside covers to provide a link to the history of the field.

SUPPLEMENTARY MATERIALS

EconActive Student Software

Prepared by David L. Carr (American University), the EconActive Student Software—downloadable from the text Web site—allows students to get interactive and involved in their own learning process. For each chapter of the textbook, EconActive contains a chapter summary with guided tutorials, multiple-choice and true-false quizzes, In the News stories, and an electronic glossary. In addition, EconActive includes Java-powered interactive graphs. The power of Java allows students to manipulate variables on a graph and immediately see the effects of those changes on the graph. This method of hands-on interaction illustrates and reinforces economic relationships in a way that static graphs and explanations cannot. The interactive graphs and the other materials on the EconActive Software are designed to reinforce student mastery and success with the section-by-section approach.

Student Web Site

The Student Web Site at **http://sexton.swcollege.com** provides access to many learning tools. The Student Web Site allows students to access PowerPoint presentations, online quizzes, Web-interactive applications, and many other resources they can use to test their understanding of key economic concepts. Online multiple-choice quizzes provide students with immediate feedback, while Web-interactive applications enhance the applications in the textbook.

In addition, students can also access South-Western's Economics Resource Center at **http://economics.swcollege.com.** This unique, rich, and robust online resource provides customer service and product information, learning tips and tools, information about careers in economics, access to all of our text-supporting Web sites and other cutting-edge educational resources such as our highly regarded EconNews, EconDebate, EconData, and EconLinks online features.

Supplements for the Instructor

Printed Test Bank Tanja Carter and Gary Galles (both of Pepperdine University) have *thoroughly* updated the test bank questions.

Computerized Test Bank ExamView allows for quick test creation. All items in the test bank are available in computerized test bank software format. Questions and answers may be added, edited, or deleted. Instructors can easily vary the sequence of questions in order to create multiple versions of the same test. Answer keys are generated quickly with each version of the test. The program is available for Mac and Windows on CD-ROM.

In addition, a Word version of the test bank is available for those instructors who wish to take advantage of this option.

Instructor's Manual and Test Bank Prepared by Gary Galles (Pepperdine University), the Instructor's Manual follows the textbook's concept-by-concept approach in two parts: chapter outlines and teaching tips. The Teaching Tips section provides analogies, illustrations, and examples to help instructors reinforce each section of the text. The answers to the end-of-chapter text questions can be found in the Instructor's Manual. The test bank includes approximately 150 test questions per chapter, consisting of multiple-choice, true/false, and short-answer questions.

Lecture Presentation in PowerPoint This PowerPoint presentation covers all the essential sections presented in each chapter of the book. Graphs, tables, lists, and concepts are animated sequentially, much as one might develop them on the blackboard. Additional examples and applications are used to reinforce major lessons. The slides are crisp, clear, and colorful. Instructors may adapt or add slides to customize their lectures.

Instructor's Web Site The Instructor's portion of the Web site to accompany *Essentials of Economics* contains electronic versions of many of the valuable instructor resources described previously. Adopters of the textbook may obtain a password from their local sales representative for access to Word versions of the Instructor's Manual and Test Bank along with other valuable teaching resources, such as Class Act. Class Act allows instructors to manage classes online with a syllabus generator, gradebook, and quizzes, which can be selected from the book's Test Bank.

South-Western Economics Resource Center A unique, rich, and robust online resource for economics instructors (and students as well), **http://economics.swcollege.com,** provides customer service and product information, teaching and learning tips and tools, information about careers in economics, access to all of our text-supporting Web sites, and other cutting-edge educational resources such as our highly regarded EconNews, EconDebate, EconData, and EconLinks online features.

WebCT Course WebCT-based courseware is available for both the micro and macro portions of the textbook, allowing students and instructors to interact outside of the classroom. Instructors have the option of hosting the content on their campus Web server, where they can customize the courseware to their preferences, or accessing existing content on our company's server. With a few clicks of the mouse, the virtual classroom offers instructors a simple method of assigning and receiving homework, tracking grades, and watching as students progress. Test banks that accompany the texts are also available in the courseware, allowing for online tests and instant grading. Students will appreciate the notes provided for each chapter, self-quizzes, Web-based applications, and chat rooms, as well as the ability to track their grades and complete class projects in an online environment.

Acknowledgments

I would like to extend special thanks to the following colleagues for their valuable insight during the manuscript phase of this project. I owe a debt of gratitude to Philip Graves, University of Colorado; Gary Galles, Pepperdine University; Tanja Carter, Pepperdine University; Richard Vedder, Ohio University; Dwight Lee, University of Georgia; Robert M. Escudero, Pepperdine University; Ron Batchelder, Pepperdine University; Cober Plucker, Pepperdine University; Robert Clower, University of South Carolina; and Gary M. Walton, University of California, Davis.

I am truly indebted to the excellent team of professionals at South-Western Publishing. My appreciation goes to Mike Worls, acquisitions editor; Andy McGuire, developmental editor; and Kara ZumBahlen, production editor. Also special thanks to Mike Roche, vice president; Mike Mercier, publisher; Lisa Lysne, executive marketing manager; and the South-Western sales representatives. I sincerely appreciate your hard work and effort.

In addition, my family deserves special gratitude—my wife, Julie, my daughters, Elizabeth and Katherine, and my son, Tommy. They are an inspiration to my work. Also, special thanks to my brother Bill for all of his work that directly and indirectly helped this project come to fruition.

Thanks to all of my colleagues who reviewed this material along the way. Your comments were very important to me.

Jack Adams, University of Arkansas, Little Rock
David Anderson, Centre College
Sisay Asefa, Western Michigan University
James Q. Aylsworth, Lakeland Community College
Todd Behr, East Stroudsburg University
Carolyn Bodkin, Trident Technical College
G. E. Breger, University of South Carolina
Nancy Burnett, University of Wisconsin
Steven T. Call, Metropolitan State College of Denver
Rebecca Campbell, Southwest Texas State University
Randall C. Campbell, Louisiana State University
James R. Carlson, Manatee Community College
Jack A. Chambless, Valencia Community College
Gilbert L. Christopher, Jr., Wingate University
Jim F. Couch, University of North Alabama
Kenneth M. Cross, Southwest Virginia Community College
Andrew J. Dane, Angelo State University
Diana Denison, Red Rocks Community College
John W. Dorsey, University of Maryland
Michael I. Duke, Blinn College
David Eaton, Murray State University
Mary E. Edwards, St. Cloud State University
Robert M. Escudero, Pepperdine University
Steve Floyd, Manatee Community College
Gary Galles, Pepperdine University

Phil Graves, University of Colorado
Gary Greene, Manatee Community College
Tina J. Harvell, Blinn College
Emily P. Hoffman, Western Michigan University
Cedric Howie, Schoolcraft College
Stanley Keil, Ball State University
Ronald Kessler, British Columbia Institute of Technology
Saleem Khan, Bloomsburg University
Philip King, San Francisco State University
John Leadley, Western Oregon University
Thomas Maloy, Muskegon Community College
Akbar Marvasti, University of Houston, Downtown
Pete Mavrokordatas, Tarrant County Junior College
Bret McMurran, Chaffey College
W. Douglas Morgan, University of California, Santa Barbara
Brian T. Parker, Blinn College
Thomas Porebski, Trinton College
Tom Potiowsky, Portland State University
Fred J. Ruppel, Eastern Kentucky University
Sue Lynn Sasser, William Woods University
Mark Strazicich, University of North Texas
Lea Templer, College of the Canyons
Stephan Weiler, Colorado State University
Donald A. Wells, University of Arizona
James N. Wetzel, Virginia Commonwealth University
Howard Whitney, Franklin University
Tim Wulf, Parkland College
Zenon X. Zygmont, Western Oregon University

Brief Contents

Detailed Contents

CHAPTER 16
FISCAL POLICY 339

CHAPTER 17
MONEY AND THE BANKING SYSTEM 371

CHAPTER 18
THE FEDERAL RESERVE SYSTEM AND MONETARY POLICY 395

chapter 1

The Role and Method of Economics

section 1.1

Economics: A Brief Introduction

- Why study economics?
- What is economics?
- What is scarcity?

WHY STUDY ECONOMICS?

As you begin your first course in economics, you may be asking yourself why you're here. What does economics have to do with your life? While there are many good reasons to study economics, perhaps the best reason is that many issues in our lives are at least partly economic in character. For example, a good understanding of economics would allow you to answer such questions as: Why do 10 A.M. classes fill up quicker than 8 A.M. classes during registration? Why is it difficult to find a taxicab after a play on a cold and rainy night in New York City? Why is it so hard to find an apartment in cities such as San Francisco, Berkeley, and New York? Why is teenage unemployment always higher than adult unemployment? Why are the prices of prescription drugs so high? What are the costs of unanticipated inflation? Will higher taxes on cigarettes reduce the number of people smoking? Why do professional athletes make so much money? Why are unemployment rates higher in some parts of the country than in others? Why don't we just get rid of the penny? Why do U.S. auto producers like tariffs (taxes) on imported cars? The study of economics improves your understanding of these and many other concerns.

Another reason to study economics is that it may teach you how to "think better"—economics helps develop a disciplined method of thinking about problems. While economics may not always give you clear-cut answers, it will give you something even more powerful: the economic way of thinking. The problem-solving tools you will develop by studying economics will prove valuable to you both in your personal and professional life, regardless of your career choice. A student of economics becomes aware that, at a basic level, much of economic life involves choosing among alternative courses of action—making choices between our conflicting wants and desires in a world of limited resources. Economics provides some clues as to how to intelligently evaluate these options and determine the most appropriate choices in given situations.

When you come across this Web icon in your book, go to the Sexton Web site at **http://sexton.swcollege.com** and click on the links that will take you to fun, useful, and interesting economics or economics-related sites.

ECONOMICS—A WORD WITH MANY DIFFERENT MEANINGS

Some individuals think economics involves the study of the stock market and corporate finance, and it does—in part. Others think that economics is concerned with the wise use of money and other matters of personal finance, and it is—in part. Still others think that economics involves forecasting or predicting what business conditions will be in the future, and again, it does—in part.

A Unique Way of Looking at Human Behavior

Economics is a unique way of analyzing many areas of human behavior. Indeed, the range of topics to which economic analysis is applied is quite broad! Many researchers have discovered that the economic approach to human behavior sheds light on social problems that have been with us for a long time: discrimination, education, crime, divorce, political favoritism, and many more. In fact, economics is front-page news almost every day, whether it involves politicians talking about tax cuts, inflation, interest rates, or unemployment; business executives talking about restructuring their companies to cut costs; or the average citizen trying to figure out how to make ends meet each month. Economics is all of this and more.

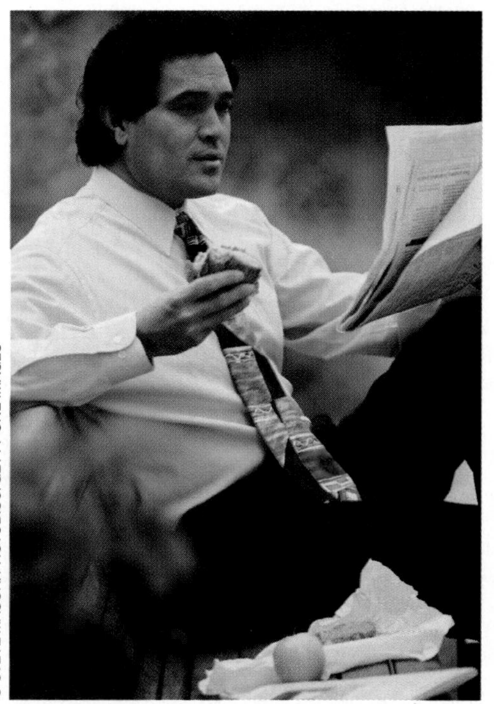
© STEVE MASON/PHOTODISC/GETTY ONE IMAGES

The front pages of our daily newspapers are filled with articles related to economics—either directly or indirectly. News headlines might read: Fuel Prices Soar; Should Social Security Be Revamped?; Stocks Rise; Stocks Fall; President Vows to Increase National Defense Spending; Health Costs Continue to Rise.

Growing Wants and Scarce Resources

Precisely defined, **economics** is the study of the allocation of our limited resources to satisfy our unlimited wants. **Resources** are inputs, such as land, human effort and skills, and machines and factories, used to produce goods and services. The problem is that our wants exceed our limited resources, a fact that we call **scarcity.** Scarcity forces us to make choices on how to best use our limited resources. This is **the economic problem:** Scarcity forces us to choose, and choices are costly because we must give up other opportunities that we value. This economizing problem is evident in every aspect of our lives. Choosing between a trip to the grocery store or the mall, or between finishing a research paper or going to a movie, can be understood more easily when one has a good handle on the "economic way of thinking."

economics
the study of the allocation of our limited resources to satisfy our unlimited wants

resources
inputs used to produce goods and services

scarcity
this occurs when our wants exceed our limited resources

the economic problem
scarcity forces us to choose, and choices are costly because we must give up other opportunities that we value

ECONOMICS IS ALL AROUND US

Although many things that we desire in life are considered to be "non-economic," economics concerns anything that is considered worthwhile to some human being. For instance, love, sexual activity, and religion have value for most people. Even these have an economic dimension. Consider religion, for example. Concern for spiritual matters has led to the development of institutions such as churches and temples that provide religious and spiritual services. These services are goods that many people desire. Love and sex likewise have received economists' scrutiny. One product of love, the institution of the family, is an important economic decision-making unit. Also, sexual activity results in the birth of children, one of the most important "goods" that humans desire.

Even time has an economic dimension. In fact, perhaps the most precious single resource is time. We all have the same limited amount of time per day, and how we divide our time between work and leisure (including perhaps study, sleep, exercise, etc.) is a distinctly economic matter. If we choose more work, we must sacrifice leisure. If we choose to study, we must sacrifice time with friends, or time spent sleeping or watching TV. Virtually everything we decide to do, then, has an economic dimension.

Living in a world of scarcity means trade-offs. And it is important that we know what these trade-offs are so we can make better choices about the options available to us.

In The NEWS

AMERICANS SCORE POORLY ON ECONOMIC LITERACY

—LYNN BRENNER

AVERAGE AMERICAN GRADE: F

The National Council of Economic Education tested 1,010 adults and 1,085 high school students on their knowledge of basic economic principles.

Grade	Among Adults (percent)	Among High School Students (percent)
A	6	3
B	10	7
C	15	11
D	20	13
F	49	66

- On average, adults got a grade of 57 percent on a test on the basics of economics. Among high school students, the average grade was 48 percent.
- Almost two-thirds of those tested did not know that in times of inflation money does not hold its value.
- Only 58 percent of the students understood that when the demand for a product goes up but the supply doesn't, its price is likely to increase.
- Half of the adults and about two-thirds of the students didn't know that the stock market brings people who want to buy stocks together with those who want to sell them.
- Just over one in three Americans realize that society must make choices about how to use resources.

SOURCE: Lynn Brenner, "What We Need to Know About Money," *Parade Magazine,* April 18, 1999, pp. 4–7. Reprinted with permission from *Parade,* copyright © 1999.

Section Check

1. Economics is a problem-solving science.
2. Economics is the study of the allocation of our limited resources to satisfy our unlimited wants.
3. Resources are inputs used to produce goods and services.
4. Our unlimited wants exceed our resources, so we must make choices.

---

1. Why is economics worth studying?
2. What is the definition of economics?
3. Why does scarcity force us to make choices?
4. Why are choices costly?
5. Why do even "non-economic" issues have an economic dimension?

section 1.2 Economics as a Science

- How is economics similar to other social sciences?
- What are macroeconomics and microeconomics?
- Are microeconomic tools important to macroeconomists?

ECONOMICS IS A SOCIAL SCIENCE

Like psychology, sociology, anthropology, and political science, economics is considered a social science. Economics, like the other social sciences, is concerned with reaching generalizations about human behavior. Economics is the study of people. It is the social science that studies the choices people make in a world of limited resources.

Economics and the other social sciences often complement one another. For example, a political scientist might examine the process that led to the adoption of a certain tax policy, while an economist might analyze the impact of that tax policy. Or while a psychologist may try to figure out what makes the criminal mind work, an economist might study the factors causing a change in the crime rate. Social scientists, then, may be studying the same issue but from different perspectives.

MACROECONOMICS AND MICROECONOMICS

Conventionally, we distinguish two main branches of economics, macroeconomics and microeconomics. **Macroeconomics** deals with the **aggregate,** or total economy; it looks at economic problems as they influence the whole of society. Topics covered in macroeconomics include discussions of inflation, unemployment, business cycles, and economic growth. **Microeconomics,** by contrast, deals with the smaller units within the economy, attempting to understand the decision-making behavior of firms and households and their interaction in markets for particular goods or services. Microeconomic topics include discussions of health care, agricultural subsidies, the price of everyday items such as running shoes, the distribution of income, and the impact of labor unions on wages. To put it simply, microeconomics looks at the trees while macroeconomics looks at the forest.

macroeconomics
the study of the whole economy including the topics of inflation, unemployment, and economic growth

aggregate
the total amount—such as the aggregate level of output

microeconomics
the study of household and firm behavior and how they interact in the marketplace

Section Check

1. Economics is concerned with reaching generalizations about human behavior.
2. Economics provides tools to intelligently evaluate and decide on choices.
3. Macroeconomics deals with the aggregate, or total, economy.
4. Microeconomics focuses on smaller units within the economy—firms and households, and how they interact in the marketplace.

---

1. What makes economics a social science?
2. What distinguishes macroeconomics from microeconomics?
3. Why is the market for running shoes considered a microeconomic topic?
4. Why is inflation considered a macroeconomic topic?

section 1.3

Economic Behavior

- What is self-interest?
- Why is self-interest not the same as selfishness?

SELF-INTEREST

Economists assume that individuals act *as if* they are motivated by self-interest and respond in predictable ways to changing circumstances. In other words, self-interest is a good predictor of human behavior. For example, to a worker, self-interest means pursuing a higher paying job and better working conditions. To a consumer, it means gaining a greater level of satisfaction from their limited income and time.

In The **NEWS**

ON COURAGE

—DAN MILLMAN

Many years ago when I worked as a volunteer at Stanford Hospital, I got to know a little girl named Liza who was suffering from a rare and serious disease. Her only chance of recovery appeared to be a blood transfusion from her 5-year-old brother, who had miraculously survived the same disease and had developed the antibodies needed to combat the illness. The doctor explained the situation to her little brother, and asked the boy if he would be willing to give his blood to his sister. I saw him hesitate for only a moment before taking a deep breath and saying, "Yes, I will do it if it will save Liza."

As the transfusion progressed, he lay in a bed next to his sister and smiled, as we all did, seeing the color return to her cheeks. Then his face grew pale and his smile faded. He looked up at the doctor and asked with a trembling voice, "Will I start to die right away?" Being young, the boy had misunderstood the doctor; he thought he was going to have to give her all of his blood.

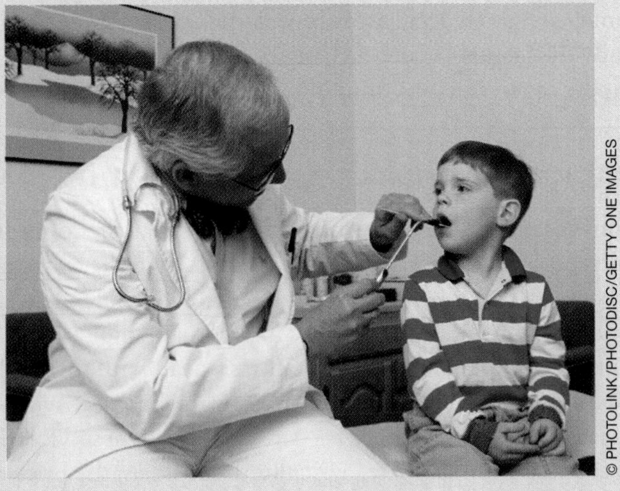

SOURCE: Dan Millman, "On Courage," *Sacred Journey of the Peaceful Warrior*. © H. K. Kramer, Inc.

CONSIDER THIS:
Some people will help others even when the costs are extraordinarily high. But more often than not, these cases of pure selflessness involve close friends or relatives. For example, we seldom observe employees asking employers to cut their wages and increase their workload to increase a company's profits. Or how often do you think customers walk into a supermarket demanding to pay more for their groceries? In short, a great deal of human behavior can be explained and predicted by assuming people pursue their own self-interest.

There is no question that self-interest is a powerful force that motivates people to produce goods and services. But self-interest can include benevolence. Think of the late Mother Teresa, who spent her whole life caring for others. One could say that it was in her self-interest, but who would consider her actions selfish? Similarly, workers may be pursuing self-interest when they choose to work harder and longer to increase their charitable giving or saving for their children's education. So, don't confuse self-interest with selfishness.

ACTION AND INACTION HAVE CONSEQUENCES

Most economists believe that it is *rational* for people to anticipate the likely future consequences of their own behavior. For example, if someone with a suspended driver's license chooses to drive an automobile illegally, we presume that the individual considered the possible consequences of this action before he made that decision. This does not necessarily mean that he will not drive, merely that he considers the consequences of that action—perhaps a serious jail sentence or an impounded car—before he makes his choice. Or if someone decides to take up smoking, she is presumed by economists to have thought about the consequences of that action. An individual may still decide to smoke, but she will have at least considered the potential results of that action. Actions have consequences. Even inaction, deciding not do something or not to make a change, has consequences: If you choose not to study, you could fail an exam; if you choose not to pay your income taxes, you could go to jail; or if you are diagnosed with high blood pressure and choose not to change your diet, you could have a stroke.

Section Check SECTION CHECK

1. Economists assume that people act as if they are motivated by self-interest and respond predictably to changing circumstances.
2. People try to anticipate the possible consequences of their actions.

---

1. What do economists mean by self-interest?
2. What does rational self-interest involve?
3. How are self-interest and selfishness different?

section 1.4

Economic Theory

- What are economic theories?
- What can we expect out of our theories?
- Why do we need to abstract?
- What is a hypothesis?
- What is empirical analysis?

ECONOMIC THEORIES

A **theory** is an established explanation that accounts for known facts or phenomena. Specifically, economic theories are statements or propositions about patterns of human behavior that are expected to take place under certain circumstances. These theories help us to sort out and understand the complexities of economic behavior. We expect a good theory to explain and predict well. A good economic theory, then, should help us to better understand and, ideally, predict human economic behavior.

theory
statements or propositions used to explain and predict behavior in the real world

ABSTRACTION IS IMPORTANT

Economic theories cannot realistically include every event that has ever occurred. This is true for the same reason that a newspaper or history book does not include every world event that has ever happened. We must abstract. A road map of the United States may not include every creek, ridge, and gully between Los Angeles and Chicago—indeed, such an all-inclusive map would be too large to be of value. However, a

How is economic theory like a map? Because of the complexity of human behavior, economists must abstract to focus on the most important components of a particular problem. This is similar to maps that highlight the important information (and assume away many minor details) to help people get from here to there.

small road map with major details will provide enough information to travel by car from Los Angeles to Chicago. Likewise, an economic theory provides a broad view, not a detailed examination, of human economic behavior.

DEVELOPING A TESTABLE PROPOSITION

hypothesis
a testable proposition

The beginning of any theory is a **hypothesis,** a testable proposition that makes some type of prediction about behavior in response to certain changes in conditions. In economic theory, a hypothesis is a testable prediction about how people will behave or react to a change in economic circumstances. For example, if the price of compact discs (CDs) increased, we might hypothesize that fewer CDs would be sold, or if the price of CDs fell, we might hypothesize that more CDs would be sold. Once a hypothesis is stated, it is tested by comparing what it predicts will happen to what actually happens.

Using Empirical Analysis

empirical analysis
the use of data to test a hypothesis

To see if our hypothesis is valid, we must engage in an **empirical analysis.** That is, we must examine the data to see if our hypothesis fits well with the facts. If the hypothesis is consistent with real-world observations, it is accepted; if it does not fit well with the facts, it is "back to the drawing board."

Determining whether a hypothesis is acceptable is more difficult in economics than it is in the natural or physical sciences. Chemists, for example, can observe chemical reactions under laboratory conditions. They can alter the environment to meet the assumptions of the hypothesis and can readily manipulate the variables (chemicals, temperatures, and so on) crucial to the proposed relationship. Such controlled experimentation is seldom possible in economics. The laboratory of economists is usually the real world. Unlike a chemistry lab, economists cannot easily control all the other variables that might influence human behavior.

FROM HYPOTHESIS TO THEORY

After gathering their data, economic researchers must then evaluate the results to determine whether the hypothesis is supported or refuted. If supported, the hypothesis can then be tentatively accepted as an economic theory.

Economic theories are always on probation. A hypothesis is constantly being tested against empirical findings. Do the observed findings support the prediction? When a hypothesis survives a number of tests, it is accepted until it no longer predicts well.

Section Check

1. Economic theories are statements used to explain and predict patterns of human behavior.
2. We must abstract and focus on the most important components of a particular problem.
3. A hypothesis makes a prediction about human behavior and is then tested.
4. We use empirical analysis to examine the data and see if our hypothesis fits well with the facts.

---

1. What are economic theories?
2. What is the purpose of a theory?
3. Why must economic theories be abstract?
4. What is a hypothesis? How do we determine if it is tentatively accepted?

section 1.5

Problems to Avoid in Scientific Thinking

- What is the *ceteris paribus* assumption?
- If events are associated with one another, does that mean one event caused the other to happen?
- What is the fallacy of composition?

In our discussion of economic theory, we have not yet mentioned that there are certain problems that may hinder scientific and logical thinking. In this section, we will discuss several potential problems to avoid in economic thinking: violation of the *ceteris paribus* assumption, confusing association and causation, and the fallacy of composition.

VIOLATION OF THE *CETERIS PARIBUS* ASSUMPTION

One condition common to virtually all theories in economics is usually expressed by use of the Latin expression ***ceteris paribus.*** This roughly means "let everything else be equal" or "holding everything else constant." In trying to assess the effect of one variable on another, we must isolate their relationship from other events that might also influence the situation that the theory tries to explain or predict. To make this clearer, we will illustrate this concept with a couple of examples.

ceteris paribus *holding all other things constant*

Suppose you develop your own theory describing the relationship between studying and exam performance: If I study harder, I will perform better on the test. That sounds logical, right? Holding other things constant *(ceteris paribus),* this is likely to be true. However, what if you studied harder but inadvertently overslept the day of the exam? What if you were so sleepy during the test that you could not think clearly? Or what if you studied the wrong material? While it may look like additional studying did not improve your performance, the real problem may lie in the impact of other variables, such as sleep deficiency or how you studied.

Researchers must be careful to hold other things constant *(ceteris paribus).* For example, in 1936, cars were inexpensive by modern standards, yet few were purchased; in 1949, cars were much more expensive, but more were bought. This statement appears to imply that people prefer to buy more when prices are higher. However, we know from ample empirical observations that this is not the case—buyers are only willing to buy more at lower prices, *ceteris paribus.* The reason people bought more cars at the higher prices was that several other important variables were not held constant over this period (the *ceteris paribus* assumption): the purchasing power of dollars, the income of potential car buyers, and the quality of cars.

CONFUSING CORRELATION AND CAUSATION

Without a theory of causation, no scientist could sort out and understand the enormous complexity of the real world. But one must always be careful not to confuse correlation with causation. In other words, the fact that two events usually occur together (**correlation**) does not necessarily mean that one caused the other to occur (**causation**). For example, say a groundhog awakes after a long winter of hibernation, climbs out of his hole, sees his shadow and then six weeks of bad weather ensue. Did the groundhog cause

correlation *two events that usually occur together*

causation *when one event brings on another event*

In The NEWS

HEAVY METAL MUSIC AND TEEN SUICIDE

—KAREN R. SCHEEL

Many parents and mental health professionals have watched the rising rate of adolescent suicide and the growing popularity of heavy metal music among teenagers and wondered, with some concern, if there is any connection between the two phenomena. A new study . . . offers the first direct assessment of the suicidal risk of American adolescent heavy metal fans compared to that of peers who do not like heavy metal music. For the study, 121 midwestern public high school students (mean age 17.2) were given two psychological assessments, the Reasons for Living Inventory (RFL) and the Suicide Risk Questionnaire (SRQ) (both measures of risk for suicide), and their musical preferences were assessed.

Compared with fans of country, pop/mainstream, rock, and rap music, heavy metal fans had lower scores on the RFL (indicating greater risk of suicide) and they were more likely to say they occasionally or seriously thought about killing themselves (74 percent versus 35 percent for females; 42 percent versus 15 percent for males).

But the author cautions that while these findings "do suggest that a teenager's liking of heavy metal music may be a useful 'red flag' for suicidal vulnerability for psychologists and other professionals who work with adolescents," she adds that these findings should not be thought of as indicative of imminent suicidal risk and that they "are not suggestive of any important causal effects of heavy metal listening on suicidality."

SOURCE: Presentation: "Adolescent Heavy Metal Fans: At Increased Risk for Suicide?" by Karen R. Scheel, University of Iowa, Session 2173 (B-14), August 10, 1996. © 1996 by the American Psychological Association. Adapted with permission.

CONSIDER THIS:
Note how the researcher cautions against any determination of causality. Perhaps the causality runs in the other direction: Kids that are at greater risk for suicide may like heavy metal music. Perhaps some other variables are causing the correlation, like genetic predisposition, peer pressure, environment, or a host of other things.

the bad weather? Similarly, Cal Ripkin's streak of consecutive baseball games played started in 1982—the same year that the Weather Channel began on television. Does that mean that the two events are systematically related? It is highly unlikely.

Perhaps the causality may run in the opposite direction. While a rooster may always crow before the sun rises, it does not cause the sunrise; rather the early light from the sunrise causes the rooster to crow.

People tend to drive more slowly when the roads are covered with ice. In addition, more traffic accidents occur when the roads are icy. So does driving slower cause the number of accidents to rise? No, it is the icy roads that lead to both lower speeds and increased accidents.

© AP PHOTO/BOB CHILD

Why Is There a Positive Correlation Between Ice Cream Sales and Crime?

Did you know that when ice cream sales rise, so do crime rates? What do you think causes the two events to occur together? Some might think that the sugar "high" in the ice cream causes the higher crime rate. Excess sugar in a snack was actually used in court testimony in a murder case—the so-called "Twinkie defense." However, it is more likely that crime peaks in the summer because of weather, more people on vacations (leaving their homes vacant), teenagers out of school, and so on. It just happens that ice cream sales also peak in those months because of weather. The lesson: One must always be careful not to confuse correlation with causation and to be clear on the direction of the causation.

THE FALLACY OF COMPOSITION

One must also be careful with problems associated with aggregation (summing up all the parts), particularly **the fallacy of composition.** This fallacy states that even if something is true for an individual, it is not necessarily true for many individuals as a group. For example, say you are at a football game and you decide to stand up to get a better view of the playing field. This works as long as no one else stands up. But what would happen if everyone stood up at the same time? Then, standing up would not let you see better. Hence, what may be true for an individual does not always hold true in the aggregate. The same can be said of arriving to class early to get a better parking place—what if everyone arrived early? Or studying harder to get a better grade in a class that is graded on a curve—what if everyone studied harder? All of these are examples of the fallacy of composition.

fallacy of composition *the incorrect view that what is true for the individual is always true for the group*

Section Check

1. In order to isolate the effects of one variable on another, we use the *ceteris paribus* assumption.
2. The fact that two events are related does not mean that one caused the other to occur.
3. What is true for the individual is not necessarily true for the group.

---

1. Why do economists hold other things constant *(ceteris paribus)?*
2. What is the relationship between correlation and causation?
3. What types of misinterpretations result from confusing correlation and causation?
4. What is the fallacy of composition?
5. If U.S. consumers bought more gasoline in 2000, when prices averaged $1.60 per gallon, than they did in 1970, when prices averaged $0.80 per gallon, does that mean that people want more gas at higher prices? Why or why not?
6. If you can sometimes get a high grade on a test without studying, does that mean that additional studying does not lead to higher grades? Explain your answer.

section 1.6

Positive and Normative Analysis

- What is positive analysis?
- What is normative analysis?
- Why do economists disagree?

POSITIVE ANALYSIS

Most economists view themselves as scientists seeking the truth about the way people behave. They make speculations about economic behavior, and then (ideally) they try to assess the validity of those predictions based on human experience. Their work emphasizes how people *do* behave, rather than how people *should* behave. In the role of scientist, an economist tries to observe objectively patterns of behavior without reference to the appropriateness or inappropriateness of that behavior. This objective, value-free approach, utilizing the scientific method, is called **positive analysis.** In positive analysis, we want to know the impact of variable A on variable B. We want to be able to test a hypothesis. For example, the following is a positive statement: If rent controls are imposed, vacancy rates will fall. This statement is testable. A positive statement does not have to be a true statement, but it does have to be a testable statement.

positive analysis
an objective testable statement—how the economy is

However, keep in mind that it is doubtful that even the most objective scientist can be totally value-free in his or her analysis. An economist may well emphasize data or evidence that supports his hypothesis, putting less weight on other evidence that might be contradictory. This, alas, is human nature. But a good economist/scientist strives to be as fair and objective as possible in evaluating evidence and in stating conclusions based on the evidence.

NORMATIVE ANALYSIS

Like everyone, economists have opinions and make value judgments. When economists, or anyone else for that matter, express opinions about some economic policy or statement, they are indicating in part how they believe things should be, not just facts as to the way things are. **Normative analysis** expresses opinions about the desirability of various actions. Normative statements involve judgments about what should be or what ought to happen. For example, one could judge that incomes should be more equally distributed. If there is a change in tax policy that makes incomes more equal, there will be positive economic questions that can be investigated, such as how work behavior will change. But we cannot say, as scientists, that such a policy is good or bad; rather, we can point to what will likely happen if the policy is adopted.

normative analysis
a subjective, non-testable statement—how the economy should be

POSITIVE VERSUS NORMATIVE STATEMENTS

The distinction between positive and normative analysis is important. It is one thing to say that everyone should have universal health care, a normative statement, and quite another to say that universal health care would lead to greater worker productivity, a testable positive statement. It is important to distinguish between positive and normative analysis because many controversies in economics revolve around policy considerations that contain both. When economists start talking about how the economy should work rather than how it does work, they have entered the normative world of the policymaker.

DISAGREEMENT IS COMMON IN MOST DISCIPLINES

While economists differ frequently on economic policy questions, there is probably less disagreement than the media would have you believe. Disagreement is common in most disciplines: Seismologists differ over predictions of earthquakes or volcanic eruption; historians can be at odds over the interpretation of historical events; psychologists disagree on proper ways to rear children; and nutritionists debate the merits of large doses of vitamin C.

The majority of disagreements in economics stem from normative issues, as differences in values or policy beliefs result in conflict. As we discussed earlier in this chapter, economists may emphasize specific facts over other facts when trying to develop support for their own hypothesis. As a result, disagreements can result when one economist gives weight to facts that have been minimized by another, and vice versa.

Freedom Versus Fairness

Some economists are concerned about individual freedom and liberty, thinking that any encroachment on individual decision making is, other things equal, bad. People with this

In The NEWS

ECONOMISTS DO AGREE

Almost 80 percent of economists agree that these statements are correct:

1. A ceiling on rents (rent control) reduces the quantity and quality of rental housing available (93 percent agree).
2. Tariffs and import quotas usually reduce general economic welfare (93 percent agree).
3. A minimum wage increases unemployment among the young and unskilled (79 percent agree).
4. Cash payments increase the welfare of recipients to a greater degree than do transfers-in-kind of equal cash value (84 percent agree).
5. Fiscal policy (e.g., tax cuts and/or government expenditure increase) has a significant stimulative impact on a less than fully employed economy (90 percent agree).
6. A large budget deficit has an adverse effect on the economy (83 percent agree).
7. Effluent taxes and marketable pollution permits represent a better approach to pollution control than imposition of pollution ceilings (78 percent agree).

SOURCE: Adapted from Richard M. Alston, J. R. Kearl, and Michael B. Vaughn, "Is There Consensus Among Economists in the 1990s?" *American Economic Review,* May 1992, pp. 203–209.

philosophic bent are inclined to be skeptical of any increased government involvement in the economy.

On the other hand, some economists are concerned with what they consider an unequal, "unfair," or unfortunate distribution of income, wealth, or power, and view governmental intervention as desirable in righting injustices that they believe exist in a market economy. To these persons, the threat to individual liberty alone is not sufficiently great to reject governmental intervention in the face of perceived economic injustice.

The Validity of an Economic Theory

Aside from philosophic differences, there is a second reason why economists may differ on any given policy question. Specifically, they may disagree as to the validity of a given economic theory for the policy in question. Suppose two economists have identical philosophical views that have led them to the same conclusion: To end injustice and hardship, unemployment should be reduced. To reach the objective, the first economist believes the government should lower taxes and increase spending, while the second economist believes increasing the amount of money in public hands by various banking policies will achieve the same results with fewer undesirable consequences. The two economists differ because the empirical evidence for economic theories about the cause of unemployment appears to conflict. Some evidence suggests government taxation and spending policies are effective in reducing unemployment, while other evidence suggests that the prime cause of unnecessary unemployment lies with faulty monetary policy. Still other evidence is consistent with the view that, over long periods, neither approach mentioned here is of much value in reducing unemployment, and that unemployment will be part of our existence no matter what macroeconomic policies we follow.

ECONOMISTS DO AGREE

Although you may not believe it after reading the previous discussion, economists don't always disagree. In fact, according to a survey among members of the American Economic Association, most economists agree on a wide range of issues, including rent control, import tariffs, export restrictions, the use of wage and price controls to curb inflation, and the minimum wage (see "In the News: Economists Do Agree").

Section Check

1. Positive analysis is objective and value-free.
2. Normative analysis involves value judgments and opinions about the desirability of various actions.
3. Disagreement is common in most disciplines.
4. Most disagreement among economists stems from normative issues.

---

1. What is positive analysis? Must positive analysis be testable?
2. What is normative analysis? Is normative analysis testable?
3. Why is the positive/normative distinction important?
4. Why are there policy disagreements among economists?
5. Is the statement, "UFOs land in my backyard at least twice a week," a positive statement? Why or why not?
6. Is there any way to determine scientifically if the "rich" pay their "fair share" of taxes? Why or why not?

Summary

Economics is the study of the allocation of our limited resources to satisfy our unlimited wants. Resources are defined as the inputs, such as land, human effort and skills, and machines and factories, that are used to produce goods and services. We all face "the economic problem"—that is, our wants exceed our limited resources, a fact that we call scarcity. Scarcity forces us to choose, and choices are costly because we must give up other opportunities that we value, but economics provides the tools to intelligently evaluate and decide on choices. Another reason to study economics is that many issues around us are economic in character. A good working knowledge of economics is important for everyone, whether they are consumers, workers, or politicians.

There are two branches of economics: microeconomics and macroeconomics. Microeconomics focuses on smaller units within the economy—firms and households; macroeconomics deals with the aggregate, or total, economy. Macroeconomics looks at the forest, while microeconomics looks at the trees.

Economists assume that it is rational for people to act in their own self-interest and try to improve their lives. In doing so, people try to anticipate the likely consequences of their actions as well as their inaction.

Economic theories are statements about patterns of human behavior. In our testing of theories we use empirical analysis to examine the data and see if our hypothesis fits well with the facts. When studying economics we must be careful of some pitfalls: violating the *ceteris paribus* assumption, confusing causation and correlation, and the fallacy of composition. It is also important when studying economics to understand the difference between positive analysis, which is testable and objective ("what is"), and normative analysis, which is subjective ("what should or ought to be").

Key Terms and Concepts

economics 3
resources 3
scarcity 3
the economic problem 3
macroeconomics 5
aggregate 5
microeconomics 5
theory 7
hypothesis 8
empirical analysis 8
ceteris paribus 9
correlation 9
causation 9
fallacy of composition 11
positive analysis 12
normative analysis 12

Review Questions

1. Explain the causal links of the following events:
   - **a.** The people in the last row of the lecture hall always seem to get the lowest grade. Does this mean that seat selection determines exam grades?
   - **b.** For years the stock market would rise the year after the National Football League beat the American Football League in the Super Bowl. Did the Super Bowl determine the fate of the stock market?
2. Why should we use the *ceteris paribus* assumption in these statements?
   - **a.** Car prices increased and people bought more cars as their incomes rose.
   - **b.** The price of generic shampoo fell and people bought less of it as their income rose.
3. After reading this chapter, see if you can come up with a list of ten topics where you think the economic way of thinking would be helpful in your life.
4. Which of the following topics do you think could benefit from the economic way of thinking, and why?
   - **a.** health care
   - **b.** the environment
   - **c.** politics
   - **d.** the law
   - **e.** sports
   - **f.** the media
   - **g.** finance
5. Answer the following questions:
   - **a.** What is the difference between self-interest and selfishness?
   - **b.** Why does inaction have consequences?
   - **c.** Why is observation and prediction more difficult in economics than in chemistry?
   - **d.** Why do economists look at group behavior rather than at individual behavior?
6. Using the map analogy from the chapter, talk about the importance of abstraction. How do you abstract when taking notes in class?
7. Identify which of the following economic statements are positive and which are normative:
   - **a.** A tax increase will increase unemployment.
   - **b.** The government should reduce funding for welfare programs.
   - **c.** Tariffs on imported wine will lead to higher prices for domestic wine.
   - **d.** A decrease in the capital gains tax rate will increase investment.
   - **e.** Goods purchased out of state on the internet should be subject to state sales taxes.
   - **f.** A reduction in interest rates will cause inflation.
8. Evaluate the following statement: "As long as there is scarcity, there will always be poverty."
9. The following statement represents which fallacy in thinking, and why: "I earn $12 per hour. If I am able to earn $12 per hour, everyone should be able to find work for at least that wage rate."
10. Go to the Sexton Web site for this chapter at **http://sexton.swcollege.com** and click on the American Economic Association Job Openings for Economists Web site and peruse the most recent job listings. What types of jobs are available to those trained in the economic way of thinking?
11. Visit the editorial section of the *Washington Post* Online (go to the Sexton site and click on *Washington Post* Online) and read a few recent editorials. See if you can identify any positive or normative statements in these op-ed pieces.

Appendix

Working with Graphs

GRAPHS ARE AN IMPORTANT ECONOMIC TOOL

Sometimes the use of visual aids, such as graphs, greatly enhances our understanding of a theory. It is much the same as finding your way to a friend's house with the aid of a map rather than with detailed verbal or written instructions. Graphs are important tools for economists. They allow us to understand better the workings of the economy. To economists, a graph can be worth a thousand words. This text will use graphs throughout to enhance the understanding of important economic relationships. This appendix provides a guide on how to read and create your own graphs.

Y-axis
the vertical axis on a graph

X-axis
the horizontal axis on a graph

The most useful graph for our purposes is one that merely connects a vertical line (the ***Y*-axis**) with a horizontal line (the ***X*-axis**), as seen in Exhibit 1. The intersection of the two lines occurs at the origin, which is where the value of both variables is equal to zero. In Exhibit 1, the graph has four quadrants or "boxes." In this textbook we will be primarily concerned with the shaded box in the upper right-hand corner. This portion of the graph deals exclusively with positive numbers. Always keep in mind that moving to the right on the horizontal axis and up along the vertical axis each lead to higher values.

USING GRAPHS AND CHARTS

pie chart
a circle subdivided into proportionate slices that represent various quantities that add up to 100 percent

Exhibit 2 presents three common types of graphs. The **pie chart** in Exhibit 2(a) shows what college students earn. That is, each slice in the pie chart represents the percent of college students in a particular earnings category. Therefore, pie charts are used to show the relative size of various quantities that add up to a total of 100 percent.

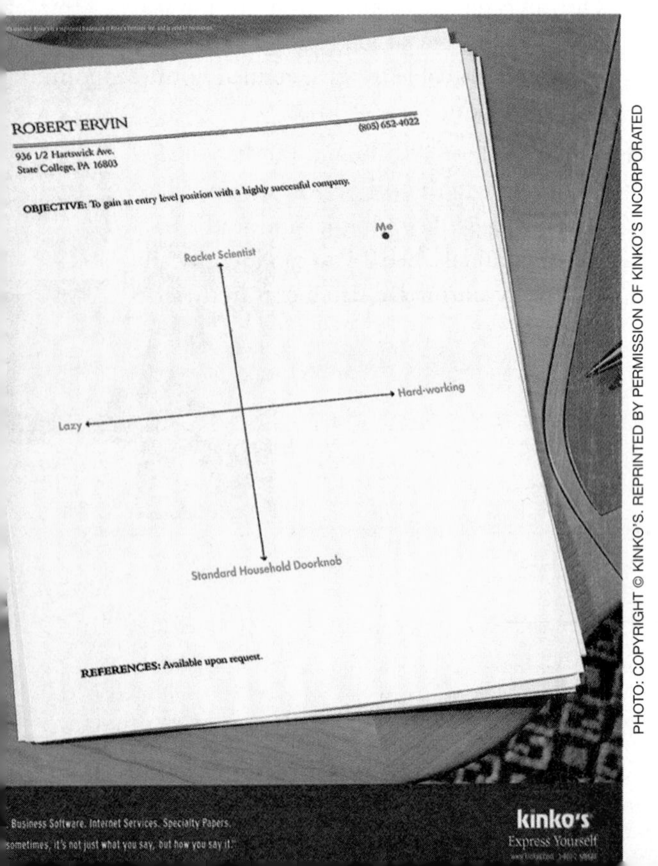

Graphs can summarize important data. This Kinko's ad of a clever resumé shows how to communicate important information to a potential employer.

appendix Exhibit 1 Plotting a Graph

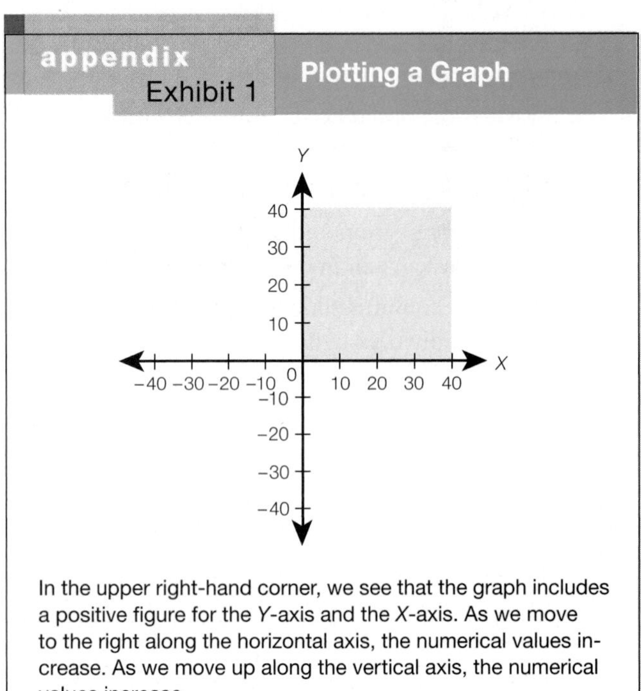

In the upper right-hand corner, we see that the graph includes a positive figure for the *Y*-axis and the *X*-axis. As we move to the right along the horizontal axis, the numerical values increase. As we move up along the vertical axis, the numerical values increase.

Exhibit 2(b) is a **bar graph** that shows the most popular tourist attractions in the United States. The height of the line represents the annual attendance at these popular tourist attractions. Bar graphs are used to show a comparison of the size of quantities of similar items.

bar graph
represents data using vertical bars rising from the horizontal axis

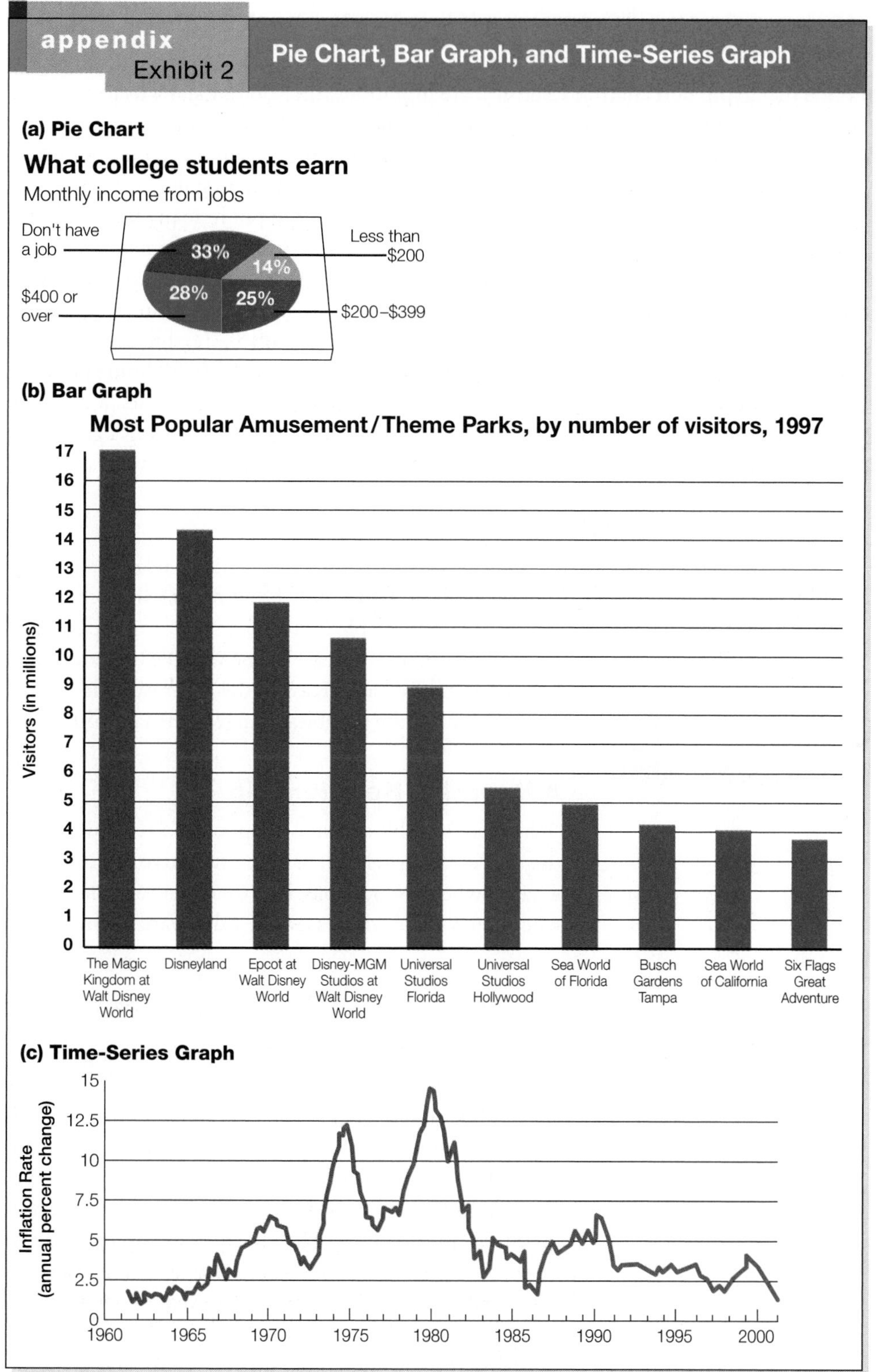

time-series graph
a type of line chart that plots data trends over time

Exhibit 2(c) is a **time-series graph.** This type of graph shows changes in the value of a variable over time. This is a visual tool that allows us to observe important trends over a certain time period. In Exhibit 2(c) we see a graph that shows trends in the inflation rate over time. The horizontal axis shows us the passage of time, and the vertical axis shows us the inflation rate (annual percent change). From the graph, we can see the trends in the inflation rate from 1961 to 2000.

USING GRAPHS TO SHOW THE RELATIONSHIP BETWEEN TWO VARIABLES

variable
something that is measured by a number, such as your height

While the graphs and chart in Exhibit 2 are important, they do not allow us to show the relationship between two variables (a **variable** is something that is measured by a number, such as your height). To more closely examine the structure of and functions of graphs, let us consider the story of Katherine, an avid inline skater who has aspirations of winning the Z Games next year. To get there, however, she will have to put in many hours of practice. But how many hours? In search of information about the practice habits of other skaters, she logged onto the Internet, where she pulled up the results of a study conducted by ESPM 3 that indicated the score of each Z Games competitor and the amount of practice time per week spent by each skater. The results of this study (see Exhibit 3) indicated that skaters had to practice 10 hours per week to receive a score of 4.0, 20 hours per week to receive a score of 6.0, 30 hours per week to get a score of 8.0, and 40 hours per week to get a perfect score of 10. What does this information tell Katherine? By using a graph, she can more clearly understand the relationship between practice time and overall score.

positive relationship
when two variables change in the same direction

negative relationship
when two variables change in opposite directions

A Positive Relationship

The study on scores and practice times revealed what is called a direct relationship, also called a positive relationship. A **positive relationship** means that the variables change in the same direction. That is, an increase in one variable (practice time) is accompanied by an increase in the other variable (overall score), or a decrease in one variable (practice time) is accompanied by a decrease in the other variable (overall score). In short, the variables change in the same direction.

appendix Exhibit 3 A Positive Relationship

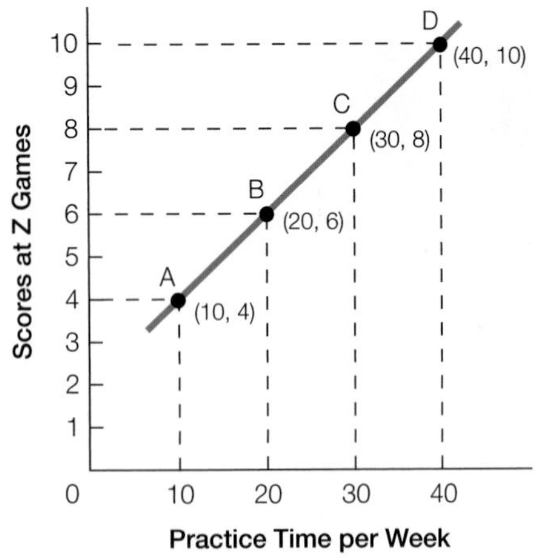

The inline skaters' practice times and scores in the competition are plotted on the graph. Each participant is represented by a point. The graph shows that those skaters who practiced the most scored the highest. This is called a positive, or direct, relationship.

A Negative Relationship

When two variables change in opposite directions, we say they are inversely related, or have a **negative relationship.** That is, when one variable rises, the other variable falls, or when one variable decreases, the other variable increases.

THE GRAPH OF A DEMAND CURVE

Let us now examine one of the most important graphs in all of economics—the demand curve. In Exhibit 4, we see Emily's individual demand curve for compact discs. It shows the price of CDs on the vertical axis and the quantity of CDs purchased per month on the horizontal axis. Every point in the space shown represents a price and quantity combination. The downward-sloping line, labeled demand curve, shows the different combinations of price and quantity purchased. Note that the higher you go up on the vertical (price) axis, the smaller the quantity purchased on the horizontal (quantity) axis, and the lower the price on the vertical axis, the greater the quantity purchased.

In Exhibit 4, we see that moving up the vertical price axis from the origin, the price of CDs increases from $5 to $25 in increments of $5. Moving out along the horizontal quantity axis, the quantity purchased increases from zero to five CDs per month. Point A represents a price of $25 and a quantity of one CD, point B represents a price of $20 and a quantity of two CDs, point C, $15 and a quantity of three CDs, and so on. When we connect all the points, we have what economists call a curve. As you can see, curves are sometimes drawn as straight lines for ease of illustration. Moving down along the curve, we see that as the price falls, a greater quantity is demanded; moving up the curve to higher prices, a smaller quantity is demanded. That is, when CDs become less expensive, Emily buys more CDs. When CDs become more expensive, Emily buys fewer CDs, perhaps choosing to go to the movies or buy a pizza instead.

appendix Exhibit 4 — A Negative Relationship

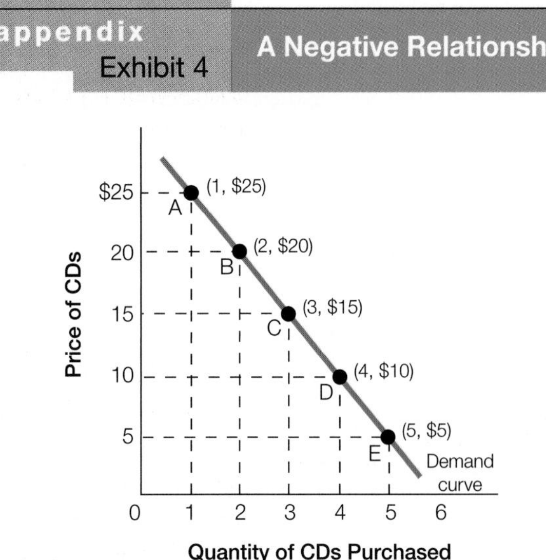

The downward slope of the curve means that price and quantity purchased are inversely, or negatively, related: When one increases, the other decreases. That is, moving down along the demand curve from point A to point E, we see that as price falls, the quantity purchased increases. Moving up along the demand curve from point E to point A, we see that as the price increases, the quantity purchased falls.

USING GRAPHS TO SHOW THE RELATIONSHIP BETWEEN THREE VARIABLES

Although only two variables are shown on the axes, graphs can be used to show the relationship between three variables. For example, say we add a third variable—income—to our earlier example. Our three variables are now income, price, and quantity purchased. If Emily's income rises, say she gets a raise at work, she is now able and willing to buy more CDs than before at each possible price. As a result, the whole demand curve shifts outward (rightward) compared to the old curve. That is, with the new income, she uses some of it to buy more CDs. This is seen in the graph in Exhibit 5(a). On the other hand, if her income falls, say she quits her job to go back to school, she now has less income to buy CDs. This causes the whole demand curve to shift inward (leftward) compared to the old curve. This is seen in the graph in Exhibit 5(b).

appendix Exhibit 5 — Shifting a Curve

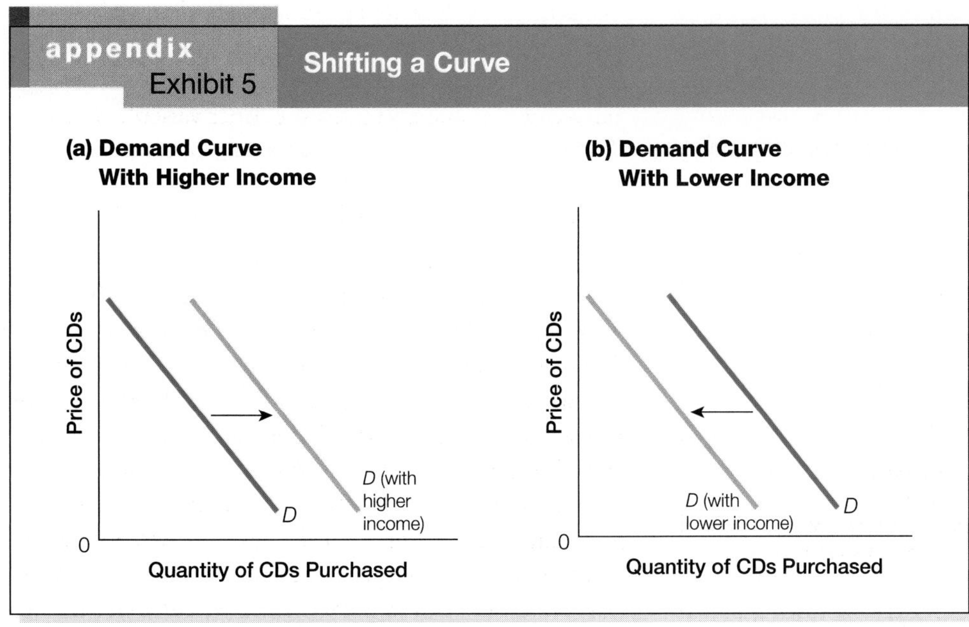

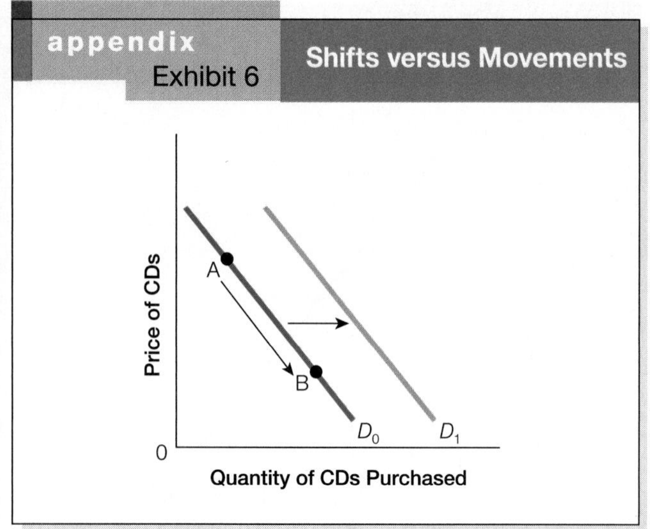

The Difference Between a Movement Along and a Shift in the Curve

It is important to remember the difference between a movement between one point and another along a curve and a shift in the whole curve. A change in one of the variables on the graph, like price or quantity purchased, will cause a movement along the curve, say from point A to point B as shown in Exhibit 6. A change in one of the variables not shown (held constant in order to show only the relationship between price and quantity), like income in our example, will cause the whole curve to shift. The change from D_0 to D_1 in Exhibit 6 shows such a shift.

SLOPE

slope
the ratio of rise (change in the Y variable) over the run (change in the X variable)

In economics, we sometimes refer to the steepness of the lines or curves on graphs as the **slope.** A slope can be either positive (upward sloping) or negative (downward sloping). A curve that is downward sloping represents an inverse, or negative, relationship between the two variables and slants downward from left to right, as seen in Exhibit 7(a). A curve that is upward sloping represents a direct, or positive, relationship between the two variables and slants upward from left to right, as seen in Exhibit 7(b). The numeric value of the slope shows the number of units of change of the *Y*-axis variable for each unit of change in the *X*-axis variable. Slope provides the direction (positive or negative) as well as the magnitude of the relationship between the two variables.

Measuring the Slope of a Linear Curve

A straight-line curve is called a linear curve. The slope of a linear curve between two points measures the relative rates of change of two variables. Specifically, the slope of a linear curve can be defined as the ratio of the change in the *Y* value to the change in the *X* value. The slope can also be expressed as the ratio of the rise to the run, where the rise is the change in the *Y* variable (along the vertical axis) and the run is the change in the *X* variable (along the horizontal axis).

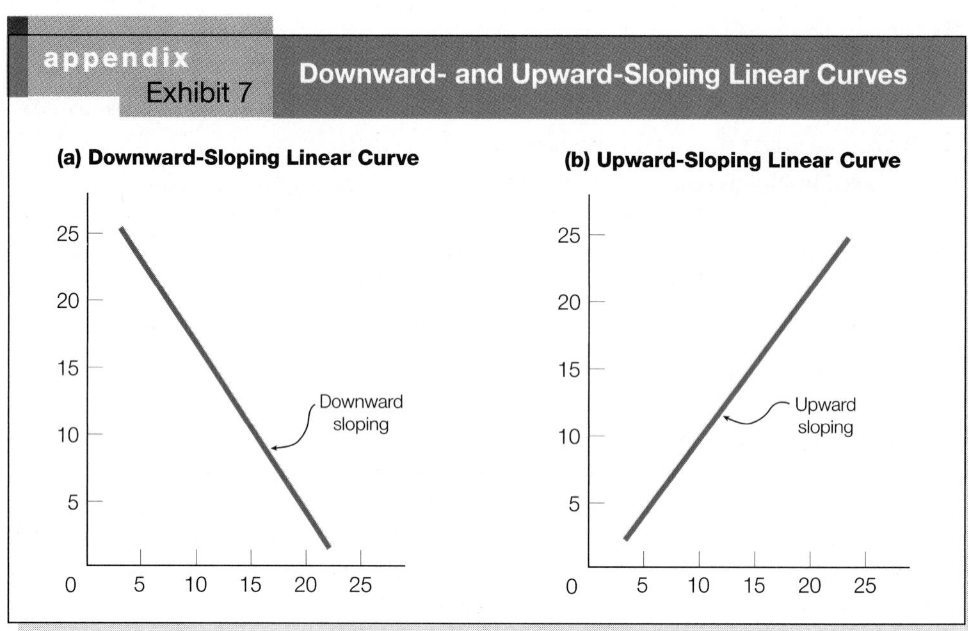

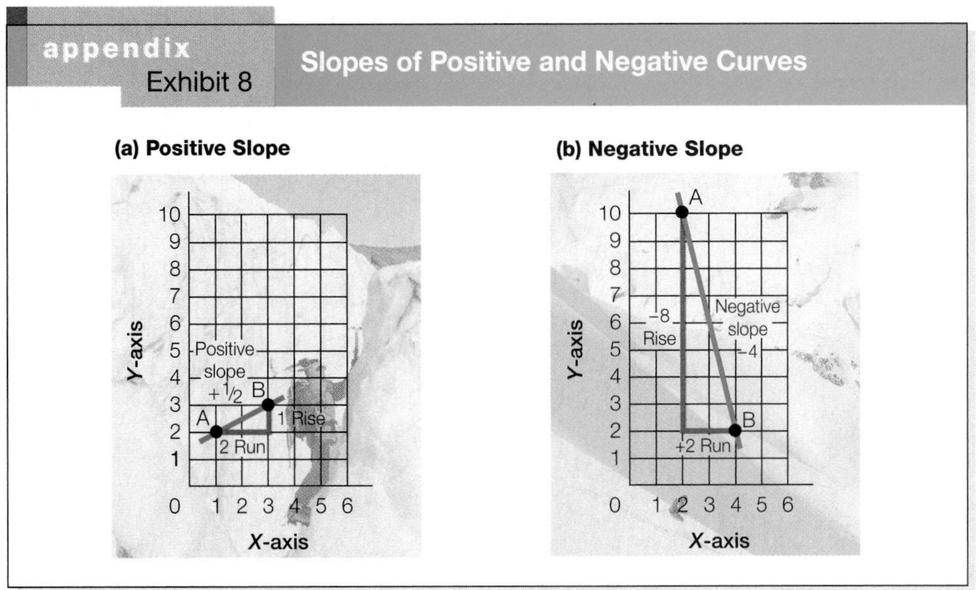

In Exhibit 8, we show two linear curves, one with a positive slope and one with a negative slope. In Exhibit 8(a), the slope of the positively sloped linear curve from point A to B is 1/2, because the rise is 1 (from 2 to 3) and the run is 2 (from 1 to 3). In Exhibit 8(b), the negatively sloped linear curve has a slope of −4, a rise of −8 (a fall of 8 from 10 to 2) and a run of 2 (from 2 to 4), which gives us a slope of −4 (−8/2). Note the appropriate signs on the slopes: The negatively sloped line carries a minus sign and the positively sloped line, a plus sign.

Finding the Slope of a Nonlinear Curve

In Exhibit 9, we show the slope of a nonlinear curve. A nonlinear curve is a line that actually curves. Here the slope varies from point to point along the curve. However, we can find the slope of this curve at any given point by drawing a straight line tangent to that point on the curve. A tangency is when a straight line just touches the curve without actually crossing it. At point A, we see that the positively sloped line that is tangent to the curve has a slope of 1—the line rises one unit and runs one unit. At point B, the line is horizontal, so it has zero slope. At point C, we see a slope of −2, because the negatively sloped line has a rise of −2 units (a fall of two units) for every one unit run.

Remember, many students have problems with economics simply because they fail to understand graphs, so make sure that you understand this material before going on to chapter 3.

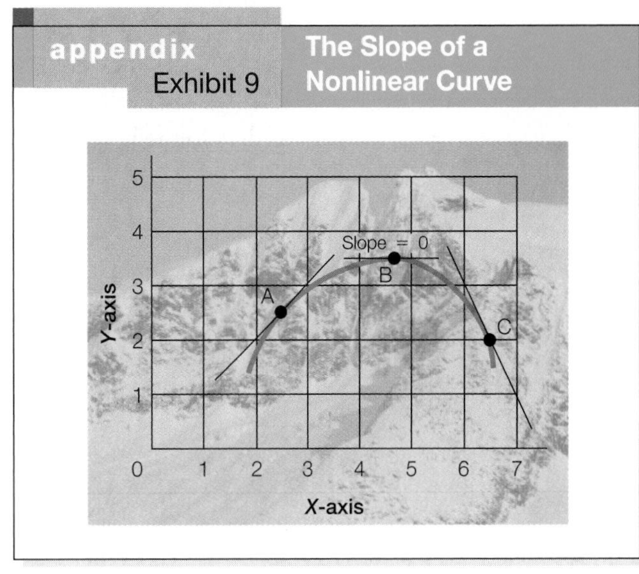

Key Terms and Concepts

Y-axis 16	bar graph 17	positive relationship 18
X-axis 16	time-series graph 18	negative relationship 18
pie chart 16	variable 18	slope 20

chapter 1 Study Guide

Fill in the Blanks

1. Economics is the study of the allocation of ______________ resources to satisfy ______________ wants for goods and services.
2. ______________ is the problem that our wants exceed our limited resources.
3. Resources are ______________ used to produce goods and services.
4. The economic problem is that ______________ forces us to choose, and choices are costly because we must give up other opportunities that we ______________.
5. Living in a world of scarcity means ______________.
6. ________________ deals with the aggregate (the forest), or total economy, while ________________ deals with the smaller units (the trees) within the economy.
7. Economists assume that individuals act as if they are motivated by ______________ and respond in ______________ ways to changing circumstances.
8. Economists believe that it is ______________ for people to anticipate the likely future consequences of their behavior.
9. Actions have ______________.
10. Economic ______________ are statements or propositions used to ______________ and ______________ patterns of human economic behavior.
11. Because of the complexity of human behavior, economists must ______________ to focus on the most important components of a particular problem.
12. A ______________ in economic theory is a testable prediction about how people will behave or react to a change in economic circumstances.
13. ______________ analysis is the use of data to test a hypothesis.
14. In order to isolate the effects of one variable on another, we use the ______________ assumption.
15. When two events usually occur together, it is called ______________.
16. When one event brings on another event, it is called ______________.
17. The ____________________ is the incorrect view that what is true for an individual is always true for the group.
18. The objective, value-free approach to economics, utilizing the scientific method, is called ______________ analysis.
19. ______________ analysis involves judgments about what should be or what ought to happen.
20. "A tax increase will lead to a lower rate of inflation" is a ______________ economic statement.

True or False

1. Choices are costly because we must give up other opportunities that we value.
2. When our limited wants exceed our unlimited resources, we face scarcity.
3. If we valued leisure more highly, the opportunity cost of working would be lower.

4. Economics is a social science because it is concerned with reaching generalizations about human behavior.

5. Microeconomics would deal with the analysis of a small individual firm, while macroeconomics would deal with very large global firms.

6. Self-interest cannot include benevolence.

7. According to the National Council of Economic Education, most adults tested in the United States performed well on economic literacy.

8. Rationality implies that someone with a suspended driver's license would not drive.

9. For a person to be rational implies that he or she always makes the right choice.

10. Economic theories do not abstract from very many particular details of situations so they can better focus on every aspect of the behavior to be explained.

11. Determining whether an economic hypothesis is acceptable is more difficult than is the case in the natural or physical sciences in that, unlike a chemist in a chemistry lab, economists cannot control all the other variables that might influence human behavior.

12. A positive statement must be both testable and true.

13. Normative analysis involves subjective, non-testable statements.

14. The majority of disagreements in economics stem from normative issues.

15. A hypothesis is a normative statement.

Multiple Choice

1. If a good is scarce,
   a. it only needs to be limited.
   b. it is not possible to produce any more of the good.
   c. it is desirable but limited.
   d. there will always be a shortage of the good at the current price.

2. Which of the following is true of resources?
   a. Their availability is unlimited.
   b. They are the inputs used to produce goods and services.
   c. Increasing the amount of resources available could eliminate scarcity.
   d. Both b and c.

3. If scarcity were not a fact,
   a. people could have all the goods and services they wanted for free.
   b. it would no longer be necessary to make choices.
   c. poverty, defined as the lack of a minimum level of consumption, would also be eliminated.
   d. all of the above would be true.

4. What do economists mean when they state that a good is scarce?
   a. There is a shortage of the good at the current price.
   b. It is impossible to expand the availability of the good.
   c. People will want to buy more of the good regardless of price.
   d. Our wants exceed our limited resources.

5. Economics is concerned with
   a. the choices people must make because resources are scarce.
   b. human decision makers and the factors that influence their choices.
   c. the allocation of limited resources to satisfy virtually unlimited desires.
   d. all of the above.

6. Scarcity would cease to exist as an economic problem if
   a. we learned to cooperate and not compete with each other.
   b. there were new discoveries of an abundance of natural resources.
   c. output per worker increased.
   d. none of the above.

7. Which of the following would *not* reflect self-interested behavior?
   a. worker pursuing a higher paying job and better working conditions
   b. consumer seeking a higher level of satisfaction with her current income
   c. Trying to help others more because the cost of doing so is higher
   d. Mother Teresa using her Nobel Prize money to care for the poor
   e. none of the above

8. If people are self-interested,
   a. they will always choose work over leisure.
   b. they will never choose work over leisure.
   c. as their preferences for leisure time increase, they are likely to work more.
   d. as the wages they are offered increase, they are likely to work more.
   e. both c and d are true.

9. When economists assume that people act rationally, it means they:
   a. always make decisions based on complete and accurate information.
   b. make decisions that will not be regretted later.
   c. make decisions based on what they believe is best for themselves using available information.
   d. make decisions based solely on what is best for society.
   e. commit no errors in judgment.

10. "As a rational person, you would expect individuals to *always* avoid actions that are illegal."
    a. This is a true statement because most people don't want to suffer the penalties associated with criminal behavior.
    b. This is a true statement because most individuals are good citizens and prefer not to commit crimes.
    c. This is a false statement because it is expected that individuals will consider the consequences of their actions and that some will choose to commit illegal acts anyway.
    d. This is a false statement because only people with certain genetic predispositions are likely to commit crimes.

11. When we look at a particular segment of the economy, such as a given industry, we are studying
    a. macroeconomics.
    b. microeconomics.
    c. normative economics.
    d. positive economics.

12. Which of the following is most likely a topic of discussion in macroeconomics?
   a. an increase in the price of a pizza
   b. a decrease in the production of VCRs by a consumer electronics company
   c. an increase in the wage rate paid to automobile workers
   d. a decrease in the unemployment rate
   e. the entry of new firms into the software industry

13. An economic theory
   a. should be as detailed as possible in order to model the complexity of an economy.
   b. is an abstraction from reality.
   c. attempts to explain but not predict.
   d. is unrealistic and therefore of dubious usefulness in explaining what occurs in a complex economy.

14. Economists use theories to
   a. abstract from the complexities of the world.
   b. understand economic behavior.
   c. explain and help predict human behavior.
   d. do all of the above.
   e. do none of the above.

15. The importance of the *ceteris paribus* assumption is that it
   a. allows one to separate normative economic issues from positive economic ones.
   b. allows one to generalize from the whole to the individual.
   c. allows one to analyze the relationship between two variables apart from the influence of other variables.
   d. allows one to hold all variables constant so the economy can be carefully observed in a suspended state.

16. Which of the following statements can explain why correlation between Event A and Event B may not imply causality from A to B?
   a. The observed correlation may be coincidental.
   b. There may be a third variable that is responsible for causing both events.
   c. Causality may run from Event B to Event A instead of in the opposite direction.
   d. All of the above can explain why the correlation may not imply causality.

17. Ten-year-old Tommy observes that people who play football are larger than average and tells his mom that he's going to play football because it will make him big and strong. Tommy is:
   a. committing the fallacy of composition.
   b. violating the *ceteris paribus* assumption.
   c. mistaking correlation for causation.
   d. committing the fallacy of decomposition.

18. Which of the following correlations is likely to involve primarily one variable causing the other, rather than a third variable causing them both?
   a. The amount of time a team's third string plays in the game tends to be greater, the larger the team's margin of victory.
   b. Higher ice cream sales and higher crime rates both tend to increase at the same time.
   c. A lower price of a particular good and a higher quantity purchased tend to occur at the same time.
   d. The likelihood of rain tends to be greater after you have washed your car.

19. Which of the following is a statement of positive analysis?
   a. New tax laws are needed to help the poor.
   b. Teenage unemployment should be reduced.
   c. We should increase Social Security payments to the elderly.
   d. An increase in tax rates will reduce unemployment.
   e. It is only fair that firms protected from competition by government-granted monopolies pay higher corporate taxes.

20. "Mandating longer sentences for any criminal's third arrest will lead to a reduction in crime. That is the way it ought to be, as such people are a menace to society." This quotation
   a. contains positive statements only.
   b. contains normative statements only.
   c. contains both normative and positive statements.
   d. contains neither normative nor positive statements.

Problems

1. Do any of the following statements involve fallacies? If so, which ones do they involve?
   a. Because sitting in the back of classrooms is correlated with getting lower grades in the class, students should always sit closer to the front of the classroom.
   b. Historically, the stock market rises in years the NFC team wins the Super Bowl and falls when the AFC wins the Super Bowl; I am rooting for the NFC team to win for the sake of my investment portfolio.
   c. When a basketball team spends more to get better players, it is more successful, which proves that all the teams should spend more to get better players.
   d. Gasoline prices were higher last year than in 1970, yet people purchased more gas, which contradicts the law of demand.
   e. An increase in the amount of money I have will make me better off, but an increase in the supply of money in the economy will not make Americans as a group better off.

2. Are the following statements normative or positive, or do they contain both normative and positive statements?
   a. A higher income-tax rate would generate increased tax revenues. Those extra revenues should be used to give more government aid to the poor.
   b. The study of physics is more valuable than the study of sociology, but both should be studied by all college students.
   c. An increase in the price of corn will decrease the amount of corn purchased. However, it will increase the amount of wheat purchased.
   d. A decrease in the price of butter will increase the amount of butter purchased, but that would be bad because it would increase Americans' cholesterol levels.
   e. The birth rate is reduced as economies urbanize, but that also leads to a decreased average age of developing countries' populations.

3. Are the following topics ones that would be covered in microeconomics or macroeconomics?
   a. the effects of an increase in the supply of lumber on the home-building industry
   b. changes in the national unemployment rate
   c. the effect of interest rates on the machine-tool industry
   d. the effect of interest rates on the demand for investment goods in society
   e. the way a firm maximizes profits

chapter 2

The Economic Way of Thinking

2.1 SCARCITY
Can all of our wants be satisfied in a world of limited resources?

2.2 OPPORTUNITY COST
Can we have our cake and eat it too?

2.3 MARGINAL THINKING
What is the rule of rational choice?

2.4 INCENTIVES MATTER
Do people respond to incentives?

2.5 SPECIALIZATION AND TRADE
How can specialization and trade lead to greater wealth?

2.6 MARKET PRICES COORDINATE ECONOMIC ACTIVITY
How do the market economy and the price system coordinate economic activity?

section 2.1

Scarcity

- What are goods and services?
- What are tangible and intangible goods?
- What are economic goods?

KNOW A FEW PRINCIPLES WELL

Most of economics is really knowing certain principles well and knowing when and how to apply them. In this chapter, some important tools are presented that will help you understand the economic way of thinking. These few basic ideas will repeatedly occur throughout the text. If you develop a good understanding of these principles and master the problem-solving skills inherent in them, they will serve you well for the rest of your life.

SCARCITY

scarcity
exists when human wants (material and non-material) exceed available resources

Economics is concerned primarily with **scarcity**—how we satisfy our unlimited wants in a world of limited resources. We may want more "essential" items like food, clothing, schooling, and health care. We may want many other items, like vacations, cars, computers, and concert tickets. We may want more friendship, love, knowledge, and so on. We also may have many goals—perhaps an A in this class, a college education, and a great job. Unfortunately, people are not able to fulfill all of their wants—material desires and nonmaterial desires. And as long as human wants exceed available resources, scarcity will exist.

labor
the physical and human effort used in the production of goods and services

land
the natural resources used in the production of goods and services

capital
the equipment and structures used to produce goods and services

human capital
the productive knowledge and skill people receive from education and on-the-job training

entrepreneurship
the process of combining labor, land, and capital together to produce goods and services

SCARCITY AND RESOURCES

The scarce resources used in the production of goods and services can be grouped into four categories: labor, land, capital, and entrepreneurship.

Labor is the total of both physical and mental effort expended by people in the production of goods and services.

Land includes the "gifts of nature" or the natural resources used in the production of goods and services. Trees, animals, water, minerals and so on are all considered to be "land" for our purposes, along with the physical space normally thought of as land.

Capital is the equipment and structures used to produce goods and services. Office buildings, tools, machines, and factories are all considered capital goods. When we invest in factories, machines, research and development, or education, we increase the potential to create more goods and services in the future. Capital also includes **human capital,** the productive knowledge and skill people receive from education and on-the-job training.

Entrepreneurship is the process of combining labor, land, and capital together to produce goods and services. Entrepreneurs make the tough and risky decisions about what and how to produce goods and services. Entrepreneurs are always looking for new ways to improve production techniques or to create new products. They are lured by the chance to make a profit. It is this opportunity to make a profit that leads entrepreneurs to take risks.

However, entrepreneurs are not necessarily a Bill Gates (Microsoft), a Larry Ellison (Oracle), or a Henry Ford (Ford Motor Company). In some sense, we are all entrepreneurs when we try new products or when we find better ways to manage our households or our study time. Rather than money, then, our profits might take the form of greater enjoyment, additional time for recreation, or better grades.

GOODS AND SERVICES

Goods are those items that we value or desire. Goods tend to be tangible—objects that can be seen, held, heard, tasted, or smelled. But there are also goods that we cannot reach out and touch, called intangible goods. **Intangible goods** include fairness for all, friendship, knowledge, security, and health. While some intangible goods have no price tags, a *USA Today* poll showed that the wealthy would be willing to pay top dollar, if they could, for a place in heaven ($640,000), true love ($487,000), and a great intellect ($407,000).

Services are intangible acts for which people are willing to pay, such as legal services, medical services, hospital care. Services are intangible because they are less overtly visible, but they are certainly no less valuable than goods.

All goods and services, whether tangible or intangible, are produced from scarce resources and can be subjected to economic analysis. Scarce goods created from scarce resources are called **economic goods.** If there are not enough economic goods for all of us, we will have to compete for those scarce goods. That is, scarcity ultimately leads to competition for the available goods and services, a subject we will return to often in the text.

goods
items we value or desire

intangible goods
goods that we cannot reach out and touch, like friendship and knowledge

service
an intangible act that people want, like treatment from a doctor or a dentist

economic good
a scarce good—a good that is desirable but limited

ARE THOSE WHO WANT MORE GREEDY?

We all want more tangible and intangible goods and services. In economics, we assume that more goods lead to greater satisfaction. However, because economics assumes that we want more goods, it does not mean that economics also presumes that we are selfish and greedy. Many people give much of their income and time to charitable or religious organizations. The way people allocate their income and time reveals their preferences for a good. The fact that people are willing to give up their money and time for what they believe to be important causes reveals quite conclusively that charitable endeavors are a desirable good. Clearly, then, many desires, like building new friendships or helping charities, can hardly be defined as selfish, yet these are desires that many people share. In other words, "self-interest" is not the same as "selfishness" or "greed."

EVERYONE FACES SCARCITY

We all face scarcity because we cannot have all of the goods and services that we desire. However, because we all have different wants and desires, scarcity affects everyone differently. For example, a child in a developing country may face a scarcity of food and clean drinking water, while a rich person may face a scarcity of garage space for his growing antique car collection. Likewise, a harried middle-class working mother may find time for exercise particularly scarce, while a pharmaceutical company may be concerned with the scarcity of the natural resources it uses in its production process. While its effects vary, no one can escape scarcity.

EVEN THE RICH FACE SCARCITY

We often hear it said of rich people that "He has everything" or "She can buy anything she wants." Actually, even the richest person must live with scarcity and must, at some point, choose one want or desire over another, and, of course, we all have only 24 hours in a day! The

Providing charity is a desire or want—many people want to help others. In this ad, we see a picture of a child who is for a brief moment able to forget about his life-threatening illness.

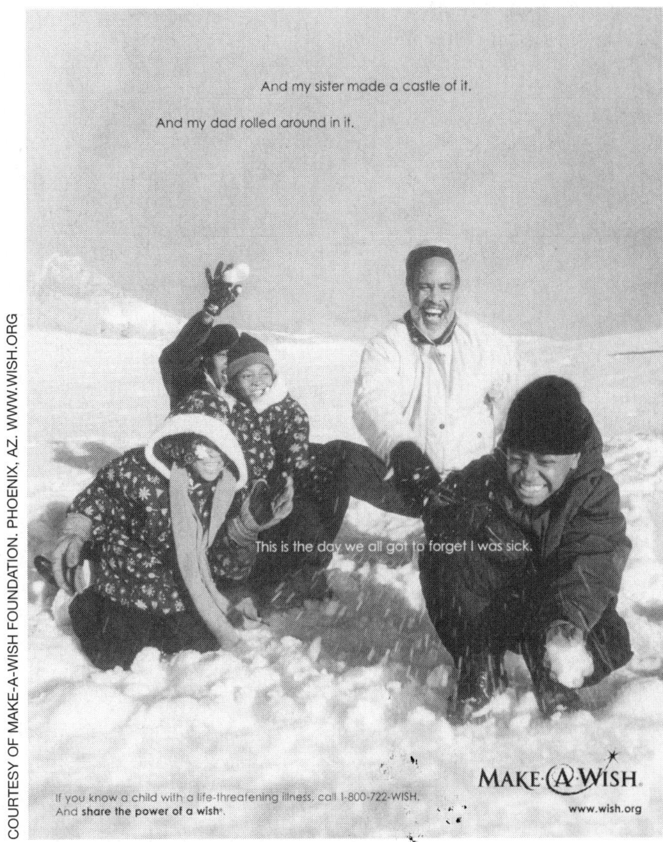

COURTESY OF MAKE-A-WISH FOUNDATION, PHOENIX, AZ. WWW.WISH.ORG

© REUTERS NEWMEDIA/CORBIS

Not even millionaire lottery winners can escape scarcity. The problem is that as we get more affluent, we learn of new luxuries to provide us with satisfaction. Even a lottery winner may become less content as the excitement wears off and begin looking for new satisfactions.

problem is that as we get more affluent, we learn of new luxuries to provide us with satisfaction. Wealth, then, creates a new set of wants to be satisfied. There is no evidence that people would not find a valuable use for additional income, no matter how rich they become. Even the wealthy individual who decides to donate all of her money to charity faces the constraints of scarcity. If she had greater resources, she could do still more for others. As Johnny Carson (Jay Leno's *Tonight Show* predecessor) reportedly once said, "Having more money does not mean having fewer problems; the problems just have more zeros after the dollar sign."

SCARCITY AND GROWING EXPECTATIONS

It is probably clear by now that scarcity never has and never will be eradicated. The same creativity that permits new methods to produce goods and services in greater quantities also reveals new wants. Fashions are always changing. Clothes and shoes that are "in" one year will surely be "out" the next. New wants quickly replace old ones. Thus, a small, black-and-white television set, which provided so much enjoyment for viewers raised on radio, most people now consider an inadequate form of entertainment. Two generations ago, only the well-to-do had telephones; today telephones are provided to some welfare recipients on the grounds that they are a "necessity." It is also possible, while people seem to be happier when they can buy more goods and services, over a period of time a rising quantity of goods and services may not increase human happiness. Why? There are several possibilities, but it is very possible that our wants grow as fast, if not faster, than our ability to meet those wants, so we still feel scarcity as much or more than we did before.

Section Check

1. We all have many wants and goals.
2. Scarcity exists when our wants exceed the available resources.
3. Scarce resources can be categorized as: land (all of our natural resources), labor (the physical and mental efforts expended in the production of goods and services), capital (the equipment and structures used to produce goods and services, and the productive knowledge and skill people receive from education and on-the-job traning) and entrepreneurship (the process of combining land, labor, and capital into production of goods and services).
4. Goods and services are things that we value.
5. Goods can be tangible (physical) or intangible (love, compassion, and intelligence).
6. Economic goods are goods created from limited resources.
7. We all face scarcity—rich and poor alike.
8. Our wants grow over time, so scarcity will never be eliminated.

---

1. What must be true for something to be an economic good?
2. Does wanting more tangible and intangible goods and services make us selfish?
3. Why does scarcity affect everyone?
4. How and why does scarcity affect each of us differently?
5. Why do you think economists often refer to training that increases the quality of workers' skills as "adding to human capital"?
6. What are some ways students act as entrepreneurs as they seek higher grades?
7. Why might sunshine be scarce in Seattle but not in Tucson?
8. Why can't a country become so technologically advanced that its citizens won't have to choose?

section 2.2

Opportunity Cost

- Why do we have to make choices?
- What do we give up when we have to choose?
- Why are "free" lunches not free?

SCARCITY AND CHOICES

We may want nice homes, two luxury cars in every garage, wholesome and good tasting food, a personal trainer, and a therapist, all enjoyed in a pristine environment with zero pollution. If we had unlimited resources, and thus an ability to produce all of the goods and services anyone wanted, we would not have to choose among those desires. If we did not have to make meaningful economic choices, the study of economics would not be necessary. The essence of economics is to understand fully the implications that scarcity has for wise decision making. This suggests another way to define economics: *Economics is the study of the choices we make among our many wants and desires.*

TO CHOOSE IS TO LOSE

We are all faced with scarcity and, as a consequence, we must make choices. Because none of us can "afford" to buy everything we want, each time we do decide to buy one good or service, we reduce our ability to buy other things we would also like to have. If you buy a new car this year, you may not be able to afford your next best choice—the vacation you've been planning. You must choose. The cost of the car to you is the value of the vacation that must be forgone. The highest or best forgone opportunity resulting from a decision is called the **opportunity cost.** For example, time spent running costs time that could have been spent doing something else that is valuable—perhaps spending time with friends or studying for an upcoming exam. Another way to put this is that "to choose is to lose" or "an opportunity cost is an opportunity lost." To get more of anything that is desirable, you must accept less of something else that you also value.

opportunity cost
the value of the best forgone alternative that was not chosen

THE OPPORTUNITY COST OF GOING TO COLLEGE OR HAVING A CHILD

The average person often does not correctly consider opportunity costs when thinking about costs. For example, the cost of going to college is not just the direct costs of tuition and books. It also includes the opportunity cost of your time, which for many people is the greatest part of their costs. Specifically, the time spent going to school is time that could have been spent on a job earning, say, $25,000 a year. And how often do people consider the cost of raising a child to the age of 18? There are the obvious costs: food, visits to the doctor, clothes, piano lessons, time spent at soccer practices, and so on. According to the Department of Agriculture, raising a child to the age of 18 costs $250,000 (on average). But there are also other substantial opportunity costs incurred in rearing a child. Consider the opportunity cost if one parent chooses to give up his or her job to stay at home. Then, the time spent in child rearing is time that could have been used making money and pursuing a career.

IS THAT REALLY A FREE LUNCH, A FREEWAY, OR A FREE BEACH?

The expression *"there's no such thing as a free lunch"* clarifies the relationship between scarcity and opportunity cost. Suppose the school cafeteria is offering "free" lunches today. While the lunch is free to you, is it really free from society's perspective? The answer is no, because some of society's scarce resources will have been used in the preparation of the lunch. The issue is whether the resources that went into creating that lunch could have been used to produce something else of value. Clearly, the scarce resources that went into the production of the lunch like the labor and materials (food-service workers, lettuce, meat, plows, tractors, fertilizer, and so forth) could have been used in other ways. They had an opportunity cost, and thus were not free. Whenever you hear the word "free"—freeways, free beaches, free libraries, free admission, and so on—an alarm should go off in your head. Very few things are free in the sense that they use none of society's scarce resources. So what does a free lunch really mean? It is, technically speaking, a "subsidized" lunch—a lunch using society's scarce resources, but one for which you personally do not have to pay.

Section Check

1. Scarcity means we all have to make choices.
2. When we are forced to choose, we give up the next highest-valued alternative.
3. Opportunity cost is what you give up when you make a choice.

---

1. Would we still have to make choices even if we had unlimited resources? Why or why not ?
2. What is given up when we make a choice?
3. What do we mean by opportunity cost?
4. Why is there no such thing as a free lunch?
5. Why was the opportunity cost of staying in college higher for Tiger Woods than for most undergraduates?
6. Why is the opportunity cost of the time spent getting an MBA typically lower for a 22-year-old straight out of college than for a 45-year-old experienced manager?

section 2.3

Marginal Thinking

- What do we mean by marginal thinking?
- What is the rule of rational choice?
- Why do we use the word "expected" with marginal benefits and costs?

CHOICES ARE PRIMARILY MARGINAL—NOT ALL OR NOTHING

Most choices involve how *much* of something to do, rather than whether or not to do something. It is not *whether* you eat, but *how much* you eat. Hopefully, the question is not *whether* to study this semester but instead *how much* to study this semester. For example, "If I studied a little more, I might be able to improve my grade," or "If I had a little better concentration when I was studying, I could improve my grade." This is what economists call **marginal thinking** because the focus is on the additional, or marginal, choices. Marginal choices involve the effects of adding or subtracting from the current situation. In short, it is the small (or large) incremental changes to a plan of action.

marginal thinking *focusing on the additional, or marginal, choices; marginal choices involve the effects of adding or subtracting from the current situation, the small (or large) incremental changes to a plan of action*

Always watch out for the difference between average and marginal costs. Suppose an airline had 10 unoccupied seats on a flight from Los Angeles to New York and the average cost was $400 per seat (the total cost divided by the number of seats—$100,000/250). If there are 10 people on standby, each willing to pay $300, should the airline sell them the tickets? Yes! The unoccupied seats earn nothing for the airline. What are the additional (marginal) costs of a few more passengers? The marginal costs are minimal—slight wear and tear on the airplane, handling some extra baggage, and 10 extra in-flight meals. In this case, thinking at the margin can increase total profits, even if it means selling at less than the average cost of production.

Another good example of marginal thinking is auctions. Prices are bid up marginally as the auctioneer calls out one price after another. When a bidder views the new price (the marginal cost) to be greater than the value she places on the good (the marginal benefit), she withdraws from further bidding.

In trying to make themselves better off, people alter their behavior if the expected marginal benefits from doing so outweigh the expected marginal costs—this is the **rule of rational choice.** The term *expected* is used with marginal benefits and costs because the world is uncertain in many important respects, so the actual result of changing behavior may not always make people better off—but on average it will. However, as a matter of rationality, people are assumed to engage only in behavior that they think ahead of time will make them better off. That is, individuals will only pursue an activity if expected marginal benefits are greater than the expected marginal costs, or $E(MB) > E(MC)$. This fairly unrestrictive and realistic view of individuals seeking self-betterment can be used to analyze a variety of social phenomena.

rule of rational choice *individuals will pursue an activity if the expected marginal benefits are greater than the expected marginal costs*

Zero Pollution Would Be Too Costly

Let's use the concept of marginal thinking to evaluate pollution levels. We all know the benefits of a cleaner environment, but what would we have to give up—that is, what marginal costs would we have to incur—in order to achieve zero pollution? A lot! You could not drive a car, fly in a plane, or even ride bikes, especially if everybody else was riding bikes too (because congestion is a form of pollution). How would you get to school or work, or go to the movies or the grocery store? Everyone would have to grow their own food because transporting, storing, and producing food uses machinery and equipment that pollute. And even growing your own food would be a problem because many plants emit natural pollutants. We could go on and on. The point is *not* that we shouldn't be concerned about the environment; rather, we have to weigh the expected marginal benefits of a cleaner environment against the expected marginal costs of a cleaner environment. This is not to say the environment should not be cleaner, only that zero pollution levels would be far too costly in terms of what we would have to give up.

What would you be willing to give up to eliminate the rush-hour congestion you face? One study estimates that gridlock costs Americans roughly the equivalent of $78 billion a year in lost wages and wasted fuel. According to the Texas Transportation Institute, the number of hours drivers wasted each year sitting in traffic in the most congested U.S. cities are: Los Angeles, 56; Seattle and Atlanta, 53; Houston, 50; Washington, D.C. and Dallas, 46; San Francisco and Boston, 42; Detroit, 41; and New York and Chicago, 34.

Optimal (Best) Levels of Safety

Just as we can have optimal (or best) levels of pollution that are greater than zero, it is also true for crime and safety. Take crime. What would it cost society to have zero crime? It would be prohibitively costly to divert a tremendous amount of our valuable resources towards the total elimination of crime. In fact, it would be impossible to eliminate crime totally. But it would also be costly to reduce crime significantly. Since lower crime rates are costly, society must decide how much it is willing to give up: The additional resources for crime prevention can only come from limited resources, which could be used to produce something else possibly valued even more.

The same is true for safer products. Nobody wants defective tires on their cars, or cars that are unsafe and roll over at low speeds. However, there are optimal amounts of safety that are greater than zero too. The issue is not safe versus unsafe products but rather *how much* safety do consumers want. It is not risk versus no-risk but rather *how much* risk are we willing to take? Additional safety can only come at higher costs. To make all products perfectly safe would be impossible, so we must weigh the benefits and costs of safer products. In fact, according to one study by Sam Peltzman, a University of Chicago economist, additional safety regulations in cars (mandatory safety belts, padded dashboards) in the late 1960s may have had little impact on highway fatalities. Peltzman found that making cars safer led to more reckless driving and more accidents. While the safety regulations did result in fewer deaths per automobile accident, the total number of deaths remained unchanged because there were more accidents.

Reckless driving has benefits—getting somewhere more quickly—but it also has costs—possibly causing an accident or even a fatality. Rational people will compare the marginal benefits and marginal costs of safer driving and make the choices that they believe will get them to their destination safely. We would expect that even thrill-seekers would slow down if there were higher fines and/or increased law enforcement. It would change the benefit–cost equation for reckless driving (as would bad brakes, bald tires, and poor visibility). On the other hand, compulsory seat belts and airbags might cause motorists to drive more recklessly.

Section Check

1. Economists are usually interested in the effects of additional, or marginal, changes in a given situation.
2. People try to make themselves better off.
3. People make decisions based on what they expect to happen.
4. The rule of rational choice states that individuals will pursue an activity if they expect the marginal benefits to be greater than the marginal costs, or $E(MB) > E(MC)$.
5. The optimal (best) levels of pollution, crime, and safety are greater than zero.

---

1. What are marginal choices? Why does economics focus on them?
2. What is the rule of rational choice?
3. Why does rational choice involve expectations?
4. Why do students often stop taking lecture notes when a professor announces that the next few minutes of material will not be on any future test or assignment?
5. If you decide to speed to get to a doctor's appointment and then get into an accident as a result, does your decision to speed invalidate the rule of rational choice? Why or why not?
6. If pedestrians felt far safer using crosswalks to cross the street, how could adding crosswalks increase the number of pedestrian accidents?
7. Imagine driving a car with daggers sticking out of the steering wheel—pointing directly at your chest. Why would you drive more safely?

section 2.4

Incentives Matter

- Can we predict how people will respond to changes in incentives?
- What are positive incentives?
- What are negative incentives?

PEOPLE RESPOND TO INCENTIVES

In acting rationally, people are responding to incentives. That is, they are reacting to the changes in expected marginal benefits and expected marginal costs. In fact, much of human behavior can be explained and predicted as a response to incentives. Consider the economic view of crime. Why do criminals engage in their "occupation"? Presumably because the "job," even with its risks, is preferred to alternative forms of employment. For criminals, the benefits of their actions are higher and/or the opportunity costs of them are lower than is the case for non-criminals. In some cases, criminals cannot get a legitimate job at a wage they would find acceptable, so the cost of crime in terms of other income forgone may be quite low. At other times, the likelihood of being caught is small, so the expected cost is negligible. Also, for some, the moral cost of a crime is low, while for others it is high. The benefits, in terms of wealth gained, are clear. If the expected gains or benefits from committing a crime outweigh the expected costs, the activity is pursued. For most policy purposes, the primary concern is not what causes the level of crime to be what it is but, rather, what causes the level of crime to change. The changes in the crime rate in recent decades can be largely explained in terms of such a benefit–cost framework. If the benefits of crime rise, say, in the form of larger real "hauls," and/or if the costs fall due to a reduced likelihood of being caught or of being imprisoned if caught, then economists would expect the amount of crime to rise. Likewise, economists would expect the crime rate to fall in response to increased police enforcement, stiffer punishments, or an increase in the employment rate. Whether this analysis tells the complete story is debatable, but the use of the economic framework in thinking about the problem provides valuable insight.

APPLICATION

DO INCENTIVES MATTER?

Q: The penalty for drug trafficking in Singapore is death. Do you think there would be more drug traffickers in Singapore if the mandatory sentence was five years with parole for good behavior?

A: Singapore's tough drug-trafficking penalty would clearly impact the cost–benefit ratios of would-be smugglers. Lighter sentences would probably result in more drug smuggling, because the overall cost of breaking the law would be reduced. Go to the Sexton Web page and click on "Singapore's Strict Laws and Penalties" where you'll see visitors are warned about the penalties for a variety of offenses that might be considered minor in the United States, "including jaywalking, littering and spitting, as well as the importation and sale of chewing gum. Singapore imposes a mandatory caning sentence on males for vandalism offenses. Caning may also be imposed for immigration violations and other offenses. Penalties for possession, use, or trafficking in illegal drugs are strict, and convicted offenders can expect jail sentences and fines. Singapore has a mandatory death penalty for many narcotics offenses."

In The **NEWS**

CHEATING IN SCHOOL: FOCUSING ON INTEGRITY

Nationwide, most forms of cheating remain at or near record levels.

- Men admit to more cheating than women; fraternity and sorority members more than nonmembers; students with lower grade-point averages say they cheat more than those with higher grade-point averages.
- Students pursuing degrees in journalism and communications, business and engineering reported cheating more than those in the sciences, social sciences or humanities.
- Only 9.7 percent of students reported "plagiarizing a paper in any way using the Internet," suggesting that such cheating is not as rampant as some fear.

SOURCE: "Cheating: Focusing on Integrity," *LA Times*, February 15, 2000, p. A-1.

CONSIDER THIS:
Can we predictably alter human behavior by changing the incentive structure—the expected marginal benefits and/or the expected marginal costs? For example, what do you think would happen to the amount of cheating if more effective ways of catching cheaters were implemented or if much harsher penalties were implemented? Honor codes also seem to deter cheating. In each of these situations, we have changed the cost–benefit ratio and would expect behavior to change in predictable directions.

POSITIVE AND NEGATIVE INCENTIVES

positive incentives
incentives that either reduce costs or increase benefits resulting in an increase in the activity or behavior

negative incentives
incentives that either increase costs or reduce benefits resulting in a decrease in the activity or behavior

Almost all of economics can be reduced to incentive [*E(MB)* versus *E(MC)*] stories, where consumers and producers are driven by incentives that affect expected costs or benefits. Prices, wages, profits, taxes, and subsidies are all examples of economic incentives. Incentives can be classified into two types: positive and negative. **Positive incentives** are those that either increase benefits or reduce costs and thus result in an increased level of the related activity or behavior. **Negative incentives,** on the other hand, either reduce benefits or increase costs, resulting in a decreased level of the related activity or behavior. For example, a tax on cars that emit lots of pollution (an increase in costs) would be a negative incentive that would lead to a reduction in emitted pollution. On the other hand, a subsidy (the opposite of a tax) to hybrid cars—part electric, part internal combustion—would be a positive incentive that would encourage greater production and

© AP PHOTO/HO

A subsidy on hybrid electric vehicles (HEVs) would be a positive incentive that would encourage greater production and consumption of these vehicles. A wide variety of incentives are offered at the federal, state and local levels to encourage the expanded use of Alternative Fuel Vehicles (AFVs). The claim is that the new hybrids will cut emissions pollutants by a third. Honda's Insight is expected to go 700 miles on a single tank of gas; the Toyota Prius is expected to go about 450 miles.

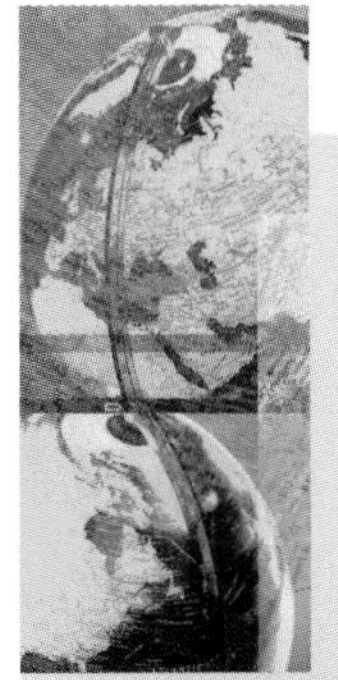

Global WATCH

DRUNK DRIVING DRAWS GLOBAL WRATH

—PETER GRIER

Alcohol and automobiles are a combustible combination all over the world. Cultural attitudes towards drinking and driving do differ from nation to nation. Penalties vary widely, too: In Bulgaria and El Salvador, driving under the influence can bring the death penalty. In Turkey, offenders may be simply driven 10 miles from town, dumped, and forced to walk home under police escort.

Americans may think that Europe has a more relaxed attitude toward drinking and driving than does the United States. In general, that is not the case. Thirty-one U.S. states set the level at which a driver is declared legally drunk at 0.10 percent alcohol in his or her bloodstream. Others have a lower limit of 0.08. However, this may soon change; if states do not adopt legal limits of 0.08 percent by October 1, 2003, they will face reductions in highway construction funds.

European nations tend to have lower blood-alcohol limits. Countries that set the bar at 0.08 include Austria, Canada, Denmark, Great Britain, Ireland, and Spain. France's legal limit is 0.05 (0.08 percent could mean time in jail). Other nations with this relatively low limit include Belgium, Finland, Greece, the Netherlands, and Norway. Sweden is at 0.02 percent. And while research is sketchy, it appears fewer drivers get behind the wheel drunk in Europe than do in the United States. One study conducted in the late 1980s indicated that about 8 percent of U.S. drivers on the road at night had blood-alcohol levels of 0.05 or higher. The comparable number from France was 5 percent; for Britain, 3 percent; and for the Nordic countries, a remarkably low 1 percent.

SOURCE: "Drunk Driving Draws Global Wrath," *The Christian Science Monitor,* September 3, 1997. Reproduced with permission.

CONSIDER THIS:
The Nordic countries (Finland, Norway, and Sweden) all have lower legal blood-alcohol limits than the United States, and at least one study shows that lower blood-alcohol rates and tougher punishments are deterring many from drinking and driving. How many drunk drivers do you think are on the road in Bulgaria and El Salvador?

consumption of hybrid cars. Human behavior is influenced in predictable ways by such changes in economic incentives, and economists use this information to predict what will happen when the benefits and costs of any choice are changed. In short, economists study the incentives and consequences of particular actions.

Section Check

1. People respond to incentives in predictable ways.
2. A negative incentive increases costs or reduces benefits, thus discouraging consumption or production.
3. A positive incentive decreases costs or increases benefits, thus encouraging consumption or production.

---

1. What is the difference between positive incentives and negative incentives?
2. According to the rule of rational choice, would you do more or less of something if its expected marginal benefits increased? Why?
3. According to the rule of rational choice, would you do more or less of something if its expected marginal costs increased? Why?
4. How does the rule of rational choice imply that young children are typically more likely to misbehave at a supermarket checkout counter than at home?
5. Why do many parents refuse to let their children have dessert before they eat the rest of their dinner?

section 2.5

Specialization and Trade

- What is the relationship between opportunity cost and specialization?
- What are the advantages of specialization in production?

WHY DO PEOPLE SPECIALIZE?

specializing
concentrating in the production of one, or a few, goods

comparative advantage
producing a good or service at a lower opportunity cost than other producers

As you look around, you can see that people specialize in what they produce. They tend to dedicate their resources to one primary activity, whether it be child-rearing, driving a cab, or making bagels. Why is this? The answer, short and simple, is opportunity costs. By concentrating their energies on only one, or a few activities, individuals are **specializing.** This allows them to make the best use of (and thus gain the most benefit from) their limited resources. A person, a region, or a country can gain by specializing in the production of the good in which they have a comparative advantage. That is, if they can produce a good or service at a lower opportunity cost than others, we say that they have a **comparative advantage** in the production of that good or service.

Michael Jordan, arguably the greatest basketball player of all time, left basketball to play baseball in 1993. According to Steve Wulf, a writer for *Sports Illustrated,* "try as he might, Michael Jordan has found baseball beyond his grasp." Michael Jordan discovered the hard way that he had a comparative advantage in basketball. He returned to basketball the following year and the rest is history.

WE ALL SPECIALIZE

We all specialize to some extent and rely on others to produce most of the goods and services we want. The work that we choose to do reflects our specialization. For example, we may specialize in selling or fixing automobiles. The wages from that work can then be used to buy goods from a farmer who has chosen to specialize in the production of food.

APPLICATION

COMPARATIVE ADVANTAGE

Q: Should an attorney who types 100 words per minute hire an administrative assistant to type her legal documents, even though he can only type 50 words per minute? If the attorney does the job, she can do it in five hours; if the administrative assistant does the job, it takes him ten hours. The attorney makes $100 an hour, and the administrative assistant earns $10 an hour. Which one has the comparative advantage (the lowest opportunity cost) in typing documents?

A: If the attorney types her own documents, it will cost $500 ($100 per hour × 5 hours). If she has the administrative assistant type her documents, it will cost $100 ($10 per hour × 10 hours). Clearly, then, the lawyer should hire the administrative assistant to type her documents, because the administrative assistant has the comparative advantage (lowest opportunity cost) in this case, despite being half as good in absolute terms.

Likewise, the farmer can use the money earned from selling his produce to get his tractor fixed by someone who specializes in that activity.

Specialization is evident not only among individuals but among regions and countries as well. In fact, the story of the economic development of the United States and the rest of the world involves specialization. Within the United States, the Midwest with its wheat, the coastal waters of the Northeast with its fishing fleets, and the Northwest with its timber are each examples of regional specialization.

THE ADVANTAGES OF SPECIALIZATION

In a small business, employees may perform a wide variety of tasks—from hiring to word processing to marketing. As the size of the company increases, each employee can perform a more specialized job, with a consequent increase in output per worker. The primary advantages of specialization are that employees acquire greater skill from repetition, they avoid wasted time in shifting from one task to another, and they do the types of work for which they are best suited, and it promotes the use of specialized equipment for specialized tasks.

The advantages of specialization are seen throughout the workplace. For example, in larger firms, specialists conduct personnel relations and accounting is in the hands of full-time accountants instead of someone with half a dozen other tasks. The owner of a small retail store selects the location for the store primarily through guesswork, placing it where she believes sales would be high or where an empty, low-rent building is available. In contrast, larger chains have store sites selected by experts who have experience in analyzing the factors that make different locations relatively more desirable, like traffic patterns, income levels, demographics, and so on.

SPECIALIZATION AND TRADE LEAD TO GREATER WEALTH AND PROSPERITY

Trade, or voluntary exchange, directly increases wealth by making both parties better off (or they wouldn't trade). It is the prospect of wealth-increasing exchange that leads to productive specialization. That is, trade increases wealth by allowing a person, a region, or a nation to specialize in those products that it produces at a lower opportunity cost and to trade for those products that others produce at a lower opportunity cost. For example, say the United States is better at producing wheat than Brazil, and Brazil is better at producing coffee than the United States. The United States and Brazil would each benefit if the United States produces wheat and trades some of it to Brazil for coffee. Coffee growers in the United States could grow coffee in expensive greenhouses, but it would result in higher coffee costs and prices, while leaving fewer resources available for employment in more productive jobs, such as wheat production. This is true for individuals, too. Imagine Tom had 10 pounds of tea and Katherine had 10 pounds of coffee. However, Tom preferred coffee to tea and Katherine preferred tea to coffee. So if Tom traded his tea to Katherine for her coffee, both parties would be better off. Trade simply reallocates existing goods, and voluntary exchange increases wealth by making both parties better off or they would not agree to trade.

Section Check

1. We all specialize.
2. Specialization is important for individuals, businesses, regions, and nations.
3. Specialization and trade increase wealth.
4. The person, region, or country that can produce a good or service at a lower opportunity cost than other producers has a comparative advantage in the production of that good or service.

---

1. Why do people specialize?
2. What do we mean by comparative advantage?
3. Why does the combination of specialization and trade make us better off?
4. If you can mow your lawn in half the time it takes your spouse or housemate to do it, do you have a comparative advantage in mowing the lawn?
5. If you have a current comparative advantage in doing the dishes, and you then became far more productive than before in completing yard chores, could that eliminate your comparative advantage? Why or why not?
6. Could a student who gets a C in one class but a D or worse in everything else have a comparative advantage in that class over someone who gets a B in that class but an A in everything else? Explain, using the concept of opportunity cost.

section 2.6 Market Prices Coordinate Economic Activity

- How does a market system allocate scarce resources?
- What are the important signals that market prices communicate?
- What are the effects of price controls and price supports?
- What are unintended consequences?
- What is a market failure?

HOW DOES THE MARKET SYSTEM WORK TO ALLOCATE RESOURCES?

In a world of scarcity, competition is inescapable, and one method of allocating resources among competing uses is the market system. The market system provides a way for millions of producers and consumers to allocate scarce resources. Buyers and sellers indicate their wants through their actions and inaction in the marketplace, and it is this collective "voice" that determines how resources are allocated. But how is this information communicated? Market prices serve as the language of the market system. By understanding what these market prices mean, you can get a better understanding of the vital function that the market system performs.

MARKET PRICES PROVIDE IMPORTANT INFORMATION

Market prices communicate important information to both buyers and sellers. These prices communicate information about the relative availability of products to buyers, and they provide sellers with critical information about the relative value that consumers place on those products. In effect, market prices provide a way for both buyers and sellers to communicate about the relative value of resources. This communication results in a shifting of resources from those uses that are less valued to those that are more valued. We will see how this works beginning in chapter 4.

The basis of market economy is the voluntary exchange and the price system that guide people's choices and produces solutions to the questions of what goods to produce and how to produce those goods and distribute them.

Take something as simple as the production of a pencil. Where did the wood come from? Perhaps, the Northwest or Georgia. The graphite may have come from the mines in Michigan and the rubber maybe from Malaysia. The paint, the glue, the metal piece that holds the eraser—who knows? The point is that market forces coordinated this activity among literally thousands of people, some of whom live in different countries and speak different languages. The market system brought these people together to make a pencil that sells for 25 cents at your bookstore. It all happened because the market system provided the incentive for people to pursue activities that benefit others. This same process produces millions of goods and services around the world from automobiles and computers to pencils and paper clips.

In countries that do not rely on the market system, there is no clear communication between buyers and sellers. In the former Soviet Union, where quality was virtually nonexistent, there were shortages of quality goods and surpluses of low-quality goods. For example, there were thousands of tractors without spare parts and millions of pairs of shoes that were left on shelves because the sizes did not match those of the population.

WHAT EFFECT DO PRICE CONTROLS HAVE ON THE MARKET SYSTEM?

Government policies called **price controls** sometimes force prices above or below what they would be in a market economy. Unfortunately, these controls often impose harm on the same people they are trying to help, in large part by short-circuiting the market's information transmission function. That is, price controls effectively strip the market price of its meaning for both buyers and sellers (which we will see in chapter 4). A sales tax will also distort price signals leading to a misallocation of resources (which we will see in chapter 6).

price controls
government mandated minimum or maximum prices

MARKET FAILURE

The market mechanism is a simple but effective and efficient general means of allocating resources among alternative uses. When the economy fails to allocate resources efficiently on its own, however, it is known as **market failure.** For example, a steel mill might put soot and other forms of "crud" into the air as a by-product of making steel. When it does this, it imposes costs on others not connected with using or producing steel from the steel mill. The soot may require homeowners to paint their homes more often, entailing a cost. And studies show that respiratory diseases are greater in areas with more severe air pollution, imposing costs and often shortening life itself. In addition, the steel mill might discharge chemicals into a stream, thus killing wildlife and spoiling recreational activities for the local population. In this case, the steel factory does not bear the cost of its polluting actions and emits too much pollution. In other words, by transferring the pollution costs onto society, the firm has lowered its costs of production and is now producing more than the ideal output—this is inefficient because it is an overallocation of resources.

market failure
when the economy fails to allocate resources efficiently on its own

Markets can also produce too little of a good, like research for example. The government might decide to subsidize promising scientific research that may benefit many people—like cancer research.

Whether the market economy has produced too little (underallocation) or too much (overallocation), the government can improve society's well-being by intervening. The case of market failure will be taken up in more detail in chapter 6.

In addition, we cannot depend on the market economy to always communicate accurately. Some firms may have market power to distort prices in their favor. For example, the only regional cement company in the area has the ability to charge a higher price and provide lower-quality services than if the company was in a highly competitive market. In this case, the lack of competition can lead to higher prices and reduced product quality. And without adequate information, unscrupulous producers may be able to misrepresent their products to the disadvantage of unwary consumers.

Does the Market Distribute Income Fairly?

Sometimes a painful tradeoff exists between how much an economy can produce efficiently and how that output is distributed–the degree of equality. There is no guarantee that the market economy will provide everyone with the adequate amounts of food, shelter, and health care. That is, not only does the market determine what goods are going to be produced, and in what quantities, but it also determines the distribution of output among members of society. For example, in the 1920s, the wealthiest 1 percent of income recipients received some 15 percent of the nation's income, and the top 5 percent received 30 percent, while the poorest 20 percent received only about 5 percent. Given these conditions, it is not surprising that many believed that community welfare could be increased by taking some income from the very rich and distributing it to the poor or even to the middle class.

As with other aspects of government intervention, the equity argument can generate some sharp disagreements. What is "fair" for one person may seem highly "unfair" to someone else. While one person may find it terribly unfair for some individuals to earn many times the amount that other individuals who work equally hard earn, another person may find it highly unfair to ask one group, the relatively rich, to pay a much higher proportion of their income in taxes than another group.

Section Check

SECTION CHECK

1. Scarcity forces us to allocate our limited resources.
2. Market prices provide important information to buyers and sellers.
3. Price controls distort market signals.
4. A market failure is said to occur when the economy fails to allocate resources efficiently.

---

1. Why must every society choose some manner by which to allocate its scarce resources?
2. How does a market system allocate resources?
3. What do market prices communicate to others in society?
4. How do price controls undermine the market as a communication device?
5. Why can markets sometimes fail to allocate resources efficiently?

Summary

This chapter introduced six powerful ideas for the economic way of thinking. Mastering these ideas will help you not only with economics, but throughout your life.

Economics is about scarcity—unlimited wants and limited resources. We all face scarcity, rich and poor alike, and our wants grow over time, so scarcity will never be eliminated.

Scarcity forces us to make choices and those choices mean that we have costs called opportunity costs.

Economists are usually interested in the effects of additional, or marginal, changes in a given situation. We assume that people are acting rationally when they try to make themselves better off. That is, a rational person will generally pursue an activity if he perceives the marginal benefits to be greater than the marginal costs, or $E(MB) > E(MC)$—this is sometimes called the rule of rational choice.

Economists predict that people will change their behavior in predictable ways when responding to changes in incentives. For example, a negative incentive, like a higher tax, increases costs or reduces benefits, thus discouraging consumption or production. A positive incentive, like a subsidy, decreases costs or increases benefits, thus encouraging consumption or production.

Trade is generally mutually beneficial, whether it is between two individuals or two countries. The person, region, or country that can produce a good or service at a lower opportunity cost than other producers has a comparative advantage in the production of that good or service. Trade allows individuals or countries to do what they do best—specialize. Specialization and trade increase wealth.

Through voluntary exchange and the price system, the market system guides people's choices and produces solutions to the questions of what goods to produce and how to produce those goods and distribute them.

Key Terms and Concepts

scarcity 24
labor 24
land 24
capital 24
human capital 24
entrepreneurship 24
goods 25
intangible goods 25
service 25
economic good 25
opportunity cost 27
marginal thinking 29
rule of rational choice 29
positive incentives 32
negative incentives 32
specializing 34
comparative advantage 34
price controls 37
market failure 37

Review Questions

1. Which of the following goods are scarce?
   - **a.** garbage
   - **b.** salt water in the ocean
   - **c.** clothes
   - **d.** clean air in a big city
   - **e.** dirty air in a big city
   - **f.** a public library

2. List some things that you need. Then ask yourself if you would still want some of those things if the price were five times higher. Would you still want them if the price were ten times higher?

3. List the opportunity costs of the following:
   - **a.** going to college
   - **b.** missing a lecture
   - **c.** withdrawing and spending $100 from your savings account, which earns 5 percent interest annually
   - **d.** going snowboarding on the weekend before final examinations

4. Which of the following activities require marginal thinking and why?
   - **a.** studying
   - **b.** eating
   - **c.** driving
   - **d.** shopping
   - **e.** getting ready for a night out
5. Which of the following are positive incentives? Negative incentives? Why?
   - **a.** a fine for not cleaning up after your dog defecates in the park
   - **b.** a trip to Hawaii paid for by your parents or significant other for earning an "A" in your economics course
   - **c.** a higher tax on cigarettes and alcohol
   - **d.** a subsidy for installing solar panels on your house
6. Which region has a comparative advantage in the following goods:
   - **a.** Wheat: Colombia or the United States
   - **b.** Coffee: Colombia or the United States
   - **c.** Timber: Iowa or Washington
   - **d.** Corn: Iowa or Washington
7. Why is it important that the country or region with the lower opportunity cost produce the good? How would you use the concept of comparative advantage to argue for reducing restictions on trade between countries?
8. Imagine that you are trying to decide whether or not to cross a street without using the designated crosswalk at the traffic signal. What are the expected marginal benefits of crossing? the expected marginal costs? How would the following conditions change your benefit–cost equation?
   - **a.** The street was busy.
   - **b.** The street was empty and it was 3 A.M.
   - **c.** You were in a huge hurry.
   - **d.** There was a police officer 100 feet away.
   - **e.** The closest crosswalk was a mile away.
   - **f.** The closest crosswalk was ten feet away.
9. Go to the Sexton Web site at **http://sexton.swcollege.com** and click on "Netscape" to find out about Netscape's Instant Messenger program designed to allow you to chat with people anytime you are online. Is there an opportunity cost of using this service? Explain. Or click on "Games.com" and play one of the many "free" solo or interactive games there. Is there an opportunity cost of playing games on this site? Explain.

http://

chapter 2 Study Guide

Fill in the Blanks

1. As long as human ____________ exceed available ____________, scarcity will exist.

2. The scarce resources that are used in the production of goods and services can be grouped into four categories: ____________, ____________, ____________, and ____________ .

3. Capital includes human capital, the ________________ people receive from ________________.

4. Entrepreneurs are always looking for new ways to improve ________________ or ____________, driven by the lure of a positive incentive—____________.

5. Scarcity ultimately leads to ____________ for the available goods and services.

6. Because we all have different ____________, scarcity affects everyone differently.

7. Economics is the study of the ____________ we make among our many ________________.

8. The highest or best forgone alternative resulting from a decision is called the ____________.

9. Most choices involve ____________ something to do rather than whether or not to do something.

10. Economists emphasize ____________ thinking because the focus is on additional, or ____________, choices, which involve the effects of ____________ or ____________ the current situation.

11. The rule of rational choice is that in trying to make themselves better off, people alter their behavior if the ________________ to them from doing so outweigh the ________________ they will bear.

12. In acting rationally, people respond to ____________.

13. If the benefits of some activity ____________ and/or if the costs ____________, economists expect the amount of that activity to rise. Likewise, if the benefits of some activity ____________ and/or if the costs ____________, economists expect the amount of that activity to fall.

14. People ____________ by concentrating their energies on the activity to which they are best suited because individuals incur ____________ opportunity costs as a result.

15. If a person, a region, or a country can produce a good or service at a lower opportunity cost than others can, we say that they have a ________________ in the production of that good or service.

16. The primary advantages of specialization are that employees acquire greater _____ from repetition, they avoid _______ time in shifting from one task to another, and they do the types of work for which they are ______ suited.

17. Market prices serve as the ____________ of the market system. They communicate information about the ________________ to buyers, and they provide sellers with critical information about the ________________ that buyers place on those products. This communication results in a shifting of resources from those uses that are ____________ valued to those that are ____________ valued.

18. The basis of a market economy is ____________ exchange and the ____________ system that guides people's choices about questions of what goods to produce and how to produce those goods and distribute them.

19. ____________ can lead the economy to fail to allocate resources efficiently, as in the cases of pollution and scientific research.

True or False

1. In economics, labor includes more than physical effort, and land includes more than what people usually think of as land.
2. Entrepreneurship is the process of combining labor, land, and capital together to produce goods and services.
3. Entrepreneurs make up only a small part of the decision makers in an economy.
4. Even intangible goods can be subjected to economic analysis.
5. Even the wealthy individual who decides to donate all of her money to charity faces the constraints of scarcity.
6. Increases in production could enable us to eliminate scarcity.
7. If we had unlimited resources, we would not have to choose among our desires.
8. Scarcity implies that "there's no such thing as a free lunch."
9. The actual result of changing behavior following the rule of rational choice will always make people better off.
10. In terms of the rule of rational choice, zero levels of pollution, crime, and safety would be far too costly in terms of what we would have to give up to achieve them.
11. Most choices in economics are all or nothing.
12. Good economic thinking requires thinking about average amounts rather than marginal amounts.
13. Positive incentives are those that either increase benefits or reduce costs, resulting in an increase in the level of the related activity or behavior; negative incentives either reduce benefits or increase costs, resulting in a decrease in the level of the related activity or behavior.
14. The safety issue is generally not whether a product is safe, but rather how much safety consumers want.
15. People can gain by specializing in the production of the good in which they have a comparative advantage.
16. Without the ability to trade, people would not tend to specialize in those areas where they have a comparative advantage.
17. Voluntary trade directly increases wealth by making both parties better off, and it is the prospect of wealth-increasing exchange that leads to productive specialization.
18. Government price controls can short-circuit the market's information transmission function.
19. When the economy produces too little or too much of something, the government can potentially improve society's well-being by intervening.

20. Not only does the market determine what goods are going to be produced and in what quantities, but also it determines the distribution of output among members of society.

Multiple Choice

1. Which of the following is part of the economic way of thinking?
   a. When an option becomes less costly, individuals will become more likely to choose it.
   b. Costs are incurred whenever scarce resources are used to produce goods or services.
   c. The value of a good is determined by its cost of production.
   d. Both a and b are part of the economic way of thinking.

2. Ted has decided to buy a burger and fries at a restaurant but is considering whether to buy a drink as well. If the price of a burger is $2.00, fries are $1.00, drinks are $1.00, and a value meal with all three costs $3.40, the marginal cost to Ted of the drink is
   a. $1.00.
   b. $0.40.
   c. $1.40.
   d. $3.40.
   e. impossible to determine from the above information.

3. If a country wanted to maximize the value of its output, each job should be carried out by the person who
   a. has the highest opportunity cost.
   b. has a comparative advantage in that activity.
   c. can complete the particular job most rapidly.
   d. enjoys that job the least.

4. Who would be most likely to drop out of college before graduation?
   a. an economics major who wishes to go to graduate school
   b. a math major with a B+ average
   c. a chemistry major who has just been reading about the terrific jobs available for those with chemistry degrees
   d. a star baseball player who has just received a multi-million-dollar major league contract offer after his sophomore year

5. "If I hadn't been set up on this blind date tonight, I would have saved $50 and spent the evening watching TV." The opportunity cost of the date is
   a. $50.
   b. $50, plus the cost to you of giving up a night of TV.
   c. smaller, the more you enjoy the date.
   d. higher, the more you like that night's TV shows.
   e. described by both b and d.

6. Say you had an 8 A.M. economics class, but you would still come to campus at the same time even if you skipped your economics class. The cost of coming to the economics class would include:
   a. the value of the time it took to drive to campus.
   b. the cost of the gasoline it took to get to campus.
   c. the cost of insuring the car for that day.
   d. both a and b.
   e. none of the above.

7. Which of the following would be likely to raise your opportunity cost of attending a big basketball game this Sunday night?
   a. A friend calls you up and offers you free tickets to a concert by one of your favorite bands on Sunday night.
   b. Your employer offers you double your usual wage to work this Sunday night.
   c. Late Friday afternoon, your physics professor makes a surprise announcement that there will be a major exam on Monday morning.
   d. All of the above.

8. Which of the following demonstrates marginal thinking?
   a. deciding to never eat meat
   b. deciding to spend one more hour studying economics tonight because you think the improvement on your next test will be large enough to make it worthwhile to you
   c. deciding to go to a sociology class you usually skip because there is a guest lecturer you are really interested in hearing that day
   d. both b and c

9. If resources and goods are free to move across states, and if Florida producers choose to specialize in growing grapefruit and Georgia producers choose to specialize in growing peaches, then we could reasonably conclude that
   a. Georgia has a comparative advantage in producing peaches.
   b. Florida has a comparative advantage in producing peaches.
   c. the opportunity cost of growing peaches is lower in Georgia than in Florida.
   d. the opportunity cost of growing grapefruit is lower in Florida than in Georgia.
   e. all of the above except b are true.

10. If a driver who had no change and whose cell-phone battery was dead got stranded near a pay phone and chose to buy a quarter and a dime from a passerby for a dollar bill,
   a. the passerby was made better off and the driver was made worse off by the transaction.
   b. both the passerby and the driver were made better off by the transaction.
   c. the transaction made the driver worse off by 65 cents.
   d. both a and c are true.

11. Which of the following is not true?
   a. Voluntary exchange is expected to be advantageous to both parties to the exchange.
   b. What one trader gains from a trade, the other must lose.
   c. If one party to a potential voluntary trade decides it does not advance his interests, he can veto the potential trade.
   d. The expectation of gain motivates people to engage in trade.

12. Which of the following is true?
   a. Scarcity and poverty are basically the same thing.
   b. The absence of scarcity means that a minimal level of income is provided to all individuals.
   c. Goods are scarce because of greed.
   d. Even in the wealthiest of countries, the desire for material goods is greater than productive capabilities.

13. An example of a capital resource is
  a. stock in a computer software company.
  b. the funds in a CD account at a bank.
  c. a bond issued by a company selling electric generators.
  d. a dump truck.
  e. an employee of a moving company.

14. Which of the following statements is true?
  a. The opportunity cost of a decision is always expressed in monetary terms.
  b. The opportunity cost of a decision is the value of the best forgone alternative.
  c. Some economic decisions have zero opportunity cost.
  d. The opportunity cost of attending college is the same for all students at the same university but may differ among students at different universities.
  e. None of the above statements is true.

15. The opportunity cost of attending college is likely to include all except which of the following?
  a. the cost of required textbooks
  b. tuition fees
  c. the income you forgo in order to attend classes
  d. the cost of haircuts received during the school term
  e. the cost of paper and pencils needed to take notes

16. The opportunity cost of an airplane flight
  a. differs across passengers only to the extent that each traveler pays a different airfare.
  b. is identical for all passengers and equal to the number of hours a particular flight takes.
  c. differs across passengers to the extent that both the airfare paid and the highest valued use of travel time vary.
  d. is equal to the cost of a bus ticket, the next best form of alternative transportation to flying.

17. Lance's boss offers him twice his usual wage rate to work tonight instead of taking his girlfriend on a romantic date. This offer will likely
  a. not affect the opportunity cost of going on the date.
  b. reduce the opportunity cost of going on the date because giving up the additional work dollars will make his girlfriend feel even more appreciated.
  c. increase the opportunity cost of going on the date.
  d. not be taken into consideration by Lance when deciding what to do tonight.

18. Which of the following best defines rational behavior?
  a. analyzing the total costs of a decision
  b. analyzing the total benefits of a decision
  c. undertaking an activity as long as the total benefit of all activities exceeds the total cost of all activities
  d. undertaking activities whenever the marginal benefit exceeds the marginal cost
  e. undertaking activities as long as the marginal benefit exceeds zero

19. The expected marginal benefit to you from purchasing a new sport-utility vehicle is $20,000. The price of the new sport-utility vehicle is $22,000.
  a. If you are acting rationally, you will borrow $2,000 and purchase a new sport-utility vehicle.
  b. You will not purchase the new sport-utility vehicle at this time if you are acting rationally.
  c. If you do not purchase the new sport-utility vehicle, your net loss will be $2,000.
  d. If you are acting rationally, you will not purchase a sport-utility vehicle until the marginal cost of doing so falls to $20,000.

20. Gallons of milk at a local grocery store are priced at one for \$4 or two for \$6. The marginal cost of buying a second gallon of milk equals

a. \$6.
b. \$4.
c. \$3.
d. \$2.
e. \$0.

21. Which of the following statements is most consistent with the rule of rational choice?

a. The Environmental Protection Agency should strive to eliminate virtually all air and water pollution.
b. When evaluating new prescription drugs, the Food and Drug Administration should weigh each drug's potential health benefits against the potential health risks posed by known side effects.
c. Police forces should be enlarged until virtually all crime is eliminated.
d. Manufacturers of automobiles should seek to make cars safer, no matter the costs involved.

22. Kelly is an attorney and also an excellent typist. She can type 120 words per minute, but she is pressed for time because she has all the legal work she can handle at \$75.00 per hour. Kelly's friend Todd works as a waiter and would like some typing work (provided that he can make at least his wage as a waiter, which is \$25.00 per hour). Todd can type only 60 words per minute.

a. Kelly should do all the typing because she is faster.
b. Todd should do the typing as long as his earnings are more than \$25.00 and less than \$37.50 per hour.
c. Unless Todd can match Kelly's typing speed, he should remain a waiter.
d. Todd should do the typing, and Kelly should pay him \$20.00 per hour.
e. Both a and c are correct.

Problems

1. Assume the total benefits to Mark from trips to a local amusement park during the year are given by the following schedule: 1 trip, \$60; 2 trips, \$115; 3 trips, \$165; 4 trips, \$200; 5 trips, \$225; 6 or more trips, \$240.

a. What is Mark's marginal benefit of the third trip? the fifth trip?
b. If the admission price to the amusement park were \$45 per day, how many times would Mark be willing and able to go in a year? What if the price were \$20 per day? Explain.
c. If the amusement park offered a year-long pass for \$200 rather than a per-day admission, would Mark be willing to buy one? If so, how many times would he go? Explain.

2. Assume the total cost of producing widgets was \$4,200 for 42 units; \$4,257 for 43 units; \$4,332 for 44 units; and \$4,420 for 45 units.

a. What is the marginal cost of producing the forty-third unit? the forty-fifth unit?
b. If the widget producer could sell however many he could produce at \$60 per unit, how many would he choose to produce? If he could sell however many he could produce at \$80 per unit? Explain.

chapter 3

Scarcity, Trade-Offs, and Economic Growth

3.1 THE THREE ECONOMIC QUESTIONS EVERY SOCIETY FACES
What are the three basic economic questions that every society has to answer?

3.2 THE CIRCULAR FLOW MODEL
What is the circular flow model?

3.3 THE PRODUCTION POSSIBILITIES CURVE
Why is the production possibilities curve useful?

3.4 ECONOMIC GROWTH AND THE PRODUCTION POSSIBILITIES CURVE
What do we have to sacrifice today to achieve greater economic growth?

section 3.1

The Three Economic Questions Every Society Faces

- What is to be produced?
- How are the goods to be produced?
- For whom are the goods produced?

SCARCITY AND THE ALLOCATION OF RESOURCES

Collectively, our wants far outstrip what can be produced from nature's scarce resources. So how should we allocate those scarce resources? Some methods of resource allocation might seem bad and counterproductive, like the "survival of the fittest" competition that exists on the floor of the jungle. Physical violence has been used since the beginning of time, as people, regions, and countries attacked one another to gain control over resources. One might argue that government should allocate scarce resources on the basis of equal shares or according to need. However, this approach poses problems because of diverse individual preferences, the problem of ascertaining needs, and the negative work and investment incentives involved. In reality, society is made up of many approaches to resource allocation. For now, we will focus on one form of allocating goods and services found in most countries—the market system.

Because of scarcity, certain economic questions must be answered, regardless of the level of affluence of the society or its political structure. We will consider three fundamental questions that inevitably must be faced: (1) What is to be produced? (2) How are the goods to be produced? (3) For whom are the goods produced? These questions are unavoidable in a world of scarcity.

WHAT IS TO BE PRODUCED?

How do individuals control production decisions in market-oriented economies? Questions arise such as "should we produce lots of cars and just a few school buildings, or relatively few cars and more school buildings?" The answer to these and other such questions is that people "vote" in economic affairs with their dollars (or pounds or yen). This concept is called **consumer sovereignty.** Consumer sovereignty explains how individual consumers in market economies determine what is to be produced.

consumer sovereignty
consumers vote with their dollars in a market economy; this explains what is produced

Televisions, VCRs, cellular telephones, pagers, camcorders, and computers, for example, became part of our lives because consumers "voted" hundreds of dollars apiece on these goods. As they bought more color TVs, consumers "voted" fewer dollars on black and white TVs. Similarly, record albums gave way to tapes and CDs as consumers voted for these items with their dollars.

How Different Types of Economic Systems Answer the Question "What Is To Be Produced?"

Economies are organized in different ways to answer the question of what is to be produced. The dispute over the best way to answer this question has inflamed passions for centuries. Should central planning boards make the decisions, as in North Korea and Cuba? Sometimes these highly centralized economic systems are referred to as **command economies.** Under this type of regime, decisions about how many tractors or automobiles to produce are largely determined by a government official or committee associated with the central planning organization. That same group decides on the number and size of school build-

command economies
economies where the government uses central planning to coordinate most economic activities

ings, refrigerators, shoes, and so on. Other countries, including the United States, much of Europe, and, increasingly, Asia and elsewhere, have largely adopted a decentralized decision-making process where literally millions of individual producers and consumers of goods and services determine what goods, and how many of them, will be produced. A country that uses such a decentralized decision-making process is often referred to as a **market economy.** Actually, no nation has a pure market economy. Most countries, including the United States, are said to have a **mixed economy.** In such economies, the government and the private sector together determine the allocation of resources.

market economy
an economy that allocates goods and services through the private decisions of consumers, input suppliers, and firms

mixed economy
an economy where government and the private sector determine the allocation of resources

HOW ARE THE GOODS TO BE PRODUCED?

All economies, regardless of their political structure, must decide how to produce the goods and services that they want—because of scarcity. Goods and services can generally be produced in several ways. For example, a ditch can be dug by many workers using their hands, by a few workers with shovels, or by one person with a backhoe. Someone must decide which method is most appropriate. The larger the quantity of the good and the more elaborate the form of capital, the more labor that is saved and is thus made available for other uses. (Remember, goods like shovels or large earthmoving machines used to produce goods and services are called capital.) From the example, you might be tempted to conclude that it is desirable to use the biggest, most elaborate form of capital. But would you really want to plant your spring flowers with huge earthmoving machinery? That is, the most capital-intensive method of production may not always be the best. The best method is the least-cost method.

What Is the Best Form of Production?

The best or "optimal" form of production will usually vary from one economy to the next. For example, earthmoving machinery is used in digging large ditches in the United States and Europe, while in developing countries, such as India, China, or Pakistan, shovels are often used. Similarly, when a person in the United States cuts the grass, he or she may use a power lawn mower, whereas in a developing country, a hand mower might be used or grass might not be cut at all. Why do these "optimal" forms of production vary so drastically?

APPLICATION

MARKET SIGNALS

Q: Adam was a college graduate with a double major in economics and art. A few years ago, Adam decided that he wanted to pursue a vocation that utilized both of his talents. In response, he shut himself up in his studio and created a watercolor collection, "Graphs of Famous Recessions." With high hopes, Adam put his collection on display for buyers. After several years of displaying his econ art, however, the only one interested in the collection was his 8-year-old sister, who wanted the picture frames for her room. Recognizing that Adam was having trouble pursuing his chosen occupation, Adam's friend Karl told him that the market had failed. What do you think? Is Karl right?

A: No. Markets provide important signals, and the signal being sent in this situation is that Adam should look for some other means of support—something that society values. Remember the function of consumer sovereignty in the marketplace. Clearly, consumers were not voting for Adam's art.

"We feel he's either going to be an artist or an economist."

labor intensive
production that uses a large amount of labor

capital intensive
production that uses a large amount of capital

Compared to capital, labor is relatively cheap and plentiful in India but relatively scarce and expensive in the United States. In contrast, capital (machines and tools, mainly) is comparatively plentiful and cheap in the United States but scarcer and more costly in India. That is, in India, production would tend to be more **labor intensive,** or labor driven. In the United States, production would tend to be more **capital intensive,** or capital driven. Each nation tends to use the production processes that conserve its relatively scarce (and thus relatively more expensive) resources and use more of its relatively abundant resources.

FOR WHOM ARE THE GOODS PRODUCED?

COURTESY OF ROBERT SEXTON

Actor Kurt Russell gets paid a lot of money because he controls a scarce resource: his talent and name recognition. As we will see in the next chapter, people's talents and other goods and services in limited supply relative to demand will command high prices. He also has good taste in his reading material!

In every society, some mechanism must exist to determine how goods and services are to be distributed among the population. Who gets what? Why do some people get to consume or use far more goods and services than others? This question of distribution is so important that wars and revolutions have been fought over it. Both the French and Russian Revolutions were concerned fundamentally with the distribution of goods and services. Even in societies where political questions are usually settled peacefully, the question of the distribution of income is an issue that always arouses strong emotional responses. As we shall see, in a market economy with private ownership and control of the means of production, the amount of goods and services one is able to obtain depends on one's income, which depends on the quantity and quality of the scarce resources the individual controls. For example, Tiger Woods makes a lot of money because he has unique and marketable skills as a golfer. This may or may not be viewed as "fair," an issue we shall look at in detail later in this book.

Section Check

1. Every economy has to decide what to produce.
2. In a decentralized market economy, millions of buyers and sellers determine what and how much to produce.
3. In a mixed economy, the government and the private sector determine the allocation of resources.
4. The best form of production is the one that conserves the relatively scarce (more costly) resources and uses more of the abundant (less costly) resources.
5. When capital is relatively scarce and labor plentiful, production tends to be labor intensive.
6. When capital is relatively abundant and labor relatively scarce, production tends to be capital intensive.
7. In a market economy, the amount of goods and services one is able to obtain depends on one's income.
8. The amount of one's income depends on the quantity and the quality of the scarce resources that the individual controls.

---

1. Why does scarcity force us to decide what to produce?
2. How is a command economy different from a market economy?
3. How does consumer sovereignty determine production decisions in a market economy?
4. Do you think that what and how much an economy produces depends on who will get the goods and services produced in that economy? Why or why not?
5. Why do consumers have to "vote" for a product with their dollars for it to be a success?
6. Why must we choose among multiple ways of producing the goods and services we want?
7. Why might production be labor intensive in one economy, but be capital intensive in another?
8. If a tourist from the United States on an overseas trip notices that other countries don't produce crops "like they do back home," would he be right to conclude that farmers in the other country produce crops less efficiently than U.S. farmers?
9. In what way does scarcity determine income?

section 3.2

The Circular Flow Model

- What are product markets?
- What are factor markets?
- What is the circular flow model?

How do we explain how the millions of people in an economy interact when it comes to buying, selling, producing, working, hiring and so on? There is a continuous flow of goods and services bought and sold between the producers of goods and services, which we call firms, and households, the buyers of goods and services. There is also a continuous flow of income from firms to households as firms buy inputs to produce the goods and services they sell. In our simple economy, these exchanges take place in product markets and factor markets.

PRODUCT MARKETS

Product markets are the markets for consumer goods and services. In the simple circular flow model there are two decision makers—firms and households. In the product market, households are buyers and firms are sellers. Households buy the goods and services that firm produce and sell. The payments from the households to the firm, for the purchases of goods and services, flow to the firm at the same time as goods and services flow to the household.

product markets
the market where households are buyers and firms are sellers of goods and services

FACTOR MARKETS

Factor or **input markets** are where households sell the use of their inputs (capital, land, labor, and entrepreneurship) to firms. In the factor markets, households are the sellers and firms are the buyers. Households receive money payments from firms as compensation for the labor, land, capital, and entrepreneurship needed to produce goods and services. These payments take the form of wages (salaries), rent, interest payments, and profits.

factor (or input) markets
the market where households sell the use of their inputs (capital, land, labor, and entrepreneurship) to firms

THE SIMPLE CIRCULAR FLOW MODEL

The simple **circular flow model of income and output** is illustrated in Exhibit 1. In the top half of the exhibit, the product market, households purchase goods and services that firms have produced. In the lower half of the exhibit, the factor (or input) market, households sell the inputs that firms use to produce goods and services. Households receive income (wages, rent, interest and profit) from firms for the inputs used in production (capital, land, labor, and entrepreneurship).

circular flow model of income and output
an illustration of the continuous flow of goods, services, inputs and payments between firms and households

Let's take a simple example to see how the circular flow model works. Suppose a teacher's supply of labor generates personal income in the form of wages (the factor market), which she can use to buy automobiles, vacations, food, and other goods (the product market). Suppose she buys an automobile (product market); the automobile dealer now has revenue to pay for his inputs (factor market)—wages to workers, purchase of new cars to replenish his inventory, rent for his building, and so on. So we see that in the

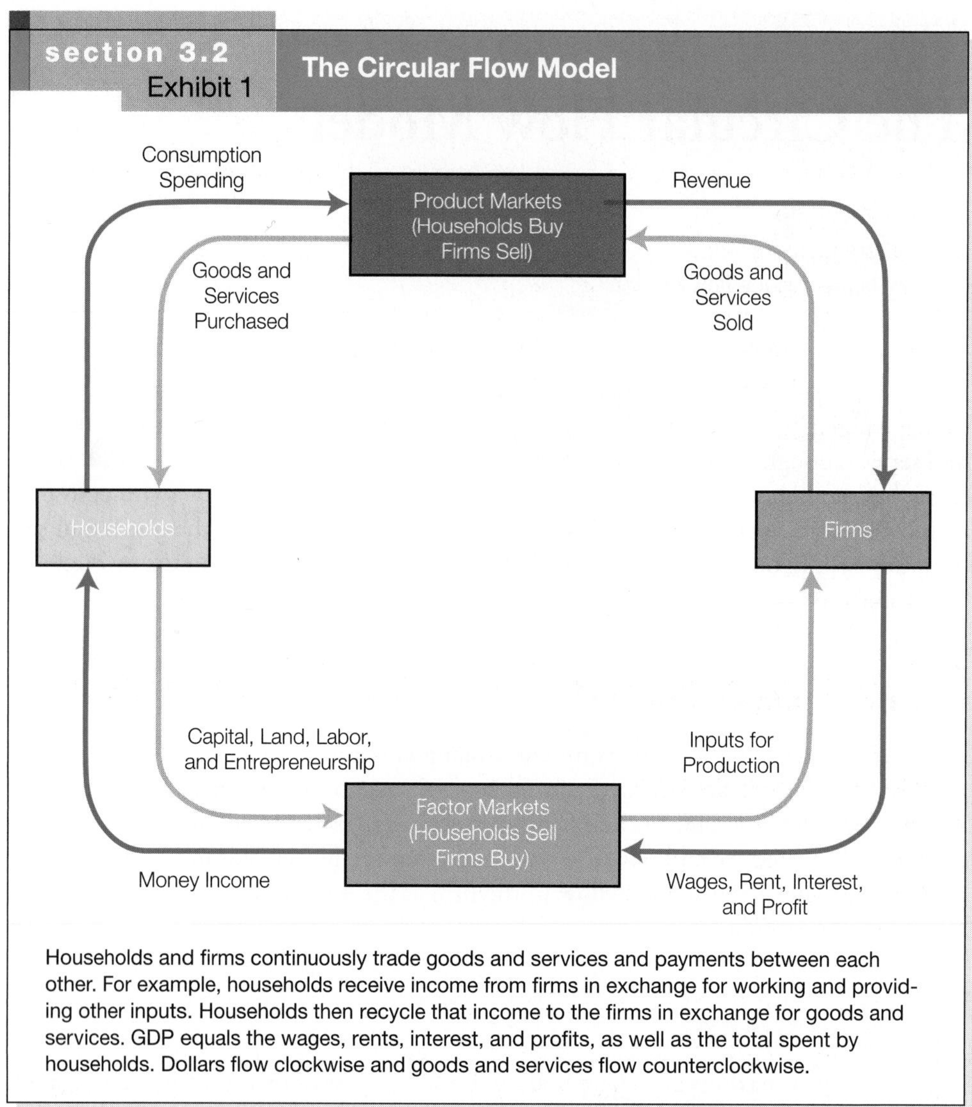

Households and firms continuously trade goods and services and payments between each other. For example, households receive income from firms in exchange for working and providing other inputs. Households then recycle that income to the firms in exchange for goods and services. GDP equals the wages, rents, interest, and profits, as well as the total spent by households. Dollars flow clockwise and goods and services flow counterclockwise.

simple circular flow model that income flows from firms to households (factor markets) and spending flows from households to firms (product markets). The simple circular flow model shows how households and firms interact in product markets and in factor markets and how product markets and factor markets are interrelated.

The circular flow model can become much more complex but here it is presented merely to introduce the major markets and players in the economy. For example, the model can be extended to show the role of government, financial, and foreign markets. Our simple model also does not show how firms and households send some of their income to the government for taxes or how households save some of their income for savings. Households are not the only buyers in the economy—firms, government, and foreigners buy some of the goods and services.

Section Check

1. In the product market, households are buyers and firms are sellers.
2. In the factor markets, households are the sellers and firms are the buyers.
3. Wages, rent, interest, and profits are the payments for the labor, land, capital, and entrepreneurship needed to produce goods and services. These transactions are carried out in factor, or input, markets.
4. The circular flow model illustrates the flow of goods, services, and payments among firms and households.

---

1. Why does the circular flow of money move in the opposite direction from the flow of goods and services?
2. What is bought and sold in factor markets?
3. What is bought and sold in product markets?

section 3.3

The Production Possibilities Curve

- What is a production possibilities curve?
- What is the law of increasing opportunity costs?
- What are unemployed resources?
- What are underemployed resources?
- What is efficiency?

THE PRODUCTION POSSIBILITIES CURVE

The economic concepts of scarcity, choice, and trade-offs can be illustrated visually by the use of a simple graph called a production possibilities curve. The **production possibilities curve** represents the potential total output combinations of any two goods for an economy, given the inputs and technology available to the economy. That is, it illustrates an economy's potential for allocating its limited resources in producing various combinations of goods, in a given time period.

production possibilities curve
the potential total output combinations of any two goods for an economy

A Straight-Line Production Possibilities Curve—Grades in Economics and History

What would the production possibilities curve look like if you were "producing" grades in two of your classes—say, economics and history? In Exhibit 1, we draw a hypothetical production possibilities curve for your expected grade in economics, on the vertical axis and your expected grade in history, on the horizontal axis. Assume, because of a part-time restaurant job, you choose to study 10 hours a week and that you like both courses and are equally adept at studying for both courses.

We see in Exhibit 1 that the production possibilities curve is a straight line. For example, if all 10 hours are spent studying economics, the expected grade in economics is 95 percent (an A) and the expected grade in history is 55 percent (an F). Of course, this is assuming you can study zero hours a week and still get a 55 percent average or study the full 10 hours a week and get a 95 percent average. Moving down the production possibilities curve, we see that as you spend more of your time studying history, and less on economics, you can raise your expected grade in history but only at the expense of lowering section 3.3 Exhibit 1 **Production Possibilities Curve: "Producing" Grades in Economics and History**

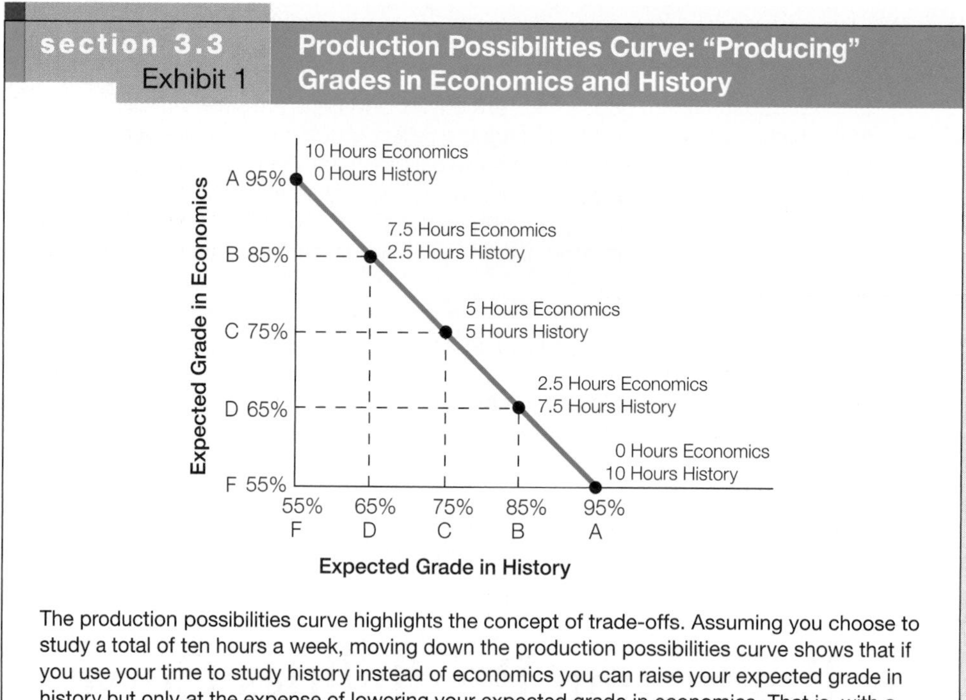

The production possibilities curve highlights the concept of trade-offs. Assuming you choose to study a total of ten hours a week, moving down the production possibilities curve shows that if you use your time to study history instead of economics you can raise your expected grade in history but only at the expense of lowering your expected grade in economics. That is, with a straight-line production possibilities curve, the opportunity costs are constant.

your expected grade in economics. Specifically, moving down along the straight-line production possibility curve, the trade-off is one lower percentage point in economics for one higher percentage point in history.

Of course, if you increase your study time it would be possible to expect higher grades in both courses. But that would be on a new production possibilities curve; along this production possibilities curve we are assuming that technology and the number of study hours are given. In the next section, the coverage is expanded to cover the more realistic case of a bowed production possibilities curve.

The Bowed Production Possibilities Curve

To more clearly illustrate the production possibilities curve, imagine an economy that produces just two goods, food and shelter. The fact that we have many goods in the real world makes actual decision making more complicated, but it does not alter the basic principles being illustrated. Each point on the production possibilities curve shown in Exhibit 2 represents the potential amounts of food and shelter that can be produced in a given time period, given the quantity and quality of resources available in the economy for production.

Note in Exhibit 2 that if we devoted all of our resources to making shelters, we could produce 10 units of shelters, but no food (point A). If, on the other hand, we chose to devote all of our resources to food, we could produce 80 units of food, but no shelters (point E).

In reality, nations would rarely opt for production possibility A or E, preferring instead to produce a mixture of goods. For example, the economy in question might produce 9 units of shelter and 20 units of food

If you only have so many hours a week to study, studying more for economics and less for history may hurt your grade in history, *ceteris paribus.* Life is full of trade-offs.

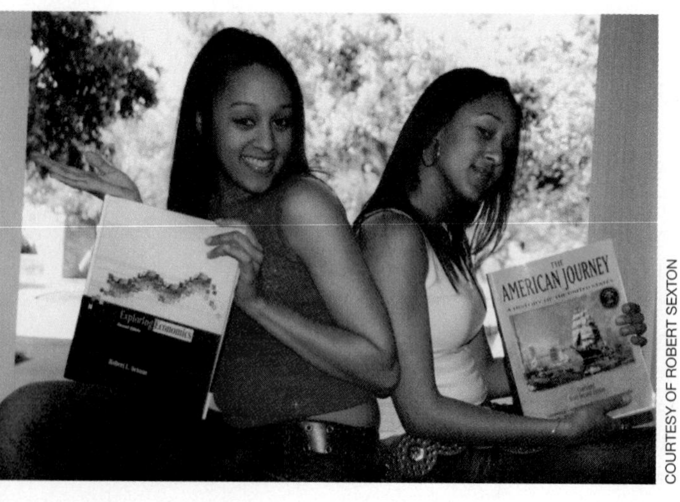

COURTESY OF ROBERT SEXTON

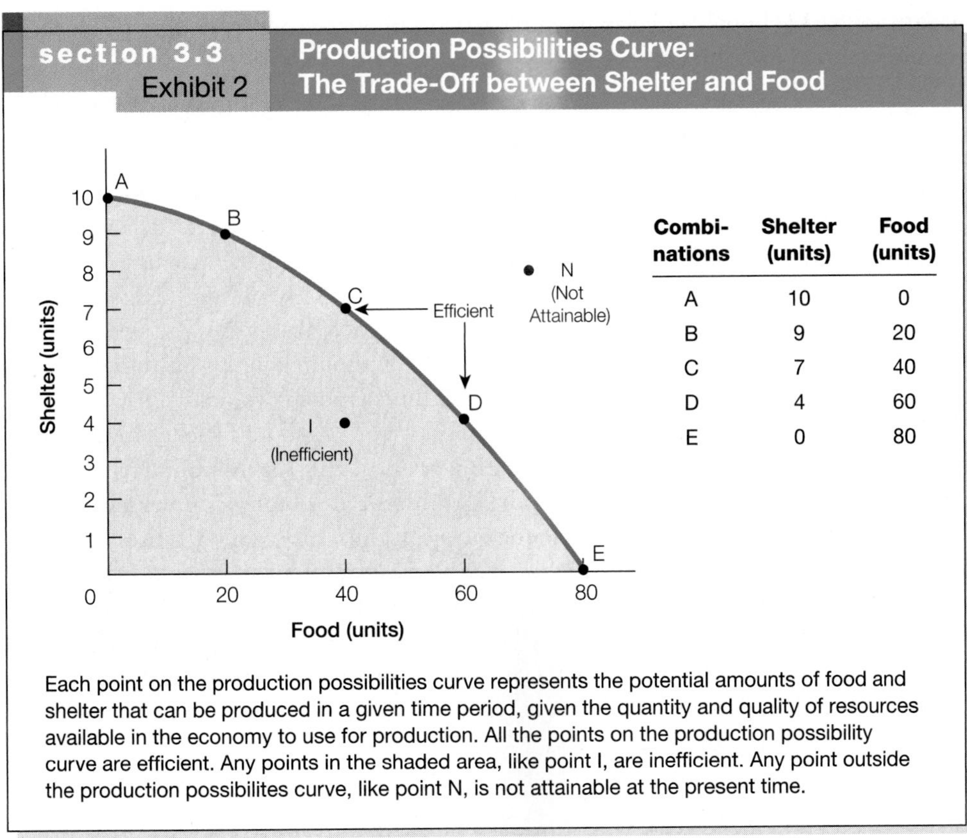

Combinations	Shelter (units)	Food (units)
A	10	0
B	9	20
C	7	40
D	4	60
E	0	80

Each point on the production possibilities curve represents the potential amounts of food and shelter that can be produced in a given time period, given the quantity and quality of resources available in the economy to use for production. All the points on the production possibility curve are efficient. Any points in the shaded area, like point I, are inefficient. Any point outside the production possibilites curve, like point N, is not attainable at the present time.

(point B), or perhaps 7 units of shelter and 40 units of food (point C). Still other combinations along the curve, such as point D, are possible.

Off the Production Possibilities Curve

The economy cannot operate at point N (not attainable) during the given time period because there are presently not enough resources to produce that level of output. However, it is possible the economy can operate inside the production possibilities curve, at point I (inefficient). If the economy is operating at point I, or any other point inside the production possibilities curve, it is not at full capacity, and is operating inefficiently. In short, the economy is not using all of its scarce resources efficiently; as a result, actual output is less than potential output.

USING RESOURCES EFFICIENTLY

Most modern economies have resources that are idle, at least for some period of time—like during periods of high unemployment. If those resources were not idle, people would have more scarce goods and services available for their use. Unemployed resources create a serious problem. For example, consider an unemployed coal miner who is unable to find work at a "reasonable" wage, or those unemployed in depressed times when factories are already operating below capacity. Clearly, the resources of these individuals are not being used efficiently.

The fact that factories can operate below capacity suggests that it is not just labor resources that should be most effectively used. Rather, all resources entering into production must be used effectively. However, for several reasons, social concern focuses on labor. First, labor costs are the largest share of production costs. Also, unemployed or underemployed laborers (whose resources are not being used to their full potential) may have mouths to feed at home, while an unemployed machine does not (although the owner of the unemployed machine may).

INEFFICIENCY AND EFFICIENCY

efficiency
getting the most from society's scarce resources

Suppose for some reason there is widespread unemployment or resources are not being put to their best uses. The economy would then be operating at a point, such as I, inside the production possibilities curve where the economy is operating inefficiently. At point I, 4 units of shelter and 40 units of food are being produced. By putting unemployed resources to work or by putting already employed resources to better uses, we could expand the output of shelter by 3 units (moving to point C) without giving up any units of food. Alternatively, we could boost food output by 20 units (moving to point D) without reducing shelter output. We could even get more of both food and shelter moving to a point on the curve between C and D. Increasing or improving the utilization of resources, then, can lead to greater output of all goods. An efficient use of our resources means more of everything we want can be available for our use. Thus, **efficiency** requires society to use its resources to the fullest extent—getting the most from our scarce resources; that is, there are no wasted resources. If resources are being used efficiently, that is, at some point along a production possibilities curve, then more of one good or service requires the sacrifice of another good or service. Efficiency does not tell us which point along the production possibilites curve is *best,* but it does tell us that points inside the curve cannot be best because some resources are wasted.

THE LAW OF INCREASING OPPORTUNITY COSTS

Note that in Exhibits 2 and 3, the production possibilities curve is not a straight line like that in Exhibit 1. It is concave from below (that is, bowed outward from the origin). Looking at the figures, you can see that at very low food output, an increase in the amount of food produced will lead to only a small reduction in the units of shelter produced. For example, increasing food output from 0 to 20 (moving from point A to point B on the curve) requires the use of resources capable of producing 1 unit of shelter. This means

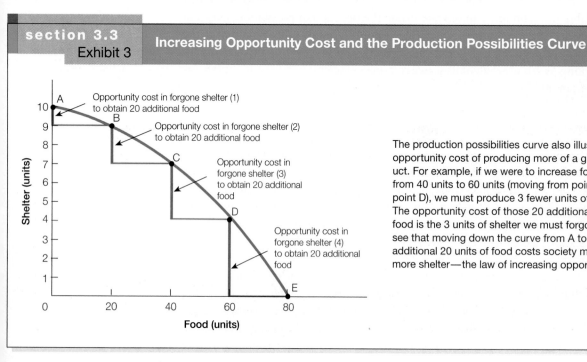

section 3.3 Exhibit 3 Increasing Opportunity Cost and the Production Possibilities Curve

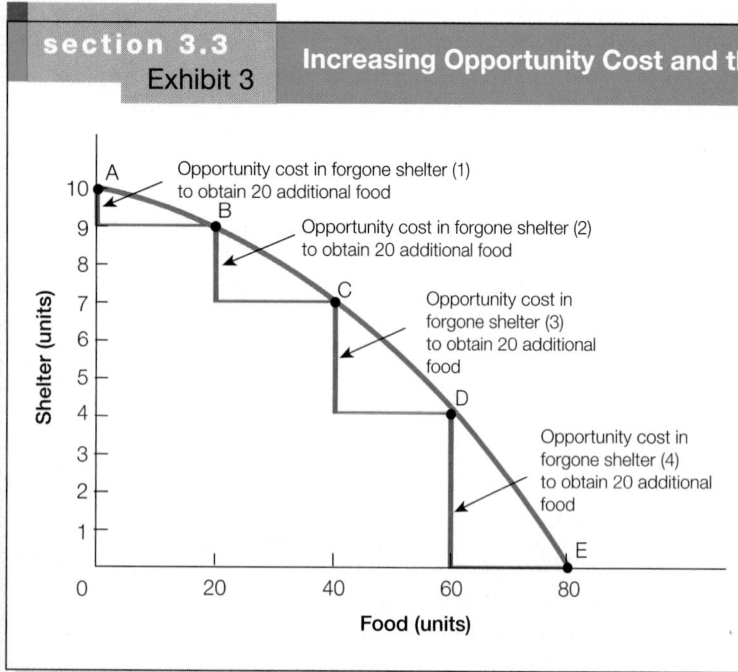

The production possibilities curve also illustrates the opportunity cost of producing more of a given product. For example, if we were to increase food output from 40 units to 60 units (moving from point C to point D), we must produce 3 fewer units of shelter. The opportunity cost of those 20 additional units of food is the 3 units of shelter we must forgo. We can see that moving down the curve from A to E, each additional 20 units of food costs society more and more shelter—the law of increasing opportunity cost.

that for the first 20 units of food, 1 unit of shelter must be given up. When food output is higher, however, more units of shelter must be given up when switching additional resources from the production of shelter to food. Moving from point D to point E, for example, an increase in food output of 20 (from 60 to 80) reduces the production of shelters from 4 to 0. At this point, then, the cost of those 20 additional units of food is 4 units of shelter, considerably more than the 1 unit of shelter required in the earlier scenario. This difference shows us that opportunity costs have not remained constant, but have risen, as more units of food and fewer units of shelter are produced. It is this increasing opportunity cost, then, that is represented by the bowed production possibilities curve.

What Is the Reason for the Law of Increasing Opportunity Cost?

increasing opportunity cost
the opportunity cost of producing additional units of a good rises as society produces more of that good

The basic reason for the **increasing opportunity cost** is that some resources and skills cannot be easily adapted from their current uses to alternative uses. For example, at low levels of food output, additional increases in food output can be obtained easily by switching relatively low skilled carpenters from making shelters to producing food. However, to

APPLICATION

THE PRODUCTION POSSIBILITIES CURVE

Q: Imagine that you are the overseer on a small island that only produces two goods, cattle and wheat. About a quarter of the land is not fertile enough for growing wheat, so cattle graze on it. What would happen if you tried to produce more and more wheat, extending your planting even to the less-fertile soil?

A: This is the law of increasing opportunity costs in action. As you planted more and more of your acreage in wheat, we would move into some of the rocky, less-fertile land and, consequently, wheat yields on the additional acreage would fall. If we tried to plant the entire island with wheat, we would find that some of the rocky less-fertile acreage would yield virtually no extra wheat. It would, however, have been great for cattle grazing—a large loss. Thus, the opportunity cost of using that marginal land for wheat rather than cattle grazing would be very high. The law of increasing opportunity cost occurs because resources are not homogeneous (identical) and are not equally adaptable for producing cattle and wheat; some acres are more suitable for cattle grazing, while others are more suitable for wheat growing. This is seen in Exhibit 4, where the vertical lines represent the opportunity cost of growing 10 more bushels of wheat in terms of cattle production sacrificed. You can see that as wheat production increases, the opportunity costs in terms of lost cattle production rises.

section 3.3 Exhibit 4 — Opportunity Costs for Cattle and Wheat

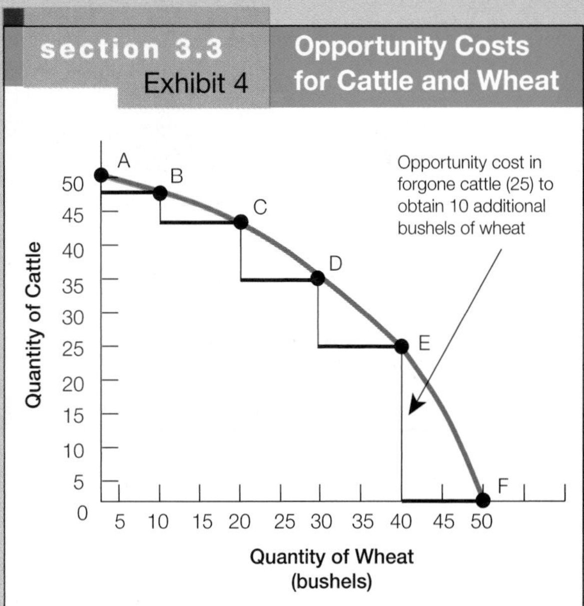

The opportunity cost of each 10 bushels of wheat in terms of forgone cattle is measured by the vertical distances. As we move from A to F, the opportunity cost of wheat in terms of forgone cattle rises.

get even more food output, workers that are less well-suited or appropriate for producing food (i.e., they are better adapted to making shelter) must be released from shelter making in order to increase food output. For example, a skilled carpenter may be an expert at making shelters but a very bad farmer, because he lacks the training and skills necessary in that occupation. So, using the skilled carpenter to farm results in a relatively greater opportunity cost than using the poor carpenter to farm. Hence, the production of additional units of food becomes increasingly costly as progressively even lower skilled farmers (but good carpenters) convert to farming.

Section Check

1. The production possibilities curve represents the potential total output combinations of two goods available to a society given its resources and existing technology.
2. If the economy is operating within the production possibilities curve, the economy is operating inefficiently; this means that actual output is less than potential output.
3. Efficiency requires society to use its resources to the fullest extent—no wasted resources.
4. A bowed production possibilities curve means that the opportunity costs of producing additional units of a good rise as society produces more of that good (the law of increasing opportunity costs).

---

1. What does a production possibilities curve illustrate?
2. How are opportunity costs shown by the production possibilities curve?
3. Why do the opportunity costs of added production increase with output?
4. How does the production possibilities curve illustrate increasing opportunity costs?
5. Why are we concerned with widespread amounts of unemployed or underemployed resources in a society?
6. What do we mean by efficiency, and how is it related to underemployment of resources?
7. How are efficiency and inefficiency illustrated with a production possibilities curve?
8. Will a country that makes being unemployed illegal be more productive than one that does not? Why or why not?
9. If a 68-year-old U.S. worker chooses not to work at all, does that mean that the United States is functioning inside its production possibilities curve? Why or why not?

section 3.4

Economic Growth and the Production Possibilities Curve

- How much should we sacrifice today to get more in the future?
- How do we show economic growth on the production possibilities curve?

GENERATING ECONOMIC GROWTH

How have some nations been able to rapidly expand their output of goods and services over time, while others have been unable to increase their standards of living at all?

section 3.4
Exhibit 1
Economic Growth and Production Possibilities

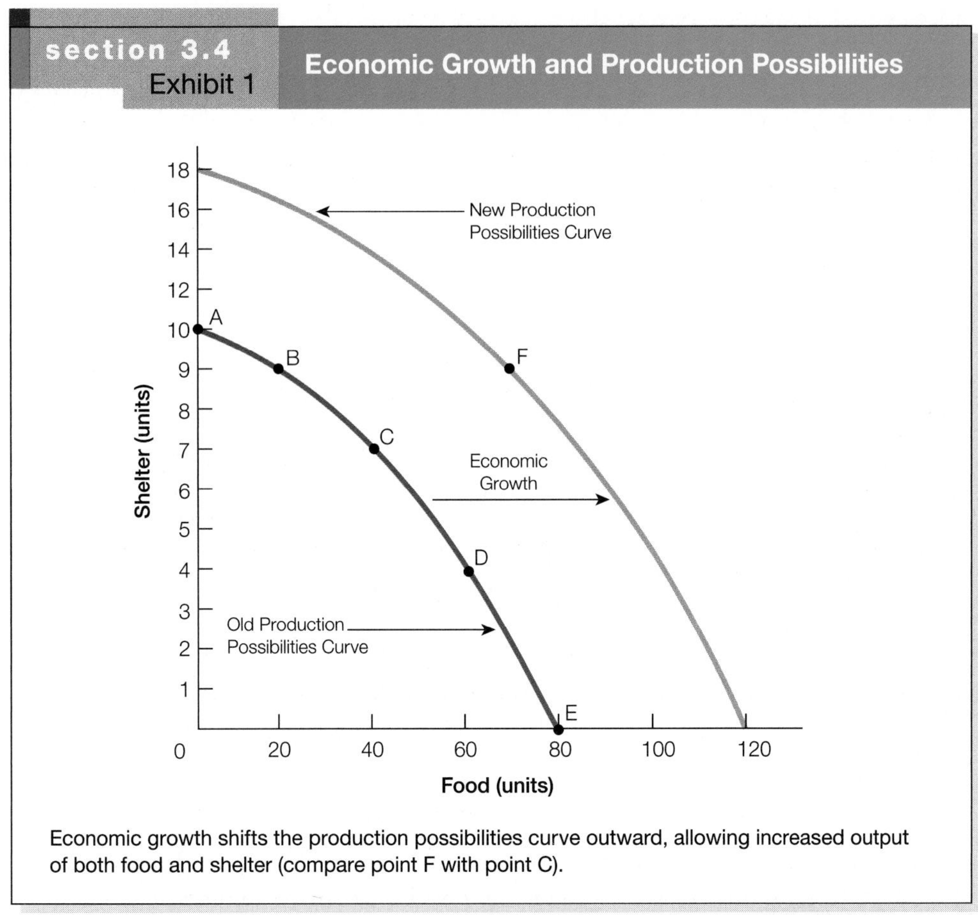

Economic growth shifts the production possibilities curve outward, allowing increased output of both food and shelter (compare point F with point C).

The economy can only grow with qualitative or quantitative changes in the factors of production—land, labor, capital, and entrepreneurship. Advancement in technology, improvements in labor productivity, or new sources of natural resources (such as previously undiscovered oil) could all lead to outward shifts of the production possibilities curve.

This idea can be clearly illustrated by using the production possibilities curve (Exhibit 1). In terms of the production possibilities curve, economic growth means an outward shift in the possible combinations of goods and services produced. With growth comes the possibility to have more of both goods than were previously available. Suppose we were producing at point C (7 units of shelter, 40 units of food) on our original production possibilities curve. Additional resources and/or new methods of using them (technological progress) can lead to new production possibilities creating the potential for more of all goods (or more of some with no less of others). These increases would push the production possibilities curve outward. For example, if you invest in human capital, such as training the workers making the shelters, it will increase the productivity of those workers. As a result, they will produce more units of shelters. This means, ultimately, that fewer resources will be used to make shelters, freeing them to be used for farming—resulting in more units of food. Notice that at point F (future) on the new curve, it is possible to produce 9 units of shelter and 70 units of food, more of both goods than were previously produced, at point C.

GROWTH DOESN'T ELIMINATE SCARCITY

With all of this discussion of growth, it is important to remember that growth, or increases in a society's output, does not make scarcity disappear. Even when output has

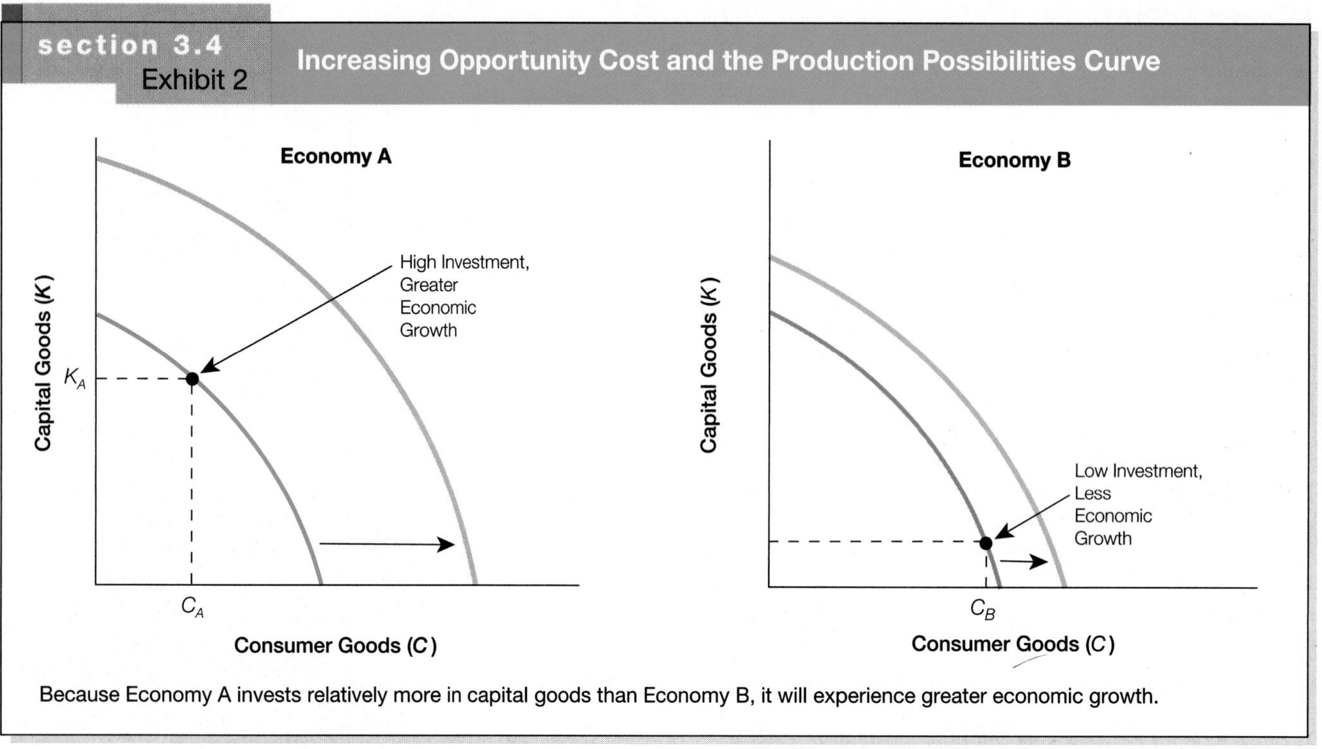

Because Economy A invests relatively more in capital goods than Economy B, it will experience greater economic growth.

grown more rapidly than population so that people are made better off, they still face trade-offs: At any point along the production possibilities curve, in order to get more of one thing, you must give up something else. There are no free lunches on the production possibilities curve.

Capital Goods versus Consumption Goods

Economies that choose to invest more of their resources for the future will grow faster than those that don't. To generate economic growth, a society must produce fewer consumer goods—like video games, DVD players, cell phones, cars, and so on—in the present and produce more capital goods. The society that devotes a larger share of its productive capacity to capital goods (machines, factories, tools, and education), rather than consumption goods (video games, stereos, and vacations), will experience greater economic growth. It must sacrifice some present consumption of consumer goods and services in order to experience growth in the future. Why? Investing in capital goods, like computers and other new technological equipment, as well as upgrading skills and knowledge, expands the ability to produce in the future. It shifts the economy's production possibilities outward, increasing the future production capacity of the economy. That is, the economy that invests more now (consumes less now) will be able to produce, and therefore consume, more in the future. In Exhibit 2, we see that Economy A invests more in capital goods than Economy B. Consequently, Economy A's production possibilities curve shifts out further than Economy B's over time.

SUMMING UP THE PRODUCTION POSSIBILITIES CURVE

http://

The production possibilities curve shown in Exhibit 3 illustrates the choices faced by an economy that makes military goods and consumer goods. How are the economic concepts of scarcity, choice, opportunity costs, efficiency, and economic growth illustrated in

section 3.4 Exhibit 3

Production Possibilities Curve

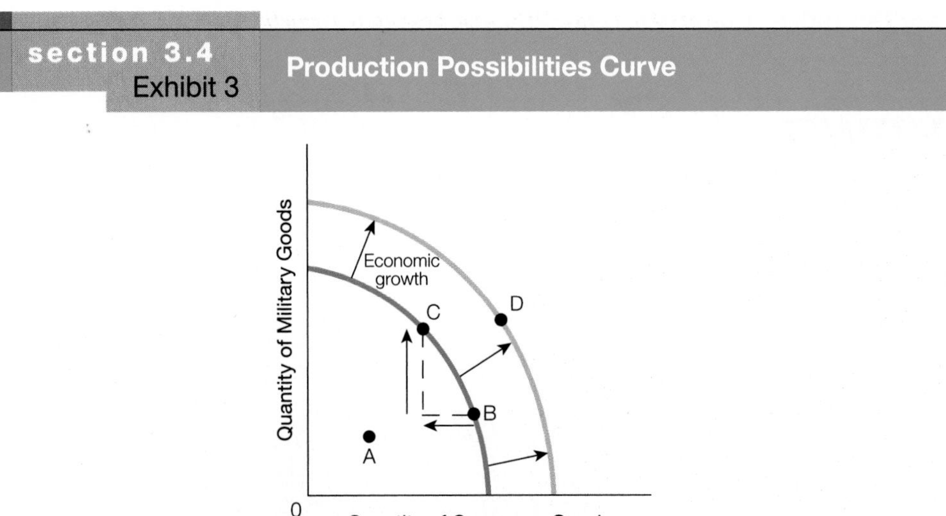

Point A, inside the initial production possibilities curve, represents inefficiency. Points B and C, on the curve, are efficient points and represent two possible output combinations. Point D can only be attained with economic growth, illustrated by the outward shift in the production possibilities curve.

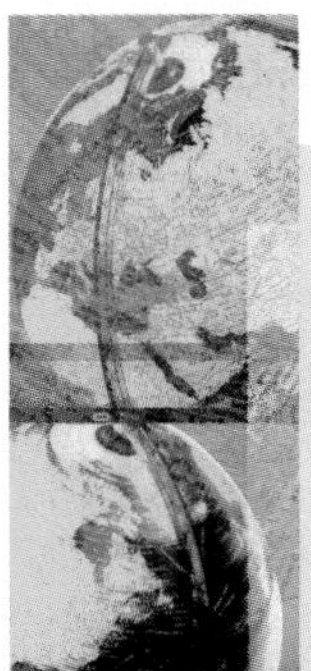

Global WATCH

CORRELATION OF INVESTMENT AND GROWTH

section 3.4 Exhibit 4

Correlation of Investment and Growth

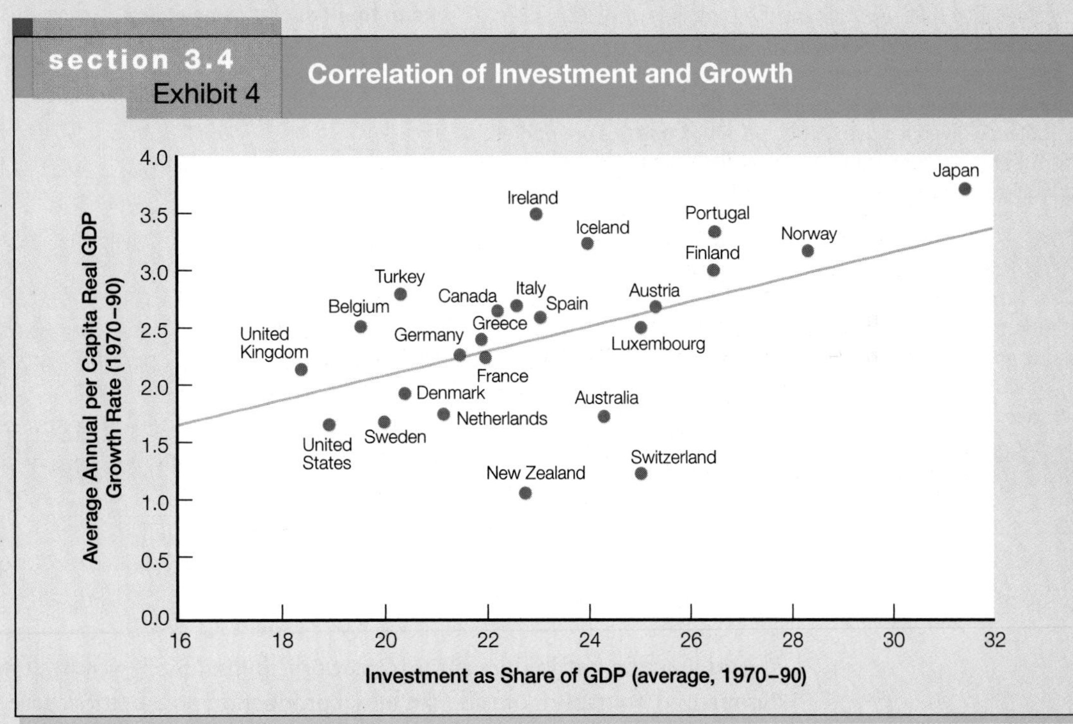

CONSIDER THIS:
Exhibit 4 shows that there is a close relationship between investment in capital goods and economic growth. Investment means that a country has to sacrifice some current consumption for the future—investment in machinery, training, and technology. Most economists agree that investment in capital (like new machinery, education, and technology) is an important component of economic growth.

In The NEWS

TOURISM VERSUS ECOSYSTEMS

BY JON KRAKAUER

Canada's main transcontinental railway and transcontinental highway roll side-by-side down the length of Banff's main valley. On the busiest weekends, the road is clotted with cars, RVs, and tour buses, and a brown haze of exhaust fumes veils the celebrated vistas. Within the park lie three ski resorts and the town of Banff—home to 7,000 permanent residents. On the typical summer day, the townies may see 25,000 tourists streaming through their streets.

One local businessman and town council member remarked, "Environmentalists love to talk gloom and doom—but all you have to do is drive five miles out of town and you're in the middle of miles and miles of nothing but nature. You get tired of looking at all these big bare mountains; what's wrong with putting a restaurant or a little chalet up there to make it nicer for the people who come here?"

One thing that is wrong with it, according to a biologist who has studied wildlife throughout the Rocky Mountains, is that the human presence in Banff is wreaking havoc on the area's fragile makeup. "I'd say the park is in very, very poor condition compared with what it was 10 years ago, 20 years ago, 30 years ago," declared the biologist. "There's been a major decline in most of our large predators—black bears, grizzlies, wolverines, lynx, cougars. Such species are one of our best indicators of overall ecological health, and the way things are going, most of these animals will not survive here."

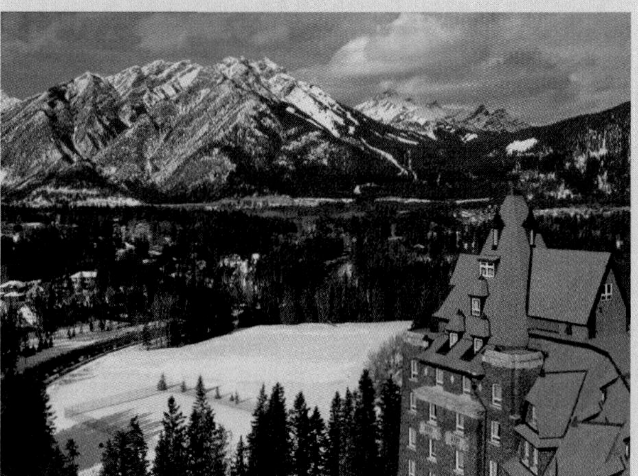

Can Banff currently have more tourism and a better environment? Society can choose high environmental quality but only at the cost of lower tourism or more tourism and commercialization at the expense of the ecosystem, but society must choose. It involves a trade-off, and in this case Canada must presently choose between tourism and ecosystems.

SOURCE: Adapted from "Rocky Times in Banff," *National Geographic*, July 1995, pp. 46-69.

CONSIDER THIS:

The principal point of this article is that there are trade-offs that require choice and those choices have costs. In order to totally preserve the ecosystem of Banff, it would mean far fewer tourists and commercial ventures. In this case, society must make a value judgment. If Banff is developed further, what will be the cost to future generations who will not be able to appreciate the visual splendors of this special "hamlet" nestled in the Canadian Rockies? On the other hand, how can you possibly accommodate the growing numbers of daily visitors without building additional restaurants, motels, and so on? Society must choose.

this production possibilities curve framework? In Exhibit 3, we can show scarcity because resource combinations outside the initial production possibilities curve, like point D, are unattainable without economic growth. If the economy is operating efficiently, we are somewhere on that production possibilities curve, like point B or point C. However, if the economy is operating inefficiently, we are operating inside that production possibilities curve, like point A. We can also see in this graph that to get more military goods you must give up consumer goods—that is, there is an opportunity cost. Finally, we see that over time, with economic growth, the whole production possibilities curve can shift outward, making point D now attainable.

Section Check

1. Economies must decide how much current consumption they are willing to sacrifice for greater growth in the future.
2. Economic growth is represented by an outward shift of the production possibilities curve.
3. Economic growth increases the possibility of producing more of all goods.
4. Despite economic growth, scarcity inevitably remains a fact of life.

---

1. What is the essential question behind issues of economic growth?
2. What is the connection between sacrifices and economic growth?
3. How is economic growth shown in terms of production possibilities curves?
4. Why doesn't economic growth eliminate scarcity?
5. What would happen to the production possibilities curve in an economy where a new innovation greatly increased its ability to produce shelter but did not change its ability to produce food?
6. If people reduced their saving (thus reducing the funds available for investment), what would that do to society's production possibilities curve over time?

Summary

Every economy has to decide what goods to produce, how to produce the goods, and how to distribute the goods. In a decentralized market economy millions of buyers and sellers determine what to produce. In a mixed economy, the government and the private sector determine the allocation of resources and answer the three basic economic questions: what, how, for whom?

The circular flow model illustrates the flow of goods, services, and payments among businesses and households. In the product market, households purchase goods and services that firms have produced. In the factor (or input) market, households sell the inputs that firms use to produce goods and services. Households receive income (wages, rent, interest, and profit) from firms for their inputs (capital, land, labor and entrepreneurship) used in production.

Economic concepts such as scarcity, choice, and tradeoffs can be illustrated using the production possibilities curve. The production possibilities curve represents the potential total output combinations of two goods available to a society. If the economy is operating within the production possibilities curve, the economy is operating inefficiently. A bowed (or concave from the origin) production possibility curve means that the opportunity costs of producing additional units of a good rise as society produces more of that good (the law of increasing opportunity costs).

The best form of production is the one that conserves the relatively scarce (more costly) resources and uses more of the abundant (less costly) resources. When capital is relatively scarce and labor plentiful, production tends to be labor intensive. When capital is relatively abundant and labor relatively scarce, production tends to be capital intensive.

In a market economy, the amount of output one is able to obtain depends on one's income. The amount of one's income depends on the quantity and the quality of the scarce resources that the individual controls.

When there is widespread unemployment and resources are not being put to their best uses, the economy is operating inside the production possibilities curve—an inefficient use of society's resources. Efficiency requires society to use its resources to the fullest extent—no wasted resources.

Economies must decide how much current consumption they are willing to sacrifice for greater growth in the future. Economic growth is represented by an outward shift of the production possibilities curve.

Key Terms and Concepts

consumer sovereignty 42
command economies 42
market economy 43
mixed economy 43
labor intensive 44
capital intensive 44
product markets 45
factor (or input) markets 45
circular flow model of income and output 45
production possibilities curve 47
efficiency 50
increasing opportunity cost 51

Review Questions

1. What is the significance of the three basic economic questions?

2. How would the following events be shown using a production possibilities curve for shelter and food?

a. The economy is experiencing double-digit unemployment.

b. Economic growth is increasing at over 5 percent per year.

c. Society decides it wants less shelter and more food.

d. Society decides it wants more shelter and less food.

3. Using the table below, answer the following questions:

Combinations

	A	B	C	D	E
Guns	1	2	3	4	5
Butter	20	18	14	8	0

a. What are the assumptions for a given production possibilities curve?

b. What is the opportunity cost of one gun when moving from point B to point C? When moving from point D to E?

c. Do these combinations demonstrate constant or increasing opportunity costs?

4. Economy A produces more capital goods and fewer consumer goods than Economy B. Which economy will grow more rapidly? Draw two production possibilities curves, one for Economy A and one for Economy B. Demonstrate graphically how one economy can grow more rapidly than the other.

5. How does education add to a nation's capital stock?

6. How does a technological advance that increases the efficiency of shoe production affect the production possibilities curve between shoes and pizza? Is it possible to produce more shoes and pizza or just more shoes? Explain.

7. A politician running for President of the United States promises to build new schools and new space stations during the next 4 years without sacrificing any other goods and services. Explain using a production possibilities curve between schools and space stations under what conditions the politician would be able to keep his promise.

8. In 1991, the United States and several allies waged war on Iraq. Illustrate a production possibilities curve showing Iraq's ability to produce tanks and milk both pre-war and post-war.

9. Visit the Sexton Web site at **http://sexton.swcollege.com** and click on the "CIA World Factbook" link. Look up information about the economy of North Korea. According to the CIA's *The World Factbook,* does North Korea more closely fit the description of a command economy or market economy? Why?

13. If resources are being used efficiently, at a point along a production possibilities curve, more of one good or service requires the sacrifice of another good or service as a cost.

14. The basic reason for increasing opportunity cost is that some resources and skills cannot be easily adapted from their current uses to alternative uses.

15. Investing in capital goods will increase the future production capacity of an economy, so an economy that invests more now (consumes less now) will be able to produce, and therefore consume, more in the future.

16. An economy can grow despite a lack of qualitative and quantitative improvements in the factors of production.

17. Economic growth means a movement along an economy's production possibilities curve in the direction of producing more consumer goods.

18. From a point inside the production possibilities curve, in order to get more of one thing, an economy must give up something else.

Multiple Choice

1. Which of the following is not a question that all societies must answer?
   - **a.** How can scarcity be eliminated?
   - **b.** What goods and services will be produced?
   - **c.** Who will get the goods and services?
   - **d.** How will the goods and services be produced?
   - **e.** All of the above are questions that all societies must answer.

2. Economic disputes over the distribution of income are generally associated with which economic question?
   - **a.** Who should produce the goods?
   - **b.** What goods and services will be produced?
   - **c.** Who will get the goods and services?
   - **d.** How will the goods and services be produced?

3. Three economic questions must be determined in all societies. What are they?
   - **a.** How much will be produced? When will it be produced? How much will it cost?
   - **b.** What will the price of each good be? Who will produce each good? Who will consume each good?
   - **c.** What is the opportunity cost of production? Does the society have a comparative advantage in production? Will consumers desire the goods being produced?
   - **d.** What goods will be produced? How will goods be produced? For whom will the goods be produced?

4. The private ownership of property and the use of the market system to direct and coordinate economic activity are most characteristic of
   - **a.** a command economy.
   - **b.** a mixed economy.
   - **c.** a market economy.
   - **d.** a traditional economy.

5. The degree of government involvement in the economy is greatest in
   - **a.** a command economy.
   - **b.** a mixed economy.
   - **c.** a market economy.
   - **d.** a traditional economy.

6. When a command economy is utilized to resolve economic questions regarding the allocation of resources, then:
a. everyone will receive an equal share of the output produced.
b. the preferences of individuals are of no importance.
c. economic efficiency will be assured.
d. the role of markets will be replaced by political decision making.

7. Which of the following is true?
a. An advanced market economy would tend to use both labor-intensive and capital-intensive production methods.
b. An economy in which labor is relatively scarce would tend to use capital-intensive production methods.
c. An increase in the availability of labor relative to capital in an economy would tend to increase how labor intensive the production processes in that economy would be.
d. All of the above are true.
e. Both b and c are true.

8. In a circular flow diagram,
a. goods and services flow in a clockwise direction.
b. goods and services flow in a counterclockwise direction.
c. product markets appear at the top of the diagram.
d. factor markets appear at the left of the diagram.
e. both b and c are true.

9. Which of the following is true?
a. In the product markets, firms are buyers and households are sellers.
b. In the factor markets, firms are sellers and households are buyers.
c. Firms receive money payments from households for capital, land, labor, and entrepreneurship.
d. All of the above are true.
e. None of the above are true.

10. In the circular flow model,
a. firms supply both products and resources.
b. firms demand both products and resources.
c. firms demand resources and supply products.
d. firms supply resources and demand products.

11. A point beyond the boundary of an economy's production possibilities curve is
a. efficient.
b. inefficient
c. attainable.
d. unattainable.
e. both attainable and efficient.

Use the diagram at right to answer questions 12 through 15.

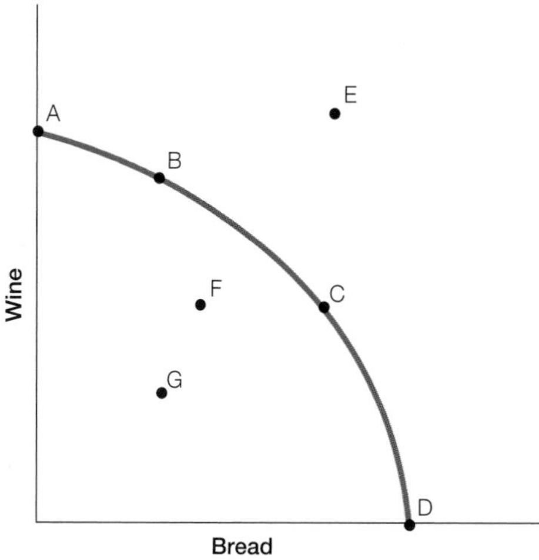

12. Currently, it is not possible to produce at

a. point A.
b. point B.
c. point E.
d. point G.
e. either point E or point G.

13. An economy is operating at full employment, and then workers in the bread industry are laid off. This change is portrayed in the movement from

a. A to B.
b. B to E.
c. C to F.
d. G to F.
e. None of the above are correct.

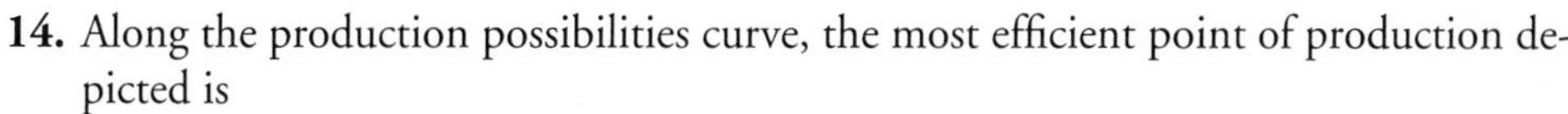

14. Along the production possibilities curve, the most efficient point of production depicted is

a. point B.
b. point C.
c. point D.
d. point G.
e. All points on the production possibilities curve are equally efficient.

15. The opportunity cost of one more unit of bread is greater at point _______ than at point ________.

a. G; B
b. C; A
c. A; C
d. None of the above. The opportunity cost of a good is constant everywhere along the production possibilities curve.

16. Which of the following is consistent with the implications of the production possibilities curve?

a. If the resources in an economy are being used efficiently, scarcity will not be a problem.
b. If the resources in an economy are being used efficiently, more of one good can be produced only if less of another good is produced.
c. Producing more of any one good will require smaller and smaller sacrifices of other goods as more of that good is being produced in an economy.
d. An economy will automatically attain that level of output at which all of its resources are fully employed.
e. Both b and c are consistent with the implications of the production possibilities curve.

17. Consider a production possibilities curve for an economy producing bicycles and video game players. It is possible to increase the production of bicycles without sacrificing video game players if

a. the production possibilities curve shifts outward due to technological progress.
b. the production possibilities curve shifts outward due to increased immigration (which enlarges the labor force).
c. the economy moves from a point inside the production possibilities curve to a point on the curve.
d. any of the above occurs.
e. either a or b, but not c, occurs.

18. What determines the position and shape of a society's production possibilities curve?

a. the physical resources of that society
b. the skills of the workforce
c. the level of technology of the society
d. the number of factories available to the society
e. all of the above

19. Which of the following is the most accurate statement about a production possibilities curve?

a. An economy can produce at any point inside or outside its production possibilities curve.
b. An economy can produce only on its production possibilities curve.
c. An economy can produce at any point on or inside its production possibilities curve, but not outside the curve.
d. An economy can produce at any point inside its production possibilities curve, but not on or outside the curve.

20. Which of the following is most likely to shift the production possibilities curve outward?

a. an increase in unemployment
b. a decrease in the stock of physical or human capital
c. a decrease in the labor force
d. a technological advance

21. Which of the following is least likely to shift the production possibilities curve outward?

a. a change in preferences away from one of the goods and toward the other
b. an invention that reduces the amount of natural resources necessary for producing a good
c. the discovery of new natural resources
d. a reduction in people's preferences for leisure

22. Inefficiency is best illustrated by which of the following?

a. forgoing civilian goods in order to produce more military goods
b. limiting economic growth by reducing capital spending
c. having high levels of unemployment of labor and other resources that could be productively employed
d. producing outside the production possibilities frontier
e. all of the above

23. Suppose Country A produces few consumption goods and many investment goods while Country B produces few investment goods and many consumption goods. Other things being equal, you would expect

a. per capita income to grow more rapidly in Country B.
b. population to grow faster in Country B.
c. the production possibilities curve for Country A to shift out more rapidly than that of Country B.
d. that if both countries started with identical production possibilities curves, in twenty years, people in Country B will be able to produce more consumer goods than people in Country A.
e. that both c and d are true.

24. A virulent disease spreads throughout the population of an economy, causing death and disability. This can be portrayed as
   a. a movement from a point on the production possibilities curve to a point inside the curve.
   b. a movement from a point on the production possibilities curve to the northeast.
   c. a movement along the production possibilities curve to the southeast.
   d. an outward shift of the production possibilities curve.
   e. an inward shift of the production possibilities curve.

25. Say that a technological change doubles an economy's ability to produce good X and triples the economy's ability to produce Y. As a result,
   a. the economy will tend to produce less X and more Y than before.
   b. the opportunity cost of producing units of Y in terms of X forgone will tend to fall.
   c. the production possibilities curve will shift out further along the *X*-axis than along the *Y*-axis.
   d. both b and c would be true.

Problems

1. Identify where the appropriate entries go in the circular flow diagram.

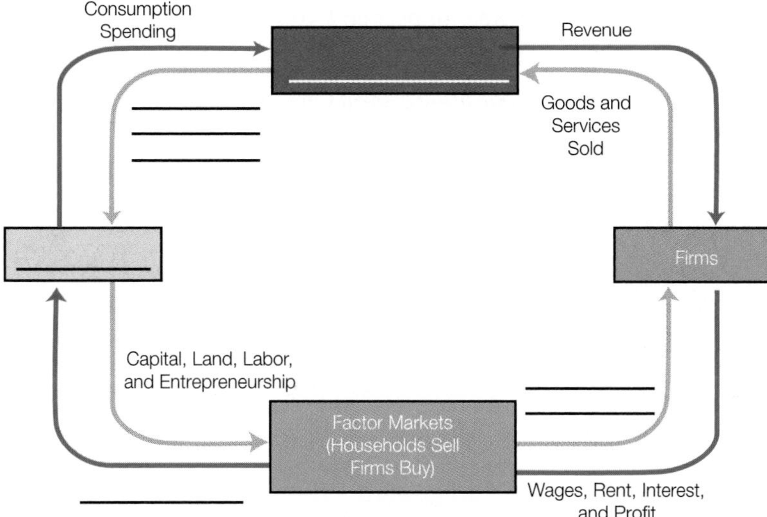

2. Assume that the production possibilities for Badlands are the following combinations of kegs of beer and sides of beef.

Beer	Beef
55	0
54	1
52	2
49	3
45	4
40	5
34	6
27	7
19	8
10	9
0	10

a. Construct the production possibilities frontier for beer and beef on the grid below.

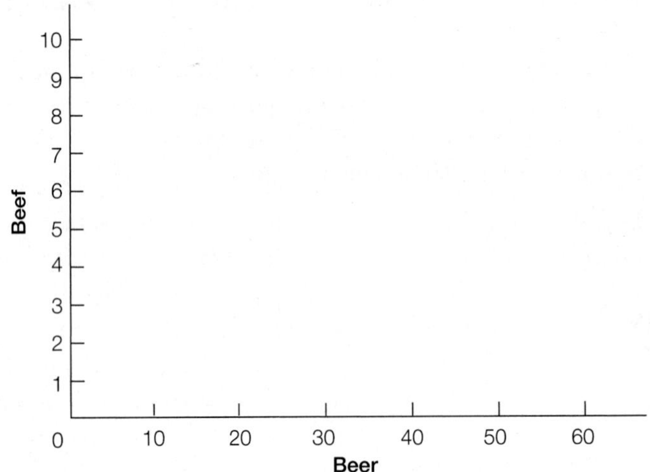

b. Given the information above, what is the opportunity cost of the fifty-fifth keg of beer in Badlands? of the sixth side of beef? of the ninth side of beef?

c. Would the combination of 40 kegs of beer and 4 sides of beef be efficient? Why or why not?

d. Is the combination of 9 kegs of beer and 10 sides of beef possible for Badlands? Why or why not?

3. Given the following production possibilities curve:

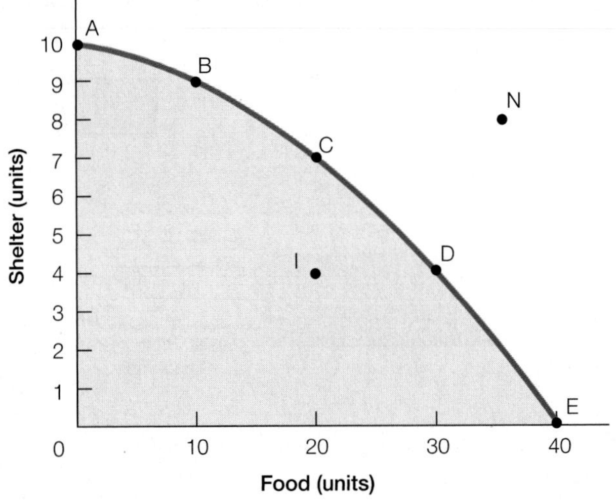

a. Does this production possibilities curve show increasing opportunity costs? Explain.

b. What is the opportunity cost of moving from point I to point D? Explain.

c. What is the opportunity cost of moving from point C to point B?

d. Which of points A–E is the most efficient? Explain.

chapter 4

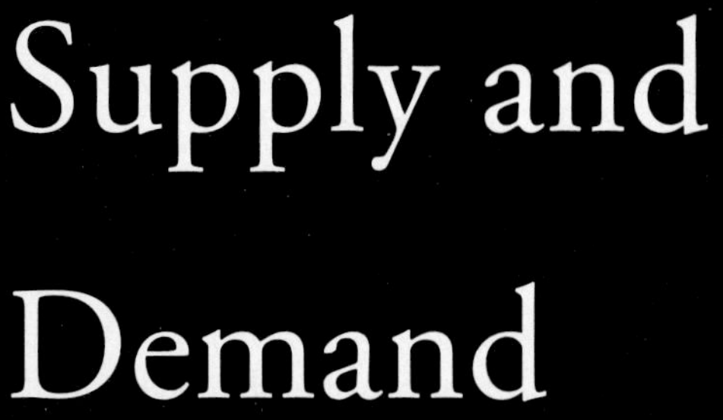

Supply and Demand

4.1 MARKETS
What is a market?

4.2 DEMAND
Why is the demand curve negatively sloped?

4.3 SHIFTS IN THE DEMAND CURVE
What are the determinants of demand?

4.4 SUPPLY
What are the determinants of supply?

4.5 MARKET EQUILIBRIUM PRICE AND QUANTITY
Why is the concept of market equilibrium such a valuable tool?

4.6 CHANGES IN EQUILIBRIUM PRICE AND QUANTITY
What happens to equilibrium price and quantity when we shift the supply or demand curve?

4.7 PRICE CONTROLS
What are price ceilings and price floors?

section

4.1

Markets

- What is a market?
- Why is it so difficult to define a market?

DEFINING A MARKET

market
the process of buyers and sellers exchanging goods and services

Although we usually think of a market as a place where some sort of exchange occurs, a market is not really a place at all. A **market** is the process of buyers and sellers exchanging goods and services. This means that supermarkets, the New York Stock Exchange, drug stores, roadside stands, garage sales, Internet stores, and restaurants are all markets.

Every market is different. That is, the conditions under which the exchange between buyers and sellers takes place can vary. These differences make it difficult to precisely define a market. After all, an incredible variety of exchange arrangements exists in the real world—organized securities markets, wholesale auction markets, foreign exchange markets, real estate markets, labor markets, and so forth.

Goods being priced and traded in various ways at various locations by various kinds of buyers and sellers further compound the problem of defining a market. For some goods, such as housing, markets are numerous but limited to a geographic area. Homes in Santa Barbara, California, for example (about 100 miles from downtown Los Angeles), do not compete directly with homes in Los Angeles. Why? Because people who work in Los Angeles will generally look for homes within commuting distance. Even within cities, there are separate markets for homes, differentiated by amenities such as bigger houses, newer houses, larger lots, and better schools.

In the stock market, there are many buyers and sellers, and profit statements and stock prices are readily available. New information is quickly understood by buyers and sellers and is incorporated into the price of the stock. When people expect a company to do better in the future, they bid up the price of that stock and if they expect the company to do poorly in the future, the price of the stock falls.

In a similar manner, markets are numerous but geographically limited for a good such as cement. Because transportation costs are so high relative to the selling price, the good is not shipped any substantial distance, and buyers are usually in contact only with local producers. Price and output are thus determined in a number of small markets. In other markets, like those for gold or automobiles, markets are global. The important point is not what a market looks like, but what it does—it facilitates trade.

BUYERS AND SELLERS

The roles of buyers and sellers in markets are important. The buyers, as a group, determine the demand side of the market. Buyers include the consumers who purchase the goods and services and the firms that buy inputs—labor, capital, and raw materials. Sellers, as a group, determine the supply side of the market. Sellers include the firms that produce and sell goods and services, and the resource owners who sell their inputs to firms—workers who "sell" their labor and resource owners who sell raw materials and capital. It is the interaction of buyers and sellers that determines market prices and output—through the forces of supply and demand.

competitive market
A market where the many buyers and sellers have very little market power—each buyer's and seller's effect on market price is negligible

In this chapter, we focus on how supply and demand works in a **competitive market.** A competitive market is one in which there are a number of buyers and sellers offering similar products and no single buyer or seller can influence the market price. That is, buyers and sellers have very little market power. Because most markets contain a large degree of competitiveness, the lessons of supply and demand can be applied to many different types of problems.

Section Check

1. Markets consist of buyers and sellers exchanging goods and services with one another.
2. Markets can be regional, national, or global.
3. Buyers determine the demand side of the market and sellers determine the supply side of the market.

---

1. Why is it difficult to define a market precisely?
2. Why do you get your produce at a supermarket rather than directly from farmers?
3. Why do the prices people pay for similar items at garage sales vary more than the prices they pay for similar items in a department store?

section 4.2

Demand

- What is the law of demand?
- What is an individual demand curve?
- What is a market demand curve?
- What is a money price?
- What is a relative price?

law of demand
the quantity of a good or service demanded varies inversely (negatively) with its price, ceteris paribus

THE LAW OF DEMAND

Some laws are made to protect us, such as "no speeding" or "no drinking and driving." Other times observed behavior is so pervasive it is called a law—like the law of demand. According to the **law of demand,** the quantity of a good or service demanded varies inversely (negatively) with its price, *ceteris paribus.* More directly, the law of demand says that, other things being equal, when the price (P) of a good or service falls, the quantity demanded (Q_D) increases, and conversely, if the price of a good or service rises, the quantity demanded decreases.

$$P\uparrow \Rightarrow Q_D\downarrow \text{ and } P\downarrow \Rightarrow Q_D\uparrow$$

The law of demand puts the concept of basic human "needs," at least as an analytical tool, to rest. Needs are those things that you must have at any price. That is, there are no substitutes. There are usually plenty of substitutes available for any good, some better than others. The law of demand, with its inverse relationship between price and quantity demanded, implies that even so-called needs are more or less urgent depending on the circumstances (opportunity costs). Whenever you hear somebody say, "I need a new car," "I need a new stereo," or "I need new clothes," always be sure to ask: What does the person really mean? At what price does that person "need" the good?

COURTESY OF ROBERT SEXTON

Need water? What if the price of water increases significantly? At the new higher price, consumers will still use almost as much water for essentials like drinking and cooking. However, they may no longer "need" to wash their cars as often, water their lawns daily, hose off their sidewalks, run the dishwasher so frequently, take long showers, or flush the toilet as often.

WHY IS THERE A NEGATIVE RELATIONSHIP BETWEEN PRICE AND THE QUANTITY DEMANDED?

The law of demand describes a negative (inverse) relationship between price and quantity demanded. When price goes up, the quantity demanded goes down, and vice versa.

substitution effect
at higher prices, buyers increasingly substitute other goods for the good that now has a higher relative price

individual demand schedule
a schedule that shows the relationship between price and quantity demanded

individual demand curve
a graphical representation that shows the inverse relationship between price and quantity demanded

But why is this so? The primary reason for this inverse relationship is the **substitution effect.** At higher prices, buyers increasingly substitute other goods for the good that now has a higher relative price. For example, if the price of orange juice increases, some consumers may substitute out of orange juice into other juices, such as apple or tomato juice, or perhaps water, milk, or coffee. This is what economists call the substitution effect of a price change. Of course, if the relative price of orange juice fell, then consumers would substitute out of other products and increase their quantity of orange juice demanded, because the lower relative price now makes it a more attractive purchase.

AN INDIVIDUAL DEMAND SCHEDULE

The **individual demand schedule** shows the relationship between the price of the good and the quantity demanded. For example, suppose Elizabeth enjoys drinking coffee. How many pounds of coffee would Elizabeth be willing and able to buy at various prices during the year? At a price of $3 a pound, Elizabeth buys 15 pounds of coffee over the course of a year. If the price is higher, at $4 per pound, she might buy only 10 pounds; if it is lower, say $1 per pound, she might buy 25 pounds of coffee during the year. Elizabeth's demand for coffee for the year is summarized in the demand schedule in Exhibit 1. Elizabeth might not be consciously aware of the amounts that she would purchase at prices other than the prevailing one, but that does not alter the fact that she has a schedule in the sense that she would have bought various other amounts had other prices prevailed. It must be emphasized that the schedule is a list of alternative possibilities. At any one time, only one of the prices will prevail, and thus a certain quantity will be purchased.

section 4.2 Exhibit 1 — Elizabeth's Demand Schedule for Coffee

Price (per pound)	Quantity Demanded (pounds per year)
$5	5
4	10
3	15
2	20
1	25

AN INDIVIDUAL DEMAND CURVE

By plotting the different prices and corresponding quantities demanded in Elizabeth's demand schedule in Exhibit 1 and then connecting them, we can create an **individual demand curve** for Elizabeth (Exhibit 2). From the curve, we can see that when the price is higher, the quantity demanded is lower, and when the price is lower, the quantity demanded is higher. The demand curve shows how the quantity demanded of the good changes as its price varies.

section 4.2 Exhibit 2 — Elizabeth's Demand Curve for Coffee

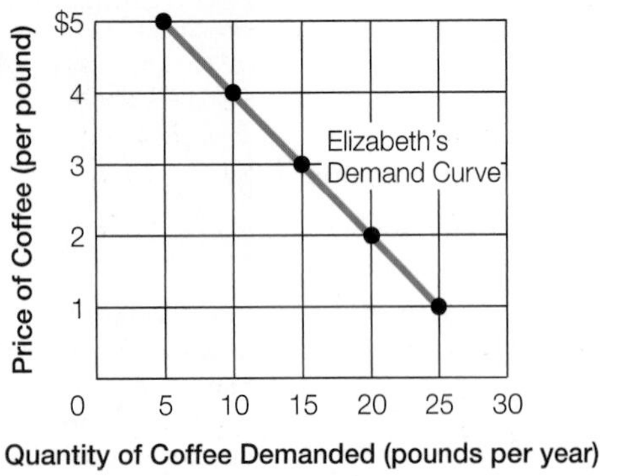

Price of Coffee (per pound): $5, 4, 3, 2, 1, 0
Elizabeth's Demand Curve
Quantity of Coffee Demanded (pounds per year): 5, 10, 15, 20, 25, 30

The dots represent various quantities of coffee that Elizabeth would be willing and able to buy at different prices in a given time period. The demand curve shows how the quantity demanded varies inversely with the price of the good when we hold everything else constant—*ceteris paribus*. Because of this inverse relationship between price and quantity demanded, the demand curve is downward sloping.

WHAT IS A MARKET DEMAND CURVE?

Although we introduced this concept in terms of the individual, economists usually speak of the demand curve in terms of large groups of people—a whole nation, a community, or a trading area. As you know, every single individual has his or her demand curve for every product. The horizontal summing of the demand curves of many individuals is called the **market demand curve.**

Suppose the consumer group is comprised of Homer, Marge, and the rest of their small community, Springfield, and that the product is still coffee. The effect of price on the quantity of coffee demanded by Marge, Homer, and the rest of Springfield is given in the demand schedule and demand curves shown in Exhibit 3. At $4 per pound, Homer would be willing and able to buy 20 pounds of coffee per year, Marge would be willing and able to buy 10 pounds and the rest of Springfield would be willing and able to buy 2,970 pounds. At $3 per pound, Homer would be willing and able to buy 25 pounds of coffee per year, Marge would be willing and able to buy 15 pounds and the rest of Springfield would be willing and able to buy 4,960 pounds. The market demand curve is simply the (horizontal) sum of the quantities Homer, Marge, and the rest of Springfield demand at each price. That is, at $4, the quantity demanded in the market would be 3,000 pounds of coffee (20 + 10 + 2,970 = 3,000), and at $3, the quantity demanded in the market would be 5,000 pounds of coffee (25 + 15 + 4,960 = 5,000).

What if this house had been on the market for a year at the same price and not sold? While no one may want this house at the current asking price, a number of people may want it at a lower price—the law of demand.

In Exhibit 4, we offer a more complete set of prices and quantities from the market demand for coffee during the year. Remember, the market demand curve shows the amounts that all the buyers in the market would be willing and able to buy at various prices. For example, if the price of coffee is $2 per pound, consumers in the market would

market demand curve
the horizontal summation of individual demand curves

section 4.2
Exhibit 3
Creating a Market Demand Curve

a. Creating a Market Demand Schedule for Coffee

	Quantity Demanded (pounds per year)						
Price (per pound)	**Homer**	**+**	**Marge**	**+**	**Rest of Springfield**	**=**	**Market Demand**
$4	20	+	10	+	2,970	=	3,000
$3	25	+	15	+	4,960	=	5,000

b. Creating a Market Demand Curve for Coffee

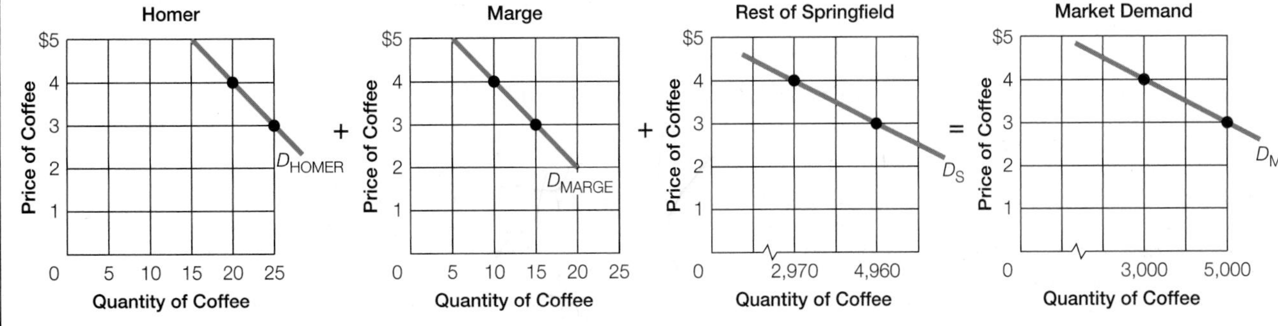

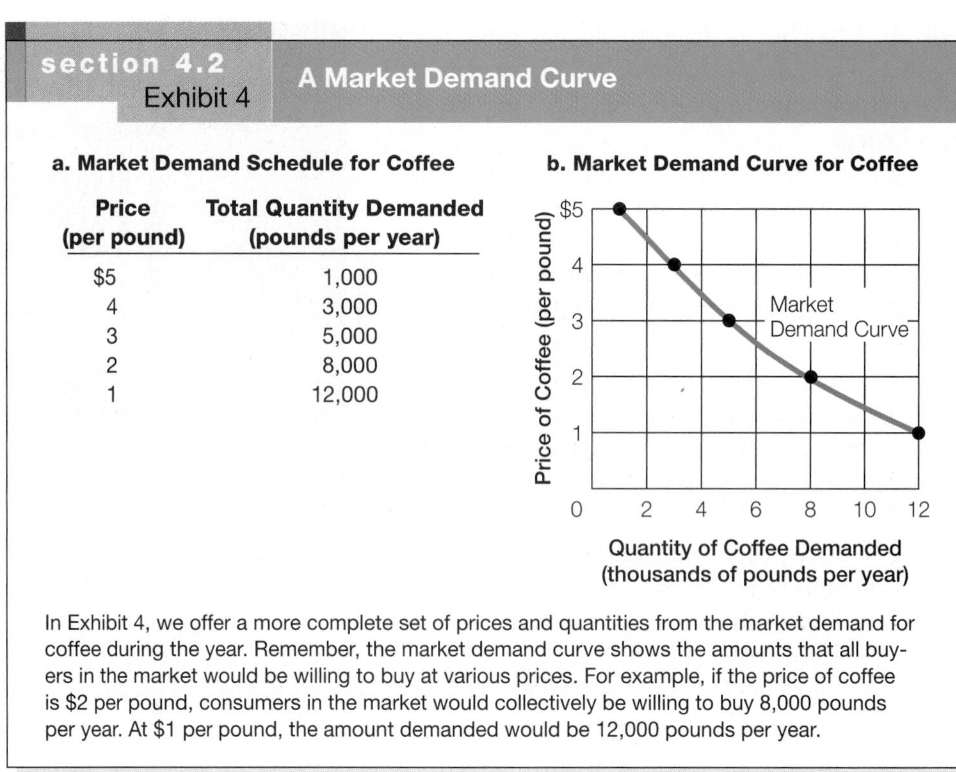

a. Market Demand Schedule for Coffee

Price (per pound)	Total Quantity Demanded (pounds per year)
$5	1,000
4	3,000
3	5,000
2	8,000
1	12,000

In Exhibit 4, we offer a more complete set of prices and quantities from the market demand for coffee during the year. Remember, the market demand curve shows the amounts that all buyers in the market would be willing to buy at various prices. For example, if the price of coffee is $2 per pound, consumers in the market would collectively be willing to buy 8,000 pounds per year. At $1 per pound, the amount demanded would be 12,000 pounds per year.

collectively be willing and able to buy 8,000 pounds per year. At $1 per pound, the amount demanded would be 12,000 pounds per year.

A MONEY PRICE

money price
the price that one pays in dollars and cents, sometimes called an absolute or nominal price

Over the past 50 years, few goods have fallen in **money price**—that is, the price that you or I would pay in dollars and cents. The money price is sometimes called the *absolute* or *nominal price,* expressed in dollars of current purchasing power. Some well-known examples of falling money prices include cellular telephones, DVD players, digital cameras, and home computers, but the evidence indicates that most prices have risen in money terms.

MONEY PRICES VERSUS RELATIVE PRICES

relative price
the price of one good relative to other goods

Money prices themselves are of little importance to most economic decisions in a world where virtually all prices are changing. It is **relative price,** the price of one good relative to other goods, that is crucial.

Suppose you were exploring the U.S. inflation rate of the 1960s and 1970s. You found that from 1960 to 1973, the price of gasoline at the pump rose markedly, but the quantities of gasoline demanded did not fall. Is this a flaw in the law of demand? No. While it is true that gasoline prices in dollars rose significantly over this period, so did just about everything else—including wages. As it turns out, the relative price of gasoline, the price of gasoline as compared to that of other goods, did not change much over this period. Thus, we would not expect this to cause a fall in the quantity demanded (holding other things constant, especially income). That is, because the relative price did not rise, we would not expect a fall in gasoline consumption.

Section Check

SECTION CHECK

1. The law of demand states that when the price of a good falls (rises), the quantity demanded rises (falls), *ceteris paribus.*
2. An individual demand curve is a graphical representation of the relationship between the price and the quantity demanded.
3. The market demand curve shows the amount of a good that all the buyers in the market would be willing and able to buy at various prices.
4. The money price is what one pays in terms of dollars and cents.
5. The relative price is the price of one good relative to another.

---

1. What is an inverse relationship?
2. How do lower prices change buyers' incentives?
3. How do higher prices change buyers' incentives?
4. What is an individual demand schedule?
5. What difference is there between an individual demand curve and a market demand curve?
6. Why does the amount of dating on campus tend to decline just before and during final exams?
7. How are money prices and relative prices different?
8. Why are economists so concerned about relative prices?
9. The money price of most goods has risen over time. What does that mean?
10. Motel 6 began by charging $6 per night for a room back in the 1960s but now charges about $40 per night. What must have happened to the overall price level for the relative price of its motel rooms to have fallen?

section 4.3

Shifts in the Demand Curve

- What is the difference between a change in demand and a change in quantity demanded?
- What are the determinants of demand?
- What are substitutes and complements?
- What are normal and inferior goods?
- How does the number of buyers affect the demand curve?
- How do changes in taste affect the demand curve?
- How do changing expectations affect the demand curve?

A CHANGE IN DEMAND VERSUS A CHANGE IN QUANTITY DEMANDED

Economists think consumers are influenced by the prices of goods when they make their purchasing decisions. At lower prices, people prefer to buy more of a good than at higher prices, holding other factors constant. Why? Primarily, it is because many goods are substitutes for one another. For example, an increase in the price of coffee might tempt some buyers to switch from buying coffee to buying tea or soft drinks.

Understanding this relationship between price and quantity demanded is so important that economists make a clear distinction between it and the various other factors that

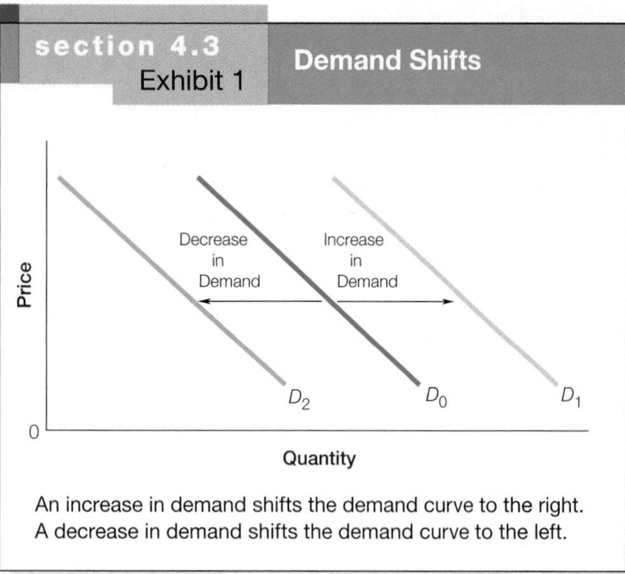

An increase in demand shifts the demand curve to the right. A decrease in demand shifts the demand curve to the left.

can influence consumer behavior. A change in a good's price is said to lead to a **change in quantity demanded.** That is, it "moves you along" a given demand curve. The demand curve is drawn under the assumption that all other things are held constant, except the price of the good. However, economists know that price is not the only thing that affects the quantity of a good that people buy. The other factors that influence the demand curve are called *determinants of demand* and a change in these other factors *shifts the entire demand curve.* These determinants of demand are called demand shifters and they lead to a **change in demand.**

SHIFTS IN DEMAND

An increase in demand shifts the demand curve to the right; a decrease in demand shifts the demand curve to the left, as seen in Exhibit 1. Some of the possible demand shifters are: the prices of related goods; income; number of buyers; tastes; and expectations. We will now look more closely at each of these variables.

change in quantity demanded
a change in a good's price leads to a change in quantity demanded, a move along a given demand curve

change in demand
the prices of related goods, income, number of buyers, tastes, and expectations can change the demand for a good. That is, a change in one of these factors shifts the entire demand curve

substitute
an increase (a decrease) in the price of one good causes the demand curve for another good to shift to the right (left)

THE PRICES OF RELATED GOODS

In deciding how much of a good or service to buy, consumers are influenced by the price of that good or service, a relationship summarized in the law of demand. However, consumers are also influenced by the prices of *related* goods and services—substitutes and complements.

Substitutes

Suppose you go into a store to buy a couple of six packs of Coca-Cola and you see that Pepsi is on sale for half its usual price. Is it possible that you might decide to buy Pepsi instead of Coca-Cola? Economists argue that this is the case, and empirical tests have confirmed that people are responsive to both the price of the good in question and the prices of related goods. In this example, Pepsi and Coca-Cola are said to be substitutes. Two goods are **substitutes** if an increase (a decrease) in the price of one good causes an increase (a decrease) in the demand for another good, a direct (or positive) relationship.

Because personal tastes differ, what are substitutes for one person may not be so for another person. Furthermore, some substitutes are better than others. For most people, good substitutes include butter and margarine, movie tickets and video rentals, jackets and sweaters, and two $10 bills and a $20 bill.

In an attempt to change its image from a gambling town to a family friendly town, several new Las Vegas hotels have been built to simulate European cities, including Paris and Venice. If the price of European travel becomes more expensive, some travelers might substitute Paris Las Vegas, or the Venetian (Las Vegas), for their European counterparts.

APPLICATION

SUBSTITUTE GOODS

Q: Can you describe the change we would expect to see in the demand curve for Pepsi if the relative price for Coca-Cola increased significantly?

A: If the price of one good increases and, as a result, an individual buys more of another good, the two related goods are substitutes. That is, buying more of one reduces purchases of the other. In Exhibit 2(a), we see that as the price of Coca-Cola increased—a movement up along your demand curve for it—you increased your demand for Pepsi, resulting in a shift in the demand for Pepsi (Exhibit 2(b)). If you hated a particular brand of soft drink, however, it might not matter if someone was giving it away, but that is highly unlikely. The substitution effect varies among individuals, but in the aggregate we can recognize substitutes fairly well.

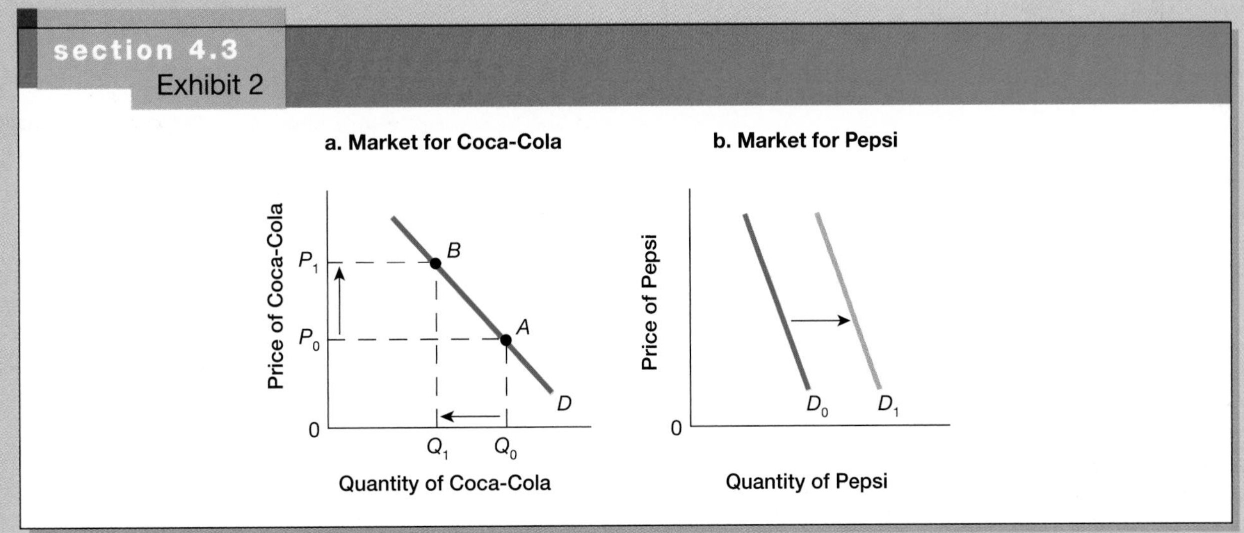

Complements

If an increase (a decrease) in the price of one good causes a decrease (an increase) in the demand of another good (an inverse or negative relationship), the two goods are called **complements.** Complements are goods that "go together," often consumed and used simultaneously, such as skis and bindings, hot dogs and buns, DVDs and DVD players, or printers and ink cartridges. For example, if the price of motorcycles rises and it causes the demand for motorcycle helmets to fall (shift to the left), the two goods are complements. Or if a decrease in the price of stereo equipment leads to an increase in the demand (a rightward shift) for compact discs, then stereos and CDs are complements.

complement
an increase (a decrease) in the price of one good shifts the demand curve for another good to the left (right)

Substitutes	**Complements**
$P_{\text{GOOD A}} \uparrow \Rightarrow \uparrow D_{\text{GOOD B}}$	$P_{\text{GOOD A}} \uparrow \Rightarrow \downarrow D_{\text{GOOD B}}$
$P_{\text{GOOD A}} \downarrow \Rightarrow \downarrow D_{\text{GOOD B}}$	$P_{\text{GOOD A}} \downarrow \Rightarrow \uparrow D_{\text{GOOD B}}$

APPLICATION

COMPLEMENTARY GOODS

Q: As he looked over the rackets hanging on the wall of the local sports shop, an aspiring young tennis player, Clay Kort, noticed that the price of the rackets was much higher (due to cost increases) than last month. Clay predicted that this increase in the relative price of tennis rackets would probably lead to a reduced demand for tennis balls. Do you agree with Clay?

A: Clay realized that there would be fewer tennis players on the courts if tennis rackets increased in price. In Exhibit 3(a), we see that as the price of tennis rackets increases, the quantity of tennis rackets demanded falls. And with fewer tennis rackets being purchased, we would also expect people to decrease their demand (a leftward shift) for tennis balls (Exhibit 3(b)). There are many other examples of complements in athletic equipment: skis and bindings, golf clubs and golf balls, bows and arrows, and so on.

section 4.3
Exhibit 3

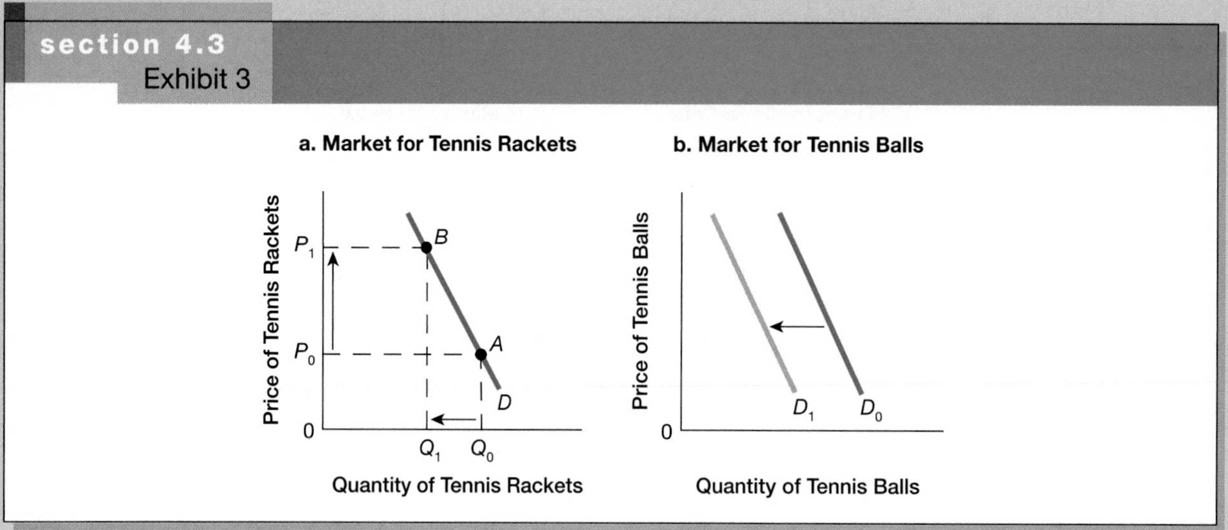

INCOME

Economists have observed that generally the consumption of goods and services is positively related to the income available to consumers. Empirical studies support the notion that as individuals receive more income they tend to increase their purchases of most goods and services. Other things held equal, rising income usually leads to an increase in the demand for goods (a rightward shift of the demand curve), and decreasing income usually leads to a decrease in the demand for goods (a leftward shift of the demand curve).

normal good
if income increases, the demand for a good increases; if income decreases, the demand for a good decreases

inferior good
if income increases, the demand for a good decreases; if income decreases, the demand for a good increases

Normal and Inferior Goods

If demand for a good increases when incomes rise and decreases when incomes fall, the good is called a **normal good.** Most goods are normal goods. Consumers will typically buy more CDs, clothes, pizzas, and trips to the movies as their incomes rise. However, if demand for a good decreases when incomes rise and increases when incomes fall, the good is called an **inferior good.** For example, for most people inferior goods might include do-it-yourself haircuts, used cars, thrift-shop clothing, mail-order dentures, store-brand products, and so on. The term *inferior* in this sense does not refer to the quality of the good in question but shows that when income changes, demand changes in the opposite direction (inversely).

APPLICATION

NORMAL AND INFERIOR GOODS

Q: Chester owns a furniture shop. If there was a recent boom in the economy (higher average income per person and fewer people unemployed), can Chester expect to sell more furniture?

A: Yes, furniture is generally considered a normal good, so a rise in income will increase the demand for furniture (Exhibit 4(a)). However, if Chester sells unfinished, used, or lower-quality furniture, the demand for his products may fall, as higher incomes allow customers to buy furniture that is finished, new, or is of higher quality. Chester's furniture would then be an inferior good (Exhibit 4(b)).

section 4.3
Exhibit 4

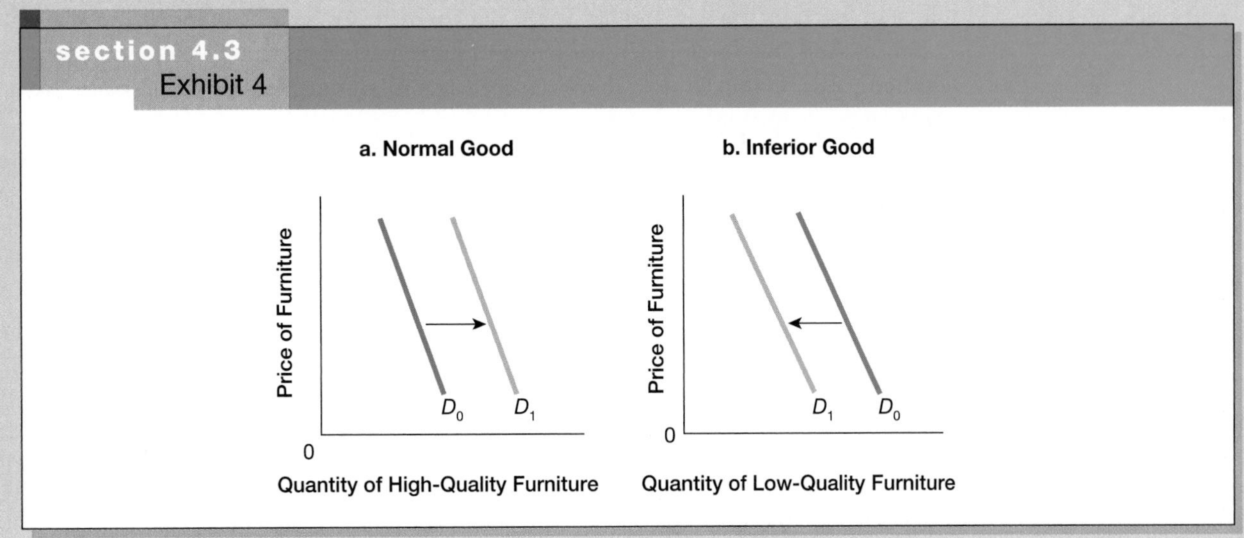

For example, if people's incomes rise and they increase their demand for movie tickets, we say that movie tickets are a normal good. But if people's incomes fall and they increase their demand for bus rides, we say bus rides are an inferior good. Whether goods are normal or inferior, the point here is that income influences demand—usually positively, but sometimes negatively.

Normal Good	Inferior Good
Income ↑ ⇒ Demand ↑	Income ↑ ⇒ Demand ↓
Income ↓ ⇒ Demand ↓	Income ↓ ⇒ Demand ↑

For most people, do-it-yourself haircuts are an inferior good. That is, an increase in income will lead to a reduction in do-it-yourself haircuts.

NUMBER OF BUYERS

The demand for a good or service will vary with the size of the potential consumer population. The demand for wheat, for example, rises as population increases, because the added population wants to consume wheat products, like bread or cereal. Marketing experts, who closely follow the patterns of consumer behavior with regards to a particular good or service, are usually vitally concerned with the "demographics" of the product—the vital statistics of the potential consumer population, including size, income, and age characteristics. For example, market researchers for baby food companies keep a close watch on the birth rate.

TASTES

The demand for a good or service may increase or decrease suddenly with changes in fashions or fads. Taste changes may be triggered by advertising or promotion, by a news story, by the behavior of some popular public figure, and so on. Taste changes are particularly noticeable in apparel. Skirt lengths, coat lapels, shoe styles and tie sizes change frequently.

Changes in preferences naturally lead to shifts in demand. Much of the predictive power of economic theory, however, stems from the assumption that tastes are relatively stable, at least over a substantial period of time. Tastes *do* change, though. A person may grow tired of one type of recreation or food and try another type. Changes in occupation, number of dependents, state of health, and age also tend to alter preferences. The birth of a baby may cause a family to spend less on recreation and more on food and clothing. Illness increases the demand for medicine and lessens purchases of other goods. A cold winter increases the demand for fuel. Changes in customs and traditions also affect preferences, and the development of new products draws consumer preferences away from other goods. Compact discs have replaced record albums, just as inline skates have replaced traditional roller skates.

Two more examples of things that have risen in popularity in recent years are tattoos and body piercing; the demand for these services has been pushed to the right. According to *U.S. News and World Report*, tattooing has emerged as one of the country's fastest-growing retail businesses. These brightly lighted establishments are springing up near suburban malls, colleges, and even on the main streets of small towns.

EXPECTATIONS

Sometimes the demand for a good or service in a given time period will dramatically increase or decrease because consumers expect the good to change in price or availability at some future date. For example, in the summer of 1997, many buyers expected coffee harvests to be lower because of El Niño. As a result of their expectations of higher future coffee prices, buyers increased their current demand for coffee. That is, the current demand for coffee shifted to the right.

According to a *Wall Street Journal* article, many firewood dealers across the country saw a large increase in the demand for firewood in *anticipation* of the Y2K problem that never materialized. Other examples, such as waiting to buy a home computer because price reductions may be even greater in the future, are also common. Or, if you expect to earn additional income next month, you may be more willing to dip into your current savings to buy something this month.

CHANGES IN DEMAND VERSUS CHANGES IN QUANTITY DEMANDED REVISITED

Economists put particular emphasis on the impact on consumer behavior of a change in the price of a good. We are interested in distinguishing between consumer behavior related to the price of a good itself (movement *along* a demand curve) from behavior related to other factors changing (shifts of the demand curve).

As indicated earlier, if the price of a good changes, we say that this leads to a *"change in quantity demanded."* If one of the other factors (determinants) influencing consumer behavior changes, we say there is a *"change in demand."* The effects of some of the determinants that cause a change in demand (shifters) are reviewed in Exhibit 5.

Exhibit 5

Possible Demand Shifters

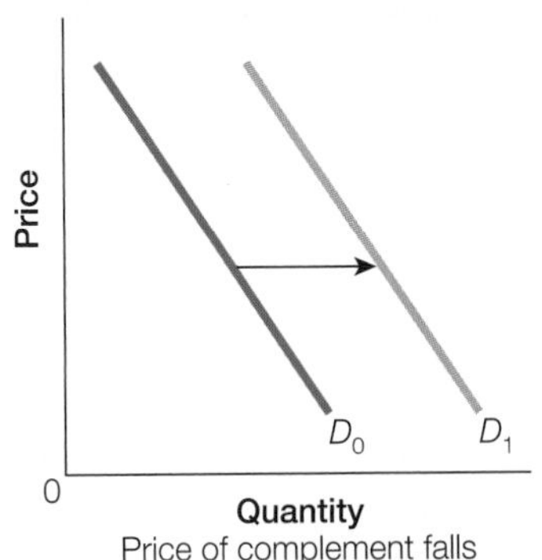

Price of complement falls or price of substitute rises

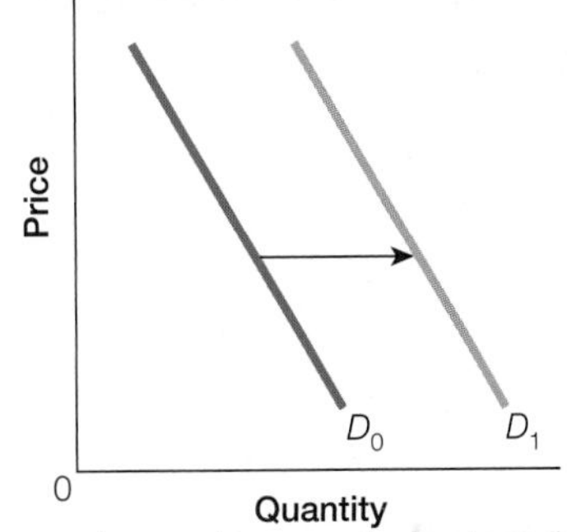

Income increases (normal good)

Price

D_1 D_0

0

Quantity

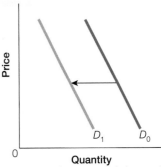

Income increases (inferior good)

Price

D_0

0

Quantity

Increase in the number of buyers in the market

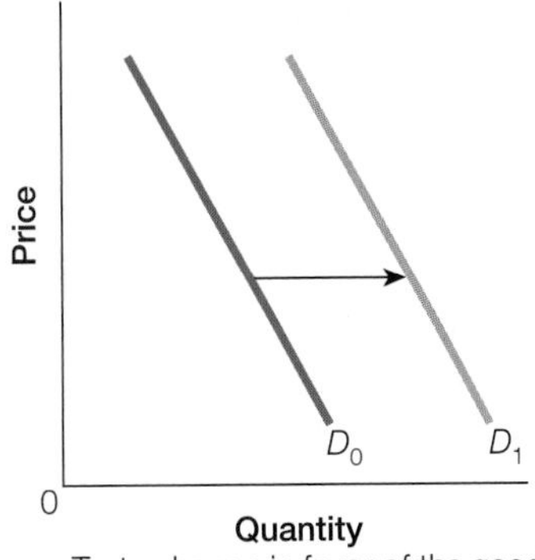

Taste change in favor of the good

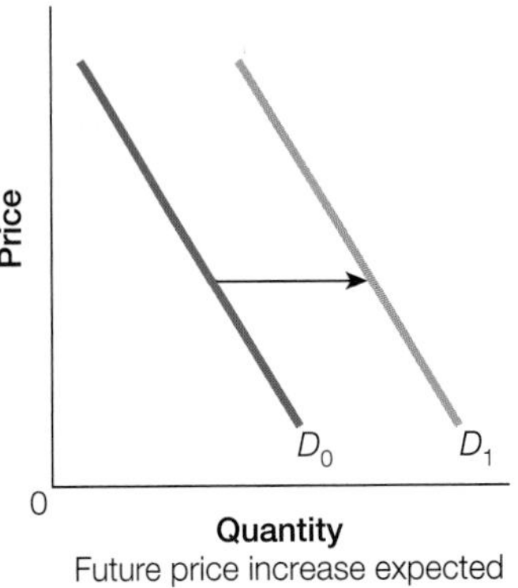

Future price increase expected

APPLICATION

CHANGES IN DEMAND VERSUS CHANGES IN QUANTITY DEMANDED

Q: How would you use a graph to demonstrate the two following scenarios? (1) Someone buys more CDs because the price of CDs has fallen; and (2) a student buys more CDs because she just got a 20 percent raise at work giving her additional income.

A: In Exhibit 6, the movement from A to B is called *an increase in quantity demanded,* and the movement from B to A is called a *decrease in quantity demanded*. Economists use the phrase "increase or decrease in quantity demanded" to describe movements along a given demand curve. However, the change from A to C is called an *increase in demand,* and the change from C to A is called a *decrease in demand*. The phrase "increase or decrease in demand" is reserved for a shift in the whole curve. So if an individual buys more CDs because the price fell, we say there was an increase in quantity demanded. However, if she buys more CDs even at the current price, say $15, we say there is an increase in demand. In this case, the increase in income was responsible for the increase in demand, as she chose to spend some of her new income on CDs.

section 4.3

Exhibit 6

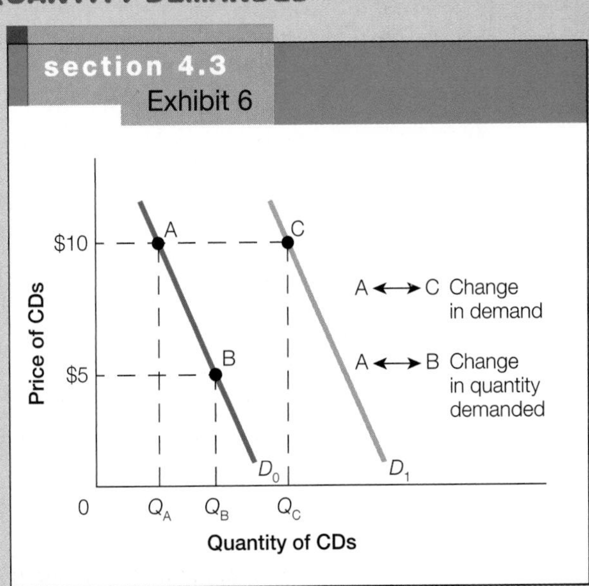

Section Check

1. A change in the quantity demanded describes a movement along a given demand curve in response to a change in the price of the good.
2. A change in demand shifts the entire demand curve. An increase in demand shifts the demand curve to the right; a decrease shifts it to the left.
3. A change in the price of a substitute shifts the demand curve for the good in question. The relationship is direct.
4. A change in the price of a complement shifts the demand curve for the good in question. The relationship is inverse.
5. Changes in income cause demand curve shifts. For normal goods the relationship is direct; for inferior goods it is inverse.
6. The position of the demand curve will vary according to the number of consumers in the market.
7. Taste changes will shift the demand curve.
8. Changes in expected future prices and income can shift the current demand curve.

---

1. What is the difference between a change in demand and a change in quantity demanded?
2. If the price of zucchini increases and it causes the demand for yellow squash to rise, what do we call the relationship between zucchini and yellow squash?
3. If incomes rise and, as a result, demand for jet skis increases, how do we describe that good?
4. How do expectations about the future influence the demand curve?
5. Would a change in the price of ice cream cause a change in the demand for ice cream? Why or why not?
6. Would a change in the price of ice cream likely cause a change in the demand for frozen yogurt, a substitute?
7. If plane travel is a normal good and bus travel is an inferior good, what will happen to the demand curves for plane and bus travel if people's incomes increase?

section 4.4

Supply

- What is the law of supply?
- What is an individual supply curve?
- What is a market supply curve?
- What is the difference between a change in supply and a change in quantity supplied?
- What are the major supply shifters?

THE LAW OF SUPPLY

In a market, the answer to the fundamental question, "What do we produce, and in what quantities?" depends on the interaction of both buyers and sellers. Demand is only half the story. The willingness and ability of suppliers to provide goods are equally important factors that must be weighed by decision makers in all societies. As in the case of demand, factors other than the price of the good are also important to suppliers, such as the cost of inputs or advances in technology. As with demand, the price of the good is an important factor. While behavior will vary among individual suppliers, economists expect, other things being equal, that the quantity supplied will vary directly with the price of the good, a relationship called the **law of supply.** According to the law of supply, the higher the price of the good (P), the greater the quantity supplied (Q_S), and the lower the price of the good, the smaller the quantity supplied.

$$P\uparrow \Rightarrow Q_S\uparrow \text{ and } P\downarrow \Rightarrow Q_S\downarrow$$

The relationship described by the law of supply is a direct, or positive, relationship, because the variables move in the same direction.

© DIGITAL STOCK/CORBISIMAGES

In order to get more oil, drillers must sometimes drill deeper or go into unexplored areas, and they still may come up with a dry hole. If it costs more to increase oil production, then oil prices would have to rise in order for producers to increase their output.

A POSITIVE RELATIONSHIP BETWEEN PRICE AND QUANTITY SUPPLIED

Firms supplying goods and services want to increase their profits, and the higher the price per unit, the greater the profitability generated by supplying more of that good. For example, if you were a coffee grower, wouldn't you much rather be paid \$5 a pound than \$1 a pound?

There is another reason that supply curves are upward sloping. The law of increasing opportunity costs demonstrated that when we hold technology and input prices constant, producing additional units of a good will require increased opportunity costs. That is, when we produce more of anything, we use the most efficient resources first (those with the lowest opportunity cost) and then draw on less efficient resources (those with higher opportunity cost) as more of the good is produced. So if costs are rising for producers as they produce more units, they must receive a higher price to compensate them for their higher costs. In short, increasing production costs mean that suppliers will require higher prices to induce them to increase their output.

law of supply
the higher (lower) the price of the good, the greater (smaller) the quantity supplied

AN INDIVIDUAL SUPPLY CURVE

To illustrate the concept of an **individual supply curve,** consider the amount of coffee that an individual supplier, John Valdez, is willing and able to supply in one year. The law of supply can be illustrated, like the law of demand, by a table or graph. John's supply schedule for coffee is shown in Exhibit 1(a). The price–quantity supplied combinations

individual supply curve
a graphical representation that shows the positive relationship between the price and the quantity supplied

section 4.4 Exhibit 1 An Individual Supply Curve

a. John's Supply Schedule for Coffee

Price (per pound)	Quantity Supplied (pounds per year)
\$5	80
4	70
3	50
2	30
1	10

b. John's Supply Curve for Coffee

section 4.4 Exhibit 2 A Market Supply Curve

a. Market Supply Schedule for Coffee

	Quantity Supplied (pounds per year)				
Price	**John**	+	**Other Producers**	=	**Market Supply**
$5	80	+	7920	=	8,000
4	70	+	6930	=	7,000
3	50	+	4950	=	5,000
2	30	+	2970	=	3,000
1	10	+	990	=	1,000

b. Market Demand Curve for Coffee

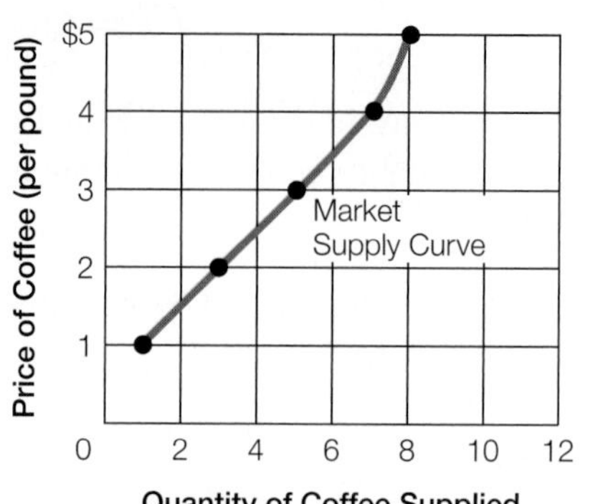

The dots on this graph indicate different quantities of coffee that producers would be willing and able to supply at various prices. The line connecting those combinations is the market supply curve.

were then plotted and joined to create the individual supply curve shown in Exhibit 1(b). Note that the individual supply curve is upward sloping as you move from left to right. At higher prices, it will be more attractive to increase production. Existing firms, or growers, will produce more at higher prices than at lower prices.

THE MARKET SUPPLY CURVE

market supply curve *a graphical representation of the amount of goods and services that suppliers are willing and able to supply at various prices*

The **market supply curve** may be thought of as the horizontal summation of the supply curves for individual firms. The market supply schedule, which reflects the total quantity supplied at each price by all of the coffee producers, is shown in Exhibit 2(a). Exhibit 2(b) illustrates the resulting market supply curve for this group of coffee producers.

A CHANGE IN QUANTITY SUPPLIED VERSUS A CHANGE IN SUPPLY

Changes in the price of a good lead to changes in quantity supplied by suppliers, just as changes in the price of a good lead to changes in quantity demanded by buyers. Similarly, a change in supply, whether an increase or a decrease, will occur for reasons other than changes in the price of the product itself, just as changes in demand are due to factors (determinants) other than the price of the good. In other words, a change in the price of the good in question is shown as a movement along a given supply curve, leading to a change in quantity supplied. A change in any other factor that can affect supplier behavior (input prices, the prices of related products, expectations, number of suppliers, technology, regulation, taxes and subsidies, and weather) results in *a shift in the entire supply curve,* leading to a change in supply.

SHIFTS IN SUPPLY

An increase in supply shifts the supply curve to the right; a decrease in supply shifts the supply curve to the left, as seen in Exhibit 3. We will now look at some of the possible determinants of supply—factors that determine the position of the supply curve—in greater depth.

INPUT PRICES

Suppliers are strongly influenced by the costs of inputs used in the production process, such as steel used for automobiles or microchips used in computers. For example, higher labor, materials, energy, or other input costs increase the costs of production, causing the supply curve to shift to the left at each and every price. If input prices fall, this will lower the costs of production, causing the supply curve to shift to the right—more will be supplied at each and every price.

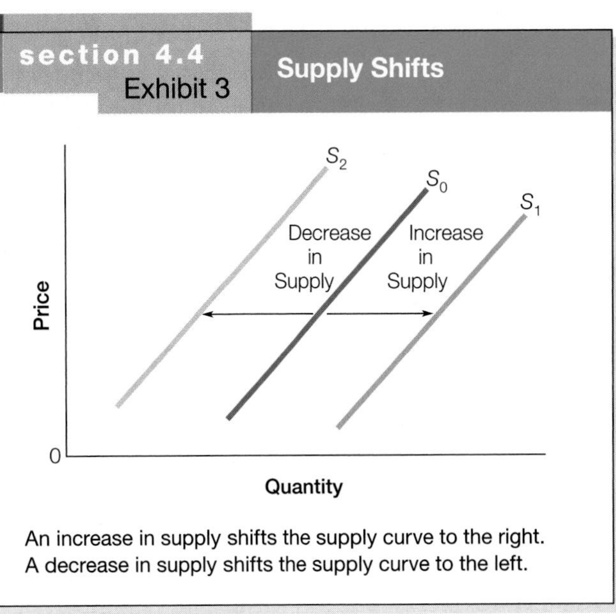

An increase in supply shifts the supply curve to the right. A decrease in supply shifts the supply curve to the left.

THE PRICES OF RELATED PRODUCTS

Suppose you own your own farm, on which you plant cotton and barley. Then, the price of barley falls and farmers reduce the quantity supplied of barley, as seen in Exhibit 4(a). What effect would the lower price of barley have on your cotton production? Easy—it would increase the supply of cotton. You would want to produce relatively less of the crop that had fallen in price (barley) and relatively more of the now more attractive other crop (cotton). Cotton and barley are *substitutes in production* because both goods can be produced using the same resources. This example demonstrates why the price of related products is important as a supply shifter as well as a demand shifter. Producers tend to substitute the production of more profitable products for that of less profitable products. This is desirable from society's perspective as well, because more profitable products tend to be those considered more valuable by society, while less profitable products are usually considered less valuable. Hence, the lower price in the barley market has caused an increase in supply (a rightward shift) in the cotton market, as seen in Exhibit 4(b).

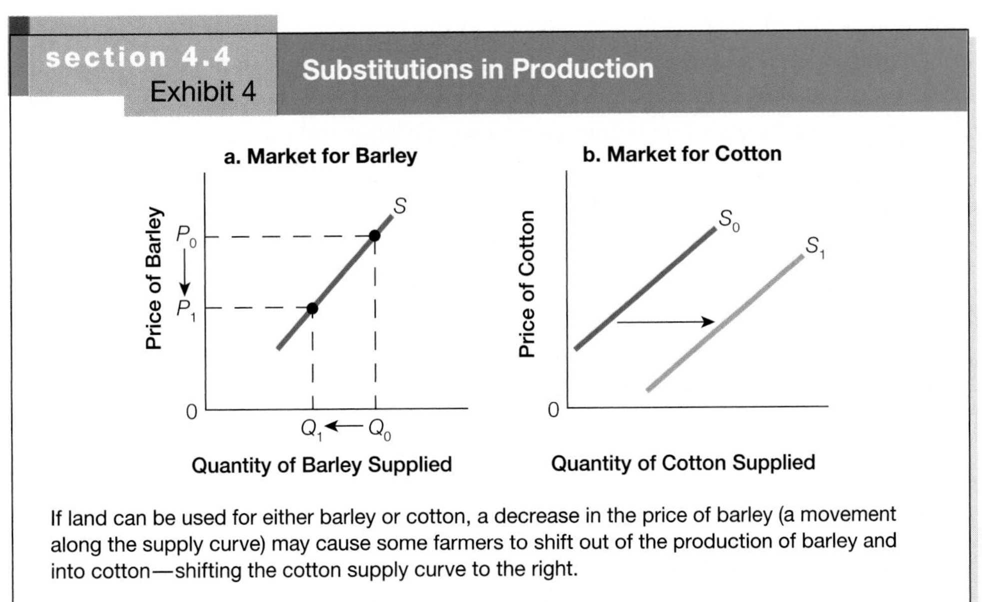

If land can be used for either barley or cotton, a decrease in the price of barley (a movement along the supply curve) may cause some farmers to shift out of the production of barley and into cotton—shifting the cotton supply curve to the right.

EXPECTATIONS

Another factor shifting supply is suppliers' expectations. If producers expect a higher price in the future, they will supply less now than they otherwise would have, preferring to wait and sell when their goods will be more valuable. For example, if an oil producer expected the future price of oil to be higher next year, he might decide to store some of his current production of oil for next year when the price would be higher. Similarly, if producers expect now that the price will be lower later, they will supply more now.

NUMBER OF SUPPLIERS

We are normally interested in market demands and supplies (because together they determine prices and quantities) rather than in the behavior of individual consumers and firms. As we discussed earlier, the supply curves of individual suppliers can be summed horizontally to create a market supply curve. An increase in the number of suppliers leads to an increase in supply, denoted by a rightward shift in the supply curve. An exodus of suppliers has the opposite impact, a decrease in supply, which is indicated by a leftward shift in the supply curve.

TECHNOLOGY

Most of us think of prices as constantly rising, given the existence of inflation, but, in fact, decreases in costs often occur because of technological progress, and such advances can lower prices. Human creativity works to find new ways to produce goods and services using fewer or less costly inputs of labor, natural resources, or capital. In recent years, despite generally rising prices, the prices of electronic equipment such as computers, cellular telephones, and DVD players have fallen dramatically. At any given price this year, suppliers are willing to provide many more (of a given quality of) computers than in the 1970s, simply because technology has dramatically reduced the cost of providing them. Graphically, the increase in supply is indicated by a shift to the right in the supply curve.

REGULATION

Supply may also change because of changes in the legal and regulatory environment in which firms operate. Government regulations can influence the costs of production to the firm, leading to cost-induced supply changes similar to those just discussed. For example, if new safety or anti-pollution requirements increase labor and capital costs, the increased cost will result, other things equal, in a decrease in supply, shifting the supply curve to the left, or up. An increase in a government-imposed minimum wage may have a similar effect by raising labor costs and decreasing supply in markets that employ many low-wage workers. However, deregulation can shift the supply curve to the right.

TAXES AND SUBSIDIES

Certain types of taxes can also alter the costs of production borne by the supplier, causing the supply curve to shift to the left at each price. The opposite of a tax (a subsidy) can lower the firm's costs and shift the supply curve to the right. For example, the government sometimes provides farmers with subsidies to encourage the production of certain agricultural products.

WEATHER

In addition, weather can certainly affect the supply of certain commodities, particularly agricultural products and transportation services. A drought or freezing temperatures will almost certainly cause the supply curves for many crops to shift to the left, while exceptionally good weather can shift a supply curve to the right.

A major disaster like a flood or a hurricane can reduce the supply of crops and livestock. Occasionally floods have spilled over the banks of the Mississippi River, but in the summer of 1993, the rainfall would not quit. Both the Mississippi and Missouri Rivers reached record levels; water was everywhere—bursting through levees and destroying crops and animals.

CHANGE IN SUPPLY VERSUS CHANGE IN QUANTITY SUPPLIED—REVISITED

If the price of a good changes, we say this leads to a change in the quantity supplied. If one of the other factors influences sellers' behavior, we say this leads to a change in supply. For example, if production costs rise because of a wage increase or higher fuel costs, other things remaining constant, we would expect a decrease in supply—that is, a leftward shift in the supply curve. Alternatively, if some variable, like lower input prices, causes the costs of production to fall, the supply curve will shift to the right. Exhibit 5 illustrates the effect of some of the determinants that cause shifts in the supply curve.

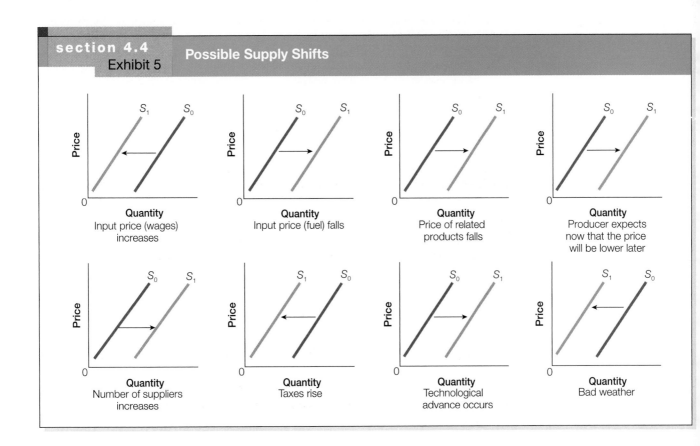

section 4.4 Exhibit 5 — Possible Supply Shifts

Price / Quantity, S_1 S_0 — Input price (wages) increases

Price / Quantity, S_0 S_1 — Input price (fuel) falls

Price / Quantity, S_0 S_1 — Price of related products falls

Price / Quantity, S_0 S_1 — Producer expects now that the price will be lower later

Price / Quantity, S_0 S_1 — Number of suppliers increases

Price / Quantity, S_1 S_0 — Taxes rise

Price / Quantity, S_0 S_1 — Technological advance occurs

Price / Quantity, S_1 S_0 — Bad weather

APPLICATION

CHANGE IN SUPPLY VERSUS CHANGE IN QUANTITY SUPPLIED

Q: How would you graph the two following scenarios: (1) the price of cotton has risen; and (2) good weather has caused an unusually abundant cotton harvest?

A: In the first scenario, there is an increase in the price of cotton, so there is a change in quantity supplied (i.e., a movement along the supply curve). In the second scenario, the good weather causes the supply curve for cotton to shift to the right. This is called a change in supply (not quantity supplied). A shift in the whole supply curve is caused by one of the other variables, not by a change in the price of the good in question.

As shown in Exhibit 6, the movement from A to B is called an increase in quantity supplied, and the movement from B to A is called a decrease in quantity supplied. However, the change from B to C is called an increase in supply and the movement from C to B is called a decrease in supply.

section 4.4
Exhibit 6

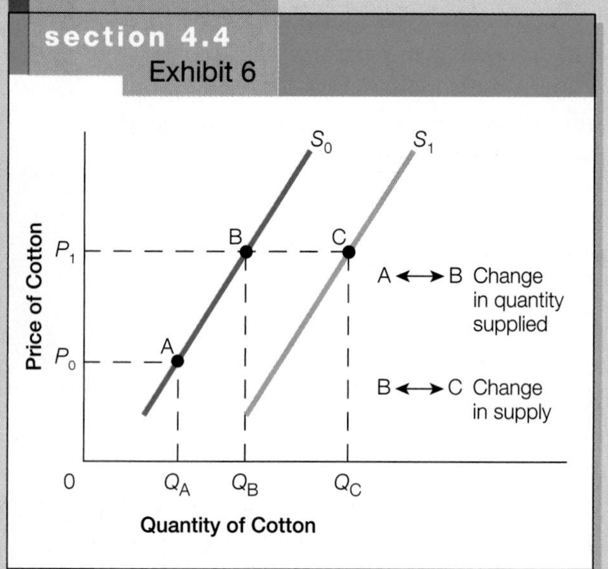

Section Check

1. The law of supply states that the higher (lower) the price of the good, the greater (smaller) the quantity supplied.
2. There is a positive relationship between price and quantity supplied because profit opportunities are greater at higher prices and because the higher production costs of increased output mean that suppliers will require higher prices.
3. The market supply curve is a graphical representation of the amount of goods and services that suppliers are willing and able to supply at various prices.
4. A movement along a given supply curve is caused by a change in the price of the good in question. As we move along the supply curve, we say there is a change in the quantity supplied.
5. A shift of the entire supply curve is called a change in supply.
6. An increase in supply shifts the supply curve to the right; a decrease shifts it to the left.
7. Input prices, the prices of related products, expectations, the number of suppliers, technology, regulation, taxes and subsidies, and weather can all lead to changes in supply.

---

1. What are the two reasons why a supply curve is positively sloped?
2. What is the difference between an individual supply curve and a market supply curve?
3. What is the difference between a change in supply and a change in quantity supplied?
4. If a seller expects the price of a good to rise in the near future, how will that affect his current supply curve?
5. Would a change in the price of wheat change the supply of wheat? Would it change the supply of corn, if wheat and corn can be grown on the same type of land?
6. If a guitar manufacturer had to increase its wages in order to keep its workers, what would happen to the supply of guitars as a result?
7. What happens to the supply of baby-sitting services in an area when many teenagers get their driver's licenses at about the same time?

section 4.5

Market Equilibrium Price and Quantity

- What is the equilibrium price?
- What is the equilibrium quantity?
- What is a shortage?
- What is a surplus?

Enough has been said for now about demand and supply separately. Bearing in mind our discussion of the "fuzzy" nature of many real-world markets, we now bring the market supply and demand together.

EQUILIBRIUM PRICE AND QUANTITY

The price at the intersection of the market demand curve and the market supply curve is called the **equilibrium price** and the quantity is called the **equilibrium quantity.** At the equilibrium price, the amount that buyers are willing and able to buy is exactly equal to the amount that sellers are willing and able to produce. If the market price is above or below the equilibrium price, there will be shortages or surpluses. However, the actions of many buyers and sellers will move the price back to the equilibrium level. Let us see how this happens.

equilibrium price
the price at the intersection of the market supply and demand curves; at this price the quantity demanded equals the quantity supplied

equilibrium quantity
the quantity at the intersection of the market supply and demand curves; at the equilibrium quantity, the quantity demanded equals the quantity supplied

SHORTAGES AND SURPLUSES

The equilibrium market solution is best understood with the help of a simple graph. Let's return to the coffee example we used in our earlier discussions of supply and demand. Exhibit 1 combines the market demand curve for coffee with the market supply curve. At $3 per pound, buyers are willing to buy 5,000 pounds of coffee and sellers are willing to

section 4.5 Exhibit 1 — A Hypothetical Market Supply and Demand Schedule for Coffee

Price	Quantity Supplied	Quantity Demanded	Difference	State of Market
$5	8,000	1,000	7,000	Surplus
4	7,000	3,000	4,000	Surplus
3	5,000	5,000	0	Equilibrium
2	3,000	8,000	−5,000	Shortage
1	1,000	12,000	−11,000	Shortage

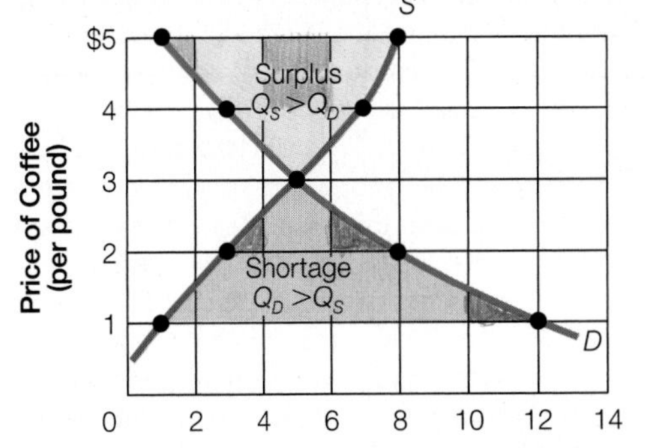

The equilibrium is $3 per pound and 5,000 pounds of coffee, where quantity demanded and quantity supplied are equal. At higher prices, quantity supplied exceeds quantity demanded, resulting in a surplus. Below $3, quantity demanded exceeds quantity supplied, leading to a shortage.

supply 5,000 pounds of coffee. Neither may be "happy" about the price, because the buyers would like a lower price and the sellers would like a higher price. But both buyers and sellers are able to carry out their purchase and sales plans at that $3 price. However, at any other price, either suppliers or demanders would be unable to trade as much as they would like.

As you can see in Exhibit 1, at $4 per pound, the quantity of coffee demanded would be 3,000 pounds but the quantity supplied would be 7,000 pounds. At that price, a **surplus** or excess quantity supplied would exist. That is, at this price, growers would be willing to sell more coffee than demanders would be willing to buy. To cut growing inventories, frustrated suppliers would cut their price and cut back on production. And as price falls, consumers would buy more, ultimately eliminating the unsold surplus and returning the market to the equilibrium.

What would happen if the price of coffee were cut to $1 per pound? The yearly quantity demanded of 12,000 pounds would be greater than the 1,000 pounds that producers would be willing to supply at that low price. So, at $1 per pound, a **shortage** or excess quantity demanded would exist. Because of the coffee shortage, frustrated buyers would be forced to compete for the existing supply, bidding up the price. The rising price would have two effects: (1) producers would be willing to increase the quantity supplied; and (2) the higher price would decrease the quantity demanded. Together, these two effects would ultimately eliminate the shortage, returning the market to the equilibrium.

surplus
a situation where quantity supplied exceeds quantity demanded

shortage
a situation where quantity demanded exceeds quantity supplied

APPLICATION

SHORTAGES

Q: Imagine that you own a butcher shop. Recently, you have noticed that at about noon, you run out of your daily supply of chicken. Puzzling over your predicament, you hypothesize that you are charging less than the equilibrium price for your chicken. Should you raise the price of your chicken? Explain using a simple graph.

A: If the price you are charging is below the equilibrium price (P_E), you can draw a horizontal line from that price straight across Exhibit 2 and see where it intersects the supply and demand curves. The point where this horizontal line intersects the demand curve indicates how much chicken consumers are willing to buy at that below-equilibrium price (P_{BE}). Likewise, the intersection of this horizontal line with the supply curve indicates how much chicken producers are willing to supply at P_{BE}. From this, it is clear that a shortage (or excess quantity demanded) exists, because consumers want more chicken (Q_D) than producers are willing to supply (Q_S) at this relatively low price. This excess quantity demanded results in competition among buyers, which will push prices up and reduce or eliminate the shortage. That is, it would make sense to raise your price on the chicken. As price moves upward toward the equilibrium price, consumers are willing to purchase less (some will substitute fish, steak, and ground round), and producers will have an incentive to supply more chicken.

section 4.5
Exhibit 2

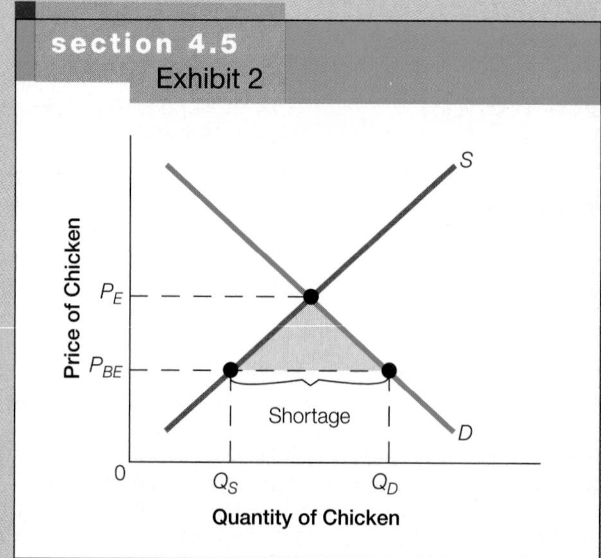

In The NEWS

JUST THE TICKET FOR SUPER BOWL FANS

TEMPE, Ariz.—You can't help but admire the power and influence of the Super Bowl. What else can close down Miami's freeways for hours on a Sunday afternoon for a parade of VIP limos? What else can cause a sacred Indian burial ground to be plowed up, without resistance, for a glitzy football theme park lasting just one week? Stronger than a sovereign nation, the National Football League rules in most situations. But the free market is the one force that eludes the NFL offense, despite its determined efforts.

The Super Bowl is a high-demand, limited-supply event. This year, in Tempe, there are some 80,000 seats for the 30th playing of football's crowning moment. The NFL has done such a good marketing job that half of the United States wants to attend. Yet the league has no intention of allowing them in. Market control is the NFL goal.

For the first 29 Super Bowls, ticket prices for all stadium seats were the same regardless of location. So much for the market! This year's game has differential prices ($200, $250, and $350), "to more adequately reflect differences in seat quality," a league spokesman says. But with present market prices ranging from $1,000 to $3,000, the NFL has not priced to what the market will bear. Even with the NFL in charge, scalping is inevitable. So many want seats, and some who receive official tickets are willing to sell them. Each year hundreds of ticket scalpers from across the United States descend on the host city a week before the game to trade from temporary command posts in motel rooms. Scalpers always appear at the stadium even when the probability of arrest is high.

Rather than ramming ahead into the force of the market, the NFL should try a reverse. Scalpers should be allowed to operate license-free at one location on game day. Phoenix pioneered such an ordinance for the 1995 NBA All-Star Game, and as we outlined on this page last year, the results have overwhelmingly benefited the customers. Search costs are minimized. Prices are lower. The nuisance effects of congested street corners, aggressive sellers, and fights are gone. Counterfeit tickets are almost nonexistent. The common area will simply make shopping easier for those rabid fans who are willing to pay what it takes to achieve a once-in-a-lifetime dream.

The NFL, alas, has no plans for a reverse. League rules prohibit anyone affiliated with the NFL from scalping Super Bowl tickets. Also, the host city is required to have an anti-scalping ordinance enforced at the event.

The Super Bowl's status as the top sporting event in the United States means that the vast majority of tickets never reach the open market. Yet the human spirit coupled with market forces still emerges as fans and scalpers search for each other. Just outside the stadium, within the shadow of the mighty NFL, they will meet. Neither ordinances nor screening can stop them. Even the NFL can't sack the laws of supply and demand.

SOURCE: Stephen Happel and Marianne Jennings, "Just the Ticket for Super Bowl Fans," p. A-22, *The Wall Street Journal,* January 25, 1996.

Section Check

1. The intersection of the supply and demand curve shows the equilibrium price and equilibrium quantity in a market.
2. A surplus is a situation where quantity supplied exceeds quantity demanded.
3. A shortage is a situation where quantity demanded exceeds quantity supplied.
4. Shortages and surpluses set in motion actions by many buyers and sellers that will move the market toward the equilibrium price and quantity unless otherwise prevented.

---

1. How does the intersection of supply and demand indicate the equilibrium price and quantity in a market?
2. What can cause a change in the supply and demand equilibrium?
3. What must be true about the equilibrium price charged for a shortage to occur?
4. What must be true about the equilibrium price charged for a surplus to occur?
5. Why do market forces tend to eliminate both shortages and surpluses?
6. If tea prices were above their equilibrium level, what force would tend to push tea prices down? If tea prices were below their equilibrium level, what force would tend to push tea prices up?

section 4.6

Changes in Equilibrium Price and Quantity

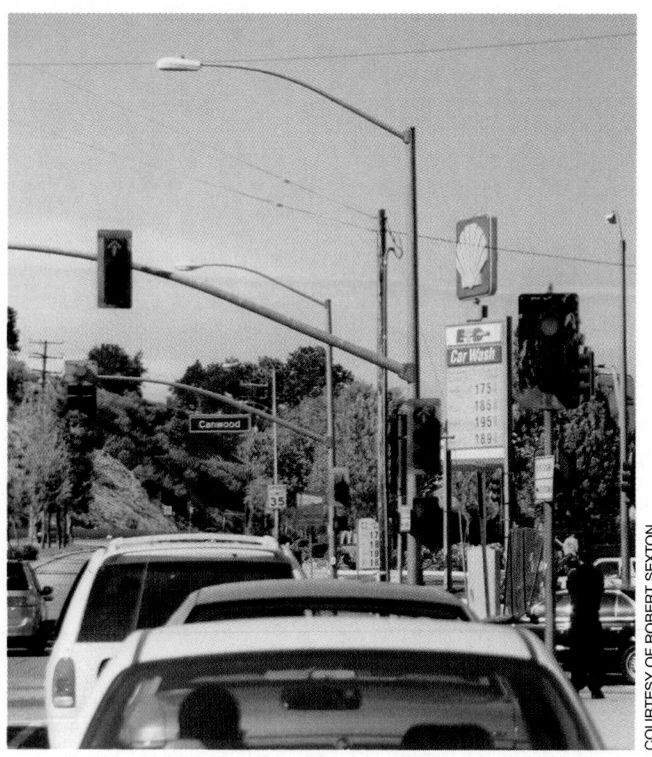

COURTESY OF ROBERT SEXTON

- What happens to equilibrium price and quantity when the demand curve shifts?
- What happens to equilibrium price and quantity when the supply curve shifts?
- What happens when both supply and demand shift in the same time period?
- What is an indeterminate solution?

When one of the many determinants of demand or supply changes, the demand and supply curves will shift leading to changes in the equilibrium price and equilibrium quantity. We first consider a change in demand.

A CHANGE IN DEMAND

A shift in the demand curve—caused by a change in the price of a related good (substitutes or complements), income, the number of buyers, tastes, or expectations—results in a change in both equilibrium price and equilibrium quantity. But how and why does this happen? This result can be most clearly explained through the use of an example. Gasoline prices are typically higher in the summer than in the winter because more people travel during the summer months than during the winter months. Therefore, the demand for gasoline increases during the summer. The greater demand for gasoline during the summer sends prices upward, *ceteris paribus.* As shown in Exhibit 1, the rightward shift of the demand curve results in an increase in both equilibrium price and quantity.

section 4.6 Exhibit 1 **Higher Gasoline Prices in the Summer**

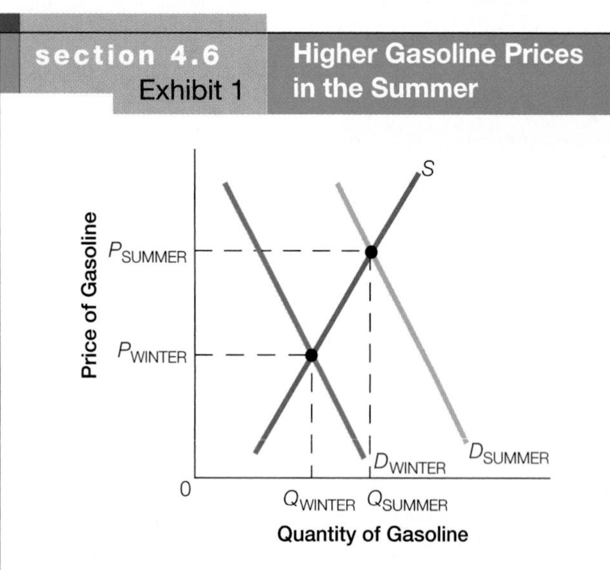

The demand for gasoline is generally higher in the summer than in the winter. The increase in demand during the summer, coupled with a fixed supply, means a higher price and a greater quantity.

A CHANGE IN SUPPLY

Like a shift in demand, a shift in the supply curve will also influence both equilibrium price and equilibrium quantity, assuming that demand for the product has not changed. For example, why are strawberries less expensive in summer than in winter? Assuming that consumers' tastes and income are fairly constant throughout the year, the answer lies on the supply side of the market. The supply of strawberries is higher during the summer because strawberries are in season. As shown in Exhibit 2, this increase in supply shifts the supply curve to the right, resulting in a lower equilibrium price (from P_{WINTER} to P_{SUMMER}) and a greater equilibrium quantity (from Q_{WINTER} to Q_{SUMMER}).

section 4.6
Exhibit 2

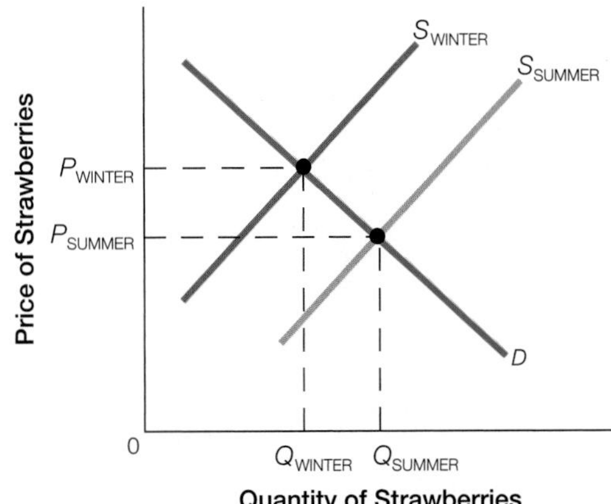

In the summer the supply of fresh strawberries is greater and this leads to a lower equilibrium price and a greater equilibrium quantity, *ceteris paribus.* In the winter, the supply of fresh strawberries is lower and this leads to a higher equilibrium price and a lower equilibrium quantity, *ceteris paribus.*

APPLICATION

CHANGE IN DEMAND

Q: In ski resorts like Aspen, hotel prices are higher in January and February (in-season when there are more skiers) than in May (off-season when there are fewer skiers). Why is this the case?

A: In the (likely) event that supply is not altered significantly, demand is chiefly responsible for the higher prices in the prime skiing months. In Exhibit 3, we see that the demand is higher in-season (February) than out of season (May). For example, at the Hotel Jerome in Aspen, the price of a Deluxe King is $525 in February and $215 in May. To see complete list of seasonal rates go to http://www.hoteljerome.com/room.html.

section 4.6
Exhibit 3

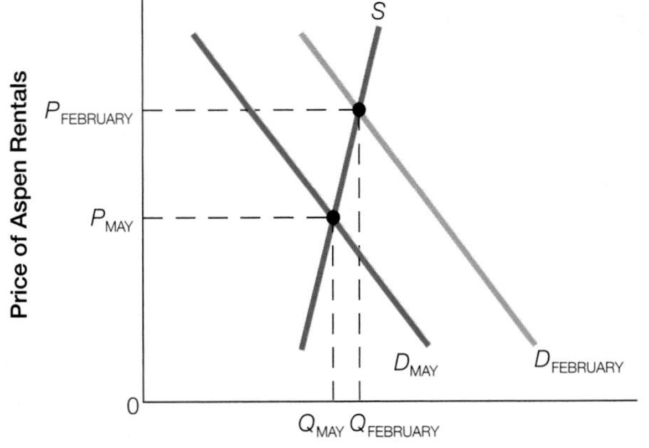

In The NEWS

BAD WEATHER PUTS THE SQUEEZE ON ORANGE CROP

The ice is starting to melt on California orange and lemon trees, and growers are cautiously optimistic that the worst of a freeze that has hobbled the state's citrus industry is over.

© T. O'KEEFE/PHOTOLINK/PHOTODISC/GETTY ONE IMAGES

Early morning temperatures Saturday hovered around 30 degrees in central California after a week in which they bottomed out at a fruit-killing 21 degrees.

With industry officials considering the region's $90 million lemon crop a total loss, the challenge comes in finding salvageable fruit hanging among oranges that are frozen through, their juice sacs burst.

Growers were banking on a slow warm-up to allow some table oranges to heal and save them from a profitless season.

"I think everyone is still holding out hope that some fruit will be good," said Terry Barker, who believes he lost almost his entire crop of navel oranges in Woodlake.

"Some guys just shut off their (wind) machines and gave up," Barker said Saturday after getting his first full night's sleep in several days.

But "you'll find people in farming are basically optimists. You hate to lose a crop, you really do. You plan on it. You realize these things happen and you just have to go on."

The past week's low temperatures are expected to seriously hurt California's $1.5 billion citrus industry, of which $853 million last year came from the oranges and lemons that have borne the brunt of the freeze.

California grows about 80 percent of the nation's fresh oranges that are used for eating.

The state's industry needed two years to recover from a 1990 freeze that destroyed nearly 90 percent of the citrus crop.

Eighty-five packing houses were shut down, leading to 12,000 layoffs. The state estimates at least $591 million in damage this year to oranges, lemons, and tangerines, although farmers said Saturday that they expected to rebound next year.

Hundreds of workers have already been laid off by a handful of packing houses. A trickle-down effect may well hit harvesters and truckers.

"'There's going to be obviously a boatload of people out of work, that's for sure," said Shann Blue, director of grower services for California Citrus Mutual, a trade group.

In "a lot of these small cities in the San Joaquin Valley, revenue is driven by the citrus industry," he said. "They're going to feel it, from car dealers to restaurants, if their money comes from people in the citrus business."

SOURCE: Associated Press, December 27, 1998

CONSIDER THIS:
The unfavorable weather conditions caused a reduction in supply. A decrease in supply, *ceteris paribus,* will lead to a higher price and a reduction in the quantity sold.

CHANGES IN BOTH SUPPLY AND DEMAND

We have discussed that as part of the continual adjustment process that occurs in the marketplace supply and demand can each shift in response to many different factors, with the market then adjusting toward the new equilibrium. We have, so far, only considered what happens when just one such change occurs at a time. In these cases, we learned that the results of these adjustments in supply and demand on the equilibrium price and quantity are predictable. However, very often supply and demand will both shift in the same time period. Can we predict what will happen to equilibrium prices and equilibrium quantities in these situations?

As you will see, when supply and demand move at the same time, we can predict the change in one variable (price or quantity), but we are unable to predict the direction of the effect on the other variable with any certainty. This change in the second variable, then, is said to be indeterminate, because it cannot be determined without additional in-

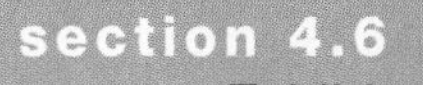

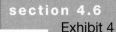

section 4.6 Exhibit 4 **Shifts in Supply and Demand**

a. A Little Increase in Supply and a Big Decrease in Demand

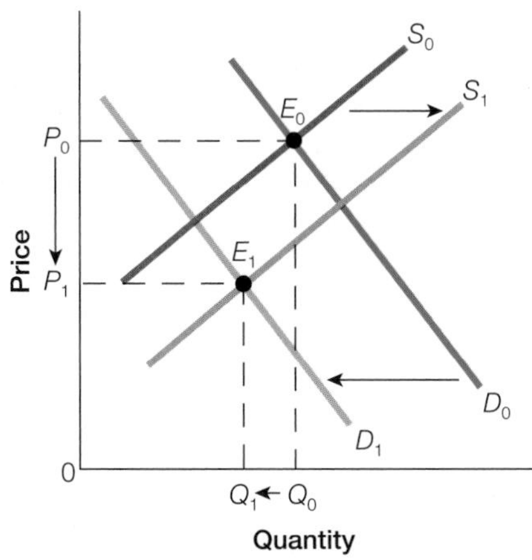

If the decrease in demand (leftward shift) is greater than the increase in supply (rightward shift), the equilibrium price and equilibrium quantity will fall.

b. A Big Increase in Supply and a Little Decrease in Demand

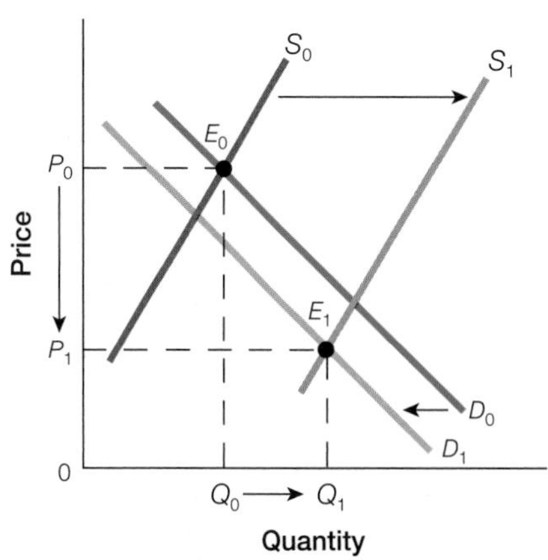

If the increase in supply (rightward shift) is greater than the decrease in demand (leftward shift), the equilibrium price will fall and the equilibrium quantity will rise.

formation about the size of the relative shifts in supply and demand. This concept will become clearer to you as we work through the following example.

An Increase in Supply and a Decrease in Demand

When considering this scenario, it might help you to break it down into its individual parts. As you learned in the last section, an increase in supply (a rightward shift in the supply curve) results in a decrease in the equilibrium price and an increase in the equilibrium quantity. A decrease in demand (a leftward movement of the demand curve), on the other hand, results in a decrease in both the equilibrium price and the equilibrium quantity. These shifts are shown in Exhibit 4(a). Taken together, then, these changes will clearly result in a decrease in the equilibrium price, because both the increase in supply and the decrease in demand work to push this price down. This drop in equilibrium price (from P_0 to P_1) is shown in the movement from E_0 to E_1.

The effect of these changes on equilibrium price is clear, but how does the equilibrium quantity change? The impact on equilibrium quantity is indeterminate, because the increase in supply increases the equilibrium quantity and the decrease in demand decreases it. In this scenario, the change in the equilibrium quantity will vary depending on the relative changes in supply and demand. If, as shown in Exhibit 4(a), the decrease in demand is greater than the increase in supply, the equilibrium quantity will decrease. If, however, as shown in Exhibit 4(b), the increase in supply is greater than the decrease in demand, the equilibrium quantity will increase.

THE COMBINATIONS OF SUPPLY AND DEMAND SHIFTS

The eight possible changes in demand and/or supply are presented in Exhibit 5, along with the resulting changes in equilibrium quantity and equilibrium price. While you could memorize the impact of the various possible changes in demand and supply, it

section 4.6 Exhibit 5 — **The Effect of Changing Demand and/or Supply**

If Demand	and Supply	then Equilibrium Quantity	and Equilibrium Price
1. Increases	Stays unchanged	Increases	Increases
2. Decreases	Stays unchanged	Decreases	Decreases
3. Stays unchanged	Increases	Increases	Decreases
4. Stays unchanged	Decreases	Decreases	Increases
5. Increases	Increases	Increases	Indeterminate*
6. Decreases	Decreases	Decreases	Indeterminate*
7. Increases	Decreases	Indeterminate*	Increases
8. Decreases	Increases	Indeterminate*	Decreases

*May increase, decrease, or remain the same, depending on the size of the change in demand relative to the change in supply.

would be more profitable to draw a graph, such as shown in Exhibit 6, whenever a situation of changing demand and/or supply arises. Remember that an increase in either demand or supply means a rightward shift in the curve, while a decrease in either means a leftward shift. Also, when both demand and supply change, one of the two equilibrium values, price or quantity, will change in an indeterminate manner (can increase or decrease) depending on the relative magnitude of the changes in supply and demand.

section 4.6 Exhibit 6 — **The Combinations of Supply and Demand Shifts**

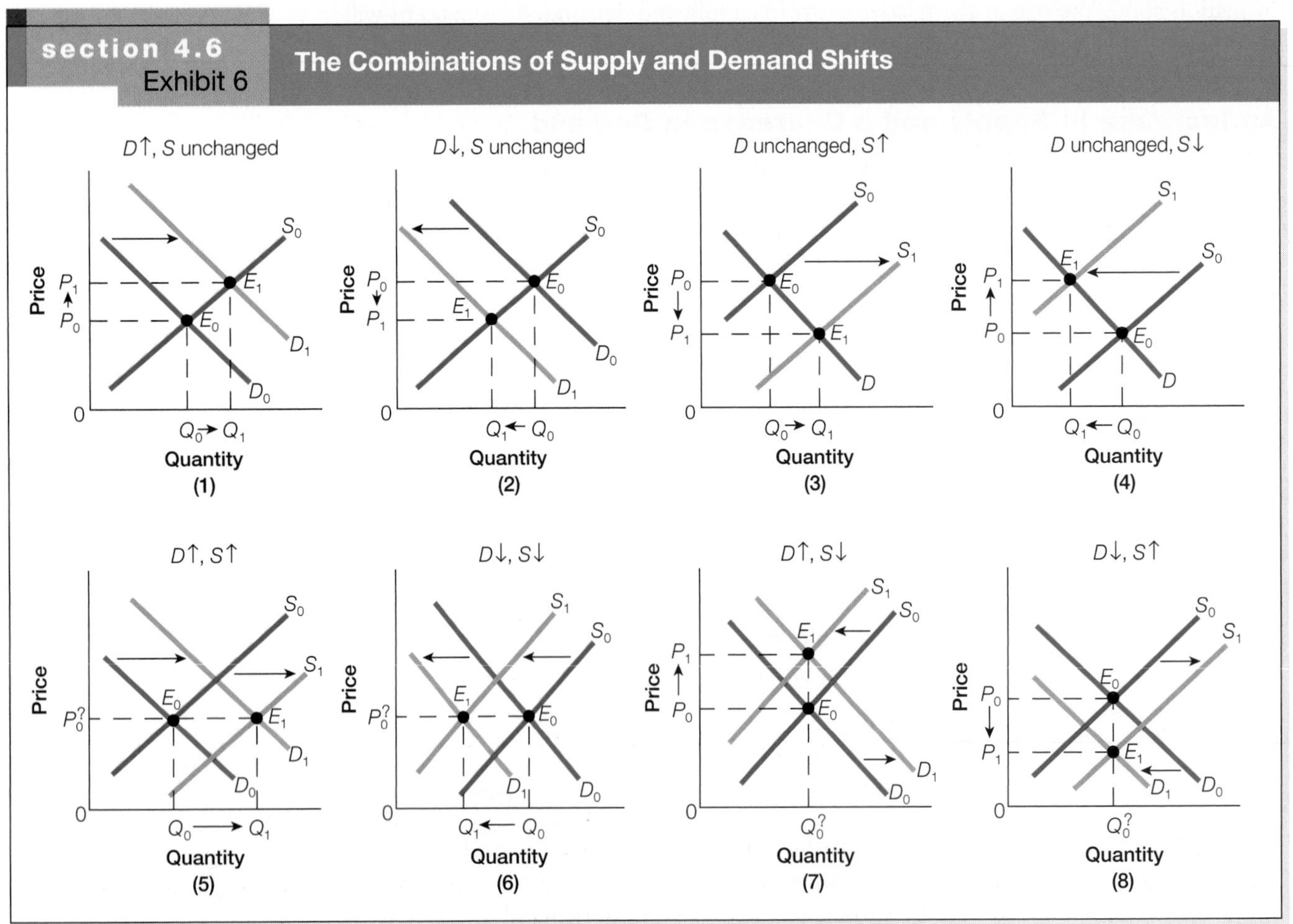

Section Check

1. Changes in demand and supply will cause a change in the equilibrium price and/or quantity, *ceteris paribus.*
2. Changes in supply will cause a change in the equilibrium price and/or quantity, *ceteris paribus.*
3. Supply and demand curves can shift simultaneously in response to changes in both supply and demand determinants.
4. When there are simultaneous shifts in both supply and demand curves, we will be able to determine one, but not both, of the variables. Either the equilibrium price or the equilibrium quantity will be indeterminate without more information.

---

1. When demand increases, does that create a shortage or a surplus at the original price?
2. What happens to equilibrium price and quantity as a result of a demand increase?
3. When supply increases, does that create a shortage or a surplus at the original price?
4. Assuming the market is already at equilibrium, what happens to equilibrium price and quantity as a result of a supply increase?
5. Why do heating-oil prices tend to be higher in the winter?
6. Why are evening and weekend long-distance calls cheaper than weekday long-distance calls?
7. What would have to be true for both supply and demand to shift in the same time period?
8. When both supply and demand shift, what added information do we need to know in order to determine in which direction the indeterminate variable changes?
9. If both buyers and sellers of grapes expect grape prices to rise in the near future, what will happen to grape prices and sales today?
10. If demand for peanut butter increases and supply decreases, what will happen to equilibrium price and quantity?

section 4.7

Price Controls

- What are price controls?
- What are price ceilings?
- What are price floors?

PRICE CONTROLS

While nonequilibrium prices can occur naturally in the private sector, reflecting uncertainty, they seldom last for long. Governments, however, may impose non-equilibrium prices for significant time periods. Price controls involve the use of the power of the state to establish prices different from the equilibrium prices that would otherwise prevail. The motivations for price controls vary with the market under consideration. For example, a **price ceiling,** a legal maximum price, is often set for goods deemed important to low-income households like housing. Or a **price floor,** a legal minimum price, may be set on wages because wages are the primary source of income for most people.

price ceiling
a legally established maximum price

price floor
a legally established minimum price

Price controls are not always implemented by the federal government. Local governments (and, more rarely, private companies) can and do impose local price controls. One fairly well-known example is rent controls. The inflation of the late 1970s meant rapidly rising rents, and some communities, such as Santa Monica, California, decided to do something about it. In response, they limited how much landlords could charge for rental housing.

PRICE CEILINGS: RENT CONTROL

Rent control experiences can be found in many cities across the country. San Francisco, Berkeley, and New York City all have had some form of rent control. While the rules may vary from city to city and over time, generally the price (or rent) of an apartment remains fixed over the tenure of an occupant, except for allowable annual increases tied to the cost of living or some other price index. When an occupant moves out, the owners can usually, but not always, raise the rent to a near-market level for the next occupant. The controlled rents for existing occupants, however, are generally well below market rental rates.

Results of Rent Controls

Rent controls distort market signals and lead to shortages. In addition, they often do not even help the intended recipients—low-income households. The actress Mia Farrow reputedly lived in a ten-room, rent-controlled apartment overlooking Central Park in New York City and paid less than 20 percent of the estimated market price. Most people living in rent-controlled apartments have a good deal, one that they would lose by moving as their family circumstances or income changes. Tenants thus are reluctant to give up their governmentally granted right to a below-market-rent apartment. In addition, because the rents received by landlords are constrained and below market levels, the rate of return (roughly, the profit) on housing investments falls compared to that on other forms of real estate not subject to rent controls, like office rents or mortgage payments on condominiums. Hence, the incentive to construct new housing is reduced. Where rent controls are truly effective, there is generally little new construction going on and a shortage of apartments that persists and grows over time.

Also, when landlords are limited in what rent they can charge, there is little incentive to improve or upgrade apartments, such as by putting in new kitchen appliances or new carpeting, in order to get more rent. In fact, there is some incentive to avoid routine maintenance, thereby lowering the cost of apartment ownership to a figure approximating the controlled rental price, although the quality of the housing stock will deteriorate over time.

Another impact of rent control is that it promotes housing discrimination. Where rent controls do not exist, a prejudiced landlord might willingly rent to someone he believes is undesirable, simply because the undesirable family is the only one willing to pay the requested rent (and the landlord is not willing to lower the rent substantially to get a desirable family, since this could translate into the loss of thousands of dollars in income). With rent controls, many families are likely to want to rent the controlled apartment, some desirable and some undesirable as seen by the landlord, simply because the rent is at a below-equilibrium price. The landlord can indulge in his "taste" for discrimination without any additional financial loss beyond that required by the controls.

Consequently, he will be more likely to choose to rent to a desirable family, perhaps a family without children or pets, rather than an undesirable one, perhaps one with lower income and so a greater risk of non-payment.

Exhibit 1 shows the impact of rent control. If the price ceiling is set below the market price, the quantity demanded will increase to Q_D from Q^* and the quantity supplied will fall to Q_S from Q^*. The rent control policy will therefore create a shortage, the difference between Q_S and Q_D.

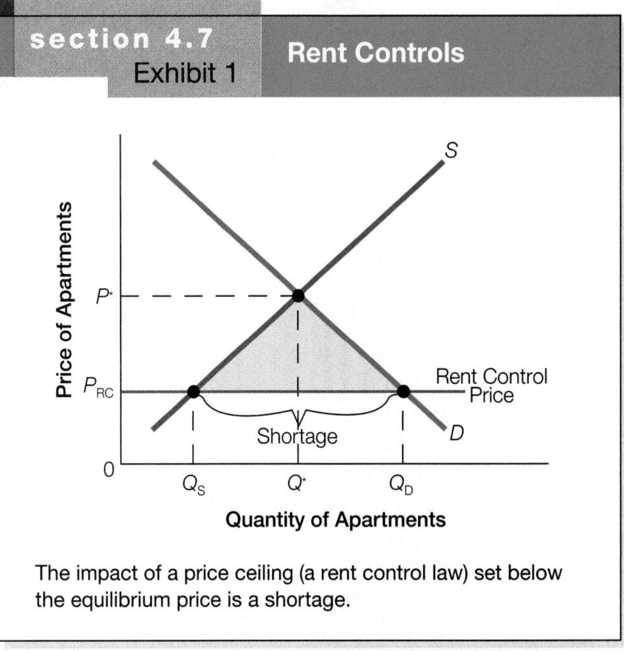

The impact of a price ceiling (a rent control law) set below the equilibrium price is a shortage.

PRICE FLOORS: THE MINIMUM WAGE

The argument for a minimum wage is simple: Existing wages for workers in some types of labor markets do not allow for a very high standard of living, and a minimum wage allows those workers to live better than before. Ever since 1938, when the first minimum wage was established (at 25 cents per hour), the federal government has, by legislation, made it illegal to pay most workers an amount below the current legislated minimum wage.

Let us examine graphically the impact of a minimum wage on low-skilled workers. In Exhibit 2, suppose the government sets the minimum wage, W_{MIN}, above the market equilibrium wage, W_E. In Exhibit 2, we see that the price floor is binding. That is, there is a surplus of low-skilled workers at W_{MIN}, because the quantity of labor supplied is greater than the quantity of labor demanded. The reason for the surplus of low-skilled workers (unemployment) at W_{MIN}, is that more people are willing to work than employers are willing and able to hire.

Notice that not everyone loses from a minimum wage. Those workers who continue to hold jobs now have higher incomes, those workers between 0 and Q_D in Exhibit 2. However, many low-skilled workers suffer from a minimum wage—they either lose their jobs or are unable to get them in the first place, those between Q_D and Q_S in Exhibit 2. Although studies disagree somewhat on the precise magnitudes, they largely agree that minimum wage laws do create some unemployment, and that the unemployment is concentrated among teenagers—the least-experienced and least-skilled members of the labor force.

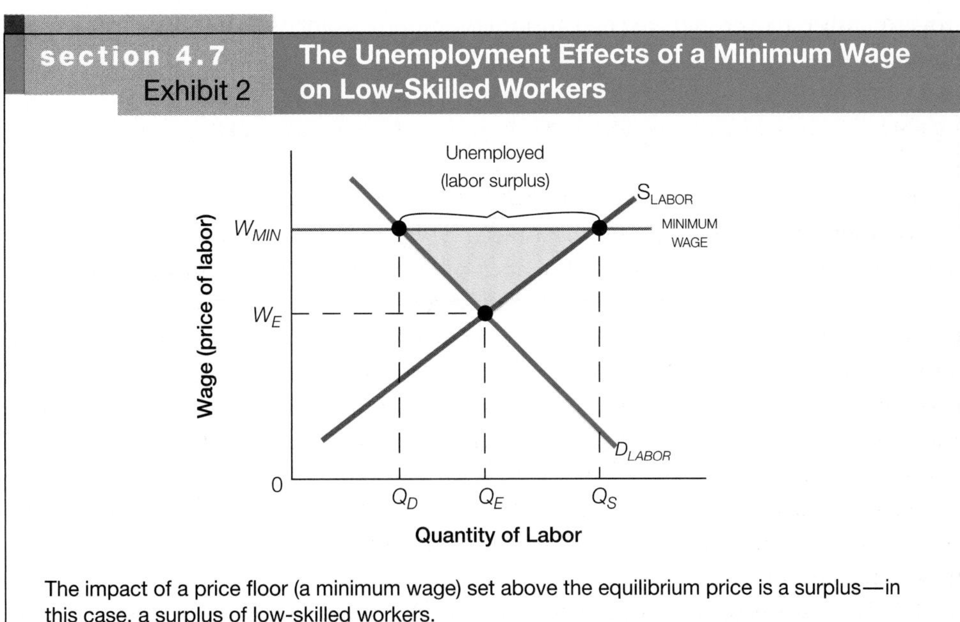

The impact of a price floor (a minimum wage) set above the equilibrium price is a surplus—in this case, a surplus of low-skilled workers.

What do you think would happen to the number of low-skilled workers getting jobs if we raised the minimum wage to $50 an hour?

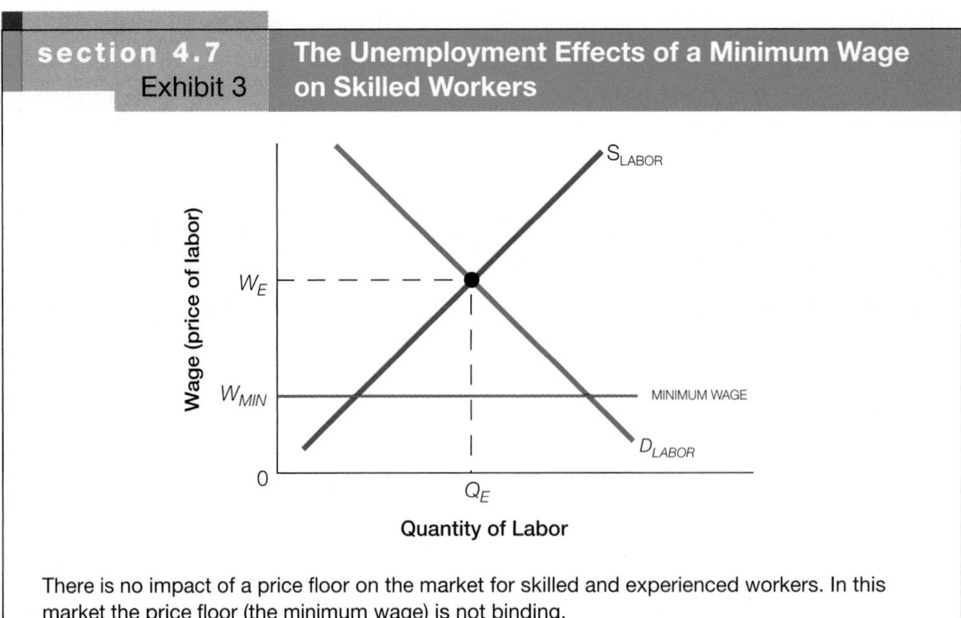

There is no impact of a price floor on the market for skilled and experienced workers. In this market the price floor (the minimum wage) is not binding.

Most U.S. workers are not affected by the minimum wage because in the market for their skills, they earn wages that exceed the minimum wage. For example, a minimum wage will not affect the unemployment rate for physicians. In Exhibit 3, we see the labor market for skilled and experienced workers. In this market the minimum wage (the price floor) is not binding because these workers are earning wages that far exceed the minimum wage—W_E is much higher than W_{MIN}.

The above analysis does not "prove" minimum wage laws are "bad" and should be abolished. To begin with, there is the empirical question of how much unemployment is caused by minimum wages. Secondly, some might believe that the cost of unemployment resulting from a minimum wage is a reasonable price to pay for assuring that those with jobs get a "decent" wage. The analysis does point out, however, that there is a cost to having minimum wages, and the burden of the minimum wage falls not only on low-skilled workers and employers but also on consumers of products made more costly by the minimum wage.

UNINTENDED CONSEQUENCES

unintended consequences
the secondary effects of an action that may occur after the initial effects

When markets are altered for policy reasons it is wise to remember that the actual results of actions are not always as initially intended or result in **unintended consequences.** As economists, we must always look for the secondary effects of an action that may occur along with the initial effects. For example, the government is often well-intentioned when it adopts price controls to help low-skilled workers, or tenants in search of affordable housing; however, such policies can also cause unintended consequences, which may completely undermine the intended effects. For example, rent controls may have an immediate effect of lowering rents, but secondary effects may well include very low vacancy rates, discrimination against low-income and large families, and deterioration of the quality of rental units. Similarly, a sizeable increase in the minimum-wage rate may help many low-skilled workers or apprentices, but will result in higher unemployment and/or a reduction in fringe benefits, such as vacations and discounts to employees. Society has to make tough decisions, and if the government subsidizes some program or groups of people in one area, then something must always be given up somewhere else. The "law of scarcity" cannot be repealed!

Section Check

1. Price controls involve government mandates to keep prices above or below the market-determined equilibrium price.
2. Price ceilings are government-imposed maximum prices.
3. If price ceilings are set below the equilibrium price, shortages will result.
4. Price floors are government-imposed minimum prices.
5. If price floors are set above the equilibrium price, surpluses will result.
6. The law of unintended consequences states that the results of certain actions may not always be as clear as they initially appear.

---

1. How is rent control an example of a price ceiling?
2. What predictable effects result from price ceilings such as rent control?
3. How is the minimum wage law an example of a price floor?
4. What predictable effects result from price floors like the minimum wage?
5. What may happen to the amount of discrimination against groups such as families with children, pet owners, smokers, or students when rent control is imposed?
6. Why does rent control often lead to condominium conversions?
7. What is the law of unintended consequences?
8. Why is the law of unintended consequences so important in making public policy?

Summary

Economists use the tools of supply and demand to study markets. A market is the process of buyers and sellers exchanging goods and services.

The law of demand states that when the price of a good falls (rises), the quantity demanded rises (falls), *ceteris paribus.* A change in the price of the good leads to a change in quantity demanded. A change in the price of related goods (substitutes and complements), income, number of buyers, tastes, and expectations can lead to a change in demand.

The law of supply states that the higher (lower) the price of the good, the greater (smaller) the quantity supplied. A change in the price of the good leads to a change in the quantity supplied. Input prices, the prices of related products, expectations, the number of suppliers, technology, regulation, taxes and subsidies, and weather can all lead to a change in supply.

The intersection of the supply and demand curve determines the equilibrium price and equilibrium quantity in a market. At the equilibrium price, quantity supplied equals quantity demanded. When the market price is above the equilibrium price, there will be a surplus, which causes the market price to fall. When the market price is below the equilibrium price, there will be a shortage, which causes the market price to rise. That is, shortages and surpluses set in motion forces that tend to move the market toward the equilibrium price and quantity.

Changes in demand and supply will cause a change in the equilibrium price and/or quantity.

Price controls (price ceilings and price floors) can lead to persistent shortages and surpluses. A price ceiling, like rent control, is a legal maximum price. If a price ceiling is set below the equilibrium price, it will lead to a shortage. A price floor, like a minimum wage, is a legal minimum price. If a price is set above the equilibrium price, it will lead to a surplus of low-skilled workers.

Key Terms and Concepts

market 60
competitive market 60
law of demand 61
substitution effect 62
individual demand schedule 62
individual demand curve 62
market demand curve 63
money price 64
relative price 64
change in quantity demanded 66
change in demand 66
substitute 66
complements 67
normal good 68
inferior good 68
law of supply 73
individual supply curve 73
market supply curve 74
equilibrium price 79
equilibrium quantity 79
surplus 80
shortage 80
price ceiling 87
price floor 87
unintended consequences 90

Review Questions

1. Using the demand curve, show the effect of the following events on the market for beef:
   - **a.** Consumer income increases.
   - **b.** The price of beef increases.
   - **c.** There is an outbreak of "mad cow" disease.
   - **d.** The price of chicken (a substitute) increases.
   - **e.** The price of barbecue grills (a complement) increases.
2. Draw the supply and demand curves for the following goods. If the price of the first good listed rises, what will happen to the demand for the second good and why?
   - **a.** hamburger and ketchup
   - **b.** Coca-Cola and Pepsi
   - **c.** camera and film
   - **d.** golf clubs and golf balls
   - **e.** skateboard and razor scooter
3. Using supply and demand curves, show the effect of each of the following events on the market for wheat.
   - **a.** The Midwestern United States (a major wheat producing area) suffers a flood.
   - **b.** The price of corn decreases (assume that many farmers can grow either corn or wheat).
   - **c.** The Midwest has great weather.
   - **d.** The price of fertilizer declines.
   - **e.** More individuals start growing wheat.
4. If a price is above the equilibrium price, explain the forces that bring the market back to the equilibrium price and quantity. If a price is below the equilibrium price, explain the forces that bring the market back to the equilibrium price and quantity.
5. The market for baseball tickets at your college stadium, which seats 2,000, is the following:

Price	Q_D	Q_S
$2	4,000	2,000
$4	2,000	2,000
$6	1,000	2,000
$8	500	2,000

   - **a.** What is the equilibrium price?
   - **b.** What is unusual about the supply curve?
   - **c.** At what price would there be a shortage?
   - **d.** At what price is there a surplus?
   - **e.** Suppose that the addition of new students (all big baseball fans) next year will add 1,000 to the quantity demanded at each price. What will this do to next year's demand curve? What is the new equilibrium price?
6. Show the impact of each of the following events in the oil market.
   - **a.** OPEC becomes more effective in limiting the supply of oil.
   - **b.** OPEC becomes less effective in limiting the supply of oil.
   - **c.** The price for natural gas (a substitute for heating oil) rises.
   - **d.** New oil discoveries occur in Alaska.
   - **e.** Electric and hybrid cars are subsidized; prices fall.

7. Which of the following will cause an increase in the quantity of cell phones demanded? In the demand for cell phones?
   a. The price of cell phones falls.
   b. Your income increases.
   c. The price of cell phone service (a complement) increases.
   d. The price of pagers (a substitute) falls.
8. What would be the impact of a rental price ceiling set above the equilibrium rental price for apartments? Below the equilibrium rental price?
9. What would be the impact of a price floor set above the equilibrium price for dairy products? Below the equilibrium price?
10. Why do both price floors and price ceilings reduce the quantity of goods traded in those markets?
11. Why do 10 a.m. classes fill up before 8 a.m. classes during class registration? Use the supply and demand curves to help explain your answers.
12. Visit the Sexton Web site at **http://sexton.swcollege.com** and click on "*Consumer Reports.*"
   a. Locate this month's product recalls under the "Recalls" section. What do you think will happen to the demand for products that have been recalled for repairs?

   b. What do you think happens to the demand for cars that receive *Consumer Reports* highest rating?

NOTE: You can't actually access the ratings without paying for a membership. You can access the Recalls section for free.

Fill in the Blanks

1. A ______________ is the process of buyers and sellers ______________ goods and services.

2. The important point about a market is what it does—it facilitates ______________.

3. ______________, as a group, determine the demand side of the market. ______________, as a group, determine the supply side of the market.

4. A ______________ market consists of many buyers and sellers where no single buyer or seller can influence the market price.

5. According to the law of demand, other things being equal, when the price of a good or service falls, the ______________ increases.

6. The primary reason for the inverse relationship between price and quantity demanded in the law of demand is the ______________ effect.

7. An ______________ reveals the different amounts of a particular good a person would be willing and able to buy at various possible prices in a particular time interval, other things being equal.

8. The ______________ for a product is the horizontal summing of the demand curves of the individuals in the market.

9. The ______________ price of a good is the price you would pay for it in dollars and cents, expressed in dollars of current purchasing power. The ______________ price of a good is its price in terms of other goods.

10. A change in ______________ leads to a change in quantity demanded, illustrated by ______________ a demand curve.

11. A change in demand is caused by changes in any of the other factors (besides the good's price) that would affect how much of the good is purchased: the ______________, ______________, the ______________ of buyers, ______________, and ______________.

12. An increase in demand is represented by a ______________ shift in the demand curve; a decrease in demand is represented by a ______________ shift in the demand curve.

13. Two goods are called ______________ if an increase in the price of one causes an increase in the demand for the other.

14. For normal goods an increase in income leads to a(n) ______________ in demand, and a decrease in income leads to a(n) ______________ in demand, other things being equal.

15. An increase in the expected future price of a good or an expected future income increase may ______________ current demand.

16. According to the law of supply, the higher the price of the good, the greater the ______________, and the lower the price of the good, the smaller the ______________.

17. The quantity supplied is positively related to the price because firms supplying goods and services want to increase their ______________ and because increasing ______________ costs mean that the suppliers will require ______________ prices to induce them to increase their output.

18. An individual supply curve is a graphical representation that shows the _____________ relationship between the price and the quantity supplied.

19. The market supply curve is a graphical representation of the amount of goods and services that suppliers are _____________ and _____________ to supply at various prices.

20. Possible supply determinants (factors that determine the position of the supply curve) are _____________ prices; _____________; _____________ of suppliers; and _____________, _____________, _____________, and _____________.

21. If input prices fall, this will _____________ the costs of production, causing the supply curve to shift to the _____________.

22. The price at the intersection of the market demand curve and the market supply curve is called the _____________ price, and the quantity is called the _____________ quantity.

23. A situation where quantity supplied is greater than quantity demanded is called a _____________.

24. A situation where quantity demanded is greater than quantity supplied is called a _____________.

25. At a price greater than the equilibrium price, a _____________, or excess quantity supplied, would exist. Sellers would be willing to sell _____________ than demanders would be willing to buy. Frustrated suppliers would _____________ their price and _____________ on production, and consumers would buy _____________, returning the market to equilibrium.

26. An increase in demand results in a _____________ equilibrium price and a _____________ equilibrium quantity.

27. A decrease in supply results in a _____________ equilibrium price and a _____________ equilibrium quantity.

28. If demand decreases and supply increases, but the decrease in demand is greater than the increase in supply, the equilibrium quantity will _____________.

29. If supply decreases and demand increases, the equilibrium price will _____________ and the equilibrium quantity will _____________.

30. A price _____________ is a legally established maximum price; a price _____________ is a legally established minimum price.

31. Rent controls distort market signals and lead to _____________ of rent-controlled apartments.

32. The quality of rent-controlled apartments would tend to _____________ over time.

33. An increase in the minimum wage would tend to create _____________ unemployment for low-skilled workers.

34. The secondary effects of an action that may occur after the initial effects are called _____________.

True or False

1. The differences in the conditions under which the exchange between buyers and sellers occurs make it difficult to precisely define a market.

2. All markets are effectively global in scope.

3. The law of demand puts the concept of basic human "needs" to rest as an analytical tool because there are usually plenty of substitutes available for any good.

4. There is an inverse or negative relationship between price and quantity demanded.

5. The market demand curve is the vertical summation of individual demand curves.

6. A relative price is the price of one good relative to the price of other goods.

7. A change in a good's price does not change its demand.

8. A change in demand is illustrated by a shift in the entire demand curve.

9. Because personal tastes differ, what are substitutes for one person may not be substitutes for another person.

10. Two goods are complements if an increase in the price of one causes an increase in the demand for the other.

11. Those goods for which falling income leads to decreased demand are called inferior goods.

12. Either an increase in the number of buyers or an increase in tastes or preferences for a good or service will increase the market demand for a good or service.

13. A decrease in the price of ice cream would cause an increase in the demand for frozen yogurt, a substitute.

14. The law of supply states that, other things being equal, the quantity supplied will vary directly (a positive relationship) with the price of the good.

15. The market supply curve for a product is the vertical summation of the supply curves for individual firms.

16. A change in the price of a good leads to a change in the quantity supplied, but not a change in its supply.

17. An increase in supply leads to a movement up along the supply curve.

18. A decrease in supply shifts the supply curve to the left.

19. Just as demanders will demand more now if the price of a good is expected to rise in the near future, sellers will supply more now if the price of a good is expected to rise in the near future.

20. Both technological progress and cost-increasing regulations will increase supply.

21. If the quantity demanded does not equal quantity supplied, a shortage will always occur.

22. At the equilibrium price the quantity demanded equals the quantity supplied.

23. A decrease in demand results in a lower equilibrium price and a higher equilibrium quantity.

24. An increase in supply results in a lower equilibrium price and a higher equilibrium quantity.

25. An increase in supply, combined with a decrease in demand, will decrease the equilibrium price but result in an indeterminate change in the equilibrium quantity.

26. If supply increases and demand decreases, but the increase in supply is greater than the decrease in demand, the equilibrium quantity will decrease.

27. An increase in both demand and supply increases the equilibrium quantity.

28. Neither a price ceiling at the equilibrium price nor a price floor at the equilibrium price would have any effect on the market price or quantity exchanged.

29. A price ceiling decreases the quantity of a good exchanged, but a price floor increases the quantity of a good exchanged.

30. A minimum wage (price floor) is likely to be binding in the market for experienced and skilled workers.

Multiple Choice

1. Which of the following is a market?
   a. a garage sale
   b. a restaurant
   c. the New York Stock Exchange
   d. an eBay auction
   e. all of the above

2. In a competitive market,
   a. there are a number of buyers and sellers.
   b. sellers, but not buyers, have significant control over the market price.
   c. no single buyer or seller can appreciably affect the market price.
   e. both a and c are true.

3. If the demand for milk is downward sloping, then an increase in the price of milk will result in a(n)
   a. increase in the demand for milk.
   b. decrease in the demand for milk.
   c. increase in the quantity of milk demanded.
   d. decrease in the quantity of milk demanded.
   e. decrease in the supply of milk.

4. Which of the following would not cause a change in the demand for cheese?
   a. an increase in the price of crackers, which are consumed with cheese
   b. an increase in the income of cheese consumers
   c. an increase in the population of cheese lovers
   d. an increase in the price of cheese
   e. none of the above

5. If the dollar price of good A rises by 15 percent while the prices of other goods rise an average of 25 percent, then good A's nominal price has _____ and its relative price has _______________.
   a. risen, risen
   b. risen, fallen
   c. fallen, risen
   d. fallen, fallen

6. *Ceteris paribus*, an increase in the price of DVD players would tend to
   a. decrease the demand for DVD players.
   b. increase the price of televisions, a complement to DVD players.
   c. increase the demand for DVD players.
   d. increase the demand for VCRs, a substitute for DVD players.
   e. decrease the quantity of DVD players supplied.

7. CNN announces that bad weather in Central America has greatly reduced the number of cocoa bean plants and as a result, the price of chocolate is expected to rise soon. As a result,
   a. the current market demand for chocolate will decrease.
   b. the current market demand for chocolate will increase.
   c. the current quantity demanded for chocolate will decrease.
   d. there is no change in the current market for chocolate, but there will be after the current crop of cocoa bean plants is processed into chocolate.

8. An upward-sloping supply curve shows that
   a. buyers are willing to pay more for particularly scarce products.
   b. suppliers expand production as the product price falls.
   c. suppliers are willing to increase production of their goods if they receive higher prices for them.
   d. buyers are willing to buy more as the product price falls.
   e. buyers are not affected either directly or indirectly by the sellers' costs of production.

9. All of the following factors will affect the supply of shoes except one. Which will not affect the supply of shoes?
   a. higher wages for shoe factory workers
   b. higher prices for leather
   c. a technological improvement that reduces waste of leather and other raw materials in shoe production
   d. an increase in consumer income

10. Which of the following would cause the quantity of wheat bread demanded to increase, but not the demand for wheat?
   a. a reduction in the price of rye, used to produce rye bread
   b. a new scientific study demonstrating that wheat bread reduces the risk of colon cancer
   c. a decrease in the price of rye bread
   d. an increase in the number of farmers growing wheat
   e. an increase in the price of wheat flour

11. Which of the following is not a determinant of supply?
   a. input prices
   b. technology
   c. tastes
   d. expectations
   e. the prices of related products

12. A market will experience a ________ in a situation where quantity supplied exceeds quantity demanded and a _______ in a situation where quantity demanded exceeds quantity supplied.
   a. shortage; shortage
   b. surplus; surplus
   c. shortage; surplus
   d. surplus; shortage

13. If incomes are rising, in the market for an inferior good,
   a. its price will rise, and the quantity exchanged will rise.
   b. its price will rise, and the quantity exchanged will fall.
   c. its price will fall, and the quantity exchanged will rise.
   d. its price will fall, and the quantity exchanged will fall.

14. If a farmer were choosing between growing wheat on his own land and growing soybeans on his own land,

- **a.** an increase in the price of soybeans would increase his supply of soybeans.
- **b.** an increase in the price of soybeans would increase his supply of wheat.
- **c.** an increase in the price of soybeans would decrease his supply of soybeans.
- **d.** an increase in the price of soybeans would decrease his supply of wheat.
- **e.** an increase in the price of soybeans would not change his supply of either wheat or soybeans.

15. If many cooks view butter and margarine to be substitutes, and the price of butter rises, then in the market for margarine

- **a.** the equilibrium price will rise, while the change to equilibrium quantity is indeterminate.
- **b.** the equilibrium price will rise, and the equilibrium quantity will decrease.
- **c.** both the equilibrium price and quantity will rise.
- **d.** the equilibrium price will fall, and the equilibrium quantity will fall.
- **e.** the equilibrium price will fall, and the equilibrium quantity will increase.

16. If you observed that the market price of a good rose while the quantity exchanged fell, which of the following could have caused the change?

- **a.** an increase in supply
- **b.** a decrease in supply
- **c.** an increase in demand
- **d.** a decrease in demand
- **e.** none of the above

17. If both supply and demand decreased, but supply decreased more than demand, the result would be

- **a.** a higher price and a lower equilibrium quantity.
- **b.** a lower price and a lower equilibrium quantity.
- **c.** no change in the price and a lower equilibrium quantity.
- **d.** a higher price and a greater equilibrium quantity.
- **e.** a lower price and a greater equilibrium quantity.

18. If the equilibrium price of widgets is $22, and then a price floor of $20 is imposed by the government, as a result,

- **a.** there will be no effect on the widget market.
- **b.** there will be a shortage of widgets.
- **c.** there will be a surplus of widgets.
- **d.** the price of widgets will decrease.

19. Which of the following is true?

- **a.** A price ceiling reduces the quantity exchanged in the market, but a price floor increases the quantity exchanged in the market.
- **b.** A price ceiling increases the quantity exchanged in the market, but a price floor decreases the quantity exchanged in the market.
- **c.** Both price floors and price ceilings reduce the quantity exchanged in the market.
- **d.** Both price floors and price ceilings increase the quantity exchanged in the market.

20. Which of the following will most likely occur with a 20 percent increase in the minimum wage?

- **a.** higher unemployment rates among the experienced and skilled workers
- **b.** higher unemployment rates among the young and low-skilled workers
- **c.** lower unemployment rates for the young and low-skilled workers
- **d.** the price floor (minimum wage) will be binding in the young and low-skilled labor market but not in the experienced and skilled labor market
- **e.** both b and d

Problems

1. Assume the following information for the demand and supply curves for good Z.

Demand		Supply	
Price	**Quantity Demanded**	**Price**	**Quantity Supplied**
$10	10	$1	10
9	20	2	15
8	30	3	20
7	40	4	25
6	50	5	30
5	60	6	35
4	70	7	40
3	80	8	45
2	90	9	50
1	100	10	55

   a. Draw the corresponding supply and demand curves.
   b. What is the equilibrium price and quantity traded?
   c. If the price were $9, would there be a shortage or a surplus? How large?
   d. If the price were $3, would there be a shortage or a surplus? How large?
   e. If the demand for Z increased by 15 units at every price, what would the new equilibrium price and quantity traded be?
   f. Given the original demand for Z, if the supply of Z were increased by 15 units at every price, what would the new equilibrium price and quantity traded be?

Price

0

Quantity

2. Refer to the following supply and demand curve diagram.
   a. Starting from an initial equilibrium at E, what shift or shifts in supply and/or demand could move the equilibrium price and quantity to each of points A through I?
   b. Starting from an initial equilibrium at E, what would happen if there were both an increase in the price of a substitute good and a decrease in income, if it is a normal good?
   c. Starting from an initial equilibrium at E, what would happen if there were both an increase in the price of an input and an advance in technology?
   d. If a price floor is imposed above the equilibrium price, which of A through I would tend to be the quantity supplied, and which would tend to be the quantity demanded? Which would be the new quantity exchanged?
   e. If a price ceiling is imposed below the equilibrium price, which of A through I would tend to be the quantity supplied, and which would tend to be the quantity demanded? Which would be the new quantity exchanged?

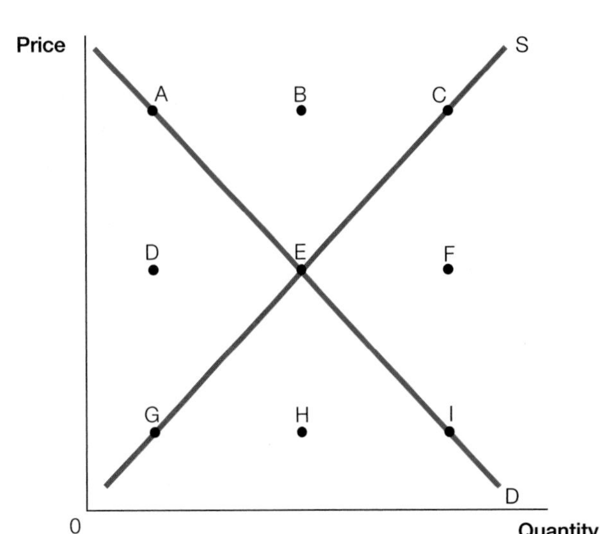

3. Draw a supply and demand curve diagram with a price floor above the equilibrium price, and indicate the quantity supplied and quantity demanded at that price and the resulting surplus.

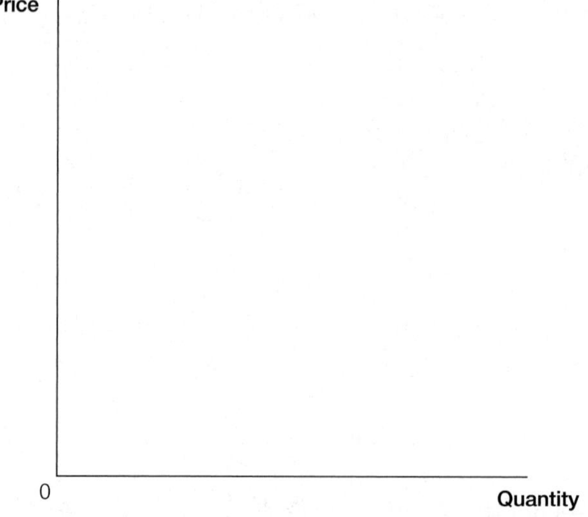

a. What happens to the quantity supplied, the quantity demanded, and the surplus if the price floor is raised? if it is lowered?
b. What happens to the quantity supplied, the quantity demanded, and the surplus if, for a given price floor, the demand curve shifts to the right?
c. What happens to the quantity supplied, the quantity demanded, and the surplus if, for a given price floor, the supply curve shifts to the right?

4. Draw a supply and demand curve diagram with a price ceiling below the equilibrium price, and indicate the quantity supplied and quantity demanded at that price, and the resulting shortage.

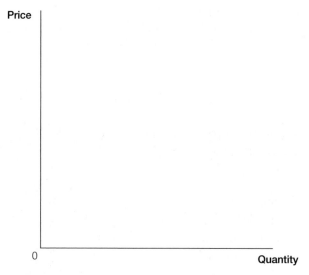

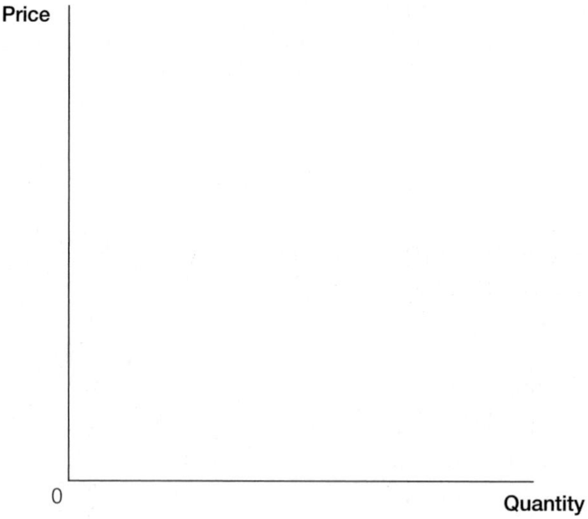

a. What happens to the quantity supplied, the quantity demanded, and the shortage if the price ceiling is raised? if it is lowered?
b. What happens to the quantity supplied, the quantity demanded, and the shortage if, for a given price ceiling, the demand curve shifts to the right?
c. What happens to the quantity supplied, the quantity demanded, and the shortage if, for a given price ceiling, the supply curve shifts to the right?

chapter 5

Elasticities, Consumer Behavior, and Welfare

section 5.1

Price Elasticity of Demand

- What are price elasticities of demand?
- How do we measure consumers' responses to price changes?
- What determines the price elasticity of demand?

WHAT IS THE PRICE ELASTICITY OF DEMAND?

price elasticity of demand
a measure of the responsiveness of quantity demanded to a change in price

In learning and applying the law of demand, we have established the basic fact that quantity demanded changes inversely with changes in price, *ceteris paribus*. But how much does quantity demanded change? The extent to which a change in price impacts quantity demanded may vary considerably from product to product and over the various price ranges for the same product. The **price elasticity of demand** measures the responsiveness of quantity demanded to a change in price. More specifically, price elasticity is defined as the percentage change in quantity demanded divided by the percentage change in price:

$$\text{Price elasticity of demand } (E_D) = \frac{\text{Percentage change in quantity demanded}}{\text{Percentage change in price}}$$

Note that, following the law of demand, there is an inverse relationship between price and quantity demanded. For this reason, price elasticity of demand is, in theory, always negative. In practice, however, this quantity is always expressed in absolute value terms, as a positive number, for simplicity.

IS THE DEMAND CURVE ELASTIC OR INELASTIC?

It is important to understand the basic intuition behind elasticities. This can be easily understood by focusing on the percentage changes in quantity demanded and price.

Think of elasticity as an elastic rubber band. If the quantity demanded is very responsive to even a small change in price, we call it elastic. On the other hand, if even a huge change in price results in only a small change in quantity demanded, then the demand is said to be *inelastic*. For example, if a 10 percent increase in the price leads to a 50 percent reduction in the quantity demanded, we say that demand is *elastic* because the quantity demanded is very sensitive to the price change.

$$E_D = \frac{\%\Delta Q_D}{\%\Delta P} = \frac{50\text{ percent}}{10\text{ percent}} = 5$$

Demand is elastic in this case, because a 10 percent change in price led to a larger (50 percent) change in quantity demanded.

Alternatively, if a 10 percent increase in the price leads to a 1 percent reduction in quantity demanded, we say that demand is *inelastic* because the quantity demanded did not respond much to the price reduction.

$$E_D = \frac{\%\Delta Q_D}{\%\Delta P} = \frac{1\text{ percent}}{10\text{ percent}} = .10$$

Demand is inelastic in this case, because a 10 percent change in price led to a smaller (1 percent) change in quantity demanded.

THE RANGES OF ELASTICITY

Economists refer to a variety of demand curves based on the magnitude of their elasticity. A demand curve or a portion of a demand curve can be elastic, or inelastic, or unit elastic. A demand curve is:

Elastic ($E_D > 1$) if Percentage change in $Q_D >$ Percentage change in P

Inelastic ($E_D < 1$) if Percentage change in $Q_D <$ Percentage change in P

Unit elastic ($E_D = 1$) if Percentage change in $Q_D =$ Percentage change in P

If bus fares increase, will ridership fall a little or a lot? It all depends on the price elasticity of demand. If the price elasticity of demand is elastic, a \$.50 price increase will lead to a relatively large reduction in bus travel as riders find viable substitutes. If the price elasticity of demand is inelastic, a \$.50 price increase will lead to a relatively small reduction in bus ridership as riders are not able to find good alternatives to bus transportation.

Elastic Demand Segments

Elastic demand segments are those with an elasticity that is numerically *greater* than one ($E_D > 1$). In this case, a given percentage increase in price, say 10 percent, leads to a larger percentage change in quantity demanded, say 20 percent, as seen in Exhibit 1(a). If the curve was perfectly elastic, a small percentage increase in price would cause the quantity demanded to fall dramatically to zero. For example, say there are two side-by-side roadside fruit stands selling the same quality of oranges. If one stand has lower prices, then the higher-priced fruit stand would soon be selling no oranges. In Exhibit 1(b), a perfectly elastic demand curve (horizontal) is illustrated. Economists define the elasticity of demand in this case as infinity, because the quantity demanded is infinitely responsive to even a very small percentage change in price.

elastic demand segment
a portion of the demand curve where the percentage change of quantity demanded is greater than the percentage change in price ($E_D > 1$)

section 5.1 Exhibit 1 — Elastic Demand

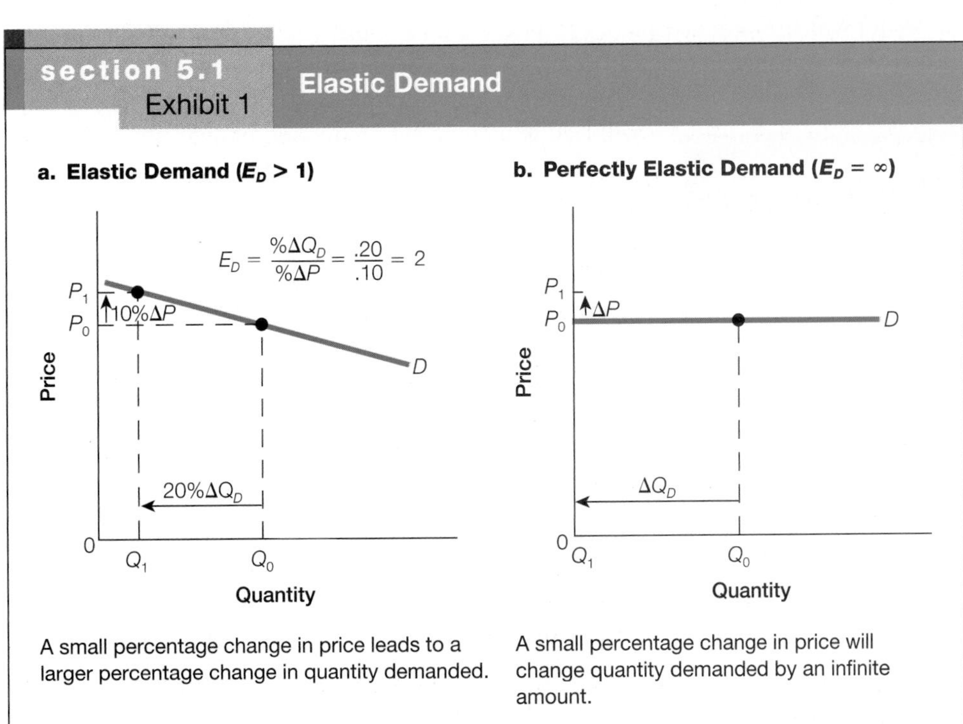

A small percentage change in price leads to a larger percentage change in quantity demanded.

A small percentage change in price will change quantity demanded by an infinite amount.

section 5.1 Exhibit 2 Inelastic Demand

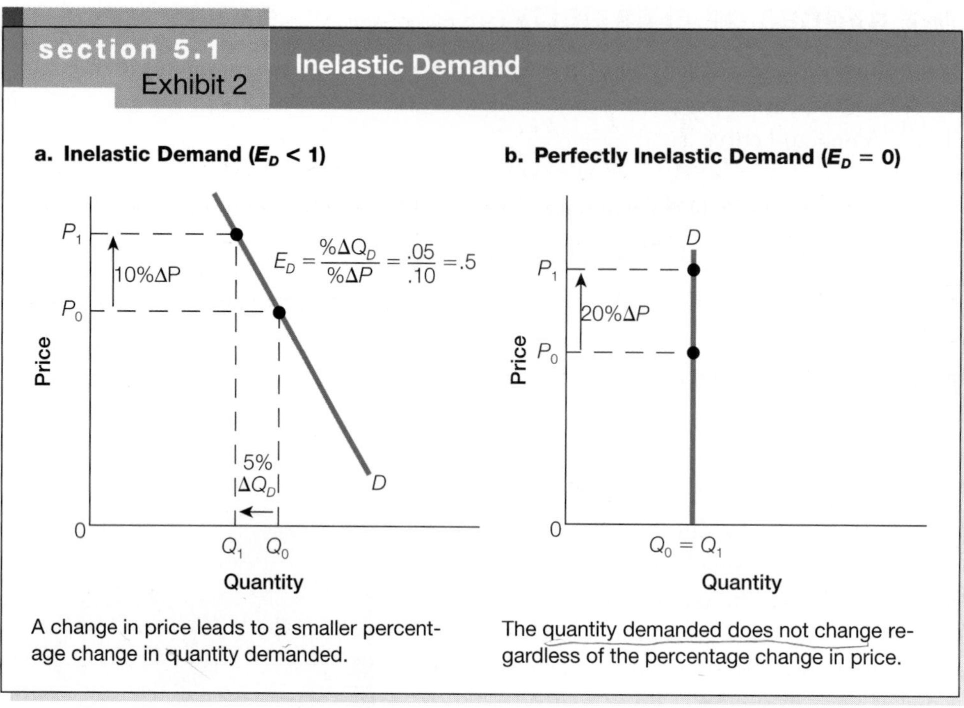

A change in price leads to a smaller percentage change in quantity demanded.

The quantity demanded does not change regardless of the percentage change in price.

inelastic demand segment
a portion of the demand curve where the percentage change in quantity demanded is less than the percentage change in price ($E_D < 1$)

unit elastic demand
demand with a price elasticity of 1; the percentage change in quantity demanded is equal to the percentage change in price

Inelastic Demand Segments

Inelastic demand segments are those with elasticity *less* than one ($E_D < 1$). In this case, a given percentage (for example, 10 percent) change in price is accompanied with a smaller (for example, 5 percent) reduction in quantity demanded, as seen in Exhibit 2(a). If the demand curve is perfectly inelastic, the quantity demanded is the same regardless of the price, as illustrated in Exhibit 2(b).

Unit Elastic Demand Segments

Goods for which E_D equals one ($E_D = 1$) are said to be **unit elastic demand.** In this case, the percentage change in quantity demanded is the same as the percentage change in price that caused it. For example, a 10 percent increase in price will lead to a 10 percent reduction in quantity demanded. This is illustrated in Exhibit 3.

section 5.1 Exhibit 3 Unit Elastic Demand

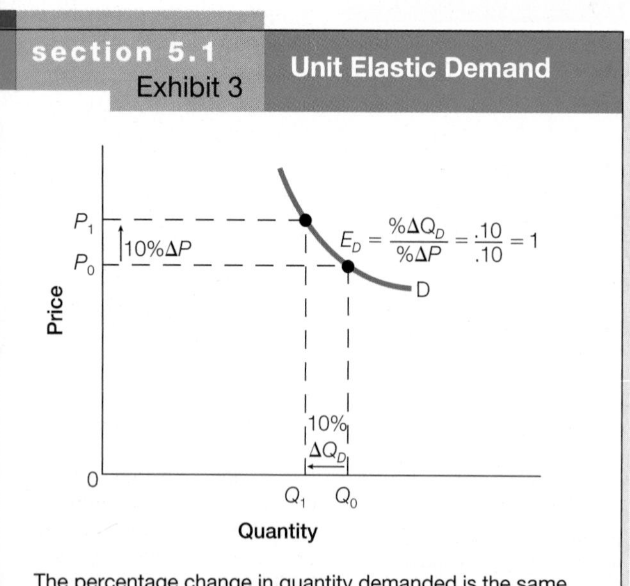

The percentage change in quantity demanded is the same as the percentage change in price that caused it (E_D = 1).

THE DETERMINANTS OF THE PRICE ELASTICITY OF DEMAND

As you have learned, the elasticity of demand for a specific good refers to movements along its demand curve as its price changes. A lower price will increase quantity demanded, and a higher price will reduce quantity demanded. But what factors will influence the magnitude of the change in quantity demanded in response to a price change? That is, what will make the demand curve relatively more elastic (where Q_D is responsive to price changes), and what will make the demand curve relatively less elastic (where Q_D is less responsive to price changes)?

For the most part, the price elasticity of demand depends on the following factors: (1) the availability of close substitutes, (2) the proportion of income spent on the good, and (3) the amount of time that has elapsed since the price change.

Availability of Close Substitutes

Goods *with* close substitutes tend to have more elastic demands. Why? Because if the price of such a good increases, consumers can easily switch to other now relatively lower-priced substitutes. There are many examples, such as butter and margarine, one brand of root beer as opposed to another, or different brands of gasoline, where the ease of substitution will make demand quite elastic for most individuals. Goods *without* close substitutes, such as insulin for diabetics, cigarettes for chain smokers, heroin for addicts, or emergency medical care for those with appendicitis or broken legs, tend to have inelastic demands.

The degree of substitutability may also depend on whether the good is a necessity or a luxury. Goods that are necessities, like food, cannot be easily substituted for and thus tend to have lower elasticities than luxury items, like jewelry.

Narrowly Defined Goods

When the demand for a good is broadly defined, it tends to be less elastic than when it is narrowly defined. For example, the elasticity of demand for food, a very broad category, tends to be inelastic because there are very few substitutes for food. But for a certain type of food, like pizza, a narrowly defined good, it is much easier to find a substitute—perhaps tacos, burgers, salads, burritos, or chili fries. That is, the demand for a particular type of food is more elastic because there are more and better substitutes than for food as an entire category.

Proportion of Income Spent on the Good

The smaller the proportion of income spent on a good, the lower its elasticity of demand. If the amount spent on a good relative to income is small, then the impact of a change in its price on one's budget will also be small. As a result, consumers will respond less to price changes for these goods than for similar percentage changes in large-ticket items, where a price change could have a potentially large impact on the consumer's budget. For example, a 50 percent increase in the price of salt will have a much smaller impact on consumers' behavior than a similar percentage increase in the price of a new automobile. Similarly, a 50 percent increase in the cost of private university tuition will have a greater impact on students' (and sometimes parents') budgets than a 50 percent increase in textbook prices.

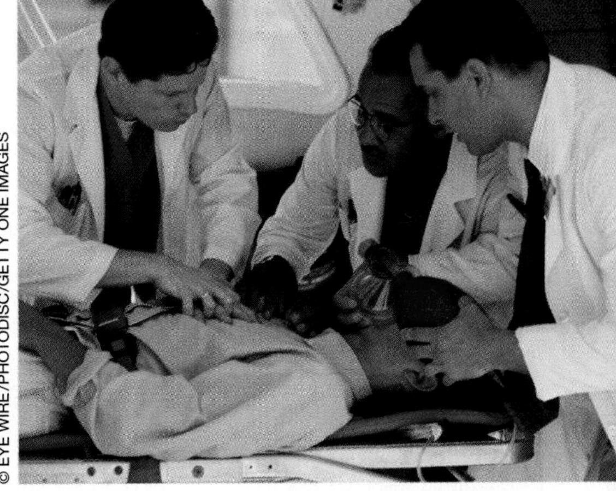

Unlike more tangible items (such as food or cars), there are few substitutes for a physician and medical care when you have an emergency. Because the number of available substitutes is limited, the demand for emergency medical care is relatively inelastic.

Time

For many goods, the more time that people have to adapt to a new price change, the greater the elasticity of demand. Immediately after a price change, consumers may be unable to locate very good alternatives or easily change their consumption patterns. But the more time that passes, the more time consumers have to find or develop suitable substitutes and to plan and implement changes in their patterns of consumption. For example, drivers may not respond immediately to an increase in gas prices, perhaps believing it to be temporary. However, if the price persists over a longer period, we would expect people to drive less, buy more fuel-efficient cars, move closer to work, carpool, take the bus, or even bike to work. Hence, for many goods, especially nondurable goods (goods that do *not* last a long time), the short-run demand curve is generally less elastic than the long-run demand curve, as illustrated by Exhibit 4.

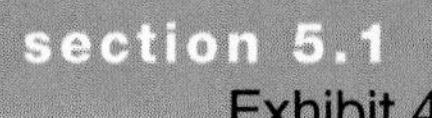

Short-Run and Long-Run Demand Curves

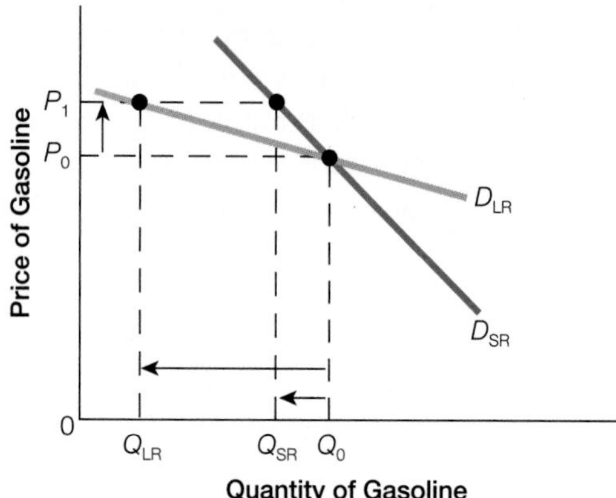

For many goods, like gasoline, price is much more elastic in the short run than the long run because buyers take time to change their consumption patterns. In the short run, the increase in price from P_0 to P_1 has only a small effect on the quantity demanded for gasoline. In the long run, the effect of the price increase will be much larger.

In The NEWS

TEEN SMOKING: PRICE MATTERS

What's the best way to curb teen smoking? Raise taxes on cigarettes. So says a new National Bureau of Economic Research study that explores the reasons behind the jump in teen smoking in the 1990s.

Teen smoking declined in the 1980s. But from 1991 through 1997, the rate of smoking among teenagers rose by a third. The NBER study, by Jonathan Gruber of the economics department of Massachusetts Institute of Technology, shows the sharp reduction in the retail price of cigarettes in the early 1990s accounts for roughly 30 percent of the increase in teen smoking in the years that followed.

The impact of higher prices varies by socioeconomic status. Both African-American teens and those with less educated parents are more sensitive to the price of cigarettes than are white youths and those with more educated parents, according to the study.

Gruber also finds that while there is "some evidence" that limiting teen access to cigarettes reduces smoking, the cost of tobacco plays a greater role. In addition, he says, there is no "consistent evidence" that rules against smoking in public places reduce the rate of teen smoking.

PHOTO: © EMMA LEE/LIFEFILE/PHOTODISC/GETTY ONE IMAGES

SOURCE: *Businessweek* Online: March 6, 2000 Issue, www.businessweek.com.

CONSIDER THIS:

Some studies have shown that a 10 percent increase in the price of cigarettes will lead to a 7 percent reduction in youth smoking. In this price range, however, demand is still inelastic at −0.7. Of course, proponents of higher taxes to discourage underage smoking would like to see a more elastic demand, where a 10 percent increase in the price of cigarettes would lead to a more than 10 percent reduction in quantity demanded.

Section Check

SECTION CHECK

1. Price elasticity of demand measures the percentage change in quantity demanded divided by the percentage change in price.
2. If the demand for a good is price elastic in the relevant range, quantity demanded is very responsive to a price change. If the demand for a good is relatively price inelastic, quantity demanded is not very responsive to a price change.
3. The price elasticity of demand depends on: (1) the availability of close substitutes, (2) the proportion of income spent on the good, and (3) the amount of time that buyers have to respond to a price change.

---

1. What question is the price elasticity of demand designed to answer?
2. How is the price elasticity of demand calculated?
3. What is the difference between a relatively price elastic demand curve and a relatively price inelastic demand curve?
4. What is the relationship between the price elasticity of demand and the slope at a given point on a demand curve?
5. What factors tend to make demand curves more price elastic?
6. Why would a tax on a particular brand of cigarettes be less effective at reducing smoking than a tax on all brands of cigarettes?
7. Why is the price elasticity of demand for products at a 24-hour convenience store likely to be lower at 2 a.m. than at 2 p.m.?
8. Why is the price elasticity of demand for turkeys, in general, likely to be lower at Thanksgiving than at other times of the year, but the price elasticity of demand for turkeys at a particular store is likely to be greater?

section 5.2

Total Revenue and Price Elasticity of Demand

- What is total revenue?
- What is the relationship between total revenue and the price elasticity of demand?
- Does the price elasticity of demand vary along a linear demand curve?

HOW DOES THE PRICE ELASTICITY OF DEMAND IMPACT TOTAL REVENUE?

The price elasticity of demand for a good also has implications for total revenue. **Total revenue** (*TR*) is simply the price of the good (*P*) times the quantity of the good sold (*Q*): $TR = P \times Q$. In Exhibit 1, we see that when the demand is price elastic ($E_D > 1$), total revenues will rise as the price declines, because the percentage increase in the quantity demanded is greater than the percent reduction in price. For example, if the price of a good is cut in half (say from \$10 to \$5) and the quantity demanded more than doubles (say from 40 to 100), total revenue will rise from \$400 (\$10 × 40 = \$400) to \$500 (\$5 × 100 = \$500). Equivalently, if the price rises from \$5 to \$10 and the quantity demanded falls from 100 to 40 units, then total revenue falls from \$500 to \$400. As this example illustrates, if the demand curve is relatively elastic, total revenue varies inversely with a price change.

total revenue
the price of the good times the quantity of the good sold

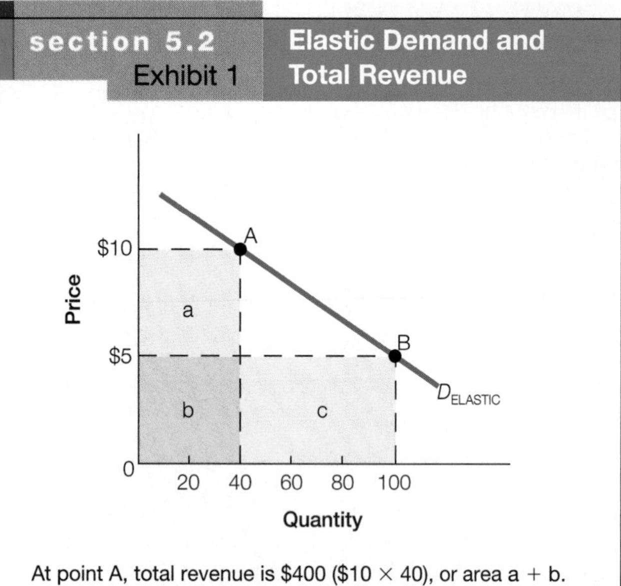

At point A, total revenue is $400 ($10 × 40), or area a + b. At point B, the total revenue is $500 ($5 × 100), or area b + c. Total revenue has increased by $100. We can also see in the graph that total revenue has increased because the area b + c is greater than area a + b, or c > a.

section 5.2 Exhibit 2 — Inelastic Demand and Total Revenue

At point A, total revenue is $300 ($10 × 30), or area a + b. At point B, the total revenue is $200 ($5 × 40), or area b + c. Total revenue has fallen by $100. We can also see in the graph that total revenue has decreased because area a + b is greater than area b + c, or a > c.

You can see from the following what happens to total revenue when demand is price elastic. (Note: The size of the price and quantity arrows represents the size of the percentage changes.)

When Demand Is Price Elastic

$$\Downarrow TR = \uparrow P \times \Downarrow Q$$

or

$$\Uparrow TR = \downarrow P \times \Uparrow Q$$

On the other hand, if demand for a good is relatively inelastic ($E_D < 1$), the total revenue will be lower at lower prices than at higher prices, because a given price reduction will be accompanied by a proportionately smaller increase in quantity demanded. For example, as seen in Exhibit 2, if the price of a good is cut, say from $10 to $5, and the quantity demanded less than doubles—say it increases from 30 to 40—total revenue will fall from $300 ($10 × 30 = $300) to $200 ($5 × 40 = $200). Equivalently, if the price increases from $5 to $10 and the quantity demanded falls from 40 to 30, total revenue will increase from $200 to $300. To summarize, then, if the demand curve is inelastic, total revenue will vary directly with a price change.

When Demand Is Price Inelastic

$$\Uparrow TR = \Uparrow P \times \downarrow Q$$

or

$$\Downarrow TR = \Downarrow P \times \uparrow Q$$

In this case, the "net" effect on total revenue is reversed but easy to see. (Again, the size of the price and quantity arrows represents the size of the percentage changes.)

PRICE ELASTICITY CHANGES ALONG A LINEAR DEMAND CURVE

As we have already shown (page 97), the slopes of demand curves can be used to estimate their *relative* elasticities of demand: The steeper one demand curve is relative to another, the more inelastic it is relative to the other. However, beyond the extreme cases of perfectly elastic and perfectly inelastic curves, great care must be taken when trying to estimate the degree of elasticity of one demand curve from its slope. In fact, as we shall see, a straight-line demand curve with a constant slope will change elasticity continuously as you move up or down it.

We can easily demonstrate that the elasticity of demand varies along a linear demand curve by using what we already know about the interrelationship between price and total revenue. Exhibit 4 shows a linear (constant slope) demand curve. In Exhibit 4(a), we

APPLICATION

ELASTICITIES AND TOTAL REVENUE

Q: Is a poor (great) wheat harvest bad (good) for all farmers? (Hint: Assume that demand for wheat is inelastic—the demand for food is generally inelastic.)

A: Without a simultaneous reduction in demand, a reduction in supply results in higher prices. With that, if demand for the wheat is inelastic over the pertinent portion of the demand curve, the price increase will cause farmers' total revenues to rise. As shown in Exhibit 3(a), if demand for the crop is inelastic, an increase in price would cause farmers to lose the revenue indicated by area c. They would, however, experience an increase in revenue equal to area a, resulting in an overall increase in total revenue equal to area a − c. Clearly, if some farmers lose their entire crop because of, say, bad weather, they are worse off; but *collectively* farmers can profit from events that reduce crop size—and they do, because the demand for most agricultural products is inelastic. Interestingly, if all farmers were hurt equally, say, losing one-third of their crop, each farmer would be better off. Of course, consumers would be worse off because the price of agricultural products would be higher. Alternatively, what if phenomenal weather has led to record wheat harvests or a technological advance has led to more productive wheat farmers? Either event would increase the supply from S_0 to S_1 in Exhibit 3(b). The increase in supply leads to a lower price, from P_0 to P_1. Because the demand for wheat is inelastic, the quantity sold of wheat rises less than proportionately to the fall in the price. That is, in percentage terms the price falls more than the quantity demanded rises. Each farmer is selling a few more bushels of wheat but the price of each bushel has fallen even more, so collectively wheat farmers will experience a decline in total revenue despite the good news.

section 5.2
Exhibit 3

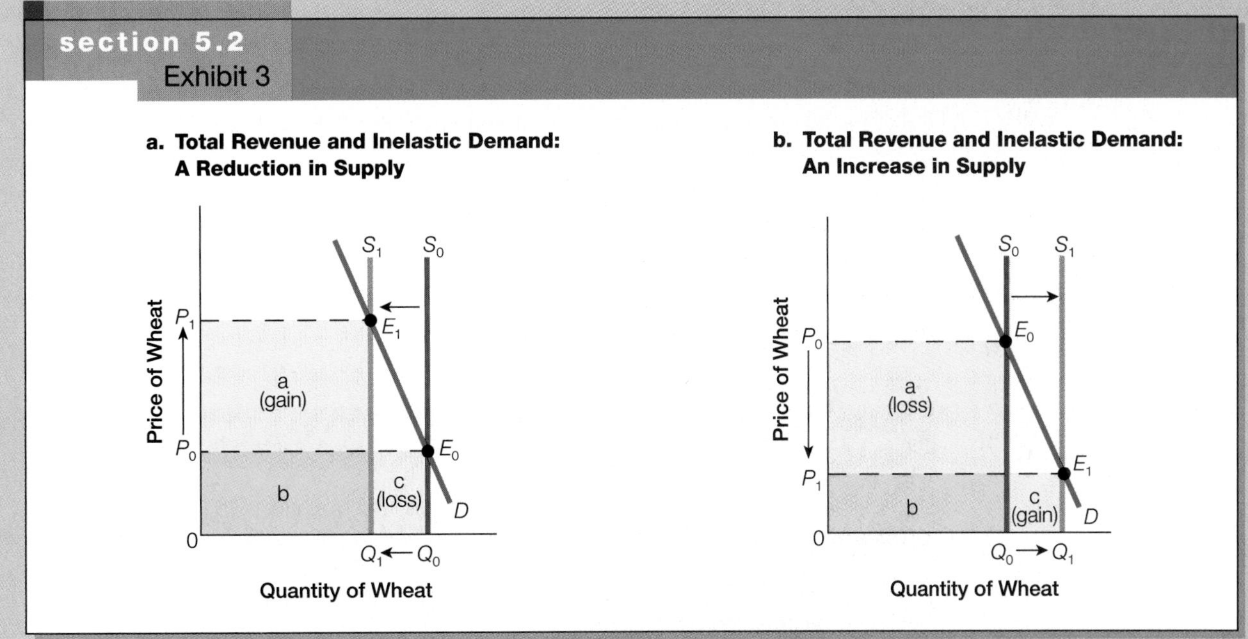

see that when the price falls on the upper half of the demand curve from P_0 to P_1, and quantity demanded increases from Q_0 to Q_1, total revenue increases. That is, the new area of total revenue (area b + c) is larger than the old area of total revenue (area a + b). It is also true that if price increased in this region (from P_1 to P_0), total revenue would fall, because b + c is greater than a + b. In this region of the demand curve, then, there is a negative relationship between price and total revenue. As we discussed earlier, this is a characteristic of an elastic demand curve ($E_D > 1$).

Exhibit 4(b) illustrates what happens to total revenue on the lower half of the same demand curve. When the price falls from P_2 to P_3 and the quantity demanded increases

section 5.2 Exhibit 4

Price Elasticity along a Linear Demand Curve

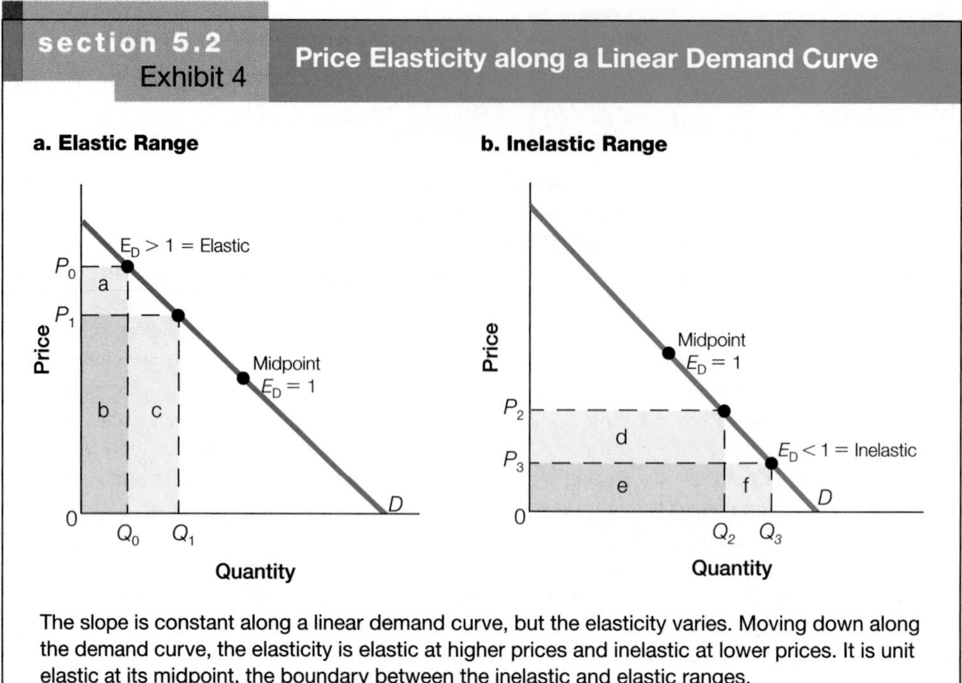

The slope is constant along a linear demand curve, but the elasticity varies. Moving down along the demand curve, the elasticity is elastic at higher prices and inelastic at lower prices. It is unit elastic at its midpoint, the boundary between the inelastic and elastic ranges.

from Q_2 to Q_3, total revenue actually decreases, because the new area of total revenue (area e + f) is less than the old area of total revenue (area d + e). Likewise, it is clear that an increase in price from P_3 to P_2 would increase total revenue. In this case, there is a positive relationship between price and total revenue, which, as we discussed, is characteristic of an inelastic demand curve ($E_D < 1$). Together, parts (a) and (b) of Exhibit 4 illustrate that, although the slope remains constant, the elasticity of a linear demand curve changes along the length of the curve—from relatively elastic at higher price ranges to relatively inelastic at lower price ranges.

Section Check

1. Total revenue is the price of the good times the quantity sold ($TR = P \times Q$).
2. If demand is price elastic ($E_D > 1$), total revenue will vary inversely with a change in price.
3. If demand is price inelastic ($E_D < 1$), total revenue will vary in the same direction as a change in price.
4. A linear demand curve is more price elastic at higher price ranges and more price inelastic at lower price ranges, and it is unit elastic at the midpoint: $E_D = 1$.

---

1. Why does total revenue vary inversely with price if demand is price elastic?
2. Why does total revenue vary directly with price if demand is price inelastic?
3. Why is a linear demand curve more price elastic at higher price ranges and price inelastic at lower price ranges?
4. If demand for some good was perfectly price inelastic, how would total revenue from its sales change as its price changed?
5. Assume that both you and Art, your partner in a picture-framing business, want to increase your firm's total revenue. You argue that in order to achieve this goal, you should lower your prices; Art, on the other hand, thinks that you should raise your prices. What assumptions are each of you making about your firm's price elasticity of demand?

section 5.3

Price Elasticity of Supply

- What is the price elasticity of supply?
- How does time affect the supply elasticity?
- How does the relative elasticity of supply and demand determine the tax burden?

WHAT IS THE PRICE ELASTICITY OF SUPPLY?

According to the law of supply, there is a positive relationship between price and quantity supplied, *ceteris paribus.* But by how much does quantity supplied change as price changes? It is often helpful to know the degree to which a change in price changes the quantity supplied. The **price elasticity of supply** measures how responsive the quantity sellers are willing and able to sell is to changes in the price. In other words, it measures the relative change in the quantity supplied that results from a change in price. Specifically, the price elasticity of supply (E_S) is defined as the percentage change in the quantity supplied divided by the percentage change in price, or

price elasticity of supply *the measure of the sensitivity of the quantity supplied to changes in price of a good*

$$E_S = \frac{\text{Percentage change in the quantity supplied}}{\text{Percentage change in price}}$$

Calculating the Price Elasticity of Supply

The price elasticity of supply is calculated in much the same manner as the price elasticity of demand. Consider, for example, the case in which it is determined that a 10 percent increase in the price of artichokes results in a 25 percent increase in the quantity of artichokes supplied after, say, a few harvest seasons. In this case, the price elasticity is +2.5 (+10 percent ÷ +25 percent = +2.5). This coefficient indicates that each 1 percent increase in the price of artichokes induces a 2.5 percent increase in the quantity of artichokes supplied.

The Ranges of the Price Elasticity of Supply

Economists delineate several ranges of the price elasticity of supply. As with the elasticity of demand, these ranges center on whether the elasticity coefficient is greater than or less than one. Goods with a supply elasticity that is greater than one ($E_S > 1$) are said to be relatively elastic in supply. With that, a 1 percent change in price will result in a greater than 1 percent change in quantity supplied. In our earlier example, artichokes were elastic in supply, because a 1 percent price increase resulted in a 2.5 percent increase in quantity supplied. An example of an elastic supply curve is shown in Exhibit 1(a).

Goods with a supply elasticity that is less than one ($E_S < 1$) are said to be inelastic in supply. This means that a 1 percent change in the price of these goods will induce a proportionately smaller change in the quantity supplied. This situation is shown in the supply curve in Exhibit 1(b).

Finally, there are two extreme cases of price elasticity of supply: perfectly inelastic supply and perfectly elastic supply. In a condition of perfectly inelastic supply, an increase in price will not change the quantity supplied. For example, in a sports arena in the short run (that is, in a period too brief to adjust the structure), the number of seats available will be almost fixed, say at 20,000 seats. Additional portable seats might be available, but for the most part, even if there is a higher price, there will only be 20,000 seats available.

section 5.3
Exhibit 1

The Price of Elasticity of Supply

a. Elastic Supply ($E_S > 1$)

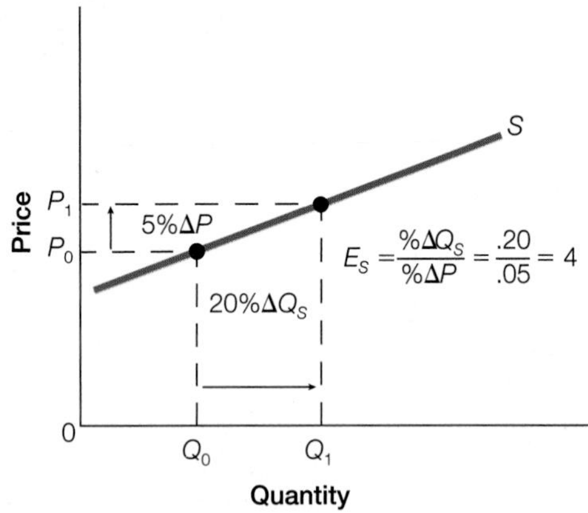

A change in price leads to a larger percentage change in quantity supplied.

b. Inelastic Supply ($E_S < 1$)

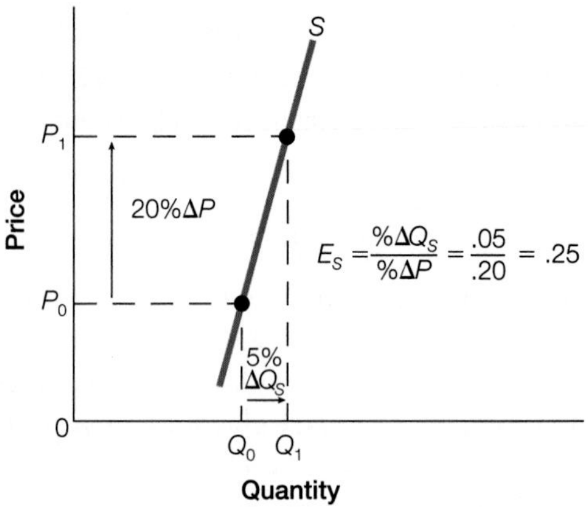

A change in price leads to a smaller percentage change in quantity supplied.

c. Perfectly Inelastic Supply ($E_S = 0$)

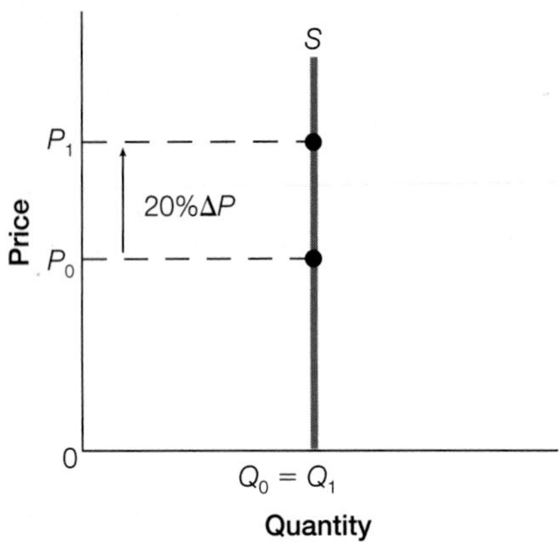

The quantity supplied does not change regardless of the change in price.

d. Perfectly Elastic Supply ($E_S = \infty$)

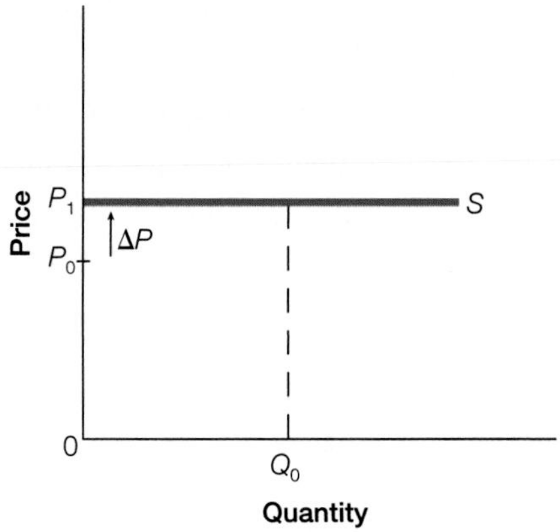

Even a small percentage change in price will change quantity supplied by an infinite amount.

We say that the elasticity of supply is zero, which describes a perfectly inelastic supply curve. Famous paintings, like Van Gogh's *Starry Night,* provide another example; there is only one original in existence and, therefore, only one can be supplied, regardless of price. An example of this condition is shown in Exhibit 1(c).

At the other extreme is a perfectly elastic supply curve, where the elasticity equals infinity as seen in Exhibit 1(d). In a condition of perfectly elastic supply, nothing will be supplied at any price up to a certain level, but at some higher price, sellers would be willing to supply whatever quantity buyers wished to buy. In this case, if the price is below the market price at P_0, the quantity supplied will fall to zero. But at P_1, sellers will sell all that buyers wish to buy. However, most cases fall somewhere between the two extremes of perfectly elastic and perfectly inelastic.

© PHOTODISC/GETTY ONE IMAGES

Immediately after harvest season is over, the supply of pumpkins is inelastic. That is, even if the price for pumpkins rises, say 10 percent, the amount of pumpkins produced will be very small until the next harvest season. Some pumpkins may be grown in greenhouses (at a much higher price to consumers), but most farmers will wait until the next growing season.

How Does Time Impact Supply Elasticities?

Time is usually critical in supply elasticities (as well as in demand elasticities), because it is more costly for producers to bring forth and release resources in a shorter period of time. For example, the higher wheat prices may cause farmers to grow more wheat, but big changes cannot occur until the next growing season. That is, immediately after harvest season, the supply of wheat is relatively inelastic, but over a longer period that extends over the next growing period, the supply curve becomes much more elastic. Hence, supply tends to be more elastic in the long run than the short run, as shown in Exhibit 2.

ELASTICITIES AND TAXES: COMBINING SUPPLY AND DEMAND ELASTICITIES

The relative elasticity of supply and demand determines the distribution of the tax burden for a good. As we shall see, if demand has a lower elasticity than supply in the relevant tax region, the largest portion of the tax is paid by the consumer. However, if demand is relatively more elastic than supply in the relevant tax region, the largest portion of the tax is paid by the producer.

In Exhibit 3, we see that when the 50 cent tax is imposed on a good, the supply curve shifts vertically by the amount of the tax (just as if an input price rose 50 cents). In the case where demand is relatively less elastic than supply in the relevant region, almost the whole tax is passed on to the consumer, *ceteris paribus.* For example, in Exhibit 3(a), the supply curve is relatively more elastic than the demand curve. In response to the tax, the consumer pays $1.40 per unit, 40 cents more than the consumer paid before the tax increase. The producer, however, receives 90 cents per unit, which is 10 cents less than she received before the tax. In Exhibit 3(b), demand is relatively more elastic than the supply in the relevant region. Here, we see that the greater burden of the same 50 cent tax falls on the producer, *ceteris paribus.* That is, the producer is now responsible for 40 cents of the tax, while the consumer only pays 10 cents. In general, then, the tax burden falls on the side of the market that is less elastic. Note that who actually pays the tax at the time of the purchase has nothing to do with who incurs the ultimate burden of the taxation—that depends on the relative elasticity.

section 5.3 Exhibit 2 — Short-Run and Long-Run Supply Curves

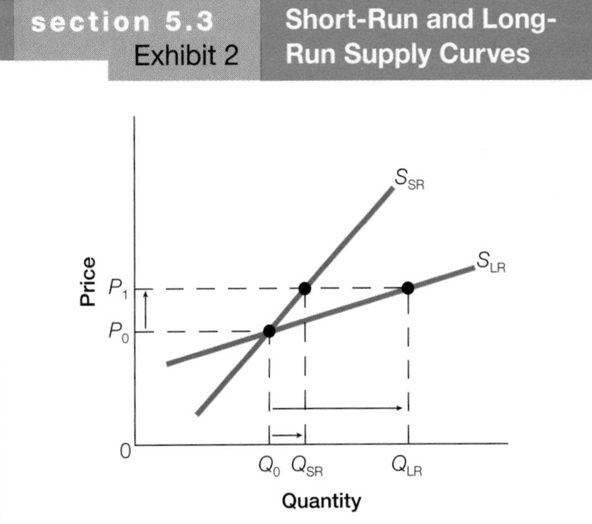

For most goods, supply is more elastic in the long run than in the short run. For example, if price increases, firms have an incentive to produce more but are constrained by the size of their plants. In the long run, they can increase their capacity and produce more.

section 5.3
Exhibit 3

Elasticity and the Burden of Taxation

a. Demand Is Relatively Less Elastic than Supply

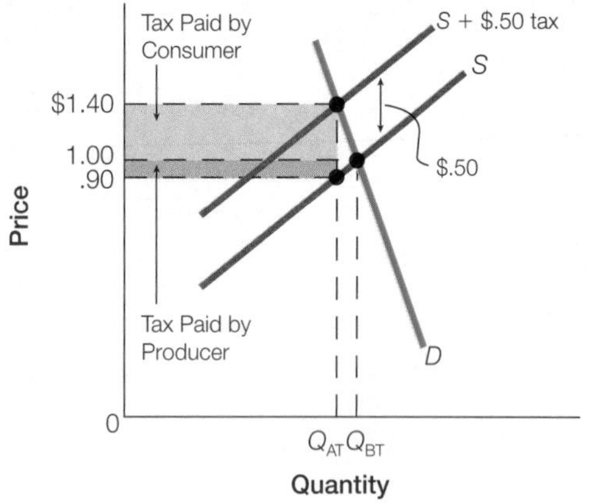

b. Demand Is Relatively More Elastic than Supply

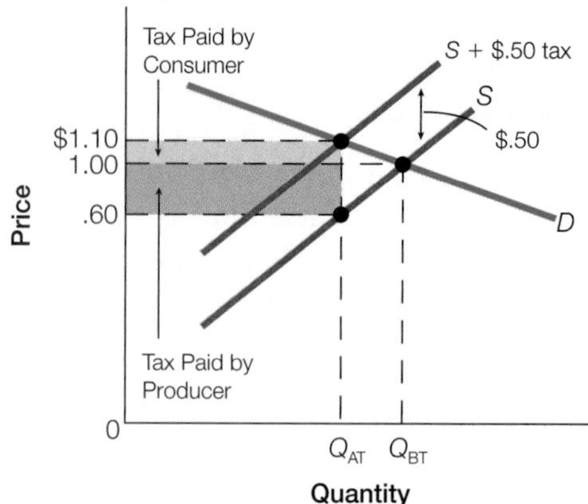

When demand is less elastic (or more inelastic) than supply, the tax burden falls primarily on consumers, as shown in Exhibit 3(a). When demand is more elastic than supply, as shown in Exhibit 3(b), the tax burden falls primarily on producers.

In The NEWS

DRUGS ACROSS THE BORDER

"They are just limited by their imagination," said a U.S. official who closely monitors Mexican trafficking groups. "Money is no obstacle at all." Trafficking schemes run the gamut from the mundane to the Byzantine. In recent years, drug mafias have bought 727-style planes and built a fleet of two-man submarines to move drugs into the United States. They have secreted loads in propane tanks and containers of hazardous materials, in small cans of tuna fish and five-gallon drums of jalapeño peppers. One trafficking group fashioned a special mold that was successfully used to ship cocaine from Mexico through the United States and into Canada completely sealed inside the walls of porcelain toilets.

The groups are using satellite-linked navigation and positioning aids to coordinate airplane drops to boats waiting in the Caribbean and to trucks in the Arizona and Texas deserts. They are using small planes equipped with ordinary car radar detectors to probe radar coverage along the border, then slipping other drug-laden aircraft through the gaps before U.S. officials can react. They are racing hauls of drugs up the coast in 22-foot-long powerboats with massive engines, digging holes in the Gulf beaches of Texas and burying their loads like hidden treasure for pickup at a later date.

Among the more ambitious drug-smuggling methods in recent years was the construction of tunnels under the border at Douglas, Arizona, and Otay Mesa, California, used to smuggle tons of cocaine into the United States until they were shut down following a tip from an informant.

SOURCE: © Copyright 1997, The Washington Post Company. John Ward Anderson and William Branigin, "Border Plagued by Drug Traffickers," *Post Foreign Service,* November 2, 1997, Page A01.

IN THE NEWS *(continued)*

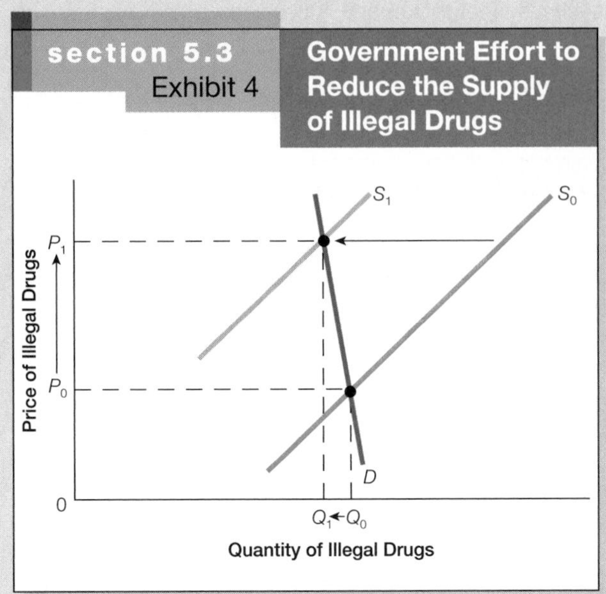

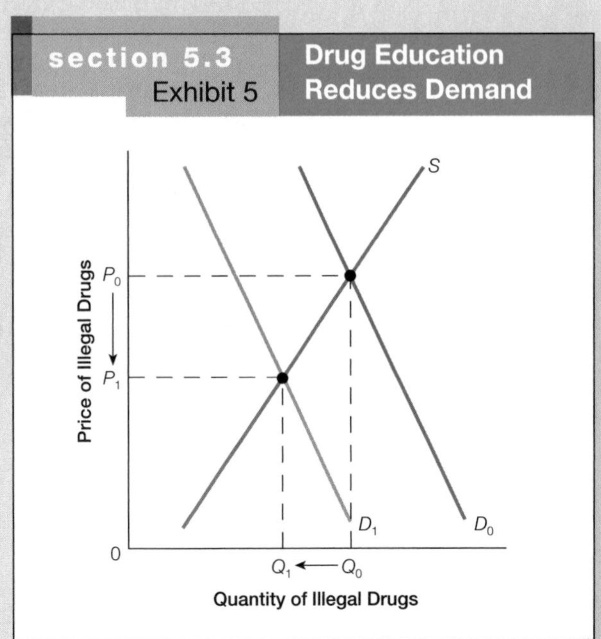

CONSIDER THIS:

The United States spends billions of dollars a year to halt the importation of illegal drugs across the border. Although these efforts are clearly targeted at suppliers, who really pays the higher enforcement and evasion costs? The government crackdown has increased the probability of apprehension and conviction for drug smugglers. That increase in risk for suppliers increases their cost of doing business—raising the cost of importing and distributing illegal drugs. This would shift the supply curve for illegal drugs to the left, from S_0 to S_1, as seen in Exhibit 4. For most drug users—addicts, in particular—the price of drugs like cocaine and heroin lies in the highly inelastic region of the demand curve. Because the demand for drugs is relatively inelastic in this region, the seller would be able to shift most of this cost onto the consumer (think of it like the tax shift just discussed). That is, enforcement efforts increase the price of illegal drugs, but only a small reduction in quantity demanded results from this price increase. Increased enforcement efforts may have unintended consequences due to the fact that buyers bear the majority of the burden of this price increase. Tighter smuggling controls may, in fact, result in higher levels of burglary, muggings, and white-collar crime, as more cash-strapped buyers search for alternative ways of funding their increasingly expensive habit. In addition, with the huge financial rewards in the drug trade, tougher enforcement and higher illegal drug prices could lead to even greater corruption in law enforcement and the judicial system.

This is not to say that we should abandon our efforts against illegal drugs. Illegal drugs can impose huge personal and social costs—billions of dollars of lost productivity and immeasurable personal tragedy. However, solely targeting the supply side can have unintended consequences. Policy makers may get their best results by focusing on a reduction in demand—changing user preferences. For example, if drug education leads to a reduction in the demand for drugs, the demand curve will shift to the left—reducing the price and the quantity of illegal drugs exchanged, as seen in Exhibit 5. The remaining drug users, at Q_1, will now pay a lower price, P_1. This lower price for drugs will lead to fewer drug-related crimes, *ceteris paribus.*

It is also possible that the elasticity of demand for illegal drugs may be more elastic in the long run than the short run. In the short run, as the price rises, the quantity demanded falls less than proportionately because of the addictive nature of illegal drugs (this is also true for goods like tobacco and alcohol). However, in the long run, the demand for illegal drugs may be more elastic; that is, the higher price may deter many younger, and poorer, people from experimenting with illegal drugs.

Section Check

1. The price elasticity of supply measures the relative change in the quantity supplied that results from a change in price.
2. If the supply price elasticity is greater than one, it is elastic; if it is less than one, it is inelastic.
3. Supply tends to be more elastic in the long run than the short run.
4. The relative elasticity of supply and demand determines the distribution of the tax burden for a good.

---

1. What does it mean to say that the elasticity of supply for one good is greater than that for another?
2. Why does supply tend to be more elastic in the long run than in the short run?
3. How do the relative elasticities of supply and demand determine who bears the greater burden of a tax?

section 5.4

Consumer Behavior

- What is utility?
- Can we make interpersonal utility comparisons?
- What is the law of diminishing marginal utility?

Individuals do not just follow simple patterns of behavior. They take action in response to recognized opportunities to advance their goals. This assumption that individuals act to advance their goals—known as the rule of rational choice—merely implies that whatever individuals do, they do with a purpose. In economics we assume that each individual seeks to maximize his or her own well-being or satisfaction.

UTILITY

utility
the relative measurement of satisfaction gleaned from the consumption of goods and services

util
a measure of utility equal to "one unit" of satisfaction

In an attempt to more clearly define the relationship between consumer choice and resource allocation, economists developed the concept of **utility** to allow them to study the relative levels of satisfaction that consumers get from the consumption of goods and services. Suppose we could measure satisfaction and one **util** was equivalent to one unit of satisfaction. Economists could then indicate relative levels of consumer satisfaction that result from alternative choices. For a java junkie, for example, a first cup of coffee might generate 150 utils of satisfaction while a first cup of tea might only generate 20 utils, because coffee is preferred to tea for this person.

Inherently, utility varies from individual to individual depending on specific preferences. For example, Jason might get 50 utils of satisfaction from eating his first piece of apple pie, while Brittany may only derive 4 utils of satisfaction from her first piece of apple pie.

UTILITY IS A PERSONAL MATTER

Economists recognize that it is not really possible to make *interpersonal utility comparisons.* That is, they know that it is impossible to compare the relative satisfactions of different persons. The relative satisfactions gained by two people drinking cups of coffee, for example, simply cannot be measured in comparable terms. Likewise, while it might be tempting to believe that a poorer person would derive greater utility from finding a $100 bill than a richer person, the temptation should be resisted. We simply cannot prove it. The poorer person may be "monetarily" poor because money and material things are not important to him, and the rich person may have become richer because of his lust for the things money can buy.

TOTAL UTILITY AND MARGINAL UTILITY

Economists recognize two different dimensions of utility: total utility and marginal utility. **Total utility** is the total amount of satisfaction derived from the consumption of a certain number of units of a good or service. In comparison, **marginal utility** is the additional satisfaction generated by the last unit of a good that is consumed. In other words, marginal utility measures the increase in satisfaction derived from the last unit of a good that has been consumed, beyond the amount of satisfaction that has been generated by the consumption of previous units of the good in a particular time period. For example, eating four slices of pizza in an evening might generate a total of 36 utils of satisfaction. The first three slices of pizza might generate a total of 35 utils, while the last slice generates only 1 util. In this case, the total utility of eating four slices of pizza is 36 utils, and the marginal utility of the fourth slice is 1 util. Notice in Exhibit 1(a) how marginal utility falls as consumption increases, while in Exhibit 1(b), total utility increases as consumption increases (there is more total utility after the fourth slice of pizza than after the third); but notice that the increase from each additional unit (slice) is less than the unit before.

total utility
the aggregate level of satisfaction that results from consumption of a given number of goods and services

marginal utility
the amount of satisfaction that results from the consumption of the last unit of good or service

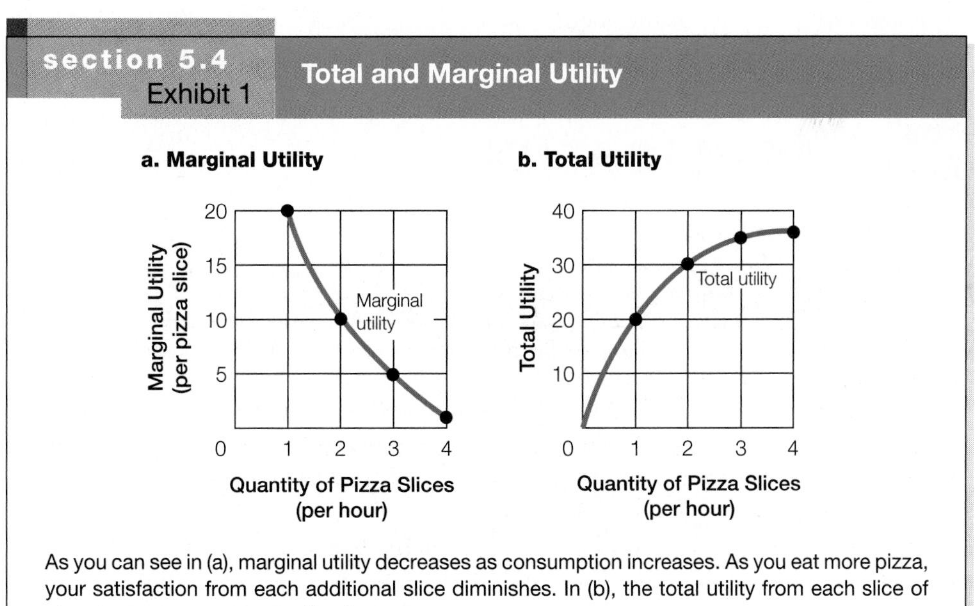

As you can see in (a), marginal utility decreases as consumption increases. As you eat more pizza, your satisfaction from each additional slice diminishes. In (b), the total utility from each slice of pizza increases as consumption increases.

DIMINISHING MARGINAL UTILITY

Although economists believe that total utility increases with additional consumption, they also argue that the incremental satisfaction—the marginal utility—that results from the consumption of additional units tends to decline as consumption increases. In other words, each successive unit of a good that is consumed generates less satisfaction than did the previous unit. This concept is traditionally referred to as the **law of diminishing marginal utility.** Exhibit 1(a) demonstrates this graphically, where the marginal utility curve has a negative slope.

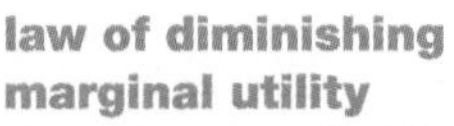
law of diminishing marginal utility
the economic principle that states that consumers will experience less satisfaction for each additional unit of good consumed

It follows from the law of diminishing marginal utility that as a person uses more and more units of a good to satisfy a given want, the intensity of the want, and the utility derived from further satisfying that want, diminishes. For example, as you eat four pieces of pepperoni pizza in an hour, your desire for another piece of pepperoni pizza, and thus the satisfaction you get from satisfying that desire, diminishes with each slice that is eaten. Think about it: If you are starving, your desire for that first piece of pizza will be great, but as you eat, you gradually become more and more full, reducing your desire for yet another piece.

"It's been fun, Dave, but I think we're entering the diminished marginal utility phase of our relationship."

THE LAW OF DEMAND AND THE LAW OF DIMINISHING MARGINAL UTILITY

The law of demand states that when the price of a good is reduced, the quantity of that good demanded will increase. But why is this the case? By examining the law of diminishing marginal utility in action, we can determine the basis for this relationship between price and quantity demanded. Indeed, the demand curve merely translates marginal utility into dollar terms. That is, marginal utility measures how much we value a particular good. The more marginal utility a buyer receives from a good, the more he or she is willing to pay for it. And because successive units yield less satisfaction, the buyer will not be as willing to pay for additional units of the good.

APPLICATION

DIMINISHING MARGINAL UTILITY

Q: Why do most individuals take only one newspaper from covered, coin-operated newspaper racks when it would be so easy to take more? Do you think potato chips, candy, or sodas could be sold profitably in the same kind of dispenser? Why or why not?

A: While ethical considerations keep some people from taking additional papers, the law of diminishing marginal utility is also at work here. The second newspaper adds practically zero utility to most individuals on most days, so there is typically no incentive to take more than one. The exception to this case might be on Sundays, when supermarket coupons are present. In that instance, while the marginal utility is still lower for the second paper than the first, the marginal utility of the second paper may be large enough to tempt some individuals to take additional copies.

On the other hand, if you put your money in the vending machine and had access to many bags of potato chips, candy bars, or sodas, the temptation to take more than one might be too great for some. After all, the potato chip bags will still be good tomorrow. Therefore, vending machines with foods and drinks only dispense one item at a time, because it is likely that, for most people, the marginal utility gained from another unit of food or drink is higher than that for a second newspaper.

Section Check

SECTION CHECK

1. Utility is the amount of satisfaction an individual receives from consumption of a good or service.
2. Economists recognize that it is not possible to make interpersonal utility comparisons.
3. Total utility is the amount of satisfaction derived from all units of goods and services consumed. Total utility increases as consumption increases.
4. Marginal utility is the change in utility from consuming one additional unit of a good or service.
5. According to the law of diminishing marginal utility, as a person consumes additional units of a given good, marginal utility declines.

---

1. How do economists define utility?
2. Why can't interpersonal utility comparisons be made?
3. What is the relationship between total utility and marginal utility?
4. Why could you say that a millionaire gets less marginal utility from a second piece of pizza than from the first piece, but you couldn't say whether she got more or less marginal utility from a second piece of pizza than someone else who has a much lower level of income?
5. Are you likely to get as much marginal utility from your last piece of chicken at an all-you-can-eat restaurant as at a restaurant where you pay $2 per piece of chicken?

section 5.5

Consumer and Producer Surplus

- What is consumer surplus?
- What is producer surplus?
- How do we measure the total gains from trade?

CONSUMER SURPLUS

What a consumer actually pays for a unit of a good is usually less than the amount she is *willing* to pay. For example, you would be willing and able to pay far more than the market price for a rope ladder to get out of a burning building. You would be willing to pay more than the market price for a tank of gasoline if you had run out of gas on a desolate highway in the desert. **Consumer surplus** is the monetary difference between the amount a consumer is willing and able to pay for an additional unit of a good and what the consumer actually pays—the market price. Consumer surplus for the whole market is the sum of all the individual consumers who have purchased the good.

consumer surplus
the difference between the price a consumer is willing and able to pay for an additional unit of a good and the price the consumer actually pays; for the whole market it is the sum of all the individual consumer surpluses

MARGINAL WILLINGNESS TO PAY FALLS AS MORE IS CONSUMED

Suppose it is a very hot day and iced tea is going for $1 per glass, but a consumer is willing to pay $4 for the first glass, $2 for the second glass, and $0.50 for the third glass, reflecting the law of demand. How much consumer surplus will this consumer receive?

section 5.5 Exhibit 1 **Consumer Surplus for Iced Tea**

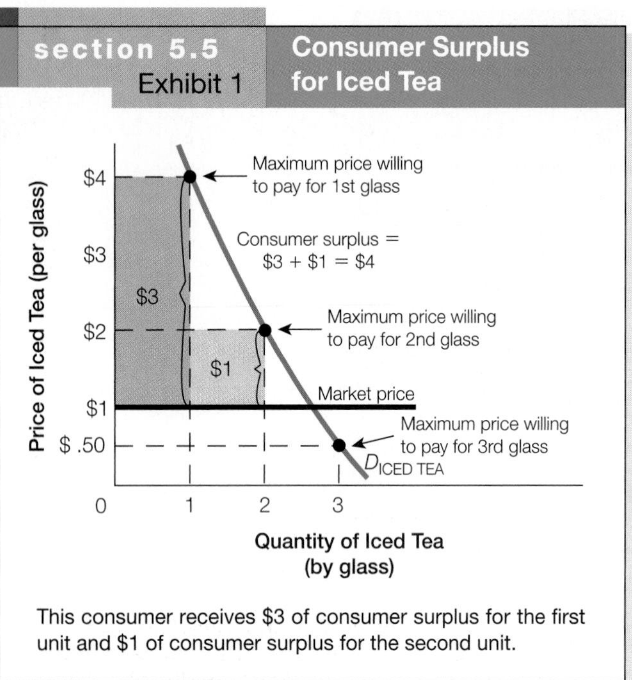

This consumer receives $3 of consumer surplus for the first unit and $1 of consumer surplus for the second unit.

First, it is important to note the general fact that if the consumer is a buyer of several units of a good, the earlier units will have greater marginal value and therefore create more consumer surplus, because *marginal willingness to pay* falls as greater quantities are consumed in any period (the law of diminishing marginal utility). This is demonstrated by the consumer's willingness to pay $4 and $2 successively for the first two glasses of iced tea. Thus, the consumer will receive $3 of consumer surplus for the first glass ($4 − $1) and $1 of consumer surplus for the second glass ($2 − $1), for a total of $4, as seen in Exhibit 1. The consumer will not be willing to purchase the third glass, because it would provide less value than its price warrants ($.50 versus $1.00) and reduce consumer surplus as a result.

In Exhibit 2, this is shown as the area under the market demand curve and above the market price (area A). Areas A and B together represent *total* willingness-to-pay for Q units of the good, while area B is the amount the consumer is required to pay for that quantity ($P \times Q$). The difference is consumer surplus, the shaded area, A.

Imagine it is 115 degrees in the shade. Do you think you would get more consumer surplus from your first glass of iced tea than you would from a fifth glass?

PRICE CHANGES AND CHANGES IN CONSUMER SURPLUS

Imagine that the price of your favorite beverage fell because of an increase in supply. Wouldn't you feel better off? An increase in supply and a lower price will increase your consumer surplus for each of the units you were already consuming, and will also increase consumer surplus from increased purchases at the lower price. Conversely, a decrease in supply will cause an increase in price and will lower the amount of consumer surplus.

Exhibit 3 shows the gain in consumer surplus associated with a technological advance that shifts the supply curve to the right. As a result, equilibrium price falls (from P_0 to P_1) and quantity rises (from Q_0 to Q_1). Consumer surplus then increases from area P_0AB to area P_1AC, or a gain in consumer surplus of P_0BCP_1. The increase in consumer surplus has two parts. First, there is an increase in consumer surplus because Q_0 can now be purchased at a lower price; this amount of additional consumer surplus is illustrated by area P_0BDP_1 in Exhibit 3. Second, the lower price makes it advantageous for buyers to expand their purchases from Q_0 to Q_1. The net benefit to buyers from expanding their consumption from Q_0 to Q_1 is illustrated by the area BCD.

producer surplus
the difference between what a producer is paid for a good and the cost of producing that unit of the good; for the market, it is the sum of all the individual sellers' producer surpluses—the area above the market supply curve and below the market price

PRODUCER SURPLUS

As we have just seen, the difference between what a consumer would be willing and able to pay for a quantity of a good and what a consumer actually has to pay is called consumer surplus. The parallel concept for producers is called producer surplus. **Producer surplus** is the difference between what a producer is paid for a good and the cost of producing that unit of the good. Because some units can be produced at a cost that is lower than the market price, the seller receives a surplus, or a net benefit, from producing those units. For example, in Exhibit 4, the market price is $5. Say the firm's cost is $2 for the first unit; $3 for the second unit; $4 for the third unit; and $5 for the fifth unit. Since pro-

section 5.5 Exhibit 2 — Consumer Surplus

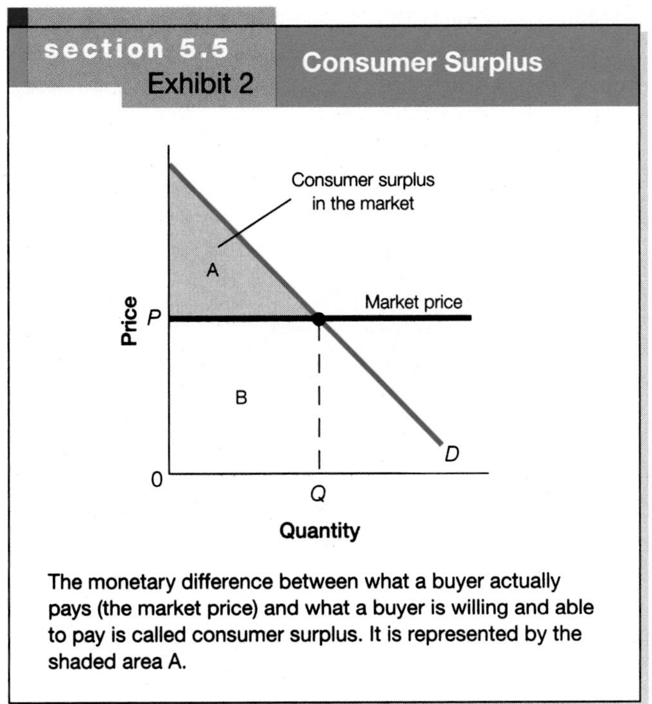

The monetary difference between what a buyer actually pays (the market price) and what a buyer is willing and able to pay is called consumer surplus. It is represented by the shaded area A.

section 5.5 Exhibit 3 — The Impact of an Increase in Supply on Consumer Surplus

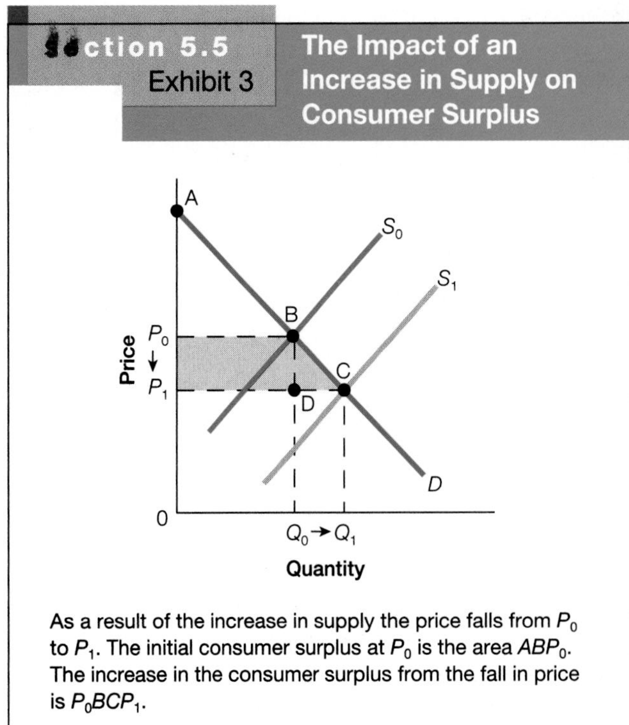

As a result of the increase in supply the price falls from P_0 to P_1. The initial consumer surplus at P_0 is the area ABP_0. The increase in the consumer surplus from the fall in price is P_0BCP_1.

ducer surplus for a particular unit is the difference between the market price and the seller's cost of producing that unit, producer surplus would be as follows: The first unit would yield \$3, the second unit would yield \$2, the third unit would yield \$1, while the fourth unit would add no more to producer surplus, as the market price equals the seller's cost.

For the market, producer surplus is obtained by summing all the producer surplus of all the sellers—the area above the market supply curve and below the market price. Producer surplus is a measurement of how much sellers gain from trading in the market.

Suppose there is an increase in demand and the market price rises, say from P_0 to P_1; the seller now receives a higher price per unit, so additional producer surplus is generated. In Exhibit 5, we see the additions to producer surplus. Part of the added surplus (area P_0DBP_1) is due to a higher price for the quantity already being produced (up to Q_0) and part (area DCB) is due to the expansion of output made profitable by the higher price (from Q_0 to Q_1).

section 5.5 Exhibit 4 — Producer Surplus

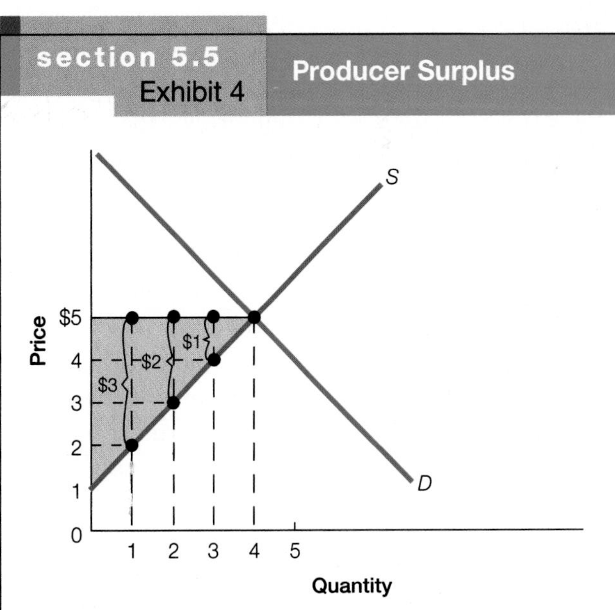

For each unit, producer surplus measures the difference between what sellers are paid and the seller's costs of production. The sum of the producer surplus is illustrated by the shaded area above the supply curve and below the market price.

MARKET EFFICIENCY AND PRODUCER AND CONSUMER SURPLUS

With the tools of consumer and producer surplus, we can better analyze the total gains from exchange. The demand curve represents a collection of maximum prices that consumers are willing and able to pay for additional quantities section 5.5 Exhibit 5 — The Impact of an Increase in Demand on Producer Surplus

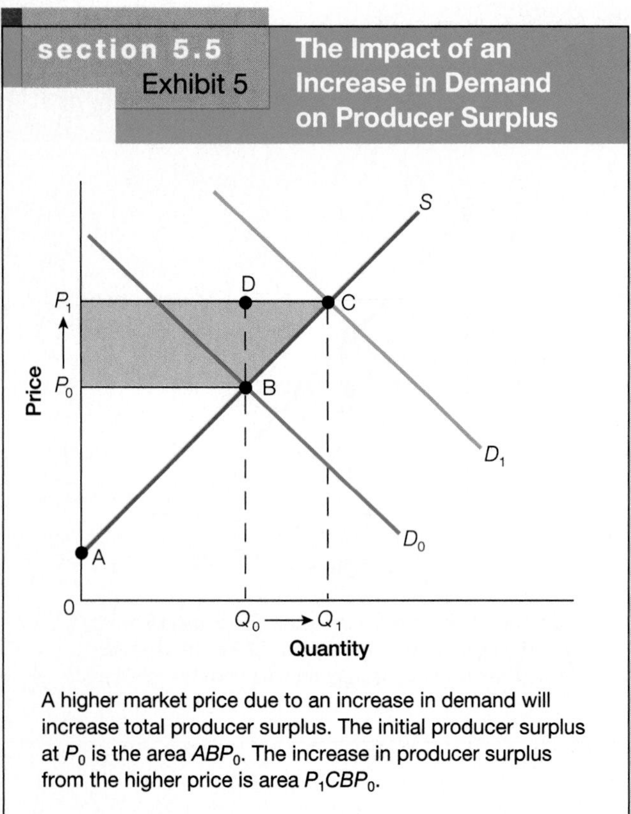

A higher market price due to an increase in demand will increase total producer surplus. The initial producer surplus at P_0 is the area ABP_0. The increase in producer surplus from the higher price is area P_1CBP_0.

section 5.5 Exhibit 6 — Consumer and Producer Surplus

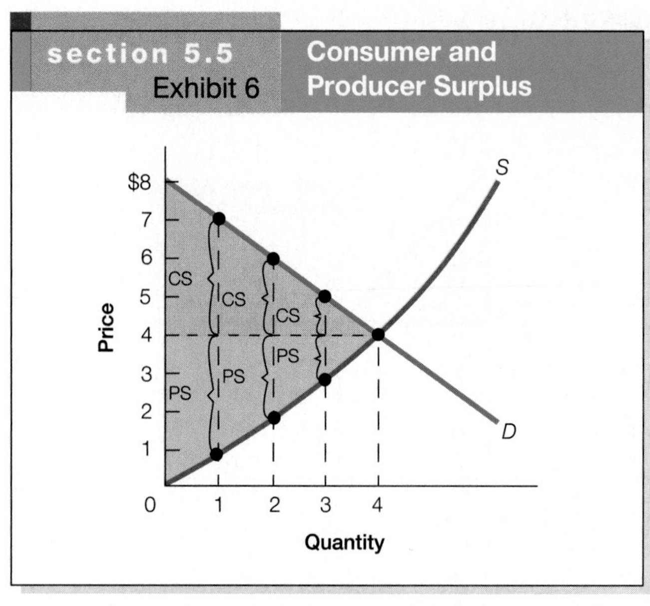

of a good or service. The supply curve represents a collection of minimum prices that suppliers require to be willing and able to supply each additional unit of a good or service, as seen in Exhibit 6. For example, for the first unit of output, the buyer is willing to pay up to $7 and the seller would have to receive at least $1 to produce that unit. However, the equilibrium price is $4, as indicated by the intersection of the supply and demand curves. It is clear that the two would gain from getting together and trading that unit because the consumer would receive $3 of consumer surplus ($7 − $4) and the producer would receive $3 of producer surplus ($4 − $1). Both would also benefit from trading the second and third units of output—in fact, both would benefit from trading every unit up to the market equilibrium output. That is, buyers purchase each good, except for the very last unit, for less than the maximum amount that they would have been willing to pay; sellers receive, except for the very last unit, more than the minimum amount that they would have been willing to accept to supply the good. Once the equilibrium output is reached at the equilibrium price, all of the mutually beneficial trade opportunities between the suppliers and the demanders will have taken place, and the sum of consumer surplus and producer surplus is maximized. Both buyers and sellers are better off from each of the units traded than they would have been if they had not exchanged them.

total welfare gains *the sum of consumer and producer surplus*

It is important to recognize that, in this case, the **total welfare gains** to the economy from trade in this good is the sum of the consumer and producer surplus created. That is, consumers benefit from additional amounts of consumer surplus and producers benefit from additional amounts of producer surplus. Improvements in welfare come from additions to both consumer and producer surplus. In competitive markets, where there are large numbers of buyers and sellers, at the market equilibrium price and quantity, the net gains to society are as large as possible.

Section Check

1. The difference between how much a consumer is willing and able to pay and how much a consumer has to pay for a unit of the good is called consumer surplus.
2. An increase in supply will lead to a lower price and an increase in consumer surplus; a decrease in supply will lead to a higher price and a decrease in consumer surplus.
3. Producer surplus is the difference between what a producer is paid for a good and the cost of producing that good.
4. An increase in demand will lead to a higher market price and an increase in producer surplus; a decrease in demand will lead to a lower market price and a decrease in producer surplus.
5. Total welfare gains from trade to the economy can be measured by the sum of consumer and producer surplus.

---

1. What is consumer surplus?
2. Why do the first units consumed at a given price add more consumer surplus than the last units consumed?
3. When market supply increases, why does a decrease in a good's price increase the consumer surplus from consumption of that good?
4. Why might the consumer surplus from purchases of diamond rings be less than the consumer surplus from purchases of far less expensive stones?
5. What is producer surplus?
6. Why do the first units produced at a given price add more producer surplus than the last units sold?
7. When market demand increases, why does an increase in a good's price increase the producer surplus from production of that good?
8. Why might the producer surplus from sales of diamond rings, which are very expensive, be less than the producer surplus from sales of far less expensive stones?

section 5.6

The Welfare Effects of Taxes

- What are the welfare effects of a tax?
- What is a deadweight loss?
- What are the welfare effects of price controls?

In the last section we used the tools of consumer and producer surplus to measure the efficiency of a competitive market; that is, how the equilibrium price and quantity in a competitive market leads to the maximization of aggregate welfare (both buyers and sellers). Now we can use the same tools, consumer and producer surplus, to measure the welfare effects of various government programs—taxes and price controls. When economists use the term **welfare effects** of a government policy they are referring to the gains and losses associated with government intervention. This should not be confused with the way we commonly use the term referring to a welfare recipient who is getting aid from the government.

welfare effects
the gains and losses associated with government intervention in markets

section 5.6 Exhibit 1 — The Supply and Demand of a Tax

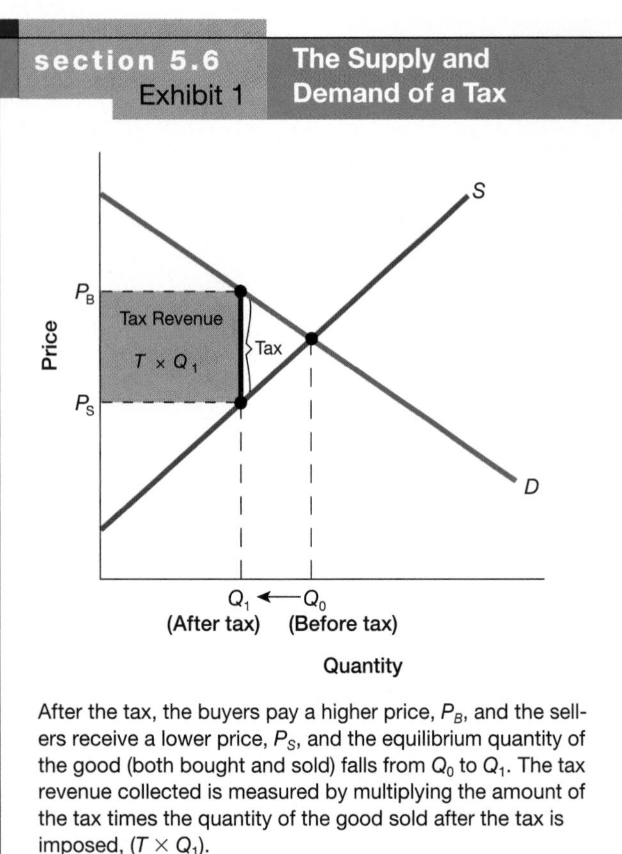

After the tax, the buyers pay a higher price, P_B, and the sellers receive a lower price, P_S, and the equilibrium quantity of the good (both bought and sold) falls from Q_0 to Q_1. The tax revenue collected is measured by multiplying the amount of the tax times the quantity of the good sold after the tax is imposed, $(T \times Q_1)$.

USING CONSUMER AND PRODUCER SURPLUS TO FIND THE WELFARE EFFECTS OF A TAX

To simplify the explanation of elasticity and the tax incidence, we will not complicate the illustration by shifting the supply curve (tax levied on sellers) or demand curve (tax levied on buyers), as we did in Section 5.3. We will simply show the result a tax must cause. The tax is illustrated by the vertical distance between the supply and demand curve at the new after-tax output—shown as the bold vertical line in Exhibit 1. After the tax, the buyers pay a higher price, P_B, and the sellers receive a lower price, P_S, and the equilibrium quantity of the good (both bought and sold) falls from Q_0 to Q_1. The tax revenue collected is measured by multiplying the amount of the tax times the quantity of the good sold after the tax is imposed, $(T \times Q_1)$.

In Exhibit 2, we can now use consumer and producer surplus to measure the amount of welfare loss associated with a tax. First, consider the amount of consumer and producer surplus before the tax. Before the tax is imposed, the price is P_0 and the quantity is Q_0; at that price and output, the amount of consumer surplus is area a + b + c, and the amount of producer surplus is area d + e + f. To get the total surplus, or total welfare, we add consumer and producer surplus, that is area a + b + c + d + e + f. And because there is no tax, tax revenues are zero.

After the tax, the price the buyer pays is P_B, and the price the seller receives is P_S, and the output falls to Q_1. As a result of the higher price and lower output from the tax, consumer surplus is now smaller, area a. After the tax, sellers now receive a lower price, so producer surplus is now smaller, area f. However, some of the loss in consumer and producer surplus is transferred in the form of tax revenues to the government that can be used to reduce other taxes, fund public projects, or be redistributed to others in society. This is a transfer of society's resources, but not a loss from society's perspective. The net loss to society can be found by measuring the difference between the loss in consumer surplus, area b + c, and the loss in producer surplus, area d + e, and the gain in tax revenue, area b + d. The reduction in total surplus is area c + e, or the shaded area in Exhibit 2. We call this the **deadweight loss** from the tax—the reduction in producer and consumer surplus minus the tax revenue transferred to the government.

deadweight loss
the elimination of a benefit to society (consumers and producer) because of a government initiative such as a tax

This deadweight loss occurs because the tax reduces the quantity exchanged below the original output level, Q_0, reducing the size of the total surplus realized from trade. The problem is that the tax distorts market incentives: The price to buyers is higher than before the tax so they consume less and the price to sellers is lower than before the tax so they produce less. This leads to deadweight loss, or market inefficiencies, the waste associated with not producing the efficient level of output. That is, the tax causes a deadweight loss because it prevents some mutual beneficial trade between buyers and sellers.

ELASTICITY AND THE SIZE OF THE DEADWEIGHT LOSS

The size of the deadweight loss from a tax, as well as how the burdens are shared between buyers and sellers, depends on the price elasticities of supply and demand. In Exhibit 3(a) we can see that, other things equal, the less elastic the demand curve, the smaller the deadweight loss. Similarly, the less elastic the supply curve, other things equal, the smaller

section 5.6 Exhibit 2 — Welfare Effects of a Tax

	Before Tax	After Tax	Change
Consumer Surplus	a + b + c	a	−(b + c)
Producer Surplus	d + e + f	f	−(d + e)
Tax Revenue ($T \times Q_1$)		b + d	b + d
Total Welfare	a + b + c + d + e + f	a + b + d + f	−(c + e)

The net loss to society of a tax can be found by measuring the difference between the loss in consumer surplus, area b + c, and the loss in producer surplus, area d + e, and the gain in tax revenue, area b + d. The deadweight loss from the tax is the reduction in the consumer and producer surplus minus the tax revenue transferred to the government, −(c + e).

section 5.6 Exhibit 3 — Elasticity and Deadweight Loss

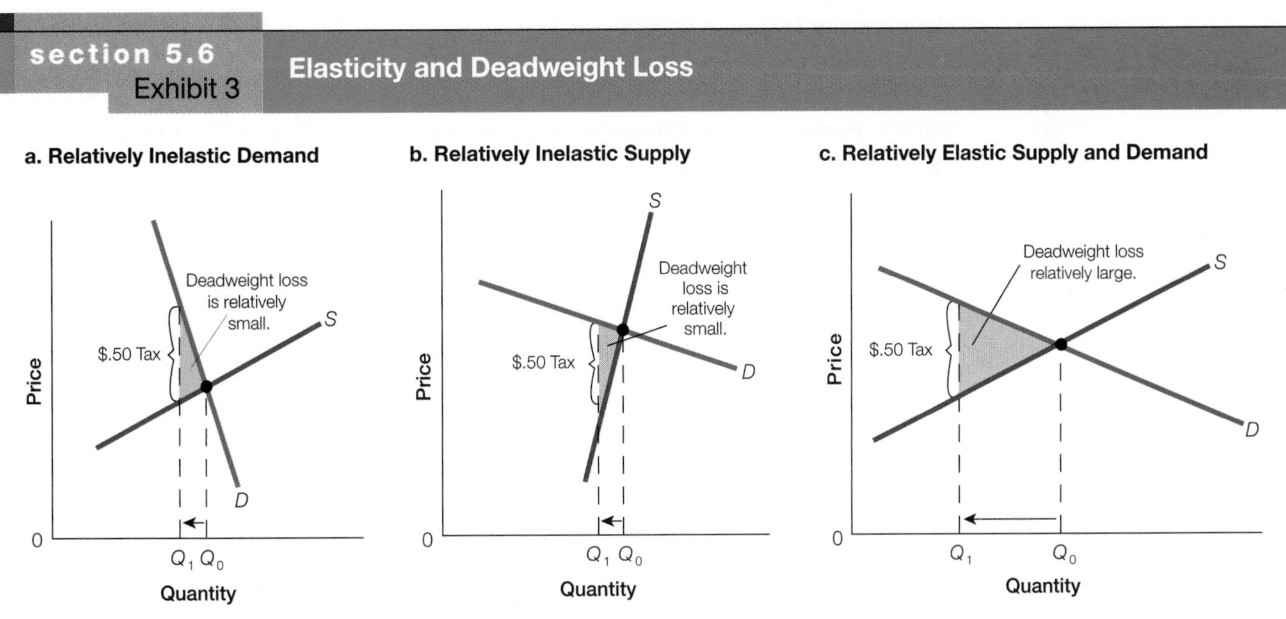

In Exhibit 3(a) and (b) we see when one of the two curves is relatively price inelastic, the deadweight loss from the tax is relatively small. However, when the supply and/or demand curves become more elastic, the deadweight loss will be larger, because a given tax will reduce the quantity exchanged by a greater amount, as seen in Exhibit 3(c). The more elastic the curves are the greater the change in output and the larger the deadweight loss.

the deadweight loss, as in Exhibit 3(b). However, when the supply and/or demand curves become more elastic, the deadweight loss will be larger, because a given tax will reduce the quantity exchanged by a greater amount, as seen in Exhibit 3(c). Recall that elasticities measure how responsive buyers and sellers are to price changes. That is, the more elastic the curves are, the greater the change in output and the larger the deadweight loss.

Elasticity differences can help us understand tax policy. Goods that are heavily taxed often have a relatively inelastic demand curve in the short run, such as alcohol, cigarettes, and gasoline. This means that the tax burden falls primarily on the buyer. It also means that the deadweight loss to society is smaller for the tax revenue raised than if the demand curve were more elastic. That is, since consumers cannot find many close substitutes in the short run, these buyers reduce their consumption only slightly at the higher after-tax price. While the deadweight loss is smaller, it still is positive, because the reduced after-tax price received by sellers and the increased after-tax price paid by buyers reduces the quantity exchanged below the previous market equilibrium level.

PRICE CEILINGS AND WELFARE EFFECTS

As we saw in chapter 4, price controls involve the use of the power of the government to establish prices different from the equilibrium market price that would otherwise prevail. The motivations for price control vary with the markets under consideration. A maximum, or ceiling, is often set for goods deemed "important," like housing. A minimum price, or floor, may be set on wages, because wages are the primary source of income for most people, or on agricultural products, to guarantee that producers will get a certain minimum price for their products.

If a price ceiling (that is, a legally established maximum price) is binding and set below the equilibrium price at P_{MAX}, the quantity demanded will be greater than the quantity supplied at that price and shortage will occur. At this price, buyers will compete for the limited supply, Q_1.

We can see the welfare effects of the price ceiling by observing the change in consumer and producer surplus from the implementation of the price ceiling in Exhibit 4. Before the price ceiling the buyer receives area a + b + c of consumer surplus at price P_0 and quantity Q_0. However, after the price ceiling is implemented at P_{MAX}, consumers can now buy the good at a lower price but cannot buy as much as before (they can now only buy Q_1 instead of Q_0). Because consumers can now buy Q_1 at a lower price, they gain area d of consumer surplus after the price ceiling. However, they lose area c of consumer surplus because they can only purchase Q_1 rather than Q_0 of output. So the change in consumer surplus is d − c.

The price the seller receives for Q_1 is P_{MAX} (the ceiling price), so producer surplus falls from area d + e + f before the price ceiling to area f after the price ceiling, for a loss of area −(d + e). On net, the price ceiling has caused a deadweight loss of −(c + e).

PRICE FLOORS

Since the Great Depression, several agricultural programs have been promoted as assisting small-scale farmers. Such a price support system guarantees a minimum price, such as promising a dairy farmer a price of $4 per pound for cheese. The reasoning is that the equilibrium price of $3 is too low and would not provide enough revenue for the small-volume farmers to maintain a "decent" standard of living. A price floor sets a minimum price that is the lowest price consumers are willing and able to pay for a good. This situation is depicted in Exhibit 5.

With the support price at $4, consumers are willing and able to purchase Q_D and dairy farmers are willing and able to sell $Q_S - Q_D$ units of cheese. The value of this

section 5.6 Exhibit 4 — Welfare Effects of a Price Ceiling

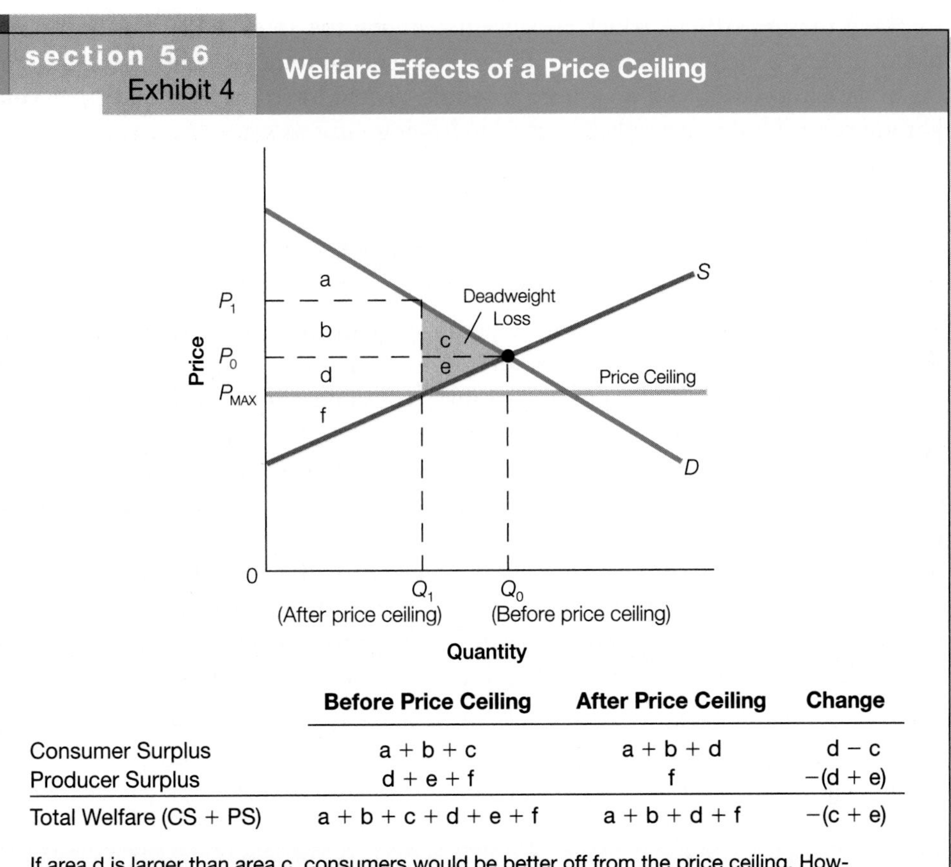

	Before Price Ceiling	After Price Ceiling	Change
Consumer Surplus	a + b + c	a + b + d	d − c
Producer Surplus	d + e + f	f	−(d + e)
Total Welfare (CS + PS)	a + b + c + d + e + f	a + b + d + f	−(c + e)

If area d is larger than area c, consumers would be better off from the price ceiling. However, any possible gain to consumers will be more than offset by the losses to producers, −(d + e). Price ceilings cause a deadweight loss of −(c + e).

section 5.6 Exhibit 5 — Agriculture Price Supports

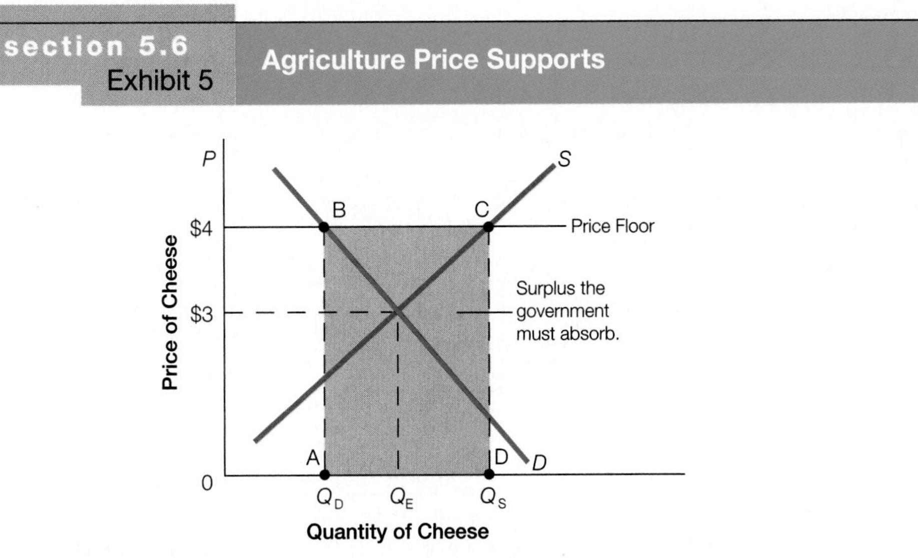

With the support price at \$4, consumers would like to purchase Q_D and farmers would like to sell Q_S. The government must absorb the surplus of ABCD. In sum, the consumer pays a higher price and higher taxes (that is, the government has to pay for the buying and storing of the extra cheese), and the cheese producer benefits by selling at a higher-than-equilibrium price. This is especially beneficial to farmers and owners of larger dairy farms, because this translates into an even greater subsidy.

surplus is the area ABCD, which the government absorbs. In sum, the consumer pays a higher price and higher taxes (that is, the government has to pay for the buying and storing of the extra cheese) and the cheese producers benefit by selling at a higher than equilibrium price. This is especially beneficial to larger producers since this translates into an even greater subsidy.

THE WELFARE EFFECTS OF A PRICE FLOOR WHEN THE GOVERNMENT BUYS UP THE SURPLUS

Who gains and who loses under price support programs when the government buys up the surplus? In Exhibit 6, the equilibrium price and quantity without the price floor is at P_0 and Q_0, respectively. Without the price floor, consumer surplus is area a + b + c and producer surplus is area e + f for a total surplus of a + b + c + e + f.

After the price floor is in effect, price rises to P_1 and output falls to Q_1 and consumer surplus falls from area a + b + c to area a, a loss of b + c, and producer surplus increases from area e + f to area b + c + d + e + f, a gain of b + c + d. If that was the end of the story, we would say that since producers gained b + c + d more than consumers lost b + c, and on net society would benefit by area d from the implementation of the price floor. However, that is *not* the end of the story. The government (taxpayers) must pay for the surplus it buys, area c + d + f + g + h + i. That is, the cost to government, area

section 5.6 Exhibit 6 Welfare Effects of a Price Floor when Government Buys the Surplus

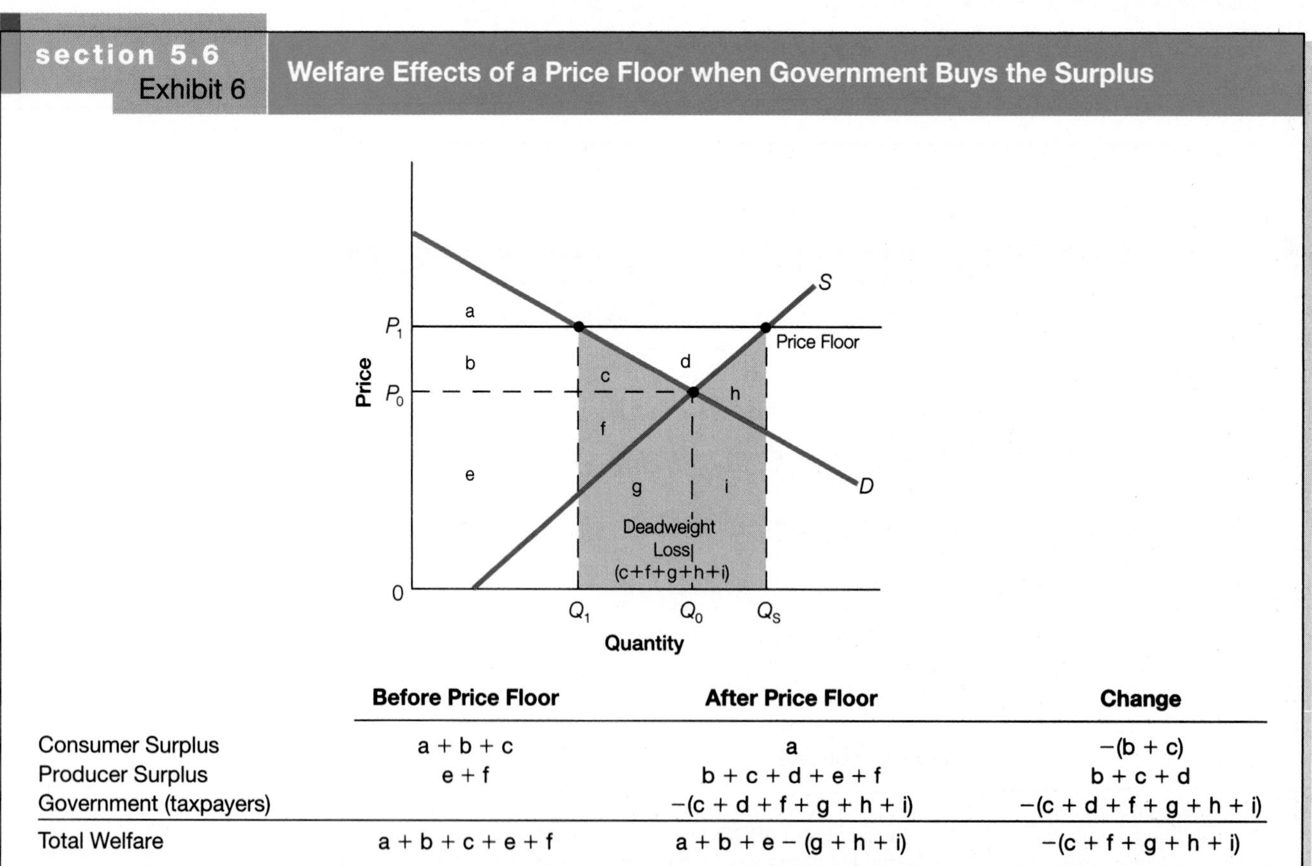

	Before Price Floor	After Price Floor	Change
Consumer Surplus	a + b + c	a	−(b + c)
Producer Surplus	e + f	b + c + d + e + f	b + c + d
Government (taxpayers)		−(c + d + f + g + h + i)	−(c + d + f + g + h + i)
Total Welfare	a + b + c + e + f	a + b + e − (g + h + i)	−(c + f + g + h + i)

After the price floor is implemented, the price rises to P_1 and output fallls to Q_1; there is a loss in consumer surplus of b + c but a gain in producer surplus of b + c + d. However, this is not the end of the story because the cost to the government (taxpayers), c + d + f + g + h + i, is greater than the gain to producers, area d, so there is a deadweight loss of c + f + g + h + i.

c + d + f + g + h + i, is greater than the gain to producers, area d. On net, there is a deadweight loss from the price floor of c + f + g + h + i. Why? Consumers are consuming less than the previous market equilibrium output, eliminating mutually beneficial exchanges, while sellers are producing more than is being consumed, with the excess production stored, destroyed, or exported.

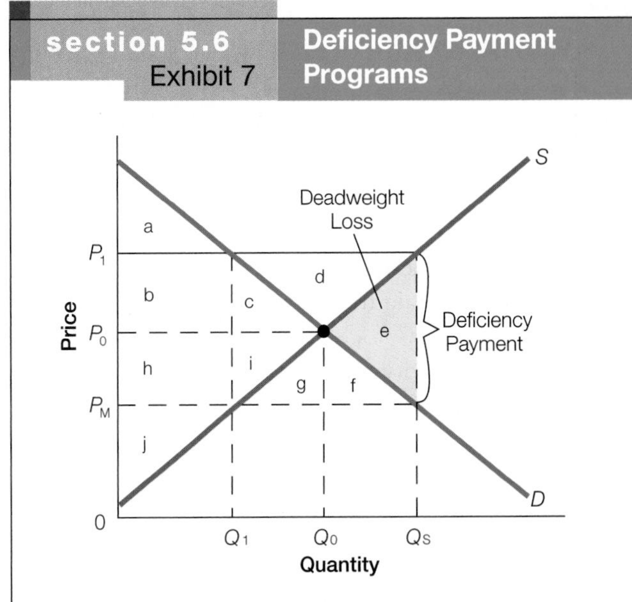

Another possibility is the deficiency payment program. In Exhibit 7, if the government sets the target price at P_1, producers will supply Q_S and sell all they can at the market price, P_M. The government then pays the producers a "deficiency payment" (DP), the vertical distance between the price the producers receive, P_M, and the price they were guaranteed, P_1. Producer surplus increases from area jhi to area jhibcd—producers can sell a greater quantity at a higher price. Consumer surplus increases from area abc to area abchigf—consumers can buy a greater quantity at a lower price. The cost to government ($Q_S \times$ DP), area bcdehigf, is greater than the gains in producer and consumer surplus, area bcdhigf and the deadweight loss is area e. The deadweight loss occurs because the program increases the output beyond the efficient level of output, Q_0. From Q_0 to Q_S, the marginal cost to sellers for producing the good (the height of the supply curve) is greater than the marginal benefit to consumers (the height of the demand curve).

Compare area e in Exhibit 7 with the much larger deadweight loss for price supports in Exhibit 6. The deficiency payment program does not lead to the production of crops that will not be consumed, or to the storage problem we saw with the previous price support program in Exhibit 6.

Section Check

SECTION CHECK

1. Taxes distort market incentives—the price to buyers is higher than before the tax so they consume less and the price to sellers is lower than before the tax so they produce less. This leads to deadweight loss, or market inefficiencies—the waste associated with not producing the efficient output.
2. The size of the deadweight loss from a tax, as well as how the burdens are shared between buyers and sellers, depends on the elasticities of supply and demand.
3. There is a deadweight loss from a price ceiling because the efficient level of output is not produced.
4. There is a deadweight loss from a price floor because consumers are consuming less than the efficient output, eliminating mutually beneficial exchanges, and sellers are producing more than is being consumed.

---

1. Could a tax be imposed without a welfare cost?
2. How does the elasticity of demand represent the ability of buyers to "dodge" a tax?
3. If both supply and demand were very elastic, how large would the effect be on the quantity exchanged, the tax revenue, and the welfare costs of the tax?
4. What impact would a larger tax have on the quantity exchanged in a market? What will happen to the size of the deadweight loss?
5. What would be the effect of a price floor if the government does not buy up the surplus?

Summary

The price elasticity of demand measures how responsive a change in quantity demanded is to a price change. If the quantity demanded is very responsive to a price change, demand is said to be price elastic in the relevant range. If the quantity demanded is not very responsive to a price change, demand is said to be price inelastic in the relevant region.

The price elasticity of demand is calculated by finding the percentage change in quantity demanded divided by the percentage change in price. If the price elasticity of demand is greater than 1, demand is price elastic ($E_D > 1$); if the price elasticity of demand is less than 1, demand is price inelastic ($E_D < 1$); if the price elasticity of demand is 1, demand is unit elastic.

The price elasticity of demand depends on: (1) the availability of close substitutes, (2) the proportion of income spent on the good, and (3) the amount of time that buyers have to respond to a price change.

If demand is elastic, total revenue will vary inversely with a price change. If demand is inelastic, total revenue will vary in the same direction as a change in price. Along a linear demand curve, price is more elastic at higher price ranges and more price inelastic at lower price ranges. It is unit elastic at the midpoint.

Total utility is the amount of satisfaction derived from all units of goods and services consumed. Total utility increases as consumption increases. Marginal utility is the change in utility from consuming an additional unit of a good or service. According to the law of diminishing marginal utility, as a person consumes additional units of a given good, marginal utility declines.

The difference between a consumer's willingness to pay and how much a consumer actually pays is called consumer surplus; it is the area below the demand curve and above the market price. Producer surplus is the difference between what the seller receives for the good—the market price and the seller's cost of production. It is the area below the market price and above the supply curve.

Total welfare gains from trade to the economy can be measured by the sum of consumer and producer surplus.

The size of the deadweight loss from a tax, as well as how the burdens are shared between buyers and sellers, depends on the elasticities of supply and demand. Price ceilings and price floors lead to a deadweight loss because the efficient level of output is not produced.

Key Terms and Concepts

price elasticity of demand 96
elastic demand segment 97
inelastic demand segment 98
unit elastic demand 98
total revenue 101
price elasticity of supply 105
utility 110
util 110
total utility 111
marginal utility 111
law of diminishing marginal utility 112
consumer surplus 113
producer surplus 114
total welfare gains 116
welfare effects 117
deadweight loss 118

Review Questions

1. The San Francisco Giants seek to boost revenues from ticket sales next season. You are hired as an economic consultant and asked to advise the Giants whether to raise or lower ticket prices next year. If the elasticity of demand for Giants game tickets is estimated to be -1.6, what would you advise? If the elasticity of demand equals -0.4?
2. How might your elasticity of demand for copying and binding services vary if your work presentation is next week versus in two hours?

3. Indicate whether a pair of products are substitutes, complements, or neither based upon the following estimates for the cross price elasticity of demand:
   a. 0.5
   b. −0.5
4. For each of the following pairs, identify which one is likely to exhibit more elastic demand:
   a. shampoo; Paul Mitchell Shampoo
   b. air travel prompted by an illness in the family; vacation air travel
   c. paperclips; an apartment rental
   d. prescription heart medication; generic aspirin
5. If the elasticity of demand for hamburgers equals −1.5 and the quantity demanded equals 40,000, predict what will happen to the quantity demanded of hamburgers when the price increases by 10 percent. If the price falls by 5 percent, what will happen?
6. Evaluate the following statement: "Along a downward-sloping linear demand curve, the slope and therefore the elasticity of demand are both constant."
7. A movie production company faces a linear demand curve for its film and it seeks to maximize total revenue from the film's distribution. At what level should the price be set? Where demand is elastic, inelastic, or unit elastic? Explain.
8. Isabella always spends $50 on red roses each month and simply adjusts the quantity she purchases as the price changes. What can you say about Isabella's elasticity of demand for roses?
9. If the government's goal is to raise tax revenue, which of the following are good markets to tax?
   a. luxury yachts
   b. alcohol
   c. movies
   d. gasoline
   e. grapefruit juice
10. Elasticity of demand in the market for one-bedroom apartments is 2.0, elasticity of supply is 0.5, the current market price is $1000, and the equilibrium number of one-bedroom apartments is 10,000. If the government imposes a price ceiling of $800 on this market, predict the size of the resulting apartment shortage.
11. Suppose it is "All-You-Can-Eat" Night at your favorite restaurant. Once you've paid $9.95 for your meal, how do you determine how many helpings to consume? Should you continue eating until your food consumption has yielded $9.95 worth of satisfaction? What happens to the marginal utility from successive helpings as consumption increases?
12. Which of the following do you think are good markets for the government to tax if the goal is to boost tax revenue? Which will lead to the least amount of deadweight loss? Why?
    a. luxury yachts
    b. alcohol
    c. motor homes
    d. cigarettes
    e. gasoline
    f. pizza
13. Using a graph, show the changes to consumer and producer surplus from a price ceiling on natural gas. Label the deadweight loss.
14. If a freeze ruined this year's lettuce crop, show what would happen to consumer surplus.
15. If demand for apples increased as result of a news story that highlighted the health benefits of two apples a day, what would happen to producer surplus?
16. How is total surplus (the sum of consumer and producer surplus) related to the efficient level of output? Using a supply and demand curve, demonstrate that producing less than the equilibrium output will lead to an inefficient allocation of resources—a deadweight loss.
17. Use consumer and producer surplus to show the deadweight loss from a subsidy (producing more than the equilibrium output). (Hint: Remember that taxpayers will have to pay for the subsidy.)
18. Go to the Sexton Web site at **http://sexton.swcollege.com** and click on the "American Petroleum Institute" and find a forecast for gasoline prices in the near future. If gasoline prices are projected to temporarily increase (decrease) in the near future, how will that affect your short-term consumption? How will your consumption vary over the long run if a price change is expected to be permanent?
19. Go to the Sexton Web site at **http://sexton.swcollege.com** and click on "Papa John's Pizza." Think about when you are most likely to go to this site. Suppose you were studying late one night and you were craving a Papa John's pizza. How much consumer surplus would you receive? How much consumer surplus would you receive from a pizza that was delivered immediately after you finished a five-course Thanksgiving dinner? Where would you be more likely to eat more pizza in a single sitting, at home or at a crowded party (particularly if you are not sure how many pizzas have been ordered)? Use marginal utility analysis to answer this last question.

Fill in the Blanks

1. The price elasticity of demand measures the responsiveness of quantity ____________ to a change in price.
2. The price elasticity of demand is defined as the percentage change in ____________ divided by the percentage change in ____________.
3. If the price elasticity of demand is elastic, it means the quantity demanded changes by a relatively ____________ amount than the price change.
4. If the price elasticity of demand is inelastic, it means the quantity demanded changes by a relatively ____________ amount than the price change.
5. A demand curve or a portion of a demand curve can be relatively ____________, ____________, or relatively ____________.
6. For the most part, the price elasticity of demand depends on the availability of ____________, the ____________ spent on the good, and the amount of ____________ people have to adapt to a price change.
7. The elasticity of demand for a Ford automobile would likely be ____________ elastic than the demand for automobiles, because there are more and better substitutes for a certain type of car than for a car itself.
8. The smaller the proportion of income spent on a good, the ____________ its elasticity of demand.
9. The more time that people have to adapt to a new price change, the ____________ the elasticity of demand. The more time that passes, the more time consumers have to find or develop suitable ____________ and to plan and implement changes in their patterns of consumption.
10. When demand is price elastic, total revenues will ____________ as the price declines because the percentage increase in the ____________ is greater than the percentage reduction in price.
11. When demand is price inelastic, total revenues will ____________ as the price declines because the percentage increase in the ____________ is less than the percentage reduction in price.
12. When the price falls on the ____________ half of a straight-line demand curve, demand is relatively ____________. When the price falls on the lower half of a straight-line demand curve, demand is relatively ____________.
13. The price elasticity of supply measures the sensitivity of the quantity ____________ to the changes in the price of the good.
14. The price elasticity of supply is defined as the percentage change in the ____________ divided by the percentage change in ____________.
15. Goods with a supply elasticity that is greater than 1 are called relatively ____________ in supply.
16. When supply is inelastic, a 1 percent change in the price of a good will induce a ____________ 1 percent change in the quantity supplied.
17. Time is usually critical in supply elasticities because it is ____________ costly for producers to bring forth and release resources in a shorter period of time.

18. The relative ____________ determines the distribution of the tax burden for a good.

19. If demand is relatively ____________ elastic than supply in the relevant region, the largest portion of a tax is paid by the producer.

20. The assumption that individuals act to advance their goals—known as the rule of ____________—merely implies that whatever individuals do is done with a ____________.

21. ____________ utility is the aggregate level of satisfaction that results from consumption of a given number of goods and services.

22. ____________ utility is the additional satisfaction generated by the last unit of a good that is consumed.

23. Total utility ____________ with additional consumption, but the marginal utility that results from the consumption of additional units tends to ____________ as consumption increases.

24. The law of ____________ is the economic principle that states that consumers will experience less satisfaction for each additional unit of good consumed.

25. The monetary difference between the price a consumer is willing and able to pay for an additional unit of a good and the price the consumer actually pays is called ____________.

26. Consumer surplus for the whole market is shown graphically as the area under the market ____________ (willingness to pay for the units consumed) and above the ____________ (what must be paid for those units).

27. A lower market price due to an increase in supply will ____________ consumer surplus.

28. ____________ is the difference between what a producer is paid for a good and the cost of producing that unit of the good.

29. Part of the added producer surplus when the price rises, as a result of an increase in demand, is due to a higher price for the quantity ____________ being produced, and part is due to the expansion of ____________ made profitable by the higher price.

30. The demand curve represents a collection of ____________ prices that consumers are willing and able to pay for additional quantities of a good or service, while the supply curve represents a collection of ____________ prices that suppliers require to be willing to supply additional quantities of that good or service.

31. The total welfare gain to the economy from trade in a good is the sum of the ____________ and ____________ created.

32. In competitive markets where there are large numbers of buyers and sellers at the market equilibrium price and quantity, the net gains to society are ____________ as possible.

33. After a tax is imposed, consumers pay a ____________ price and lose the corresponding amount of consumer surplus as a result. Producers receive a ____________ price after tax and lose the corresponding amount of producer surplus as a result. The government ____________ the amount of the tax revenue generated, which is transferred to others in society.

34. The size of the deadweight loss from a tax, as well as how the burdens are shared between buyers and sellers, depends on the relative ____________.

True or False

1. If a small change in quantity demanded results from a huge change in price, then demand is said to be elastic.
2. A segment of a demand curve has an elasticity less than 1 if the percentage change in quantity demanded is less than the percentage change in price that caused it.
3. A perfectly elastic demand curve would be horizontal, but a perfectly inelastic demand curve would be vertical.
4. Along a segment of a demand curve that was unit elastic, quantity demanded would change by 10 percent as a result of 10 percent change in the price.
5. Goods with close substitutes tend to have more elastic demands, and goods without close substitutes tend to have less elastic demand.
6. We would expect that the elasticity of demand for Ford automobiles would be greater than the demand for insulin by diabetics.
7. Based on the percentage of a person's budget devoted to a particular item, you would expect that the elasticity of demand for salt would be greater than the elasticity of demand for attending a university.
8. The short-run demand curve is generally more elastic than the long-run demand curve.
9. Along a demand curve, if the price rises and total revenue falls as a result, then demand must be relatively elastic along that range of the demand curve.
10. If demand is inelastic, the price and total revenue will move in opposite directions along the demand curve.
11. A straight-line demand curve will have a constant elasticity of demand along its length.
12. The price elasticity of supply measures the relative change in the quantity supplied that results from a change in price.
13. When supply is relatively elastic, a 10 percent change in price will result in a greater than 10 percent change in quantity supplied.
14. A perfectly elastic supply curve would be vertical, but a perfectly inelastic supply curve would be horizontal.
15. Goods with a supply elasticity that is less than 1 are called relatively inelastic in supply.
16. Unlike demand, supply tends to be more elastic in the long run than the short run.
17. If demand has a lower elasticity than supply in the relevant region, the largest portion of a tax is paid by the producer.
18. Who bears the burden of a tax has nothing to do with who actually pays the tax at the time of the purchase.
19. In economics we assume that each individual seeks to maximize his or her own well-being or satisfaction.

20. It is not possible to compare the relative satisfactions of different persons because utility varies from individual to individual depending on specific preferences.

21. The law of diminishing marginal utility is that each successive unit of a good that is consumed generates less additional satisfaction than did the previous unit.

22. If the consumer is a buyer of several units of a good, the earlier units will have greater marginal value and therefore create more consumer surplus because marginal willingness to pay falls as greater quantities are consumed in any period.

23. A lower price will increase your consumer surplus for each of the units you were already consuming and will also increase consumer surplus from increased purchases at the lower price.

24. Because some units can be produced at a cost that is lower than the market price, the seller receives a surplus, or net benefit, from producing those units.

25. Producer surplus is shown graphically as the area under the demand curve and above the supply curve.

26. If the market price of a good falls as a result of a decrease in demand, additional producer surplus is generated.

27. At the market equilibrium both consumers and producers benefit from trading every unit up to the market equilibrium output.

28. Once the equilibrium output is reached at the equilibrium price, all of the mutually beneficial trade opportunities between the suppliers and the demanders will have taken place, and the sum of consumer and producer surplus is maximized.

29. The deadweight loss of a tax is the difference between the lost consumer surplus and producer surplus and the tax revenue generated.

30. The deadweight loss of a tax occurs because the tax reduces the quantity exchanged below the original output level, reducing the size of the total surplus realized from trade.

31. Other things being equal, the more elastic the demand curve, or the more elastic the supply curve, the smaller the deadweight loss.

32. If either the supply or demand curves become more inelastic, a given tax will reduce the quantity exchanged by a greater amount.

33. Those goods that are heavily taxed often have a relatively inelastic demand curve in the short run so that the burden falls mainly on the buyer, and the deadweight loss to society is smaller than if the demand curve were more elastic.

Multiple Choice

1. Price elasticity of demand is defined as the ____________ change in quantity demanded divided by the ____________ change in price.
   a. total; percentage
   b. percentage; marginal
   c. marginal; percentage
   d. percentage; percentage
   e. total; total

2. Demand is said to be ______________ when the quantity demanded is not very responsive to changes in price.
   a. independent
   b. inelastic
   c. unit elastic
   d. elastic

3. For a given decrease in price, the greater is the elasticity of demand, the greater is the resulting
   a. increase in quantity demanded.
   b. increase in demand.
   c. decrease in quantity demanded.
   d. decrease in demand.

4. When demand is inelastic,
   a. price elasticity of demand is less than 1.
   b. consumers are not very responsive to changes in price.
   c. the percentage change in quantity demanded resulting from a price change is less than the percentage change in price.
   d. all of the above are correct.

5. Which of the following will not tend to increase the elasticity of demand for a good?
   a. an increase in the availability of close substitutes
   b. an increase in the amount of time people have to adjust to a change in the price
   c. an increase in the proportion of income spent on a good
   d. All of the above will increase the elasticity of demand for a good.

6. Which of the following would tend to have the most elastic demand curve?
   a. automobiles
   b. Chevrolet automobiles
   c. Both a and b would be the same.
   d. none of the above

7. Iron Mike's steel mill finds that a 10 percent increase in its price leads to a 14 percent decrease in the quantity it is able to sell. The demand curve for the mill's output is
   a. elastic.
   b. inelastic.
   c. unit elastic.
   d. perfectly elastic.

8. Price elasticity of demand is said to be greater
   a. the shorter the period of time consumers have to adjust to price changes.
   b. the longer the period of time consumers have to adjust to price changes.
   c. when there are fewer available substitutes.
   d. when the elasticity of supply is greater.

9. If recent sharp increases in the price of insulin have had only a small effect on the amount of insulin purchased, then the demand for insulin is
   a. elastic.
   b. inelastic.
   c. unit elastic.
   d. perfectly elastic.

10. The price elasticity of demand coefficient for herbal tea is estimated to be equal to 0.5. It is expected, therefore, that a 10 percent decrease in price would lead to ______________ in the quantity of herbal tea demanded.

a. a 5 percent decrease
b. a 5 percent increase
c. a 10 percent decrease
d. a 10 percent increase
e. a 0.5 percent increase

11. The long-run demand curve for gasoline is likely to be

a. more elastic than the short-run demand curve for gasoline.
b. more inelastic than the short-run demand curve for gasoline.
c. the same as the short-run demand curve for gasoline.
d. more inelastic than the short-run supply of gasoline.

12. Demand curves for goods tend to become more inelastic

a. when there are more good substitutes for the good available.
b. when the good makes up a larger portion of a person's income.
c. when people have less time to adapt to a given price change.
d. when any of the above is true.
e. in none of the above situations.

13. When the local symphony recently raised its ticket price for its summer concerts in the park, the symphony was surprised to see that its total revenue had actually decreased. The reason was that the elasticity of demand for tickets was

a. unit elastic.
b. unit inelastic.
c. inelastic.
d. elastic.

14. For a given increase in price, the greater is the elasticity of supply, the greater is the resulting

a. decrease in quantity supplied.
b. decrease in supply.
c. increase in quantity supplied.
d. increase in supply.

15. If the demand for gasoline is highly inelastic and the supply is highly elastic, and then a tax is imposed on gasoline, it will be paid

a. largely by the sellers of gasoline.
b. largely by the buyers of gasoline.
c. equally by the sellers and buyers of gasoline.
d. by the government.

16. An increase in demand will increase the price but not the quantity sold in a market if

a. supply is perfectly elastic.
b. supply is perfectly inelastic.
c. supply is relatively elastic.
d. supply is relatively inelastic.

17. The total utility from consuming five slices of pizza is 11, 18, 24, 29, and 32 utils, respectively. The marginal utility of the third slice of pizza is

a. 11.
b. 7.
c. 18.
d. 6.
e. 53.

18. Which of the following is not true about utility?

a. Utility varies from individual to individual.
b. Total utility is the total amount of satisfaction derived from the consumption of a certain number of units of a good or a service.
c. Marginal utility tends to decline, the more of a good or service is consumed.
d. When marginal utility is at its maximum, total utility is zero.

Use the following demand schedule to answer questions 19 and 20.

Fred's demand schedule for DVDs is as follows: At $30 each, he would buy 1; at $25, he would buy 2; at $15, he would buy 3; and at $10, he would buy 4.

19. If the price of DVDs equals $20, the consumer surplus Fred receives from purchasing DVDs would be

a. $10.
b. $15.
c. $20.
d. $55.
e. $90.

20. If the price of DVDs equals $25, the consumer surplus Fred receives from purchasing DVDs would be

a. $0.
b. $5.
c. $25.
d. $55.
e. $70.

21. Which of the following is not true about consumer surplus?

a. Consumer surplus is the difference between what consumers are willing to pay and what they actually pay.
b. Consumer surplus is shown graphically as the area under the demand curve but above the market price.
c. An increase in the market price due to a decrease in supply will increase consumer surplus.
d. A decrease in market price due to an increase in supply will increase consumer surplus.

22. Which of the following is not true about producer surplus?

a. Producer surplus is the difference between what sellers are paid and their cost of producing those units.
b. Producer surplus is shown graphically as the area under the market price but above the supply curve.
c. An increase in the market price due to an increase in demand will increase producer surplus.
d. All of the above are true about producer surplus.

23. At the market equilibrium price and quantity, the total welfare gains from trade are measured by
   a. the total consumer surplus captured by consumers.
   b. the total producer surplus captured by producers.
   c. the sum of consumer surplus and producer surplus.
   d. the consumer surplus minus the producer surplus.

24. Taxes on goods with _______________ demand curves will tend to raise more tax revenue for the government than taxes on goods with _______________ demand curves.
   a. elastic; unit elastic
   b. elastic; inelastic
   c. inelastic; elastic
   d. unit elastic; inelastic

25. After the imposition of a tax,
   a. consumers pay a higher price, including the tax.
   b. consumers lose consumer surplus.
   c. producers receive a lower price after taxes.
   d. producers lose producer surplus.
   e. all of the above occur.

26. Other things being equal, for a given tax, if the demand curve is less elastic,
   a. the greater the tax revenue raised and the greater the deadweight cost of the tax.
   b. the greater the tax revenue raised and the smaller the deadweight cost of the tax.
   c. the less the tax revenue raised and the greater the deadweight cost of the tax.
   d. the less the tax revenue raised and the smaller the deadweight cost of the tax.

Problems

1. If the midpoint on a straight-line demand curve is at a price of $7, what can we say about the elasticity of demand for a price change from $12 to $10? What about from $6 to $4?

2. If the local bus company raises its price per rider from $0.50 to $0.75 and its total revenues rise, what can we say about its elasticity of demand? What if total revenues fall as a result of the price increase?

3. Suppose Carrie's utility function for clams is as follows: If she consumes 1 clam, she gets 5 units of total utility; for 2 clams, she gets 9 units of total utility; for 3 clams, she gets 12 units of total utility; for 4 clams, she gets 14 units of total utility; for 5 clams, she gets 15 units of total utility; and for 6 clams, she gets 13 units of total utility.
   a. What is Carrie's marginal utility for each of the clams?
   b. Would Carrie ever choose to consume the sixth clam? Why or why not?

4. Suppose Phil's supply curve for widgets is as follows: At $20, he will supply 1; at $30, he will supply 2; at $40, he will supply 3; at $50, he will supply 4; and at $60, he will supply 5.
   a. If the price of widgets is $40, what is his producer surplus?
   b. If the price of widgets rises from $40 to $50, how much will his producer surplus change?

Use the diagram at right to answer the following questions (5a–d).

5. a. At the equilibrium price before the tax is imposed, what area represents consumer surplus? What area represents producer surplus?

b. Say that a tax of $T per unit is imposed in the industry. What area now represents consumer surplus? What area represents producer surplus?

c. What area represents the deadweight cost of the tax?

d. What area represents how much tax revenue is raised by the tax?

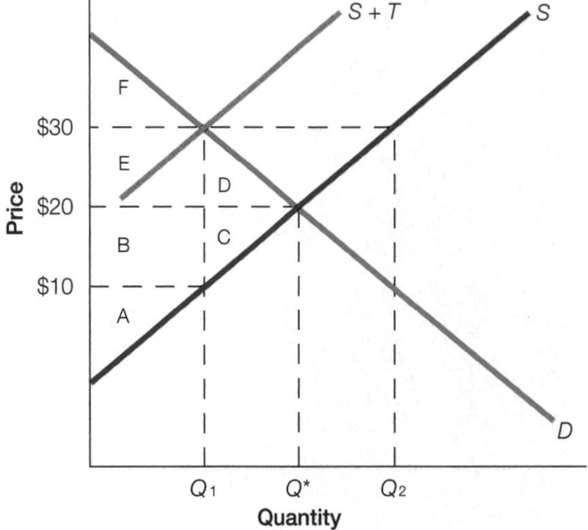

chapter 6

Externalities, Public Goods, and Public Choice

6.1 **EXTERNALITIES**
What are externalities?

6.2 **PUBLIC GOODS**
What is a public good?

6.3 **PUBLIC CHOICE**
Is politics influenced by self-interest?

section 6.1

Externalities

- What is a negative externality?
- How are negative externalities internalized?
- What is a positive externality?
- How are positive externalities internalized?

externalities
a benefit or cost from consumption or production that spills over on to those that are not consuming or producing the good

negative externality
occurs when costs spill over to an outside party that is not involved in producing or consuming the good

positive externality
occurs when benefits spill over to an outside party that is not involved in producing or consuming the good

The forces represented by supply and demand perform an extremely complicated and valuable function. However, these market forces do not always produce the "right" amount of all goods and services. That is, sometimes the market system fails to produce efficient outcomes because of side effects economists call **externalities.** An externality is said to occur whenever there are physical impacts (benefits or costs) of an activity on individuals not directly involved in the activity. If the impact on the outside party is negative, it is called a **negative externality;** if the impact is positive, it is called a **positive externality.**

NEGATIVE EXTERNALITIES

The classic example of a negative externality is pollution from an air-polluting factory, such as a steel mill. If the firm uses clean air in production and returns dirty air to the atmosphere, it has created a negative externality. The polluted air has "spilled over" to outside parties. Now people in the neighboring communities may experience higher incidences of disease, dirtier houses, and other property damage. Such damages are real costs, but because no one owns the air, the firm does not have to pay for its use, unlike the other resources the firm uses in production. A steel mill has to pay for labor, capital, energy, and raw materials, because it must compensate the owners of those inputs for their use. If a firm can avoid paying the cost it imposes on others—the external costs—it has lowered its own costs of production, but not the true cost to society.

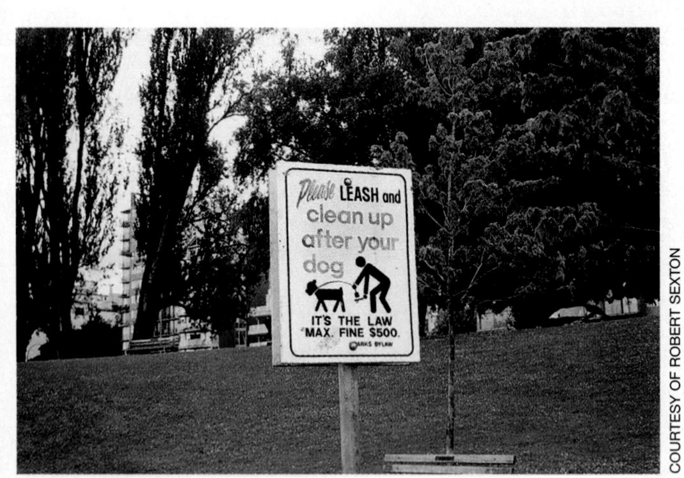

COURTESY OF ROBERT SEXTON

There is nothing worse than having a public place spoiled by the inconsiderate behavior of others. Some laws, such as this "pooper scooper" law, are intended to minimize negative externalities in public areas.

Examples of negative externalities are numerous: the roommate who plays his stereo too loud at 2:00 a.m.; the neighbor's dog that barks all night long or leaves "messages" on your front lawn; the gardener who runs his leaf blower on full power at 7:00 a.m. on a Saturday.

Graphing Negative External Costs

Let's take another look at the steel industry. In Exhibit 1, we see the market for steel. Notice that at each level of output, the first supply curve, $S_{PRIVATE}$, is lower than the second, S_{SOCIAL}. The reason for this is simple: $S_{PRIVATE}$ only includes the private costs to the firm—the capital, entrepreneurship, land, and labor for which it must pay. However, S_{SOCIAL} includes all of those costs, plus the external costs that production imposes on others. That is, if the firm could somehow be required to compensate those damaged, it would increase the cost of production for the firm and cause a leftward shift in the supply curve. In Exhibit 1, we see that if the government stepped in and made the firm pay for the external costs, then the output of steel would fall to Q_{SOCIAL}, the social optimal (or best) level of output. From society's standpoint, Q_{SOCIAL} is the best level of output because it represents all the costs (private + external costs) associated with the production of this good. If the suppliers of steel are not aware of or are not responsible for the external costs, they will tend to produce too much from society's standpoint. This means that there is an *overallocation* of scarce resources to the production of this good.

section 6.1 Exhibit 1 **Negative Externalities**

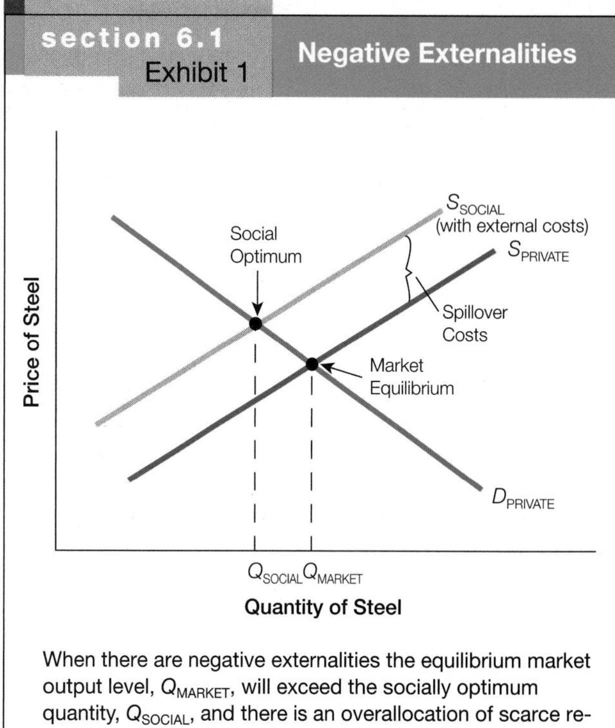

When there are negative externalities the equilibrium market output level, Q_{MARKET}, will exceed the socially optimum quantity, Q_{SOCIAL}, and there is an overallocation of scarce resources in the production of this good.

WHAT CAN THE GOVERNMENT DO TO CORRECT FOR NEGATIVE EXTERNALITIES?

The government can intervene in market decisions in an attempt to take account of these negative externalities. It may do this by estimating the amount of those external costs and then taxing the manufacturer by that amount, forcing the manufacturer to internalize (bear) the costs.

Pollution Taxes

Pollution taxes are designed to internalize negative externalities. If government could impose a pollution tax equal to the exact size of the external cost, then the firm would produce at the socially desired level of output, Q_{SOCIAL}. That is, the tax would shift the supply curve for steel leftward to S_{SOCIAL} and would provide an incentive for the firm to produce at the social optimum level of output. Additionally, tax revenues would be generated that could be used to compensate those who had suffered damage from the pollution, or that could be used in some other productive way.

Americans deposit large amounts of solid wastes as litter on beaches, campgrounds, highways, and vacant lots. Some of this is removed by government agencies, and some of it biodegrades over many years. There are several solutions to the litter problem. Stiffer fines and penalties and more aggressive monitoring could be employed. Alternatively, through education and civic pride, individuals and groups could be encouraged to pick up trash.

Regulation

Alternatively, the government could use regulation. The government might simply prohibit certain types of activities causing pollution, or might force firms to reduce their emissions. The purchase and use of new pollution-control devices can also increase the cost of production and shift the supply curve to the left, from $S_{PRIVATE}$ to S_{SOCIAL}.

POSITIVE EXTERNALITIES

Unlike negative externalities, positive externalities benefit others. For some goods, the individual consumer receives all of the benefits. If you buy a hamburger, for example, you get all of its benefits. But take for example a company that landscapes its property with beautiful flowers and sculptures. The landscaping may create a positive externality for those who walk or drive by the company grounds. Or consider education. Certainly, when you "buy" an education, you receive many of its benefits: greater future income, more choice of future occupations, and the consumption value of knowing more about life as a result of classroom (and extracurricular) learning. These benefits, however, great as they may be, are not all of the benefits associated with your education. You may be less likely to be unemployed or commit crimes, or you may end up curing cancer or solving some other social problem. These nontrivial benefits are the positive external benefits of education.

The government frequently subsidizes education. Why? Presumably because the private market does not provide enough. It is argued that the education of a person benefits not only that person, but all of society, because a more informed citizenry can make more intelligent collective decisions that benefit everyone. Another example: Why do public health departments sometimes offer "free" inoculations against certain communicable diseases, such as influenza? Partly because by protecting one group of citizens, everyone gets some protection; if the first citizen does not get the disease, it prevents that person from passing it on to others. Many governmental efforts in the field of health and education are justified on the basis of perceived positive externalities. Of course, because positive externalities are often difficult to measure, it is hard to empirically demonstrate whether many governmental educational and health programs achieve their intended purpose.

Graphing Positive External Benefits

Let's take the case of a new vaccine against the common cold. The market for the vaccine is shown in Exhibit 2. The demand curve $D_{PRIVATE}$ represents the prices and quantities that buyers would be willing to pay in the private market to reduce their probability of catching the common cold. The supply curve shows the amounts that suppliers would offer for sale at different prices. However, at the equilibrium market output, Q_{MARKET}, we are far short of the socially optimum level of output for vaccination s, Q_{SOCIAL}. Why? Many people benefit from the vaccines, including those who do not have to pay for them; they are now less likely to be infected because others took the vaccine. If we could add the benefits derived by nonpaying consumers, the demand curve would shift to the right, from $D_{PRIVATE}$ to D_{SOCIAL}. The greater level of output, Q_{SOCIAL}, that would result if D_{SOCIAL} were the observed demand reflects the socially optimal output level. However, because producers are unable to collect payments from all of those who are benefiting from the good or service, the market has a tendency to underproduce. In this case, the market is not producing enough vaccinations from society's standpoint. In this case, there is an *underallocation* of resources because from society's standpoint we are producing too little of this good or service (producing Q_{MARKET} rather than Q_{SOCIAL}).

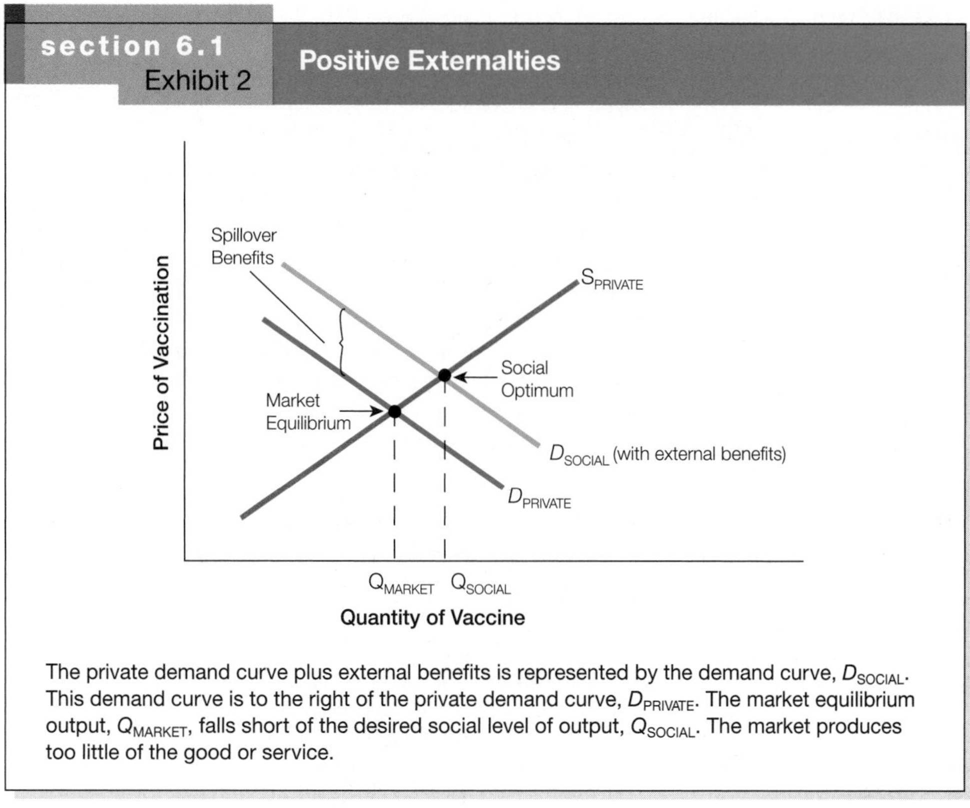

The private demand curve plus external benefits is represented by the demand curve, D_{SOCIAL}. This demand curve is to the right of the private demand curve, $D_{PRIVATE}$. The market equilibrium output, Q_{MARKET}, falls short of the desired social level of output, Q_{SOCIAL}. The market produces too little of the good or service.

WHAT CAN THE GOVERNMENT DO TO CORRECT FOR POSITIVE EXTERNALITIES?

How could society correct for this market failure? Two particular methods of achieving the higher preferred output are subsidies and regulation.

Subsidies

Government could give a subsidy—either give refunds to individuals who receive an inoculation or provide an incentive for businesses to give their employees "free" inoculations at the office. If the subsidy was exactly equal to external benefits of inoculation, the demand curve would shift from $D_{PRIVATE}$ to D_{SOCIAL}, resulting in an efficient level of output, Q_{SOCIAL}.

Regulation

The government could also pass a regulation requiring each person to get an inoculation. This would also shift the demand curve to the right toward the efficient level of output.

In summary, when there are positive externalities, the private market supplies too little of the good in question (such as education or inoculations for communicable diseases). When there are negative externalities, the market supplies too much. In either case, buyers and sellers are receiving the wrong signals. The producers and consumers are not doing what they do because they are evil; rather, whether well-intentioned or ill-intentioned, they are behaving according to the incentives they face. The free market, then, works fine in providing most goods, but it functions less well without regulations, taxes, and subsidies in providing others.

In The NEWS

MESSAGE IN A BOTTLENECK: IS IT TIME TO START CHARGING RUSH-HOUR COMMUTERS?

BY BETSY STREISAND

It's not your imagination. Every year, your commute to work probably is taking longer. Since 1986, car travel has increased almost 40 percent, while highway capacity has barely grown. As a result, most interstate routes in major metropolitan areas are jammed during rush hours. Gridlock costs Americans roughly the equivalent of $51 billion a year in lost wages and wasted fuel. And the situation is only going to get worse.

But there may be a way to avoid total gridlock: "peak-period pricing," or, in plain English, tolls. Now, the government gives away precious road space for free, virtually guaranteeing backups. Charging drivers during peak times would naturally reduce the traffic.

This simple idea isn't new. But it hasn't been adopted on a single public road because politicians know it would be career suicide to force Americans to pay for something they've long had for free. Instead, they embrace solutions that are more politically palatable than they are effective. They include:

BUILDING MORE ROADS

Sounds good. But additional roads inevitably produce what traffic expert Anthony Downs in his book *Stuck in Traffic* calls "triple convergence." More commuters come—from other roads, from mass transit and from new developments. Soon, the new roads are as crowded as the old. Los Angeles is a monument to this phenomenon.

BOLSTERING MASS TRANSIT

Even if Americans could learn to rely on buses and trains—and that's a huge *if*—workplaces are now so spread out in the suburbs that connecting all the dots with buses or other transports in affordable and convenient routes is nearly impossible. This makes perfect sense. Suburbs were designed with drivers in mind. If the number of mass-transit users miraculously doubled, they still would constitute only 10 percent of commuters.

DEVELOPING "SMART CARS" AND HIGHWAYS

The federal government is spending millions a year to develop an intelligent-vehicle highway system. It would involve a network of road sensors and computers that would feed traffic information to car TV screens, warning of trouble spots. Sounds impressive, in a Jetsons sort of way. But its limitations are obvious: Drivers will head for open roads, relocating but not reducing congestion.

Which brings us to the more drastic solution of putting a price on the rush-hour commute. Peak-period pricing would turn all major metropolitan arteries into toll roads, with prices high enough to keep traffic moving steadily. During slow times, tolls would be cut or eliminated. Tolls could be collected easily, thanks to new technology that lets sensors read signals from small transponders inside the car. Fees would be debited from prepaid accounts. In theory, drivers who didn't want to pay would change their commuting hours, car pool, or use mass transit.

California was the first state to construct toll lanes, or "express lanes" on a freeway. Rather than becoming "Lexus Lanes" for well-off commuters, as expected, express lanes are a mirror of the freeway as a whole, attracting drivers from all income brackets, according to surveys by the California Private Transportation Co. For many working parents, a $2.50 toll is preferable to steep overtime charges for day care. The fast lanes also are popular with independent contractors and other workers who are paid by the job. True, some low-income workers can't afford the toll. But if the system were public, the government could subsidize their commutes with deposits into their toll accounts drawn from toll proceeds.

SOURCE: Betsy Streisand, "Message in a bottleneck: Is it time to start charging rush-hour commuters?" *U.S. News and World Report,* December 30, 1996. http://www.usnews.com.

CONSIDER THIS:

If a road is crowded, it creates a negative externality. That is, when one person enters a road, it causes all other people to drive a little more slowly. Highway space is overused because we pay so little for it. At least at some particular times like at rush hours, if we charge a zero money price, there will be a shortage of highway space, as seen in Exhibit 3. A toll raises the price and brings the market closer to equilibrium.

section 6.1
Exhibit 3

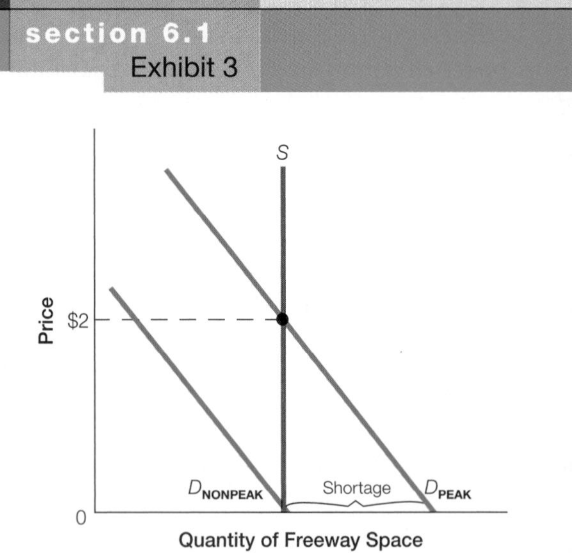

The supply of highway space is fixed in the short run, so the supply curve is perfectly inelastic. The demand varies considerably during the day. For example, the demand at peak hours (7 a.m.–8:30 a.m. and 4:00 p.m.–6:30 p.m.) is much higher that at nonpeak hours. At some price, the shortage during peak hours will disappear. In this example, it is at $2.

NON-GOVERNMENTAL SOLUTIONS TO EXTERNALITIES

Sometimes the externality problems can be handled by individuals without the intervention of government, and people may decide to take steps on their own to minimize negative externalities. Moral and social codes may prevent some people from littering, driving gas-guzzling cars, or using gas-powered mowers and log-burning fireplaces. The same self-regulation also applies to positive externalities. Philanthropists, for example, frequently donate money to public and private schools. In part, this must be because they view the positive externalities from education as a good buy for their charitable dollars.

COURTESY OF ROBERT SEXTON

People may take steps on their own to minimize negative externalities. For example, some people might use battery-powered mowers, or even old-fashioned push mowers, rather than gasoline mowers.

Section Check

1. If a market activity has a negative physical impact on an outside party, that side effect is called a negative externality.
2. The government can use taxes or other forms of regulation to correct the overallocation problem associated with negative externalities.
3. If a market activity has a positive physical impact on an outside party, that side effect is called a positive externality.
4. The government can provide subsidies or other forms of regulation to correct the underallocation problem associated with positive externalities.

---

1. Why are externalities also called spillover effects?
2. How are externalities related to property rights?
3. How do external costs affect the price and output of a polluting activity?
4. How can the government intervene to force producers to internalize external costs?
5. How does internalizing the external costs improve efficiency?
6. How do external benefits affect the output of an activity that causes them?
7. How can the government intervene to force external benefits to be internalized?
8. Why do most cities have more stringent noise laws for the early morning and late evening hours than for during the day?

section 6.2

Public Goods

- What is a public good?
- What is the free-rider problem?
- Why does the government provide public goods?

WHAT IS A PUBLIC GOOD?

Externalities are not the only culprit behind resource misallocations. A **public good** is another source of market failure. As used by economists, this term refers not to how particular goods are purchased—by a government agency rather than some private economic

public good
a good that has two properties: nonrivalrous in consumption and nonexcludability

private good
a good with rivalrous consumption and excludability

agent—but to the properties that characterize them. A **private good** such as a cheeseburger has two critical properties in this context. First, if you buy it, it is yours—nobody else can have it (unless you let them, in which case you no longer have it). Second, the user of a private good receives all the benefits of its consumption. Consumption of a private good is therefore rivalrous.

nonrivalrous
occurs when everyone can consume the good simultaneously; one person's usage of it does not diminish another's ability to use it

nonexcludable
once the good is produced it is prohibitively costly to exclude anyone from consuming the good

Unlike private goods, the consumption of public goods is both nonexcludable and nonrivalrous. One example of a public good is national defense. Whatever the level of national defense, we all benefit from it (consumption is **nonrivalrous**). That is, once the military has its defense in place, everyone is protected simultaneously. In addition, it is prohibitively costly to exclude anyone from consuming national defense. For example, if you lived at 16 Main Street and you weren't willing to pay to be protected, it would be too costly to exclude you because it is too difficult to exclude anyone from consuming a public good (consumption is **nonexcludable**).

Another example of a public good is a flood control project. A flood control project would allow all the people who live in the flood plain area to enjoy the protection of the new program simultaneously. It would also be very difficult to exclude someone who lived in the middle of the project who said she did not want to pay. That is, the good is nonrivalrous in consumption and it is difficult to exclude any consumer once the project is produced. This is what makes the good so difficult to produce privately. Some would know they could derive the benefits from the program without paying for them, because once it is produced, it is too difficult to exclude them. Some would try to take a *free ride*—derive benefits for something they did not pay for.

PUBLIC GOODS AND THE FREE-RIDER PROBLEM

Public goods are closely related to externalities and to the free-rider problem. Suppose the quality of the air where you live is undesirable, so you clean it up. Perhaps you reduce your own pollution by replacing a cleaner wood-burning stove for your old, highly polluting one, or even by placing a huge filter upwind of your home. Because air quality is largely a public good, you know that others will benefit. It might well be advantageous from society's perspective for the air to be cleaned up in this way, but what incentive do your neighbors have to pay for the benefits they will receive? The answer, of course, is very little. They know that if you choose to clean up the air, they cannot be prevented from receiving the benefits.

free rider
deriving benefits from something not paid for

Let's return to our public good example of national defense. Suppose the private protection of national defense is actually worth $100 to you. Assume that there are a 100 million households in the United States that each are willing to make a $100 contribution for national defense. This would add up to $10 billion. You might write a check for $100. Or you might reason as follows: "if I don't give $100 and everybody else does, I will be equally well protected plus derive the benefits of the $100 in my pocket." Taking the latter course represents a rational attempt to be a **free rider.** The rub is that if everyone attempts to take a free ride, the ride will not exist.

On both the supply and the demand side, it is clear that we are likely to get too little of public goods without some intervention—indeed, we may get zero! On the supply side, nonexcludability precludes charging consumers for benefits received. As a result, producers are not able to cover their costs of producing public goods from revenues. On the demand side, individual consumers have an incentive to be free riders, further reducing the likelihood that goods having benefits greater than costs will be produced. Public goods, then, are not profitable to produce.

As a result of the nonexclusion provision of public goods, the free-rider problem prevents the private market from supplying the efficient amount of the public goods. The government may be able to step in to overcome the free-rider problem. For example, if national defense has total benefits that are greater than total costs, the government can provide defense and have all taxpayers pay for it. Without the government supplying national defense, some households may choose not to pay for it, knowing that it is too difficult to keep them from receiving the benefits of protection.

Government provides important public goods, such as national defense. Voters may disagree on whether we have too much or too little, but most agree that we must have national defense. If national defense was provided privately and people were asked to pay for the use of national defense, many would free ride knowing they could derive the benefits of the good without paying for it.

THE DIFFICULTY WITH PROVIDING PUBLIC GOODS—ASSESSING ACCURATE BENEFITS AND COSTS

The government providing public goods still presents problems. When evaluating the desire for a public good, the government cannot accurately assess the desires of all those affected. In its assessment of the desire for a public good, the government must, just like other suppliers of goods, complete a benefit–cost analysis that weighs the benefits of providing the good against the cost that must be incurred to provide that good.

Consider the case of a new highway. Before it builds the highway, the appropriate government agency will undertake a benefit–cost analysis of the situation. In this case, it must evaluate consumers' willingness to pay for the highway against the costs that will be incurred for construction and maintenance. However, those individuals who want the highway have an incentive to exaggerate their desire for it. At the same time, individuals who will be displaced or otherwise harmed by the highway have an incentive to exaggerate the harm that will be done to them. Together, these elements make it difficult for the government to assess benefits and costs accurately. Ultimately, their evaluations are reduced to educated guesses about the net impact of the highway on all parties concerned.

Section Check

1. A public good is both nonrivalrous in consumption (one person's usage of it does not diminish another's ability to use it) and nonexclusive (no one can be excluded from using it).
2. A free rider is someone who attempts to enjoy the benefits of a good without paying for it.
3. The government provides public goods because the free-rider problem results in underproduction of these goods in the marketplace.

---

1. How are public goods different from private goods?
2. Why does the free-rider problem arise in the case of public goods?
3. How does the free-rider problem relate to property rights?
4. In what way can government provision of public goods solve the free-rider problem?
5. Why is it difficult for the government to determine the proper amount of a public good to produce?

section 6.3

Public Choice

- What is public choice theory?
- What are the similarities between the private (market) sector and the public (government) sector?
- What are the differences between the private (market) sector and the public (government) sector?

As we have discussed in this chapter, when the market fails, as in the externality or the public good case, it may be necessary for government to intervene and make public choices. However, just because markets have failed to generate efficient results doesn't necessarily mean that government can do a better job. Public choice theory presents one explanation for this.

PUBLIC CHOICE ANALYSIS

public choice analysis *the principles of economics applied to the political process*

Public choice analysis is the application of economic principles to the political process. Public choice economists believe that government actions are an outgrowth of individual behavior. Specifically, they assume that the behavior of individuals in politics, like those in the marketplace, will be influenced by self-interest. Bureaucrats, politicians, and voters make choices that they believe will yield them expected marginal benefits that are greater than their expected marginal costs. There are, of course, differences between the private sector and the public sector in the "rules of the game" but the self-interest assumption is central to the analysis of behavior in both arenas.

SCARCITY AND COMPETITION IN THE PUBLIC SECTOR

The self-interest assumption is not the only similarity between the market and public sectors. For example, scarcity is present in the public sector as well as the private sector. Public schools and public libraries come at the expense of something else. Competition is also present in the public sector as different government agencies compete for government funds and lobbyists compete with each other to get favored legislation passed.

DIFFERENCES BETWEEN THE PRIVATE SECTOR AND THE PUBLIC SECTOR

While there are similarities between the private sector and the public sector, there are also differences. For example, the amount of information that is necessary to make an efficient decision is much greater in the public sector than the private sector. In the private sector, about the only information that potential buyers need to know is how much they are willing to pay for the good and how much the seller is willing to accept for the good. The market price informs buyers how much is necessary to entice the seller to supply the good. Only one question remains: Is the good worth more to consumers than they are willing to pay? If so, consumers will purchase the good; if not, consumers will not purchase the good.

Information is much more difficult to obtain when a political good is being considered. The problem is that political decisions usually affect many people. For example, if voters decide to increase national defense, everyone will receive more and pay higher taxes

In The **NEWS**

WILD PITCH

BY ROGER G. NOLL

WASHINGTON—Even at a time when major league sports have become a cartoon of financial excess, the proposed new home for the Yankees is breathtaking in its audacity. Excluding land value, a multipurpose mausoleum on Manhattan's West Side would cost a billion dollars.

Independent studies of sports facilities invariably conclude that they provide no significant economic benefits. A sports team does increase overall income in a community slightly, but the increase never offsets the stadium's financing and operating costs. And because a team has relatively few (but very highly paid) employees, it usually causes overall employment in a city to fall because it can drive other entertainment businesses to cut back or close.

Stadiums are bad investments, which is why the teams themselves are never willing to pay for them. New York City would generate more cash by putting the money in a savings account.

Why do cities pour hundreds of millions into new stadiums? With intense competition for sports franchises, not even New York can keep a team without subsidizing it. New Jersey and New York have at various times fought over the Giants, Jets, Yankees, and Mets. The sad thing is that the states need not be competitors: Fans could easily support a third team in both football and baseball. But each league is a monopoly, doing what monopolists do best: making the product scarce to hike up the price.

© ERIC RIBERRG/AP PHOTO

There is a far cheaper way to keep the Yankees. Bribe them. A new stadium could give the Yankees an additional $10 million in profits each year. So instead of spending $80 million annually to finance and operate a new stadium, New York could just hand the Yankees $10 million. Or, even better, the city could pay $100,000 for each game won, with a million-dollar bonus for winning the pennant.

This plan would save the city money, improve the Yankee's bottom line and benefit fans, who would be less likely to have a team that collapsed in the stretch.

(Roger G. Noll is professor of economics at Stanford University.)

SOURCE: Roger G. Noll, *New York Times,* April 11, 1996, p. A17.

CONSIDER THIS:

Many big cities have either built or are planning on building large sports arenas, largely at the taxpayers' expense. According to proponents, the new sports arenas will bring recognition and fame to the city, and this will benefit everyone who lives in the city because they will be living in a more prestigious community. Hence, everyone in the city should contribute to the sports arena, whether they go to the games or not.

However, the people who receive the primary benefits from a better sports arena are first, the owners, second, the players, and third, those who frequent it to watch ball games. Further, it's easy to prevent a fan from receiving this benefit if he (or she) doesn't pay at the gate. The assertion that everyone would benefit from the arena whether they go to the games or not must be questioned. A sports arena will generate growth and congestion that many people will find undesirable. To these people, being forced to pay for a big sports center makes no sense.

Perhaps some people who never go to a sporting event may feel a little bit better just knowing they can. This is what economists call option demand. But does this justify commandeering funds from everyone in the city to build a sports arena? What about fine restaurants? Certainly fine restaurants enhance the reputation of the city. Many people are happy to know that one is nearby, waiting to serve them, whether they visit it or not. But most people would find a proposal to publicly finance restaurants very farfetched. If desirable side effects justified government subsidies, well-kept yards, car washes, toothpaste, deodorants, and smiles would all qualify for a handout.

Regardless of the desirability of requiring the public to pay for certain projects, it should be noted that special-interest groups expend a lot of effort to get subsidies for those projects from which they receive enjoyment and profit. Many of these efforts have been successful; the sports arena example is only one of many. The more "cultured," and usually wealthier, members of many cities have managed to obtain government support for symphonies, operas, ballet, and the performing arts in general. The stated justification for requiring everyone to pay for entertainment that caters primarily to the tastes of the rich is similar to that given for subsidizing sports arenas. Supposedly, everyone in a community will benefit, even those who prefer to sit home with a can of beer and watch all-star wrestling on television.

for the additional national defense. However, for such a political decision to result in an efficient result, it will require that we have information on everyone's preferences, not just those of an individual buyer and an individual seller.

INDIVIDUAL-CONSUMPTION-PAYMENT LINK

In private markets, when a shopper goes to the supermarket to purchase groceries, the shopping cart is filled with many different goods that the consumer presumably wants and is willing to pay for; this reflects the *individual-consumption-payment link.* The link between what a person wants and what a person has to pay for breaks down when there is an assortment of political goods that have been decided on by majority rule. These political goods might include such items as additional national defense, additional money for the space program, new museums, new public schools, increased foreign aid, and so on. While individuals might be willing to pay for some of those goods, it is unlikely that they will want to consume or pay for all of them that have been placed in the political shopping cart. However, if the majority has decided that these political goods are important, individuals will have to purchase the goods through higher taxes, whether they value the goods or not.

Section Check

SECTION CHECK

1. Public choice analysis uses economic principles to study the political process.
2. The self-interest assumption is not the only similarity between the market and public sectors. Scarcity and competition are present in both the public sector and the private sector. Public schools and public libraries are scarce goods; different government agencies compete for government funds; and lobbyists compete with each other to get favored legislation passed.
3. There are differences between the market sector and the public sector. The amount of information that is necessary to make an efficient decision is much greater in political markets than private markets.
4. In private markets, when a shopper goes to the supermarket to purchase groceries, the shopping cart is filled with many different goods that the consumer presumably wants, known as the individual-consumption-payment link. This link breaks down when there are political goods. If the majority has decided that these political goods are important, individuals will have to purchase the goods through higher taxes, whether they value the goods or not.

---

1. What principles does the public choice analysis of government behavior share with the economic analysis of market behavior?
2. What are the differences between the public and private sectors?
3. What are the similarities between the private and public sectors?

Summary

If a market activity has a negative physical impact on an outside party, that side effect is called a negative externality. The government can use taxes or other forms of regulation to correct the overallocation problem associated with negative externalities. If a market activity has a positive physical impact on an outside party, that side effect is called a positive externality. The government can provide subsidies or other forms of regulation to correct the underallocation problem associated with positive externalities.

A public good is both nonrivalrous in consumption (one person's usage of it does not diminish another's ability to use it) and nonexclusive (no one can be excluded from using it). A free rider is someone who attempts to enjoy the benefits of a good without paying for it. The government provides public goods because the free rider problem results in underproduction of these goods in the marketplace.

Public choice theory is the theory that the behavior of individuals in politics, like that in the marketplace, is influenced by self-interest.

Key Terms and Concepts

externalities 128
negative externality 128
positive externality 128
public good 133
private good 134
nonrivalrous 134
nonexcludable 134
free rider 134
public choice analysis 136

Review Questions

1. Indicate which of the following activities create a positive externality, a negative externality, or no externality at all:
   a. during a live theater performance, an audience member's cell phone loudly rings.
   b. you are given a flu shot.
   c. you purchase and drink a soda during a break from class.
   d. a college fraternity and sorority clean up trash along a two-mile stretch on the highway.
   e. a firm dumps chemical waste into a local water reservoir.
   f. the person down the hall in your dorm plays a Britney Spears CD loudly while you are trying to sleep.

2. Is a lighthouse a public good if it benefits many ship owners? What if it primarily benefits ships going to a port nearby?

3. What kind of problems does the government face when trying to perform a benefit–cost analysis of whether and/or how much of a public project to produce?

4. How does a TV broadcast have characteristics of a public good? What about cable services like HBO?

5. How can you be forced to pay for something you do not want to "buy" in the political sector? Can this sometimes be good?

6. Why do you think economics professors are more informed than average citizens about public policy issues?

7. Visit the Sexton Web site at **http://sexton.swcollege.com** and click on the "Environmental Protection Agency's Air Quality Web site." Click on "Where I Live" and find out about the current air quality in areas of California (particularly Metropolitan Los Angeles and Metropolitan Riverside Counties) and Washington state. Do you think that automobile owners in Washington should be subject to the same smog control restrictions as drivers in these two areas of Southern California? How about Wyoming or Montana? Why or why not?

chapter 6 Study Guide

Fill in the Blanks

1. Sometimes the market system fails to produce efficient outcomes because of side effects economists call EXTERNALITIES.

2. Whenever there are physical impacts of an activity on individuals not directly involved in the activity, if the impact on the outside party is negative, it is called a NEGATIVE EXTERN.; if the impact is positive, it is called a POSITIVE EXTERN.

3. If a firm can avoid paying the external costs it imposes on others, it LOWERS its own costs of production but not the TRUE cost to society.

4. If the government taxed a manufacturer by the amount of those external costs it imposes on others, it would force the manufacturer to RAISE the costs.

5. The benefits of a product or service that spill over to an outside party that is not involved in producing or consuming the good are called POSITIVE EXTERN.

6. If suppliers are unaware of or are not responsible for the external costs created by their production, there is an OVERALLOCATION of scarce resources to the production of the good.

7. Because producers are unable to collect payments from all of those that are benefiting from the good or service, the market has a tendency to OVERPRODUCE goods with external benefits.

8. In either the case of external benefits or external costs, buyers and sellers are receiving the wrong signals: The apparent benefits or costs of some actions differ from the TRUE SOCIAL benefits or costs.

9. Unlike the consumption of private goods, the consumption of public goods is both NONEXCLUDABLE and NONRIVOULOUS.

10. If once a good is produced it is prohibitively costly to exclude anyone from consuming the good, consumption of that good is called NON EXCLUDABLE.

11. If everyone can consume a good simultaneously, it is NON RIVOULOUS.

12. When individuals derive the benefits of a good without paying for it, it is called a FREE RIDE.

13. Public goods and externalities can lead to the FREE RIDER problem because people have little incentive to pay for the benefits they will receive, as they cannot be prevented from receiving the benefits.

14. The government may be able to overcome the free-rider problem by PROVIDING the public good and imposing taxes to pay for it.

15. Public choice theory is the application of ECONOMIC principles to politics.

16. Public choice economists believe that the behavior of individuals in politics, like those in the marketplace, will be influenced by SELF INTEREST.

17. The amount of information that is necessary to make an efficient decision is much GREATER in political markets than in private markets.

18. In private markets, there is an individual PAYMENT link, where the goods one gets reflect what one is willing to pay for.

True or False

1. An externality is said to occur whenever there are physical impacts (benefits or costs) of an activity on individuals not directly involved in the activity.

2. Negative externalities are real costs, but because no one owns the air, unlike the other resources a firm uses in production, a firm does not have to pay for its use.

3. In the case of external costs, firms tend to produce too little from society's standpoint, causing an efficiency loss due to an underallocation of scarce resources to the production of the good.

4. If government could impose a pollution tax equal to the exact size of the external costs imposed by a firm, then the firm would produce at the socially desired level of output.

5. The tax revenues raised by a pollution tax could be used to compensate those who have suffered damages from the pollution.

6. Alternatives to pollution taxes include the government prohibiting certain types of activities causing pollution and forcing firms to clean up their emissions.

7. Because the decision makers involved ignore some of the real social benefits, the private market does not provide enough of goods that generate external benefits.

8. In the case of external benefits, if we could add the benefits that are derived by nonpaying consumers, the demand curve would shift to the right, increasing output.

9. In the case of external benefits, a tax equal to external benefits would result in an efficient level of output.

10. Externality problems always require the intervention of government.

11. In the case of goods where all those affected benefit simultaneously and it is prohibitively costly to exclude anyone from consuming them, market failures tend to arise.

12. In the case of public goods, when people act as free riders, some goods having benefits greater than costs will not be produced.

13. In the case of public goods, the government accurately assesses the benefits and costs of those affected, and the resulting output is at its most efficient level.

14. In those areas where markets have failed to generate efficient results, the government will always do a better job.

15. In public choice analysis, bureaucrats, politicians, and voters are assumed to make choices that they believe will yield to the public expected marginal benefits greater than their expected marginal costs.

16. Scarcity and competition are present in the public sector as well as in the private sector.

17. The individual consumption-payment link breaks down when goods are decided on by majority rule.

Multiple Choice

1. The presence of negative externalities leads to a misallocation of societal resources because
   a. whenever external costs are imposed on outside parties, the good should not be produced at all.
   b. less of the good than is ideal for society is produced.
   c. there are some costs associated with production that the producer fails to take into consideration.
   d. the government always intervenes in markets when negative externalities are present, and the government is inherently inefficient.

2. A tax equal to the external cost on firms that emit pollutants would
   a. provide firms with the incentive to increase the level of activity creating the pollution.
   b. provide firms with the incentive to decrease the level of activity creating the pollution.
   c. provide firms with little incentive to search for less environmentally damaging production methods.
   d. not reduce pollution levels at all.

3. In the case of a good whose production generates negative externalities,
   a. those not directly involved in the market transactions are harmed.
   b. internalizing the externality would tend to result in a lower price of the good.
   c. too little of the good tends to be produced.
   d. a subsidy would be the appropriate government corrective action.
   e. all of the above are true.

4. If firms were required to pay the full social costs of the production of goods, including both private and external costs, other things being equal, there would probably be
   a. an increase in production.
   b. a decrease in production.
   c. a greater misallocation of resources.
   d. a decrease in the market price of the product.

5. Which of the following will most likely generate positive externalities?
   a. a hot dog vendor
   b. public education
   c. an automobile
   d. a city bus
   e. a polluting factory

6. Socially inefficient outcomes may occur in markets where there are
   a. free riders.
   b. negative externalities present.
   c. asymmetric information problems.
   d. positive externalities present.
   e. any of the above.

7. In the case of externalities, appropriate government corrective policy would be
   a. taxes in the case of external benefits and subsidies in the case of external costs.
   b. subsidies in the case of external benefits and taxes in the case of external costs.
   c. taxes in both the case of external benefits and the case of external costs.
   d. subsidies in both the case of external benefits and the case of external costs.
   e. none of the above; the appropriate thing to do would be to do nothing.

8. If Don beautifully paints the outside of his house and landscapes his front yard,
   a. he probably has raised the value of his home but not that of his neighbors' homes.
   b. he probably has raised the value of his home and the value of his neighbors' homes.
   c. he probably has raised the value of his neighbors' homes but not the value of his own home.
   d. he is unlikely to capture all the social benefits of his actions.
   e. both b and d are true.

9. Which of the following is true?
   a. Consumption of a public good by one individual reduces the availability of the good for others.
   b. It is extremely difficult to limit the benefits of a public good to the people who pay for it.
   c. Public goods are free whenever the government produces them.
   d. From an efficiency standpoint, a market economy will generally supply too much of a public good.
   e. None of the above are correct.

10. Which of the following is not true?
    a. The government may be able to overcome the free-rider problem with public goods by providing the public goods and imposing taxes to pay for them.
    b. The nature of public goods is such that the government cannot accurately assess the benefits and costs of those affected.
    c. National defense and flood control are illustrations of public goods.
    d. Just as in the case of external costs, public goods tend to be underprovided by the private sector.

11. Public goods are
    a. nonexcludable and nonrivalrous.
    b. nonexcludable and rivalrous.
    c. excludable and rivalrous.
    d. excludable and nonrivalrous.

12. Public goods
    a. can be consumed only by those who have paid for them.
    b. can be consumed by people whether they have paid for their production or not.
    c. can be consumed only by free riders.
    d. tend to be underprovided by the private market.
    e. are characterized by both b and d.

13. The amount of information that is necessary to make an efficient choice is generally _______ in the public sector than in the private sector.
    a. less
    b. more
    c. the same
    d. none of the above

Problems

1. Draw a standard supply and demand diagram for widgets, and indicate the equilibrium price and output.

2. Assuming that the production of widgets generates external costs, illustrate the effect of the producer being forced to pay a tax equal to the external costs generated, and indicate the equilibrium output.

3. If instead of generating external costs, widget production generates external benefits, illustrate the effect of the producer being given a subsidy equal to the external benefits generated, and indicate the equilibrium output.

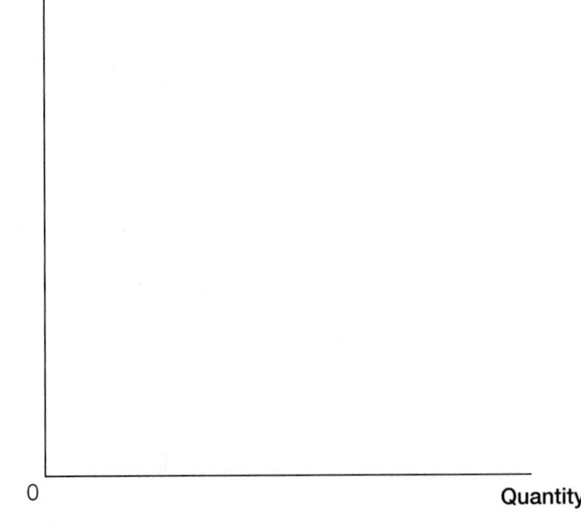

chapter 7

Production and Costs

section 7.1

Profits: Total Revenues Minus Total Costs

- What are explicit and implicit costs?
- What are accounting profits?
- What are economic profits?
- Do firms really maximize profits?

THE CONCEPT OF COSTS

As we discussed in chapter 2, costs exist because resources are scarce and have competing uses—to produce more of one good means forgoing the production of another good. The cost of producing a good is measured by the worth of the most valuable alternative that was given up to obtain the resource. As you may recall this is called the *opportunity cost.*

In chapter 3, the production possibilities curve highlighted this trade-off. Recall that the opportunity cost of producing additional shelter was the units of food that had to be sacrificed. Other examples of opportunity costs abound: Paper used in this text could have been used in other books or for hundreds of other uses and the steel used in the construction of a new building could have been used in the production of an automobile or a washing machine.

But what exactly makes up a firm's costs? Let's look at the two distinct components that make up the firm's costs: explicit costs and implicit costs.

EXPLICIT COSTS

explicit costs
the opportunity costs of production that require a monetary payment

Explicit costs are the input costs that require a monetary payment—the out-of-pocket expenses that pay for labor services, raw materials, fuel, transportation, utilities, advertising, and so on. It is important to note that the explicit costs are opportunity costs to the firm. For example, money spent on electricity cannot be used for advertising. Remember in a world of scarcity, we are always giving up something to get something else. Trade-offs are pervasive. The costs that we have discussed so far are relatively easy to measure and an economist and an accountant would most likely arrive at the same amounts. But that will generally not be the case.

IMPLICIT COSTS

implicit costs
the opportunity costs of production that do not require a monetary payment

Some of the firm's (opportunity) costs of production are implicit. **Implicit costs** do not require an outlay of money. This is where the economist's and the accountant's idea of costs diverge because accountants do not include implicit costs. For example, whenever an investment is made, opportunities to invest elsewhere are forgone. This lost opportunity is an implicit cost that economists include in the total cost of the firm, even though no money is expended. A typical farmer or small business owner may perform work without receiving formal wages, but the value of the alternative earnings forgone represents an implicit opportunity cost to the individual. Because other firms could have used the resources, what the resources could have earned elsewhere is an implicit cost to the firm. It is important to emphasize that whenever we are talking about costs—explicit or implicit—we are talking about opportunity costs.

PROFITS

Economists generally assume that the ultimate goal of the firm is to maximize **profits.** In other words, firms try to maximize the difference between what they give up for their inputs—their total costs (explicit and implicit)—and the amount they receive for their goods and services—their total revenue. Like revenues and costs, profits refer to flows over time. When we say that a firm earned $5 million in profits, we must clarify the time period in which the profits were earned—a week, month, year, and so on.

COURTESY OF ROBERT SEXTON

As the owner of this salon, what explicit and implicit costs might he incur? His explicit costs include chairs, rent for the shop, scissors, the rinse sinks, electricity, blower dryers, and so on. The implicit costs include the salary he could make at another job or the leisure he could enjoy if he retired.

ARE ACCOUNTING PROFITS THE SAME AS ECONOMIC PROFITS?

A firm can make a profit in the sense that the total revenues that it receives exceed the explicit costs that it incurs in the process of doing business. We call these **accounting profits**—profits as accountants record them are based on total revenues and explicit costs. In other words, accounting profits do not include implicit costs.

Economists prefer an alternative way of measuring profits; they are interested in total revenue minus all costs (both explicit and implicit). In their calculating a firm's costs, economists include the implicit costs—as well as the explicit costs—when calculating the total costs of the firm.

Summing up, measured in terms of accounting profits, like those reported in real-world financial statements, a firm has a profit if its total revenues exceed explicit costs. In terms of **economic profits,** a firm has a profit if its total revenues exceed its total opportunity cost—both its explicit costs and implicit costs. Exhibit 1 illustrates the difference between accounting profits and economic profits.

profits
the difference between total revenue and total cost

accounting profits
total revenues minus total explicit costs

economic profits
total revenue minus explicit and implicit costs

APPLICATION

EXPLICIT AND IMPLICIT COSTS

Q: True or False? If a company owns its own building in a growing urban area, it can protect itself from rising rents.

A: False; the company cannot avoid implicit costs. If the company owned the building and rents increased, so would the opportunity cost of owning the building. That is, by occupying the building, the company is giving up the new higher rents it could receive from renters if it leased out the space. That is, even though the firm pays zero rent by owning the building, the rent that it could receive by leasing it to another company is a very real economic cost (but not an accounting cost) to the firm.

© T/MAKER COMPANY

section 7.1 Exhibit 1 — Accounting Profits versus Economic Profits

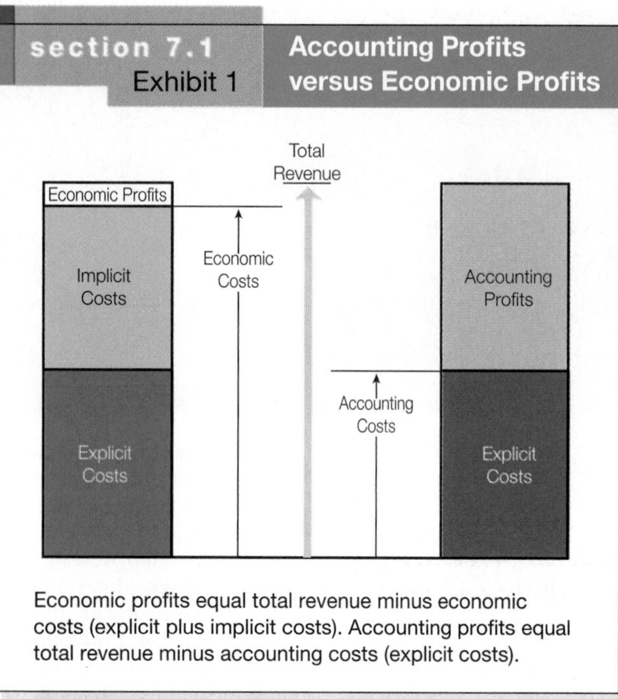

Economic profits equal total revenue minus economic costs (explicit plus implicit costs). Accounting profits equal total revenue minus accounting costs (explicit costs).

A ZERO ECONOMIC PROFIT IS A NORMAL PROFIT

As we just discussed, an economic profit is less than an accounting profit because economic profits include implicit as well as explicit costs. In fact, an economist considers a zero economic profit a normal profit. Recall that zero economic profit means that the firm is covering both explicit and implicit costs—the total opportunity costs of its resources. In other words, the firm's total revenue is sufficient to compensate the time and money that owners have put in the business. This is clearly different than making zero accounting profits, because then revenues would not cover the implicit costs. (We will return to this important point in the next chapter.)

SUNK COSTS

sunk costs
costs that have been incurred and cannot be recovered

We have just seen how opportunity costs are often hidden, as in the case of implicit costs. However, there is another type of cost that should be discussed—sunk costs. **Sunk costs** have already been incurred and cannot be recovered. Suppose, for example, that you bought a CD that looked interesting, but when you got home and played it you wished you hadn't. Now your friend comes over and says he likes that CD and will buy it from you for $5. You say, "no way" because you paid $15 for the CD. Are you acting rationally? Economists believe that what you paid for the CD is now irrelevant. Now, you must decide whether you would rather have the $5 or the CD. If you decide to keep the CD, the cost is the $5 you could have received from your friend—the rest is sunk.

Or suppose a donut shop has a one-year lease and after three months the owner decides that the shop would do much better by relocating to a new mall that has just opened. Should the donut shop just stay put until the end of the year because it is legally obligated to pay the 12-month lease? No, the nonrefundable lease payment is sunk and

APPLICATION

ACCOUNTING PROFITS AND ECONOMIC PROFITS

Q: Emily, an energetic 10-year-old, set up a lemonade stand in front of her house. One Saturday, she sold 50 cups of lemonade at 50 cents apiece to her friends, who were hot and thirsty from playing. These sales generated $25 in total revenues for Emily. Emily was pleased, because she knew that her total costs—lemonade mix, cups, and so on—were only $5. As she was closing up shop for the day, her neighbor, an accountant, stopped by to say hello. Emily told him about her successful day. He said, "What a great job! You made a $20 profit!" Excited, Emily rushed into the house to tell her mother, an economist, the great news. Will Emily's mother agree with the accountant's calculation of Emily's profits? If not, why?

A: No, Emily's mother will not agree with the accountant, because he forgot to include the implicit costs when calculating Emily's profits. That is, he neglected to take into account what Emily could have been doing with her time if she had not been selling lemonade. For example, she could have been playing with her friends, cleaning her room, or perhaps helping her friends make money at their garage sale. These lost opportunities are implicit costs that should be included in the calculation of Emily's economic profits.

irrelevant to the decision to relocate. The decision to relocate should be based on the prospects of future profits regardless of the length of the current lease. In short, sunk costs are irrelevant for any future action because they have already been incurred and cannot be recovered.

Section Check

SECTION CHECK

1. Total cost consists of explicit costs and implicit costs.
2. Explicit costs are the opportunity costs of production that require a monetary payment.
3. Some opportunity costs of the firm are implicit—they do not represent an outlay of money or a contractual obligation.
4. Profits are the difference between the total revenues of a firm and its total costs.
5. Accounting profits are revenues minus explicit costs.
6. Economic profits are revenue minus total opportunity costs—both explicit and implicit costs.
7. Sunk costs are irretrievable and irrelevant to the firm.

---

1. What is the difference between explicit costs and implicit costs?
2. Why are both explicit costs and implicit costs relevant in making economic decisions?
3. How do we measure profits?
4. Why is it important to look at all the opportunity costs of production?
5. If you turn down a job offer of $45,000 per year to work for yourself, what is the opportunity cost of working for yourself?

section 7.2

Production in the Short Run

- What is the difference between the short run and the long run?
- What is a production function?
- What is diminishing marginal product?

THE SHORT RUN VERSUS THE LONG RUN

Of fundamental importance for cost and production behavior is the extent to which a firm is able to adjust inputs as it varies output. Since it takes more time to vary some inputs than others, we must distinguish between the short run and the long run. The **short run** is defined as a period too brief for some inputs to be varied. For example, the current size of a plant cannot be altered and new equipment cannot be obtained or built overnight. If demand increases for the firm's product and the firm chooses to produce more output in the short run, it must do so with its existing equipment and factory. Inputs like buildings and equipment that do not change with output are called *fixed* inputs.

short run
a period too brief for some production inputs to be varied

The **long run** is a period of time in which the firm can adjust all inputs. That is, in the long run all inputs to the firm are *variable,* and will change as output changes. The long run can vary considerably from industry to industry. For a chain of coffeehouses that

long run
a period over which all production inputs are variable

wants to add a few more stores, the long run may only be a few months. In other industries, like the automobiles or steel, the long run might be a couple of years, as a new plant or factory in this type of industry will take much longer to build.

PRODUCTION IN THE SHORT RUN

total product (*TP*) *the total output of a good produced by the firm*

Suppose that Moe's Bagel Shop has just one input that is variable, labor, while the size of the bagel shop is fixed in the short run. What will happen to **total product (*TP*),** the total amount of output (bagels) generated by Moe's shop, as the level of the variable input, labor, is increased? Common sense suggests that total product will start at a low level and increase—perhaps rapidly at first, and then more slowly—as the amount of the variable input increases. It will continue to increase until the quantity of the variable input (labor) becomes so large in relation to the quantity of other inputs—like the size of the bagel shop—that further increases in output become more and more difficult or even impossible. In the second column of Exhibit 1, we see that as we increase the number of workers in Moe's Bagel Shop, Moe is able to produce more bagels. The addition of the first worker results in a total output of 10 bagels per hour. When Moe adds a second worker, bagel output climbs to 24, an increase of 14 bagels per hour. Total product continues to increase even with the sixth worker hired, but you can see that it has slowed considerably, with the sixth worker only increasing total product by one bagel per hour. Beyond this point, additional workers may even result in a decline in total bagel output as workers bump into each other in the small bagel shop. This outcome is evident both in the table in Exhibit 1, as well as in the total product curve shown in Exhibit 2(a).

section 7.2 Exhibit 1 — Moe's Production Function with One Variable, Labor

Variable Input Labor (Workers)	Total Output (Bagels per hour) Q	Marginal Product of Labor (Bagels per hour) $\Delta Q/\Delta V$
0	0	
		10
1	10	
		14
2	24	
		12
3	36	
		10
4	46	
		4
5	50	
		1
6	51	

section 7.2 Exhibit 2 — Total Product and Marginal Product

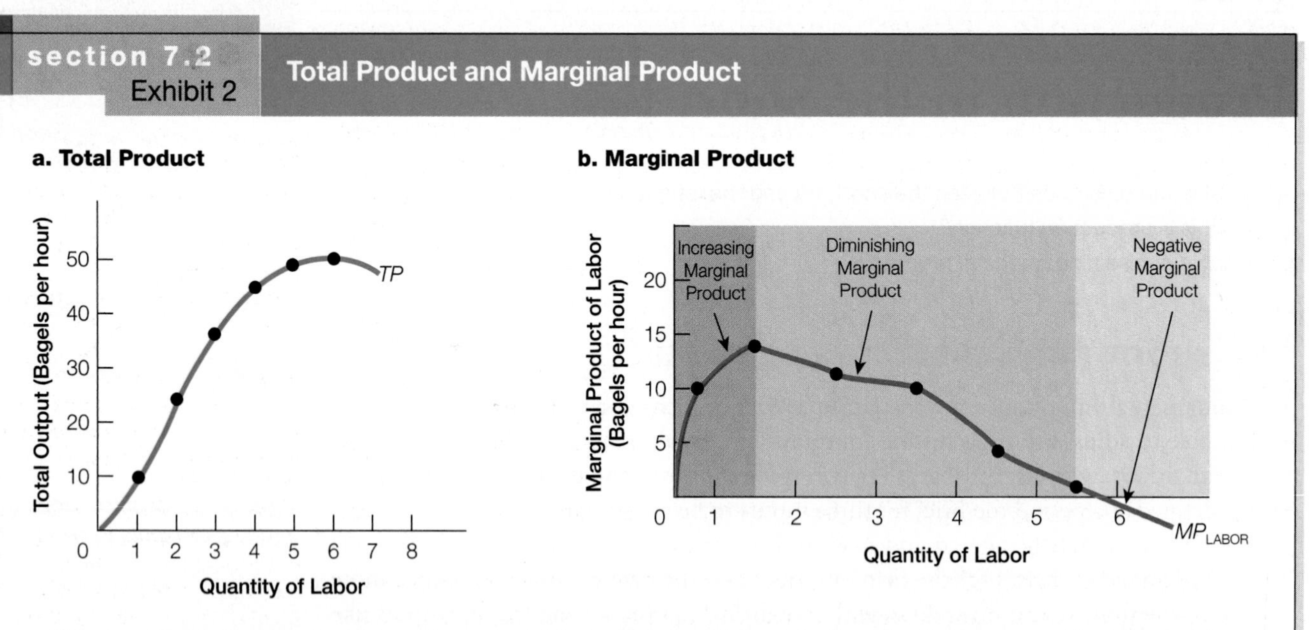

In 2(a) we see that total output increases as the amount of the variable input, labor, is increased—usually more rapidly at first and then more slowly. In 2(b), we see that the marginal product first rises (increasing marginal product) as workers are added to the fixed input (for example, a machine), which is thus used more efficiently. Then the marginal product falls; the crowding of the fixed input with more and more workers causes marginal product to fall. Lastly, negative marginal product occurs where additional inputs cause output to fall.

DIMINISHING MARGINAL PRODUCT

The **marginal product (*MP*)** of any single input is defined as the change in total product resulting from a small change in the amount of input used. This concept is shown in the final column in Exhibit 1, and is illustrated by the *MP* curve in Exhibit 2(b). As you can see in Exhibit 2(b), the *MP* curve first rises and then falls.

marginal product (*MP*)
the change in total output of a good that results from a unit change in input

The Rise in Marginal Product

The initial rise in the marginal product is the result of more effective use of fixed inputs (the bagel shop) as the number of workers increases (due to specialization and division of labor). For example, certain types of capital equipment may require a minimum number of workers for efficient operation, or perhaps any operation at all. With a small number of workers (the variable factors), some machines cannot operate at all, or only at a very low level of efficiency. As additional workers are added, machines are brought into efficient operation, and thus the marginal product of the workers rises. Similarly, if one person tried to operate a large department store alone—doing work of all types necessary in the store—her energies would be spread so thinly in so many directions that total output (sales) might be less than if she were operating a smaller store (working with less capital). As successive workers are added, up to a certain number, each worker adds more to total product than the previous one and the marginal product rises. This is seen in the shaded area of Exhibit 2(b) labeled increasing marginal product.

diminishing marginal product
as a variable input increases, with other inputs fixed, a point will be reached where the additions to output will eventually decline

The Fall in Marginal Product

But why does marginal product then fall? The answer is **diminishing marginal product,** which stems from the crowding of the fixed input. Specifically, as the amount of a variable input is increased, the amount of other (fixed) inputs being held constant, a point ultimately will be reached beyond which marginal product will decline. Beyond this point, output increases, but at a decreasing rate. It is the crowding of the fixed input with more and more workers that causes the decline in the marginal product. Too many workers in a store make it more difficult for customers to shop; too many workers in a factory get in each other's way. Adding more and more of a variable input to a fixed input will eventually lead to diminishing marginal product.

How many workers could be added to this jackhammer and still be productive (not to mention safe)? If more workers are added, how much output would be derived from each additional worker? There may be slightly more total output from the second worker because the second worker will be using the jackhammer while the first worker is taking a break from "the shakes." However, the fifth or sixth worker would clearly not create any additional output, as workers would just be standing around for their turn. That is, the marginal product (additional output) would eventually fall because of diminishing marginal product.

The point of this discussion is that production functions conform to the same general pattern as that shown by Moe's Bagel Shop in the third column of Exhibit 1 and illustrated in Exhibit 2(b). In the third column of Exhibit 1, we see that as we increase the number of workers in Moe's Bagel Shop, Moe is able to produce more bagels. The first worker is able to produce 10 bagels per hour. When Moe adds a second worker, total bagel output climbs to 24, an increase of 14 bagels per hour. However, when Moe hires a third worker, bagel output still increases, but a third worker's marginal production (12 bagels per hour) is less than that of the second worker. In fact, the marginal product continues to drop as more and more workers are added to the bagel shop. This is diminishing marginal product at work. Note that it is not because the third worker is not as "good" as the second worker that marginal product fell. Even with identical workers, the increased "crowding" of the fixed input causes marginal output to eventually fall.

A firm never *knowingly* allows itself to reach the point where the marginal product becomes negative, the situation in which the use of additional variable input units actually reduces total product. In such a situation, there are so many units of the variable input—inputs with positive opportunity costs—that efficient use of the fixed input units is impaired. In such a situation, *reducing* the number of workers would actually *increase* total product.

Section Check

1. The short run is defined as a period too brief for some inputs to be varied. Inputs like buildings and equipment that do not change with output are called fixed inputs.
2. The long run is a period of time long enough to allow the firm to adjust all inputs. That is, in the long run all costs are variable and will change as output changes.
3. The production function describes the maximum amount of a product that a firm can produce with any combination of inputs, using existing technology.
4. A diminishing marginal product occurs when the amount of a variable input keeps increasing while the amount of fixed inputs holds constant; eventually, the marginal product declines.

---

1. What is the difference between fixed and variable inputs?
2. Why are all inputs variable in the long run?
3. What relationship does a production function represent?
4. What is diminishing marginal product? What causes it?

section 7.3 Costs in the Short Run

- What are fixed costs?
- What are variable costs?
- What is average fixed, average variable, and average total cost?
- What is marginal cost?

In the last section we learned about the relationship between a firm's inputs and its level of output. But that is only one part of the discussion; we must also consider how much it will cost the firm to use each of these inputs in production. In this section, we will examine the short-run costs of the firm—what they are and how they vary with the output levels that are produced. The short-run total costs of a business fall into two distinct categories: fixed costs and variable costs.

FIXED COSTS, VARIABLE COSTS, AND TOTAL COSTS

fixed costs
costs that do not vary with the level of output

total fixed costs (*TFC*)
the sum of the firm's fixed costs

variable costs
costs that vary with the level of output

Fixed costs are those that do not vary with the level of output. For example, the rent on buildings or equipment is usually fixed at least for some period of time; whether the firm produces lots of output or little output, the rent stays the same. Insurance premiums, property taxes, and interest payments on debt used to finance capital equipment are other examples of fixed costs—they have to be paid even if no output is produced. In the short run, fixed costs cannot be avoided. The only way a firm can avoid a fixed cost is by going out of business. The sum of the firm's fixed costs is called the **total fixed cost (*TFC*).**

Variable costs vary with the level of output. As more variable inputs like labor and raw materials are added, output increases. The variable cost, the expenditures for wages and raw materials, increases as output increases. The sum of the firm's variable costs is called **total variable cost (*TVC*).** The sum of the total fixed costs and total variable costs is called the firm's **total cost (*TC*).**

total variable cost (*TVC*)
the sum of the firm's variable costs

total cost (*TC*)
the sum of the firm's total fixed costs and total variable costs

AVERAGE TOTAL COST

While we are often interested in the total amount of costs incurred by the firm, sometimes we find it convenient to discuss these costs on a per-unit-of-output, or an average, basis. For example, if Pizza Shack Company has $1,600 in total fixed cost and $2,400 in total variable cost, its total cost is $4,000. If it produces 800 pizzas in the time period in question, its total cost per unit of output equals $5 ($4,000 total cost divided by 800 units of output). We call this per-unit cost the **average total cost (*ATC*).** Likewise, we might talk about the fixed cost per unit of output, or **average fixed cost (*AFC*).** In the case of Pizza Shack, the average fixed cost, or *AFC,* would equal $2 ($1,600 is the fixed cost divided by 800 units of output). Similarly, we can speak of per-unit variable cost, or **average variable cost (*AVC*).** In this example, the average variable cost would equal $3 ($2,400 is the variable cost divided by 800 units of output).

average total cost (*ATC*)
a per-unit cost of operation; total cost divided by output

average fixed cost (*AFC*)
a per-unit measure of fixed costs; fixed costs divided by output

average variable cost (*AVC*)
a per-unit measure of variable costs; variable costs divided by output

MARGINAL COST

To this point, six different short run cost concepts have been introduced: total cost, total fixed cost, total variable cost, average total cost, average fixed cost, and average variable cost. All of these concepts are relevant to a discussion of firm behavior and profitability. However, the most important single cost concept has yet to be mentioned: marginal (or additional) cost. You may recall this concept from chapter 2, where we highlighted the importance of using marginal analysis—that is, analysis that focuses on *additional* or marginal choices. Specifically, **marginal cost (*MC*)** shows the change in total costs associated with a change in output by one unit ($\Delta TC/\Delta Q$). Put a bit differently, marginal cost is the costs of producing one more unit of output. As such, marginal costs are really just a very useful way to view variable costs—costs that vary as output varies. Marginal cost represents the added labor, raw materials, and miscellaneous expenses that are

marginal cost (*MC*)
the change in total costs resulting from a one-unit change in output

APPLICATION

MARGINAL COST VERSUS AVERAGE TOTAL COST

Q: Suppose an oil producer's average total cost of producing a barrel of oil has been $20 a barrel and the oil producer can sell that oil to a distributor for $23 a barrel. On average, this seems like a profitable business. Should the oil producer expand production given this profitability?

A: Not necessarily. It is marginal cost that is critical. The next barrel of oil might cost $30 to produce because the well may be drying up or the company might have to drill deeper to get additional oil, making it even more costly to retrieve. It is possible that the *marginal cost* of the additional barrels of oil may be greater than the market price and, thus, no longer profitable.

incurred in making an additional unit of output. Marginal cost is the additional, or incremental, cost associated with the "last" unit of output produced.

HOW ARE THESE COSTS RELATED?

Exhibit 1 summarizes the definitions of the seven different short-run cost concepts introduced in this chapter. To further clarify these concepts and to illustrate the relationships between them, we will now return to our discussion of the costs faced by Pizza Shack.

Exhibit 2 presents the costs incurred by Pizza Shack at various levels of output. Note that the total fixed cost is the same at all output levels and that at very low output levels (four or fewer units in the example), total fixed cost is the dominant portion of total costs. At high output levels (eight or more units in the example), total fixed cost becomes quite small relative to total variable cost. As the firm increases its output, it spreads its total fixed cost across more units; as a result, average fixed cost declines continuously.

section 7.3 Exhibit 1 — A Summary of the Short-Run Cost Concepts

Concept	Abbreviation	Definition
Total fixed cost	*TFC*	Costs that are the same at all output levels (e.g., insurance, rent)
Total variable cost	*TVC*	Costs that vary with the level of output (e.g., hourly labor, raw materials)
Total cost	*TC*	The sum of the firm's total fixed costs and total variable costs at a level of output ($TC = TFC + TVC$).
Marginal cost	*MC*	The added cost of producing one more unit of output; change in *TC* associated with one more unit of output ($\Delta TC/\Delta Q$).
Average total cost	*ATC*	*TC* per unit of output; *TC* divided by output (TC/Q).
Average fixed cost	*AFC*	*TFC* per unit of output; *TFC* divided by output (TFC/Q).
Average variable cost	*AVC*	*TVC* per unit of output; *TVC* divided by output (TVC/Q).

section 7.3 Exhibit 2 — Cost Calculations for Pizza Shack Company

Hourly Output (Q)	Total Fixed Cost (TFC)	Total Variable Cost (TVC)	Total Cost ($TC = TVC + TFC$)	Marginal Cost ($MC = \Delta TC/\Delta Q$)	Average Fixed Cost ($AFC = TFC/Q$)	Average Variable Cost ($AVC = TVC/Q$)	Average Total Cost ($ATC = TC/Q$ or $AFC + ATC$)
0	$40	$ 0	$ 40		—	—	—
				$10			
1	40	10	50		$40.00	$10.00	$50.00
				8			
2	40	18	58		20.00	9.00	29.00
				7			
3	40	25	65		13.33	8.33	21.66
				10			
4	40	35	75		10.00	8.75	18.75
				12			
5	40	47	87		8.00	9.40	17.40
				13			
6	40	60	100		6.67	10.00	16.67
				15			
7	40	75	115		5.71	10.71	16.42
				20			
8	40	95	135		5.00	11.88	16.88
				25			
9	40	120	160		4.44	13.33	17.77
				30			
10	40	150	190		4.00	15.00	19.00

It is often easier to understand the cost concepts by examining graphs that show the levels of the various costs at different output levels. The graph in Exhibit 3 shows the first three cost concepts: fixed, variable, and total costs. The total fixed cost (*TFC*) curve is always a horizontal line because, by definition, fixed costs are the same at all output levels—even at zero level of output. In Exhibit 3, notice that $TVC = 0$ when $Q = 0$; if there is no output being produced, there are no variable costs.

The total cost (*TC*) curve is the summation of the total variable cost (*TVC*) and total fixed cost (*TFC*) curves. Because the total fixed cost curve is horizontal, the total cost curve lies above the total variable cost curve by a fixed (vertical) amount.

Exhibit 4 shows the average fixed cost curve, the average variable cost curve, the average total cost curve, and the associated marginal cost curve. In this exhibit, note how the average fixed cost (*AFC*) curve constantly declines, approaching but never reaching zero. Remember, the *AFC* is simply TFC/Q so as output expands, *AFC* declines, because the total fixed cost is being spread over successively larger volumes of output. Also observe how the marginal cost (*MC*) curve crosses the average variable cost (*AVC*) and average total cost (*ATC*) curves at their lowest points. At higher output levels, high marginal costs pull up the average variable cost and average total cost curves, while at low output levels, low marginal costs pull the curves down. In the next section, we will explain why the marginal cost curve intersects the average variable cost curve and the average total cost curve at their minimum points.

section 7.3 Exhibit 3 — Total and Fixed Costs

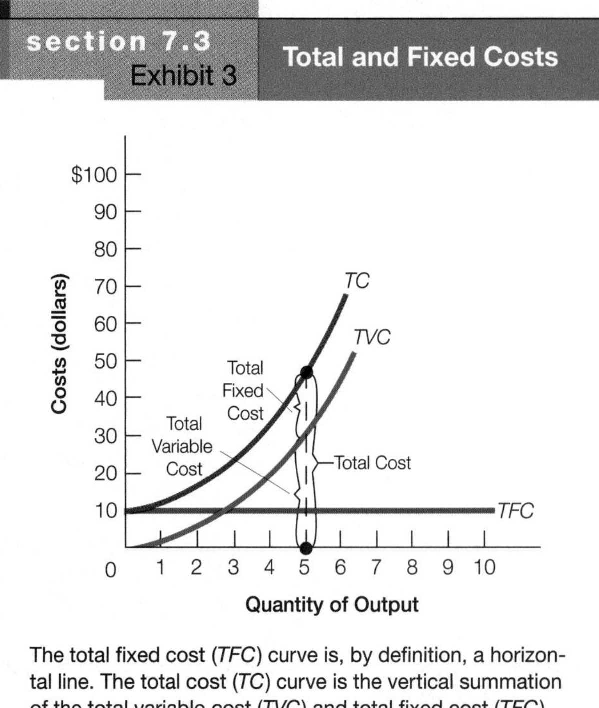

The total fixed cost (*TFC*) curve is, by definition, a horizontal line. The total cost (*TC*) curve is the vertical summation of the total variable cost (*TVC*) and total fixed cost (*TFC*) curves. Notice that *TVC* = zero when *Q* = 0 and that *TFC* = $10 even when there is no output being produced.

section 7.3 Exhibit 4 — Average and Marginal Costs

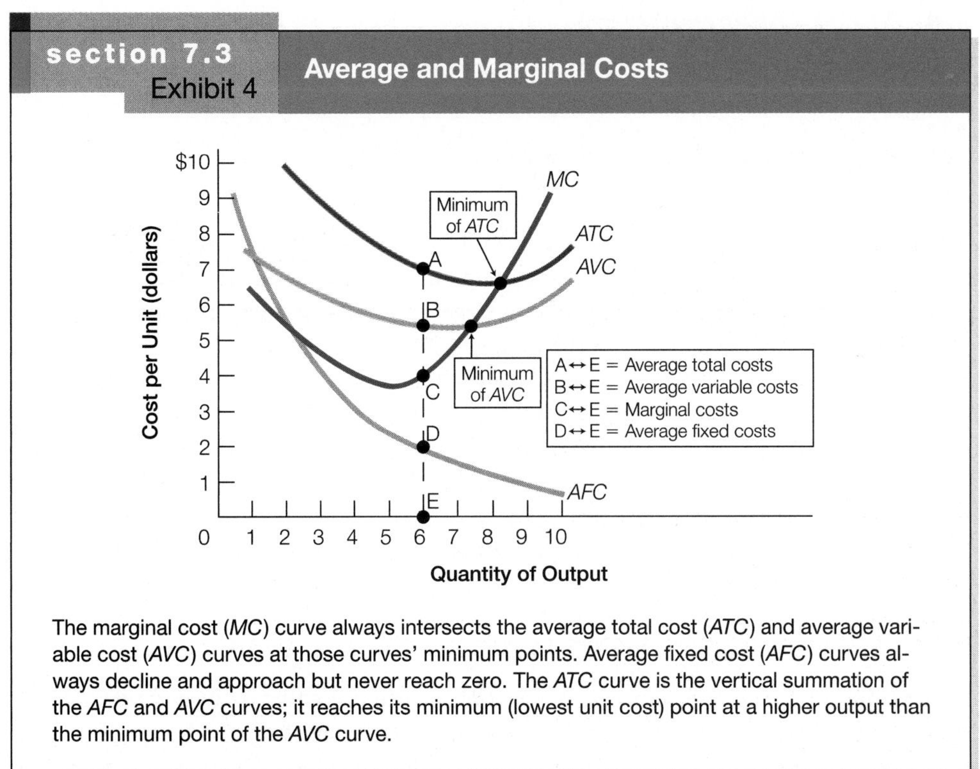

The marginal cost (*MC*) curve always intersects the average total cost (*ATC*) and average variable cost (*AVC*) curves at those curves' minimum points. Average fixed cost (*AFC*) curves always decline and approach but never reach zero. The *ATC* curve is the vertical summation of the *AFC* and *AVC* curves; it reaches its minimum (lowest unit cost) point at a higher output than the minimum point of the *AVC* curve.

Section Check

SECTION CHECK

1. Fixed costs do not change with the level of output.
2. Variable costs are not fixed. Variable costs change as the level of output changes.
3. Average total cost (*ATC*) is total cost divided by output.
4. Average fixed cost (*AFC*) is fixed cost divided by output.
5. Average variable cost (*AVC*) is variable cost divided by output.
6. Marginal cost (*MC*) is the added cost of producing one more unit of output; it is the change in total cost associated with one more unit of output. It is this cost that is relevant to decisions to produce more or less.

---

1. What is the difference between fixed cost and variable cost?
2. How are average fixed cost, average variable cost, and average total cost calculated?
3. Why is marginal cost the relevant cost to consider when one is deciding whether to produce more or less of a product?
4. If the average variable cost curve were constant over some range of output, why would the average total cost be falling over that range of output?
5. If your season batting average going into a game was .300 (three hits per ten at bats) and you got two hits in five at bats during the game, would your season batting average rise or fall as a result?

section 7.4

The Shape of the Short-Run Cost Curves

- Why is the average total cost curve U-shaped?
- When marginal cost is greater than average cost, what happens to the average?

THE RELATIONSHIP BETWEEN MARGINAL AND AVERAGE AMOUNTS

The relationship between the marginal and the average is simply a matter of arithmetic; when a number (the marginal cost) being added into a series is smaller than the previous average of the series, the new average will be lower than the previous one. Likewise, when the marginal number is larger than the average, the average will rise. For example, if you have taken two economics exams and received a 90 percent on your first exam and 80 percent on your second exam, you have an 85 percent average. If after some serious studying, you get a 100 percent on the third exam (the marginal exam), what happens to your average? It rises to 90 percent. Because the marginal is greater than the average, it "pulls" the average up. However, if the score on your third (marginal) exam is lower, a 70 percent, your average will fall to 80 percent because the marginal is below the average.

WHY IS THE AVERAGE TOTAL COST CURVE U-SHAPED?

The average total cost curve is usually U-shaped, as seen in Exhibit 1. Why is this? At very small levels of output and very large levels of output, average total cost is very high. The reason for the high average total cost when the firm is producing a very small amount of section 7.4 Exhibit 1 **U-Shaped Average Total Cost Curve**

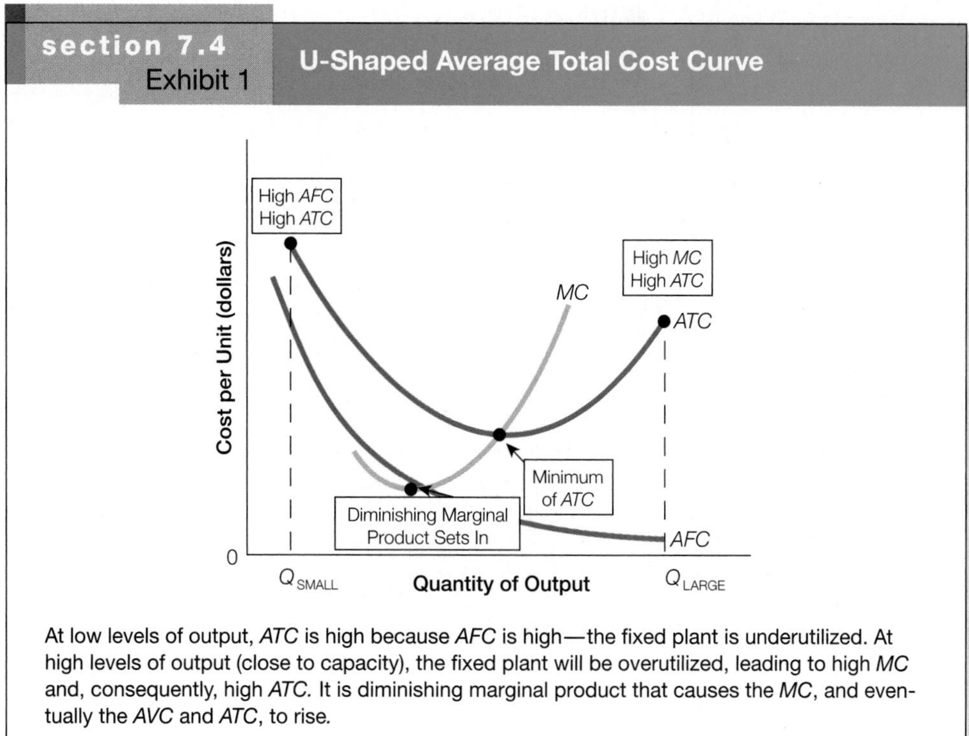

At low levels of output, *ATC* is high because *AFC* is high—the fixed plant is underutilized. At high levels of output (close to capacity), the fixed plant will be overutilized, leading to high *MC* and, consequently, high *ATC*. It is diminishing marginal product that causes the *MC*, and eventually the *AVC* and *ATC*, to rise.

output is the high average fixed cost—when the output rate of the plant is small relative to its capacity the plant is being underutilized. But as the firm expands output beyond this point, the average total cost falls. Why? Remember that $ATC = AFC + AVC$ and average fixed cost always falls when output expands, because the fixed costs are being spread over more units of output. Thus, it is the declining *AFC* that is primarily responsible for the falling *ATC*.

The average total cost rises at high levels of output because of diminishing marginal product. For example, as more and more workers are put to work using a fixed quantity of machines, the result may be crowded working conditions and/or increasing maintenance costs as equipment is used more intensively, or older, less-efficient machinery is called upon to handle the greater output. In fact, diminishing marginal product sets in at the very bottom of the marginal cost curve, as seen in Exhibit 1. That is, it is diminishing marginal product that causes the marginal cost to increase, eventually causing the average variable cost and the average total cost curves to rise. At very large levels of output, where the plant approaches full capacity, the fixed plant is overutilized, and this leads to high marginal cost that causes a high average total cost.

THE RELATIONSHIP BETWEEN MARGINAL COST AND AVERAGE VARIABLE AND AVERAGE TOTAL COST

Certain relationships exist between marginal cost and average variable and average total costs. For example, when average variable cost is falling, marginal cost must be less than average variable cost; and when average variable cost is rising, marginal cost is greater than average variable cost. Marginal cost is equal to average variable cost at the lowest point of the average variable cost curve, as seen in Exhibit 2. In the lefthand (shaded) portion of Exhibit 2, marginal cost is less than average variable cost and the average is falling. On the righthand side, marginal cost is greater than average variable cost and the average is

section 7.4 Exhibit 2 — Marginal Cost and Average Variable Cost

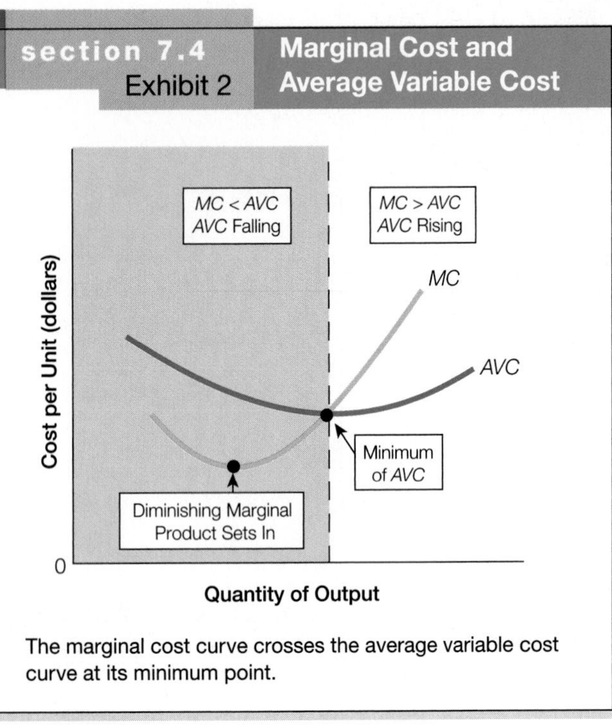

The marginal cost curve crosses the average variable cost curve at its minimum point.

section 7.4 Exhibit 3 — Marginal Cost and Average Total Cost

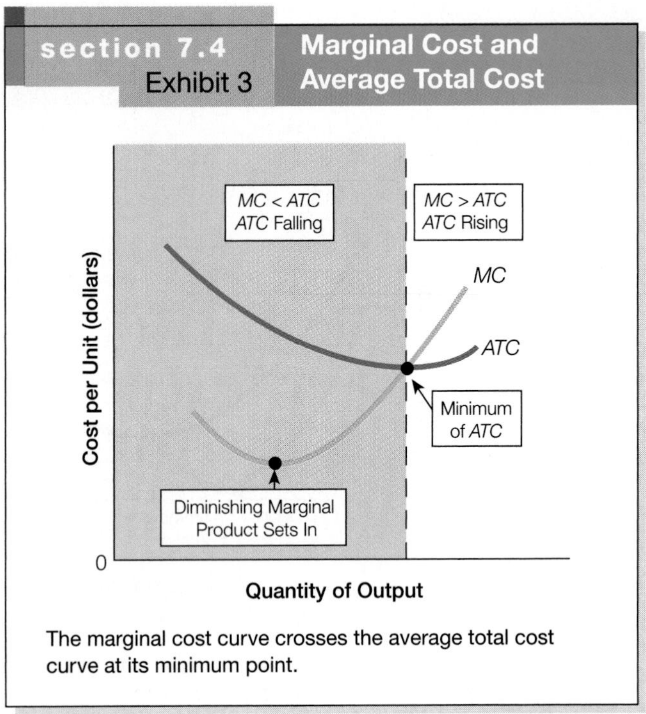

The marginal cost curve crosses the average total cost curve at its minimum point.

rising. The same relationship holds for the marginal cost curve and the average total cost curve. In the lefthand (shaded) portion of Exhibit 3, marginal cost is less than average total cost and the average is falling. On the righthand side, marginal cost is greater than average total cost and the average is rising.

APPLICATION

MARGINAL VERSUS AVERAGE AMOUNTS

Q: If a small horse-racing jockey decided to join your economics class of ten students, what would happen to the *average* height of the class?

A: The *marginal* addition, the jockey, would presumably be smaller than the *average* person in the class, so the *average* height in the class would fall. Now, if the star 7-foot center on the men's basketball team joined your class, the *average* height would rise, as the newer marginal member would be presumably taller than the average person. In sum, if the margin is greater (less) than the average, the average will rise (fall).

© SPURLOCK PHOTOGRAPHY

If Shaquille O'Neal joined your class of 10 students, what would happen to the average class height?

Section Check

1. Average total cost declines as output expands, but then increases again as output expands still further beyond a certain point.
2. When marginal cost is less than average variable cost, average variable cost must be falling; when marginal cost is less than average total cost, average total cost must be falling.
3. When marginal cost is greater than average variable cost, average variable cost must be rising; when marginal cost is greater than average total cost, average total cost must be rising.

---

1. What is the primary reason that average total cost falls as output expands over low output ranges?
2. Why does average total cost rise at some point as output expands further?
3. If marginal cost is less than average total cost, why does *ATC* fall? If *MC* is greater than *ATC*, why does the *ATC* rise?

section 7.5

Cost Curves: Short Run and Long Run

- What are economies of scale?
- What are diseconomies of scale?
- What are constant returns to scale?

LONG-RUN VERSUS SHORT-RUN COST CURVES

Over long enough periods of time, firms can vary all of their productive inputs. For example, time provides an opportunity to substitute lower-cost capital, like larger plants or newer, more sophisticated equipment, for more expensive labor inputs. However, in the short run, a company cannot vary its plant size and equipment. These inputs are fixed in the short run, so the firm can only expand output by employing more variable inputs (e.g., workers and raw materials) in order to get extra output from the existing factory. For example, if a company has to pay lots of workers overtime wages to get expanded output in the short run, over longer periods, new highly automated machinery may be introduced that conserves on expensive labor. That is, in the long run (perhaps several years), the company can expand the size of its factories, build new ones, or shut down unproductive ones.

Creating the Long-Run Average Total Cost Curve

In Exhibit 1, the firm has three possible plant sizes—a small plant, $SRATC_1$, a medium-sized plant, $SRATC_2$, and a large plant, $SRATC_3$. As we move along the *LRATC* (the blue line) in Exhibit 1, the factory size changes with the quantity of output. Certain relationships among the successive curves should be emphasized. For very small output levels, q_1, costs are lowest with plant size $SRATC_1$, point A. Costs with plant size $SRATC_2$ (larger plant size) are relatively high for these low levels of output because the plant's fixed costs are far too high for low levels of output; machinery, buildings, and so on would be poorly utilized. In Exhibit 1, we can see that if q_1 output is produced with plant size $SRATC_2$, the plant would be operating below capacity, point B, and the cost would be higher at

By having several screens in one complex, the cinema company can cut down on advertising and employee costs as well as rent. Because of economies of scales, it may be less expensive to have eight screens in one building with one concession area than eight separate theaters, each with one screen and a concession area.

section 7.5 Exhibit 1 — Short- and Long-Run Average Total Costs

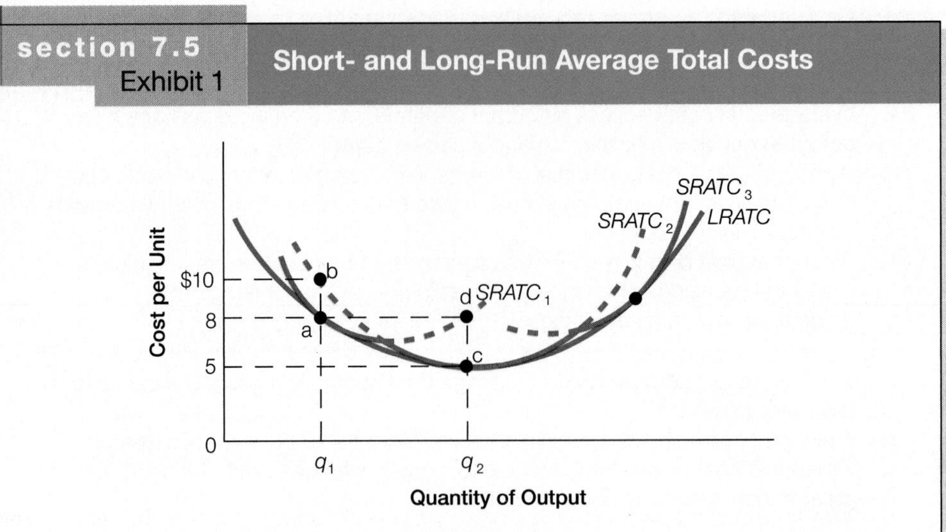

In the short run, some inputs are fixed, like the size of the physical plant or certain machinery. In the long run, firms can increase their capital inputs (fixed in the short run) as well as their inputs that are variable in the short run, in some cases lowering average costs per unit. The curve thus has a shallower U-shape than the short-run average total cost curves. In the long run, all inputs are variable. The *LRATC* is the solid blue line that traces out the three different possible plant sizes, $SRATC_1$, $SRATC_2$, and $SRATC_3$. The *LRATC* shows the lowest average total cost for producing each output in the long run.

$10 per unit rather than at $8 per unit, at point A. However, if the firm planned to produce output level q_2, costs with plant size $SRATC_2$ are lower that those with $SRATC_1$. If output levels in this range were produced with the smaller plant, $SRATC_1$, the plant would be operating beyond designed capacity, point d, and the cost would be higher at $8 per unit rather than at $5 per unit, at point c. That is, plant $SRATC_2$, designed for a larger volume of output than the small plant, would minimize costs for producing quantity q_2.

If a straight line were extended upward from the horizontal output axis on a graph containing the various *SRATC* curves for different-sized plants, the point at which it first struck an *SRATC* curve would indicate the relevant value of *LRATC* for that output level. Thus, in Exhibit 1, for low levels of output, q_1, the lowest average cost point is on curve $SRATC_1$; at output, q_2, it is on $SRATC_2$, and so on. The *LRATC* curve is identical with *SRATC* at the solid scalloped portion of the three short-run cost curves. When there are many possible plant sizes, the successive *SRATC* curves will be close to one another, and the *LRATC* curve will be smooth and U-shaped like the dark solid blue line in Exhibit 1.

The *LRATC* curve is often called a *planning curve,* since it represents the cost data relevant to the firm when it is planning policy relating to scale of operations, output, and price over a long period of time. At a particular time, a firm already in operation has a certain plant and must base its current price and output decisions on the costs with the existing plant. However, when the firm considers the possibility of adjusting its scale of operations, long-run cost estimates are necessary.

economies of scale
occur in an output range where LRATC falls as output increases

constant returns to scale
occur in an output range where LRATC does not change as output varies

diseconomies of scale
occur in an output range where LRATC rises as output expands

THE SHAPE OF THE LONG-RUN ATC CURVE

By examining the long-run average total cost in Exhibit 2, we can see three possible production patterns. In Exhibit 2(a), when *LRATC* falls as output expands, we say that there are **economies of scale** present. In Exhibit 2(b) when the *LRATC* does not vary with output, the firm is facing **constant returns to scale.** And in Exhibit 2(c) when *LRATC* rises as output expands, we say that the firm is facing **diseconomies of scale.**

section 7.5 Exhibit 2 — Economies of Scale, Constant Returns to Scale, and Diseconomies of Scale

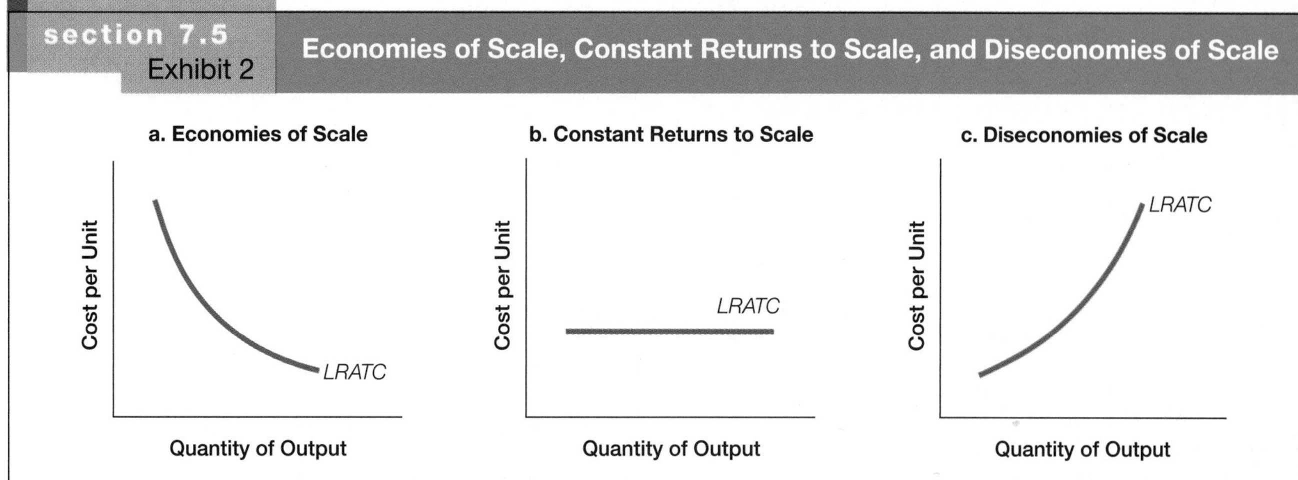

At very low output levels, some reduction of average costs per unit are obtainable by expanding output; in those output ranges, economies of scale exist, as seen in Exhibit 2(a). If the *LRATC* is flat, the average per unit costs will be constant over this range of output, and the firm is experiencing constant returns to scale, as seen in Exhibit 2(b). At higher output ranges, average costs per unit will start rising if the firm enters an output range characterized by diseconomies of scale, as seen in Exhibit 2(c).

The typical firm in an industry may well experience economies of scale at low levels of output, constant returns to scale at higher levels of output, and diseconomies of scale at still higher levels of output, as seen in Exhibit 3. At the **minimum efficient scale,** a plant has exhausted its economies of scale and the long-run average total costs are minimized. This is shown in Exhibit 3. In this constant returns to scale range (the flat portion of the *LRATC*), firms of differing size can compete on a roughly equal basis as far as costs are concerned—that is, they have no cost advantage over firms that are operating at the minimum efficient scale.

minimum efficient scale
the output level where economies of scale are exhausted and constant returns to scale begin

WHY DO ECONOMIES AND DISECONOMIES OF SCALE OCCUR?

As we have just seen, economies of scale exist when there is a reduction in the firm's long-run average costs as output expands. This may occur because a firm can use mass production techniques like assembly line production or capture gains from labor specialization that might not be possible if the firm were producing at lower levels of output. For example, workers might experience greater proficiency gains if they concentrated on a few specific tasks rather than on many different tasks.

Recall that diseconomies of scale exist when there is an increase in the firm's long-run average costs as output expands. This may occur as the firm finds it increasingly difficult to handle the complexities of large-scale management. For example, information and coordination problems tend to increase when a firm becomes very large.

section 7.5 Exhibit 3 — A Typical Long-Run *ATC*

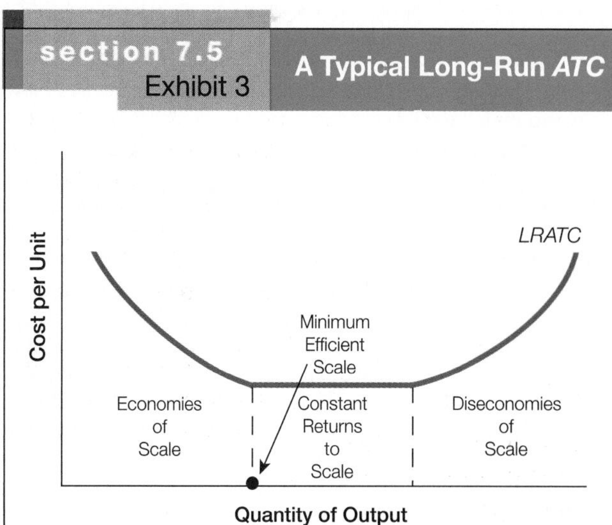

All firms are different but most firms will probably have a long-run *ATC* that declines at low levels of output and then remains constant and eventually will rise at the higher levels of output. The minimum efficient scale is the lowest level of output at which average total costs are minimized.

SHIFTING THE COST CURVES

Any cost curve is based on the assumption that input prices and technology are constant. When these factors change, the cost curves of the firm will shift. For example, in Exhibit 4(a)

In The NEWS

THE COST REVOLUTION

The payoffs from the microprocessor and its spillovers are part of daily life for just about every American . . . because they embody a sweeping capacity to lower the cost of producing goods and services. . . . Technology impacts prices in several ways. Direct costs fall as Information Age tools make it cheaper to produce goods and services. . . . Most important, the microprocessor and its spillovers transform the structure of long-term average costs, not just for New Economy enterprises but for the nation as a whole.

Corporate America invests heavily in computers, shelling out hundreds of billions of dollars in the 1990s for PCs, servers, software, and peripherals. The investment pays off as computers boost the speed, accuracy, and efficiency of just about everything businesses do—from the design studio to the factory floor, from the checkout counter to the accounting department. Information systems shorten supply chains, allowing timely delivery and automated reordering that slash inventory and paperwork costs . . . the new technology is often powerful enough to allow many companies to lower prices, a trend most evident in the computer and electronics industries.

In 1985, when Ford Motor Co. wanted data on how cars withstood accidents, it spent $60,000 to slam a vehicle into a barrier. Today, Ford's supercomputers can simulate the same collision in 15 minutes for $200. In the future, the cost of a frontal "crash" in cyberspace will be down to just $10.

In the airline business, the Final Approach Spacing Tool, air traffic control software developed for NASA, makes takeoffs and landings more efficient. The system has already cut two minutes off the average landing time at Dallas/Fort Worth International Airport. When fully operational nationwide, it will save airlines almost $1 billion a year in jet fuel.

Wal-Mart, the nation's largest retailer, cut up to 20 percent off the cost of operating a delivery truck by installing computers, global positioning gear and cell phones in 4,300 vehicles. Supercomputers produce a thousand fold improvement in seismic data, allowing BP Amoco to find oil for under $1 a barrel, down from nearly $10 a barrel in 1991. Processing an Internet transaction costs a bank just a penny, compared with $1.14 with a pen, paper, and teller.

The economics of the Industrial Age centered on the cost structure of yesterday's major industries—manufacturing, mining, agriculture, and construction. Their costs may fall as output increases, but not for long. Well before demand is satisfied, enterprises exhaust economies of scale and start bidding up prices for scarce inputs. Production costs for additional units rise, slowly at first but then more rapidly.

The Information Age gave birth to companies and industries with a decidedly different cost structure. Their output exhibits increasing returns to scale (economies of scale) over a wide range of products. Instead of rising with additional output, average costs continue to slope downward. Goods and services become cheaper to produce as the size of the market increases. This gives companies a powerful incentive for aggressive pricing, including quantity discounts.

Information Age enterprises need more customers to recoup their investment in new-product development. Today, bigger is often better, which helps explain the surge in mergers and acquisitions in the 1990s. Companies combine to capture the advantages that come from downward sloping long-run average cost curves.

Telecommuting

The ability to work productively at home has jumped, thanks to the spread of personal computers, e-mail, fax machines, cell phones, and the Internet. Roughly 30 million adults currently use the Internet at home for business purposes. The proportion of workers with flexible schedules has risen sharply, from just 15 percent in 1991 (when the World Wide Web was introduced) to nearly 30 percent today. Roughly 20 million Americans now telecommute, working at least one day per month from home during normal business hours. Studies show that telecommuting saves businesses roughly $10,000 annually for a worker earning $44,000—a savings in lost work time and employee retention costs, plus gains in worker productivity. By freeing us from the 8-to-5 company office so we can work when and where we do it best, technology has cut the cost of getting the job done nearly a quarter.

Laparoscopic Surgery

Approximately 600,000 people in America had their gallbladders removed last year, 95 percent of them with a new technique known as laparoscopic cholecystectomy. . . . Patients can resume normal activities in just one week, compared with six weeks or more with yesterday's highly invasive surgery. The 85 percent reduction in lost work time isn't the only savings. The procedure itself costs roughly 10 percent less in hospital and physician fees. Similar savings apply to laparoscopic procedures involving the stomach, appendix, esophagus, abdomen, colon and other organs.

SOURCE: W. Michael Cox and Richard Alm, *1999 Annual Report: The New Paradigm*, Federal Reserve Bank of Dallas. Reprinted with permission.

we see how a per-unit tax increases the marginal cost of each unit of output, shifting the *MC* curve and *ATC* up by the tax amount. The tax does not affect the firm's fixed cost because it is a tax on units produced. If a license to operate fee increased, it would act like a fixed cost and affect only the average total cost curve—shifting *ATC* up by the amount of the fee increase. A lower wage rate or improved technology will reduce marginal costs, shifting *MC* downward along with *ATC*, as in Exhibit 4(b).

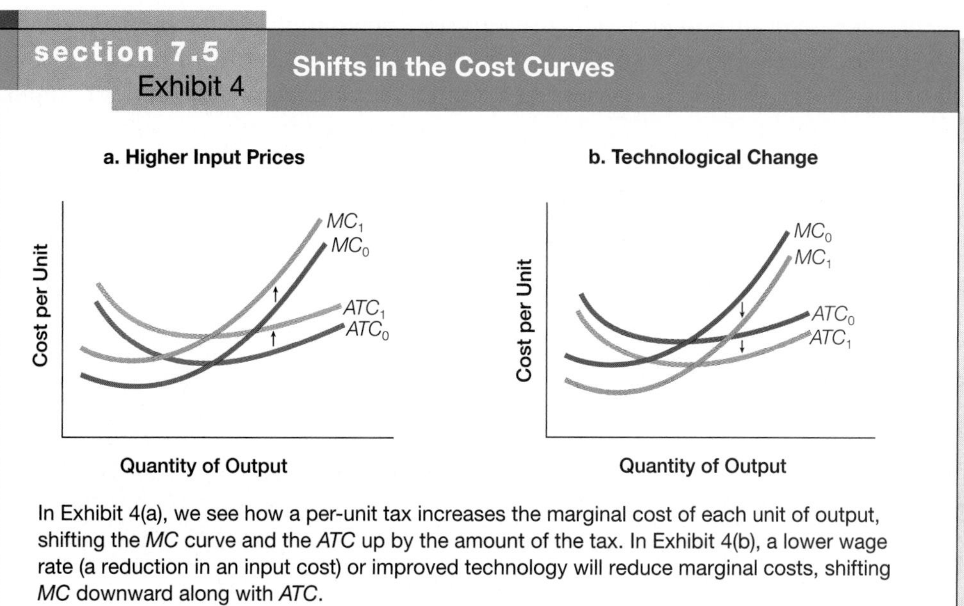

In Exhibit 4(a), we see how a per-unit tax increases the marginal cost of each unit of output, shifting the *MC* curve and the *ATC* up by the amount of the tax. In Exhibit 4(b), a lower wage rate (a reduction in an input cost) or improved technology will reduce marginal costs, shifting *MC* downward along with *ATC*.

Section Check

1. At low output levels, when all inputs can be varied, some firms will experience economies of scale, where their per-unit costs are decreasing as output increases.
2. Firms that expand all inputs beyond a certain point will encounter diseconomies of scale, incurring rising per-unit costs as output grows in the long run.
3. In intermediate output ranges, firms may exhibit roughly constant returns to scale; in this range, their per-unit costs remain stable as output increases.

---

1. What are economies of scale, diseconomies of scale, and constant returns to scale?
2. How might cooking for a family dinner be subject to falling average total cost in the long run as the size of the family grows?

Summary

It is important for a firm to consider its total opportunity costs—that is both its explicit costs and implicit costs. Explicit costs are the opportunity costs of production that require a monetary payment such as a firm paying wages to its workers. Some opportunity costs are implicit—they do not represent an outlay of money or a contractual obligation, like the forgone rent a business would incur if it decided to use all of the office space in its own building rather than renting it out.

Profits are the difference between the total revenues of a firm and its total costs. Accounting profits are based on revenues minus explicit costs. Economic profits occur when the firm is covering its total opportunity cost—both explicit and implicit costs. Firms try to maximize the value of a stream of future profits.

The production function describes the maximum amount of a product that a firm can produce with any combination of inputs, using existing technology. Diminishing marginal product states that as the amount of a variable input is increased, the amount of other (fixed) inputs being held constant, a point ultimately will be reached where the additions to output will decline.

Fixed costs are expenses that stay constant regardless of the level of output. Variable costs change as the level of output changes. Marginal cost is the added cost of producing one more unit of output; it is the change in total cost associated with one more unit of output. It is this cost that is relevant to decisions to produce more or less. When marginal costs are less than average total costs, average total costs must be falling. When marginal costs are greater than average total costs, average total costs must be rising.

In the long run, at low output levels, some firms will experience economies of scale, where their per-unit costs are decreasing as output increases. At a higher level of output, firms may experience constant returns to scale; in this range, their per-unit costs remain stable as output increases. At an even higher level of output, firms may experience diseconomies of scale, rising per-unit costs as output grows.

Key Terms and Concepts

explicit costs 142
implicit costs 142
profits 143
accounting profits 143
economic profits 143
sunk costs 144
short run 145
long run 145
total product (*TP*) 146
marginal product (*MP*) 147
diminishing marginal product 147
fixed costs 148
total fixed costs (*TFC*) 148
variable costs 148
total variable cost (*TVC*) 149
total cost (*TC*) 149
average total cost (*ATC*) 149
average fixed cost (*AFC*) 149
average variable cost (*AVC*) 149
marginal cost (*MC*) 149
economies of scale 156
constant returns to scale 156
diseconomies of scale 156
minimum efficient scale 157

Review Questions

1. What happens to the cost of growing strawberries on your own land if a housing developer offers you three times what you thought your land was worth?
2. As a farmer, you work for yourself using your own tractor, equipment, and farm structures, and you cultivate your own land. Why might it be difficult to calculate your profits from farming?
3. Say that your firm's total product curve includes the following data: 1 worker can produce 8 units of output; 2 workers, 20 units; 3 workers, 34 units; 4 workers, 50 units; 5 workers, 60 units; 6 workers, 70 units; 7 workers, 76 units; 8 workers, 78 units; and 9 workers, 77 units.
   a. What is the marginal product of the seventh worker?
   b. When does the law of diminishing product set in?
   c. Under these conditions, would you ever choose to employ nine workers?
4. Why does the law of diminishing marginal product imply the law of increasing costs?
5. What is likely to happen to your marginal costs when adding output requires working beyond an eight-hour day, if workers must be paid time-and-a-half wages beyond an eight-hour day?
6. A one-day ticket to visit the Screaming Coasters theme park costs $36, but you can also get a two-consecutive-day ticket for $40. What is the average cost per day for the two-day ticket? What is the marginal cost of the second consecutive day?
7. As a movie exhibitor, you can choose between paying a flat fee of $5,000 to show a movie for a week or paying a fee of $2 per customer. Will your choice affect your fixed and variable costs? How?
8. If your university pays lecture notetakers $20 per hour to take notes in your economics class, and then sells subscriptions for $15 per student, is the cost of the lecture notetaker a fixed or variable cost of selling an additional subscription?
9. How might a university cafeteria cooking for 400 students rather than for 3 students be subject to economies of scale in the long run?
10. Go to the Sexton Web site at **http://sexton.swcollege.com** and click on "Costco." Do you think that Costco (a large discount warehouse store) obtains economies of scale? How is Costco able to undercut the prices of many small stores? Does selling products on-line help capture economies of scale?

chapter 7 Study Guide

Fill in the Blanks

1. Profits are defined as TOTAL REVENUES minus TOTAL COST.
2. The cost of producing a good is measured by the worth of the MOST VALUABLE alternative that was given up to obtain the resource.
3. Explicit costs are input costs that require a MONATARY payment.
4. Whenever we talk about costs—explicit or implicit—we are talking about OPPORTUNITY cost.
5. Economists generally assume that the ultimate goal of a firm is to MAXIMIZE profits.
6. Accounting profits equal actual revenues minus actual expenditures of cash (explicit costs), so they do not include IMPLICIT costs.
7. Economists consider a zero economic profit a normal profit because it means that the firm is covering both IMPLICIT and EXPLICIT costs—the total opportunity cost of its resources.
8. SUNK costs are costs that have already been incurred and cannot be recovered.
9. Because it takes more time to vary some inputs than others, we must distinguish between the SHORT run and the LONG run.
10. The long run is a period of time in which the firm can adjust ALL inputs.
11. In the long run, all costs are VARIABLE costs and will change as output changes.
12. The total product schedule shows the total amount of OUTPUT generated as the level of the variable input increases.
13. The marginal product of any single input is the change in total product resulting from a SMALL change in the amount of that input used.
14. As the amount of a variable input is increased, the amount of other fixed inputs being held constant, a point ultimately will be reached beyond which marginal product will decline. This is called DIMINISHING MARGINAL PRODUCT.
15. The short-run total costs of a business fall into two distinct categories: FIXED costs and VARIABLE costs.
16. Fixed costs are costs that DON'T CHANGE with the level of output.
17. In the short run, fixed costs cannot be avoided without GOING OUT OF BUSINESS.
18. The sum of a firm's fixed costs is called its TOTAL FIXED COST.
19. Costs that are not fixed are called VARIABLE costs.
20. The sum of a firm's variable costs is called its TOTAL VARIABLE COST.
21. The sum of a firm's total FIXED costs and total VARIABLE costs is called its total cost.
22. Average total cost equals TOTAL COST divided by the LEVEL OF OUTPUT produced.
23. Average fixed cost equals TOTAL FIXED COST divided by the LEVEL OF OUTPUT produced.

24. ________ equals total variable cost divided by the level of output produced.

25. Marginal costs are the ________ costs associated with the "last" unit of output produced.

26. A fixed cost curve is always a ________ line because, by definition, fixed costs are the same at all output levels.

27. The reason for high average total costs when a firm is producing a very small amount of output is the high ________ costs.

28. The average total cost curve rises at high levels of output because of ________ product.

29. When *AVC* is falling, *MC* must be ________ than *AVC;* and when *AVC* is rising, *MC* must be ________ than *AVC.*

30. In the ________ run, a company cannot vary its plant size and equipment, so the firm can only expand output by employing more ________ inputs.

31. The *LRATC* curve is often called a ________ curve because it represents the cost data relevant to a firm when it is planning policy relating to scale of operations, output, and price over a long period of time.

32. When *LRATC* falls as output expands, there are ________ of scale. When the *LRATC* does not vary with output, the firm faces ________ to scale. When the *LRATC* rises as output expands, there are ________ of scale.

33. At the ________ scale, a plant has exhausted its economies of scale and the long-run average total costs are minimized.

34. Any particular cost curve is based on the assumption that ________ prices and ________ are constant.

35. ________ may occur as a firm finds it increasingly difficult to handle the complexities of large-scale management.

True or False

1. Explicit costs include both wages paid to workers and the opportunity cost of using one's own land, labor, or capital.

2. Because implicit costs do not represent an explicit outlay of money, they are not real costs.

3. When economists say firms try to maximize profits, they mean that firms try to maximize the difference between what they receive for their goods and services—their total revenue—and what they give up for their inputs—their total costs (explicit and implicit).

4. Economic profits equal actual revenues minus all explicit and implicit costs.

5. Economists consider a zero economic profit to be less than a normal profit rate.

6. Earning zero economic profit is different from earning zero accounting profit.

7. Sunk costs are irrelevant for any future action.

8. The short run is defined as a period too brief for some inputs to be varied.

9. In the long run, the inputs that do not change with output are called fixed inputs or fixed factors of production.

10. The long run can vary considerably in length from industry to industry.

11. Total product will typically start at a low level and increase slowly at first and then more rapidly as the amount of the variable input increases.

12. Marginal product first rises as the result of more effective use of fixed inputs and then falls.

13. Diminishing marginal product stems from the crowding of the fixed inputs with more and more of the variable input.

14. A firm never knowingly allows itself to reach the point where the marginal product becomes negative.

15. If a firm were producing at the level where the marginal product of an input was negative, its profits would be lower as a result.

16. Fixed costs for a given period have to be paid only if a firm produces output in that period.

17. Variable costs vary with the level of output, while fixed costs do not.

18. Marginal cost shows the change in total costs associated with a change in output by one unit, or the costs of producing one more unit of output.

19. Marginal costs are really just a useful way to view changes in fixed costs as output changes.

20. The total cost curve is the summation of the total variable cost and total fixed cost curves.

21. The average fixed cost curve is always a horizontal line, since fixed costs do not change with output.

22. The marginal cost curve crosses the average variable cost and average total cost curves at those curves' lowest points.

23. At output levels where average total cost is rising, marginal cost must be greater than average total cost.

24. The average fixed cost curve declines whether the marginal cost curve is rising or falling.

25. The average total cost curve is usually U-shaped.

26. It is the declining average variable cost curve that is primarily responsible for the falling segment of the average total cost curve.

27. Diminishing marginal product first sets in at the minimum point of the average total cost curve.

28. Diminishing marginal product causes the marginal cost curve to increase, eventually causing the average variable cost and average total cost curves to rise.

29. *MC* is equal to *AVC* at the lowest point on the *AVC* curve, and it is equal to *ATC* at the lowest point on the *ATC* curve.

30. Over long enough time periods, firms can vary all of their productive inputs.

31. As we move along the *LRATC*, the factory size changes with the quantity of output.

32. A typical firm experiences economies of scale at low levels of output, constant returns to scale at higher levels of output, and diseconomies of scale at still higher levels of output.

33. Diseconomies of scale may exist because a firm can use mass production techniques or capture gains from further labor specialization not possible at lower levels of output.

34. When input prices or technology changes, the cost curves of a firm will shift.

35. A lower wage will reduce *MC*, *AVC*, and *ATC*.

Multiple Choice

1. An explicit cost
   a. is an opportunity cost.
   b. is an out-of-pocket expense.
   c. does not require an outlay of money.
   d. is characterized by both a and b.
   e. is characterized by both a and c.

2. Which of the following is *false?*
   a. Explicit costs are input costs that require a monetary payment.
   b. Implicit costs do not represent an explicit outlay of money.
   c. Both implicit and explicit costs are opportunity costs.
   d. Sunk costs are irrelevant for any future action.
   e. All of the above are true.

3. Which of the following is *false?*
   a. Profits are a firm's total revenue minus its total costs.
   b. Accounting profits are actual revenues minus actual expenditures of money.
   c. Economic profits are actual revenues minus all explicit and implicit costs.
   d. If a firm has any implicit costs, its economic profits exceed its accounting profits.
   e. All of the above are *true.*

4. The crucial difference between how economists and accountants analyze the profitability of a business has to do with whether or not ______________ are included when calculating total production costs.
   a. implicit costs
   b. cash payments
   c. sunk costs
   d. explicit costs

5. Which of the following is *true?*
   a. If a firm's implicit costs are zero, accounting profits equal economic profits.
   b. If a firm's implicit costs are positive, accounting profits exceed economic profits.
   c. If a firm's implicit costs are positive, economic profits exceed accounting profits.
   d. Both a and b are true.
   e. Both a and c are true.

6. Cassie produces and sells 300 jars of homemade jelly each month for $3 each. Each month, she pays $200 for jars, pays $150 for ingredients, and uses her own time, with an opportunity cost of $300. Her economic profits each month are
   a. $250.
   b. $400.
   c. $550.
   d. $600.
   e. minus $350.

7. Sunk costs
   a. should be included when weighing the marginal costs of production against the marginal benefits received.
   b. have already been incurred and cannot be recovered.
   c. plus variable costs equal the total costs of production.
   d. are relevant to future decisions and should be carefully considered.

8. The short run
   a. is a period too brief for any inputs to be varied.
   b. is a period in which there are no fixed costs.
   c. is normally a period of one year.
   d. is none of the above.

9. The long run
   a. is a period in which a firm can adjust all its inputs.
   b. can vary in length from industry to industry.
   c. is a period in which all costs are variable costs.
   d. is characterized by all of the above.

10. The long-run production period
    a. is a time when all inputs are variable.
    b. varies in length according to how capital goods are specialized.
    c. is likely longer for a steel manufacturer than for a retailer who sells watches off a cart at the local mall.
    d. is characterized by all of the above.

11. Which of the following most accurately describes the long-run period?
    a. The long run is a period of time in which a firm is unable to vary some of its factors of production.
    b. In the long run, a firm is able to expand output by utilizing additional workers and raw materials, but not physical capital.
    c. The long run is of sufficient length to allow a firm to alter its plant capacity and all other factors of production.
    d. The long run is of sufficient length to allow a firm to transform economic losses into economic profits.
    e. Both a and b most accurately describe the long-run period.

12. Production in the short run
    a. is subject to the law of diminishing marginal product.
    b. involves some fixed factors.
    c. can be increased by employing another unit of a variable input, as long as the marginal product of that input is positive.
    d. is characterized by all of the above.
    e. is characterized by none of the above.

13. A production function shows the relationship between
    a. variable inputs and fixed inputs.
    b. variable inputs and output.
    c. costs and output.
    d. inputs and costs.
    e. production and sales revenue.

14. Diminishing marginal product
    a. occurs in the long run but not in the short run.
    b. occurs in the short run but not in the long run.
    c. occurs both in the long run and the short run.
    d. occurs in neither the long run nor the short run.

15. Diminishing marginal productivity in a frozen-pizza company means that
   a. hiring additional workers causes the total output of pizza to fall.
   b. hiring additional workers does not change the total output of pizza produced.
   c. hiring additional workers adds fewer and fewer pizzas to total output.
   d. the average total cost of production must be decreasing.

16. If the marginal product of a firm's only variable input is negative,
   a. its total product is growing at a decreasing rate.
   b. it will use more of the variable input until its marginal product is again positive.
   c. it will reduce its use of the variable input.
   d. its total product is minimized.
   e. none of the above would be true.

17. Total fixed costs
   a. do not vary with the level of output.
   b. cannot be avoided in the short run without going out of business.
   c. do not exist in the long run.
   d. are characterized by all of the above.

18. Which of the following is most likely a variable cost for a business?
   a. the loan payment on funds borrowed when a new building is constructed
   b. payments for electricity
   c. the lease payment on a warehouse used by the business
   d. the opportunity cost of the heavy equipment installed in a factory

19. The change in total cost that results from the production of one additional unit of output is called
   a. marginal revenue.
   b. average variable cost.
   c. marginal cost.
   d. average total cost.
   e. average fixed cost.

20. Which short-run curve typically declines continuously as output expands?
   a. average variable cost
   b. average total cost
   c. average fixed cost
   d. marginal cost
   e. none of the above

21. Which of the following is true?
   a. The short-run *ATC* exceeds the short-run *AVC* at any given level of output.
   b. If the short-run *ATC* curve is rising, the short-run *AVC* curve is also rising.
   c. The short-run *AFC* is always falling with increased output, whether the short-run *MC* curve is greater or less than short-run *AFC*.
   d. If short-run *MC* is less than short-run *AVC*, short-run *AVC* is falling.
   e. All of the above are true.

22. Which of the following is false in the short run?
   a. *ATC* is usually U-shaped.
   b. Declining *AFC*s are the primary reason *ATC* decreases at low levels of output.
   c. *ATC* increases at high levels of output because of diminishing marginal product.
   d. Diminishing marginal product sets in at the minimum point of *ATC*.
   e. All of the above are true in the short run.

23. Typically, what is the shape of the average total cost curve for a firm in the short run?
 a. Typically, an average total cost curve is U-shaped.
 b. Typically, an average total cost curve constantly slopes upward as output expands and eventually approaches an infinite dollar amount at high rates of output.
 c. Typically, an average total cost curve is a vertical line.
 d. Typically, an average total cost curve slopes downward as output expands and approaches the *X*-axis when output is very large.

24. Which of the following is true in the short run?
 a. *MC* equals *ATC* at the lowest point of *ATC*.
 b. *MC* equals *AVC* at the lowest point of *AVC*.
 c. When *AVC* is at its minimum point, *ATC* is falling.
 d. When *ATC* is at its minimum point, *AVC* is rising.
 e. All of the above are true.

25. Which of the following is always true?
 a. When marginal cost is less than average total cost, average total cost is increasing.
 b. When average fixed cost is falling, marginal cost must be less than average fixed cost.
 c. When average variable cost is falling, marginal cost must be greater than average variable cost.
 d. When marginal cost is greater than average total cost, average total cost is increasing.

26. When marginal product is increasing,
 a. marginal cost is increasing.
 b. marginal cost is decreasing.
 c. average variable cost is increasing.
 d. average total cost is increasing.
 e. total cost is decreasing.

27. Luke Spacewalker realizes that his space taxi service is operating in the region of diminishing marginal product. As he provides more taxi service in the short run, what will happen to the marginal cost of providing the additional service?
 a. It is impossible to say anything about marginal cost with the information provided.
 b. Marginal cost will decrease.
 c. Marginal cost will increase.
 d. Marginal cost will stay the same.

28. If Bob's Burger Barn's city permit to operate rose by $3,000 per year,
 a. that would shift its *MC* curve upward.
 b. that would shift its *AVC* curve upward.
 c. that would shift its *ATC* curve upward.
 d. that would shift its *MC*, *AVC*, and *ATC* curves upward.

29. If a firm's *ATC* is falling in the long run, then
 a. it is subject to economies of scale over that range of output.
 b. it is subject to diseconomies of scale over that range of output.
 c. it is subject to constant return to scale over that range of output.
 d. it has reached the minimum efficient scale of production.
 e. both c and d are true.

30. In the long run,
  a. the average fixed cost curve is U-shaped.
  b. average fixed cost exceeds the average variable cost of production.
  c. all costs are variable.
  d. all costs are fixed.
  e. none of the above are correct.

31. When there are economies of scale in production,
  a. long-run average total cost declines as output expands.
  b. long-run average total cost increases as output expands.
  c. marginal cost increases as output expands.
  d. the marginal product of an input diminishes with increased utilization.

32. The lowest level of output at which a firm's goods are produced at minimum long-run average total cost is called
  a. the point of zero marginal cost.
  b. the point of diminishing returns.
  c. the minimum total product.
  d. the minimum efficient scale.
  e. plant capacity.

Problems

1. Fill in the rest of the production function for Candy's Candies from the information provided.

Labor (workers)	Total Product (pounds)	Marginal Product (pounds)
0	________	________
1	20	________
2	44	________
3	62	________
4	________	12
5	________	6
6	78	________

  a. Candy's Candies begins to experience diminishing marginal product with which worker?
  b. Does Candy's Candies ever experience negative marginal product? If so, with the addition of which worker?

2. Use the graph below to answer the following questions.
   a. Curve A represents which cost curve?
   b. Curve B represents which cost curve?
   c. Curve C represents which cost curve?
   d. Curve D represents which cost curve?
   e. Why must curve D pass through the minimum points of both curve B and curve C?
   f. What significance does the point where curve A intersects curve D have?

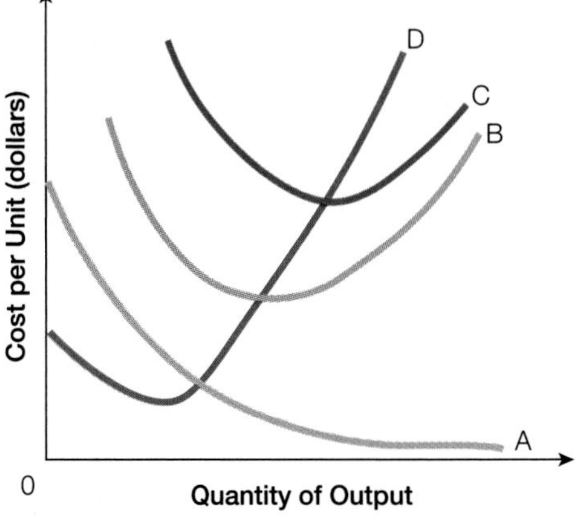

3. Fill in the rest of the cost function for Bob's Beautiful Bowling Balls.

Output	Total Fixed Costs	Total Variable Costs	Total Costs	Average Fixed Cost	Average Variable Cost	Average Total Cost	Marginal Cost
1	$200	$60	$______	$______	$______	$______	$______
2	______	100	______	______	______	______	______
3	______	120	______	______	______	______	______
4	______	128	______	______	______	______	______
5	______	180	______	______	______	______	______
6	______	252	______	______	______	______	______
7	______	316	______	______	______	______	______
8	______	436	______	______	______	______	______

Competition

8.1 THE FOUR DIFFERENT MARKET STRUCTURES
What are the characteristics of the four market structures?

8.2 AN INDIVIDUAL PRICE TAKER'S DEMAND CURVE
Why can't an individual price taker charge more than the market price?

8.3 PROFIT MAXIMIZATION
What is the profit-maximizing output level for a perfectly competitive firm?

8.4 SHORT-RUN PROFITS AND LOSSES
How can you determine if a perfectly competitive firm is generating a short-run profit or loss?

8.5 LONG-RUN EQUILIBRIUM
What is the long-run response to economic profits in perfect competition?

8.6 LONG-RUN SUPPLY
What are constant- and increasing-cost industries?

section 8.1

The Four Different Market Structures

- What are the four market structures?
- What are the characteristics of a perfectly competitive firm?
- What is a price taker?

Economists have identified four different market structures in which firms operate: perfect competition, monopoly, monopolistic competition, and oligopoly. Each structure or environment has certain key characteristics that distinguish it from the other structures. In practice it is sometimes difficult to decide precisely which structure a given firm or industry most appropriately fits, since the dividing line between the structures is not entirely crystal clear.

Perfect Competition

A competitive market is a market situation where there are a large number of buyers and sellers—perhaps thousands or very conceivably millions. In addition, no single firm produces more than an extremely small proportion of total output. This means that no single firm can influence the market price or quantity. Firms are price takers; they must accept the price for the product as determined by the forces of demand and supply. Individually, they are too small and powerless to alter prices.

perfect competition
a market with many buyers and sellers, selling homogeneous goods, easy market entry and exit, and no firm can affect the market price

Firms in **perfect competition** sell a homogeneous or standardized product. In the wheat market, which approximates the conditions of perfect competition, it is not possible to determine any significant and consistent qualitative differences in the wheat produced by different farmers. New firms can easily enter the market.

Monopoly

monopoly
a firm that is the single seller of a product without close substitutes

On the other end of the continuum of market environments is pure **monopoly.** This is a market structure where there is a single seller—the seller sets the price that will maximize their profits. An example might be the local cable company in your town. However, even that industry, which once had monopoly power, is losing market share to satellite dishes, which have become an attractive substitute for a number of buyers.

Monopolistic Competition

monopolistic competition
a market structure with many firms selling differentiated products

Monopolistic competition falls between perfect competition and monopoly. Monopolistic competition is a market structure where firms have both an element of competition and an element of monopoly power. Because each firm's product is differentiated at least slightly from that of other competitors, it has some monopoly power. For example, in a given city of 100,000 there may be 100 gasoline service stations, each slightly different in the brand of gas that they sell, the services that they provide, the hours that they stay open, the location of the stations, and whether or not they provide repair work. However, because there are so many competing stations vying for your business it also has an element of competitive markets.

Oligopoly

Like monopolistic competition, **oligopoly** also falls between perfect competition and monopoly. Oligopoly exists when a *few* firms produce similar or identical goods, as opposed to one firm (monopoly) or many (competitive market). Unlike pure monopoly, oligopoly allows for some competition between firms; unlike competition, individual firms have a significant share of the total market for the good being produced.

oligopoly
a market structure with only a few sellers offering similar or identical products

The oligopolist is very conscious of the actions of competing firms. In this respect, the oligopoly structure differs from others. In perfect competition, farmer Jones does not worry about what farmer Smith does, since neither of them is big enough to have any influence on overall market conditions. In monopoly, there is no other firm to worry about. In true monopolistic competition, there are many relatively small firms, so again a firm usually does not worry much about the impact on it of the behavior of a competing firm. In oligopoly, though, a firm's behavior is closely related to that of its competitors. General Motor's pricing decisions influence the pricing decisions of Ford, Chrysler and other manufacturers, including ones located in other countries. The oligopolist does have some control over price and thus is a price-searcher. Note that the oligopoly may involve a standardized product (like steel, aluminum, or crude oil) or a differentiated one (automobiles, refrigerators, TV sets).

Can the owner of this orchard charge a noticeably higher price for the same quality of apples? What if she charges a lower price for the same quality apples? How many apples can she sell at the market price?

Economists often distinguish the perfectly competitive market from the imperfectly competitive markets of monopoly, monopolistic competition, and oligopoly. The differences between each of these markets will become more clear as we look at each model separately in the chapters to come. Because we will often compare perfect competition to the other market structures, it is a good starting point for our study of the four market models. Let us take a closer look now at the perfectly competitive model.

A PERFECTLY COMPETITIVE MARKET

This chapter examines perfect competition, a market structure characterized by (1) many buyers and sellers, (2) an identical (homogeneous) product, and (3) easy market entry and exit. Let's examine these characteristics in greater detail.

Many Buyers and Sellers

In a perfectly competitive market there are *many buyers and sellers* trading identical goods. Because each firm is so small in relation to the industry, its production decisions have no impact on the market—each regards price as something over which it has little control. This is why perfectly competitive firms are called **price takers.** That is, they must take the price given by the market because their influence on price is insignificant. If the price of apples in the apple market is $2 a pound, then individual apple farmers will receive $2 per pound for their apples. Similarly, no single buyer of apples can influence the price of apples because each buyer purchases only a small amount of the apples traded. We will see how this works in more detail in Section 8.3.

price taker
a perfectly competitive firm takes the price that it is given by the intersection of the market demand and market supply curve

COURTESY OF THE CHICAGO BOARD OF TRADE

At the Chicago Board of Trade (CBOT), prices get set by thousands of buyers interacting with thousands of sellers. The goods in question are typically standardized (e.g., grade A winter wheat) and information is readily available. For example, if a news story breaks on an infestation of the cotton crop, the price of cotton will rise immediately. CBOT price information is used to determine the value of a particular commodity all over the world.

Identical (Homogeneous) Products

Consumers believe that all firms in perfectly competitive markets *sell identical (or homogeneous) products.* For example, in the wheat market, it is not possible to determine any significant and consistent qualitative differences in the wheat produced by different farmers. Wheat produced by Farmer Jones looks, feels, smells, and tastes like that produced by Farmer Smith. In short, a bushel of wheat is a bushel of wheat. The products of all the firms are considered to be perfect substitutes.

Easy Entry and Exit

Product markets characterized by perfect competition have no significant *barriers to entry or exit.* This means that it is fairly easy for entrepreneurs to become suppliers of the product or, if they are already producers, to stop supplying the product. "Fairly easy" does not mean that any person on the street can instantly enter the business, but rather that the financial, legal, educational, and other barriers to entering the business are modest, so that large numbers of people can overcome the barriers and enter the business if they so desire in any given time period. If buyers can easily switch from one seller to another and sellers can easily enter or exit the industry, then we have met the perfectly competitive condition of easy entry and exit. Because of this easy market entry, perfectly competitive markets generally consist of a large number of small suppliers.

A perfectly competitive market is approximated most closely in highly organized markets for securities and agricultural commodities, such as the New York Stock Exchange or the Chicago Board of Trade. Wheat, corn, soybeans, cotton, and many other agricultural products are sold in perfectly competitive markets. While the assumptions for a perfectly competitive firm may seem a bit unrealistic, it is important to note that studying the model of perfect competition is useful because there are many markets that resemble perfect competition—that is, markets where firms face very elastic (flat) demand curves and relatively easy entry and exit. It also gives us a standard of comparison. In other words, we can make comparisons with the perfectly competitive model to help us evaluate what is going on in the real world.

Section Check

1. There are four main market structures: perfect competition, monopoly, monopolistic competition, and oligopoly.
2. A perfectly competitive market is characterized by many buyers and sellers, an identical (homogeneous) product, and easy market entry and exit.
3. Consumers believe that all firms in perfectly competitive markets sell virtually identical (homogeneous) products. The products of all the firms are considered to be perfect substitutes.
4. Because there are so many buyers and so many sellers, neither buyers nor sellers have any control over price in perfect competition. They must take the going price and are called price takers.
5. Perfectly competitive markets have no significant barriers to entry. That is, the barriers are significantly modest so that many sellers can enter or exit the industry.

---

1. Why do perfectly competitive markets involve homogeneous goods?
2. Why does the absence of significant barriers to entry tend to result in a large number of suppliers?
3. Why does the fact that perfectly competitive firms are "small" relative to the market make them price takers?
4. Why is the market for used furniture unlikely to be perfectly competitive?

section
8.2

An Individual Price Taker's Demand Curve

- Why won't individual price takers raise or lower their prices?
- Can individual price takers sell all they want at the market price?
- Will the position of individual price takers' demand curves change when market price changes?

AN INDIVIDUAL FIRM'S DEMAND CURVE

Perfectly competitive firms are price takers; that is, they must sell at the market-determined price, where the market price and output are determined by the intersection of the market supply and demand curves, as seen in Exhibit 1(a). Individual wheat farmers know that they cannot dispose of their wheat at any figure higher than the current market price; if they attempt to charge a higher price, potential buyers would simply make their purchases from other wheat farmers. And they certainly would not knowingly charge a lower price, because they could sell all they want at the market price.

Likewise, in a perfectly competitive market, individual sellers can change their output and it will not alter the market price. This is possible because of the large number of sellers who are selling identical products. Each producer provides such a small fraction of the total supply that a change in the amount they offer does *not* have a noticeable effect

section 8.2 Exhibit 1 — Market and Individual Firm Demand Curves in Perfect Competition

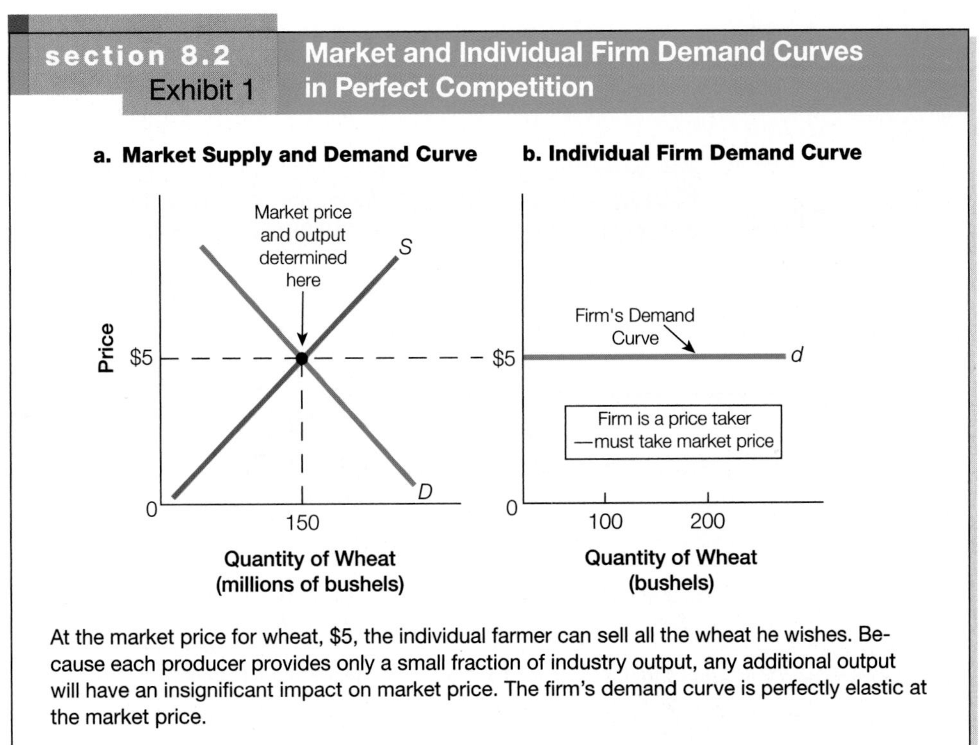

At the market price for wheat, $5, the individual farmer can sell all the wheat he wishes. Because each producer provides only a small fraction of industry output, any additional output will have an insignificant impact on market price. The firm's demand curve is perfectly elastic at the market price.

on market equilibrium price. In a perfectly competitive market, then, an individual firm can sell as much as it wishes to place on the market at the prevailing price; the demand, as seen by the seller, is perfectly elastic.

It is easy to construct the demand curve for an individual seller in a perfectly competitive market. Remember, she won't charge more than the market price because no one will buy it, and she won't charge less because she can sell all she wants at the market price. Thus, the farmer's demand curve is horizontal over the entire range of output that she could possibly produce. If the prevailing market price of the product is $5, the farmer's demand curve will be represented graphically by a horizontal line at the market price of $5, as shown in Exhibit 1(b).

A CHANGE IN MARKET PRICE AND THE FIRM'S DEMAND CURVE

To say that producers under perfect competition regard price as a given is not to say that price is constant. The *position* of the firm's demand curve varies with every change in the market price. In Exhibit 2, we see that when the market price for wheat increases, say as a result of an increase in market demand, the price-taking firm will receive a higher price for all of its output. Or when the market price decreases, say as a result of a decrease in market demand, the price-taking firm will receive a lower price for all of its output.

In effect, sellers are provided with current information about market demand and supply conditions as a result of price changes. It is an essential aspect of the perfectly competitive model that sellers respond to the signals provided by such price movements, so they must alter their behavior over time in the light of actual experience, revising their production decisions to reflect changes in market price. In this respect, the perfectly competitive model is very straightforward; it does not assume any knowledge on the part of individual buyers and sellers about market demand and supply—they only have to know the price of the good they sell.

section 8.2 Exhibit 2 — Market Prices and the Position of a Firm's Demand Curve

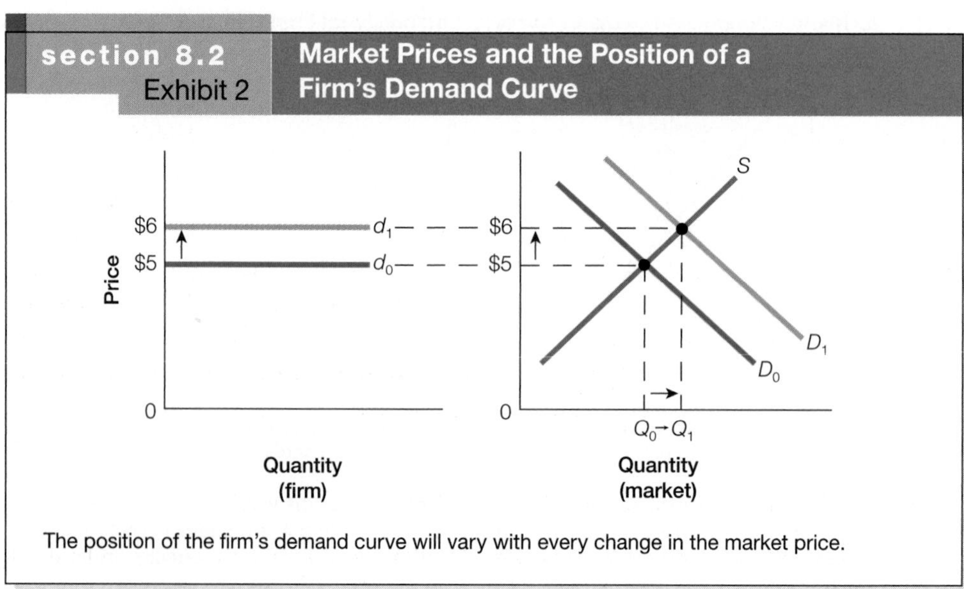

The position of the firm's demand curve will vary with every change in the market price.

Section Check

1. An individual seller won't sell at a higher price than the going price because buyers can purchase the same good from someone else at the going price.
2. Individual sellers won't sell for less than the going price because they are so small relative to the market that they can sell all they want at the going price.
3. The position of the individual firm's demand curve varies directly with the market price.

---

1. Why would a perfectly competitive firm not try to raise or lower its price?
2. Why can we represent the demand curve of a perfectly competitive firm as perfectly elastic (horizontal) at the market price?
3. How does an individual perfectly competitive firm's demand curve change when the market price changes?
4. If the marginal cost facing every producer of a product shifted up, would the position of the perfectly competitive firm's demand curve be likely to change as a result? Why or why not?

section 8.3

Profit Maximization

- What is total revenue?
- What is average revenue?
- What is marginal revenue?
- Why does the firm maximize profits where marginal revenue equals marginal costs?

REVENUES IN A PERFECTLY COMPETITIVE MARKET

The objective of the firm is to maximize profits. To maximize profits the firm wants to produce the amount that maximizes the difference between its total revenues and total costs. In this section, we will examine the different ways to look at revenue in a perfectly competitive market: total revenue, average revenue, and marginal revenue.

TOTAL REVENUE

Total revenue (*TR*) is the revenue that the firm receives from the sale of its products. Total revenue from a product equals the price of the good (P) times the quantity (q) of units sold ($TR = P \times q$). For example, if a farmer sells 10 bushels of wheat a day for $5 a bushel, his total revenue is $50 ($5 × 10 bushels). (Note: We will use the small letter q to denote the single firm's output and reserve the large Q for the output of the entire market. For example, q would be used to represent the output of one lettuce grower, while Q would be used to represent the output of all lettuce growers in the lettuce market.)

total revenue (*TR*)
the product price times the quantity sold

AVERAGE REVENUE AND MARGINAL REVENUE

Average revenue (*AR*) equals total revenue divided by the number of units sold of the product (TR/q, or $[P \times q]/q$). For example, if the farmer sells 10 bushels at $5 a bushel,

average revenue (*AR*)
total revenue divided by the number of units sold

section 8.3 Exhibit 1 **Revenues for a Perfectly Competitive Firm**

Quantity (q)	Price (P)	Total Revenue ($TR = P \times q$)	Average Revenue ($AR = TR/q$)	Marginal Revenue ($MR = \Delta TR/\Delta q$)
1	$5	$ 5	$5	
				$5
2	5	10	5	
				5
3	5	15	5	
				5
4	5	20	5	
				5
5	5	25	5	

total revenue is $50 and average revenue is $5 ($50/10 bushels = $5 per bushel). So, in perfect competition, average revenue is equal to price of the good.

marginal revenue (*MR*) *the increase in total revenue resulting from a one-unit increase in sales*

Marginal revenue (*MR*) is the additional revenue derived from the production of one more unit of the good. In other words, marginal revenue represents the increase in total revenue that results from the sale of one more unit. In a perfectly competitive market, because additional units of output can be sold without reducing the price of the product, marginal revenue is constant at all outputs and equal to average revenue. For example, if the price of wheat per bushel is $5, the marginal revenue is $5. Because total revenue is equal to price multiplied by quantity ($TR = P \times q$), as we add one additional unit of output, total revenue will always increase by the amount of the product price, $5. Marginal revenue facing a perfectly competitive firm is equal to the price of the good.

In perfect competition, then, we know that marginal revenue, average revenue, and price are all equal: $P = MR = AR$. These relationships are clearly illustrated in the calculation presented in Exhibit 1.

section 8.3 Exhibit 2 **Finding the Profit-Maximizing Level of Output**

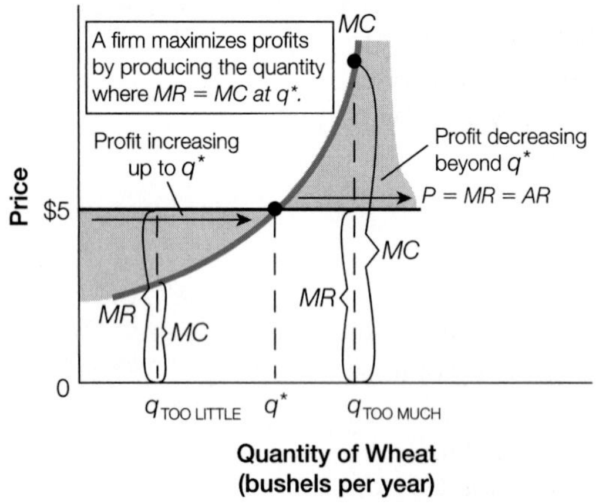

At any output below q^*, like at $q_{\text{TOO LITTLE}}$, the marginal revenue (MR) from expanding output exceeds the added costs (MC) of that output, so additional profits can be made by expanding output. Beyond q^*, like at $q_{\text{TOO MUCH}}$, marginal costs exceed marginal revenue, so output expansion is unprofitable and output should be reduced. The profit-maximizing level of output is at q^*, where the profit-maximizing output rule is followed—the firm should produce the level of output where $MR = MC$.

HOW DO FIRMS MAXIMIZE PROFITS?

Now that we have discussed both the firm's costs curves (chapter 7) and the firm's revenues, we are ready to see how a firm maximizes its profits. A firm's profits equal its total revenues minus its total costs. But at what output level will a firm produce and sell in order to maximize profits? There are two methods for identifying this output, the marginal approach and the total cost–total revenue approach. In all types of market environments, firms will maximize profits at that output that maximizes the difference between total revenue and total costs, which is at the same output level where marginal revenue equals marginal costs.

EQUATING MARGINAL REVENUE AND MARGINAL COST

The importance of equating marginal revenue and marginal costs is seen in Exhibit 2. As output expands beyond zero up to q^*, the marginal revenue derived from each unit of the expanded output exceeds the marginal cost of that unit of output, so the expansion of output creates additional profits. This addition to profit is shown as the left-most shaded section in Exhibit 2. As long as marginal revenues exceed marginal costs, profits continue to grow. For example, if the firm decides to produce $q_{\text{TOO LITTLE}}$, the firm sacrifices potential profits because the marginal revenue from producing more output is greater than the marginal cost. Only at q^*, where $MR = MC$, is the output level just right—not too large, not too small. Further expansion of output beyond q^* will lead to losses on the additional output (decrease the firm's overall profits) because $MC > MR$. For example, if the firm produces $q_{\text{TOO MUCH}}$, the firm incurs losses on that output produced beyond q^*; the firm should reduce its output. Only at output q^*, where $MR = MC$, can we find the profit-maximizing level of output. The **profit-maximizing output rule** says a firm should always produce at the level of output where its $MR = MC$.

profit-maximizing output rule
a firm should always produce at the level of output where MR = MC

THE MARGINAL APPROACH

We can use the data in Exhibit 3 to find Farmer John's profit-maximizing position. In the table in Exhibit 3, columns 5 and 6 show the marginal revenue and marginal cost, respectively. We see that output levels of one and two bushels produce outputs that have marginal revenues that exceed marginal cost—John certainly wants to produce those units and more. That is, as long as marginal revenue exceeds marginal costs, producing and selling those units add more to revenues than to costs; in other words, they add to profits. However, once he expands production beyond four units of output, John's marginal revenues are less that his marginal revenues and his profits begin to fall. Clearly, Farmer John should not produce beyond four bushels of wheat.

THE TOTAL COST–TOTAL REVENUE APPROACH

Let us take another look at profit maximization using the table in Exhibit 3. Comparing columns 2 and 3, the calculations of total revenues and total costs, respectively, we see that Farmer John maximizes his profits at output levels of three or four bushels, where he will make profits of $4. In column 4, Profit, you can see that there is no higher level of profit at any of the other output levels.

In the next section we will use the profit-maximizing output rule to see what happens when changes in the market cause the price to fall below average total cost and even below average variable costs. We will introduce the three-step method to determine whether the firm is making an economic profit, minimizing its losses, or should temporarily shut down.

section 8.3 Exhibit 3 **Cost and Revenue Calculations for a Perfectly Competitive Firm**

Quantity (1)	Total Revenue (2)	Total Cost (3)	Profit ($TR - TC$) (4)	Marginal Revenue ($\Delta TR/\Delta q$) (5)	Marginal Cost ($\Delta TC/\Delta q$) (6)
0	$ 0	$ 2	$−2		
				$5	$2
1	5	4	1		
				5	3
2	10	7	3		
				5	4
3	15	11	4		
				5	5
4	20	16	4		
				5	6
5	25	22	3		

Section Check

SECTION CHECK

1. Total revenue is price times the quantity sold ($TR = P \times q$).
2. Average revenue is total revenue divided by the quantity sold ($AR = TR/q = P$).
3. Marginal revenue is the change in total revenue from the sale of an additional unit of output ($MR = \Delta TR/\Delta q$). In a competitive industry, the price of the good equals both the average revenue and the marginal revenue.
4. As long as marginal revenue exceeds marginal costs, the seller should expand production because producing and selling those units adds more to revenues than to costs, or increases profits. However, if marginal revenue is less than marginal cost, the seller should decrease production.
5. The profit-maximizing output rule says a firm should always produce where $MR = MC$.

---

1. How is total revenue calculated?
2. How is average revenue derived from total revenue?
3. How is marginal revenue derived from total revenue?
4. Why is marginal revenue equal to price for a perfectly competitive firm?

section 8.4

Short-Run Profits and Losses

- How do we determine if a firm is generating an economic profit?
- How do we determine if there is an economic loss?
- How do we determine if a firm is making zero economic profits?
- Why doesn't a firm produce when price is below average variable costs?

In the previous section, we discussed two methods of determining the profit-maximizing output level for a perfectly competitive firm. However, producing at this profit-maximizing level does not mean that a firm is actually generating profits; it merely means that a firm is maximizing its profit opportunity at a given price level. How do we know if a firm is actually making economic profits or losses?

THE THREE-STEP METHOD

What Is the Three-Step Method?

Determining whether a firm is generating economic profits, economic losses, or zero economic profits at the profit-maximizing level of output, q^*, can be done in three easy steps. First, we will walk through these steps, and then we will apply the method to three different situations for a hypothetical firm in the short run in Exhibit 1.

1. Find where marginal revenues equal marginal costs and proceed straight down to the horizontal quantity axis to find q^*, the profit-maximizing output level.

2. At q^*, go straight up to the demand curve and then to the left to find the market price, P^*. Once you have identified P^* and q^*, you can find total revenue at the profit-maximizing output level, because $TR = P \times q$.
3. The last step is to find total costs. Again, go straight up from q^* to the average total cost (ATC) curve and then left to the vertical axis to compute the average total cost *per unit.* If we multiply average total costs by the output level, we can find the total costs ($TC = ATC \times q$).

If total revenue is greater than total costs at q^*, the firm is generating economic profits. And if total revenue is less than total costs at q^*, the firm is generating economic losses. Remember, the cost curves include implicit and explicit costs—that is, we are covering the opportunity costs of our resources. So even if there are zero economic profits, no tears should be shed, because the firm is covering both its implicit and explicit costs. Because firms are also covering their implicit costs, or what they could be producing with these resources in another endeavor, economists sometimes call this zero economic profit *a normal rate of return.* That is, the owners are doing as well as they could elsewhere, in that they are getting the normal rate of return on the resources they invested in the firm.

The Three-Step Method in Action

In Exhibit 1, there are three different short-run equilibrium positions; in each case, the firm is producing at a level where marginal revenue equals marginal costs. Each of these alternatives shows that the firm is maximizing profits or minimizing losses in the short run.

Assume that there are three alternative prices—\$6, \$5, and \$4—for a firm with given costs. In Exhibit 1(a), the firm receives \$6 per unit at an equilibrium level of output ($MR = MC$) of 120 units. Total revenue ($P \times q^*$) is \$6 × 120, or \$720. The average total costs at 120 units of output is \$5, and the total cost ($ATC \times q^*$) is \$600. Following the three-step method, we can calculate that this firm is earning total economic profits of \$120.

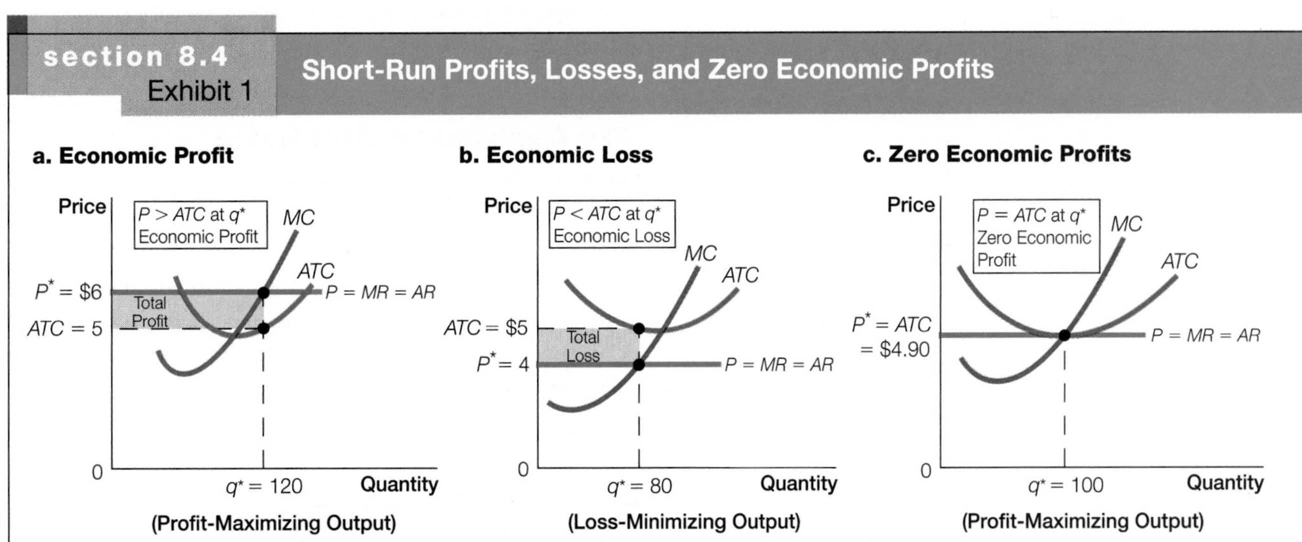

In Exhibit 1(a), the firm is earning short-run economic profits of \$120; in (b), the firm is suffering losses of \$80. In Exhibit 1(c), the firm is making zero economic profits, with the price just equal to the average total cost in the short run.

In Exhibit 1(b), the market price has fallen to $4 per unit. At the equilibrium level of output, the firm is now producing 80 units of output at an average total cost of $5 per unit. The total revenue is now $320 ($4 × 80), and the total costs are $400 ($5 × 80). We can see that the firm is now incurring total economic losses of $80.

In Exhibit 1(c), the firm is earning zero economic profits, or a normal rate of return. The market price is $4.90, and the average total cost is $4.90 per unit for 100 units of output. In this case, economic profits are zero, because total revenue, $490, minus total cost, $490, is equal to zero. This firm is just covering all its costs, both implicit and explicit.

EVALUATING ECONOMIC LOSSES IN THE SHORT RUN

A firm generating an economic loss faces a tough choice: Should it continue to produce or shut down its operation? To make this decision, we need to add another variable to our discussion of economic profits and losses: average variable costs. Variable costs are those costs that vary with output, such as wages, raw material, transportation, and electricity. If a firm cannot generate enough revenues to cover its variable costs, then it will have larger losses if it operates than if it shuts down (losses in that case = fixed costs). Thus, a firm will not produce at all unless the price is greater than its average variable costs.

Operating at a Loss

At price levels greater than or equal to average variable costs, a firm may continue to operate in the short run even if average total costs—variable and fixed costs—are not completely covered. That is, the firm may continue to operate even though it is experiencing an economic loss. Why? Because fixed costs continue whether the firm produces or not; it is better to earn enough to cover a portion of fixed costs rather than earn nothing at all.

In Exhibit 2, price is less than average total costs but more than average variable costs. In this case, the firm produces in the short run, but at a loss. To shut down would make this firm worse off, because it can cover at least *some* of its fixed costs with the excess of revenue over its variable costs.

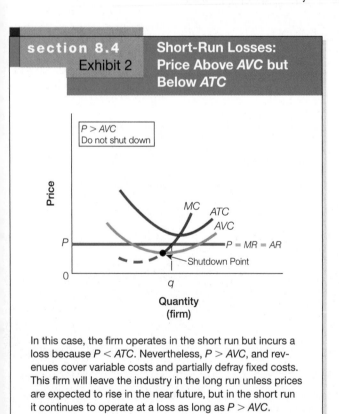

section 8.4 Exhibit 2 — Short-Run Losses: Price Above *AVC* but Below *ATC*

P > AVC
Do not shut down

Price; MC; ATC; AVC; P; P = MR = AR; Shutdown Point; 0; q; Quantity (firm)

In this case, the firm operates in the short run but incurs a loss because $P < ATC$. Nevertheless, $P > AVC$, and revenues cover variable costs and partially defray fixed costs. This firm will leave the industry in the long run unless prices are expected to rise in the near future, but in the short run it continues to operate at a loss as long as $P > AVC$.

The Decision to Shut Down

Exhibit 3 illustrates a situation in which the price a firm is able to obtain for its product is below its average variable costs at all ranges of output. In this case, the firm is unable to cover even its variable costs in the short run. Because the firm is losing even more than the fixed costs it would lose if it shut down, it is more logical for the firm to cease operations. So if $P < AVC$, the firm can cut its losses by shutting down.

The Short-Run Supply Curve

As we have just seen, at all prices above minimum *AVC*, a firm produces in the short run even if average total cost (*ATC*) is not completely covered, and at all prices below

section 8.4 Exhibit 3 — Short-Run Losses: Price Below *AVC*

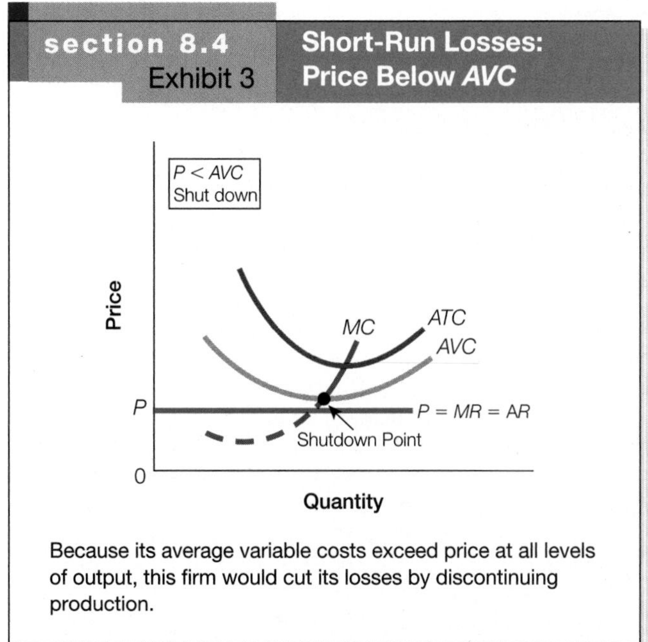

Because its average variable costs exceed price at all levels of output, this firm would cut its losses by discontinuing production.

section 8.4 Exhibit 4 — The Firm's Short-Run Supply Curve

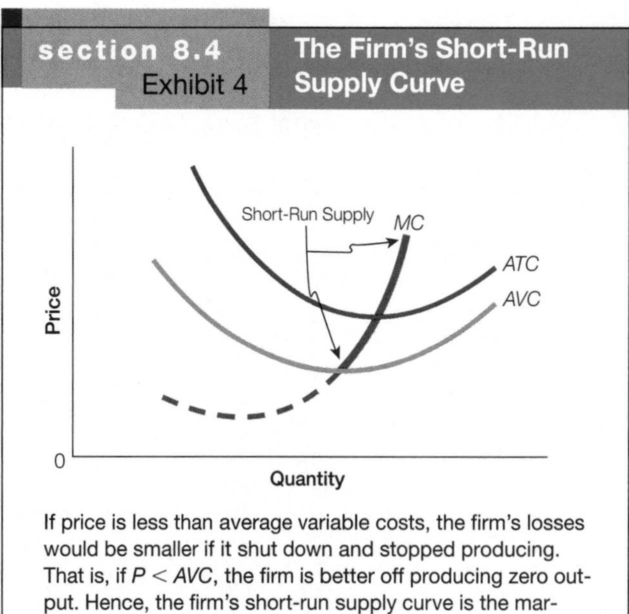

If price is less than average variable costs, the firm's losses would be smaller if it shut down and stopped producing. That is, if $P < AVC$, the firm is better off producing zero output. Hence, the firm's short-run supply curve is the marginal cost curve above average variable cost.

the minimum *AVC* the firm shuts down. The firm produces above the minimum of the *AVC* even if it is incurring economic losses because it can still earn enough in total revenues to cover all of its average variable costs and a portion of its fixed costs—this is better than not producing and earning nothing at all.

In graphical terms, the **short-run supply curve** of an individual competitive seller is identical with that portion of the *MC* curve that lies above the minimum of the *AVC* curve. As a cost relation, this curve shows the marginal cost of producing any *given output;* as a supply curve, it shows the *equilibrium output* that the firm will supply at various prices in the short run. The thick line in Exhibit 4 is the firm's supply curve—the portion of *MC* above its intersection with *AVC*. The declining portion of the *MC* curve has no significance for supply, because if the price falls below average variable costs, the firm is better off shutting down—producing no output. Beyond the point of lowest *AVC*, the marginal costs of successively larger amounts of output are progressively greater, so the

short-run supply curve
As a cost relation, this curve shows the marginal cost of producing any given output; as a supply curve, it shows the equilibrium output that the firm will supply at various prices in the short run.

COURTESY OF ROBERT SEXTON

Since the demand for summer camps will be lower during the off-season, it is likely that revenues may be too low for the camp to cover its variable costs and the owner will choose to shut down. Remember, the owner will still have to pay the fixed costs: property tax, insurance, the costs associated with the building and land. However, if the camp is not in operation during the off-season, the owner will at least not have to pay the variable costs: salary for the camp staff, food, and electricity.

APPLICATION

EVALUATING SHORT-RUN ECONOMIC LOSSES

Q: Rosa is one of many florists in a medium-size urban area. That is, we assume that she works in a market similar to a perfectly competitive market and operates, of course, in the short run. Rosa's cost and revenue information is provided in the table below. Based on this information, what should Rosa do in the short run, and why?

A: Fixed costs are unavoidable unless the firm goes out of business. Rosa really has two decisions in the short run—either to operate or to shut down temporarily. In Exhibit 5, we see that Rosa makes $2,000 a day in total revenues but her daily costs (fixed and variable) are $2,500. She has to pay her workers, pay for the fresh flowers, and pay for the fuel used by the drivers in picking up and delivering the flowers. She must also pay the electricity bill to heat her shop and keep her refrigerators going to protect her fresh flowers. That is, every day, poor Rosa is losing $500, but she still might want to operate the shop despite the loss. Why? Rosa's average variable costs (flowers, transportation fuel, daily wage earners, and so on) cost her $1,500 a day, and her fixed costs (insurance, property taxes, rent for the building, and refrigerator payments) are $1,000 a day. Now, if Rosa does not operate, she will save on her average variable costs—$1,500 a day—but she will be out the $2,000 a day she makes in revenues from selling her flowers. So every day she operates, she is better off than if she had not operated at all. That is, if the firm can cover average variable costs, it is better off operating than not operating. Suppose Rosa's *AVC* was $2,100 a day. Then Rosa should not operate, because every day she does, she is $100 worse off than if she shut down altogether.

Why does Rosa even bother operating if she is making a loss? Perhaps the economy is in a recession and the demand for flowers is temporarily down, but Rosa thinks things will pick up again in the next few months. If Rosa is right and demand picks up, her prices and marginal revenue will rise and she may then have a chance to make short-run economic profits.

COURTESY OF ROBERT SEXTON

If Rosa cannot cover her fixed costs, will she continue to operate?

section 8.4 Exhibit 5 — Rosa's Daily Revenue and Cost Schedule

Total Revenue	**$2,000**
Total Costs	**2,500**
Variable Costs	1,500
Fixed Costs	1,000

firm will supply larger and larger amounts only at higher prices. The absolute maximum that the firm can supply, regardless of price, is the maximum quantity that it can produce with the existing plant.

DERIVING THE SHORT-RUN MARKET SUPPLY CURVE

short-run market supply curve
the horizontal summation of the individal firms' supply curves in the market

The **short-run market supply curve** is the horizontal summation of the individual firms' supply curves (that is, the portion of the firms' *MC* above *AVC*) in the market, providing that input prices are not affected by increased production of existing firms (a topic we cover in Section 8.6). Because the short run is too brief for new firms to enter the market, the market supply curve is the horizontal summation of *existing* firms. For example, in Exhibit 6, at P_0, each of the 1,000 identical firms in the industry produce 50 bushels of wheat per day at point a, in Exhibit 6(a) and the quantity supplied in the market is 50,000 bushels of wheat, point A, in Exhibit 6(b). We can again sum horizontally at P_1;

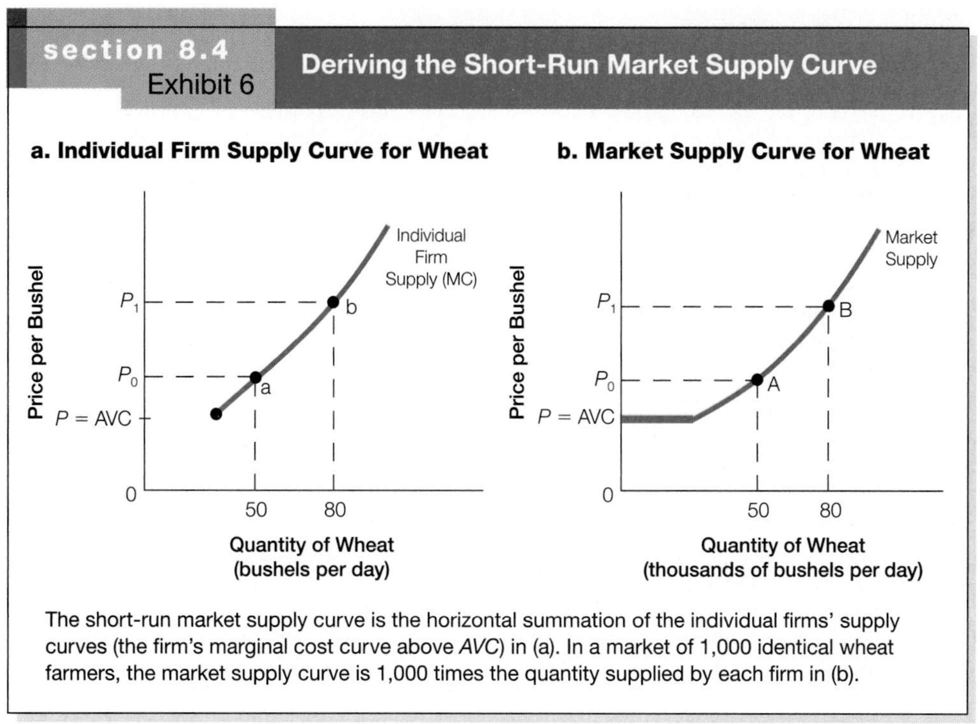

The short-run market supply curve is the horizontal summation of the individual firms' supply curves (the firm's marginal cost curve above *AVC*) in (a). In a market of 1,000 identical wheat farmers, the market supply curve is 1,000 times the quantity supplied by each firm in (b).

the quantity supplied for each of the 1,000 identical firms is 80 bushels of wheat per day at point b in Exhibit 6(a), so the quantity supplied for the industry is 80 thousand bushels of wheat per day, point B in Exhibit 6(b). Continuing this process gives us the market supply curve for the wheat market. In a market of 1,000 identical wheat farmers, the market supply curve is 1,000 times the quantity supplied by each firm, as long as the price is above *AVC*.

APPLICATION

REVIEWING THE SHORT-RUN OUTPUT DECISION

Exhibit 7 shows the firm's short-run output at these various market prices: P_1, P_2, P_3, and P_4.

At a market price of P_1, the firm would not cover its average variable costs—the firm would produce zero output because the firm's losses would be smaller if it shut down and stopped producing. At a market price of P_2, the firm would produce at the loss-minimizing output of q_2 units. It would operate rather than shut down because it could cover all of its average variable costs and some of its fixed costs. At a market price of P_3, the firm would produce q_3 units of output and make zero economic profits (a normal rate of return). At a market price of P_4, the firm would produce q_4 units of output and be making short-run economic profits.

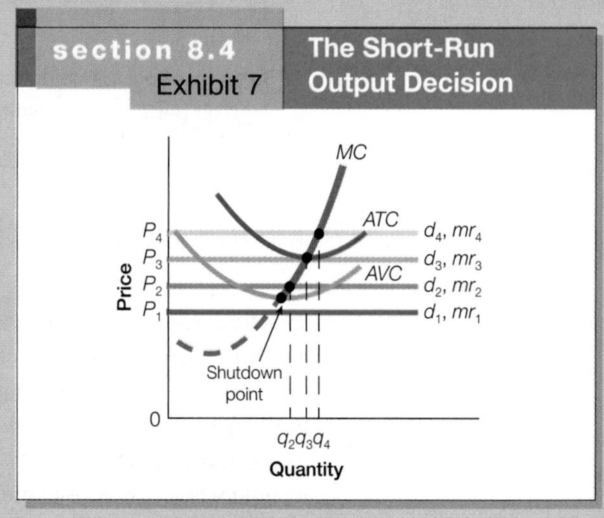

Section Check

1. The profit-maximizing output level is found by equating $MR = MC$ at q^*. If at that output the firm's price is greater than its average total costs, it is making an economic profit.
2. If at the profit-maximizing output level, q^*, the price is less than the average total cost, the firm is incurring an economic loss.
3. If at the profit-maximizing output level, q^*, the price is equal to average total cost, the firm is making zero economic profits; that is, the firm is covering both its implicit and explicit costs (making a normal rate of return).
4. If the price falls below average variable cost, the firm is better off shutting down than operating in the short run because it would incur greater losses from operating than from shutting down.

---

1. How is the profit-maximizing output quantity determined?
2. How do we determine total revenue and total cost for the profit-maximizing output quantity?
3. If a profit-maximizing, perfectly competitive firm is earning a profit because total revenue exceeds total cost, why must the market price exceed average total cost?
4. If a profit-maximizing, perfectly competitive firm is earning a loss because total revenue is less than total cost, why must the market price be less than average total cost?
5. If a profit-maximizing, perfectly competitive firm is earning zero economic profits because total revenue equals total cost, why must the market price be equal to the average total cost for that level of output?
6. Why would a profit-maximizing, perfectly competitive firm shut down rather than operate if price was less than its average variable costs?
7. Why would a profit-maximizing, perfectly competitive firm continue to operate for a period of time if price was greater than average variable cost but less than average total cost?

section 8.5

Long-Run Equilibrium

- If there are profits being earned in an industry, will this encourage the entry of new firms?
- Why do perfectly competitive firms make zero economic profits in the long run?

ECONOMIC PROFITS AND LOSSES DISAPPEAR IN THE LONG RUN

If farmers are able to make economic profits producing wheat, what will their response be in the long run? Farmers will increase the resources that they devote to the lucrative business of producing wheat. Suppose Farmer John is making an economic profit (he is earning an above-normal rate of return) producing wheat. To make even more profits, he may take land out of producing other crops and plant more wheat. Other farmers or people who are holding land for speculative purposes might also decide to plant wheat on their land.

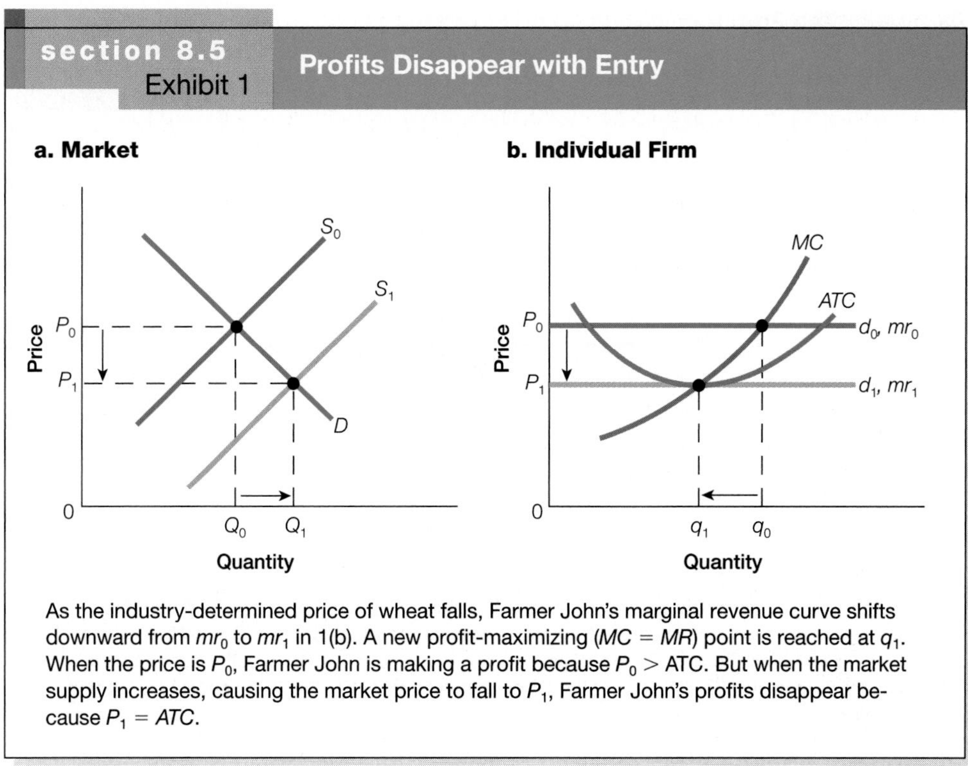

As the industry-determined price of wheat falls, Farmer John's marginal revenue curve shifts downward from mr_0 to mr_1 in 1(b). A new profit-maximizing ($MC = MR$) point is reached at q_1. When the price is P_0, Farmer John is making a profit because $P_0 >$ ATC. But when the market supply increases, causing the market price to fall to P_1, Farmer John's profits disappear because $P_1 = ATC$.

As the word gets out that wheat production is proving profitable, there will be a supply response—the market supply curve will shift to the right as more firms enter the industry and existing firms expand as in Exhibit 1(a). With this shift, the quantity of wheat supplied at any given price is greater than before. It may take a year or even longer, of course, for the complete supply response to take place, simply because it takes some time for information to spread on profit opportunities, and still more time to plant, grow, and harvest the wheat. Note that the impact of increasing supply, other things equal, is to reduce the equilibrium price of wheat. Suppose that, as a result of the supply response, the price of wheat falls from P_0 to P_1.

The impact of the change in the market price of wheat, over which John has absolutely no control, is very simple. If his costs have not changed, he will move from making a profit ($P_0 > ATC$) to zero economic profits ($P_1 = ATC$), as seen in Exhibit 1(b). In long-run equilibrium, perfectly competitive firms make zero economic profits. Remember, zero economic profits means that the firm is actually earning a normal return on the use of its capital. Zero economic profits is an equilibrium or stable situation because any positive economic (above-normal) profits signal resources into the industry, beating down prices and thus revenues to the firm; any economic losses signal resources to leave the industry, leading to supply reductions that lead to increased prices and higher firm revenues to the remaining firms. Only at zero economic profits is there no tendency for firms to either enter or leave the industry.

THE LONG-RUN EQUILIBRIUM FOR THE COMPETITIVE FIRM

The long-run competitive equilibrium for a perfectly competitive firm is graphically illustrated in Exhibit 2. At the equilibrium point (where $MC = MR$), short-run and long-run average total costs are also equal. The average total cost curves touch the marginal cost and marginal revenue (demand) curves at the equilibrium output point. Because the marginal revenue curve is also the average revenue curve, average revenues and average

section 8.5 Exhibit 2 **The Long-Run Competitive Equilibrium**

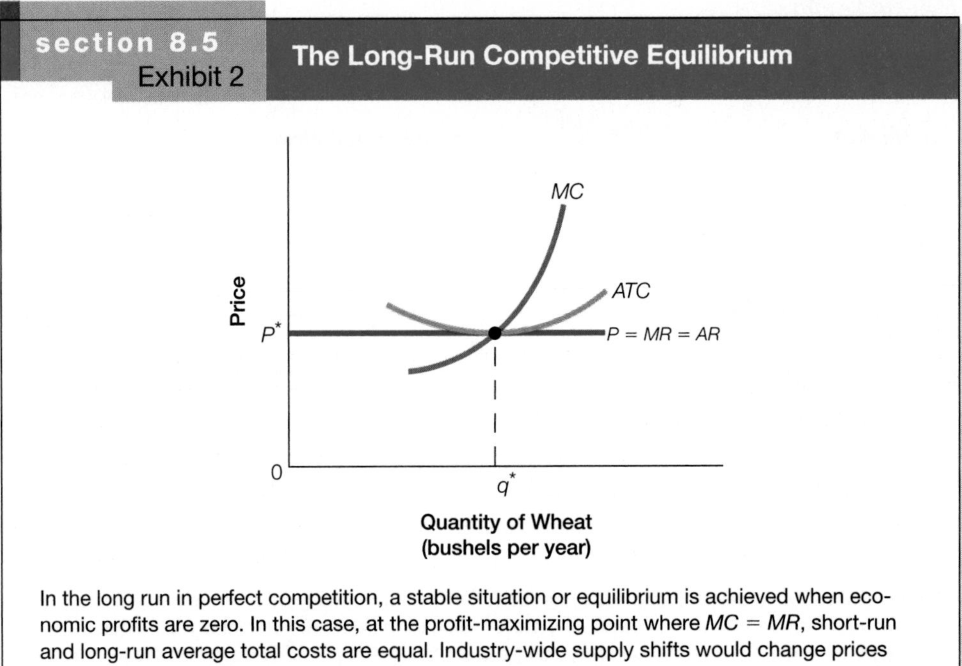

In the long run in perfect competition, a stable situation or equilibrium is achieved when economic profits are zero. In this case, at the profit-maximizing point where $MC = MR$, short-run and long-run average total costs are equal. Industry-wide supply shifts would change prices and average revenues and wipe out any losses or profits that develop in the short run, leading to the situation depicted above.

total costs are equal at the equilibrium point. The long-run equilibrium in perfect competition depicted in Exhibit 2 has an interesting feature. Note that the equilibrium output occurs at the lowest point on the average total cost curve. As you may recall, this occurs because the marginal cost curve must intersect the average total cost curve at the latter curve's lowest point. Hence, the equilibrium condition in the long run in perfect competition is for firms to produce at that output that minimizes average total costs. At this long-run equilibrium, new firms have no incentive to enter the market and existing firms have no incentive to exit the market.

Section Check

1. Economic profits will encourage entry of new firms, which will shift the market supply curve to the right.
2. Any positive economic profits signal resources into the industry, driving down prices and revenues to the firm.
3. Any economic losses signal resources to leave the industry, leading to supply reduction, higher prices, and increased revenues.
4. Only at zero economic profits is there no tendency for firms to either enter or exit the industry.

---

1. Why do firms enter profitable industries?
2. Why does entry eliminate positive economic profits in a perfectly competitive industry?
3. Why do firms exit unprofitable industries?
4. Why does exit eliminate economic losses in a perfectly competitive industry?
5. Why is a situation of zero economic profits a stable long-run equilibrium situation for a perfectly competitive industry?

section 8.6

Long-Run Supply

- What are constant-cost industries?
- What are increasing-cost industries?

The preceding sections have considered the costs of an individual, perfectly competitive firm as it varies output, on the assumption that the prices paid for inputs (costs) are given. However, when the output of an entire industry changes, the likelihood is greater of changes occurring in costs. But how will the changes in the number of firms in an industry affect the input costs of individual firms? In this section we develop the long-run supply curve (*LRS*). As we will see, the shape of the long-run supply curve depends on the extent to which input costs change when there is entry or exit of firms in the industry. We will look at two possible types of industries when considering long-run supply: constant-cost industries and increasing-cost industries.

A CONSTANT-COST INDUSTRY

In a **constant-cost industry,** the prices of inputs do not change as output is expanded. The industry may not use inputs in sufficient quantities to affect input prices. For example, say the firms in the industry use a lot of unskilled labor but the industry is small. So, as output expands, the increase in demand for unskilled labor will not cause the market wage for unskilled labor to rise. Similarly, suppose a paper clip maker decides to double its output. It is highly unlikely that its demand for steel will have an impact on steel prices because its demand for the input is so small.

constant-cost industry
an industry where input prices (and cost curves) do not change as industry output changes

Once long-run adjustments are complete, by necessity each firm operates at the point of lowest long-run average total costs, because supply shifts with entry and exit, eliminating profits. Therefore, each firm supplies the market the quantity of output that it can produce at the lowest possible long-run average total cost.

In Exhibit 1, we can see the impact of an unexpected increase in market demand. Suppose that recent reports show that blueberries can lower cholesterol, lower blood pressure, and significantly reduce the risk of all cancers. The increase in market demand for blueberries leads to a price increase from P_0 to P_1 as the firm increases output from q_0 to q_1, and blueberry industry output increases from Q_0 to Q_1 as seen in Exhibit 1(b). The increase in market demand generates a higher price and positive profits for existing firms in the short run. The existence of economic profits will attract new firms into the industry, causing the short-run supply curve to shift from S_0 to S_1 and lowering price until excess profits are zero. This shift results in a new equilibrium, point C in Exhibit 1(c). Because the industry is one of constant costs, industry expansion does not alter firms' cost curves, and the industry long-run supply curve is horizontal. That is, the long-run equilibrium price is at the same level that prevailed before demand increased; the only long-run effect of the increase in demand is an increase in industry output, as more firms enter that are just like existing firms as Exhibit 1(c) indicates. However, the long-run supply curve does not have to be horizontal.

AN INCREASING-COST INDUSTRY

In the **increasing-cost industry,** a more likely scenario, the cost curves of the individual firms rise as the total output of the industry increases. Increases in input prices (upward shifts in cost curves) occur as larger quantities of factors are employed in the industry.

increasing-cost industry
an industry where input prices rise (and cost curves rise) as industry output rises

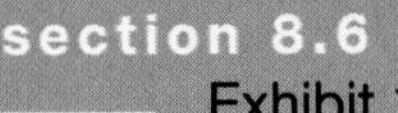

Demand Increase in a Constant-Cost Industry

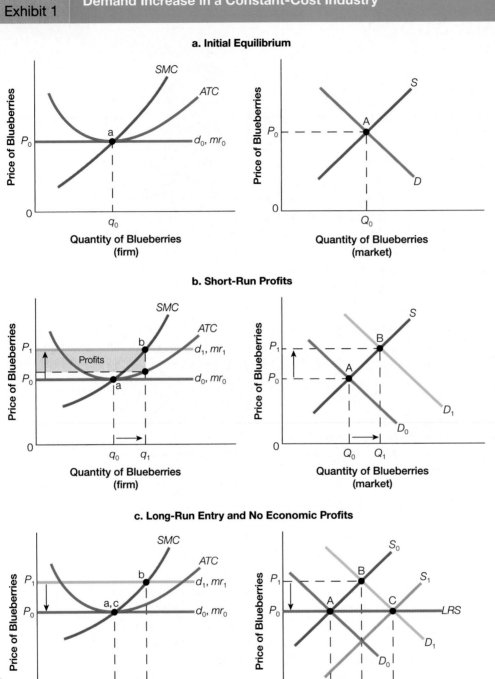

a. Initial Equilibrium

b. Short-Run Profits

c. Long-Run Entry and No Economic Profits

An unexpected increase in market demand for blueberries leads to an increase in the market price in (b). The new market price leads to positive profits for existing firms, which attracts new firms into the industry, shifting market supply from S_0 to S_1 in (c). This increased short-run industry supply curve intersects D_1 at point C. Each firm (of a new larger number of firms) is again producing at q_0 and earning zero economic profit.

When an industry utilizes a large portion of an input whose total supply is not huge, input prices will rise when the industry uses more of the input.

Increasing cost conditions are typical of "extractive" industries, such as agriculture, fishing, mining, and lumbering, which utilize large portions of the total supply of specialized natural resources such as land or mineral deposits. As the output of such an industry expands, the increased demand for the resources raises the prices that must be paid for their use. Because additional resources of given quality cannot be produced, greater supplies can be obtained (if at all) only by luring them away from other industries, or by using lower-quality (and less-productive, thus higher-cost) resources.

Wheat production is a typical example of an increasing-cost industry. As the output of wheat increases, the demand for land suitable for the production of wheat rises, and thus the price paid for the use of land of any given quality increases.

If there were a construction boom in a fully employed economy, would it be more costly to get additional resources like workers and raw materials? Yes, if this is an increasing-cost industry, the industry can only produce more output if it gets a higher price because the firm's costs of production rise as output expands. As new firms enter and output expands the increase in demand for inputs causes the price of inputs to rise—the cost curves of all construction firms shift upward as the industry expands. The industry can produce more output but only at a higher price, enough to compensate the firm for the higher input costs. In an increasing-cost industry, the long-run supply curve is upward sloping.

For example, in Exhibit 2, we see that an unexpected increase in the market demand for wheat will shift the market demand curve from D_0 to D_1. Consequently, price will increase from P_0 to P_1 in the short run. The typical firm (farm) will have positive short-run profits and expand output from q_0 to q_1. With the presence of short-run economic profits, new firms will enter the industry, shifting the short-run market supply curve to the right from S_0 to S_1. The prices of inputs, like farm land, fertilizer, seed, farm machinery, and so on will be bid up by competing farmers causing the firm's marginal and average cost curves

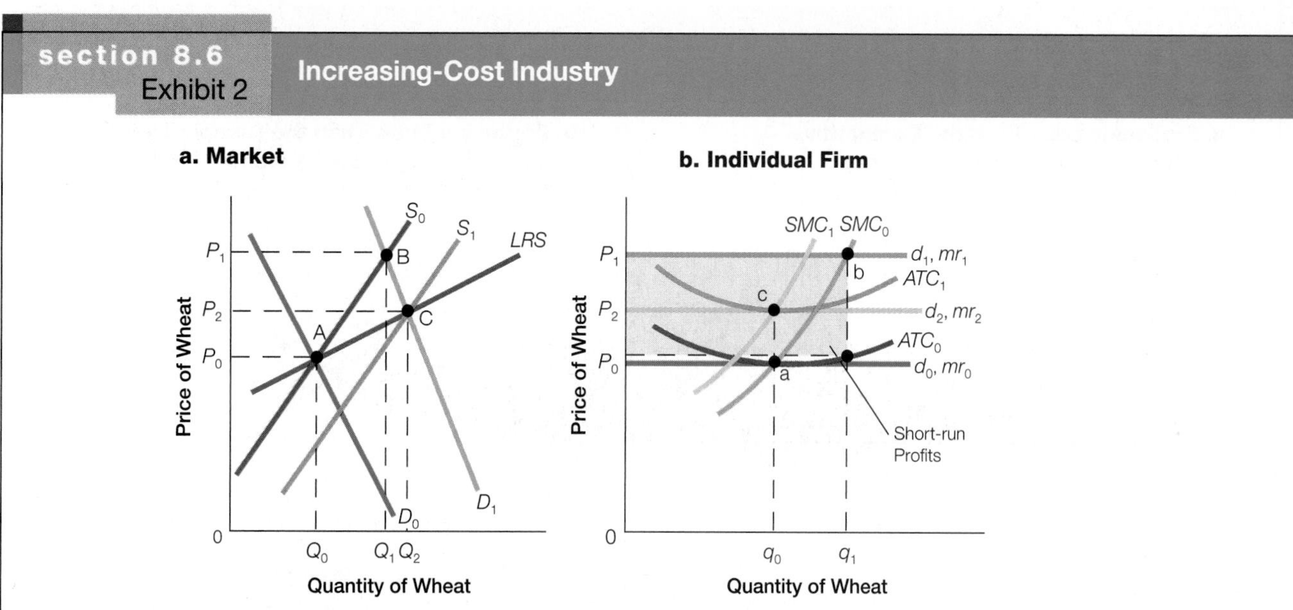

In (a) the unexpected increase in demand for wheat shifts the demand curve from D_0 to D_1. The increase in demand leads to higher prices from P_0 to P_1. In (b) firms increase output from q_0 to q_1 and experience short-run economic profits. The short-run economic profits induce other firms to enter the industry. This causes the short-run supply curve to shift right, from S_0 to S_1. As new firms enter and output expands, the increase in demand for inputs causes the price of inputs to rise, leading to higher cost curves for the firm—SMC_0 to SMC_1 and ATC_0 to ATC_1. The new long-run equilibrium is at P_2 and q_0. The *LRS* is positively sloped. This means the industry must receive a higher market price to produce more output, Q_2, because the increased output causes input prices to rise.

to rise from ATC_0 to ATC_1 and from SMC_0 to SMC_1. The new long-run equilibrium would be at a higher price, P_2 and a greater industry output, Q_3. The long-run supply curve (*LRS*) has a positive slope; that is, the industry must receive a higher price to produce more output because the cost of production rises (cost curves shift up) as the industry expands, thus the name increasing-cost industry.

Whether the industry is one of constant cost or increasing cost, the basic point is the same. The long-run supply is usually more elastic than the short-run supply because in the long run, firms can enter and exit the industry.

PERFECT COMPETITION AND ECONOMIC EFFICIENCY

We say that the output that results from equilibrium conditions of market demand and market supply in perfectly competitive markets is *economically efficient.* Only at this outcome can maximum output be obtained from our scarce resources. Let us return to the consumer and producer surplus graphs developed in chapter 5 (in section 5.5) to see how the competitive firm achieves economic efficiency.

At the intersection of market supply and market demand we find the competitive equilibrium price, P^*, and the competive equilibrium output, Q^*. In competitive markets, market supply equals market demand and $P = MC$. When $P = MC$, buyers value the last unit of output by the same amount that it cost sellers to produce it. If buyers value the last unit by more than the marginal cost of production, resources are not being allocated efficiently, like at Q_0, in Exhibit 3. Think of the demand curve as the marginal benefit curve ($D = MB$) and the supply curve as the marginal cost curve ($S = MC$). According to the rule of rational choice, we should pursue an activity as long as the expected marginal benefits are greater than the expected marginal costs. For example in Exhibit 3,

section 8.6 Exhibit 3 — Allocative Efficiency and Perfect Competition

a. Producing Less Than the Competitive Level of Output Lowers Welfare

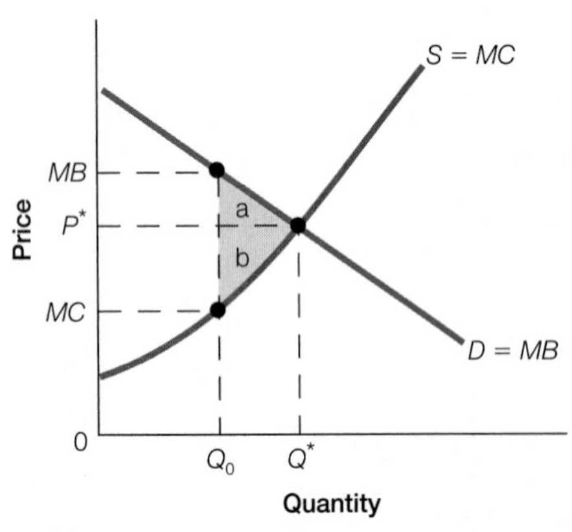

b. Producing More Than the Competitive Level of Output Lowers Welfare

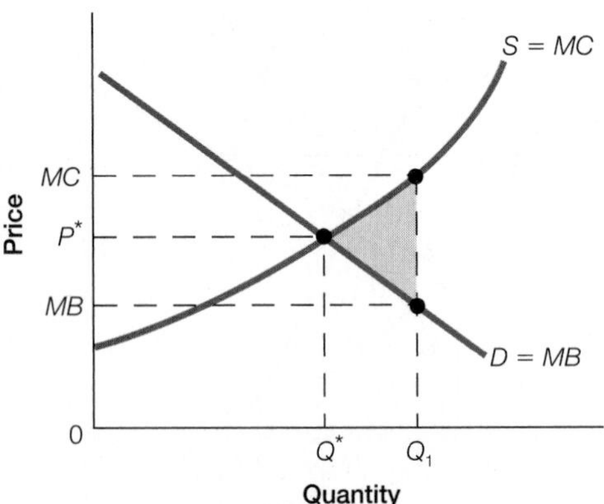

The demand curve measures the marginal benefits to the consumer and the supply curve measures the marginal cost to the sellers. At P^* and Q^*, resources are being allocated efficiently—the marginal benefits of those resources are equal to the marginal cost of those resources. At this point the sum of consumer and producer surplus is maximized. If Q_0 is produced, then the marginal benefits from producing additional units are greater than the marginal costs. Society gains from expanding output up to the point where $MB = MC$ at Q^*. If output is expanded beyond Q^*, $MC > MB$, society gains from a reduction in output, back to Q^*.

In The NEWS

INTERNET CUTS COSTS AND INCREASES COMPETITION

The Internet makes it easier for buyers and sellers to compare prices. It cuts out the middlemen between firms and customers. It reduces transaction costs. And it reduces barriers to entry. To understand this, go back to Ronald Coase, an economist, who argued in 1937 that the main reason why firms exist (as opposed to individuals acting as buyers and sellers at every stage of production) is to minimize transaction costs. Since the Internet reduces such costs, it also reduces the optimal size of firms. Small firms can buy in services from outside more cheaply. Thus, in overall terms, barriers to entry will fall.

In these ways, then, the Internet cuts costs, increases competition and improves the functioning of the price mechanism. It thus moves the economy closer to the textbook model of perfect competition, which assumes abundant information, zero transaction costs, and no barriers to entry. The Internet makes this assumption less far-fetched. By improving the flow of information between buyers and sellers, it makes markets more efficient, and so ensures that resources are allocated to their most productive use. The most important effect of the "new" economy, indeed, may be to make the "old" economy more efficient.

It is hard to test this conclusion, but some studies seem to support it. Prices of goods bought online, such as books and CDs, are, on average, about 10 percent cheaper (after including taxes and delivery) than in conventional shops, though the non-existent profits of many electronic retailers make this evidence inconclusive. Competition from the Internet is also forcing traditional retailers to reduce prices. The Internet offers even clearer savings in services such as banking. According to Lehman Brothers, a transfer between bank accounts costs $1.27 if done by a bank teller, 27 cents via a cash machine, and only one cent over the Internet.

The biggest economic impact of the Internet is likely to come from business-to-business (B2B) e-commerce. GartnerGroup forecasts that global B2B turnover could reach $4 trillion in America in 2003, compared with less than $400 billion of online sales to consumers.

B2B e-commerce cuts companies' costs in three ways. First, it reduces procurement costs, making it easier to find the cheapest supplier and cutting the cost of processing transactions. Second, it allows better supply-chain management. And third, it makes possible tighter inventory control, so that firms can reduce their stocks or even eliminate them. Through these three channels B2B e-commerce reduces firms' production costs, by increasing efficiency or by squeezing suppliers' profit margins.

SOURCE: Internet Economics, "A Thinker's Guide," pp. 64–66. *The Economist*, April 1, 2000. www.economist.com.

at Q_0, we see that the sum of consumer and producer surplus is not maximized—and welfare (the sum of consumer and producer surplus) would rise if production were expanded from Q_0 to Q^*. Notice that there would be gains in both consumer surplus (area a) and producer surplus (area b) if production were increased from Q_0 to Q^*. That is, at Q_0, resources are not being allocated efficiently and output should be expanded.

We can also produce too much output. For example, if output is expanded beyond Q^* in Exhibit 3, the cost to sellers for producing the good is greater than the mar-ginal benefits to consumers. Society would gain from a reduction in output back to Q^*.

Once the competitive equilibrium is reached, the buyers' marginal benefit equals the sellers' marginal cost and the sum of consumer and producer surplus is maximized. If the buyers and sellers are the only ones affected by the perfectly competitive outcome (that is, no positive or negative externalities), than total welfare (the sum of consumer and producer surplus) is maximized and resources are allocated efficiently.

Section Check

1. In constant-cost industries, the cost curves of the firm are not affected by changes in the output of the entire industry. Such industries must be very small demanders of resources in the market.
2. In an increasing-cost industry, the cost curves of the individual firms rise as total output increases. This case is the most typical.

---

1. What must be true about input costs as industry output expands for a constant-cost industry?
2. What must be true about input costs as industry output expands for an increasing-cost industry?
3. What would be the long-run equilibrium result of an increase in demand in a constant-cost industry?
4. What would be the long-run equilibrium result of an increase in demand in an increasing-cost industry?

Summary

There are four main market structures: perfect competition, monopoly, monopolistic competition, and oligopoly. Many markets may come close to approximating perfect competition in the sense that they act as if their demand curves are very elastic (flat). The characteristics of a perfectly competitive market are: many buyers and sellers, an identical (homogeneous) product, and easy market entry and exit.

The short-run profit-maximizing output level is found by equating $MR = MC$. If at that output the firm's price is greater than its average total costs, it is making an economic profit. If at the profit-maximizing output level, q^*, the price is less than the average total cost, the firm is incurring an economic loss. If at the profit-maximizing output level, q^*, the price is equal to average total cost, the firm is making zero economic profits; that is, the firm is covering both its implicit and explicit costs (making a normal rate of return). If the price falls below average variable cost, the firm is better off shutting down than operating in the short run.

Economic profits will encourage entry of new firms, which will shift the market supply curve to the right. Any positive economic profits signal resources into the industry, driving down prices and revenues to the firm. Any economic losses signal resources to leave the industry, leading to supply reduction, higher prices, and increased revenues. Only at zero economic profits is there no tendency for firms to either enter or exit the industry. In long-run competitive equilibrium there are no economic profits and there is no incentive to enter or exit the industry.

In constant-cost industries, the cost curves of the firm are not affected by changes in the output of the entire industry. Such industries must be very small demanders of resources in the market. In an increasing-cost industry, the cost curves of the individual firms rise as total output increases. This case is the most typical.

Key Terms and Concepts

perfect competition 162
monopoly 162
monopolistic competition 162
oligopoly 163
price taker 163
total revenue (*TR*) 167
average revenue (*AR*) 167
marginal revenue (*MR*) 168
profit-maximizing output rule 169
short-run supply curve 173
short-run market supply curve 174
constant-cost industry 179
increasing-cost industry 179

Review Questions

1. Which of the following are most likely to be perfectly competitive?
   a. the Chicago Board of Trade
   b. fast food industry
   c. the computer software industry
   d. the New York Stock Exchange
   e. clothing industry

2. Illustrate the *SRATC, AVC, SRMC,* and *MR* curves for a perfectly competitive firm that is operating at a loss. What is the output level that minimizes losses? Why is it more profitable to continue producing in the short run rather than shut down?

3.

Output	Total Cost	Total Revenue
0	30	0
1	45	25
2	65	50
3	90	75
4	120	100
5	155	125

Given the data above, determine *AR, MR, P* and the short-run profit-maximizing (loss-minimizing) level of output.

4. Explain why the following conditions are typical under perfect competition in the long run.
   a. $P = MC$
   b. $P =$ minimum ATC

5. Graph and explain the adjustments to long-run equilibrium when there is a decrease in market demand in a constant-cost industry.

6. Evaluate the following statements. Determine whether each is true or false and explain your answer.
   a. If economic profits are zero, firms will exit the industry in the long run.
   b. A firm cannot maximize profits without minimizing costs.
   c. If a firm is minimizing costs, it must be maximizing profits.

7. What is meant by the term "perfect competition"? Is it possible for a situation that does not conform to the assumptions of perfect competition to still be described by the perfectly competitive price theory? Discuss.

8. Discuss the following questions.
   a. Why must price cover *AVC* if firms are to continue to operate?
   b. If firms are covering *AVC* but not all of their fixed costs, will they continue to operate in the short run? Why or why not?
   c. Why is it possible for price to remain above average total cost in the short run but not the long run?

9. Say that there are a large number of small producers in an industry but very large barriers to entry to new firms. After a large, permanent increase in industry demand, would producers in the industry again earn zero economic profits in long-run equilibrium?

10. What affect would happen to the equilibrium output if there was a specific tax on a competitive firm? Graph the curve. What happens to the marginal cost curve? The average total cost curve?

11. Go to the Sexton Web site at **http://sexton.swcollege.com** and click on "eBay" and take a look around at all of the goods. How does this market resemble perfect competition?

Fill in the Blanks

1. Economists have identified four different market structures in which firms operate: ______________, ______________, ______________, and ______________.

2. Perfect competition is a market structure involving a ______________ number of buyers and sellers, a ______________ product, and ______________market entry and exit.

3. Perfectly competitive firms are ______________, who must accept the market price as determined by the forces of demand and supply.

4. In ______________, there is a single seller who sets the price that will maximize the seller's profits.

5. In monopolistic competition, there is an element of monopoly power because each firm's product is ______________ from that of other competitors, but because there are ______________ competitors, it also has an element of competition.

6. In oligopoly, ______________ firms, as opposed to one firm or many, produce similar or identical goods.

7. Because perfectly competitive markets have ______________ buyers and sellers, each firm is so ______________ in relation to the industry that its production decisions have no impact on the market.

8. Because consumers believe that all firms in a perfectly competitive market sell ______________ products, the products of all the firms are perfect substitutes.

9. Because of ______________ market entry and exit, perfectly competitive markets generally consist of a ______________ number of small suppliers.

10. In a perfectly competitive industry each producer provides such a ______________ fraction of the total supply that a change in the amount he or she offers does not have a noticeable effect on the market price.

11. Since perfectly competitive sellers can sell all they want at the market price, their demand curve is ______________ at the market price over the ______________ range of output that they could possibly produce.

12. The objective of a firm is to maximize profits by producing the amount that maximizes the difference between its ______________ and ______________.

13. Total revenue for a perfectly competitive firm equals the ______________ times the ______________.

14. ______________ equals total revenue divided by the number of units of the product sold.

15. ______________ is the additional revenue derived from the sale of one more unit of the good.

16. In perfect competition, we know that ______________ and price are equal.

17. There are two methods for identifying a firm's profit-maximizing output: the ______________ approach and the ______________ approach.

18. In all types of market environments, firms will maximize profits at that output that maximizes the difference between ______________ and ______________, which is the same output level where ______________ equals ______________.

19. At the level of output chosen by a competitive firm, total cost equals ______ ______ times quantity, while total revenue equals ______ times quantity.

20. If total revenue is greater than total costs at its profit-maximizing output level, a firm is generating ______. If total revenue is less than total costs, the firm is generating ______. If total revenue equals total cost, the firm is earning ______.

21. If a firm cannot generate enough revenues to cover its ______ costs, then it will have larger losses if it operates than if it shuts down in the short run.

22. The loss a firm would bear if it shuts down would be equal to ______.

23. When price is less than ______ but more than ______, a firm produces in the short run, but at a loss.

24. The short-run supply curve of an individual competitive seller is identical with that portion of the ______ curve that lies above the minimum of the ______ curve.

25. The short-run market supply curve is the horizontal summation of the individual firms' supply curves, providing that ______ are not affected by increased production of existing firms.

26. If perfectly competitive producers are currently making economic profits, the market supply curve will shift to the right over time as more firms ______ and existing firms ______.

27. As entry into the profitable industry pushes down the market price, producers will move from a situation where price ______ average total cost to one where price ______ average total cost.

28. Only at ______ is there no tendency for firms either to enter or leave the business.

29. The long-run equilibrium output in perfect competition occurs at the lowest point on the average total cost curve, so the equilibrium condition in the long run in perfect competition is for firms to produce at that output that minimizes ______.

30. The shape of the long-run supply curve depends on the extent to which ______ change when there is entry or exit of firms in the industry.

31. In a constant-cost industry, the prices of inputs ______ as output is expanded.

32. In an increasing-cost industry, the cost curves of the individual firms ______ as the total output of the industry increases.

33. The output that results from equilibrium conditions of market demand and market supply in perfectly competitive markets is economically ______.

34. Once the competitive equilibrium is reached, the sum of ______ and ______ is maximized.

True or False

1. Each market structure has certain key characteristics that distinguish it from the other structures.

2. In practice, it is sometimes difficult to decide precisely which market structure a given firm or industry most appropriately fits.

3. In perfect competition, no single firm produces more than an extremely small proportion of output, so no firm can influence the market price.

4. At the other end of the continuum of market environments from perfect competition is pure monopoly, where there is a single seller.

5. Despite each firm's product being differentiated at least slightly from that of other competitors in monopolistic competition, none has any monopoly power.

6. Unlike monopoly, oligopoly allows for some competition between firms; unlike competition, individual firms have a significant share of the total market for the good being produced.

7. As in the other market structures, an oligopolist is very conscious of the actions of competing firms.

8. Unlike a perfectly competitive firm, an oligopolist has some control over price and thus is a price-searcher.

9. It would be possible to have perfect competition without easy market entry and exit, but that market structure requires that firms sell an identical or homogeneous product.

10. Perfectly competitive firms are price takers because their influence on price is insignificant.

11. It is difficult for entrepreneurs to become suppliers of a product in a perfectly competitive market structure.

12. A perfectly competitive market is approximated most closely in highly organized markets for securities and agricultural commodities.

13. A perfectly competitive firm cannot sell at any figure higher than the current market price and would not knowingly charge a lower price, because the firm could sell all it wants at the market price.

14. In a perfectly competitive market, individual sellers can change their output and it will not alter the market price.

15. In a perfectly competitive industry, the market demand curve is perfectly elastic at the market price.

16. Because perfectly competitive firms are price takers, each firm's demand curve remains unchanged even when the market price changes.

17. The perfectly competitive model does not assume any knowledge on the part of individual buyers and sellers about market demand and supply—they only have to know the price of the good they sell.

18. In a perfectly competitive market, marginal revenue is constant and equal to the market price.

19. For a perfectly competitive firm, as long as the price derived from expanded output exceeds the marginal cost of that output, the expansion of output creates additional profits.

20. Producing at the profit-maximizing output level means that a firm is actually earning economic profits.

21. A competitive firm earning zero economic profit will be unable to continue in operation over time.

22. A firm will not produce at all unless the price is greater than its average variable costs.

23. A perfectly competitive firm will operate in the short run only at price levels greater than or equal to average total costs.

24. The *MC* curve above minimum *AVC* shows the marginal cost of producing any given output, as well as the equilibrium output that the firm will supply at various prices in the short run.

25. Because the short run is too brief for new firms to enter the market, the market supply curve is the vertical summation of the supply curves of existing firms.

26. As new firms enter an industry where sellers are earning economic profits, the result will include a reduction in the equilibrium price.

27. In long-run equilibrium, perfectly competitive firms make zero economic profits, earning a normal return on the use of their capital.

28. For a perfectly competitive firm, the long-run equilibrium will be the point at which price equals marginal cost as well as short-run average total cost and long-run average cost.

29. In a constant-cost industry, the industry does not use inputs in sufficient quantities to affect input prices.

30. In a constant-cost competitive industry, industry expansion does not alter a firm's cost curves, and the industry long-run supply curve is upward sloping.

31. In a constant-cost competitive industry, the only long-run effect of an increase in demand is an increase in industry output.

32. When an industry utilizes a large portion of an input, input prices will rise when the industry uses more of that input as it expands output, which will shift firms' cost curves upward.

Multiple Choice

1. Which market structure has the largest number of firms?
   a. perfect competition
   b. monopolistic competition
   c. oligopoly
   d. monopoly

2. Which of the following is *false?*
   a. Monopolistically competitive firms produce differentiated products.
   b. Oligopolistic firms produce a substantial fraction of the output of their industry.
   c. A monopoly is the single seller of a product without a close substitute.
   d. Only a perfectly competitive firm has no power to influence the market price for its product.
   e. All of the above are *true.*

3. Which of the following is *false* about perfect competition?
   a. Perfectly competitive firms sell homogeneous products.
   b. There is easy entry into, and exit from, a perfectly competitive industry.
   c. A perfectly competitive firm must take the market price as given.
   d. A perfectly competitive firm produces a substantial fraction of the industry output.
   e. All of the above are *true.*

4. An individual perfectly competitive firm
   a. may increase its price without losing sales.
   b. is a price maker.
   c. has no perceptible influence on the market price.
   d. sells a product that is differentiated from those of its competitors.

5. When will a perfectly competitive firm's demand curve shift?
   a. never
   b. when the market demand curve shifts
   c. when new producers enter the industry in large numbers
   d. when either b or c occurs

6. In a market with perfectly competitive firms, the market demand curve is ________ and the demand curve facing each individual firm is ________.
   a. upward sloping; horizontal
   b. downward sloping; horizontal
   c. horizontal; downward sloping
   d. horizontal; upward sloping
   e. horizontal; horizontal

7. The marginal revenue of a perfectly competitive firm
   a. decreases as output increases.
   b. increases as output increases.
   c. is constant as output increases and equal to price.
   d. increases as output increases and is equal to price.

8. A perfectly competitive firm seeking to maximize its profits would want to maximize the difference between
   a. its marginal revenue and its marginal cost.
   b. its average revenue and its average cost.
   c. its total revenue and its total cost.
   d. its price and its marginal cost.
   e. either a or d.

9. If a perfectly competitive firm's marginal revenue exceeded its marginal cost,
   a. it would cut its price in order to sell more output and increase its profits.
   b. it would expand its output but not cut its price in order to increase its profits.
   c. it is currently earning economic profits.
   d. both a and c are true.
   e. both b and c are true.

10. A perfectly competitive firm maximizes its profit at an output in which
   a. total revenue exceeds total cost by the greatest dollar amount.
   b. marginal cost equals the price.
   c. marginal cost equals marginal revenue.
   d. all of the above are true.

11. In perfect competition, at a firm's short-run profit-maximizing output,
- **a.** its marginal revenue equals zero.
- **b.** its average revenue could be greater or less than average cost.
- **c.** its marginal revenue will be falling.
- **d.** both b and c will be true.

12. In perfect competition, at the firm's short-run profit-maximizing output, which of the following need *not* be true?
- **a.** Marginal revenue equals marginal cost.
- **b.** Price equals marginal cost.
- **c.** Average revenue equals average cost.
- **d.** Average revenue equals marginal revenue.
- **e.** All of the above would have to be true.

13. The minimum price at which a firm would produce in the short run is the point at which
- **a.** price equals the minimum point on its marginal cost curve.
- **b.** price equals the minimum point on its average variable cost curve.
- **c.** price equals the minimum point on its average total cost curve.
- **d.** price equals the minimum point on its average fixed cost curve.

14. A profit-maximizing perfectly competitive firm would never operate at an output level at which
- **a.** it would lose more than its total fixed costs.
- **b.** it was not earning a positive economic profit.
- **c.** it was not earning a zero economic profit.
- **d.** it was not earning an accounting profit.

15. If a perfectly competitive firm finds that price is greater than *AVC* but less than *ATC* at the quantity where its marginal cost equals the market price,
- **a.** the firm will produce in the short run but may eventually go out of business.
- **b.** the firm will produce in the short run, and new entrants would tend to enter the industry over time.
- **c.** the firm will immediately shut down.
- **d.** the firm will be earning economic profits.
- **e.** both b and d are true.

Use the following diagram to answer questions 16–19.

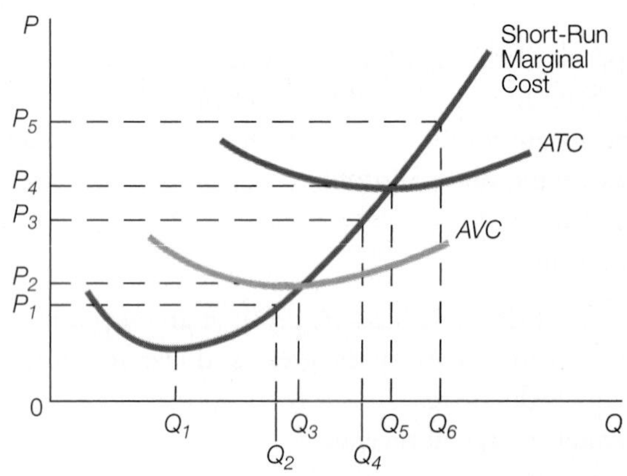

16. When the market price equals P_1, the firm should produce output

a. Q_1.
b. Q_2.
c. Q_3.
d. Q_4.
e. none of the above

17. When the market price equals P_3, the firm should produce output

a. Q_3, operating at a loss.
b. Q_4, operating at a loss.
c. Q_4, earning an economic profit.
d. Q_5, operating at a loss.
e. Q_5, earning a normal profit.

18. When the market price equals P_4, the firm should produce output

a. Q_4, operating at a loss.
b. Q_4, earning an economic profit.
c. Q_5, operating at a loss.
d. Q_5, earning a normal profit.
e. Q_5, earning a positive economic profit.

19. When the market price equals P_5, the firm should produce output

a. Q_5, operating at a loss.
b. Q_5, earning an economic profit.
c. Q_6, operating at a loss.
d. Q_6, earning a normal profit.
e. Q_6, earning a positive economic profit.

20. The short-run supply curve of a perfectly competitive firm is

a. its *MC* curve.
b. its *MC* curve above the minimum point of *AVC.*
c. its *MC* curve above the minimum point of *ATC.*
d. none of the above.

21. Darlene runs a fruit-and-vegetable stand in a medium-sized community where there are many such stands. Her weekly total revenue equals $3,000. Her weekly total cost of running the stand equals $3,500, consisting of $2,500 of variable costs and $1,000 of fixed costs. An economist would likely advise Darlene to

a. shut down as quickly as possible in order to minimize her losses.
b. keep the stand open because it is generating an economic profit.
c. keep the stand open for a while longer because she is covering all of her variable costs and some of her fixed costs.
d. keep the stand open for a while longer because she is covering all of her fixed costs and some of her variable costs.

22. The entry of new firms into an industry will very likely

a. shift the industry supply curve to the right.
b. cause the market price to fall.
c. reduce the profits of existing firms in the industry.
d. do all of the above.

23. Which of the following statements concerning equilibrium in the long run is incorrect?
  a. Firms will exit the industry if economic profits equal zero.
  b. Firms are able to vary their plant sizes in the long run.
  c. Economic profits are eliminated as new firms enter the industry.
  d. The market price equals both marginal cost and average total cost.

24. In long-run equilibrium under perfect competition, price does not equal which of the following?
  a. long-run marginal cost
  b. minimum average total cost
  c. average fixed cost
  d. marginal revenue
  e. average revenue

25. If the domino-making industry is a constant-cost industry, one would expect the long-run result of an increase in demand for dominos to include
  a. a greater number of firms and a higher price.
  b. a greater number of firms and the same price.
  c. the same number of firms and a higher price.
  d. the same number of firms and the same price.

26. In an increasing-cost industry, an unexpected increase in demand would lead to what result in the long run?
  a. higher costs and a higher price
  b. higher costs and a lower price
  c. no change in costs or prices
  d. impossible to determine from the information given

27. If input prices rise as industry output expands, then a perfectly competitive firm's marginal cost and average cost curves will
  a. shift upward.
  b. shift downward.
  c. not shift. As the firm increases production, however, costs increase as the firm moves upward to the right along these curves.
  d. not shift. As the firm increases production, however, costs decrease as the firm moves downward to the left along these curves.

Problems

1. Use the diagram below to answer a, b, and c.

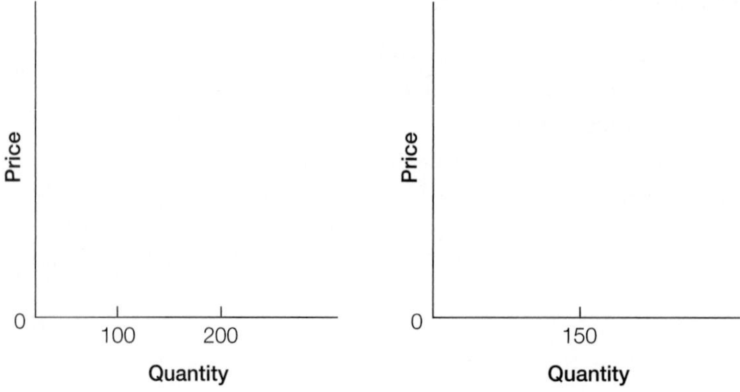

a. Illustrate the relationship between a perfectly competitive firm's demand curve and the market supply and demand curve.
b. Illustrate the effects of an increase in market demand on a perfectly competitive firm's demand curve.
c. Illustrate the effects of a decrease in market demand on a perfectly competitive firm's demand curve.

2. Complete the following table for a perfectly competitive firm, and indicate its profit-maximizing output.

Quantity	Price	Total Revenue	Marginal Revenue	Total Cost	Marginal Cost	Total Profit
6	10	____	____	30	3	30
7	____	____	____	35	____	____
8	____	____	____	42	____	____
9	____	____	____	51	____	____
10	____	____	____	62	____	____
11	____	____	____	75	____	____
12	____	____	____	90	____	____

3. Use the following diagram to answer a–d.

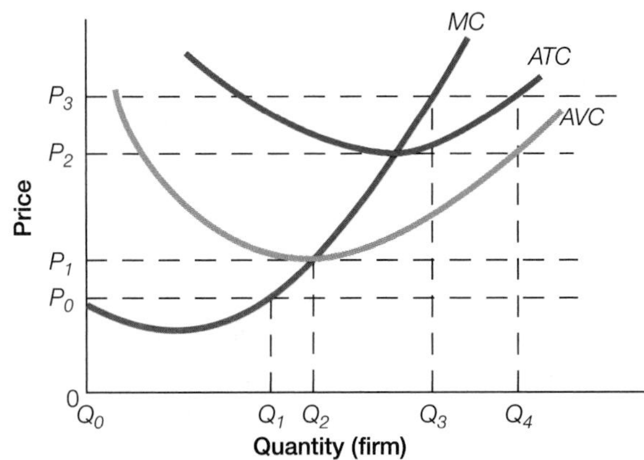

a. How much would a perfectly competitive firm produce at each of the indicated prices?
b. At which prices is the firm earning economic profits? zero economic profits? negative economic profits?
c. At which prices would the firm shut down?
d. Indicate what this firm's supply curve would be.

4. Use the following diagrams to answer a and b.

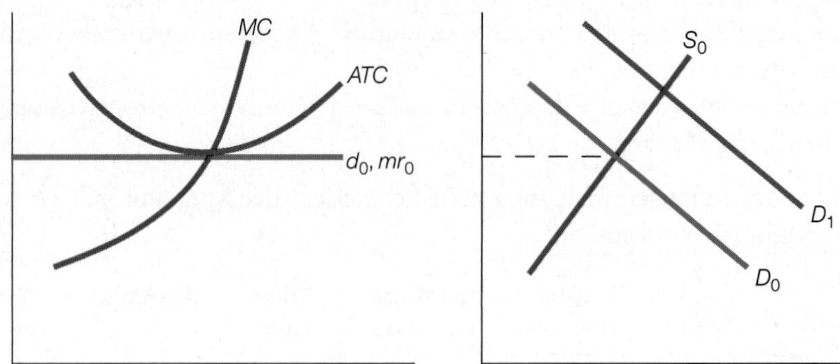

a. Show the effect of the increase in demand on the perfectly competitive firm's price, marginal revenue, output, and profits in the short run.

b. Show the long-run effects of the increase in demand for the industry, and the effects on a perfectly competitive firm's price, marginal revenue, output, and profits.

chapter 9

Monopoly

9.1 MONOPOLY: THE PRICE MAKER
How do you find equilibrium price and output in monopoly?

9.2 DEMAND AND MARGINAL REVENUE IN MONOPOLY
Why are the demand and marginal revenue curves different in monopoly?

9.3 THE MONOPOLIST'S EQUILIBRIUM
How does the monopolist decide what output to produce?

9.4 MONOPOLY AND WELFARE LOSS
What are the welfare costs of a monopoly?

9.5 MONOPOLY POLICY
What are three common approaches that are used to deal with the monopoly problem?

9.6 PRICE DISCRIMINATION
What is price discrimination?

section 9.1

Monopoly: The Price Maker

- What is a monopoly?
- Why is pure monopoly rare?
- What are the sources of monopoly power?
- What is a natural monopoly?

WHAT IS A MONOPOLY?

monopoly
exists when there is only one supplier of a product that has no close substitute and there are natural and legal barriers to entry that prevent competition

http://

A true or pure **monopoly** exists where there is only one seller of a product for which no close substitute is available and there are natural or legal barriers to entry that prevent competition. In a monopoly, the firm and "the industry" are one and the same. Consequently, the firm sets the price of the good, because the firm faces the industry demand curve and can pick the most profitable point on that demand curve. Monopolists are price makers (rather than price takers) who try to pick the price that will maximize their profits.

PURE MONOPOLY IS A RARITY

Few goods and services truly have only one producer. One might think of a small community with a single bank, a single newspaper, or even a single grocery store. Even in these situations, however, most people can bank out of town, use a substitute financial institution, buy out-of-town newspapers or read them on the Web, go to a nearby town to buy groceries, and so on. Near-monopoly conditions exist, but absolute total monopoly is rather unusual.

One area where there is typically only one producer of goods and services within a market area is public utilities. In any given market, usually only one company provides natural gas or supplies water. Moreover, governments themselves provide many services for which they are often the sole providers—sewer services, fire and police protection, and military protection. Most of these situations resemble a pure monopoly. Again, however, for most of the above cited goods and services, substitute goods and services are available. People heating their home with natural gas can switch to electric heat (or vice versa). In some areas, one can even substitute home-collected rain water or well water for that provided by the local water company.

While the purist might correctly deny the existence of monopoly, the number of situations where monopoly conditions are closely approximated are numerous enough to make the study of monopoly more than a theoretical abstraction; moreover, the study of monopoly is useful in clarifying certain desirable aspects of perfect competition.

BARRIERS TO ENTRY

There are several ways that a monopolist may make it virtually impossible for other firms to overcome barriers to entry. For example, a monopolist might prevent potential rivals from entering the market through legal barriers, economies of scale, or by controlling important inputs.

Legal Barriers

In the case of legal barriers, the government might franchise only one firm to operate an industry, as is the case for postal services in most countries. The government can also provide licensing designed to ensure a certain level of quality and competence. Many trade industries require government licensing, such as hair stylists, bartenders, contractors, electricians, and plumbers.

Also, the government could give a company a patent to encourage inventive activity. It can cost millions of dollars to develop a new drug or a computer chip and without a patent to recoup some of these costs, there would certainly be less inventive activity. As long as the patent is in effect the company has the potential to enjoy monopoly profits for many years. After all, why would a firm engage in costly research if any company could free ride off their discovery and produce and sell the new drug or computer chip?

section 9.1 Exhibit 1 **Economies of Scale**

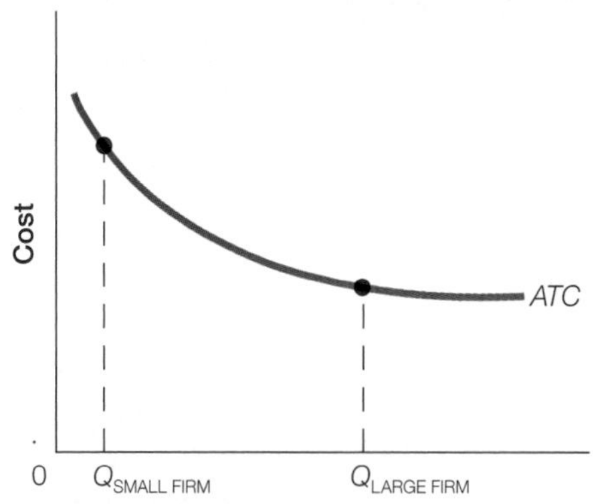

Exhibit 1 shows a firm that has economies of scale over the relevant range of output with declining average total costs. If one firm can produce the total output at a lower cost than several small firms, it is called a natural monopoly.

Economies of Scale

The situation in which one large firm can provide the output of the market at a lower cost than two or more smaller firms is called a **natural monopoly.** With a natural monopoly, it is more efficient to have one firm produce the good. The reason for the cost advantage is economies of scale; that is, *ATC* falls as output expands throughout the relevant output range, as seen in Exhibit 1. Public utilities, like water, gas, and electricity, are often given exclusive monopoly rights because the government believes they are natural monopolies.

natural monopoly
a firm that can produce at a lower cost than a number of smaller firms could

Control Over an Important Input

Another barrier to entry could occur if a firm had control over an important input. For example, from the late nineteenth century to the early 1940s, the Aluminum Company of America (Alcoa) had a monopoly in the production of aluminum. Their monopoly power was guaranteed because of their control over an important ingredient in the production of aluminum—bauxite. Similarly, the DeBeers company of South Africa has monopoly power because they control roughly 75 percent of the world's output of diamonds. In some sense, Kobe Bryant, the star L.A. Lakers basketball player, has a monopoly because he has unique control over his special basketball talents.

Section Check

1. A pure monopoly exists where there is only one seller of a product for which no close substitute is available.
2. Pure monopolies are rare because there are few goods and services where only one producer exists.
3. Sources of monopoly power include: legal barriers, economies of scale, and the control over important inputs.
4. A natural monopoly occurs when one firm can provide the good or service at a lower cost than two or more smaller firms.

---

1. Why does monopoly depend on the existence of barriers to entry?
2. Why is a pure monopoly a rarity?
3. Why does the government grant some companies like public utilities monopoly power?

section 9.2

Demand and Marginal Revenue in Monopoly

- How does the demand curve for a monopolist differ from that of a perfectly competitive firm?
- Why is marginal revenue less than price in monopoly?

In monopoly, the market demand curve may be regarded as the demand curve for the firm's product because the monopoly firm *is* the market for that particular product. The demand curve indicates the quantities that the firm can sell at various possible prices. In monopoly, the demand curve for the firm's product declines as additional units are placed on the market—the demand curve is downward sloping. In monopoly, the firm cannot set both its price and the quantity it sells. That is, a monopolist would love to sell a larger quantity at a high price, but it can't. If the monopolist reduces output, the price will rise; if the monopolist expands output, the price will fall.

Recall that in perfect competition, because there are many buyers and sellers of homogeneous goods (resulting in a perfectly elastic demand curve), competitive firms can sell all they want at the market price. They face a horizontal demand curve. The firm takes the price of its output as determined by the market forces of supply and demand. Monopolists, on the other hand, face a downward-sloping demand curve and if the monopolist wants to expand output, it must accept a lower price. The two demand curves are displayed side by side in Exhibit 1.

section 9.2 Exhibit 1 — Comparing Demand Curves: Perfect Competition versus Monopoly

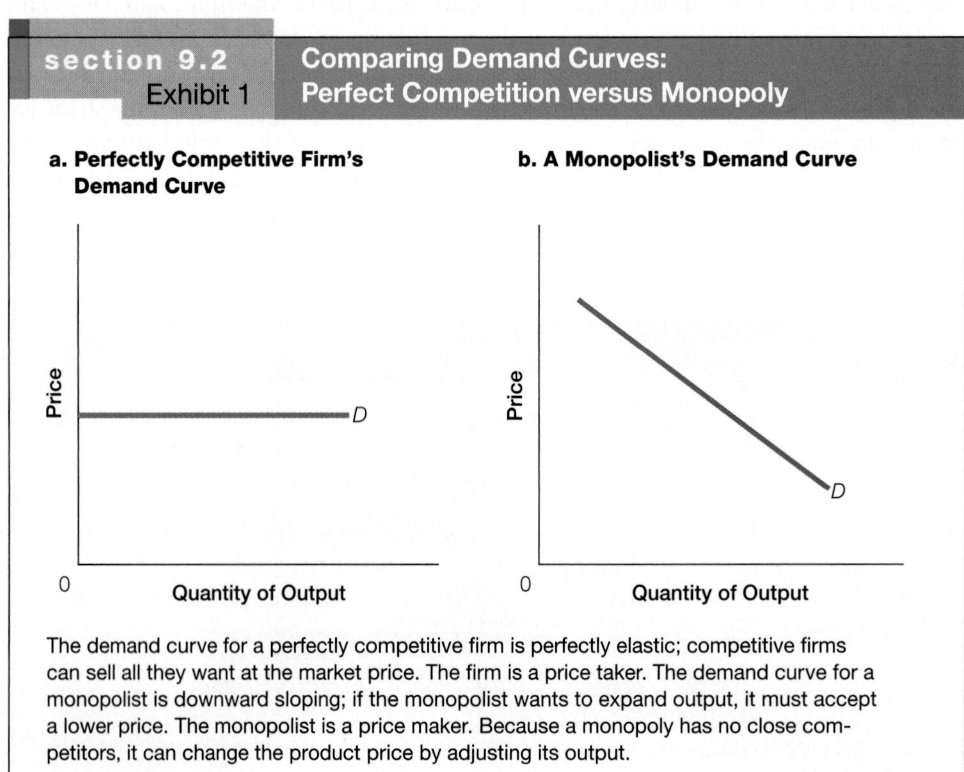

The demand curve for a perfectly competitive firm is perfectly elastic; competitive firms can sell all they want at the market price. The firm is a price taker. The demand curve for a monopolist is downward sloping; if the monopolist wants to expand output, it must accept a lower price. The monopolist is a price maker. Because a monopoly has no close competitors, it can change the product price by adjusting its output.

section 9.2 Exhibit 2 **Total, Marginal, and Average Revenue**

Price	Quantity	Total Revenues ($TR = P \times Q$)	Marginal Revenue ($MR = \Delta TR/\Delta Q$)	Average Revenue ($AR = TR/Q$)
$6	0	—	—	—
5	1	$5		$5
4	2	8	$3	4
3	3	9	1	3
2	4	8	−1	2
1	5	5	−3	1

In Exhibit 2, we see the price of the good, the quantity of the good, the *total revenue* ($TR = P \times Q$), and the *average revenue,* the amount of revenue the firm receives per unit sold ($AR = TR/Q$). The average revenue is just the price per unit sold, which is exactly equal to the market demand curve and the *marginal revenue*—the amount of revenue the firm receives from selling an additional unit ($MR = \Delta TR/\Delta Q$).

In Exhibit 3, we see that the marginal revenue curve for a monopolist lies below the demand curve. Why is this the case? Suppose the firm initially sets its price at $5. It only sells one unit a day and its total revenue is $5. Now to increase sales it decides to drop the price to $4. Sales increase to two units a day and total revenue increases to $8. The firm's marginal revenue is only $3. Why? When the firm cuts the price in order to induce the second customer to buy, it now gains only $4 from the first customer even though she is willing to pay $5. That is, because both customers are now paying $4, the company is re-

section 9.2 Exhibit 3 **Demand and Marginal Revenue for the Monopolist**

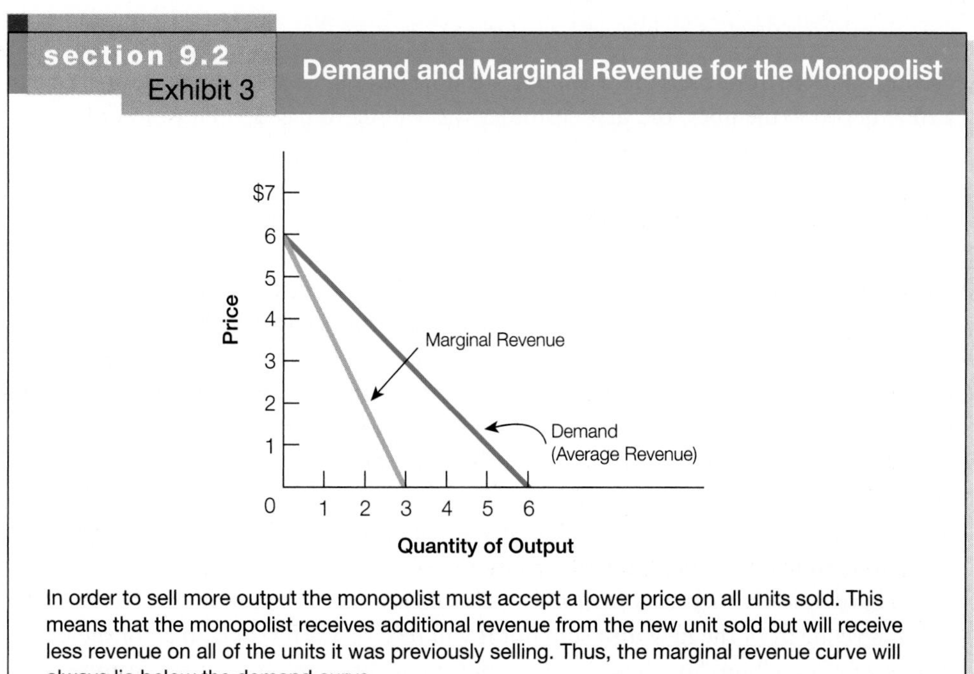

In order to sell more output the monopolist must accept a lower price on all units sold. This means that the monopolist receives additional revenue from the new unit sold but will receive less revenue on all of the units it was previously selling. Thus, the marginal revenue curve will always lie below the demand curve.

APPLICATION

DEMAND AND MARGINAL REVENUE

Q: Using the concepts of total revenue and marginal revenue, show why marginal revenue is less than price in a monopoly situation. Suppose a monopolist wants to expand output from one unit to two units. In order to sell two units rather than one, the monopolist must lower its price from $10 to $8—see Exhibit 4. Will the marginal revenue be less than the price?

A: In Exhibit 4 we see that to sell two units we have to lower the price on both units to $8. That is, the seller doesn't receive $10 from unit one, and $8 for unit two, but rather, receives $8 for both units. So what happens to marginal revenue? There are two parts to this answer. One, there is a loss in revenue, $2, from selling the first unit at $8 instead of $10. Two, there is a gain in revenue from selling the additional output—the second unit at $8. So the marginal revenue is $6 ($8 − $2), which is less than the price of the good, $8. The monopolist's marginal revenue will always be less than price because of the downward-sloping demand curve.

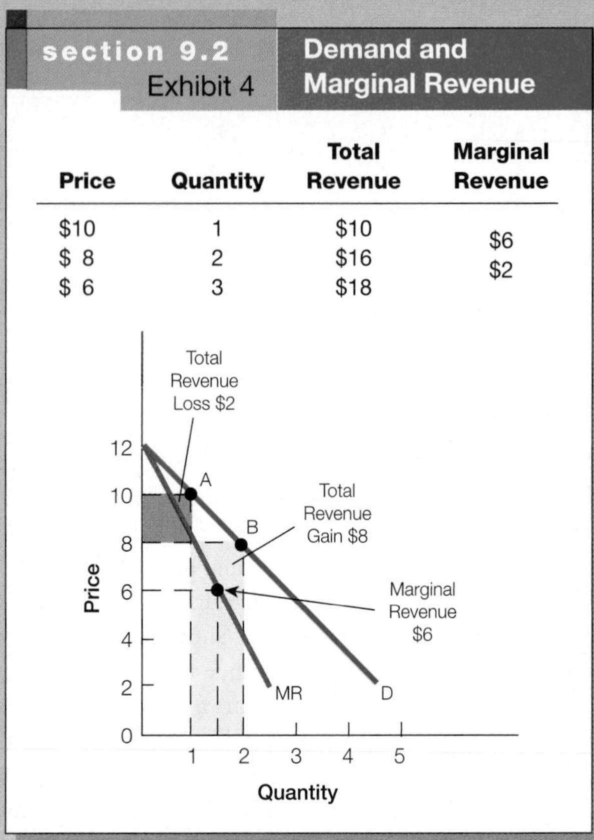

section 9.2 Exhibit 4 — Demand and Marginal Revenue

Price	Quantity	Total Revenue	Marginal Revenue
$10	1	$10	
$ 8	2	$16	$6
$ 6	3	$18	$2

ceiving $4 more from customer two, but it is now earning $1 less from customer one for a total of $8. Remember, the first customer was willing to pay $5. Thus, in order to get revenue from marginal customers, the firm has to lower the price.

In order to induce a third daily customer to purchase the good, the firm must cut its prices to $3. In doing so, it gains $3 in revenue from the new, third customer, but it loses $2 in revenue because each of the first two customers are now paying $1 less than previously. The marginal revenue is $1 ($3 − $2), less than the price of the good ($3).

Finally, in order to get a fourth customer, the firm has to cut the price to $2. The firm finds that in doing so, it actually loses additional revenue, because the new revenue received from the fourth customer ($2) is more than offset by losses in revenues from the first three customers, $3, because each customer pays $1 less than before.

Hence, *the marginal revenue is always less than the price*—that is, the marginal revenue curve will always lie below the demand curve as shown in Exhibit 3. Recall in perfect competition, the firm could sell all it wanted at the market price and the price was equal to marginal revenue. However, in monopoly, if the seller wants to expand output it will have to lower its price on *all* units. This means that the monopolist receives additional revenue from the new unit sold but it will receive less revenue on all of the units it was previously selling. So when the monopolist cuts price to attract new customers, the old customers benefit.

It is important to note that while a monopolist can set its price anywhere it wants, it will not set its price as high as possible—be careful not to confuse ability with incentive. As we will see in the next section, some prices along the demand curve will not be profitable for a firm. In other words, profits may be enhanced by either lowering the price or raising it.

MONOPOLISTS' PRICE IN THE ELASTIC PORTION OF THE DEMAND CURVE

The relationship between the elasticity of demand and marginal and total revenue are shown in Exhibit 5. In Exhibit 5(a), elasticity varies along a linear demand curve. Recall from chapter 5 that above the midpoint, the demand curve is elastic ($e > 1$); below the midpoint, it is inelastic ($e < 1$); and at the midpoint, it is unit elastic ($e = 1$). How does elasticity relate to total and marginal revenue? In the elastic portion of the curve, when the price falls, total revenue rises in Exhibit 5(b), so that marginal revenue is positive. In the inelastic region of the demand curve, when the price falls, total revenue falls in Exhibit 5(b), so that marginal revenue is negative. At the midpoint of the linear demand curve, the total revenue curve reaches its highest point, as seen in Exhibit 5(b), so that $MR = 0$.

For example, suppose the price falls on the top half of the demand curve in Exhibit 5(a) from \$90 to \$80; total revenue increases from \$90 (\$90 × 1) to \$160 (\$80 × 2); the marginal revenue is positive at \$70. Because a reduction in price leads to an increase in total revenue, the demand curve is elastic in this region. Now, suppose the price falls from \$20 to \$10 on the lower portion of the demand curve; total revenue falls from \$160 (\$20 × 8) to \$90 (\$10 × 9); the marginal revenue is negative at −\$70. Because a reduction in price leads to a decrease in total revenue, the demand curve is inelastic in this region.

A monopolist will never knowingly operate in the inelastic portion of its demand curve, because increased output will lead to lower total revenue in this region. Not only are total revenues falling, but total costs will rise as you produce more output. Similarly, if a monopolist was to lower its output, it could increase its total revenue and lower its total costs (because it costs less to produce fewer units), leading to greater economic profits.

a. Demand and Marginal Revenue

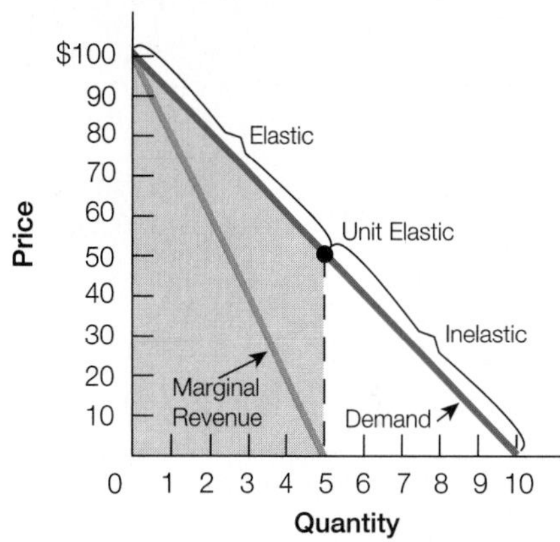

b. Total Revenue

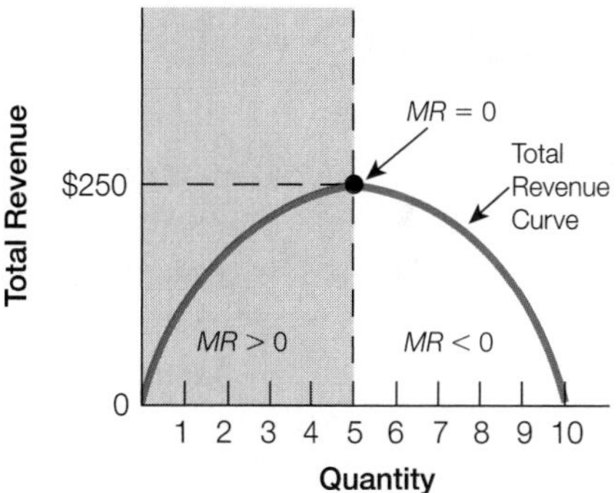

In Exhibit 5(a) we see that along a linear demand curve, the elastic segment lies above the midpoint, the inelastic segment lies below the midpoint, and at the midpoint the demand is unit elastic. When demand is elastic, a decline in price will increase total revenue; when demand is inelastic, a decline in price will lead to a decrease in total revenue. In Exhibit 5(b), we see that over the range from 0 to 5 units, total revenue is rising, so that marginal revenue is positive. Over the range from 5 units to 10 units, total revenue is falling, so that marginal revenue is negative. At 5 units of output, total revenue is maximized at \$250 (\$50 × 5), so that marginal revenue is zero.

Section Check

1. The monopolist's demand curve is downward sloping because it is the market demand curve. To produce and sell another unit of output, the firm must lower its price on all units. As a result, the marginal revenue curve lies below the demand curve.
2. The monopolist cannot set both price and the quantity it sells. If the monopolist reduces output, the price will rise, and if the monpolist expands output, the price will fall.
3. The monopolist's marginal revenue will always be less than price because there is a downward-sloping demand curve. In order to sell more output, the monopolist must accept a lower price on all units sold. This means that the monopolist receives additional revenue from the new unit sold but he will receive less revenue on all of the units he was previously selling.
4. The monopolist will operate in the elastic portion of its demand curve.

---

1. Why are the market and the firm's demand curves the same for a monopoly?
2. Why is a monopoly a price maker but a perfectly competitive firm a price taker?
3. Why is marginal revenue less than price for a profit-maximizing monopolist?
4. Why would a monopolist never knowingly operate in the inelastic portion of its demand curve?

section 9.3 The Monopolist's Equilibrium

- How does the monopolist decide what output to produce?
- How does the monopolist decide what price to charge?
- How do we know if the monopolist is making a profit?
- How do we know if the monopolist is incurring a loss?
- Can the monopolist's economic profits last into the long run?

HOW DOES A MONOPOLIST DETERMINE THE PROFIT-MAXIMIZING OUTPUT?

In the last section we saw how a monopolist could choose any point along a demand curve. But the monopolist's decision on what level of output to produce depends on more than the marginal revenue derived at various outputs. The firm faces production costs, and the monopolist, like the perfect competitor, will maximize profits at that output where $MR = MC$. This point is demonstrated graphically in Exhibit 1.

As you can see in Exhibit 1, at output level Q_1, the marginal revenue exceeds the marginal cost of that production, so it is profitable for the monopolist to expand output. Profits continue to grow until output Q^* is reached. Beyond that output, say Q_2, the marginal cost of production exceeds the marginal revenue from production, so profits decline. The monopolists should cut production back to Q^*. Therefore, the equilibrium output is Q^*. At this output, marginal costs and marginal revenues are equal.

THREE-STEP METHOD FOR MONOPOLISTS

Let us return to the three-step method we used in chapter 8. Determining whether a firm is generating economic profits, economic losses, or zero economic profits at the profit-maximizing level of output, Q^*, can be done in three easy steps.

1. Find where marginal revenues equal marginal costs and proceed straight down to the horizontal quantity axis to find Q^*, the profit-maximizing output level.
2. At Q^*, go straight up to the demand curve then to the left to find the market price, P^*. Once you have identified P^* and Q^*, you can find total revenue at the profit-maximizing output level, because $TR = P \times Q$.
3. The last step is to find total costs. Again, go straight up from Q^* to the average total cost (ATC) curve then left to the vertical axis to compute the average total cost *per unit*. If we multiply average total costs by the output level, we can find the total costs ($TC = ATC \times Q$).

section 9.3 Exhibit 1 — Equilibrium Output and Price for a Pure Monopolist

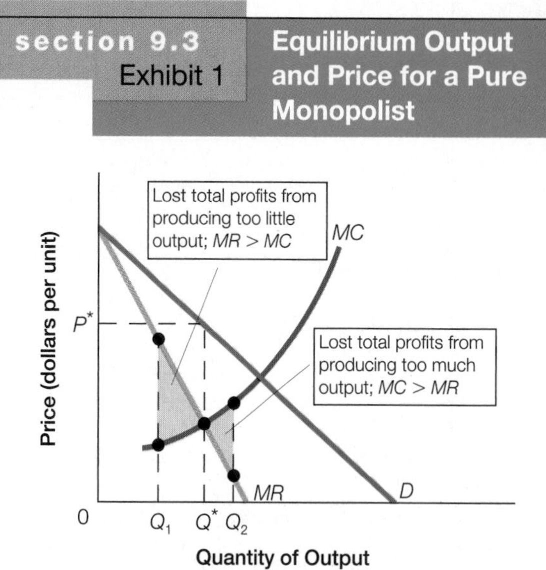

The monopolist maximizes profits at that quantity where $MR = MC$, at Q^*. At Q^* the monopolist finds P^* by extending a vertical line up to the demand curve and over to the vertical axis to find the price. Rather than charging a price equal to marginal cost or marginal revenue at their intersection, however, the monopolist charges the price that customers are willing to pay for that quantity as indicated on the demand curve at P^*. At Q_1, $MR > MC$ and the firm should expand output. At Q_2, $MC > MR$ and the firm should cut back its production.

PROFITS FOR A MONOPOLIST

Exhibit 1 does not show what profits, if any, the monopolist is actually making. This is rectified in Exhibit 2, which shows the equilibrium position of a monopolist, this time adding an average total cost (ATC) curve. As we just discussed, the firm produces where $MC = MR$, or output Q^*. At output Q^* and price P^*, the firm's total revenue is equal to P^*AQ^*0, which is $P^* \times Q^*$. At output Q^*, the firm's total cost is CBQ^*0, which is $ATC \times Q^*$. In Exhibit 2, we see that total revenues are greater than total costs so the firm has a total profit of area P^*ABC.

In perfect competition, profits in an economic sense will persist only in the short run, because in the long run, new firms will enter the industry, increasing industry supply, and thus driving down the price of the good. With this, profits are eliminated. In monopoly, however, profits are not eliminated, because one of the conditions for monopoly is that barriers to entry exist. Other firms cannot enter, so economic profits persist in the long run.

section 9.3 Exhibit 2 — A Monopolist's Profits

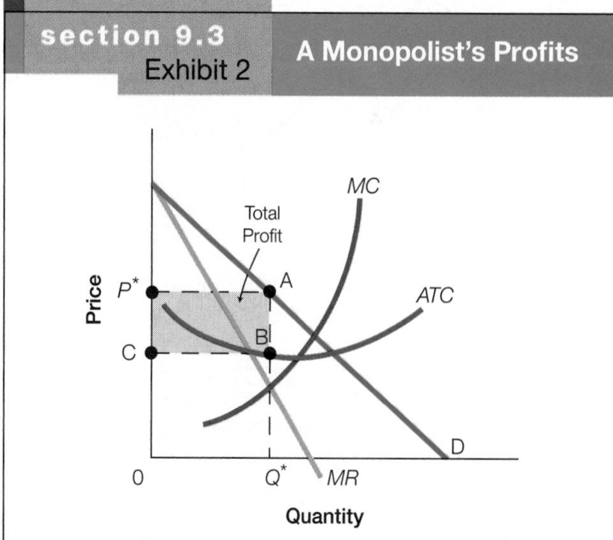

The intersection of MR and MC determines Q^*, the profit-maximizing level of output. The demand curve shows the price that can be charged for Q^*. Total profits equal the area P^*ABC—the difference between total revenues (P^*AQ^*0) and total costs (CBQ^*0).

LOSSES FOR A MONOPOLIST

It is easy to imagine a monopolist ripping off consumers by charging prices resulting in long-run economic profits.

section 9.3 Exhibit 3 **A Monopolist's Losses**

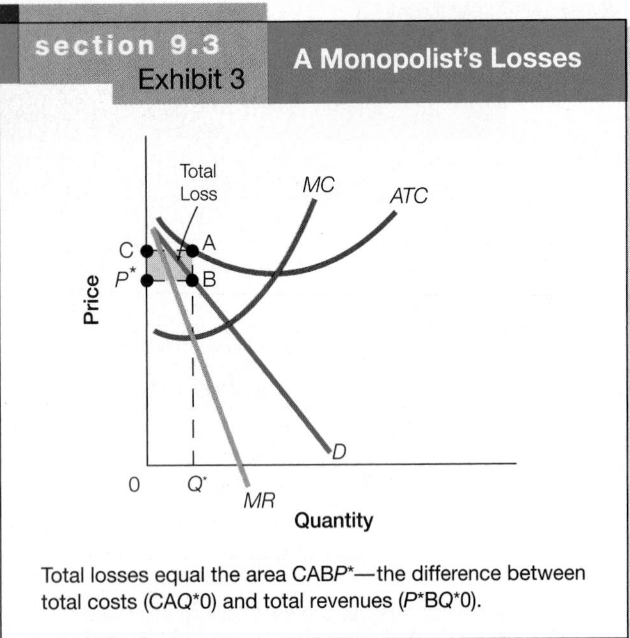

Total losses equal the area CABP*—the difference between total costs (CAQ*0) and total revenues (P*BQ*0).

However, there are also many companies with monopoly power that have gone out of business. Imagine that you received a patent on a bad idea like a roof ejection seat for a helicopter, or that you had the sole rights to turn an economics textbook into a screenplay for a motion picture. While you may be the sole supplier of a product, that does not guarantee that consumers will demand your product. There may be no close substitute for your product, but there is always competition for the consumer dollar—other goods may provide greater satisfaction. Exhibit 3 illustrates loss in a monopoly situation. In this graph, notice that the demand curve is well below the average total cost curve. In this case, the monopolist will incur a loss because there is insufficient demand to cover average total costs at any price and output combination along the demand curve. At Q^*, total costs, CAQ^*0, are greater than total revenues, P^*BQ^*0, so the firm incurs a total loss of CABP^* in Exhibit 3.

In summary, if total revenue is greater than total costs at Q^*, the firm is generating total economic profits. And if total revenue is less than total costs at Q^*, the firm is generating total economic losses. If total revenue is equal to total costs at Q_2, the firm is earning zero economic profits. Remember, the cost curves include implicit and explicit costs—so in this case, we are covering the total opportunity costs of our resources and are earning a normal profit or rate of return.

section 9.3 Exhibit 4 **Impact of Patent Protection on Equilibrium Price and Quality**

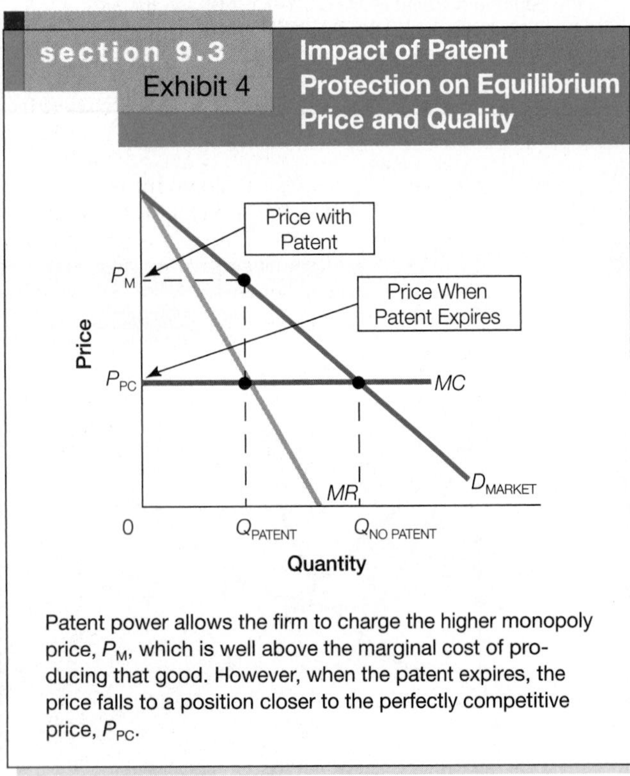

Patent power allows the firm to charge the higher monopoly price, P_M, which is well above the marginal cost of producing that good. However, when the patent expires, the price falls to a position closer to the perfectly competitive price, P_{PC}.

PATENTS

One form of monopoly power conferred by governments is provided by patents and copyrights. A patent puts the government's police power behind the patent holder's exclusive right to make a product for a period of time (20 years) without anyone else being able to make an identical product. As Exhibit 4 suggests, this gives the supplier at least temporary monopoly power over that good or service. This allows the firm with the patent to price its product well above marginal costs, at P_M. Notice the marginal cost curve is flat. The reason for this is that most of the cost of drugs is in the development stage. Once the drug is available for the market, the marginal costs are close to constant—flat. When patents expire, the price of the patented good or service usually falls substantially with the entry of competing firms. The price will fall towards the perfectly competitive price P_{PC} and the output will increase towards $Q_{NO\ PATENT}$.

Why does the government give inventors this limited monopoly power, raising the prices of pharmaceutical drugs and other "vital" goods? The rationale is simple. Without patents, inventors would have little incentive to incur millions of dollars in research and development expenses to create new products (e.g., life-saving drugs) if others could immediately copy the idea and manufacture the products without incurring the research expenses. Similarly, copyrights stimulate creative activity of other kinds, giving writers the incentive to write books that earn royalties and are not merely copied freely. Just as the enormous number of computer programs written for home computers reflects the fact that program writers receive royalties from the sale of each copy sold; that is why they and the firms they work for vehemently oppose unauthorized copying of their work.

Without patents, would some life-saving drugs have been invented? Some drugs cost millions of dollars in research. Without the protection of a patent, the firm may not have been able to make profits from its inventive activity for very long, which is why the government issues patents that last up to 20 years. However, after the patent expires, many popular drugs soon lose their protection; Prozac lost its patent in February 2001 and Claritin will lose its patent in April 2004. In most cases, less costly generic drugs hit the market soon after the patent expiration and prices then move closer to the competitive price, although perhaps not all the way to the competitive level, as some companies are able to keep customers through brand loyalty.

Section Check

1. The monopolist, like the perfect competitor, maximizes profits at that output where marginal revenue equals marginal cost.
2. The monopolist sets the price according to the demand for the product at the profit-maximizing output.
3. Monopoly profits can be found by comparing price per unit and average total cost per unit at Q^*. If $P > ATC$, there are economic profits. If $P < ATC$, there are economic losses.
4. Monopolists' profits can last into the long run, because in monopoly, there are barriers to entry.

---

1. What is a monopolist's principle for choosing the profit-maximizing output?
2. How do you find the profit-maximizing price for a monopolist?
3. For a monopolist making positive economic profits, what must be true about the relationship between price and average total cost?
4. For a monopolist making negative economic profits, what must be true about the relationship between price and average total cost?
5. Why, unlike perfectly competitive firms, can a monopolist continue to earn positive economic profits in the long run?

section 9.4

Monopoly and Welfare Loss

- How does monopoly lead to inefficiencies?
- What is the welfare loss in monopoly?
- Does monopoly retard innovation?

DOES MONOPOLY PROMOTE INEFFICIENCY?

Monopoly is often considered to be bad. But what is the basis in economic theory for concerns about the establishment of monopoly power? There are two main objections to

section 9.4 Exhibit 1 **Perfect Competition versus Monopoly**

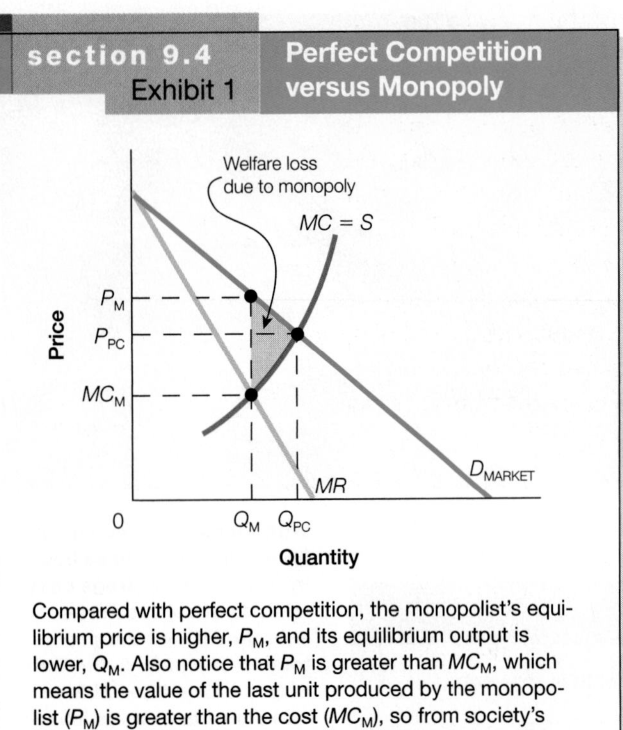

Compared with perfect competition, the monopolist's equilibrium price is higher, P_M, and its equilibrium output is lower, Q_M. Also notice that P_M is greater than MC_M, which means the value of the last unit produced by the monopolist (P_M) is greater than the cost (MC_M), so from society's point of view the monopolist is producing too little output.

monopoly. First, on equity grounds, many people feel that it is not "fair" for monopoly owners to have persistent economic profits when they work no harder than other firms. However, to most economists, the more serious objection is that monopolies result in market inefficiencies. That is, monopoly leads to a lower output and to higher prices than would exist under perfect competition. To demonstrate why this is so, see Exhibit 1. In monopoly, the firm produces output Q_M and charges a price of P_M. Suppose, however, that we had perfect competition and that the industry was characterized by many small firms that could produce output with the same efficiency (at the same cost) as one large firm. Then the marginal cost curve shown in Exhibit 1 could be the sum of the individual marginal cost curves of the individual firms, and the upward portion of that curve might be considered the industry supply curve.

Equilibrium price and quantity would be determined where the marginal cost (or supply) curve intersects with the demand curve, at output Q_{PC} and price P_{PC}. Thus, the competitive equilibrium solution provides for more output and lower prices than the solution prevailing in monopoly. This provides the major efficiency objection to monopoly: Monopolists charge higher prices and produce less output. This may also be viewed as "unfair," in that consumers are burdened more than under the alternative competitive arrangement.

Welfare Loss in Monopoly

In addition to the monopolist producing lower levels of output at higher prices, notice that the monopolist produces at an output where the price (P_M) is greater than the marginal cost (MC_M). Because $P > MC$, it means that the value to society from the last unit produced is greater than its costs (MC_M). That is, the monopoly is *not* producing enough of the good from society's perspective. We call the shaded area in Exhibit 1 the welfare loss due to monopoly.

The actual amount of the welfare loss in monopoly is of considerable debate among economists. Estimates vary between one-tenth of 1 percent to 6 percent of national income. The variation depends on the researchers' estimates of elasticity of demand, whether firm or industry data was used, whether adjustments for profits were made (for the inclusion of royalties and intangibles), and last, whether the researcher included some proxy for scarce resources used in attempting to create a monopoly.

DOES MONOPOLY RETARD INNOVATION?

Another argument against monopoly is that a lack of competition tends to retard technological advancement. Monopolists become comfortable, reaping their monopolistic profits, so they do not work hard at product improvement, technical advances designed to promote efficiency, and so forth. The American railroad is sometimes cited as an example of this situation. Early in the last century, railroads had a strong amount of monopoly power, but they did not spend much on research or development; they did not aggressively try to improve rail transport. As a consequence, technical advances in other transport modes—like cars, trucks, and airplanes—led to a loss of monopoly power, as transportation substitutes came into existence.

However, the notion that monopoly retards all innovation can be disputed. Many near-monopolists are, in fact, important innovators. Companies like Microsoft, International Business Machines (IBM), Polaroid, and Xerox have all, at one time or another, had very strong market positions, in some instances approaching monopoly secured by patent protection, but they were also important innovators. Indeed, innovation helps firms initially obtain a degree of monopoly status, as patents can give a monopoly new products and/or cost-saving technology. Even the monopolist wants more profits, and any innovation that lowers costs or expands revenues creates profits for the monopolist. In addition, because patents expire, a monopolist may be expected to innovate in order to obtain additional patents and preserve its monopoly power. Therefore, the incentive to innovate may well exist in monopolistic market structures.

Section Check

1. Monopoly results in smaller output and a higher price than would be the case under perfect competition.
2. The monopolist produces at an output where $P > MC$. This means the value to society of the last unit produced is greater than its cost. In other words, the monopoly is not producing enough output from society's standpoint.
3. Monopoly may lead to greater concentration of economic power and could retard innovation.

---

1. Why does the reduced output under monopoly cause inefficiency?
2. Does monopoly power retard innovation? Why or why not?
3. What does the welfare cost of monopoly represent? How is it measured?
4. How can economies of scale lead to monopoly? How can it result in monopoly increasing rather than decreasing market output relative to the competitive market structure?
5. Can monopoly be the result of a new innovation that leaves consumers better off than before? Why or why not?

Monopoly Policy

section 9.5

- What is the objective of antitrust policy?
- What is regulation?
- What is average cost pricing?

Because monopolies pose certain problems with respect to efficiency, equity, and power, the public, through its governments, must decide how to deal with the phenomenon. Three major approaches to dealing with the monopoly problem are commonly used: antitrust policies, regulation, and public ownership. We will discuss the first two of these approaches here; the topic of government-run monopolies is covered later in this section.

© DOUG MENUEZ/PHOTODISC/GETTY ONE IMAGES

Ivy League schools have been charged with illegally colluding to fix the price of scholarships. Ivy League schools wanted to make sure they did not get into a "scholarship war," so the participating schools collectively met and fixed scholarship packages. Students would then pick their schools on the basis of academic quality, not the size of scholarship package. These activities guaranteed that any student applying to more than one of these schools would receive the same financial package.

It should be pointed out that in these discussions, the word "monopoly" is sometimes used in a loose, general sense to refer to imperfectly competitive markets, not just to "pure" monopoly.

ANTITRUST POLICIES

Perhaps the most obvious way to deal with monopoly is to make it illegal. The government can bring civil lawsuits or even criminal actions against business people or corporations engaged in monopolistic practices. By imposing both monetary and nonmonetary costs on monopolists (the fear of lawsuits or even jail sentences), antitrust policies reduce the profitability of monopoly.

Keeping Firms from Getting Too Big

Antitrust efforts in the 1960s and 1970s turned increasingly against conglomerate-type mergers, where firms acquired firms producing goods in other industries. More traditional-type antitrust suits against firms with dominant market positions within a single industry also continued. Most notably, a monumental suit was brought against IBM that alleged it had a near-monopoly role in the computer business. More recently, Netscape has claimed that the same monopoly power exists with Microsoft.

Promoting More Price Competition

Many professional associations have restricted the promotion of price competition by prohibiting advertising among their members. Recently, both the FTC and the Justice Department have successfully attacked these types of restrictions on price competition on the grounds that they violate the antitrust laws. They have been spurred on in their efforts by consumer groups who have noticed that prices tend to be much lower where price competition is allowed to flourish. Thus, optometrists were prodded to advertise the price of eyeglasses; pharmacists, the price of commonly prescribed drugs; and even lawyers, the price of a divorce.

HAVE ANTITRUST POLICIES BEEN SUCCESSFUL?

The success of antitrust policies can be debated. Surely very few giant monopolies have been disbanded as a consequence of antitrust policies. Studies have shown that there was little change in the degree of monopoly/oligopoly power in the first 100 years or so of U.S. antitrust legislation. Manufacturing, as a whole, has actually become more concentrated; that is, there are now fewer firms in the industry. However, it is very likely that at least some anticompetitive practices have been prevented simply by the existence of laws prohibiting monopoly-like practices. While the laws have probably been enforced in an imperfect fashion, on balance, they have probably successfully impeded monopoly influences to some degree.

GOVERNMENT REGULATION

Government regulation is an alternative approach to dealing with monopolies. Under regulation, a company would not be allowed to charge any price it wants. Suppose the government does not want to break up a natural monopoly in the water or the power in-

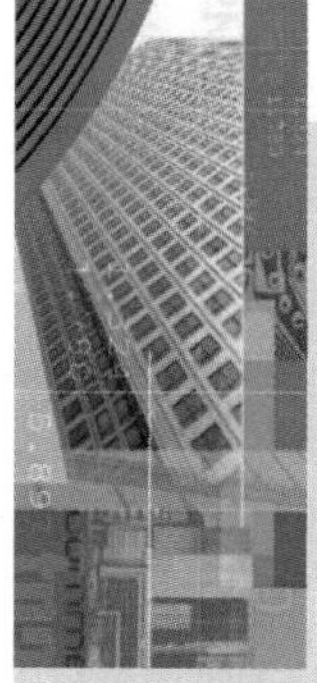

In The NEWS

IS MICROSOFT A MONOPOLY?

Government prosecutors have argued that Microsoft has engaged in a pattern of using its monopoly power to crush rivals and prevent real competition from developing. In June 2001, a federal appeals court unanimously threw out a lower court order to break up Microsoft into two companies. However, the appeals court did find that the company had repeatedly abused its monopoly power in the software business. It now looks like a Microsoft break up is unlikely.

What does Larry Ellison, the Oracle Software magnate, think of the Microsoft antitrust case? "So they make all the stuff for free and drive Netscape out of business. They thought Netscape was an incredibly dangerous company. They thought that the browser would become the platform for the next-generation application. As it turns out, I think they were mistaken. They should have been shooting at us [Oracle], when they were shooting at Netscape. In fact, we used to refer to Netscape as the heat-shield. They were so busy destroying Netscape, they kind of lost sight of what we were doing. And in the Internet, it's not about the desktop software. It's about the server software. The irony of all of this is they broke into the wrong bank.

"They repeatedly broke the law. They said to Compaq: If you want to get a good price for Windows, you better not put Netscape on that computer. That is using an existing monopoly, Windows, to obtain a new monopoly in browsers. That's an explicit violation of the Sherman Antitrust Act. They did it over and over again."

SOURCE: http://www.businessweek.com/2001/01_09/b3721108.htm February 26, 2001.

CONSIDER THIS:

It appears that the Microsoft case has less to do with the degree of monopoly power and more to do with the abuse of that power. Specifically, antitrust is about the *actions* taken to form, extend, or maintain the monopoly. However, we have to ask the question: are consumers necessarily worse off as a result of a few powerful computer companies that temporarily dominate the industry? There may be economies of scale in production and technology. Furthermore, the monopoly might well be short-lived. And are the barriers to entry in the computer industry insurmountable? The history of the computer industry has several success stories of individuals with great ideas that have successfully broken into the industry. In addition, Microsoft and Intel are at least partially responsible for making computer power what it is today. A Dell computer with Intel Pentium 4 and Microsoft Windows 2000, available for under $1,000, could not be matched in performance 10 years ago at many times that price.

However, it is important to remember that if the computer market was more competitive, prices might have gone down even faster and the quality of the products might be even higher. For example, look what happened to long-distance rates when Sprint and MCI entered the long-distance telephone market. And just because prices are falling now, will they continue to fall if markets do not become more competitive in the future?

dustry. Remember that natural monopolies occur when one large firm can produce as much output as many smaller firms but at a lower average cost per unit. The government may decide to regulate the monopoly price, but what price does it let the firm charge? The goal is to achieve the efficiency of large-scale production without permitting the high monopoly prices and low output that can promote allocative *inefficiency.*

The basic policy dilemma that regulators often face in attempting to fix maximum prices can be rather easily illustrated. Consider Exhibit 1. Without regulation, say the profit-maximizing monopolist operates at point A, at output Q_M and price P_M. At that output, the price exceeds the average total cost, so economic profits exist. However, the monopolist is producing relatively little output and is charging a relatively high price, and it is producing at a point where price is above marginal cost. This is not the best point from society's perspective.

Allocative Efficiency

From society's point of view, what would be the best price and output position? As we discussed in chapter 8, the best position is at the competitive equilibrium output where $P = MC$. This is because the equilibrium price represents the marginal value of output. The marginal cost represents society's opportunity costs in making the good as opposed to something else. Where price equals marginal cost, society matches marginal value and marginal cost or achieves **allocative efficiency;** this is seen at point C in Exhibit 1.

allocative efficiency
production where the price of a good equals marginal cost

section 9.5 Exhibit 1 Marginal Cost Pricing versus Average Cost Pricing

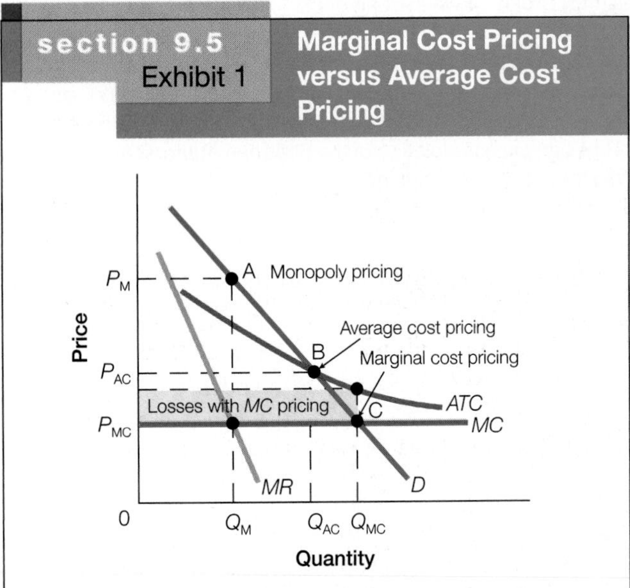

The marginal cost (MC) curve is less than the average total cost curve (ATC) for a natural monopolist as the average cost falls. If the monopolist is unregulated, it could produce a relatively small level of output, Q_M, at a relatively high price, P_M. If regulators require the natural monopolist to use marginal cost pricing, the monopoly will lose money, because P_{MC} is less than average total costs. Average cost pricing (at point B) would permit firms to make a normal rate of return, where $P_{AC} = ATC$. The monopolist's unregulated output at point A is not optimal from society's standpoint, and the optimal output at point C is not feasible.

Can the Regulated Monopolist Operate at $P = MC$?

Unfortunately, the natural monopoly cannot operate profitably at the allocative efficient point, where $P = MC$, indicated at point C on Exhibit 1. At point C, the intersection of the demand and marginal cost curves, average total costs are greater than price. The optimal output, then, is an output that produces losses for the producer. Any regulated business that produced for long at this "optimal" output would go bankrupt; it would be impossible to attract new capital to the industry.

Therefore, the "optimal" output from a welfare perspective really is not viable because losses are incurred. The regulators cannot force firms to price their product at P_{MC} and to sell Q_{MC} output, because the firm would go out of business. Indeed, in the long run, the industry's capital would deteriorate as investors failed to replace old capital when it became worn out or obsolete. If the monopolist's unregulated output at point A is not optimal from society's standpoint, and the short-run optimal output at point C is not feasible from the monopolist's standpoint, where should the regulated monopolist be allowed to operate?

One option to the problem is the government could subsidize the losses associated with marginal cost pricing. However, the burden will ultimately fall on the taxpayers, as the government will have to raise the money to pay for the losses.

The Compromise: Average Cost Pricing

A compromise between monopoly pricing and marginal cost pricing is found at point B on Exhibit 1, output Q_{AC}, which is somewhere between the excessively low output and high prices of an unregulated monopoly and the excessively large output and low prices achieved when prices are equated with marginal cost pricing. At point B, price equals average total costs. The monopolist is permitted to price the product where economic profits are zero, meaning that there is a normal economic profit or rate of return, like firms experience in perfect competition in the long run. This compromise is called **average cost pricing.**

average cost pricing
to set the price equal to average total cost

In the real world, regulators often permit utilities to receive a "fair and reasonable" return that is a rough approximation to that suggested by average cost pricing, at point B. Point B would seem "fair" in that the monopolist is receiving rewards equal to those that a perfect competitor would ordinarily receive—no more and no less. Point B permits more output at a significantly lower price than would occur if the monopolist were unregulated, point A, even though output is still somewhat less and price somewhat more than that suggested by point C, the social optimum or best position.

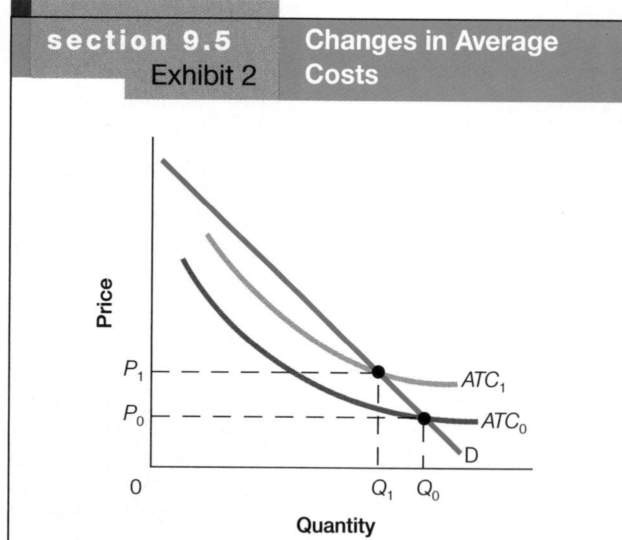

An increase in average total costs leads to a higher price and lower output (P_1Q_1); lower average total costs leads to a lower price and greater output (P_0Q_0). However, both situations lead to a normal rate of return. Because the regulated firm has little incentive to minimize costs, average total costs would have a tendency to rise.

DIFFICULTIES IN AVERAGE COST PRICING

Accurate Calculations of Costs

The actual implementation of a rate (price) that permits a "fair and reasonable" return is more difficult than the analysis suggests. The calculations of costs and values are difficult. In reality, the firm may not know exactly what its demand and cost curves look like. This forces regulatory agencies to use profits, another somewhat ambiguous target, as a guide. If profits are "too high," lower the price, and if profits are "too low," raise the price.

No Incentives to Keep Costs Down

Another problem is that average cost pricing gives the monopolists no incentive to reduce costs. That is, if the firm's costs rise from ATC_0 to ATC_1 in Exhibit 2, the price will rise from P_0 to P_1. And if costs fall, the firm's price will fall. In either scenario, the firm will still be earning a normal rate of return. This is equivalent to saying that if the regulatory agency sets the price at any point where the *ATC* curve intersects the demand curve, the firm will earn a normal rate of return. So if the agency is going to set the price wherever *ATC* intersects the demand curve, why not let your average costs rise? Let your employees fly first class and dine in the finest restaurants. While you are at it, why not buy concert tickets and season tickets to sporting events? Regulators have tackled this problem by allowing the regulated firm to keep some of the profits that come from lower costs; that is, they do not adhere strictly to average cost pricing.

Special Interest Groups

Also, in the real world, consumer groups are constantly battling for lower rates, while the utilities themselves are lobbying for higher rates so that they can approach the monopoly profits indicated by point A on Exhibit 1. Decisions are not always made in a calm, objective, dispassionate atmosphere free of outside involvement. It is precisely the political economy of rate setting that disturbs some critics of this approach of dealing with the monopoly problem. For example, it is possible that a rate-making commissioner could become friendly with a utility company, believing that he can obtain a nice job after his tenure as a regulator is over. The temptation is great for the commissioner to be generous to the utilities. On the other hand, there may be a tendency for regulators to bow to pressure from consumer groups. A politician who wants to win votes can almost always succeed by attacking utility rates and promising rate "reform" (lower rates). If zealous rate regulators listen too closely to the consumer groups and push rates down to a level indicated by point C in Exhibit 1, the industry might be too unstable to attract capital for expansion.

Section Check

1. Antitrust policies are government policies designed to reduce the profitability of a monopoly and push production closer to the social optimum.
2. Privately-owned monopolies may be allowed to operate but under regulation of a government agency.
3. Average cost pricing sets price equal to average total cost, where the demand curve intersects average total costs.

---

1. What alternative ways of dealing with the monopoly problem are commonly used?
2. How do antitrust laws promote more price competition?
3. What price and output are ideal for allocative efficiency for a regulated natural monopolist? Why is an unregulated natural monopolist unlikely to pick this solution?
4. What is average cost pricing? How is it different from marginal cost pricing?
5. What are some difficulties encountered when regulators try to implement average cost pricing on natural monopolies?
6. Why might a job with a regulated natural monopolist that is allowed to earn a "fair and reasonable" return tend to have more perks (noncash forms of compensation) than a comparable job in a nonregulated firm?

section 9.6

Price Discrimination

- What is price discrimination?
- Why does price discrimination exist?
- Does price discrimination work when reselling is easy?

PRICE DISCRIMINATION

price discrimination
the practice of charging different consumers different prices for the same good or service

Sometimes, producers will charge different customers different prices for the same good or service when the cost of providing that good or service does not differ among the customers. This is called **price discrimination.** For example, kids pay less for the movies than adults; senior citizens get discounts on hotels, restaurants, museums, and zoos; most vacation travelers fly between places for less than business travelers; some patients of a doctor may pay more for treatment than others because of their income or insurance coverage; and so on.

Note that price discrimination is possible only with monopoly or where members of a small group of firms (firms that are not price takers) follow identical pricing policies. When there are a large number of competing firms, discrimination is less likely because competitors tend to undercut the high prices charged those discriminated against.

WHY DOES PRICE DISCRIMINATION EXIST?

Price discrimination results from the profit-maximization motive. In our graphical analysis of monopoly, we suggested that there was a demand curve for the product and a corresponding marginal revenue curve. Sometimes, however, different groups of people have

APPLICATION

PRICE DISCRIMINATION AND BUSINESS TRAVELERS

Q: Why do business travelers generally pay more for their flights than vacation travelers?

© JACK HOLLINGSWORTH/PHOTODISC/ GETTY ONE IMAGES

A: The airline industry has found that business travelers have a more inelastic demand for air travel than vacationers and students do. The airlines know that business travelers are generally unwilling to stay over for the weekend (away from home, family, or their favorite golf course), only spend a day or two at their destination, and often do not make their reservations far in advance. All of which means the business traveler has a more inelastic demand curve for flights (fewer substitutes). If the airlines cut prices for business travelers, airline revenues would fall. Personal travelers (perhaps vacationers) are operating on a much more elastic demand curve—they are much more flexible. For these travelers, many substitutes are available, such as other modes of transportation, different times (non-peak times), and so on. Clearly the airlines can make more money by separating the market according to each group's elasticity of demand rather than charging all users the same price.

different demand curves and therefore react differently to price changes. A producer can make more money by charging those different buyers different prices. For example, if the price of a movie is increased from $5 to $8, many kids who would attend at $5 may have to stay home at $8, as they (and perhaps their parents) balk at paying the higher price. The impact on attendance of raising prices may be less, however, for adults, who have higher incomes in the first place and for whom the ticket price may represent a smaller part of the expenses of an evening out.

Thus, there is a different demand curve for those, say, under 16, as opposed to those who are older. Specifically, the elasticity of demand with respect to price is greater for children than for adults. This means that there is a different marginal revenue curve for children than for adults. Assume, for simplicity, that the marginal cost is constant. The profit-maximizing movie theater owner will price where the constant marginal costs equal marginal revenue for each group. As you can see in Exhibit 1(a), the demand curve for kids is rather elastic, perhaps not too different than the perfectly elastic demand curve of perfect competition, where marginal revenue is equal to price. The adult demand curve, shown in Exhibit 1(b), is more downward sloping at any given price and quantity (relatively inelastic), meaning the marginal revenue curve lies well below the demand curve at most output levels. Thus, the price charged adults is way above the point where marginal revenue equals marginal costs, whereas for kids, the price is not as much above the point where marginal revenue equals marginal costs. But in order for price discrimination to be feasible, the seller must be able to successfully distinguish members of targeted groups.

RESALE PREVENTION: THE KEY TO PRICE DISCRIMINATION

For price discrimination to work, the person buying the product at a discount must have difficulty in reselling the product to customers being charged more. Otherwise, those getting the item cheaply would want to buy extra amounts of the product at the discounted price (increasing demand and thus the profit-maximizing price for the discounted prod-

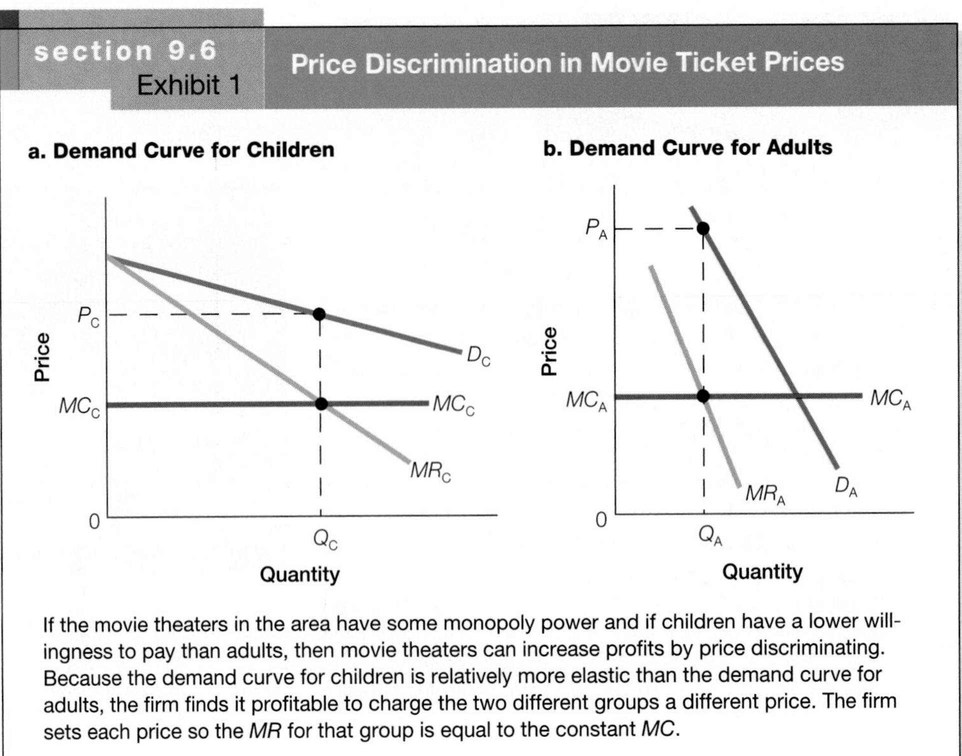

If the movie theaters in the area have some monopoly power and if children have a lower willingness to pay than adults, then movie theaters can increase profits by price discriminating. Because the demand curve for children is relatively more elastic than the demand curve for adults, the firm finds it profitable to charge the two different groups a different price. The firm sets each price so the *MR* for that group is equal to the constant *MC*.

uct) and sell it at a profit to others. In turn, this would reduce the number of customers paying the higher price (thus reducing demand and lowering the profit-maximizing price for that group). Price differentials between groups will erode if reselling is easy. Usually, price discrimination is limited to services and to some goods where it is inherently difficult to resell or where the producer can effectively prevent resale. For example, the

APPLICATION

PRICE DISCRIMINATION AND COUPONS

Q: Tara loves to go through the Sunday paper and cut out supermarket coupons. How do you think Tara's coupon-clipping habits apply to the concept of price discrimination?

A: Often, the key to price discrimination is observing the difference in demand curves for different customers. For example, Tara, who spends an hour looking through the Sunday paper for coupons, will probably have a relatively more elastic demand curve than, say, a busy and wealthy physician or executive.

movie theater operator can simply refuse to admit adults who show a child's admission ticket, and airlines can put restrictions on a ticket indicating the conditions under which it may be used by passengers.

PRICE DISCRIMINATION AND TIME

A publisher can price discriminate when publishing both hardback and paperback editions of a book because people differ in their willingness to pay. You will likely pay a lot more for a hardcover book than a paperback book. Why? While a hardcover book is only slightly more expensive to publish, the real reason for the price differential between hardcover and softcover books is the price elasticity of demand. Some people are willing to pay a higher price to be among the first to read a book or see a movie; their demand curve is relatively inelastic, as in Exhibit 1(b). Other individuals have a more elastic demand curve for these goods and are willing to wait for the book to come out in paperback or the movie to reach the video store, as in Exhibit 1(a). Other customers, like libraries, find that paperbacks are not durable enough to be good substitutes for hardbacks. Sellers are able to profit from this difference in elasticities of demand by charging more to those who are more willing to pay and charging a lower price to those who are less willing to pay. This is called **intertemporal price discrimination.**

QUANTITY DISCOUNTS

Another form of price discrimination occurs when customers buy in large quantities. This is often the case with public utilities and wholesalers, but even stores will sell a six-pack of soda for less than six single cans. Or the local bagel shop might sell you a baker's dozen, where you may get 13 bagels for the price of 12. This type of price discrimination allows the producer to charge a higher price for the first unit than for, say, the twentieth unit. If the monopolist charged the same price for all of the units that she charged for the twentieth unit, then consumers would have a lot more consumer surplus. That is, instead of charging the lower price for all the units, this form of price discrimination allows the producer to extract some consumer surplus.

intertemporal price discrimination
groups of consumers are charged different prices in different time periods

Section Check

1. When producers charge different prices for the same good or service when no cost differences exist, it is called price discrimination.
2. Price discrimination occurs if demand differs among buyers and the seller can successfully identify group members, because producers can make profits by charging different prices to each group.
3. Price discrimination would not work well if the person buying the product could easily resell the product to another customer at a higher, profitable price.

---

1. How do we define price discrimination?
2. Why does price discrimination arise from the profit-maximization motive?
3. What principle will a profit-maximizing monopolist use in trying to price discriminate among different groups of customers?
4. Why will a price-discriminating monopolist charge a higher price to relatively inelastic demanders than to relatively elastic demanders?
5. Why is preventing resale the key to successful price discrimination?
6. Why is it generally easier to price discriminate for services than for goods?

Summary

A pure monopoly exists where there is only one seller of a product for which no close substitute is available, but they are rare because there are few goods and services where only one producer exists. Barriers to entry tend to be very high in monopoly. Sources of monopoly power include legal barriers, economies of scale, and control over important resources.

The monopolist's demand curve is downward sloping because it is the market demand curve. To produce and sell another unit of output, the firm must lower its price on all units. As a result, the marginal revenue curve lies below the demand curve. The monopolist, like the perfect competitor, maximizes profits at that output where marginal revenue equals marginal cost.

Monopoly profits can be found by comparing price per unit and average total cost per unit at Q^*. If $P > ATC$, there are economic profits. If $P < ATC$, there are economic losses. Monopolists' profits can last into the long run, because in monopoly, there are barriers to entry.

Monopoly results in smaller output and a higher price than would be the case under perfect competition. The monopolist produces at an output where $P > MC$. This means the value to society of the last unit produced is greater than its cost. In other words, the monopoly is not producing enough output from society's standpoint.

Antitrust policies can reduce the profitability of a monopoly and push production closer to the social optimum. A natural monopoly occurs when one firm can provide the good or service at a lower cost than two or more smaller firms. Under these conditions, a number of small firms may be less efficient than one large firm, particularly if the latter is regulated.

Price discrimination occurs when producers charge different prices for the same good or service when no cost differences exist. Price discrimination occurs if demand differs among buyers and the seller can successfully identify group members because producers can make profits by charging different prices to different groups. Price discrimination would not work well if the person buying the product could easily resell the product to another customer at a higher, profitable price.

Key Terms and Concepts

monopoly 188
natural monopoly 189
allocative efficiency 202
average cost pricing 202
price discrimination 204
intertemporal price discrimination 207

Review Questions

1. Which of the following could be considered a monopoly:
   a. Kate Hudson (an actress)
   b. DeBeers diamonds
   c. the only doctor in a small town
   d. Ford Motor Company

2.

Quantity	Price Demanded
4	$35
5	30
6	25
7	20
8	15

Output	Total Cost
4	$ 20
5	30
6	45
7	65
8	100

Given the data in the tables, determine the short-run profit-maximizing (loss-minimizing) level of output and price for the monopolist. Fixed cost equals $10.

3. Is it optimal for the monopolist to operate on the inelastic portion of the demand curve? Why or why not?
4. If economic profits were zero, would a monopolist ever stay in business? Why might it be possible for a monopolist to earn positive economic profits in the long run?
5. What is meant by "the welfare loss" of monopoly? Why is there no welfare loss if a monopolist successfully practices perfect price discrimination?

6. Suppose an industry experiences decreasing average costs of production over the relevant range of market demand. Discuss the merits of a regulation requiring the natural monopolist to price where demand equals marginal cost and service all willing customers. What about where demand equals average cost? Are any practical difficulties likely to be encountered with either regulatory program?

7.

Price	Quantity	Fixed Cost	Variable Cost
$100	0	$60	$ 0
90	1	60	25
80	2	60	40
70	3	60	50
60	4	60	70
50	5	60	100
40	6	60	140
30	7	60	190
20	8	60	250

A simple monopolist with the above fixed and variable cost schedules maximizes profits at what level of output?

8. During the fall and spring, Disneyland charges different prices to locals than it does to those from out of town. Why? What if the locals could easily resell their tickets?

9.

"Super Duper" Cuts Hair Salon	
Permanent Price	
Long Hair	$100
Short Hair	$ 75

Does the above price schedule reflect price discrimination? Why or why not?

10. Explain why a computer store offering significant student discounts may require student buyers to sign an agreement not to purchase another computer from the store for a period of six months.

11. Explain how each of the following are a form of price discrimination.

a. a student discount at the movie theater

b. long-distance phone service that costs 15 cents per minute for the first 10 minutes, and 5 cents per minute after 10 minutes

c. a psychic charges each customer his or her maximum reservation price for palm readings

d. a senior citizen breakfast discount at a local restaurant

e. coupon discounts on laundry detergent

12. In October of 1999, Coca-Cola announced that it may test a new vending machine that was temperature sensitive. The price of the soft drinks in the machines would be higher on hot days. The Miami Herald story read "Soda jerks." How is this a form of price discrimination? How can the placement of the vending machines create a monopoly? What if other vending machines are close by and are not owned by Coca-Cola?

13. Compare the size of the welfare (deadweight) loss under monopoly where there is perfect price discrimination and under the standard case of simple monopoly. Explain.

14. Visit the Sexton Web site at **http://sexton.swcollege.com** and click on "U.S. Patent and Trademark Office" and search for the number of drug patents issued (key search word: drug). Currently the length of a U.S. patent from date of issue is 20 years. What do you think would happen to research and development of drugs in the United States if patent lives were much shorter or if no patents were issued at all? How does the protection of intellectual property rights through patents and copyrights encourage economic growth?

chapter 9 Study Guide

Fill in the Blanks

1. A true or pure monopoly exists where there is only ONE seller of a product for which no close substitute is available.

2. Monopolists are PRICEMAKERS rather than price takers.

3. A monopolist's barriers to entry can include LEGAL BARRIERS, ECONOMICS OF SCALE, and CONTROL OF IMP. INPUTS.

4. LEGAL BARRIERS TO ENTRY include franchising, licensing, and patents.

5. The situation in which one large firm can provide the output of the market at a lower cost than two or more smaller firms is called a NATURAL MONOPOLY.

6. A barrier to entry is control over an important INPUT, such as Alcoa's control over bauxite in the 1940s and DeBeers' control over much of the world's output of diamonds.

7. In monopoly, the market demand curve may be regarded as the demand curve for the FIRM because it is the market for that particular product.

8. If a monopolist reduces output, the price will RISE; and if the monopolist expands output, the price will FALL.

9. In monopoly, if the seller wants to expand output, it will have to lower its price on ALL units.

10. The monopolist, like the perfect competitor, will maximize profits at that output where MR = *MC*.

11. The monopolist, unlike the perfect competitor, will not maximize profits at that output where PRICE = *MC*.

12. If at a monopolist's profit-maximizing price and output, the price is less than AVERAGE TOTAL COST, the monopolist is generating economic losses.

13. In monopoly, economic profits are not eliminated by entry because one of the conditions for monopoly is that BARRIERS TO ENTRY exist.

14. Patents and copyrights are examples of MONOPOLY power designed to provide an incentive to develop new products.

15. The major efficiency objection to monopoly is that a monopolist charges HIGHER prices and produces LESS output than would exist under perfect competition.

16. A monopolist produces at an output where the price is GREATER than its marginal cost, so the value to society from the last unit produced is GREATER than its marginal cost.

17. An argument against monopoly is that a lack of competition tends to retard TECHNOLOGICAL advance, but, in fact, many near-monopolists are important innovators.

18. Three major approaches to dealing with the monopoly problem are commonly used: ANTI-TRUST policies, REGULATION, and PUBLIC ownership.

19. It is very likely that at least some anticompetitive practices have been prevented by ANTI-TRUST policies simply by their prohibition of monopoly-like practices.

20. The goal of government regulation as an alternative approach to dealing with monopolies is to achieve the efficiency of large-scale production without permitting the HIGH monopoly prices and LOW output that can cause allocative inefficiency.

21. From society's point of view, allocative efficiency occurs where the price of the good is equal to MARGINAL COST. But with natural monopoly, at the "optimal" level of output for allocative efficiency, LOSSES are incurred.

22. A compromise between unregulated monopoly and marginal cost pricing is AVERAGE COST pricing, where the monopolist is permitted to price the product where price equals AVERAGE TOTAL COST.

23. Average cost pricing REDUCES the incentives for a monopolist to find ways to reduce its costs.

24. PRICE DISCRIMINATION occurs when sellers charge different customers different prices for the same good or service when the cost does not differ.

25. When there are a number of competing firms, price discrimination is LESS likely because competitors tend to undercut the HIGH prices charged those discriminated against.

26. A profit-maximizing seller will charge a HIGHER price for more inelastic demanders and a LOWER price for more elastic demanders.

27. The profit-maximizing rule for a price-discriminating monopolist is to price where MARGINAL REVENUE equals MARGINAL COST for each different group of demanders.

28. For price discrimination to work, the person buying the product at a discount must have difficulty in RESELLING the product to customers being charged more.

29. QUANTITY DISCOUNTS, which allow sellers to charge a higher price for the first unit than for later units, are another form of price discrimination.

30. Quantity discounts allow the price-discriminating producer to extract additional CONSUMER SURPLUS from customers.

True or False

1. For a pure monopoly the firm and the industry are one and the same.

2. A monopoly firm is a price maker, and it will pick a price that is the highest point on its demand curve.

3. Pure monopolies are a rarity because few goods and services truly have only one producer.

4. The cost advantage of a natural monopoly is due to economies of scale throughout the relevant output range.

5. As in perfect competition, in monopoly the demand curve for the firm's product is downward sloping.

6. The marginal revenue curve for a monopolist lies below the demand curve.

7. For a monopoly to get revenue from marginal customers, the firm has to lower the price so that marginal revenue is always less than price.

8. When a monopolist cuts price to attract new customers, its existing customers benefit.

9. Along the inelastic portion of the demand curve, when the price falls, total revenue rises, so that marginal revenue is positive.

10. Along the elastic portion of the demand curve, when the price falls, total revenue rises so that marginal revenue is positive.

11. A monopolist will never knowingly operate in the inelastic portion of its demand curve because increased output will lead to lower total revenue and higher total cost in that region.

12. For a monopolist, the profit-maximizing price is indicated by the height of the demand curve at the profit-maximizing quantity of output.

13. If at a monopolist's profit-maximizing price and output, the price is greater than average total cost, the monopolist is generating economic losses.

14. Economic profits cannot persist in the long run for a monopolist.

15. A monopolist will incur a loss if there is insufficient demand to cover average total costs at any price and output combination along its demand curve.

16. Having monopoly guarantees economic profits.

17. Perfect competition leads to lower output and higher prices than would exist under monopoly.

18. Monopoly creates a welfare loss because a monopoly does not produce enough of a good from society's perspective.

19. There is widespread agreement among economists about the size of the welfare loss from monopoly.

20. By imposing monetary and nonmonetary costs on monopolists, antitrust policies aim to reduce the profitability of monopoly.

21. Government regulation of monopolies aims to achieve the efficiency of large-scale production without permitting the monopolists to charge monopoly prices, which would reduce output.

22. With natural monopoly, the efficient, or optimal, output is one that produces zero economic profits for the producer where price equals marginal cost.

23. Any regulated business that produced for long at the optimal, or efficient, output would go bankrupt.

24. Under average cost pricing, a regulated monopoly is permitted to earn a normal return, as firms experience in perfect competition in the long run.

25. Price discrimination is possible only with monopoly or where members of a small group of firms follow identical pricing policies.

26. When different groups of customers have predictably different elasticities of demand, a monopolist could earn higher profits by charging those different buyers different prices, if it could prevent resale of the product among customers.

27. Price differentials between groups will erode if reselling is easy, which is why price discrimination is usually limited to services and to some goods where it is inherently difficult to resell or where the producer can effectively prevent resale.

Multiple Choice

1. Pure monopoly is defined as
   a. an industry in which there is a single seller.
   b. a market structure in which there are many substitute products.
   c. a market in which there are many rival firms competing for sales.
   d. a market structure in which there is a single buyer.

2. For a true, or pure, monopoly,
   a. there is only one seller of the product.
   b. no close substitutes are available.
   c. the firm and the industry are the same.
   d. it must be virtually impossible for other firms to overcome barriers to entry.
   e. all of the above are true.

3. Which of the following is inconsistent with monopoly?
   a. a single seller
   b. economies of scale
   c. $MR < P$
   d. free entry and exit
   e. selling in the elastic portion of the demand curve in order to maximize profits

4. For a natural monopoly, which of the following is *false?*
   a. It is more efficient to have a single firm produce the good.
   b. Production of the good must involve economies of scale throughout the relevant output range.
   c. It would typically result from a firm's possession of an exclusive patent.
   d. One large firm can produce at lower cost than two or more smaller firms.

5. Which of the following is potentially a barrier to entry into a product market?
   a. patent protection on the design of the product
   b. economies of scale in the product market
   c. government licensing of the product's producers
   d. the control of a crucial input necessary to produce the product
   e. all of the above

6. A profit-maximizing monopolist sets
   a. the product price where marginal cost equals marginal revenue.
   b. output where marginal cost equals marginal revenue.
   c. output where marginal cost equals average revenue.
   d. output where demand equals average total cost.
   e. price equal to the highest dollar amount that any customer is willing to pay.

7. For a monopolist,
   a. its demand curve is downward sloping.
   b. its marginal revenue is less than price.
   c. existing economic profits can be sustained over time.
   d. all of the above are true.

8. If a profit-maximizing monopolist is currently charging a price on the inelastic portion of its demand curve, it should
   a. raise price and decrease output.
   b. lower price and increase output.
   c. reduce both output and price.
   d. hold output constant and raise price.
   e. do none of the above.

9. If a monopolist had a zero marginal cost of production, it would maximize profits by choosing to produce a quantity where
   a. demand was inelastic.
   b. demand was unit elastic.
   c. demand was elastic.
   d. It is impossible to determine where along a demand curve such a monopolist would choose to produce.

10. Tom is the monopoly provider of a town's TV cable service, whose current subscription price is $20.00 per month. In order to attract one more subscriber, he has to lower his price to $19.95. What is true of Tom's marginal revenue from that additional subscriber?
   a. Tom's marginal revenue equals $19.95.
   b. Tom's marginal revenue is greater than $19.95.
   c. Tom's marginal revenue is less than $19.95.
   d. Tom's marginal revenue is between $19.95 and $20.00.

11. Rob owns the only race-car track in the entire region. When he lowers his price, the track attracts more customers, but its total revenue falls. Which of the following is true of Rob?
   a. He is a monopolist operating on the inelastic region of his demand curve.
   b. He is a monopolist operating on the elastic region of his demand curve.
   c. He would not choose to lower his price in such a situation.
   d. He is a price taker.
   e. Both a and c are true of Rob.

12. Which of the following is *not* true about a profit-maximizing monopolist?
   a. The monopolist faces the downward-sloping market demand curve.
   b. The monopolist always earns an economic profit.
   c. The price of output exceeds marginal revenue.
   d. The monopolist chooses output where marginal revenue equals marginal cost.
   e. All of the above are true.

13. Which of the following is true for a firm that is a monopolist?
   a. The firm will definitely make an economic profit in the short run.
   b. The firm will produce a smaller quantity of output than what would be best from the viewpoint of ideal economic efficiency.
   c. The additional revenue that can be generated from an increase in output will exceed the firm's price.
   d. The firm can charge whatever it wants for its product since consumers have no alternatives.

14. Monopolists are like perfectly competitive firms in that
   a. both maximize profits at the output level where marginal revenue equals marginal cost.
   b. both could be earning either positive profits or losses in the short run.
   c. both are in industries with downward-sloping demand curves.
   d. all of the above are true of both of them.
   e. a and b are true of both of them, but not c.

15. Monopoly is unlike perfect competition in that
   a. a monopolist's price is greater than marginal cost.
   b. there are no barriers to entry into a monopoly industry.
   c. a monopolist earns an economic profit only if its price is greater than *ATC.*
   d. all of the above are ways monopoly is unlike perfect competition.
   e. a and b, but not c, are ways monopoly is unlike perfect competition.

16. A price-taking firm and a monopolist are alike in that
   a. price equals marginal revenue for both.
   b. both maximize profits by choosing an output where marginal revenue equals marginal cost, provided that price exceeds average variable cost.
   c. price exceeds marginal cost at the profit-maximizing level of output for both.
   d. in the long run, both earn zero economic profits.

17. Which of the following is true of perfect competition but not true of monopoly?
   a. The firm's average total cost curve is U-shaped.
   b. Marginal revenue is equal to price.
   c. A profit-maximizing firm chooses output where marginal revenue equals marginal cost.
   d. Profits may exist in the short run.

18. Objections to monopolies do *not* include which of the following?
   a. They reduce output below the efficient level of output that would be produced in perfect competition.
   b. They reduce the price below what would be charged in perfect competition.
   c. They charge a price that is greater than marginal cost.
   d. They create a welfare cost.
   e. All of the above are objections to monopolies.

19. A natural monopoly is defined as an industry in which
   a. one firm can produce the entire industry output at a lower average cost than can a larger number of firms.
   b. a single firm controls crucial inputs to the production process.
   c. one firm is very large relative to other firms that could enter the industry.
   d. a single seller exists as a result of patent protection.

20. If regulators set a price according to marginal cost pricing, the firm will
   a. earn positive economic profits.
   b. make zero economic profits.
   c. suffer an economic loss.
   d. earn the same level of profits as it would absent regulation.

21. Average cost pricing for a natural monopoly will
   a. result in the socially efficient level of output.
   b. result in a less than socially efficient level of output.
   c. result in a greater than socially efficient level of output.
   d. result in the firm suffering economic losses.
   e. result in the firm earning economic profit.

22. Under average cost pricing by a natural monopoly,
   a. price is greater than marginal cost.
   b. there will be a welfare cost.
   c. the producer will earn a normal rate of return.
   d. there is little or no incentive for the producer to hold down costs.
   e. all of the above are true.

23. Which of the following is not a limitation that regulators face when they implement average cost pricing?
   a. Average cost pricing provides little or no incentive for firms to keep costs down.
   b. The accurate calculation of a firm's costs is difficult.
   c. Decisions are political and often influenced by special interests.
   d. All of the above are limitations faced by regulators implementing average cost pricing.

24. A price-discriminating monopolist will
   a. price where marginal revenue equals marginal cost for each different group of demanders.
   b. charge a higher price for more inelastic demanders.
   c. have to face customers who have a difficult time reselling the good to others who were charged more.
   d. do all of the above.

25. A price-discriminating monopolist will tend to charge a lower price to students if it believes that student demand is
   a. more elastic than that of other demanders.
   b. more inelastic than that of other demanders.
   c. unit elastic.
   d. graphically represented by a vertical curve.

26. Which of the following is not true of successful price discriminators?
   a. They could make greater profits by charging everyone a higher, uniform price.
   b. Their customers must have different elasticities of demand.
   c. Their customers must have difficulty reselling the good to other customers.
   d. They must have monopoly power.

27. Price discrimination may be a rational strategy for a profit-maximizing monopolist when
   a. there is no opportunity for reselling across market segments.
   b. there is a substantial opportunity for reselling across market segments.
   c. consumers are unable to be segmented into identifiable markets.
   d. the elasticity of demand is the same across all customers.

Problems

1. Fill in the missing data in the table below for a monopolist.

Quantity	Price	Total Revenue	Marginal Revenue	Demand Elastic or Inelastic?
1	11	______	______	______
2	10	______	______	______
3	9	______	______	______
4	8	______	______	______
5	7	______	______	______
6	6	______	______	______
7	5	______	______	______
8	4	______	______	______
9	3	______	______	______
10	2	______	______	______
11	1	______	______	______

2. Assume that the monopolist in problem 1 had fixed costs of $10 and a constant marginal cost of $4 per unit. Add columns to the above table for Total Cost, Marginal Cost, and Profit.

3. Use the following diagram to answer a–c.

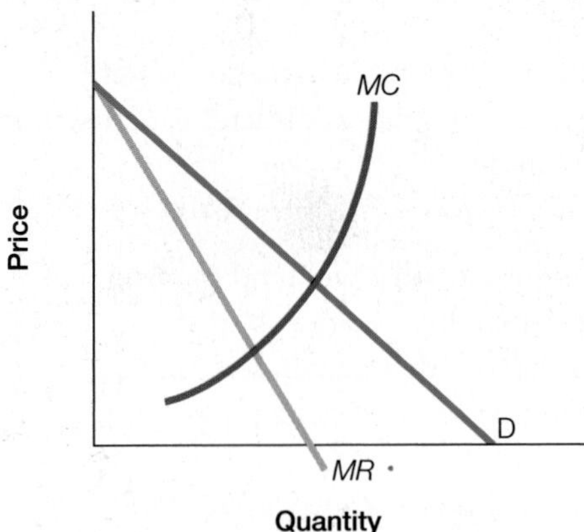

a. Assuming the monopolist indicated in the diagram produced at all, indicate its profit-maximizing quantity and price.
b. Add an *ATC* curve that would show this monopolist earning an economic profit.
c. Add an *ATC* curve that would show this monopolist earning an economic loss.

4. Use the following diagram to answer a–c.

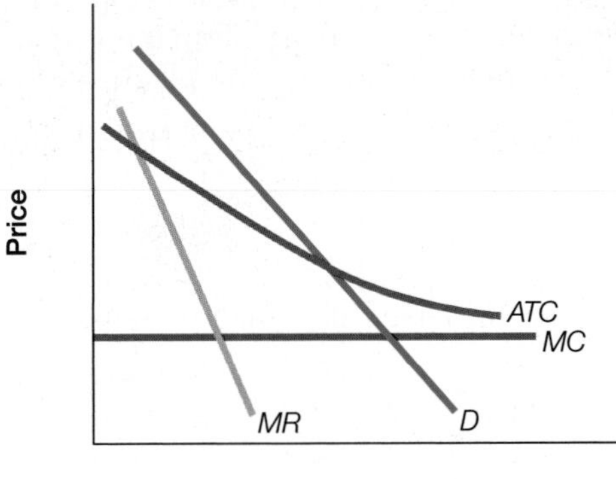

a. Indicate the efficient result on the graph above.
b. Illustrate the profits or losses from the efficient result in a.
c. Show the average cost-pricing solution. What profits are earned with that approach?

chapter 10

Input Markets and the Distribution of Income

section 10.1

Input Markets

- How is income distributed among workers, landowners, and the owners of capital?
- What is derived demand?

MARKETS FOR THE FACTORS OF PRODUCTION

Approximately 75 percent of national income goes to wages and salaries for labor services. But how are salary levels among those individuals determined? After laborers take their share, the remaining 25 percent of national income is compensation received by the owners of land and capital and the entrepreneurs who employ those resources to produce valued goods and services. How can we explain the variations in these forms of income, such as rent on houses, offices, or factories, or interest on borrowed money? The answer is supply and demand. In this chapter, we will see how supply and demand determine the prices paid to workers, landowners, and capital owners.

In labor markets, actor Mel Gibson can make over $20 million a film. Baseball player Alex Rodriguez of the Texas Rangers signed a contract for over $20 million a year—for ten years. Singer Britney Spears' income is many times larger than that of the average college professor or medical doctor. Female models make more than male models, yet male basketball players make more than female basketball players. Why is this the case? To understand why some workers receive such vastly different compensation for their labor than others we must focus on the workings of supply and demand in the labor market.

DETERMINING THE PRICE OF A PRODUCTIVE FACTOR: DERIVED DEMAND

derived demand
the demand for an input is derived from the consumer's demands for a good or service

Output (goods and services) markets and input markets have one major difference. In input or factor markets, the demand for an input is called a **derived demand.** That is, the demand for an input like labor is derived from the demand for the good or service. So consumers do *not* demand the labor directly—it is the goods and services that labor produces that consumers demand. For example, the chef at a restaurant is paid, and her skills are in demand, because she produces what the customer wants—a meal. The "price" of any productive factor is directly related to consumer demand for the final good or service.

Section Check

SECTION CHECK

1. Supply and demand determine the prices paid to workers, landowners, and capital owners.
2. In factor or input markets, demand is derived from consumers' demand for the final good or service that the input produces.

---

1. Why is the demand for productive inputs derived from the demand for the outputs those inputs produce?
2. Why is the demand for tractors and fertilizer derived from the demand for agricultural products?

In The **NEWS**

DEMAND, NOT HIGHER SALARIES, DRIVES UP BASEBALL TICKET PRICES

BY BILL SHAIKIN

Teams that blame escalating salaries for escalating ticket prices are simply using players as a handy scapegoat, University of Chicago economist Allen Sanderson says. . . . "Player salaries have virtually no impact on ticket prices. Ticket prices are set by what the market will bear. After that, it's a matter of who gets the money, [Dodger owner] Rupert Murdoch or Kevin Brown [Dodger's $105 million pitcher]."

Remember supply and demand from your economics class? A team would raise ticket prices, regardless of player salaries, only if it believed fans would pay the higher prices. In economic jargon, a team would raise ticket prices only if it believed a demand would remain strong at the higher prices for a fixed supply of seats.

"If I'm an owner and I have to justify this to my season-ticket holders, I have to blame somebody," Sanderson said. "I can't stand up and say, 'The ticket prices are going up 19% next year because you'll pay it. . . .'"

Virtually all economists would support this application of the basic economic theory of supply and demand.

"Anyone who has studied the industry would tell you this is what's going on," Noll said. "Revenues drive everything, including the degree of vitriol in collective bargaining." [Roger Noll is a Stanford economist and a specialist on Sports Economics.]

So owners, defending price increases, point fingers at players. But when three national theater chains increased movie prices recently, executives did not point fingers at actors. "There was certainly no reference to . . . we have to do this because Jack Nicholson and Tom Cruise and Michelle Pfeiffer have such high salaries," Sanderson said. "I've never heard anyone say, 'If Tom Cruise would work for $10 million [a movie] instead of $20 million, my ticket would be $6 instead of $7. . . .'"

"Every sports fan, if he wants to see why player salaries are so high should go look in the mirror," Noll said. "If fans were not willing to pay a lot, salaries would not be so high. Everything starts with what consumers are willing to pay."

SOURCE: Bill Shaikin, "Face Value," *Los Angeles Times,* April 1, 1999, p. D1. Copyright 2000, *Los Angeles Times.* Reprinted by permission.

CONSIDER THIS:

Baseball salaries are a derived demand. It is the customers' demand for a baseball game that drives baseball salaries. This is the same reason why top women's tennis players make more than top women (and men) professional bowlers.

section 10.2

Supply and Demand in the Labor Market

- What is the marginal revenue product for an input?
- What is the marginal resource cost of hiring another worker?
- Why is the demand curve for labor downward sloping?
- What is the shape of the supply curve of labor?

WILL HIRING THAT INPUT ADD MORE TO REVENUE THAN COSTS?

marginal revenue product (*MRP*)
marginal product times the price of the product

marginal resource cost (*MRC*)
the amount that an extra input adds to the firm's total costs

Because firms are trying to maximize their profits, they try (by definition) to make the *difference* between total revenue and total cost as large as possible. An input's attractiveness, then, varies with what the input can add to the firm's revenues relative to what the input adds to costs. The demand for labor is determined by its **marginal revenue product (*MRP*)**, which is the additional revenue that a firm obtains from one more unit of input. Why? Suppose a worker adds $500 per week to a firm's sales by his productivity; he produces 100 units that add $5 each to firm revenue. In order to determine if the worker adds to the firm's profits, we would need to calculate the marginal resource cost associated with the worker. The **marginal resource cost (*MRC*)** is the amount that an extra input adds to the firm's total costs. In this case, the marginal resource cost is the wage the employer has to pay to entice an extra worker. Assume that the marginal resource cost of the worker, the market wage, is $350 per worker a week. In our example, the firm would find its profits growing by adding one more worker, because the marginal benefit (*MRP*) associated with the worker, $500, would exceed the marginal cost (*MRC*) of the worker, $350. So we can see that just by adding another worker to its labor force, the firm would increase its weekly profits by $150 ($500 − $350). Even if the market wage were $490 per week, the firm could slightly increase its profits by hiring the employee because the marginal revenue product, $500, is greater than the added labor cost, $490. At wage payments above $500, however, the firm would not be interested in the worker because the marginal resource cost would exceed the marginal revenue product, making additional hiring unprofitable.

section 10.2 Exhibit 1 — The Marginal Revenue Product of Labor

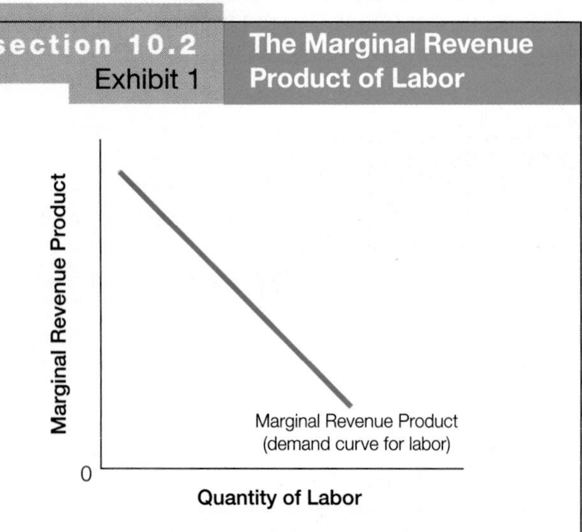

The value of the marginal revenue product of labor ($MP \times P$) shows how the marginal revenue product depends on the number of workers employed. The curve is downward sloping because of the diminishing marginal product of labor.

THE DEMAND CURVE FOR LABOR SLOPES DOWNWARD

The downward-sloping demand curve for labor indicates a negative relationship between wage and the quantity of labor demanded. Higher wages will decrease the quantity of labor demanded, while lower wages will increase the quantity of labor demanded. But why does this relationship exist?

The major reason for the downward-sloping demand curve for labor (illustrated in Exhibit 1) is the law of diminishing marginal product. Remember that the law of diminishing marginal product states that as increasing quantities of some variable input (say labor) are added to fixed quantities of another input (say, land or capital), output will rise, but at some point it will increase by diminishing amounts.

Consider a farmer who owns a given amount of land. Suppose he is producing wheat, and the relationship between his output and his labor force requirements is that indicated in Exhibit 2. Output expands as more workers are hired to cultivate the land, but the growth in output steadily slows, meaning the added output associated with one more worker declines as more workers are added. For example, in Exhibit 2 when a third worker is hired, total wheat output increases from 5,500 bushels to 7,000 bushels, an increase of 1,500 bushels in terms of marginal product. However, when a fourth worker is added, total wheat output only increases from 7,000 bushels to 8,000 bushels, or a marginal increase of 1,000 bushels. Note that the reason for this is *not* that the workers being added are steadily inferior in terms of ability or quality relative to the first workers. Indeed, for simplicity, we assume that each worker has exactly the same skills and productive capacity. But as more workers are added, each additional worker has fewer of the fixed resources with which to work and marginal product falls. For example, the fifth worker might just cultivate the same land more intensively. The work of the fifth worker, then, might only slightly improve output. That is, the **marginal product (*MP*)**—the number of physical units of added output from the addition of one additional unit of input—falls.

section 10.2 Exhibit 2 — Diminishing Marginal Productivity on a Hypothetical Farm

Units of Labor Input (workers)	Total Wheat Output (bushels per year)	Marginal Product of Labor (bushels per year)
0	—	
		3,000
1	3,000	
		2,500
2	5,500	
		1,500
3	7,000	
		1,000
4	8,000	
		500
5	8,500	
		300
6	8,800	
		200
7	9,000	

marginal product (*MP*) *the number of physical units of added output from the addition of one additional unit of input*

As we discussed earlier, the marginal revenue product (*MRP*) is the change in total revenue associated with an additional unit of input. The marginal revenue product is equal to the marginal product, the units of output added by a worker, multiplied by marginal revenue, in this case the price of the output (e.g., $10 per bushel of wheat).

$$MRP = MP \times P$$

(Note that in this case the price of the output, wheat, is the same at all outputs because the farmer is a price taker in a competitive market.)

The marginal revenue product of labor declines because of the diminishing marginal product of labor when additional workers are added. This is illustrated in Exhibit 3, which shows various output and revenue levels for a wheat farmer using different quantities of labor. We see in Exhibit 3 that the marginal product, or the added physical volume of output, declines as the number of workers grows because of diminishing marginal product. Thus, the fifth worker adds only 60 bushels of wheat per week, compared with 100 bushels for the first worker.

HOW MANY WORKERS WILL AN EMPLOYER HIRE?

Profits are maximized if the firm hires only to the point where the wage equals the expected marginal revenue product; that is, the firm will hire up to the last unit of input for which the marginal revenue product is expected to exceed the wage. Because the demand curve for labor and the value of the marginal revenue product show the quantity of labor that a firm demands at a given wage in a competitive market, we say that the marginal revenue product (*MRP*) is the same as the demand curve for labor for a competitive firm.

Using the data in Exhibit 3, if the market wage is $550 per week, it would pay for the grower to employ five workers. The fifth worker's marginal revenue product ($600) exceeds the wage, so profits are increased $50 by adding the worker. Adding a sixth

section 10.2 Exhibit 3

Marginal Revenue Product, Output, and Labor Inputs

Quantity of Labor	Total Output (bushels per week)	Marginal Physical Product of Labor (bushels per week)	Product Price (dollars per bushel)	Marginal Revenue of Labor	Wage Rate (*MRC*) (dollars per week)	Marginal Profit (*MRP* – *W*)
0	0					
		100	$10	$1,000	$500	$450
1	100					
		90	10	900	500	350
2	190					
		80	10	800	500	250
3	270					
		70	10	700	500	150
4	340					
		60	10	600	500	50
5	400					
		50	10	500	500	– 50
6	450					
		40	10	400	500	–150
7	490					
		30	10	300	500	–250
8	520					

worker would be unprofitable, though, as that worker's marginal revenue product of $500 is less than the wage of $550. Hiring the sixth worker would reduce profits by $50.

But what if the market wage increases from $550 to $650? In this case, hiring the fifth worker becomes unprofitable, because the marginal resource cost, $650, is now greater than the marginal revenue product of $600. That is, a higher wage rate, *ceteris paribus,* lowers the employment levels of individual firms.

In a competitive labor market, many firms are competing for workers and no single firm is big enough by itself to have any significant effect on the level of wages. The firm is a wage taker. The ability to hire all you wish at the prevailing wage is analogous to perfect competition in output markets, where a firm could sell all it wanted at the going price.

In Exhibit 4, when the firm hires less than q^* workers, the marginal revenue product exceeds the market wage, so adding workers expands profits. With more than q^* work-

The Competitive Firm's Hiring Decision

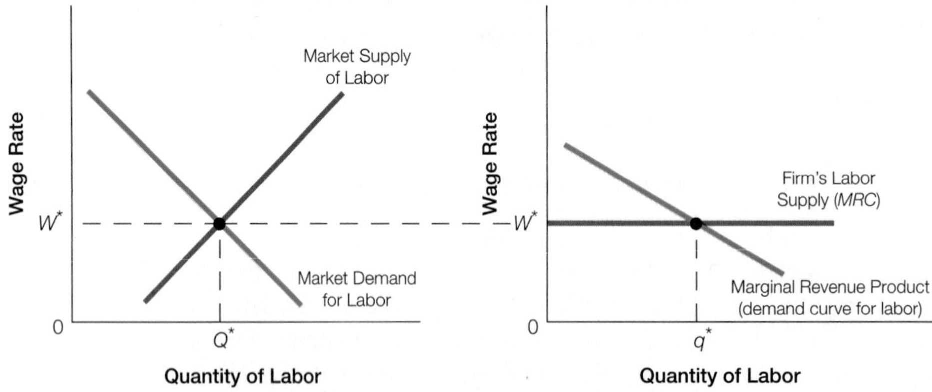

A competitive firm can hire any number of potential workers at the market-determined wage; it is a price (wage) taker. At employment levels less than q^*, additional workers add profits. At employment levels beyond q^*, additional workers are unprofitable; at q^*, profits are maximized.

section 10.2
Exhibit 5

The Market Supply Curve of Labor

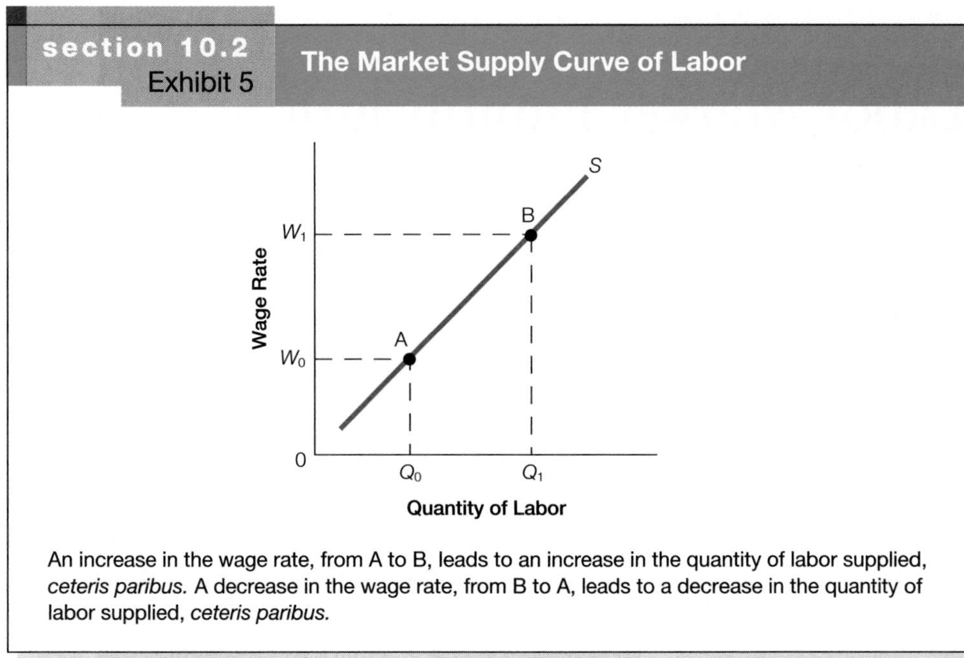

An increase in the wage rate, from A to B, leads to an increase in the quantity of labor supplied, *ceteris paribus.* A decrease in the wage rate, from B to A, leads to a decrease in the quantity of labor supplied, *ceteris paribus.*

ers, though, the "going wage" exceeds marginal revenue product, and hiring additional workers lowers profits. With q^* workers, profits are maximized.

THE MARKET LABOR SUPPLY CURVE

How much work effort are individuals collectively willing and able to supply in the marketplace? This is the essence of the market supply curve. Just as was the case in our earlier discussion of the law of supply, a positive relationship exists between the wage rate and the quantity of labor supplied. As the wage rate rises, the quantity of labor supplied increases, *ceteris paribus;* as the wage rate falls, the quantity of labor supplied falls, *ceteris paribus.* This positive relationship is consistent with the evidence that the total quantity of labor supplied by *all* workers increases as the wage rate increases, as shown in Exhibit 5.

Section Check

1. The demand curve for labor is downward sloping because of diminishing marginal product. That is, if additional labor is added to a fixed quantity of land or capital equipment, output will increase, but eventually by smaller amounts.
2. The value of the marginal product of labor is the marginal product times the price of the output.
3. Along a market supply curve, a higher wage rate will increase the quantity supplied of labor and a lower wage rate will decrease the quantity supplied of labor.

---

1. What is the value of marginal product?
2. Would a firm hire another worker if the value of marginal product exceeded the market wage rate? Why or why not?
3. Why does the marginal product of labor eventually fall?
4. Why does diminishing marginal product mean that the value of marginal product will eventually fall?
5. Why is a firm hiring in a competitive labor market a price (wage) taker for a given quantity of labor?

section 10.3

Labor Market Equilibrium

- How are the equilibrium wage and employment determined in labor markets?
- What shifts the labor demand curve?
- What shifts the labor supply curve?

DETERMINING EQUILIBRIUM IN THE LABOR MARKET

The equilibrium wage and quantity in the labor market is determined by the intersection of labor demand and labor supply. Referring to Exhibit 1, the equilibrium wage, W^*, and equilibrium employment level, Q^*, are found at that point where the quantity of labor demanded equals the quantity of labor supplied. At any wage higher than W^*, like at W_1, the quantity of labor supplied exceeds the quantity of labor demanded, resulting in a surplus of labor. In this situation, unemployed workers would be willing to undercut the established wage in order to get jobs, pushing the wage down and returning the market to equilibrium. Likewise, at a wage below the equilibrium level, like at W_2, quantity demanded would exceed quantity supplied, resulting in a labor shortage. In this situation, employers would be forced to offer higher wages in order to hire as many workers as they would like. Note that only at the equilibrium wage are both suppliers and demanders able to exchange the quantity of labor they desire.

SHIFTS IN THE LABOR DEMAND CURVE

In chapter 4, we demonstrated that the determinants of demand can shift the demand curve for a good or service. In the case of an input such as labor, two important factors

section 10.3 Exhibit 1

Supply and Demand in the Labor Market

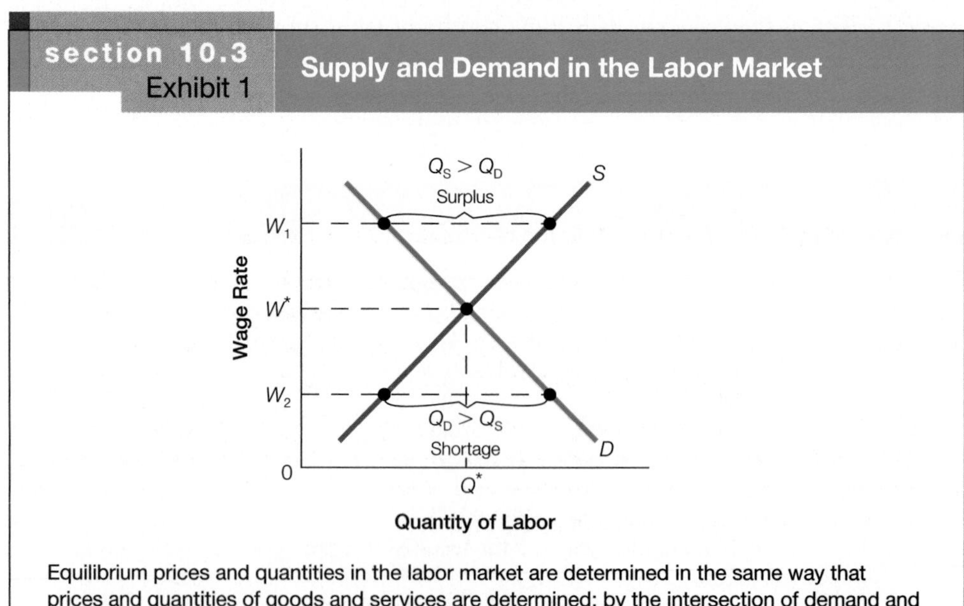

Equilibrium prices and quantities in the labor market are determined in the same way that prices and quantities of goods and services are determined: by the intersection of demand and supply. At wages above the equilibrium wage, like W_1, quantity supplied exceeds quantity demanded, and potential workers will be willing to supply their labor services for an amount lower than the prevailing wage. At a wage lower than W^*, like W_2, potential demanders will overcome the resulting shortage of labor by offering workers a wage greater than the prevailing wage. In both cases, wages are pushed toward the equilibrium value.

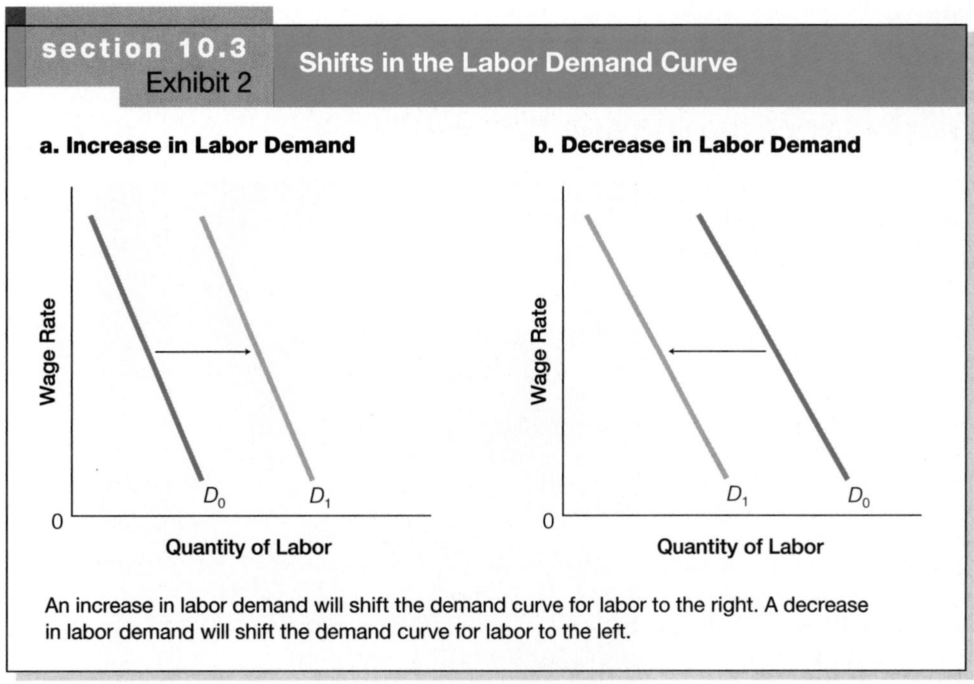

An increase in labor demand will shift the demand curve for labor to the right. A decrease in labor demand will shift the demand curve for labor to the left.

can shift the demand curve: increases in labor productivity, such as due to technological advances; or changes in the output price of the good, such as due to increased demand for the firm's product. Exhibit 2 highlights the impact of these changes.

Changes in Labor Productivity

Workers can increase productivity if they have more capital or land with which to work, if technological improvements occur, or if they acquire additional skills or experience. This increase in productivity will increase the marginal product of the labor and shift the demand curve for labor to the right from D_0 to D_1 in Exhibit 2. However, if labor productivity falls, then marginal product will fall and the demand curve for labor will shift to the left.

Changes in the Demand for the Firm's Product

The greater the demand for the firm's product, the greater the firm's demand for labor or any other variable input (the "derived demand" discussed earlier). The reason for this is that the higher demand for the firm's product increases the firm's marginal revenue, which increases marginal revenue product. That is, the greater demand for the product will cause prices to rise, and the price of the product is part of the value of the labor to the firm ($MRP = MP \times P$)—so the rising product price shifts the labor demand curve to the right. Of course, if demand for the firm's product falls, the labor demand curve will shift to the left as marginal revenue product falls.

SHIFTING THE LABOR SUPPLY CURVE

In chapter 4, we learned that changes in the determinants of supply can shift the supply curve for goods and services to the right or left. Likewise, several factors can cause the labor supply curve to shift. These factors include immigration and population growth, the

APPLICATION

LABOR SUPPLY AND DEMAND

Q: Why do teachers, who provide a valuable service to the community, make millions and millions of dollars less than star basketball players?

A: It is the marginal revenue product of additional teachers and the supply of teachers that determine the market wage (regardless of how we perceive the job's importance). A teacher's marginal revenue product is likely to be well below $5 million a year. Most people probably think that teachers are more important than star basketball players, yet teachers make a lot less money. Of course, the reason for this is simple supply and demand. A lot of people enjoy watching star basketball players but only a few individuals have the skill to perform at that level. While demand for teachers is also large, there is also a relatively large number of potential suppliers. As seen in Exhibit 3, this translates into a much lower wage for teachers than for star basketball players.

© MARK TERRILL/AP PHOTO

section 10.3
Exhibit 3

a. Labor Market for Star Basketball Players

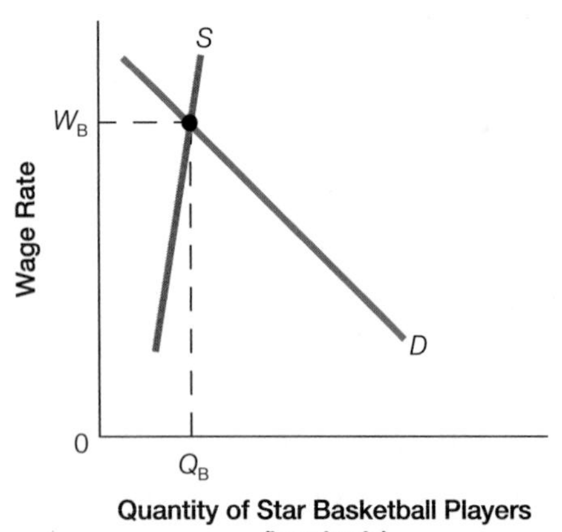

b. Labor Market for Teachers

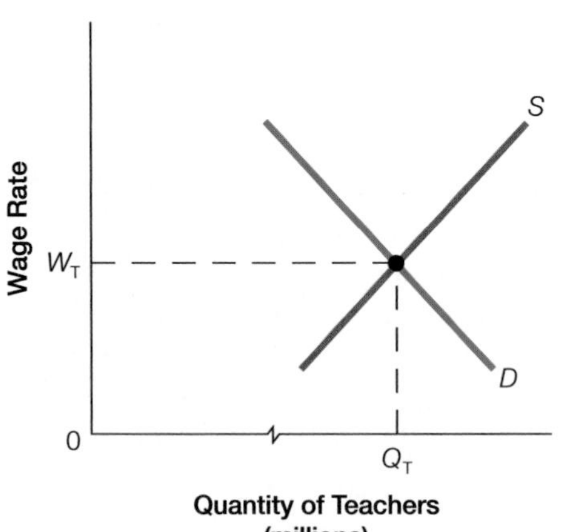

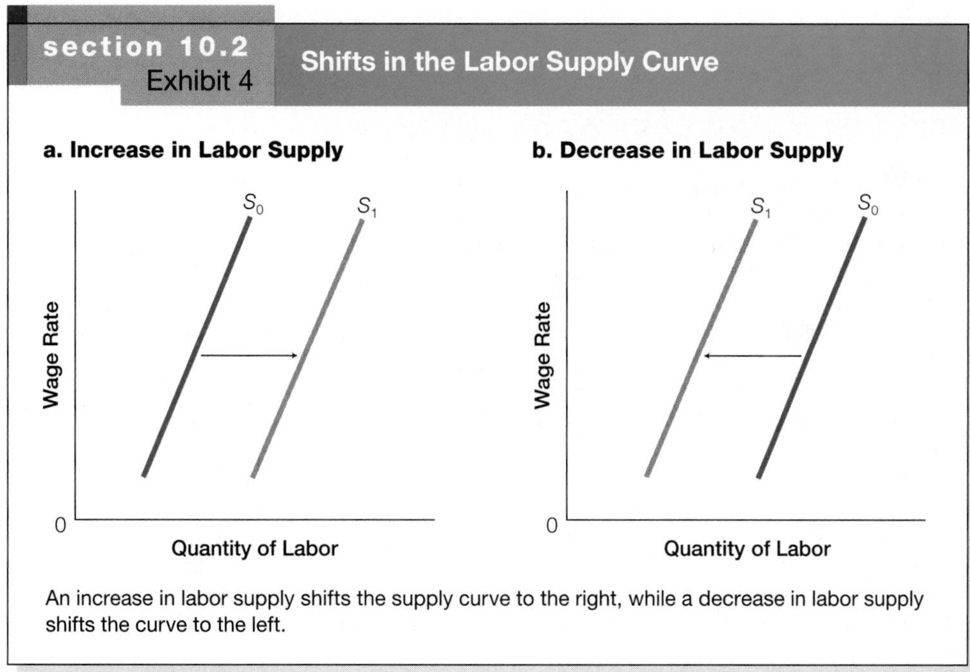

An increase in labor supply shifts the supply curve to the right, while a decrease in labor supply shifts the curve to the left.

number of hours workers are willing to work at a given wage (worker tastes or preferences), nonwage income, and amenities. Exhibit 4 illustrates the impact of these factors on the labor supply curve.

Immigration and Population Growth

If new workers enter the labor force, it will shift the labor supply curve to the right, as from S_0 to S_1 in Exhibit 4(a). Of course, if workers leave the country—and thus the labor force—or the relevant population declines, it will cause the supply curve to shift to the left, as shown in Exhibit 4(b).

Number of Hours People Are Willing to Work (Worker Preferences)

If people become willing to work more hours at a given wage (due to changes in worker tastes or preferences), the labor supply curve will shift to the right, shown in the movement from S_0 to S_1 in Exhibit 4(a). If they become willing to work fewer hours at a given wage, the labor supply curve will shift to the left, as shown in Exhibit 4(b).

Nonwage Income

Increases in income from other sources than employment can cause the labor supply curve to shift to the left. For example, if you just won $20 million in your state's Super Lotto, you might decide to take yourself out of the labor force. Likewise, a decrease in nonwage income might push a person back into the labor force, thus shifting the labor supply curve to the right.

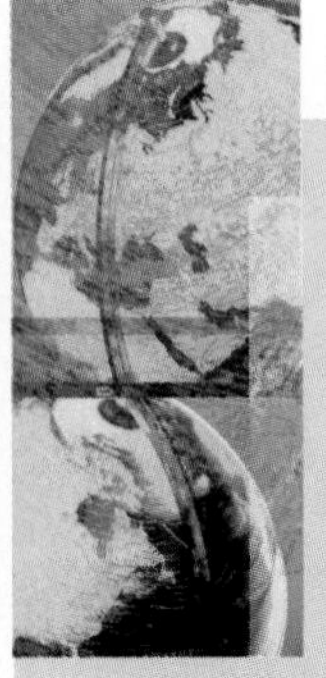

Global WATCH

CAUSE, CONSEQUENCE, AND CURE OF CHILD LABOR

In 1995, at least 120 million children aged between 5 and 14 performed full-time work, many in excess of ten hours a day. When part-time work is included, the number of working children in the world rises to a staggering 250 million! In 1995, the proportion of working children aged 10-14 was 26 percent in Africa and 13 percent in Asia. To make matters worse, many children work in hazardous or unhygienic conditions, risking accident, injury, or health deterioration. Full-time work also prevents children from obtaining an education, trapping them in a vicious circle of despair.

While the incidence of child labor is at least headed in the right direction, it still is a very serious problem, and has outraged many developed countries. A natural reaction to this plight has been to seek different kinds of bans of child labor. For example, *"Harkin's bill"*—passed in the United States in 1997—bans the import of goods produced using child labor. Other initiatives have placed the decision in consumers' hands, by requiring that product labels specify the absence of child labor in the production of imported goods. While these initiatives are often well intended, many developing countries have criticized them on the basis that they disguise an ulterior motive: protectionism against cheap labor.

In several articles, Kaushik Basu of Cornell University and the World Bank claims that many proposed initiatives at curbing child labor do not adequately consider the impact on working children themselves whose welfare they are intended to improve. . . . His research shows that the popular sector-specific ban—in which industries that use child labor are prevented from exporting their goods to developed countries—can make working children worse off. Children who are unable to work in export-related industries may turn to welding or, worse, prostitution. Sadly, a UNICEF study has found that 5,000–7,000 young Nepalese girls moved from the carpet industry to prostitution as a result of such bans. . . .

The problem in many poor countries today is that families depend on their children's wages for survival. A ban on child labor could push many families to the brink of starvation, given that social programs are nonexistent. The author believes that while isolated cases of child abuse do exist—where children are sent to work, so that parents do not have to—parents generally send their children to work only when compelled by poverty, not due to malice. There is no other way to explain the prevalence of child labor as a mass phenomenon. . . .

According to Basu, the long-run consequences of child labor have largely been neglected. Having forgone schooling, a working child will generally be less productive in his adult life. Consequently, his wages will be low as an adult, increasing the likelihood that he will be compelled to send his children to work as well. Basu refers to this vicious cycle as a "child labor trap." In light of this dreadful possibility, he suggests that "if an economy is caught in a child labor trap, what is needed is a large effort to educate one generation. . . ."

Basu believes that a labor market can be in a "good" or "bad" equilibrium. In a "good" equilibrium—characteristic of developed countries—children do not work, and adult wages are relatively high. This is so because children are poor substitutes for adults as jobs require high levels of skill. This is not true of developing countries, where jobs are menial, and children are good substitutions for adults, such as in making hand-knotted carpets. . . .

The author cautions that the impact of banning child labor in a given country has to be studied empirically before jumping to conclusions. Remember that an outright ban can sometimes result in starvation instead. In the latter circumstance, the interest of the working children may be better served by combining light work with schooling. In fact, a study of Peruvian families has shown that, in some cases, a limited amount of part-time work makes it possible for children to attend school.

SOURCE: *Economic Intuition*, Spring 2000, pp. 5–6. © 2000 *Economic Intuition,* Montreal, Canada.

Amenities

Amenities associated with a job or a location—like good fringe benefits, safe and friendly working conditions, a child-care center, and so on—will make for a more desirable work atmosphere, *ceteris paribus.* These amenities would cause an increase in the supply of labor, resulting in a rightward shift, such as from S_0 to S_1 in Exhibit 4(a). If job conditions deteriorate, it would lead to a reduction in the labor supply, shifting the labor supply curve to the left, as shown in Exhibit 4(b).

Section Check

1. The intersection of the labor demand curve and the labor supply curve determine wages in the labor market.
2. The labor demand curve can shift if there is a change in productivity or a change in the demand for the final product.
3. The labor supply curve can shift if there are changes in immigration or population growth, workers' preferences, nonwage income, or amenities.

---

1. If wages were above their equilibrium level, why would they tend to fall toward the equilibrium level?
2. If wages were below their equilibrium level, why would they tend to rise toward the equilibrium level?
3. Why do increases in technology or increases in the amounts of capital or other complementary inputs increase the demand for labor?
4. Why can any of the demand shifters for output markets shift the demand for labor and other inputs used to produce that output in the same direction?
5. Explain why increases in immigration or population growth, increases in workers' willingness to work at a given wage, decreases in nonwage income, or increases in workplace amenities will increase the supply of labor.
6. What would happen to the supply of labor if nonwage incomes increased and workplace amenities also increased over the same time period?
7. Why are wages in different fields not necessarily related to how important people think those jobs are?
8. If the private-market wage of engineers was greater than that of sociologists, what would happen if a university tried to pay all of its faculty the same salary?

section 10.4

Labor Unions

- Why do labor unions exist?
- What is the impact of unions on wages?
- Can unions increase productivity?

WHY ARE THERE LABOR UNIONS?

The supply and demand curves for labor can help us better understand the impact of labor unions. Labor unions like the United Auto Workers (UAW) and the United Farm Workers (UFW) were formed to increase their members' wages and to improve working conditions. On behalf of the union members, the union negotiates with firms through a process called **collective bargaining.** Why is this necessary? The argument is that when economies begin to industrialize and urbanize, firms become larger and often the "boss" becomes more distant from the workers. In small shops or on farms, workers usually have a close relationship with an owner-employer, but in larger enterprises, the workers may only know a supervisor, and have no direct contact with either the owner or upper management. Workers realize that acting together, as a union of workers, gives them more collective bargaining power than acting individually.

collective bargaining
negotiations between representatives of employers and unions

WHERE ARE LABOR UNIONS FOUND?

The growth in union membership certainly has slowed since 1947, and relative to the labor force as a whole, membership has declined by a fairly significant amount, from a peak

of 25.5 percent in 1953 to only about 16 percent today (and less than 10 percent of private-sector employment). The recent sluggish absolute growth (and relative decline) in labor union membership probably reflects, to a considerable extent, structural shifts in the occupations of American workers. Unions have traditionally found it difficult to organize workers in white-collar jobs, in the service industries, and in southern and western states. By contrast, blue-collar manufacturing positions in the north and east, especially in large firms, have been unionized to a considerable extent. One reason for this is that workers' tasks typically are standardized, making such workers better able to negotiate as a group. Yet in the past 30 years, manufacturing has moved increasingly to the south and west, and automation has led to a declining proportion of the workforce in manufacturing. Many of the fastest-growing occupations are in the service industries, which are characterized by small firms where workers' tasks are far more varied, making it harder for workers to organize to negotiate as a group. In addition, unions are less appealing to these job holders, partly because they work more closely with management or owners.

Unionization efforts have been particularly successful in the public sector. In education, teachers organizations like the National Education Association (NEA) have converted from being primarily professional organizations concerned with improving education to being powerful labor unions. The NEA is now, by some measures, the most powerful union in the country.

UNION IMPACT ON LABOR SUPPLY AND WAGES

Labor unions influence the quantity of union labor hired and the wages at which they are hired primarily through their ability to alter the supply of labor services from what would exist if workers acted independently. One way to do this, of course, is by raising barriers to entry into a given occupation. For example, by restricting membership, unions can reduce the quantity of labor supplied to industry employers from what it otherwise would be, and as a result, wages in that occupation would increase from W_0 to W_1, as shown in Exhibit 1(a). As you can see in the shift from Q_0 to Q_1 in Exhibit 1(a), while some union

section 10.4 Exhibit 1 The Effect of Unions on Wages

a. Union Sector

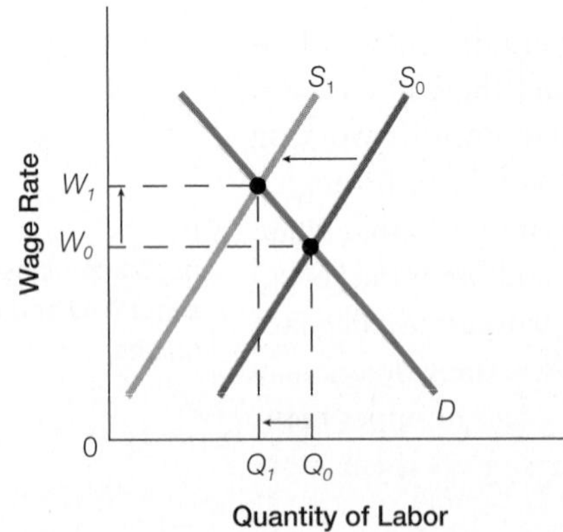

b. Nonunion Sector

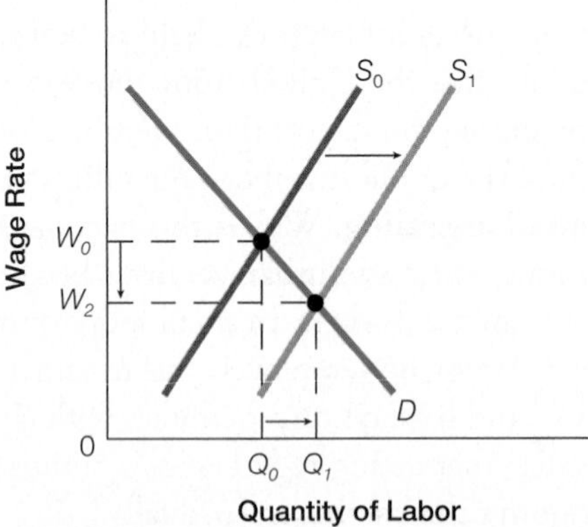

Through restrictive membership practices and other means, a union can reduce the labor supply in its industry, thereby increasing the wage rate they can earn (from W_0 to W_1) but reducing employment (from Q_0 to Q_1) as shown in Exhibit 1(a). However, as workers unable to get jobs in the union sector join the nonunion sector, the supply of labor in the nonunion sector increases (from Q_0 to Q_1), lowering wages in those industries (from W_0 to W_2) as shown in Exhibit 1(b).

workers will now receive higher wages, others will become unemployed. Many economists believe that this is why wages are approximately 15 percent higher in union jobs, even when nonunion workers have comparable skills. Of course, some of these gains will be appropriated by the unions in the form of dues, initiation fees, and the like, so the workers themselves will not receive the full benefit.

WAGE DIFFERENCES FOR SIMILARLY SKILLED WORKERS

Suppose you had two labor sectors: the union sector and the nonunion sector. If unions are successful in obtaining higher wages either through bargaining, threatening to strike, or by restricting membership, wages will rise and employment will fall in the union sector, as seen in Exhibit 1(a). With a downward-sloping demand curve for labor, higher wages mean that less labor is demanded in the union sector. Those workers that are equally skilled but are unable to find union work will seek nonunion work, thus increasing supply in that sector and, in turn, lowering wages in the nonunion sector. This effect is shown in Exhibit 1(b). Thus, comparably skilled workers will experience higher wages in the union sector (W_1) than in the nonunion sector (W_2).

CAN UNIONS LEAD TO INCREASED PRODUCTIVITY?

Harvard economists, Richard Freeman and James Medoff, argue that unions might actually increase worker productivity by increasing marginal productivity. Their argument is that unions provide a collective voice that workers can use to communicate their discontents more effectively. This might lower the number of union workers that quit their jobs. Resignations can be particularly costly for firms, because they have often invested in training and job-specific skills for their employees. In addition, by handling worker's grievances, unions may increase worker motivation and morale. The combined impact of fewer resignations and improved morale could boost productivity.

However, this improvement in worker productivity in the labor sector should show up on the bottom line—the profit statement of the firm. While the evidence is still preliminary, it appears that unions tend to lower the profitability of firms, not raise it.

Section Check

1. Workers realize that acting together gives them collective bargaining power.
2. Labor unions try to increase their members' wages and improve working conditions.
3. Through restrictive membership, a union can reduce the labor supply in the market for union workers, thus reducing employment and raising wages. This increases the supply of workers in the nonunion sector, shifting supply to the right and lowering wages for nonunion workers.

---

1. How can acting together as a group increase workers' bargaining power?
2. Why are service industries harder to unionize than manufacturing industries?
3. How do union restrictions on membership or other barriers to entry affect the wages of members?
4. What would increasing unionization do to the wages of those who were not in unions?
5. How can unions potentially increase worker productivity?
6. Why does data indicating that unionization tends to lower firm profits weaken the argument that the primary effect of unionization is increased worker productivity?

section 10.5

Land and Rent

- How is the price of land determined?
- What are economic rents?

THE SUPPLY OF AND DEMAND FOR LAND

In the first four sections of this chapter we focused on supply and demand in the labor market. We saw how wages were determined in labor markets and how firms determined how much labor to use and the forces of supply and demand in the union market for workers. However, firms must also decide on the other inputs of production—land and capital: how much capital to employ or how much land to acquire.

You might think of the term *rent* as something you pay at the end of the month to compensate the owner for the use of a house or an apartment. But economists use this term in a narrower sense. **Economic rent** is the price paid for land or any other factor that has a fixed supply—a perfectly inelastic supply curve. For example, for the most part, the total supply of land in the country can be viewed as fixed—that is the supply of land is perfectly inelastic and not at all responsive to prices. As much land will be available at zero price as at a very high price. The supply curve does not shift. Only so much land is available.

economic rent
the payment for the use of any resource above its opportunity cost

In Exhibit 1, we see that the price of using land is determined by demand and supply considerations. Because the supply curve is completely inelastic, the demand curve determines the price of the land. If the demand is high, D_H, the rental price of the land is high, at R_H; if the demand for the land is low, D_L, the rental price of the land is low at R_L. Only changes in the demand for land will change the price of land.

section 10.5 Exhibit 1 — Supply and Demand in the Land Market

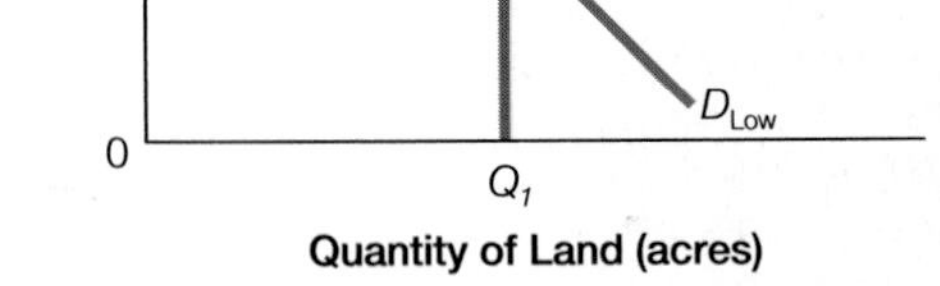

The supply and demand curves for land determine the amount paid to landowners.

What causes high rents?

Rents are high because of a high demand for land, but what causes the demand for land to be high? It is derived from the demand for the products being produced. Suppose there is an effective advertising campaign that promises that cotton is going to keep us looking and feeling cooler. That is, the price of cotton is now higher because of the higher demand for cotton as a result of the advertising campaign. If the supply of land suitable for raising cotton is fixed, an increase in the demand for cotton raises the demand (or the *MRP*) of land, driving up rents.

That is the same reason that rents are very high for stores in trendy locations. Rents are bid up as prospective tenants compete with each other for the desirable location. The reason for the bidding wars for the busy locations is that each prospective tenant sees the potential for greater revenue there than elsewhere.

ECONOMIC RENT TO LABOR

The concept of economic rent does not only apply to land. It is a very powerful tool for understanding labor. For example, we often assume that workers are homogenous, all contain similar skills. Likewise, when we theorize about the compensation for the use of land and natural resources, we also often assume that the quality of land or the resource is the same throughout the market area in question. In fact, of course, there are differences between human beings, between parcels of land, and between units of capital equipment. These differences between productive resources give rise to variations in productivity and thus to variations in compensation.

Why can a star athlete sometimes command a salary of $15 to 20 million a year, while more ordinary athletes earn far less? Why can a world-famous heart surgeon, a famous comedian, or a well-known popular music star earn work-related compensation that may be 50 or more times as great as that received by a "typical" worker?

One reason is that there is a great demand for their services. Lots of people are willing to pay high prices to hear the Dave Matthews Band; a famous heart surgeon may have all the patients she could possibly operate on, even at a price of thousands of dollars per operation. The second reason is that the resources that command such a large amount of compensation are in highly limited supply. There is only one Dave Matthews Band; no one can quite precisely match the qualities that make this band so successful. If you are suffering from a severe heart disease that is potentially curable by surgery, you would like to go to "the best" surgeon. By definition, there can be only one "best" surgeon or only a few who can be "one of the top heart surgeons in the country." The limit on supply is the largest single factor in explaining the high salaries of certain people. If we could train exact duplicates of rock stars or the famed heart surgeons, the incomes of those rock stars and surgeons would fall, as an increase in supply would lead to a lower equilibrium wage.

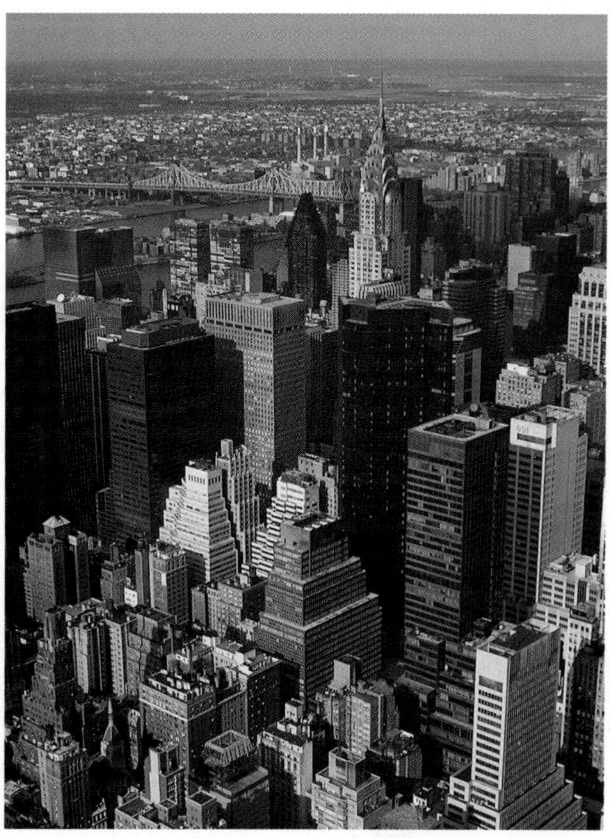

Why is the price of land so expensive in New York City? The supply of land is fixed in the short run. That is, no matter whether the price is high or low, there is only so much land available in New York City. It is the demand for living, shopping, theatres, museums, and restaurants that is high. This, in turn, increases the demand for land, which drives up the price of land.

People who receive their income because of a distinct, unique skill or talent are collecting economic rent—compensation for a resource whose supply is perfectly inelastic over the relevant range of prices. That means the amount of, say, labor services provided will be the same if the annual compensation is $50,000 or $250,000. Or if the famed heart surgeon could only get $5,000 per operation instead of $20,000, she would still operate. Only at a very low payment, say $500, might the surgeon decide that the compensation was inadequate. At very high levels of compensation, increases in compensation do not increase the amount of services provided by such people. In addition, it does not bring new suppliers unless they have precisely the qualities or skills necessary to do the job. The inelasticity of supply (e.g., Julia Roberts, Tiger Woods, Mariah Carey, or Madonna), gives the owners of the resource in limited supply some monopoly-like powers that allow them to earn extraordinary incomes.

Another way of looking at economic rent is that it represents the payment that the resource owner receives beyond what he or she would receive using the resource in its next most attractive use. The heart surgeon will do the surgery if the price is $5,000 or $20,000, but at a fee level, of say, $500 she might decide that alternative employment (e.g., general practice) is more rewarding. Thus, the economic rent is only that part of her fee above the $500 that could be earned by pursuing alternative forms of employment. Above $500, the surgeon's supply curve is perfectly inelastic, below that it varies with the level of compensation.

Economic rent is the payment of any resource above its opportunity cost—the amount necessary to induce the resource to be supplied. Nearly every resource owner has some ability or skill that allows them to earn at least a little economic rent. College professors' additional training and background typically allow them to earn several thousand dollars a year more than they could earn in the next most remunerative employment, say, high school teaching. If college teaching was not available, they might supply their services to high schools for perhaps $25,000 less.

Section Check

1. The intersection of the supply and demand curves for land determines the price of land, the compensation to land owners.
2. At the profit-maximizing level, the price of land will equal the value of the marginal product of land.
3. Economic rent represents the payment that the resource owner receives beyond its opportunity cost.

---

1. If the supply of land was perfectly inelastic, how much would the price of land rise if the price of crops raised on the land doubled, other things equal? What if the supply of land was less than perfectly inelastic?
2. What would happen to the economic rent earned by Madonna if her alternative earning opportunities outside singing improved? What would it do to her willingness to record and play concerts?
3. How does the existence of professional basketball leagues other than the NBA affect the economic rents earned by NBA players?

section 10.6

Capital and Interest

- How is the price of capital determined?
- How does a potential investor decide whether to purchase capital or not?

SUPPLY AND DEMAND IN THE CAPITAL MARKET

Resources like capital can be "leased" or "rented" for some stipulated period of time. For example, we might want to analyze the market for a certain type of machine that can be used in making running shoes. Following the law of demand, the lower the rental price of a shoe-making machine (which would lower the cost of making running shoes), the greater the quantity of shoe machines demanded. Following the law of supply, the greater the rental price of the machine, the more willing owners of shoe machines are to supply them to entrepreneurs.

interest
the cost of borrowed funds

Rather than renting a shoe machine, a shoemaker may borrow funds and buy his own machine. In this case, the manufacturer is borrowing funds for the purpose of acquiring capital. The cost of the borrowed funds is usually called **interest.** At lower interest rates, the cost of financing the purchase of the shoe machine is lower. If a machine costs $1,000 and the interest rate being charged is 10 percent, the interest cost of a shoe machine is $100 a year ($1,000 × .10); if the relevant interest rate is 8 percent, interest costs are only $80 a year ($1,000 × .08). At lower interest rates, then, capital costs are lower, and the quantity of funds demanded is greater. Likewise, fund lenders will derive greater income the greater the interest rate, so the benefits to them of making a loan increase as interest rates (the "price" of funds) rise. Thus, the quantity of funds supplied is positively related to interest rates.

The graph in Exhibit 1 is virtually the same whether we are renting the capital equipment or borrowing to pay for that capital. The intersection of the upward-sloping supply curve for capital and the downward-sloping demand curve for capital determines the price of capital.

section 10.6 Exhibit 1 — The Supply and Demand for Capital Goods

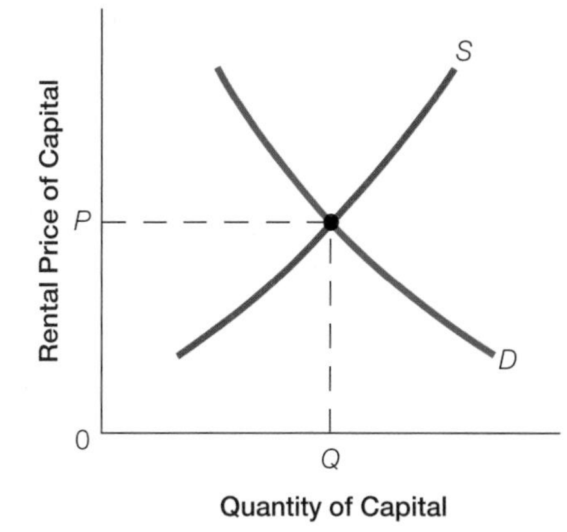

The demand curve for capital is downward sloping, reflecting the fact that as more capital is employed, the value of the marginal product of capital falls. The supply curve for capital is upward sloping, implying that owners of capital will be more willing to supply at higher prices. The price of capital is found at the intersection of the supply and demand curves.

THE CAPITAL INVESTMENT DECISION

One of the most important decisions a firm makes is investment in new capital. A lot of money will be invested in factory equipment and machines that are expected to last for many years. The firm making the investment decision must consider the price that it must pay *now* for the new capital compared with the additional revenue the capital should generate *over time*. That is, the firm must compare current cost with future benefits. To figure out how much those future benefits are worth today, economists use a concept called **present value.**

How Do We Determine the Present Value?

present value
a concept used to figure out how much future benefits are worth today

The present value of future income is the value of having that future income now. That is, a dollar today is worth more than a dollar in the future. People prefer to have money now rather than later, which is why they are willing to pay interest to borrow it. The present value of receiving $1,000 a year from now can be calculated by using the present value equation:

$$PV = \frac{\$X}{(1 + r)^t}$$

Where $X = \$1{,}000$; $t =$ years from now; and $r =$ current market interest rate. So the present value of $1,000 one year from now at the current market interest rate of 5 percent is:

$$\$1{,}000/(1.05)^1 = \$952.38$$

The present value of $1,000 two years from now at a current market interest rate of 5 percent is:

$$\$1{,}000/(1.05)^2 = \$907.03$$

To illustrate, suppose we are restaurant owners contemplating the purchase of a jukebox that we think will produce additional annual earnings of $1,000 a year for ten years, at which time it will be obsolete (worthless). In this case, let us assume that we can get 10 percent annually on the use of our funds in some comparable alternative investment, which is our discount rate. Because the discount rate varies from person to person, a good proxy is the market rate of interest. We can now calculate the present value of earnings to be received in each year (first, second, third, and so on) and sum them. Since these multiyear computations can be tedious, Exhibit 2 provides a summary of present values for annuities. For example, $1,000 per year over 10 years at 10 percent interest yields a discounted present value of $6,145 ($1,000 × 6.1446). If the price of the jukebox were only $5,000, we would buy it (invest); if the price were $7,000, however, the marginal cost of $7,000 would exceed the present expected value, $6,140, so we would not invest.

section 10.6
Exhibit 2

Present Value Table

Year	3%	6%	8%	10%	15%	Year
1	0.9709	0.9434	0.9259	0.9091	0.8696	1
2	1.9135	1.8334	1.7833	1.7355	1.6257	2
3	2.8286	2.6730	2.5771	2.4869	2.2832	3
4	3.7171	3.4651	3.3121	3.1699	2.8550	4
5	4.5797	4.2124	3.9927	3.7908	3.3522	5
6	5.4172	4.9173	4.6229	4.3553	3.7845	6
7	6.2303	5.5824	5.2064	4.8684	4.1604	7
8	7.0197	6.2098	5.7466	5.3349	4.4873	8
9	7.7861	6.8017	6.2469	5.7590	4.7716	9
10	8.5302	**7.3601**	6.7101	**6.1446**	5.0188	**10**
11	9.2526	7.8869	7.1390	6.4951	5.2337	11
12	9.9540	8.3838	7.5361	6.8137	5.4206	12
13	10.6350	8.8527	7.9038	7.1034	5.5831	13
14	11.2961	9.2950	8.2442	7.3667	5.7245	14
15	11.9379	9.7122	8.5595	7.6061	5.8474	15
16	12.5611	10.1059	8.8514	7.8237	5.9542	16
17	13.1661	10.4773	9.1216	8.0216	6.0472	17
18	13.7535	10.8276	9.3719	8.2014	6.1280	18
19	14.3238	11.1581	9.6036	8.3649	6.1982	19
20	14.8775	11.4699	9.8181	**8.5136**	6.2593	20
30	19.6004	13.7648	11.2578	9.4269	6.5660	30

However, if interest rates were to fall to 6 percent, the expected present value of the flow of future earnings would grow to $7,360 ($1,000 × 7.3601), and we probably would make the investment even if the machine cost $7,000. Thus, falling interest rates lead to greater investment. In short, we see that an investor will buy capital if the expected discounted present value of the capital exceeds the current price.

THE INTERDEPENDENCE OF INPUT MARKETS

For simplicity, we have treated the labor, capital, and land markets independently. In reality, these markets are interconnected. For example, if wages rise or the rental price of capital falls, machines might be substituted for some workers.

APPLICATION

WINNING BIG

Q: If you won $10 million in the lottery and were given a choice of a lump sum payment or payment over a 20-year period, which would you choose?

A: Suppose you did win $10 million in the state lottery and your state will pay you this money over a 20-year period—$500,000 a year or you can get a lump sum payment up front. What is the actual present value of this $10 million lottery prize? Using a 10 percent interest rate, the present value over a 20-year period is $4,256,800. That is, using the present value table in Exhibit 2 we multiply $500,000 × 8.5136 = $4,256,800. If you want it up front, it is certainly less than $10 million. Oh yes, there are taxes too.

Section Check

SECTION CHECK

1. The intersection of the demand and supply curves for capital determine the rental price of capital.
2. Firms making the investment decision must consider the price they must pay *now* for the new capital with the additional revenue from the capital that the firm anticipates to make *over time*. That is, the firm must compare current cost with future benefits.

---

1. Why is the demand curve for capital downward sloping?
2. Why is the supply curve for capital upward sloping?
3. If a new machine could earn a 12 percent rate of return for your firm, and you could borrow the funds to finance it at an interest rate of 15 percent per year, would you borrow the money to buy it? Why or why not?
4. What happens to the present value of a stream of payments of $1,000 per year as the interest rate falls?

section 10.7

Income Distribution

- What has happened to the income distribution since 1935?
- Are the income distribution statistics accurate?
- How significant is income mobility?
- How much income inequality is there in other countries?

The ultimate purpose of producing goods and services is to satisfy the material wants of people. Up to this point, we have examined the process by which society decides which wants to satisfy in a world characterized by scarcity; we have examined the question of how goods are produced; and we have examined the question of how society can fully utilize its productive resources. We have not, however, looked carefully into the question of for whom society produces consumer goods and services. Why are some people able to consume much more than others? Exhibit 1 shows a breakdown of mean household income. This is one way to look at the income distribution.

section 10.7 Exhibit 1 — Mean Household Income by Quintile

Quintile	Income
Lower Quintile	$ 10,190
Second Quintile	25,334
Third Quintile	42,361
Fourth Quintile	65,729
Highest Quintile	141,620

SOURCE: U.S. Bureau of the Census, 2001.

THE RECORD SINCE 1935

Exhibit 2 illustrates the changing distribution of measured income in the United States since 1935. As you can see in this table, the proportion of income received by the richest Americans (top 5 percent) declined sharply after 1935 but has been edging back up since the 1980s. The proportion received by the poorest Americans (the lowest 20 percent) has remained virtually unchanged since 1935. Most of the observed changes occurred between 1935 and 1950, probably reflecting the impact of the Great Depression

section 10.7
Exhibit 2

Before-Tax Income Shares

Year	Lowest Fifth	Second Fifth	Third Fifth	Fourth Fifth	Highest Fifth	Highest 5%
1935	4.1%	9.2%	14.1%	20.9%	51.7%	26.5%
1950	4.5	12.0	17.4	23.4	42.7	17.3
1960	4.8	12.2	17.8	24.0	41.3	15.9
1970	5.4	12.2	17.6	23.8	40.9	15.6
1980	5.3	11.6	17.6	24.4	41.1	14.6
1990	4.6	10.8	16.6	23.8	44.3	17.4
2000	4.3	9.8	15.5	22.8	47.4	20.8

SOURCE: U.S. Bureau of Census.

and new government programs in the 1930s, as well as World War II. From 1950 to 1980, there was little change in the overall distribution of income. Two significant changes have occurred since the 1980s: The lowest one-fifth of families have seen their share of measured income fall from 5.3 to 4.3 percent of all income, and the top one-fifth of families have seen their share of measured income rise from 41.1 to 47.4 percent of all income.

ARE WE OVERSTATING THE DISPARITY IN THE DISTRIBUTION OF INCOME?

Failing to take into consideration differences in age, certain demographic factors, institutional factors, and government redistributive activities have all been identified as elements that influence income distribution data and may suggest that we might be overstating inequality.

Differences in Age

At any moment in time, middle-age people tend to have higher incomes than both younger and older people. Middle age is when most people are at their peak in terms of productivity and participate in the labor force to a greater extent than the very old or very young. Put differently, if every individual earned exactly the same total income over his or her lifetime, there would still be some observed inequality at any given moment in time, simply because people earn more in middle age.

Inequality resulting from this demographic difference overstates the true inequality in the lifetime earnings of people. A typical 50-year-old male earns nearly twice the income of a male in his early 20s and nearly one-third more than workers over 65. Since 1950, the proportion of individuals that are either very young or very old has grown, meaning that in a relative sense, more people are in lower-income age groups.

Other Demographic Trends

Other demographic trends, like the increased number of divorced couples and the rise of two-income families (and DINKs—Double Income, No Kids), have also caused the measured distribution of income (which is measured in terms of household income) to appear more unequal. For example, in the 1950s, the overwhelming majority of families had single incomes. In the 1990s, a family that decides to have two breadwinners instead of one might be making $70,000 or $80,000 a year instead of, say, $40,000 a year; thus, they would move into a higher-income quintile and create greater apparent income inequality. At the same time, divorces create two households instead of one, lowering income per household for divorced couples; thus, they move into lower-income quintiles, also creating greater apparent income inequality.

Government Activities

Other scholars have argued that the impact of increased government activity should be considered in evaluating the measured income distribution.[1] Government-imposed taxes burden different income groups in different ways. Also, government programs benefit some groups of income recipients more than others. For example, it has been argued that state-subsidized higher education has benefited the high- and middle-income groups more than the poor (because far more students from these income groups go to college), as have such things as government subsidies to airports and airlines, operas, and art museums. Some programs, though, clearly aid the poor more than the rich. Food stamps, school lunch programs, housing subsidies, Medicaid, and several other programs provide recipients with **in-kind transfers**—that is, transfers given in a nonmonetary form. When these in-kind transfers are included, many economists conclude that they have served to reduce levels of inequality significantly from the levels suggested by aggregate income statistics.

in-kind transfers
transfers given in goods and services rather than cash

On balance, the evidence suggests that inequality of money income in the United States declined from 1935 to 1950, then remained rather stable until 1980. Since then, the distribution of income has become less equal. However, if we consider age distribution, institutional factors, and in-kind transfer programs, it is safe to say that the income distribution is considerably more equal than it appears in Exhibit 2.

MOVING UP AND DOWN THE ECONOMIC LADDER

Most Americans experience significant fluctuations in their economic well-being from one year to the next. According to a Census Bureau study in the mid-1990s, about three-fourths of the population see their economic well-being go either up or down by at least 5 percent from one year to the next. Economic well-being can be affected by changes in personal and family circumstances, such as work experience, marital status, household composition, as well as changes in earnings.

WHY DO SOME EARN MORE THAN OTHERS?

There are many reasons why some people make more income than others. Some reasons for the differences in the income include differences in age, skill, education, training, and preferences toward risk and leisure.

Age

The amount of income people earn varies over their lifetimes. Younger people with few skills tend to make little income when they begin their working careers. Income rises as

[1] Edgar Browning, "The Trend Towards Equality in the Distribution of Income," *Southern Economic Journal*, July 1976, pp. 912–923; Frank Levy, *Dollars and Dreams* (New York: Norton, 1987), p. 195.

workers gain experience and on-the-job training. As productivity increases, workers can command higher wages. These wage earnings generally increase up to the age of 50 and fall dramatically at retirement age, around 65.

Skills and Human Capital

Some workers are just more productive than others and therefore earn higher wages. The greater productivity may be a result of innate skills or of improvements in human capital, such as training and education. Still others, like star athletes and rock stars, have specialized talents that are in huge demand, so they make more money than those with fewer skills or with skills that are in less demand.

Worker Preferences

Aside from skills, education, and training, people have different attitudes about and preferences regarding their work. Workaholics (by definition) work longer hours and so they earn more than others with comparable skills. Some earn more because they work more intensely than others. Still others may choose jobs that pay less but have more amenities—flexible hours, favorable job location, generous benefit programs, child care, and so on. And some may choose to work less and spend more time pursuing leisure activities, like traveling, hobbies, or spending time with family and friends. It is not for us to say that one preference is better than another but simply to recognize that these choices lead to differences in earnings.

Job Preferences

Finally, some of the differences in income are the result of the risks or undesirable features of some occupations. Police officers and firefighters are paid higher wages because of the dangers associated with their jobs. The same would be true for window washers on skyscrapers and painters on the Golden Gate bridge. Coal miners and garbage collectors are paid more than other workers with comparable skill levels because of the unpleasantness of the jobs. In short, some workers have higher earnings because they are compensated for the difficult, risky, or unappealing nature of their jobs.

Section Check

1. From 1935 to 1980, the distribution of income became more equal. However, since 1980, there has been increased inequality.
2. Nonmonetary income and privileges to the well-to-do may understate the disparity in income inequality, while demographics, institutional factors, and government programs may overstate the disparity in income inequality.
3. High-income and low-income earners will always be with us, but they will likely be different people.

---

1. Why might patterns in the measured income distribution give an incorrect impression?
2. Why might measured income shares understate the degree of income inequality?
3. Why might measured income shares overstate the degree of income inequality?
4. How does the fraction of the population that is middle aged, rather than young or old, affect measurements of income inequality?
5. How does the growth of both two-earner families and divorced couples increase measured income inequality?
6. Why is it important to take account of the substantial mobility of families within the income distribution over time when evaluating the degree of income inequality in the United States?

The Economics of Discrimination

section 10.8

- What is job-entry discrimination?
- What is wage discrimination?
- Do earnings differences reflect discrimination or differences in productivity?
- How can we remedy discrimination?

When a worker is denied employment on the basis of some biological feature, such as sex or race, without any regard to her productivity, it is called **job-entry discrimination. Wage discrimination** is where a worker is given employment at a wage lower than that of other workers, based on something other than productivity.

job-entry discrimination *denial of employment based upon a non-economic factor, such as race, religion, sex, or ethnicity*

wage discrimination *employment at wages lower than that of other workers based on an attribute other than productivity differences, such as race or sex*

JOB-ENTRY DISCRIMINATION

In a world where sex and race have absolutely no bearing whatsoever on the employment circumstances of people (e.g., talent, education, willingness and ability to work, move, etc.), every occupation would, apart from random variations, have a workforce with the same sex and race proportions as the population at large. Thus, on average 51 percent of employees in each occupation would be expected to be female, if women constituted 51 percent of the population, and approximately 12 percent or so would be blacks and other racial minorities, reflecting the proportion of nonwhites to the total population.

In fact, the proportion of females working (46 percent) is slightly less than the proportion of men. Likewise, the proportion of blacks in the workforce is lower than would

Education level has a great impact on earnings potential. Young adults who have completed a bachelor's degree earn substantially more than those with a high school diploma—earnings rise roughly 50 percent for males and 90 percent for females. Income gaps between males and females decline with increasing levels of education. Between 1980 and 2000, the earnings of those with a bachelor's degree or higher rose faster than those who had only completed high school.

be expected given the general population percentages. Looking first at females, their less than proportionate presence in the workforce might be viewed as a matter of choice; some women may prefer to be engaged in full-time household production rather than work outside the house. On the other hand, others argue that this attitude reflects ingrained sexism and that there is no inherent reason that the adult male member of the household should not stay at home with the kids as much as the female member. In any case, the proportion of women to men in the workforce has dramatically increased over time—women were only 38 percent of the labor force in 1970 and now they are over 46 percent.

Also, a higher proportion of white males have relatively high-paying jobs, while females and nonwhites make up a relatively larger proportion of employees working in unskilled jobs with low pay and relatively little prestige.

WAGE DISCRIMINATION

A strong statistical correlation exists between lifetime earnings and years of schooling. High-school graduates earn roughly two-thirds of the salary of college graduates.

Overall, white women make 25 to 30 percent less than white men. White males also typically earn 25 to 30 percent more than black males. At least part of this wage differential can be explained by differences in educational attainment and does not simply reflect racial prejudice on the part of employers. Blacks and women on average may have acquired fewer years of schooling, less training, and fewer years of experience. For example, although almost 25 percent of whites have a college degree, less than 14 percent of blacks and 10 percent of Hispanics have completed four years of college. Also, compared to 26 percent of men, less than 22 percent of women have completed four years of college. Among females, black women earned 10 percent less than white women. While a major reason women and nonwhites earn less than white males is that they occupy jobs that are lower paying due to their lower skills, it is also possible that they earn less because of wage discrimination—being paid less for a job strictly because of their race or sex.

DISCRIMINATION OR DIFFERENCES IN PRODUCTIVITY?

Merely demonstrating that wages are lower for blacks and females does not in itself prove wage discrimination, although it is consistent with the notion that discrimination occurs. Likewise, just because there are fewer female lawyers than males is not proof that discrimination exists. However, if occupational and wage differentials are not caused by discrimination, what are the causes?

Several scholars have developed statistical models that argue that a great deal of the earnings differentials across the sexes and races can be explained by differences in productivity. In other words, employers hire and pay workers roughly an amount equal to their perceived contributions (marginal revenue product). Now, if it happens that the marginal revenue product of blacks and women is lower on average than that of white men, even within occupational groups, then one could argue that employers are not discriminating on the basis of race or sex, but rather on the basis of expected productivity. Assuming this is at least partly true, why might white male workers be more productive than other workers?

Productivity Differences: An Environmental Explanation

The first explanation is that various environmental factors have prevented blacks, Hispanics, and females from gaining the training and skills necessary to achieve high productivity. In the past, blacks and Hispanics often received less schooling than whites, and the quality of that schooling has often been lower. Females, because they are far more likely to interrupt their careers to have and care for children, often have less work experience than their male counterparts. This, too, may lower their productivity relative to males. This environmental explanation of productivity differences does not rule out discrimination, but rather argues that past discrimination's perverse influences on the environment of females and nonwhites has caused them to have an inferior endowment of human capital now, even if present-day employers were color- and sex-blind in terms of paying workers.

WHY DO PEOPLE DISCRIMINATE?

Why would any employer want to discriminate against an employee on the basis of race or sex? It might appear that discrimination is totally inconsistent with the economist's view of the rational utility-maximizing person. After all, if a firm really wants to maximize profits, it should hire the best person available per dollar of wage expenditure, regardless of the age, sex, race, or other attribute of the worker.

Let us take a look to see why there may be discrimination.

Reducing Information Costs

To some extent, discrimination may reflect information costs. Suppose an employer has previously hired ten green workers and ten blue workers for a certain type of work, and eight of the green workers performed well while only two of the blue workers did. (The poorer blue worker performance may have reflected poorer training and educational backgrounds). In this situation, the employer might prefer to hire a green employee for the next job opening, because past experience suggests that the probability is greater that the green worker will perform well. In this case, the color of the worker is used as a screening device, a means of narrowing the list of job candidates.

It costs money and time to evaluate the prospects of every applicant, and race is an imperfect but cheap way of doing some of the screening. The fact that using color of workers as a screening device discriminates against good blue workers is not a major concern to a profit-maximizing employer. The information cost reduction from hiring on the basis of color may exceed the perceived benefits from the identification of good blue workers.

Personal Preferences

Beyond this, though, it is a fact that some people prefer association with others with certain racial and/or sexual attributes. These people may have developed these preferences out of an ignorance, developing bigotry and racism, but the preferences are there nonetheless. The utility gained from having the desired racial mix might exceed the loss in income from not having the best employees. A racially prejudiced person might prefer making $900,000 a year in profits from a business with, say, an all white labor force to making \$1,000,000 with a racially mixed force. In the words of the pioneer in the economics of discrimination, Nobel laureate Gary Becker of the University of Chicago, the person has acquired a "taste" for discrimination, just as one might acquire a taste for certain goods. That is, an employer may be willing to trade away some income in order to satisfy the taste for discrimination.

THE COSTS OF DISCRIMINATION

It is also true that in competitive industries, firms who discriminate may lose out ultimately to those firms that do not. The nondiscriminating firm can hire the unfavored but equally competent workers and have a cost advantage over employers who discriminate. This cost advantage may allow the nondiscriminating firm to undercut its discriminating competitors' prices and either force them out of business or make them change their hiring practices. That is, in the long run, competition has the potential to reduce discrimination.

REMEDYING DISCRIMINATION

The primary means used to address economic discrimination in the United States is affirmative action programs, in which employers are strongly encouraged to hire more minority group workers in occupations where those groups are now relatively underrepresented. The second aspect of affirmative action is correcting wage and salary inequities. Beyond this, some of the possible environmental causes of productivity differences between racial and sex groups have been addressed, such as through compensatory education programs (e.g., Head Start), increased efforts to increase minority enrollments in colleges and universities, and so on. There is some evidence that these various efforts have met with some success, as the proportion of employees from minority groups in higher-paying occupations has increased in recent years, and blatant wage and salary discrimination has become less frequent. Still, the economic differences between different races and sexes are rather large.

Affirmative action job hiring programs are controversial. Affirmative action may increase the probability that someone will be hired on some basis other than productivity. While this may be desirable from the standpoint of equalizing opportunities between demographic groups, it also can serve to lower society's output as a whole and profits to firms. Also, the "reverse discrimination" equity argument is raised. For example, with respect to productivity, a firm may be forced to hire a minority worker with a marginal revenue product of \$80, instead of a non-minority worker whose marginal revenue product may be \$100 (perhaps because of more years of schooling). Society ultimately loses \$20 in output (the difference in the value of marginal output). Moreover, if the firm that hires the minority worker has to pay the prevailing wage (say \$90) to avoid wage discrimination charges, hiring that worker will lower profits. With that, the firm might decide to not hire anyone, knowing that affirmative action pressures prevent them from hiring the profitable non-minority worker (whose marginal revenue product exceeds the prevailing wage by \$10) instead of the minority worker (whose hiring will reduce profits by \$10).

Employer actions to protect profits, then, might negate some or all the expected gains from affirmative action programs. An alternative approach to one using implicit quotas would be to subsidize employers for hiring minority workers. Some would regard this approach as a gift or bailout for business enterprise more than a help to minorities, and thus oppose the approach. The subsidy approach would, however, provide employers with greater incentive to increase minority job opportunities.

Section Check

1. If a worker is denied employment on the basis of some noneconomic factor like race, religion, sex, or ethnic origin, it is called job-entry discrimination.
2. If a worker is hired at a wage lower than that of other workers on some basis other than productivity differences, it is called wage discrimination.
3. If a firm really wants to maximize profits, it should minimize costs by hiring the best persons available per dollar of wage expenditure, regardless of the age, sex, race, or other attribute of the worker.
4. Discrimination may occur because of information costs or because some workers may prefer to associate with persons with certain racial and/or sexual attributes.
5. Remedies to discrimination might include affirmative action and education programs.

---

1. What is the difference between job-entry discrimination and wage discrimination?
2. Explain how earnings differences could reflect either discrimination or productivity differences.
3. What is the environmental explanation for differences in earnings across the sexes and races?
4. How do firms' incentives to maximize profits tend to reduce the extent of discrimination?
5. How can discrimination reflect imperfect information and the costs of acquiring more information about potential employees?
6. Say you now hire only purple workers. If purple workers strongly prefer to work with one another instead of with other groups, why might you prefer to hire a less-productive purple worker than a more-productive non-purple worker at the same wage?
7. Why would subsidizing employers for hiring minority workers rather than imposing implicit hiring quotas give employers greater incentives to expand minority job opportunities?

section 10.9

Poverty

- How do we define poverty?
- How many people live in poverty?
- What is relative income?

At several points in the previous discussion, the words "rich" and "poor" have been used without being defined. Of particular interest is the question of poverty. Our concern over income distribution largely arises because most people believe that those with low incomes have lower satisfaction than those with higher incomes. Thus, the "poor" people are those who, in a material sense, suffer relative to other people. It is desirable, therefore, to define and measure the extent of poverty in the United States.

DEFINING POVERTY

The federal government measures poverty by using a set of money income thresholds that vary by family size to detect who is poor. If the family's total income is less than the

poverty rate
the percentage of population that falls below a determined income

poverty line
the income threshold at which an absolute level of poorness is established

established family threshold, then that family, and every individual in it, is considered poor. The poverty threshholds are adjusted annually for inflation. The **poverty rate** is the percentage of the population who fall below this absolute level called the **poverty line.** The official poverty rate for the United States is currently set at three times the cost of providing a nutritionally adequate diet—slightly less than $20,000 for a family of four. The official poverty definition may overstate the level of poverty because it does not include noncash benefits (such as public housing, medicaid, and food stamps).

The amount of poverty fell steadily in the 1960s, was steady in the 1970s, and rose during the recession in the early 1980s. The poverty rate then fell slightly during the rest of the 1980s and rose again during the recession of 1990–1991. As you would expect, when the economy is in a recession, unemployment rises and poverty tends to increase. Exhibit 1 provides some statistics on the U.S. poverty rate.

According to the Census Bureau, the poverty rate dropped from 12.7 percent in 1998 to 11.3 percent in 2000, close to the record low of 11.1 set in 1973. "Every racial and ethnic group experienced a drop in both the number of poor and the percent in poverty, as did children, the elderly and people ages 25 to 44," said Daniel Weinberg, chief of the Census Bureau's Housing and Household Economic Statistics Division. "Declines in poverty were concentrated in metropolitan areas, particularly central cities."

The Census Bureau reported that 31.1 million were poor in 2000, 1.1 million fewer than in 1999. Also, the percentage of people 65 and over who were living in poverty reached a measured low of 10.2 percent in 2000 and the percentage of the people under 18 living in poverty was the lowest since 1979. With the exception of whites, the poverty rates for the major racial and ethnic groups set or equaled historic lows.

With a definition of poverty that is determined at some fixed, real income level (that is, an income that has been adjusted for inflation), poverty over time should decline and, indeed, largely disappear, because real incomes generally rise over time with economic growth. Unless lower income groups do not share at all in the rising incomes of the population, some reduction in poverty is inevitable. Thus, one cure for poverty, as defined by some absolute income or standard or living criterion, is economic growth. The greater the rate of economic growth, the more rapidly poverty will be eradicated.

section 10.9 Exhibit 1 **Number of Poor and Poverty Rate: 1959 to 2000**

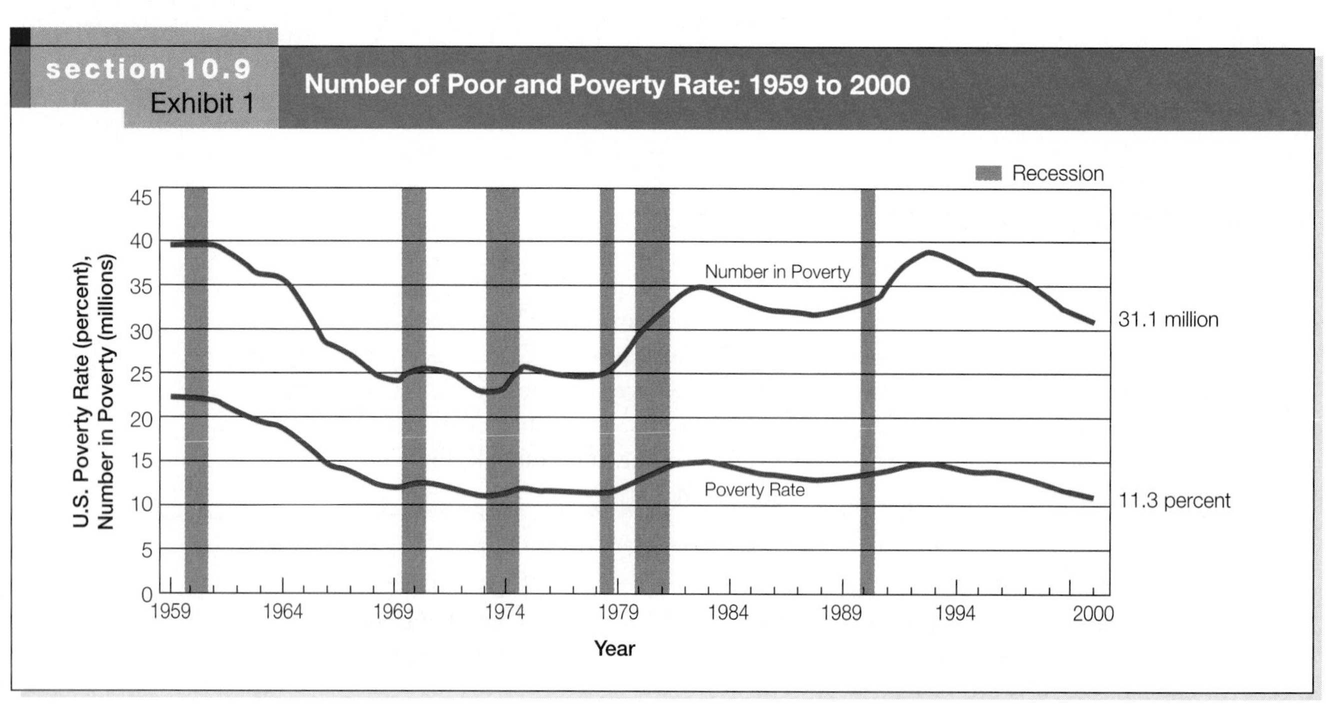

In The NEWS

DEFINING POVERTY UP

BY W. MICHAEL COX AND RICHARD ALM

America could soon get a lot poorer. The Census Bureau is experimenting with a new formula that would raise the poverty threshold for a family of four to $19,500 from $16,660. Through a simple change of definition . . . 12 million Americans might become "poor" overnight. It's true that existing measures of poverty are riddled with flaws. The poverty rate tells us how many Americans earn low incomes, not what they're able to buy. Households in the bottom fifth of the income distribution consume well beyond their earnings. In 1997 an average low-income household made $7,086 a year before taxes. Consumption—what the poor spent, not what they earned—totaled $14,670.

How can poor families consume more than they earn? Many supplement their income through welfare, Food Stamps, unemployment benefits, Medicare, Medicaid, school lunches, rent subsidies and other programs, all of which the statistics leave uncounted. And the poverty statistics ignore wealth, which can be more important than current income. Workers temporarily laid off don't get paychecks, but they often have savings to fall back on. Although many retirees earn low incomes, their houses, cars and furnishings are paid for, and they've got nest eggs. In 1993, 302,000 families with incomes of less than $20,000 lived in homes worth more than $300,000. But over the years, the poor have gained access to more goods. Government statistics show that poor households own many of the consumer goods usually associated with middle-class life in the United States.

The percentage of poor households with washing machines rose to 72 percent in 1996 from 58 percent in 1984. Ownership of dryers went to 50 percent from 36 percent. Two-thirds of poor families had microwave ovens in 1996, up from one in eight a decade ago. Ninety-seven percent of poor households have color televisions, and three-fourths have videocassette recorders. Almost three-quarters of poor families own at least one car. Spending patterns help explain how the poor can afford more of the trappings of middle-class life yet still not escape the poverty statistics. Among households below the poverty line, outlays for food, clothing and shelter were 37 percent of consumption in 1995, compared with 52 percent two decades earlier, 57 percent in 1950 and 75 percent in 1920. Thus poor households have considerably more discretionary income than they once did.

The crux of the debate over the proposed new statistics is the purpose of measuring poverty. As originally conceived, the poverty statistics were meant to be diagnostic. They emerged in the mid-1960s as a benchmark for President Johnson's "war on poverty." What we wanted to know then—what we should still want to know today—is whether we're reducing the number of families struggling to obtain the basic necessities of life.

In 1993, University of Texas economist Daniel Slesnick recalculated the poverty rate based on spending rather than income. To remove the vagaries of inflation, he established the poverty threshold at three times the cost of a nutritionally adequate diet for all members of a household. Mr. Slesnick's results show that the proportion of poor in the U.S., measured by consumption, has fallen steadily, from 31 percent in 1949 to 13 percent in 1965 to 2 percent at the end of the 1980s.

SOURCE: W. Michael Cox and Richard Alm, "Defining Poverty Up," *Wall Street Journal,* November 2, 1999, p. A26. *Wall Street Journal,* eastern edition [staff-produced copy only] by W. Michael Cox and Richard Alm.

AN ALTERNATIVE DEFINITION OF POVERTY

Many "poor" individuals in the United States, using the official definition, would be considered well off, even "rich," in many less-developed countries. For example, $15,000 of income a year, while not much in the United States, would make you rich in a country like Ethiopia. Conversely, many Americans with incomes now considered just above the poverty line might be considered "poor" a generation from now, even though their income will permit them to buy far more than what today are considered to be necessities of life. Why?

To most people, being "poor" means having less income and purchasing power than most other people living in the same community or nation. A person is "poor" if her income is low relative to the incomes of most other people in the same geographical area, and "rich" if her income exceeds that of most other people in the area. Poverty is therefore often thought of as a *relative income* concept, rather than being determined by some ability to buy some specific fixed basket of goods and services.

Alternative definitions of poverty have been suggested based on relative income measures. For instance, families that earn less than one-half the median (or middle) family income could be considered poor. Over time, as economic growth proceeds, the income necessary to avoid being considered poor by this measure increases. Using this definition, then, poverty cannot be eradicated by economic growth, but only by income redistribution. Even from an equity or fairness point of view, few people favor total income equality, because income needs presumably vary with family size and possibly with the ages of the family members and the cost of living in different cities. Even some of the poor might not favor such policies of equality, because their kids would—in such a system—have less of a chance of "making good." It is clear, then, that "poverty" in a relative income sense will always be with us. We can perhaps reduce the consequences of being poor by policies that raise the incomes of lowest-income persons to levels closer to the median, but we cannot raise everyone's income to a level equal to or above that median; that is an economic, as well as a statistical, impossibility.

Section Check

1. One method of defining poverty is to determine an absolute income level that is necessary to provide the basic necessities of life in minimum quantities. The poverty rate, then, would be the proportion of persons who fail to earn the minimum income standard.
2. An alternative definition of poverty is a relative income measure. For instance, families that earn less than one-half the median (or middle) family income are considered poor. Using this definition, poverty cannot be eradicated by economic growth, but only by income redistribution.

---

1. How are absolute and relative measures of poverty different?
2. Why could economic growth potentially eliminate absolute measures of poverty but not relative measures of poverty?
3. Some people have argued that poverty could be eliminated by "rich" countries. Can both absolute and relative poverty be eliminated by "rich" countries? Why or why not?

Summary

The price and output in the markets for labor, land, and capital are determined by the intersection of the supply and demand curves. In factor or input markets, demand is derived from consumers' demand for the final good or service that the input produces.

The marginal revenue product of an input is the marginal product times the price of the output. The demand curve for labor is downward sloping because of the diminishing marginal product of labor. That is, if additional labor is added to a fixed quantity of land or capital equipment, output will increase, but eventually by smaller amounts.

Wages in the labor market are determined by the intersection of the labor demand curve and the labor supply curve. The labor demand curve can shift if there is a change in productivity or a change in the demand for the final product. The labor supply curve can shift if there are changes in immigration or population growth, workers' preferences, nonwage income, or amenities.

Real wages are determined by the intersection of the labor demand and labor supply curves. If the demand for labor rises more rapidly than the supply of labor, real wages will rise. If the supply of labor rises more rapidly than the demand for labor, real wages will fall.

Through restrictive membership, a union can reduce the labor supply in the market for union workers, thus reducing employment and raising wages. This increases the supply of workers in the nonunion sector, shifting supply to the right and lowering wages for nonunion workers.

The intersection of the supply and demand curves for land determines the price of land or the compensation to landowners. Economic rent represents the payment that resource owners receive beyond what they would receive using the resource in its next most attractive use.

Firms making the investment decision must consider the price they must pay *now* for the new capital with the additional revenue from the capital that the firm anticipates to make *over time*. That is, the firm must compare current cost with future benefits.

From 1935 to 1980, the distribution of income became more equal. However, since 1980, inequality has increased. Demographics, institutional factors, and government programs may overstate the disparity in income inequality. High-income and low-income earners will always be with us, but they will likely be different people. Income inequality between nations is substantial.

If a worker is denied employment on the basis of some noneconomic factor like race, religion, sex, or ethnic origin, it is called job-entry discrimination. If workers are given employment at wages lower than that of other workers on some basis other than productivity differences, it is called wage discrimination. If a firm really wants to maximize profits, it should minimize costs by hiring the best persons available per dollar of wage expenditure, regardless of the age, sex, race, or other attribute of the worker.

Discrimination may occur because of information costs or because some workers may prefer to associate with people with certain racial and/or sexual attributes. Remedies to discrimination might include affirmative action and education programs.

One method of defining poverty is to determine an absolute income level that is necessary to provide the basic necessities of life in minimum quantities. The poverty rate, then, would be the proportion of people who fail to earn the minimum income standard.

An alternative definition of poverty is a relative income measure. For example, families that earn less than one-half the median (or middle) family income are considered poor. Using this definition, poverty cannot be eradicated by economic growth, but only by income redistribution.

Key Terms and Concepts

derived demand 212
marginal revenue product (*MRP*) 214
marginal resource cost (*MRC*) 214
marginal product (*MP*) 215
collective bargaining 223
economic rent 226
interest 228
present value 229
in-kind transfers 233
job-entry discrimination 235
wage discrimination 235
poverty rate 240
poverty line 240

Review Questions

1. At right is a table showing the Total Output each week of workers on a perfectly competitive cherry farm. The equilibrium price of a pound of cherries is $4. Complete the Marginal Product of Labor and the Value of Marginal Product of Labor columns in the table.

2. Using the same table, how many workers will the farmer hire if the equilibrium wage rate is $550 per week? $650 per week?

3. What happens to the demand curve for labor when the equilibrium price of output increases?

Quantity of Labor	Total Output	Marginal Product of Labor	Value of Marginal Product of Labor
0	—	______	______
1	250	______	______
2	600	______	______
3	900	______	______
4	1125	______	______
5	1300	______	______
6	1450	______	______
7	1560	______	______

4. Which of the following groups are likely to benefit from legislation substantially increasing the minimum wage? Explain why.
   a. unskilled workers seeking jobs but lacking experience and education
   b. skilled workers whose current wages are above the minimum wage
   c. manufacturers of machinery that saves labor in industries employing large amounts of unskilled labor
   d. unskilled workers who have a criminal record
   e. a teenager seeking his first job
   f. unskilled workers who retain employment after the minimum wage is raised
   g. regions where almost everybody already earns substantially more than the minimum wage
5. If a competitive firm is paying $8 per hour (with no fringe benefits) to its employees, what would tend to happen to its equilibrium wage if the company began to give on-the-job training or free health insurance to its workers? What would happen to its on-the-job training and health insurance for its workers if the government mandated a minimum wage of $9 an hour?
6. Would the owner of University Pizza Parlor hire another worker for $60 per day if that worker added 40 pizzas a day and each pizza added $2 to University Pizza Parlor's revenues? Why or why not?
7. What would happen to the demand for unskilled labor if there was an increase in the demand for hamburgers and fries?
8. Professional athletes command and receive higher salaries than teachers. Yet teachers, not athletes, are considered essential to economic growth and development. If this is in fact the case, why do athletes receive higher salaries than teachers?
9. The availability of jobs at higher real wages motivates many people to migrate illegally to the United States. Other things equal, what impact would a large influx of illegal (or legal) immigrants have on real wages? What impact would it have on the real wages in the immigrant's home country?
10. The Dean at Middle State University knows that poets generally earn less than engineers in the private market; that is, the equilibrium wage for engineers is higher than that for poets. Suppose that all colleges and universities except for Middle State University pay their professors according to their potential private market wage. The administration at Middle State believes that salaries should be equal across all disciplines because its professors work equally hard and because all of the professors have similar degrees—Ph.D.'s. As a result, Middle State opts to pay all of its professors a mid-range wage, W_{MS}. What do you think is likely to happen to the engineering and poetry programs at Middle State?
11. An entrepreneur considers the following investment opportunity: for an investment of $500 today he can earn a return of $200 per year over the next three years. Should he undertake the investment if the interest rate is 8 percent? 10 percent?
12. How might each of the following affect the distribution of income in the near term:
    a. a massive influx of low-skilled immigrants
    b. a new baby boom occurs
    c. the babies in (b) enter their twenties
    d. the babies in (b) reach age 65 or older
13. What factors might explain the differential in average income between males and females?
14. How might a significant reduction in the divorce rate affect the distribution of income?
15. Visit the Sexton Web site at **http://sexton.swcollege.com** and click on "Bureau of Labor and Statistics National Compensation Survey" and compare the mean hourly earnings of white-collar workers and blue-collar workers in the Los Angeles area. What factors contribute to this difference in earnings?
16. Visit the Sexton Web site and click on the "World Bank" link and download the PDF file titled "World Development Indicators: Poverty and Inequality." Compare the income distribution in Denmark and Guatemala. What factors might account for the differences in income distribution between these two countries?
17. What is the definition of poverty in the United States? Visit the Sexton Web site and click on "Census Bureau" and look up the latest poverty threshold for a single person under the age of 65. How do you think that definition compares with most other parts of the world?

Fill in the Blanks

1. In input or factor markets, the demand for an input is a DERIVED demand—DERIVED from consumers' demand for the good or service.

2. The demand for labor is determined by its MARGINAL REVENUE PRODUCT, which is the additional revenue that a firm obtains from one more unit of input.

3. The MARGINAL RESOURCE COST is the amount that an extra input adds to a firm's total costs.

4. A firm would find its profits growing by adding one more worker when the MRP associated with the worker exceeds the MRC of the worker.

5. The law of diminishing marginal product reflects the fact that by adding increasing quantities of a VARIABLE input (for example, labor) to fixed quantities of another input, output will rise, but at some point it will increase by DIMINISHING amounts.

6. Profits are maximized if a firm hires only to the point where the wage equals the expected MRP.

7. As the wage rate rises, the quantity of labor supplied INCREASES, *ceteris paribus;* as the wage falls, the quantity of labor supplied FALLS, *ceteris paribus.*

8. At a wage below the equilibrium level, quantity DEMAND would exceed quantity SUPPLIED, resulting in a labor SHORTAGE. In this situation, employers would be forced to offer higher wages in order to hire as many workers as they would like.

9. Increases in the demand curve for labor may arise from INCREASES in labor productivity or from INCREASES in the price of the good.

10. Workers can increase productivity if they have more CAPITAL or land with which to work, if TECHNOLOGY improvements occur, or if they acquire additional SKILLS or experience.

11. If labor productivity falls, then the demand curve for labor will shift to the LEFT.

12. If new workers enter the labor force, the labor supply curve will shift to the RIGHT.

13. If unions are successful in raising union wages, the result will be LOWER wages in the nonunion sector.

14. If the demand for land is high, the rental price of land is HIGH; if demand is low, the rental price of land is LOW.

15. Those who receive their income because of a distinct, unique skill are collecting ECONOMIC RENT—compensation for a resource whose supply is perfectly inelastic over the relevant range of prices.

16. The PRESENT VALUE of future income is the value of having that future income now.

17. An investor will buy capital if the expected discounted present value of the capital EXCEED the current price.

18. Failing to take into consideration differences in AGE, certain DEMOGRAPHIC factors, INSTITUTIONAL factors, and government REDISTRIBUTIVE activities have all been identified as elements that influence the income distribution data and suggest that we might be overstating inequality.

19. At any moment in time, middle-aged persons tend to have HIGHER incomes than younger and older persons because they are at an age when their PRODUCTIVITY is at a peak and they are participating in the LABOR FORCE to a greater extent.

20. Reasons that some people make more money than others include differences in AGE, SKILL, EDUCATION, TRAINING, and PREFERENCE toward risk and leisure.

21. JOB-ENTRY discrimination occurs when a worker is denied employment on the basis of some factor without regard to the productivity of the worker.

22. A great deal of the earnings differentials across the sexes and races can be explained by differences in PRODUCTIVITY.

23. In competitive industries, firms who do not discriminate can hire the unfavored but equally competent workers and have a COST advantage, allowing them to UNDERCUT discriminating competitors' prices.

24. The primary means used to address economic discrimination in the United States is AFFIRMATIVE ACTION programs, in which employers are strongly encouraged to hire more minority group workers in occupations where those groups are now relatively underrepresented and to correct wage and salary inequities.

25. The poverty rate for the United States is currently set at THREE TIMES the cost of providing a nutritionally adequate diet.

26. The greater the rate of economic growth, the MORE rapidly poverty will be eradicated.

27. Using a relative definition of poverty, poverty cannot be eradicated by economic growth but only by INCOME REDISTRIBUTION.

True or False

1. By far the largest fraction of national income goes to wages and salaries for labor services.

2. The "price" of a productive factor is directly related to consumer demand for the final good or service.

3. In a competitive labor market, a firm's marginal resource cost is the market wage.

4. Hiring an additional worker would lower profits when the marginal resource cost is less than the marginal revenue product.

5. The law of diminishing marginal product states that as increasing quantities of a variable input (for example, labor) are added to fixed quantities of another input, output will rise, but at some point it will increase by diminishing amounts.

6. The marginal revenue product of labor declines, even in the case of competitive output markets, because of the diminishing marginal product of labor.

7. A profit-maximizing firm will hire up to the last unit of input for which the wage is expected to exceed the marginal revenue product.

8. In a competitive labor market, a firm can hire all the labor it wishes at the prevailing wage.

9. Only at the equilibrium wage are both suppliers (workers) and demanders (employers) of labor able to exchange the quantity of labor they desire.

10. Decreases in the demand curve for labor may arise from decreases in labor productivity or from increases in the price of the good produced by that labor.

11. An increase in the demand for a good will increase the demand for labor.

12. A decrease in the nonwage income of workers would shift the labor supply curve to the right.

13. The wage premium paid to union workers shows that all workers benefit from the activity of unions.

14. If unions are successful in obtaining higher wages, it causes employment to rise in the union sector but to fall in the nonunion sector.

15. Because the supply curve is completely inelastic, only changes in the demand for land will change the price of land.

16. The concept of economic rent only applies to land.

17. A firm will invest in a new piece of capital when its price is less than the present value of additional net revenue it is expected to provide the firm over time.

18. While there have been changes in the distribution of measured income, there remains substantial income inequality.

19. Even if every individual earned exactly the same income over his or her lifetime, there would still be inequality at any given moment in time.

20. The increased proportion of the U.S. population that is either very young or very old has tended to decrease the observed inequality in the distribution of income.

21. Both the increased number of divorced couples and the rise of two-income families have caused the measured distribution of income to appear more unequal.

22. The impact of increased government activity should be considered in evaluating the measured income distribution, because government-imposed taxes burden different income groups differently and many government programs benefit some groups of income recipients more than others.

23. The income distribution is considerably more unequal than it appears.

24. The people that make up a given income group are not always the same people because there is substantial movement between income groups.

25. Other things being equal, workers who prefer more amenities at work or more time for leisure earn less.

26. Wage discrimination occurs when workers are given employment at wages lower than other workers on some basis other than productivity differences.

27. Only a weak statistical correlation exists between lifetime earnings and years of schooling.

28. The fact that average wages are lower for blacks and females proves wage discrimination.

29. To some extent, discrimination may reflect information costs.

30. In the long run, competition has the potential to reduce discrimination.

31. Affirmative action can lead to "reverse discrimination."

32. If employers were subsidized for hiring minority workers, they would have greater incentive to increase minority job opportunities.

33. The poverty rate reflects a relative standard for poverty.

34. Economic growth could eliminate poverty in an absolute sense but not poverty in a relative sense.

35. Many "poor" individuals in the United States, using the official definition, would be considered well off, even "rich," in many less-developed countries.

Multiple Choice

1. Which of the following is *false* about input markets?
   - **a.** The greatest fraction of national income goes to wages and salaries for labor services.
   - **b.** The price and quantity of an input traded depends on its supply and demand.
   - **c.** The demand for an input is a derived demand.
   - **d.** The price of an input tends to increase when the demand for the output produced by the input increases.
   - **e.** All of the above are *true.*

2. Marginal revenue product
   - **a.** is the additional revenue that a firm obtains by employing one more unit of an input.
   - **b.** will increase if an input's productivity increases.
   - **c.** will decrease if the price of the output produced by the input falls.
   - **d.** is characterized by all of the above.

3. The marginal resource cost of an input
   - **a.** is the amount an added unit of an input adds to a firm's total cost.
   - **b.** exceeds the market wage in a competitive industry.
   - **c.** is less than the market wage in a competitive industry.
   - **d.** is characterized by both a and b.
   - **e.** is characterized by both a and c.

4. If an additional salesclerk is hired to work in a furniture store, the clerk's sales efforts will contribute $700 to the store's total revenue. The store's profits will rise if the additional salesclerk is hired whenever the cost of hiring the clerk is ______ in wages and other costs.
   - **a.** $700
   - **b.** less than $700
   - **c.** more than $700
   - **d.** There is not enough information to make a determination.

5. A firm will increase its profits by adding one more unit of an input when
  a. $MRP < MRC$.
  b. $MRP = MRC$.
  c. $MRP > MRC$.
  d. none of the above

6. Assuming competitive markets, a worker's contribution to revenue is given by
  a. the production function.
  b. the marginal revenue product of labor.
  c. the marginal resource cost of labor.
  d. the marginal product minus marginal cost.

7. In a competitive labor market,
  a. a firm is a wage taker.
  b. a firm can hire all the labor it wishes to at the market wage.
  c. a firm hires a small fraction of the total market quantity of labor supplied.
  d. a firm hires a substantial fraction of the total market quantity of labor supplied.
  e. all of the above except d are true.

8. *MRP* falls as more labor is hired in a perfectly competitive market because
  a. *MRC* increases as more labor is hired.
  b. the price of the output produced falls as more inputs are hired and more output is produced.
  c. of the law of diminishing marginal product.
  d. of all of the above.

9. In a competitive labor market in equilibrium,
  a. a firm's $MRP = MP \times MR$.
  b. a firm's $MRP = MP \times P$.
  c. a firm's $MRP = MRC$.
  d. a firm's $wage = MRC$.
  e. all of the above are true.

10. At any wage higher than the equilibrium wage, the quantity of labor supplied _______ the quantity of labor demanded, resulting in a _______ of labor.
  a. exceeds, surplus
  b. exceeds, shortage
  c. is less than, surplus
  d. is less than, shortage

11. An increase in the demand for labor can result from
  a. increases in the price of the good produced by the labor.
  b. technological improvements.
  c. improvements in labor productivity.
  d. an increase in the amount of capital available for use by workers.
  e. any of the above.

12. Which of the following results in a rightward shift of the market demand curve for labor?
  a. an increase in labor productivity
  b. an increase in demand for the firm's product
  c. an increase in a firm's product price
  d. all of the above

13. The market supply of labor resources is affected by
   a. the number of hours workers are willing to work.
   b. the amount of immigration allowed.
   c. changes in a nation's working-age population.
   d. all of the above.

14. Differences in monetary wages across jobs may result from
   a. differences in job amenities.
   b. differences in on-the-job hazards.
   c. differences in working conditions.
   d. differences in fringe benefits.
   e. all of the above.

15. If labor unions successfully negotiate wage increases for their members,
   a. the wages of nonunion workers increase as well.
   b. the wages in nonunion sectors decrease.
   c. employment likely falls in the union sector.
   d. both a and c occur.
   e. both b and c occur.

16. An increase in the demand for land will
   a. increase the economic rent to land.
   b. increase the price of land.
   c. increase the quantity of land supplied.
   d. do all of the above.
   e. do a and b, but not c.

17. At high levels of interest, borrowers will want to borrow ______ and suppliers of funds will want to supply ______.
   a. more; less
   b. less; more
   c. less; less
   d. more; more

18. An investor will buy a piece of capital if the expected present value of the benefits ______ the current price.
   a. exceeds
   b. is less than
   c. is equal to
   d. none of the above

19. The present value of a future stream of income gets larger
   a. the lower the interest rate.
   b. the longer that stream of income lasts.
   c. the larger amount that is received in each future period.
   d. when any of the above occur.

20. Which of the following is true?
   a. There is substantial income inequality in the U.S., and there has been little change in the distribution of measured income in the past few decades.
   b. There is substantial income inequality in the U.S., but there have been appreciable changes in the distribution of measured income in the past few decades.
   c. There is very little income inequality in the U.S., and there has been little change in the distribution of measured income in the past few decades.
   d. There is very little income inequality in the U.S., but there have been appreciable changes in the distribution of measured income in the past few decades.

21. The measured distribution of income may appear more unequal as a result of

a. an increased number of divorced couples.
b. an increased proportion of young people in the population.
c. an increased proportion of older people in the population.
d. an increase in the number of two-income families.
e. all of the above.

22. Evidence suggests that levels of inequality of income _______ from 1935 to 1950, then _______ until 1980, and have since _______.

a. increased, decreased, increased
b. increased, remained relatively stable, decreased
c. decreased, increased, decreased
d. decreased, remained relatively stable, increased
e. increased, decreased, remained relatively stable

23. Which of the following is likely to improve a person's income?

a. increasing productivity
b. investing in human capital
c. possessing a special talent or skill
d. being highly motivated to succeed
e. all of the above

24. Schooling and other types of training

a. are regarded as investment in human capital.
b. are an important cause of income differentials.
c. involve workers sacrificing current income in order to enjoy higher future income.
d. are characterized by all of the above.

25. Which of the following is true?

a. Job-entry discrimination occurs when a person is denied employment on some basis other than productivity, while wage discrimination involves paying equally productive workers different wages.
b. Wage discrimination occurs when a person is denied employment on some basis other than productivity, while job-entry discrimination involves paying equally productive workers different wages.
c. Both wage and job-entry discrimination involve denying some persons employment on some basis other than productivity.
d. Both wage and job-entry discrimination involve paying equally productive workers different wages.
e. None of the above are true.

26. The poverty rate

a. is the proportion of the persons who fall below the poverty line.
b. is set at two times the cost of providing a nutritionally adequate diet.
c. may understate the degree of poverty by not counting noncash government benefits as income.
d. All of the above are true.
e. None of the above are true.

Problems

1. Fill in the missing data on the following chart.

Workers	Total Corn Output	Marginal Product of Labor
1	4,000	______
2	10,000	______
3	15,000	______
4	______	3,000
5	______	1,000
6	______	−1,000

2. Fill in the missing data on the following chart for a perfectly competitive firm.

Workers	Total Output	Marginal Physical Product	Price	Marginal Revenue Product	Wage	Marginal Profit
1	200	______	20	______	2,200	______
2	380	______	20	______	2,200	______
3	540	______	20	______	2,200	______
4	680	______	20	______	2,200	______
5	800	______	20	______	2,200	______
6	900	______	20	______	2,200	______
7	980	______	20	______	2,200	______
8	1,040	______	20	______	2,200	______

3. Indicate which point could correspond to the equilibrium wage and quantity hired

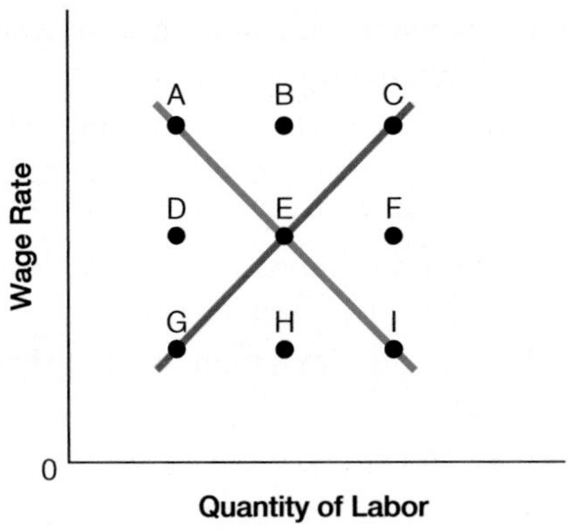

a. at the initial equilibrium.
b. if the price of the output produced by the labor increased.
c. if the price of the output produced by the labor decreased.
d. if there were an increase in immigration.
e. if there were a reduction in the quality of workplace amenities.
f. if worker productivity increased and there were an increase in workers' non-wage incomes.
g. if worker productivity decreased and there were a decrease in population.
h. if there were an increase in the price of output produced by the labor and an increase in the number of hours workers were willing to work.
i. if there were a decrease in the price of output produced by the labor and a decrease in workers' nonwage incomes.

4. Use the following diagram to answer a–c.

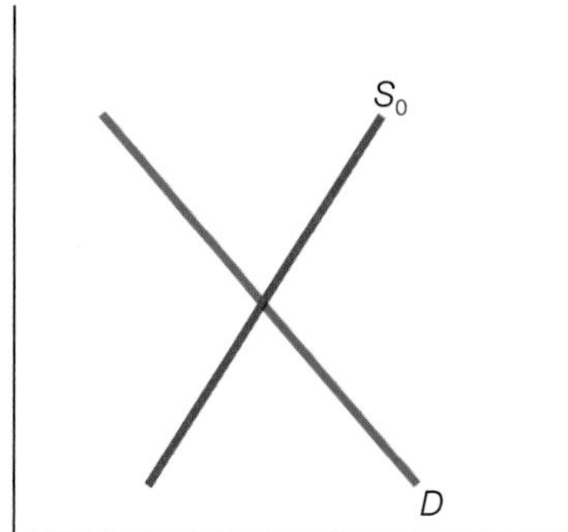

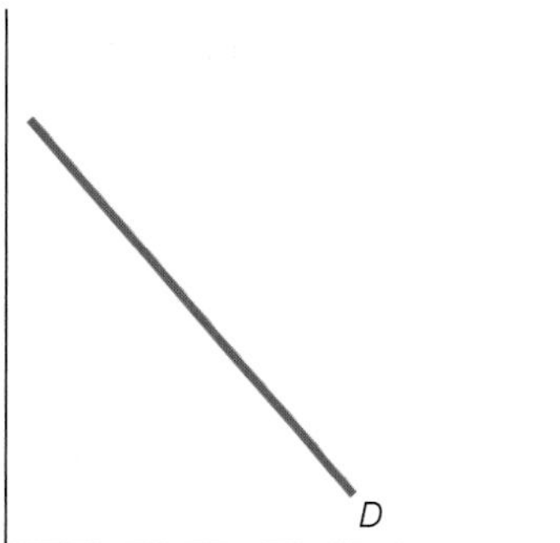

a. If unions were unable to have any effect on wages, draw the supply curve for the nonunion market.

b. If unions now are able to restrict the supply of labor in the union sector, indicate what would happen in both the union and nonunion sectors.

c. What happens to the union wage and the number of union workers hired in b? What happens to the nonunion wage and the number of nonunion workers hired in b?

5. Use the present value table in the text (p. 230) to answer the following questions:

a. What is the present value of $1,000 to be received at the end of each of three years from now at a 6 percent interest rate?

b. What is the present value of $100 to be received at the end of each of 20 years from now at a 10 percent interest rate?

c. If the interest rate were 10 percent, would you rather have $10,000 at the end of each of 13 years from now or $80,000 today?

d. If the interest rate were 3 percent, would you rather have $1,000 at the end of each of 8 years from now or $500 at the end of each of 17 years from now?

6. Explain at least three reasons why the official data on the distribution of income may overstate the actual degree of income inequality.

7. Answer the following questions regarding discrimination.

a. Define and give an example of job-entry discrimination.

b. Define and give an example of wage discrimination.

c. How can discrimination arise as a result of information costs?

d. What is the argument for why, in competitive industries, firms that discriminate could be outcompeted as a result?

8. Can economic growth reduce poverty? How does the answer depend on whether we are using an absolute or relative measure of poverty?

chapter 11

Introduction to the Macroeconomy

section 11.1

Macroeconomic Goals

- What are the most important macroeconomic goals in the United States?
- Are these goals universal?
- How has the United States shown its commitment to these goals?

THREE MAJOR MACROECONOMIC GOALS

Recall from chapter 1 that macroeconomics is the study of the whole economy—the study of the forest, not the trees. A macroeconomist may study the changes in the inflation rate or the unemployment rate, the impact of changing monetary policy or fiscal policy on output and the inflation, or alternate policies that may contribute to long-term economic growth.

Nearly every society has been interested in three major macroeconomic goals: (1) maintaining employment of human resources at relatively high levels, meaning that jobs are relatively plentiful and financial suffering from lack of work and income is relatively uncommon; (2) maintaining prices at a relatively stable level so that consumers and producers can make better decisions; and (3) achieving a high rate of economic growth, meaning a growth in real per capita total output over time. We use the term **real gross domestic product (RGDP)** to measure output or production. The term *real* is used to indicate that the output is adjusted for the general increase in prices over time. Technically gross domestic product (GDP) is defined as the total value of all final goods and services produced in a given time period such as a year or a quarter. In fact the 1990s saw an extraordinary economic expansion: rising rates of economic growth, a falling unemployment rate, and a falling inflation rate, as seen in Exhibit 1.

real gross domestic product (RGDP)
the total value of all final goods and services produced in a given time period such as a year or a quarter, adjusted for inflation

section 11.1 Exhibit 1 — U.S. Economic Growth, Unemployment Rates, and Inflation Rates: 1991–2001

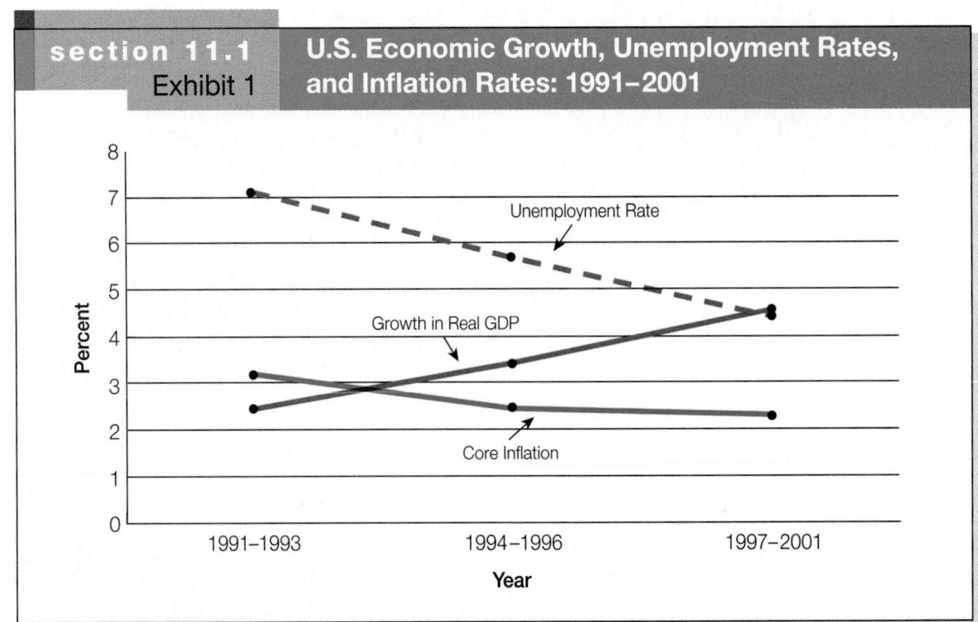

WHAT OTHER GOALS ARE IMPORTANT?

In addition to these primary goals, concern has been expressed at various times and places about other economic issues, some of which are essentially microeconomic in character. For example, concern about the "quality of life" has prompted some societies to try to reduce "bads" such as pollution and crime, and increase goods and services such as education and health services. Another goal has been "fairness" in the distribution of income or wealth. Still another goal pursued in many nations at one time or another has been self-sufficiency in the production of certain goods or services. For example, in the 1970s, the United States implemented policies that reduced U.S. reliance on other nations for supplies of oil, partly for reasons of national security.

HOW DO VALUE JUDGMENTS AFFECT ECONOMIC GOALS?

In stating that nations have economic goals, we must acknowledge that nations are made up of individuals. Individuals within a society may differ considerably in their evaluation of the relative importance of certain issues, or even whether certain "problems" are really problems after all. For example, economic growth, viewed positively by most persons, is not considered so favorably by others. While some citizens may think the income distribution is just about right, others might think it provides insufficient incomes to the poorer members of society; still others think it involves taking too much income from the relatively well-to-do and thereby reduces incentives to carry out productive, income-producing activities.

ACKNOWLEDGING OUR GOALS: THE EMPLOYMENT ACT OF 1946

Many economic problems—particularly those involving unemployment, price instability, and economic stagnation—are pressing concerns for the U.S. government. In fact, it was the concern over both unemployment and price instability that led to the passage of the **Employment Act of 1946,** which requires the U.S. government to pursue unemployment policies that are also consistent with price stability. This was the first formal acknowledgment of these primary macroeconomic goals. In other words, the government was holding itself accountable for short-run economic fluctuations.

Employment Act of 1946
a commitment by the federal government to hold itself accountable for short-run economic fluctuations

Section Check

1. The most important U.S. macroeconomic goals are full employment, price stability, and economic growth.
2. Individuals each have their own reasons for valuing certain goals more than others.
3. The United States showed its commitment to the major macroeconomic goals with the Employment Act of 1946.

---

1. What are the three major economic goals of most societies?
2. What is the Employment Act of 1946? Why was it significant?

section 11.2

Employment and Unemployment

- What are the consequences of unemployment?
- What is the unemployment rate?
- Does unemployment affect everyone equally?
- What causes unemployment?
- How long are people typically unemployed?

THE CONSEQUENCES OF HIGH UNEMPLOYMENT

Nearly everyone agrees that it is unfortunate when a person who wants a job cannot find one. A loss of a job can mean financial insecurity and a great deal of anxiety. High rates of unemployment in a society can increase tensions and despair. A family without income from work undergoes great suffering; as its savings fade, it wonders where it is going to obtain the means to survive. Society loses some potential output of goods when some of its productive resources—human or non-human—remain idle, and potential consumption is also reduced. Clearly, then, there is a loss in efficiency when people willing to work and productive equipment remain idle. That is, other things equal, relatively high rates of unemployment are viewed almost universally as undesirable.

WHAT IS THE UNEMPLOYMENT RATE?

unemployment rate
the percent of the population aged 16 and older who are willing and able to work, but are unable to obtain a job

labor force
the number of people aged 16 and over who are available for employment

When discussing unemployment, economists and politicians refer to the **unemployment rate.** In order to calculate the unemployment rate, you must first understand another important concept—the **labor force.** The labor force is the number of people over the age of 16 who are available for employment, regardless of whether or not they are currently employed, as seen in Exhibit 1. The civilian labor force figure excludes all those in the armed services and those in prison or mental hospitals. Those outside of the labor force

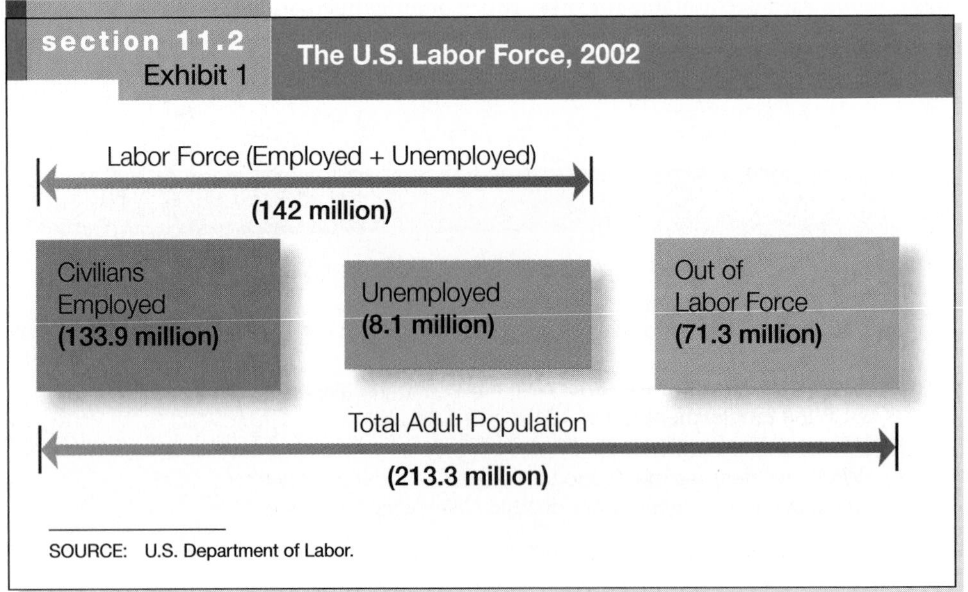

also include homemakers, retirees, and full-time students. These groups are excluded from the labor force because they are not considered currently available for employment.

When we say that the unemployment rate is 5 percent, we mean that 5 percent of the population over the age of 16 who are willing and able to work are unable to get a job. The 5 percent means that 5 out of 100 people in the total labor force are unemployed. To calculate the unemployment rate, we simply divide the number of unemployed by the number in the civilian labor force.

$$\text{Unemployment rate} = \text{Number of unemployed}/\text{Civilian labor force}$$

In March 2002, the number of civilians unemployed in the United States was 8.1 million and the civilian labor force totaled 142 million. Using this data, we can calculate that the unemployment rate in March 2002 was 5.7 percent.

$$\text{Unemployment rate} = 8.1\text{ million}/142\text{ million} = .057 \times 100 = 5.7\text{ percent}$$

THE WORST CASE OF U.S. UNEMPLOYMENT

By far the worst employment downturn in U.S. history was the Great Depression, which began in late 1929 and continued until 1941. Unemployment rose from only 3.2 percent of the labor force in 1929 to more than 20 percent in the early 1930s, and double-digit unemployment persisted through 1941. The debilitating impact of having millions of productive people out of work led Americans (and people in other countries as well) to say "Never again." Some economists would argue that modern macroeconomics, with its emphasis on the determinants of unemployment and its elimination, truly began in the 1930s.

VARIATIONS IN THE UNEMPLOYMENT RATE

Exhibit 2 shows the unemployment rates over the last 40 years. Unemployment since 1960 has ranged from a low of 3.5 percent in 1969 to a high of 9.7 percent in 1982. Un-

section 11.2 Exhibit 2 Unemployment Rates

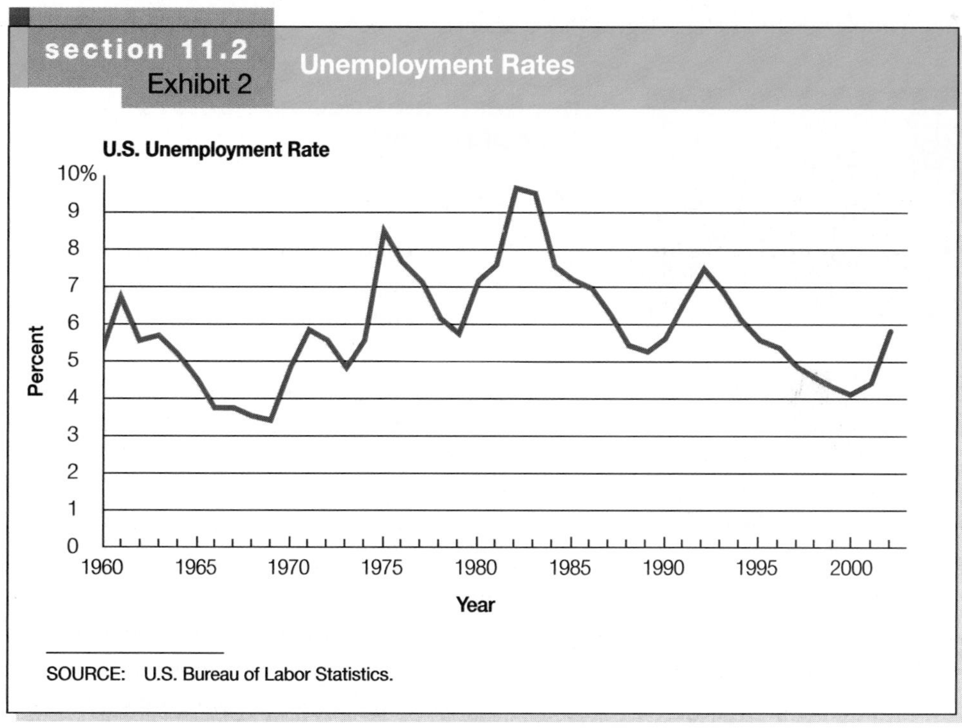

SOURCE: U.S. Bureau of Labor Statistics.

employment in the worst years is twice or more than what it is in good years. Before 1960, variations in unemployment were more pronounced.

ARE UNEMPLOYMENT STATISTICS ACCURATE REFLECTIONS OF THE LABOR MARKET?

discouraged worker
an individual who has left the labor force because he/she could not find a job

In periods of prolonged recession, some individuals think that the chances of landing a job are so bleak that they quit looking. These people are called **discouraged workers.** Individuals who have not actively sought work for four weeks are not counted as unemployed; instead, they fall out of the labor force. Also, people looking for full-time work who grudgingly settle for a part-time job are counted as "fully" employed, yet they are only "partly" employed. However, at least partially balancing these two biases in government employment statistics is the number of people who are overemployed—that is, working overtime or extra jobs. Also, there are a number of jobs in the underground economy (drugs, prostitution, gambling, and so on) that are not reported at all. In addition, many people may claim they are actually seeking work when, in fact, they may just be going through the motions so that they can continue to collect unemployment compensation or receive other government benefits.

WHO ARE THE UNEMPLOYED?

Unemployment usually varies greatly between different segments of the population and over time.

Education as a Factor in Unemployment

According to the Bureau of Labor Statistics, the unemployment rate across sex and race among college graduates is significantly lower than for those without a high-school diploma. In April 2002, the unemployment rate for individuals without a high-school diploma was 9.0 percent, versus 4.7 percent for college graduates. Also, college graduates have lower unemployment rates than those with some college education, but who have not completed a bachelor's degree (5.7 percent).

Teenagers have the highest rates of unemployment. Do you think it would be easier for them to find jobs if they had more experience and higher skill levels?

Age, Sex, and Race as Factors in Unemployment

The incidence of unemployment varies widely among the population. Unemployment tends to be greater among the very young, among blacks and other minorities, and among less-skilled workers. Adult female unemployment tends to be higher than adult male unemployment.

Considering the great variations in unemployment for different groups in the population, we calculate separate unemployment rates for groups classified by sex, age, race, family status, and type of occupation. Exhibit 3 shows unemployment rates for various groups in 2002. Note that the variation around the average unemployment rate for the total population of 5.7 percent was considerable. The unemployment rate for blacks and Hispanics was much higher than the rate for whites, a phenomenon that has persisted throughout the post–World War II period. Unemployment among teenagers was much higher than adult unemployment, at 16.4 percent. Some would re-

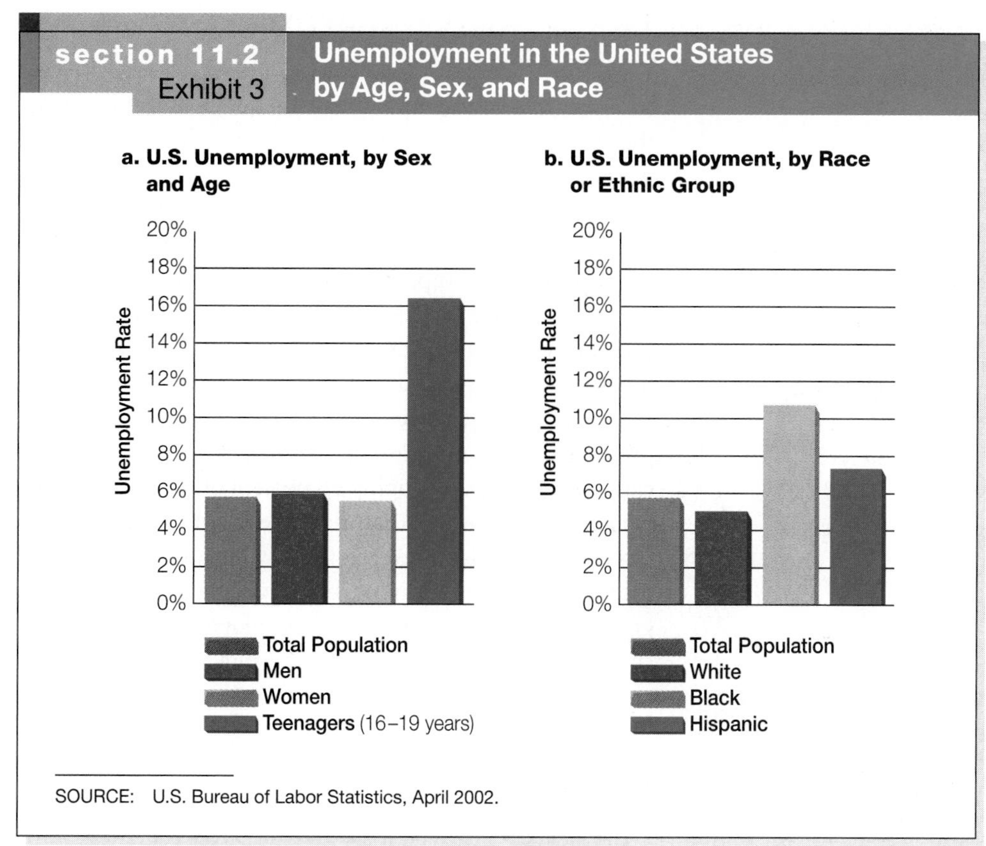

SOURCE: U.S. Bureau of Labor Statistics, April 2002.

gard teenage unemployment a lesser evil than unemployment among adults, because most teenagers have parents or guardians on whom they can rely for subsistence.

REASONS FOR UNEMPLOYMENT

According to the Bureau of Labor Statistics, there are four main categories of unemployed workers: **job losers** (temporarily laid off or fired), **job leavers** (quit), **reentrants** (worked before and now reentering the labor force), and **new entrants** (entering the labor force for first time—primarily teenagers). It is a common misconception that most workers are unemployed because they have lost their jobs. While job losers may typically account for 50 to 60 percent of the unemployed, a sizeable fraction is due to job leavers, new entrants, and reentrants, as seen in Exhibit 4.

job loser
an individual who has been temporarily laid off or fired

job leaver
a person that quits his or her job

reentrant
an individual who worked before and is now reentering the labor force

new entrant
an individual who has not held a job before but is now seeking employment

HOW MUCH UNEMPLOYMENT?

While unemployment is painful to those who have no source of income, reducing unemployment is not costless. In the short run, a reduction in unemployment may come at the expense of a higher rate of inflation, especially if the economy is close to full capacity, where resources are almost fully employed. Also, trying to match employees with jobs quickly may lead to significant inefficiencies because of mismatches between the worker's skill level and the level of skill required for a job. For example, the economy would be wasting resources subsidizing education if people with a Ph.D. in biochemistry were driving taxis or tending bar. That is, the skills of the employee may be higher than that necessary for the job, resulting in what economists call **underemployment.** Alternatively, employees may be placed in jobs beyond their abilities, which would also lead to inefficiencies.

underemployment
a situation in which laborers have skills higher than necessary for a job

section 11.2 Exhibit 4 Reasons for Unemployment

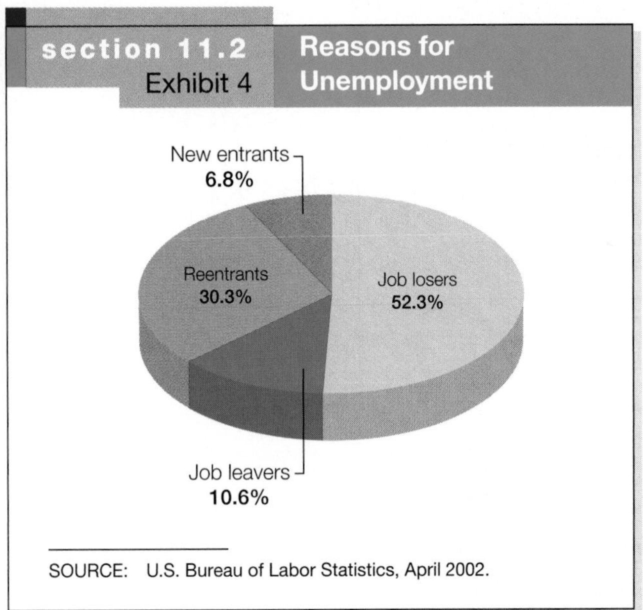

SOURCE: U.S. Bureau of Labor Statistics, April 2002.

section 11.2 Exhibit 5 Duration of Unemployment

Duration	Percent Unemployed
Less than 5 weeks	37.6%
5 to 14 weeks	29.5
15 to 26 weeks	16.6
27 weeks and over	16.3

SOURCE: U.S. Bureau of Labor Statistics, April 2002.

THE AVERAGE DURATION OF UNEMPLOYMENT

The *duration* of unemployment is equally as important as the amount of unemployment. The financial consequences of a head of household being unemployed four or five weeks are usually not extremely serious, particularly if the individual is covered by an unemployment compensation system. The impact becomes much more serious if a person is unemployed for several months. Therefore, it is useful to look at the average duration of unemployment to discover what percent of the labor force is unemployed for more than a certain time period, say 15 weeks. Exhibit 5 presents data on the duration of unemployment. As you can see in this table, roughly 38 percent of the unemployed were out of work less than five weeks, and 16 percent of the total unemployed were out of work for more than six months. The duration of unemployment tends to be greater when the amount of unemployment is high, and smaller when the amount of unemployment is low. Unemployment of any duration, of course, means a potential loss of output. This loss of current output is permanent; it is not made up when unemployment starts falling again.

LABOR FORCE PARTICIPATION RATE

The percentage of the population that is in the labor force is what economists call the **labor force participation rate.** Since 1950, there has been an increase in the labor force participation rate from 59.2 percent to 67.1 percent. Most of that change occurred between 1970 and 1990. The increase in the labor force participation rate can be attributed in large part to the entry of the baby boomers into the labor force and a 14.2 percentage point increase in the women's labor force participation rate.

labor force participation rate
the percentage of the population in the labor force

Over the last 50 years, the number of women working has shifted dramatically, reflecting the changing role of women in the workforce. In Exhibit 6, we see that in 1950 only 33 percent of women were working or looking for work. Today that figure is roughly 60 percent. In 1950 over 85 percent of men were working or looking for work. Today the labor force participation rate for men has fallen to roughly 74 percent, as many men stay in school longer and opt to retire earlier.

section 11.2 Exhibit 6 Labor Force Participation Rates for Men and Women

	1950	1960	1970	1980	1990	2002
Total	59.2%	59.4%	60.4%	63.8%	66.4%	66.6%
Men	86.4	83.3	79.7	77.4	76.1	73.8
Women	33.9	37.7	43.3	51.5	57.5	59.8

SOURCE: U.S. Department of Labor Statistics.

Section Check

1. The consequences of unemployment to society include a reduction in potential output and consumption—a decrease in efficiency.
2. The unemployment rate is found by taking the number of people officially unemployed and dividing by the number in the civilian labor force.
3. Unemployment rates are the highest for minorities, the young, and less-skilled workers.
4. There are four main categories of unemployed workers: job losers, job leavers, reentrants, and new entrants.
5. The duration of unemployment tends to be greater (smaller) when the amount of unemployment is high (low).

---

1. What happens to the unemployment rate when the number of unemployed people increases, *ceteris paribus?* When the labor force grows, *ceteris paribus?*
2. How might the official unemployment rate understate the "true" degree of unemployment? How might it overstate it?
3. Why might the fraction of the unemployed who are job leavers be higher in a period of strong labor demand?
4. Suppose you live in a community of 100 people. If 80 people, over 16 years old, are in the labor force, and 8 are unemployed, what is the unemployment rate in that community?
5. What would happen to the unemployment rate if a substantial group of unemployed people started going to school full time? What would happen to the size of the labor force?
6. What happens to the unemployment rate when people become discouraged workers? Does anything happen to employment in this case?

section 11.3

Different Types of Unemployment

- What are the three types of unemployment?
- What is frictional unemployment?
- What is structural unemployment?
- What is cyclical unemployment?
- What is the natural rate of unemployment?

In examining the status of and changes in the unemployment rate, it is important to recognize that there are numerous types of unemployment. In this section, we will examine these different types of unemployment and evaluate the relative impact of each on the overall unemployment rate.

FRICTIONAL UNEMPLOYMENT

Some unemployment results from people being temporarily between jobs. For example, consider an advertising executive who was fired in Chicago on March 1 and is now actively looking for similar work in San Francisco. This is an example of **frictional unemployment.** Of course, not all unemployed workers were fired from their jobs; some may voluntarily quit their jobs. In either case, frictional unemployment is short term and re-

frictional unemployment
unemployment from normal turnovers in the economy, such as when individuals change from one job to another

sults from the normal turnover in the labor market, such as when people change from one job to another.

SHOULD WE WORRY ABOUT FRICTIONAL UNEMPLOYMENT?

Geographic and occupational mobility are considered good for the economy because they generally lead human resources to go from activities of relatively low productivity or value to areas of higher productivity, increasing output in society as well as the wage income of the mover. Hence, frictional unemployment, while not good in itself, is a by-product of a healthy phenomenon, and because it is often short-lived, it is generally not viewed as a serious problem. While the amount of frictional unemployment varies somewhat over time, it is unusual for it to be much less than 2 percent of the labor force. Actually, frictional unemployment tends to be somewhat greater in periods of low unemployment, when job opportunities are plentiful. This high level of job opportunities stimulates mobility, which, in turn, creates some frictional unemployment.

STRUCTURAL UNEMPLOYMENT

structural unemployment
unemployment persisting due to lack of skills necessary for available jobs

A second type of unemployment is structural unemployment. Like frictional unemployment, **structural unemployment** is related to occupational movement or mobility, or in this case, to a lack of mobility. Structural unemployment occurs when workers lack the necessary skills for jobs that are available or have particular skills that are no longer in demand. For example, if a machine operator in a manufacturing plant loses his job, he could still remain unemployed despite the openings for computer programmers in his community. The quantity of unemployed workers conceivably could equal the number of job vacancies, but the unemployment persists because the unemployed lack the appropriate skills. Given the existence of structural unemployment, it is wise to look at both unemployment and job vacancy statistics in assessing labor market conditions. Structural unemployment, like frictional unemployment, reflects the dynamic dimension of a changing economy. Over time, new jobs open up that require new skills, while old jobs that required different skills disappear. It is not surprising, then, that many people advocate government-subsidized retraining programs as a means of reducing structural unemployment.

What type of unemployment would occur if these coal miners lost their jobs as a result of a reduction in demand for coal and needed retraining to find other employment? Usually structural unemployment occurs because of poor skills or long-term changes in demand. Consequently, it generally lasts for a longer period of time than frictional unemployment. In this picture, both might come into play.

The dimensions of structural unemployment are debatable, in part because of the difficulty in precisely defining the term in an operational sense. Structural unemployment varies considerably—sometimes it is very low and at other times, like the 1970s and early 1980s, it is high. To some extent, in this latter period, jobs in the traditional sectors like automobile manufacturing and oil production gave way to jobs in the computer and biotechnology sectors. Consequently, structural unemployment was higher.

IMPERFECTIONS AND UNEMPLOYMENT

Some unemployment is actually normal and important to the economy. Frictional and structural unemployment is simply unavoidable in a vibrant economy. To a considerable extent, one can view both frictional and structural unemployment as phenomena resulting from imperfections in the labor market. For example, if individuals seeking jobs and employers seeking workers had better information about each other, the amount of frictional unemployment would be considerably lower. It takes time for suppliers of labor to find the demanders of labor services, and it takes time and money for labor resources to acquire the necessary skills. But because information is not costless, and because job search also is costly, the bringing of demanders and suppliers of labor services together does not occur instantaneously.

CYCLICAL UNEMPLOYMENT

Often, unemployment is composed of more than just frictional and structural unemployment. In years of relatively high unemployment, some joblessness may result from short-term cyclical fluctuations in the economy. We call this **cyclical unemployment.** Whenever the unemployment rate is greater than the natural rate, or during a recession, there is cyclical unemployment.

cyclical unemployment
unemployment due to short-term cyclical fluctuations in the economy

REDUCING CYCLICAL UNEMPLOYMENT

Most economists believe cyclical unemployment is the most volatile form of unemployment. Given its volatility and dimensions, governments, rightly or wrongly, have viewed unemployment resulting from inadequate demand to be especially correctable through government policies. Most of the attempts to solve the unemployment problem have placed an emphasis on increasing aggregate demand to counter recessions. Attempts to reduce frictional unemployment by providing better labor market information and to reduce structural unemployment through job retraining have also been made, but these efforts have received fewer resources and much less attention from policy makers.

THE NATURAL RATE OF UNEMPLOYMENT

It is interesting to observe that over the period during which annual unemployment data are available, the median, or "typical," annual unemployment rate has been at or slightly above 5 percent. Some economists call this typical unemployment rate the **natural rate of unemployment.** When unemployment rises well above 5 percent, we have abnormally high unemployment; when it falls below 5 percent, we have abnormally low unemployment. The natural rate of unemployment of approximately 5 percent roughly equals the sum of frictional and structural unemployment when they are at a maximum. Thus, one can view unemployment rates below the natural rate as reflecting the existence of a below-average level of frictional and structural unemployment. When unemployment rises above the natural rate, however, it reflects the existence of cyclical unemployment. In short, the natural rate of unemployment is the unemployment rate when there is neither a recession nor a boom.

natural rate of unemployment
the median or "typical" unemployment rate, equal to the sum of frictional and structural unemployment when they are at a maximum

APPLICATION

CYCLICAL UNEMPLOYMENT

Q: Are layoffs more prevalent during a recession than a recovery? Do most resignations occur during a recovery?

A: Layoffs are more likely to occur during a recession. When times are bad, employers are often forced to let workers go. Resignations are relatively more prevalent during good economic times, because there are more job opportunities for those seeking new jobs.

Global WATCH

UNEMPLOYMENT AROUND THE GLOBE, 2001

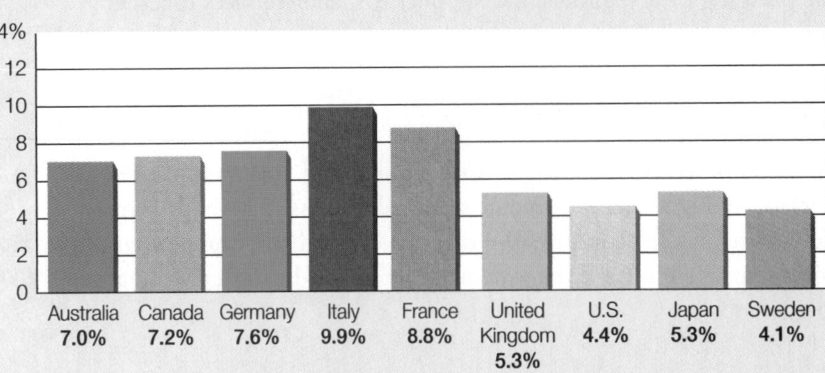

CONSIDER THIS:
Many developed countries had higher unemployment rates than the United States in 2001. Generous unemployment benefits and sluggish economic growth in European countries have helped cause the higher unemployment rates.

SOURCE: International Monetary Fund, 2001. Reprinted by permission from International Monetary Fund. www.imf.org

Today, however, economists, for the most part, have come to accept a current range somewhere between 4.5 and 5.5 percent for the natural rate of unemployment. The natural rate of unemployment can change over time as technological, demographic, institutional, and other conditions vary. For example, as baby boomers have aged, the natural rate has fallen because middle-aged workers generally have lower unemployment rates than younger workers. Thus, the natural rate is not fixed because it can change with demographic changes over time.

Full Employment and Potential Output

When all of the economy's labor resources and other resources like capital are fully employed, the economy is said to be producing its potential level of output. That is, the amount these resources could produce if they were fully employed. Literal full employment of labor means that the economy is providing employment for all who are willing and able to work with no cyclical unemployment. It also means that capital and land are fully employed. That is, at the natural rate of unemployment, all resources are fully employed and the economy is producing its **potential output** and there is no cyclical unemployment. This does not mean the economy will always be producing at its potential output of resources. For example, when the economy is experiencing cyclical unemployment, the unemployment rate is greater than the natural rate. It is also possible that the economy can temporarily exceed the natural rate as workers take on overtime or moonlight by taking on extra employment.

potential output
is the amount of real output the economy would produce if its labor and other resources were fully employed—that is, at the natural rate of unemployment

UNEMPLOYMENT INSURANCE

Losing a job can lead to considerable hardships, and unemployment insurance is designed to partially offset the severity of the unemployment problem. The program does not cover

In The NEWS

A LIGHT THAT NEVER GOES OUT

(CNN)—Lighthouses have been called the most altruistic structures ever built. After almost 300 years of guiding ships along the U.S. coasts and Great Lakes, their usefulness is waning. But they have never lost their power to ignite poetry in those who visit them.

"Lighthouses are to America what castles are to Europe. They're among the oldest standing structures in (the U.S.)," says Tim Harrison, editor of the Maine-based *Lighthouse Digest*.

When the United States became a country, 12 lighthouses kept vigil over settled shores, according to Wayne Wheeler, founder of the U.S. Lighthouse Society. Over the years, he says more than 2,000 light stations were built. Today, the National Park Service estimates about 634 lighthouses remain, 405 of which are in service.

Automation has virtually eliminated the romantic tradition of lighthouse keepers—salty, solitary souls guiding ships safely through treacherous storms. And electronic pings are replacing the mournful drone of the foghorn calling sailors home.

SOURCE: CNN Interactive, Destinations, April 19, 1997.

CONSIDER THIS:
Just like elevator operators and service station attendants, now lighthouse keepers have given way to automation. In a world of scarcity, lighthouse keepers can now be employed producing something that is more valuable from society's perspective.

those that were fired or quit their jobs. To qualify recipients must have worked a certain length of time and lost their jobs because the employer no longer needed their skills. The typical compensation is half salary for 26 weeks. While the program is intended to ease the pain of unemployment, it also leads to prolonged periods of unemployment, as job seekers stay unemployed for longer periods of time searching for new jobs.

For example, some unemployed people may show little drive in seeking new employment, because unemployment insurance lowers the opportunity cost of being unemployed. Say a worker making $400 a week when employed receives $220 in compensation when unemployed; as a result, the cost of losing his job is not $400 a week in forgone income, but only $180. It has been estimated that the existence of unemployment compensation programs may raise overall unemployment rates by as much as 1 percent.

Without employment insurance, job seekers would more likely take the first job offered even if did not match their preferences or skill levels. A longer job search might mean a better match but at the expense of lost production and greater amounts of tax dollars.

Will new technology in one industry displace workers in the whole economy? No. There may be some job loss of specific jobs or within certain industries. But the overall effect of technological improvements is the release of scarce resources for the expansion of output and employment in other areas and ultimately more economic growth and a higher standard of living.

DOES NEW TECHNOLOGY LEAD TO GREATER UNEMPLOYMENT?

Although many believe that technological advances inevitably result in the displacement of workers, this is not necessarily the case. New inventions are generally cost saving, and these cost savings will generally generate higher incomes for producers, and lower prices and better products for consumers, benefits that will ultimately result in the growth of other industries. If the new equipment is a substitute for labor, then it might displace workers. For example, many fast-food restaurants have substituted self-service beverage bars for workers. However, new capital equipment requires new workers to manufacture and repair the new equipment. The most famous example of this is the computer, which was supposed to displace thousands of workers. Although it did displace workers, the total job growth it generated exceeded the number of lost jobs. The problem is that it is easy to just see the initial effect of technological advances (displaced workers), without recognizing the implications of that invention for the whole economy over time.

Section Check

1. The three types of unemployment are frictional unemployment, structural unemployment, and cyclical unemployment.
2. Frictional unemployment results when a person moves from one job to another as a result of normal turnovers in the economy.
3. Structural unemployment results when people who are looking for jobs lack the required skills for the jobs that are available or a long-term change in demand occurs.
4. Cyclical unemployment is caused by a recession.
5. Imperfections in the labor market and institutional factors result in higher rates of unemployment.
6. When cyclical unemployment is almost completely eliminated, our economy is said to be operating at full employment, or at a natural rate of unemployment.
7. Some unemployed persons may show little drive in seeking new employment, given the existence of unemployment compensation. Unemployment compensation lowers the opportunity cost of being unemployed.

---

1. Why do we want some frictional unemployment?
2. Why might a job retraining program be a more useful policy to address structural unemployment than to address frictional unemployment?
3. What is the traditional government policy "cure" for cyclical unemployment?
4. Does new technology increase unemployment?
5. What types of unemployment are present at full employment (at the natural rate of unemployment)?
6. Why might frictional unemployment be higher in a period of plentiful jobs (low unemployment)?
7. If the widespread introduction of the automobile caused a productive maker of horse-drawn carriages to lose his job, would he be structurally or frictionally unemployed?
8. If a fall in demand for domestic cars causes autoworkers to lose their jobs in Michigan, while there are plenty of jobs for lumberjacks in Montana, what kind of unemployment results?
9. Why would higher unemployment compensation in a country such as France lead to higher rates of unemployment?

section 11.4

Inflation

- Why is the overall price level important?
- How has the price level behaved this century?
- Who are the winners and losers during inflation?
- Can wage earners avoid the consequences of inflation?

STABLE PRICE LEVEL AS A DESIRABLE GOAL

Just as full employment brings about economic security of one kind, an overall stable **price level** increases another form of security. Most prices in the U.S. economy tend to rise over time. The continuing rise in the *overall* price level is called **inflation.** Even when the level of prices is stable, some prices will be rising while others are falling. However, when inflation is present, the goods and services with rising prices will outweigh the goods and services with lower prices. Without stability in the price level, consumers and producers will experience more difficulty in coordinating their plans and decisions. When the *overall* price level is falling, there is **deflation.** The average price level in the U.S. economy fell throughout the late nineteenth century.

price level
the average level of prices in the economy

inflation
a rise in the overall price level, which decreases the purchasing power of money

deflation
a decrease in the overall price level, resulting in an increase of the purchasing power of money

In general, the only thing that can cause a *sustained* increase in the rate of inflation is a high rate of growth in money, a topic we will discuss thoroughly in the coming chapters.

THE PRICE LEVEL OVER THE YEARS

Unanticipated and sharp changes in the price level are almost universally considered to be "bad" and to require a policy remedy. What is the historical record of changes in the overall U.S. price level? Exhibit 1 shows changes in the **consumer price index (CPI),** the standard measure of inflation, from 1914 to 2002. Can you believe that in 1940 stamps

consumer price index (CPI)
a measure of the trend in prices of a basket of consumable goods and services that serves to gauge inflation

section 11.4 Exhibit 1 — The Price Level in the United States, 1914–2002

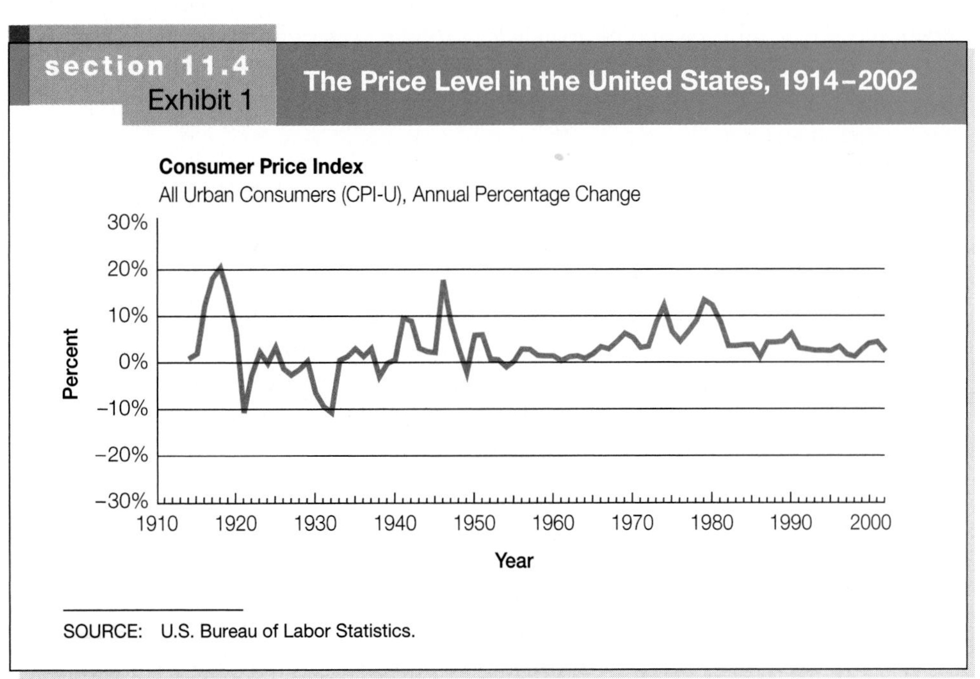

SOURCE: U.S. Bureau of Labor Statistics.

were three cents per letter, postcards were a penny, the median price of a house was $2,900, and the price of a new car was $650?

WHO LOSES WITH INFLATION?

Inflation brings about changes in real incomes of persons, and these changes may be either desirable or undesirable. Suppose you retire on a fixed pension of $2,000 per month. Over time, the $2,000 will buy less and less if prices generally rise. Your real income—your income adjusted to reflect changes in purchasing power—falls. Inflation lowers income in real terms for people on fixed-dollar incomes. Likewise, inflation can hurt creditors. Suppose you loaned someone $1,000 in 1985 and were paid back $1,000 plus interest in 2003. The $1,000 in principal you were paid back actually is worth less in 2003 than it was in 1985 because inflation has eroded the purchasing power of the dollar. Thus, inflation erodes the real wealth of the creditor. Another group that sometimes loses from inflation, at least temporarily, are people whose incomes are tied to long-term contracts. If inflation begins shortly after a labor union signs a three-year wage agreement, it may completely eat up the wage gains provided by the contract. The same applies to businesses that agree to sell a quantity of something, say coal, for a fixed price for a given number of years.

If some people lose because of changing prices, others must gain. The debtor pays back dollars worth less in purchasing power than those she borrowed. Corporations that can quickly raise the prices on their goods may have revenue gains greater than their increases in costs, providing additional profits. Wage earners sometimes lose from inflation because wages may rise at a slower rate than the price level. The redistributional impact of inflation is not the result of conscious public policy; it just happens.

The uncertainty that inflation creates can also discourage investment and economic growth. Moreover, inflation can raise one nation's price level relative to that in other countries. In turn, this can make financing the purchase of foreign goods difficult, or can decrease the value of the national currency relative to that of other countries. In its extreme form, inflation can lead to a complete erosion in faith in the value of the pieces of paper we commonly call money. In Germany after both World Wars, prices rose so fast that people in some cases finally refused to take paper money, insisting instead on payment in goods or metals whose prices tend to move predictably with inflation. Unchecked inflation can feed on itself and ultimately lead to hyperinflation of 300 percent or more per year. We saw these rapid rates of inflation in Argentina in the 1980s and Brazil in the 1990s.

UNANTICIPATED INFLATION DISTORTS PRICE SIGNALS

In periods of high and variable inflation, households and firms have a difficult time distinguishing between changes in the relative prices of individual goods and services and changes in the general price level of all goods and services. Inflation distorts the information that flows from price signals. Does the good have a higher price because it has become relatively more scarce, and therefore more valuable relative to other goods, or did the price rise along with all other prices because of inflation? This muddying of price information undermines good decision making.

MENU AND SHOE-LEATHER COSTS

Another cost of inflation is that incurred by firms as a result of being forced to change prices more frequently. For example, a restaurant may have to print new menus, or a department or mail-order store may have to print new catalogs to reflect changing prices.

Global WATCH

AVERAGE ANNUAL INFLATION RATES, SELECTED COUNTRIES

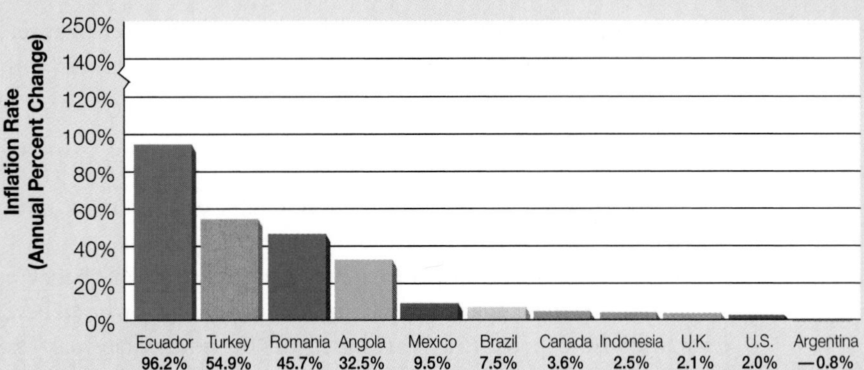

CONSIDER THIS:
While a few countries are still experiencing very high rates of inflation, some emerging countries (Mexico, Brazil, Indonesia, and Argentina) have lowered their inflation rates.

SOURCE: *World Bank, 2000–2001,* International Monetary Fund. Reprinted by permission from International Monetary Fund. www.imf.org

These costs are called **menu costs,** and they are the costs of changing posted prices. In some South American economies in the 1980s, inflation increased at over 300 percent per year, with prices changing on a daily, or even hourly, basis in some cases. Imagine how large the menu costs could be in an economy such as that!

menu costs
the cost imposed on a firm from changing listed prices

There is also the **shoe-leather cost** of inflation: the cost of going to and from the bank (and thus wearing out the leather on your shoes) to check on your assets. Specifically, high rates of inflation erode the value of a currency; this means that people will want to hold less currency—perhaps going to the ATM once a week rather than twice a month. That is, the higher inflation rates lead to higher nominal interest rates and this may induce more individuals to put money in the bank rather than allowing it to depreciate in their pockets. The effects of shoe-leather costs of inflation, like menu costs, are very modest in

shoe-leather cost
the cost incurred when individuals reduce their money holdings because of inflation

APPLICATION

INFLATION

Q: Evaluate the following three statements: Inflation means 1) that people have less money to spend, 2) that there are less goods available, and 3) that one must pay more money for goods purchased.

A: Of the three statements, only one is correct: With inflation, we must, on average, pay more money for the goods we purchase. Inflation does not necessarily mean we have fewer goods but rather that, on net, these goods have higher price tags. Inflation does not necessarily mean that people have less money to spend. Employees and unions will bargain for higher wages when there is inflation.

countries with low inflation rates but can be quite large in countries where inflation is substantial.

INFLATION AND INTEREST RATES

nominal interest rate
the reported interest rate that is not adjusted for inflation

real interest rate
the nominal interest rate minus the inflation rate; also called the inflation-adjusted interest rate

The interest rate is usually reported as the **nominal interest rate.** We determine the actual **real interest rate** by taking the nominal rate of interest and subtracting the inflation rate.

$$\text{Real interest rate} = \text{Nominal interest rate} - \text{Inflation rate}$$

For example, if the nominal interest rate was 5 percent and the inflation rate was 3 percent, then the real interest rate would be 2 percent.

If people can correctly anticipate inflation, they will behave in a manner that will largely protect them against loss. Consider the creditor who believes that the overall price level will rise 6 percent a year, based on the immediate past experience. Would that creditor lend money to someone at a 5 percent rate of interest? No. A 5 percent rate of interest means that a person borrowing $1,000 now will pay back $1,050 ($1,000 plus 5 percent of $1,000) one year from now. But if prices go up 6 percent, it will take $1,060 to buy what $1,000 does today. ($1,060 is 6 percent more than $1,000.) Thus, the person who lends at 5 percent will get paid back an amount ($1,050) that is less than the purchasing power of the original loan ($1,060) at the time it was paid back. The real interest rate, then, would actually be negative. Hence, to protect themselves, lenders will demand a rate of interest large enough to compensate for the deteriorating value of the dollar.

section 11.4 Exhibit 2 Nominal Interest Rates

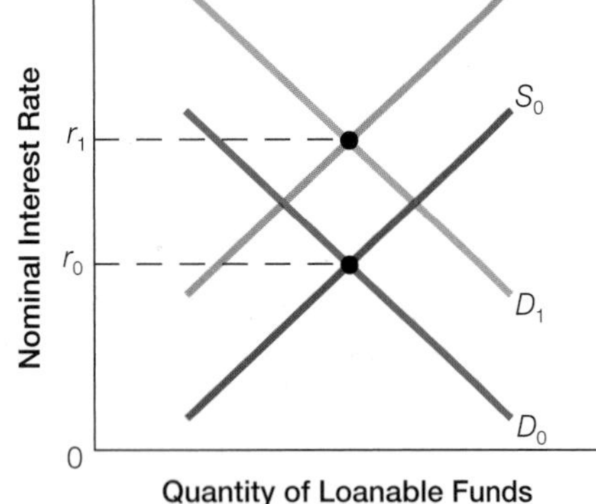

Nominal interest rates are determined by the intersection of the demand and supply curves for loanable funds. The lower the interest rate (price), the greater the quantity of loanable funds demanded, *ceteris paribus;* the higher the interest rate, the greater the quantity of loanable funds supplied by individuals and institutions like banks, *ceteris paribus.* Expected inflation shifts the supply curve left and the demand curve right, both of which tend to increase nominal (money) interest rates.

ANTICIPATED INFLATION AND THE NOMINAL INTEREST RATE

The economic theory behind the behavioral responses of creditors and debtors to anticipated inflation is straightforward and can be expressed in a simple diagram (Exhibit 2). An interest rate is, in effect, the price that one pays for the use of funds. Like other prices, interest rates are determined by the interaction of demand and supply forces. The lower the interest rate (price), the greater the quantity of loanable funds demanded, *ceteris paribus;* the higher the interest rate (price), the greater the quantity of loanable funds supplied by individuals and institutions like banks, *ceteris paribus.* Suppose that in an environment where prices in general are expected to remain stable in the near future, the demand for loanable funds is depicted by D_0 and the supply of such funds is indicated by S_0. In this scenario, the equilibrium price, or interest rate, will be r_0, where the quantity demanded equals the quantity supplied.

When people start expecting future inflation, creditors such as banks will become less willing to lend funds at any given interest rate, because they fear they will be repaid in dollars of lesser value than those they loaned. This is depicted by a leftward shift in the supply curve of loanable funds (a decrease in supply) to S_1. Likewise, demanders of funds (borrowers) are more anxious to borrow, because they think they will pay their loans back in dollars of lesser purchasing power than the dollars they borrowed. Thus, the demand for funds increases from D_0 to D_1. Both the decrease in supply and the increase in demand push up the interest rate to a new equilibrium, r_1. Whether the equilibrium quantity of loanable funds will increase or decrease depends on the relative sizes of the shifts in the respective curves.

DO CREDITORS ALWAYS LOSE DURING INFLATION?

Usually lenders are able to anticipate inflation with reasonable accuracy. For example, in the late 1970s, when the inflation rate was over 10 percent a year, nominal interest rates on a 90-day Treasury bill were relatively high. In 2002, with low inflation rates, the nominal interest rate was relatively low. If the inflation rate is anticipated accurately, new creditors will not lose nor will debtors gain from a change in the inflation rate. However, nominal interest rates and real interest rates do not always run together. For example, in periods of high *unexpected* inflation, the nominal interest rates can be very high while the real interest rates may be very low or even negative.

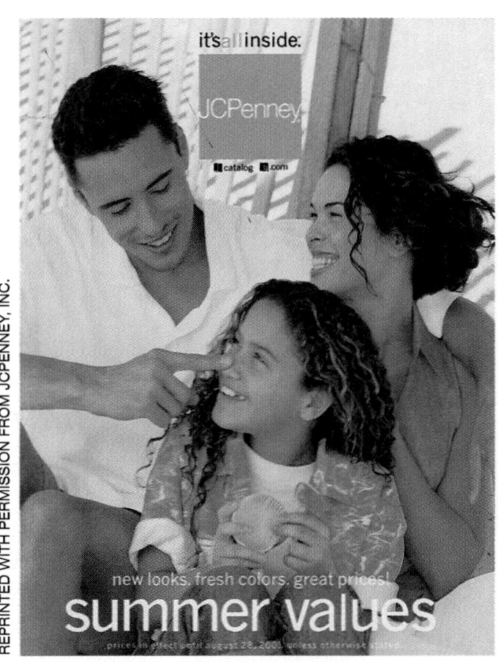

REPRINTED WITH PERMISSION FROM JCPENNEY, INC.

What if JCPenney was selling its clothes through its catalogs in a country with very high and unexpected changes in the inflation rate? How often would JCPenney have to print new catalogs? Would this be costlier than selling in an environment with low and anticipated inflation rates?

PROTECTING OURSELVES FROM INFLATION

Increasingly, groups try to protect themselves from inflation by using cost-of-living clauses in contracts. With these clauses, laborers automatically get wage increases that reflect rising prices. The same is true of many pensioners, including those on Social Security. Personal income taxes also are now indexed (adjusted) for inflation. However, some of the tax code is still not indexed for inflation. This can affect the incentives to work, save, and invest.

Some economists have argued that we should go one step further and index everything, meaning that all contractual arrangements would be adjusted frequently to take account of changing prices. Such an arrangement might reduce the impact of inflation, but it would also entail additional contracting costs (and not every good—notably currency—can be indexed). An alternative approach has been to try to stop inflation through various policies relating to the amount of government spending, tax rates, or the amount of money created. **Wage and price controls**—legislation limiting wage and price increases—offer still another approach to the inflation problem.

wage and price controls
legislation used to combat inflation by limiting changes in wages and prices

APPLICATION

ANTICIPATED INFLATION AND INTEREST RATES

Q: Suppose you had a 30-year, fixed-interest mortgage on a home, which you purchased six years ago. In the meantime, the inflation rate has fallen considerably and probably will not reach that higher level again. Did you get a good interest rate on your loan?

A: No. You will be paying a higher interest rate to borrow money than others who have borrowed money more recently. Now, of course, you could refinance to get a lower interest rate, but you would need to calculate how much you would save on your loan and compare it to the cost of refinancing to determine whether that would be worth doing.

Section Check

1. Unanticipated inflation causes unpredictable transfers of wealth and reduces the efficiency of the market system by distorting price signals.
2. Inflation generally hurts creditors and those on fixed incomes and pensions; debtors generally benefit from inflation.
3. The nominal interest rate is the actual amount of interest you pay. The real interest rate is the nominal rate minus the inflation rate.
4. Wage earners attempt to keep pace with inflation by demanding higher wages each year or by indexing their annual wage to inflation.

---

1. How does price level instability increase the difficulties buyers and sellers have in coordinating their plans?
2. What will happen to the nominal interest rate if the real interest rate rises, *ceteris paribus?* What if expected inflation increases, *ceteris paribus?*
3. Say you owe money to the Big River Bank. Will you gain or lose from an unanticipated decrease in inflation?
4. How does a variable interest rate loan "insure" the lender against unanticipated increases in inflation?
5. Why will neither creditors nor debtors lose from inflation if it is correctly anticipated?
6. How can inflation make people turn to exchange by barter (trading goods for goods)?
7. What would happen in the loanable funds market if suppliers of loanable funds expect a substantial fall in inflation, while demanders of funds expect a substantial rise in inflation?

section 11.5

Economic Fluctuations

- What are short-term economic fluctuations?
- What are the four stages of a business cycle?
- Is there a difference between a recession and a depression?
- Can an economy be in a recession while still growing?

SHORT-TERM FLUCTUATIONS IN ECONOMIC GROWTH

business cycles
short-term fluctuations in the economy relative to the long-term trend in output

The aggregate amount of economic activity in the United States and most other nations has increased markedly over time, even on a per capita basis, indicating economic growth. Short-term fluctuations in the level of economic activity also occur. We sometimes call these short-term fluctuations **business cycles.** Exhibit 1 illustrates the distinction between long-term economic growth and short-term economic fluctuations. Over a long period of time, the line representing economic activity slopes upwards, indicating increasing real output. Over short time periods, however, there are downward, as well as upward, output changes. Business cycles refer to the short-term ups and downs in economic activity, not to the long-term trend in output, which in modern times has been upward.

expansion
when output (real GDP) is rising significantly—the period between the trough of a recession and the next peak

THE PHASES OF A BUSINESS CYCLE

A business cycle has four phases—expansion, peak, contraction, and trough—as illustrated in Exhibit 2. The period of **expansion** is when output (real GDP) is rising signifi-

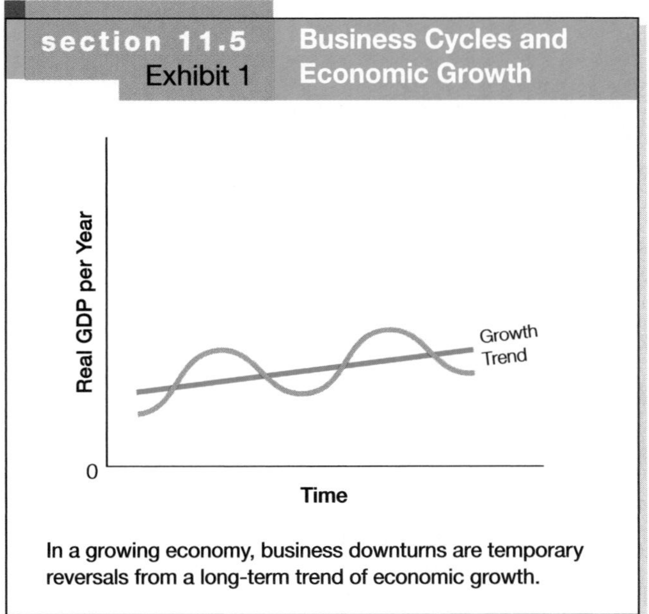

In a growing economy, business downturns are temporary reversals from a long-term trend of economic growth.

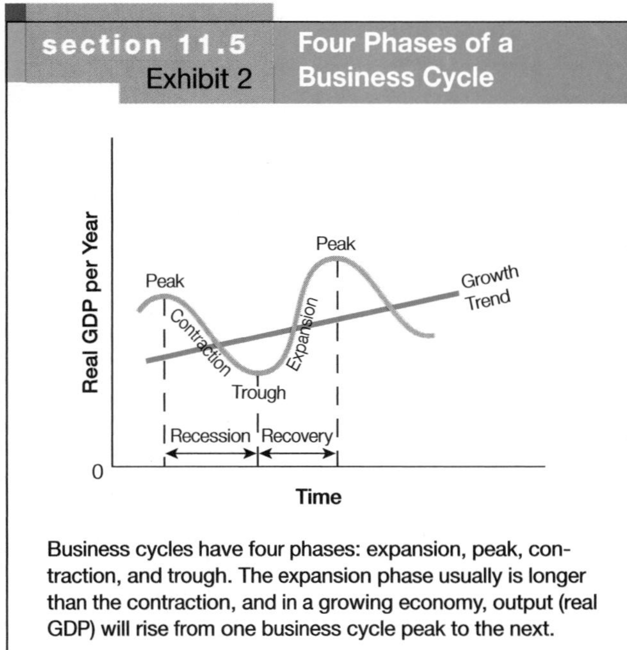

Business cycles have four phases: expansion, peak, contraction, and trough. The expansion phase usually is longer than the contraction, and in a growing economy, output (real GDP) will rise from one business cycle peak to the next.

cantly. Usually during the expansion phase, unemployment is falling and both consumer and business confidence is high. Thus, investment is rising, as well as expenditures for expensive durable consumer goods, such as automobiles and household appliances. The **peak** is the point in time when the expansion comes to an end, when output is at the highest point in the cycle. The contraction is a period of falling real output, and is usually accompanied by rising unemployment and declining business and consumer confidence. The **contraction** phase is measured from the peak to the trough. Investment spending and expenditures on consumer durable goods fall sharply in a typical contraction. This contraction phase is also called **recession,** a period of significant decline in output and employment (lasting more than a few months). The **trough** is the point in time when output stops declining; it is the moment when business activity is at its lowest point in the cycle. Unemployment is relatively high at the trough, although the actual maximum amount of unemployment may not occur exactly at the trough. Often, unemployment remains fairly high well into the expansion phase. The expansion phase is measured from the trough to the peak.

peak
is the point in time when the expansion comes to an end, when output is at the highest point in the cycle

contraction
when the economy is slowing down—measured from the peak to the trough

recession
a period of significant decline in output and employment

trough
the trough is the point in time when output stops declining; it is the moment when business activity is at its lowest point in the cycle

HOW LONG DOES A BUSINESS CYCLE LAST?

There is no uniformity to a business cycle's length. This is why economists often call them economic fluctuations rather than business cycles, since there is not the regularity that a cycle implies. In both the 1980s and 1990s, the expansions were quite long by historical standards. The contraction phase is one of recession, a decline in business activity. Severe recessions are called **depressions.** Likewise, a prolonged expansion in economic activity is sometimes called a **boom.** Exhibit 3 shows the record of U.S. business cycles since 1854. Note in Exhibit 3 that contractions seem to be getting shorter over time. The National Bureau of Economic Research (NBER) Business Cycle Dating Committee determined that a recession began in March 2001, ending an expansion that lasted from March 1991 to March 2001. The attacks of September 11 clearly deepened the contraction and may have been instrumental in turning a contraction into a recession.

depressions
severe recessions, or contraction in output

boom
periods of prolonged economic expansion

section 11.6 Exhibit 3

A Historical Record of U.S. Business Cycles, 1854–2001

Trough	Expansion (Months)	Peak	Contraction (Months)
December 1854	30	June 1857	18
December 1858	22	October 1860	8
June 1861	46 (Civil War)	April 1865	32
December 1867	18	June 1869	18
December 1870	34	October 1873	65
March 1879	36	March 1882	38
May 1885	22	March 1887	13
April 1888	27	July 1890	10
May 1891	20	January 1893	17
June 1894	18	December 1895	18
June 1897	24	June 1899	18
December 1900	21	September 1902	23
August 1904	33	May 1907	13
June 1908	19	January 1910	24
January 1912	12	January 1913	23
December 1914	44 (World War I)	August 1918	7
March 1919	10	January 1920	18
July 1921	22	May 1923	14
July 1924	7	October 1926	13
November 1927	21	August 1929	43 (Depression)
March 1933	50	May 1937	13 (Depression)
June 1938	80 (World War II)	February 1945	8
October 1945	37	November 1948	11
October 1949	45 (Korean War)	July 1953	10
May 1954	39	August 1957	8
April 1958	24	April 1960	10
February 1961	106 (Vietnam War)	December 1969	11
November 1970	36	November 1973	16
March 1975	58	January 1980	6
July 1980	12	July 1981	16
November 1982	92	July 1990	8
March 1991	120	March 2001	—

SOURCE: http://www.nber.org/cycles.html; U.S. Department of Commerce, *Survey of Current Business, March 2001,* Table C-51.

Between 1982 and 2000 the economy has experienced a very long boom with only a brief eight month recession in 1990–1991. The expansion of the 1990s has become the longest in history. According to Nobel laureate Paul Samuelson, "the old-fashioned business cycle, in its virulence, should be as gone as the old-fashioned diphtheria and pre-penicillin diseases."

SEASONAL FLUCTUATIONS AFFECT ECONOMIC ACTIVITY

While the determinants of cyclical fluctuations in the economy are the major thrust of the next several chapters, it should be mentioned that some fluctuation in economic activity reflects seasonal patterns. Business activity, whether measured by production or by the sale of goods, tends to be high in the two months before the winter holidays, and somewhat lower in summertime, when many families are on vacation. Within individual industries, of course, seasonal fluctuations in output often are extremely pronounced, agriculture being the best example. Often, key economic statistics, like unemployment rates, are seasonally adjusted, meaning the numbers are modified to take account of normal seasonal fluctuations. Thus, seasonally adjusted unemployment rates in summer months are below actual unemployment rates, because employment is normally high in summertime due to the inflow of school-age workers into the labor force.

POLITICAL BUSINESS CYCLES

Studies have shown there is a strong correlation between the performance of the economy and the fate of an incumbent president's (or an incumbent president's party) bid for reelection. In fact, the 1992 presidential election sheds light on this hypothesis. President George Bush lost his reelection bid shortly after the economy had struggled through the 1990–1991 recession. Some scholars have speculated that if the election had taken place a few months later when the economic data looked a lot stronger, President Bush would have been reelected.

If this correlation between the strength of the economy and a successful reelection bid does exist, then it would be in the best interest of the incumbent to do everything in his power to stimulate the economy in the period leading up to the election. This might take the form of trying to pressure the Federal Reserve System into using monetary policy to lower the interest rate or pressing Congress to cut taxes or increase government spending—anything that might generate more spending and thus greater employment. Of course, the negative side to all of this is that although the incumbent may get reelected, the economy may have been overstimulated, causing inflationary problems.

However, the evidence of a political business cycle is mixed. It is possible that the 1972 presidential election might have been a political business cycle as the economy was pushed beyond potential GDP with expansionary monetary policy, but the elections of 1980 and 1992 occurred during recessions. This indicates that no one successfully tried to overstimulate the economy prior to those elections. And in 1980, Ronald Reagan defeated Jimmy Carter at least partly because Carter's appointment to the Fed, Paul Volker, pursued a contractionary monetary policy to fight the high inflation rates of the late 1970s. The expected result was a recession that most likely lost the 1980 election for Carter.

FORECASTING CYCLICAL CHANGES

The farmer and the aviator rely heavily on weather forecasters for information on climatic conditions in planning their activities. Similarly, businesses, government agencies, and to a lesser extent, consumers, rely on economic forecasts to learn of forthcoming developments in the business cycle. If it looks like the economy will continue in an expansionary phase, businesses might expand production to meet a perceived forthcoming need; if it looks like contraction is coming, perhaps they will be more cautious.

Forecasting Models

Using theoretical models, which will be discussed in later chapters, economists gather statistics on economic activity in the immediate past, including, for example, consumer expenditures, business inventories, the supply of money, governmental expenditures, tax revenues, and so on. Using past historical relationships between these factors and the overall level of economic activity (which form the basis of the economic theories), they formulate *econometric models.* Statistics from the immediate past are plugged into the model and forecasts are made. Because human behavior changes and we cannot correctly make assumptions about certain future developments, our numbers are imperfect and our econometric models are not always accurate. Like the weather forecasts, although the econometric models are not perfect, they are helpful.

Leading Economic Indicators

leading economic indicators
factors that economists at the Commerce Department have found that typically change before changes in economic activity

One less sophisticated but very useful forecasting tool is watching trends in **leading economic indicators.** Some types of economic activity change before the economy as a whole changes. If in March these activities show an increase after having declined for several months, past experience suggests the entire output will start rising after a few months, perhaps in July or August. About a dozen such leading indicators exist, including the lengths of the average workweek, the magnitude of the nation's money supply, prices of common stocks, the number of new businesses formed, and new orders for plant and equipment. The Department of Commerce combines all of these into an index of leading indicators. If the index rises sharply for two or three months, it is likely (but not certain) that increases in the overall level of activity will follow.

Since the development of the leading economic indicators some 60 years ago, the composite index of leading economic indicators has never failed to give some warning of an economic downturn. Unfortunately, the lead time has varied widely. The composite index turned down 23 months prior to the 1957–1958 recession but gave only a three-month warning before the 1981–1982 slump. This variance in lead time can cause particular policy problems. Specifically, the use of leading economic indicators to predict future trends can make policy decisions less accurate. For example, if the federal government responds with policies to combat the recession as soon as the leading economic indicators begin predicting a recession, then the recession that would have occurred may fail to materialize. On the other hand, a self-fulfilling prophecy may result if businesses respond with cutbacks in orders for plant and equipment as soon as the leading economic indicators begin predicting a recession.

While the economic indicators do provide a warning of a likely downturn, they do not provide accurate information on the depth or the duration of the downturn.

Section Check

1. Business cycles (or economic fluctuations) are short-term fluctuations in the amount of economic activity, relative to the long-term growth trend in output.
2. The four phases of a business cycle are expansion, peak, contraction, and trough.
3. Recessions occur during the contraction phase of a business cycle. Severe, long-term recessions are called depressions.
4. The economy often goes through short-term contractions even during a long-term growth trend.

---

1. Why would you expect unemployment to tend to fall during an economy's expansionary phase and to rise during a contractionary phase?
2. Why might a politician want to stimulate the economy prior to a reelection bid?
3. Why is the output of investment goods and durable consumer goods more sensitive to the business cycle than that of most goods?
4. Why might the unemployment rate fall only after output starts recovering during the expansion phase of the business cycle?

Summary

The most important macroeconomic goals are full employment, price stability, and economic growth. The United States showed its commitment to the major macroeconomic goals with the Employment Act of 1946. The consequences of unemployment to society include a reduction in potential output and consumption—a decrease in efficiency. The unemployment rate is found by taking the number of people officially unemployed and dividing by the number in the labor force. Unemployment rates are the highest for minorities, the young, and less-skilled workers.

There are four main categories of unemployed workers: job losers, job leavers, reentrants, and new entrants. The duration of unemployment tends to be greater (smaller) when the amount of unemployment is high (low). The three types of unemployment are frictional unemployment, structural unemployment, and cyclical unemployment. Frictional unemployment results from people moving from one job to another. Structural unemployment results when people who are looking for jobs lack the required skills for the available jobs. Cyclical unemployment is caused by a recession. The natural rate of unemployment is attributable to structural and frictional unemployment only, no cyclical unemployment is thought to be present.

Price stability provides security in the marketplace by ensuring constant purchasing power of a nation's currency. Inflation generally hurts creditors and those on fixed incomes and pensions; debtors generally benefit from unexpected inflation while creditors generally are hurt. Inflation distorts price signals, leads to shoe-leather costs and menu costs, arbitrarily redistributes wealth, and discourages long-term planning and investment. The nominal interest rate is the actual amount of interest you pay. The real interest rate is the nominal rate minus the inflation rate.

Business cycles are short-term fluctuations in economic activity, relative to the long-term trend in output. The four phases of a business cycle are expansion, peak, contraction, and trough. Recessions occur during the contraction phase of a business cycle. Severe, long-term recessions are called depressions.

Key Terms and Concepts

real gross domestic product (RGDP) 246
Employment Act of 1946 247
unemployment rate 248
labor force 248
discouraged worker 250
job loser 251
job leaver 251
reentrant 251
new entrant 251
underemployment 251
labor force participation rate 252
frictional unemployment 253
structural unemployment 254
cyclical unemployment 255
natural rate of unemployment 255
potential output 256
price level 259
inflation 259
deflation 259
consumer price index (CPI) 259
menu costs 261
shoe-leather cost 261
nominal interest rate 262
real interest rate 262
wage and price controls 263
business cycles 264
expansion 264
peak 265
contraction 265
recession 265
trough 265
depressions 265
boom 265
leading economic indicators 268

Review Questions

1. Which of the following individuals would economists consider unemployed?
   a. Sam looked for work for several weeks, but has now given up his search and is going back to college.
   b. A fourteen-year-old wants to mow lawns for extra cash but is unable to find neighbors willing to hire him.
   c. A factory worker is temporarily laid off but expects to be called back to work soon.
   d. A receptionist, who works only 20 hours per week, would like to work 40 hours per week.
   e. A high-school graduate spends his days backpacking across the country rather than seeking work.
2. Identify whether each of the following reflects seasonal, structural, frictional, or cyclical unemployment.
   a. A sales employee is laid off due to slow business after consumer spending falls.
   b. An automotive worker is replaced by robotic equipment on the assembly line.
   c. A salesperson quits a job in California and seeks a new sales position after moving to New York.
   d. An employee is fired due to poor job performance and searches the want ads each day for work.
3. Calculate the unemployment rate for an economy using the following data:

Number of employed:	80 million
Number of unemployed:	15 million
Number of discouraged workers:	5 million
Total adult population:	160 million

4. Unemployment benefits in many European countries tend to be both more generous and available for longer periods of time than in the United States. What impact do you think this is likely to have on the unemployment rate in a country? Why?
5. How can unions result in higher unemployment rates? How would the results differ for someone who wants to be employed in the union sector than for someone who currently has a job in the union sector?
6. You borrow $10,000 at a nominal interest rate of 6 percent. What is the real rate of interest when the inflation rate is
   a. 2 percent.
   b. 6 percent.
   c. 8 percent.
7. You borrow money at a fixed rate of interest to finance your college education. If the rate of inflation unexpectedly slows down between the time you take out the loan and the time you begin paying it back, is there a redistribution of income? What if you already expected the inflation rate to slow at the time you took out the loan? Explain.
8. How does an adjustable rate mortgage agreement protect lenders against inflation? Who bears the inflation risk?
9. In 2000, a proposal was made in Santa Monica, California, to raise the minimum wage in the hotel and shopping district to a "living" wage of $10.69 per hour. Predict the impact of such legislation on unemployment in the hotel and shopping industry in Santa Monica. What would you expect to happen to the unemployment rate in neighboring areas?
10. http:// Visit the Sexton Web site at **http://sexton.swcollege.com** and click on "Conference Board" to find out the latest information about leading economic indicators. Based on the latest trend in the data, what can you predict about the outlook for employment in the economy?

Fill in the Blanks

1. There are three major macroeconomic goals: maintaining employment at ______________ levels; maintaining prices at a ______________ level; and achieving a ______________ rate of economic growth.

2. Concern over both unemployment and price instability led to the passage of the ______________, in which the United States committed itself to policies designed to reduce unemployment in a manner consistent with price stability.

3. With high rates of unemployment, society loses some potential ______________ of goods and services.

4. The unemployment rate is the number of people officially ______________ divided by ______________.

5. The labor force is the number of people over the age of 16 who are either ______________ or ______________.

6. ______________ workers, who have not actively sought work for four weeks, are not counted as unemployed; instead, they fall out of the ______________.

7. Some people working overtime or extra jobs might be considered to be ______________employed.

8. There are four main categories of unemployed workers: job ______________ (temporarily laid off or fired), job ______________ (quit), ______________ (worked before and now reentering labor force), and ______________ entrants (entering the labor force for first time).

9. ______________ typically account for the largest fraction of those unemployed.

10. In the short run, a reduction in unemployment may come at the expense of a higher rate of ______________, especially if the economy is close to full capacity.

11. Trying to match employees with jobs quickly may lead to significant inefficiencies because of ______________ between a worker's skill level and the level of skill required for a job.

12. The duration of unemployment tends to be greater when the amount of unemployment is ______________ and smaller when the amount of unemployment is ______________.

13. The percentage of the population that is in the labor force is called the ______________ rate.

14. Frictional unemployment is ______________ term and results from the ______________ turnover in the labor market.

15. Frictional unemployment tends to be somewhat ______________ in periods of low unemployment, when job opportunities are plentiful.

16. If individuals seeking jobs and employers seeking workers had better information about each other, the amount of frictional unemployment would be considerably ______________.

17. ______________ unemployment reflects the existence of persons who lack the necessary skills for jobs that are available.

18. ______________ unemployment is the most volatile form of unemployment.

19. Most of the attempts to solve the unemployment problem have placed an emphasis on increasing ____________.

20. Job-retraining programs have the potential to reduce ____________ unemployment.

21. The natural rate of unemployment roughly equals the sum of ____________ and ____________ unemployment when they are at a maximum.

22. One can view unemployment rates below the ____________ rate as reflecting the existence of a below-average level of frictional and structural unemployment.

23. The natural rate of unemployment is the median, or "typical," unemployment rate, equal to the sum of ____________ and ____________ unemployment when they are at a maximum.

24. The natural rate of unemployment may change over time as ____________, ____________, ____________, and other conditions vary.

25. When all of the economy's labor resources and other resources, like capital, are fully employed, the economy is said to be producing its ____________ level of output.

26. When the economy is experiencing cyclical unemployment, the unemployment rate is ____________ than the natural rate.

27. The economy can ____________ exceed potential output as workers take on overtime or moonlight by taking on extra employment.

28. Without price stability, consumers and producers will experience more difficulty in ____________ their plans and decisions.

29. In general, the only thing that can cause a sustained increase in the rate of inflation is a ____________ rate of growth in money.

30. The ____________ is the standard measure of inflation.

31. Retirees on fixed pensions, creditors, and those whose incomes are tied to long-term contracts can be hurt by inflation because inflation ____________ the purchasing power of the money they receive.

32. The ____________ that inflation creates can discourage investment and economic growth.

33. Inflation can ____________ one nation's price level relative to price levels in other countries, which can lead to difficulties in financing the purchase of foreign goods or to a decline in the value of the national currency relative to that of other countries.

34. In periods of high and variable inflation, households and firms have a difficult time distinguishing changes in ____________ prices from changes in the general price level, distorting the information that flows from price signals.

35. ____________ costs are the costs of changing posted prices.

36. ____________ costs are the costs of checking on your assets.

37. The real interest rate equals the ____________ interest rate minus the ____________ rate.

38. The ______________ the interest rate, the greater the quantity of funds people will demand, *ceteris paribus;* the ______________ the interest rate, the greater the quantity of loanable funds supplied, *ceteris paribus.*

39. When creditors start expecting future inflation, there will be a ______________ shift in the supply curve of loanable funds. Likewise, demanders of funds (borrowers) are more anxious to borrow because they think they will pay their loans back in dollars of lesser purchasing power than the dollars they borrowed. Thus, the demand for funds increases.

40. If the inflation rate is ______________ anticipated, new creditors do not lose, nor do debtors gain, from inflation.

41. Groups try to protect themselves from inflation by using ______________ clauses in contracts.

42. Business cycles refer to the ______________-______________ fluctuations in economic activity, not to the ______________-______________ trend in output.

43. A business cycle has four phases: ______________, ______________, ______________, and ______________.

44. Expansion occurs when output is ______________ significantly, unemployment is ______________, and both consumer and business confidence is ______________.

45. The ______________ is when an expansion comes to an end, when output is at the highest point in the business cycle; while the ______________ is the point in time when output stops declining, when business activity is at its lowest point in the business cycle.

46. Seasonally adjusted unemployment rates in summer months are ______________ actual unemployment rates because unemployment is normally ______________ in summertime as a result of the inflow of school-age workers into the labor force.

47. It can be in the best interest of the incumbent to stimulate the economy in the period leading up to an ______________.

48. Businesses, government agencies, and to a lesser extent, consumers rely on economic ______________ to learn of forthcoming developments in the business cycles.

49. If the index of ______________ increases sharply for two or three months, it is likely (but not certain) that increases in the overall level of activity will follow.

50. While the leading economic indicators do provide a warning of a likely downturn, they do not provide accurate information on the ______________ or ______________ of the downturn.

True or False

1. Economic growth means a growth in real, per capita total output over time.

2. Individuals, because they may differ considerably in their evaluation of the relative importance of certain issues, may disagree about whether certain "problems" are really problems after all.

3. Economic growth is considered positively by all persons.

4. Other things being equal, relatively high rates of unemployment are almost universally viewed as bad.

5. The unemployment rate is the number of people officially unemployed divided by a country's population aged 16 or over.

6. The civilian labor force figure excludes those in the armed services, prison, or mental hospitals, as well homemakers, retirees, and full-time students, because they are not considered currently available for employment.

7. By far the worst employment downturn in U.S. history was the Great Depression.

8. Before 1960, variations in unemployment tended to be more pronounced than since 1960.

9. Discouraged workers, who have not actively sought work for four weeks, are counted as unemployed.

10. People looking for full-time work who grudgingly settle for a part-time job are counted as employed, even though they are only "partly" employed.

11. Some people working in the underground economy may be counted in labor statistics as unemployed, while others may be counted as not in the labor force.

12. Unemployment rates are usually very similar across different segments of the population, but they vary substantially over time.

13. In the short run, a reduction in unemployment may come at the expense of a higher rate of inflation.

14. The duration of unemployment tends to be greater when the amount of unemployment is low, and smaller when the amount of unemployment is high.

15. Unemployment means a loss of potential output.

16. When the baby-boom generation began entering the labor force, it raised the labor force participation rate.

17. Frictional unemployment results from persons being temporarily between jobs.

18. Frictional unemployment, while not good in itself, is a by-product of a healthy phenomenon, and because it is short lived, it is not generally viewed as a serious problem.

19. Structural employment can arise because jobs that require particular skills disappear.

20. Structural unemployment is easily measured and stable over time.

21. Cyclical unemployment may result from an insufficient level of demand for goods and services.

22. Given its volatility and dimensions, governments have viewed unemployment resulting from inadequate demand to be especially correctable through government policies.

23. The natural rate of unemployment roughly equals the sum of frictional and cyclical unemployment when they are at a maximum.

24. When unemployment rises above the natural rate, it reflects the existence of cyclical unemployment.

25. The natural rate of unemployment does not change over time.

26. At the natural rate of unemployment, the economy is producing its potential output.

27. When the economy is experiencing cyclical unemployment, the unemployment rate is less than the natural rate.

28. In both inflation and deflation, a country's currency unit changes in purchasing power.

29. Unanticipated and sharp price changes are almost universally considered to be a "bad" thing that needs to be remedied by some policy.

30. Debtors lose from inflation.

31. Wage earners will lose from inflation if wages rise at a slower rate than the price level.

32. Inflation brings about changes in real incomes of persons.

33. Menu costs and shoe-leather costs are modest, regardless of the rate of inflation.

34. The real interest rate equals the nominal interest rate plus the inflation rate.

35. If people correctly anticipate inflation, they will behave in a manner that will largely protect them against loss.

36. When people start expecting future inflation, creditors become less willing to lend funds at any given interest rate because they fear they will be repaid in dollars of lesser value than those they loaned.

37. When borrowers of funds start expecting future inflation, the demand for funds decreases.

38. When both suppliers and demanders of funds begin to expect inflation, it will push up the interest rate to a new higher equilibrium level.

39. In periods of high unexpected inflation, the nominal interest rate can be very high while the real interest rate is low or even negative.

40. In a growing economy, real GDP will tend to rise from one business-cycle peak to the next.

41. In an expansion, investment is rising, but expenditures for expensive durable consumer goods are falling.

42. A contraction is a period of falling real output and is usually accompanied by rising unemployment and declining business and consumer confidence.

43. Unemployment falls substantially as soon as the economy enters the expansion phase of the business cycle.

44. There is no uniformity to a business cycle's length.

45. There is a strong correlation between the performance of the economy and the fate of an incumbent's bid for reelection.

46. Econometric forecasts are generally highly accurate.

47. Since the development of the index of leading economic indicators, it has never failed to give some warning of an economic downturn.

48. The lead time between a change in the index of economic indicators and changes in business conditions has varied widely.

Multiple Choice

1. Which is *not* one of society's major economic goals?
   a. maintaining employment at high levels
   b. maintaining prices at a stable level
   c. maintaining a high rate of economic growth
   d. All of the above are major economic goals of society.

2. The three major macroeconomic goals of nearly every society are
   a. maintaining stable prices, reducing interest rates, and achieving a high rate of economic growth.
   b. maintaining high levels of employment, increasing the supply of money, and achieving a high rate of economic growth.
   c. maintaining stable prices, maintaining high levels of employment, and achieving high rates of economic growth.
   d. achieving high rates of economic growth, reducing unemployment, and reducing interest rates.

3. With regard to macroeconomic goals, which is *not* true?
   a. Individuals differ considerably in their evaluation of the relative importance of certain issues.
   b. Individuals disagree on whether certain "problems" are really problems.
   c. Virtually everyone views economic growth positively.
   d. Some individuals disagree about the appropriate distribution of income.
   e. All of the above *are* true.

4. Economic growth is measured by changes in
   a. nominal GDP.
   b. the money supply.
   c. real GDP per capita.
   d. the rate of unemployment.
   e. none of the above.

5. High rates of unemployment
   a. can lead to increased tensions and despair.
   b. result in the loss of some potential output in society.
   c. reduce the possible level of consumption in society.
   d. represent a loss of efficiency in society.
   e. All of the above are true.

6. The unemployment rate is the number of people officially unemployed divided by
   a. the civilian labor force.
   b. the noninstitutional population.
   c. the total population.
   d. the number of people employed.
   e. none of the above.

7. The labor force consists of
   a. discouraged workers, employed workers, and those actively seeking work.
   b. all persons over the age of 16 who are working or actively seeking work.
   c. all persons over the age of 16 who are able to work.
   d. all persons over the age of 16 who are working, plus those not working.
   e. discouraged workers, part-time workers, and full-time workers.

8. The civilian labor force includes which of the following groups?
   a. those in the armed forces
   b. those who are currently working part-time
   c. full-time students
   d. retirees
   e. all of the above

9. Discouraged workers
   a. are considered unemployed.
   b. are considered as not in the labor force.
   c. are considered as in the labor force.
   d. are considered as both unemployed and in the labor force.
   e. are considered as unemployed but not in the labor force.

10. Which of these groups tends to have the lowest unemployment rate?
   a. teenagers
   b. those with some college education
   c. college graduates
   d. those with a high-school diploma, but no college experience

11. The largest fraction of those counted as unemployed is due to
   a. job losers.
   b. job leavers.
   c. new entrants.
   d. reentrants.

12. In Littletown, there are 1,000 people over the age of 16; 800 are in the labor force, and 600 are employed. The unemployment rate is
   a. 33 percent.
   b. 25 percent.
   c. 20 percent.
   d. 75 percent.
   e. none of the above.

13. The official unemployment rate may overstate the extent of unemployment because
   a. it excludes discouraged workers.
   b. it counts part-time workers as fully employed.
   c. it does not count those with jobs in the underground economy as employed.
   d. it includes those who claim to be looking for work as unemployed, even if they are just going through the motions in order to get government benefits.
   e. of both c and d.

14. The unemployment rate may underestimate the true extent of unemployment if
   a. employees increase the number of hours they work overtime.
   b. many people become discouraged and cease looking for work.
   c. there are a large number of people working in the underground economy.
   d. any of the above occur.

15. If unemployment benefits increase and that leads more people to claim to be seeking work when they are not really seeking work, the measured unemployment rate would
   a. rise.
   b. fall.
   c. be unaffected.
   d. change in an indeterminate direction.

16. After looking for a job for more than eight months, Kyle has become frustrated and stopped looking. Economists view Kyle as

a. unemployed.
b. part of the labor force, but neither employed nor unemployed.
c. a discouraged worker.
d. cyclically unemployed.
e. both b and c.

17. Persons who do not have jobs and who do not look for work are considered

a. unemployed.
b. out of the labor force.
c. underemployed.
d. overemployed.
e. part of the underground economy.

18. If the unemployment rate is 6 percent and the number of persons unemployed is 6 million, the number of people employed is equal to

a. 100 million.
b. 94 million.
c. 106 million.
d. 6 million.
e. none of the above.

19. According to the Bureau of Labor Statistics, the four main categories of unemployed workers are

a. discouraged workers, part-time workers, the cyclically unemployed, and the frictionally unemployed.
b. discouraged workers, job losers, new entrants, and the underemployed.
c. new entrants, job losers, job leavers, and reentrants.
d. job losers, job leavers, the structurally unemployed, and the frictionally unemployed.

20. Frictional unemployment is

a. unemployment that is due to normal turnover in the labor market.
b. unemployment caused by automation in the workplace.
c. unemployment caused by lack of training and education.
d. unemployment that is due to the friction of competing ideological systems.
e. all of the above.

21. Unemployment caused by a contraction in the economy is called

a. frictional unemployment.
b. cyclical unemployment.
c. structural unemployment.
d. seasonal unemployment.

22. A federal program aimed at retraining the unemployed workers of the declining auto and steel industries is designed to reduce which type of unemployment?

a. seasonal
b. cyclical
c. structural
d. frictional

23. When unemployment rises above the natural rate, it reflects the existence of ______ unemployment.

a. frictional
b. structural
c. seasonal
d. cyclical

24. When an economy is operating at full employment,

a. the unemployment rate will equal zero.
b. frictional unemployment will equal zero.
c. cyclical unemployment will equal zero.
d. structural unemployment will equal zero.
e. both b and d are correct.

25. The natural rate of unemployment would increase when which of the following increases?

a. frictional unemployment
b. structural unemployment
c. cyclical unemployment
d. any of the above
e. either frictional or structural unemployment

26. If a nation's labor force receives a significant influx of young workers,

a. the natural rate of unemployment is likely to increase.
b. the natural rate of unemployment is likely to decrease.
c. the natural rate of unemployment is unlikely to change.
d. frictional unemployment will likely decrease to zero.

27. Which of the following is false?

a. At the natural rate of unemployment, the economy is considered to be at full employment.
b. At full employment, the economy is producing at its potential output.
c. If unemployment is greater than its natural rate, the economy is producing at greater than its potential output.
d. If we are at less than full employment, some cyclical unemployment exists.

28. When would consumers and producers experience increased difficulty in coordinating their plans and decisions?

a. in a period of inflation
b. in a period of deflation
c. in either a period of inflation or deflation
d. none of the above

29. Inflation can harm

a. retirees on fixed pensions.
b. borrowers who have long-term fixed interest rate loans.
c. wage earners whose incomes grow slower than inflation.
d. either a or c.
e. all of the above.

30. Inflation will be least harmful if

a. interest rates are not adjusted accordingly when inflation occurs.
b. worker wages are set by long-term contracts.
c. it is correctly anticipated and interest rates adjust accordingly.
d. it is not fully anticipated.

31. Unexpected inflation generally benefits
   a. lenders.
   b. borrowers.
   c. the poor.
   d. people on fixed incomes.

32. The costs of inflation include
   a. menu costs.
   b. shoe-leather costs.
   c. a distortion of price signals.
   d. all of the above.

33. If the nominal interest rate is 9 percent and the inflation rate is 3 percent, the real interest rate is
   a. 3 percent.
   b. 6 percent.
   c. 9 percent.
   d. 12 percent.
   e. 27 percent.

34. What is the real interest rate paid on a loan bearing 7 percent nominal interest per year if the inflation rate is 6 percent?
   a. 13 percent
   b. 7 percent
   c. 6 percent
   d. 1 percent

35. If people correctly anticipate inflation, it will
   a. benefit borrowers.
   b. benefit lenders.
   c. benefit neither borrowers nor lenders.
   d. harm both borrowers and lenders.

36. If there is an increase in the expected future rate of inflation, it will
   a. increase the supply of funds.
   b. decrease the supply of funds.
   c. increase the demand for funds.
   d. decrease the demand for funds.
   e. do both b and d.

37. A business cycle reflects changes in economic activity, particularly real GDP. The stages of a business cycle in order are
   a. expansion, peak, contraction, and trough.
   b. expansion, trough, contraction, and peak.
   c. contraction, recession, expansion, and boom.
   d. trough, expansion, contraction, and peak.

38. In the contraction phase of the business cycle,
   a. output is rising.
   b. unemployment is falling.
   c. consumer and business confidence is high.
   d. investment is rising.
   e. none of the above are true.

39. The contractionary phase of the business cycle is characterized by
  a. reduced output and increased unemployment.
  b. reduced output and reduced unemployment.
  c. increased output and increased unemployment.
  d. increased output and reduced unemployment.

Problems

1. Answer the following questions about unemployment.
   a. If a country had a noninstitutional population of 200 million and a labor force of 160 million, and 140 million people were employed, what is its labor force participation rate and its unemployment rate?
   b. If 10 million new jobs were created in the country, and it attracted 20 million of the people previously not in the labor force into the labor force, what would its new labor force participation rate and its unemployment rate be?
   c. Beginning from the situation in a, if 10 million unemployed people became discouraged and stopped looking for work, what would its new labor force participation rate and its unemployment rate be?
   d. Beginning from the situation in a, If 10 million current workers retired, but their jobs were filled by others still in the labor force, what would its new labor force participation rate and its unemployment rate be?

2. Answer the following questions about reasons for unemployment.
   a. In a severe recession, explain what would tend to happen to the number of people in each of the following categories:

      job losers
      job leavers
      reentrants
      new entrants

   b. In very good economic times, why might job leavers, reentrants, and new entrants all increase?

3. Answer the following questions about inflation.
   a. What would be the effect of unexpected inflation on each of the following?

      retirees on fixed incomes
      workers
      debtors
      creditors
      shoe-leather costs
      menu costs

   b. How would your answers change if the inflation was expected?

4. Answer the following questions about the nominal and real interest rate.
   a. What would be the real interest rate if the nominal interest rate were 14 percent and the inflation rate were 10 percent? if the nominal interest rate were 8 percent and the inflation rate were 1 percent?
   b. What would happen to the real interest rate if the nominal interest rate went from 9 percent to 15 percent when the inflation rate went from 3 percent to 10 percent? if the nominal interest rate went from 11 percent to 7 percent when the inflation rate went from 8 percent to 4 percent?

chapter 12

Measuring Economic Performance

12.1 **NATIONAL INCOME ACCOUNTING: MEASURING ECONOMIC PERFORMANCE**
How can we measure our nation's economic performance?

12.2 **THE EXPENDITURE APPROACH TO MEASURING GDP**
What are the four categories of purchases in the expenditure approach?

12.3 **THE INCOME APPROACH TO MEASURING GDP**
How do we compute GDP using the income approach?

12.4 **PROBLEMS IN CALCULATING AN ACCURATE GDP**
What factors make it difficult to calculate GDP accurately?

12.5 **PROBLEMS WITH GDP AS A MEASURE OF ECONOMIC WELFARE**
How does GDP fail to measure economic welfare accurately?

section 12.1

National Income Accounting: Measuring Economic Performance

- What reasons are there for measuring our economy's performance?
- What is gross domestic product?
- What are the different methods of measuring GDP?

WHY DO WE MEASURE OUR ECONOMY'S PERFORMANCE?

There is a great desire to measure the success, or performance, of our economy. Are we getting "bigger" (and hopefully better) or "smaller" (and worse) over time? Aside from intellectual curiosity, the need to evaluate the magnitude of our economic performance is important to macroeconomic policy makers, who want to know how well the economy is performing so that they can set goals and develop policy recommendations.

Measurement of the economy's performance is also important to private businesses because inaccurate measurement can lead to bad decision making. Traders in stocks and bonds are continually checking economic statistics—buying and selling in response to the latest economic data.

WHAT IS NATIONAL INCOME ACCOUNTING?

national income accounting
a uniform means of measuring economic performance

To fulfill the desire for a reliable method of measuring economic performance, **national income accounting** was born early in the twentieth century. The establishment of a uniform means of accounting for economic performance was such an important accomplishment that one of the first Nobel prizes in economics was given to the late Simon Kuznets, a pioneer of national income accounting in the United States.

Several measures of aggregate national income and output have been developed, the most important of which is gross domestic product (GDP). We will examine GDP and other indicators of national economic performance in detail later in this chapter.

WHAT IS GROSS DOMESTIC PRODUCT?

gross domestic product (GDP)
the measure of economic performance based on the value of all final goods and services produced in a given period

The measure of aggregate economic performance that gets the most attention in the popular media is **gross domestic product (GDP),** which is defined as the value of all final goods and services produced within a country during a given period of time. By convention, that period of time is almost always one year. But let's examine the rest of this definition. What is meant by "final good or service" and "value"?

Measuring the Value of Goods and Services

Value is determined by the market prices at which goods and services sell. Underlying the calculations, then, are the various equilibrium prices and quantities for the multitude of goods and services produced.

What Is a Final Good or Service?

The word "final" means that the good is ready for its designated ultimate use. Many goods and services are intermediate goods or services, that is, used in the production of other goods. For example, suppose United States Steel Corporation produces some steel that it sells to General Motors Corporation for use in making an automobile. If we counted the value of steel used in making the car as well as the full value of the finished auto in the GDP, we would be engaging in **double counting**—adding the value of the steel in twice, first in its raw form and second in its final form, the automobile.

double counting
adding the value of a good or service twice by mistakenly counting intermediate goods and services in GDP

MEASURING GROSS DOMESTIC PRODUCT

Economic output can be calculated primarily two ways: the expenditure approach and the income approach. Although these methods differ, their result, GDP, is the same, apart from minor "statistical discrepancies." In the following two sections, we will examine each of these approaches in turn.

Section Check

1. We measure our economy's status in order to see how its performance has changed over time. These economic measurements are important to government officials, private businesses, and investors.
2. National income accounting, pioneered by Simon Kuznets, is a uniform means of measuring national economic performance.
3. Gross domestic product (GDP) is the value of all final goods and services produced within a country during a given time period.
4. Two different ways to measure GDP are the expenditure approach and the income approach.

---

1. Why does GDP measure only final goods and services produced, rather than all goods and services produced?
2. Why aren't all of the expenditures on used goods in an economy included in the current GDP?
3. Why do GDP statistics include real estate agents' commissions from selling existing homes and used car dealers' profits from selling used cars but not the value of existing homes and used cars when they are sold?
4. Why are sales of previously existing inventories of hula hoops not included in the current year's GDP?

The paper used in this book is an intermediate good; it is the book, the final good, that is included in the GDP.

section 12.2

The Expenditure Approach to Measuring GDP

- What are the four categories of purchases included in the expenditure approach?
- What are durable and nondurable goods?
- What are fixed investments?
- What types of government purchases are included in the expenditure approach?
- How are net exports calculated?

THE EXPENDITURE APPROACH TO MEASURING GDP

expenditure approach
calculation of GDP by adding the expenditures of market participants on final goods and services over a given period

One approach to measuring GDP is the **expenditure approach.** With this method, GDP is calculated by adding up how much market participants spend on final goods and services over a period of time. For convenience and for analytical purposes, economists usually categorize spending into four categories: consumption, identified symbolically by the letter *C;* investment, *I;* government purchases, *G;* and net exports (which equals exports (X) minus imports (M), or ($X - M$). Following the expenditure method, then

$$GDP = C + I + G + (X - M)$$

CONSUMPTION (*C*)

consumption
purchases of final goods and services

Consumption refers to the purchase of consumer goods and services by households. For most of us, a large percentage of our income in a given year goes for consumer goods and services. The consumption category does not include purchases by business or government. As Exhibit 1 indicates, in 2001, consumption expenditures totaled over \$7 trillion (\$7,002 billion). This figure was 68 percent of GDP. In that respect, the 2001 data were fairly typical. In every year since 1929, when GDP accounts began to be calculated annually, consumption has been more than half of total expenditures on goods and services (even during World War II).

Consumption spending, in turn, is usually broken down into three subcategories, nondurable goods, durable consumer goods, and services.

What Are Nondurable and Durable Goods?

nondurable goods
tangible items that are consumed in a short period of time, such as food

durable goods
longer-lived consumer goods, such as automobiles

Nondurable goods include tangible consumer items that are typically consumed or used up in a relatively short period of time. Food and clothing are examples, as are such quickly consumable items as drugs, toys, magazines, soap, razor blades, light bulbs, and so on. Nearly everything purchased in a supermarket or drug store is a nondurable good.

Durable goods include longer-lived consumer goods, the most important single category of which is automobiles and other consumer vehicles. Appliances, stereos, and furniture are also included in the durable goods category. On occasion, it is difficult to decide whether a good is durable or nondurable, and the definitions are, therefore, somewhat arbitrary.

The distinction between durables and nondurables is important because consumer buying behavior is somewhat different for each of these categories of goods. In boom periods, when GDP is rising rapidly, expenditures on durables often increase dramatically, while in years of stagnant or falling GDP, sales of durable goods often plummet. By con-

section 12.2 Exhibit 1 2001 U.S. GDP by Type of Spending

Category	Amount (billions of current dollars)	Percent of GDP
Gross domestic product	\$10,227	
Consumption (*C*)	7,002	68%
Investment (*I*)	1,789	17
Government purchases (G)	1,811	18
Net exports of goods and services (*X* − *M*)	−375	−3

SOURCE: U.S. Bureau of Economic Analysis, *Survey of Current Business.*

trast, sales of nondurables like food tend to be more stable over time because purchases of such goods are more difficult to shift from one time period to another. You can "make do" with your car for another year, but not your lettuce.

What Are Services?

Services are intangible items of value, as opposed to physical goods. Education, health care, domestic housekeeping, professional football, legal help, automobile repair, haircuts, airplane transportation—all of these are services. In recent years, service expenditures have been growing faster than spending on goods; the share of total consumption going for services increased from 35 percent in 1950 to almost 60 percent by 2001. As incomes have risen, service industries such as health, education, financial, and recreation have grown dramatically.

services
intangible items of value provided to consumers, such as education

INVESTMENT (*I*)

Investment, as used by economists, refers to the creation of capital goods—inputs like machines and tools whose purpose is to produce other goods. This definition of investment deviates from the popular use of that term. It is common for people to say that they invested in stocks, meaning that they have traded money for a piece of paper, called a stock certificate, that says they own a share in some company. Such transactions are not investment as defined by economists (i.e., an increase in capital goods), even though they might provide the enterprises selling the stock the resources for new capital goods, which *would* be counted as investment by economists.

investment
the creation of capital goods to augment future production

There are two categories of investment purchases measured in the expenditures approach: fixed investment and inventory investment.

Fixed Investments

Fixed investments include all spending on capital goods—sometimes called **producer goods**—such as machinery, tools, and factory buildings. All of these goods increase future production capabilities. Residential construction is also included as an investment expenditure in GDP calculations. The construction of a house allows for a valuable consumer service—shelter—to be provided, and is thus considered an investment. Residential construction is the only part of investment that is tied directly to household expenditure decisions.

fixed investments
all new spending on capital goods by producers

producer goods
capital goods that increase future production capabilities

Inventory Investment

Inventory investment includes all purchases by businesses that add to their inventories—stocks of goods kept on hand by businesses to meet customer demands. Every business needs inventory and, other things equal, the greater the inventory, the greater the amount of goods and services that can be sold to a consumer in the future. Thus, inventories are considered a form of investment. Consider a grocery store. If the store expands and increases the quantity and variety of goods on its shelves, future sales can rise. An increase in inventories, then, is presumed to increase the firm's future sales, and this is why we say it is an investment.

inventory investment
purchases that add to the stocks of goods kept by the firm to meet consumer demand

How Stable Are Investment Expenditures?

In recent years, investment expenditures have generally been around 15 percent of gross domestic product. Investment spending is the most volatile category of GDP, however, and tends to fluctuate considerably with changing business conditions. When the economy is booming, investment purchases tend to increase dramatically. In downturns, the reverse

© EYEWIRE/GETTY ONE IMAGES

Did you know that the estimate of vehicle miles traveled for the year 2000 was 2.688 trillion miles? The Federal Highway Administration is working with its partners in the state transportation departments to improve the larger National Highway System (NHS) of 160,000 miles. The Federal-Aid Highway Program, begun in 1916, operates today with a budget of nearly $30 billion a year and is linked closely to the federal transit program.

happens. In the first year of the Great Depression, investment purchases declined by 37 percent. U.S. expenditures on capital goods have been a smaller proportion of GDP in most recent years than in many other developed nations. This fact worries some people who are concerned about U.S. GDP growth compared to other countries, because investment in capital goods is directly tied to a nation's future production capabilities.

GOVERNMENT PURCHASES IN GDP (*G*)

The part of government purchases that is included in GDP is expenditures on goods and services. For example, the government must pay the salaries of its employees, and it must also make payments to the private firms with which it contracts to provide various goods and services, such as highway construction companies and weapons manufacturers. All of these payments would be included in GDP. However, transfer payments are not included in government purchases, because that spending does not go to purchase newly produced goods or services, but is merely a transfer of income among that country's citizens (which is why such expenditures are called transfer payments). The government purchase proportion of GDP has grown rapidly over the last 30 years.

EXPORTS (*X* − *M*)

Some of the goods and services that are produced in the United States are exported for use in other countries. The fact that these goods and services were made in the United States means that they should be included in a measure of U.S. production. Thus, we include the value of exports when calculating GDP. At the same time, however, some of our expenditures in other categories (consumption and investment in particular) were for foreign-produced goods and services. These imports must be excluded from GDP in order to obtain an accurate measure of American production. Thus, GDP calculations measure net exports, which equals total exports (X) minus total imports (M). Net exports are a small proportion of GDP and are often negative for the United States.

Section Check

1. The expenditure approach to measuring GDP involves adding up the purchases of final goods and services by market participants.
2. Four categories of spending are used in the GDP calculation: consumption (*C*), investment (*I*), government purchases (*G*), and net exports (*X* − *M*).
3. Consumption includes spending on nondurable consumer goods, tangible items that are usually consumed in a short period of time; durable consumer goods, longer-lived consumer goods; and services, intangible items of value that do not involve physical production.
4. Fixed investment includes all spending on capital goods, such as machinery, tools, and buildings. Inventory investment includes the net expenditures by businesses to increase their inventories.
5. Purchases of goods and services are the only part of government spending included in GDP. Transfer payments are not included in these calculations, because that spending is not a payment for a newly produced good or service.
6. Net exports are calculated by subtracting total imports from total exports.

---

1. What would happen to GDP if consumption purchases (*C*) and net exports (*X* − *M*) both rose, holding other things equal?
2. Why do you think economic forecasters focus so much on consumption purchases and their determinants?
3. Why are durable goods purchases more unstable than nondurable goods purchases?
4. Why does the investment component of GDP include purchases of new capital goods but not purchases of corporate stock?
5. If Mary received a welfare check this year, would that transfer payment be included in this year's GDP? Why or why not?
6. Could inventory investment or net exports ever be negative?

section 12.3

The Income Approach to Measuring GDP

- How is national income calculated?
- What are factor payments?
- What does personal income measure?

THE INCOME APPROACH TO MEASURING GDP

In the last section, we outlined the expenditure approach to GDP calculation. There is, however, also an alternative method called the **income approach.** This approach involves summing the incomes received by producers of goods and services.

income approach
calculation of GDP based on the summation of incomes received by the owners of resources used in the production of goods and services

When someone makes an expenditure for a good or service, that spending creates income for someone else. For example, if you buy $10 in groceries at the local supermarket, your $10 in spending creates $10 in income for the grocery store owner. The owner, then, must buy more goods to stock her shelves as a consequence of your consumer purchases; in addition, she must pay her employees, her electricity bill, and so on. Consequently, much of the $10 spent by you will eventually end up in the hands of someone other than the grocer. The basic point, however, is that someone (one person or many) receives the $10 you spent, and that receipt of funds is called income. Therefore, by adding up all of the incomes received by producers of goods and services, we can also calculate the gross domestic product, because output creates income of equal value.

FACTOR PAYMENTS

factor payments
wages (salaries), rent, interest payments, and profits paid to the owners of productive resources

gross national product (GNP)
the difference between net income of foreigners and GDP

depreciation
annual allowances set aside to replace worn-out capital

net national product (NNP)
GNP minus depreciation

indirect business taxes
taxes, such as sales tax, that are levied on goods and services sold

national income (NI)
a measure of income earned by owners of the factors of production

Incomes received by people providing goods and services are actually payments to the owners of productive resources. These payments are sometimes called **factor payments.** Factor payments include wages for the use of labor services, rent for land, payments for the use of capital goods in the form of interest, and profits for entrepreneurs who put labor, land, and capital together. However, before we can measure income we must make three adjustments to GDP. First, we must look at the net income of foreigners—the income earned abroad by U.S. firms or citizens minus the income earned by foreign firms or citizens in the United States. This difference between net income of foreigners and GDP is called **gross national product (GNP).** In the United States, the difference between GDP and GNP is small because net income of foreigners is a small percentage of GDP.

The second adjustment we make to find national income is to deduct depreciation from GNP. **Depreciation** payments are annual allowances set aside for the replacement of worn-out plant and equipment. After we have subtracted depreciation, we have **net national product (NNP).**

The final adjustment is to subtract **indirect business taxes.** The best example of an indirect business tax is a sales tax. For example, a compact disc may cost $14.95 plus a tax of $1.20, for a total of $16.15. The retail distributor (record store), record producer, and others will share $14.95 in proceeds, even though the actual equilibrium price is $16.15. In other words, the output (compact disc) is valued at $16.15, even though recipients only get $14.95 in income. Besides sales taxes, other important indirect business taxes include excise taxes (e.g., taxes on cigarettes, automobiles, and liquor) and gasoline taxes.

Now we can measure **national income (NI),** which is a measure of the income earned by owners of resources—factor payments. Accordingly, national income includes payments for labor services (wages, salaries, and fringe benefits), for use of land and buildings (rent), money lent to finance economic activity (interest), and payments for use of capital resources (profits). In Exhibit 1, the five primary categories of national income are presented with their proportions of national income: employee compensation, proprietor's income (self-employed business owners), rents, interest income, and corporate profits.

In Exhibit 2, we see the circular flow of income and expenditures. People earn income from producing goods and services (aggregate income) and then spend on goods and services (aggregate expenditures), $C + I + G + (X - M)$. The main point is that buyers have sellers—that is, aggregate expenditures are equal to aggregate income.

section 12.3 Exhibit 1 National Income, by Type of Income

	Amount (billions of current dollars)	Percent of Total
National income	$8165	
Employee compensation	5854	71%
Proprietor's income	726	9
Rents	138	2
Interest income	578	7
Corporate profits	869	11

SOURCE: U.S. Bureau of Economic Analysis, *Survey of Current Business*.

PERSONAL INCOME AND DISPOSABLE PERSONAL INCOME

Often, we are interested in the income people *receive* rather than the income they *earn,* because the income re-

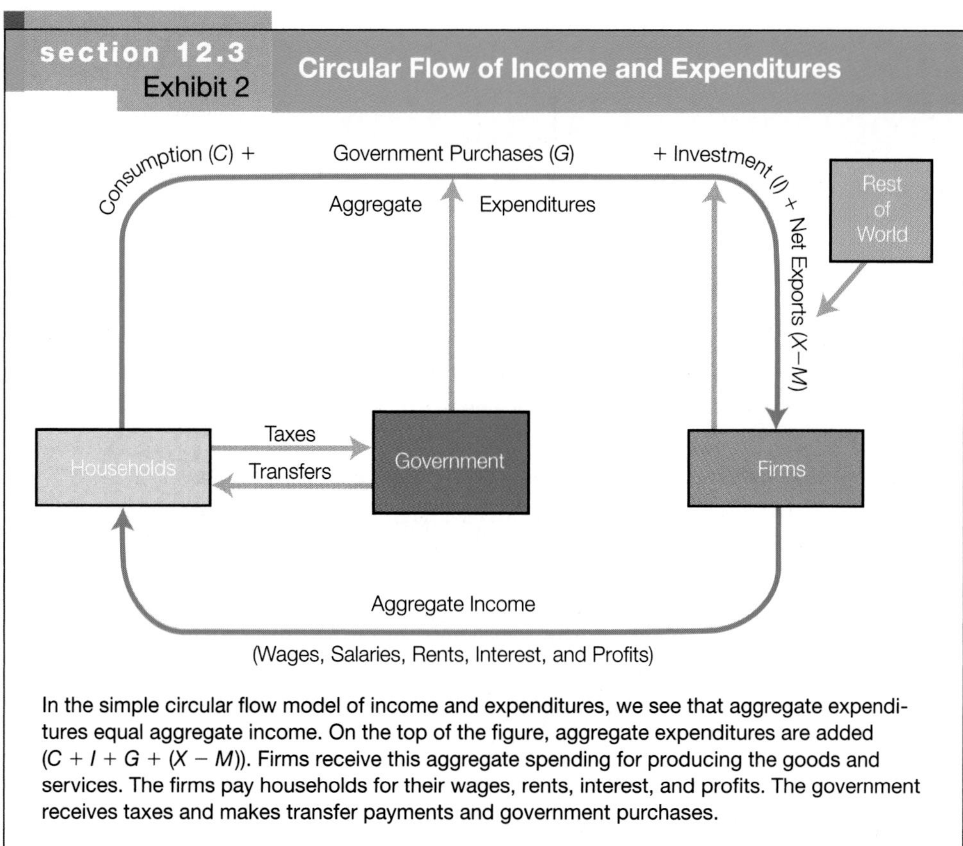

In the simple circular flow model of income and expenditures, we see that aggregate expenditures equal aggregate income. On the top of the figure, aggregate expenditures are added ($C + I + G + (X - M)$). Firms receive this aggregate spending for producing the goods and services. The firms pay households for their wages, rents, interest, and profits. The government receives taxes and makes transfer payments and government purchases.

ceived reflects the total amount available for spending before taxes. **Personal income (PI)** measures the amount of income received by households (including transfer payments) before income taxes. **Disposable personal income** is the personal income available to individuals after taxes.

personal income (PI)
the amount of income received by households before personal taxes

disposable personal income
the personal income available after personal taxes

Section Check

1. The income approach to measuring GDP involves summing the incomes received by the producers of goods and services. These payments to the owners of productive resources are also known as factor payments.
2. To find national income we must subtract from GDP: (1) indirect business taxes, such as sales taxes, and (2) depreciation, payments set aside for the replacement of worn-out capital, and (3) net income of foreigners in the United States.
3. National income (NI) is measured by adding together the payments to the factors of production—wages, rent, interest, and profit.
4. Personal income (PI) measures the amount of income received by households (including transfer payments) before personal taxes.
5. Disposable personal income is the personal income available after personal taxes.

---

1. Why should we expect the total expenditures that go into GDP to equal total income in an economy?
2. What two nonincome expense items does the income approach take into consideration?
3. How is personal income different from national income?

section 12.4

Problems in Calculating an Accurate GDP

- What are the problems with GDP in measuring output?
- What is the purpose of a price level index?
- What inherent problems exist with a price level index?
- What is per capita GDP?

PROBLEMS IN CALCULATING AN ACCURATE GDP

The primary problem in calculating accurate GDP statistics becomes evident when attempts are made to compare the GDP over time. Between 1970 and 1978, a period of relatively high inflation, GDP in the United States rose over 100 percent. What great progress! Unfortunately, however, the "yardstick" used in adding together the values of different products, the U.S. dollar, also changed in value over this time period. A dollar in 1979, for example, would certainly not buy as much as a dollar in 1970, because the *overall* price level for goods and services increased.

HOW DO WE SOLVE THIS PROBLEM?

One solution to this problem would be to use physical units of output—which, unlike the dollar, don't change in value from year to year—as our measure of total economic activity. The major problem with this approach is that different products have different units of measurement. How do you add together tons of steel, bushels of wheat, kilowatts of electricity, gallons of paint, cubic feet of natural gas, miles of air passenger travel, number of games of bowling, and number of magazines sold? In order to compare GDP values over time, a common or standardized unit of measure, which only money can provide, must be used in the calculations.

A PRICE LEVEL INDEX

price index
a measurement that attempts to provide a measure of the trend in prices paid for a certain bundle of goods and services over a given period

consumer price index (CPI)
provides a measure of the trend in prices of a basket of consumable goods and services that serves to gauge inflation

GDP deflator
a price index that helps to measure the average price level of all final consumer goods and services produced

The dollar, then, is the yardstick of value that we can use to correct the inflation-induced distortion of the GDP. We must adjust for the changing purchasing power of the dollar by constructing a **price index.** Essentially, a price index attempts to provide a measure of the trend in prices paid for a certain bundle of goods and services over time. The price index can be used to deflate the nominal or current dollar GDP values to a real GDP expressed in dollars of constant purchasing power.

THE CONSUMER PRICE INDEX (CPI) AND THE GDP DEFLATOR

There are many different types of price indices. The most well-known index, the **consumer price index (CPI),** measures the trend in the prices of certain goods and services purchased for consumption purposes. The CPI may be most relevant to households trying to evaluate their changing financial position over time.

The **GDP deflator** corrects GDP statistics for changing prices in even broader terms. The GDP deflator measures the average level of prices of all final goods and services produced in the economy.

In The NEWS

THE BOX-OFFICE LEADERS

Everyone knows that *Titanic* is one of the biggest box-office hits of all time. But where would it rank if the grosses of old-time releases were adjusted for inflation?

	All-Time Leaders		Gross Receipts	Inflation-Adjusted Gross Receipts
1	*Gone With the Wind* (MGM)*	1939	$198,654,225	$1,001,690,000
2	*Star Wars* (Fox)*	1977	$460,987,469	$865,910,000
3	*The Sound of Music* (Fox)	1965	$158,671,368	$694,990,000
4	*E.T.* (Univ)*	1982	$399,804,539	$654,360,000
5	*Titanic* (Para)	1997	$600,743,440	$639,830,000
6	*The Ten Commandments* (Para)	1956	$65,500,000	$639,320,000
7	*Jaws* (Univ)	1975	$260,000,000	$625,050,000
8	*Doctor Zhivago* (MGM)	1965	$111,721,910	$590,960,000
9	*The Jungle Book* (BV)*	1967	$141,800,000	$528,650,000
10	*Snow White and the Seven Dwarfs* (RKO/BV)*	1937	$184,925,486	$518,850,000

*Gross totals include reissues, which will affect gross receipts.

SOURCE: stats-a-mania at http://www.teako170.com/inflation.html. Used with permission from www.teako170.com.

HOW IS A PRICE INDEX CREATED?

Constructing a price index is complicated. To begin with, there are literally thousands of goods and services in our economy; attempting to include all of them in an index would be cumbersome, make the index expensive to compute, and would take a long period of time to gather necessary price data. Therefore, a "bundle" or "basket" of representative goods and services is selected by the index calculators (the Bureau of Labor Statistics of the U.S. Department of Labor for consumer and wholesale price indices; the Office of Business Economics of the Department of Commerce for the GDP deflator).

According to the Bureau of Labor Statistics, the CPI is based on prices of food, clothing, shelter, and fuels, transportation fares, charges for doctors' and dentists' services, drugs, and other goods and services that people buy for day-to-day living. Prices are collected in 87 urban areas across the country from about 50,000 housing units and approximately 23,000 retail establishments—department stores, supermarkets, hospitals, filling stations, and other types of stores and service establishments.

Calculating a Simple Price Index

Suppose a consumer typically buys 24 loaves of bread and 12 gallons of milk in a year. The following table indicates the prices of bread and milk and the cost of the consumer's typical market basket in the years 2001 to 2003. Using the numbers from the table and the following formula, we can calculate a price index to measure the inflation rate.

$$\text{Price Index} = \frac{\text{cost of market basket in current year}}{\text{cost of market basket in base year}} \times 100$$

Year	Price of Bread	Price of Milk	Cost of Market Basket
2001	$1.00	$2.00	(24 × $1.00) + (12 × $2.00) = $48.00
2002	1.15	2.10	(24 × 1.15) + (12 × 2.10) = 52.80
2003	1.40	2.20	(24 × 1.40) + (12 × 2.20) = 60.00

The year 2001 is designated as the base year, so its value is arbitrarily set equal to 100.

Year	Price Index
2001	$48/$48 × 100 = 100
2002	$52.80/$48 × 100 = 110
2003	$60/$48 × 100 = 125

A comparison of the price indices shows that between 2001 and 2002, prices increased an average of 10 percent (110 − 100). In addition, between 2001 and 2003, 25 percent inflation occured (125 − 100).

$$\text{Price Index} = \frac{\text{cost of market basket in 2003}}{\text{cost of market basket in 2001 (base year)}} \times 100 = \frac{\$60}{\$48} \times 100 = 125$$

That is, the price index for 2003 compared to 2001 is 125. So using our price index formula we can say that prices are 25 percent higher in 2003 than they were in 2001, the base year.

Unfortunately for our ability to calculate inflation, not all prices move by the same amount or in the same direction, so an average of the many price changes must be calculated. This is complicated by several factors. First, goods and services change in quality over time, so the observed price change may, in reality, reflect a quality change in the product rather than the purchasing power of the dollar. A $300 television set today is dramatically better than a television set in 1950. Second, new products come on the market and occasionally old products disappear. For example, color TV sets did not exist in 1950 but are a major consumer item now. How do you calculate changes in prices over time when some products did not even exist in the earlier period?

Clearly, calculating a price index is not a simple, direct process. As you can see from the *In the News* article (p. 284), many factors can potentially distort the CPI.

REAL GDP

Once the price index has been calculated, the actual procedure for adjusting nominal, or current dollar, GDP to get real GDP is not complicated. For convenience, an index number of 100 is assigned to some base year. The base year is arbitrarily chosen—it can be any year.

The formula for converting any year's nominal GDP into real GDP (in base year dollars) is as follows:

$$\text{Real GDP} = \frac{\text{Nominal GDP}}{\text{Price level index}} \times 100$$

Say the GDP deflator (price level index) was expressed in terms of 1996 prices (1996 = 100), and the index figure for 2002 was 115. This means that prices were 15 percent higher in 2002 than they were in 1996. Now, in order to correct the 2002 nominal GDP, we take the nominal GDP figure for 2002, suppose it is $10,000 billion, and divide it by the price level index, 115, which results in a quotient of $86.95 billion. We then multiply this number by 100, giving us $8,695 billion, which is the 2002 GDP in 1996 dollars (that is, 2002 real GDP, in terms of a 1996 base year).

APPLICATION

BABE RUTH'S SALARY ADJUSTED FOR INFLATION

Q: To many baseball purists Babe Ruth was the greatest player of the game, but how did his salary compare with the highest salary in baseball today? When Babe Ruth made $80,000 a year in 1931, he was asked by the press if he knew that his salary exceeded that of President Herbert Hoover. Ruth said, "Yes, I know. But I had a better year than President Hoover did." By the beginning of the 2001 season, Alex Rodriguez, the shortstop for the Texas Rangers, was the highest paid major league baseball player—at an annual salary of $22 million. Now let us compare the two figures by adjusting Ruth's salary to 2001 dollars.

A: The Bureau of Labor Statistics computes CPI all the way back to 1913. The average CPI for the year of 1931, when Babe Ruth made $80,000, was 15.2. The average CPI for the year 2001 was 177. We can simply convert the Babe's salary into current dollars by performing the following:

$$\text{Babe's salary in 1931} \quad \$80{,}000 \times \frac{\text{Price level in 2001}}{\text{Price level in 1931}}$$

$$= \$80{,}000 \times \frac{177}{15.2} = \$931{,}578$$

So the Babe would be making $931,578 a year. Not bad, but not even close to the stars of the game today. At $22 million, Alex Rodriguez would be making roughly 24 times Babe's salary.

LEFT PHOTO: © AP PHOTO, RIGHT PHOTO: © AP PHOTO/JIM MONE

How much more would Alex Rodriguez of the Texas Rangers make than the Sultan of Swat (Babe Ruth) if we adjusted for inflation?

IS REAL GDP ALWAYS LESS THAN NOMINAL GDP?

In modern times, inflation has been prevalent. For many readers of this book, the price level (as measured by the consumer price index) has risen in every single year of their lifetimes, because the last year of a declining price level was 1955. Therefore, the adjustment of nominal (money) GDP to real GDP will tend to reduce the growth in GDP suggested by nominal GDP figures. Given the distortions introduced by inflation, most news reports about GDP today speak of real GDP changes, although this is not always made explicit.

In The NEWS

A BETTER CPI

BY ALISON WALLACE AND BRIAN MOTLEY

The monthly consumer price index (CPI) is the most oft-cited measure of inflation and one of the most important and closely watched statistics in the U.S. economy. It is an indicator of how well the Federal Reserve is doing in achieving and maintaining low inflation, and it also is used to determine cost-of-living adjustments for many government programs, collective bargaining contracts, and individual income tax brackets.

Since 1995, the Bureau of Labor Statistics (BLS) has been eliminating biases that cause the index to overstate inflation, and further changes will come in January 1999. These changes are expected to create a more reliable index and by 1999 will have lowered measured CPI inflation by more than half a percentage point. Although this may seem like a small change, the effect of these changes is permanent so that measured inflation will be lower by this amount in all future years.

It is important that the CPI should measure inflation accurately or that the degree of bias be known. Macroeconomic policymakers such as the Fed then can take appropriate steps to keep inflation low, and the public can be informed about their successes and failures in achieving their goal. Also, if the CPI does not measure inflation correctly, cost-of-living adjustments based on it will have different effects from those desired when the commitments to make these adjustments were made. For example, adjusting Social Security benefits based on an upwardly biased CPI may shift spending power from the young toward the old.

The BLS has been studying possible biases in the CPI for a long time. The issue gained national prominence in 1996 when the Congress commissioned a panel of experts on price measurement issues, chaired by Michael Boskin of Stanford University, to examine biases in the CPI. Their report, "Toward a More Accurate Measure of the Cost of Living," identified four major sources of bias and estimated that they caused the CPI to overstate inflation by 1.1 percentage points per year at that time.

Substitution Bias. Substitution bias occurs because the CPI measures the price changes of a fixed basket of goods and services and thus does not capture the savings that households enjoy when they change their spending in response to relative price changes of goods and services. For example, a rise in the price of beef leads people to buy more chicken in order to keep their food costs down. . . .

COURTESY OF ROBERT SEXTON

If people prefer buying in bulk at discount stores, will the CPI accurately measure inflation? The success of discount stores has grown over the last few years, indicating that for some customers the reduction in customer service often associated with these megastores does not offset the lower prices, introducing an upward bias into the index. One estimate suggests that this bias raises the CPI by 0.1 percentage point a year.

IN THE NEWS *(continued)*

Outlet Bias. This type of bias is similar to substitution bias, but refers to *where* households shop rather than to *what* they purchase. Over the past 15 years, for example, the growth of discount stores has helped consumers lower their expenditures by offering high-volume purchases at reduced prices. The expansion of these establishments has not been adequately represented in the CPI, thus creating an upward bias of prices estimated at 0.1 percentage point per year. A similar problem may arise in the future as shopping online becomes more widespread.

New Product Bias. This bias occurs because new products, such as VCRs and cellular phones, are not introduced into the index until they are commonplace items. This means that the substantial price decreases and quality increases that occur during the early years following introduction are not captured by the index. A problem of dealing with this bias is that the BLS can never know in advance which of the many new products introduced each year will be successful and hence worthy of inclusion in the CPI.

Quality Bias. This bias arises because some of any increase in the price of an item may be due to an improvement in quality, rather than being a pure price increase. For example, when car prices rise, this may be due to the addition of seat belts, air bags, or anti-smog devices, or to pure price inflation. In the case of cars, the BLS often uses the price of the new item as an optional feature before it becomes standard equipment as an indicator of what the improvement is worth to consumers. Quality improvements in other areas—such as medical care—are more difficult to measure so that bias is more likely to occur. And features of a product that become mandatory—such as seat belts, which buyers are forced to purchase even if they would prefer not to—are particularly difficult to handle.

The BLS began to address the bias in the CPI even before the Boskin Commission was convened. For example, in 1995 the BLS introduced a new sampling procedure to determine which outlets to visit to obtain price data for specific items and what weights to apply to those item prices. The old procedure put too much weight on items that were temporarily cheap at that outlet, so when their prices rose back to their normal level, this registered as an increase in inflation. That same year, the BLS also revised sampling methods to remove the effects of substituting between brand drugs and generic drugs. . . . Spurred by the work of the Boskin Commission, the BLS introduced further changes to confront substitution and outlet bias.

Since the Fed uses the CPI as an indicator of price inflation, a more accurate index should make anti-inflationary monetary policy more effective. The public will have a better indicator to check how well the Fed is doing its job. If we want our tax and transfer system to be invariant to inflation, an accurate CPI is essential so that the task of adjusting tax and transfer payments to price changes can be done quickly, easily, and without undue dispute.

Ongoing research is necessary to identify biases in the CPI. Changes to this index are inevitable as the BLS strives to maintain an accurate measure of inflation in our dynamic economy. By 1999, about half of the bias identified by the Boskin Commission will have been removed. Although the changes may be inconvenient—because they make the current index less comparable with the past index—they will lead to an improved measure of actual inflation and, thus, a better CPI.

SOURCE: Alison Wallace and Brian Motley, *Economic Letter,* "A Better CPI," The Federal Reserve Bank of San Francisco, February 5, 1999 http://www.frbsf.org. Reprinted from the Federal Reserve Bank of San Francisco Economic Letter. The opinions expressed in this article do not necessarily reflect the views of the management of the Federal Reserve Bank of San Francisco, or of the Board of Governors of the Federal Reserve System.

REAL GDP PER CAPITA

The measure of economic well-being, or standard of living, most often used is **real gross domestic product per capita.** We use a measure of real GDP for reasons already cited. To calculate real GDP per capita, we divide the real GDP by the total population to get the value of real output of final goods and services per person. *Ceteris paribus,* people prefer more goods to fewer, so a higher GDP per capita would seemingly make people better off, improving their standard of living. Economic growth, then, is usually considered to have occurred anytime the real GDP per capita has risen. In Exhibit 1, we see that in the United States the real gross domestic per capita has grown sharply from 1958 to 2002. Real GDP per capita is almost three times larger in 2002 than it was in 1958. However, the growth in real GDP per capita is not steady, as seen by the shaded areas that represent recessions in Exhibit 1. Falling real GDP per capita can bring on many human hardships like rising unemployment, lower profits, stock market losses, and bankruptcies.

real gross domestic product per capita
real output of goods and services per person

section 12.5
Exhibit 1

U.S. Real Gross Domestic Product Per Capita

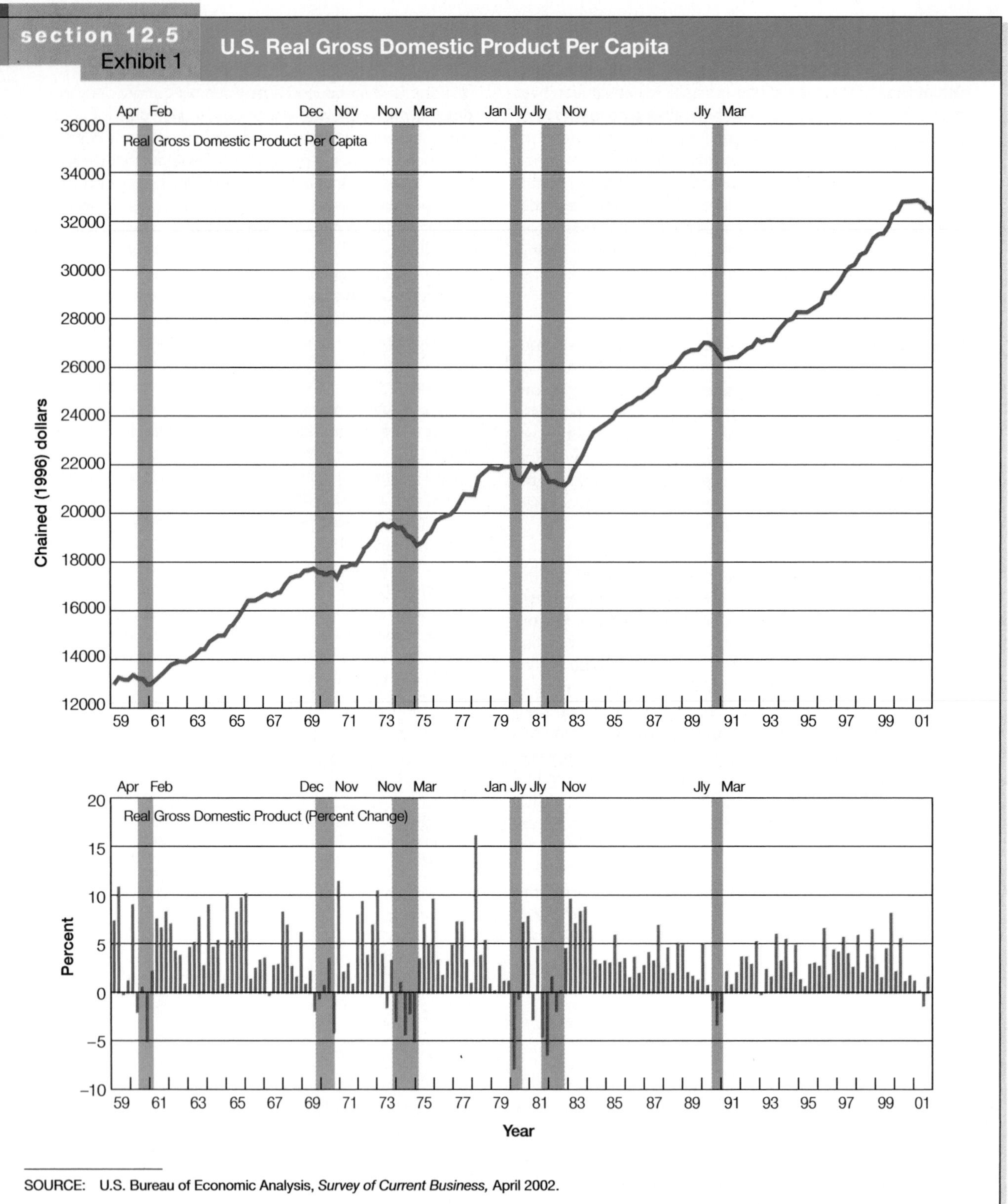

SOURCE: U.S. Bureau of Economic Analysis, *Survey of Current Business,* April 2002.

WHY IS THE MEASURE OF PER CAPITA GDP SO IMPORTANT?

Because one purpose of using GDP as a crude welfare measure is to relate output to human desires, we need to adjust for population change. If we do not take population growth into account, we can be misled by changes in real GDP values. For example, in some less-developed countries in some time periods, real GDP has risen perhaps 2 percent a year but the population has grown just as fast. In these cases, the real output of goods and services per person has remained virtually unchanged, but this would not be apparent in an examination of real GDP trends alone.

Section Check

1. It is difficult to compare real GDP over time because of the changing value of money over time.
2. A price index allows us to compare prices paid for goods and services over time by creating a measure of how many dollars it would take to maintain a constant purchasing power over time. The consumer price index (CPI) is the most well-known index.
3. The GDP deflator is a price index that measures the average level of prices of all final goods and services produced in the economy.
4. The consumer price index fails to account for increased quality of goods, introduction of new goods, or changes in the relative quantities of goods purchased.
5. Per capita GDP is real output of goods and services per person. In some cases, real GDP may increase, but per capita GDP may actually drop as a result of population growth.

---

1. If we overestimated inflation over time, would our calculations of real GDP growth likely be over- or underestimated?
2. Why does the consumer price index tend to overstate inflation if the quality of goods and services is rising over time?
3. Why would the growth in real GDP overstate the growth of output per person in a country with a growing population?
4. Why doesn't the consumer price index accurately adjust for the cost-of-living effects of a tripling in the price of bananas relative to the prices of other fruits?

section 12.5

Problems with GDP as a Measure of Economic Welfare

- What are some of the deficiencies of GDP as a measure of economic welfare?
- What are nonmarket transactions?
- What is the underground economy?

As we have noted throughout this chapter, real GDP is often used as a measure of the economic welfare of a nation. The accuracy of this measure for that purpose is, however, questionable, because several important factors are excluded from its calculations. These

Are her household production efforts included in GDP? Some estimate that nonmarket activities like household and family work account for roughly 20 percent of GDP. If a family hires someone to clean the house, provide child-care, mow the lawn, or cook, this is included in GDP; when members of the household provide these services, it is not. Neglecting household production in GDP distorts measurements of economic growth and leads to potential policy problems. Is it time to include household activities in GDP? An estimate of the value of these services could be obtained by calculating the cost to buy these services in the marketplace.

factors include nonmarket transactions, the underground economy, leisure, externalities, and the quality of the goods purchased.

NONMARKET TRANSACTIONS

Nonmarket transactions include the provision of goods and services outside of traditional markets for which no money is exchanged. We simply do not have reliable enough information on this output to include it in the GDP. The most important single nonmarket transaction omitted from the GDP is the services of housewives (or househusbands). These services are not sold in any market, so they are not entered into the GDP, but they are nonetheless performed. For example, if a single woman hires a tax accountant, those payments enter into the calculation of GDP. Suppose, though, that the woman marries her tax accountant. Now the woman no longer pays her husband for his accounting services. Reported GDP falls after the marriage, although output does not change.

In less-developed countries, where a significant amount of food and clothing output is produced in the home, the failure to include nonmarket economic activity in GDP is a serious deficiency. Even in the United States, homemade meals, housework, and the vegetables and flowers produced in home gardens are excluded, even though they clearly represent an output of goods and services.

THE UNDERGROUND ECONOMY

It is impossible to know for sure the magnitude of the underground economy, which includes unreported income from both legal and illegal sources. For example, illegal gambling and prostitution are not included in the GDP, leading to underreporting of an unknown dimension. The reason these activities are excluded, however, has nothing to do with the morality of the services performed, but rather results from the fact that most payments made for these services are neither reported to governmental authorities nor go through normal credit channels. Likewise, cash payments made to employees "under the table" slip through the GDP net. The estimates of the size of the underground economy vary from less than 4 percent to more than 20 percent of GDP. It also appears that a good portion of this unreported income comes from legal sources, such as self-employment.

MEASURING THE VALUE OF LEISURE

The value that individuals place on leisure is omitted in calculating GDP. Most of us could probably get a part-time job if we wanted to, earning some additional money by working in the evening or on weekends. Yet we choose not to do so. Why? The opportunity cost is too high—we would have to forgo some leisure. If you work on Saturday nights, you cannot see your friends, go to parties, see concerts, watch television, or go to the movies. The opportunity cost of the leisure is the income forgone by not working. For example, if people start taking more three-day weekends, GDP will surely fall, but can we necessarily say that the standard of living will fall? GDP will fall but economic well-being may rise.

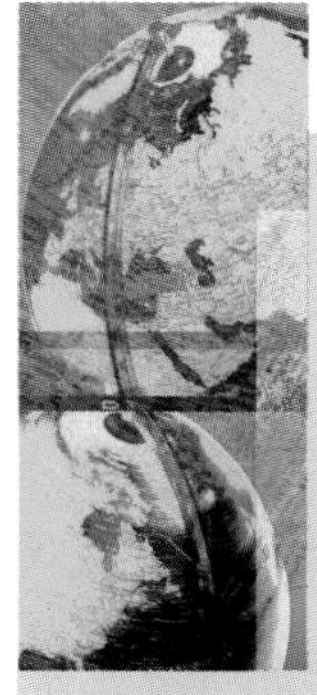

Global WATCH

GROWING UNDERGROUND

Underground economies are large and growing rapidly in most countries. High taxes and labor market regulations are the reasons why 17 percent of economic activity goes unreported in OECD countries, while corruption explains the large black market in some developing ones.

By definition, national income statistics capture economic activity reported by individuals and corporations. A large and growing portion of economic activity, however, goes unrecorded in most countries. This "underground" economy consists of legal activities that are concealed, mainly for reasons of tax evasion. Underground activity grew during the 1970s, when government became pervasive in national economies. As tax rates were raised to finance public spending programs, an increasing number of individuals risked dodging taxes. It is only since the 1980s that economists have attempted to estimate the size of underground economies. This is an inherently difficult task.

Nevertheless, it is important to estimate the size and growth of all economic activity, not only the reported kind. For one thing, cross-country comparisons of per capita income depend on it. By one account, Italy would be one of the richest European countries if its large black market were included alongside reported income. More importantly, GDP growth figures and unemployment rates may be severely distorted if a sudden increase in taxes pushes more people underground. Accurate statistics about overall economic activity and true unemployment are essential for effective economic policy decisions.

An article in the *Journal of Economic Literature* takes a closer look at the size, causes, and consequences of underground economies. Its authors, Friedrich Schneider of the University of Linz and Dominick Enste of the University of Cologne, claim that no cross-country comparison of underground economies has yet been undertaken. In their research, the authors compare the relative size of underground economies for 76 countries, and track their growth over time. They point out that even though estimates of underground economies are naturally inexact, economists generally agree that they are growing in most countries. Moreover, underground economies vary significantly in size, from a small fraction of "official" GDP (Switzerland), to nearly three-quarters of economic output (Nigeria, Egypt, and Thailand).

But first, what drives people underground? The authors argue that underground activity grows when tax rates rise. This is most noticeable in Scandinavian countries where governments have created some of the most generous public programs over the past few decades, and have consequently witnessed a substantial rise in their underground economies. This unsurprising claim is substantiated by the data. Norway, for example, has seen its underground economy grow from a negligible 1.5 percent of GNP in 1960 to a staggering 18 percent in 1995 (based on the currency demand approach). The high fiscal burden in other Scandinavian countries has led to a similar growth in their underground economies. In contrast, countries with relatively small public sectors—such as Switzerland and the United States—have developed much smaller underground markets.

The study shows that underground economies have grown in all OECD countries over the past few decades, representing an alarming 17 percent of reported GDP by 1997. In countries like Spain, Portugal, Italy, Belgium, and Greece, the estimated size of unreported economic activity stood at 22 to 30 percent. "In the European Union at least 20 million workers and in OECD countries about 35 million work in the unofficial economy. Moreover, the amount doubled within 20 years."

The authors find evidence that fewer regulations (that are properly enforced), lower tax rates, and a better rule of law lead to smaller underground economies, and consequently generate higher tax revenues. These factors are absent in many countries of Latin America, where underground economies amount to one-quarter to one-third of official GNP, and in the former Soviet Union, where underground economies stand at more than one-third of reported income.

SOURCE: Friedrich Schneider and Dominick H. Enste, "Shadow Economies: Size, Causes and Consequences," *Journal of Economic Literature*, March 2000 and *Economic Intuition,* Summer 2000.

Leisure, then, has a positive value that does not show up in the GDP accounts. To put leisure in the proper perspective, ask yourself if you would rather live in Country A, which has a per capita GDP of $25,000 a year and a 30-hour work week, or Country B, with a $25,000 per capita GDP and a 50-hour work week. Most would choose Country A. The problem that this omission in GDP poses can be fairly significant in international comparisons, or when one looks at one nation over time. Because the amount of leisure varies considerably, usually falling with rising GDP, it suggests an understatement of economic growth.

In The NEWS

AN INVALUABLE ENVIRONMENT

Environmentalists have long felt cross with the way governments measure national incomes and wealth. These figures for GDP, they point out, fail to value a country's environmental assets, such as fine public parks. They treat the use of natural capital differently from that of man-made capital: a country that depletes its stock of production equipment grows poorer, while one that chops down its forests appears to grow richer. And they treat the costs of cleaning up environmental damage as an addition to national income without subtracting the environmental loss caused by the damage in the first place.

© DOUG MENUEZ/PHOTODISC/GETTY ONE IMAGES

The answer might seem obvious: adjust national accounts to take account of changes in the environment. Statisticians have labored for more than a decade to find ways to do this. The difficulties of creating environmental statistics that are comparable to national income and wealth statistics are serious. GDP is measured in money, but putting monetary values on environmental assets is a black art. Some assets, such as timber, may have a market value, but that value does not encompass the trees' role in harboring rare beetles, say, or their sheer beauty. Methods for valuing such benefits are controversial. To get round these problems, the U.N. guidelines suggest measuring the cost of repairing environmental damage. But some kinds of damage, such as extinction, are beyond costing, and others are hard to estimate.

For economists, the average value of a good or service is usually less important than the marginal value—the cost or benefit of one more unit. Marginal value, however, is a tricky concept to bring into environmental analysis. It may be clear that the cost of wiping out an entire species of beetle would be high, but what value should be attached to the extermination of a few hundred bugs?

Putting environmental concepts into economic terms raises other difficulties as well. Geography weighs differently: a ton of sulphur dioxide emitted in a big city may cause more harm than the same ton emitted in a rural area, while a dollar's worth of output counts the same wherever it is produced. And the exploitation of natural resources may not always have a cost. Is a country depleting resources if it mines a ton of coal? All other things equal, the mining of that ton might raise the value of the coal that remains in the ground, leaving the value of coal assets unchanged.

SOURCE: "An Invaluable Environment", *The Economist*, April 18, 1998, p. 75. http://www.economist.com/displaystory.cfm?story_ID=160621. www.economist.com.

CONSIDER THIS:
GDP doesn't measure everything that contributes or detracts from our well-being; it is very difficult to measure the value of those effects. Environmentalists believe that national income accounts should adjust for changes in the environment. But this leads to many conceptual problems, such as measuring the marginal values of goods and services not sold in markets, and adjusting for geographical differences in environmental damage. The critical issue is whether there are important trends in "uncounted" goods and services that result in questionable conclusions about whether we are getting better or worse off.

GDP AND EXTERNALITIES

As we discussed in earlier chapters, positive and negative externalities can result from the production of some goods and services. As a result of these externalities, the equilibrium prices of these goods and services—the figure used in GDP calculations—does not reflect their true values to society (unless, of course, the externality has been internalized). For example, if a steel mill produces 100,000 more tons of steel, GDP increases; GDP does not, however, decrease to reflect damages from the air pollution that resulted from

In The NEWS

TIME WELL SPENT

BY W. MICHAEL COX AND RICHARD ALM

As America exits the twentieth century, we'd be hard-pressed to find a five and dime store. Penny candy now goes for a nickel or more. Five cents no longer buys a good cigar. Dime novels can't be found. Even a 3¢ stamp costs 32¢. Over the century, prices have gone up. The buying power of a dollar is down. We know this from statistical measures of inflation. We know it also from Grandpa's stories about paying 15¢ for a ticket to *Gone with the Wind* or 19¢ for a gallon of gasoline. Even a casual observer of the U.S. economy can see that the prices of milk, bread, houses, clothes, cars, and many other goods and services rise from year to year.

The cost of living is indeed going up—in money terms. What really matters, though, isn't what something costs in money; it's what it costs in time. Making money takes time, so when we shop, we're really spending time. The real cost of living isn't measured in dollars and cents but in the hours and minutes we must work to live. American essayist Henry David Thoreau (1817–62) noted this in his famous book, *Walden:* "The cost of a thing is the amount of . . . life which is required to be exchanged for it, immediately or in the long run."

The shortcoming of money prices is that they mean little apart from money wages. A pair of stockings cost just 25¢ a century ago. This sounds wonderful until we learn that a worker of the era earned only 14.8¢ an hour. So paying for the stockings took 1 hour 41 minutes of work. Today a better pair requires only about 18 minutes of work. Put another way, stockings cost an 1897 worker today's equivalent of $22, whereas now a worker pays only about $4. If modern Americans had to work as hard as their forebears did for everyday products, they'd be in a continual state of sticker shock—$67 scissors, $913 baby carriages, $2,222 bicycles, $1,202 telephones.

The best way to measure the cost of goods and services is in terms of a standard that doesn't change—time at work, or real prices. There's a regular pattern to real prices in our dynamic economy.

Americans come in all shapes and sizes. We differ in height and weight, gender, race, and age. We vary in talents, skills, education, experience, determination, and luck. Quite naturally, our paychecks differ, too. Some of us scrape by at minimum wage, while movie stars, corporate chieftains, and athletes sometimes make millions of dollars a year.

Calculations of the work time needed to buy goods and services use the average hourly wage for production and nonsupervisory workers in manufacturing. A century ago this figure was less than 15¢ an hour. By 1997 it had hit a record $13.18, a livable wage, but nothing worthy of Lifestyles of the Rich and Famous. What's most important about this wage is that it roughly represents what's earned by the great bulk of American society.

In calculating our cost of living, a good place to start is with the basics—food, shelter, and clothing. In terms of time on the job, the cost of a half-gallon of milk fell from 39 minutes in 1919 to 16 minutes in 1950, 10 minutes in 1975 and 7 minutes in 1997. A pound of ground beef steadily declined from 30 minutes in 1919 to 23 minutes in 1950, 11 minutes in 1975 and 6 minutes in 1997. Paying for a dozen oranges required 1 hour 8 minutes of work in 1919. Now it takes less than 10 minutes, half what it did in 1950. The money price of a 3-pound fryer chicken rose from $1.23 in 1919 to $3.15 in 1997, but its cost in work time fell from 2 hours 37 minutes to just 14 minutes. A sample of a dozen food staples—a market basket broad enough to provide three squares a day—shows that what required 9.5 hours to buy in 1919 and 3.5 hours in 1950 now takes only 1.6 hours.

SOURCE: W. Michael Cox and Richard Alm, *1997 Annual Report: Time Well Spent,* Federal Reserve Bank of Dallas. Reprinted with permission.

CONSIDER THIS:
According to Michael Cox and Richard Alm, the real cost of living as measured in the hours and minutes we must work to live is surely falling. That is, what does it cost to buy a particular good or service in terms of time on the job? Many goods like microwaves, cellular phones, and camcorders have fallen in money prices. This, coupled with higher wages and better quality, has been a real boon to the consumer.

the production of that additional steel. Likewise, additional production of a vaccine would be reflected in the GDP, but the positive benefit to society members other than the purchaser would not be included in the calculation. In other words, while GDP measures the goods and services produced, it does not adequately measure the "goods" and "bads" that result from the production processes.

QUALITY OF GOODS

GDP can also miss important changes in the improvements in the *quality* of goods and services. For example, there is a huge difference between the quality of a computer bought today and one that was bought ten years ago, but it will not lead to an increase in measured GDP. The same is true of many goods from cellular phones to automobiles to medical care.

Section Check

1. There are several factors that make it difficult to use GDP as a welfare indicator, including nonmarket transactions, the underground economy, leisure, and externalities.
2. Nonmarket transactions are the exchange of goods and services that do not occur in traditional markets, and so no money is exchanged.
3. The underground economy is the unreported production and income that come from legal and illegal activities.
4. The presence of positive and negative externalities makes it difficult to measure GDP accurately.

---

1. Why do GDP measures omit nonmarket transactions?
2. How would the existence of a high level of nonmarket activities in one country impact real GDP comparisons between it and other countries?
3. If we choose to decrease our hours worked because we value the additional leisure more, would the resulting change in real GDP accurately reflect the change in our well-being? Why or why not?
4. How do pollution and crime affect GDP? How do pollution- and crime-control expenditures impact GDP?

Summary

Gross domestic product (GDP) is the value of all final goods and services produced within a country during a given time period. Two different ways to measure GDP are the expenditure approach and the income approach. The expenditure approach to measuring GDP involves adding up the purchases of final goods and services by market participants. The four categories of spending used in the GDP calculation are consumption (C), investment (I), government purchases (G), and net exports ($X-M$).

The income approach to measuring GDP involves summing the incomes received by the producers of goods and services. These payments received by owners of productive resources are known as factor payments.

National income (NI) is measured by adding together the payments earned by the owners of the factors of production—wages, rent, interest, and profit. Personal income (PI) measures the amount of income *received* by households before personal taxes.

It is difficult to compare real GDP over time because of the changing value of money over time. A price index allows us to compare prices paid for goods and services over time by creating a measure of how many dollars it would take to maintain a constant purchasing power over time. The consumer price index (CPI) is the most well-known index. The GDP deflator is a price index that measures the average level of prices of all final goods and services produced in the economy. The consumer price index fails to fully account for increased quality in goods, introduction of new goods, or changes in the relative quantities of goods purchased.

Several factors make it difficult to use GDP as a welfare indicator, including nonmarket transactions, the underground economy, leisure, and externalities. Nonmarket transactions are the exchange of goods and services that do not occur in traditional markets, and so no money is exchanged. The underground economy is the unreported production and income that come from legal and illegal activities. Also, the presence of positive and negative externalities makes it difficult to measure GDP accurately.

Key Terms and Concepts

national income accounting 272
gross domestic product (GDP) 272
double counting 273
expenditure approach 273
consumption 274
nondurable goods 274
durable goods 274
services 275
investment 275
fixed investments 275
producer goods 275
inventory investment 276
income approach 277
factor payments 278
gross national product (GNP) 278
depreciation 278
net national product (NNP) 278
indirect business taxes 278
national income (NI) 278
personal income (PI) 279
disposable personal income 279
price index 280
consumer price index (CPI) 280
GDP deflator 280
real gross domestic product per capita 285

Review Questions

1. Which of the following are included in GDP calculations?
   a. cleaning services performed by Molly Maid corporation
   b. lawn mowing services performed by a neighborhood child
   c. drugs sold illegally on a local street corner
   d. prescription drugs manufactured in the U.S. and sold at a local pharmacy
   e. a rug woven by hand in Turkey
   f. air pollution that diminishes the quality of the air you breathe
   g. toxic waste cleanup performed by a local company
   h. car parts manufactured in the United States for assembly of a car in Mexico
   i. a purchase of 1,000 shares of IBM stock
   j. monthly Social Security payment received by a retiree
2. To which U.S. GDP expenditure category does each of the following correspond?
   a. Department of Motor Vehicles services
   b. automobiles exported to Europe
   c. a refrigerator
   d. a newly constructed four-bedroom house
   e. a restaurant meal
   f. additions to inventory at a furniture store
   g. F-16 fighter jets built by a U.S. aerospace corporation and contracted for by the government
   h. a new steel mill
3. The expenditures on tires by the Ford Motor Company are not included directly in GDP statistics while consumer expenditures on replacement tires are included. Why?
4. Using any relevant information below, calculate GDP via the expenditure approach.

Inventory Investment	$50 billion
Fixed Investment	$120 billion
Consumer durables	$420 billion
Consumer nondurables	$275 billion
Interest	$140 billion
Indirect business taxes	$45 billion
Government wages and salaries	$300 billion
Government purchases of goods and services	$110 billion
Imports	$80 billion
Exports	$40 billion
Profits	$320 billion
Services	$600 billion

5. Nominal GDP in Nowhereland in 1999 and 2000 is as follows:

NGDP 1999	NGDP 2000
$4 trillion	$4.8 trillion

   Can you say that the production of goods and services in Nowhereland has increased between 1999 and 2000? Why or why not?
6. Calculate a price index for 2000, 2001, and 2002 using the following information about prices. Let the market basket consist of one pizza, two sodas, and

three video rentals. Let the year 2000 be the base year (with an index value of 100).

Year	Price of a Pizza	Price of a Soda	Price of a Video Rental
2000	$9.00	$0.50	$2.00
2001	$9.50	$0.53	$2.24
2002	$10.00	$0.65	$2.90

How much inflation occurred between 2000 and 2001? Between 2000 and 2002?

7. Calculate real GDP for the years 1996 to 2000 using the following information:

Year	Nominal GDP	Price Index	Real GDP
1996	$7,200 billion	100	
1997	$7,500 billion	102	
1998	$8,000 billion	110	
1999	$9,000 billion	114	
2000	$9,600 billion	120	

8. Evaluate the following statement: "Real GDP in the United States is higher than real GDP in Canada. Therefore the standard of living in the U.S. must be higher than in Canada."

9. Population and real GDP in Country A are as follows:

Year	Population	Real GDP
1980	1.25 million	$4,000 million
1990	1.6 million	$6,750 million
2000	1.8 million	$9,000 million

Calculate real GDP per capita in 1980, 1990, and 2000. Does real output per person increase or decrease over time?

10. Visit the Sexton Web site at **http://sexton.swcollege.com** and click on "Bureau of Economic Analysis" and locate the latest estimates of U.S. real GDP and the breakdown of expenditures on consumption (personal consumption expenditures), investment (gross private domestic investment), government (government consumption expenditures), and net exports.

In addition, look in the "Regional" section and locate the Real Gross State Production of your home state for the most recent year it is available.

chapter 12 Study Guide

Fill in the Blanks

1. ______________ accounting was created to provide a reliable, uniform method of measuring economic performance.

2. ______________ is defined as the value of all final goods and services produced in a country in a period of time, almost always one year.

3. A ______________ good or service is one that is ready for its designated ultimate use, in contrast to ______________ goods or services that are used in the production of other goods.

4. There are two primary ways of calculating economic output: the ______________ approach and the ______________ approach.

5. With the ______________ approach, GDP is calculated by adding up the expenditures of market participants on final goods and services over a period of time.

6. For analytical purposes, economists usually categorize expenditures into four categories: ______________, ______________, ______________, and ______________.

7. Consumption spending is usually broken down into three subcategories: ______________ goods, ______________ consumer goods, and ______________.

8. Consumption refers to the purchase of consumer goods and services by ______________.

9. The most important single category of consumer durable goods is consumer ______________.

10. Sales of nondurable consumer goods tend to be ______________ stable over time than sales of durable goods.

11. Investment, as used by economists, refers to the creation of ______________ goods whose purpose is to ______________.

12. The two categories of investment purchases measured in the expenditures approach are ______________ investment and ______________ investment.

13. When the economy is booming, investment purchases tend to ______________ dramatically.

14. ______________ payments are not included in government purchases because that spending does not go to purchase newly produced goods or services.

15. Imports must be ______________ from GDP in order to obtain an accurate measure of domestic production.

16. The ______________ approach to measuring GDP involves summing the incomes received by producers of goods and services.

17. Output creates ______________ of equal value.

18. Factor payments include ______________ for the use of labor services, ______________ for land, ______________ payments for the use of capital goods, and ______________ for entrepreneurs who put labor, land, and capital together.

19. The incomes received by persons providing goods and services are actually payments to the owners of ______________ resources and are sometimes called ______________ payments.

20. ____________ must be subtracted from gross domestic product to get net national product (NNP).

21. ____________ income is the personal income available to individuals after taxes.

22. We must adjust for the changing purchasing power of the dollar by constructing a price ____________.

23. The most well-known price index is the ____________, which provides a measure of the trend in the prices of goods and services purchased for consumption purposes.

24. The GDP deflator measures the average level of prices of all ____________ goods and services produced in the economy.

25. The CPI is the price index that is most relevant to ____________ trying to evaluate their changing financial position over time

26. A price index is equal to the cost of the chosen market basket in the ____________ year, divided by the cost of the same market basket in the ____________ year, times 100.

27. The formula for converting any year's nominal GDP into real GDP (in base year dollars) is real GDP equals ____________ divided by the ____________, times 100.

28. To calculate real per capita GDP, we divide ____________ GDP by the ____________ to get the value of real output of final goods and services per person.

29. We do not have ____________ enough information on the output of nonmarket transactions to include it in the GDP.

30. The most important nonmarket transactions omitted from GDP are services provided directly ____________.

31. The value that individuals place on leisure is ____________ in calculating GDP.

True or False

1. Measuring the performance of our economy is important to private businesses and to macroeconomic policy makers in setting goals and developing policy recommendations.

2. All goods and services exchanged in the current period are included in this year's GDP.

3. The value of a good or service is determined by the market prices at which goods and services sell.

4. If we counted the value of intermediate goods as well as the full value of the final products in GDP, we would be double counting.

5. Although the expenditure approach and the income approach differ, their result, GDP, is the same, apart from minor "statistical discrepancies."

6. Following the expenditure method, $GDP = C + I + G + X$.

7. The distinction between whether a good is durable or nondurable is clear and easy to apply.

8. In boom periods, expenditures on consumer durables often increase more than expenditures on nondurables.

9. As incomes have risen, expenditures on services have been growing slower than expenditures on goods.

10. The share of total consumption going for services now exceeds 50 percent.

11. Purchases of stock are included as part of investment in the national income accounts.

12. Fixed investments include all spending on capital goods, as well as on residential construction.

13. Investment spending is the most volatile category of GDP.

14. Government expenditures on goods and services as a proportion of GDP have grown slowly over the last 30 years.

15. Because exports are consumed in other countries, they are omitted from measures of domestic GDP.

16. Net exports are a small proportion of GDP and are often negative for the United States.

17. When someone makes an expenditure for a good or service, that spending creates income for someone else.

18. The net income of foreigners must be subtracted from GDP to get GNP.

19. National income is a measure of the income earned by owners of resources and available for spending after taxes.

20. The primary problem in calculating accurate U.S. GDP statistics is that the "yardstick" used in adding together the values of different products, the U.S. dollar, changes in value over time.

21. A price index can be used to deflate current dollar GDP to real GDP expressed in dollars of constant purchasing power.

22. The consumer price index measures the average level of prices of all final goods and services produced in the economy.

23. Our ability to accurately calculate inflation is complicated by changing qualities of goods and services over time and the creation of new products.

24. There are many factors that could potentially distort the CPI.

25. Nominal GDP equals real GDP divided by the price level index, times 100.

26. In periods of inflation, real GDP will tend to be greater than nominal GDP growth.

27. The measure of economic welfare most often cited is real per capita gross domestic product.

28. In a country with a growing population, real GDP per capita could be falling at the same time that real GDP was rising.

29. Nonmarket transactions, the underground economy, and the value of leisure are all omitted from official measures of GDP.

30. Real GDP is a highly accurate measure of the economic welfare of a nation.

31. Marrying one's housekeeper would leave reported GDP unchanged.

32. In less-developed countries, where a significant amount of food and clothing output is produced in the home, the failure to include nonmarket economic activity in GDP is a serious deficiency.

33. Almost all of the underground economy represents income from illegal sources, such as drug dealing.

34. GDP is decreased to reflect pollution resulting from production.

35. There are severe defects with real GDP as a welfare measure. Nonetheless, at the present time, there is no alternative measure that is generally accepted as better.

Multiple Choice

1. GDP is defined as the
- **a.** value of all final goods and services produced in a country in a period of time.
- **b.** value of all final goods produced in a country in a period of time.
- **c.** value of all goods and services produced in a country in a period of time.
- **d.** value of all final services produced in a country in a period of time.

2. GDP measures
- **a.** the value of all intermediate goods produced domestically within a given period.
- **b.** the value of all final goods and services sold in an economy within a given period.
- **c.** the value of all final goods and services produced domestically within a given period.
- **d.** the government's domestic product.

3. An example of an intermediate product is
- **a.** the purchase of tires by Ford Motor Company to put on its Ford Explorers.
- **b.** the purchase of wood by a home construction firm.
- **c.** the purchase of leather by a shoe manufacturer.
- **d.** All of the above are examples of intermediate products.

4. Which of the following is *not* included in the calculated gross domestic product?
- **a.** a new Ford Expedition sport-utility vehicle
- **b.** dinner at Burger King
- **c.** a construction firm's purchase of lumber to build a four-bedroom home
- **d.** the purchase of a newly constructed home

5. GDP is calculated including
- **a.** intermediate products but not final products.
- **b.** manufactured goods but not services.
- **c.** final products but not intermediate products.
- **d.** only goods purchased by consumers in a given year.

6. The expenditure measure of GDP accounting adds together
- **a.** consumption, interest, government purchases, and net exports.
- **b.** consumption, government purchases, wages and salaries, and net exports.
- **c.** consumption, investment, government purchases, and net exports.
- **d.** wages and salaries, rent, interest, and profit.
- **e.** wages and salaries, rent, investment, and profit.

7. Which category of consumption spending tends to be the most unstable over the business cycle?
   a. nondurable consumer goods
   b. durable consumer goods
   c. services
   d. All of these categories of consumer spending are highly unstable over the business cycle.

8. Which of the following are most likely classified by economists as consumer durable goods?
   a. stocks, bonds, EE savings bonds, CDs (certificates of deposit)
   b. automobiles, furniture, CD players
   c. drugs, toys, magazines, books
   d. food, clothing, shelter

9. Investment includes
   a. fixed investment.
   b. fixed investment plus government investment.
   c. fixed investment plus additions to business inventories.
   d. fixed investment plus subtractions from business inventories.
   e. fixed investment plus government investment plus additions to business inventories.

10. Included in the investment category under the expenditure approach to GDP accounting is (are)
    a. additions to inventory.
    b. machines and tools.
    c. newly constructed residential housing.
    d. all of the above.

11. Which of the following is *not* included in government purchases?
    a. government purchases of investment goods
    b. transfer payments
    c. government spending on services
    d. None of the above is included in government purchases.
    e. Neither b nor c is included in government purchases.

12. A negative amount of net exports in the GDP expenditures accounting means
    a. exports are less than imports.
    b. imports are less than exports.
    c. the sum of this period's exports and imports has declined from the previous period.
    d. net exports have declined from the previous period.
    e. none of the above.

13. We can be certain that net exports fall if
    a. both exports and imports rise.
    b. both exports and imports fall.
    c. exports rise and imports fall.
    d. exports fall and imports rise.
    e. either b or d occurs.

14. French perfume that is purchased in the United States is accounted for in which expenditure category of U.S. GDP?

a. consumption
b. investment
c. government purchases
d. net exports
e. none of the above

15. If the United States imported $1.5 billion worth of goods and services and sold $2.9 billion worth of goods and services outside its borders, net exports would equal

a. −$4.4 billion.
b. $4.4 billion.
c. $1.4 billion.
d. −$1.4 billion.
e. none of the above.

16. The largest category of GDP is ________, and the most unstable category of GDP is ________.

a. consumption, consumption
b. government, investment
c. consumption, investment
d. consumption, government purchases
e. investment, consumption

17. Which of the following will be counted as part of this year's U.S. GDP?

a. goods produced last year but not sold until this year
b. goods produced this year by an American working in Paris
c. purchases of Cisco Systems stock (not issued this year) that take place this March
d. sales of used lawn mowers that take place this year
e. none of the above

18. In the income approach to measuring GDP, factor payments do *not* include

a. wages and salaries for the use of labor services.
b. rent for land.
c. interest payments for the use of capital goods.
d. profits for entrepreneurs.
e. All of the above are included as factor payments.

19. Which of the following is *not* considered a factor payment?

a. wages
b. interest
c. rent
d. profit
e. transfer payments

20. What is *not* subtracted from GDP to get national income?

a. the net income of foreigners
b. depreciation
c. indirect business taxes
d. personal income taxes
e. All of the above are subtracted from GDP to get national income.

21. Disposable income is
   a. a measure of the market value of total output.
   b. a measure of the income households have to spend before paying taxes.
   c. a measure of the income households have to spend after paying taxes.
   d. a measure of household income from investment income, such as dividends and capital gains.

22. Disposable personal income will increase when
   a. taxes rise and transfer payments rise.
   b. taxes rise and transfer payments fall.
   c. taxes fall and transfer payments rise.
   d. taxes fall and transfer payments fall.

23. The CPI is a measure of
   a. the overall cost of goods and services produced in the economy.
   b. the overall cost of inputs purchased by a typical producer.
   c. the overall cost of goods and services bought by a typical consumer.
   d. the overall cost of stocks on the New York Stock Exchange.

24. If the consumer price index was 100 in the base year and 110 in the following year, the inflation rate was
   a. 110 percent.
   b. 100 percent.
   c. 11 percent.
   d. 10 percent.

25. The current cost of a market basket of goods is $6,000. The cost of the same basket of goods in the base year was $4,000. The current price index is
   a. 600.
   b. 160.
   c. 150.
   d. 133.
   e. 66.7.

26. The CPI overestimates changes in the cost of living because
   a. the growth of discount stores where consumers can obtain goods at discount prices has not been adequately represented in the construction of the CPI.
   b. the CPI does not adequately deal with changes in the quality of products over time.
   c. the CPI deals with a fixed market basket and doesn't capture the savings households enjoy when they substitute cheaper alternatives in response to a price change.
   d. of all of the above.

27. Nominal GDP is
   a. the base year market value of all final goods and services produced domestically during a given period.
   b. the current year market value of all final goods and services produced domestically during a given period.
   c. usually less than real GDP.
   d. the current year market value of domestic production of intermediate goods.
   e. none of the above.

28. Nominal GDP differs from real GDP in that
  a. nominal GDP tends to increase when total production of output in the economy increases, while real GDP does not.
  b. nominal GDP is measured in base year prices, while real GDP is measured in current year prices.
  c. nominal GDP is measured in current year prices, while real GDP is measured in base year prices.
  d. real GDP excludes taxes paid to the government, while nominal GDP does not.

29. The consumer price index
  a. takes government purchases into account, unlike the GDP deflator.
  b. takes business investment purchases into account, unlike the GDP deflator.
  c. equals 100 in the base year, unlike the GDP deflator.
  d. is generally used to adjust nominal GDP to calculate real GDP.
  e. None of the above is true.

30. Real GDP in base year dollars equals
  a. nominal GDP divided by the price index, times 100.
  b. nominal GDP divided by the price index.
  c. nominal GDP times the price index.
  d. nominal GDP times the price index, divided by 100.
  e. none of the above.

31. Suppose that nominal GDP in 2000 equals $8,000 trillion, and in 2001, nominal GDP equals $8,500 trillion. It can be concluded that
  a. total production of output decreased from 2000 to 2001.
  b. total production of output increased from 2000 to 2001.
  c. the economy experienced inflation from 2000 to 2001.
  d. the economy experienced deflation from 2000 to 2001.
  e. None of the above is true.

32. If real GDP increases and population increases, then real GDP per capita
  a. will rise.
  b. will fall.
  c. will remain unchanged.
  d. could either rise, fall, or remain unchanged.

33. If nominal GDP rises from $5 billion to $6 billion, when the GDP deflator goes from 100 to 120, real GDP
  a. rises.
  b. falls.
  c. stays the same.
  d. could either be rising or falling.

34. Important factors that are excluded from GDP measurements include
  a. leisure.
  b. the underground economy.
  c. nonmarket transactions.
  d. the value of changes in the environment.
  e. all of the above.

35. Which of the following is measured in per capita GDP?
  a. leisure
  b. underground economic transactions
  c. the services of homemakers
  d. external benefits and costs
  e. none of the above

36. If country A had a bigger underground economy than country B, and country A's citizens worked fewer hours per week than the citizens of country B, other things being equal, then
  a. GDP comparisons between the countries would overstate the economic welfare of country A compared to B.
  b. GDP comparisons between the countries would understate the economic welfare of country A compared to B.
  c. it is impossible to know which direction GDP comparisons between the countries would be biased as measures of the economic welfare of the two countries.
  d. it would not introduce any bias in using GDP to compare economic welfare between the countries.
  e. none of the above would be true.

Problems

1. Answer the following questions about GDP.
  a. What is the definition of GDP?
  b. Why does GDP measure only the final value of goods and services?
  c. Why does GDP measure only the value of goods and services produced within a country?
  d. How does GDP treat the sales of used goods?
  e. How does GDP treat sales of corporate stock from one stockholder to another?

2. Fill in the missing data for the following table (in billions).

Consumption: __________

Consumption of durable goods: $1,200

Consumption of nondurable goods: $1,800

Consumption of services: $2,400

Investment: __________

Fixed investment: $800

Inventory investment: $600

Government expenditures on goods and services: $1,600

Government transfer payments: $500

Exports: $500

Imports: $650

Net exports: __________

GDP: __________

3. Fill in the missing data for the following table.

Year	GDP deflator	Nominal GDP (in billions)	Real GDP (in billions)
1997	90.9	$7,000	______
1998	100	______	$8,000
1999	______	$10,000	$8,000
2000	140	$14,000	______
2001	150	______	$12,000

4. Say that the bundle of goods purchased by a typical consumer in the base year consisted of 20 gallons of milk, at a price of $1 per gallon, and 15 loaves of bread, at a price of $2 per loaf. What would the price index be in a year in which

a. milk cost $2 per gallon and bread cost $1 per loaf?
b. milk cost $3 per gallon and bread cost $2 per loaf?
c. milk cost $2 per gallon and bread cost $4 per loaf?

chapter 13

Economic Growth in the Global Economy

13.1 **ECONOMIC GROWTH**
What is economic growth?

13.2 **DETERMINANTS OF ECONOMIC GROWTH**
What changes lead to economic growth?

13.3 **RAISING THE LEVEL OF ECONOMIC GROWTH**
What can the government do to increase the level of economic growth?

section 13.1

Economic Growth

- What is economic growth?
- What is the Rule of 70?

SHORT RUN VERSUS LONG RUN

John Maynard Keynes, one of the most influential economic thinkers of all times, once said that "in the long run, we are all dead." The reason Keynes said this is that he was primarily concerned with explaining and reducing short-term fluctuations in the level of business activity. He wanted to smooth out the business cycle, largely because of the implications that cyclical fluctuations had for buyers and sellers in terms of unemployment and price instability. No one would deny that Keynes's concerns were important and legitimate.

At the same time, however, Keynes's flippant remark about the long run ignores the fact that human welfare is greatly influenced by long-term changes in a nation's capacity to produce goods and services. Emphasis on short-run economic fluctuations ignores the longer-term dynamic changes that affect output, leisure, real incomes, and lifestyles.

What are the determinants of long-run economic change in our ability to produce goods and services? What are some of the consequences of rapid economic change? Why are some nations rich while others are poor? Does growth in output improve our economic welfare? These are a few questions that we need to explore.

economic growth
an upward trend in the real per capita output of goods and services

section 13.1 Exhibit 1 — Economic Growth and the Shifting Production Possibilities Curve

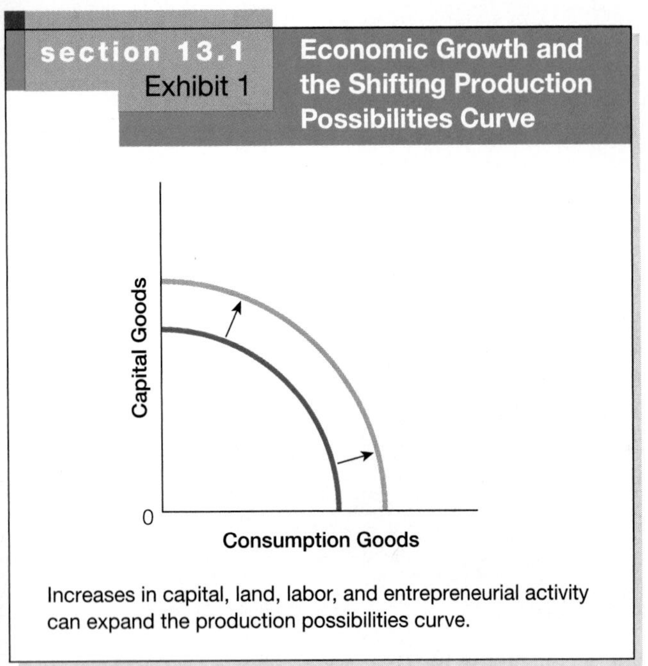

Increases in capital, land, labor, and entrepreneurial activity can expand the production possibilities curve.

DEFINING ECONOMIC GROWTH

Economic growth is usually measured by the annual percent change in real output of goods and services per capita (real GDP per capita). In chapter 3, we introduced the production possibilities curve. Along the production possibilities curve, the economy is producing at its potential output. How much the economy will produce at its potential output, sometimes called its *natural rate of output,* depends on the quantity and quality of an economy's resources, including labor, capital (like factories, machinery, tools, and productive skills), and natural resources (land, coal, timber, oil, iron, and so on). In addition, technology can increase the economy's production capabilities. As shown in Exhibit 1, improvements in and greater stocks of land, labor, capital, and entrepreneurial activity will shift the production possibilities curve out. Another way of saying that economic growth has shifted the production possibilities curve out is to say that it has increased potential output.

THE RULE OF 70

If Nation A and Nation B start off with the same size population and the same level of real GDP but grow at only slightly different rates over a long period of time, will it make much of a difference? Yes. In the first year or two the differences will be small but even over a decade the differences will be large, and huge after 50 to 100 years. And the final impact will be a much higher standard of living in the nation with the greater economic growth, *ceteris paribus.*

A simple formula, called the Rule of 70, shows how long it will take a nation to double its output at various growth rates. If you take a nation's growth rate and divide it into 70, you will have the approximate time it will take to double the income level. For example, if a nation grows at 3.5 percent per year, then the economy will double every 20 years (70/3.5). However, if an economy only grows at 2 percent per year, then the economy will double every 35 years (70/2). And at a 1 percent annual growth rate, it will take 70 years to double income (70/1). So even a small change in the growth rate of a nation will have a large impact over a lengthy period.

In Exhibit 2, we see the growth rates in real per capita GDP for selected industrial countries. Because of differences in growth rates, some countries will become richer than others over time. With relatively slower economic growth, today's richest countries will not be the richest for very long. And with even slight improvements in economic growth, today's poorest countries will not remain poor for very long.

section 13.1 Exhibit 2 **Growth in Real per Capita GDP, Selected Industrial Countries**

	Ten-Year Averages	
	1982–1991	**1992–2001**
United States	2.3%	2.1%
Japan	3.5	0.9
Germany	2.4	1.4
France	2.0	1.7
Italy	2.1	1.8
United Kingdom	2.4	2.5
Canada	1.1	2.1

SOURCE: International Monetary Fund, *World Economic Outlook,* September 2000. Printed by permission from International Monetary Fund. www.imf.org

Because of past economic growth the "richest" or "most-developed" countries today have many times the market output of the "poorest" or "least-developed" countries. Put differently, the most-developed countries produce and market more output in a day than the least-developed countries do in a year. The international differences in income, output, and wealth are indeed striking and have caused a great deal of friction between developed and less-developed countries. The United States and the nations of the European Union have had sizeable increases in real output over the past two centuries, but even in 1800 most of these nations were better off in terms of market output than such contemporary impoverished countries as Ethiopia, India, or Nepal.

PRODUCTIVITY: THE KEY TO A HIGHER STANDARD OF LIVING

Will the standard of living in the United States rise, level off, or even decline over time? The answer depends on productivity growth. **Productivity** is the amount of goods and services a worker can produce per hour. Productivity is especially important because it determines a country's standard of living. For example, slow growth of capital investment can lead to lower labor productivity and, consequently, lower wages. On the other hand, increases in productivity and higher wages can occur as a result of carefully crafted economic policies, such as tax policies that stimulate investment or programs that encourage research and development.

productivity
the amount of goods and services a worker can produce per hour

The link between productivity and the standard of living can most easily be understood by recalling our circular flow model in Section 12.3. The circular flow model showed that aggregate expenditures are equal to aggregate income. In other words, the aggregate values of all goods and services produced in the economy must equal the payments made to the factors of production—the wages and salaries paid to workers, the rental payment to capital, the profits, and so on. That is, the only way an economy can increase its rate of consumption in the long run is if it increases the amount it produces. But why are some countries so much better than others at producing goods and services? We will see the answer in the next section, as we examine the determinants of productivity—quantity and quality of labor resources, physical capital, and techonological advances.

Section Check

SECTION CHECK

1. Economic growth is usually measured by the annual percent change in real output of goods and services per capita. Improvements in and greater stocks of land, labor, capital, and entrepreneurial activity will lead to greater economic growth and shift the production possibilities curve outward.
2. According to the Rule of 70, if you take a nation's growth rate and divide it into 70, you have the approximate time it will take to double the income level.

---

1. Why does the production possibilities curve shift out with economic growth?
2. Even if "in the long run we are all dead," are you glad that earlier generations of Americans worked and invested for economic growth?
3. If long-run consequences were not important, would many students go to college or participate in internship programs without pay?
4. When the Dutch "created" new land with their system of dikes, what did it do to their production possibilities curve? Why?

section 13.2

Determinants of Economic Growth

- What factors contribute to economic growth?
- What is human capital?

FACTORS THAT CONTRIBUTE TO ECONOMIC GROWTH

Many separate explanations of the process of economic growth have been proposed. Which is correct? None of them, by themselves, can completely explain economic growth. However, each of the explanations may be part of a more complicated reality. Economic growth is a complex process involving many important factors, no one of which completely dominates. We can list at least several factors that nearly everyone would agree have contributed to economic growth in some or all countries.

1. The quantity and quality of labor resources (labor and human capital)
2. Increase in the use of inputs provided by the land (natural resources)
3. Physical capital inputs (machines, tools, buildings, inventories)
4. Technological knowledge (new ways of combining given quantities of labor, natural resources, and capital inputs), allowing greater output than previously possible

Labor

We know that labor is needed in all forms of productive activity. But other things being equal, an increase in the quantity of labor inputs does not necessarily increase output per capita. For example, if the increase in the quantity of labor input is due to an increase in population, per capita growth might not occur because the increase in output could be offset by the increase in population. However, if a greater proportion of the population works (that is, the labor force participation rate rises) or if workers put in longer hours, output per capita will increase—assuming that the additional work activity adds something to output.

Qualitative improvements in workers (learning new skills, for example) can also enhance output. Indeed, it has become popular to view labor skills as "**human capital**" that can be augmented or improved by education and on-the-job training. Human capital has to be produced like physical capital with teachers, schoolrooms, libraries, computer labs, and time devoted to studying.

human capital
the accumulation of investments in education and on-the-job training

Natural Resources

The abundance of natural resources, like fertile soils, and other raw materials, like timber and oil, can enhance output. Many scholars have cited the abundance of natural resources in the United States as one reason for its historical success. Canada and Australia are endowed with a large natural resource base and high per capita incomes. Resources are, however, not the whole story, as is clear with reference to Japan or especially Hong Kong, both of which have had tremendous success with relatively few natural resources. Similarly, Brazil has a large and varied natural resource base yet its income per capita is relatively low compared to many developed countries. It appears that a natural resource base can affect the initial development process but sustained growth is influenced by other factors. However, most economists would agree that a limited resource base does pose an important obstacle to economic growth.

Physical Capital

Even in primitive economies, workers usually have some rudimentary tools to further their productive activity. Take the farmer who needs to dig a ditch to improve drainage in his fields. If he used just his bare hands, it might take a lifetime to complete the job. If he used a shovel, he could dig the ditch in hours or days. But with a big earth-moving machine, he could do it in minutes. There is nearly universal agreement that capital formation has played a significant role in the economic development of nations.

Countries that do not keep up with technology will generally be unable to keep up their economic growth and standard of living. If a country is technologically backward, it will lose global competitiveness and often rely on a narrow range of exports that will eventually lose their profitability in the global economy. For example, a country that relied on exporting copper may lose its market as other countries around the world convert their phone and cable lines to fiber optics.

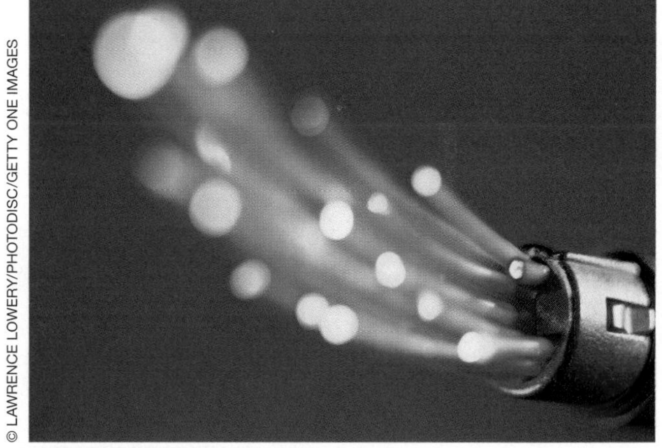

Technological Advances

Technological advances stem from human ingenuity and creativity in developing new ways of combining the factors of production to enhance the amount of output from a given quantity of resources. The process of technological advance involves invention and innovation. **Innovation** is the adoption of the product or process. For example, in the United States, the invention and innovation of the cotton gin, the Bessemer steel-making process, and the railroad were important stimuli to economic growth. New technology, however, must be introduced into productive use by managers or entrepreneurs who must weigh the perceived estimates of benefits of the new technology against estimates of costs. Thus, the entrepreneur is an important economic factor in the growth process.

Technological advance permits us to economize on one or more inputs used in the production process. It can permit savings of labor, such as when a new machine does the work of many workers. When this happens, technology is said to be embodied in capital and to be labor saving. Technology, however, can also be land (natural resource) saving or even capital saving. For example, nuclear fission has permitted us to build power plants that economize on the use of coal, a natural resource. The reduction in transportation time that accompanied the invention of the railroad allowed businesses to reduce the capital they needed in the form of inventories. Because goods could be obtained more quickly, businesses could reduce the stock kept on their shelves.

innovation
applications of new knowledge that create new products or improve existing products

In The NEWS

THE NEW ECONOMY?

BY JOHN BROWNING AND SPENCER REISS

Working with information is very different from working with the steel and glass from which our grandparents built their wealth. Information is easier to produce and harder to control than stuff you can drop on your foot. For a start, computers can copy it and ship it anywhere, almost instantly and almost for free. Production and distribution, the basis of industrial power, can increasingly be taken for granted. Innovation and marketing are all.

So an information economy is more open—it doesn't take a production line to compete, just a good idea. But it's also more competitive. Information is easy not just to duplicate, but to replicate. Successful firms have to keep innovating to keep ahead of copycats nipping at their heels. The average size of companies shrinks. New products and knockoffs alike emerge in months rather than years, and market power is increasingly based on making sense of an overabundance of ideas rather than rationing scarce material goods. Each added connection to a network's pool of knowledge multiplies the value of the whole. . . . The result: new rules of competition, new sorts of organization, new challenges for management.

Some zealots talk about a New Economy, capital N, capital E, all too easily caricatured as "there won't be inflation anymore, because of technological change." Alas, as Stanford economist Paul Romer has reminded us, "If a majority of the Fed's board of governors decided to have 20 percent inflation, they could have it in a year, possibly in months." Then there's the idea that recessions are things of the past. This comes up at the end of every expansion.

SOURCE: John Browning and Spencer Reiss, "Encyclopedia of the New Economy," *Wired*. http://www.hotwired.com/special/ene/index.html?word=intro_two. © *Wired*.

CONSIDER THIS:
The move to the information economy is shaping the way we think about the future. However, it is difficult to accurately measure the gains computers and telecoms are generating. Almost 75 percent of all computers are used in the service sector, like finance and health. In these areas, productivity gains have been difficult to measure. In addition, many of the benefits come in the form of quality or convenience, like 24-hour-a-day automated bank tellers. Some of these quality-of-life improvements are not accurately measured in macroeconomic data.

Section Check

1. The factors that contribute to economic growth are increased quantity and quality of labor, natural resources, physical capital, and technological advances.
2. Labor can be improved through investment in human capital—that is, education, on-the-job training, and experience can improve the quality of labor.

---

1. Why is no single factor capable of completely explaining economic growth patterns?
2. Why might countries with relatively scarce labor be leaders in labor-saving innovations? In what area would countries with relatively scarce land likely be innovative leaders?
3. Why could an increase in the price of oil increase real GDP growth in oil-exporting countries like Saudi Arabia and Mexico, while decreasing growth in oil-importing countries like the United States and Japan?
4. How is Hong Kong a dramatic example of why abundant natural resources are not necessary to rapid economic growth?

section 13.3

Raising the Level of Economic Growth

- Why is the saving rate so important to increasing economic growth?
- Why is research and development so important to economic growth?
- Why are property rights so important to increasing economic growth?
- What impact will free trade have on economic growth?
- Why is education so important to economic growth?

THE IMPACT OF ECONOMIC GROWTH

Economic growth means more than an increase in the real income (output) of the population. A number of other important changes accompany changes in output. Some have even claimed that economic growth stimulates political freedom or democracy, but the correlation here is far from conclusive. While there are rich democratic societies and poor authoritarian ones, the opposite also holds. That is, some features of democracy, such as majority voting and special interest groups, may actually be growth retarding. For example, if the majority decides to vote in large land reforms and wealth transfers, this will lead to higher taxes and market distortions that will reduce incentives for work, investment, and ultimately economic growth. However, there are a number of policies that a nation can pursue to increase economic growth

SAVING RATES, INVESTMENT, CAPITAL STOCK, AND ECONOMIC GROWTH

One of the most important determinants of economic growth is the saving rate. In order to consume more in the future, we must save more now. Generally speaking, higher levels of saving will lead to higher rates of investment and capital formation and, therefore, to greater economic growth. Individuals can either consume or save their income. If individuals choose to consume all of their income, there will be nothing left for saving, which businesses could use for investment purposes to build new plants or replace worn-out or obsolete equipment. With little investment in capital stock, there will be little economic growth. Capital can also increase as a result of capital injections from abroad (foreign direct investments), but the role of national saving rates in economic growth is of particular importance.

Exhibit 1 clearly shows that sustained rapid economic growth is associated with high rates of saving and investment around the world. However, investment alone does not guarantee economic growth. Economic growth hinges on the quality and the type of investment as well as on investments in human capital and improvements in technology.

RESEARCH AND DEVELOPMENT

Some scholars believe that the importance of **research and development (R&D)** is understated. The concept of R&D is broad indeed—it can include new products, management improvements, production innovations, or simply learning-by-doing. However, it is clear that investing in R&D and rewarding innovators with patents have paid big dividends in the past 50 to 60 years. Some would argue that even larger rewards for research

research and development (R&D)
activities undertaken to create new product and processes that will lead to technological progress

section 13.3 Exhibit 1 — Saving Rates and GDP Growth during High-Growth Periods in Selected Economies

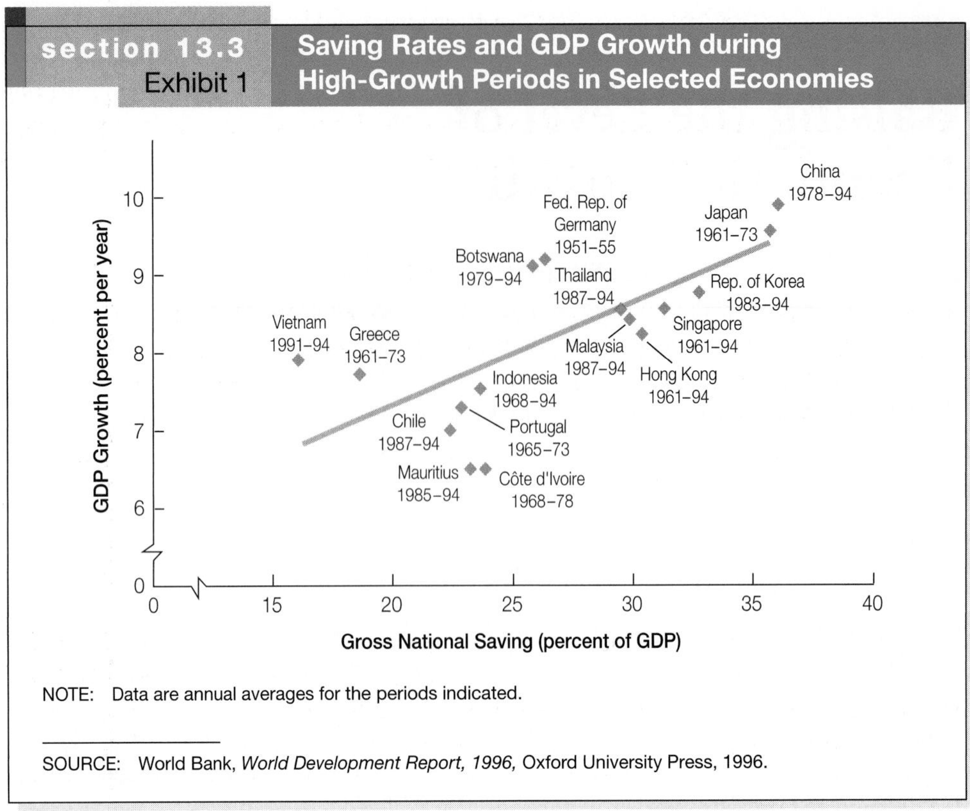

NOTE: Data are annual averages for the periods indicated.

SOURCE: World Bank, *World Development Report, 1996,* Oxford University Press, 1996.

and development would spur even more rapid economic growth. In addition, an important link exists between research and development and capital investment. As already noted, when capital depreciates over time, it is replaced with new equipment that embodies the latest technology. Consequently, R&D may work hand-in-hand with investment to improve growth and productivity.

Free trade and a stable monetary environment are important to economic growth but governance is important too. The government has to protect private property and individual rights and enforce contracts, otherwise globalization can lead to corruption and violence. Russians have high levels of education but the failure of the legal system has led to a dismal economic performance.

THE PROTECTION OF PROPERTY RIGHTS IMPACTS ECONOMIC GROWTH

Economic growth rates tend to be higher in countries where the government enforces property rights. Property rights give owners the legal right to keep or sell their property—land, labor, or capital. Without property rights, life would be a huge "free-for-all," where people could take whatever they wanted; in this scenario, protection for property, such as alarm systems and private security services, would have to be purchased.

In most developed countries, property rights are effectively protected by the government. However, in developing countries, this is not usually the case. And if the government is not enforcing these rights, the private sector must respond in costly ways that stifle economic growth. For example, an unreliable judiciary system means that entrepreneurs are often forced to rely on informal agreements that are difficult to enforce. As a result, they may have to pay bribes to get things done, and even then, they may not get the promised services. Individuals will have to buy private security or pay "organized crime" for protection against crime and corruption. In addition, landowners and business owners might be fearful of coups or takeovers from a new government, which might confiscate their property altogether. In short, if government is not adequately protecting property rights, the incentive to invest will be hindered, and political instability, corruption, and lower rates of economic growth will be likely.

FREE TRADE AND ECONOMIC GROWTH

Allowing free trade can also lead to greater output because of the principle of comparative advantage. Essentially, the principle of comparative advantage suggests that if two nations or individuals with different resource endowments and production capabilities specialize in producing a smaller number of goods and services and engage in trade, both parties will benefit. Total output will rise. This will be discussed in greater detail in the chapter on international trade.

EDUCATION

Education, investment in human capital, may be just as important as improvements in physical capital. At any given time, an individual has a choice between current work and investment activities like education that can increase future earning power. People accept reductions in current income to devote current effort to education and training. In turn, a certain return on the investment is expected, for in later years they will earn a higher wage rate (the amount of the increase depending on the nature of the education and training as well as individual natural ability). For example, in the United States, a person with a college education can be expected to earn almost twice as much per year as a high school graduate.

One argument for government subsidizing education is that this investment can increase the skill level of the population and raise the standard of living. However, even if the individual does not benefit financially from increased education, society may benefit culturally and in other respects from having its members highly educated. For example, more education may lead to lower crime rates, new ideas that may benefit the society at large, and more informed voters.

© ROBERT CAPUTO/AURORA/PICTUREQUEST

Better education in poor countries is a relatively inexpensive method to enrich the lives of those in poorer countries. Education allows these countries to produce more advanced goods and services and enjoy in the wealth created from trading in the global economy. Taiwan, India, and Korea are now all part of the high-tech global economy but most of Africa, with the lowest levels of education, has been left behind.

With economic growth, illiteracy rates falls and formal education grows. Exhibit 2 shows the adult literacy rates for selected countries. The correlation between per capita output and the proportion of the population that is able to read or write is striking. Improvements in literacy stimulate economic growth by reducing barriers to the flow of information; when information costs are high, out of ignorance many resources flow to or remain in uses that are rather unproductive. Moreover, education imparts skills that are directly useful in raising labor productivity, whether it is mathematics taught to a sales clerk, engineering techniques taught to a college graduate, or just good ideas that facilitate production and design.

However, in developing, poor countries, the higher opportunity costs of education present an obstacle. Children in developing countries are an important part of the labor force starting at a young age. But children who are attending school cannot help in the field—planting, harvesting, fence building, and many other tasks that are so important

section 13.3 Exhibit 2 Literacy and Economic Development

Country	Output Per Capita	Adult Literacy Rates
United States	$30,200	97%
Japan	24,500	99
Italy	21,500	97
Brazil	6,300	81
India	1,600	52
Haiti	1,070	53
Ethiopia	530	28

NOTE: The literacy rates are based on the ability to read and write at an elementary school level.

SOURCE: *Time Almanac, 2000.*

in the rural areas of developing countries. A child's labor contribution to the family is far less important in a developed country. Thus the higher opportunity cost of an education in developing countries is one of the reasons that school enrollments are lower.

Education may also be a consequence of economic growth, because as incomes rise, people's tendency to consume education increases. People increasingly look to education for more than the acquisition of immediately applicable skills. Education becomes a consumption good as well as a means of investing in human capital.

Section Check

1. Generally speaking, higher levels of saving will lead to higher rates of investment and capital formation and, therefore, to greater economic growth.
2. Larger rewards for research and development would spur even more rapid economic growth.
3. Economic growth rates tend to be higher in countries where the government enforces property rights more vigorously.
4. Allowing free trade can also lead to greater output because of the principle of comparative advantage.
5. Education, investment in human capital, is important to improving standards of living and economic growth.

---

1. Why does knowing what factors are correlated with economic growth not tell us what causes economic growth?
2. How does increasing the capital stock lead to economic growth?
3. How do higher saving rates affect long-run economic growth?
4. Why would you expect an inverse relationship between self-sufficiency and real GDP per capita?
5. If a couple was concerned about their retirement, why could that lead them to have more children if they lived in an agricultural society but fewer children if they were in an urban society?
6. Why is the effective use of land, labor, capital, and entrepreneurial activities dependent on the protection of property rights?

Summary

Economic growth is usually measured by the annual percent change in real output of goods and services per capita—real GDP per capita. The factors that contribute to economic growth are increased quantity and quality of labor, natural resources, physical capital, and technological advances

Higher savings rates generally lead to greater investment and capital formation, which lead to economic growth. Research and development can spur more rapid economic growth. Economic growth rates tend to be higher in countries where the government enforces property rights vigorously. Freer trade can also lead to greater output because of specialization and trade. Education, investment in human capital, is important to improving standards of living and economic growth.

Key Terms and Concepts

economic growth 296
productivity 297
human capital 299
innovation 299
research and development (R&D) 301

Review Questions

1. Which of the following best measures economic growth?
   - **a.** change in nominal GDP
   - **b.** the change in real GDP
   - **c.** the annual percentage change in real GDP
   - **d.** the annual percentage change in nominal GDP per capita
   - **e.** the annual percentage change in real GDP per capita
   - **f.** the inflation rate
2. Which of the following will shift the U.S. production possibilities curve out?
   - **a.** the discovery of new oil reserves
   - **b.** increased immigration of scientists and engineers to the United States
   - **c.** a nuclear war that destroys both people and structures
   - **d.** producing fewer bagels in order to produce more tractors
   - **e.** producing fewer strawberries in order to produce more corn
3. Explain why choosing between consumer goods and capital goods in the current period is really an intertemporal choice between present and future consumption.
4. Suppose that two poor countries experience different growth rates over time. Country A's real GDP per capita grows at a rate of 7 percent per year on average while Country B's real GDP per capita grows at a rate of only 3 percent per annum. Predict how the standard of living will vary between these two countries over time as a result of divergent growth rates.
5. Estimate the number of years needed for an economy's real GDP per capita to double if the annual growth rate in real GDP per capita is
   - **a.** 10 percent.
   - **b.** 5 percent.
   - **c.** 2 percent.
   - **d.** 0.5 percent.
6. What is the difference between "labor" and "human capital"? How does one increase human capital?

7. What is the implication for an economic system with weak enforcement of patent and copyright laws? Why does weak property right enforcement create an incentive problem?
8. Which of the following are likely to improve the productivity of labor and thereby lead to economic growth?
   a. on-the-job experience
   b. vocational school
   c. a decrease in the amount of capital per worker
   d. improvements in management of resources
9. Visit the Sexton Web site at **http://sexton.swcollege.com** and click on "CIA Factbook" and compare the real GDP per capita, growth rate in the real GDP, life expectancy at birth, birth rate, death rate, and literacy across the following countries: the United States, Thailand, and Haiti. How do you think economic growth affects birth rates, death rates, and literacy (and vice versa)?

Fill in the Blanks

1. John Maynard Keynes was primarily concerned with explaining and reducing ____________ fluctuations in the level of business activity.
2. Many would argue that in the long run, economic growth is a ____________ determinant of people's well-being.
3. Economic growth is usually measured by the annual percent change in ____________.
4. How much the economy will produce at its potential output depends on the ____________ and ____________ of an economy's resources.
5. ____________ in technology can increase the economy's production capabilities.
6. A nation with ____________ economic growth will end up with a much higher standard of living, *ceteris paribus.*
7. The Rule of 70 says that the number of years necessary for a nation to double its output is approximately equal to the nation's ____________ rate divided into 70.
8. The international differences in income, output, and wealth are striking and have caused a great deal of friction between ____________ and ____________ countries.
9. There are several factors that nearly everyone agrees have contributed to economic growth in some or all countries: (1) growth in the quantity and quality of ____________ resources used (human capital); (2) increase in the use of inputs provided by the ____________ (natural resources); (3) growth in physical ____________ inputs (machines, tools, buildings, inventories); (4) ____________ advances (new ways of combining given quantities of labor, natural resources, and capital inputs) allowing greater output than previously possible.
10. If the labor force participation rate in a country ____________or if workers put in ____________ hours, output per capita will tend to increase.
11. It has become popular to view labor as ____________ capital that can be augmented or improved by education and on-the-job training.
12. There is nearly universal agreement that ____________ formation has played a significant role in the economic development of nations.
13. ____________ is the adoption of a new product or process.
14. Technological advance permits us to economize on ____________, ____________, or even ____________.
15. Generally speaking, higher levels of saving will lead to ____________ levels of investment and capital formation and, therefore, to ____________ economic growth.
16. Investment alone does not guarantee economic growth, which hinges on the ____________ and the ____________ of investment as well.
17. Research and development can result in ____________ products, management ____________, production ____________, or learning by ____________.

18. Economic growth rates tend to be higher in countries where the government enforces ______________.

19. If a country's government is not enforcing property rights, the private sector must respond in ______________ ways that ______________ economic growth.

20. ______________ can lead to greater output because of the principle of comparative advantage.

21. Accepting a ______________ in current income to acquire education and training can ______________ future earning ability, which can raise the standard of living.

22. With economic growth, illiteracy rates ______________ and formal education ______________.

23. Improvements in literacy stimulate economic growth by ______________ barriers to the flow of information and ______________ labor productivity.

24. One problem of providing enough education in poorer countries is that because children in developing countries are an important part of the labor force at a young age, there is a ______________ opportunity cost of education in terms of forgone contribution to family income.

True or False

1. Human welfare is greatly influenced by long-term changes in a nation's capacity to produce goods and services.

2. Emphasis on the short run of the business cycle can ignore the longer-term dynamic changes that affect output and real incomes.

3. Economic growth is usually measured by the annual percent change in the nominal output of goods and services per capita.

4. Along the production possibilities curve, the economy is producing at its potential output, sometimes called its natural level of output.

5. Another way of saying that economic growth has shifted the production possibilities curve out is that it has increased potential output.

6. Greater stocks of land, labor, or capital can shift out the production possibilities curve.

7. The Rule of 70 says that the number of years necessary for a nation to double its output is approximately equal to the nation's growth rate divided by 70.

8. The "richest" or "most-developed" countries today have many times the per capita output of the "poorest" or "least-developed" countries.

9. Economic growth is a complex process involving many important factors, no one of which completely dominates.

10. If there were an increase in the quantity of physical capital in a country at the same time that the quantity or quality of labor resources used fell, that country would experience economic growth as a result.

11. Technological advances, even if there is no change in the quantity or quality of the labor resources used, tend to lead to economic growth.

12. An increase in labor input does not necessarily increase output per capita.
13. A limited resource base is no obstacle to economic growth.
14. Both the initial development process and the sustained growth of an economy are dependent on a large natural resource base.
15. Technological advances involve both invention and innovation.
16. Because new technology must be introduced into productive use by someone who must weigh estimates of the benefits of the new technology against estimates of the costs, the entrepreneur is an important economic factor in the growth process.
17. Technological advance permits us to economize on labor, land, or even capital.
18. One of the most important determinants of economic growth is the saving rate.
19. Investment alone does not guarantee economic growth.
20. There is an important link between research and development and capital investment, in that when capital depreciates over time, it is replaced with new equipment that embodies the latest technology.
21. In most developed countries, property rights are effectively protected by the government, but in developing countries, this is not normally the case.
22. Free-trade policies will tend to increase the value of total output in an economy.
23. The correlation between per capita output and the proportion of the population that is unable to read or write is very small.
24. Education is both a consequence of economic growth and a cause of economic growth.

Multiple Choice

1. John Maynard Keynes, who once said that "in the long run, we are all dead," was primarily concerned with
   a. long-run economic growth.
   b. long-run price stability.
   c. redirecting short-run fluctuations in the business cycle.
   d. Keynes was equally concerned with all these issues.
2. Economists typically measure economic growth by tracking
   a. the employment rate.
   b. the unemployment rate.
   c. the expansion index.
   d. real GDP per capita.
   e. nominal GDP.
3. Economic growth refers to a(n) _________ in the output of goods and services in an economy. The greater the economic growth, the _________ goods citizens and their descendants will have to consume.
   a. decrease; less
   b. decrease; more
   c. increase; more
   d. increase; less

4. Economic growth is usually measured by the annual percent change in
   a. nominal GDP.
   b. nominal GDP per capita.
   c. real GDP.
   e. real GDP per capita.

5. How much the economy can produce at its natural rate of output depends on
   a. technology.
   b. the quantity of available natural resources.
   c. the productivity of labor.
   d. the stock of available capital.
   e. all of the above.

6. The natural level of real output in a country will tend to fall if
   a. technology advances.
   b. an increasing fraction of the population retires.
   c. increased investment adds to the capital stock.
   d. existing supplies of natural resources are depleted.
   e. either b or d occurs.

7. The standard of living will decline if
   a. nominal GDP grows at a faster rate than real GDP.
   b. nominal GDP grows at a slower rate than real GDP.
   c. the rate of population growth exceeds the rate of growth of real GDP.
   d. the rate of population growth is less than the rate of growth of real GDP.

8. An economy's production possibilities curve will shift outward over time if
   a. technological progress occurs.
   b. the stock of available capital decreases.
   c. emigration results in a decrease in the supply of available labor.
   d. the productivity of labor increases.
   e. either a or d occurs.

9. Which of the following would *not* result in increasing the natural rate of output in a country?
   a. increasing current consumption by reducing current saving
   b. draining swampland to allow cultivation
   c. improving the transportation system
   d. raising the fraction of resources that the country devotes to education
   e. All of the above *would* tend to increase the natural rate of output in a country.

10. Which one of the following will cause the production possibilities curve to shift outward?
   a. improved public education
   b. improved health-care systems
   c. larger budgets for research, development, and exploration
   d. all of the above

11. According to the Rule of 70, if a nation grows at a rate of 5 percent per year, it will take roughly ________ for national income to double.
   a. 10 years
   b. 7 years
   c. 70 years
   d. 14 years
   e. none of the above

12. A country will roughly double its GDP in 10 years if its annual growth rate is
- **a.** 5 percent.
- **b.** 7 percent.
- **c.** 10 percent.
- **d.** 12 percent.
- **e.** 20 percent.

13. According to the Rule of 70,
- **a.** if a country is growing at 7 percent per year, its output will double in approximately 10 years.
- **b.** if a country is growing at 3.5 percent per year, its output will double in approximately 20 years.
- **c.** if a country is growing at 1 percent per year, its output will double in approximately 70 years.
- **d.** all of the above are true.
- **e.** none of the above are true.

14. According to the Rule of 70, if a country's growth rate doubled, the amount of time before its output doubled would be
- **a.** quartered.
- **b.** halved.
- **c.** doubled.
- **d.** quadrupled.

15. In the long run, the most important determinant of a nation's standard of living is
- **a.** its rate of productivity growth.
- **b.** its ability to export cheap labor.
- **c.** its ability to control the nation's money supply.
- **d.** its endowment of natural resources.

16. Per capita real output would tend to rise, other things being equal,
- **a.** if the labor force participation rate in the country rose.
- **b.** if the population rose.
- **c.** if the population fell and the labor force participation rate in the country fell.
- **d.** in all of the above cases.
- **e.** in none of the above cases.

17. If there were both an increase in the capital stock and an increase in technology in a country, other things being equal, the country's potential output would
- **a.** rise.
- **b.** fall.
- **c.** remain unchanged.
- **d.** change in an indeterminate direction.

18. If a country reduced its spending on education and used the resources to build capital goods, economic growth in that country
- **a.** would tend to rise.
- **b.** would tend to fall.
- **c.** would tend to remain the same.
- **d.** could rise, fall, or remain the same.

19. Technological advances can be
- **a.** labor saving.
- **b.** capital saving.
- **c.** land (natural resource) saving.
- **d.** any of the above.

20. If Goodland's population grows faster than Badland's population, but Badland's labor force participation rate is growing faster than that in Goodland, other things being equal,
   a. real GDP will be growing faster in Badland.
   b. real GDP per capita will be growing faster in Badland.
   c. real GDP will be growing faster in Goodland.
   d. real GDP per capita will be growing faster in Goodland.
   e. both b and d will be true.

21. If a country increased its saving rate,
   a. its current consumption would have to fall.
   b. its current consumption would have to rise.
   c. its future consumption possibilities will fall.
   d. its future consumption possibilities will rise.
   e. both a and d will occur.

22. Which of the following statements is incorrect?
   a. One of the most important determinants of economic growth is a nation's saving rate.
   b. Injections of foreign capital from abroad may contribute to a nation's economic growth.
   c. Economic growth depends on the quality and type of investments made.
   d. Economic growth rates tend to be lower in countries where property rights are better enforced by government.

23. High rates of saving and investment in a country
   a. guarantee rapid economic growth.
   b. tend to increase economic growth but do not guarantee it.
   c. will result in greater economic growth if they are accompanied by advances in technology than if they are not.
   d. will result in greater economic growth if they are accompanied by more investment in human capital than if they are not.
   e. will result in all of the above except a.

24. Which of the following is considered a factor that contributes to economic growth?
   a. government protection of property rights
   b. increased specialization of labor
   c. research and development
   d. improved efficiencies through economies of scale
   e. all of the above

25. Economic growth tends to be greater in countries where
   a. the government effectively protects property rights.
   b. more resources are devoted to research and development.
   c. there is greater freedom to trade freely.
   d. any of the above is true.

26. During the Klondike gold rush, the first prospectors in the region arrived before any government authority was established. They followed a long goldfield tradition and created "miners' laws," which described how gold claims could be staked and how these claims would be enforced. The creation of "miners' laws" showed that these prospectors recognized the importance of which of the following factors that affect economic growth?
   a. increasing physical capital
   b. economies of scale
   c. well-defined and enforced property rights
   d. technological advance

27. In a country that has an unstable government or judiciary, would you expect to see more entrepreneurial activity, or less?
  a. Less, because in an unstable economy there are fewer entrepreneurs.
  b. Less, because there would be an unreliable infrastructure for protecting property rights.
  c. More, because there would be fewer governmental restrictions.
  d. More, because in general there would be less taxation of commercial and research activities.

28. Investment in human capital
  a. is of minor importance to economic growth.
  b. can be acquired through on-the-job training.
  c. is an important source of economic growth.
  d. does not affect economic growth; only physical capital does.
  e. is characterized by both b and c.

29. Other things being equal, the higher the rate of savings across countries,
  a. the higher the rate of change of real GDP per capita.
  b. the lower the rate of change of real GDP per capita.
  c. the lower the productivity of labor.
  d. the lower the rate of investment.

30. Reduced levels of illiteracy
  a. are, in part, a cause of economic growth.
  b. are, in part, caused by economic growth.
  c. are, in part, both a cause of economic growth and caused by economic growth.
  d. are largely unrelated to economic growth.

Problems

1. Answer the following questions.
  a. According to the Rule of 70, how many years will it take a country to double its output at each of the following annual growth rates?

0.5 percent:	____ years
1 percent:	____ years
1.4 percent:	____ years
2 percent:	____ years
2.8 percent:	____ years
3.5 percent:	____ years
7 percent:	____ years

  b. If a country had $100 billion of real GDP today, what would its real GDP be in 50 years if it grows at an annual growth rate of

1.4 percent?	__________
2.8 percent?	__________
7 percent?	__________

2. Which direction would the following changes alter GDP growth and per capita GDP growth in a country (increase, decrease, or indeterminate), other things being equal?

	Real GDP Growth	**Real GDP Growth per Capita**
An increase in population	________	________
An increase in labor force participation	________	________
An increase in population and labor force participation	________	________
An increase in current consumption	________	________
An increase in technology	________	________
An increase in illiteracy	________	________
An increase in tax rates	________	________
An increase in productivity	________	________
An increase in tariffs on imported goods	________	________
An earlier retirement age in the country	________	________
An increase in technology and a decrease in labor force participation	________	________
An earlier retirement age and an increase in the capital stock	________	________

chapter 14

Aggregate Demand

section
14.1

The Determinants of Aggregate Demand

- What is aggregate demand?
- What is consumption?
- What is investment?
- What is government purchases?
- What are net exports?

WHAT IS AGGREGATE DEMAND?

aggregate demand (*AD*) *the total demand for all the final goods and services in the economy*

Aggregate demand (*AD*) is the sum of the demand for all final goods and services in the economy. It can also be seen as the quantity of real GDP demanded at different price levels. The four major components of aggregate demand are consumption (C), investment (I), government purchases (G), and net exports ($X - M$). Aggregate demand, then, is equal to $C + I + G + (X - M)$.

CONSUMPTION (*C*)

Consumption is by far the largest component in aggregate demand. Expenditures for consumer goods and services typically absorb almost 70 percent of total economic activity, as measured by GDP. Understanding the determinants of consumption, then, is critical to an understanding of the forces leading to changes in aggregate demand, which in turn, change total output and income.

Does Higher Income Mean Greater Consumption?

The notion that the higher a nation's income, the more it spends on consumer items, has been validated empirically. At the level of individuals, most of us spend more money when we have higher incomes. But what matters most to us is not our total income but our after-tax or *disposable income.* Moreover, other factors might explain consumption. Some consumer goods are "lumpy"; that is, the expenditures for these goods must come in big amounts rather than in small dribbles. Thus, in years in which a consumer buys a new car, takes the family on a European trip, or has major surgery, consumption may be much greater in relation to income than in years in which the consumer does not buy such high-cost consumer goods or services. Interest rates also affect consumption because they affect savings. At higher real interest rates, people save more and consume less. At lower real interest rates, people save less and consume more.

average propensity to consume (*APC*) *the fraction of total disposable income that households spend on consumption*

marginal propensity to consume (*MPC*) *the additional consumption resulting from an additional dollar of disposable income*

The Average and Marginal Propensity to Consume

Households typically spend a large portion of their disposable income and save the rest. The fraction of their total disposable income that households spend on consumption is called the **average propensity to consume (*APC*).** For example, a household that consumes \$450 out of \$500 disposable income has an *APC* of 0.9 (\$450/\$500). However, households tend to behave differently with additional income than with their income as a whole. How much increased consumption results from an increase in income? That depends upon the **marginal propensity to consume (*MPC*),** which is the additional consumption that results from an additional dollar of disposable income. If consumption goes from \$450 to \$600 when disposable income goes from \$500 to \$700, what is the marginal propensity to consume out of disposable income? First, we calculate the change in consumption: \$600 − \$450 = \$150. Next, we calculate the change in income: \$700 − \$500 = \$200. The marginal propensity to consume, then, equals change in consumption divided by change in disposable income. In this example,

$$MPC = \text{Consumption}/\text{Disposable Income} = \$150/\$200 = 3/4 = 0.75$$

For each additional dollar in after-tax income over this range, this household consumes three-fourths of the addition, or 75 cents.

INVESTMENT (*I*)

Because investment spending (purchases of investment goods) is an important component of aggregate demand, which in turn is a determinant of the level of GDP, changes in investment spending are often responsible for changes in the level of economic activity. If consumption is determined largely by the level of disposable income, what determines the level of investment expenditures? As you may recall, investment expenditures is the most unstable category of GDP; it is sensitive to changes in economic, social, and political variables. In 2001, investment was roughly 16 percent of GDP.

Many factors are important in determining the level of investment. Good business conditions "induce" firms to invest, because a healthy growth in demand for products in the future is likely based on current experience. We will consider the key variables that influence investment spending in the next section.

GOVERNMENT PURCHASES (*G*)

Government purchases, another component of aggregate demand, is spending by the federal, state, and local governments on the purchases of new goods and services produced. Most of the purchases at the federal level are for the military. In 2001, the federal government accounted for slightly more than 17 percent of total spending. Government purchases at the state and local levels include education, highways, and police protection. While volatile shifts in government purchases are less frequent than volatile shifts in investment spending, they do occasionally occur, often at the beginning or end of wars.

NET EXPORTS (*X* − *M*)

The interaction of the U.S. economy with the rest of the world is becoming increasingly important. Up to this point, for simplicity, we have not included the foreign sector. However, international trade must be incorporated into the framework. Models that include international trade effects are called **open economy** models.

open economy
a type of model that includes international trade effects

Remember, exports are goods and services that we sell to foreign customers, like movies, wheat, or Ford Mustangs; imports are goods and services that we buy from foreign companies, like BMWs, French wine, or Sony TVs. Exports and imports can alter aggregate demand. It makes no difference to sellers if buyers are in this country or in some other country. A buyer is a buyer, foreign or domestic, so exports (X) must be added to the demand side of our equation. But what about goods and services that are consumed here but not produced by the domestic economy? When U.S. consumers, investors, or the government buy foreign goods and services, there is no direct impact on the total demand for U.S. goods and services, so imports (M) must be subtracted from our equation.

net exports
the difference between the value of exports and the value of imports

Exports minus imports is what we call **net exports.** If exports are greater than imports, we have positive net exports ($X > M$). If imports are greater than exports, net exports are negative ($X < M$).

The impact that net exports ($X - M$) have on aggregate demand is similar to the impact that government purchases has on aggregate demand. Suppose the United States has no trade surplus and no trade deficit—zero net exports. Now say that foreign consumers start buying more U.S. goods and services while U.S. consumers continue to buy imports at roughly the same rate. This will lead to *positive net exports* ($X > M$) and result in greater demand for U.S. goods and services, a higher level of aggregate demand. From a policy standpoint, this might explain why countries that are currently in a recession might like to run a trade surplus by increasing exports.

Of course, it is also possible that a country could run a trade deficit. Again let us assume that the economy was initially in a position with zero net exports. A trade deficit, or *negative net exports* ($X < M$), *ceteris paribus,* would lower U.S. aggregate demand.

Section Check

SECTION CHECK

1. Aggregate demand is the sum of the demand for all final goods and services in the economy. It can also be seen as the quantity of real GDP demanded at different price levels.
2. The four major components of aggregate demand are consumption (C), investment (I), government purchases (G), and net exports ($X - M$). Aggregate demand, then, is equal to $C + I + G + (X - M)$.
3. Empirical evidence suggests that consumption increases directly with any increase in income.
4. The additional consumption spending stemming from an additional dollar of disposable income is called the marginal propensity to consume (*MPC*).
5. Changes in investment spending are often responsible for changes in the level of economic activity.
6. Government purchases are made up of federal, state, and local purchases of goods and services.
7. Trade deficits lower aggregate demand, other things equal; trade surpluses increase aggregate demand, other things equal.

---

1. What are the major components of aggregate demand?
2. If consumption is a direct function of disposable income, how would an increase in personal taxes or a decrease in transfer payments affect consumption?
3. Would you spend more or less on additional consumption if your marginal propensity to consume increased?
4. What would an increase in exports do to aggregate demand, other things equal? An increase in imports? An increase in both imports and exports, where the change in exports was greater in magnitude?

section 14.2

The Investment and Saving Market

- What is the investment demand curve?
- What is the saving supply curve?
- How is the real interest rate determined?

If we put the investment demand for the whole economy and national savings together, we can establish the real interest rate in the saving and investment market. We begin by revisiting investment, and then follow with the introduction of the saving supply curve and equilibrium.

Exhibit 1 shows the investment demand curve for all the firms in the whole economy. The investment demand (*ID*) curve is downward sloping, reflecting the fact that investment spending varies inversely with the real interest rate—the amount borrowers pay for their loans. At high real interest rates, firms will only pursue those few investment activities with even higher expected rates of return. As the real interest rate falls, additional projects with lower expected rates of return become profitable for firms, and the quantity of investment demanded rises. In other words, the investment demand curve shows the dollar amount of investment forthcoming at different real interest rates. Because lower interest rates stimulate the quantity of investment demanded, governments often try to combat recessions by lowering interest rates.

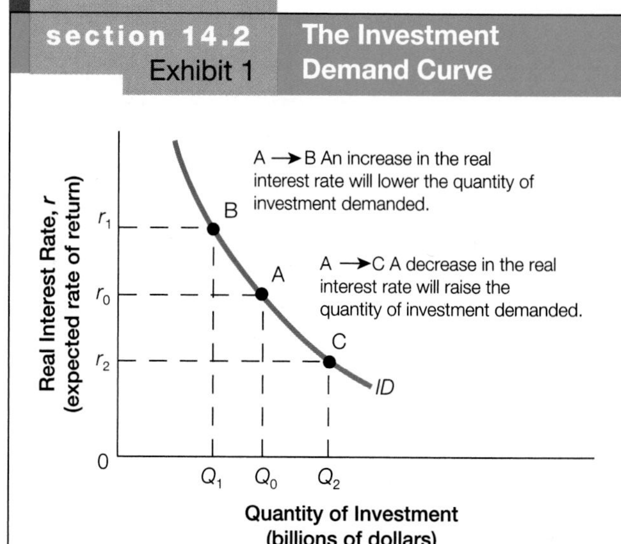

There is an inverse relationship between the real interest rate and the quantity of investment demanded. At higher real interest rates, firms will only pursue those investment activities with the highest expected return and the quantity of investment demanded will fall—a movement from point A to point B. As the real interest rate falls, projects with lower expected returns become potentially profitable for firms and the quantity of investment demanded rises—a movement from point A to point C.

SHIFTING THE INVESTMENT DEMAND CURVE

Several other determinants will shift the investment demand curve. If firms expect higher rates of return on their investments, for a given interest rate, the *ID* curve will shift to the right, as seen in Exhibit 2. If firms expect lower rates of return on their investments, for a given interest rate, the *ID* curve will shift to the left, also seen in Exhibit 2. Possible investment demand curve shifters include changes in technology, inventory, expectations, and business taxes.

Technology

Product and process innovation can cause the *ID* curve to shift out. For example, the development of new machines that can improve the quality and the quantity of products or lower the costs of production will increase the rate of return on investment, independent of the interest rate. The same is true for new products like handheld computers, the Internet, genetic applications in medicine, or HDTV. Imagine how many different firms increased their investment demand during the computer revolution.

Inventories

When inventories are high and goods are stockpiled in warehouses all over the country, there is a lower expected rate of return on new investment—*ID* shifts to the left. Firms with excess inventories of finished goods have very little incentive to invest in new capital. Alternatively, if inventories are depleted below the levels desired by firms, the expected rate of return on new investment increases, as firms look to replenish their shelves to meet the growing demand—*ID* shifts to the right.

Expectations

If higher expected sales and a higher profit rate are forecast, firms will invest in plant and equipment and the *ID* curve shifts to the right—more investment will be desired at a given interest rate. If lower expected sales and a lower profit rate are forecasted, the *ID* curve shifts to the left—fewer investments will be desired at a given interest rate.

Business Taxes

If business taxes are lowered—such as with an investment tax credit—potential after-tax profits on investment projects will increase and shift the *ID* curve to the right. Higher business taxes will lead to lower potential after-tax profits on investment projects and shift the *ID* curve to the left.

THE SUPPLY OF NATIONAL SAVING

http://

The supply of national saving is composed of both private saving and public saving. Households, firms, and the government can supply savings. The supply curve of savings is upward sloping, as seen in Exhibit 3. At a higher real interest rate, there is a greater quantity of sav-

section 14.2 Exhibit 2 — Shifts in the Investment Demand Curve

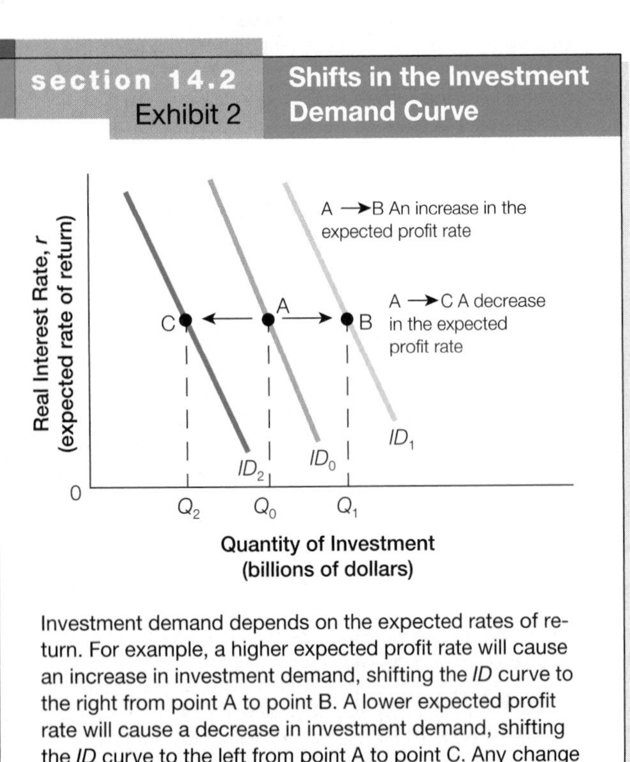

Investment demand depends on the expected rates of return. For example, a higher expected profit rate will cause an increase in investment demand, shifting the *ID* curve to the right from point A to point B. A lower expected profit rate will cause a decrease in investment demand, shifting the *ID* curve to the left from point A to point C. Any change in technology, inventory, expectations, and business taxes can cause the investment demand curve to shift.

section 14.2 Exhibit 3 — Saving Supply Curve

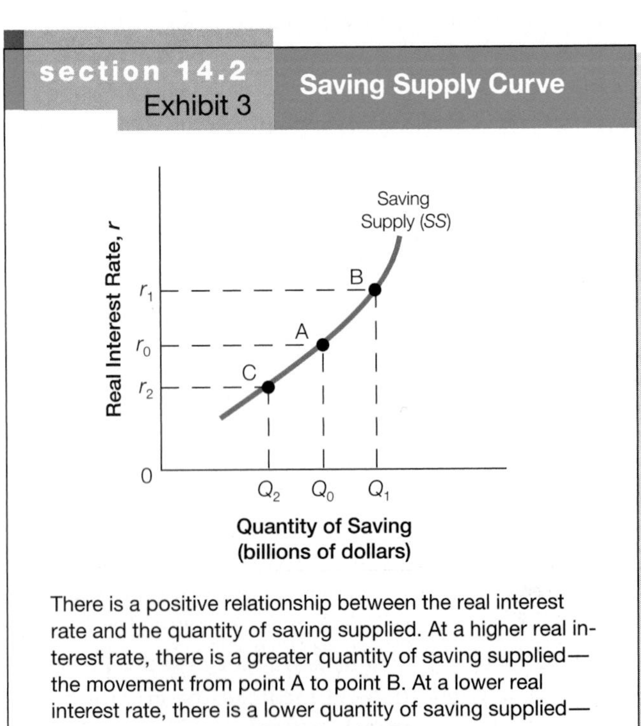

There is a positive relationship between the real interest rate and the quantity of saving supplied. At a higher real interest rate, there is a greater quantity of saving supplied—the movement from point A to point B. At a lower real interest rate, there is a lower quantity of saving supplied—the movement from point A to point C.

ings supplied. Think of the interest rate as the reward for saving and supplying funds to financial markets. At a lower real interest rate, a lower quantity of savings is supplied.

As with the investment demand curve, there are non-interest determinants of the saving supply curve. For example, if disposable (after-tax) income were to rise, the supply of savings would shift to the right—more savings would occur at any given interest rate. If disposable income fell, there would be less saving at any given interest rate. Also, if you expected lower future earnings, you would tend to save more now at any given interest rate—shifting the saving supply curve to the right. If you expected higher future earnings, you would tend to consume more and save less now, knowing that more income is right around the corner—shifting the saving supply curve to the left. In Exhibit 4, we see that an increase in disposable income or lower expected future earnings shifts the saving supply curve to the right. A decrease in disposable income or higher expected future earnings will shift the saving supply curve to the left.

In equilibrium, desired investment equals desired national saving at the intersection of the investment demand curve and the saving supply curve. The real equilibrium interest rate is shown by the intersection of these two curves, as seen in Exhibit 5. If the real interest rate, r_1, is above the equilibrium real interest rate, r_E, forces within the economy would tend to restore the equilibrium. At a higher than real equilibrium interest rate, the quantity of savings supplied would be greater that quantity of investment demanded—there would be a surplus of savings at this real interest rate. As savers (lenders) compete against each other to attract investment demanders (borrowers), the real interest rate falls. Alternatively if the real interest rate, r_2, is below the equilibrium real interest rate, r_E, the quantity of investment demanded is greater than the quantity of saving supplied at that interest rate—a shortage of saving occurs. As investment demanders (borrowers) compete against each other for the available saving, the real interest rate is bid up to r_E.

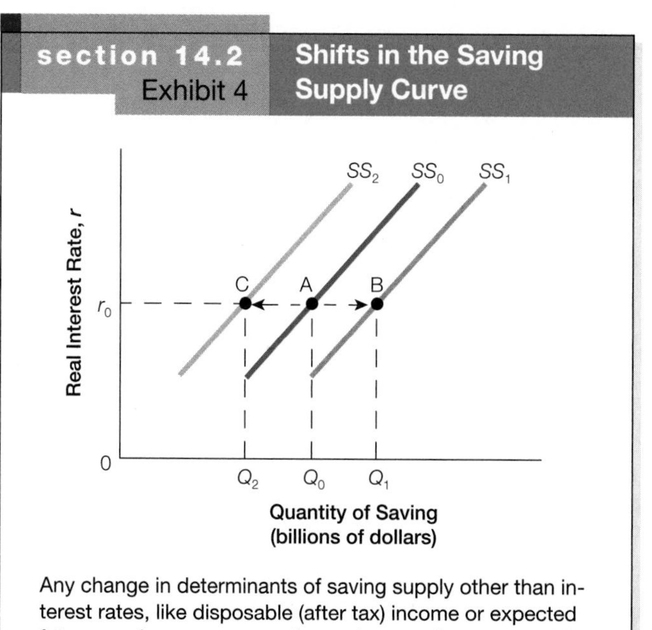

Any change in determinants of saving supply other than interest rates, like disposable (after tax) income or expected future earnings, can cause the saving supply curve to shift. An increase in disposable income or lower expected future earnings shifts the saving supply curve to the right, from point A to point B. A decrease in disposable income and higher expected future earnings will shift the saving supply curve to the left, from point A to point C.

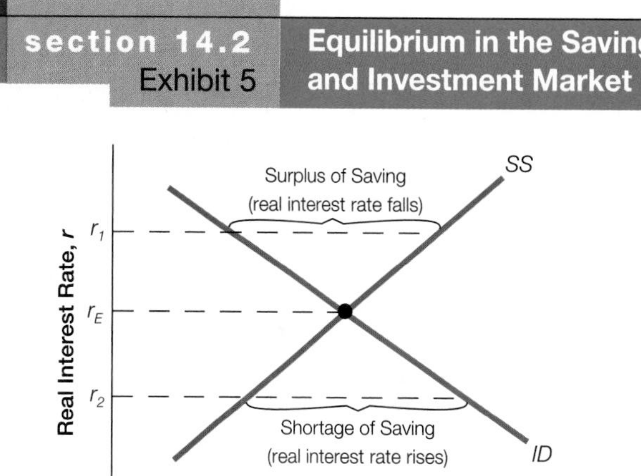

Desired investment equals desired national saving at the intersection of the investment demand curve and the saving supply curve, the equilibrium in the saving and investment market. The intersection of these two curves shows the real equilibrium interest rate. At higher than the real equilibrium interest rate, the quantity of savings supplied would be greater that quantity of investment demanded; there would be a surplus of savings at this real interest rate. As savers (lenders) compete against each other to attract investment demanders (borrowers), the real interest rate falls. If the real interest rate, r_2, is below the equilibrium real interest rate, r_E, the quantity of investment demanded is greater than the quantity of saving supplied at that interest rate and a shortage of saving occurs. As investment demanders (borrowers) compete against each other for the available saving, the real interest rate is bid up to r_E.

Section Check

SECTION CHECK

1. The investment demand curve is downward sloping, reflecting the fact that the quantity of investment demanded varies inversely with the real interest rate.
2. At high real interest rates, firms will only pursue those few investment activities with still higher expected rates of return. At lower real interest rates, projects with lower expected rates of return become profitable for firms, and the quantity of investment demanded rises.
3. Technology, inventories, expectations, and business taxes can shift the investment demand curve at a given real interest rate.
4. The supply of national saving is composed of both private saving and public saving.
5. The supply curve of saving is upward sloping. At a higher real interest rate, there is an increase in the quantity of saving supplied. At a lower real interest rate, there is a decrease in the quantity of saving supplied.
6. Two non-interest determinants of the saving supply curve are disposable (after tax) income and expected future earnings.
7. In equilibrium, desired investment equals desired national saving at the intersection of the investment demand curve and the saving supply curve. If the real interest rate is above the equilibrium real interest rate, the quantity of saving supplied is greater than the quantity of investment demanded at that interest rate; lenders will compete against each other to attract borrowers and the real interest rate falls. If the real interest rate is below the equilibrium real interest rate, the quantity of investment demanded is greater than the quantity of saving supplied at that interest rate; borrowers compete with each other for the available saving and drive the real interest rate up.

---

1. Why does the investment demand curve slope downward?
2. What factors can shift the investment demand curve?
3. Why does the saving supply curve slope upward?
4. What factors can shift the saving supply curve?
5. How is the real interest rate determined?
6. How are shortages and surpluses eliminated in the investment and saving market?

section 14.3

The Aggregate Demand Curve

- How is the aggregate demand curve different from the demand curve for a particular good?
- Why is the aggregate demand curve downward sloping?

aggregate demand curve
graph that shows the inverse relationship between the price level and RGDP demanded

The **aggregate demand curve** reflects the total amount of real goods and services that all groups together want to purchase in a given time period. In other words, it indicates the quantities of real gross domestic product demanded at different price levels. Note that this is different from the demand curve for a particular good presented in chapter 4, which looked at the relationship between the relative price of a good and the quantity demanded.

HOW IS THE QUANTITY OF REAL GDP DEMANDED AFFECTED BY THE PRICE LEVEL?

The aggregate demand curve slopes downward, which means that there is an inverse (or opposite) relationship between the price level and real gross domestic product (RGDP) demanded. Exhibit 1 illustrates this relationship, where the quantity of RGDP demanded is measured on the horizontal axis and the overall price level is measured on the vertical axis. As we move from point A to point B on the aggregate demand curve, we see that an increase in the price level causes RGDP demanded to fall. Conversely, if there is a reduction in the price level, a movement from B to A, quantity demanded of RGDP increases. Why do purchasers in the economy demand less real output when the price level rises, and more real output when the price level falls?

section 14.3 Exhibit 1 — The Aggregate Demand Curve

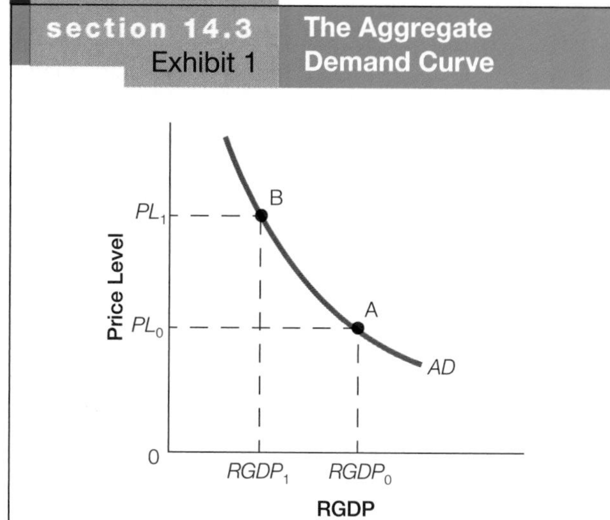

The aggregate demand curve slopes downward, reflecting an inverse relationship between the overall price level and the quantity of real GDP demanded. When the price level increases, the quantity of RGDP demanded decreases; when the price level decreases, the quantity of RGDP demanded increases.

WHY IS THE AGGREGATE DEMAND CURVE NEGATIVELY SLOPED?

Three complementary explanations exist for the negative slope of the aggregate demand curve: the real wealth effect, the interest rate effect, and the open economy effect.

The Real Wealth Effect

Imagine that you are living in a period of high inflation on a fixed pension that is not indexed for the changing price level. As the cost of goods and services rises, your monthly pension check remains the same. Therefore, the purchasing power of your pension will continue to decline as long as inflation is occurring. The same would be true of any asset of fixed dollar value, like cash. If you had $1,000 in cash stashed under your bed while the economy suffered a serious bout of inflation, the purchasing power of your cash would be eroded by the extent of the inflation. That is, an increase in the price level reduces real wealth and would consequently decrease your planned purchases of goods and services, lowering the quantity of RGDP demanded.

In the event that the price level falls, the reverse would hold true. A falling price level would increase the real value of your cash assets, increasing your purchasing power and increasing RGDP. The connection can be summarized as follows:

$$\uparrow \text{Price level} \Rightarrow \downarrow \text{Real wealth} \Rightarrow \downarrow \text{Purchasing power} \Rightarrow \downarrow \text{RGDP demanded}$$

and

$$\downarrow \text{Price level} \Rightarrow \uparrow \text{Real wealth} \Rightarrow \uparrow \text{Purchasing power} \Rightarrow \uparrow \text{RGDP demanded}$$

The Interest Rate Effect

The effect of the price level on interest rates can also cause the aggregate demand curve to have a negative slope. Suppose the price level increases. As a result, most goods and services will now have a higher price tag. Consequently, consumers will wish to hold more dollars in order to purchase those items that they want to buy, which will increase the demand for money. If the demand for money increases and the Federal Reserve System, the controller of the money supply, does not alter the money supply, then interest rates will rise. In other words, if the demand for money increases relative to the supply, then the demanders of dollars will bid up the price of those dollars—the interest rate. At higher interest rates, the opportunity cost of borrowing rises, and fewer interest-sensitive investments will be profitable, reducing the quantity of investment goods demanded. Businesses contemplating replacing worn-out equipment or planning to expand capacity may cancel or delay their investment decisions unless interest rates decline again. Also, at the higher interest rate, many consumers may give up plans to buy new cars, boats, or houses. That is, the higher interest rate also has a consumption link. The net effect of the higher interest rate, then, is that it will result in fewer investment goods demanded and, consequently, a lower RGDP demanded.

On the other hand, if the price level fell, and people demanded less money as a result, then interest rates would fall. Lower interest rates would trigger greater investment spending, and a larger real GDP demanded would result. We can summarize this process as follows:

↑Price level ⇒ ↑Money demand (Money supply unchanged) ⇒ ↑Interest rate ⇒ ↓Investments ⇒ ↓RGDP demanded

and

↓Price level ⇒ ↓Money demand (Money supply unchanged) ⇒ ↓Interest rate ⇒ ↑Investments ⇒ ↑RGDP demanded

The Open Economy Effect of Changes in the Price Level

Many goods and services are bought and sold in global markets. If the prices of goods and services in the domestic market rise relative to those in global markets due to a higher domestic price level, consumers and businesses will buy more from foreign producers and less from domestic producers. Because real GDP is a measure of domestic output, the reduction in the willingness of consumers to buy from domestic producers leads to a lower real GDP demanded at the higher domestic price level. And if domestic prices of goods and services fall relative to foreign prices, more domestic products will be bought, increasing real GDP demanded. This relationship can be shown as follows:

↑Price level ⇒ ↓Demand for domestic goods ⇒ ↓RGDP demanded

and

↓Price level ⇒ ↑Demand for domestic goods ⇒ ↑RGDP demanded

Section Check

1. An aggregate demand curve shows the inverse relationship between the amounts of real goods and services (RGDP) that is demanded at each possible price level.
2. The aggregate demand curve is downward sloping because of the real wealth effect, the interest rate effect, and the open economy effect.

---

1. Why is the aggregate demand curve downward sloping?
2. How does an increased price level reduce the quantities of investment goods and consumer durables demanded?
3. What is the real wealth effect, and how does it imply a downward-sloping aggregate demand curve?
4. What is the interest rate effect, and how does it imply a downward-sloping aggregate demand curve?
5. What is the open economy effect, and how does it imply a downward-sloping aggregate demand curve?

section 14.4

Shifts in the Aggregate Demand Curve

- What variables shift the aggregate demand curve to the right?
- What variables shift the aggregate demand curve to the left?
- What is the difference between a movement along and a shift in the aggregate demand curve?

DOES A CHANGE IN THE PRICE LEVEL SHIFT THE AGGREGATE DEMAND CURVE?

As for the supply and demand curves of chapter 4, there can be both shifts in and movements along the aggregate demand curve. In the previous section, we discussed three factors—the real wealth effect, the interest rate effect, and the foreign market effect—that result in the downward slope of the aggregate demand curve. Each of these factors, then, generates a movement *along* the aggregate demand curve, because the general price level changed. In this section, we will discuss some of the many factors that can cause the aggregate demand curve to shift to the right or left.

The whole aggregate demand curve can shift to the right or left, as seen in Exhibit 1. Put simply, if some non-price level determinant causes total spending to increase, then the aggregate demand curve will shift to the right. If a non-price level determinant causes the level of total spending to decline, then the aggregate demand curve will shift to the left. Now let's look at some specific factors that could cause the aggregate demand curve to shift.

section 14.4 Exhibit 1 Shifts in the Aggregate Demand Curve

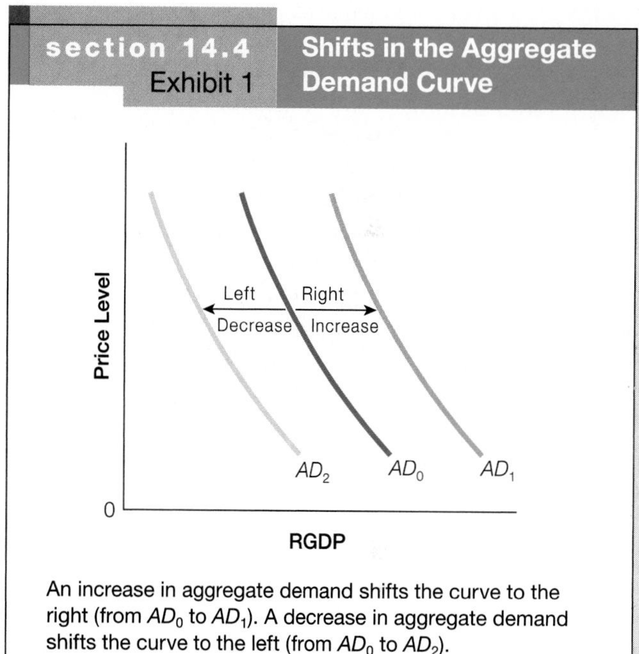

An increase in aggregate demand shifts the curve to the right (from AD_0 to AD_1). A decrease in aggregate demand shifts the curve to the left (from AD_0 to AD_2).

AGGREGATE DEMAND CURVE SHIFTERS

Anything that changes the amount of total spending in the economy (holding price levels constant) will impact the aggregate demand curve. An increase in any component of GDP (C, I, G, and $X - M$) can cause the aggregate demand curve to shift rightward. Conversely, decreases in C, I, G, or $(X - M)$ will shift aggregate demand leftward.

Changing Consumption (*C*)

A whole host of changes could alter consumption patterns. For example, an increase in consumer confidence, an increase in wealth, or a tax cut each can increase consumption and shift the aggregate demand curve to the right. An increase in population would also increase the aggregate demand, as there are now more consumers spending more money on goods and services.

APPLICATION

CHANGES IN AGGREGATE DEMAND

Q: Any aggregate demand category that has the ability to change total purchases in the economy will shift the aggregate demand curve. That is, changes in consumption purchases, investment purchases, government purchases, or net export purchases shift the aggregate demand curve. For each component of aggregate demand (*C*, *I*, *G*, and *X* – *M*) list some changes that can increase aggregate demand. Then, list some changes that can decrease aggregate demand.

A: Below we list some aggregate demand curve shifters.

INCREASES IN AGGREGATE DEMAND (RIGHTWARD SHIFT)

Consumption (*C*)
- —lower personal taxes
- —a rise in consumer confidence
- —greater stock market wealth
- —an increase in transfer payments

Investment (*I*)
- —lower real interest rates
- —optimistic business forecasts
- —lower business taxes

Government Purchases (*G*)
- —an increase in government purchases

Net Exports (*X* – *M*)
- —income increases abroad, which will likely increase the sale of domestic goods (exports)

DECREASES IN AGGREGATE DEMAND (LEFTWARD SHIFT)

Consumption (*C*)
- —higher personal taxes
- —a fall in consumer confidence
- —reduced stock market wealth
- —a reduction in transfer payments

Investment (*I*)
- —higher real interest rates
- —pessimistic business forecasts
- —higher business taxes

Government Purchases (*G*)
- —a reduction in government purchases

Net Exports (*X* – *M*)
- —income falls abroad, which will lead to a reduction in the sales of domestic goods (exports)

Of course, the aggregate demand curve could shift to the left due to decreases in consumption demand. For example, if consumers sensed that the economy was headed for a recession or if the government imposed a tax increase, this would result in a leftward shift of the aggregate demand curve. Because consuming less is saving more, an increase in savings, *ceteris paribus,* will shift aggregate demand to the left. Consumer debt may also be a reason that some consumers might put off additional spending. In fact, some economists believe that part of the 1990–1992 recession was due to consumer debt that had built up during the 1980s. Aside from maxing out their credit cards, some individuals also lost equity in their homes and, consequently, had a reduction in their wealth and purchasing power—again shifting aggregate demand to the left.

Changing Investment (*I*)

Investment is also an important determinant of aggregate demand. Increases in the demand for investment goods occur for a variety of reasons. For example, if business confidence increases or real interest rates fall, business investment will increase and aggregate demand will shift to the right. A reduction in business taxes would also shift the aggregate demand curve to the right, because businesses would now retain more of their profits to invest. However, if interest rates or business taxes rise, then we would expect to see a leftward shift in aggregate demand.

In The NEWS

THE CONSUMER CONFIDENCE INDEX: A BRIEF DESCRIPTION OF THE CONSUMER CONFIDENCE SURVEY

The Consumer Confidence Survey measures the level of confidence individual households have in the performance of the economy. Survey questionnaires are mailed to a representative nationwide sample of 5,000 households, of which approximately 3,500 respond. Households are asked five questions that include (1) a rating of current business conditions in the household's area, (2) a rating of expected business conditions in six months, (3) current job availability in the area, (4) expected job availability in six months, and (5) expected family income in six months. The responses are seasonally adjusted. An index is constructed for each response and then a composite index is fashioned based on the responses. Two other indexes, one for an assessment of the present situation and one for expectations about the future, are also constructed. Expectations account for 60 percent of the index, while the current situation is responsible for the remaining 40 percent. In addition, indexes for the present and expected future economic situations are calculated for each of the nine census divisions. In the base year, 1985, the value of the index was 100.

The Conference Board also tracks consumer buying plans over the next six months. Among the items tracked are automobiles, homes, vacations, and major appliances. If the economy experiences a long-term expansion, buying intentions may eventually decline even if the jobless rate stays low, because of the satisfaction of pent-up demand. Conversely, if inflation begins to accelerate, spending plans may increase for the short term as consumers buy now to avoid paying higher prices later.

section 14.4 Exhibit 2 Losing Confidence, 2001–2002

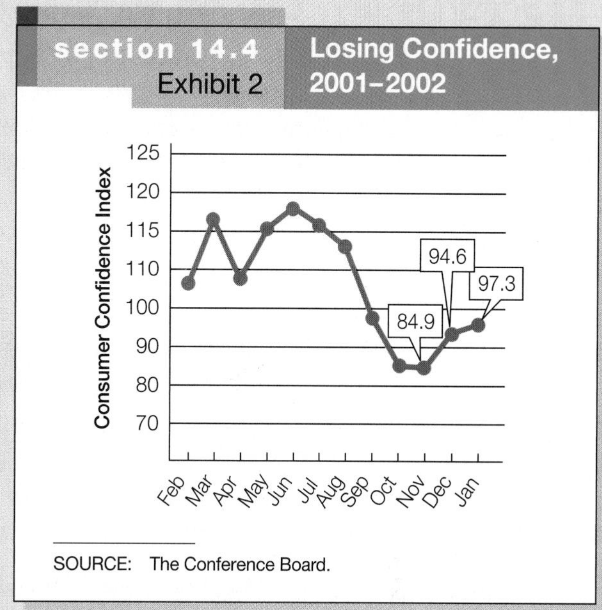

SOURCE: The Conference Board.

Consumer confidence correlates closely with joblessness, inflation, and real incomes. The growth of help wanted advertising (a measure of job prospects) is also correlated with strong consumer confidence. Rising stock market prices also boost consumer confidence.

SOURCE: Dismal Sciences.

CONSIDER THIS

The consumer confidence index has the potential to reflect important aggregate demand shifters. For example, if inflation is expected, consumers may increase their spending now. This would shift the aggregate demand curve to the right. Also, if the consumer confidence survey shows that consumer and business confidence in the economy is rising, we would also expect to see an increase in aggregate demand. Stock market wealth would increase consumption and shift the aggregate demand curve to the right. Of course, if the consumer confidence survey showed pessimism and signs of a downturn, we would expect the aggregate demand curve to shift to the left. In short, consumer and business perceptions of the economy are often important aggregate demand shifters and can have significant impact on price level, real output, and employment as a result.

The consumer confidence index is a critical piece of information because consumer spending fuels over two-thirds of the U.S. economy. The Federal Reserve cut short-term interest rates 11 times in 2001 in an effort to make borrowing easier and keep consumers spending in light of a recession that began in March 2001 and the terror attacks of September 11.

Changing Government Purchases (*G*)

Government purchases is also part of total spending and therefore must impact aggregate demand. An increase in government purchases, other things equal, shifts the aggregate demand curve to the right, while a reduction shifts aggregate demand to the left.

Changing Net Exports ($X - M$)

Global markets are also important in a domestic economy. For example, if major trading partners are experiencing economic slowdowns (such as occurred in the Asian market in the late 1990s), then they will demand fewer U.S. imports. This causes U.S. net exports ($X - M$) to fall, shifting aggregate demand to the left. Alternatively, an economic boom in the economies of major trading partners may lead to an increase in our exports to them, causing net exports ($X - M$) to rise and aggregate demand to increase.

Section Check

1. A change in the price level causes a movement along the aggregate demand curve, not a shift in the aggregate demand curve.
2. Aggregate demand is made up of total spending, or $C + I + G + (X - M)$. Any change in these factors will cause the aggregate demand curve to shift.

---

1. How is the distinction between a change in demand and a change in quantity demanded the same for aggregate demand as for the demand for a particular good?
2. What happens to aggregate demand if the demand for consumption goods increases, *ceteris paribus?*
3. What happens to aggregate demand if the demand for investment goods falls, *ceteris paribus?*
4. Why would an increase in the money supply tend to increase expenditures on consumption and investment, *ceteris paribus?*

Summary

Aggregate demand is the sum of the demand for all goods and services in the economy. It can also be seen as the quantity of real GDP demanded at different price levels. The four major components of aggregate demand are consumption (C), investment (I), government purchases (G), and net exports ($X - M$). Aggregate demand, then, is equal to $C + I + G + (X - M)$.

Empirical evidence suggests that consumption increases directly with any increase in disposable income. The additional consumption spending stemming from an additional dollar of disposable income is called the marginal propensity to consume (MPC).

At high real interest rates, firms will only pursue those few investment activities with still higher expected rates of return. At lower real interest rates, projects with lower expected rates of return become profitable for firms, and the quantity of investment demanded rises. In equilibrium in the saving and investment market, desired investment equals desired national saving at the intersection of the investment demand curve and the saving supply curve. At high real interest rates, firms will only pursue those few investment activities with still higher expected rates of return. At lower real interest rates, projects with lower expected rates of return become profitable for firms, and the quantity of investment demanded rises.

An aggregate demand curve shows the inverse relationship between the price level and RGDP demanded. The aggregate demand curve is downward sloping because of the real wealth effect, the interest rate effect, and the open economy effect. A change in the price level causes a movement along the aggregate demand curve, not a shift in the aggregate demand curve. Aggregate demand is made up of total spending, or $C + I + G + (X - M)$. Any change in these factors will cause the aggregate demand curve to shift.

Key Terms and Concepts

aggregate demand (*AD*) 308
average propensity to consume (*APC*) 308
marginal propensity to consume (*MPC*) 308
open economy 309
net exports 310
aggregate demand curve 314

Review Questions

1. Suppose an elderly person draws upon past savings and spends more each month than she receives from Social Security. What economic theory is illustrated by the behavior of this person?
2. If retailers such as Wal-Mart and Target find that inventories are rapidly being depleted, would it have been caused by a rightward or leftward change in the aggregate demand curve? What are the likely consequences for output and investment?
3. Evaluate the following statement: "A higher price level decreases the purchasing power of the dollar and reduces RGDP."
4. How does a higher price level in the U.S. economy affect purchases of imported goods? Explain.
5. Which of the following both decreases consumption *and* shifts the aggregate demand curve to the left?
   - **a.** an increase in financial wealth
   - **b.** an increase in taxes
   - **c.** an increase in the price level
   - **d.** a decrease in interest rates
6. Predict how each of the following would impact investment expenditures.
   - **a.** inventory levels are depleted
   - **b.** banks scrutinize borrower credit more carefully and interest rates rise
   - **c.** decreasing profit rates over the last few quarters
   - **d.** factories operate at 60 percent capacity, down from 80 percent
7. Identify which expenditure category each of the following will directly impact, and also which direction the U.S. aggregate demand curve will shift as a result.
   - **a.** income increases abroad
   - **b.** a decrease in interest rates
   - **c.** Congress passes a permanent tax cut
   - **d.** Firms become more optimistic about the outlook for the economy
   - **e.** Stocks traded on the NASDAQ market lose 40 percent of their value in one month's time
8. Explain how a recession in Latin America may affect aggregate demand in the U.S. economy.
9. Visit the Sexton Web site at **http://sexton.swcollege.com** and click on "Government Printing Office." Look up the latest Economic Indicators and examine business capacity utilization rates. Is the recent trend in capacity utilization rates in an upward or downward direction? On that basis, what might you predict about investment and aggregate demand in the economy?
10. Visit the Sexton Web site, click on "Conference Board" and find the latest figures for the Consumer Confidence Index (CCI). What does the recent trend in the Consumer Confidence Index bode for aggregate demand in the macroeconomy?

Fill in the Blanks

1. Aggregate demand (*AD*) refers to the quantity of ______________ at different price levels.
2. ______________ is by far the largest component of *AD*.
3. The higher a nation's income, the ______________ it spends on consumption.
4. At higher real interest rates, consumers save ______________ and consume ______________.
5. The additional consumption that results from an additional dollar of disposable income is the ______________ propensity to consume.
6. If a person with $10,000 in total disposable income spent $6,000 on consumption, her average propensity to consume would be equal to ______________.
7. Government purchases tend to be a ______________ volatile category of aggregate demand than investment.
8. Models that include international trade effects are called ______________ models.
9. Exports minus imports equals ______________.
10. If we put the investment demand for the whole economy and national savings together, we can establish the ______________ interest rate in the saving and investment market.
11. The ______________ curve shows the dollar amount of investment forthcoming at different real interest rates.
12. The investment demand curve is ______________ sloping, reflecting the fact that investment spending varies ______________ with the real interest rate.
13. As the real interest rate ______________, additional projects with lower expected rates of return become profitable for firms, and the quantity of investment demanded ______________.
14. Governments often try to combat recessions by ______________ interest rates.
15. If firms expect lower rates of return on their investments, for a given interest rate, the investment demand curve will shift to the ______________.
16. The development of new machines that can ______________ the quality and the quantity of products or ______________ the costs of production will increase the rate of return on investment.
17. When inventories are high, there is a ______________ expected rate of return on new investment, and the investment demand curve shifts to the ______________.
18. If higher expected sales and a higher profit rate are forecast, the investment demand curve shifts to the ______________.
19. Higher business taxes will lead to ______________ potential after-tax profits on investment projects and shift the investment demand curve to the ______________.
20. The supply curve of savings is ______________ sloping.
21. At a lower real interest rate, a ______________ quantity of savings is supplied.
22. If disposable income fell, there would be ______________ saving at any given interest rate.

23. If you expected lower future earnings, you would tend to save ____________ now at any given interest rate—shifting the saving supply curve to the ____________.

24. In equilibrium, desired ____________ equals desired national saving.

25. The equilibrium ____________ interest rate is determined by the intersection of the investment demand curve and the saving supply curve.

26. At a higher-than-equilibrium real interest rate, the quantity of savings supplied would be ____________ than the quantity of investment demanded—there would be a ____________ of savings at this real interest rate.

27. The *AD* curve slopes ____________, which means that there is an ____________ relationship between the price level and real gross domestic product (RGDP) demanded.

28. Three complementary explanations exist for the negative slope of the aggregate demand curve: the ____________ effect, the ____________ effect, and the ____________ effect.

29. As the price level decreases, the real value of people's cash balances ____________ so that their planned purchases of goods and services ____________.

30. The real wealth effect can be summarized as follows: A higher price level → ____________ real wealth → ____________ purchasing power → ____________ RGDP demanded.

31. At a higher price level, consumers will wish to hold ____________ dollars in order to purchase those items that they want to buy, which will ____________ the demand for money.

32. At higher interest rates, the opportunity cost of borrowing ____________, and ____________ interest-sensitive investments will be profitable, which will result in a ____________ quantity of RGDP demanded.

33. The interest rate effect process can be summarized as follows: A higher price level → ____________ money demand (money supply unchanged) → ____________ the interest rate → ____________ investments → ____________ RGDP demanded.

34. If the prices of goods and services in the domestic market rise relative to those in global markets due to a higher domestic price level, consumers and businesses will buy ____________ from foreign producers and ____________ from domestic producers.

35. The open economy effect can be summarized as follows: A decreased price level → ____________ the demand for domestic goods → ____________ RGDP demanded.

36. The real wealth effect, the interest rate effect, and the open economy effect all contribute to the ____________ slope of the *AD* curve.

37. An increase in any component of GDP (C, I, G, and $X - M$) can cause the *AD* curve to shift ____________.

38. If consumers sensed the economy was headed for a recession or the government imposed a tax increase, this would result in a ____________ shift of the *AD* curve.

39. Since consuming less is saving more, an increase in savings, *ceteris paribus,* would shift *AD* to the ____________.

40. A reduction in business taxes would shift *AD* to the ____________, while an increase in real interest rates or business taxes would shift *AD* to the ____________.

41. An increase in government purchases, other things being equal, shifts *AD* to the ____________.

42. If major trading partners are experiencing economic slowdowns, then they will demand ____________ imports from the U.S., shifting *AD* to the ____________.

True or False

1. Aggregate demand (*AD*) = Consumption (*C*) + Investment (*I*) + Government purchases (*G*) + Net exports ($X - M$).
2. Because consumption is such a stable part of GDP, analyzing its determinants is not very important to an understanding of the forces leading to changes in aggregate demand.
3. At the level of individuals, consumption increases with after-tax, or disposable, income.
4. The fraction of their total disposable income that households spend on consumption is called the marginal propensity to consume.
5. If a person's consumption spending went from $8,000 to $14,000 when his total disposable income went from $10,000 to $20,000, his marginal propensity to consume would be 0.7.
6. Good business conditions tend to increase the level of investment by firms.
7. A $1 million increase in exports has a smaller direct effect on aggregate demand than a $1 million increase in government purchases.
8. Either an increase in exports or a decrease in imports would increase net exports.
9. *Ceteris paribus,* negative net exports would decrease aggregate demand.
10. The investment demand curve is upward sloping, reflecting the fact that investments are more profitable when they yield higher real interest rates.
11. As the real interest rate falls, additional projects with lower expected rates of return become profitable for firms, and the demand for investment curve shifts right.
12. If firms expect higher rates of return on their investments, for a given interest rate, the investment demand curve will shift to the right.
13. Either changes in technology or business taxes can shift the investment demand curve.
14. The development of new products can increase the rate of return on investment and cause the investment demand curve to shift to the right.
15. Firms with excess inventories of finished goods have an increased incentive to invest in new capital to put those inventories to productive use.
16. If firms' inventories are depleted below the levels desired, the economy would tend to move down along its investment demand curve.

17. If lower expected sales and a lower profit rate are forecast, fewer investments will be desired at a given interest rate.

18. If business taxes are lowered, potential after-tax profits on investment projects will increase and shift the investment demand curve to the right.

19. Households, firms, and the government can all supply savings in the economy.

20. At a higher real interest rate, the supply of savings shifts to the right.

21. If disposable (after-tax) income were to rise, more savings would occur at any given interest rate.

22. If you expected higher future earnings, you would tend to both consume more and save more now.

23. If the real interest rate is above the equilibrium real interest rate, forces within the economy would tend to restore the equilibrium.

24. If the real interest rate is below the equilibrium real interest rate, the quantity of investment demanded is greater than the quantity of saving supplied at that interest rate, and a shortage of saving occurs.

25. If the real interest rate is above the equilibrium real interest rate, investment demanders (borrowers) will compete against each other for the available saving, bidding the real interest rate up.

26. The aggregate demand (*AD*) curve indicates the quantities of nominal GDP demanded at different price levels.

27. The *AD* curve is downward sloping for the same reasons that the demand curve for a particular product is downward sloping.

28. An increase in the price level causes the quantity of RGDP demanded to fall.

29. The real wealth effect reflects the fact that the real (adjusted for inflation) value of any asset of fixed dollar value, like cash, falls as the price level increases.

30. A lower price level, other things being equal, will lead to increased real wealth and an increase in the quantity of RGDP demanded.

31. At a higher price level, if the money supply does not increase, then interest rates will fall, other things being equal.

32. If the price level fell, interest rates would fall, which would trigger greater investment and consumer durable spending.

33. A lower price level, other things being equal, would decrease money demand and the interest rate, and increase both the level of investment and the quantity of RGDP demanded.

34. If domestic prices of goods and services fall relative to foreign prices, more domestic products will be bought, increasing RGDP demanded.

35. An increased price level will tend to increase the demand for domestic goods and increase RGDP demanded.

36. The real wealth effect, the interest rate effect, and the open economy effect all shift the *AD* curve.

37. A change in the price level will not change aggregate demand.

38. Decreases in any of *C, I, G,* or $X - M$ for reasons other than changes in the price level will shift *AD* leftward.

39. An increase in consumer confidence, an increase in wealth, or a tax cut can each increase consumption and shift *AD* to the right.

40. An increase in consumer debt, other things being equal, would tend to shift *AD* to the left.

41. If either business confidence increases or real interest rates rise, business investment will increase and *AD* will shift to the right.

42. A reduction in government purchases shifts *AD* to the left.

43. An economic boom in the economies of major trading partners may lead to an increase in U.S. exports to them, causing net exports to rise and *AD* to increase.

Multiple Choice

1. The largest component of aggregate demand is
- **a.** government purchases.
- **b.** net exports.
- **c.** consumption.
- **d.** investment.

2. A reduction in personal income taxes, other things being equal, will
- **a.** leave consumers with less disposable income.
- **b.** decrease aggregate demand.
- **c.** leave consumers with more disposable income.
- **d.** increase aggregate demand.
- **e.** do both c and d.

3. Aggregate demand is the sum of ______.
- **a.** $C + I + G$
- **b.** $C + I + G + X$
- **c.** $C + I + G + (X - M)$
- **d.** $C + I + G + (X + M)$

4. The marginal propensity to consume (*MPC*) is defined as
- **a.** the additional consumption that results from a one-dollar increase in disposable income.
- **b.** the fraction of total disposable income that households spend on consumption.
- **c.** the fraction of total disposable income that households save.
- **d.** the additional disposable income households earn in a given period.

5. Empirical evidence suggests that consumption ______ with any ______.
- **a.** decreases, increase in income
- **b.** decreases, tax cut
- **c.** increases, decrease in consumer confidence
- **d.** increases, increase in income
- **e.** Both a and b are true

6. Investment (I) includes
- **a.** the amount spent on new factories and machinery.
- **b.** the amount spent on stocks and bonds.
- **c.** the amount spent on consumer goods that last more than one year.
- **d.** the amount spent on purchases of art.
- **e.** all of the above.

7. If private consumption in the United States were 67 percent of GDP, investment were 16 percent, government purchases were 13 percent, exports were 12 percent, and imports were 8 percent, net exports would be equal to ______ percent of GDP.
   a. 4
   b. −4
   c. 20
   d. −20
   e. none of the above

8. If our exports of final goods and services increase more than our imports, other things being equal, aggregate demand will
   a. increase.
   b. be negative.
   c. decrease by the change in net exports.
   d. stay the same.
   e. do none of the above.

9. Bill's disposable income goes from $100,000 in 2001 to $200,000 in 2002, and his consumption spending goes from $80,000 in 2001 to $140,000 in 2002. Which of the following statements about Bill is true?
   a. Bill's *APC* rose between 2001 and 2002.
   b. Bill's *MPC* is equal to 0.7.
   c. Bill's *MPC* is equal to 0.6.
   d. Both a and b are true.
   e. Both a and c are true.

10. If Rhonda's taxes rose by $20,000, other things being equal,
   a. her consumption would fall by $15,000 if her MPC were equal to 0.75.
   b. her consumption would fall by $15,000 if her APC were equal to 0.75.
   c. her consumption would rise by $15,000 if her MPC were equal to 0.75.
   d. her consumption would rise by $15,000 if her APC were equal to 0.75.

11. A given change in disposable income would have the greatest effect on consumption with which of the following marginal propensities to consume?
   a. 0.2
   b. 0.4
   c. 0.6
   d. 0.8

12. Which of the following changes in disposable income would lead to the greatest increase in consumption?
   a. a $20,000 increase in disposable income, if *MPC* equals 0.5
   b. a $12,000 increase in disposable income, if *MPC* equals 0.75
   c. a $15,000 increase in disposable income, if *MPC* equals 0.6
   d. a $30,000 increase in disposable income, if *MPC* equals 0.25

13. An appreciable increase in interest rates would, other things being equal,
   a. decrease consumption.
   b. increase consumption.
   c. increase saving.
   d. do both a and b.
   e. do both a and c.

14. Increases in investment will tend to occur when

a. businesses decide to proceed with an investment on the basis of increases in income or output.

b. the level and rate of change of profits increase.

c. investors become more optimistic in their expectations toward the future.

d. any of the above occur.

15. Investment increases

a. when interest rates are higher.

b. when firms have very high capital utilization rates.

c. when tax rates on businesses are reduced.

d. when firms hold higher amounts of inventory than they desire.

e. when either b or c occurs.

16. If the country is experiencing rapid economic growth and increasing personal incomes, the expected result is that consumption will ______ and investment will ______.

a. increase; decrease

b. decrease; decrease

c. increase; increase

d. decrease; increase

e. increase; decrease

17. A decrease in interest rates is likely to result in

a. a decrease in consumption spending.

b. a decrease in investment spending.

c. an increase in investment spending.

d. an increase in consumption spending.

e. both c and d.

18. At lower real interest rates,

a. people save more.

b. people save less.

c. people consume more.

d. people consume less.

e. both b and c are true.

19. I. The investment demand curve for the economy is downward sloping.
II. The supply of national saving curve for the economy is upward sloping.

a. I and II are both true.

b. I and II are both false.

c. I is true, and II is false.

d. I is false, and II is true.

20. Which of the following will *not* increase the investment demand curve?

a. the introduction of new profitable technology investment opportunities

b. business inventories that have fallen far below desired levels

c. a decrease in real interest rates

d. business expectations of higher future sales and profits

e. none of the above

21. A combination of the discovery of profitable new technology investment opportunities and inventories that have fallen far below desired levels

a. would increase the investment demand curve.

b. would decrease the investment demand curve.

c. would leave the investment demand curve unchanged.

d. could either increase or decrease the investment demand curve.

22. A combination of higher business taxes, reduced expected future profitability of businesses, and a reduction in the level of new profitable technology investment opportunities
   a. would increase the investment demand curve.
   b. would decrease the investment demand curve.
   c. would leave the investment demand curve unchanged.
   d. could either increase or decrease the investment demand curve.

23. Which of the following would increase the supply of national saving curve?
   a. an increase in disposable income
   b. a decrease in disposable income
   c. an increase in expected future earnings
   d. Both a and c would increase the supply of national saving curve.
   e. Both b and c would increase the supply of national saving curve.

24. If at a given interest rate the quantity of savings supplied is greater than the quantity of investment demanded,
   a. there is a surplus of savings, and real interest rates will rise.
   b. there is a surplus of savings, and real interest rates will fall.
   c. there is a shortage of savings, and real interest rates will rise.
   d. there is a shortage of savings, and real interest rates will fall.

25. An increase in the investment demand curve would
   a. increase real interest rates.
   b. decrease real interest rates.
   c. increase the dollar amount of investment.
   d. decrease the dollar amount of investment.
   e. do both a and c.

26. A decrease in the supply of national saving curve would
   a. increase real interest rates.
   b. decrease real interest rates.
   c. increase the dollar amount of investment.
   d. do both a and c.
   e. do both b and c.

27. The aggregate demand curve
   a. is negatively sloped.
   b. demonstrates an inverse relationship between the price level and real gross domestic product demanded.
   c. shows how real gross domestic product demanded changes with the changes in the price level.
   d. All of the above are correct.

28. As the price level increases, other things being equal,
   a. aggregate demand decreases.
   b. the quantity of real gross domestic product demanded increases.
   c. the quantity of real gross domestic product demanded decreases.
   d. aggregate demand increases.
   e. both a and c occur.

29. According to the real wealth effect, if you are living in a period of falling price levels on a fixed income (that is not indexed), the cost of the goods and services you buy ______ and your real income ______.

a. decreases; decreases
b. increases; increases
c. decreases; remains the same
d. decreases; increases

30. As the price level decreases, real wealth ______, purchasing power ______, and the quantity of RGDP demanded ______.

a. increases; decreases; increases
b. increases; increases; increases
c. decreases; decreases; decreases
d. decreases; decreases; increases
e. increases; decreases; decreases

31. As the price level increases, money demand (money supply unchanged) ______, interest rates ______, investments ______, and the quantity of RGDP demanded ______.

a. increases; decrease; increase; decreases
b. increases; increase; increase; decreases
c. decreases; decrease; decrease; increases
d. decreases; decrease; increase; increases
e. increases; increase; decrease; decreases

32. What is the open economy effect?

a. If prices of the goods and services in the domestic market rise relative to those in global markets due to a higher domestic price level, consumers and businesses will buy less from foreign producers and more from domestic producers.
b. People are allowed to trade with anyone, anywhere, anytime.
c. It is the ability of firms to enter or leave the marketplace—easy entry and exit with low entry barriers.
d. If prices of the goods and services in the domestic market rise relative to those in global markets due to a higher domestic price level, consumers and businesses will buy more from foreign producers and less from domestic producers, other things being equal.

33. Which of the following helps explain the downward slope of the aggregate demand curve?

a. the real wealth effect
b. the interest effect
c. the open economy effect
d. all of the above
e. none of the above

34. Which of the following will result as part of the interest rate effect when the price level rises?

a. Money demand will increase.
b. Interest rates will increase.
c. The dollar amount of investment will decrease.
d. A lower quantity of real GDP will be demanded.
e. All of the above will result.

35. Which of the following will *not* decrease when the price level falls?
a. money demand
b. the real interest rate
c. the real level of investment
d. a and b
e. b and c

36. A decrease in the U.S. price level will
a. increase U.S. exports.
b. increase U.S. imports.
c. increase RGDP demanded in the United States.
d. both a and c.
e. both b and c.

37. An economic bust or severe downturn in the Japanese economy will likely result in a(n)
a. decrease in U.S. exports and U.S. aggregate demand.
b. increase in U.S. exports and U.S. aggregate demand.
c. decrease in U.S. imports and U.S. aggregate demand.
d. increase in U.S. imports and U.S. aggregate demand.

38. Which of the following will cause consumption, and as a result, aggregate demand, to decrease?
a. a tax increase
b. a fall in consumer confidence
c. reduced stock market wealth
d. rising levels of consumer debt
e. all of the above

39. A massive increase in interstate highway construction will affect aggregate demand through which sector? Will this increase or decrease aggregate demand?
a. investment, increase
b. government purchases, increase
c. government purchases, decrease
d. consumption, decrease

40. An increase in government purchases, combined with a decrease in investment, would have what effect on aggregate demand?
a. *AD* would increase.
b. *AD* would decrease.
c. *AD* would stay the same.
d. *AD* could either increase or decrease, depending on which change was of greater magnitude.

41. An increase in consumption, combined with an increase in exports, would have what effect on aggregate demand?
a. *AD* would increase.
b. *AD* would decrease.
c. *AD* would stay the same.
d. *AD* could either increase or decrease, depending on which change was of greater magnitude.

42. What would happen to aggregate demand if the federal government increased military purchases and state and local governments decreased their road-building budgets at the same time?
   a. *AD* would increase because only federal government purchases affect *AD*.
   b. *AD* would decrease because only state and local government purchases affect *AD*.
   c. *AD* would increase if the change in federal purchases were greater than the change in state and local purchases.
   d. *AD* would decrease if the change in federal purchases were greater than the change in state and local purchases.

43. If exports and imports both decrease, but exports decrease more than imports,
   a. *AD* would decrease.
   b. *AD* would increase.
   c. *AD* would be unaffected.
   d. *AD* could either increase or decrease.

44. If exports increased and imports decreased,
   a. *AD* would decrease.
   b. *AD* would increase.
   c. *AD* would be unaffected.
   d. *AD* could either increase or decrease.

Problems

1. Assume that Melanie had $200,000 of income and spent $180,000 on consumption in 2001 and had $300,000 of income and spent $240,000 on consumption in 2002.
   a. What was Melanie's average propensity to consume in 2001?
   b. What was Melanie's average propensity to consume in 2002?
   c. What is Melanie's marginal propensity to consume?
   d. If Melanie's income went up to $400,000 in 2003, how much would she be likely to spend on consumption that year? What would be her average propensity to consume?
   e. If Melanie's income went down to $100,000 in 2003, how much would she be likely to spend on consumption that year? What would be her average propensity to consume?

2. Describe what the effect on aggregate demand would be, other things being equal, if
   a. exports increase.
   b. both imports and exports decrease.
   c. consumption decreases.
   d. investment increases.
   e. investment decreases and government purchases increase.
   f. the price level increases.
   g. the price level decreases.

3. In the saving and investment market,
   a. what happens to the investment demand curve when the real interest rate declines?
   b. what happens to the investment demand curve when firms' inventories are rising above what the firms desire?
   c. what happens to the investment demand curve when technological advances give rise to popular new products?
   d. what happens to the saving supply curve when the real interest rate increases?
   e. what happens to the saving supply curve when disposable income increases?

4. 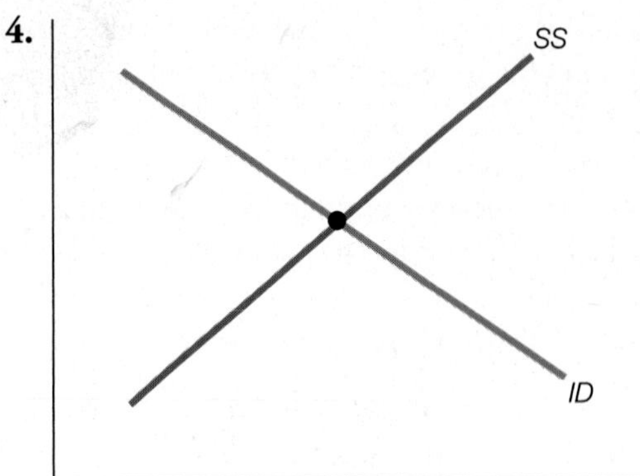

Label the axes for the saving and investment market. Then, explain and illustrate what would happen in the saving and investment market if

a. businesses become more optimistic about future business conditions.
b. individuals become less optimistic about their future incomes.
c. business taxes increase.
d. individuals' disposable incomes increase.

5. Fill in the blanks in the following explanations.

a. The real wealth effect is described by the following: An increase in the price level leads to a(n) ______ in real wealth, which leads to a(n) ______ in purchasing power, which leads to a(n) ______ in RGDP demanded.

b. The interest rate effect is described by the following: A decrease in the price level leads to a(n) ______ in money demand, which leads to a(n) ______ in the interest rate, which leads to a(n) ______ in investments, which leads to a(n) ______ in RGDP demanded.

c. The open economy effect is described by the following: An increase in the price level leads to a(n) ______ in the demand for domestic goods, which leads to a(n) ______ in RGDP demanded.

chapter 15

Aggregate Supply and Macroeconomic Equilibrium

15.1 **THE AGGREGATE SUPPLY CURVE**
What do the short-run and long-run aggregate supply curves represent?

15.2 **SHIFTS IN THE AGGREGATE SUPPLY CURVE**
What causes the aggregate supply curves to shift?

15.3 **MACROECONOMIC EQUILIBRIUM**
What are demand-pull and cost-push inflation?

section 15.1

The Aggregate Supply Curve

- What does the aggregate supply curve represent?
- Why do producers supply more as the price level increases in the short run?
- Why is the long-run aggregate supply curve vertical at the natural rate of output?

WHAT IS THE AGGREGATE SUPPLY CURVE?

aggregate supply curve (*AS*) *the total quantity of final goods and services suppliers are willing and able to supply at a given price level*

short-run aggregate supply curve *the graphical relationship between RGDP and the price level when output prices can change but input prices are unable to adjust*

long-run aggregate supply curve *the graphical relationship between RGDP and the price level when output prices and input prices can fully adjust to economic changes*

The **aggregate supply curve (*AS*)** is the relationship between the total quantity of final goods and services that suppliers are *willing* and *able* to produce and the overall price level. The aggregate supply curve represents how much RGDP suppliers are willing to produce at different price levels. In fact, there are two aggregate supply curves—a **short-run aggregate supply curve** and a **long-run aggregate supply curve.** The short-run relationship refers to a period when output can change in response to supply and demand, but input prices have not yet been able to adjust. For example, nominal wages are assumed to adjust slowly in the short run. The long-run relationship refers to a period long enough for the prices of outputs and all inputs to fully adjust to changes in the economy.

WHY IS THE SHORT-RUN AGGREGATE SUPPLY CURVE POSITIVELY SLOPED?

In the short run, the aggregate supply curve is upward sloping, as shown in Exhibit 1. This means that at a higher price level, producers are willing to supply more real output, and at lower price levels, they are willing to supply less real output. Why would producers be willing to supply more output just because the price level increases? There are two possible explanations: the profit effect and the misperception effect.

section 15.1 Exhibit 1 The Short-Run Aggregate Supply Curve

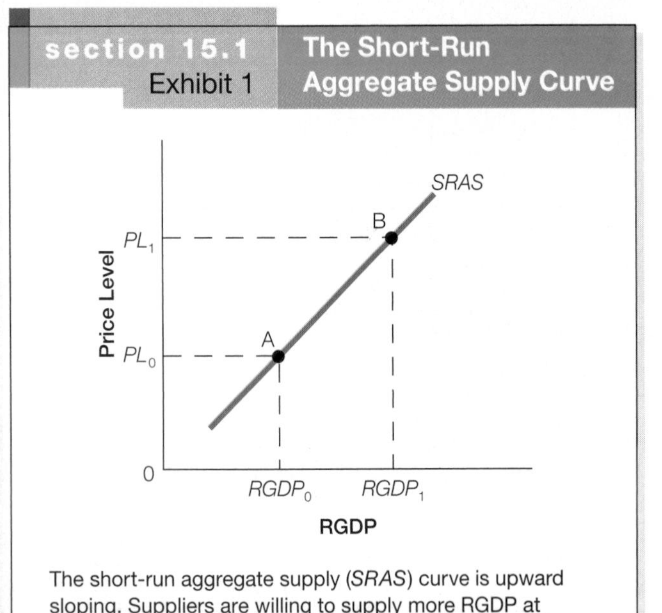

The short-run aggregate supply (*SRAS*) curve is upward sloping. Suppliers are willing to supply more RGDP at higher price levels and less at lower price levels, other things equal.

The Profit Effect

To many firms, input costs—like wages and rents—are relatively constant in the short run. The slow adjustments of input prices are due to contracts that do not adjust quickly to output price level changes. So when the price level rises, output prices rise relative to input prices (costs), raising producers' short-run profit margins. This is the short-run profit effect. The increased profit margins make it in the producers' self-interest to expand production and sales at higher price levels.

If the price level falls, output prices fall and producers' profits tend to fall. Again, this is because many input costs, such as wages and other contracted costs, are relatively constant in the short run. When output price levels fall, producers find it more difficult to cover their input costs and, consequently, reduce their level of output.

The Misperception Effect

The second explanation of the upward-sloping short-run aggregate supply curve is that producers can be fooled by price changes in the short run. For example, say a cotton rancher sees the price of his cotton rising. If he thinks that the relative price of his cotton is rising (i.e., that cotton is becoming more valuable in real terms), he will supply more. In actuality, however, it might be that it was not just cotton prices that were rising; the prices of many other goods and services could also be rising at the same time as a result of an increase in the price level. The relative price of cotton, then, was not actually rising, although it appeared so in the short run. In this case, the producer was fooled into supplying more based on the *short-run misperception* of relative prices. In other words, producers may be fooled into thinking that the relative price of the item they are producing is rising, so they increase production.

If the price of cotton rises, along with the average of all other prices, cotton ranchers may be fooled into supplying more cotton to the market. This is what we call the misperception effect and it is a possible reason for an upward-sloping, short-run aggregate supply curve.

WHY IS THE LONG-RUN AGGREGATE SUPPLY CURVE VERTICAL?

Along the short-run aggregate supply curve, we assume that wages and other input prices are constant. This is not the case in the long run, which is a period long enough for the price of all inputs to fully adjust to changes in the economy. When we move along the long-run supply curve, then we are looking at the relationship between RGDP produced and the price level, once input prices have been able to respond to changes in output prices. Along the long-run aggregate supply (*LRAS*) curve, two sets of prices are changing—the price of outputs and the price of inputs. That is, along the *LRAS* curve, a 10 percent increase in the price of goods and services is matched by a 10 percent increase in the price of inputs. The long-run aggregate supply curve, then, is insensitive to the price level. As you can see in Exhibit 2, the *LRAS* curve is drawn as perfectly vertical, reflecting the fact that the level of RGDP producers are willing to supply is not affected by changes in the price level. Note that the vertical long-run aggregate supply curve will always be positioned at the natural rate of output, where all resources are fully employed ($RGDP_{NR}$). That is, in the long run, firms will always produce at the maximum level allowed by their capital, labor, and technological inputs, regardless of the price level.

The long-run equilibrium level is where the economy will settle when undisturbed and when all resources are fully employed. Remember that the economy will always be at the intersection of aggregate supply and aggregate demand but that will not always be at the natural rate of output, $RGDP_{NR}$. Long-run equilibrium will only occur where the aggregate supply and aggregate demand curves intersect along the long-run aggregate supply curve at the natural, or potential, rate of output.

section 15.1 Exhibit 2 — The Long-Run Aggregate Supply Curve

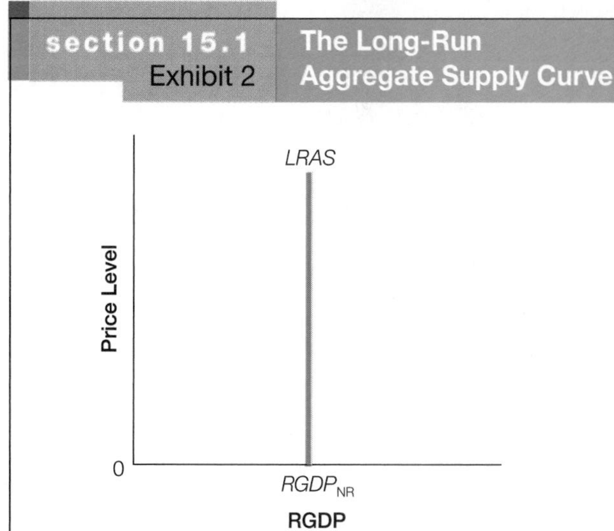

Along the long-run aggregate supply curve, the level of RGDP does not change with the price level. The position of the *LRAS* curve is determined by the natural rate of output, $RGDP_{NR}$, which reflects the levels of capital, land, labor, and technology in the economy.

Section Check

1. The short-run aggregate supply curve measures how much RGDP suppliers are willing to produce at different price levels.
2. In the short run, producers supply more as the price level increases because wages and other input prices tend to change more slowly than output prices. For this reason, producers can make a profit by expanding production when the price level rises. Producers also may be fooled into thinking that the relative price of the item they are producing is rising, so they increase production.
3. In the long run, the aggregate supply curve is vertical. In the long run, input prices change proportionally with output prices. The position of the *LRAS* curve is determined by the level of capital, land, labor, and technology at the natural rate of output, $RGDP_{NR}$.

---

1. What relationship does the short-run aggregate supply curve represent?
2. What relationship does the long-run aggregate supply curve represent?
3. Why is focusing on producers' profit margins helpful in understanding the logic of the short-run aggregate supply curve?
4. Why is the short-run aggregate supply curve upward sloping, while the long-run aggregate supply curve is vertical at the natural rate of output?
5. What would the short-run aggregate supply curve look like if input prices always changed instantaneously as soon as output prices changed? Why?
6. If the price of cotton increased 10 percent when cotton producers thought other prices were rising 5 percent over the same period, what would happen to the quantity of RGDP supplied in the cotton industry? What if cotton producers thought other prices were rising 20 percent over the same period?

section 15.2 Shifts in the Aggregate Supply Curve

- Which factors of production affect the short-run and the long-run aggregate supply curve?
- What factors exclusively shift the short-run aggregate supply curve?

SHIFTING LONG-RUN AND SHORT-RUN SUPPLY CURVES

We will now examine the determinants that can shift the short run and the long run aggregate supply curve to the right or left, as shown in Exhibit 1. Any change in the quantity of any factor of production available—capital, land, labor, or technology—can cause a shift in both the long-run and short-run aggregate supply curves. We will now see how these factors can change the position of the aggregate supply curve.

How Capital Affects Aggregate Supply

Changes in the stock of capital will alter the amount of goods and services the economy can produce. Investing in capital improves the quantity and quality of the capital stock, which lowers the cost of production in the short run. This in turn shifts the short-run aggregate supply curve rightward, and allows output to be permanently greater than before, shifting the long-run aggregate supply curve rightward, *ceteris paribus.*

Changes in human capital can also alter the aggregate supply curve. Investments in human capital may include educational or vocational programs or on-the-job training. All of these investments in human capital cause productivity to rise. As a result, the short-run aggregate supply curve shifts to the right, because a more skilled workforce lowers the cost of production; in turn the *LRAS* curve shifts to the right because greater output is achievable on a permanent, or sustainable, basis, *ceteris paribus*.

Technology and Entrepreneurship

Bill Gates of Microsoft, Steve Jobs of Apple Computer, and Larry Ellison of Oracle are just a few examples of entrepreneurs who, through inventive activity, have developed innovative technology. Computers and specialized software have led to many cost savings—ATMs, bar code scanners, biotechnology, and increased productivity across the board. These activities shift both the short-run and long-run aggregate supply curves outward by lowering costs and expanding real output possibilities.

section 15.2 Exhibit 1 Shifts in Both Short-Run and Long-Run Aggregate Supply

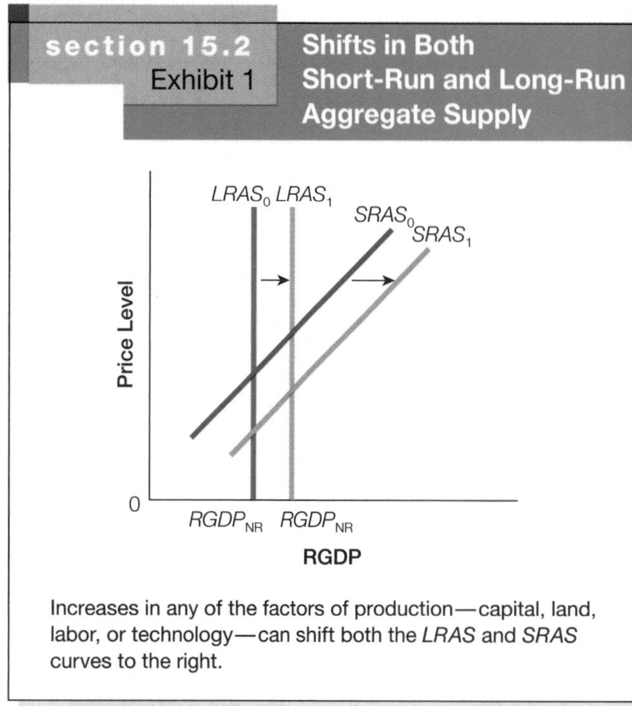

Increases in any of the factors of production—capital, land, labor, or technology—can shift both the *LRAS* and *SRAS* curves to the right.

Land (Natural Resources)

Remember that land is an all-encompassing definition that includes all natural resources. An increase in natural resources, such as successful oil exploration, would presumably lower the costs of production and expand the economy's sustainable rate of output, shifting both the short-run and long-run aggregate supply curves to the right. Likewise, a decrease in natural resources available would result in a leftward shift of both the short-run and long-run aggregate supply curves. For example, in the 1970s and early 1980s when the OPEC cartel was strong and effective at raising world oil prices, the *AS* curve shifted to the left, as the members of the cartel deliberately reduced the production of oil.

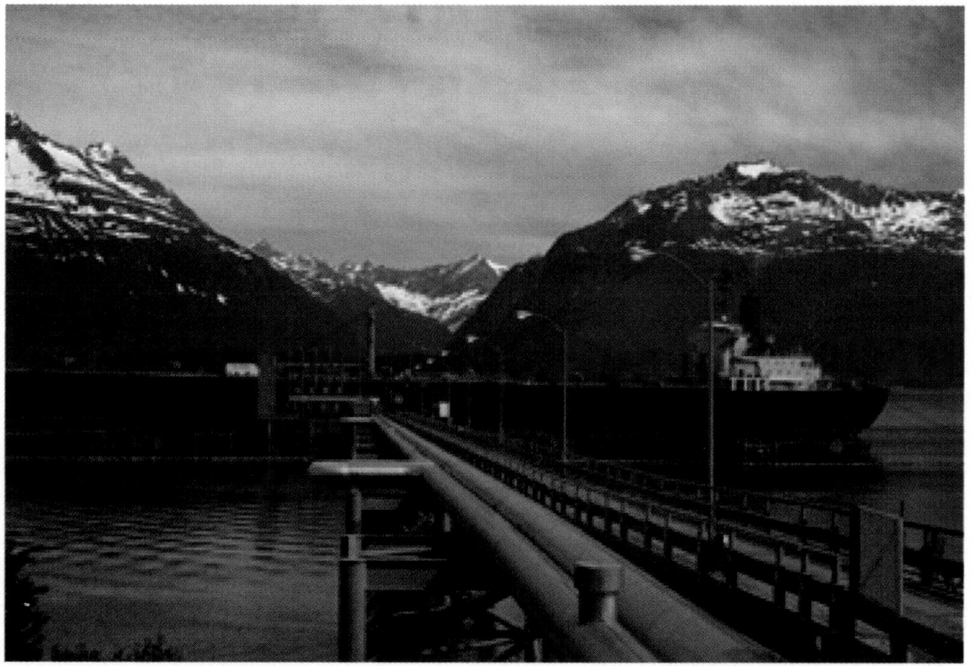

Exploring and finding new oil supplies can shift the *SRAS* and *LRAS* curves. With gas prices soaring, legislation has been introduced to allow drilling in Alaska's Arctic National Wildlife Refuge (ANWR), which could contain up to 16 billion barrels of recoverable oil. However, even if drilling were approved, it would take ten years before production would begin. Proponents of drilling say that this would open a small portion of the 1.5 million-acre coastal plain, but opponents argue that opening ANWR to oil development would disturb the breeding ground of thousands of caribou, polar bears, swans, snow geese, musk ox, and other species. There is that problem of scarcity and tradeoffs again.

The Labor Force

The addition of workers to the labor force, *ceteris paribus,* can increase aggregate supply. For example, during the 1960s, women and baby boomers entered the labor force in large numbers. This increase tended to depress wages and increase short-run aggregate supply, *ceteris paribus.* The expanded labor force also increased the economy's potential output, increasing long-run aggregate supply.

Government Regulations

Increases in government regulations can make it more costly for producers. This increase in production costs results in a leftward shift of the short-run aggregate supply curve, and a reduction in society's potential output shifts the long-run aggregate supply curve to the left as well. Likewise, a reduction in government regulations on businesses would lower the costs of production and expand potential real output, causing both the *SRAS* and *LRAS* curves to shift to the right.

WHAT FACTORS SHIFT SHORT-RUN AGGREGATE SUPPLY ONLY?

Some factors shift the short-run aggregate supply curve but do not impact the long-run aggregate supply curve. The most important of these factors are changes in input prices, temporary natural disasters, and other unexpected supply shocks. Exhibit 2 illustrates the impact of these factors on short-run aggregate supply.

Input Prices

The price of factors, or inputs, that go into producing outputs will affect only the short-run aggregate supply curve if they don't reflect permanent changes in the supplies of some factors of production. For example, if wages increase without a corresponding increase in

section 15.2 Exhibit 2 — **Shifts in Short-Run Aggregate Supply but Not Long-Run Aggregate Supply**

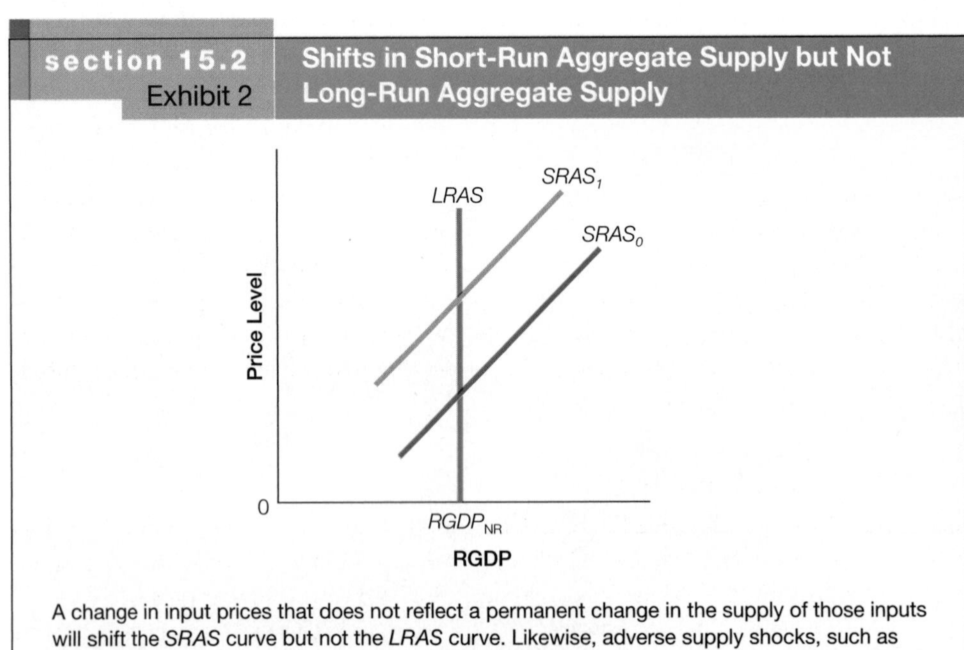

A change in input prices that does not reflect a permanent change in the supply of those inputs will shift the *SRAS* curve but not the *LRAS* curve. Likewise, adverse supply shocks, such as those caused by natural disasters, may cause a temporary change that will only impact short-run aggregate supply.

APPLICATION

SHIFTS IN THE SHORT-RUN AGGREGATE SUPPLY CURVE

Q: Why do wage increases (and other input prices) impact the short-run aggregate supply but *not* the long-run aggregate supply?

A: Remember, in the short run, wages and other input prices are assumed to be constant along the *SRAS* curve. If the firm has to pay more for its workers or any other input, its costs will rise. That is, the *SRAS* curve will shift to the left. This is shown in Exhibit 3 in the shift from $SRAS_0$ to $SRAS_1$. The reason the *LRAS* curve will not shift is that unless these input prices reflect permanent changes in input supply, those changes will only be temporary, and output will not be permanently or sustainedly different as a result. Other things equal, if an input price is to be permanently higher relative to other goods, its supply must have decreased, but that would mean that potential real output, and hence long-run aggregate supply, would also shift left.

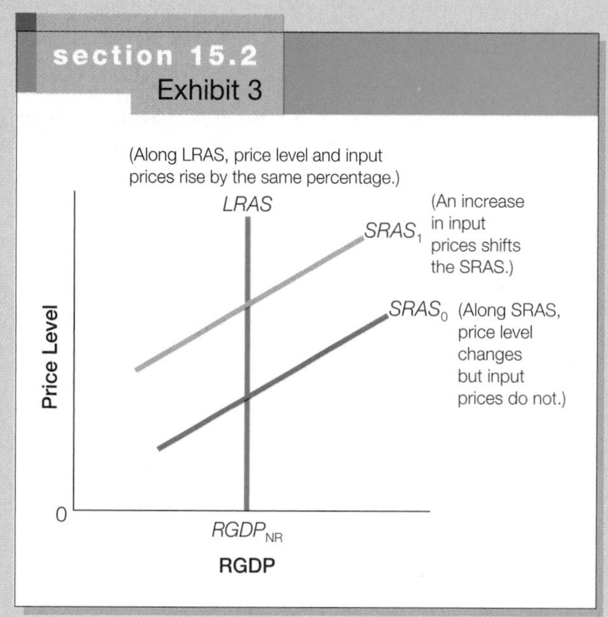
section 15.2
Exhibit 3
(Along LRAS, price level and input prices rise by the same percentage.)
LRAS
SRAS1
(An increase in input prices shifts the SRAS.)
SRAS0
(Along SRAS, price level changes but input prices do not.)
Price Level
0
RGDPNR
RGDP

labor productivity, then it will become more costly for suppliers to produce goods and services at every price level, causing the *SRAS* curve to shift to the left. As Exhibit 3 shows, long-run aggregate supply will not shift because with the same supply of labor as before, potential output does not change. If the price of steel rises, automobile producers will find it more expensive to do business, because their production costs will rise, again resulting in a leftward shift in the short-run aggregate supply curve. The *LRAS* curve will not shift, however, as long as the capacity to make steel has not been reduced.

It is supply and demand in factor markets (like capital, land, and labor) that causes input prices to change. The reason that changes in input prices only affect short-run aggregate supply and not long-run aggregate supply, unless they reflect permanent changes in the supplies of those inputs, lies in our definition of long-run aggregate supply. Recall that the long-run aggregate supply curve is vertical at the natural level of real output, determined by the supplies of the various factors of production. A fall in input prices, which shifts the short-run aggregate supply curve to the right, only shifts long-run aggregate supply to the right if potential output has risen, and that only occurs if the supply of those inputs is increased.

Temporary natural disasters like droughts can destroy crops and leave land parched like in the picture above. This may shift the *SRAS* curve but not the *LRAS* curve. The drought of 1998–2000 was a natural disaster that cost American agriculture roughly $6 to $8 billion a year. The bands of dry conditions ranged from Arizona to Florida in the south; Montana, Wyoming, and North Dakota in the north; and Nebraska to Indiana in the midwest.

Temporary Supply Shocks

Major widespread flooding, earthquakes, droughts, and other natural disasters can increase the costs of production. Any of these disasters could cause the short-run aggregate supply curve to shift to the left, *ceteris paribus.* However, once the temporary effects of these disasters have been felt, no appreciable change in the economy's productive capacity has occurred, so the long-run aggregate supply doesn't shift as a result. Other temporary supply shocks, such as disruptions in trade due to war or labor strikes, will have similar effects on short-run aggregate supply.

Section Check

1. Any increase in the quantity of any of the factors of production—capital, land, labor, or technology—available will cause both the long-run and short-run aggregate supply curves to shift to the right. A decrease in any of these factors will shift both of the aggregate supply curves to the left.
2. Changes in input price and temporary supply shocks shift the short-run aggregate supply curve but do not affect the long-run aggregate supply curve.

---

1. Which of the aggregate supply curves will shift in response to a change in the price level? Why?
2. Why do lower input costs increase the level of RGDP supplied at any given price level?
3. What would discovering huge new supplies of oil and natural gas do to the short-run and long-run aggregate supply curves?
4. What would happen to the short-run and long-run aggregate supply curves if the government required every firm to file explanatory paperwork each time a decision was made?
5. What would happen to the short-run and long-run aggregate supply curves if the capital stock grew and available supplies of natural resources expanded over the same period of time?
6. How can a change in input prices change the short-run aggregate supply curve but not the long-run aggregate supply curve? How could it change both long-run and short-run aggregate supply?
7. What would happen to short- and long-run aggregate supply if unusually good weather led to bumper crops of most agricultural products?
8. If OPEC temporarily restricted the world output of oil, what would happen to short- and long-run aggregate supply? What would happen if the output restriction was permanent?

section 15.3 Macroeconomic Equilibrium

- What is short-run macroeconomic equilibrium?
- What are recessionary and inflationary gaps?
- What is demand-pull inflation?
- What is cost-push inflation?
- How does the economy self-correct?
- What is wage and price inflexibility?

DETERMINING MACROECONOMIC EQUILIBRIUM

The short-run equilibrium level of real output and the price level are shown by the intersection of the aggregate demand curve and the short-run aggregate supply curve. When this equilibrium occurs at the potential output level, the economy is operating at full employment on the long-run aggregate supply curve, as seen in Exhibit 1. Only a short-run equilibrium that is at potential output is also a long-run equilibrium. Short-run equilibrium can change when the aggregate demand curve or the short-run aggregate supply curve shifts rightward or leftward, but the long-run equilibrium level of RGDP only changes when the *LRAS* curve shifts. Sometimes, these supply or demand changes are anticipated; at other times, however, the shifts occur unexpectedly. Economists call these unexpected shifts *shocks.*

shocks
unexpected aggregate supply or aggregate demand changes

section 15.3 Exhibit 1 Long-Run Macroeconomic Equilibrium

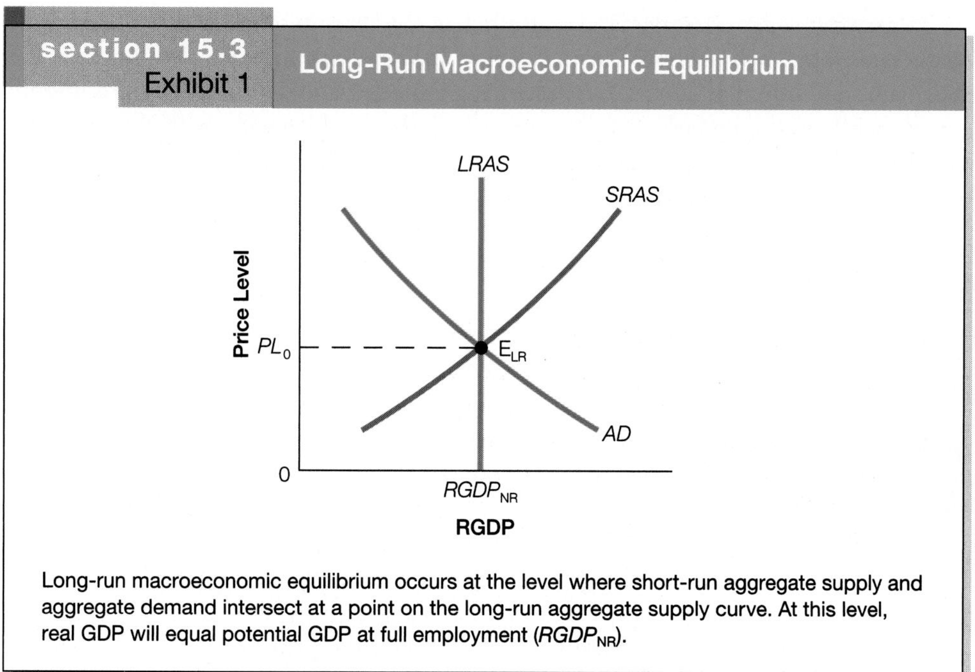

Long-run macroeconomic equilibrium occurs at the level where short-run aggregate supply and aggregate demand intersect at a point on the long-run aggregate supply curve. At this level, real GDP will equal potential GDP at full employment ($RGDP_{NR}$).

contractionary gap
the output gap that occurs when the actual output is less than the potential output

expansionary gap
the output gap that occurs when the actual output is greater than the potential output

CONTRACTIONARY AND EXPANSIONARY GAPS

As we just demonstrated, equilibrium will not always occur at full employment. In fact, equilibrium can occur at less that the potential output of the economy, $RGDP_{NR}$ (a **contractionary gap**), temporarily beyond $RGDP_{NR}$ (an **expansionary gap**), or at potential GDP. Exhibit 2 shows these three possibilities. In (a) we have a contractionary gap at the short-run equilibrium, E_{SR}, at $RGDP_0$. When RGDP is less than $RGDP_{NR}$ there is a con-

section 15.3 Exhibit 2 Contractionary and Expansionary Gaps

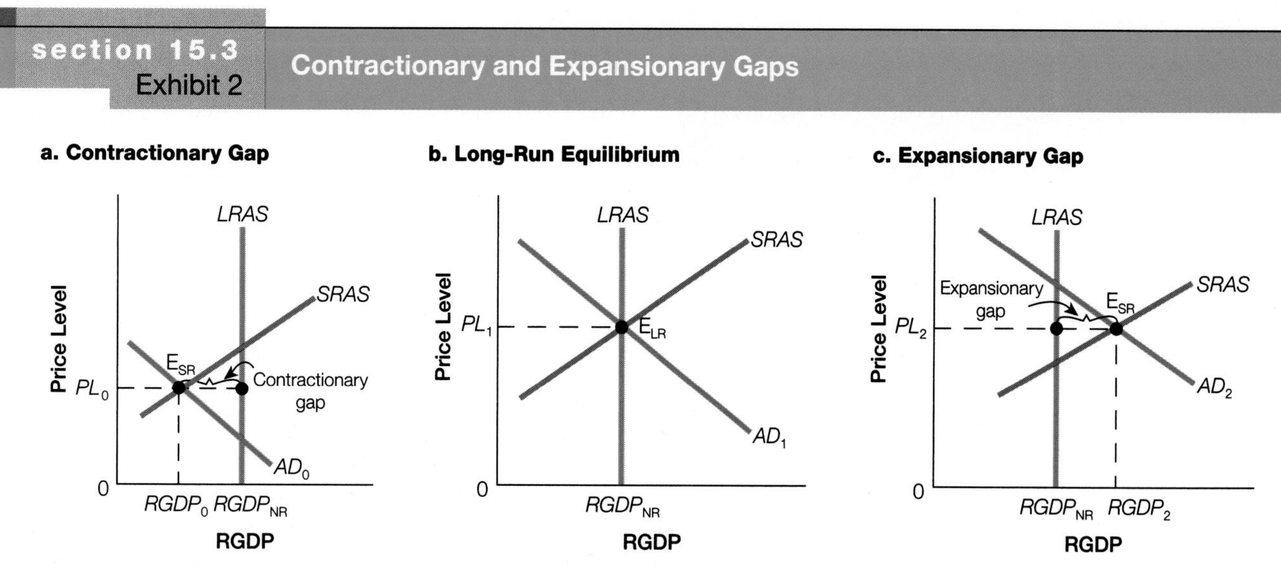

In (a), the economy is currently in short-run equilibrium at E_{SR}. At this point, $RGDP_0$ is less than $RGDP_{NR}$. That is, the economy is producing less than its potential output and the economy is in a contractionary gap. In (c), the economy is currently in short-run equilibrium at E_{SR}. At this point $RGDP_2$ is greater than $RGDP_{NR}$. The economy is temporarily producing more than its potential output and we have an expansionary gap. In (b) the economy is producing its potential output at the $RGDP_{NR}$. At this point the economy is in long-run equilibrium and is not experiencing an expansionary or contractionary gap.

tractionary gap—aggregate demand is insufficient to fully employ all of society's resources so unemployment will be above the normal rate. In (c) we have an expansionary gap at the short-run equilibrium, E_{SR}, at $RGDP_2$, where aggregate demand is so high that the economy is temporarily operating beyond full capacity ($RGDP_{NR}$), which will usually lead to inflationary pressure so unemployment will be below the normal rate. In (b) the economy is just right where AD_1 and *SRAS* intersect at $RGDP_{NR}$—the long-run equilibrium position.

demand-pull inflation
a price level increase due to an increase in aggregate demand

stagflation
a situation in which lower growth and higher prices occur together

cost-push inflation
a price level increase due to a negative supply shock or increases in input prices

DEMAND-PULL INFLATION

Demand-pull inflation occurs when the price level rises as a result of an increase in aggregate demand. Consider the case in which an increase in consumer optimism results in a corresponding increase in aggregate demand. Exhibit 3 shows that an increase in aggregate demand causes an increase in the price level and an increase in real output. The movement is along *SRAS* from point E_0 to point E_1. This causes an expansionary gap. Recall that there is an increase in output as a result of the increase in the price level in the short run, because firms have an incentive to increase real output when the prices of the goods they are selling are rising faster than the costs of the inputs they use in production.

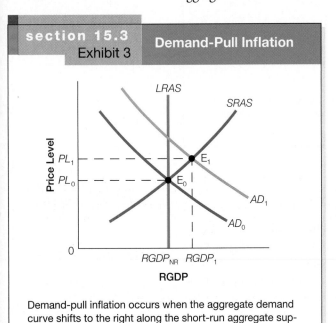

section 15.3 Exhibit 3 — Demand-Pull Inflation

LRAS, SRAS, Price Level, PL_1, PL_0, E_1, E_0, AD_1, AD_0, 0, $RGDP_{NR}$, $RGDP_1$, RGDP

Demand-pull inflation occurs when the aggregate demand curve shifts to the right along the short-run aggregate supply curve.

Note that E_1 in Exhibit 3 is positioned beyond $RGDP_{NR}$—an expansionary gap. It seems peculiar that the economy can operate beyond its potential, but this is possible, temporarily, as firms encourage workers to work overtime, extend the hours of part-time workers, hire recently retired employees, reduce frictional unemployment through more extensive searches for employees, and so on. However, this level of output and employment *cannot* be sustained in the long run.

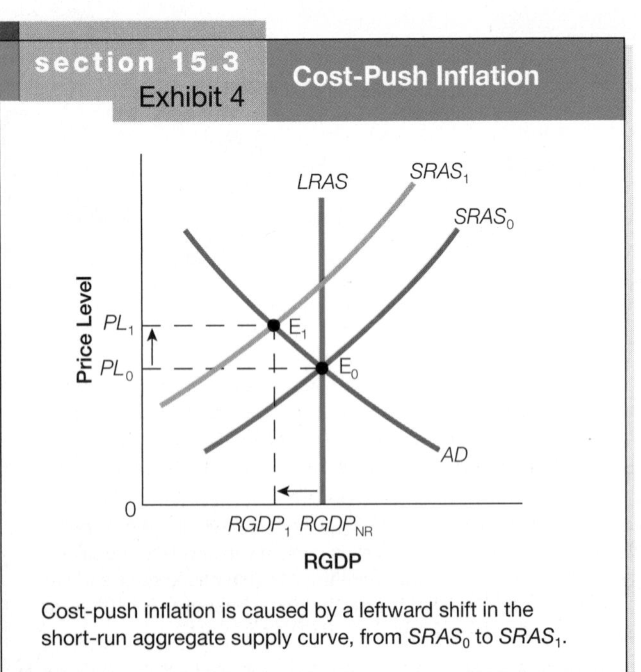

Cost-push inflation is caused by a leftward shift in the short-run aggregate supply curve, from $SRAS_0$ to $SRAS_1$.

COST-PUSH INFLATION

The 1970s and early 1980s witnessed a phenomenon known as **stagflation,** where lower growth and higher prices occurred together. Some economists believe that this was caused by a leftward shift in the aggregate supply curve, as seen in Exhibit 4. If the aggregate demand curve did not increase considerably but the price level increased significantly, then the inflation was caused by supply-side forces. This is called **cost-push inflation.**

The increase in oil prices was the primary culprit responsible for the leftward shift in the aggregate supply curve. As we discussed in the last section, an increase in input prices can cause the short-run aggregate supply curve to shift to the left, and this spelled big trouble for the U.S. economy—higher price levels, lower output, and higher rates of unemployment. The impact of cost-push inflation is illustrated in Exhibit 4.

In Exhibit 4, we see that the economy is initially at full employment equilibrium at point E_0. Now suppose there is a sudden increase in input prices, such as the increase in the price of oil. This increase would shift the *SRAS* curve to the left—from $SRAS_0$ to $SRAS_1$. As a result of the shift in short-run aggregate supply, the price level rises to PL_1 and real output falls from $RGDP_{NR}$ to $RGDP_1$ (point E_1). Now firms demand fewer workers as a result of the higher input costs that cannot be passed on to the consumers. The result is higher prices, lower real output, and more unemployment—and it leads to a contractionary gap.

WHAT HELPED THE UNITED STATES RECOVER IN THE 1980S?

As far as energy prices are concerned, oil prices fell during the 1980s because OPEC lost some of its clout due to internal problems. In addition, many non-OPEC oil producers increased production. The net result was a rightward shift in the aggregate supply curve. Holding aggregate demand constant, this rightward shift in the aggregate supply curve leads to a lower price level, greater output, and lower rates of unemployment—moving the economy back towards E_0 in Exhibit 4.

ANOTHER CAUSE OF A CONTRACTIONARY GAP

Just as cost-push inflation can cause a contractionary gap, so can a decrease in aggregate demand. For example, consider the case in which consumer confidence plunges and the stock market "tanks." As a result, aggregate demand would fall, shown in Exhibit 5 as the shift from AD_0 to AD_1, and the economy would be in a new short-run equilibrium at point E_1. Now, households, firms, and governments are buying fewer goods and services at every price level. In response to this drop in demand, output would fall from $RGDP_{NR}$ to $RGDP_1$, and the price level would fall from PL_0 to PL_1. So in the short run, this fall in aggregate demand causes higher unemployment and a reduction in output—and it too can lead to a contractionary gap.

ADJUSTING TO A CONTRACTIONARY GAP

Many recoveries from a contractionary gap occur because of increases in aggregate demand—perhaps consumer and business confidence picks up or the government lowers taxes and/or lowers interest rates to stimulate the economy. That is, there is eventually a rightward shift in the aggregate demand curve that takes the economy back to potential output—$RGDP_{NR}$.

However, it is possible that the economy could *self-correct* through declining wages and prices. In Exhibit 6, at E_1 at PL_1 and $RGDP_1$, the economy is in a contractionary gap—the economy is producing less than its potential

section 15.3 Exhibit 5 — Short-Run Decrease in Aggregate Demand

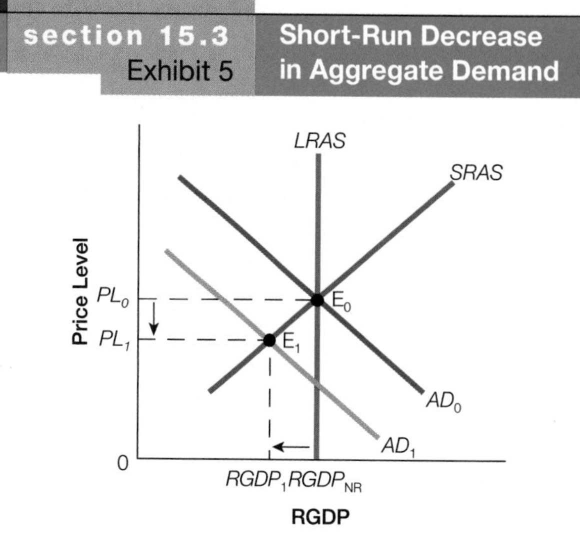

A fall in aggregate demand from a drop in consumer confidence can cause a short-run change in the economy. The decrease in aggregate demand (shown in the movement from point E_0 to E_1) causes lower output and higher unemployment in the short run.

section 15.3 Exhibit 6 — Adjusting to a Contractionary Gap

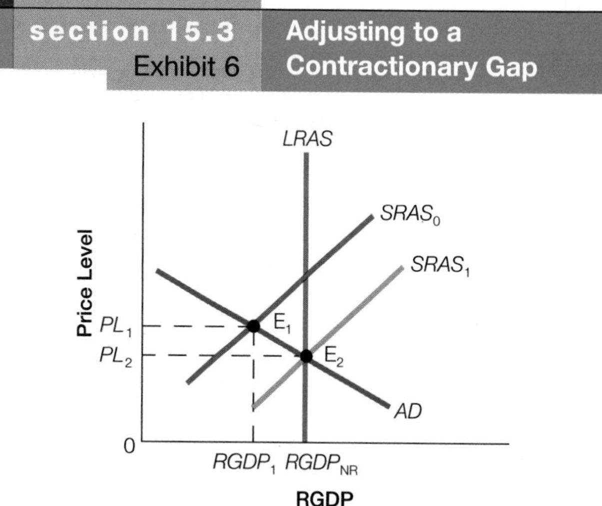

At point E_1, the economy is in a contractionary gap. However, the economy may self-correct as laborers and other input suppliers are now willing to accept lower wages and prices for the use of their resources. This results in a reduction in production costs that shifts the short-run supply curve from $SRAS_0$ to $SRAS_1$. Eventually, the economy returns to a long-run equilibrium at point E_2, at $RGDP_{NR}$, and a lower price level, PL_2. However, if wages and other input prices are sticky, the economy's adjustment mechanism might take many months to totally self-correct.

output. At this lower level of output, firms lay off workers to avoid inventory accumulation. In addition, firms may cut prices to increase demand for their products. Unemployed workers and other input suppliers may also bid down wages and prices. That is, laborers and other input suppliers are now willing to accept lower wages and prices for the use of their resources, and the resulting reduction in production costs shifts the short-run supply curve from $SRAS_0$ to $SRAS_1$. Eventually, the economy returns to a long-run equilibrium at E_2 at $RGDP_{NR}$, and a lower price level, PL_2.

SLOW ADJUSTMENTS TO A CONTRACTIONARY GAP

wage and price inflexibility
the tendency for prices and wages to only adjust slowly downward to changes in the economy

Many economists believe that wages and prices may be very slow to adjust, especially downward. This downward **wage and price inflexibility** may lead to prolonged periods of a contractionary gap.

For example, in Exhibit 6 we see that the economy is in a recession at E_1 at $RGDP_1$. The economy will eventually self-correct to $RGDP_{NR}$ at E_2, as workers and other input owners accept lower wages and prices for their inputs, shifting the *SRAS* curve to the right from $SRAS_0$ to $SRAS_1$. However, if wages and other input prices are sticky, the economy's adjustment mechanism might take many months to totally self-correct.

WHAT CAUSES WAGES AND PRICES TO BE STICKY DOWNWARD?

Empirical evidence supports several reasons for the downward stickiness of wages and prices. Firms may not be able to legally cut wages because of long-term labor contracts (particularly with union workers) or a legal minimum wage. Efficiency wages may also limit a firm's ability to lower wage rates. Menu costs may cause price inflexibility as well.

Efficiency Wages

In economics, it is generally assumed that as productivity rises, wages will rise, and that workers can raise their productivity through investments in human capital like education and on-the-job training. However, some economists believe that in some cases, *higher wages will lead to greater productivity.*

In the efficiency wage model, employers pay their employees more than the equilibrium wage, as a means to increase efficiency. Proponents of this theory suggest that higher-than-equilibrium wages may attract the most productive workers, lower job turnover and training costs, and improve morale. Because the efficiency wage rate is greater than the equilibrium wage rate, the quantity of labor that would be willingly supplied is greater than the quantity of labor demanded, resulting in greater amounts of unemployment.

However, aside from creating some additional unemployment, it may also cause wages to be inflexible downward. For example, in the event that there is a decrease in aggregate demand, firms that pay efficiency wages may be reluctant to cut wages in the fear that it could lead to lower morale, greater absenteeism, and general productivity losses. In short, if firms are paying efficiency wages, they may be reluctant to lower wages in a recession, leading to downward wage inflexibility.

Menu Costs

As we explained in chapter 11, there is a cost to changing prices in an inflationary environment. Thus the higher price level in an inflationary environment is often reflected slowly, as restaurants, mail-order houses, and department stores change their prices gradually so that they incur fewer *menu costs* (the costs of changing posted prices) in printing new catalogs, new mailers, new advertisements, and so on. Since businesses are not likely to change these prices instantly, we can say that some prices are sticky, or slow to change. For example, many outputs, like steel, are inputs in the production of other products, like automobiles. As a result, these prices are slow to change.

Suppose that there was an unexpected reduction in the money supply that led to a decrease in aggregate demand. This could lower the price level. While some firms may adjust to the change quickly, others may move more slowly because of menu costs. The potential result is that their prices may become too high (above equilibrium); sales and output will fall, causing a potential recession.

If some firms are not responding quickly to changes in demand, there must be a reason, and to some economists, menu costs are at least part of that reason.

ADJUSTING TO AN EXPANSIONARY GAP

In Exhibit 7, the economy is currently in an expansionary gap where $RGDP_0$ is greater than $RGDP_{NR}$. Because the price level is now higher than workers anticipated, workers become disgruntled with wages that have not yet adjusted to the new price level (if prices have risen, but wages have not risen as much, real wages have fallen). Recall that along the *SRAS* curve, wages and other input prices are assumed to be constant. Therefore, workers' and input suppliers' purchasing power falls as output prices rise. Real (adjusted for inflation) wages have fallen. Consequently, workers and other suppliers demand higher prices to be willing to supply their inputs. As input prices respond to the higher level of output prices, the short-run aggregate supply curve shifts to the left, from $SRAS_0$ to $SRAS_1$. Suppliers will continually seek higher prices for their inputs until they reach the long-run equilibrium, at point E_1 in Exhibit 7. At point E_1, input suppliers' purchasing power is now restored at the long-run equilibrium, at $RGDP_{NR}$, and a new higher price level, PL_1.

section 15.3 Exhibit 7 — Adjusting to an Expansionary Gap

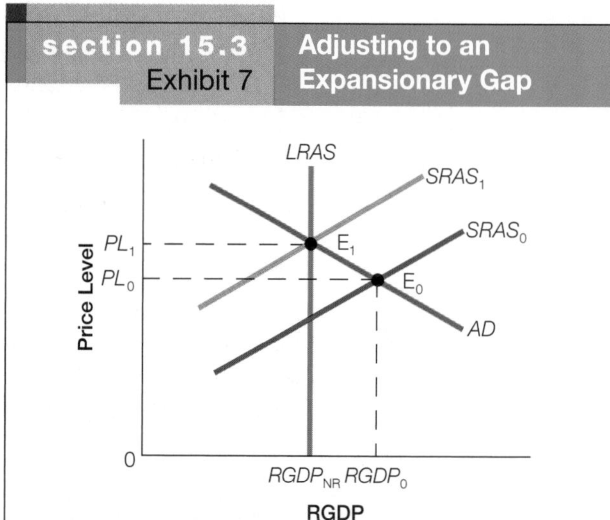

The economy is currently in an expansionary gap, where $RGDP_0$ is greater than $RGDP_{NR}$. Because the price level is now higher than workers anticipated, workers become disgruntled with wages that have not yet adjusted to the new price level. Consequently, workers and other suppliers demand higher prices to be willing to supply their inputs. As input prices respond to the higher level of output prices, the short-run aggregate supply curve shifts to the left, from $SRAS_0$ to $SRAS_1$. Suppliers will continually seek higher prices for their inputs until they reach the long-run equilibrium, at point E_1. At point E_1, input suppliers' purchasing power is now restored at the natural rate, $RGDP_{NR}$, at a new higher price level, PL_1.

HOW PRECISE IS THE AGGREGATE SUPPLY AND DEMAND MODEL?

In this chapter, we have been shifting the aggregate supply and aggregate demand curves around as if we knew exactly what we were doing. But it is very important to mention that the *AD/AS* model is a crude tool.

In the supply and demand curves covered in chapter 4, we saw how this simple tool is very rich in explanatory power. But even supply and demand analysis does not always provide precise estimates of the shifts or of the exact price and output changes that accompany those shifts. However, while supply and demand analysis is not perfect, it does provide a framework to predict the direction that certain important variables will change under different circumstances.

The same is true in the *AD/AS* model, but it is less precise because of the complexities and interrelationships that exist in the macroeconomy. The slopes of the aggregate demand and aggregate supply curves, the magnitudes of the shifts, and the interrelationship of the variables are to some extent a mystery. For example, if a reduction in aggregate demand leads to lower RGDP and, as a result, there are fewer workers that are willing to look for work, it impacts the aggregate supply curve. There are other examples of the interdependence of the aggregate demand and aggregate supply curves that make this analysis not completely satisfactory. Nevertheless, the framework still provides important insights into the workings of the macroeconomy.

Section Check

SECTION CHECK

1. Short-run macroeconomic equilibrium is shown by the intersection of the aggregate demand curve and the short-run aggregate supply curve. A short-run equilibrium is also a long-run equilibrium only if it is at potential output on the long-run aggregate supply curve.
2. If short-run equilibrium occurs at less that the potential output of the economy, $RGDP_{NR}$, there is a contractionary gap. If short-run equilibrium temporarily occurs beyond $RGDP_{NR}$, there is an expansionary gap.
3. Demand-pull inflation occurs when the price level rises as a result of an increase in aggregate demand.
4. Cost-push inflation is caused by a leftward shift in the short-run aggregate supply curve.
5. It is possible that the economy could *self-correct* through declining wages and prices. For example, during a recession, laborers and other input suppliers are willing to accept lower wages and prices for the use of their resources, and the resulting reduction in production costs increases the short-run supply curve. Eventually, the economy returns to the long-run equilibrium, at $RGDP_{NR}$, and a lower price level.
6. Wages and other input prices may be very slow to adjust, especially downward. This downward wage and price inflexibility may lead to prolonged periods of recession.
7. Firms might not be willing to lower nominal wages in the short run for several reasons, leading to downward wage and price inflexibility or sticky prices. Firms may not be able to legally cut wages because of long-term labor contracts (particularly with union workers) or due to a legal minimum wage. In addition, efficiency wage and menu costs may lead to sticky wages and prices.

---

1. What is a contractionary gap?
2. What is an expansionary gap?
3. What is demand-pull inflation?
4. What is cost-push inflation?
5. Starting from long-run equilibrium on the long-run aggregate supply curve, what happens to the price level, real output, and unemployment as a result of cost-push inflation?
6. How would a drop in consumer confidence impact the short-run macroeconomy?
7. What would happen to the price level, real output, and unemployment in the short run if world oil prices fell sharply?
8. What are sticky prices and wages?
9. How does the economy self-correct?

Summary

The short-run aggregate supply curve measures how much RGDP suppliers will be willing to produce at different price levels given fixed input prices. In the short run, producers supply more as the price level increases because wages and other input prices tend to be slower to change than output prices. For this reason, they can make a profit by expanding production when the price level rises. Producers also may be fooled into thinking that the relative price of the item they are producing is rising, so they increase production.

In the long run, the aggregate supply curve is vertical. In the long run, input prices change proportionally with output prices. The position of the *LRAS* curve is determined by the level of capital, land, labor, and technology at the natural rate of output, $RGDP_{NR}$. Any increase in the quantity of any of the factors of production—capital, land, labor, or technology—available will cause both the long-run and short-run aggregate supply curves to shift to the right. A decrease in any of these factors will shift both of the aggregate supply curves to the left. Changes in input price and temporary supply shocks shift the short-run aggregate supply curve but do not affect the long-run aggregate supply curve.

Short-run macroeconomic equilibrium is shown by the intersection of the aggregate demand curve and the short-run aggregate supply curve. A short-run equilibrium is also a long-run equilibrium only if it is at potential output on the long-run aggregate supply curve. If short-run equilibrium occurs at less that the potential output of the economy, $RGDP_{NR}$, there is a contractionary gap. If short-run equilibrium temporarily occurs beyond $RGDP_{NR}$, there is an expansionary gap.

Demand-pull inflation occurs when the price level rises as a result of an increase in aggregate demand. A contractionary gap can be caused by cost-push inflation, which is caused by a leftward shift in the short-run aggregate supply curve. A contractionary gap may also occur as a result of insufficient aggregate demand. It appears that most recoveries from contractions occur because of increases in aggregate demand. However, it is possible that the economy could *self-correct* through declining wages and other input prices. Eventually, the economy returns to a long-run equilibrium.

Wages and prices may be very slow to adjust, especially downward. This downward wage and price inflexibility may lead to prolonged periods of recession. Firms might not be willing to lower nominal wages in the short run for several reasons, leading to downward wage inflexibility or sticky prices. Firms may not be able to legally cut wages because of long-term labor contracts (particularly with union workers) or due to a legal minimum wage. In addition, efficiency wage and menu costs may lead to sticky wages and prices.

Key Terms and Concepts

aggregate supply curve (*AS*) 324
short-run aggregate supply curve 324
long-run aggregate supply curve 324
shocks 330
contractionary gap 331
expansionary gap 331
demand-pull inflation 332
stagflation 332
cost-push inflation 332
wage and price inflexibility 334

Review Questions

1. You operate a business in which you manufacture furniture. You are able to increase your furniture prices by 5 percent this quarter. You assume that the demand for your furniture has increased and begin increasing furniture production. Only later do you realize that prices in the macroeconomy are rising generally at a rate of 5 percent per quarter. This is an example of what effect? What does it imply about the slope of the short-run aggregate supply curve?

2. What would each of the following do to the short-run aggregate supply curve?
   a. a decrease in wage rates
   b. passage of more stringent environmental and safety regulations affecting businesses
   c. technological progress
   d. an increase in consumer optimism
3. What would each of the following do to the long-run aggregate supply curve?
   a. advances in medical technologies
   b. increased immigration of skilled workers
   c. an increase in wage rates
   d. an epidemic involving a new strain of the flu kills hundreds of thousands of people
4. Indicate whether the following events affect short-run aggregate supply or long-run aggregate supply and the direction of impact.
   a. Unusually cold weather in California freezes many of the states current crops.
   b. A devastating earthquake in Northern California destroys hundreds of buildings and kills thousands of people.
   c. Economywide wage increases.
   d. Advances in computers and wireless technologies improve the efficiency of production.
5. How does an increase in aggregate demand affect output, unemployment, and the price level in the short run?
6. How does an increase in short-run aggregate supply affect output, unemployment, and the price level in the short run?
7. Distinguish cost-push from demand-pull inflation. Provide an example of an event or shock to the economy that would cause each.
8. Which of the following lead to stagflation, assuming an economy currently operating at full employment?
   a. an increase in spending on education
   b. striking workers demand and receive nominal wage increases
   c. a decrease in federal spending on a missile defense program
   d. an increase in OPEC oil production quotas
   e. a decrease in OPEC oil production quotas
9. Is it ever possible for an economy to operate above the full-employment level in the short term? Explain.
10. Visit the Sexton Web site at **http://sexton.swcollege.com** and click on "The Economist." Peruse the headline stories and locate one likely reflecting a change in macroeconomic equilibrium. Is a shift in aggregate demand, short-run aggregate supply, and/or long-run aggregate supply indicated? Explain using a diagram.

chapter 15 Study Guide

Fill in the Blanks

1. The _____________ curve is the relationship between the total quantity of final goods and services that suppliers are willing and able to produce and the overall price level.

2. There are two aggregate supply curves—a _____________ aggregate supply curve and a _____________ aggregate supply curve.

3. The short-run relationship refers to a period when _____________ can change in response to supply and demand, but _____________ prices have not yet been able to adjust.

4. In the short run, the aggregate supply curve is _____________ sloping.

5. In the short run, at a higher price level, producers are willing to supply _____________ real output, and at lower price levels, they are willing to supply _____________ real output.

6. The two explanations for why producers would be willing to supply more output when the price level increases are the _____________ effect and the _____________ effect.

7. When the price level rises in the short run, output prices _____________ relative to input prices (costs), _____________ producers' short-run profit margins.

8. If the price level falls, output prices _____________, producers' profits will _____________, and producers will _____________ their level of output.

9. If the overall price level is rising, producers can be fooled into thinking that the _____________ price of their output is rising, so they will supply _____________ in the short run.

10. The long run is a period long enough for the price of _____________ to fully adjust to changes in the economy.

11. Along the *LRAS* curve, two sets of prices are changing—the prices of _____________ and the prices of _____________.

12. The level of RGDP producers are willing to supply in the long run is _____________ by changes in the price level.

13. The vertical *LRAS* curve will always be positioned at the _____________ of output.

14. The long-run equilibrium level is where the economy will settle when undisturbed and all resources are _____________ employed.

15. Long-run equilibrium will only occur where *AS* and *AD* intersect along the _____________.

16. The underlying determinant of shifts in short-run aggregate supply is _____________.

17. _____________ production costs will motivate producers to produce less at any given price level, shifting the short-run aggregate supply curve _____________.

18. A permanent increase in the available amount of capital, entrepreneurship, land, or labor can shift the *LRAS* and *SRAS* curves to the _____________.

19. A decrease in the stock of capital will _____________ real output in the short run and _____________ real output in the long run, *ceteris paribus.*

20. Investments in human capital would cause productivity to ____________.

21. A ____________ in the amount of natural resources available would result in a leftward shift of both *SRAS* and *LRAS.*

22. An increase in the number of workers in the labor force, *ceteris paribus,* tends to ____________ wages and ____________ short-run aggregate supply.

23. ____________ output per worker causes production costs to rise and potential real output to fall, resulting in a ____________ shift in both *SRAS* and *LRAS.*

24. A ____________ in government regulations on businesses would lower the costs of production and expand potential real output, causing both *SRAS* and *LRAS* to shift to the right.

25. The most important of the factors that shift *SRAS* but do not impact *LRAS* are change in ____________ prices and ____________.

26. If the price of steel rises, it will shift *SRAS* ____________, while the *LRAS* will ____________ as long as the capacity to make steel has not been reduced.

27. A fall in input prices, which shifts *SRAS* right, shifts *LRAS* right only if ____________ has risen, and that only occurs if the ____________ of those inputs is increased.

28. ____________ supply shocks, such as natural disasters, can increase the costs of production.

29. Only a short-run equilibrium that is at ____________ output is also a long-run equilibrium.

30. The short-run equilibrium level of real output and the price level are determined by the intersection of the ____________ curve and the ____________ curve.

31. The long-run equilibrium level of RGDP changes only when the ____________ curve shifts.

32. Economists call unexpected shifts in supply or demand ____________.

33. When short-run equilibrium occurs at less than the potential output of the economy, it results in a ____________ gap.

34. ____________ inflation occurs when the price level rises as a result of an increase in aggregate demand.

35. Demand-pull inflation causes an ____________ in the price level and an ____________ in real output in the short run, illustrated by a movement up along the *SRAS* curve.

36. Demand-pull inflation causes an ____________ gap.

37. When *AD* increases, real (adjusted for inflation) wages ____________ in the short run.

38. In response to an inflationary gap in the short run, real wages and other real input prices will tend to ____________, which is illustrated by a ____________ shift in the *SRAS* curve.

39. ____________ is the situation in which lower economic growth and higher prices occur together.

40. An increase in input prices can cause the *SRAS* curve to shift to the ____________, resulting in ____________ price levels, ____________ real

output, and ______________ rates of unemployment in the short run.

41. Starting with the economy initially at full employment equilibrium, a sudden increase in oil prices would result in ______________ unemployment and in real output ______________ than potential output in the short run.

42. Falling oil prices would result in a ______________ shift in the *SRAS* curve.

43. Holding *AD* constant, falling oil prices would lead to ______________ prices, ______________ output, and ______________ rates of unemployment in the short run.

44. An economy can self-correct from a recessionary gap through ______________ wages and prices.

45. The long-run result of a fall in aggregate demand is an equilibrium ______________ potential output and a ______________ price level.

46. Wages and prices may be sticky downward because of ______________ labor contracts, a legal ______________ wage, employers paying ______________ wages, and ______________ costs.

47. If the economy is currently in an inflationary gap, with output greater than potential output, the price level is ______________ than workers anticipated.

48. The ______________ of the *AD* and *AS* curves makes the *AD*/*AS* analysis not completely satisfactory.

True or False

1. The aggregate supply curve represents how much RGDP suppliers will be willing to produce at different price levels.
2. Nominal wages are assumed to adjust quickly in the short run.
3. The long-run relationship refers to a period long enough for the prices of outputs and all inputs to fully adjust to changes in the economy.
4. In the short run, the aggregate supply curve is vertical.
5. In the short run, the slow adjustments of input prices are due to the longer-term input contracts that do not adjust quickly to price-level changes.
6. When price level rises in the short run, it will increase producers' profit margins and make it in the producers' self-interest to expand their production.
7. If the price level falls, input prices, producers' profits, and real output will fall in the short run.
8. When the price level falls, producers can be fooled into supplying more based on a short-run misperception of relative prices.
9. Along the short-run aggregate supply curve, we assume that wages and other input prices have time to adjust.
10. Along the long-run aggregate supply curve, we are looking at the relationship between RGDP produced and the price level, once input prices have been able to respond to changes in output prices.
11. Along the *LRAS* curve, a 10 percent increase in the price of goods and services is matched by a 10 percent increase in the price of inputs.

12. Along the *LRAS* curve, the economy is assumed to be at full employment.

13. In the long run, the economy will produce at the maximum sustainable level allowed by its capital, labor, and technological inputs, regardless of the price level.

14. Long-run equilibrium occurs wherever *SRAS* and *AD* intersect.

15. The economy can be in short-run equilibrium without being in long-run equilibrium.

16. *Ceteris paribus,* lower production costs will motivate producers to produce more at any given price level, shifting *AS* rightward.

17. Any permanent change in the quantity of any factor of production available—capital, entrepreneurship, land, or labor—can cause a shift in the long-run aggregate supply curve but not the short-run aggregate supply curve.

18. Less and lower-quality capital will shift both the short-run aggregate supply curve and the long-run aggregate supply curve to the left.

19. Added investments in human capital would shift the short-run aggregate supply curve right but leave the long-run aggregate supply curve unchanged.

20. If entrepreneurs can find ways to lower the costs of production, then the short-run and long-run aggregate supply curves both shift to the right.

21. Successful oil exploration would leave *LRAS* unchanged because it would not change the total amount of oil in the earth.

22. An expanded labor force increases the economy's potential output, increasing *LRAS.*

23. Increases in government regulations that make it more costly for producers shift *SRAS* left but leave *LRAS* unchanged.

24. The price of factors, or inputs, that go into producing outputs will affect only *SRAS* if they don't reflect permanent changes in the supplies of some factors of production.

25. If wages increase without a corresponding increase in labor productivity, *SRAS* will shift to the left, but *LRAS* will not shift because with the same supply of labor as before, potential output does not change.

26. Changes in input prices only affect *SRAS* if they reflect permanent changes in the supplies of those inputs.

27. Adverse supply shocks can increase the costs of production, shifting *SRAS* to the left; but once the temporary effects of these disasters have been felt, no appreciable change in the economy's productive capacity occurs, so *LRAS* doesn't shift as a result.

28. In long-run equilibrium, the economy operates at full employment, regardless of the level of the aggregate demand curve.

29. Short-run equilibrium can change only when the short-run aggregate supply curve shifts.

30. A change in aggregate demand will change RGDP in the short-run equilibrium, but not in the long run.

31. When short-run equilibrium occurs beyond the economy's level of potential output, it results in an expansionary gap.

32. Demand-pull inflation causes a contractionary gap.

33. Demand-pull inflation causes the prices of the goods producers sell to rise faster than the costs of the inputs they use in production.

34. The economy can never operate beyond its potential output.

35. Short-run real output beyond potential output (and employment beyond full employment) cannot be sustained in the long run.

36. In response to an expansionary gap in the short run, real wages and other real input prices will tend to rise.

37. When an increase in *AD* causes an expansionary gap in the short run, the only long-run difference from the initial equilibrium is the new, higher price level.

38. A leftward shift in the aggregate supply curve can cause cost-push inflation.

39. The primary culprits responsible for the leftward shift in *SRAS* in the 1970s were oil price decreases.

40. Starting with the economy initially at full employment equilibrium, a sudden increase in oil prices would result in a contractionary gap.

41. Holding *AD* constant, falling oil prices would lead to lower prices, lower output, and lower rates of unemployment.

42. A fall in *AD* would reduce real output and the price level and increase unemployment in the short run—a contractionary gap.

43. In a recession, unemployed workers and other input suppliers will bid down wages and prices, and the resulting reduction in production costs shifts the short-run aggregate supply curve to the right.

44. Downward wage stickiness may lead to prolonged periods of recession in response to decreases in aggregate demand by making the economy's adjustment mechanism slower.

45. If the economy is currently in a contractionary gap, with output less than potential output, the price level is higher than workers anticipated.

46. When aggregate demand increases, workers' and input suppliers' purchasing power falls in the short run, but input suppliers' purchasing power is restored at a higher price level in the long run.

47. The *AD/AS* model is a very precise tool for analyzing the economy.

Multiple Choice

1. The short-run aggregate supply curve slopes
   a. downward because firms can sell more, and hence, will produce more when prices are lower.
   b. downward because firms find it costs less to purchase labor and other inputs when prices are lower, and hence, they produce more.
   c. upward because when the price level rises, output prices rise relative to input prices (costs), raising profit margins and increasing production and sales.
   d. upward because firms find that it costs more to purchase labor and other inputs when prices are higher, and hence, they must produce and sell more in order to make a profit.

2. If the price level rises, what will happen to the quantity of RGDP produced along the long-run aggregate supply curve?
   a. It will increase.
   b. It will usually increase, but not always.
   c. Nothing will happen to it.
   d. It will decrease.
   e. It will usually decrease, but not always.

3. If the price level rises, what happens to the level of real GDP supplied?
   a. It will increase in both the short run and the long run.
   b. It will increase in the short run but not in the long run.
   c. It will decrease in both the short run and the long run.
   d. It will decrease in the short run but not in the long run.
   e. It will usually decrease, but not always.

4. What is the typical response of firms to an increase in the price of what they sell, for given input prices?
   a. an increase in output
   b. an increase in hiring factors of production
   c. an increase in the profit level of firms
   d. an increase in employment in the industry
   e. all of the above

5. The short run is
   a. a time period in which the prices of output cannot change, but in which the prices of inputs have time to adjust.
   b. a time period in which output prices can change in response to supply and demand, but in which all input prices have not yet been able to completely adjust.
   c. a time period in which neither the prices of output nor the prices of inputs are able to change.
   d. any time period of less than a year.

6. The profit effect is explained in the text as follows:
   a. When the price level decreases, output prices rise relative to input prices (costs), raising producers' short-run profit margins.
   b. At equilibrium prices, when costs rise, profit margins are able to float with them and be passed along.
   c. The profit effect is only a long-run phenomenon.
   d. When the price level rises, output prices rise relative to input prices (costs), raising producers' short-run profit margins.

7. The text's explanation for the misperception effect for an upward-sloping short-run aggregate supply curve is based on
   a. falling profit margins as the price level rises.
   b. rising costs of production as the price level rises.
   c. fixed-wage labor contracts.
   d. the fact that producers may be fooled into thinking that the relative price of the item they are producing is rising, so they increase production.

8. In the short run, a decrease in the price level
   a. increases output prices relative to input prices.
   b. increases the profit margins of many producers.
   c. decreases RGDP supplied.
   d. decreases unemployment rates.
   e. does none of the above.

9. Which of the following would shift the long-run aggregate supply curve if it changed?
   - **a.** the level of capital in the economy
   - **b.** the amount of land in the economy
   - **c.** the amount of labor in the economy
   - **d.** the technology in the economy
   - **e.** any of the above

10. The short-run aggregate supply curve will shift to the left, other things being equal, if
   - **a.** energy prices fall.
   - **b.** technology and productivity increase in the nation.
   - **c.** there is a short-term increase in input prices.
   - **d.** the capital stock of the nation increases.

11. An increase in input prices causes
   - **a.** the short-run aggregate supply curve to shift outward, which means the quantity supplied at any price level declines.
   - **b.** the short-run aggregate supply curve to shift inward, which means the quantity supplied at any price level declines.
   - **c.** the short-run aggregate supply curve to shift inward, which means the quantity supplied at any price level increases.
   - **d.** the short-run aggregate supply curve to shift outward, which means the quantity supplied at any price level increases.

12. How will an increase in money wages affect the short-run aggregate supply curve?
   - **a.** It will shift left (a decrease in short-run aggregate supply).
   - **b.** It will shift left (an increase in short-run aggregate supply).
   - **c.** It will shift right (a decrease in short-run aggregate supply).
   - **d.** It will shift right (an increase in short-run aggregate supply).

13. An unusual series of rainstorms washes out the grain crop in the upper plains states, severely curtailing the availability of corn and wheat, as well as soybeans. What effect would this have on aggregate supply?
   - **a.** It would shift the *SRAS* left, but not the *LRAS*.
   - **b.** It would shift both the *SRAS* and the *LRAS* left.
   - **c.** It would shift the *SRAS* right, but not the *LRAS*.
   - **d.** It would shift both the *SRAS* and the *LRAS* right.

14. Any permanent increase in the quantity of any of the factors of production—capital, land, labor, or technology—available, will cause the
   - **a.** *SRAS* to shift to the left and *LRAS* to remain constant.
   - **b.** *SRAS* to shift to the right and *LRAS* to remain constant.
   - **c.** both *SRAS* and *LRAS* to shift to the right.
   - **d.** both *SRAS* and *LRAS* to shift to the left.

15. Which of the following could be expected to shift the short-run aggregate supply curve upward?
   - **a.** a rise in the price of oil
   - **b.** a natural disaster
   - **c.** wage increases without increases in labor productivity
   - **d.** all of the above

16. A temporary positive supply shock will shift ______; a permanent positive supply shock will shift ______.
   - **a.** *SRAS* and *LRAS* right; *SRAS* and *LRAS* right
   - **b.** *SRAS* but not *LRAS* right; *SRAS* and *LRAS* right
   - **c.** *SRAS* and *LRAS* right; *SRAS* but not *LRAS* right
   - **d.** *SRAS* but not *LRAS* right; *SRAS* but not *LRAS* right

17. A year of unusually good weather for agriculture would
- **a.** increase *SRAS* but not *LRAS*.
- **b.** increase *SRAS* and *LRAS*.
- **c.** decrease *SRAS* but not *LRAS*.
- **d.** decrease *SRAS* and *LRAS*.

18. When there is a temporary sharp increase in the price of oil, which curve(s) will shift left?
- **a.** *SRAS*
- **b.** *LRAS*
- **c.** neither *SRAS* nor *LRAS*
- **d.** both *SRAS* and *LRAS*

19. Inflation that occurs due to a decrease in aggregate supply is called
- **a.** cost-push.
- **b.** demand-pull.
- **c.** inflationary push.
- **d.** none of the above.

20. Assuming a constant level of aggregate demand, the short-run effects of an adverse supply shock include
- **a.** an increase in the price level and a decrease in real output.
- **b.** an increase in the price level and an increase in real output.
- **c.** a decrease in the price level and an increase in real output.
- **d.** a decrease in the price level and a decrease in real output.

21. Cost-push inflation occurs when
- **a.** the aggregate demand curve shifts right at a faster rate than short-run aggregate supply.
- **b.** the short-run aggregate supply curve shifts left while aggregate demand is fixed.
- **c.** the aggregate demand curve shifts left and aggregate supply is fixed.
- **d.** the short-run aggregate supply curve shifts right.

22. A recession could result from
- **a.** a decrease in aggregate demand.
- **b.** an increase in long-run aggregate supply.
- **c.** an increase in aggregate demand.
- **d.** an increase in short-run aggregate supply.
- **e.** none of the above.

23. When *SRAS* and *AD* intersect at the natural level of real output, it is
- **a.** a short-run equilibrium and a long-run equilibrium.
- **b.** a short-run equilibrium but not necessarily a long-run equilibrium.
- **c.** a long-run equilibrium but not necessarily a long-run equilibrium.
- **d.** not necessarily either a short-run equilibrium or a long-run equilibrium.

24. Where *SRAS* and *AD* currently intersect at a real output level greater than the natural level of real output,
- **a.** it is a short-run equilibrium, and real output will tend to fall from its current level as it adjusts to long-run equilibrium.
- **b.** it is a short-run equilibrium, and real output will tend to rise from its current level as it adjusts to long-run equilibrium.
- **c.** it is a short-run disequilibrium, and real output will tend to fall from its current level as it adjusts to long-run equilibrium.
- **d.** it is a short-run disequilibrium, and real output will tend to rise from its current level as it adjusts to long-run equilibrium.

25. Starting from long-run equilibrium, an increase in aggregate demand will cause
- **a.** an expansionary gap in the short run.
- **b.** a contractionary gap in the short run.
- **c.** an expansionary gap in the short run and the long run.
- **d.** a contractionary gap in the short run and the long run.
- **e.** neither an expansionary nor a contractionary gap in the short run or the long run.

26. When there is a contractionary gap,
- **a.** real output exceeds the natural level of output, and unemployment exceeds its natural rate.
- **b.** real output exceeds the natural level of output, and unemployment is less than its natural rate.
- **c.** real output is less than the natural level of output, and unemployment exceeds its natural rate.
- **d.** real output is less than the natural level of output, and unemployment is less than its natural rate.

27. Which of the following could begin an episode of demand-pull inflation?
- **a.** an increase in consumer optimism
- **b.** a faster rate of economic growth by a major trading partner country
- **c.** expectations of higher rates of return in investment
- **d.** any of the above
- **e.** none of the above

28. If real output is currently less than the natural level of real output, a decrease in aggregate demand will
- **a.** make the current expansionary gap larger.
- **b.** make the current expansionary gap smaller.
- **c.** make the current contractionary gap larger.
- **d.** make the current contractionary gap smaller.

29. In the short run, demand-pull inflation
- **a.** increases both unemployment and the price level.
- **b.** increases unemployment but not the price level.
- **c.** increases the price level but not unemployment.
- **d.** decreases unemployment and increases the price level.

30. In a stagflation situation,
- **a.** unemployment increases, and the price level increases.
- **b.** unemployment increases, and the price level decreases.
- **c.** unemployment decreases, and the price level increases.
- **d.** unemployment decreases, and the price level decreases.

31. A sharp fall in oil prices will cause a(n) _____; a sudden increase in the wages demanded by workers will cause a(n) _____.
- **a.** contractionary gap; expansionary gap
- **b.** contractionary gap; contractionary gap
- **c.** expansionary gap; expansionary gap
- **d.** expansionary gap; contractionary gap

32. Starting from long-run equilibrium, an increase in aggregate demand
- **a.** causes an expansionary gap.
- **b.** results in a lower price level.
- **c.** increases unemployment.
- **d.** does all of the above.
- **e.** does b and c, but not a.

33. During the self-correction process after a fall in aggregate demand,
   a. the price level increases, and real output increases.
   b. the price level increases, and real output decreases.
   c. the price level decreases, and real output increases.
   d. the price level decreases, and real output decreases.

34. Which of the following can contribute to slowing the adjustment to a contractionary gap?
   a. efficiency wages
   b. the minimum wage
   c. menu costs
   d. all of the above
   e. b and c, but not a

35. An unexpected increase in aggregate demand will
   a. increase real wages in the short run but not the long run.
   b. increase real wages in the short run and the long run.
   c. decrease real wages in the short run but not the long run.
   d. decrease real wages in the short run and the long run.

Problems

1. How will each of the following changes alter aggregate supply?

Change	Short-Run Aggregate Supply	Long-Run Aggregate Supply
An increase in aggregate demand	________	________
A decrease in aggregate demand	________	________
An increase in the stock of capital	________	________
A reduction in the size of the labor force	________	________
An increase in input prices (that does not reflect permanent changes in their supplies)	________	________
A decrease in input prices (that does reflect permanent changes in their supplies)	________	________
An increase in usable natural resources	________	________
A temporary adverse supply shock	________	________
Increases in the cost of government regulations	________	________

2. Use the following diagram to answer questions a and b.

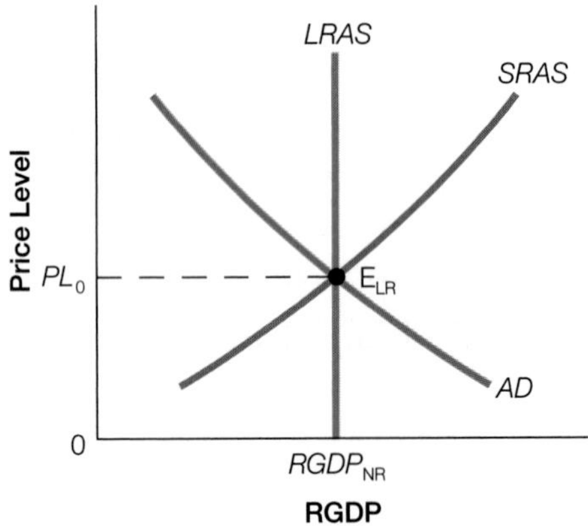

a. On the exhibit provided, illustrate the short-run effects of an increase in aggregate demand. What happens to the price level, real output, employment, and unemployment?

b. On the exhibit provided, illustrate the long-run effects of an increase in aggregate demand. What happens to the price level, real output, employment, and unemployment?

3. Use the following diagram to answer questions a and b.

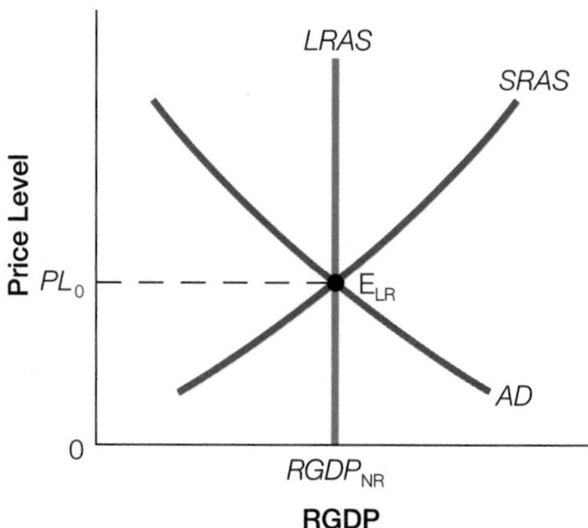

a. On the exhibit provided, illustrate the short-run effects of a decrease in aggregate demand. What happens to the price level, real output, employment, and unemployment?

b. On the exhibit provided, illustrate the long-run effects of a decrease in aggregate demand. What happens to the price level, real output, employment, and unemployment?

4. Use the following diagram to answer questions a and b.

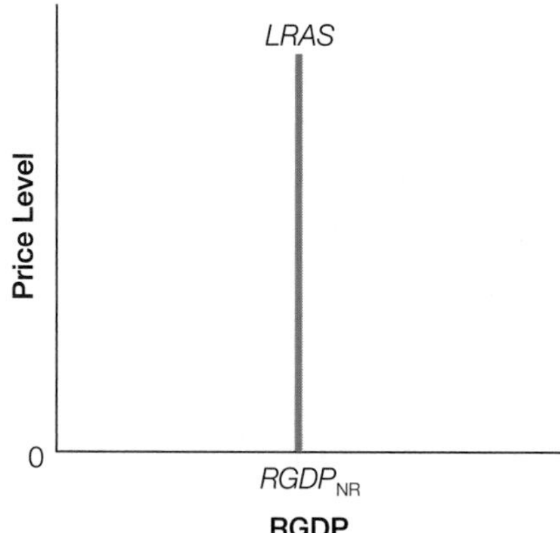

a. Illustrate a contractionary gap on the diagram provided.

b. Given the illustration in a, illustrate and explain the eventual long-run equilibrium in this case.

5. Use the following diagram to answer questions a and b.

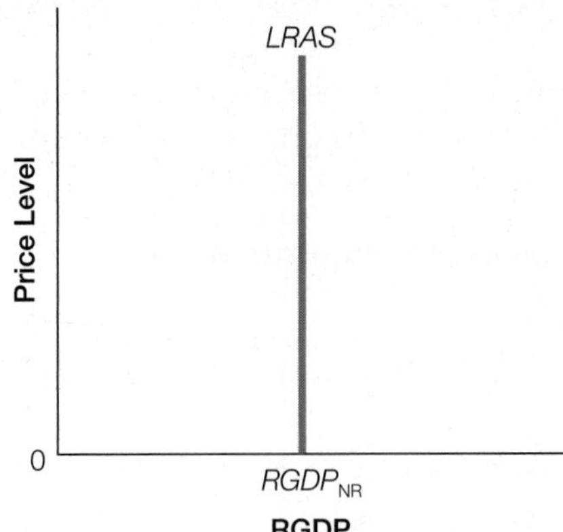

a. Illustrate an expansionary gap on the diagram provided.
b. Given the illustration in a, illustrate and explain the eventual long-run equilibrium in this case.

chapter 16

Fiscal Policy

section
16.1

Fiscal Policy

- What is fiscal policy?
- How does expansionary fiscal policy affect the government's budget?
- How does contractionary fiscal policy affect the government's budget?

FISCAL POLICY

fiscal policy
use of government purchases, taxes, and transfer payments to alter equilibrium output and prices

Fiscal policy is the use of government purchases, taxes, and transfer payments to alter RGDP and the price level. Sometimes it is necessary for the government to use fiscal policy to stimulate the economy during a contraction (or recession) or to try to curb an expansion in order to bring inflation under control. In the early 1980s, large tax cuts helped the U.S. economy out of a recession. In the 1990s, Japan used large government spending programs to help pull itself out of a recessionary slump. In 2001, a large tax cut was implemented to combat an economic slowdown and to promote long-term economic growth in the United States. When should the government use such policies and how well do they work are just a couple of the questions we will answer in this chapter.

budget deficit
government spending exceeds tax revenues for a given fiscal year

budget surplus
tax revenues are greater than government expenditures for a given fiscal year

When government spending (for purchases of goods and services and transfer payments) exceeds tax revenues, there is a **budget deficit.** When tax revenues are greater than government spending, a **budget surplus** exists. A balanced budget, where government expenditures equal tax revenues, may seldom occur unless efforts are made to deliberately balance the budget as a matter of public policy.

FISCAL STIMULUS AFFECTS THE BUDGET

expansionary fiscal policy
use of fiscal policy tools to foster increased output by increasing government purchases, lowering taxes, and/or increasing transfer payments

contractionary fiscal policy
use of fiscal policy tools to reduce output by decreasing government purchases, increasing taxes, and/or reducing transfer payments

When the government wishes to stimulate the economy by increasing aggregate demand, it will increase government purchases of goods and services, increase transfer payments, lower taxes, or use some combination of these approaches. Any of those options will increase the budget deficit (or reduce the budget surplus). Thus, **expansionary fiscal policy** is associated with increased government budget deficits. Likewise, if the government wishes to dampen a boom in the economy by reducing aggregate demand, it will reduce its purchases of goods and services, increase taxes, reduce transfer payments, or use some combination of these approaches. Thus, **contractionary fiscal policy** will tend to create or expand a budget surplus, or reduce a budget deficit, if one exists.

Section Check

SECTION CHECK

1. Fiscal policy is the use of government purchases of goods and services, taxes, and transfer payments to affect aggregate demand and to alter RGDP and the price level.
2. Expansionary fiscal policies will increase the budget deficit (or reduce a budget surplus) through greater government spending, lower taxes, or both.
3. Contractionary fiscal policies will create a budget surplus (or reduce a budget deficit) through reduced government spending, higher taxes, or both.

---

1. If, as part of its fiscal policy, the federal government increased its purchases of goods and services, would that be an expansionary or contractionary tactic?
2. If the federal government decreased its purchases of goods and services, would the budget deficit increase or decrease?
3. If the federal government increased taxes or decreased transfer payments, would that be an expansionary or contractionary fiscal policy?
4. If the federal government increased taxes or decreased transfer payments, would the budget deficit increase or decrease?
5. If the federal government increased government purchases and lowered taxes at the same time, would the budget deficit increase or decrease?

Government: Spending and Taxation

section 16.2

- How does government finance its spending?
- On what does the public sector spend its money?
- What are progressive and regressive taxes?

GROWTH IN GOVERNMENT

While it is true that government spending has changed little since 1970, the composition of government spending has changed considerably. National defense spending has fallen from roughly 9 percent of GDP in 1968 to 3.5 percent in 2001. However, in the aftermath of September 11, and the addition of homeland security, we are already starting to see increases in defense spending. Areas of government growth can be partly determined by looking at statistics of the types of government spending. Exhibit 1 shows categories of government spending as a proportion of total spending.

Other areas had rapid spending growth as well. Educational expenditures, for example, tripled in the 1960s alone. By the mid-1970s and for the first time in the nation's history, roughly half of government spending was for social concerns such as education, health, and public housing. In the 1980s and 1990s, we saw a continued increase in income transfer payments including Social Security, welfare, and unemployment compensation.

Exhibit 1(a) shows that 38 percent of federal government spending went to Social Security and income security programs. Another 21 percent was spent on health care and Medicare (for the elderly). The rest of federal expenditures include national defense (17 percent), interest on the national debt (11 percent), and miscellaneous items such as foreign aid, education, agriculture, transportation, and housing (13 percent).

section 16.2
Exhibit 1

Government Expenditures

a. Federal Expenditures, 2001

b. State and Local Expenditures, 1999

SOURCE: *Economic Report of the President, 2002.*

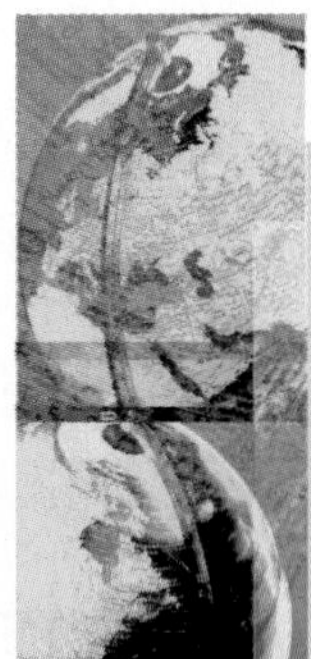

Global WATCH

A GLOBAL COMPARISON OF TAXATION

section 16.2
Exhibit 2

A Global Comparison of Taxation

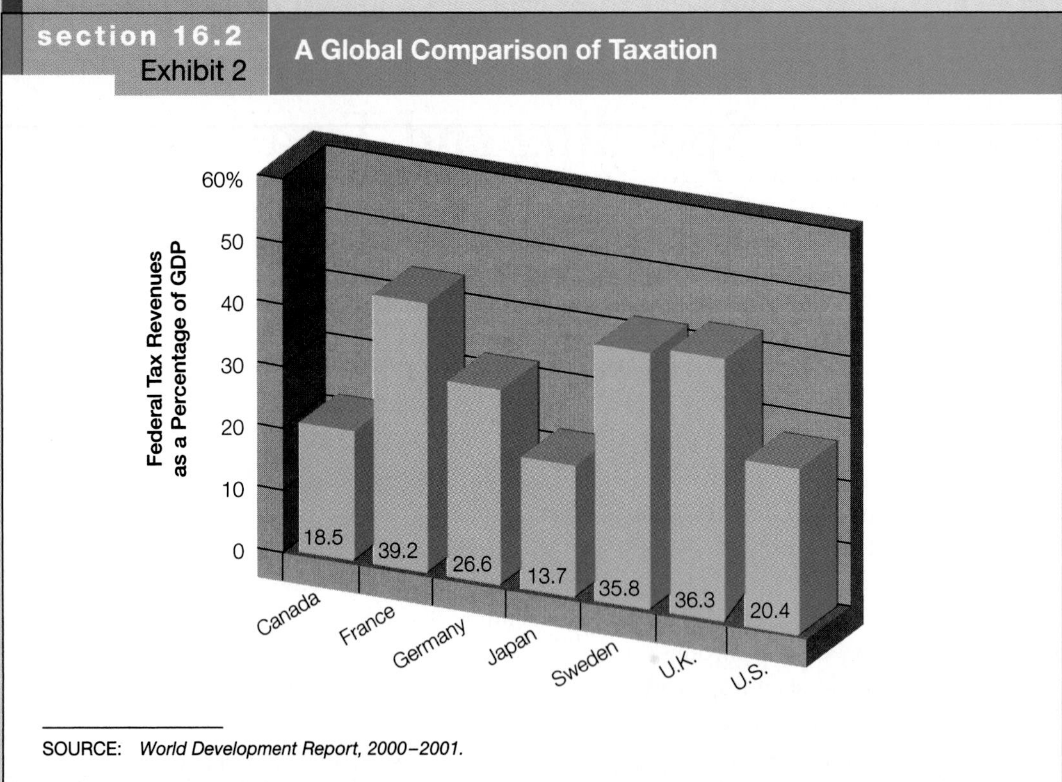

SOURCE: *World Development Report, 2000–2001.*

CONSIDER THIS:
In Exhibit 2, we see that taxpayers in other parts of the developed world have a heavier tax burden than those in the United States.

Exhibit 1(b) shows that state and local spending is highly different from federal spending. Education and public welfare account for 50 percent of the state and local expenditures. Other areas of state and local spending include highways, utilities, and police and fire protection.

GENERATING GOVERNMENT REVENUE

Governments have to pay their bills like any person or institution that spends money. But how do they obtain revenue? Two major avenues are open: taxation and borrowing.

TYPES OF TAXATION

In most years, a large majority of government activity is financed by taxation. What kinds of taxes are levied on the American population?

At the federal level, most taxes or levies are on income. Exhibit 3 shows that about 60 percent of tax revenues come in the form of income taxes on individuals and corporations, called personal income taxes and corporate income taxes, respectively. Most of the remaining revenues come from payroll taxes, which are levied on work-related income—payrolls. These taxes are used to pay for Social Security and compulsory insurance plans like Medicare. This tax is split between employees and the employers. The Social Security share of federal taxes has steadily risen as the proportion of the population over 65 has grown and as Social Security benefits have been increased. Consequently, payroll taxes have risen significantly in recent years. Other taxes on items like gasoline, liquor, and tobacco products provide for a small proportion of government revenues, as do customs duties, estate and gift taxes, and some minor miscellaneous taxes and user charges. The United States federal government relies more heavily on income-based taxes than nearly any other government in the world. Most other governments rely more heavily on sales taxes, excise taxes, and customs duties.

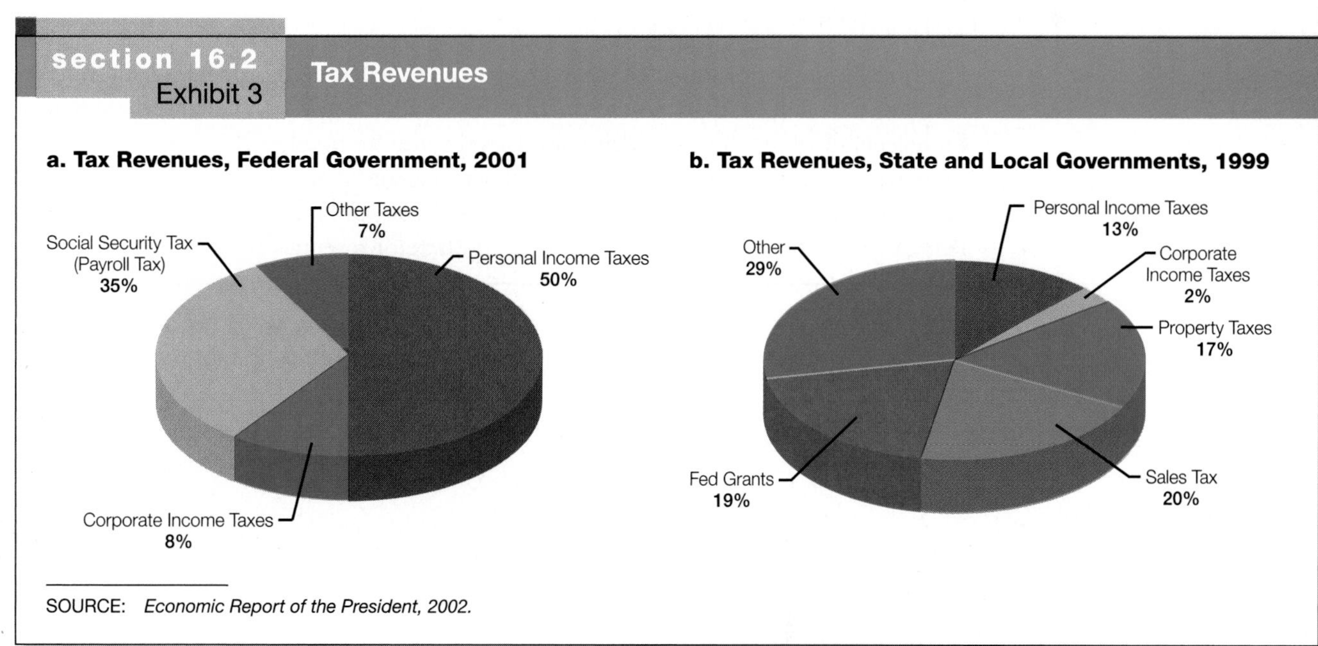

SOURCE: *Economic Report of the President, 2002.*

A Progressive Tax

progressive tax
the amount of an individual's tax rises as a proportion of income, as the person's income rises

http://

One impact of substantial taxes on income is that the effective "take home" income of Americans is significantly altered by the tax system. **Progressive taxes,** of which the federal income tax is one example, are designed so that those with higher incomes pay a greater proportion of their income in taxes. A progressive tax is one tool that the government can use to redistribute income. It should be noted, however, that certain types of income are excluded from income for taxation purposes, such as interest on municipal bonds, and income in kind—like foods stamps or Medicare.

A Regressive Tax

regressive tax
the amount of an individual's tax falls as a proportion of income, as the person's income rises

Payroll taxes, the second most important income source for the federal government, are actually a **regressive tax;** that is, they take a greater proportion of the income of lower-income groups than higher-income groups. The reasons for this are simple. Social Security, for example, is imposed as a fixed proportion (now 7.65 percent on employees and an equal amount on employers) of wage and salary income up to $80,000 in 2001. Also, wealthy persons have relatively more property income that is not subject to payroll taxes. Adding together individual income and payroll taxes, the federal tax system is probably only slightly progressive. The same would hold if other taxes were included.

An Excise Tax

excise tax
a sales tax on individual products such as alcohol, tobacco, and gasoline

Some consider an **excise tax**—a sales tax on individual products such as alcohol, tobacco, and gasoline—to be the most unfair type of tax because it is generally the most regressive. This type of tax on specific items will impose a far greater burden, as a percentage of income, on the poor and middle class than on the wealthy, because low-income families pay a greater proportion of their income on these taxes than do high-income families.

In addition, excise taxes may lead to economic inefficiencies. By isolating a few products and subjecting them to discriminatory taxation, consumption taxes subject economic choices to political manipulation and lead to inefficiency.

FINANCING STATE AND LOCAL GOVERNMENT ACTIVITIES

Historically, the major source of state and local revenue has been property taxes. In recent decades, state and local governments have relied increasingly on sales and income taxes for revenues (see Exhibit 3). Today, sales taxes account for roughly 20 percent of revenues, property taxes account for 17 percent, and personal and corporate income taxes account for 15 percent of revenues. Another 19 percent of state and local revenues come from the federal government in grants. The remaining share of revenues comes from license fees and user charges (e.g., payment for utilities, occupational license fees, tuition fees) and other taxes.

In The NEWS

THE STATUS OF SOCIAL SECURITY

BY PAUL BARNES

Most Americans have a great investment in Social Security. 27.6 million people receive Social Security retirement benefits every month, and if you include those collecting Social Security because they are disabled, 44 million people, or one out of every five Americans, are receiving Social Security benefits. Ninety-six percent of all workers are covered by the program, and at this time, 25 million people pay into the system through payroll Social Security taxes.

WHO IS ELIGIBLE FOR SOCIAL SECURITY?

Anyone who has worked and paid Social Security taxes for at least 10 years over their lifetime, and is at least age 62, is eligible. Also, if you are the spouse of someone who has worked and paid Social Security taxes for at least 10 years, you may be eligible—even if you never worked.

However, a spouse will only collect 50 percent of the working spouse's Social Security. But both can collect at the same time.

A couple of things to remember. Full retirement age is now 65. That's the age you have to be to retire and receive full benefits. You can retire early, but you will only receive partial benefits—currently 80 percent—but it's slowly going down over the next 27 years to 70 percent of full benefits, if you retire early.

However, the retirement age is slowly going up. The full retirement age is going up from 65 to 67 over the next 27 years. So, for instance, if you are 62 now, you will have to wait until you are 65 years and 2 months until you can retire with full benefits.

HOW MUCH WILL I GET EVERY MONTH?

The average Social Security benefit is $800.00 a month. The maximum right now is $1,400.00. That means, for the average earner, you will get about 42 percent of your current earnings. For a low earner, you'll get about 57 percent of your current earnings, and for a high earner you'll get about 27 percent of your current earnings.

The amount of your benefit is determined based on your average earnings over your lifetime as a worker—usually about 35 years.

It's important to note that your Social Security benefit will periodically be adjusted for the cost of living (COLA). The amount of the increase is based on the consumer price index (CPI).

WILL SOCIAL SECURITY BE THERE WHEN THE BABY BOOMERS NEED IT?

Absolutely. Right now, Social Security is solvent through the year 2034 and is building reserves to help fund it for the baby boomer generation. The slow increase in the retirement age (as noted above) is part of a plan enacted in the 80s to keep the fund solvent, and more is expected to be done.

SOURCE: by Paul Barnes, Deputy Commissioner of the Social Security Administration, http://www.msnbc.com/news

section 16.2
Exhibit 4 On the Road to Ruin

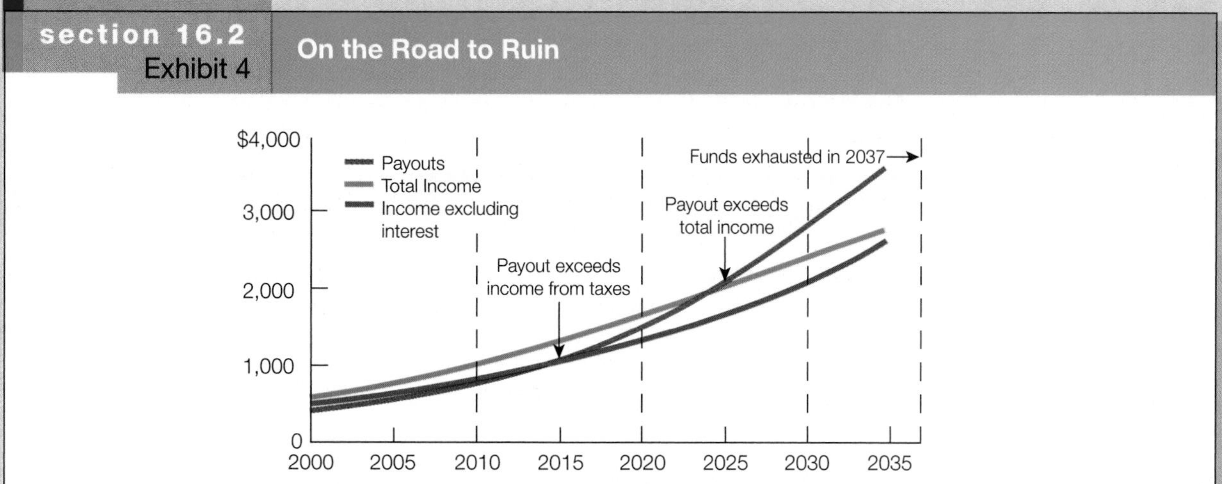

In Exhibit 4, we see that the Social Security Trust Fund is expected to go broke in 2037 unless the retirement system is restructured. Shown above are projections, using intermediate cost assumptions, of the amount of income going into the trust fund and the amount of money going out, in billions of dollars.

(continued)

IN THE NEWS *(CONTINUED)*

CONSIDER THIS:

Rumor has it that most young people believe that there is a greater chance that they will see an unidentified flying object (UFO) in their lifetime than a Social Security payment. We are often told that Social Security is a retirement program. However, it is really a tax plan that transfers money from workers to the elderly. Social Security is a pay-as-you-go system—payments to current retirees are derived from payroll taxes imposed on current workers

In Exhibit 4, you can see that the Social Security Trust Fund is slowly going broke, and if it not fixed, it is predicted to go belly up by 2037 (and some say serious problems could occur as soon as 2016). At that point, retirees would only get 75 percent of their promised benefits. The problem is that many baby boomers will begin to retire in the next several years and there will simply not be enough workers to pay for these new retirees. In addition, demographers' forecasts of declining birth rates and longer life expectancies only make matters worse.

As the ratio of retirees to workers grows, the Social Security system will either have to cut benefits, increase taxes, cut government spending in other areas, reform the current system, or some combination of the above. So what can we do? Several options have been recently proposed to reform the Social Security system: The government could invest part of Social Security funds in the stock market, or they could put part of the payroll tax in a personal retirement savings account and allow individuals to manage their own accounts; or allow individuals a choice of the current system or private social security.

The reason why the government is interested in investing part of Social Security in the stock market is that historically the returns are much greater in the stock market. The real rate of return (indexed for inflation) is roughly 7 percent in the stock market as compared to only 2 percent for government bonds. However, one of the drawbacks of government investment in the stock market is that there is the potential for political abuse. With such a large amount of funds, there may be the temptation for the government to favor some firms and punish others. An alternative would be to put some of the payroll tax in an individual retirement plan and let individuals manage their own funds—perhaps choosing from a list of mutual funds.

A third option might be to let individuals choose to continue with the current Social Security system or contribute a minimum of say 10 or 20 percent of their wages to private investment fund. This has been tried in a number of Central and South American countries. In Chile, almost 90 percent of workers chose to leave the government Social Security program to invest privately.

Critics of the private plan argue that it is risky and individuals may make poor investment decisions and that the government may ultimately have to pay for their mistakes. However, if the government were to approve only low- to moderate-risk mutual funds, with their diverse portfolios, this should offset most of the risk associated with this criticism.

Section Check

1. Over a third of federal spending goes towards pensions and income security programs.
2. A progressive tax takes a greater proportion of the income of higher-income groups than of lower-income groups.
3. A regressive tax takes a greater proportion of the income of lower-income groups than of higher-income groups.

---

1. What options are available for a government to finance its spending?

section 16.3

The Multiplier Effect

- What is the multiplier effect?
- How does the marginal propensity to consume affect the multiplier effect?
- How does investment interact with the multiplier effect?

CHANGES IN RGDP

The RGDP will change anytime the amount of any one of the four forms of purchases—consumption, investment, government purchases, and net exports—changes. If, for any reason, people generally decide to purchase more in any of these categories out of given income, aggregate demand will shift rightward. If they decide to purchase less, there will be a reduction in aggregate demand.

Any one of the components of purchases of goods and services (C, I, G, or $X - M$) can initiate changes in aggregate demand, and thus a new short-run equilibrium. Changes in total output are often brought about by alterations in investment plans, because investment purchases are a relatively volatile category of expenditures. However, if policy makers are unhappy with the present short-run equilibrium GDP, perhaps because they consider unemployment too high, they can deliberately manipulate the level of government purchases in order to obtain a new short-run equilibrium value. Similarly, by changing taxes or transfer payments, they can alter the amount of disposable income of households and thus bring about changes in consumption purchases.

THE MULTIPLIER EFFECT

Usually when an initial increase in purchases of goods or services occurs, the ultimate increase in total purchases will tend to be greater than the initial increase; this is called the **multiplier effect.** But how does this effect work? Suppose the government increases its defense budget by $10 billion to buy aircraft carriers. When the government purchases the aircraft carriers, not only does it add to the total demand for goods and services directly, it also provides $10 billion in added income to the companies that actually construct the aircraft carriers. Those companies will then hire more workers and buy more capital equipment and other inputs in order to produce the new output. The owners of these inputs therefore receive more income because of the increase in government purchases. And what will they do with this additional income? While behavior will vary somewhat among individuals, collectively they will probably spend a substantial part of the additional income on additional consumption purchases, pay some additional taxes incurred because of the income, and save a bit of it as well. The **marginal propensity to consume (*MPC*)** is the fraction of additional disposable income that a household consumes rather than saves.

multiplier effect
a chain reaction of additional income and purchases that results in total purchases that are greater than the initial increase in purchases

marginal propensity to consume (*MPC*)
is the fraction of additional disposable income that a household consumes rather than saves

THE MULTIPLIER EFFECT AT WORK

Suppose that out of every dollar in *added* disposable income generated by increased investment purchases, individuals collectively spend two-thirds, or 67 cents, on consumption purchases. In other words, the *MPC* is 2/3. The initial $10 billion increase in government purchases causes both a $10 billion increase in aggregate demand and an income increase of $10 billion to suppliers of the inputs used to produce aircraft carriers; the owners of those inputs, in turn, will spend an additional $6.67 billion (two-thirds of $10 billion) on additional consumption purchases. A chain reaction has been started. The added $6.67 billion in consumption purchases by those deriving income from the initial investment brings a $6.67 billion increase in aggregate demand and in new income to suppliers of the inputs that produced the goods and services. These persons, in turn, will spend some two-thirds of their additional $6.67 billion in income, or $4.44 billion on consumption purchases. This means $4.44 billion more in aggregate demand and income to still another group of people, who will then proceed to spend two-thirds of that amount, or $2.96 billion, on consumption purchases.

The chain reaction continues, with each new round of purchases providing income to a new group of people who in turn increase their purchases. As successive changes in consumption purchases occur, the feedback becomes smaller and smaller. The added income generated and the number of resulting consumer purchases get smaller, because some of the increase in income goes to savings and tax payments that do not immediately flow into greater investment or government expenditure. As Exhibit 1 indicates, the fifth change in consumption purchases is indeed much smaller than the first change in consumption purchases. What is the total impact of the initial increase in purchases on additional purchases and income? We can find that out using the multiplier formula, calculated as follows:

$$\text{Multiplier} = 1/(1 - MPC)$$

In this case,

$$\text{Multiplier} = 1/(1 - 2/3) = 1/(1/3) = 3$$

An initial increase in purchases of goods or services of $10 billion will increase total purchases by $30 billion ($10 billion × 3), as the initial $10 billion in investment purchases also generates an additional $20 billion in consumption purchases.

CHANGES IN THE *MPC* AFFECT THE MULTIPLIER PROCESS

Note that the larger the marginal propensity to consume, the larger the multiplier effect, because relatively more additional consumption purchases out of any given income in-

section 16.3 Exhibit 1 — The Multiplier Process

Change in government purchases	$10.00 billion—direct effect on *AD*	
First change in consumption purchases	6.67 billion (2/3 of 10)	The sum of the indirect effect on *AD*, through induced additional consumption purchases, is equal to $20 billion
Second change in consumption purchases	4.44 billion (2/3 of 6.67)	
Third change in consumption purchases	2.96 billion (2/3 of 4.44)	
Fourth change in consumption purchases	1.98 billion (2/3 of 2.96)	
Fifth change in consumption purchases	1.32 billion (2/3 of 1.98)	
	$30 billion = Total effect on purchases (*AD*)	

crease generates relatively larger secondary and tertiary income effects in successive rounds of the process. For example, if the *MPC* is 3/4, the multiplier is 4:

$$\text{Multiplier} = 1/(1 - 3/4) = 1/(1/4) = 4$$

If the *MPC* is only 1/2, however, the multiplier is 2:

$$\text{Multiplier} = 1/(1 - 1/2) = 1/(1/2) = 2$$

THE MULTIPLIER AND THE AGGREGATE DEMAND CURVE

As we discussed earlier, when the Defense Department decides to buy additional aircraft carriers, it affects aggregate demand. It increases the incomes of owners of inputs used to make the aircraft carriers, including profits that go to owners of the firms involved. That is the initial effect. The secondary effect, the greater income that results, will lead to increased consumer purchases. In addition, the higher profits for the firms involved in carrier construction may lead them to increase their investment purchases. So the initial effect of the government's purchases will tend to have a multiplied effect on the economy. In Exhibit 2, we see that the initial impact of a $10 billion additional purchase by the government directly shifts the aggregate demand curve from AD_0 to AD_1. The multiplier effect then causes the aggregate demand to shift out $20 billion further, to AD_2. The total effect on aggregate demand of a $10 billion increase in government purchases is therefore $30 billion, if the marginal propensity to consume equals 2/3.

section 16.3 Exhibit 2 — The Multiplier and Aggregate Demand

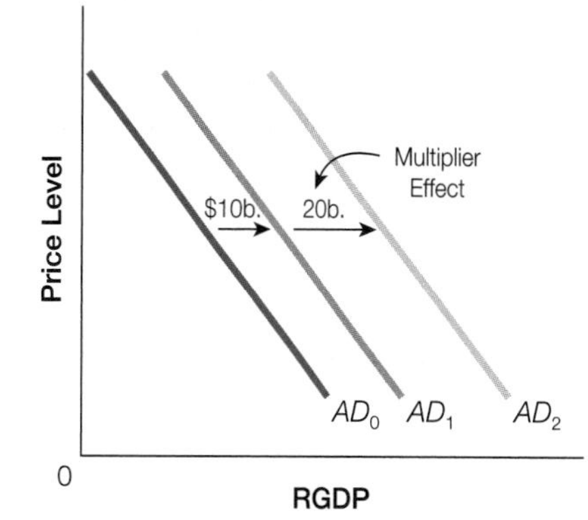

In this hypothetical example, an increase in government purchases of $10 billion for new aircraft carriers will shift the aggregate demand curve to the right by more than the $10 billion initial purchase, other things equal. It will shift aggregate demand by a total of $30 billion, to AD_2. (The shifts are shown larger than they would really be for visual ease; $30 billion is a small shift in an $10,000 billion economy.)

As another example, some have argued that the multiplier effect of a new sports stadium will lead to additional local spending that will be 3 or 4 times the amount of the initial investment. However, this is unlikely. It is important to remember that money spent on the stadium (taxpayer dollars) could also have been spent on food, clothing, entertainment, recreation and many other goods and services. So the expenditure on the stadium comes at the expense of other consumer expenditures. In addition, the multiplier is most effective when it brings idle resources into production. If all resources are fully employed, the expansion in demand and the multiplier effect will lead to a higher price level, not increases in employment and RGDP.

TIME LAGS, SAVING, TAXES, AND IMPORTS REDUCE THE SIZE OF THE MULTIPLIER

The multiplier process is not instantaneous. If you get an additional $100 in income today, you may spend two-thirds of that on consumption purchases eventually, but you may wait six months or even longer to do it. Such time lags mean that the ultimate increase in purchases resulting from an initial increase in purchases may not be achieved for a year

In The **NEWS**

BOEING MULTIPLE-USE FIGHTER JET COMPLETES FLIGHT; DEVELOPMENTAL AIRCRAFT IN RACE FOR HUGE CONTRACT

BY CHRIS PLANTE

WASHINGTON (CNN)—A developmental version of the Boeing Joint Strike Fighter aircraft made its first flight Monday, beating competitor Lockheed-Martin to the sky in a contest for what could lead to the largest single defense contract in history.

AP PHOTO, JUDSON BOHMER

The Joint Strike Fighter is designed for use in various versions by the U.S. Air Force, Navy, and Marine Corps.

In October 2001, Lockheed-Martin won the $200 billion defense contract for the Joint Strike Fighter.

In the real world, the multiplier process is important because it may help explain why small changes in consumption, investment, and government purchases can cause larger, multiplied changes in total purchases. These increased purchases, in turn, could lead to increased real output and reduced unemployment when the economy is not already fully employed.

In this application, when the government purchased the jet fighters, we are assuming that it would not have purchased other goods and services with those same dollars instead. This is important because the purchase of the Joint Strike Fighter has the potential to lead to a net increase in demand only so far as it increases total government purchases, which, if the economy is less than fully employed, will increase real output and employment. That is, the demand for the Joint Strike Fighter, other things equal, will lead to an increase in output for Lockheed-Martin. As a result, the company that wins the contract will hire more employees, who will take their paychecks and spend some of it on clothes, restaurant meals, and other goods and services. Those purchases will result in further growth in those industries, many of which are located far from the aircraft plant. In other words, a government purchase has the potential to have an impact on the economy that is greater than the magnitude of that original purchase. This is the multiplier process at work.

However, if the aircraft purchases just replace other government purchases, the multiplied expansion in defense-related industries is offset by a multiplied contraction in industries where government purchases have fallen.

Contrast this example with government purchases of food for a school lunch program. Government purchases of school lunches rise, but private consumption falls as parents now purchase less food—perhaps by the same amount—for their children's lunches. Overall, we would expect only a small change in demand, if any, as government demand replaces private demand. In some real sense, the suppliers of apples, milk, cookies, and chips have just had the names of their customers change.

SOURCE: Chris Plante, "BOEING MULTIPLE-USE FIGHTER JET COMPLETES FLIGHT," http://www.cnn.com/2000/US/09/18/new.fighter/index.html.

or more. The extent of the multiplier effect visible within a short time period will be less than the total effect indicated by the multiplier formula. In addition, saving, taxes, and money spent on import goods (which are not part of aggregate demand for domestically produced goods and services) will reduce the size of the multiplier, because each of them reduces the fraction of a given increase in income that will go to additional purchases of domestically produced consumption goods.

It is also important to note that the multiplier effect is not restricted to changes in government purchases. The multiplier effect can apply to changes that alter spending in any of the components of aggregate demand: consumption, investment, government purchases, or net exports.

Section Check

1. The multiplier effect is a chain reaction of additional income and purchases that results in a final increase in total purchases that is greater than the initial increase in purchases.
2. An increase in the marginal propensity to consume leads to an increase in the multiplier effect.
3. Because of a time lag, the full impact of the multiplier effect on GDP may not be felt until a year or more after the initial investment.
4. An increase in government purchases will also cause an increase in aggregate income and stimulate additional consumer purchases, which will result in a magnified (or multiplying) effect on aggregate demand.

---

1. How does the multiplier effect work?
2. What is the marginal propensity to consume?
3. Why is the marginal propensity to consume always less than one?
4. Why does the multiplier effect get larger as the marginal propensity to consume gets larger?
5. If an increase in government purchases leads to a reduction in private sector purchases, why could the effect on the economy be less than indicated by the multiplier?

section 16.4

Fiscal Policy and the *AD/AS* Model

- How can government stimulus of aggregate demand reduce unemployment?
- How can government reduction of aggregate demand reduce inflation?

FISCAL POLICY AND THE *AD/AS* MODEL

The primary tools of fiscal policy, government purchases, taxes, and transfer payments, can be presented in the context of the aggregate supply and demand model. In Exhibit 1, we have used the *AD/AS* model to show how the government can use fiscal policy as either an expansionary or contractionary tool to help control the economy.

BUDGET DEFICITS AND FISCAL POLICY

As we discussed earlier, when the government purchases more, taxes less, and/or increases transfer payments, the size of the government's budget deficit will grow. While budget deficits are often thought to be bad, a case can be made for using budget deficits to stimulate the economy when it is operating at less than full capacity. Such expansionary fiscal policy may have the potential to move an economy out of a contraction (or a recession) and closer to full employment.

Expansionary Fiscal Policy at Less Than Full Employment

If the government decides to purchase more, cut taxes, and/or increase transfer payments, other things constant, total purchases will rise. That is, increased government purchases,

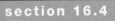

section 16.4
Exhibit 1

Expansionary Fiscal Policy

a. At Less Than Full Employment

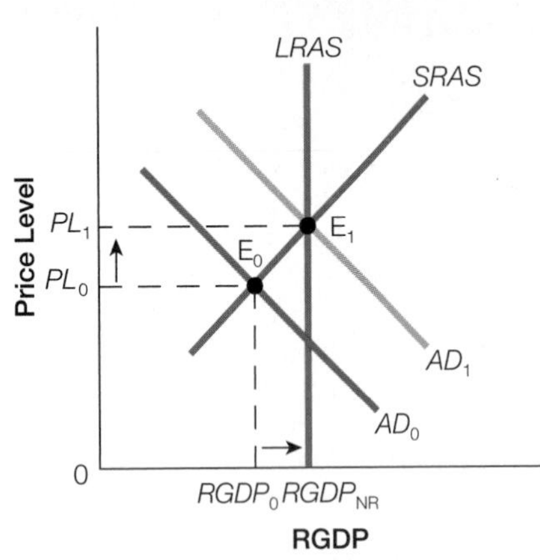

An increase in government purchases, an increase in transfer payments, and/or a tax cut at less than full employment.

b. At Full Employment

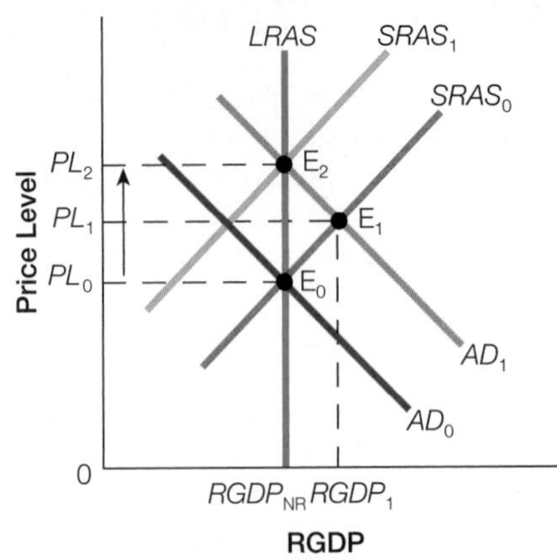

An increase in government purchases, an increase in transfer payments, and/or a tax cut at full employment.

In Exhibit 1(a), the increase in government purchases, a tax cut, and/or an increase in transfer payments leads to a rightward shift in aggregate demand. This results in a change in equilibrium from E_0 to E_1, reflecting a higher price level and a higher RGDP. Because this result is on the *LRAS* curve, it is a long-run, sustainable equilibrium. In Exhibit 1(b), we see that the same policy change will only lead to a short-run increase in RGDP at E_1. Once input owners realize that the price level has changed, they will require higher input prices, raising costs and shifting the *SRAS* curve to the left. The final long-run equilibrium at E_2 will only reflect the new higher price level, PL_2.

tax cuts, or transfer payment increases can increase consumption and investment and government purchases, shifting the aggregate demand curve to the right. The effect of this increase in aggregate demand depends on the position of the macroeconomic equilibrium prior to the government stimulus. For example, in Exhibit 1(a), the initial equilibrium is at E_0, a recession scenario, with real output below potential RGDP. Starting at this point and moving along the short-run aggregate supply curve, an increase in government purchases, a tax cut, and/or an increase in transfer payments would increase the size of the budget deficit and lead to an increase in aggregate demand, ideally from AD_0 to AD_1. The result of such a change would be an increase in the price level, from PL_0 to PL_1, and an increase in RGDP, from $RGDP_0$ to $RGDP_{NR}$. We must remember, of course, that some of this increase in aggregate demand is caused by the multiplier process, so the magnitude of the change in aggregate demand will be larger than the magnitude of the stimulus package of tax cuts, increases in transfer payments, and/or government purchases. If the policy change is of the right magnitude and timed appropriately, the expansionary fiscal policy might stimulate the economy, pull it out of the contraction and/or recession, and result in full employment at $RGDP_{NR}$.

Expansionary Fiscal Policy at Full Employment

Now suppose that the economy is currently operating at full employment—$RGDP_{NR}$. This is seen as point E_0 in Exhibit 1(b). An increase in government spending, an increase

In The NEWS

THE BUSH TAX CUT

In June 2001, Congress voted in a tax cut over ten years. With the economy in a slowdown in 2001, many economists were on board for a tax cut but for different sizes and for a variety of different reasons.

Nobel laureate economist Gary Becker, believes that the short-run effects of a tax cut to combat an economic slowdown are exaggerated. According to Becker, "more important to the long-run growth of the economy is the proposed cut of all marginal income tax rates, including lowering the top rate from 39% to 33%." Becker believes tax cuts of this nature will stimulate investment and entrepreneurial activity.

Becker acknowledges that studies by many economists lead to conflicting conclusions about the relationship between tax cuts and investment. However, Becker believes the most important effect of a tax reduction is to curtail government spending not stimulate private investment. He states "that the addiction to spending whatever revenue is available is bipartisan."

Laura D'andrea Tyson, former Clinton economic adviser, thought there should be an immediate tax cut to give a countercyclical boost to the economy. Still others argued for retroactive tax cuts to get an even greater fiscal stimulus.

Tyson acknowledged that the top 1% of income earners pay roughly 20% of the total share of federal income taxes. However, she argued the proposed Bush tax cut gave too much to the rich. As a compromise, she was in favor of changing the top marginal tax rate to 35% rather than 33%, giving more tax relief to the middle-income earners.

SOURCE: Gary Becker, "The Real Reason We Need a Tax Cut," *Business Week,* March 19, 2001, p. 28, and Laura D'andrea Tyson "Tax Cut Truths You Won't Hear from the Prez," *Business Week,* March 26, 2001, p. 28.

in transfer payments, and/or a tax cut causes an increase in aggregate demand from AD_0 to AD_1. Moving along short-run aggregate supply curve $SRAS_0$, the price level rises and real output rises to $RGDP_1$ as we reach a short-run equilibrium at E_1. This is not a long-run, or sustainable, equilibrium, however, because at this point, the high level of aggregate demand is beyond full capacity and will put pressure on input markets, sending wages and other input prices higher. The higher costs that result from these input price increases will shift the short-run aggregate supply curve leftward from $SRAS_0$ to $SRAS_1$. This, in turn, shifts the short-run equilibrium point from E_1 to E_2, which, because it is on the long-run aggregate supply curve, is a sustainable long-run equilibrium. So we see that real output returns to the full employment level, and the long-term effect is a large increase in the price level, from PL_0 to PL_2.

BUDGET SURPLUSES (OR BUDGET DEFICIT REDUCTIONS) AND FISCAL POLICY

When the government purchases less, taxes more, or decreases transfer payments, the size of the government's budget deficit will fall or the size of the budget surplus will rise, other things equal. Sometimes such a change in fiscal policy may help "cool off" the economy when it has overheated and inflation has become a serious problem. Then, contractionary fiscal policy has the potential to offset an overheated, inflationary boom.

Contractionary Fiscal Policy Beyond Full Employment

Suppose that the price level is at PL_0 and that short-run equilibrium is at E_0, as shown in Exhibit 2(a). Say that the government decides to reduce its purchases, increase taxes, or reduce transfer payments. A government purchase change may directly affect aggregate

section 16.4 Exhibit 2

Contractionary Fiscal Policy

a. Beyond Full Employment

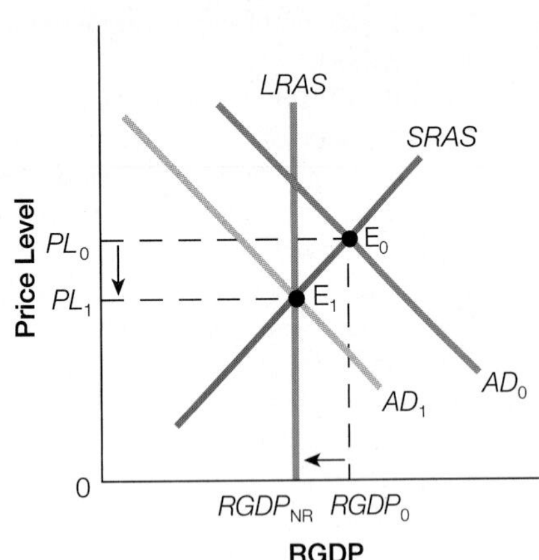

A reduction in government purchases, a decrease in transfer payments, and/or higher taxes beyond full employment.

b. At Full Employment

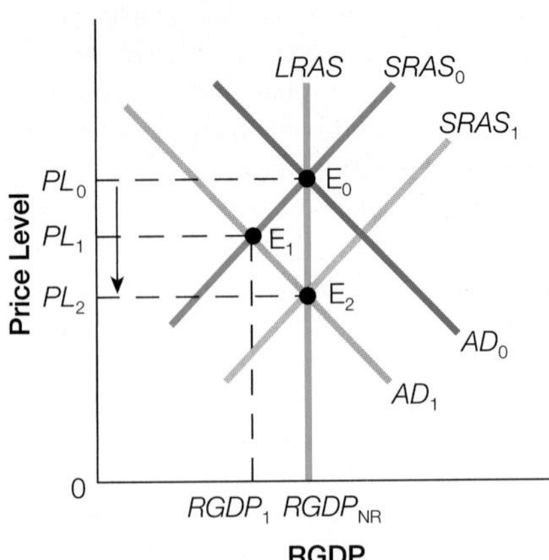

A reduction in government purchases, a decrease in transfer payments, and/or higher taxes at full employment.

In Exhibit 2(a), the reduction in government purchases, tax increase, or transfer payment decrease leads to a leftward shift in aggregate demand and a change in the short-run equilibrium from E_0 to E_1, reflecting a lower price level and a return to full employment RGDP ($RGDP_{NR}$). In Exhibit 2(b), the reduction in aggregate demand leads to a short-run equilibrium at E_1, reflecting a lower price level and real output below its full employment level. At this point, input owners change their price level expectations and are now willing to accept lower compensation. This reduces production costs and shifts short-run aggregate supply to the right, from $SRAS_0$ to $SRAS_1$. The final long-run effect is a new lower price level and real output that has returned to $RGDP_{NR}$.

demand. A tax increase on consumers or a decrease in transfer payments will reduce households' disposable incomes, reducing purchases of consumption goods and services, and higher business taxes will reduce investment purchases. The reductions in consumption, investment, and/or government purchases will shift the aggregate demand curve leftward, ideally from AD_0 to AD_1. This lowers the price level from PL_0 to PL_1 and brings RGDP back to the full employment level at $RGDP_{NR}$, resulting in a new short- and long-run equilibrium at E_1.

A Contractionary Fiscal Policy at Full Employment

Now consider Exhibit 2(b), which shows the case of an initial short- and long-run equilibrium at full employment, as indicated by point E_0, with a price level of PL_0, where AD_0 intersects both the *SRAS* curve and the *LRAS* curve. A decrease in aggregate demand from AD_0 to AD_1, which results from a reduction in government purchases, higher taxes, or lower transfer payments, leads to a short-run equilibrium at E_1, with lower prices and real output reduced below its full employment level at $RGDP_1$. As prices fall, input suppliers then revise their price-level expectations downward. That is, laborers and other input suppliers are now willing to take less for the use of their resources, and the resulting reduction in production costs shifts the short-run supply curve from $SRAS_0$ to $SRAS_1$. The resulting eventual long-run equilibrium is a reduction in the price level, with real output returning to its full employment at E_2.

Section Check

1. If the government decided to purchase more, cut taxes, and/or increase transfer payments, that would increase total purchases and shift out the aggregate demand curve.
2. If the correct magnitude of expansionary fiscal policy is used in a recession, it could potentially bring the economy to full employment at a higher price level.
3. Expansionary fiscal policy at full employment may lead to short-run increases in output and employment, but in the long run, the expansionary effect will only lead to higher price levels.
4. Contractionary fiscal policy has the potential to offset an overheated inflationary boom.

---

1. If the economy is in recession, what sorts of fiscal policy changes would tend to bring it out of recession?
2. If the economy is at a short-run equilibrium at greater than full employment, what sorts of fiscal policy changes would tend to bring the economy back to a full-employment equilibrium?
3. What effects would an expansionary fiscal policy have on the price level and real GDP, starting from a full-employment equilibrium?
4. What effects would a contractionary fiscal policy have on the price level and real GDP, starting from a full-employment equilibrium?

section 16.5

Automatic Stabilizers

- What are automatic stabilizers?
- Which automatic stabilizers are the most important?

AUTOMATIC STABILIZERS

Some changes in government transfer payments and taxes take place automatically as business cycle conditions change, without deliberations in Congress or the executive branch of the government. Changes in government transfer payments or tax collections that automatically tend to counter business cycle fluctuations are called **automatic stabilizers.**

automatic stabilizers
changes in government transfer payments or tax collections that automatically help counter business cycle fluctuations

HOW DOES THE TAX SYSTEM STABILIZE THE ECONOMY?

The most important automatic stabilizer is the tax system. For example, with the personal income tax, as incomes rise, tax liabilities also increase automatically. Personal income taxes vary directly in amount with income and, in fact, rise or fall by greater percentage terms than income itself. Big increases and big decreases in GDP are both lessened by automatic changes in income tax receipts. For example, declines in GDP and tax liabilities, increases in disposable incomes, and stimulated consumption spending partly offset the initial decline in aggregate demand.

There are, of course, other income-related payroll taxes, notably Social Security taxes. In addition, there is the corporate profit tax. Because incomes, earnings, and profits all fall during a recession, the government collects less in taxes. This reduced tax burden partially

© AP PHOTO, RON EDMONDS

Automatic stabilizers work without legislative action. The stabilizers serve as a shock absorber to the economy. But the key is that they do it quickly.

offsets the magnitude of the recession. Beyond this, the unemployment compensation program is another example of an automatic stabilizer. During recessions, unemployment is usually high and unemployment compensation payments increase, providing income that will be consumed by recipients. During boom periods, such payments will fall as the number of unemployed declines. The system of public assistance (welfare) payments tends to be another important automatic stabilizer because the number of low-income persons eligible for some form of assistance grows during recessions (stimulating aggregate demand) and declines during booms (reducing aggregate demand).

Section Check

SECTION CHECK

1. Automatic stabilizers are changes in government transfer payments or tax collections that happen automatically and with effects that vary inversely with business cycles.
2. The tax system is the most important automatic stabilizer; it has the greatest ability to smooth out swings in GDP during business cycles. Other automatic stabilizers are unemployment compensation and welfare payments.

---

1. How does the tax system act as an automatic stabilizer?
2. Are automatic stabilizers impacted by a time lag? Why or why not?
3. Why are transfer payments, such as unemployment compensation, effective automatic stabilizers?

section 16.6

Possible Obstacles to Effective Fiscal Policy

- How does the crowding-out effect limit the economic impact of increased government purchases or reduced taxes?
- How do time lags in policy implementation affect policy effectiveness?

THE CROWDING-OUT EFFECT

The multiplier effect of an increase in government purchases implies that the increase in aggregate demand will tend to be greater than the initial fiscal stimulus, other things equal. However, this may not be true, because all other things will not tend to stay equal in this case. For example, when an increase in government purchases stimulates aggregate demand, it also drives the interest rate up. In particular, when the federal government competes with private borrowers for available savings, it drives up interest rates. As a result of the higher interest rate, consumers may decide against buying a car, a home, or other interest-sensitive good, and businesses may cancel or scale back plans to expand or buy new capital equipment. In short, the higher interest rate will choke off private investment spending, and as a result, the impact of the increase in government purchases may be smaller than we first assumed. Economists call this the **crowding-out effect.**

crowding-out effect
theory that government borrowing drives up the interest rate, lowering consumption by households and investment spending by firms

In Exhibit 1, suppose there was an initial \$10 billion increase in government purchases. This by itself would shift aggregate demand right by \$10 billion times the multiplier, from AD_0 to AD_1. However, when the government borrows in the money market to pay for increases in government purchases, the interest rate increases. The higher interest rate crowds out investment spending. This causes the aggregate demand curve to shift left, from AD_1 to AD_2. Because both these processes are taking place at the same time, the net effect is an increase in aggregate demand from AD_0 to AD_2 rather than AD_0 to AD_1.

Critics of the Crowding-Out Effect

Critics of the crowding-out effect argue that the increase in government spending, particularly if the economy is in a severe recession, could actually improve consumer and business expectations and actually encourage private investment spending. It is also possible that the monetary authorities could actually increase the money supply to offset the higher interest rates from the crowding-out effect.

section 16.6 Exhibit 1 — The Crowding-Out Effect

Net Effect
LRAS
Crowding-out Effect
Fiscal Policy Effect
Price Level
AD_0 AD_2 AD_1
0
$RGDP_{NR}$
RGDP

When the government borrows to finance a deficit, this leads to a higher interest rate and lower levels of private investment spending. The lower levels of private spending can crowd out the fiscal policy effect, shifting aggregate demand to the left from AD_1 to AD_2; the net effect of the fiscal policy is AD_0 to AD_2, not the larger increase, AD_0 to AD_1.

The Crowding-Out Effect in the Open Economy

Another form of crowding out can take place in international markets. For example, when the government increases purchases, it tends to drive up interest rates (assuming the money supply is unchanged). This is the basic crowding-out effect. However, the higher U.S. interest rate will attract funds from abroad. In order to invest in the U.S. economy, foreigners will have to first convert their currencies into dollars. The increase in the demand for dollars relative to other currencies, will cause the dollar to appreciate in value, making foreign imports relatively cheaper in the United States and U.S. exports relatively more expensive in other countries. This will cause net exports $(X - M)$ to fall for two reasons. One, because of the higher relative price of the dollar, foreign imports become cheaper for those in the United States, and imports will increase. Two, because of the higher relative price of the dollar, U.S.-made goods become more expensive to foreigners, so exports fall. The increase in imports and the decrease in exports causes a reduction in net exports and a fall in aggregate demand. The net effect is that to the extent net exports are crowded out, fiscal policy has a smaller effect on aggregate demand than it would otherwise.

TIME LAGS IN FISCAL POLICY IMPLEMENTATION

It is important to recognize that in a democratic country, fiscal policy is implemented through the political process, and that process takes time. Often, the lag between the time that a fiscal response is desired and the time an appropriate policy is implemented and its effects felt is considerable. Sometimes a fiscal policy designed to deal with a contracting economy may actually take effect during a period of economic expansion, or vice versa, resulting in a stabilization policy that actually destabilizes the economy.

The Recognition Lag

Government tax or spending changes require both congressional and presidential approval. Suppose the economy is beginning a downturn. It may take two or three months before enough data are gathered to indicate the actual presence of a downturn. This is called the *recognition lag.* Sometimes a future downturn can be forecast through econometric models or by looking at the index of leading indicators, but usually decision makers are hesitant to plan policy on the basis of forecasts that are not always accurate.

The Implementation Lag

At some point, however, policy makers may decide that some policy change is necessary. At this point, experts are consulted, and congressional committees have hearings about and listen to testimony on possible policy approaches. During the consultation phase, many decisions have to be made. If, for example, a tax cut is recommended, what form should the cut take and how large should it be? Across-the-board income tax reductions? Reductions in corporate taxes? More generous exemptions and deductions from the income tax (e.g., for child care, casualty losses, education of children)? In other words, who should get the benefits of lower taxes? Likewise, if the decision is made to increase government expenditures, which programs should be expanded or initiated and by how much? These are questions with profound political consequences, so reaching a decision is not always easy and usually involves much compromise and a great deal of time.

Finally, once the House and Senate have completed their separate deliberations and have arrived at a final version of the bill, it is presented to Congress for approval. After congressional approval is secured, the bill then goes to the president for approval or veto. This is all part of what is called the *implementation lag.*

During the period 1990–91, the actual output of the economy was less than the potential output of the economy—a recessionary gap. Because automatic stabilizers resulted in lower taxes and larger transfer payments, consumption did not fall as far as it would have. However, President Clinton believed that more was needed, so he put together a stimulus package of additional government spending and tax cuts. But by the time the bill reached the floor of Congress, the recession was over, illustrating how difficult it is to time fiscal stimulus.

The Impact Lag

Even after legislation is signed into law, it takes time to bring about the actual fiscal stimulus desired. If the legislation provides for a reduction in withholding taxes, for example, it might take a few months before the changes actually show up in workers' paychecks. With respect to changes in government purchases, the delay is usually much longer. If the government increases spending for public works projects like sewer systems, new highways, or urban renewal, it takes time to draw up plans and get permissions, to advertise for bids from contractors, to get contracts, and then to begin work. And there may be further delays because of government regulations. For example, an environmental impact statement must be completed before most public works projects can begin, a process that often takes many months or even years. This is called the *impact lag.*

Timing Is Critical

The timing of fiscal policy is crucial. Because of the significant lags before the fiscal policy has its impact, the increase in aggregate demand may occur at the wrong time. For example, imagine that we are initially at AD_0 in Exhibit 2. The economy is currently suffering from low levels of output and high rates of unemployment. In response, policy makers decide to increase government purchases and implement a tax cut. But from the time when the policy makers recognized the problem to the time when the policies had a chance to work themselves through the economy, business and consumer confidence increased, shifting the aggregate demand curve rightward from AD_0 to AD_1—increasing RGDP and employment. Now when the fiscal policy takes effect, the policies will have the undesired effect of causing inflation, with little permanent effect on output and employment. This is seen in Exhibit 2, as the aggregate demand curve shifts from AD_1 to AD_2. At E_2, $RGDP_1$ and input owners will require higher input prices, shifting the *SRAS* leftward from $SRAS_0$ to $SRAS_1$ to the new long-run equilibrium at E_3.

section 16.6
Exhibit 2
Timing Expansionary Fiscal Policy

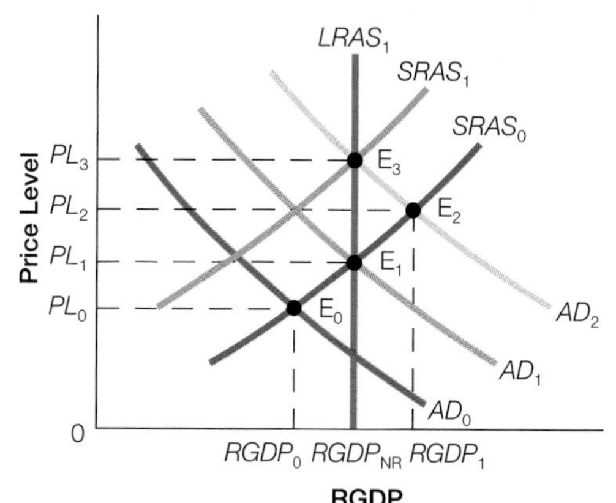

Initially, the macroeconomy is at equilibrium at point E_0. With high unemployment (at $RGDP_0$), the government decides to increase government purchases and cut taxes to stimulate the economy. This shifts aggregate demand from AD_0 to AD_1 over time, perhaps 12 to 16 months. In the meantime, if consumer confidence increases, the aggregate demand curve might shift to AD_2, leading to much higher prices (PL_3) in the long run, rather than at the target level, E_1, at price level PL_1.

Section Check

1. The crowding-out effect states that as the government borrows to pay for the deficit, it drives up the interest rates and crowds out private investment spending.
2. If crowding out causes a higher U.S. interest rate, it will attract foreign funds. In order to invest in the U.S. economy, foreigners will have to first convert their currencies into dollars. The increase in the demand for dollars relative to other currencies will cause the dollar to appreciate in value, making foreign imports relatively cheaper in the United States and U.S. exports relatively more expensive in other countries. This will cause net exports ($X - M$) to fall. This is the crowding-out effect in the open economy.
3. The lag time between when a fiscal policy may be needed and when it is actually implemented is considerable.

---

1. Why does a larger government budget deficit increase the magnitude of the crowding-out effect?
2. Why does fiscal policy have a smaller effect on aggregate demand the greater the crowding-out effect?
3. How do time lags impact the effectiveness of fiscal policy?

section 16.7

Supply-Side Fiscal Policy

- What is supply-side fiscal policy?
- How do supply-side policies affect long-run aggregate supply?
- What do its critics say about supply-side ideas?

WHAT IS SUPPLY-SIDE FISCAL POLICY?

The debate over short-run stabilization policies has been going on for some time, and there is no sign that it is close to being settled. When policy makers discuss methods to stabilize the economy, the focus since the 1930s has been on managing the economy through demand-side policies. But there is a group of economists who believe that we should be focusing on the supply side of the economy as well, especially in the long run, rather than just on the demand side. In particular, they believe that individuals will save less, work less, and provide less capital when taxes, government transfer payments (like welfare), and regulations are too burdensome on productive activities. In other words, they believe that fiscal policy can work on the supply side of the economy as well as the demand side.

IMPACT OF SUPPLY-SIDE POLICIES

Supply-siders would encourage government to reduce individual and business taxes, deregulate, and increase spending on research and development. Supply-siders believe that these types of government policies could generate greater long-term economic growth by stimulating personal income, savings, and capital formation.

section 16.7 Exhibit 1 Laffer Curve

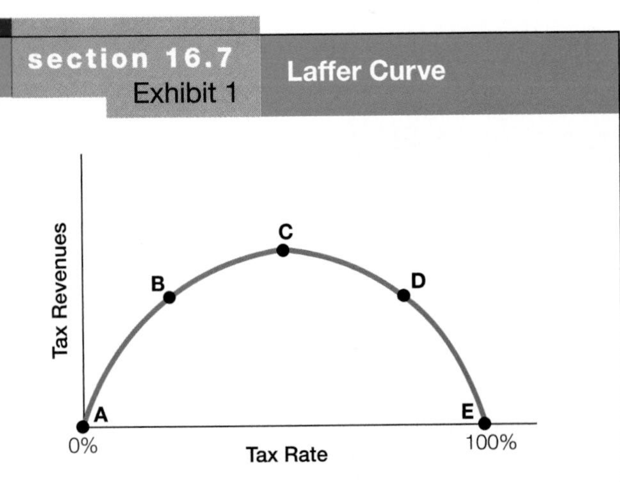

If the tax rate is set at 100 percent, point E, there will be no incentive to work or invest and tax revenues will be zero. Tax revenues will also be 0, at point A, if the tax rate is zero. If the economy has a relatively high tax rate (point D), tax revenues could be increased by lowering the tax rate, a move toward point C. However, as tax rates are lowered beyond point C, the tax revenues fall. Moving in the other direction from point B to point C, we see that tax revenues would increase with higher tax rates up to point C. At higher tax rates beyond point C, tax revenues fall.

THE LAFFER CURVE

High tax rates could conceivably reduce work incentives to the point that government revenues are lower at high marginal rates of taxation than they would be at somewhat lower rates. Economist Arthur Laffer has argued that point graphically in what has been called the Laffer Curve (Exhibit 1). When tax rates are low, increasing the federal tax rate will increase federal tax revenues as seen in the movement from point B to point C in Exhibit 1. However, at very high federal tax rates, disincentive effects and increased tax evasion may actually reduce federal tax revenue. Over this range of tax rates, lowering may actually increase federal tax revenue. This is seen as a movement from point D to point C in Exhibit 1. A very high marginal tax rate on the rich actually might reduce the incentive to work, save, and invest, and might produce, perhaps as important, illegal shifts in transactions to what has been termed the underground economy, meaning that people make cash and barter transactions that are very difficult for any tax collector to observe. If tax evasion becomes common, the equity and revenue-raising efficiency of the tax system suffers, as does general respect for the law.

While all economists believe that incentives matter, disagreement exists as to the shape of the Laffer curve and where the economy actually is on the Laffer curve.

RESEARCH AND DEVELOPMENT AND THE SUPPLY SIDE OF THE ECONOMY

Some economists believe that investment in research and development will have long-run benefits for the economy. In particular, greater research and development will lead to new technology and knowledge, which will permanently shift the short- and long-run aggregate supply curves to the right. The government could encourage investments in research and development by giving tax breaks or subsidies to firms. The challenge, of couse, is to produce *productive* R & D.

HOW DO SUPPLY-SIDE POLICIES AFFECT LONG-RUN AGGREGATE SUPPLY?

We see in Exhibit 2 that rather than being primarily concerned with short-run economic stabilization, supply-side policies are aimed at increasing both the short-run and long-run aggregate supply curves. If these policies are successful and maintained, output and employment will increase in the long run, as seen in the shift from $RGDP_{NR}$ to $RGDP'_{NR}$. Both short- and long-run aggregate supply will increase over time, as the effects of deregulation and major structural changes in plant and equipment work their way through the economy. It takes workers some time to fully respond to improved work incentives.

CRITICS OF SUPPLY-SIDE ECONOMICS

Of course, those that believe in the supply-side effects of fiscal policy have their critics. The critics are skeptical of the magnitude of the impact of lower taxes on work effort and the impact of deregulation on productivity. Critics claim that the tax cuts of the 1980s

section 16.7 Exhibit 2 — The Impact of Supply-Side Policies on Short-Run and Long-Run Aggregate Supply

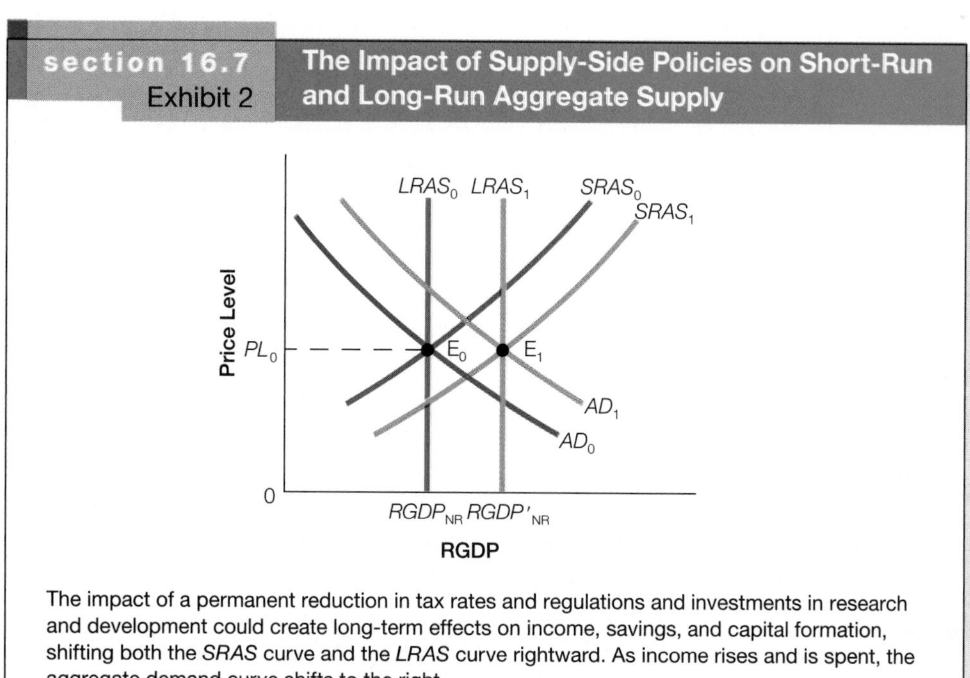

The impact of a permanent reduction in tax rates and regulations and investments in research and development could create long-term effects on income, savings, and capital formation, shifting both the *SRAS* curve and the *LRAS* curve rightward. As income rises and is spent, the aggregate demand curve shifts to the right.

led to moderate real output growth but only through a reduction in real tax revenues, inflation, and large budget deficits.

While real economic growth followed the tax cuts, the critics say that it came as a result of a large budget deficit. And what will happen to the distribution of income since most supply-side policies focus on benefits to those with capital? Also, the critics question whether people will save and invest much more if capital gains taxes are reduced (capital gains are increases in the value of an asset). How much more work effort will we see if marginal tax rates are lowered? Will the new production that occurs from deregulation be enough to offset the benefits thought by many to come from regulation?

THE SUPPLY-SIDE AND DEMAND-SIDE EFFECTS OF A TAX CUT

A tax cut can lead to greater incentives to work and save—an increase in aggregate supply (short run and long run) and to demand-side stimulus from the increased disposable income (income after taxes)—an increase in aggregate demand. But how much will the tax rate affect aggregate demand and aggregate supply? We do not know for sure, but let's look at two possible outcomes of the supply-side effects of a tax cut. In this example, we focus on the aggregate demand curve and the *SRAS* curve. Suppose the tax cut leads to a large increase in *AD* but only a small increase in *SRAS*. What happens to the price level and RGDP? The more traditional view of a fiscal policy tax cut is shown in Exhibit 3(a). In Exhibit 3(a), we see that there is an increase in RGDP from $RGDP_0$ to $RGDP_1$ and an increase in the price level from PL_0 to PL_1. The good news is that the price level rises less than it would if there was no supply-side effect to the tax cut. Without the supply-side effect from the tax cut, the price level would rise to PL_2. But what if the supply-side effect was much larger, like that in Exhibit 3(b)? It could completely offset the higher price level effect of an expansionary fiscal policy, as RGDP rises from $RGDP_0$ to $RGDP_1$, and the price level stays constant at PL_0.

For example, RGDP rose only very slowly in 1960 and 1961, and unemployment increased; by 1961, the unemployment rate of 6.7 percent approached the highest rate since

section 16.7
Exhibit 3

Two Possible Supply-Side Effects of a Tax Cut

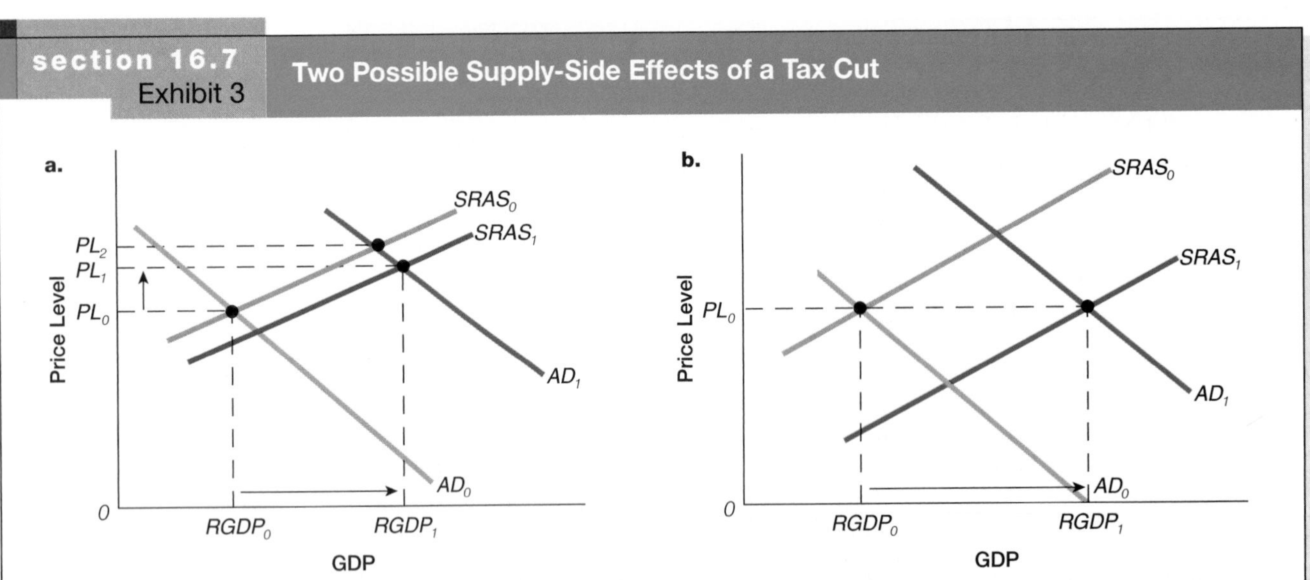

If the supply-side tax cut has a small effect on the *SRAS* but a large effect on *AD*, then RGDP increases from $RGDP_0$ to $RGDP_1$ but the price level rises from PL_0 to PL_1, as seen in Exhibit 3(a). However, if the supply-side tax cut has a large effect on *SRAS* and a large effect on *AD*, then RGDP increases from $RGDP_0$ to $RGDP_1$ and the price level is constant at PL_0, as seen in Exhibit 3(b).

the Great Depression. The new president, John F. Kennedy, was lectured on the need for countercyclical fiscal policy by his chairman of the Council of Economic Advisers, Walter Heller, and two future Nobel laureates in economics, James Tobin and Robert Solow. Kennedy accepted the view that a more expansionary policy was needed, and he advocated both some increase in government spending and a tax cut. In short, he wanted to use both fiscal policy mechanisms to shift the aggregate demand curve to the right (supply-siders also believe that the tax cut stimulated work effort). In fiscal 1962, federal government spending rose by $9 billion, or more than 9 percent, while revenues rose by only $5 billion. The doubling of the federal deficit (from $3 billion to $7 billion) provided added stimulus to the economy. The 1962 unemployment rate fell to 5.5 percent, a major drop from the previous year, and RGDP surged by more than 6 percent. Given the substantial slack in the economy, the increase in output and employment was not accompanied by massive inflation. The GDP deflator rose by only a bit over 1 percent a year in both 1961 and 1962.

In addition, President Kennedy proposed an investment tax credit plan that lowered taxes for firms that invested in new capital equipment. The impact of this move was to shift out the aggregate supply curve. The impact of these policies on the two curves was similar to that shown in Exhibit 3 (b).

Both the Kennedy tax cut and the Reagan tax cut of the early 1980s, which lowered marginal tax rates and helped the economy recover from the 1980–81 recession, likely raised the growth rate of potential GDP—shifting the *LRAS* rightward.

Fiscal policy was used infrequently in the United States and in Europe from the 1980s to late 1990s because of concern over large budget deficits. However, the budget surplus that emerged in the latter half of the 1990s opened the gate for increased government spending and the Bush tax cut in 2001. Most economists agree that taxes alter incentives and distort market outcomes, as we learned in chapter 5. Taxes clearly change people's behavior and the tax cuts that lead to the strongest incentives to work, save, and invest will lead to the greatest economic growth and will be the least inflationary.

Section Check

1. Supply-side fiscal policy advocates believe that people will save less, work less, and provide less capital when taxes, government transfer, and regulations are too burdensome.
2. Supply-side policies are designed to increase output and employment in the long run, causing the long-run and short-run aggregate supply curves to shift to the right.
3. Critics of supply-siders question the magnitude of the impact of lower taxes on work effort, saving, and investment, and the impact of deregulation on productivity.

---

1. Is supply-side economics more concerned with short-run economic stabilization or long-run economic growth?
2. Why could you say that supply-side economics is really more about after-tax wages and after-tax returns on investment than it is about tax rates?
3. Why do government regulations have the same sorts of effects on businesses as taxes?
4. Why aren't the full effects of supply-side policies seen quickly?
5. If taxes increase, what would you expect to happen to employment in the underground economy? Why?

section 16.8

The National Debt

- How is the national debt financed?
- What has happened to the federal budget balance?
- What impact does a budget deficit have on interest rates?
- What impact does a budget surplus have on interest rates?

HOW GOVERNMENT FINANCES THE DEBT

For many years, the U.S. government ran budget deficits and built up a large federal debt. How did it pay for those budget deficits? After all, it has to have some means of paying out the funds necessary to support government expenditures that are in excess of the funds derived from tax payments. One thing the government can do is simply print money—dollar bills. This approach was used to finance much of the Civil War budget deficit, both in the North and in the Confederate states. However, printing money to finance activities is highly inflationary and also undermines confidence in the government. Typically, the budget deficit is financed by issuing debt. The federal government in effect borrows an amount necessary to cover the deficit by issuing bonds, or IOUs, payable typically at some maturity date. The sum total of the values of all bonds outstanding constitutes the federal debt. Exhibit 1 shows the improvement in the federal budget balance since the early 1990s as a result of economic growth and the efforts of the president and Congress to control the growth of government spending.

section 16.8 Exhibit 1 — Federal Budget Balance, 1970–2001

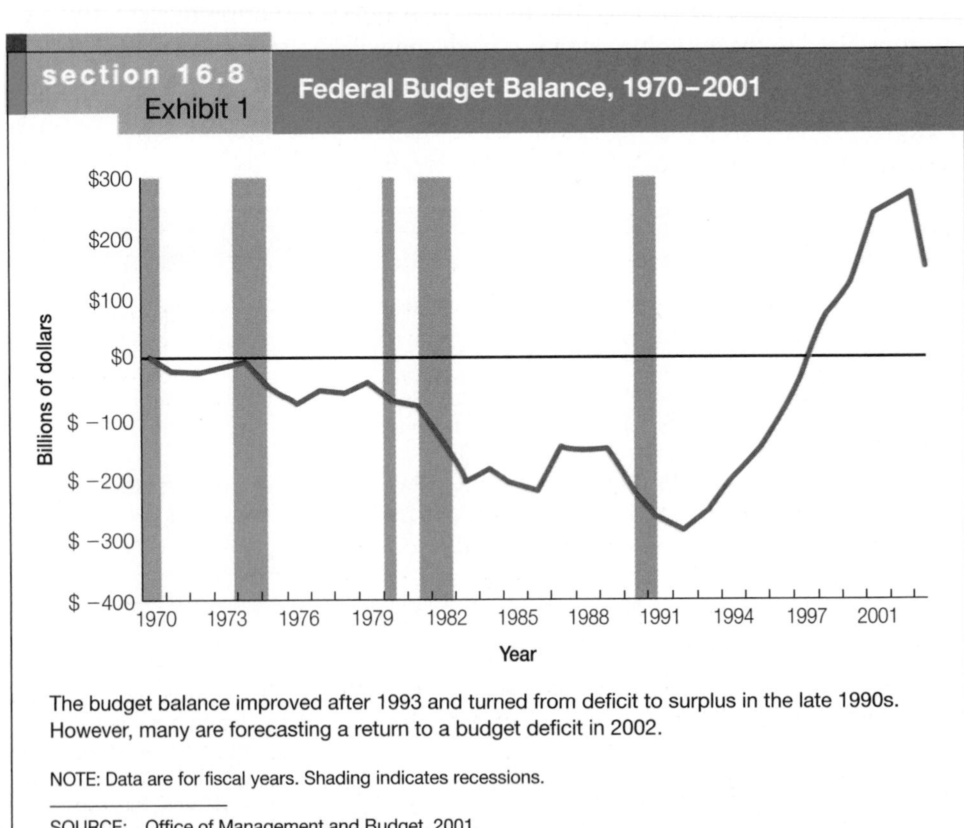

The budget balance improved after 1993 and turned from deficit to surplus in the late 1990s. However, many are forecasting a return to a budget deficit in 2002.

NOTE: Data are for fiscal years. Shading indicates recessions.

SOURCE: Office of Management and Budget, 2001.

WHY RUN A BUDGET DEFICIT?

From 1960 through 1997, the federal budget deficit was in deficit every year except one, when the government ran a small balanced surplus in 1969. Budget deficits can be important because they provide the federal government with the flexibility to respond appropriately to changing economic circumstances. For example, the government may run deficits in time of special emergencies like military involvement, earthquakes, fires, or floods. The government may also use a budget deficit to avert an economic downturn.

Historically the largest budget deficits and a growing government debt occur during war years when defense spending escalates and taxes typically do not rise as rapidly as spending. The federal government will also typically run budget deficits during recessions as taxes are cut and government spending increases. However, in the 1980s deficits and debt soared in a relatively peaceful and prosperous time. In 1980, President Reagan ran a platform of lowering taxes and reducing the size of government. While the tax cuts occurred, the reduction in the growth of government spending did not. The result was huge peacetime budget deficits and a growing national debt that continued through the early 1990s, as seen in Exhibit 1.

Recall that when the government borrows to finance a budget deficit, it causes the interest rate to rise. The higher interest rate will crowd out private investment by households and firms. And higher private investment and increases in capital formation are critical in a growing economy. But what if the government runs a budget deficit reduction (or surplus)? In the short run, deficit reduction is the same as running contractionary fiscal policy; either tax increases and/or a reduction in government purchases will shift the aggregate demand curve to the left from AD_0 to AD_1, as seen in Exhibit 2 . Unless this is offset by expansionary monetary policy (chapter 18) this will lead to a lower price level and lower RGDP. That is, in the short run an aggressive program of deficit reduction can lead to a recession.

In the long run, however, the story is different. Lowering the budget deficit, or running a larger budget surplus, leads to lower interest rates which increase private investment and stimulates higher growth in capital formation and economic growth. In fact, this is what happened in the 1990s as the budget deficit was reduced and finally turned into a budget surplus. The reduction in the deficit increased the potential rate of output, shifting the *SRAS* and *LRAS* curves rightward in Exhibit 3. The final effect was a higher RGDP and a lower price level than would have otherwise prevailed. Both investment and RGDP grew as the budget deficit shrank. The long-run effects of

section 16.8 Exhibit 2 — Reducing a Budget Deficit—The Short-Run Effects

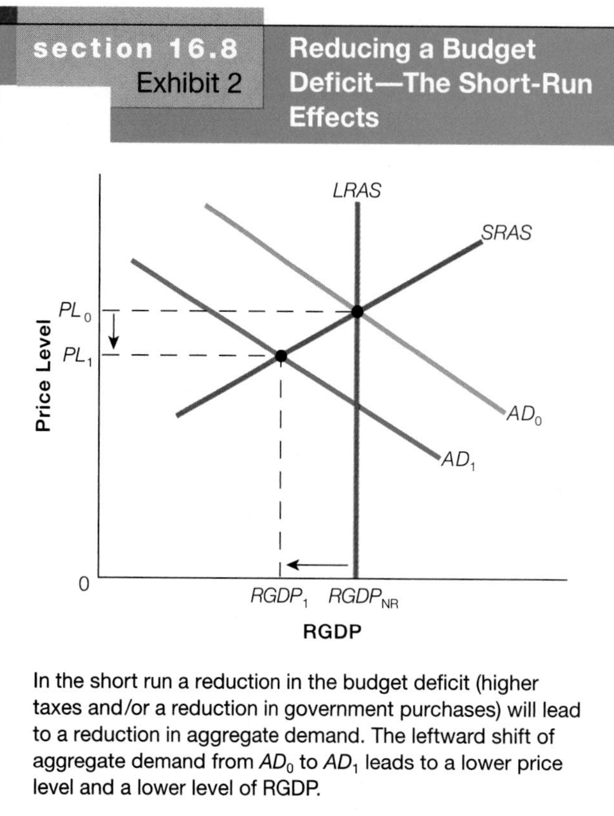

In the short run a reduction in the budget deficit (higher taxes and/or a reduction in government purchases) will lead to a reduction in aggregate demand. The leftward shift of aggregate demand from AD_0 to AD_1 leads to a lower price level and a lower level of RGDP.

section 16.8 Exhibit 3 — Reducing a Budget Deficit—The Long-Run Effects

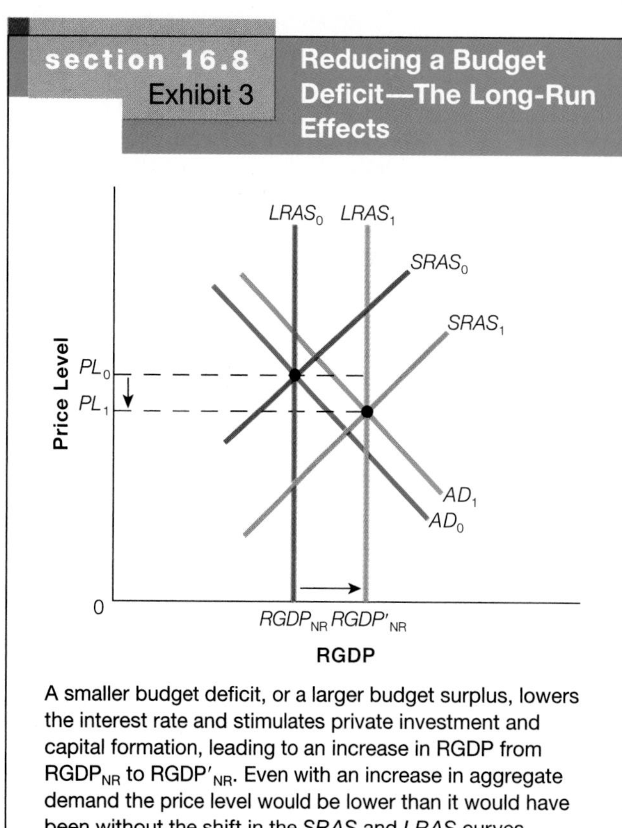

A smaller budget deficit, or a larger budget surplus, lowers the interest rate and stimulates private investment and capital formation, leading to an increase in RGDP from $RGDP_{NR}$ to $RGDP'_{NR}$. Even with an increase in aggregate demand the price level would be lower than it would have been without the shift in the *SRAS* and *LRAS* curves.

the deficit reduction are greater economic growth and a lower price level, *ceteris paribus.* The short-run recessionary effects of a budget deficit reduction can be avoided through the appropriate monetary policy as we will explore in chapter 18.

What to Do with the Budget Surplus

When the United States has a budget surplus, policy makers have to decide what to do with it. Some favor paying down the national debt, arguing this might drive interest rates down further and stimulate private investment and economic growth. Others think that we should cut taxes because as we saw in chapter 5, taxes can lead to a misallocation of resources. They argue that Congress might be tempted to spend the surplus on a small number of people, special interest groups, at the expense to many, the taxpayers. Which raises the question: Are we getting government goods and services with benefits that are greater than costs? Still others believe the surplus should be used for improvements in education and research and development that will lead to greater economic growth.

THE BURDEN OF PUBLIC DEBT

The "burden" of the debt is a topic that has long interested economists, particularly whether it falls on present or future generations. Exhibit 4 shows the burden as a percentage of GDP from 1929 to 2002. Arguments can be made that the generation of taxpayers living at the time that the debt is issued shoulders the true cost of the debt, because the debt permits the government to take command of resources that might be available for other, private uses. In a sense, the resources it takes to purchase government bonds might take away from private activities, such as private investment financed by private debt. There is no denying, however, that the issuance of debt does involve some intergenerational transfer of incomes. Long after federal debt is issued, a new generation of taxpayers is making interest payments to people of the generation that bought the bonds issued to finance that debt. If public debt is created intelligently, however, the "burden" of the debt should be less than the benefits derived from the resources acquired as a result; this is particularly true when the debt allows for an expansion in real economic activity or for the development of vital infrastructure for the future. The opportunity cost of expanded public activity may be very small in terms of private activity that must be forgone to finance the public activity, if unemployed resources are put to work. The real issue of importance is whether the government's activities have benefits that are greater than costs; whether taxes are raised, money is printed, or deficits are run are for the most part "financing issues."

Parents can offset some of the intergenerational debt by leaving larger bequests. In addition, if the parents save now to bear the cost of the burden of future taxes, the reduced consumption and increased savings will lower interest rates or more precisely offset the higher interest rate caused by the budget deficit. Many parents might not respond that way, but some might.

section 16.8 Exhibit 4 — **Public Debt, Federal Government, Selected Years**

Fiscal Year	Public Debt (billions of dollars)	Public Debt as a Percentage of GDP
1929	$16.9	18%
1940	43.0	45
1945	260.2	120
1950	256.8	94
1955	274.4	69
1960	290.5	56
1965	322.3	47
1970	380.9	38
1975	541.9	35
1980	909.1	33
1985	1,817.5	44
1990	3,206.6	56
1995	4,921.0	67.2
2000	5,629.0	57.3
2002*	5,663.7	52.2

*Estimate

SOURCE: Office of Management and Budget, 2001.

It is possible if the budget deficits led people to believe there would be higher future taxes, a budget surplus might lead them to think that would be lower future taxes—perhaps saving less and consuming more. So do we pay down the public debt or cut taxes? They may be equivalent policy prescriptions since each tends to lead to increases in consumption spending.

Section Check

SECTION CHECK

1. The budget deficit is financed by issuing debt.
2. Improvement in the federal budget balance since the early 1990s resulted from economic growth and the efforts of the president and Congress to control the growth of government spending. From 1960 through 1997, the federal budget had been in deficit every year except one, when the government ran a small balanced surplus in 1969.
3. When the government borrows to finance a budget deficit, it causes the interest rate to rise.
4. If the government runs a budget surplus this adds to national saving and lowers the interest rate and stimulates private investment and capital formation.

---

1. What will happen to the interest rate when there is a budget deficit?
2. What will happen to the interest rate when there is a budget surplus?
3. What are the intergenerational effects of a national debt?
4. What must be true for individuals in the United States to be better off as a result of an increase in the federal debt?

Summary

Fiscal policy is the use of government purchases of goods and services, taxes, and transfer payments to affect aggregate demand, GDP, and price levels. Expansionary fiscal policies will increase the budget deficit (or reduce a budget surplus) through greater government spending, lower taxes, or both. Contractionary fiscal policies will create a budget surplus (or reduce a budget deficit) through reduced government spending, higher taxes, or both.

The multiplier effect is a chain reaction of additional income and purchases that results in a final increase in total purchases that is greater than the initial increase in purchases. An increase in the marginal propensity to consume leads to an increase in the multiplier effect. Because of a time lag, the full impact of the multiplier effect on GDP may not be felt until a year or more after the initial investment. An increase in government purchases will also cause an increase in aggregate income and stimulate additional consumer purchases, which will result in a magnified (or multiplying) effect on aggregate demand.

If the government decided to purchase more, cut taxes, and/or increase transfer payments, that would increase total purchases and shift out the aggregate demand curve. If the correct magnitude of expansionary fiscal policy is used in a contraction and/or recession, it could potentially bring the economy to full employment.

Expansionary fiscal policy at full employment may lead to short-run increases in output and employment, but in the long run, the expansionary effect will only lead to higher price levels. Contractionary fiscal policy has the potential to offset an overheated inflationary boom.

Automatic stabilizers are changes in government transfer payments or tax collections that happen automatically and that have effects that vary inversely with business cycles. The tax system is the most important automatic stabilizer; it has the greatest ability to smooth out swings in GDP during business cycles. Other automatic stabilizers are unemployment compensation and welfare payments.

The crowding-out effect states that as the government borrows to pay for the deficit, it drives up the interest rates and crowds out private investment spending and consumption. If the crowding out causes a higher U.S. interest rate, it will attract foreign funds. In order to invest in the U.S.

economy, foreigners will first have to convert their currencies into dollars. The increase in the demand for dollars relative to other currencies will cause the dollar to appreciate in value, making foreign imports relatively cheaper in the United States and U.S. exports relatively more expensive in other countries. This will cause net exports ($X - M$) to fall. This is the crowding-out effect in the open economy.

The lag time between when a fiscal policy may be needed and when it is actually implemented is considerable.

Supply-side fiscal policy advocates believe that people will save less, work less, and provide less capital when taxes, government transfer, and regulations are too burdensome. Supply-side policies are designed to increase output and employment in the long run, causing the long-run and short-run aggregate supply curves to shift to the right.

Critics of supply-siders question the magnitude of the impact of lower taxes on work effort, saving, and investment and the impact of deregulation on productivity.

The government finances a budget deficit primarily by issuing debt to government agencies, private institutions, and private individuals.

Key Terms and Concepts

fiscal policy 340
budget deficit 340
budget surplus 340
expansionary fiscal policy 340
contractionary fiscal policy 340
progressive tax 344
regressive tax 344
excise tax 344
multiplier effect 347
marginal propensity to consume (*MPC*) 347
automatic stabilizers 355
crowding-out effect 357

Review Questions

1. Calculate the spending multiplier when the *MPC* equals
   a. 0.75.
   b. 0.8.
   c. 0.6.
2. Estimate the potential impact on GDP of each of the following events.
   a. an increase in government spending of $15 billion in order to build new highways
   b. a decrease in federal spending of $200 billion due to peacetime military cutbacks
   c. consumer optimism leading to a $40 billion spending increase
   d. gloomy business forecasts leading to an $18 billion decline in investment spending
3. The economy is experiencing a contractionary gap of $400 billion. If the $MPC = 0.75$, what government spending stimulus would you recommend to move the economy back to full employment? If the $MPC = 0.66$?
4. The economy is experiencing a $300 billion expansionary gap. Absent government intervention, what can you predict will happen to the economy in the long run? (Use aggregate demand–aggregate supply analysis in your answer.) If the government decides to intervene using changes in spending, would you recommend a spending increase or decrease? Of what magnitude?
5. Illustrate the impact of a tax cut using aggregate demand–aggregate supply analysis when the economy is operating above full employment. Is this a wise policy? Why or why not?
6. Can government spending that causes crowding out be detrimental to long-run economic growth? Explain.
7. What happens to the following variables during an expansion?
   a. unemployment compensation
   b. welfare payments
   c. income tax receipts
   d. government budget deficit (surplus)
8. Under current U.S. law, capital gains (the difference between the price paid for an asset and the price at which it is eventually sold) are taxed at lower rates

than ordinary stock dividends. Capital gains taxes are only owed when an asset is sold. Earnings that are not paid out as dividends are retained and used to further finance business ventures. How do you think this difference in tax rates (and the timing of tax payments) affects investment behavior, aggregate demand and aggregate supply?

9. Suppose a proportional tax system that eliminated all deductions and tax shelters replaced the current U.S. tax code. Would there be any change in the incentive to engage in tax avoidance? What about the incentive to work? (On what might that depend?) Explain.

10. Visit the Sexton Web site at **http://sexton.swcollege.com** and click on "National Budget Simulation." Complete the budget simulation (short or long version) by making your own adjustments to the U.S. federal budget. What is the resulting projected budget surplus or deficit? What impact do you think the changes you've proposed would have on the macroeconomy over time?

Fill in the Blanks

1. ______________ is the use of government purchases, taxes, and transfer payments to alter real GDP and price levels.
2. When government spending (for purchases of goods and services and transfer payments) exceeds tax revenues, there is a budget ______________.
3. When the government wishes to stimulate the economy by increasing aggregate demand, it will ______________ government purchases of goods and services, ______________ transfer payments, ______________ taxes, or use some combination of these approaches.
4. Expansionary fiscal policy is associated with ______________ government budget deficits.
5. If the government wishes to dampen a boom in the economy, it will ______________ its purchases of goods and services, ______________ taxes, ______________ transfer payments, or use some combination of these approaches.
6. Governments obtain revenue through two major avenues: ______________ and ______________.
7. By changing taxes or transfer payments, the government can alter the amount of ______________ income of households and thus bring about changes in ______________ purchases.
8. The ______________ effect explains why, when an initial increase in purchases of goods or services occurs, the ultimate increase in total purchases will tend to be greater than the initial increase.
9. When the government purchases additional goods and services, not only does it add to the total demand for goods and services directly, but the purchases also add to people's ______________.
10. When people's incomes rise because of increased government purchases of goods and services, collectively people will spend a substantial part of the additional income on additional ______________ purchases.
11. The additional consumption purchases made as a portion of one's additional income is measured by the ______________.
12. With each additional round of the multiplier process, the added income generated and the resulting consumer purchases get ______________ because some of each round's increase in income goes to ______________ and ______________ payments.
13. The ______________ is equal to 1 divided by 1 minus the marginal propensity to consume.
14. The larger the marginal propensity to consume, the ______________ the multiplier effect.
15. If the marginal propensity to consume were smaller, a given increase in government purchases would have a ______________ effect on consumption purchases.
16. The extent of the multiplier effect visible within a short time period will be ______________ than the total effect indicated by the multiplier formula.
17. Savings, taxes, and money spent on imported goods will each ______________ the size of the multiplier.

18. Increased budget _____________ will stimulate the economy when it is operating at less than full capacity.

19. The result of an expansionary fiscal policy in the short run would be an _____________ in the price level and an _____________ in RGDP.

20. Starting at a full-employment equilibrium, the only long-term effect of an increase in aggregate demand is an increase in the _____________ level.

21. Starting at a full-employment equilibrium, once the economy has returned to its long-run equilibrium after an increase in government purchases, employment will be _____________ full employment.

22. If the government wanted to use fiscal policy to help "cool off" the economy when it has overheated and inflation has become a serious problem, it would tend to _____________ government purchases, _____________ taxes, and/or _____________ transfer payments.

23. A tax _____________ on consumers will reduce households' disposable incomes, reducing purchases of _____________ goods and services, while higher business taxes will reduce _____________ purchases.

24. Contractionary fiscal policy will result in a _____________ price level and _____________ employment in the short run.

25. The multiplier effect of an increase in government purchases implies that the increase in aggregate demand will tend to be _____________ than the initial fiscal stimulus, other things being equal.

26. When the government borrows money to finance a deficit, it _____________ the overall demand for money in the money market, driving interest rates _____________.

27. The _____________ effect refers to the theory that when the government borrows money to finance a deficit, it drives interest rates up, choking off some private spending on goods and services.

28. The monetary authorities could _____________ the money supply to offset the _____________ interest rates from the crowding-out effect of expansionary fiscal policy.

29. Expansionary fiscal policy will tend to _____________ the demand for dollars relative to other currencies.

30. Expansionary fiscal policy will tend to cause net exports to _____________.

31. The larger the crowding-out effect, the _____________ the actual effect of a given change in fiscal policy.

32. Because of the _____________ in implementing fiscal policy, a fiscal policy designed to deal with a contracting economy may actually take effect during a period of economic expansion.

33. Timed correctly, contractionary fiscal policy could correct an _____________; timed incorrectly, it could cause a _____________.

34. Changes in government transfer payments or tax collections that automatically tend to counter business-cycle fluctuations are called _____________.

35. The most important automatic stabilizer is the _____________ system.

36. Big increases and big decreases in GDP are both ____________ by automatic changes in income tax receipts.

37. Because incomes, earnings, and profits all fall during a recession, the government collects ____________ in taxes. This reduced tax burden partially ____________ any contractionary fall in aggregate demand.

38. Supply side economists believe that individuals will save ____________, work ____________, and provide ____________ capital when taxes, government transfer payments (like welfare), and regulations are too burdensome on productive activities.

39. The ____________ Curve shows that high tax rates could conceivably reduce work incentives to the point that government revenues are lower at high marginal tax rates than they would be at somewhat lower rates.

40. If the demand-side stimulus from reduced tax rates is ____________ than the supply-side effects, the result will be a higher price level and a greater level of real output.

41. A budget surplus ____________ to national savings and ____________ the interest rate, ____________ private investment and capital formation.

42. Typically, a budget deficit is financed by issuing ____________.

43. Parents could offset some of the intergenerational burden of the national debt by leaving ____________ bequests.

True or False

1. The government can use fiscal policy to stimulate the economy out of a recession or to try to bring inflation under control.

2. When tax revenues are greater than government spending, a budget surplus exists.

3. A budget surplus is the most common result of government fiscal policy.

4. In recent years, the U.S. federal budget has tended to be roughly balanced over the business cycle, running surpluses in good times and offsetting deficits in bad times.

5. There has not been a budget surplus even 1 year in the last 20 years.

6. An increase in government purchases of goods and services would stimulate the economy by increasing aggregate demand.

7. An increase in taxes would increase aggregate demand.

8. Contractionary fiscal policy will tend to reduce a federal budget surplus or increase a federal budget deficit.

9. Government spending as a percentage of GDP has changed little since 1970, but the composition of government spending has changed considerably.

10. The composition of state and local spending is very different from that of federal spending.

11. A large majority of government activity is financed by borrowing.

12. Real GDP will tend to change any time the amount of consumption, investment, government purchases, or net exports changes.

13. If policy makers are unhappy about the present short-run equilibrium GDP, they can deliberately manipulate the level of government purchases in order to obtain a new short-run equilibrium value.

14. When an initial increase in government purchases of goods or services occurs, the ultimate increase in total purchases will tend to be greater than the initial increase.

15. If the marginal propensity to consume is two-thirds, a $6 million increase in disposable income to certain households will lead them to increase their consumption spending by $18 million.

16. The multiplier is equal to 1 divided by the marginal propensity to consume.

17. The multiplier would be smaller if the marginal propensity to consume were smaller.

18. If the *MPC* were equal to two-thirds, the multiplier would be equal to 3.

19. The multiplier process is virtually instantaneous.

20. Savings, taxes, and money spent on imported goods will each reduce the size of the multiplier because each of them reduces the fraction of a given increase in income that will go to additional purchases of domestically produced consumption goods.

21. Expansionary fiscal policy has the potential to move an economy out of a recession.

22. The effect of an increase in aggregate demand depends on the position of the macroeconomic equilibrium prior to the government stimulus.

23. Starting from an initial recession equilibrium, expansionary fiscal policy could potentially increase employment to the full employment level.

24. Starting from an initial recession equilibrium, a government tax increase would tend to reduce the severity of the recession.

25. An increase in government spending, an increase in transfer payments, and/or a tax cut will tend to move the economy up along its short-run aggregate supply curve.

26. Starting at a full employment equilibrium, the gains in employment that result from expansionary fiscal policy will not be sustainable in the long run.

27. Contractionary fiscal policy has the potential to offset an overheated, inflationary boom.

28. Contractionary fiscal policy will tend to increase a current government budget deficit.

29. Starting at full employment, contractionary fiscal policy could cause a recession in the short run.

30. Starting at full employment, the long-run result of contractionary fiscal policy includes a lower price level and reduced real output.

31. The crowding-out effect will tend to reduce the magnitude of the effects of increases in government purchases.

32. The crowding-out effect implies that expansionary fiscal policy will tend to reduce private purchases of interest-sensitive goods.

33. The crowding-out effect does not occur with a tax change.

34. Critics of the crowding-out effect argue that an increase in government purchases (or a tax cut), particularly if the economy is in a severe recession, could improve consumer and business expectations and actually encourage private investment spending.

35. Expansionary U.S. fiscal policy will tend to move funds out of the U.S.

36. Expansionary fiscal policy will tend to be partly crowded out by a reduction in net exports.

37. Sometimes fiscal policy designed to stabilize the economy can actually destabilize the economy.

38. Time lags in the legislative process are a serious problem in the implementation of fiscal policy.

39. After expansionary fiscal policy legislation is signed into law, it takes time to bring about the actual fiscal stimulus desired.

40. One of the advantages of automatic stabilizers is that they take place without the necessity for deliberations in Congress or the executive branch of the government.

41. Unemployment compensation and public assistance payments act as automatic stabilizers, stimulating aggregate demand during recessions and reducing aggregate demand during booms.

42. Supply-siders would encourage government to reduce individual and business taxes, deregulate, and increase spending on research and development.

43. Supply-siders' primary focus is on stabilizing aggregate demand in the short run.

44. A lower marginal tax rate will raise after-tax earnings, improving productive incentives.

45. Higher marginal tax rates will lead investors to spend more scarce resources looking for tax shelters, which harms the economy, as high-return but highly taxed investments give way to lower-return tax shelters.

46. Although all economists believe that incentives matter, there is considerable disagreement on the shape of the Laffer Curve and where the economy actually is on the Laffer Curve.

47. If greater research and development leads to new technology and knowledge, it will shift the short- and long-run aggregate supply curves to the right.

48. If tax rates are reduced, it will affect aggregate supply but not aggregate demand.

49. The sum total of the values of all bonds outstanding constitutes the federal debt.

50. Printing money to finance government activities is inflationary.

51. If public debt is created intelligently, the "burden" of the debt should be less than the benefits derived from the resources acquired as a result.

Multiple Choice

1. Traditionally, government has used ______ to influence ______.
   a. taxing and spending, the demand side of the economy
   b. spending, the supply side of the economy
   c. supply management, the demand side of the economy
   d. demand management, the supply side of the economy

2. Contractionary fiscal policy consists of
   a. increased government purchases, increased taxes, and increased transfer payments.
   b. decreased government purchases, decreased taxes, and decreased transfer payments.
   c. decreased government purchases, increased taxes, and decreased transfer payments.
   d. increased government purchases, decreased taxes, and increased transfer payments.

3. Budget deficits are created when
   a. government spending exceeds its tax revenues.
   b. government tax revenues exceed its spending.
   c. government spending equals its tax revenues.
   d. none of the above.

4. If the government wanted to move the economy out of a current recession, which of the following might be an appropriate policy action?
   a. decrease taxes
   b. increase government purchases of goods and services
   c. increase transfer payments
   d. any of the above

5. If the marginal propensity to consume is two-thirds, the multiplier is
   a. 30.
   b. 66.
   c. 1.5.
   d. 3.

6. The multiplier effect is based on the fact that ______ by one person is ______ to another.
   a. income, income
   b. expenditures, expenditures
   c. expenditures, income
   d. income, expenditures

7. The multiplier is
   a. 1/*MPC*.
   b. 1/1 − *MPC*.
   c. 1 − *MPC*/1.
   d. 1/change in *MPC*.

8. The federal government buys $20 million worth of computers from Gateway 2000. If the *MPC* is 0.60, what will be the impact on aggregate demand, other things being equal?
   a. Aggregate demand will increase $12 million.
   b. Aggregate demand will increase $13.33 million.
   c. Aggregate demand will increase $20 million.
   d. Aggregate demand will increase $50 million.
   e. Aggregate demand will not change.

9. When taxes are increased, disposable income ________, and hence, consumption ________.
   a. increases, increases
   b. increases, decreases
   c. decreases, increases
   d. decreases, decreases
   e. stays the same, stays the same

10. Starting at full employment, if *MPC* = 2/3, an increase in government purchases of $10 billion would lead *AD* to ______ and ______ real output in the long run.
   a. increase $30 billion, increase
   b. increase $30 billion, not change
   c. decrease $30 billion, decrease
   d. decrease $30 billion, not change
   e. none of the above

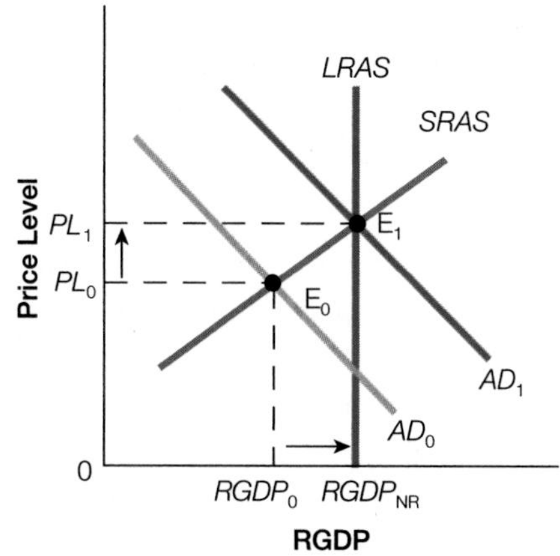

Using the graph above, answer question 11.

11. In order for the economy pictured above to get back to $RGDP_{NR}$, this economy could use
  a. decreased taxes and increased government purchases.
  b. increased taxes and increased government purchases.
  c. decreased taxes and decreased government purchases.
  d. decreased taxes and increased government purchases.

12. If government policy makers were worried about the inflationary potential of the economy, which of the following would not be a correct fiscal policy change?
  a. increase consumption taxes
  b. increase government purchases of goods and services
  c. reduce transfer payments
  d. increase the budget deficit

13. In the short run, expansionary fiscal policy can cause a rise in real GDP
  a. in combination with a rise in the price level.
  b. in combination with no rise in the price level.
  c. in combination with a reduction in the price level.
  d. in combination with a rise or a reduction in the price level, depending on the economy.

14. If the government wanted to offset the effect of a boom in consumer and investor confidence on *AD,* it might
  a. decrease government purchases.
  b. decrease taxes.
  c. decrease transfer payments.
  d. do either a or c.

15. An increase in taxes combined with a decrease in government purchases would
  a. increase *AD.*
  b. decrease *AD.*
  c. leave *AD* unchanged.
  d. have an indeterminate effect on *AD.*

16. A combination of an increase in investment and a decrease in exports would
  a. increase *AD.*
  b. decrease *AD.*
  c. leave *AD* unchanged.
  d. have an indeterminate effect on *AD.*

17. A decrease in government purchases will do which of the following in the long run?
   a. increase unemployment
   b. decrease real output
   c. decrease the price level
   d. all of the above

18. *AD* will shift to the right, other things being equal, when
   a. the government budget deficit increases because government purchases rose.
   b. the government budget deficit increases because taxes fell.
   c. the government budget deficit increases because transfer payments rose.
   d. any of the above circumstances exist.

19. Automatic stabilizers
   a. reduce the problems that lags cause, using fiscal policy as a stabilization tool.
   b. are changes in fiscal policy that act to stimulate *AD* automatically when the economy goes into a recession.
   c. are changes in fiscal policy that act to restrain *AD* automatically when the economy is growing too fast.
   d. All of the above are correct.

20. During a recession, government transfer payments automatically ______ and tax revenue automatically ______.
   a. fall, falls
   b. increase, falls
   c. increase, increases
   d. fall, increases

21. One of the real-world complexities of countercyclical fiscal policy is that
   a. fiscal policy is based on forecasts, which are not foolproof.
   b. there is a lag between a change in fiscal policy and its effect.
   c. there is uncertainty about how much of the multiplier effect will take place in a given amount of time.
   d. All of the above are correct.

22. According to the crowding-out effect, if the federal government borrows to finance deficit spending,
   a. the demand for loanable funds will decrease, driving interest rates down.
   b. the demand for loanable funds will increase, driving interest rates up.
   c. the supply for loanable funds will increase, driving interest rates up.
   d. the supply for loanable funds will decrease, driving interest rates down.

23. If U.S. budget deficits (which require the borrowing of funds) raise interest rates and attract investment funds from abroad,
   a. the foreign exchange value of the dollar will appreciate, and U.S. net exports will decrease.
   b. the foreign exchange value of the dollar will depreciate, and U.S. net exports will decrease.
   c. the foreign exchange value of the dollar will depreciate, and U.S. net exports will increase.
   d. the foreign exchange value of the dollar will appreciate, and U.S. net exports $(X - M)$ will increase.

24. When the crowding-out effect of an increase in government purchases is included in the analysis:
   a. *AD* shifts left.
   b. *AD* doesn't change.
   c. *AD* shifts right, but by more than the simple multiplier analysis would imply.
   d. *AD* shifts right, but by less than the simple multiplier analysis would imply.

25. Lower marginal tax rates stimulate people to work, save, and invest, resulting in more output and a larger tax base. This statement most closely reflects which of the following views?
   a. the Keynesian
   b. the crowding-out theory of budget deficits
   c. the aggregate demand theory
   d. the supply-side view

26. Other things being constant, an increase in marginal tax rates will
   a. decrease the supply of labor and reduce its productive efficiency.
   b. decrease the supply of capital and decrease its productive efficiency.
   c. encourage individuals to buy goods that are tax deductible instead of those that are more desired but nondeductible.
   d. do all of the above.

27. According to the Laffer Curve,
   a. decreasing tax rates on income always increase tax revenues.
   b. decreasing tax rates on income always decrease tax revenues.
   c. decreasing tax rates are more likely to increase tax revenues the higher tax rates are to start with.
   d. decreasing tax rates are more likely to increase tax revenues the lower tax rates are to start with.

28. How does the government finance budget deficits?
   a. The Federal Reserve creates new money.
   b. It issues debt to government agencies, private institutions, and private investors.
   c. It is primarily financed by foreign investors.
   d. It does nothing to finance budget deficits.

29. When government debt is financed internally, future generations will
   a. inherit a lower tax liability.
   b. inherit neither higher taxes nor interest payment liability.
   c. inherit higher taxes.
   d. none of the above.

Problems

1. Answer the following questions.
   a. If there is currently a budget surplus, what would an increase in government purchases do to it?
   b. What would that increase in government purchases do to aggregate demand?
   c. When would an increase in government purchases be an appropriate countercyclical fiscal policy?

2. Answer the following questions.
   a. If there is currently a budget deficit, what would an increase in taxes do to it?
   b. What would that increase in taxes do to aggregate demand?
   c. When would an increase in taxes be an appropriate countercyclical fiscal policy?

3. What would the multiplier be if the marginal propensity to consume was
   a. 1/3?
   b. 1/2?
   c. 3/4?

4. If there were a $20 billion increase in government purchases, other things being equal, what would be the resulting change in aggregate demand, and how much of the change would be a change in consumption, if the *MPC* were
   a. 1/3?
   b. 1/2?
   c. 2/3?
   d. 3/4?
   e. 4/5?

5. Use the following diagram to answer questions a–f.

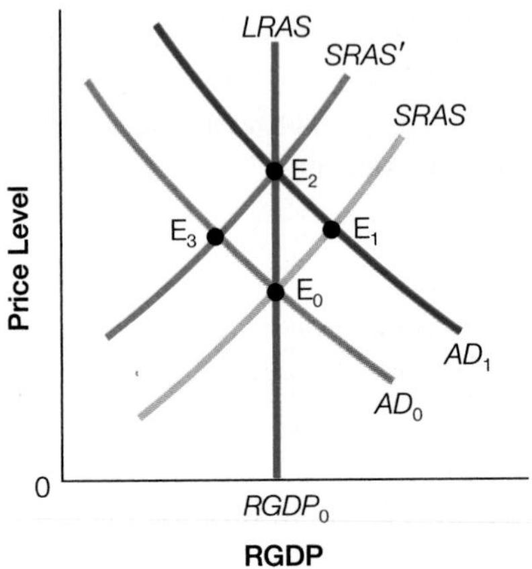

   a. At what short-run equilibrium point might expansionary fiscal policy make sense to help stabilize the economy?
   b. What would be the result of appropriate fiscal policy in that case?
   c. What would be the long-run result if no fiscal policy action was taken in that case?
   d. At what short-run equilibrium point might contractionary fiscal policy make sense to help stabilize the economy?
   e. What would be the result of appropriate fiscal policy in that case?
   f. What would be the long-run result if no fiscal policy action were taken in that case?

6. Use the following diagram to answer questions a and b.

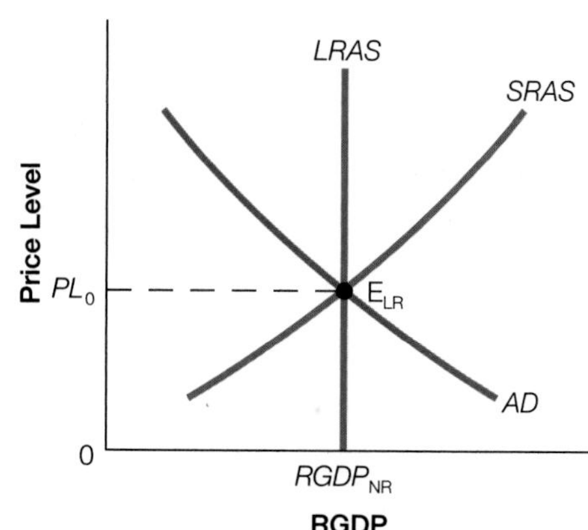

a. Starting from the initial equilibrium in the diagram, illustrate the case of a supply-side fiscal policy that left the price level unchanged in both the short run and the long run.

b. Compared to your answer in a, when would a supply-side fiscal policy result in an increase in the price level?

chapter 17

Money and the Banking System

section 17.1

What Is Money?

- What is money?
- In what forms is money held?
- What is liquidity?
- What is included in the money supply?
- What backs our money?

money
anything generally accepted in exchange for goods or services

currency
coins and/or paper created to be used to facilitate the trade of goods and services and the payment of debts

legal tender
coins and paper officially declared to be acceptable for the settlement of financial debts

fiat money
a means of exchange established by government declaration

Money is anything that is generally accepted in exchange for goods or services. In colonial times, commodities such as tobacco and wampum (Native American trinkets) were sometimes used as money. At some times and in some places, even cigarettes and whiskey have been used as money. But commodities have several disadvantages when used as money, the most important of which is that many commodities deteriorate easily after a few trades. Precious metal coins have been used for money for millennia, partly because of their durability.

CURRENCY

Currency consists of coins and/or paper that some institution or government has created to be used in the trading of goods and services and the payment of debts. Currency in the form of metal coins is still used as money throughout the world today. But metal currency has a disadvantage: It is bulky. Also, certain types of metals traditionally used in coins, like gold and silver, are not available in sufficient quantities to meet our demands for a monetary instrument. For these reasons, metal coins have for centuries been supplemented by paper currency, often in the form of bank notes. In the United States, the Federal Reserve System issues Federal Reserve Notes in various denominations, and this paper currency, along with coins, provides the basis for most transactions of relatively modest size in the United States today.

© KENT KNUDSON/PHOTOLINK/PHOTODISK/GETTYONE IMAGES

Tobacco was once used as money in colonial America, in particular in Virginia and Maryland. Tobacco was used rather than other commodities because it was resistant to spoilage. In the seventeenth century, colonists used wampum (polished shells) as lawful money. The ancient Chinese used chisels for money while other societies have used fish and cattle and, of course, gold coins as money.

CURRENCY AS LEGAL TENDER

In the United States and in most other nations of the world, metallic coins and paper currency are the only forms of **legal tender.** In other words, coins and paper money have been officially declared to be money—to be acceptable for the settlement of debts incurred in financial transactions. In effect, the government says, "We declare these instruments to be money, and citizens are expected to accept them as a medium of exchange." Legal tender is **fiat money**—a means of exchange that has been established not by custom and tradition, or because of the value of the metal in a coin, but by government fiat, or declaration.

DEMAND DEPOSITS AND OTHER CHECKABLE DEPOSITS

Most of the money that we use for day-to-day transactions, however, is not official legal tender. Rather, it is a monetary instrument that has become "generally accepted" in ex-

In The NEWS

SHOULD WE GET RID OF THE PENNY?

Americans know where to find pennies—in jars and fountains and on the countertops of convenience stores. What's not known is just what ought to be done about the nation's lowliest coin. At a House hearing last week, lobbyists for the penny—Americans for Common Cents—reported a poll showing that 73 percent of the American public wants the government to keep circulating pennies. The Treasury wants to do that, although the government's General Accounting Office reported that penny production costs taxpayers over $8 million a year. The U.S. Mint disputed this, saying penny production nets the U.S. government between $17.9 and $26.6 million.

The GAO found that only about a third of existing pennies are in circulation. And a poll commissioned by the GAO showed that most Americans (52 percent) would prefer that prices be rounded to the nearest nickel. Penny backers responded with an estimate by Penn State economist Raymond Lombra, who said that rounding prices would result in overcharges costing consumers at least $600 million extra a year.

SOURCE: "Whither the Penny?" *U.S. News & World Report*, July 29, 1999, p. 8. Copyright © 1999 *U.S. News & World Report*, L.P. Reprinted with permission.

change over the years and has now, by custom and tradition, become money. What is this instrument? It is balances in checking accounts in banks, more formally called **demand deposits.**

demand deposits
balances in bank accounts that depositors can access on demand

Demand deposits are defined as balances in bank accounts that depositors can access on demand by simply writing a check. Some other forms of accounts in financial institutions also have virtually all of the attributes of demand deposits. For example, there are also other checkable deposits that earn interest but have some restrictions, such as higher monthly fees or minimum balance requirements. These interest-earning checking accounts effectively permit the depositors to write "orders" similar to checks and assign the rights to the deposit to other persons, just as we write checks to other parties. Practically speaking, funds in these accounts are the equivalent of demand deposits and have become an important component in the supply of money. Both of these types of accounts are forms of **transaction deposits,** because they can be easily converted into currency or used to buy goods and services directly. **Traveler's checks,** like currency and demand deposits, are also easily converted into currency or used directly as a means of payment.

transaction deposits
deposits that can be easily converted to currency or used to buy goods and services directly

traveler's checks
transaction instruments easily convertible into currency

THE POPULARITY OF DEMAND DEPOSITS AND OTHER CHECKABLE DEPOSITS

Demand deposits and other checkable deposits have replaced paper and metallic currency as the major source of money used for larger transactions in the United States and in most other relatively well-developed nations for

© EYEWIRE COLLECTION/GETTY ONE IMAGES

What makes this paper and metal valuable? Paper and metal are valuable if they are acceptable to people who want to sell goods and services. Sellers must be confident that the money that they accept is also acceptable at the place where they want to buy goods and services. Imagine if money in California was not accepted as money in Texas or New York. It would certainly make it more difficult to carry out transactions.

several reasons, including ease and safety of transactions, lower transaction costs, and transaction records.

Ease and Safety of Transactions

Paying for goods and services with a check is easier (meaning cheaper) and less risky than paying with paper money. Paper money is readily transferable: If someone takes a $20 bill from you, it is gone, and the thief can use it to buy goods with no difficulty. If, however, someone steals a check that you have written to the telephone company to pay a monthly bill, that person probably will have great difficulty using it to buy goods and services, because the individual has to be able to identify himself as a representative of the telephone company. If your checkbook is stolen, a person can use your checks as money only if he can successfully forge your signature and provide some identification. Hence, transacting business by check is much less risky than using legal tender; an element of insurance or safety exists in the use of transaction deposits instead of currency.

Lower Transaction Costs

Suppose you decide that you want to buy a compact disc player that costs $81.28 from the current J.C. Penney mail-order catalogue. It is much cheaper, easier, and safer for you to send a check for $81.28 rather than four $20 bills, a $1 bill, a quarter, and three pennies. Transaction deposits are popular precisely because they lower transaction costs compared with the use of metal or paper currency. In very small transactions, the gains in safety and convenience of checks are outweighed by the time and cost required to write and process them; in these cases, transaction costs are lower with paper and metallic currency. For this reason, it is unlikely that the use of paper or metallic currency will disappear entirely.

Transaction Records

Another useful feature of transaction deposits is that they provide a record of financial transactions. Each month, the bank sends the depositor canceled checks and/or a statement recording the deposit and withdrawal of funds. In an age where detailed records are often necessary for tax purposes, this is a useful feature. Of course, it can work both ways. Paper currency transactions are also popular in business activities where participants prefer no records for tax collectors to review.

CREDIT CARDS

Credit cards are "generally acceptable in exchange for goods and services." At the same time, however, credit card payments are actually guaranteed loans available on demand to users, which merely defers customer payment for transactions using a demand deposit. Ultimately, things purchased with a credit card must be paid for with a check; monthly payments on credit card accounts are required in order to have continued use of the card. Credit cards, then, are not money, but rather a convenient means to carry out transactions that minimizes the physical transfer of checks and currency. In that sense, they are substitutes for the use of money in exchange; they also allow any given amount of money to facilitate more exchanges.

SAVINGS ACCOUNTS

Economists are not completely in agreement on what constitutes money for all purposes. Coins, paper currency, demand and other checkable deposits, and traveler's checks are certainly forms of money, because all are accepted as direct means of payment for goods and services. There is nearly universal agreement on this point. Some economists, however, argue that for some purposes "money" should be more broadly defined to include **nontransaction deposits**. Nontransaction deposits are fund accounts against which the depositor *cannot* directly write checks—hence the name. If these funds cannot be used directly as a means of payment, but must first be converted into money, then why do people hold such accounts? People use these accounts primarily because they generally pay higher interest rates than transaction deposits.

nontransaction deposits
funds that cannot be used for payment directly and must be converted into currency for general use

Two primary types of nontransaction deposits exist—savings accounts and time deposits (sometimes referred to as certificates of deposit, or CDs). Most purists would argue that nontransaction deposits are **near money** assets but not money itself. Why? Savings accounts and time deposits cannot be used directly to purchase a good or service. They are not a direct medium of exchange. For example, you cannot go into a supermarket, pick out groceries, and give the clerk the passbook to your savings account. You must convert funds from your savings account into currency or demand deposits before you can buy goods and services. So, strictly speaking, nontransaction deposits do not meet the formal definition of money. At the same time, however, savings accounts are assets that can be quickly converted into money at the face value of the account. In the jargon of finance, savings accounts are highly liquid assets. True, under federal law, commercial banks legally can require depositors to request withdrawal of funds in writing, and then can defer making payment for several weeks. But in practice, no bank prohibits instant withdrawal, although early withdrawal from some time deposits, especially certificates of deposit, may require the depositor to forgo some interest income as a penalty.

near money
nontransaction deposits that are not money, but can be quickly converted into money

MONEY MARKET MUTUAL FUNDS

Money market mutual funds are interest-earning accounts provided by brokers who pool funds into investments like Treasury bills. These funds are invested in short-term securities, and depositors are allowed to write checks against their accounts subject to certain limits. This type of fund has experienced tremendous growth over the last 20 years. Money market mutual funds are highly liquid assets. They are considered to be near money because they are relatively easy to convert into money for the purchases of goods and services.

money market mutual funds
interest-earning accounts provided by brokers that pool funds into investments like Treasury bills

STOCKS AND BONDS

Virtually everyone agrees that many other forms of financial assets, such as stocks and bonds, are not "money." Suppose you buy 100 shares of common stock in General Motors at $70 per share, for a total of $7,000. The stock is traded daily on the New York Stock Exchange and elsewhere; you can readily sell the stock and get paid in legal tender or a demand deposit. Why, then, is this stock not considered money? First, it takes a few days to receive payment for the sale of stock; the asset cannot be turned into cash as quickly as a savings deposit in a financial institution. Second and more importantly, the value of the stock fluctuates over time, and there is no guarantee that the owner of the asset can obtain its original nominal value at any moment in time. Thus, stocks and bonds are not generally considered "money."

LIQUIDITY

liquidity
the ease with which one asset can be converted into another asset or into goods and services

Money is an asset that we generally use to buy goods or services. In fact, it is so easy to convert money into goods and services that we say it is the most liquid of assets. When we speak of **liquidity** we are speaking about the ease with which one asset can be converted into another asset or goods and services. For example, to convert a stock into goods and services would prove to be somewhat more difficult—contacting your broker or going online, determining at what price to sell your stock, paying the commission for your service, and waiting for the completion of the transaction. Clearly, stocks are not as liquid an asset as money. But other assets are even less liquid, like converting your painting collection or your baseball card or Barbie collection into other goods and services.

THE MONEY SUPPLY

Because a good case can be made both for including and for excluding savings accounts, certificates of deposits (CDs), and money market mutual funds from our operational definition of the money supply for different purposes, we will compromise and do both. Economists call the narrow definition of money—currency, checkable deposits, and traveler's checks—**M1.** The broader definition of money, encompassing M1 plus savings deposits, time deposits (except for some large-denomination certificates of deposits), and money market mutual funds, is called **M2.**

M1
the narrowest definition of money; includes currency, checkable deposits, and traveler's checks

M2
a broader definition of money that includes M1 plus savings deposits, time deposits, and money market mutual funds

The difference between M1 and M2 is striking, as evidenced by the varying size of the total stock of money using different definitions as seen in Exhibit 1. M2 is more than four times the magnitude of M1. This means that people prefer to keep the bulk of their liquid assets in the form of savings accounts of various kinds.

HOW WAS MONEY "BACKED"?

Until fairly recent times, coins in most nations were largely made from precious metals, usually gold or silver. These metals had a considerable intrinsic worth: If the coins were melted down, the metal would be valuable for use in jewelry, industrial applications, dentistry, and so forth. Until 1933, the United States was on an internal **gold standard** meaning that the dollar was defined as equivalent in value to a certain amount of gold, and paper currency or demand deposits could be freely converted to gold coin. The United States left the gold standard, however, eventually phasing out gold currency. Some silver coins and paper money convertible into silver remained, but by the end of the 1960s, even this tie of the monetary system to precious metals ended. This was due in part because the price of silver soared so high that the metal in coins had an intrinsic worth greater than its face value, leading people to hoard coins or even melt them down. When there are two forms of money available, people prefer to spend the form of money that is less valuable. This is a manifestation of **Gresham's Law:** "Cheap money drives out dear money."

gold standard
defining the dollar as equivalent to a set value of a quantity of gold, allowing direct convertibility from currency to gold

Gresham's Law
the idea that "cheap money drives out dear money"; given an alternative, people prefer to spend less valuable money

section 17.1 Exhibit 1 — **Two Definitions of the Money Supply: M1 and M2**

Currency = $586.9 billion

M1: Currency + checkable deposits + traveler's checks = $1,184.8 billion

M2: M1 Savings Deposits + Time Deposits + Money Market Mutual Funds = $5,468.8 billion

SOURCE: Federal Reserve, February 2002.

In The NEWS

TINY MICRONESIAN ISLAND USES GIANT STONES AS CURRENCY

BY ART PINE

YAP, Micronesia—On this tiny South Pacific island, life is easy and the currency is hard. Elsewhere, the world's troubled monetary system creaks along; floating exchange rates wreak havoc in currency markets, and devaluations are commonplace. But on Yap the currency is as solid as a rock. In fact, it is rock. Limestone to be precise. For nearly 2,000 years the Yapese have used large stone wheels to pay for major purchases, such as land, canoes and permission to marry. Yap is a U.S. trust territory, and the dollar is used in grocery stores and gas stations. But reliance on stone money, like the island's ancient caste system and the traditional dress of loincloths and grass skirts, continues.

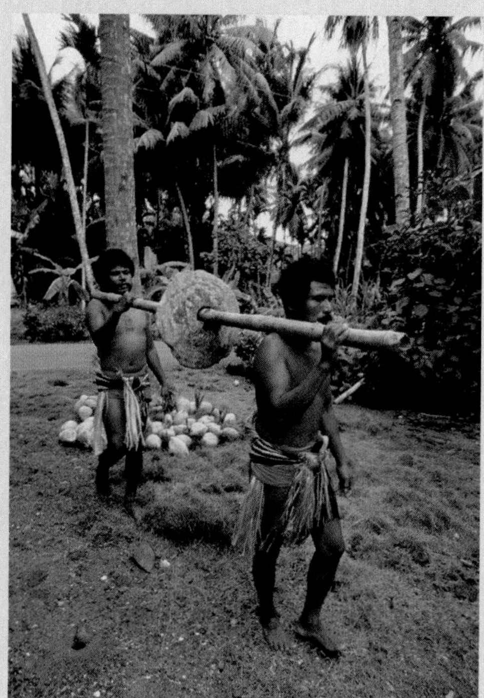

© CHARLES O'REAR/CORBIS

Buying property with stones is "much easier than buying it with U.S. dollars," says John Chodad, who recently purchased a building lot with a 30-inch stone wheel. "We don't know the value of the U.S. dollar." Others on this 37-square-mile island 530 miles southwest of Guam use both dollars and stones. Venito Gurtmag, a builder, recently accepted a four-foot-wide stone disk and $8,700 for a house he built in an outlying village.

Stone wheels don't make good pocket money, so for small transactions, Yapese use other forms of currency, such as beer. Beer is proffered as payment for all sorts of odd jobs, including construction. The 10,000 people on Yap consume 40,000 to 50,000 cases a year, mostly of Budweiser. In fact, Yapese drink so much that sales taxes on alcoholic beverages account for 25 percent of local tax revenue.

Besides stone wheels and beer, the Yapese sometimes spend "gaw," consisting of necklaces of stone beads strung together around a whale's tooth. They also can buy things with "yar," a currency made from large sea shells. But these are small change.

The people of Yap have been using stone money ever since a Yapese warrior named Anagumang first brought the huge stones over from limestone caverns on neighboring Palau, some 1,500 to 2,000 years ago. Inspired by the moon, he fashioned the stone into large circles. The rest is history.

Yapese lean the stone wheels against their houses or prop up rows of them in village "banks." Most of the stones are 2½ to 5 feet in diameter, but some are as much as 12 feet across. Each has a hole in the center so it can be slipped onto the trunk of a fallen betel-nut tree and carried. It takes 20 men to lift some wheels.

By custom, the stones are worthless when broken. You never hear people on Yap musing about wanting a piece of the rock.

There are some decided advantages to using massive stones for money. They are immune to black-market trading, for one thing, and they pose formidable obstacles to pickpockets. In addition, there aren't any sterile debates about how to stabilize the Yapese monetary system. With only about 6,600 stone wheels remaining on the island, the money-supply level stays put. "If you have it, you have it," shrugs Andrew Ken, a Yapese monetary thinker.

SOURCE: Art Pine, "Fixed Assets, Or: Why a Loan in Yap Is Hard to Roll Over—Tiny Micronesian Island Uses Giant Stones as Currency; Don't Forget Your Change," *The Wall Street Journal,* March 29, 1984, p. 1. *Wall Street Journal,* eastern edition [staff-produced copy only] by Art Pine.

WHAT REALLY BACKS OUR MONEY NOW?

Consequently, today, there is no meaningful precious metal "backing" to give our money value. Why, then, do people accept dollar bills in exchange for goods? After all, a dollar bill is a piece of generally wrinkled paper about 6 inches by 2.5 inches in size, with virtually no inherent utility or worth. Do we accept these bills because it states on the front of the bills, "This note is legal tender for all debts, public and private"? Perhaps, but we accept some forms of currency and money in the form of demand deposits without that statement.

The true backing behind money in the United States is faith that people will take it in exchange for goods and services. People accept with great eagerness these small pieces of green paper with pictures of long-deceased people with funny looking hair simply because we believe that they will be exchangeable for goods and services with an intrinsic value. If you were to drop two pieces of paper of equal size on the floor in front of 100 students, one a blank piece of paper and the other a $100 dollar bill, and then leave the room, the group would probably start fighting for the $100 dollar bill while the blank piece of paper would be ignored. Such is our faith in the green paper's practical value that some will even fight for it. As long as people have confidence in something's convertibility into goods and services, "money" will exist and no further backing is necessary.

Because governments represent the collective will of the people, they are the institutional force that traditionally defines money in the legal sense. People are willing to accept pieces of paper as money only because of their faith in the government. When people lose faith in the exchangeability of pieces of paper that the government decrees as money, even legal tender loses its status as meaningful money. Something is money only if people will generally accept it. While governments play a key role in defining money, much of it is actually created by private businesses in the pursuit of profit. A majority of U.S. money, whether M1 or M2, is in the form of deposits at privately owned financial institutions.

People who hold money, then, must not only have faith in their government, but also in banks and other financial institutions as well. If you accept a check drawn on a regional bank, you believe that bank or, for that manner, any bank will be willing to convert that check into legal tender (currency) enabling you to buy goods or services that you want to have. Thus you have faith in the bank as well. In short, our "money" is money because of confidence that we have in private financial institutions as well as our government.

Section Check

SECTION CHECK

1. Money is anything that is generally accepted in exchange for goods or services.
2. Coins, paper currency, demand and other checkable deposits, and traveler's checks are all forms of money.
3. The ease with which one asset can be converted into another asset or goods and services is called liquidity.
4. M1 is made up of currency, checkable deposits, and traveler's checks. M2 is made up of M1, plus savings accounts, time deposits, and money market mutual funds.
5. Money is no longer backed by gold. The true backing is our faith that others will accept it from us in exchange for goods and services.

---

1. If everyone in an economy accepted poker chips as payment in exchange for goods and services, would poker chips be money?
2. If you were buying a pack of gum, would using currency or a demand deposit have lower transactions costs? What if you were buying a house?
3. What is the main advantage of a transaction deposit for tax purposes? What is its main disadvantage for tax purposes?
4. Are credit cards money?
5. What are M1 and M2?
6. How have interest-earning checking accounts and overdraft protection led to the relative decline in demand deposits?

section 17.2

The Functions of Money

- Is using money better than barter?
- How does money lower the costs of making transactions?
- How does money serve as a store of value?
- Is it less risky to make loans of money or of goods?

MONEY AS A MEDIUM OF EXCHANGE

We have already indicated that the primary function of money is to serve as a **medium of exchange,** to facilitate transactions, and to lower transactions costs. That is, sellers will accept it as payment in a transaction. However, money is not the only medium of exchange; rather, it is the only medium that is generally accepted for most transactions. How would people trade with one another in the absence of money? They would **barter** for goods and services they desire.

medium of exchange
the primary function of money, which is to facilitate transactions and lower transactions costs

barter
direct exchange of goods and services without the use of money

The Barter System Is Inefficient

Under a barter system, individuals pay for goods or services by offering other goods and services in exchange. Suppose you are a farmer who needs some salt. You go to the merchant selling salt and offer her 30 pounds of wheat for 2 pounds of salt. The wheat that you use to buy the salt is not money, because the salt merchant may not want wheat and therefore may not accept it as payment. That is one of the major disadvantages of barter: The buyer may not have appropriate items of value to the seller. The salt merchant may reluctantly take the wheat that she does not want, later bartering it away to another customer for something that she does want. In any case, barter is inefficient because several trades may be necessary in order to receive the desired goods.

Moreover, barter is extremely expensive over long distances. What would it cost me, living in California, to send wheat to Maine in return for an item in the L.L.Bean

catalogue? It is much cheaper to mail a check. Finally, barter is time consuming, because of difficulties in evaluating the value of the product that is being offered for barter. For example, the person that is selling the salt may wish to inspect the wheat first to make sure that it is pure and not filled with dirt or other unwanted items. Barter, in short, is expensive and inefficient and generally prevails only where limited trade is carried out over short distances, which generally means in relatively primitive economies. The more complex the economy (e.g., the higher the real per capita GDP), the greater the economic interactions between people, and consequently, the greater the need for one or more universally accepted assets serving as money. Only in a Robinson Crusoe economy, where people live in isolated settlements and are generally self-sufficient, is the use of money unnecessary.

MONEY AS A MEASURE OF VALUE

Besides serving as a medium of exchange, money is also a measure of value. With a barter system, one does not know precisely what 30 pounds of wheat are worth relative to 2 pounds of salt. With money, a common "yardstick" exists so that the values of diverse goods and services can be very precisely compared. Thus, if wheat cost 50 cents a pound and salt costs $1 a pound, we can say that a pound of salt is valued precisely two times as much as a pound of wheat ($1 divided by 50 cents = 2). By providing a universally understood measure of value, money serves to lower the information costs involved in making transactions. Without money, a person might not know what a good price for salt is, because so many different commodities can be bartered for it. With money, there is but one price for salt, and that price is readily available as information to the potential consumer.

MONEY AS A STORE OF VALUE

Money also serves as a store of value. It can provide a means of saving or "storing" things of value in an efficient manner. The farmer in a barter society who wants to save for retirement might accumulate enormous inventories of wheat, which he would then gradually trade away for other goods in his old age. This is a terribly inefficient way to save. Storage buildings would have to be constructed to hold all of the wheat, and the interest payments that the farmer would earn on the wheat would actually be negative, as rats will eat part of it or it will otherwise deteriorate. Most important, physical goods of value would be tied up in unproductive use for many years. With money, the farmer saves pieces of paper that can be used to purchase goods and services in old age. It is both cheaper and safer to store paper rather than wheat.

MONEY AS A MEANS OF DEFERRED PAYMENT

means of deferred payment
the attribute of money that makes it easier to borrow and to repay loans

Finally, money is a **means of deferred payment.** Money makes it much easier to borrow and to repay loans. With barter, lending is cumbersome and subject to an added problem. What if a wheat farmer borrows some wheat and agrees to pay it back in wheat next year, but the value of wheat soars because of a poor crop resulting from drought? The debt will be paid back in wheat that is far more valuable than that borrowed, causing a problem for the borrower. Of course, fluctuations in the value of money can also occur, and indeed, inflation has been a major problem in our recent past and continues to be a problem in many countries. But the value of money fluctuates far less than the value of many individual commodities, so lending in money imposes fewer risks on buyers and sellers than lending in commodities.

Section Check

1. Barter is inefficient compared to money because a person may have to make several trades before receiving something that is truly wanted.
2. By providing a universally understood measure of value, money serves to lower the information costs involved in making transactions.
3. Money is both cheaper and easier to store than other goods.
4. Because the value of money fluctuates less than specific commodities, it imposes fewer risks on borrowers and lenders.

---

1. Why does the advantage of monetary exchange over barter increase as an economy becomes more complex?
2. How can uncertain and rapid rates of inflation erode money's ability to perform its functions efficiently?
3. In a world of barter, would useful financial statements, like balance sheets, be possible? Would stock markets be possible? Would it be possible to build cars?
4. Why do you think virtually all societies create something to function as money?

section 17.3

How Banks Create Money

- How is money created?
- What is a reserve requirement?
- How do reserve requirements affect how much money can be created?

FINANCIAL INSTITUTIONS

The biggest players in the banking industry are **commercial banks.** Commercial banks account for more than two-thirds of all of the deposits in the banking industry; they maintain almost all of the demand deposits and close to half of the savings accounts.

There are nearly 1,000 commercial banks in the United States. This number is in marked contrast to most other nations, where the leading banks operate throughout the country and where a large proportion of total bank assets are held in a handful of banks. Until recently, federal law restricted banks from operating in more than one state. This has now changed, and the structure of banking as we now know it will inevitably change with the emergence of interstate banking, mergers, and "hostile" takeovers.

Aside from commercial banks, the banking system includes two other important financial institutions: **savings and loan associations** and **credit unions.** Savings and loan associations provide many of the same services as commercial banks, including checkable deposits, a variety of time deposits, and money market deposit accounts. The almost 2,000 members of savings and loan associations have typically invested most of their savings deposits into home mortgages. Credit unions are cooperatives, made up of depositors with some common affiliation, like the same employer or union.

commercial banks
financial institutions organized to handle everyday financial transactions of business and household through demand deposit accounts, and saving accounts, and by making short-term commercial and consumer loans

savings and loan associations
financial institutions organized as cooperative associations organized to hold demand deposits and savings of members in the form of dividend-bearing shares and to make loans, especiallly home mortgage loans

credit unions
financial institution cooperatives made up of depositors with a common affiliation

THE FUNCTIONS OF FINANCIAL INSTITUTIONS

Financial institutions offer a large number of financial functions. For example, they often will pay an individual's monthly bills by automatic withdrawals, administer estates, rent safe deposit boxes, and so on. Most important, though, they are depositories for savings and liquid assets that are used by individuals and firms for transaction purposes. They can create money by making loans. In making loans, financial institutions act as intermediaries (the middle persons) between savers, who supply funds, and borrowers seeking funds to invest.

HOW DO BANKS CREATE MONEY?

As we have already learned, most money, narrowly defined, is in the form of transaction deposits, assets that can be directly used to buy goods and services. But how did the balance in, say, a checking account get there in the first place? Perhaps it was through a loan made by a commercial bank. When a bank lends to a person, it does not typically give the borrower cash (paper and metallic currency). Rather, it gives the person the funds by a check or by adding funds to an existing checking account of the borrower. If you go into a bank and borrow $1,000, the bank probably will simply add $1,000 to your checking account at the bank. In doing so, a new checkable deposit—money—is created.

HOW DO BANKS MAKE PROFITS?

Banks make loans and create checkable deposits in order to make a profit. How do they make their profit? By collecting higher interest payments on the loans they make than they pay their depositors for those funds. If you borrow $1,000 from Loans R Us National Bank, the interest payment you make, less the expenses the bank incurs in making the loan, including their costs of acquiring the funds, represents profit to the bank.

RESERVE REQUIREMENTS

reserve requirements
holdings of assets at the bank or at the Federal Reserve Bank as mandated by the Fed

Because the way to make more profit is to make more loans, banks want to make a large volume of loans. Stockholders of banks want the largest profits possible, so what keeps banks from making nearly infinite quantities of loans? Primarily, government regulatory authorities limit the loan issuance of banks by imposing **reserve requirements.** Banks are required to keep on hand a quantity of cash or reserve accounts with the Federal Reserve equal to a prescribed proportion of their checkable deposits.

FRACTIONAL RESERVE SYSTEM

Even in the absence of regulations restricting the creation of checkable deposits, a prudent bank would put some limit on their loan (and therefore deposit) volume. Why? For people to accept checkable deposits as money, the checks written must be generally accepted in exchange for goods and services. People will accept checks only if they know that they are quickly convertible at par (face value) into legal tender. For this reason, banks must have adequate cash reserves on hand (including reserves at the Fed that can be almost immediately converted to currency, if necessary) to meet the needs of customers who wish to convert their checkable deposits into currency or spend them on goods or services.

fractional reserve system
a system that requires banks to hold reserves equal to some fraction of their checkable deposits

Our banking system is sometimes called a **fractional reserve system,** because banks, by law as well as by choice, find it necessary to keep cash on hand and reserves at the Federal Reserve equal to some fraction of their checkable deposits. If a bank were to create $100 in demand deposits for every $1 in cash reserves that it had, the bank might well find itself in difficulty before too long. Why? Consider a bank with $10,000,000 in demand and time deposits and $100,000 in cash reserves. Suppose a couple of large companies with big accounts decide to withdraw $120,000 in cash on the same day. The bank would be unable to convert into legal tender all of the funds requested. The word would then spread that the bank's checks are not convertible into lawful money. This would cause a so-called "run on the bank." The bank would have to quickly convert some of its other assets into currency, or it would be unable to meet its obligations to convert its deposits into currency, and it would have to close.

Therefore, even in the absence of reserve regulations, few banks would risk maintaining fewer reserves on hand than they thought prudent for their amount of deposits (particularly demand deposits). Reserve requirements exist primarily to control the amount of demand and time deposits, and thus the size of the money supply; they do not exist simply to prevent bank failures.

While banks must meet their reserve requirements, they do not want to keep any more of their funds as additional reserves than necessary for safety, because cash assets do not earn any interest. In order to protect themselves but also earn some interest income, banks usually keep some of their assets in highly liquid investments such as U.S. government bonds. These types of highly liquid, interest-paying assets are often called **secondary reserves.**

secondary reserves
highly liquid, interest-paying assets held by the bank

A BALANCE SHEET

Earlier in this chapter, we learned that money is created when banks make loans. We will now look more closely at the process of bank lending and its impact on the stock of money. In doing so, we will take a closer look at the structure and behavior of our hypothetical bank, the Loans R Us National Bank. To get a good picture of the size of the bank, what it owns, and what it owes, we look at its **balance sheet,** which is sort of a financial "photograph" of the bank at a single moment in time. Exhibit 1 presents a balance sheet for the Loans R Us Bank.

balance sheet
a financial record that indicates the balance between a bank's assets and its liabilities plus capital

Assets

The assets of a bank are those things of value that the bank owns (e.g., cash, reserves at the Federal Reserve, bonds, and its buildings), including contractual obligations of individuals and firms to pay funds to the bank (loans). The largest asset item for most banks

section 17.3 Exhibit 1 — Balance Sheet, Loans R Us National Bank

Assets		Liabilities and Capital	
Cash (reserves)	$2,000,000	Transaction deposits (Checking deposits)	$5,000,000
Loans	6,100,000	Savings and time deposits	4,000,000
Bonds (U.S. govt. and municipal)	1,500,000	Total Liabilities	$9,000,000
		Capital	1,000,000
Bank building, equipment, fixtures	400,000		
Total Assets	**$10,000,000**	**Total Liabilities and Capital**	**$10,000,000**

is loans. Banks maintain most of their assets in the form of loans because interest payments on loans are the primary means by which they earn revenue. Some assets are kept in the form of non-interest-bearing cash and reserve accounts at the Federal Reserve, in order to meet legal reserve requirements (and secondly, to meet the cash demands of customers). Typically, relatively little of a bank's reserves, or cash assets, is physically kept in the form of paper currency in the bank's vault or at tellers' windows. Most banks keep a majority of their reserves as reserve accounts at the Federal Reserve. As previously indicated, banks usually also keep some assets in the form of bonds that are quickly convertible into cash if necessary (secondary reserves).

Liabilities

All banks have substantial liabilities, which are financial obligations that the bank has to other people. The predominant liability of virtually all banks is deposits. If you have money in a demand deposit account, you have the right to demand cash for that deposit at any time. Basically, the bank owes you the amount in your checking account. Time deposits similarly constitute a liability of banks.

Capital

For a bank to be healthy and solvent, its assets, or what it owns, must exceed its liabilities, or what it owes others. In other words, if the bank were liquidated and all the assets converted into cash and all the obligations to others (liabilities) paid off, there would still be some cash left to distribute to the owners of the bank, its stockholders. This difference between a bank's assets and its liabilities constitutes the bank's capital. Note that this definition of capital differs from the earlier definition, which described capital as goods used to further production of other goods (machines, structures, tools, etc.). As you can see in Exhibit 1, capital is included on the right side of the balance sheet so that both sides (assets and liabilities plus capital) are equal in amount. Any time the aggregate amount of bank assets changes, the aggregate amount of liabilities and capital also must change by the same amount, by definition.

THE REQUIRED RESERVE RATIO

required reserve ratio
the percentage of deposits that a bank must hold at the Federal Reserve Bank or in bank vaults

excess reserves
reserve levels held above that required by the Fed

Suppose for simplicity that the Loans R Us National Bank faces a reserve requirement of 10 percent on all deposits. That percentage is often called the **required reserve ratio.** But what does a required reserve ratio of 10 percent mean? This means that the bank *must* keep cash on hand or at the Federal Reserve Bank equal to one-tenth (10 percent) of its deposits. For example, if the required reserve ratio was 10 percent, banks would be required to hold $100,000 in required reserves for every $1 million in deposits. The remaining 90 percent of cash is called **excess reserves.**

Reserves in the form of cash and reserves at the Federal Reserve earn no revenue for the bank; no profit is made from holding cash. Whenever excess reserves appear, banks will invest the excess reserves in interest-earning assets, sometimes bonds but usually loans.

LOANING EXCESS RESERVES

Let's see what happens when someone deposits $100,000 at the Loans R Us Bank. We will continue to assume that the required reserve ratio is 10 percent. That is, the bank is required to hold $10,000 in required reserves for this new deposit of $100,000. The remaining 90 percent, or $90,000, becomes excess reserves, and most of this will likely become available for loans for individuals and businesses.

However, this is not the end of the story. Let us say that the bank loans all of its new excess reserves of $90,000 to an individual who is remodeling her home. At the time that the loan is made, the money supply will increase by $90,000. Specifically, no one has less money—the original depositor still has $100,000 and the bank now adds $90,000 to the borrower's checking account (demand deposit). A new demand deposit, or checking account, of $90,000 has been created. *Since demand deposits are money, the issuers of the new loan have created money.*

Furthermore, borrowers are not likely to keep the money in their checking accounts for long, since you usually take out a loan to buy something. If that loan is used for remodeling, then the borrower pays the construction company whose owner will likely deposit the money into his account at another bank to add even more funds for additional money expansion. This whole process is summarized in Exhibit 2.

IS MORE MONEY MORE WEALTH?

When banks create more money by putting their excess reserves to work, they make the economy more liquid. There is clearly more money in the economy after the loan, but is the borrower any wealthier? The answer is no. While borrowers have more money to buy goods and services, they are not any richer because the new liability, the loan, has to be repaid.

In short, banks create money when they increase demand deposits through the process of creating loans. However, the process does not stop here. In the next section, we will see how the process of loans and deposits has a multiplying effect throughout the banking industry.

section 17.3 Exhibit 2 — Fractional Reserve Banking System

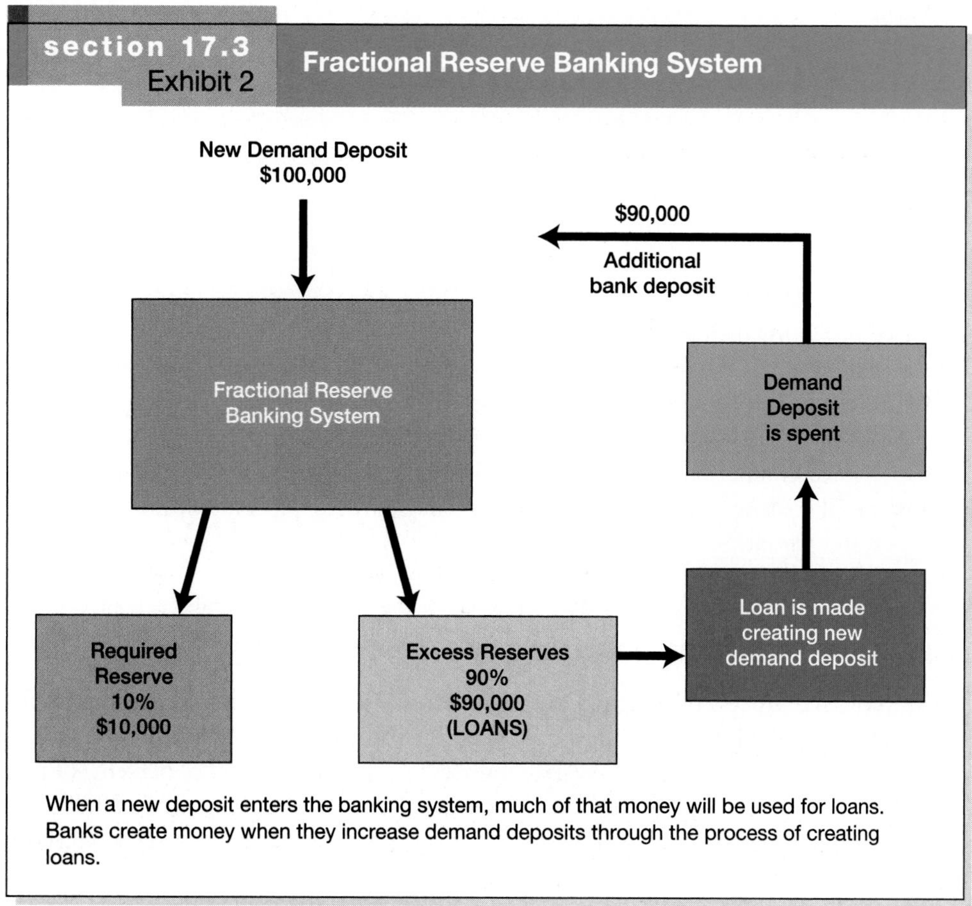

When a new deposit enters the banking system, much of that money will be used for loans. Banks create money when they increase demand deposits through the process of creating loans.

Section Check

SECTION CHECK

1. Money is created when banks make loans. Borrowers receive newly created demand deposits.
2. Required reserves are the amount of cash or reserves—equal to a prescribed proportion of their deposits—that banks are required to keep on hand or in reserve accounts with the Federal Reserve.
3. A balance sheet is a financial record that indicates the balance between a bank's assets and its liabilities plus capital.

---

1. What is happening to the number of banks now that interstate banking is allowed?
2. In what way is it true that "banks make money by making money"?
3. How do legal reserve deposit regulations lower bank profits?
4. Is a demand deposit an asset or a liability to a financial institution?
5. If the Bonnie and Clyde National Bank's only deposits were demand deposits of $20 million, and it faced a 10 percent reserve requirement, how much money would it be required to hold in reserves?
6. Suppose you found $10,000 while digging in your backyard and you deposited it in the bank. How would your new demand deposit account create a situation of excess reserves at your bank?

section 17.4

The Money Multiplier

- How does the multiple expansion of the money supply process work?
- What is the money multiplier?

THE MULTIPLE EXPANSION EFFECT

We have just learned that banks can create money (demand deposits) by making loans and that the monetary expansion of an individual bank is limited to its excess reserves. While this is true, it ignores the further effects of a new loan and the accompanying expansion in the money supply. New loans create new money directly, but they also create excess reserves in other banks, which leads to still further increases in both loans and the money supply. There is a multiple expansion effect, where a given volume of bank reserves creates a multiplied amount of money.

NEW LOANS AND MULTIPLE EXPANSIONS

To see how the process of multiple expansion works, let us extend our earlier example. Say Loans R Us Bank receives a new cash deposit of $100,000. For convenience, say the bank was only required to keep new cash reserves equal to one-tenth (10 percent) of new deposits. With that, Loans R Us is only required to hold $10,000 of the $100,000 deposit for required reserves. Thus, Loans R Us now has $90,000 in excess reserves as a consequence of the new cash deposit.

The Loans R Us Bank, being a profit maximizer, will probably put its newly acquired excess reserves to work in some fashion earning income in the form of interest. Most likely, it will make one or more new loans totaling $90,000.

When the borrowers from Loans R Us Bank get their loans, the borrowed money will almost certainly be spent on something—such as new machinery, a new house, a new car, or greater store inventories. The new money will lead to new spending.

The $90,000 spent by people borrowing from Loans R Us Bank likely will end up in bank accounts in still other banks, such as Bank A shown in Exhibit 1. Bank A now has a new deposit of $90,000 with which to make more loans and create still more money. This process continues with Bank B, Bank C, Bank D, and others. Loans R Us Bank's initial cash deposit, then, has a chain reaction impact that ultimately involves many banks and a total monetary impact that is far greater than suggested by the size of the original deposit of $100,000. That is, every new loan gives rise to excess reserves, which lead to still further lending and deposit creation. Each round of lending is smaller than the preceding one, because some (we are assuming 10 percent) of the new money created must be kept as required reserves.

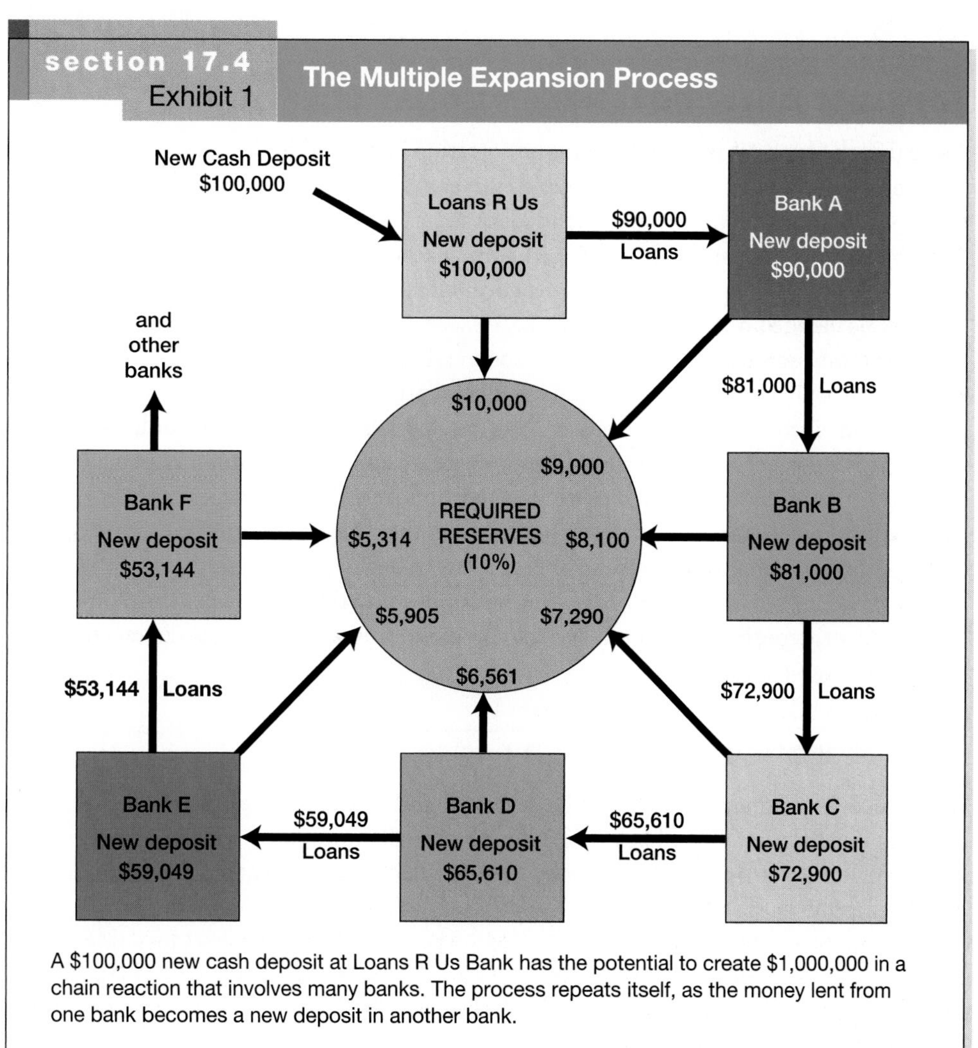

A $100,000 new cash deposit at Loans R Us Bank has the potential to create $1,000,000 in a chain reaction that involves many banks. The process repeats itself, as the money lent from one bank becomes a new deposit in another bank.

THE MONEY MULTIPLIER

money multiplier
measures the potential amount of money that the banking system generates with each dollar of reserves

The **money multiplier** measures the potential amount of money that the banking system generates with each dollar of reserves. The following formula can be used to measure the total maximum potential impact on the supply of money:

$$\text{Potential money creation} = \text{Initial deposit} \times \text{Money multiplier}$$

To find the size of the money multiplier we simply divide 1 by the reserve requirement ($1/R$). The larger the reserve requirement, the smaller the money multiplier. Thus, a reserve requirement of 25 percent, or one-fourth, means a money multiplier of four. Likewise, a reserve requirement of 10 percent, or one-tenth, means a money multiplier of 10.

In the example in Exhibit 1, where Loans R Us Bank (facing a 10 percent reserve requirement) receives a new $100,000 cash deposit, initial deposit equals $100,000. Potential money creation, then, equals $100,000 (initial deposit) multiplied by 10 (the money multiplier), or $1,000,000. Using the money multiplier, we can calculate that the total potential impact of the initial $100,000 deposit is some $1,000,000 in money being created. In other words, the final monetary impact is 10 times as great as the initial deposit. Most of this increase, $900,000, has been created by the increase in demand deposits generated when banks make loans; the remaining $100,000 is from the initial deposit.

WHY IS IT ONLY "POTENTIAL" MONEY CREATION?

Note that the expression "potential money creation" was used in describing the impact of creating loans and deposits out of excess reserves. Why "potential"? Because it is possible that some banks will choose not to lend all of their excess reserves. Some banks may simply be extremely conservative and keep some extra newly acquired cash assets in that form. When that happens, the chain reaction effect is reduced by the amount of excess reserves not loaned out.

Moreover, some borrowers may not spend all of their newly acquired bank deposits, or they may wait a considerable period of time before doing so. Others may put their borrowed funds into time deposits rather than checkable deposits, which would reduce the M1 expansion process but not the M2 money expansion process. Still others may choose to keep some of their loans as currency in their pockets. Such leakages and time lags in the bank money expansion process usually mean that the actual monetary impact of an initial deposit created out of excess reserves within a short time period is less than indicated by the money multiplier. Still, the multiplier principle does work, and a multiple expansion of deposits will generally occur in a banking system that is characterized by fractional reserve requirements.

HOW IS MONEY DESTROYED?

The process of money creation can be reversed, and in the process, money is destroyed. When a person pays a loan back to a bank, she usually does so by writing a check to the bank for the amount due. As a result, demand deposits decline, directly reducing the money supply.

Section Check

1. New loans mean new money (demand deposits), which can increase spending as well as the money supply.
2. The banking system as a whole can potentially create money equal to several times the amount of total reserves or new money equal to several times the amount of excess reserves, the exact amount determined by the money multiplier, which is equal to one divided by the reserve requirement.

---

1. Why do the money supply and the volume of bank loans both increase or decrease at the same time?
2. Why would each bank in the money supply multiple expansion process lend out a larger fraction of any new deposit it receives, the lower the reserve requirement?
3. If a particular bank with a reserve requirement of 10 percent has $30,000 in a new cash deposit, how much money could it create through making new loans?
4. Why do banks choosing to hold excess reserves or borrowers choosing to hold some of their loans in the form of currency reduce the actual impact of the money multiplier to a level below that indicated by the multiplier formula?

section 17.5

The Collapse of America's Banking System, 1920–1933

- What caused the collapse of the banking system between 1920 and 1933?
- How are bank failures avoided today?

Perhaps the most famous utterance from Franklin D. Roosevelt, the President of the United States from 1933 to 1945, was made on the day he assumed office, when he declared, "The only thing we have to fear is fear itself." Those ten words succinctly summarize the problems that led the world's leading economic power to a near total collapse in its system of commercial banking and, with that, to an abrupt and unprecedented decline in the money supply. The decline in the money supply, in turn, contributed to an economic downturn that had dire consequences for many, especially for the one-fourth of the labor force unemployed at the time of Roosevelt's first inaugural address.

WHAT HAPPENED TO THE BANKING INDUSTRY?

In 1920, there were 30,000 banks in the United States; by 1933, the number had declined to about 15,000. What happened? In some cases, bank failure reflected imprudent management or even criminal activity on the part of bank officers (stealing from the bank). More often, though, banks in rural areas closed as a consequence of having large sums of assets tied up in loans to farmers who, because of low farm prices, were not in a position to pay off the loans when they came due. Rumors spread that a bank was in trouble, and those rumors, even if false, became self-fulfilling prophecies. Bank "runs" developed and even conservatively run banks with cash equal to 15 or 20 percent of their

How does the Fed keep banks safe? One of the Fed's functions is to supervise banks and make sure that they are operating safely and soundly. The Fed examines banks' financial statements to make sure the banks are not susceptible to theft or fraud. For a variety of reasons in the 1980s the Fed was not successful and there was an extraordinary upsurge in the number of bank failures. Between 1980 and 1994 more than 1,600 banks insured by the Federal Deposit Insurance Corporation (FDIC) were closed or received FDIC financial assistance—far more than in any other period since the beginning of federal deposit insurance in the 1930s.

deposit liabilities found themselves with insufficient cash reserves to meet the withdrawal requests of panicky depositors.

The bank failures of the 1920s, while numerous, were generally scattered around small towns in the country. Confidence in banks actually generally increased in that decade, and by the fall of 1929, there were $11 in bank deposits for every $1 in currency in circulation.

The first year following the stock market crash of 1929 saw little dramatic change to the banking system, but in late 1930, a bank with the unfortunately awesome sounding name of the Bank of the United States failed, the largest bank failure in the country to that time. This failure had a ripple effect. More bank "runs" occurred as depositors began to get jittery. Banks, fearing runs, began to not lend their excess reserves, thereby aggravating a fall in the money supply reducing business investment.

As depositors converted their deposits to currency, bank reserves fell, and with that the ability of banks to support deposits. The situation improved a bit in 1932, when a newly created government agency, the Reconstruction Finance Corporation (RFC), made loans to distressed banks. By early 1933, however, the depositor confidence decline had reached such a point that the entire banking system was in jeopardy. On March 4, newly inaugurated President Roosevelt declared a national bank holiday, closing every bank in the country for nearly two weeks. Then, only the "good" banks were allowed to reopen, an action that increased confidence. By this time the deposit–currency ratio had fallen from 11 to 1 (in 1929) to 4 to 1. Passage of federal deposit insurance in mid-1933 greatly strengthened depositor confidence and led to money reentering the banks. The recovery process began.

WHAT CAUSED THE COLLAPSE?

The collapse occurred for several reasons. First, the nation had thousands of relatively small banks. Customers believed that depositor withdrawals could force a bank to close, and the mere fear of bank runs made them a reality. Canada, with relatively few banks that were mostly very large with many branches, had no bank runs. Second, governmental attempts to stem the growing distress were weak and too late. Financial aid to banks was nonexistent; the Federal Reserve System and other governmental efforts began only in 1932—well into the decline. Third, deposit insurance, which would have bolstered customer confidence, did not exist. The financial consequences of bank failures were correctly perceived by the public to be great. Fourth, growing depositor fear was enhanced by the fact that the economy was in a continuous downward spiral—there was no basis for any optimism that bank loans would be safely repaid.

BANK FAILURES TODAY

The combination of the Federal Deposit Insurance Corporation (FDIC) and the government's greater willingness to assist distressed banks has reduced the number of bank failures in recent times. Now, when a bank runs into financial difficulty, the FDIC may assist another bank in taking over the assets and liabilities of the troubled bank so that no depositor loses a cent. Thus, changes in the money supply resulting from a loss of deposits from failed banks are no longer a big problem. Better bank stability means a greater stability in the money supply, which means, as will be more explicitly demonstrated in the next chapter, a greater level of economic stability.

However, in the 1980s we did have a savings and loan crisis. Some called this the worst financial crisis since the Great Depression. The inflation of the 1970s had created a problem for many savings and loans. They had made many real estate loans in the early 1970s, when the inflation rate was relatively low—around 5 percent. Then, during most of the rest of that decade, inflation rates rose rapidly and nominal interest rates soared. The savings and loans were in a squeeze—they had to pay high interest rates to attract depositors but were earning low interest rates on their real estate loans from the early 1970s. This was a disastrous combination for many savings and loans and many of them went belly up.

Unfortunately, that was not the only problem. The government eased regulations to make it easier for savings and loans to compete for deposits with other financial institutions in the national market. Deregulation, coupled with deposit insurance, put savings and loans in a gambling mood. Many savings and loans poured money into high-risk real estate projects and other risky ventures. Depositors did not have an incentive to monitor their banks because they knew they would be protected up to $100,000 on their accounts by the government. Eventually, more than a thousand thrift institutions went bankrupt. While depositors were saved, taxpayers were not. Taxpayers ended up paying the bill for much of the savings and loan debacle—the bailout for the financial losses have been estimated to be over $150 billion. The Thrift Bailout Bill of 1989 provided funds for the bailout and new stricter provisions for banks.

Section Check

SECTION CHECK

1. The banking collapse occurred because of customers' fears and the government's weak attempt to correct the problem.
2. The creation of the Federal Deposit Insurance Corporation has largely eliminated bank runs in recent times.

---

1. How did the combination of increased holding of excess reserves by banks and currency by the public lead to bank failures in the 1930s?
2. What are the four reasons cited in the text for the collapse of the U.S. banking system in this period?
3. What is the FDIC, and how did its establishment increase bank stability and reassure depositors?

Summary

Money is anything generally accepted as a medium of exchange for goods or services. Coins, paper currency, demand and other checkable deposits, and traveler's checks are all forms of money. M1 is made up of currency and checkable deposits. M2 is made up of M1, plus savings accounts, time deposits, and money market mutual funds. Barter is inefficient compared to money because a person may have to make several trades before receiving something that is truly wanted. Money is backed by our faith that others will accept it as a medium of exchange.

Money is created when banks make loans. Borrowers receive newly created demand deposits.

Required reserves are the amount of cash or reserves—equal to a prescribed proportion of deposits—that banks are required to keep on hand or in reserve accounts with the Federal Reserve.

Banks create money by increasing demand deposits through the process of making loans. New loans mean new money (demand deposits), which can increase spending as well as the stock of money.

The banking system as a whole can potentially create money equal to several times the amount of total reserves or new money equal to several times the amount of excess reserves, the exact amount determined by the money multiplier, which is equal to one divided by the reserve requirement.

The entire banking system was in jeopardy by 1933. The banking collapse occurred because of customers' fears and the government's weak attempt to correct the problem. Today we have fewer bank failures because of the Federal Deposit Insurance Corporation (FDIC) and the government's greater willingness to help distressed banks.

Key Terms and Concepts

money 372
currency 372
legal tender 372
fiat money 372
demand deposits 373
transaction deposits 373
traveler's checks 373
nontransaction deposits 375
near money 375
money market mutual funds 375
liquidity 375
M1 376
M2 376
gold standard 376
Gresham's Law 376
medium of exchange 379
barter 379
means of deferred payment 380
commercial banks 381
savings and loan associations 381
credit unions 381
reserve requirements 382
fractional reserve system 382
secondary reserves 383
balance sheet 383
required reserve ratio 384
excess reserves 384
money multiplier 388

Review Questions

1. Explain the difficulties that an economics professor might face in purchasing a new car under a barter system.
2. Why do people who live in countries experiencing rapid inflation often prefer to hold American dollars rather than their own country's currency? Explain.
3. Which one of each of the following pairs of assets is most liquid?
   a. Microsoft stock or a traveler's check
   b. a 30-year bond or a six-month Treasury bill
   c. a certificate of deposit or a demand deposit
   d. a savings account or 10 acres of real estate
4. Indicate whether each of the following belong on the asset or liability side of a bank's balance sheet.
   a. loans
   b. holdings of government securities
   c. demand deposits
   d. vault cash
   e. deposits at the Fed
   f. bank buildings
   g. certificates of deposit
5. Calculate the money multiplier when the required reserve ratio is

a. 10 percent.

b. 2 percent.

c. 20 percent.

d. 8 percent.

6. If the required reserve ratio is 10 percent, calculate the potential change in demand deposits under the following circumstances.

a. You take $5,000 from under your mattress and deposit it in your bank.

b. You withdraw $50 from the bank and leave it in your wallet for emergencies.

c. You write a check for $2,500 drawn on your bank (Wells Fargo) to an auto mechanic who deposits the funds in his bank (Bank of America).

7. Calculate the magnitude of the money multiplier if banks were to hold 100 percent of deposits in reserve. Would banks be able to create money in such a case? Explain.

8. Examine the balance sheet for a bank below:

Assets	Liabilities
Total Reserves $500,000	Demand Deposits $2,000,000
Loans $1,600,000	Capital $1,300,000
Buildings $1,200,000	

If the required ratio is 10 percent, what are the bank's excess reserves? If the bank were to loan out those excess reserves, what is the potential expansion in demand deposits in the banking system?

9. Visit the Sexton Web site at **http://sexton.swcollege.com** and click on "FDIC" and read the FAQ (Frequently Asked Questions) sheet about deposit insurance. If you have checking accounts at two different banks, are both accounts insured? Are multiple deposits (savings and checking) at the same institution insured each up to $100,000 or for $100,000 total?

10. Visit the Sexton Web site and click on "U.S. Bureau of Engraving and Printing" and go to the "Facts and Trivia" section. Read the facts and trivia there to find out the origin of the "$" sign and the motto "In God We Trust."

chapter 17 Study Guide

Fill in the Blanks

1. The most important disadvantage of using commodities as money is that they ______________ easily after a few trades.
2. ______________ consists of coins and/or paper that some institution or government has created to be used in the trading of goods and services and the payment of debts.
3. Legal tender is ______________ money.
4. Assets in checking accounts in banks are more formally called ______________ deposits.
5. Demand deposits are deposits in banks that can be ______________ on demand by simply writing a check.
6. ______________ deposits are assets that can be easily converted into currency or used to buy goods and services directly.
7. ______________ deposits and ______________ deposits have replaced paper and metallic currency as the major source of money used for transactions in the United States.
8. Transaction deposits are a popular monetary instrument precisely because they lower ______________ costs compared with the use of metal or paper currency.
9. Credit card payments are actually guaranteed ______________, which merely defer customer payment.
10. Credit cards are not money; they are ______________ for the use of money in exchange.
11. ______________ deposits are fund accounts against which the depositor cannot directly write checks.
12. Two primary types of nontransaction deposits exist— ______________ accounts and ______________ deposits.
13. Assets that can be quickly converted into money are considered highly ______________ assets.
14. Money market mutual funds are considered ______________ money because they are relatively easy to convert into money for the purchase of goods and services.
15. ______________ includes M1, plus saving accounts, time deposits (except for some large-denomination certificates of deposits), and money market mutual funds.
16. ______________ Law states that "cheap money drives out dear money."
17. Something is money only if people will generally ______________ it.
18. Our money is money because of confidence that we have in ______________ institutions as well as in our ______________.
19. The primary function of money is to serve as a ______________.
20. The more complex the economy, the ______________ the need for one or more universally accepted assets serving as money.
21. Money is both a ______________ of value and a ______________ of value.

22. With money, a common ____________ exists so that the values of diverse goods and services can be very precisely compared.

23. The value of money fluctuates far ____________ than the value of many individual commodities.

24. The biggest players in the banking industry are ____________.

25. Aside from commercial banks, the banking system includes two other important financial institutions: ____________ and ____________.

26. Most important, financial institutions are ____________ for savings and liquid assets that are used by individuals and firms for transaction purposes.

27. In making loans, financial institutions act as intermediaries between ____________, who supply funds, and ____________ seeking funds to invest.

28. If you go into a bank and borrow $1,000, the bank probably will simply ____________ to your checking account at the bank.

29. Banks make their profit by collecting ____________ interest payments on the loans they make than they pay their depositors for those funds.

30. ____________ require banks to keep on hand a quantity of cash or reserve accounts with the Federal Reserve equal to a prescribed proportion of their checkable deposits.

31. Our banking system is sometimes called a ____________ system because banks find it necessary to keep cash on hand and reserves at the Federal Reserve equal to some fraction of their checkable deposits.

32. Money is created when banks ____________.

33. The largest asset item for most banks is ____________.

34. Most banks keep a majority of their reserves as ____________.

35. Checking account deposits and time deposits constitute ____________ of banks.

36. Any time the aggregate amount of bank ____________ changes, the aggregate amount of liabilities and capital also must change by the same amount, by definition.

37. Required reserves equal ____________ times ____________.

38. Whenever excess reserves appear, banks will convert the ____________ reserves into other ____________ assets.

39. The monetary expansion of an individual bank is limited to its ____________ reserves.

40. Potential money creation from a cash deposit equals that initial deposit times ____________.

41. The actual monetary impact of an initial deposit created out of excess reserves within a short time period is ____________ indicated by the money multiplier.

42. When a person pays a loan back to a bank, demand deposits ____________, and the money supply ____________.

43. In the Depression, as depositors converted their deposits to currency, bank reserves _____________, and the ability of banks to support deposits _____________ as a result.

44. Passage of federal _____________ in mid-1933 greatly strengthened depositor confidence in banks.

45. In the 1980s, the United States had a _____________ crisis.

True or False

1. Money is anything that is generally accepted in exchange for goods or services.
2. In the United States, the Federal Reserve System issues paper currency.
3. Checks provide the basis for most transactions of relatively modest size in the United States today.
4. Metallic coins and paper currency are the only forms of legal tender.
5. Most of the money that we use for day-to-day transactions is official legal tender.
6. Other checkable deposits that earn interest but have some restrictions have become an important component in the supply of money.
7. There is an element of insurance or safety in the use of transaction deposits instead of currency.
8. Credit cards are included in some measures of the money supply.
9. Economists are not completely in agreement on what constitutes money for all purposes.
10. People use nontransaction accounts primarily because they generally pay higher interest rates than transaction deposits.
11. Most purists would argue that nontransaction deposits are near money assets but not money itself because they are not a direct medium of exchange.
12. Liquidity refers to the ease with which one asset can be converted into another asset or goods and services.
13. Money market mutual funds have experienced tremendous growth over the last 20 years, but they are not very liquid assets.
14. M1 is substantially larger than M2.
15. M1 includes currency, checkable deposits, and traveler's checks, but not savings accounts.
16. People prefer to keep the bulk of their liquid assets as currency or in transaction accounts rather than in the form of savings accounts of various kinds.
17. When the United States was on an internal gold standard, the dollar was defined as equivalent in value to a certain amount of gold.
18. When there are two forms of money available, people prefer to spend the form of money that is more valuable.
19. As long as people have confidence in something's convertibility into goods and services, no further backing is necessary for it to serve as money.

20. When people lose faith in the exchangeability of pieces of paper that the government decrees as money, even legal tender loses its status as meaningful money.

21. A majority of U.S. money, whether M1 or M2, is in the form of deposits at privately owned financial institutions.

22. Money is the only medium of exchange that is generally accepted for most transactions.

23. Lending in money imposes more risks on buyers and sellers than lending in commodities.

24. Unlike in other nations, there are very few separate commercial banks in the United States.

25. Financial institutions can create money by making loans.

26. If you go into a bank and borrow $1,000, the bank probably will simply add $1,000 to your checking account at the bank, but it will not create new money in the process.

27. In the absence of reserve requirements, a prudent bank would still put some limit on its loan volume.

28. Reserve requirements exist primarily to eliminate bank runs.

29. While banks must meet their reserve requirements, they do not want to keep any more of their funds as additional reserves than necessary for safety, because cash assets do not earn any interest.

30. The predominant liability of virtually all banks is deposits.

31. The difference between a bank's assets and its liabilities constitutes the bank's capital, or net worth.

32. Actual reserves equal required reserves minus excess reserves.

33. Banks earn no interest on reserves, whether kept as cash on hand or in accounts with the Federal Reserve.

34. If a bank lends out its excess reserves of $90,000, at the time the loan is made, the money supply will increase by $90,000.

35. When banks create more money, they also directly create wealth.

36. New loans create new money directly, but they also create excess reserves in other banks, which leads to still further increases in both loans and the stock of money.

37. Assume that Loans R Us Bank receives a new cash deposit of $100,000. With a 10 percent required reserve ratio, this creates $10,000 of required reserves and $90,000 of excess reserves.

38. The money multiplier is 1 divided by the required reserve ratio.

39. The higher the required reserve ratio, the larger the money multiplier.

40. If some banks choose not to lend all of their excess reserves, the total amount of money created by an initial cash deposit will be smaller.

41. When a person pays a loan back to a bank, demand deposits decline, directly reducing the money supply.

42. In the Depression, there was an abrupt and unprecedented decline in the supply of money.

43. In the Depression, bank runs could leave even conservatively run banks with insufficient cash reserves to meet the withdrawal requests of panicky depositors.

44. In the Depression, banks, fearing runs, began to not lend their excess reserves, thereby aggravating a fall in the money stock.

45. In the Depression, governmental attempts to stem the growing distress in the banking system were rapid but too weak.

46. The combination of the Federal Deposit Insurance Corporation (FDIC) and the government's greater willingness to assist distressed banks has largely eliminated bank runs and failures in recent times.

Multiple Choice

1. Money's principal role is to serve as
- **a.** a standard for credit transactions.
- **b.** a medium of exchange.
- **c.** a standard for making bank loans.
- **d.** a standard for the real bills doctrine.

2. The money supply that includes currency, checkable deposits, and traveler's checks is known as
- **a.** M1.
- **b.** M2.
- **c.** M3.
- **d.** L.

3. Credit cards
- **a.** are included in the M1 definition of the money supply.
- **b.** are included in the M2 definition of the money supply.
- **c.** are included in the M3 definition of the money supply.
- **d.** are included only in the broadest definition of the money supply.
- **e.** are not included in the definition of the money supply.

4. The distinction between M1 and M2 is based on
- **a.** liquidity—the ease with which an asset can be converted into cash.
- **b.** storability—the ease with which an asset can be stored.
- **c.** divisibility—the ease with which an asset can be used to make specific payments.
- **d.** portability—the ease with which an asset can be moved to make a payment on the spot.
- **e.** all of the above.

5. Barter is inefficient compared to using money for trading because
- **a.** it is more expensive over long distances.
- **b.** potential buyers may not have appropriate items of value to sellers with which to barter.
- **c.** it is more time consuming, as it is more difficult to evaluate the products that are being offered for barter than to evaluate money.
- **d.** all of the above.
- **e.** none of the above.

6. Currency is a poor store of value when
   a. the unemployment rate is high.
   b. banks are failing at an abnormally high rate.
   c. the rate of inflation is very high.
   d. gold can be purchased at bargain prices.
   e. all of the above are correct.

7. Money makes it easier to borrow and repay loans. This function of money is referred to as
   a. a store of value.
   b. a means of deferred payment.
   c. a unit of account.
   d. a standard of value.
   e. none of the above.

8. Money is
   a. whatever is generally accepted in exchange for goods and services.
   b. an object to be consumed.
   c. a highly illiquid asset.
   d. widely used in a barter economy.

9. Without money to serve as a medium of exchange,
   a. gains from trade would be severely limited.
   b. our standard of living probably would be reduced.
   c. the transactions costs of exchange would increase.
   d. all of the above are true.

10. An increase in demand deposits combined with an equal decrease in currency in circulation would
   a. have no direct effect on M1 or M2.
   b. increase both M1 and M2.
   c. increase M1 and decrease M2.
   d. decrease M1 and increase M2.

11. Liquidity is defined as
   a. the cash value of fiat money.
   b. the value of fiat money when used to buy a good or a service.
   c. the speed at which money is spent.
   d. the ease with which money can be divided to make payments.
   e. the ease with which an asset can be converted into cash.

12. Under fractional reserve banking, when a bank lends to a customer,
   a. bank credit decreases.
   b. reserves drain away from the system.
   c. the bank is protected from a run.
   d. borrowers receive a newly created demand deposit; that is, money is created.
   e. bank profitability is decreased.

13. Required reserves of a bank are a specific percentage of their
   a. loans.
   b. cash on hand.
   c. total assets.
   d. deposits.

14. Which of the following will lead to an increase in the money supply?
   a. You pay back a $10,000 loan that you owe to your bank.
   b. Your bank gives you a $10,000 loan by adding $10,000 to your checking account.
   c. You pay $10,000 in cash for a new motorcycle.
   d. You bury $10,000 in cash in your backyard.

15. If a banking transaction created new excess reserves in the banking system, the result would tend to be
   a. an increase in the amount of loans made by banks and an increase in the supply of money.
   b. an increase in the amount of loans made by banks and a decrease in the supply of money.
   c. a decrease in the amount of loans made by banks and an increase in the supply of money.
   d. a decrease in the amount of loans made by banks and a decrease in the supply of money.

16. If many people were to suddenly deposit into their checking accounts large sums of cash previously kept in their wallets, and there were no offsetting actions by the Fed, this would result in
   a. a reduction in the U.S. money supply.
   b. a decrease in M1 but an increase M2.
   c. an increase in interest rates.
   d. an increase in reserves of banks and therefore an increase in the money supply.
   e. both a and c.

17. A reserve requirement of 20 percent means a money multiplier of
   a. 1.25.
   b. 2.
   c. 5.
   d. 20.

18. If the required reserve ratio were increased, then
   a. the money supply would tend to decrease, but the outstanding loans of banks would tend to increase.
   b. both the money supply and the outstanding loans of banks would tend to decrease.
   c. the money supply would tend to increase, but the outstanding loans of banks would tend to decrease.
   d. both the money supply and the outstanding loans of banks would tend to increase.

Problems

1. What would each of the following changes do to M1 and M2?

Change	M1	M2
An increase in currency in circulation	________	________
A decrease in demand deposits	________	________
An increase in savings deposits	________	________
An increase in credit card balances	________	________
A conversion of savings account balances into checking account balances	________	________
A conversion of savings account balances into time account balances	________	________
A conversion of checking account balances into money market mutual funds	________	________

2. What would the money multiplier be if the required reserve ratio were

5 percent? __________

10 percent? __________

20 percent? __________

25 percent? __________

50 percent? __________

3. Assume there was a new $100,000 deposit into a checking account at a bank.

a. What would be the resulting excess reserves created by that deposit if banks faced a reserve requirement of

10 percent? __________

20 percent? __________

25 percent? __________

50 percent? __________

b. How many additional dollars could that bank lend out as a result of that deposit if banks faced a reserve requirement of

10 percent? __________

20 percent? __________

25 percent? __________

50 percent? __________

c. How many additional dollars of money could the banking system as a whole create in response to such a new deposit if banks faced a reserve requirement of

10 percent? __________

20 percent? __________

25 percent? __________

50 percent? __________

4. Answer questions a and b.

a. If a bank had reserves of $30,000 and demand deposits of $200,000 (and no other deposits), how much could it lend out if it faced a required reserve ratio of

10 percent? __________

15 percent? __________

20 percent? __________

b. If the bank then received a new $40,000 deposit in a customer's demand deposit account, how much could it now lend out if it faced a required reserve ratio of

10 percent? __________

15 percent? __________

20 percent? __________

chapter 18

The Federal Reserve System and Monetary Policy

section 18.1

The Federal Reserve System

- What are the functions of a central bank?
- Who controls the Federal Reserve System?
- How is the Fed tied to Congress and the executive branch?

THE FUNCTIONS OF A CENTRAL BANK

In most countries of the world, the job of manipulating the supply of money belongs to the central bank. A central bank has many functions. First, a central bank is a "banker's bank." It serves as a bank where commercial banks maintain their own cash deposits—their reserves. Second, a central bank performs a number of service functions for commercial banks, such as transferring funds and checks between various commercial banks in the banking system. Third, the central bank typically serves as the major bank for the central government, handling, for example, its payroll accounts. Fourth, the central bank buys and sells foreign currencies and generally assists in the completion of financial transactions with other countries. Fifth, it serves as a "lender of last resort" that helps banking institutions in financial distress. Sixth, the central bank is concerned with the stability of the banking system and the supply of money, which, as you have already learned, results from the loan decisions of banks. The central bank can and does impose regulations on private commercial banks; it thereby regulates the size of the money supply and influences the level of economic activity. The central bank also implements monetary policy, which, along with fiscal policy, forms the basis of efforts to direct the economy to perform in accordance with macroeconomic goals.

Commercial banks keep reserves with the central bank. Roughly 4,000 U.S. banks are members of the Federal Reserve System. While this is less than half of the number of total banks, the member banks hold roughly 75 percent of U.S. bank deposits. Furthermore, all banks must meet the Fed's requirements, whether they are members or not.

LOCATION OF THE FEDERAL RESERVE SYSTEM

In most countries, the central bank is a single bank; for example, the central bank of Great Britain, the Bank of England, is a single institution located in London. In the United States, however, the central bank is 12 institutions, closely tied together and collectively called the Federal Reserve System. The Federal Reserve System, or Fed, as it is nicknamed, has separate banks in Boston, New York, Philadelphia, Richmond, Atlanta, Dallas, Cleveland, Chicago, St. Louis, Minneapolis–St. Paul, Kansas City, and San Francisco. As Exhibit 1 shows, these banks and their branches are spread all over the country, but they are most heavily concentrated in the Eastern states.

Each of the 12 banks has branches in key cities in its district. For example, the Federal Reserve Bank of Cleveland serves the fourth Federal Reserve district and has branches in Pittsburgh and Cincinnati. Each Federal Reserve bank has its own board of directors and, to some limited extent, can set its own policies. Effectively, however, the 12 banks act in unison on major policy issues, with control of major policy decisions resting with the Board of Governors and the Federal Open Market Committee, headquartered in Washington, D.C. The Chairman of the Federal Reserve Board of Governors (currently

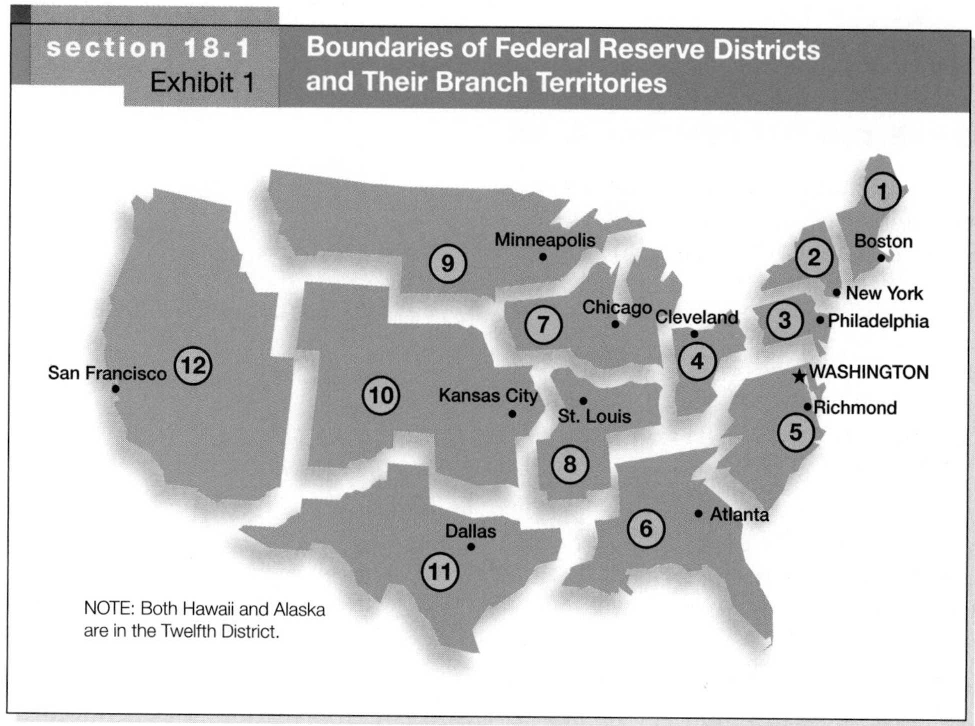

section 18.1 Exhibit 1 Boundaries of Federal Reserve Districts and Their Branch Territories

Alan Greenspan) is generally regarded as one of the most important and powerful economic policy makers in the country.

THE FED'S RELATIONSHIP TO THE FEDERAL GOVERNMENT

The Federal Reserve was created in 1913 because the U.S. banking system had so little stability and no central direction. Technically, the Fed is privately owned by the banks that "belong" to it. All banks are not required to belong to the Fed; however, since the passage of new legislation in 1980, virtually no difference exists between the requirements of member and nonmember banks.

The private ownership of the Fed is essentially meaningless, because the Board of Governors of the Federal Reserve, which controls major policy decisions, is appointed by the president of the United States, not by the stockholders. The owners of the Fed have relatively little control over its operations and receive only small fixed dividends on their modest financial stake in the system. Again, the private ownership but public control feature was a compromise made to appease commercial banks opposed to direct public (government) regulation.

THE FED'S TIES TO THE EXECUTIVE BRANCH

An important aspect of the Fed's operation is that, historically, it has had a considerable amount of independence from both the executive and legislative branches of government. True, the president appoints the seven members of the Board of Governors, subject to Senate approval, but the term of appointment is 14 years. This means that no member of the Federal Reserve Board will face reappointment from the president who initially made the appointment, because presidential tenure is limited to two four-year terms. Moreover, the terms of board members are staggered, so a new appointment is made only every two years. It is practically impossible for a single president to appoint a majority of

In The **NEWS**

INDEPENDENCE AND THE CENTRAL BANK

"There have been three great inventions since the beginning of time: fire, the wheel and central banking," quipped Will Rogers, an American humorist. Yet central banking as we know it today is an invention of the 20th century.

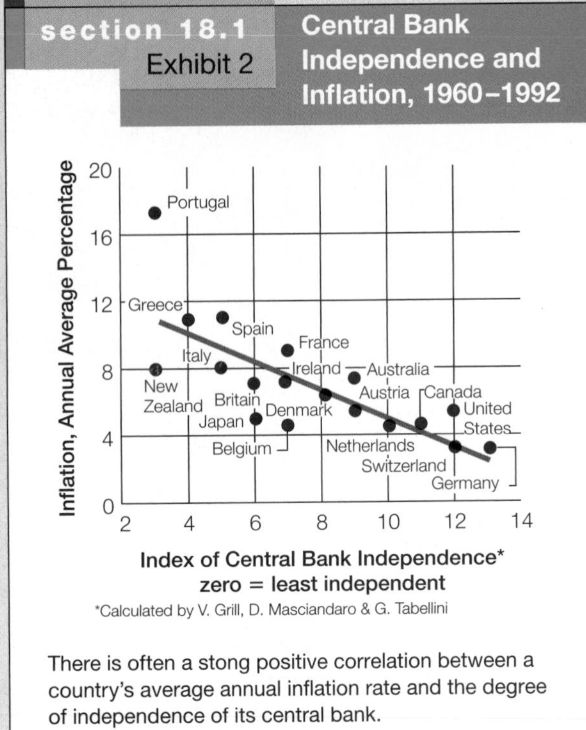

section 18.1 Exhibit 2 **Central Bank Independence and Inflation, 1960–1992**

There is often a stong positive correlation between a country's average annual inflation rate and the degree of independence of its central bank.

Central banks' original task was not to conduct monetary policy or support the banking system, but to finance government spending. The world's oldest central bank, the Bank of Sweden, was established in 1668 largely as a vehicle to finance military spending. The Bank of England was created in 1694 to fund a war with France. Even as recently as the late 1940s, a Labour chancellor of the exchequer, Stafford Cripps, took great pleasure in describing the Bank of England as "his bank." Today most central banks are banned from financing government deficits.

The United States managed without a central bank until early this century. Private banks used to issue their own notes and coins, and banking crises were fairly frequent. But following a series of particularly severe crises, the Federal Reserve was set up in 1913, mainly to supervise banks and act as a lender of last resort. Today the Fed is one of the few major central banks that is still responsible for bank supervision; most countries have handed this job to a separate agency.

At first, governments in most countries kept a tight grip on the monetary reins, telling central banks when to change interest rates. But when inflation soared, governments saw the advantage of granting central banks independence in matters of monetary policy. Short-sighted politicians might try to engineer a boom before an election, hoping that inflation would not rise until after the votes had been counted, but an independent central bank insulated from political pressures would give higher priority to price stability. If, as a result of independence, policy is more credible, workers and firms are likely to adjust their wages and prices more quickly in response to a tightening of policy, and so, the argument runs, inflation can be reduced with a smaller loss of output and jobs . . .

Several studies in the early 1990s confirmed that countries with independent central banks did indeed tend to have lower inflation rates (see Exhibit 2). And better still, low inflation did not appear to come at the cost of slower growth. . . . No central bank is completely independent. Before the ECB was set up, the German Bundesbank was the most independent central bank in the world, yet the German government chose to ignore its advice on the appropriate exchange rate for unification, and thereby stoked inflationary pressures. Some central banks, such as the Bank of England, have full independence in the setting of monetary policy, but their inflation target is set by the government.

Independent central banks are more likely to achieve low inflation than finance ministers because they have a longer time horizon. But independence is no panacea: central banks can still make mistakes. Note that Germany's Reichsbank was statutorily independent when the country suffered hyperinflation in 1923.

SOURCE: "Monetary Metamorphosis," *The Economist*, September 25, 1999. From "A Survey of the World Economy: The Navigators," pp. 1–42, appearing on p. 4.

the members of the board, and even if it were possible, members have little fear of losing their jobs as a result of presidential wrath. The Chair of the Federal Reserve Board is a member of the Board of Governors and serves a four-year term. The Chair is truly the chief executive officer of the system, and he effectively runs it with considerable help from the presidents of the 12 regional banks.

FED OPERATIONS

Many of the key policy decisions of the Federal Reserve are actually made by its Federal Open Market Committee (FOMC), which consists of the seven members of the Board of Governors; the president of the New York Federal Reserve Bank, and four other presidents of Federal Reserve Banks, who serve on the committee on a rotating basis. The FOMC makes most of the key decisions influencing the direction and size of changes in the money supply, and their regular, closed meetings are accordingly considered very important by the business community, news media, and government.

Section Check

1. Of the six major functions of a central bank, the most important is its role in regulating the money supply.
2. There are 12 Federal Reserve banks in the Federal Reserve System. Although these banks are independent institutions, they act largely in unison on major policy decisions.
3. The Federal Reserve Board of Governors and the Federal Open Market Committee are the prime decision makers for U.S. monetary policy.
4. The president of the United States appoints the members of the Federal Reserve Board of Governors to a 14-year term, with only one appointment made every two years. The president also selects the Chair of the Federal Reserve Board, who serves a four-year term. The only other government intervention in the Fed can come from legislation passed in Congress.

---

1. What are the six primary functions of a central bank?
2. What is the FOMC and what does it do?
3. How is the Fed tied to the executive branch? How is it insulated from executive branch pressure to influence monetary policy?

---

section 18.2

The Equation of Exchange

- What is the equation of exchange?
- What is the velocity of money?
- How is the equation of exchange useful?

As we discussed in the previous section, perhaps the most important function of the Federal Reserve is its ability to regulate the money supply. In order to fully understand the significant role that the Federal Reserve plays in the economy, we will first examine the role of money in the national economy.

THE EQUATION OF EXCHANGE

The role that money plays in determining equilibrium GDP, the level of prices, and real output of goods and services has attracted the attention of economists for generations. In the early part of this century, economists noted a useful relationship that helps our

equation of exchange
the money supply (M) times velocity (V) of circulation equals the price level (P) times quantity of goods and services produced in a given period (Q)

understanding of the role of money in the national economy, called the **equation of exchange.** The quantity equation can be presented as follows:

$$M \times V = P \times Q$$

where M is the money supply, however defined (usually M1 or M2), V is the velocity of money, P is the average level of prices of final goods and services, and Q is the physical quantity of final goods and services produced in a given period (usually one year).

We have previously defined MV, the velocity of money, as it refers to the "turnover" rate, or the intensity with which money is used. Specifically, V represents the average number of times that a dollar is used in purchasing final goods or services in a one-year period. Thus, if individuals are hoarding their money, velocity will be low; if individuals are writing lots of checks on their checking accounts and spending currency as fast as they receive it, velocity will tend to be high.

The expression $P \times Q$ represents the dollar value of all final goods and services sold in a country in a given year. Does that sound familiar? It should, because that is the definition of nominal gross domestic product (GDP). Thus, for our purposes, we may consider the average level of prices (P) times the physical quantity of final goods and services in a given time period (Q) to be equal to nominal GDP. We could say then, that

$$MV = \text{Nominal GDP}$$

or,

$$V = \text{Nominal GDP}/M$$

That, in fact, is the definition of velocity: The total output of goods in a year divided by the amount of money is the same thing as the average number of times a dollar is used in final goods transactions in a year.

The actual magnitude of V will depend on the definition of money that is used. For simplicity, let us use some hypothetical numbers to derive the velocity of money:

$$V = \text{Nominal GDP/M1} = \$10{,}000 \text{ billion } /\$1{,}000 \text{ billion} = 10$$

Using a broader definition of money, M2, the velocity of money equals

$$V = \text{Nominal GDP/M2} = \$10{,}000 \text{ billion}/\$4{,}000 \text{ billion} = 2.5$$

The average dollar of money, then, turns over a few times in the course of a year, with the precise number depending on the definition of money.

USING THE EQUATION OF EXCHANGE

The quantity equation of money is a useful tool when we try to assess the impact on the aggregate economy of a change in the supply of money (M). If M increases, then one of the following must happen:

1. V must decline by the same magnitude, so that $M \times V$ remains constant, leaving $P \times Q$ unchanged.
2. P must rise.
3. Q must rise.
4. P and Q must each rise some, so that the product of P and Q remains equal to MV.

In other words, if the money supply increases and the velocity of money does not change by an offsetting amount, there will be either higher prices (inflation), greater output of final goods and services, or a combination of both. If one considers a macroeconomic policy to be successful if output is increased but unsuccessful if the only effect of the policy is inflation, then an increase in *M* is an effective policy if *Q* increases but an ineffective policy if *P* increases.

Likewise, dampening the rate of increase in *M* or even causing it to decline will cause nominal GDP to fall, unless the change in *M* is counteracted by a rising velocity of money. Intentionally decreasing *M* can also either be good or bad, depending on whether the declining money GDP is reflected mainly in falling prices (*P*) or in falling output (*Q*).

Therefore, expanding the money supply, unless counteracted by increased hoarding of currency (leading to a decline in *V*), will have the same type of impact on aggregate demand as an expansionary fiscal policy—increasing government purchases, reducing taxes, or increases in transfer payments. Likewise, policies designed to reduce the money supply will have a contractionary impact (unless offset by a rising velocity of money) on aggregate demand, similar to the impact obtained from increasing taxes, decreasing transfer payments, or decreasing government purchases.

In sum, what these relationships illustrate is that monetary policy can be used to obtain the same objectives as fiscal policy. Some economists, often called monetarists, believe that monetary policy is the most powerful determinant of macroeconomic results.

HOW VOLATILE IS THE VELOCITY OF MONEY?

Economists once considered the velocity of money a given. We now know that it is not constant, but moves in a fairly predictable pattern. Thus, the connection between money supply and GDP is still fairly predictable. Historically, the velocity of money has been quite stable over a long period of time, and it has been particularly stable using the M2 definition. However, velocity is less stable when measured using the M1 definition and over shorter periods of time. For example, an increase in velocity can occur with anticipated inflation. When individuals expect inflation, they will spend their money more quickly. They don't want to be caught holding money that is going to be worth less in the future. Also, an increase in the interest rates will cause people to hold less money. That is, people want to hold less money when the opportunity cost of holding money increases. This, in turn, means that the velocity of money increases.

THE RELATIONSHIP BETWEEN THE INFLATION RATE AND THE GROWTH IN THE MONEY SUPPLY

The inflation rate tends to rise more in periods of rapid monetary expansion than in periods of slower growth in the money supply. In Exhibit 1, we see the relationship between higher money growth and higher inflation rate among different countries. During the 1990s, when there was not as much inflation worldwide as there was in the 1970s and 1980s, it was more difficult to test this relationship.

The relationship between the growth in the money supply and higher inflation is particularly strong with hyperinflation—inflation that is greater than 50 percent. The most famous case of hyperinflation was in Germany in the 1920s—inflation was roughly 300 percent *per month* for over a year. The German government incurred large amounts of debt during World War I and could not raise enough money to pay its expenses, so it printed huge amounts of money. The inflation was so bad that store owners would change their prices in the middle of the day, firms had to pay workers several times a week, and many resorted to barter. Recently, Brazil, Argentina, and Russia have all experienced hyperinflation. The cause of hyperinflation is simply excessive money growth—printing too much money.

section 18.2 Exhibit 1 — **Money Supply Growth and Inflation Rates, 1908–1996**

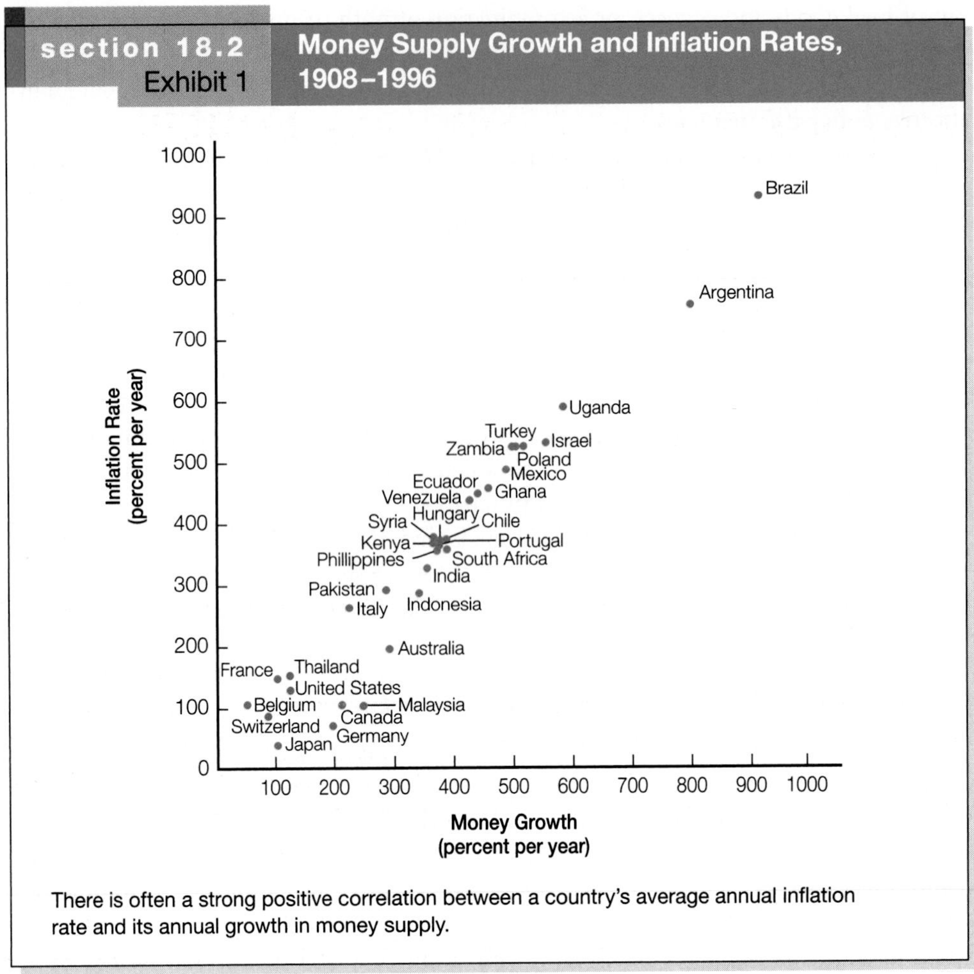

There is often a strong positive correlation between a country's average annual inflation rate and its annual growth in money supply.

Section Check

1. The equation of exchange is $M \times V = P \times Q$, where M is the money supply, V is the velocity of money, P is the average level of prices of final goods and services, and Q is the physical quantity of final goods and services produced in an economy in a given year.
2. The velocity of money (V) represents the average number of times that a dollar is used in purchasing final goods or services in a one-year period.
3. The equation of exchange is a useful tool when analyzing the effects of a change in the money supply on the aggregate economy.

---

1. If M1 is $10 billion and velocity is 4, what is the product of the price level and output? If the price level is 2, what does output equal?
2. If nominal GDP is $200 billion and the money supply is $50 billion, what must velocity be?
3. If the money supply increases and velocity does not change, what will happen to nominal GDP?
4. If velocity is unstable, does stabilizing the money supply help stabilize the economy? Why or why not?

section 18.3

Implementing Monetary Policy: Tools of the Fed

- What are the three major tools of the Fed?
- What is the purpose of the Fed's tools?
- What other powers does the Fed have?

HOW DOES THE FED MANIPULATE THE SUPPLY OF MONEY?

As noted previously, the Federal Reserve Board of Governors and the Federal Open Market Committee are the prime decision makers for U.S. monetary policy. They decide whether to expand the money supply and, it is hoped, the real level of economic activity, or to contract the money supply, hoping to cool inflationary pressures. How does the Fed control the money supply, particularly when it is the privately owned commercial banks that actually create and destroy money by making loans, as we discussed earlier?

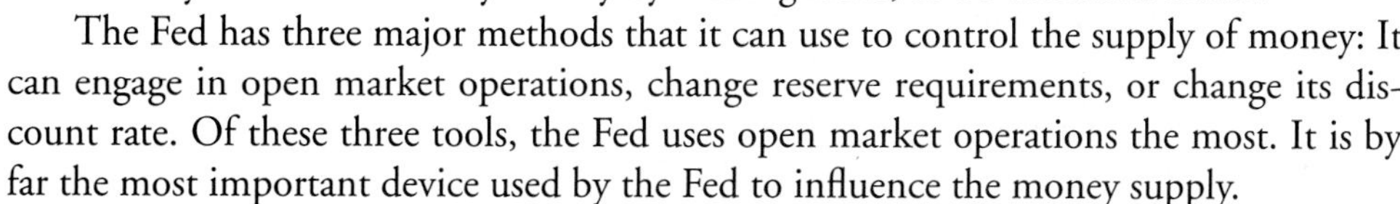

The Fed has three major methods that it can use to control the supply of money: It can engage in open market operations, change reserve requirements, or change its discount rate. Of these three tools, the Fed uses open market operations the most. It is by far the most important device used by the Fed to influence the money supply.

OPEN MARKET OPERATIONS

open market operations *purchase and sale of government securities by the Federal Reserve System*

Open market operations involve the purchase and sale of government securities by the Federal Reserve System. At its regular meetings, the Federal Open Market Committee (FOMC) decides to buy or sell government bonds. For several reasons, open market operations are the most important method the Fed uses to change the money supply. To begin, it is a device that can be implemented quickly and cheaply—the Fed merely calls an agent who buys or sells bonds. It can be done quietly, without a lot of political debate or a public announcement. It is a rather powerful tool, as any given purchase or sale of securities has an ultimate impact several times the amount of the initial transaction.

When the Fed buys bonds, it pays the seller of the bonds by a check written on one of the 12 Federal Reserve banks. The person receiving the check will likely deposit it in his or her bank account, increasing the money supply in the form of added transactions deposits. More importantly, the commercial bank, in return for crediting the account of the bond seller with a new deposit, gets cash reserves or a higher balance in their reserve account at the Federal Reserve Bank in its district.

For example, suppose the Loans R Us National Bank has no excess reserves and that one of its customers sells a bond for $10,000 through a broker to the Federal Reserve System. The customer deposits the check from the Fed for $10,000 in his or her account, and the Fed credits the Loans R Us Bank with $10,000 in reserves. Suppose the reserve requirement is 10 percent. The Loans R Us Bank, then, only needs new reserves of $1,000 ($10,000 × .10) to support its $10,000, meaning that it has acquired $9,000 in new excess reserves ($10,000 new actual reserves minus $1,000 in new required reserves). Loans R Us can, and probably will, lend out its excess reserves of $9,000, creating $9,000 in new deposits in the process. The recipients of the loans, in turn, will likely spend the money, leading to still more new deposits and excess reserves in other banks, as discussed in the previous chapter.

APPLICATION

OPEN MARKET OPERATIONS

Q: How does the money supply increase as the result of open market operations?

A: In order for people to want to put more money in banks and less in government bonds, the Fed must offer bond holders an attractive price. If the Fed's price is high enough, it will tempt some investors to sell their government bonds. When those individuals place the proceeds from the sale in the bank, new deposits are created, increasing reserves in the banking system. The excess reserves can then be loaned by the banks, creating more new deposits and increasing the excess reserves in still other banks.

In other words, the Fed's purchase of the bond directly creates $10,000 in money in the form of bank deposits, and indirectly permits up to $90,000 in additional money to be created through the multiple expansion in bank deposits. (The money multiplier is the reciprocal of 1/.10, or 10. 10 × $9,000 = $90,000.) Thus, if the reserve requirement is 10 percent, a potential total of up to $100,000 in new money is created by the purchase of one $10,000 bond by the Fed.

The process works in reverse when the Fed sells a bond. The individual purchasing the bond will pay the Fed by check, lowering demand deposits in the banking system. Reserves of the bank where the bond purchaser has a bank account will likewise fall. If the bank had zero excess reserves at the beginning of the process, it will now have a reserve deficiency. The bank must sell secondary reserves or reduce loan volume, either of which will lead to further destruction of deposits. A multiple contraction of deposits will begin.

Open Market Activities and the Equation of Exchange

Generally, in a growing economy where the real value of goods and services is increasing over time, an increase in the supply of money is needed even to maintain stable prices. If the velocity of money (V) in the equation of exchange is fairly constant and real GDP (denoted by Q in the equation of exchange) is rising between 3 and 4 percent a year (as it has over the period since 1840), then a 3 or 4 percent increase in M is consistent with stable prices. We would expect, then, that over long time expanses, the Fed's open market operations would more often lead to monetary expansion than monetary contraction. In other words, the Fed would more often purchase bonds than sell them. Moreover, in periods of rising prices, if V is fairly constant, the growth of M likely will exceed the 3 to 4 percent annual growth that appears to be consistent with long-term price stability.

THE RESERVE REQUIREMENT

While open market operations are the most important and widely utilized tool that the Fed has to achieve its monetary objectives, it is not its potentially most powerful tool. The Fed possesses the power to change the reserve requirements of member banks by altering the reserve ratio. This can have an immediate, significant impact on the ability of member banks to create money. Suppose the banking system as a whole has $500 billion in deposits and $60 billion in reserves, with a reserve ratio of 12 percent. Because $60 billion is 12 percent of $500 billion, the system has no excess reserves. Suppose now that the Fed lowers reserve requirements by changing the reserve ratio to 10 percent. Now, banks are required to keep only $50 billion in reserves ($500 billion × .10), but they still have $60 billion. Thus, the lowering of the reserve requirement gives banks $10 billion in excess reserves. The banking system as a whole can expand deposits and the money stock by a multiple of this amount, in this case 10 (10 percent equals 1/10; the banking multiplier is the reciprocal of this, or 10). The lowering of the reserve requirement in this case, then, would permit an expansion in deposits of $100 billion, which represents a 20 percent increase in the stock of money, from $500 to $600 billion.

When Does the Fed Use This Tool?

Relatively small reserve requirement changes, then, can have a big impact on the potential supply of money. The tool is so potent, in fact, that it is seldom used. In other words, the advantage of the reserve requirement is that it is a very powerful tool. However, this is also its disadvantage because a very small reduction in the reserve requirement can make a huge change in the number of dollars that are in excess reserves in banks all over the country. Such huge changes in required reserves and excess reserves have the potential to be disruptive to the economy.

Frequent changes in the reserve requirement would make it very difficult for banks to plan. For example, a banker might worry that if she makes loans now, and then the Fed raises the reserve requirement, she would not have enough reserves to meet the new reserve requirements. If she does not make loans and the Fed leaves the reserve requirement alone, she loses the opportunity to earn income on those loans.

Carpenters don't use sledge hammers to hammer small nails or tacks; the tool is too big and powerful to use effectively. Similarly, the Fed changes reserve requirements rather infrequently for the same reason, and when it does make changes, it is by very small amounts. For example, between 1970 and 1980, the Fed changed the reserve requirement twice, and less than 1 percent on each occasion.

THE DISCOUNT RATE

Banks having trouble meeting their reserve requirement can borrow funds directly from the Fed. The interest rate the Fed charges on these borrowed reserves is called the **discount rate.** If the Fed raises the discount rate, it makes it more costly for banks to borrow funds from it to meet their reserve requirements. The higher the interest rate banks have to pay on the borrowed funds, the lower the potential profits from any new loans made from borrowed reserves, and fewer new loans will be made and less money created. If the Fed wants to contract the money stock, it will raise the discount rate, making it more costly for banks to borrow reserves. If the Fed is promoting an expansion of money and credit, it will lower the discount rate, making it cheaper for banks to borrow reserves.

discount rate
interest rate that the Fed charges commercial banks for the loans it extends to them

The discount rate changes fairly frequently, often several times a year. Sometimes the rate will be moved several times in the same direction within a single year, which has a substantial cumulative effect.

The Significance of the Discount Rate

The discount rate is a relatively unimportant tool, mainly because member banks do not rely heavily on the Fed for borrowed funds in any case. There seems to be some stigma among bankers about borrowing from the Fed; borrowing from the Fed is something most bankers believe should be reserved for real emergencies. When banks have short-term needs for cash to meet reserve requirements, they are more likely to take a very short-term (often overnight) loan from other banks in the **federal funds market.** For that reason, many people pay a lot of attention to the interest rate on federal funds.

federal funds market
market in which banks provide short-term loans to other banks that need cash to meet reserve requirements

The discount rate's main significance is that changes in the rate are commonly viewed as a signal of the Fed's intentions with respect to monetary policy. Unlike open market operations, which are carried out in private, with the operations being announced in the minutes of the FOMC published only several weeks after the decisions have been made, discount rate changes are widely publicized.

HOW THE FED REDUCES THE MONEY SUPPLY

The Fed can do three things to reduce the money supply or reduce the rate of growth in the money supply: (1) sell bonds ("buy" money from the economy), (2) raise reserve requirements, or (3) raise the discount rate. Of course, the Fed could also opt to use some combination of these three tools in its approach.

These moves would tend to decrease aggregate demand, reducing nominal GDP, hopefully through a decrease in *P* rather than *Q*. These actions would be the monetary policy equivalent of a fiscal policy of raising taxes, lowering transfer payments, and/or lowering government purchases.

HOW THE FED INCREASES THE MONEY SUPPLY

If the Fed is concerned about underutilization of resources (e.g., unemployment), it would engage in precisely the opposite policies: (1) buy bonds, (2) lower reserve requirements, or (3) lower the discount rate. The Fed could also use some combination of these three approaches.

These moves would tend to increase aggregate demand, increasing nominal GDP, hopefully through an increase in *Q* (in the context of the equation of exchange) rather than *P*. Equivalent expansionary fiscal policy actions would be to reduce taxes, increase transfer payments, and/or increase government purchases.

HOW ELSE CAN THE FED INFLUENCE ECONOMIC ACTIVITY?

moral suasion
the Fed uses its influence to persuade banks to follow a particular course of action

The Fed's control of the money supply is largely exercised through the three methods outlined above, but it can influence the level and direction of economic activity in numerous less important ways as well. First, the Fed can attempt to influence banks to follow a particular course of action by the use of **moral suasion.** For example, if the Fed thinks the money supply and credit are growing too fast, it might write a letter to bank presidents urging them to be more selective in making loans, and suggesting that good banking practices mandate that banks maintain some excess reserves. During business contractions, the Fed may urge bankers to lend more freely, hoping to promote an increase in the stock of money.

The Federal Reserve also has at its command some selective controls, meaning regulatory authority over specific types of economic activity. For example, the Federal Reserve Board of Governors establishes margin requirements for the purchase of common stock. This means that the Fed specifies the proportion of the purchase price of stock that a purchaser must pay in cash. By allowing the Fed to control limits on borrowing for stock purchases, Congress believes that the Fed can limit speculative market dealings in securities and reduce instability in securities markets. (Whether the margin requirement rule has in fact helped achieve such stability is open to question.)

In the last few decades or so, the Federal Reserve regulatory authority has been extended to new areas. Beginning in 1969, the Fed began enforcing provisions of the Truth in Lending Act, which requires lenders to state actual interest rate charges when making loans. Similarly, in the mid-1970s, the Fed assumed the authority of enforcing provisions of the Equal Lending Opportunity Act, designed to eliminate discrimination against loan applicants. Note that these are not monetary tools and do not have any significant effects on output.

Section Check

SECTION CHECK

1. The three major tools of the Fed are open market operations, changing reserve requirements, and changing the discount rate.
2. If the Fed wants to stimulate the economy (increase aggregate demand), it will increase the money supply by buying government bonds, lowering the reserve ratio, and/or lowering the discount rate.
3. If the Fed wants to restrain the economy (decrease aggregate demand), it will lower the money supply by selling bonds, increasing the reserve ratio, and/or raising the discount rate.
4. The Fed has some lesser tools that can influence specific sectors of the economy, such as the authority to establish and change margin requirements on the purchase of common stock (thus hopefully controlling excess speculation).

---

1. What three main tactics could the Fed use in pursuing a contractionary monetary policy?
2. What three main tactics could the Fed use in pursuing an expansionary monetary policy?
3. Would the money supply rise or fall if the Fed made an open market purchase of government bonds, *ceteris paribus?*
4. If the Fed raised the discount rate from 12 to 15 percent, what impact would that have on the money supply?
5. What is moral suasion, and why would the Fed use this tactic?

section 18.4

Money, Interest Rates, and Aggregate Demand

- What causes the demand for money to change?
- How do changes in income change the money market equilibrium?
- How does the Fed buying and selling bonds affect RGDP in the short run?
- What is the relationship between bond prices and the interest rate?
- Why does the Fed target the interest rate rather than the money supply?
- How are the real and nominal interest rate connected in the short run?

THE MONEY MARKET

The Federal Reserve's policies with respect to the money supply have a direct impact on short-run real interest rates, and accordingly, on the components of aggregate demand. The **money market** is the market where money demand and money supply determine the equilibrium *nominal* interest rate. When the Fed acts to change the money supply by changing one of its policy variables, it alters the money market equilibrium.

money market
market in which money demand and money supply determine the equilibrium interest rate

Money has several functions, but why would people hold money instead of other financial assets? That is, what is responsible for the demand for money? Transaction purposes, precautionary reasons, and asset purposes are at least three determinants of the demand for money.

Transaction Purposes

First, the primary reason that money is demanded is for transactions purposes—to facilitate exchange. The higher one's income, the more transactions a person will make (because consumption is income related), the greater will be GDP, and the greater the demand for money for transactions purposes, other things equal.

Precautionary Reasons

Second, people like to have money on hand for precautionary reasons. If unexpected medical or other expenses require an unusual outlay of cash, people like to be prepared. The extent to which people demand cash for precautionary reasons depends partly on an individual's income and partly on the opportunity cost of holding money, which is determined by market rates of interest. The higher market interest rates, the higher the opportunity cost of holding money, and people will hold less of their financial wealth as money.

Asset Purposes

Third, money has a trait (liquidity) that makes it a desirable asset. Other things equal, people prefer more-liquid assets to less-liquid assets. That is, they would like to easily convert some of their money into goods and services. For this reason, most people wish to have some of their portfolio in money form. At higher interest rates on other assets, the amount of money desired for this purpose will be smaller because the opportunity cost of holding money will have risen.

THE DEMAND FOR MONEY AND THE NOMINAL INTEREST RATE

The quantity of money demanded varies inversely with the nominal interest rate. When interest rates are higher, the opportunity cost—in terms of the interest income on alternative assets—of holding monetary assets is higher, and persons will want to hold less money. At the same time, the demand for money, particularly for transaction purposes, is highly dependent on income levels, because the transaction volume varies directly with income. And lastly, the demand for money depends on the price level. If the price level increases, buyers will need more money to purchase their goods and services. Or if the price level falls, buyers will need less money to purchase their goods and services.

The demand curve for money is presented in Exhibit 1. At lower interest rates, the quantity of money demanded is greater, a movement from A to B in Exhibit 1. An increase in income will lead to an increase in the demand for money, depicted by a rightward shift in the money demand curve, a movement from A to C in Exhibit 1.

section 18.4 Exhibit 1 — Money Demand, Interest Rates, and Income

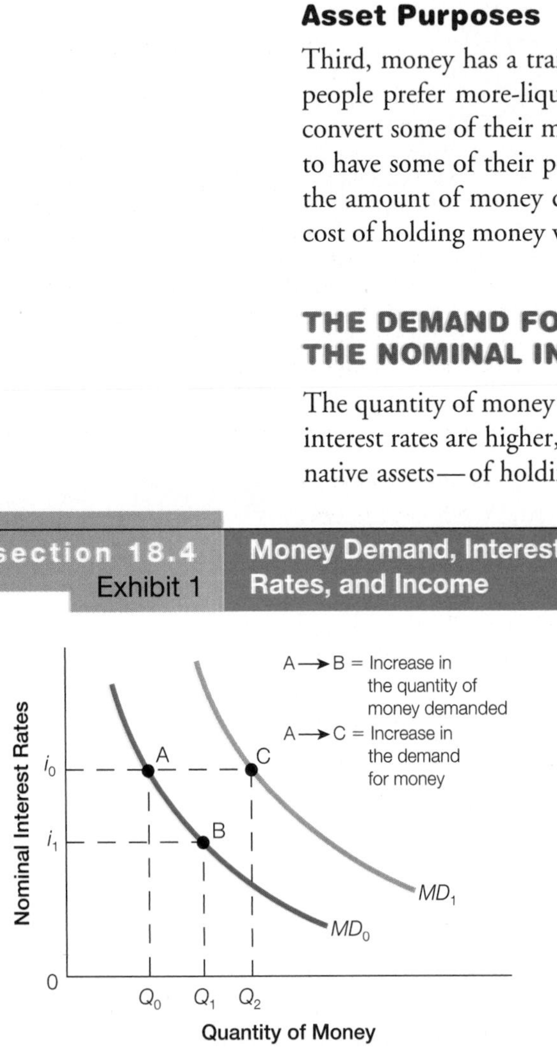

A→B = Increase in the quantity of money demanded
A→C = Increase in the demand for money

Nominal Interest Rates (i_0, i_1); Quantity of Money (Q_0, Q_1, Q_2); MD_0, MD_1

An increase in the level of income will increase the amount of money that people want to hold for transactions purposes at any given interest rate; therefore it shifts the demand for money to the right, from MD_0 to MD_1. The demand for money curve is downward sloping because at the lower nominal interest rate, the opportunity cost of holding money is lower.

WHY IS THE SUPPLY OF MONEY RELATIVELY INELASTIC?

The supply of money is largely governed by the regulatory policies of the central bank. Whether interest rates are 4 percent or 14 percent, banks seeking to maximize profits will increase lending as long as they have reserves above their desired level. Even a 4 percent return on loans provides more profit than maintaining those assets in non-interest-bearing cash or reserve accounts at the Fed. Given this fact, the money supply is effectively almost perfectly inelastic with respect to interest rates over their plausible range. Therefore, we draw the money supply curve as vertical, other things equal, in Exhibit 2, with changes in Federal Reserve policies acting to shift the money supply curve.

section 18.4 Exhibit 2 — Changes in the Money Market Equilibrium

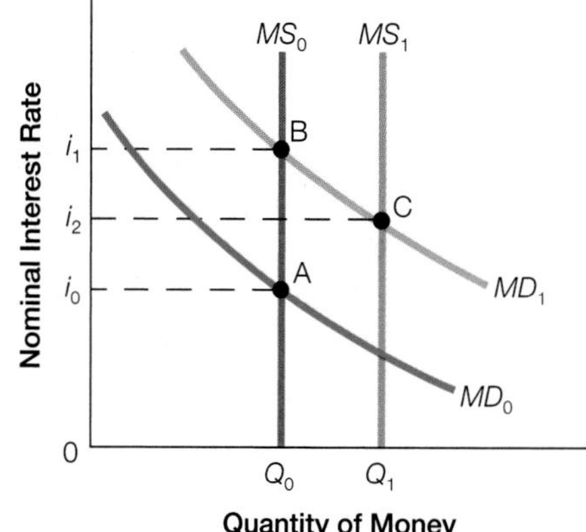

Combining the money demand and money supply curves, money market equilibrium occurs at that nominal interest rate where the quantity of money demanded equals the quantity of money supplied, initially at point A and interest rate i_0. An increase in income will shift the money demand curve to the right, from MD_0 to MD_1, raising the interest rate from i_0 to i_1 and resulting in a new equilibrium at point B. If the economy is presently at point B, an increase in the money supply resulting from expansionary monetary policies (e.g., the Fed buying bonds or lowering the discount rate or required reserves) will shift the money supply curve to the right (from MS_0 to MS_1), lowering the nominal interest rate from (from i_1 to i_2) and shifting the equilibrium to point C.

CHANGES IN MONEY DEMAND AND MONEY SUPPLY AND THE NOMINAL INTEREST RATE

Equilibrium in the money market is found by combining the money demand and money supply curve in Exhibit 2. Money market equilibrium occurs at that *nominal* interest rate, where the quantity of money demanded equals the quantity of money supplied. Initially, the money market is in equilibrium, at i_0, point A in Exhibit 2.

For example, rising national income increases the demand for money, shifting the money demand curve to the right from MD_0 to MD_1, and leading to a new higher equilibrium interest rate. If the economy is now at point B, an increase in the money supply (e.g., the Fed buys bonds) will shift the money supply curve to the right from MS_0 to MS_1, lowering the nominal rate of interest from i_1 to i_2, and shifting the equilibrium to point C.

THE FED BUYS BONDS

Suppose the economy is headed for a recession and the Fed wants to pursue an expansionary monetary policy to increase aggregate demand. It will buy bonds on the open market. The Fed increases the demand for bonds shifting the demand curve for bonds to the right and the price of bonds rises in the bond market as seen in Exhibit 3 (a). When the Fed buys bonds, bond sellers will likely deposit their check from the Fed in their bank and the money supply increases. The immediate impact of expansionary monetary policy is to decrease the interest rates, as seen in Exhibit 3(b). The lower interest rate, or the fall in the cost of borrowing money, then leads to an increase in aggregate demand for goods and services at the current price level. The lower interest rate will increase home sales, car sales, business investments, and so on. That is, when the Fed buys bonds, there is an increase in the demand for bonds and the price of bonds rises. The increase in the money supply will lead to lower interest rates and an increase in aggregate demand, as seen in Exhibit 3(c).

THE FED SELLS BONDS

Now suppose the Fed wants to contain an overheated economy—that is, pursue a contractionary monetary policy to reduce aggregate demand. It will sell bonds on the open market. The Fed increases the supply of bonds and the price of bonds falls in the bond market. This is seen in Exhibit 4(a). As we just learned, when the Fed sells bonds to the private sector, the bond purchaser takes the money out of his checking account to pay for the bond and that bank's reserves are reduced by the size of the check. This reduction in reserves leads to a reduction in the money supply or a leftward shift, as seen in the money

section 18.4 Exhibit 3 — The Fed Buys Bonds, Increases the Money Supply

a. Bond Market

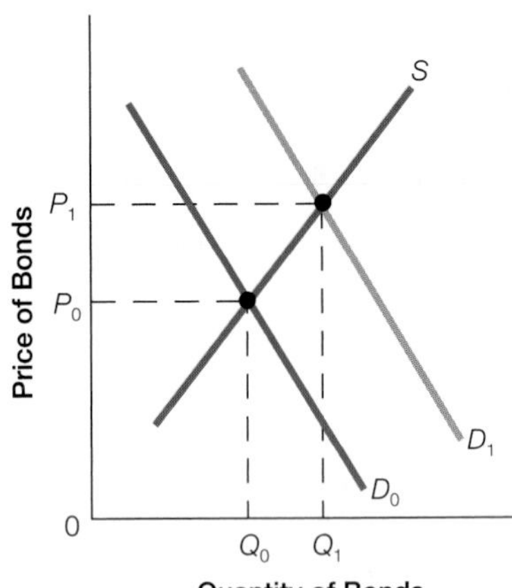

b. Money Market

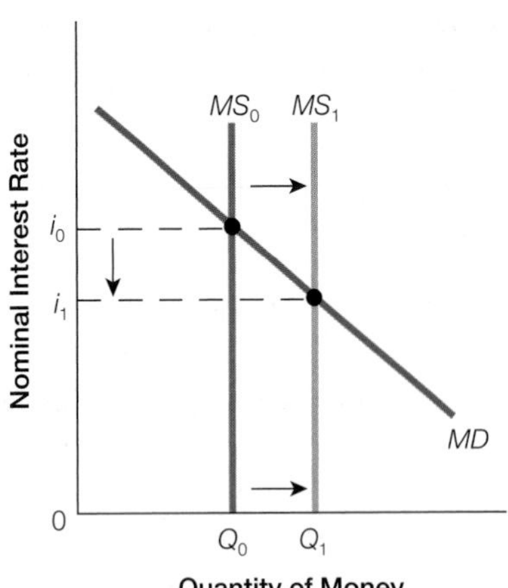

c. *AD/AS* Model

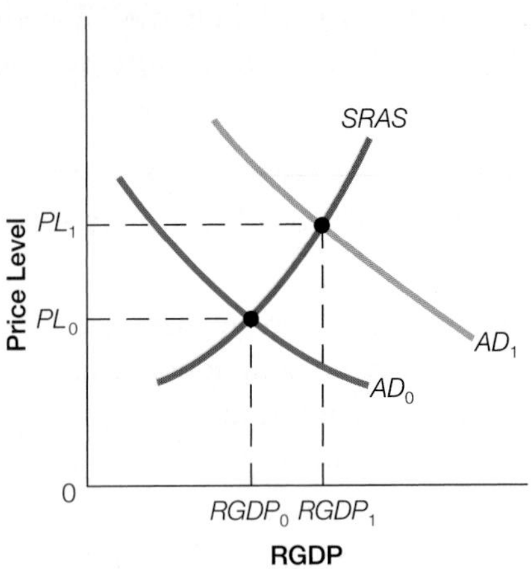

If the Fed is pursuing an expansionary monetary policy (increasing the money supply), it will increase the demand for bonds, shifting the demand curve for bonds to the right, and the price of bonds rises in the bond market as seen in Exhibit 3(a). When the Fed buys bonds, bond sellers will likely deposit their check from the Fed in their bank and the money supply increases. This will lower the interest rates, as seen in Exhibit 3(b). At lower interest rates, households and businesses will invest more and buy more goods and services, shifting the aggregate demand curve to the right, as seen in Exhibit 3(c).

section 18.4 Exhibit 4 — The Fed Sells Bonds, Decreases the Money Supply

a. Bond Market

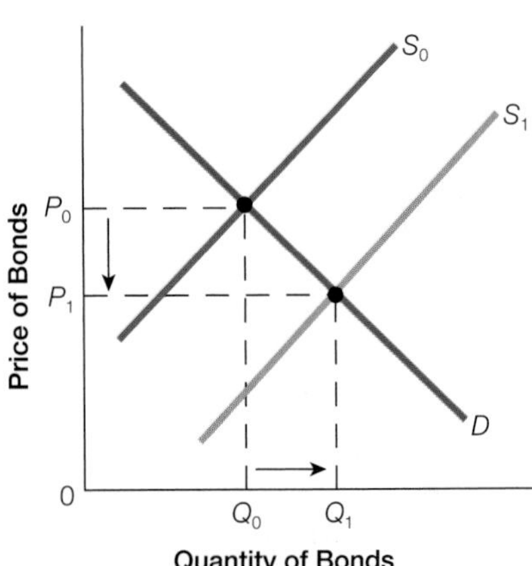

b. Money Market

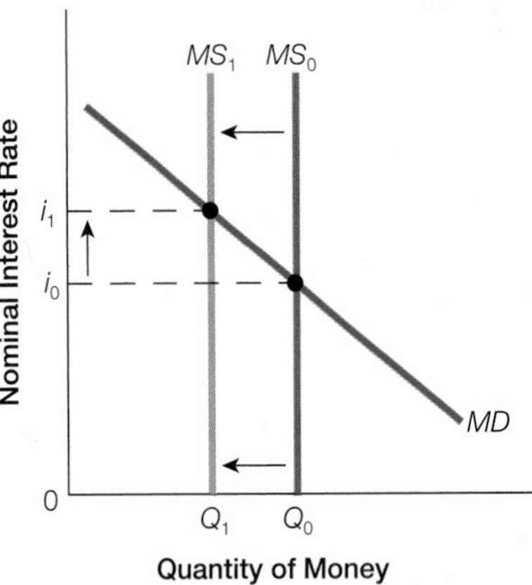

c. *AD/AS* Model

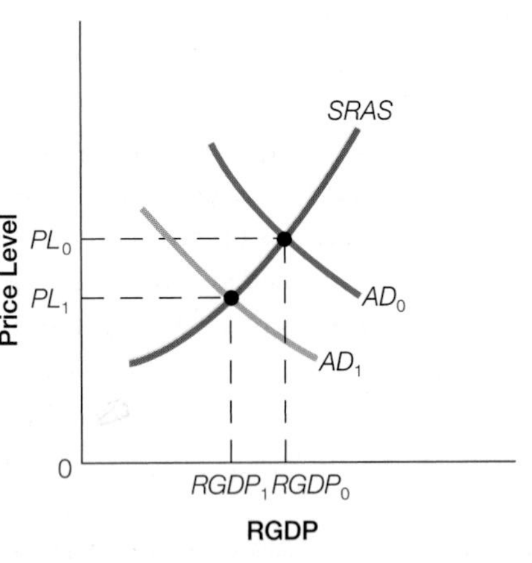

If the Fed is pursuing a contractionary monetary policy the Fed increases the supply of bonds and the price of bonds falls in the bond market. This is seen in Exhibit 4(a). When the Fed sells bonds to the private sector, the bond purchasers take the money out of their checking accounts to pay for the bonds and those banks' reserves are reduced by the size of the check. This reduction in reserves leads to a reduction in the money supply or a leftward shift, as seen in the money market in Exhibit 4(b). The reduction of the money supply leads to an increase in the interest rate in the money market. The higher interest rate, or the rise in the cost of borrowing money, then leads to a reduction in aggregate demand for goods and services, as seen in Exhibit 4(c).

market in Exhibit 4(b). The reduction of the money supply leads to an increase in the interest rate in the money market. The higher interest rate, or the rise in the cost of borrowing money, then leads to a reduction in aggregate demand for goods and services, as seen in Exhibit 4(c). That is, the higher interest rate will lead to a decrease in home sales, car sales, business investments, and so on. In sum, when the Fed sells bonds, there is an increase in the supply of bonds, and bond prices fall. When bonds are bought at the new lower price, there is a reduction in the money supply, which leads to a higher interest rate and a reduction in aggregate demand, at least in the short run.

BOND PRICES AND INTEREST RATES

Notice the relationship between the interest rate and bond prices. When the Fed sells bonds—increases the supply of bonds—bond prices fall. However, when the Fed sells bonds, the money supply is reduced, because bond buyers write checks against their banks; the reduction in the supply of money leads to higher interest rates. That is, there is an inverse correlation between the interest rate and the price of bonds. When the price of bonds rises, the interest rate falls.

This relationship also holds when the Fed buys bonds on the open market. When the Fed buys bonds, this leads to an increase in demand for bonds and bond prices rise. However, when the Fed buys bonds, bond sellers put their checks in their banks; this increases the money supply and lowers the interest rate. When the price of bonds falls, the interest rate rises.

DOES THE FED TARGET THE MONEY SUPPLY OR THE INTEREST RATE?

Some economists believe the Fed should try to control the money supply. Other economists believe the Fed should try to control the interest rate. Unfortunately, the Fed cannot do both—it must pick one or the other.

The economy is initially at point A in Exhibit 5, where the interest rate is i_0 and the quantity of money is at Q_0. Now suppose the demand for money were to increase because of an increase in national income, or an increase in the price level, or overall, people desire to hold more money. As a result, the demand curve for money would shift to the right from MD_0 to MD_1. If the Fed decides it does not want the money supply to increase, it can pursue a no monetary growth policy; this will lead to an increase in the interest rate to i_1 at point C in Exhibit 5. The Fed could also try to keep the interest rate stable at i_0, but it can only do so by increasing the growth in the money supply through expansionary monetary policy. Since the Fed cannot simultaneously pursue a no monetary growth policy and expansionary monetary policy it must choose—a higher interest rate or a greater money supply or some combination. The Fed cannot completely control both the growth in the money supply and the interest rate. If it attempts to keep the interest rate steady in the face of increased money demand, it must increase the growth in the money supply. And if it tries to keep the growth of the money supply in check in the face of increased money demand, the interest rates will rise.

section 18.4 Exhibit 5 — Fed Targeting: Money Supply versus the Interest Rate

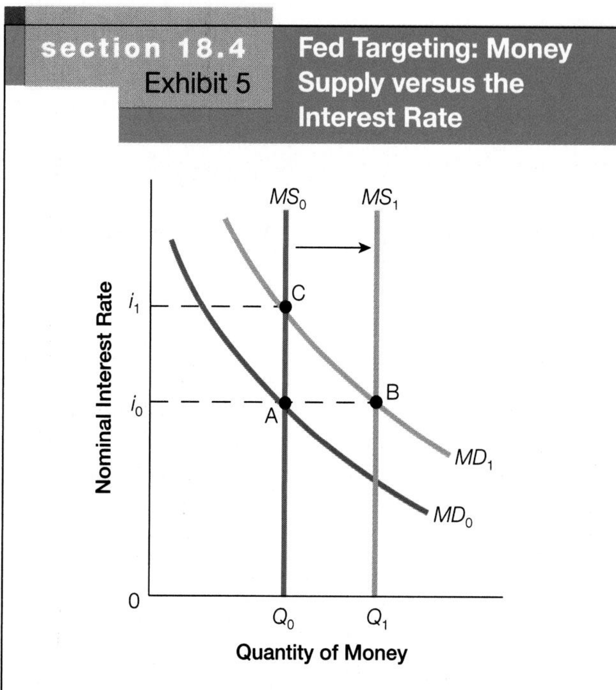

When the demand curve for money shifts out the Fed must either settle for a higher interest rate, a greater money supply, or both. The Fed cannot completely control the growth in the money supply and the interest rate. If it attempts to keep the interest rate steady, it must increase the growth in the money supply. And if it tries to keep the growth of the money supply in check, the interest rate will rise.

The Problem

The problem with targeting the money supply is that the demand for money fluctuates considerably in the short run. Focusing on the growth in the money supply when the demand for money is changing unpredictably will lead to large fluctuations in the interest rate like in the U.S. economy during the late 1970s and early 1980s. These erratic changes in the interest rate could seriously disrupt the investment climate.

Keeping interest rates in check would also create problems. For example, when the economy grows, the demand for money also grows, so the Fed would have to increase the money supply to keep interest rates from rising. And if the economy were in a recession, the Fed would have to contract the money supply to keep the money supply from falling. This would lead to the wrong policy prescription—expanding the money supply during a boom would eventually lead to inflation and contracting the money supply during a recession would make the recession even worse.

WHICH INTEREST RATE DOES THE FED TARGET?

The Fed targets the federal funds rate. Remember, the federal funds rate is the interest rate that banks charge each other for short-term loans. A bank that may be short of reserves might borrow from another bank that has excess reserves. The Fed has been targeting the federal funds rate since about 1965. At the close of the meetings of the Federal Open Market Committee (FOMC), the Fed will usually announce whether the federal funds rate target will be increased, decreased, or left alone.

Monetary policy actions can be conveyed through either the money supply or the interest rate. That is, if the Fed wants to pursue a contractionary monetary policy (a reduction in aggregate demand) this can be thought of as a reduction in the money supply or a higher interest rate. And if the Fed wants to pursue an expansionary monetary policy (an increase in aggregate demand), this can be thought of as an increase in the money supply or a lower interest rate. So why is the interest rate used? First, many economists believe the primary effects of monetary policy are felt through the interest rate. Second, the money supply is difficult to accurately measure. Third, as we mentioned earlier, changes in the demand for money can complicate money supply targets. Lastly, people are more familiar with changes in the interest rates than changes in the money supply.

DOES THE FED INFLUENCE THE REAL INTEREST RATE IN THE SHORT RUN?

In chapter 14, we saw how the equilibrium real interest rate was found at the intersection of the investment demand curve and the saving supply curve in the saving and investment market. In this chapter, we have seen how the equilibrium nominal interest rate is found at the intersection of the demand for money and the supply of money in the money market. Both are important and the saving and investment market and money markets are interconnected.

Most economists believe that in the short run the Fed can control the nominal interest rate and the real interest rate. Recall that the *real interest rate is equal to the nominal interest rate minus the expected inflation rate.* So a change in the nominal interest rate tends to change the real interest rate by the same amount because the expected inflation rate is slow to change in the short run. That is, if the expected inflation rate does not change, there is a direct relationship between the nominal and real interest rate; a one percent reduction in the nominal interest rate will generally lead to a 1 percent reduction in the real interest rate in the short run. However, in the long run, over several years after the inflation rate has adjusted, the equilibrium real interest rate is found by the intersection of the saving supply and investment demand curve.

Section Check

1. The money market is the market where money demand and money supply determine the equilibrium interest rate.
2. Money demand has three possible motives: transaction purposes, precautionary reasons, and asset purposes.
3. The quantity of money demanded varies inversely with interest rates (a movement along the money demand curve) and directly with income (a shift of the money demand curve). Monetary policies that increase the supply of money will lower interest rates in the short run, other things equal.
4. Rising incomes increase the demand for money. This will lead to a new higher equilibrium interest rate, other things equal.
5. The supply of money is effectively almost perfectly inelastic with respect to interest rates over their plausible range, as controlled by Federal Reserve policies.
6. Money market equilibrium occurs at the intersection of the money demand and money supply curves. At the equilibrium nominal interest rate, the quantity of money demanded equals the quantity of money supplied.
7. When the Fed sells bonds to the private sector, bond purchasers take the money out of their checking accounts to pay for the bonds and those banks' reserves are reduced by the size of the check. This reduction in bank reserves leads to a reduction in the money supply, which in turn leads to a higher interest rate and a reduction in aggregate demand, at least in the short run.
8. When the Fed buys bonds, bond sellers will likely deposit their check from the Fed in their bank and the money supply increases. The increase in the money supply will lead to lower interest rates and an increase in aggregate demand.
9. There is an inverse relationship between the interest rate and the price of bonds. When the price of bonds rise (falls) the interest rate falls (rises).
10. A change in the nominal interest rate tends to change the real interest rate by the same amount in the short run.
11. The Fed signals its intended monetary policy through the federal funds rate target it sets.

---

1. What are the determinants of the demand for money?
2. If the earnings available on other financial assets rose, would you want to hold more or less money? Why?
3. For the economy as a whole, why would individuals want to hold more money as GDP rises?
4. Why might people who expect a major market "correction" (a fall in the value of stock holdings) wish to increase their holdings of money?
5. How is the money market equilibrium determined?
6. Who controls the supply of money in the money market?
7. How does an increase in income or a decrease in the interest rate affect the demand for money?
8. What Federal Reserve policies would shift the money supply curve to the left?
9. Will an increase in the money supply increase or decrease the short-run equilibrium real interest rate, other things equal?
10. Will an increase in national income increase or decrease the short-run equilibrium real interest rate, other things equal?
11. What is the relationship between interest rates and aggregate demand in monetary policy?
12. When the Fed sells bonds, what happens to the price of bonds and interest rates?
13. When the Fed buys bonds, what happens to the price of bonds and interest rates?
14. Why is there an inverse relationship between bond prices and interest rates?

section 18.5

Expansionary and Contractionary Monetary Policy

- What is expansionary monetary policy?
- What is contractionary monetary policy?

EXPANSIONARY MONETARY POLICY AT LESS THAN FULL EMPLOYMENT

An increase in aggregate demand through monetary policy can lead to an increase in real GDP if the economy is currently operating at less than full employment, the output level to the left of $RGDP_{NR}$ in Exhibit 1. The initial equilibrium is E_0, the point at which AD_1 intersects the short-run aggregate supply curve. At this point, output is equal to $RGDP_0$ and the price level is PL_0. If the Fed engages in an expansionary monetary policy, it can shift the aggregate demand curve from AD_0 to AD_1, expanding output to $RGDP_{NR}$, and increasing the price level to PL_1.

For example, in the first half of 2001, the Fed slashed interest rates to their lowest levels since August 1994. Between January 2001 and August 2001, the Fed cut the federal funds rate target 11 times, clearly demonstrating that it was concerned that the economy was contracting. The economy officially fell into recession in March 2001. The Fed's actions were aimed at increasing consumer confidence, restoring stock market wealth, and stimulating investment in the midst of a downturn that was worsened by the September 11 attacks. That is, the Fed's move was designed to increase aggregate demand in an effort to increase output and employment to long-run equilibrium at E_1. The Fed's move coupled with the tax cut helped the economy weather a series of shocks. The longest expansion in U.S. history was followed by one of the shortest and shallowest recessions.

section 18.5 Exhibit 1 — Expansionary Monetary Policy at Less than Full Employment

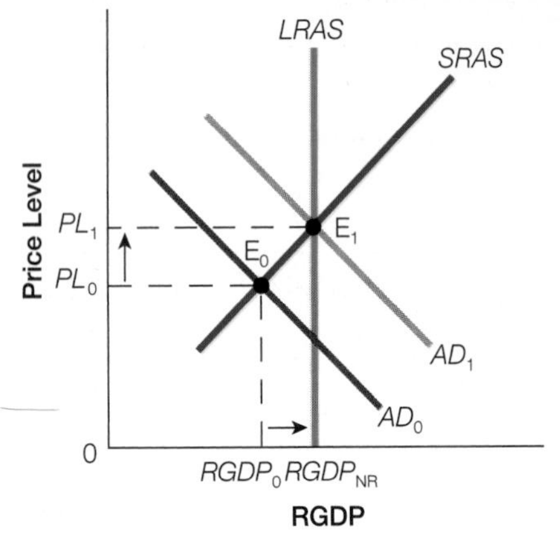

Expansionary monetary policy can shift the aggregate demand curve to the right, from AD_0 to AD_1, causing an increase in output and in the price level.

EXPANSIONARY MONETARY POLICY AT FULL EMPLOYMENT

Suppose that the Fed increases the money supply via open market operations. As a result, the money supply increases. This increase in the money supply will increase aggregate demand, shifting it from AD_0 to AD_1 as shown in Exhibit 2. However, if the economy is initially at full employment, $RGDP_{NR}$, the increase in aggregate demand moves the economy to a temporary short-run equilibrium at E_1, where the price level is PL_1 and real output is $RGDP_1$. This equilibrium at $E_1$is *not* sustainable, because the economy is beyond full capacity. This puts pressure on input markets, sending wages and other input prices higher. The higher input costs shift the short-run aggregate supply curve leftward, from $SRAS_0$ to $SRAS_1$. As a result of this shift in aggregate supply, a new equilibrium, E_2, is reached. Because this new equilibrium is on the long-run aggregate supply curve, it is a sustainable long-run equilibrium. So we see that real output returns to the full employment output level, but at a higher price level, PL_2 rather than PL_0.

section 18.5 Exhibit 2 — Expansionary Monetary Policy at Full Employment

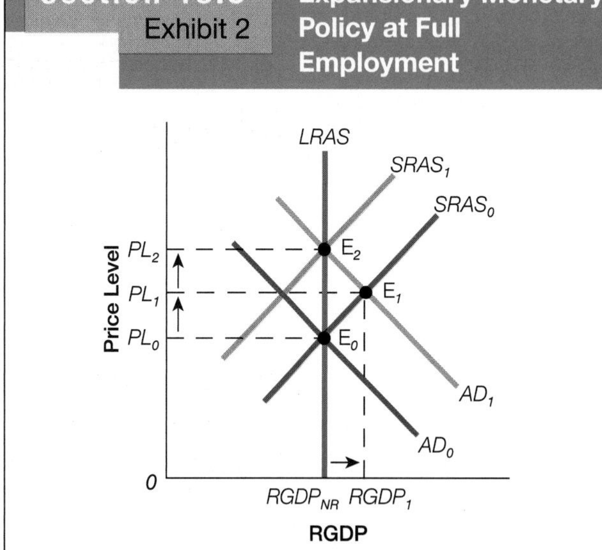

Expansionary monetary policy shifts the aggregate demand curve from AD_0 to AD_1. At the short-run equilibrium, E_1, the economy is operating beyond full capacity, which puts pressure on input markets. The higher cost in input markets causes the short-run aggregate supply curve to shift from $SRAS_0$ to $SRAS_1$. The resulting new long-run equilibrium, E_2, is at a higher price level, PL_2.

CONTRACTIONARY MONETARY POLICY BEYOND FULL EMPLOYMENT

A contractionary monetary policy (say the Fed is selling bonds) would reduce aggregate demand, shifting it from AD_0 to AD_1 in Exhibit 3. If the initial short-run equilibrium is at E_0, where the economy is temporarily beyond full employment at $RGDP_0$, an appropriate countercyclical monetary policy would shift the aggregate demand curve leftward to AD_1. At the new short-run and long-run equilibrium, E_1, monetary policy has successfully combated a potential inflationary boom.

section 18.5 Exhibit 3 — Contractionary Monetary Policy beyond Full Employment

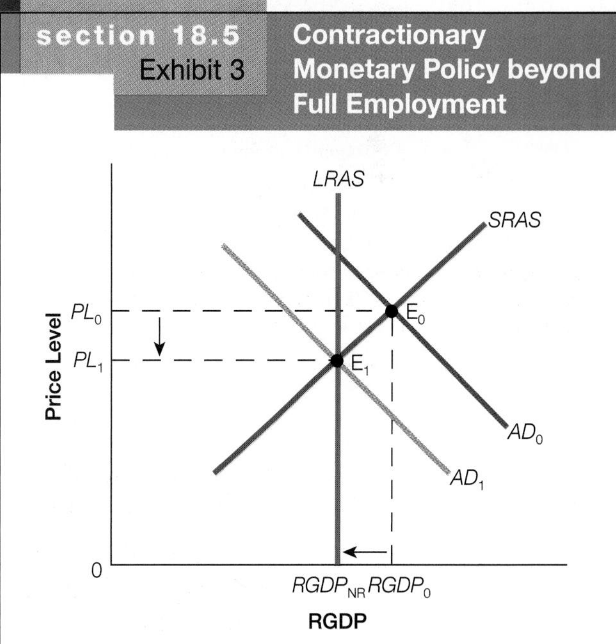

If the appropriate contractionary monetary policy is used during an overheated economy, the policy would prevent an inflationary boom.

CONTRACTIONARY MONETARY POLICY AT FULL EMPLOYMENT

If the Fed pursues a contractionary monetary policy when the economy is at full employment, the Fed's policy could cause a recession. In Exhibit 4, we start at E_0, where the economy is at both the short-run and long-run equilibrium. The contractionary monetary policy will shift the aggregate demand curve leftward from AD_0 to AD_1. In the short run we can see this leads to a recession at E_1, where RGDP is $RGDP_1$ less than full employment at $RGDP_{NR}$, and the price level falls from PL_0 to PL_1. At a lower than expected price level, owners of inputs will revise their expectations downward, input prices will fall due to high unemployment of resources, causing a rightward shift in the *SRAS* curve from $SRAS_0$ to $SRAS_1$. This self-correcting process would lead to a new long-run equilibrium at E_2—pushing the economy back to $RGDP_{NR}$ at an even lower price level, PL_2.

MONETARY POLICY IN THE OPEN ECONOMY

For simplicity we have assumed that the global economy does not impact domestic monetary policy. This is incorrect. Suppose the Fed decides to pursue an expansionary policy by buying bonds on the open market. As we have

section 18.5 Exhibit 4 — Contractionary Monetary Policy at Full Employment

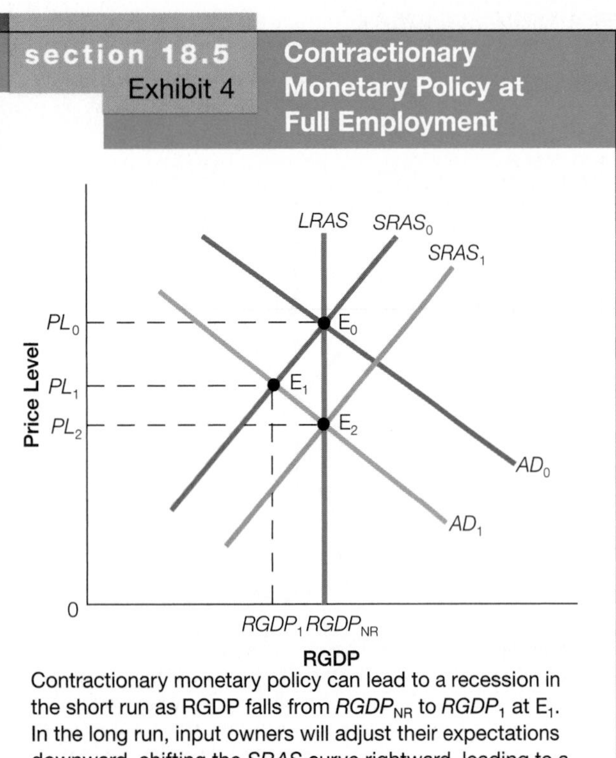

Contractionary monetary policy can lead to a recession in the short run as RGDP falls from $RGDP_{NR}$ to $RGDP_1$ at E_1. In the long run, input owners will adjust their expectations downward, shifting the *SRAS* curve rightward, leading to a new long-run equilibrium at E_2.

seen, if the Fed buys bonds on the open market, the immediate effect is that the money supply will increase and the interest rate will fall. As some domestic investors seek to invest funds in foreign markets, they will exchange dollars for foreign currency leading to a depreciation of the dollar (a decrease in the value of the dollar). The depreciation of the dollar makes the U.S. market more attractive to foreign buyers and foreign markets relatively less attractive to domestic buyers. That is, there is an increase in net exports—fewer imports and greater exports—and an increase in RGDP in the short run.

Similarly, if the Fed reduces the money supply and causes the interest rates to rise, foreign investors will convert their currencies to dollars to take advantage of the relatively higher interest rates. This will lead to an appreciation of the dollar (an increase in the value of a currency). The appreciation of the dollar will make U.S. goods and services relatively more expensive—foreigners will import less and domestic consumers will buy more exports. This leads to a decrease in net exports and a reduction in RGDP in the short run.

APPLICATION

MONEY AND THE *AD/AS* MODEL

Q: During the Great Depression in the United States, the price level fell, real GDP fell, and unemployment reached 25 percent. Investment fell, and as banks failed, the money supply fell dramatically. Can you show the effect of these changes from a vibrant 1929 economy to a battered 1932 economy using the *AD/AS* model?

A: The 1929 economy was at PL_{1929} and $RGDP_{1929}$ in Exhibit 5. The lack of consumer confidence coupled with the large reduction in the money supply and falling investment sent the aggregate demand curve reeling. As a result, the aggregate demand curve fell from AD_{1929} to AD_{1932}, real GDP fell to $RGDP_{1932}$, and the price level fell to PL_{1932}—deflation.

section 18.5 Exhibit 5

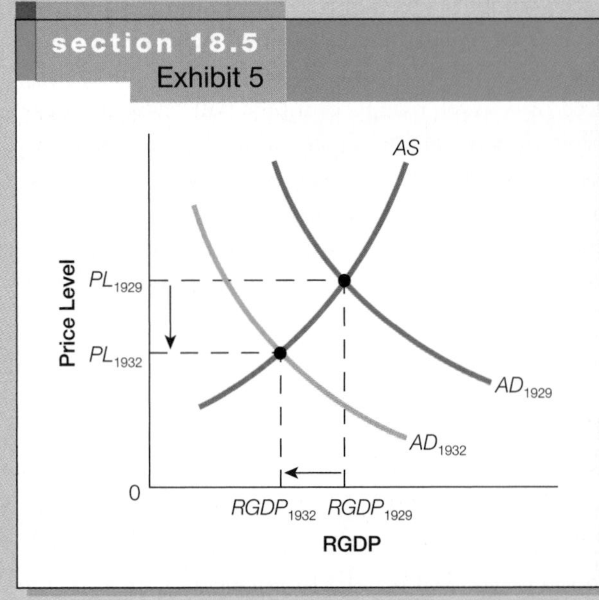

Section Check

1. An expansionary monetary policy at less than full employment can cause an increase in real GDP and price level.
2. An expansionary monetary policy at full employment can temporarily increase real GDP, but in the long run, only the price level will rise.

---

1. How will an expansionary monetary policy impact real GDP and the price level at less than full employment?
2. How will an expansionary monetary policy impact real GDP and the price level at full employment?
3. How will a contractionary monetary policy beyond full employment impact real GDP and the price level?
4. How will a contractionary monetary policy at full employment impact real GDP and the price level?

section 18.6

Problems in Implementing Monetary and Fiscal Policy

- What problems exist in implementing monetary policy?
- What problems exist in coordinating monetary and fiscal policies?

PROBLEMS IN CONDUCTING MONETARY POLICY

The lag problem inherent in adopting fiscal policy changes is much less acute for monetary policy, largely because the decisions are not slowed by the same budgetary process. The FOMC of the Federal Reserve, for example, can act quickly (in emergencies, almost instantly, by conference call) and even secretly to buy or sell government bonds, the key day-to-day operating tool of monetary policy. However, the length and variability of the impact lag before its effects on output and employment are felt are still significant and the time before the full price level effects are felt is even longer and more variable. According to the Federal Reserve Bank of San Francisco, the major effects of a change in policy on growth in the overall production of goods and services usually are felt within three months to two years. And the effects on inflation tend to involve even longer lags, perhaps one to three years or more.

HOW DO COMMERCIAL BANKS IMPLEMENT THE FED'S MONETARY POLICIES?

One limitation of monetary policy is that it ultimately must be carried out through the commercial banking system. The central bank (Federal Reserve System in the United States) can change the environment in which banks act, but the banks themselves must take the steps necessary to increase or decrease the money supply. Usually, when the Fed is trying to constrain monetary expansion, there is no difficulty in getting banks to make appropriate responses. Banks must meet their reserve requirements, and if the Fed raises bank reserve requirements, sells bonds, and/or raises the discount rate, banks must obtain the necessary cash or reserve deposits at the Fed to meet their reserve requirements. In response, banks will call in loans that are due for collection, sell secondary reserves, and so on, to obtain the necessary reserves, and in the process of collecting loans, they lower the money supply.

When the Federal Reserve wants to induce monetary expansion, however, it can provide banks with excess reserves (e.g., by lowering reserve requirements or buying government bonds), but it cannot force the banks to make loans, thereby creating new money. Ordinarily, of course, banks want to convert their excess reserves to interest-earning income by making loans. But in a deep recession or depression, banks might be hesitant to make enough loans to put all those reserves to work, fearing that they will not be repaid. Their pessimism might lead them to perceive that the risks of making loans to many normally credit-worthy borrowers outweigh any potential interest earnings (particularly at the low real interest rates that are characteristic of depressed times). Some have argued that banks maintaining excess reserves rather than loaning them out was, in fact, one of the monetary policy problems that arose in the Great Depression.

BANKS THAT ARE NOT PART OF THE FEDERAL RESERVE SYSTEM AND POLICY IMPLEMENTATION

A second problem with monetary policy relates to the fact that the Fed can control deposit expansion at member banks, but it has no control over global and nonbank institutions that also issue credit (loan money) but are not subject to reserve requirement limitations; examples are pension funds and insurance companies. Therefore, while the Fed may be able to predict the impact of its monetary policies on member bank loans, global and nonbanking institutions can alter the impact of monetary policies adopted by the Fed. Hence, there is a real question of how precisely the Fed can control the short-run real interest rates and the money supply through its monetary policy instruments.

FISCAL AND MONETARY COORDINATION PROBLEMS

Another possible problem that arises out of existing institutional policy making arrangements is the coordination of fiscal and monetary policy. Congress and the president make fiscal policy decisions, while monetary policy decision making is in the hands of the Federal Reserve System. A macroeconomic problem arises if the federal government's fiscal decision makers differ with the Fed's monetary decision makers on policy objectives or targets. For example, the Fed may be more concerned about keeping inflation low, while fiscal policy makers may be more concerned about keeping unemployment low.

ALLEVIATING COORDINATION PROBLEMS

In recognition of potential macroeconomic policy coordination problems, the Chairman of the Federal Reserve Board has participated for several years in meetings with top economic advisers of the president. An attempt is made in those meetings to reach a consensus on the appropriate policy responses, both monetary and fiscal. Still, there is often some disagreement, and the Fed occasionally works to partly offset or even neutralize the effects of fiscal policies that it views as inappropriate. Some people believe that monetary policy should be more directly controlled by the president and Congress, so that all macroeconomic policy will be determined more directly by the political process. Also, it is argued that such a move would enhance coordination considerably. Others, however, argue that it is dangerous to turn over control of the nation's money supply to politicians, rather than allowing decisions to be made by technically competent administrators who are focused more on price stability and more insulated from political pressures from the public and from special interest groups.

© EYEWIRE COLLECTION

Some economists believe that fine-tuning the economy is like driving a car with an unpredictable steering lag on a winding road.

OVERALL PROBLEMS WITH MONETARY AND FISCAL POLICY

Much of macroeconomic policy in this country is driven by the idea that the federal government can counteract economic fluctuations: stimulating the economy (with increased government purchases, tax cuts, transfer payment increases, and easy money) when it is weak, and restraining it when it is overheating. But policy makers must adopt the right policies in the right amounts at the right time for such "stabilization" to do more good than harm. And for this, government policy makers need far more accurate and timely information than experts can give them.

First, economists must know not only which way the economy is heading, but also how rapidly. And the unvarnished truth is that in our incredibly complicated world, no one knows exactly what the economy will do, no matter how sophisticated the econometric models used. It has often been said, and not completely in jest, that the purpose of economic forecasting is to make astrology look respectable.

But let's assume that economists can outperform astrologers at forecasting. Indeed, let's be completely unrealistic and assume that economists can provide completely accurate economic forecasts of what will happen if macroeconomic policies are unchanged. Even then, they could not be certain of how to best promote stable economic growth.

If economists knew, for example, that the economy was going to dip into another recession in six months, they would then need to know exactly how much each possible policy would spur activity in order to keep the economy stable. But such precision is unattainable, given the complex forecasting problems faced. Furthermore, despite assurances to the contrary, economists aren't always sure what effect a policy will have on the economy. Will an increase in government purchases quicken economic growth? It is widely assumed so. But how much? And increasing government purchases increases the budget deficit, which could send a frightening signal to the bond markets. The result can be to drive up interest rates and choke off economic activity. So even when policy makers know which direction to nudge the economy, they can't be sure which policy levers to pull, or how hard to pull them, to fine-tune the economy to stable economic growth.

But let's further assume that policy makers know when the economy will need a boost, and also which policy will provide the right boost. A third crucial consideration is how long it will take a policy before it has its effect on the economy. The trouble is that, even when increased government purchases or expansionary monetary policy does give the economy a boost, no one knows precisely how long it will take to do so. The boost may come very quickly, or many months (or even years) in the future, when it may add inflationary pressures to an economy that is already overheating, rather than helping the economy recover from a recession.

In this way, macroeconomic policy making is like driving down a twisting road in a car with an unpredictable lag and degree of response in the steering mechanism. If you turn the wheel to the right, the car will eventually veer to the right, but you don't know exactly when or how much. In short, there are severe practical difficulties in trying to fine-tune the economy. Even the best forecasting models and methods are far from perfect.

Economists are not exactly sure where the economy is or where or how fast it is going, making it very difficult to prescribe an effective policy. Even if we do know where the economy is headed, we cannot be sure how large a policy's effect will be or when it will take effect.

Unexpected Global and Technological Events

The Fed must take into account the influences of many different factors that can either offset or reinforce monetary policy. This isn't easy because sometimes these developments occur unexpectedly, and because the size and timing of their effects are difficult to estimate.

For example, during the 1997–1998 currency crisis in East Asia, economic activity in several countries in that region either slowed or declined. This led to a reduction in the aggregate demand for U.S. goods and services. In addition, the foreign exchange value of most of their currencies depreciated, and this made Asian-produced goods less expensive for us to buy and U.S.-produced goods more expensive in Asian countries. Both of these factors, considered by themselves, would reduce aggregate demand and lower output and employment. So the Fed must consider these global events in formulating their monetary policy.

Through the late 1990s, the U.S. economy has experienced a productivity surge through high-tech and other developments. This "new" economy may increase productivity growth allowing for greater economic growth without creating inflationary pressures. The Fed must estimate how much faster productivity is increasing and whether those increases are temporary or permanent. This is not an easy task.

Section Check

1. Monetary policy faces somewhat different implementation problems than fiscal policy. Both face difficult forecasting and lag problems. But the Fed can take action much more quickly. However, its effectiveness depends largely on the reaction of the private banking system to its policy changes, and those effects can be offset by global and nonbank financial institutions, over which the Fed lacks jurisdiction.
2. In the United States, monetary and fiscal policy are carried out by different decision makers, thus requiring cooperation and coordination for effective policy implementation.

---

1. Why is the lag time for adopting policy changes shorter for monetary policy than for fiscal policy?
2. Why would a banking system that wanted to keep some excess reserves rather than lending them all out hinder the Fed's ability to increase the money stock?
3. How can the activities of global and nonbank institutions weaken the Fed's influence on the money market?
4. If fiscal policy was expansionary, but the Fed wanted to counteract the fiscal policy effect on aggregate demand, what could it do?
5. What are the arguments for and against having monetary policy more directly controlled by the political process?
6. How is fine-tuning the economy like driving a car with an unpredictable steering lag on a winding road?

section 18.7

Rational Expectations

- What is the rational expectations theory?
- What do critics say about the rational expectations theory?

CAN HUMAN BEHAVIOR COUNTERACT GOVERNMENT POLICY?

Is it possible that people can anticipate the plans of policy makers and alter their behavior quickly to neutralize the intended impact of government action? For example, if workers see that the government is allowing the money supply to expand rapidly, they may quickly demand higher money wages in order to offset the anticipated inflation. In the extreme form, if people could instantly recognize and respond to government policy changes, it might be impossible to alter real output or unemployment levels through policy actions, because government policy makers could no longer surprise consumers and businesses. An increasing number of economists believe that there is at least some truth to this point of view. At a minimum, most economists accept the notion that real output and the unemployment rate cannot be altered with the ease that was earlier believed; some believe that the unemployment rate can seldom be influenced by fiscal and monetary policies.

THE RATIONAL EXPECTATIONS THEORY

The relatively new extension of economic theory that leads to this rather pessimistic conclusion regarding macroeconomic policy's ability to achieve our economic goals is called the **theory of rational expectations.** The notion that expectations or anticipations of future events are relevant to economic theory is not new; for decades, economists have incorporated expectations into models analyzing many forms of economic behavior. Only in the recent past, however, has a theory evolved that tries to incorporate expectations as a central factor in the analysis of the entire economy.

theory of rational expectations
belief that workers and consumers incorporate the likely consequences of government policy changes into their expectations by quickly adjusting wages and prices

The interest in rational expectations has grown rapidly in the last decade. Acknowledged pioneers in the development of the theory include Professor Robert Lucas of the University of Chicago and Professor Thomas Sargent of the University of Minnesota. In 1995, Professor Lucas won the Nobel Prize for his work in rational expectations.

Rational expectation economists believe that wages and prices are flexible, and that workers and consumers incorporate the likely consequences of government policy changes quickly into their expectations. In addition, rational expectation economists believe that the economy is inherently stable after macroeconomic shocks, and that tinkering with fiscal and monetary policy cannot have the desired effect unless consumers and workers are caught "off guard" (and catching them off guard gets harder the more you try to do it).

RATIONAL EXPECTATIONS AND THE CONSEQUENCES OF GOVERNMENT MACROECONOMIC POLICIES

Rational expectations theory, then, suggests that government economic policies designed to alter aggregate demand to meet macroeconomic goals are of very limited effectiveness. When policy targets become public, it is argued, people will alter their own behavior from what it would otherwise have been, in order to maximize their own utility, and in so doing, they largely negate the intended impact of policy changes. If government policy seems tilted towards permitting more inflation in order to try to reduce unemployment, people start spending their money faster than before, become more adamant in their wage and other input price demands, and so on. In the process of quickly altering their behavior to reflect the likely consequences of policy changes, they make it more difficult (costly) for government authorities to meet their macroeconomic objectives. Rather than fooling people into changing real wages, and therefore unemployment, with inflation "surprises," changes in inflation are quickly reflected into expectations with little or no effect on unemployment or real output even in the short run. As a consequence, policies intended to reduce unemployment through stimulating aggregate demand will often fail to have the intended effect. Fiscal and monetary policy, according to this view, will work only if the people are caught off guard or fooled by policies so that they do not modify their behavior in a way that reduces policy effectiveness.

ANTICIPATION OF AN EXPANSIONARY MONETARY POLICY

Consider the case in which there is an increase in aggregate demand as a result of an expansionary monetary policy. This increase is reflected in Exhibit 1 in the shift from AD_0 to AD_1. Anticipating the predictable inflationary consequences of that expansionary policy, the price level will immediately adjust to a new price level at PL_1. Consumers, producers, workers, and lenders who have anticipated the effects of the expansionary policy simply built the higher inflation rates into their product prices, wages, and interest rates. That is, consumers, producers, and workers realize that expansionary monetary policy can cause inflation if the economy is working close to capacity. Consequently, in an effort to protect themselves from the higher anticipated inflation, workers ask for higher wages, suppliers increase input prices, and producers raise their product prices. Because wages, prices, and interest rates are assumed to be flexible, the adjustments take place immediately. This increase in input costs for wages, interest, and raw materials causes the aggregate supply curve to shift up or leftward, shown as the movement from $SRAS_0$ to $SRAS_1$ in Exhibit 1. So the desired policy effect of greater real output and reduced unemployment from a shift in the aggregate demand curve is offset by an upward or leftward shift in the aggregate supply curve caused by an increase in input costs.

section 18.7 Exhibit 1 — Rational Expectations and the *AD/AS* Model

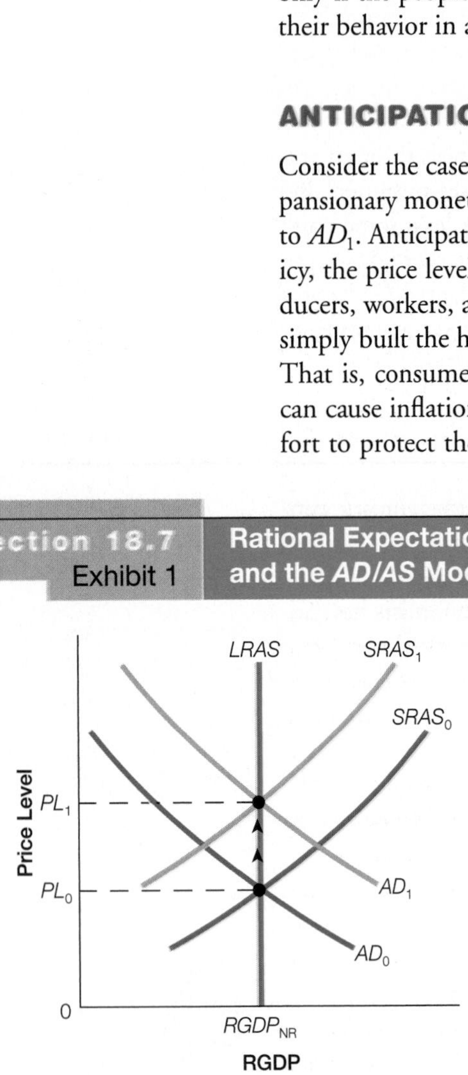

Expansionary monetary policy (or fiscal policy) will not affect RGDP if wages and prices are completely flexible as in the rational expectations model. This means that the *SRAS* curve will shift leftward from $SRAS_0$ to $SRAS_1$ at the same time as the *AD* curve. Therefore, an expansionary policy, an increase in *AD* from AD_0 to AD_1 will lead to a higher price level but no change in RGDP or unemployment.

UNANTICIPATED EXPANSIONARY POLICY

Again, consider the case in which there is an increase in aggregate demand as a result of an expansionary monetary policy. However, this time it is *unanticipated.* The increase in the money supply is reflected in Exhibit 2 in the shift from AD_0 to AD_1. This *unanticipated* change in monetary policy stimulates output and employment in the short run, as the equilibrium moves from point A to point B. At the new short-run equilibrium, the output is at $RGDP_1$ and the price level is at PL_1. This output is beyond $RGDP_{NR}$, so it is not sustainable in the long run. Because it is *unan-*

section 18.7 Exhibit 2 — **An Expansionary Policy That Is Unanticipated**

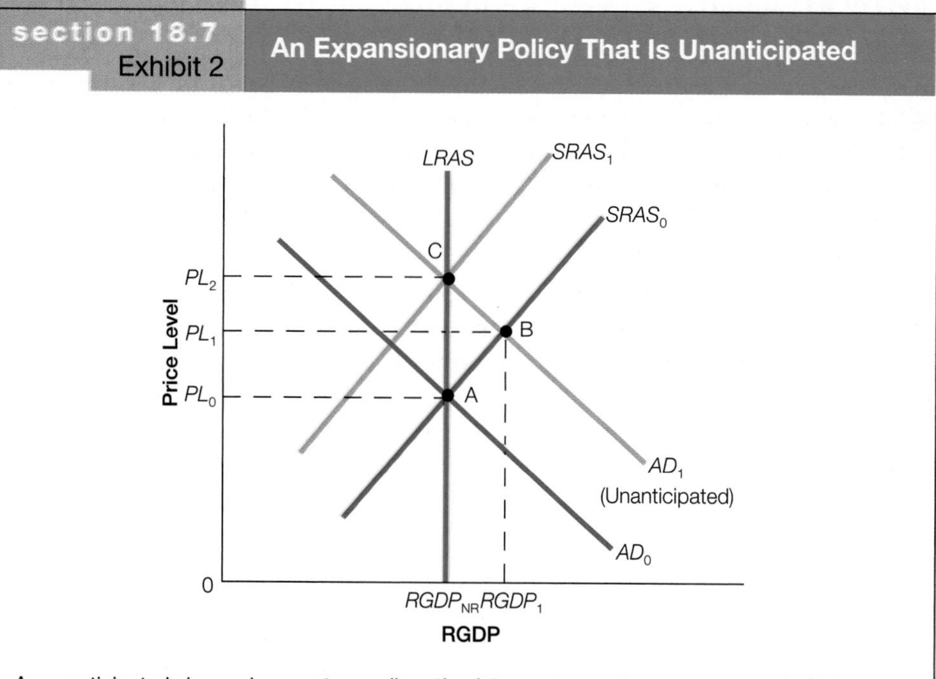

An unanticipated change in monetary policy stimulates output and employment in the short run, as the equilibrium moves from point A to point B. At the new short-run equilibrium, the output is at $RGDP_1$ and the price level is at PL_1. Because the expansionary policy is unanticipated, workers and other input owners are expecting the price level to remain at PL_0, rather than PL_1. When input owners eventually realize that the actual price level has changed, they will require higher input prices, shifting the *SRAS* from $SRAS_0$ to $SRAS_1$. At point C, we see that output has returned to $RGDP_{NR}$ but at a higher price level, PL_2. If the expansionary policy is unanticipated, it leads to a short-run expansion in output and employment. But in the long run, the only impact of the change in the expansionary policy is a higher price level.

ticipated, workers and other input owners are expecting price level to remain at PL_0, rather than PL_1. However, when input owners eventually realize that the actual price level has changed, they will require higher input prices, shifting the *SRAS* from $SRAS_0$ to $SRAS_1$. At point C, we see that output has returned to $RGDP_{NR}$ but at a higher price level, PL_2.

This means that when the expansionary policy is *unanticipated* it leads to a short-run expansion in output and employment. But in the long run, the only impact of the change in monetary policy is a higher price level—inflation. In short, when the change is correctly anticipated, there is no change in real output from an expansionary monetary (or fiscal) policy. However, if the expansionary monetary (fiscal) policy is *unanticipated* there is a short-run increase in RGDP and employment but in the long run, just a higher price level.

In fact, the only way that monetary or fiscal policy can change output in the rational expectations model is with a surprise—an *unanticipated* change. For example, on April 18, 2001, between regularly scheduled meetings of the Federal Open Market Committee, the Fed surprised financial markets with an aggressive half-point cut in the interest rate. The Fed was trying to boost consumer confidence and impact falling stock market wealth. The surprise interest rate cut sent the stock market soaring as the Dow posted its third largest single-day point gain and the Nasdaq had its fourth largest percentage gain. Fed Chairman Greenspan hoped that this would shift the *AD* curve rightward, leading to higher levels of output.

WHEN AN ANTICIPATED EXPANSIONARY POLICY CHANGE IS LESS THAN THE ACTUAL POLICY CHANGE

In the context of the rational expectations model (wages and prices are flexible), suppose people are expecting a large increase in the money supply as a result of expansionary monetary policy. This causes the *anticipated* price level to increase from PL_0 to PL_2 when the anticipated aggregate demand increases from AD_0 to AD_2, as seen in Exhibit 3. If people anticipate price level PL_2, wages and other input price adjust quickly, as the *SRAS* shifts leftward from $SRAS_0$ to $SRAS_1$. But what if the increase in the money supply ends up being less than people anticipated? Say the *actual* increase in the money supply only shifts *AD* from AD_0 to AD_1. That is, the economy moves from point A to point B rather than to point C as many had expected. This leads to a higher price level but a lower level of RGDP—a recession.

That is, a policy designed to increase output may actually reduce output if prices and wages are flexible and the expansionary effect is less than people anticipated.

CRITICS OF RATIONAL EXPECTATIONS THEORY

Of course, rational expectations theory does have its critics. Critics want to know if consumers and producers are completely informed about the impact that, say, an increase in money supply will have on the economy. In general, all citizens will not be completely informed, but key players like corporations, financial institutions, and labor organizations

section 18.7 Exhibit 3 **An Actual Expansionary Policy That Is Less Than the Anticipated Policy**

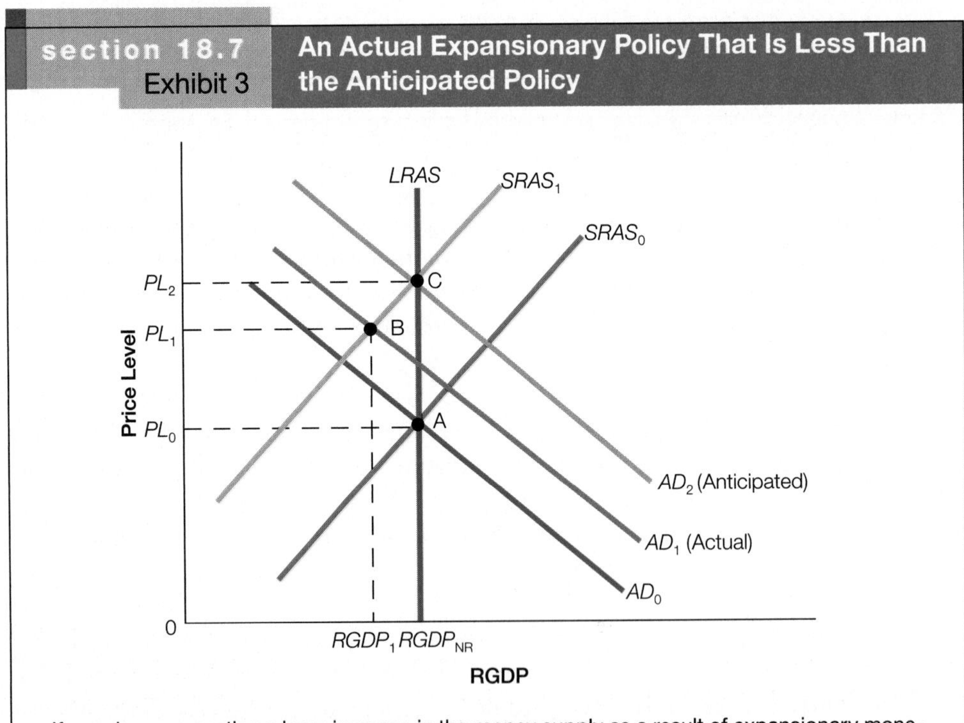

If people are expecting a large increase in the money supply as a result of expansionary monetary policy, the anticipated price level increases from PL_0 to PL_2 and the anticipated *AD* shifts from AD_0 to AD_2. Because wages and prices are completely flexible, the *SRAS* shifts leftward from $SRAS_0$ to $SRAS_1$ at the same time the *AD* curve shifts to the right. But if the actual increase in the money supply only shifts *AD* from AD_0 to AD_1, the economy moves from point A to point B rather than to point C. This leads to a higher price level but a lower level of RGDP—a recession, not the intended policy prescription.

may well be informed about the impact of these policy changes. But there are other problems, too. For example, are wages and other input prices really that flexible? That is, even if decision makers could anticipate the eventual effect of policy changes on prices, those prices may still be slow to adapt (e.g., what if you had just signed a three-year labor or supply contract when the new policy is implemented?).

Most economists reject the extreme rational expectations model of complete wage and price flexibility. In fact, most economists still believe there is a short-run trade-off between inflation and unemployment because some input prices are slow to adjust to changes in the price level. However, in the long run, the expected inflation rate adjusts to changes in the actual inflation rate at the natural rate of unemployment, $RGDP_{NR}$.

Section Check SECTION CHECK

1. Rational expectation economists believe that wages and prices are flexible and thus should be left alone. They also believe that workers and consumers form rational expectations that essentially negate the desired effect of a policy change.
2. Critics of rational expectations theory believe that most people are not truly informed about the effects of a policy change and therefore do not adjust their behavior. Additionally, they question whether prices and wages are really that flexible.

---

1. What is the rational expectations theory?
2. Why could an unexpected change in inflation change real wages and unemployment, while an expected change in inflation could not?
3. Why can the results of rational expectations be described as generating the long-run results of a policy change in the short run?
4. In a world of rational expectations, why is it harder to reduce unemployment below its natural rate but potentially easier to reduce inflation rates?
5. Even if people could quickly anticipate the consequences of government policy changes, how could long-term contracts (e.g., three-year labor agreements and 30-year fixed-rate mortgages) and the costs of changing price lists and catalogs result in unemployment still being affected by those policy changes?
6. Why do expected rainstorms have different effects on people than unexpected rainstorms?

Summary

Of the six major functions of a central bank, the most important is its role in regulating the money supply. There are 12 Federal Reserve banks in the Federal Reserve System. Although these banks are independent institutions, they act largely in unison on major policy decisions.

The Federal Reserve Board of Governors and the Federal Open Market Committee are the prime decision makers for U.S. monetary policy. The Fed is tied to the president in that he appoints the members of the Board of Governors to 14-year terms, with only one appointment made every two years. The president also selects the Chair of the Federal Reserve Board, who serves a four-year term. The only other government intervention in the Fed can come from legislation passed in Congress.

The equation of exchange is $M \times V = P \times Q$, where M is the money supply, V is the velocity of money, P is the average level of prices of final goods and services, and Q is the physical quantity of final goods and services produced in an economy in a given year.

The velocity of money (V) represents the average number of times that a dollar is used in purchasing final goods or services in a one-year period.

The equation of exchange is a useful tool when analyzing the effects of a change in the supply of money on the aggregate economy, provided that velocity is constant or at least predictable.

The three major tools of the Fed are open market operations, changing reserve requirements, and changing the discount rate. If the Fed wants to stimulate the economy, it will increase the money supply by buying government bonds, lowering the reserve ratio, and/or lowering the discount rate. If the Fed wants to restrain the economy, it will lower the money supply by selling bonds, increasing the reserve ratio, and/or raising the discount rate.

The Fed has some lesser tools that can influence specific sectors of the economy, such as the authority to establish and change margin requirements on the purchase of common stock (hopefully controlling excess speculation).

Monetary policy faces somewhat different implementation problems than fiscal policy. Both face difficult forecasting and lag problems. But the Fed can take action much more quickly. But its effectiveness depends largely on the reaction of the private banking system to its policy changes, and those effects can be offset by global and nonbank financial institutions, over which the Fed lacks jurisdiction.

In the United States, monetary and fiscal policy are carried out by different decision makers, thus requiring cooperation and coordination for effective policy implementation.

Rational expectation economists believe that wages and prices are flexible and thus should be left alone. They also believe that workers and consumers form rational expectations that essentially negate the desired effect of a policy change. Critics of rational expectations theory believe that most people are truly not informed about the effects of a policy change and therefore do not adjust their behavior. Additionally, they question whether prices and wages are really that flexible.

Key Terms and Concepts

equation of exchange 400
open market operations 403
discount rate 405
federal funds market 405
moral suasion 406
money market 407
theory of rational expectations 421

Review Questions

1. Which of the following are functions of the Federal Reserve Bank?
   - **a.** provide loans to developing economies
   - **b.** supervise member banking institutions
   - **c.** back the U.S. dollar with gold
   - **d.** provide a system for check clearing
   - **e.** regulate the money supply
   - **f.** loan money to member banks
   - **g.** act as the bank for the U.S. government
   - **h.** set interest rates on all government-issued bonds
2. Suppose that velocity and the money supply remain constant. If GDP grows at an annual rate of 5 percent, what can you predict will happen to the price level using the quantity equation of money? If GDP falls by 2 percent?
3. If the Federal Reserve Bank purchases $10 million worth of Treasury securities in the open market when the required reserve ratio is 5 percent, what is the potential change in the money supply? If the required reserve ratio is 25 percent?
4. If the Federal Reserve Bank sells a $10,000 bond to an investor, what is the potential change in the money supply?
5. The following table shows the balance sheet for the Bank of Arizona. If the required reserve ratio decreases from 10 percent to 5 percent, what happens to the "required reserves" and "excess reserves" on the bank's balance sheet? What is the potential change in the money supply?

Bank of Arizona Balance Sheet

Assets		Liabilities	
Reserves			
Required	$100,000	Demand Deposits	$1,000,000
Excess	$0	Equity Capital	$50,000
Loans	$700,000		
Securities	$250,000		

6. Answer Question 5 again for a situation where the Federal Reserve Bank increases the required reserve ratio from 10 percent to 12.5 percent. Where can the bank acquire the additional funds necessary to cover the required reserves?
7. What is the motive for holding money in each of the following cases (precautionary, transaction, or asset)?
   a. Concerned about the fluctuations of the stock market, you sell stock and keep cash in your brokerage account.
   b. You keep ten $20 bills in your earthquake preparedness kit.
   c. You go to New York City with a large sum of money in order to complete your holiday shopping.
   d. You keep $20 in your glove compartment just in case you run out of gas.
8. Money is said to be "neutral" in the long run. Using the aggregate demand–aggregate supply framework, explain why an increase in the money supply when an economy is operating at full employment affects only the price level in the long run.
9. What use of the monetary policy tools do you think would have been appropriate to help bring the U.S. economy out of the Great Depression? Explain.
10. Abraham Lincoln once said "You can fool all of the people some of the time, and some of the people all of the time, but you cannot fool all of the people all of the time." How can a central bank that conducts monetary policy "fool people" and thereby affect the level of unemployment in the economy? What happens if people begin to anticipate future monetary policy correctly based upon past experience?
11. Visit the Sexton Web site at **http://sexton.swcollege.com** and click on "Federal Open Market Committee." Read the statements and/or minutes from the last Open Market Committee meeting. What, in the Open Market Committee's view, is the current state of the macroeconomy and what course of action (if any) did the committee undertake?

Fill in the Blanks

1. In most countries, the job of manipulating the supply of money belongs to the ____________.

2. Effective control of major monetary policy decisions rests with the ____________ and the ____________ of the Federal Reserve System.

3. The Federal Reserve was created in 1913 because the U.S. banking system had little ____________ and no ____________ direction.

4. The ____________ consists of the seven members of the Board of Governors, the president of the New York Federal Reserve Bank, and four other presidents of Federal Reserve Banks, who serve on the committee on a rotating basis.

5. Perhaps the most important function of the Federal Reserve is its ability to regulate the ____________.

6. The quantity equation of money can be presented as: ____________ = ____________.

7. ____________ represents the average number of times that a dollar is used in purchasing final goods or services in a 1-year period.

8. If M increases, and V remains constant, then P must ____________, Q must ____________, or P and Q must each ____________.

9. Expanding the money supply, other things being equal, will have the same type of impact on aggregate demand as ____________ government purchases, ____________ taxes, or ____________ transfer payments.

10. Some economists, often called ____________, believe that monetary policy is the most powerful determinant of macroeconomic results.

11. Velocity is ____________ stable when measured using the M1 definition and over shorter periods of time.

12. An increase in the interest rates will cause people to hold ____________ money, which, in turn, means that the velocity of money ____________.

13. Higher rates of anticipated inflation would tend to ____________ velocity.

14. The inflation rate tends to rise ____________ in periods of rapid monetary expansion.

15. The Fed has three major methods that it can use to control the supply of money: It can engage in ____________ operations, change ____________ requirements, or change its ____________ rate.

16. ____________ are by far the most important device used by the Fed to influence the money supply.

17. Open market operations involve the purchase or sale of ____________ by ____________.

18. When the Fed buys government bonds in an open market operation, it ____________ the money supply.

19. The most a bank can lend out at a given time is equal to its ____________.

20. If the reserve requirement is 10 percent, a total of up to ____________ in new money is potentially created by the purchase of $100,000 of government bonds by the Fed.

21. When the Fed sells a bond, the reserves of the bank where the bond buyer keeps his bank account will ____________.

22. If the Fed ____________ reserve requirements, other things being equal, it will create excess reserves in the banking system.

23. An increase in the required reserve ratio would result in a ____________ in the money supply.

24. Small reserve requirement changes have a ____________ impact on the potential supply of money.

25. Banks having trouble meeting their reserve requirement can borrow reserves directly from the Fed at an interest rate called the ____________ rate.

26. If the Fed raises the discount rate, it makes it ____________ costly for banks to borrow funds from it to meet their reserve requirements, which will result in ____________ new loans being made and ____________ money created.

27. If the Fed wants to expand the money supply, it will ____________ the discount rate.

28. When banks have short-term needs for cash to meet reserve requirements, they are more likely to take a very short-term (often overnight) loan from other banks in the ____________ market than to borrow reserves directly from the Fed.

29. The Fed can do three things if it wants to reduce the money supply. It can ____________ government bonds, ____________ reserve requirements, or ____________ the discount rate.

30. An increase in the money supply would tend to ____________ nominal GDP.

31. People have three basic motives for holding money instead of other assets: for ____________ purposes, ____________ reasons, and ____________ purposes.

32. The quantity of money demanded varies ____________ with the rate of interest.

33. If the price level falls, buyers will need ____________ money to purchase their goods and services.

34. We draw the money supply curve as ____________, other things being equal, with changes in ____________ policies acting to shift the money supply curve.

35. Money market equilibrium occurs at that ____________ interest rate where the quantity of money demanded equals the quantity of money supplied.

36. Rising national income will shift the demand for money to the ____________, leading to a new ____________ equilibrium nominal interest rate.

37. An increase in the money supply will lead to ____________ interest rates and an ____________ in aggregate demand.

38. When the Fed sells bonds, it ____________ the price of bonds, ____________ interest rates, and ____________ aggregate demand in the short run.

39. If the demand for money increases, but the Fed doesn't allow the money supply to increase, interest rates will ____________, and aggregate demand will ____________.

40. When the economy grows, the Fed would have to ____________ the money supply to keep interest rates from rising.

41. The ____________ is the interest rate the Fed targets.

42. A contractionary policy can be thought of as a(n) ______________ in the money supply or a(n) ______________ in the interest rate.

43. The ______________ interest rate is determined by investment demand and saving supply; the ______________ interest rate is determined by the demand and supply of money.

44. The real interest rate is equal to ______________ minus ______________.

45. Countercyclical monetary policy would ______________ the supply of money to combat a potential inflationary boom.

46. The Fed selling bonds will lead to a(n) ______________ in the money supply, a(n) ______________ in interest rates, a(n) ______________ of the dollar, a(n) ______________ in net exports, and a(n) ______________ in RGDP in the short run.

47. The lag problem inherent in adopting fiscal policy changes is much ______________ acute for monetary policy.

48. According to the Federal Reserve Bank of San Francisco, the major effects of a change in policy on growth in the overall production of goods and services usually are felt within ______________ months to ______________ years, and the effects on inflation tend to involve even longer lags, perhaps ______________ to ______________ years or more.

49. In the process of calling in loans to obtain necessary banking reserves, banks ______________ the supply of money.

50. Ordinarily, banks want to convert excess reserves into interest-earning ______________, but in a deep recession or depression, banks might be hesitant to make enough loans to put all those reserves to work.

51. The Fed can control deposit expansion at ______________ banks, but it has no control over global and nonbank institutions that also ______________.

52. Decision making with respect to fiscal policy is made by ______________ and ______________, while monetary policy decision making is in the hands of ______________.

53. Some people believe that monetary policy should be more directly controlled by the president and Congress, so that all macroeconomic policy will be determined ______________ directly by the political process, which will ______________ policy coordination.

54. Policy makers must adopt the ______________ policies in the ______________ amounts at the ______________ time for such "stabilization" to do more good than harm.

55. When increased government purchases or expansionary monetary policy does give the economy a boost, ______________ knows precisely how long it will take to do so.

56. If people can anticipate the plans of policy makers and alter their behavior quickly, their behavior could ______________ the intended impact of government action.

57. If workers see that the government is allowing the money supply to expand rapidly, they will demand ______________ money wages in order to offset the anticipated inflation.

58. The theory of ______________ tries to incorporate expectations as a central factor in the analysis of the entire economy.

59. The theory of rational expectations leads to ____________ conclusions regarding macroeconomic policy's ability to achieve its intended economic goals.

60. Rational expectation economists believe that wages and prices are ____________ and that workers and consumers incorporate the likely consequences of government policy changes ____________ into their expectations.

61. Rational expectations theory suggests that government economic policies designed to alter aggregate demand to meet macroeconomic goals are of very ____________ effectiveness, because when policy targets become public, people will alter their own behavior from what it would otherwise have been, and in so doing, they largely ____________ the intended impact of policy changes.

62. If changes in inflation do not surprise people, they will have ____________ effect on unemployment or real output in the short run.

63. An ____________ increase in *AD* as a result of an expansionary monetary policy stimulates output and employment in the short run, but an ____________ increase in *AD* does not.

64. Unanticipated increases in *AD* expand output and employment in the ____________ run, but only increase the price level—inflation—in the ____________ run.

65. A correctly anticipated increase in *AD* from expansionary monetary or fiscal policy will ____________ real output, employment, or unemployment in the short run.

66. In the rational expectations model, people expecting expect a larger increase in *AD* than actually results from a policy change leads to a ____________ price level and a ____________ level of RGDP in the short run.

67. If some input prices are slow to adjust to changes in the price level, the extreme rational expectations model of complete wage and price flexibility will be ____________.

68. In the long run, the expected inflation rate will be ____________ the actual inflation rate at the ____________ of unemployment.

True or False

1. A central bank has only one function—controlling the supply of money in a country.
2. The central bank typically serves as the major bank for the central government.
3. The central bank implements monetary and fiscal policy for the government.
4. The 12 member banks of the Federal Reserve System act largely in unison on major monetary policy issues.
5. Banks are not all required to belong to the Fed; but there is currently virtually no difference in the requirements of member and nonmember banks.
6. Historically, the Fed has had very limited independence from the executive and legislative branches of government.
7. No member of the Federal Reserve Board will face reappointment from the president who initially made the appointment.
8. The Federal Open Market Committee makes most of the key decisions influencing the direction and size of changes in the money stock.
9. The money supply times velocity equals the price level times real GDP.

10. If individuals are writing lots of checks on their checking accounts and spending currency as fast as they receive it, velocity will tend to be low.

11. Velocity equals nominal GDP divided by the money supply.

12. The magnitude of velocity does not depend on the definition of money that is used.

13. If the money stock increases and the velocity of money does not change, there will be higher prices (inflation), greater real output of goods and services, or a combination of both.

14. Expanding the money supply, unless counteracted by increased hoarding of currency (leading to a decline in V), will have the same type of impact on aggregate demand as an expansionary fiscal policy.

15. Reducing the money supply, other things being equal, will have a contractionary impact on aggregate demand.

16. The velocity of money is a constant.

17. If velocity changes, but it moves in a fairly predictable pattern, the connection between money supply and GDP is still fairly predictable.

18. The cause of hyperinflation is excessive money growth.

19. The Fed controls the supply of money, even though privately owned commercial banks actually create and destroy money by making loans.

20. Open market purchases or sales of securities by the Fed have an ultimate impact on the money supply that is several times the amount of the purchase or sale.

21. If the Fed buys bonds in an open market operation, and the seller deposits the payment in her bank account, the money supply will increase, and there will be an increase in the bank's reserves.

22. With a 10 percent required reserve ratio, a $10,000 cash deposit in a bank would result in an increase in the bank's excess reserves by $1,000.

23. With a 10 percent required reserve ratio, a $1,000 bond purchase by the Fed directly creates $1,000 in money in the form of bank deposits, and indirectly permits up to $9,000 in additional money to be created through the multiple expansion in bank deposits.

24. The Fed selling government bonds will tend to cause a multiple expansion of bank deposits.

25. Generally, in a growing economy where the real value of goods and services is increasing over time, an increase in the supply of money is needed to maintain stable prices.

26. Changes in required reserve ratios are such a potent monetary policy tool that they are frequently used.

27. If the Fed raises the discount rate, the money supply will tend to increase.

28. The discount rate is a relatively unimportant monetary policy tool, mainly because member banks do not rely heavily on the Fed for borrowed funds.

29. The discount rate's main significance is that changes in the rate signal the Fed's intentions with respect to monetary policy.

30. If the Fed wanted to increase the money supply, it would buy bonds, lower reserve requirements, or lower the discount rate.

31. When interest rates are lower, the opportunity cost of holding monetary assets is higher.

32. The demand for money, particularly for transactions purposes, is highly dependent on income levels because the transactions volume varies directly with income.

33. At lower interest rates, the quantity of money demanded, but not the demand for money, is greater.

34. An increase in the money supply raises the equilibrium nominal interest rate.

35. The Fed buying bonds on the open market is an example of an expansionary monetary policy.

36. When the price of bonds rises, the interest rate rises.

37. The Fed cannot control both the money supply and the interest rate at the same time.

38. If the demand for money increases, and the Fed wants to keep the interest rate stable, it will have to increase the money supply.

39. Focusing on the growth in the money supply when the demand for money is changing unpredictably will lead to large fluctuations in the interest rate.

40. An expansionary policy can be thought of as an increase in the money supply or an increase in the interest rate.

41. A change in the nominal interest rate tends to change the real interest rate by the same amount in the short run because the expected inflation rate is slow to change in the short run.

42. In the long run, the real interest rate is determined by the intersection of the saving supply and investment demand curve.

43. An increase in *AD* through monetary policy can lead to only a temporary, short-run increase in real GDP, if the economy is initially operating at or above full employment, with no long-run effect on output or employment.

44. If the Fed pursues a contractionary monetary policy when the economy is at full employment, the Fed could cause a recession.

45. The Fed buying bonds on the open market will lead to an appreciation of the dollar, an increase in net exports, and an increase in RGDP in the short run.

46. The FOMC of the Federal Reserve is unable to act quickly in emergencies.

47. The length and variability of the impact lag before the effects of monetary policy on output and employment are felt longer and are more variable than for fiscal policy.

48. The Fed can change the environment in which banks act, but the banks themselves must take the steps necessary to increase or decrease the supply of money.

49. If the Fed raises bank reserve requirements, sells bonds, and/or raises the discount rate, banks will call in loans that are due for collection, sell secondary reserves, and so on to obtain the necessary reserves, and in the process of contracting loans, they lower the supply of money.

50. When the Fed is trying to constrain monetary expansion, it often has difficulty in getting banks to make appropriate responses.

51. When the Federal Reserve wants to induce monetary expansion, it can provide banks with excess reserves, but it cannot force the banks to make loans, thereby creating new money.

52. Banks maintaining excess reserves hinder attempts by the Fed to induce monetary expansion.

53. While the Fed may be able to predict the impact of its monetary policies on loans by member banks, the actions of global and nonbanking institutions can serve to partially offset the impact of monetary policies adopted by the Fed on the money and loanable funds markets.

54. There is no real question of how precisely the Fed can control the short-run real interest rates through its monetary policy instruments.

55. A macroeconomic problem arises if the federal government's fiscal decision makers differ with the Fed's monetary decision makers on policy objectives or targets.

56. The Fed occasionally works to partly offset or even neutralize the effects of fiscal policies that it views as inappropriate.

57. For government policy makers to be sure of doing more good than harm, they need far more accurate and timely information than experts can give them.

58. Economic advisers, using sophisticated econometric models, can forecast what the economy will do in the future with reasonable accuracy.

59. Even if economists could provide completely accurate economic forecasts of what will happen if macroeconomic policies are unchanged, they could not be certain of how to best promote stable economic growth.

60. Given the difficulties of timing stabilization policy, an expansionary monetary policy intended to reduce the severity of a recession may instead add inflationary pressures to an economy that is already overheating.

61. If the "new" economy increases productivity, the Fed, in trying to allow for greater economic growth without creating inflationary pressures, must estimate how much faster productivity is increasing and whether those increases are temporary or permanent.

62. If people could instantly recognize and respond to government policy changes, it might be impossible to alter real output or unemployment levels through policy actions.

63. Most economists accept the notion that real output and the unemployment rate cannot be altered with the ease that was earlier believed, and some believe that the unemployment rate can seldom be influenced by fiscal and monetary policies.

64. Rational expectation economists believe that the economy is inherently unstable after macroeconomic shocks.

65. Rational expectation economists believe that tinkering with fiscal and monetary policy cannot have the desired effect unless consumers and workers are caught off guard.

66. If people quickly alter their behavior to reflect the likely consequences of policy changes, they make it easier for government authorities to meet their macroeconomic objectives.

67. Anticipated increases in *AD* expand output and employment in the short run but only increase the price level—inflation—in the long run.

68. The only effect of a correctly anticipated increase in *AD* from expansionary monetary or fiscal policy will be an increase in the price level.

69. A policy designed to increase output may actually reduce output if prices and wages are flexible and the expansionary effect is less than people anticipated.

70. Most economists believe there is a short-run trade-off between inflation and unemployment because some input prices are slow to adjust to changes in the price level.

Multiple Choice

1. The most important role of the Federal Reserve System is
   a. raising or lowering taxes.
   b. regulating the supply of money.
   c. increasing or reducing government spending.
   d. none of the above.

2. Which of the following is *not* a function of the Federal Reserve System?
   a. being a lender of last resort
   b. being concerned with the stability of the banking system
   c. serving as a major bank for the central government
   d. setting currency exchange rates

3. The Fed is institutionally independent. A major advantage of this is that
   a. monetary policy is subject to regular ratification by congressional votes.
   b. monetary policy is not subject to control by politicians.
   c. monetary policy cannot be changed once it has been completed.
   d. monetary policy will always be coordinated with fiscal policy.
   e. monetary policy will always offset fiscal policy.

4. The P in the equation of exchange represents the
   a. profit earned in the economy.
   b. average level of prices of final goods and services in the economy.
   c. marginal level of prices.
   d. marginal propensity to spend.

5. The equation of exchange can be written as
   a. $M \times P = V \times Q$.
   b. $M \times V = P \times Q$.
   c. $M \times Q = P \times V$.
   d. $Q \times M = P \times V$.

6. If an economist divides the level of nominal GDP by the number of dollars in the money supply, she has computed
   a. the velocity of money.
   b. the price level.
   c. the level of real GDP.
   d. the economic growth rate.

7. If nominal GDP is $3,200 billion, and M1 is $800 billion, then velocity is
   a. 0.5.
   b. 2.
   c. 4.
   d. 8.
   e. 400.

8. According to the simple quantity theory of money, a change in the money supply of 6.5 percent would, holding velocity constant, lead to
   a. a 6.5 percent change in real GDP.
   b. a 6.5 percent change in nominal GDP.
   c. a 6.5 percent change in velocity.
   d. a 6.5 percent change in aggregate supply.

9. If people expect increasing inflation, what would be the expected reaction of velocity in the equation of exchange?
   a. Velocity would be expected to remain the same.
   b. Velocity would be expected to decrease.
   c. Velocity would be expected to increase.
   d. None of the above

10. If *M* increases, and *V* increases,
   a. nominal GDP increases.
   b. nominal GDP decreases.
   c. nominal GDP stays the same.
   d. there is an indeterminate effect on nominal GDP.

11. If the velocity of money (*V*) and real output (*Q*) were increasing at approximately the same rate, then
   a. it would be impossible for monetary authorities to control inflation.
   b. monetary acceleration would not lead to inflation.
   c. inflation would be closely related to the long-run rate of monetary expansion.
   d. both a and b would be true.

12. In order to increase the rate of growth of the money supply, the Fed can
   a. raise the discount rate.
   b. raise the reserve requirement.
   c. buy government securities on the open market.
   d. sell government securities on the open market.

13. The monetary policies generated by the Federal Reserve System
   a. must be consistent with fiscal policies that are formatted in Congress.
   b. are sometimes inconsistent with fiscal policies.
   c. must be ratified by Congress.
   d. must be approved by the president.

14. If the Fed buys a bond from an individual instead of a bank, what is the effect on the money supply?
   a. There will be no effect at all.
   b. The money supply will shrink.
   c. The money supply will grow by smaller amounts than if the Fed bought from a bank.
   d. The money supply will grow by larger amounts than if the Fed bought from a bank.
   e. The effect will be the same as if the Fed had bought the bond from a bank.

15. When the Fed purchases government securities from a commercial bank, the bank
   a. automatically becomes poorer.
   b. loses equity in the Fed.
   c. receives reserves that can be used to make additional loans.
   d. loses its ability to make loans.

16. If the Fed wishes to expand the money supply, it
   a. buys stocks.
   b. sells stocks.
   c. buys government securities.
   d. sells government securities.

17. If the Fed sells a U.S. government bond from a member of the public,
   a. the banking system has more reserves, and the money supply tends to grow.
   b. the banking system has fewer reserves, and the money supply tends to grow.
   c. the banking system has more reserves, and the money supply tends to fall.
   d. the banking system has fewer reserves, and the money supply tends to fall.

18. An open market purchase of government bonds by the Fed would tend to cause
   a. the money supply to fall and bond prices to go up.
   b. the money supply to rise and bond prices to go up.
   c. the money supply to rise and bond prices to go down.
   d. the money supply to fall and bond prices to go down.

19. If the Fed lowers the discount rate, what will be the effect on the money supply?
   a. The money supply will tend to increase.
   b. The money supply will tend to decrease.
   c. There will be no change—there has been no deposit to begin an expansion or contraction process.
   d. Not enough data are given to answer.

20. When the Fed sells a U.S. government security,
   a. the volume of loans issued by the banking system increases, and investment will tend to increase.
   b. the volume of loans issued by the banking system increases, and investment will tend to decrease.
   c. the volume of loans issued by the banking system decreases, and investment will tend to increase.
   d. the volume of loans issued by the banking system decreases, and investment will tend to decrease.

21. Reducing reserve requirements, other things being equal, would tend to
   a. increase the dollar volume of loans made by the banking system.
   b. increase the money supply.
   c. increase aggregate demand.
   d. all of the above.
   e. do a and b, but not c.

22. A combination of a decrease in the required reserve ratio and a decrease in the discount rate would
   a. increase the money supply.
   b. decrease the money supply.
   c. leave the money supply unchanged.
   d. have an indeterminate effect on the money supply.

23. When the money supply increases, other things being equal,
   a. real interest rates fall, and investment spending rises.
   b. real interest rates fall, and investment spending falls.
   c. real interest rates rise, and investment spending falls.
   d. real interest rates rise, and investment spending rises.

24. The money demand curve shows
   a. the various amounts of money that individuals will hold at different price levels.
   b. the various amounts of money that individuals will spend at different levels of GDP.
   c. the various amounts of money that individuals will hold at different interest rates.
   d. the quantity of bonds that the Fed will buy at different price levels.

25. If velocity is relatively stable and the central bank persistently increases the money supply faster than the rate of real output, the result will be
- **a.** unemployment.
- **b.** inflation.
- **c.** stagflation.
- **d.** recession.

26. What will happen to the demand for money if real GDP rises?
- **a.** It will decrease.
- **b.** It will be unchanged.
- **c.** It will increase.
- **d.** It depends on what happens to interest rates.

27. Contractionary monetary policy will tend to have what effect?
- **a.** increase the money supply and lower interest rates
- **b.** increase the money supply and increase interest rates
- **c.** decrease the money supply and lower interest rates
- **d.** decrease the money supply and increase interest rates

28. The combination of an increase in the discount rate and an open market sale of government securities by the Fed will tend to result in
- **a.** a higher loan volume issued by the commercial banking system.
- **b.** higher bond prices.
- **c.** a lower price level.
- **d.** a decrease in unemployment rates.

29. When money demand increases, the Fed can choose between
- **a.** increasing interest rates or increasing the supply of money.
- **b.** increasing interest rates or decreasing the supply of money.
- **c.** decreasing interest rates or increasing the supply of money.
- **d.** decreasing interest rates or decreasing the supply of money.

30. When the economy is initially at full employment,
- **a.** expansionary monetary policy can potentially result in increased real output, but only in the short run.
- **b.** expansionary monetary policy can potentially result in increased real output in both the short run and the long run.
- **c.** contractionary monetary policy can potentially result in increased real output, but only in the short run.
- **d.** contractionary monetary policy can potentially result in increased real output in both the short run and the long run.

31. The flatter the *SRAS* curve,
- **a.** the harder it is for fiscal policy to change real GDP in the short run.
- **b.** the easier it is for fiscal policy to change real GDP in the short run.
- **c.** the harder it is for monetary policy to change real GDP in the short run.
- **d.** the easier it is for monetary policy to change real GDP in the short run.
- **e.** both b and d are true.

32. If a reduction in the money supply were desired to slow inflation, the Federal Reserve might
- **a.** decrease reserve requirements.
- **b.** buy U.S. securities on the open market.
- **c.** raise the discount rate.
- **d.** do either b or c.

33. Suppose the Fed purchases $100 million of U.S. securities from the public. If the reserve requirement is 20 percent and all banks keep zero excess reserves, the total impact of this action on the money supply will be a
   a. $100 million decrease in the money supply.
   b. $100 million increase in the money supply.
   c. $200 million increase in the money supply.
   d. $500 million increase in the money supply.

34. Which of the following Federal Reserve actions would most likely help counteract an oncoming recession?
   a. an increase in reserve requirements and an increase in the discount rate
   b. the sale of government securities and an increase in the discount rate
   c. the sale of foreign currencies and an increase in reserve requirements
   d. the purchase of government securities and a reduction in the discount rate

35. The quantity of money that households and businesses will demand
   a. increases if income rises but decreases if interest rates rise.
   b. increases if income rises and increases if interest rates rise.
   c. decreases if income rises but increases if interest rates rise.
   d. decreases if income rises and decreases if interest rates rise.
   e. None of the above is true.

36. Starting from an initial long-run equilibrium, an unanticipated shift to more expansionary monetary policy would tend to increase
   a. prices and unemployment in the long run.
   b. real output in the short run, but not in the long run.
   c. real output in the long run, but not the short run.
   d. real output in both the long run and the short run.

37. The Fed unexpectedly increasing the money supply will cause an increase in aggregate demand because
   a. real interest rates will fall, stimulating business investment and consumer purchases.
   b. the dollar will depreciate on the foreign exchange market, leading to an increase in net exports.
   c. lower interest rates will tend to increase asset prices, which increases wealth and thereby stimulates current consumption.
   d. of all the above reasons.

38. Which one of the following would be the most appropriate stabilization policy if the economy is operating beyond its long-run potential capacity?
   a. an increase in the discount rate
   b. an increase in government purchases, holding taxes constant
   c. a reduction in reserve requirements
   d. a reduction in taxes, holding government purchases constant

39. In the long run, a sustained increase in growth of the money supply relative to the growth rate of potential real output will most likely
   a. cause the nominal interest rate to fall.
   b. cause the real interest rate to fall.
   c. reduce the natural rate of unemployment.
   d. increase real output growth.
   e. do none of the above.

40. Which of the following is true?
  a. An unanticipated shift to a more expansionary monetary policy will temporarily stimulate real output and employment.
  b. Once decision makers come to anticipate the inflationary side effects, expansionary monetary policy will fail to stimulate either real output or employment.
  c. The primary long-run effect of persistent growth of the money supply at a rapid rate will be inflation.
  d. All of the above are true.

41. Which of the following would cause the U.S. money supply to expand?
  a. a commercial bank calling in a loan to build up more excess reserves
  b. a commercial bank purchasing U.S. securities from the Fed as an investment
  c. a decrease in reserve requirements
  d. an increase in the discount rate

42. Which of the following would tend to reduce the price level?
  a. a commercial bank using excess reserves to extend a loan to a customer
  b. a commercial bank purchasing U.S. securities from an individual as an investment
  c. an increase in reserve requirements
  d. an increase in the discount rate
  e. a purchase of U.S. government securities by the Fed

43. Compared to fiscal policy, which of the following is an advantage of using monetary policy to attain macroeconomic goals?
  a. It takes a long time for fiscal policy to have an effect on the economy, but the effects of monetary policy are immediate.
  b. The effects of monetary policy are certain and predictable, while the effects of fiscal policy are not.
  c. The implementation of monetary policy is not slowed down by the same budgetary process as fiscal policy.
  d. The economists that help conduct monetary policy are smarter than those that help with fiscal policy.

44. An important limitation of monetary policy is that
  a. it is conducted by people in Congress who are under pressure to get reelected every two years.
  b. when the Fed tries to buy bonds, it is often unable to find a seller.
  c. when the Fed tries to sell bonds, it is often unable to find a buyer.
  d. it must be conducted through the commercial banking system, and the Fed cannot always make banks do what it wants them to do.

Problems

1. Answer questions a–e.
  a. What is the equation of exchange?
  b. In the equation of exchange, if V doubled, what would happen to nominal GDP as a result?
  c. In the equation of exchange, if V doubled and Q remained unchanged, what would happen to the price level as a result?
  d. In the equation of exchange, if M doubled and V remained unchanged, what would happen to nominal GDP as a result?
  e. In the equation of exchange, if M doubled and V fell by half, what would happen to nominal GDP as a result?

2. In which direction would the money supply change if
   a. the Fed raised the reserve requirement?
   b. the Fed conducted an open market sale of government bonds?
   c. the Fed raised the discount rate?
   d. the Fed conducted an open market sale of government bonds and raised the discount rate?
   e. the Fed conducted an open market purchase of government bonds and raised reserve requirements?

3. Using the following diagram, answer questions a and b.

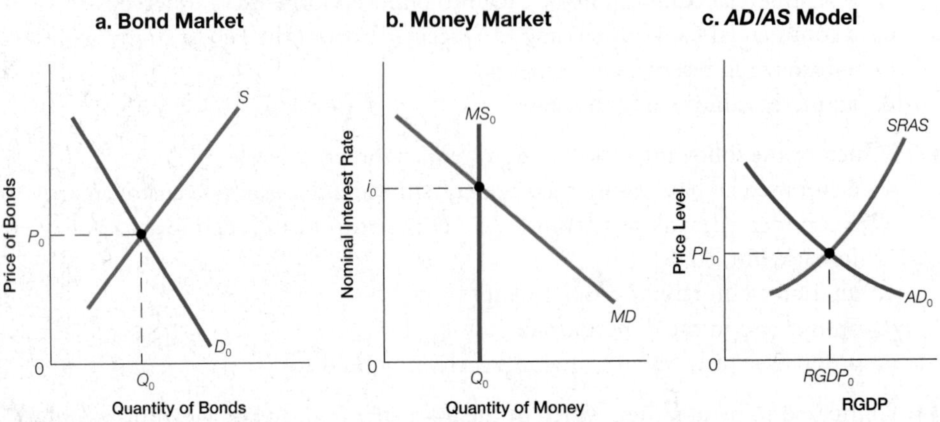

   a. Show the effects in each of the indicated markets of an open market purchase of government bonds by the Fed.
   b. Show the effects in each of the indicated markets of an open market sale of government bonds by the Fed.

4. Using the following diagram, answer questions a–c.

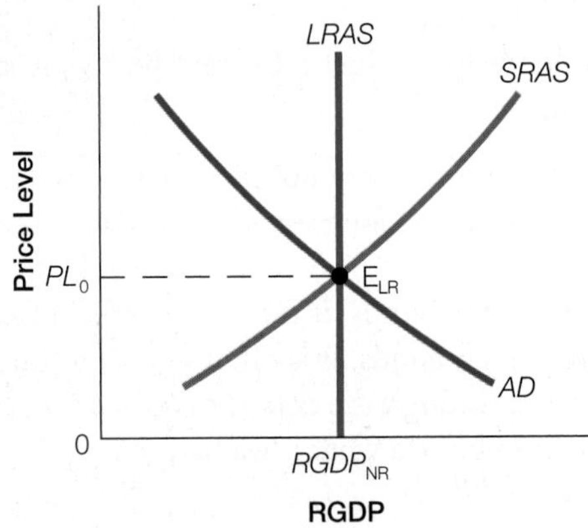

   a. On the diagram, illustrate the short-run effects of an unanticipated increase in aggregate demand caused by expanding the money supply.
   b. On the diagram, illustrate the short-run effects of an increase in aggregate demand caused by expanding the money supply, if people correctly anticipate the effects.
   c. On the diagram, illustrate the case where the short-run effect of an anticipated increase in aggregate demand leads to a recession.

chapter 19

International Trade

section 19.1

The Growth in World Trade

- What has happened to the volume of international trade over time?
- Who trades with the United States?
- What does the United States import? Export?

IMPORTANCE OF INTERNATIONAL TRADE

In a typical year, about 15 percent of the world's output is traded in international markets. Of course, the importance of the international sector varies enormously from place to place on the planet. Some nations are almost closed economies (no interaction with other economies), with foreign trade equaling only a very small proportion (perhaps 5 percent) of total output. In the United States in 1998, exports were roughly 12 percent of gross domestic product (GDP), while imports were a little higher, at over 13 percent of GDP. In Germany, by contrast, roughly 30 percent of all output produced is exported, while Ireland and Belgium each export over 70 percent of GDP.

The volume of international trade has increased substantially in the United States over the last 70 years; exports and imports have gone from less than 5 percent of GDP to almost 20 percent. Most of this change has taken place since the mid-1970s.

U.S. exports include capital goods, automobiles, industrial supplies, raw materials, consumer goods, and agricultural products. U.S. imports include crude oil and refined petroleum products, machinery, automobiles, consumer goods, industrial raw materials, food, and beverages.

TRADING PARTNERS

In its early history, U.S. international trade was largely directed towards Europe and to Great Britain in particular. Now the United States trades with a number of countries. Exhibit 1 shows the most important trading partners. The single most important U.S. trading partner is Canada, accounting for roughly one-fifth of the imports and one-fourth of the exports. Trade with Japan, Mexico, Germany, China, Taiwan, and Italy are also particularly important.

section 19.1 Exhibit 1 — Major U.S. Trading Partners

Top Five Trading Partners—Exports of Goods in 2000

Rank	Country	Percent of Total
1	Canada	23%
2	Mexico	14
3	Japan	8
4	United Kingdom	5
5	Germany	4

SOURCE: CIA, *The World Factbook 2001.*

Top Five Trading Partners—Imports of Goods in 2000

Rank	Country	Percent of Total
1	Canada	19%
2	Japan	11
3	Mexico	11
4	China	8
5	Germany	5

SOURCE: CIA, *The World Factbook 2001.*

In The NEWS

BAYWATCH IS WORLD WATCHED

BY STEVE BARTH

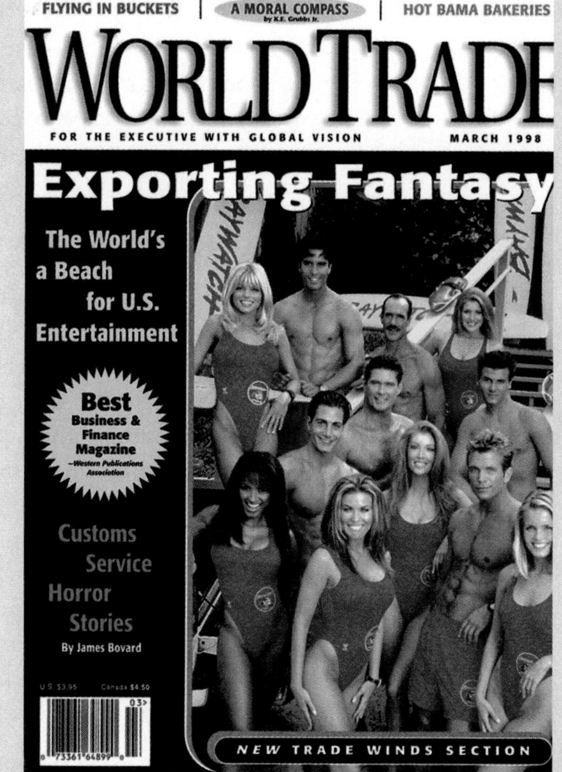

In the world of entertainment exports, the syndicated series *Baywatch* is like the Boeing 747. You can see *Baywatch* in Bangladesh, Barbados, Bolivia, Brunei, and 140 other countries. Produced by a small, independent Los Angeles production company, the weekly dose of sun, sand, sea, and skin, with muscled lifeguards rescuing drowning damsels (and vice versa), earns about $100 million per year, 67 percent of which is currently from foreign distribution.

At the Walt Disney Company in Burbank, Calif., CFO Richard Nanula says that while the Magic Kingdom has had a presence in some foreign markets for up to 50 years, the international demand for Disney products is now growing at an accelerated pace. This is especially true in film and television where international business now accounts for about 40 percent of revenue, but growth is twice that of domestic.

"The international markets really help the performance of a movie in its profit statement—substantially more than they used to," Nanula says. Overseas box office receipts used to add perhaps 20 percent to a film's gross. Now some movies, particularly animation and action/adventure, that make $100 million at home might eventually make twice as much internationally.

SOURCE: Steve Barth, "Exporting Fantasy," *World Trade,* March 1998, pp. 41–42. Reprinted with permission from *World Trade* Magazine.

CONSIDER THIS:
The international marketplace has become very important in the television and movie industry. The television program *Baywatch* has been broadcasted all over the world.

Section Check

1. The volume of international trade has increased substantially in the United States over the last 50 years. During that time, exports and imports have grown from less than 5 percent to over 12 percent of GDP.
2. Our single most-important trading partner, Canada, accounts for roughly one-fourth of our exports and almost one-fifth of our imports. Trade with Japan, Mexico, China, Germany, the United Kingdom, France, and Taiwan is also particularly important to the United States.
3. U.S. exports include capital goods, automobiles, industrial supplies, raw materials, consumer goods, and agricultural products. U.S. imports include crude oil and refined petroleum products, machinery, automobiles, consumer goods, industrial raw materials, food, and beverages.

---

1. Why is it important to understand the effects of international trade?
2. Why would U.S. producers and consumers be more concerned about Canadian trade restrictions than Swedish trade restrictions?

section 19.2

Comparative Advantage and Gains from Trade

- Does voluntary trade lead to an improvement in economic welfare?
- What is the principle of comparative advantage?
- What benefits are derived from specialization?

ECONOMIC GROWTH AND TRADE

Using simple logic, we conclude that the very existence of trade suggests that trade is economically beneficial. This is true if one assumes that people are utility maximizers and are rational, intelligent, and engage in trade on a voluntary basis. Because almost all trade is voluntary, it would seem that trade occurs because the participants feel that they are better-off because of the trade. Both participants of an exchange of goods and services anticipate an improvement in their economic welfare. Sometimes, of course, anticipations are not realized (because the world is uncertain), but the motive behind trade remains an expectation of some enhancement in utility or satisfaction by both parties.

Granted, "trade must be good because people do it," is a rather simplistic explanation. The classical economist David Ricardo is usually given most of the credit for developing the economic theory that more precisely explains how trade can be mutually beneficial to both parties, raising output and income levels in the entire trading area.

THE PRINCIPLE OF COMPARATIVE ADVANTAGE

comparative advantage *occurs when a person or a country can produce a good or service at a lower opportunity cost than others*

Ricardo's theory of international trade centers on the concept of comparative advantage. A person, a region, or a country can gain by specializing in the production of the good in which they have a comparative advantage. That is, if they can produce a good or service at a lower opportunity cost than others, we say that they have a **comparative advantage** in the production of that good or service. In other words, a country or a region should specialize in producing and selling those items that it can produce at a lower opportunity cost than other regions or countries.

Comparative advantage analysis does not mean that nations or areas that export goods will necessarily be able to produce those goods or services more cheaply than other nations in an absolute sense. What is important is *comparative* advantage, not *absolute* advantage. For example, the United States may be able to produce more cotton cloth per worker than India, but that does not mean the United States should necessarily sell cotton cloth to India. Indeed, the United States has an absolute advantage or productive superiority over India in nearly every good, given the higher levels of output per person in the United States. Yet India's inferiority in producing some goods is much less than for others. In goods where India's productivity is only slightly less than that of the United States, such as perhaps in cotton cloth, it probably has a comparative advantage over the United States. How? For a highly productive nation to produce goods in which it is only marginally more productive than other nations, the nation must take resources from the production of other goods in which its productive abilities are markedly superior. As a result, the opportunity costs in India of making cotton cloth may be less than in the United States. With that, both can gain from trade, despite potential absolute advantages for every good in the United States.

section 19.2 Exhibit 1 **Specialization and Trade**

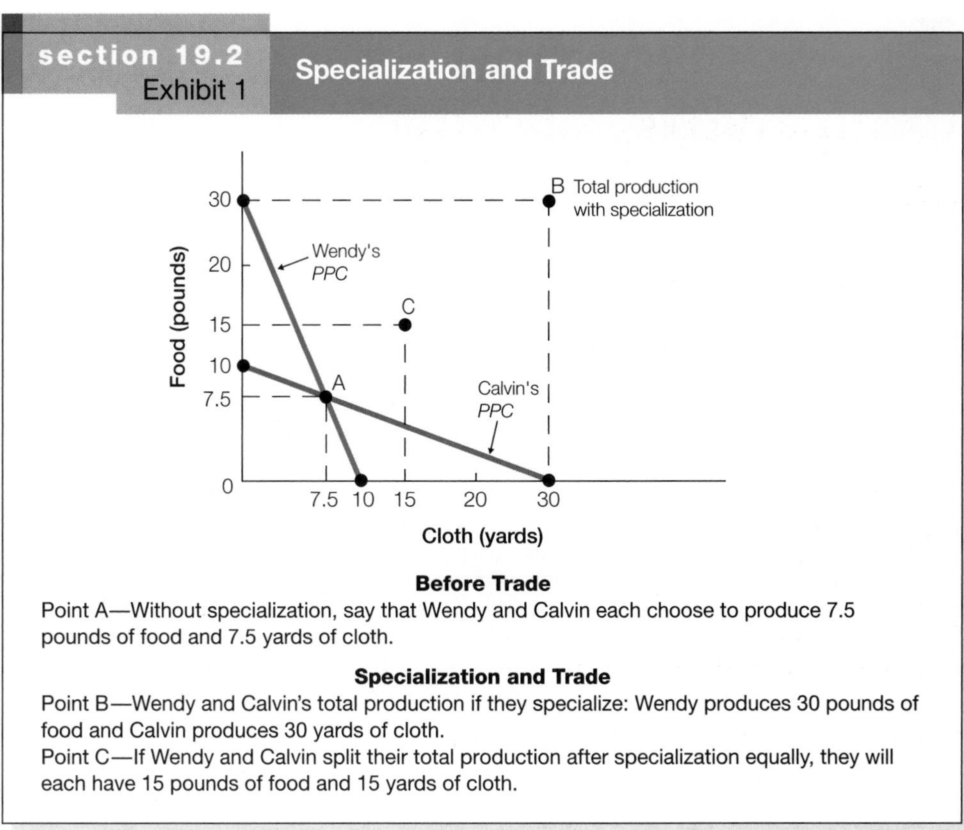

Before Trade

Point A—Without specialization, say that Wendy and Calvin each choose to produce 7.5 pounds of food and 7.5 yards of cloth.

Specialization and Trade

Point B—Wendy and Calvin's total production if they specialize: Wendy produces 30 pounds of food and Calvin produces 30 yards of cloth.

Point C—If Wendy and Calvin split their total production after specialization equally, they will each have 15 pounds of food and 15 yards of cloth.

COMPARATIVE ADVANTAGE AND THE PRODUCTION POSSIBILITIES CURVE

In Exhibit 1, we show the production possibilities curves for two individuals, Wendy and Calvin. Wendy and Calvin can produce either food or cloth. In Exhibit 1, we see that if Wendy devotes all of her resources to producing food, she can produce 30 pounds of food; if she devotes all of her resources to producing cloth, she can produce 10 yards of cloth. In Exhibit 1, we see that when Calvin uses all of his resources to produce food, he only produces 10 pounds, but when he uses all of his resources to produce cloth, he can produce 30 yards. In this example, Wendy actually has an absolute advantage in food, while Calvin has an absolute advantage in cloth. But as we shall see, it would not affect the result if Calvin could only produce 2 pounds of food and 6 yards of cloth.

For simplicity, we will assume each producer operates on a straight-line production possibilities curve (*PPC*) and each initially chooses to divide their productive resources between these products in order to produce 7.5 pounds of food and 7.5 yards of cloth, although any amount of each good within their respective PPCs could have been produced.

Wendy can produce food at a lower opportunity cost than Calvin. When Wendy produces 30 pounds of food, it costs only 10 yards of cloth. However, when Calvin produces only 10 pounds of food, it costs 30 yards of cloth. Wendy, then, is the lowest-cost producer of food, but Calvin can produce cloth at a lower opportunity cost than Wendy. When Calvin produces 30 yards of cloth, it costs him 10 pounds of food. And when Wendy produces 10 yards of cloth, it costs 30 pounds of food. Calvin, then, is the lowest-cost producer of cloth.

To demonstrate our point about comparative advantage, we have overlapped the two production possibility curves in Exhibit 1. At point A, we see that Wendy produces 7.5 pounds of food and 7.5 yards of cloth and Calvin produces 7.5 yards of cloth and

APPLICATION

COMPARATIVE ADVANTAGE AND ABSOLUTE ADVANTAGE

Q: Renee, a successful artist, can complete one painting in each 40-hour workweek. Each painting sells for $4,000. As a result of her enormous success, however, Renee is swamped in paperwork. To solve the problem, Renee hires Drake to handle all of the bookkeeping and typing associated with buying supplies, answering inquiries from prospective buyers and dealers, writing art galleries, and so forth. Renee pays Drake $300 per week for his work. After a couple of weeks in this arrangement, Renee realizes that she can handle Drake's chores more quickly than Drake does. In fact, she estimates that she is twice as fast as Drake, completing in 20 hours what it takes Drake 40 hours to complete. Should Renee fire Drake?

A: Clearly Renee has an absolute advantage over Drake in both painting and paperwork because she can do twice as much paperwork in 40 hours as Drake can, and Drake can't paint well at all. Still, it would be foolish for Renee to do both jobs. If Renee did her own paperwork, it would take her 20 hours per week, leaving her only 20 hours to paint. Because each watercolor takes 40 hours to paint, Renee's output would fall from one painting per week to one painting per two weeks.

When Drake works for her, Renee's net income is $3,700 per week ($4,000 per painting minus $300 in Drake's wages); when Drake does not work for her, it is only $2,000 per week (one painting every two weeks). While Renee is both a better painter and better at Drake's chores than Drake, it pays for her to specialize in painting, in which she has a comparative advantage, and allow Drake to do the paperwork. The opportunity cost to Renee of paperwork is high. For Drake, who lacks skills as a painter, the opportunity costs of doing the paperwork are much less.

In The NEWS

THE MIRACLE OF TRADE

It is mere common sense that if one country is very good at making hats, and another is very good at making shoes, then total output can be increased by arranging for the first country to concentrate on making hats and the second on making shoes. Then, through trade in both goods, more of each can be consumed in both places.

That is a tale of absolute advantage. . . . Each country is better than the other at making a certain good, and so profits from specialization and trade. Comparative advantage is different: a country will have it despite being bad at the activity concerned. Indeed, it can have a comparative advantage in making a certain good even if it is worse at making that good than any other country.

This is not economic theory, but a straightforward matter of definition: a country has a comparative advantage where its margin of superiority is greater, or its margin of inferiority smaller.

[W]hen people say of Africa, or Britain, or wherever, that it has no comparative advantage in anything, they are simply confusing absolute advantage (for which their claim may or may not be true) with comparative advantage (for which it is certainly false).

Why does this confusion over terms matter? Because the case for free trade is often thought to depend on the existence of absolute advantage and is therefore thought to collapse whenever absolute advantage is absent. But economics shows that gains from trade follow, in fact, from comparative advantage. Since comparative advantage is never absent, this gives the theory far broader scope than more popular critics suppose.

In particular, it shows that even countries which are desperately bad at making everything can expect to gain from international competition. If countries specialize according to their comparative advantage, they can prosper through trade regardless of how inefficient, in absolute terms, they may be in their chosen specialty.

SOURCE: "The Miracle of Trade," *The Economist*, January 27, 1996, pp. 61, 62.

7.5 pounds of food. However, if each specialized and pursued his or her comparative advantage, the goods each can produce at the lowest opportunity cost, then Wendy could produce 30 pounds of food and Calvin could produce 30 yards of cloth, point B. That is, by specializing, Wendy and Calvin have produced 30 units of each good rather than 15 units, using the same amount of total resources. Now if Wendy does not want all food and Calvin does not want all cloth, they can trade with each other. In fact, if Wendy trades half of her food for half of the cloth Calvin has produced, then each will have 15 units of food and cloth. This is 7.5 more pounds of food and 7.5 more yards of cloth than they had before specialization and trade. That is, if they choose to consume equal amounts of both products, after specialization and trade, their new consumption point is at point C—outside of their original PPCs.

By specializing in products in which it has a comparative advantage, individuals, regions and countries can increase their total production. And it is trade that allows people to specialize in those activities they do best.

Section Check

1. Voluntary trade occurs because the participants feel that they are better off because of the trade.
2. A nation, geographic area, or even a person can gain from trade if the good or service is produced relatively cheaper than anyone else can produce it. That is, an area should specialize in producing and selling those items that it can produce at a lower opportunity cost than others.
3. Through trade and specialization in products in which it has a comparative advantage, a country can enjoy a greater array of goods and services at a lower cost.

---

1. Why do people voluntarily choose to specialize and trade?
2. How could a country have an absolute advantage in producing one good or service without also having a comparative advantage in its production?
3. Why do you think the introduction of the railroad reduced self-sufficiency in the United States?
4. If you can do the dishes in two-thirds the time it takes your younger sister, do you have a comparative advantage in doing the dishes compared to her?

section 19.3

Supply and Demand in International Trade

- What is consumer surplus?
- What is producer surplus?
- Who benefits and who loses when a country becomes an exporter?
- Who benefits and who loses when a country becomes an importer?

THE IMPORTANCE OF TRADE: PRODUCER AND CONSUMER SURPLUS

Recall from chapter 5, the difference between the most a consumer would be willing to pay for a quantity of a good and what a consumer actually has to pay is called **consumer surplus.** The difference between the least a supplier is willing to supply a quantity of a

consumer surplus
the difference between what the consumer is willing and able to pay and what the consumer actually pays for a quantity of a good or service

producer surplus
the difference between the lowest price at which a supplier is willing and able to supply a good or service and the actual price received for a given quantity of a good or service

good or service for and the revenues a supplier actually receives for selling it is called **producer surplus.** With the tools of consumer and producer surplus, we can better analyze the impact of trade. Who gains? Who loses? What happens to net welfare?

The demand curve represents maximum prices that consumers are willing and able to pay for different quantities of a good or service; the supply curve represents minimum prices suppliers require to be willing to supply different quantities of that good or service. See Exhibit 1. For example, for the first unit of output, the consumer is willing to pay up to $7 and the producer would demand at least $1 for producing that unit. However, the equilibrium price is $4, as indicated by the intersection of the supply and demand curves. It is clear that the two would gain from getting together and trading that unit because the consumer would receive $3 of consumer surplus ($7 − $4) and the producer would receive $3 of producer surplus ($4 − $1). Both would also benefit from trading the second and third unit of output—in fact, from every unit up to the equilibrium output. Once the equilibrium output is reached at the equilibrium price, all of the mutually beneficial opportunities from trade between suppliers and demanders will have taken place; the sum of consumer surplus and producer surplus is maximized.

It is important to recognize that the total gains to the economy from trade is the sum of consumer and producer surplus. That is, consumers benefit from additional amounts of consumer surplus and producers benefit from additional amounts of producer surplus.

FREE TRADE AND EXPORTS—DOMESTIC PRODUCERS GAIN MORE THAN DOMESTIC CONSUMERS LOSE

Using the concepts of consumer and producer surplus, we can graphically show the net benefits of free trade. Imagine an economy with no trade, where the equilibrium price, P_{BT}, and the equilibrium quantity, Q_{BT}, of wheat are determined exclusively in the domestic economy, as seen in Exhibit 2. Say that this imaginary economy decides to engage in free trade. You can see that the world price (established in the world market for wheat), P_{WORLD}, is higher than the domestic price before trade, P_{BT}. In other words, the domestic economy has a comparative advantage in wheat, because it can produce wheat at a lower relative price than the rest of the world. So this wheat-producing country sells some wheat to the domestic market and some wheat to the world market, all at the going world price.

The price after trade (P_{AT}) is higher than the price before trade (P_{BT}). Because the world market is huge, the demand from the rest of the world at the world price (P_{WORLD}) is assumed to be perfectly elastic. That is, domestic wheat farmers can sell all the wheat they want at the world price. If you were a wheat farmer in Nebraska, would you rather sell all of your bushels of wheat at the higher world price or the lower domestic price? As a wheat farmer, you would surely prefer the higher world price. But this is not good news for domestic cereal and bread eaters, who now have to pay more for products made with wheat, because P_{AT} is greater than P_{BT}.

Graphically, we can see how free trade and exports affect both domestic consumers and domestic producers. At the higher world price, P_{AT}, domestic wheat producers are receiving larger amounts of producer surplus. Before trade, they received a surplus equal to area c; after trade, they re-

section 19.3 Exhibit 1 **Consumer and Producer Surplus**

Consumer surplus is the difference between what a consumer has to pay ($4) and what the consumer is willing to pay. For unit 1, consumer surplus is $3 ($7 − $4). Producer surplus is the difference between what a seller receives for selling a good or service ($4) and the price at which he is willing to supply that good or service. For unit 1, producer surplus is $3 ($4 − $1).

section 19.3 Exhibit 2 **Free Trade and Exports**

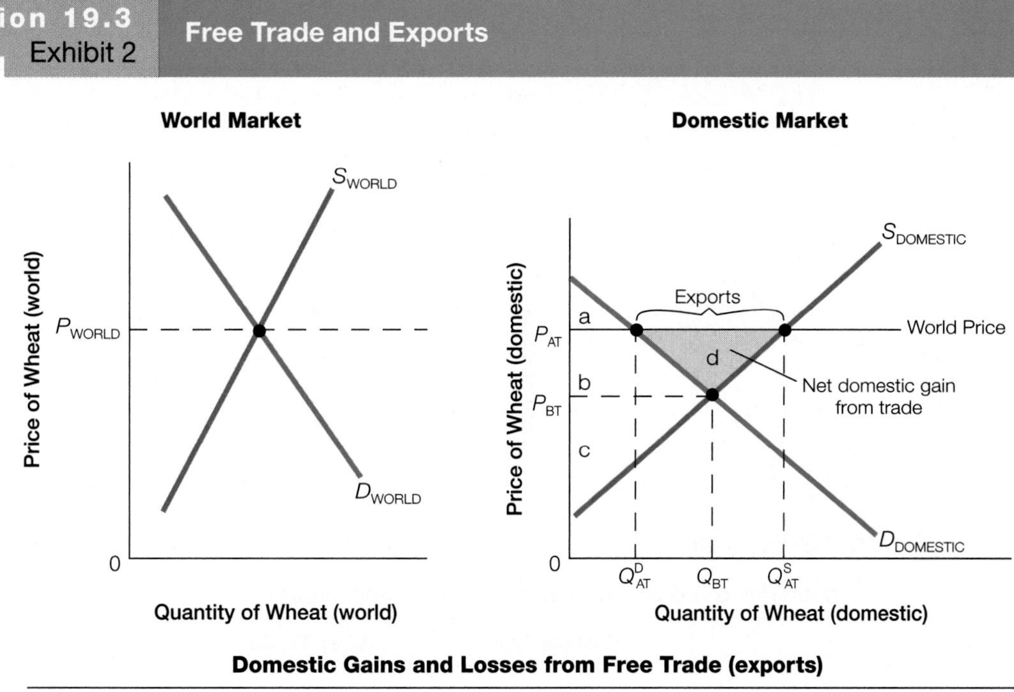

Domestic Gains and Losses from Free Trade (exports)

Area	Before Trade	After Trade	Change
Consumer Surplus (*CS*)	a + b	a	− b
Producer Surplus (*PS*)	c	b + c + d	+ (b + d)
Total Welfare from Trade (*CS* + *PS*)	a + b + c	a + b + c + d	+ d

Domestic producers gain more than domestic consumers lose from exports when there is free trade. On net, domestic wealth rises by area d.

ceived surplus b + c + d, for a net gain of area b + d. However, part of the domestic producer's gain comes at domestic consumer's expense. Specifically, consumers had a consumer surplus equal to area a + b before the trade (at P_{BT}), but they now only have area a (at P_{AT})—a loss of area b.

Area b reflects a redistribution of income, because producers are gaining exactly what consumers are losing. Is that good or bad? We can't say objectively whether consumers or producers are more deserving. However, the net benefits from allowing free trade and exports are clearly visible in area d. Without free trade, no one gets area d. That is, on net, members of the domestic society gain when domestic wheat producers are able to sell their wheat at the higher world price. While domestic wheat consumers lose from the free trade, those negative effects are more than offset by the positive gains captured by producers. Area d is the net increase in domestic wealth (the welfare gain) from free trade and exports.

FREE TRADE AND IMPORTS

Now suppose that our economy does not produce shirts as well as other countries of the world. In other words, other countries have a comparative advantage in producing shirts. This means that the domestic price for shirts is above the world price. This scenario is illustrated in Exhibit 3. At the new, lower world price, the domestic producer will supply quantity Q^S_{AT}. However, at the lower world price, the domestic producers will not produce the entire amount demanded by domestic consumers, Q^D_{AT}. At the world price, reflecting

section 19.3 Exhibit 3 — **Free Trade and Imports**

World Market

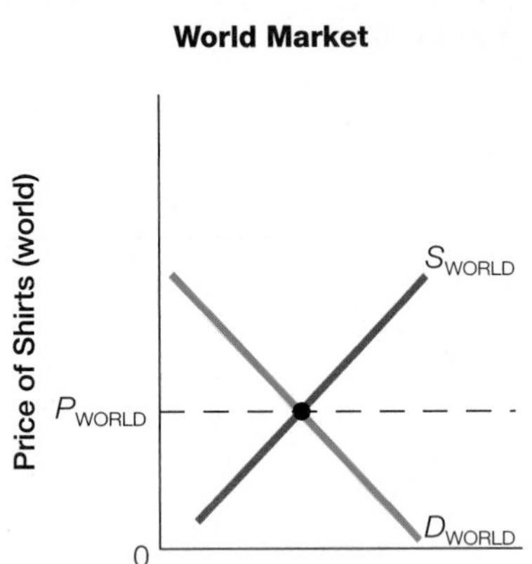

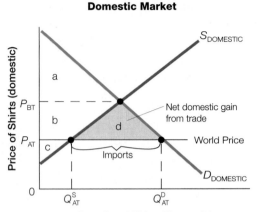

Domestic Market

Price of Shirts (domestic)
$S_{DOMESTIC}$
a
P_{BT}
b
d
Net domestic gain from trade
P_{AT}
c
World Price
Imports
$D_{DOMESTIC}$
0
Q^S_{AT}
Q^D_{AT}
Quantity of Shirts (domestic)

Domestic Gains and Losses from Free Trade (imports)

Area	Before Trade	After Trade	Change
Consumer Surplus (*CS*)	a	a + b + d	+ (b + d)
Producer Surplus (*PS*)	b + c	c	− b
Total Welfare from Trade (*CS* + *PS*)	a + b + c	a + b + c + d	+ d

Domestic consumers gain more than domestic producers lose from imports when there is free trade. On net, domestic wealth rises by area d.

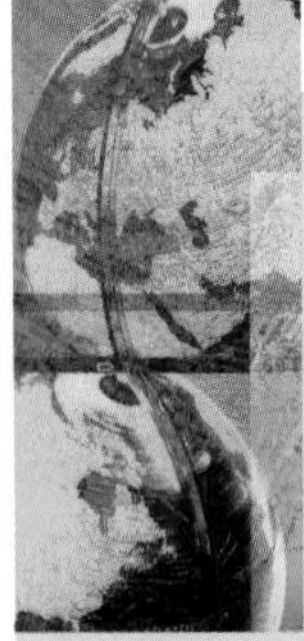

Global WATCH

BIG GAINS FOR MEXICO FROM FREE TRADE

The $229 billion worth of trade between the United States and Mexico resulting from NAFTA has improved life on both sides of the border.

- Wages have grown 150 percent for Mexican truck drivers and overall unemployment has fallen below two percent.
- Recent elections in Mexico installed a new leadership who wants to improve U.S.–Mexico political and social relations.
- Mexico has made it possible to extradite drug traffickers to face criminal charges in the United States.
- Mexico has pledged to stop publicly defending Cuba's poor human rights record.
- Although Mexican officials have pledged to find solutions to immigration problems, it is predicted that within 10 years the rising prosperity in Mexico resulting from free trade will reduce illegal immigration to the United States anyway.
- More than 200,000 new jobs have been created in the U.S. economy as a direct result of NAFTA, surpassing Clinton administration prediction.
- Americans also benefit from low-priced Mexican goods, such as produce, computers, and cars.
- Legislation is underway to allow private investment in electricity production—meaning new power plants and potential gains for power-starved areas of the United States.

SOURCE: Editorial, "Bush Border Crossing Salutes U.S.-Mexican Trade Gains," *USA Today,* February 16, 2001, and http://www.ncpa.org.

the world supply and demand for shirts, the difference between what is domestically supplied and what is domestically demanded is supplied by imports.

At the world price (established in the world market for shirts), we assume the world supply curve to the domestic market is perfectly elastic—that the producers of the world can supply all that domestic consumers are willing to buy at the going price. At the world price, Q^S_{AT} is supplied by domestic producers and the difference between Q^D_{AT} and Q^S_{AT} is imported from other countries.

Who wins and who loses from free trade and imports? Domestic consumers benefit from paying a lower price for shirts. In Exhibit 3, before trade, consumers only received area a in consumer surplus. After trade, the price fell and quantity purchased increased, causing the area of consumer surplus to increase from area a to area a + b + d, a gain of b + d. Domestic producers lose because they are now selling their shirts at the lower world price, P_{AT}. The producer surplus before trade was b + c. After trade, the producer surplus falls to area c, reducing producer surplus by area b. Area b, then, represents a redistribution from producers to consumers, but area d is the net increase in domestic wealth (the welfare gain) from free trade and imports.

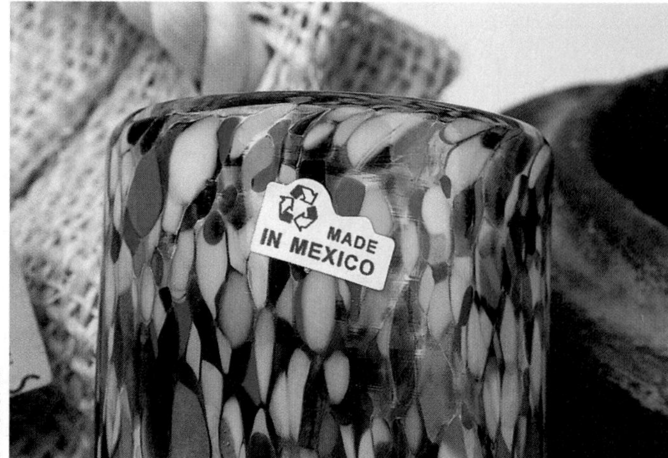

In 1993, the North American Free Trade Agreement (NAFTA) was passed. This lowered the trade barriers between Mexico, Canada, and the United States. Proponents of freer trade, especially economists, viewed the agreement as a way to gain greater wealth through specialization and trade for all three countries—one of our ten powerful ideas. Opponents thought the agreement would take away U.S. jobs and lower living standards. Or, in the words of former presidential candidate Ross Perot, that there would be "a giant sucking sound."

Section Check

1. The difference between what a consumer is willing and able to pay and what a consumer actually has to pay is called consumer surplus.
2. The difference between what a supplier is willing and able to supply and the price a supplier actually receives for selling a good or service is called producer surplus.
3. With free trade and exports, domestic producers gain more than domestic consumers lose.
4. With free trade and imports, domestic consumers gain more than domestic producers lose.

---

1. How does voluntary trade generate both producer and consumer surplus?
2. If the world price of a good is greater than the domestic price prior to trade, why does that imply that the domestic economy has a comparative advantage in producing that good?
3. If the world price of a good is less than the domestic price prior to trade, why does that imply that the domestic economy has a comparative disadvantage in producing that good?
4. When a country has a comparative advantage in the production of a good, why do domestic producers gain more than domestic consumers lose from free international trade?
5. When a country has a comparative disadvantage in the production of a good, why do domestic consumers gain more than domestic producers lose from free international trade?
6. Why do U.S. exporters, such as farmers, favor free trade more than U.S. producers of domestic products who face competition from foreign imports, such as the automobile industry?

section 19.4

Tariffs, Import Quotas, and Subsidies

- What is a tariff?
- What are the effects of a tariff?
- What are the effects of an import quota?
- What is the economic impact of subsidies?

TARIFFS

tariff
a tax on imports

A **tariff** is a tax on imported goods. Tariffs are usually relatively small revenue producers that retard the expansion of trade. They bring about higher prices and revenues to domestic producers, and lower sales and revenues to foreign producers. Moreover, tariffs lead to higher prices to domestic consumers. In fact, the gains to producers are more than offset by the loss to consumers. Let us see how this works graphically.

THE DOMESTIC ECONOMIC IMPACT OF TARIFFS

The domestic economic impact of tariffs is presented in Exhibit 1, which illustrates the supply and demand curves for domestic consumers and producers of shoes. In a typical international supply and demand illustration, the intersection of the world supply and demand curves would determine the domestic market price. However, with import tariffs, the domestic price of shoes is greater than the world price, as in Exhibit 1. We consider the world supply curve (S_{WORLD}) to domestic consumers to be perfectly elastic; that is, we can buy all we want at the world price (P_{WORLD}). At the world price, domestic producers are only willing to provide quantity Q_S, but domestic consumers are willing to buy quantity Q_D—more than domestic producers are willing to supply. Imports make up the difference.

As you can see in Exhibit 1, the imposition of the tariff shifts up the perfectly elastic supply curve from foreigners to domestic consumers from S_{WORLD} to $S_{WORLD + TARIFF}$, but it does not alter the domestic supply or demand curve. At the resulting higher domestic price ($P_{W + T}$), domestic suppliers are willing to supply more, Q'_S, but domestic consumers are willing to buy less, Q'_D. At the new equilibrium, the domestic price ($P_{W + T}$) is higher and the quantity of shoes demanded (Q'_D) is smaller. But at the new price, the domestic quantity demanded is lower and the quantity supplied domestically is greater, reducing the quantity of imported shoes. Overall, then, tariffs lead to (1) a smaller total quantity sold, (2) a higher price for shoes for domestic consumers, (3) greater sales of shoes at higher prices for domestic producers, and (4) lower sales of foreign shoes.

While domestic producers do gain more sales and higher earnings, consumers lose much more. The increase in price from the tariff results in a loss in consumer surplus, as shown in Exhibit 1. After the tariff, shoe prices rise to $P_{W + T}$, and, consequently, consumer surplus falls by area b + c + d + e, representing the welfare loss to consumers from the tariff. Area b in Exhibit 1 shows the gain to domestic producers as a result of the tariff. That is, at the higher price, domestic producers are willing to supply more shoes, representing a welfare gain to producers resulting from the tariff. As a result of the tariff revenues, government gains area d. This is the import tariff—the revenue government

section 19.4 Exhibit 1 Free Trade and Tariffs

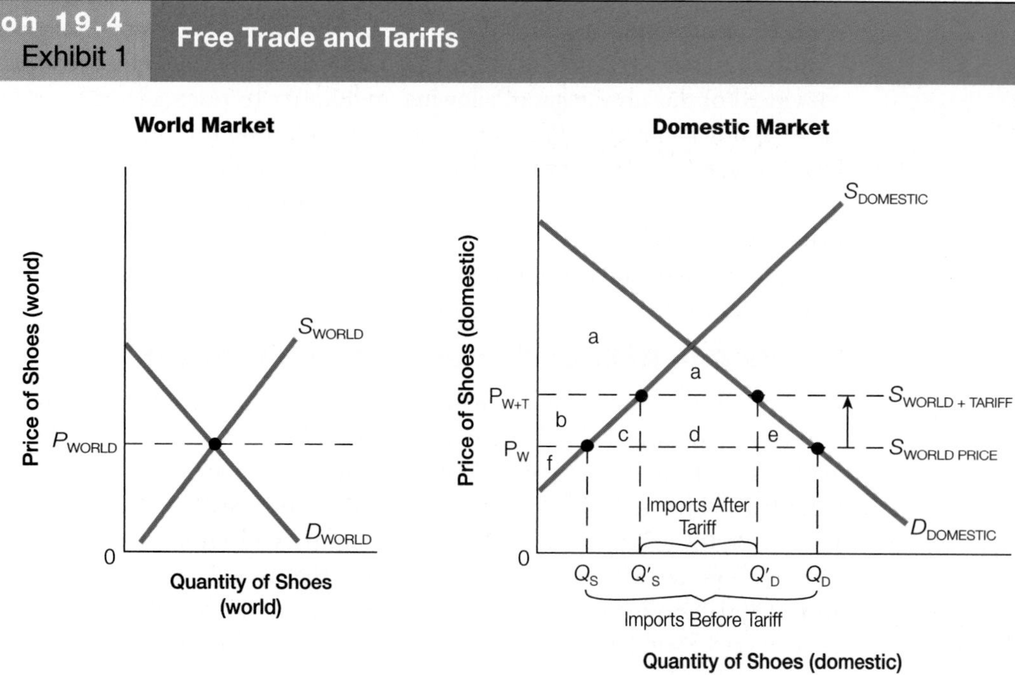

Gains and Losses from Tariffs

Area	Before Tariff	After Tariff	Change
Consumer Surplus (*CS*)	a + b + c + d + e	a	− (b + c + d + e)
Producer Surplus (*PS*)	f	b + f	+ b
Government Revenues (Tariff)	—	d	+ d
Total Welfare from Tariff (*CS* + *PS* + Tariff Revenues)	a + b + c + d + e + f	a + b + d + f	− (c + e)

In the case of a tariff, we see that consumers lose more than producers and government gain. On net, the deadweight loss associated with the new tariff is represented by area c + e.

collects from foreign countries on imports. However, we see from Exhibit 1 that consumers lose more than producers and government gain from the tariff. That is, on net, the deadweight loss associated with the tariff is represented by area c + e.

ARGUMENTS FOR TARIFFS

Despite the preceding arguments against trade restrictions, they continue to be levied. Some rationale for their existence is necessary. Three common arguments for the use of trade restrictions deserve our critical examination.

Temporary Trade Restrictions Help Infant Industries Grow

A country might argue that a protective tariff will allow a new industry to more quickly reach a scale of operation at which economies of scale and production efficiencies can be realized. That is, temporarily shielding the young industry from competition from foreign firms will allow the infant industry a chance to grow. With the early protection, these firms will eventually be able to compete effectively in the global market. It is presumed that without this protection, the industry could never get on its feet. At first hearing, the argument sounds valid, but there are many problems with it. How do you identify "infant industries" that genuinely have potential economies of scale and will quickly become efficient with protection? We do not know the long-run average total cost curves of industries, a necessary piece of information. Moreover, if firms and governments are truly convinced of the advantages of allowing an industry to reach a large scale, would it not be wise to make massive loans to the industry, allowing it to instantly begin large-scale production rather than slowly and at the expense of consumers? In other words, the goal of allowing the industry to reach its efficient size can be reached without protection. Finally, the history of infant industry tariffs suggests that the tariffs often linger long after the industry is mature and no longer in "need" of protection.

Tariffs Can Reduce Domestic Unemployment

Exhibit 1 showed how tariffs increase output by domestic producers, thus leading to increased employment and reduced unemployment in industries where tariffs were imposed. Yet the overall employment effects of a tariff imposition are not likely to be positive; the argument is incorrect. Why? First, the imposition of a tariff by the United States on, say, foreign steel is going to be noticed in the countries adversely affected by the tariff. If a new tariff on steel lowers Japanese steel sales to the United States, the Japanese likely will retaliate by imposing tariffs on U.S. exports to Japan, say, on machinery exports. The retaliatory tariff will lower U.S. sales of machinery and thus employment in the U.S. machinery industries. As a result, the gain in employment in the steel industry will be offset by a loss of employment elsewhere.

Even if the other countries did not retaliate, U.S. employment would likely suffer outside the industry gaining the tariff protection. The way that other countries pay for U.S. goods is by getting dollars from sales to the United States—imports to us. If new tariffs lead to restrictions on imports, fewer dollars will be flowing overseas in payment for imports, which means that foreigners will have fewer dollars available to buy our exports. Other things equal, this will tend to reduce our exports, thus creating unemployment in the export industries.

Tariffs Are Necessary for National Security Reasons

Sometimes it is argued that tariffs are a means of preventing a nation from becoming too dependent on foreign suppliers of goods vital to national security. That is, by making foreign goods more expensive, we can protect domestic suppliers. For example, if oil is vital to running planes and tanks, a cutoff of foreign supplies of oil during wartime could cripple a nation's defenses.

The national security argument is usually not valid. If a nation's own resources are depletable, tariff-imposed reliance on domestic supplies will hasten depletion of domestic reserves, making the country even *more* dependent on imports in the future. If we impose a high tariff on foreign oil to protect domestic producers, we will increase domestic output of oil in the short run, but in the process, we will deplete the stockpile of available reserves. Thus, the defense argument is often of questionable validity. From a defense standpoint, it makes more sense to use foreign oil in peacetime and perhaps stockpile "insurance" supplies so that larger domestic supplies would be available during wars.

import quota
a legal limit on the imported quantity of a good that is produced abroad and can be sold in domestic markets

IMPORT QUOTAS

Like tariffs, **import quotas** directly restrict imports, leading to reductions in trade and thus preventing nations from fully realizing their comparative advantage. The case for quotas is probably even weaker than the case for tariffs. Suppose that the Japanese have been sending 4 million TV sets annually to the United States but now are told that, because of quota restrictions, they can only send 3 million sets. If the Japanese manufacturers are allowed to determine how the quantity reduction is to occur, they will likely collude, leading to higher prices. Suppose that each producer is simply told to reduce sales by 25 percent. They will substantially raise the price of the sets to Americans above what the 4 million original buyers would have paid for them.

THE GOVERNMENT DOES NOT COLLECT REVENUES FROM IMPORT QUOTAS

Unlike what occurs with a tariff, the U.S. government does not collect any revenue as a result of the import quota. Despite the higher prices, the loss in consumer surplus, and the loss in government revenue, quotas come about because people often view them as being less "protectionist" than tariffs—the traditional, most maligned form of protection.

Besides the rather blunt means of curtailing imports by using tariffs and quotas, nations have devised still other, more subtle means to restrict international trade. For example, nations sometimes impose product standards, ostensibly to protect consumers against inferior merchandise. Effectively, however, sometimes those standards are simply a means to restrict foreign competition. For example, France might keep certain kinds of wine out of the country on the grounds that they were made with allegedly inferior grapes or had an inappropriate alcoholic content. Likewise, the United States might prohibit automobile imports that do not meet certain standards in terms of pollutants, safety, and gasoline mileage. Even if these standards are not intended to restrict foreign competition, the regulations may nonetheless have that impact, restricting consumer choice in the process.

THE DOMESTIC ECONOMIC IMPACT OF AN IMPORT QUOTA

The domestic economic impact of an import quota on autos is presented in Exhibit 2. The introduction of an import quota increases the price from the world price, P_W (established in the world market for autos) to P_{W+Q}. The quota causes the price to rise above the world price. The domestic quantity demanded falls and the domestic quantity supplied rises. Consequently, the number of imports is much smaller than it would be without the import quota. Compared to free trade, domestic producers are better-off but domestic consumers are worse-off. Specifically, the import quota results in a gain in producer surplus of area a and a loss in consumer surplus of area b + c + d + e. However, unlike the tariff case, where the government gains area d in revenues, the government does not gain any revenues with a quota. Consequently, the deadweight loss is even greater with quotas than with tariffs. That is, on net, the deadweight loss associated with the quota is represented by area c + d + e. Recall that the deadweight loss was only c + e for tariffs.

If tariffs and import quotas hurt importing countries, why do they exist? The reason they exist is that producers can make large profits or "rents" from tariffs and import quotas. Economists call these efforts to gain profits from government protection **rent seeking.** Because this is money, time, and effort that could have been spent producing something else rather than spent on lobbying efforts, the deadweight loss from tariffs and quotas will likely understate the true deadweight loss to society.

rent seeking
producer efforts to gain profits from government protections such as tariffs and import quotas

Free Trade and Import Quotas

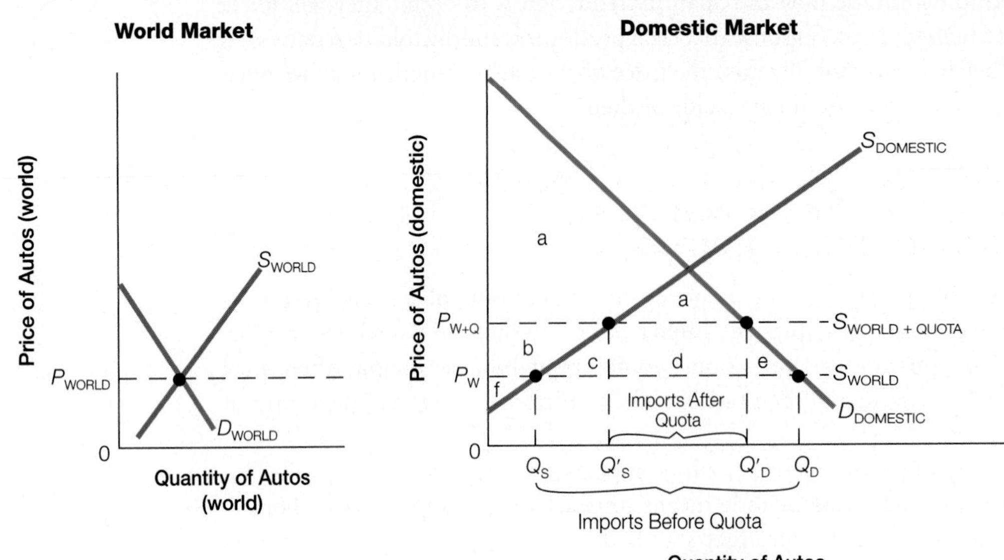

Gains and Losses from Import Quotas

Area	Before Quota	After Quota	Change
Consumer Surplus (*CS*)	a + b + c + d + e	a	− (b + c + d + e)
Producer Surplus (*PS*)	f	b + f	+ b
Total Welfare (*CS* + *PS*) from Quota	a + b + c + d + e + f	a + b + f	− (c + d + e)

With an import quota, the price rises from P_W to P_{W+Q}. Compared to free trade, consumers lose area b + c + d + e and producers gain area b. The deadweight loss from the quota is area c + d + e. Under quotas, consumers lose and producers gain. The difference in deadweight loss between quotas and tariffs is area d that the government is not able to pick up with import quotas.

THE ECONOMIC IMPACT OF SUBSIDIES

Working in the opposite direction, governments sometimes try to encourage exports by subsidizing producers. With a subsidy, revenue is given to producers for each exported unit of output. This stimulates exports. While not a barrier to trade like tariffs and quotas, objections can be raised that subsidies distort trade patterns and lead to inefficiencies. How does this happen? With subsidies, producers will export goods not because their costs are lower than that of a foreign competitor, but because their costs have been artificially reduced by government action, transferring income from taxpayers to the exporter. The subsidy does not reduce the actual labor, raw material, and capital costs of production—society has the same opportunity costs as before. A nation's taxpayers end up subsidizing the output of producers who, relative to producers in other countries, are inefficient. The nation, then, exports products in which it does not have a comparative advantage. Gains from trade in terms of world output are eliminated or reduced by such subsidies. Thus, subsidies, usually defended as a means of increasing exports and improving a nation's international financial position, are usually of dubious worth to the world economy and even to the economy doing the subsidizing.

Section Check

1. A tariff is a tax on imported goods.
2. Tariffs bring about higher prices and revenues to domestic producers, and lower sales and revenues to foreign producers. Tariffs lead to higher prices and reduce consumer surplus for domestic consumers. Tariffs result in a net loss in welfare because the loss in consumer surplus is greater than the gain to producers and the government.
3. Arguments for the use of tariffs include: tariffs help infant industries grow; tariffs can reduce domestic unemployment; new tariffs can help finance our international trade; and tariffs are necessary for national security reasons.
4. Like tariffs, import quotas restrict imports, lowering consumer surplus and preventing countries from fully realizing their comparative advantage. There is a net loss in welfare from quotas, but it is proportionately larger than for a tariff because there are no government revenues.
5. Sometimes government tries to encourage production of a certain good by subsidizing its production with taxpayer dollars. Because subsidies stimulate exports, they are not a barrier to trade like tariffs and import quotas. However, they do distort trade patterns and cause overall inefficiencies.

---

1. Why do tariffs increase domestic producer surplus but decrease domestic consumer surplus?
2. How do import tariffs increase employment in "protected" industries, but at the expense of a likely decrease in employment overall?
3. Why is the national security argument for tariffs questionable?
4. Why is the domestic argument for import quotas weaker than the case for tariffs?
5. Why would foreign producers prefer import quotas to tariffs, even if they resulted in the same reduced level of imports?
6. Why does subsidizing exports by industries that lack a comparative advantage tend to harm the domestic economy, on net?

section 19.5

The Balance of Payments

- What is the balance of payments?
- What are the three main components of the balance of payments?
- What is the balance of trade?

BALANCE OF PAYMENTS

The record of all of the international financial transactions of a nation over a year is called the **balance of payments.** The balance of payments is a statement that records all the exchanges requiring an outflow of funds to foreign nations or an inflow of funds from other nations. Just as an examination of gross domestic product accounts gives us some idea of the economic health and vitality of a nation, the balance of payments provides information about a nation's world trade position. The balance of payments is divided into three main sections: the current account, the capital account, and an "error term" called the statistical discrepancy. These are highlighted in Exhibit 1. Let us look at each of these components beginning with the current account, which is made up of imports and exports of goods and services.

balance of payments
the record of international transactions in which a nation has engaged over a year

section 19.5
Exhibit 1

U.S. Balance of Payments (Billions of Dollars)

Type of Transaction

Current Account			**Capital Account**		
1. Exports of goods	$ 772		10. U.S.-owned assets abroad	$ −581	
2. Imports of goods	−1224		11. Foreign owned assets in the United States	1,024	
3. Balance of trade (lines 1+ 2)		−452	12. Capital account balance (lines 10 + 11)		443
4. Service exports	294		13. Statistical discrepancy	1	
5. Service imports	−217		14. Net Balance (lines 9 + 12 + 13)		$0
6. Balance on goods and services (lines 3 + 4 + 5)		−375			
7. Unilateral transfers (net)	−54				
8. Investment income (net)	−15				
9. Current account balance (lines 6 + 7 + 8)		−444			

SOURCE: *Survey of Current Business.*

THE CURRENT ACCOUNT

Export Goods and the Current Account

current account
a record of a country's imports and exports of goods and services, net investment income, and net transfers

A **current account** is a record of a country's imports and exports of goods and services, net investment income, and net transfers. Any time a foreign buyer purchases a good from a U.S. producer, the foreign buyer must pay the U.S. producer for the good. Usually, the foreigner must pay for the good in U.S. dollars, because the seller wants to pay his workers and for other inputs with dollars. This requires the foreign buyer to exchange units of his currency at a foreign exchange dealer for U.S. dollars. Because the United States gains claims for foreign goods by obtaining foreign currency in exchange for the dollars needed to buy exports, all exports of U.S. goods abroad are considered a credit or plus (+) item in the U.S. balance of payments. Those foreign currencies are later exchangeable for goods and services made in the country that purchased the U.S. exports.

Import Goods and the Current Account

When a U.S. consumer buys an imported good, however, the reverse is true: The U.S. importer must pay the foreign producer, usually in that nation's currency. Typically, the U.S. buyer will go to a foreign exchange dealer and exchange dollars for units of that foreign currency. Imports are thus a debit (–) item in the balance of payments, because the dollars sold to buy the foreign currency add to foreign claims for foreign goods, which are later exchangeable for U.S. goods and services. Our imports, then, provide the means by which foreigners can buy our exports.

Services and the Current Account

While imports and exports of goods are the largest components of the balance of payments, they are not the only ones. Nations import and export services as well. A particularly important service is tourism. When U.S. tourists go abroad, they are buying foreign-produced services in addition to those purchased by citizens there. Those services include the use of hotels, sightseeing tours, restaurants, and so forth. In the current account, these services are included in imports. On the other hand, foreign tourism in the United States provides us with foreign currencies and claims against foreigners, so they are included in exports. Airline and shipping services also affect the balance of payments. When someone from Italy flies American Airlines, that person is making a payment to a U.S. company. Because the flow of international financial claims is the same, this payment is treated just like a U.S. export in the balance of payments. If an American flies on Alitalia, however, Italians acquire claims against the United States, and so it is included as a debit (import) item in the U.S. balance of payments accounts.

When a foreign tourist rides a cable car in San Francisco, how does that affect the current account? Tourism provides the United States with foreign currency, which is included in exports.

Net Transfer Payments and Net Investment Income

Other items that affect the current account are private and government grants and gifts to and from other countries. When the U.S. gives foreign aid to another country, this creates a debit in the U.S. balance of payments because it gives foreigners added claims against the United States in the form of dollars. Private gifts, such as individuals receiving money from relatives or friends in foreign countries, show up in the current account as debit items as well. Because the United States usually sends more humanitarian and military aid to foreigners than we receive, net transfers are usually in deficit.

There is also net investment income in the current account—U.S. investors hold foreign assets and foreign investors hold U.S. assets. In Exhibit 1, investment income paid to foreigners exceeded investment received from foreigners by $15 billion.

Current Account Balance

The balance on current account is the net amount of credits or debits after adding up all transactions of goods (merchandise imports and exports), services, and transfer payments (e.g., foreign aid and gifts). If the sum of credits exceeds the sum of debits, the nation is said to run a balance of payments surplus on current account. If debits exceed credits, however, the nation is running a balance of payment deficit on current account.

The Balance of Trade and the Balance of Current Account

The balance of payments of the United States is presented in Exhibit 1. Note that exports and imports of goods and services are by far the largest credits and debits. Note also that U.S. exports of goods were $452 billion less than imports of goods. The import/export goods relationship is often called the **balance of trade.** The United States, therefore, experienced a balance of trade deficit that year of $452 billion. However, some of the $452 billion trade deficit was offset by credits from a $77 billion surplus in services. That leads to a $375 billion balance of goods and services deficit. When $54 billion of net unilateral transfers (gifts and grants between the U.S. and foreigners) and $15 billion of investment income (net) from the United States is subtracted (the United States gave more to the foreigners than they gave to the United States), the total deficit on current account was $444 billion.

balance of trade
the net surplus or deficit resulting from the level of exportation and importation of merchandise

THE CAPITAL ACCOUNT

How was this deficit on current account financed? Remember that U.S. credits give us the financial means to buy foreign goods, and that our credits were $194 billion less than our debits from our imports and net unilateral transfers to foreign countries. This deficit on current account balance is settled by movements of financial, or capital, assets. These transactions are recorded in the *capital account,* so that a current account deficit is financed by a capital account surplus.

What Does the Capital Account Record?

Capital account transactions include items such as international bank loans, purchases of corporate securities, government bond purchases, and direct investments in foreign subsidiary companies. In Exhibit 1, we see that the United States purchased foreign assets of $581 billion, which was a further debit because it provided foreigners with U.S. dollars. On the other hand, foreign investments in the United States were over $1,024 billion to buy bonds, stocks and other investments. In addition, the United States and other governments buy and sell dollars. On net, foreign-owned assets in the United States made about $443 billion more than U.S. assets abroad. On balance, then, there was a surplus (positive credit) in the capital account from capital movements of $443 billion, offsetting the $444 billion deficit on current account.

The Statistical Discrepancy

In the final analysis, it is true that the balance of payments account must balance so that credits and debits are equal. Why is this so? Due to the reciprocal aspect of trade, every credit eventually creates a debit of equal magnitude. These errors are sometimes large and are entered into the balance of payments as the *statistical discrepancy.* Including the errors and omissions recorded as the statistical discrepancy, the balance of payments do balance. That is, the number of U.S. dollar demanded equals the number of U.S. dollars supplied when there is a balance of payments of zero.

Balance of Payments: A Useful Analogy

In concept, the international balance of payments is similar to the personal financial transactions of individuals. Each individual has his own "balance of payments," reflecting his trading with other economic units: other individuals, corporations, or governments. People earn income or credits by "exporting" their labor service to other economic units, or by receiving investment income (a return on capital services). Against that, they "import" goods from other economic units; we call these imports "consumption." This debit item is sometimes augmented by payments made to outsiders (e.g., banks) on loans, and so forth. Fund transfers, such as gifts to children or charities, are other debit items (or credit items for recipients of the assistance).

As individuals, if our spending on our consumption exceeds our income from our exports of our labor and capital services, we have a "deficit" that must be financed by borrowing or selling assets. If we "export" more than we "import," however, we can make new investments and/or increase our "reserves" (savings and investment holdings). Like nations, individuals who run a deficit in daily transactions must make up for it through accommodating transactions (e.g., borrowing or reducing one's savings or investment holdings) to bring about an ultimate balance of credits and debits to their personal account.

Section Check

1. The balance of payments is the record of all the international financial transactions of a nation for any given year.
2. The balance of payments is made up of the current account, the capital account, as well as an "error term" called the statistical discrepancy.
3. The balance of trade refers strictly to the imports and exports of (merchandise) goods with other nations. If our imports of foreign goods are greater than our exports, we are said to have a balance of trade deficit.

---

1. What is the balance of payments?
2. Why would a British purchaser of U.S. goods or services have to first exchange pounds for dollars?
3. How is it that U.S. imports provide foreigners the means to buy U.S. exports?
4. What would have to be true in order for the United States to have a balance of trade deficit and a balance of payments surplus?
5. What would have to be true in order for the United States to have a balance of trade surplus and a current account deficit?
6. If there are no errors or omissions in the recorded balance of payments accounts, what should the statistical discrepancy equal?
7. A Nigerian family visiting Chicago enjoys a Chicago Cubs baseball game at Wrigley Field. How would that expense be recorded in the balance of payments accounts? Why?

section 19.6

Exchange Rates

- What are exchange rates?
- How are exchange rates determined?
- How do exchange rates affect the demand for foreign goods?

THE NEED FOR FOREIGN CURRENCIES

When U.S. consumers buy goods from people in other countries, the sellers of those goods want to be paid in their own domestic currencies. The U.S. consumers, then, must first exchange U.S. dollars for the seller's currency in order to pay for those goods. American importers must, therefore, constantly buy yen, euros, pesos, and other currencies in order to finance their purchases. Similarly, people in other countries buying U.S. goods must sell their currencies to obtain U.S. dollars in order to pay for those goods.

THE EXCHANGE RATE

The price of a unit of one foreign currency in terms of another is called the **exchange rate.** If a U.S. importer has agreed to pay euros (the new currency of the European Union) to buy a cuckoo clock made in the Black Forest in Germany, she would then have to exchange U.S. dollars for euros. If it takes $1.00 to buy 1 euro, then the exchange rate is $1.00 per euro. From the German perspective, the exchange rate is 1 euro per U.S. dollar.

exchange rate
the price of one unit of a country's currency in terms of another country's currency

CHANGES IN EXCHANGE RATES AFFECT THE DOMESTIC DEMAND FOR FOREIGN GOODS

Prices of goods in their currencies combine with exchange rates to determine the domestic price of foreign goods. Suppose the cuckoo clock sells for 100 euros in Germany. What is the price to U.S. consumers? Let us assume that tariffs and other transactions costs are zero. If the exchange rate is $1 = 1 euro, then the equivalent U.S. dollar price of the cuckoo clock is 100 euros times $1 per euro, or $100. If the exchange rate were to change to $2 = 1 euro, fewer clocks would be demanded in the United States. This is because the effective U.S. dollar price of the clocks would rise to $200 (100 euros times $2 per euro). The new higher relative value of a euro compared to the dollar (or equivalently, the lower the relative value of a dollar compared to the euro) would lead to a reduction in U.S. demand for German-made clocks.

With the introduction of the euro it will be easy to compare prices for the same goods in different countries using this currency. For example, if you use mail order or shop on the Internet, it will be easier to spot the bargains between countries.

THE DEMAND FOR A FOREIGN CURRENCY

The demand for foreign currencies is a **derived demand.** This is because the demand for a foreign currency derives directly from the demand for foreign goods and services or for foreign investment. The more foreign goods are demanded, the more of that foreign currency needed to pay for those goods. Such an increased demand for the currency will push up the exchange value of that currency relative to other currencies.

derived demand
the demand for an input derived from consumers' demand for the good or service produced with that input

THE SUPPLY OF A FOREIGN CURRENCY

Similarly, the supply of foreign currency is provided by foreigners who want to buy the exports of a particular nation. For example, the more that foreigners demand U.S. products, the more of their currencies they will supply in exchange for U.S. dollars, which they use to buy our products.

DETERMINING EXCHANGE RATES

We know that the demand for foreign currencies is derived from the demand for foreign goods, but how does that affect the exchange rate? Just as in the product market, the answer lies with the forces of supply and demand. In this case, it is the supply of and demand for a foreign currency that determine the equilibrium price (exchange rate) of that currency.

APPLICATION

EXCHANGE RATES

Q: Why is a strong dollar (i.e., exchange rate for foreign currencies is low) a mixed blessing?

A: A strong dollar will lower the price of imports and make trips to foreign countries less expensive. Lower prices on foreign goods also help keep inflation in check and make investments in foreign financial markets (foreign stocks and bonds) relatively cheaper. However, it makes U.S. exports more expensive. Consequently, foreigners will buy fewer U.S. goods and services. The net effect is a fall in exports and a rise in imports—net exports fall. Note that some Americans are helped (vacationers going to foreign countries and those preferring foreign goods), while others are harmed (producers of U.S. exports, operators of hotels dependent on foreign visitors in the United States). A stronger dollar also makes it more difficult for foreign investors to invest in the United States.

section 19.6
Exhibit 1

Equilibrium in the Foreign Exchange Market

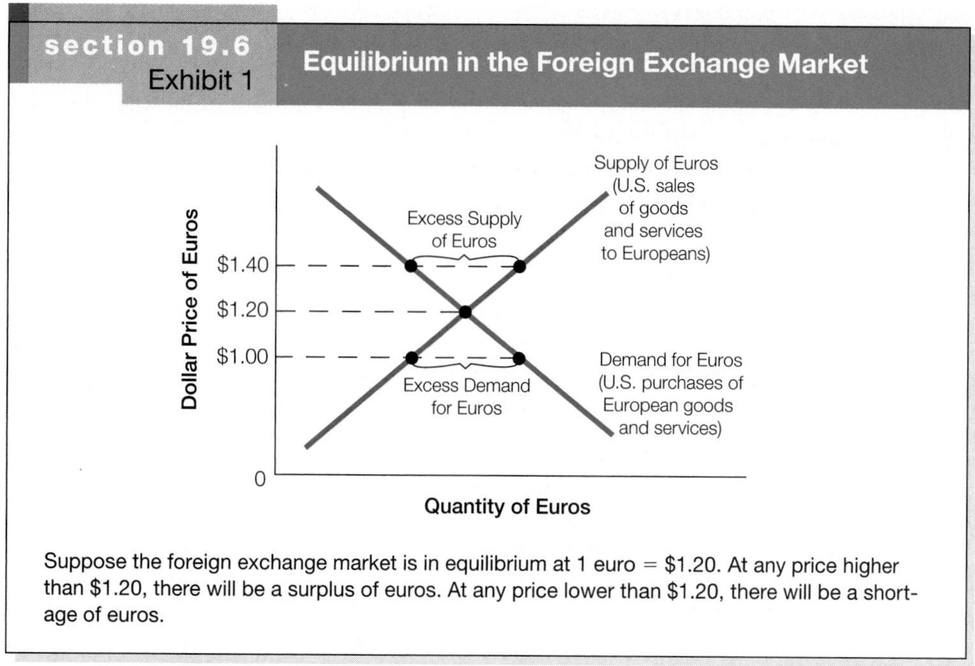

Suppose the foreign exchange market is in equilibrium at 1 euro = $1.20. At any price higher than $1.20, there will be a surplus of euros. At any price lower than $1.20, there will be a shortage of euros.

THE DEMAND CURVE FOR A FOREIGN CURRENCY

As Exhibit 1 shows, the demand curve for a foreign currency—euro, for example—is downward sloping, just as it is in product markets. In this case, however, the demand curve has a negative slope because as the price of the euro falls relative to the dollar, European products become relatively more inexpensive to U.S. consumers, who therefore buy more European goods. To do so, the quantity of euros demanded by U.S. consumers will increase to buy more European goods as the price of the euro falls. This is why the demand for foreign currencies is considered to be a derived demand.

THE SUPPLY CURVE FOR FOREIGN CURRENCY

The supply curve for a foreign currency is upward sloping, just as it is in product markets. In this case, as the price, or value, of the euro increases relative to the dollar, U.S. products will become relatively less expensive to European buyers and they will increase the quantity of dollars they demand. Europeans will, therefore, increase the quantity of euros supplied to the U.S. by buying more U.S. products. Hence, the supply curve is upward sloping.

EQUILIBRIUM IN THE FOREIGN EXCHANGE MARKET

Equilibrium is reached where the demand and supply curves for a given currency intersect. In Exhibit 1, the equilibrium price of a euro is $1.20. As in the product market, if the dollar price of euros is higher than the equilibrium price, an excess quantity of euros will be supplied at that price, or a surplus of euros. Competition among euro sellers will push the price of euros down toward equilibrium. Likewise, if the dollar price of euros is lower than the equilibrium price, an excess quantity of euros will be demanded at that price, or a shortage of euros. Competition among euro buyers will push the price of euros up toward equilibrium.

Section Check

1. The price of a unit of one foreign currency in terms of another is called the exchange rate.
2. The exchange rate for a currency is determined by the supply of and demand for that currency in the foreign exchange market.
3. If the dollar appreciates in value relative to foreign currencies, foreign goods become more inexpensive to U.S. consumers, increasing U.S. demand for foreign goods.

---

1. What is an exchange rate?
2. When a U.S. dollar buys relatively more French francs, why does the cost of imports from France fall in the United States?
3. When a U.S. dollar buys relatively fewer Austrian shillings, why does the cost of U.S. exports fall in Austria?
4. How does an increase in domestic demand for foreign goods and services increase the demand for those foreign currencies?
5. As euros get cheaper relative to U.S. dollars, why does the quantity of euros demanded by Americans increase? Why doesn't the demand for euros increase as a result?
6. Who competes exchange rates down when they are above their equilibrium value? Who competes exchange rates up when they are below their equilibrium value?

section 19.7

Equilibrium Changes in the Foreign Exchange Market

- What factors cause the demand curve for a currency to shift?
- What factors cause the supply curve for a currency to shift?

DETERMINANTS IN THE FOREIGN EXCHANGE MARKET

The equilibrium exchange rate of a currency changes many times daily. Sometimes, these changes can be quite significant. Any force that shifts either the demand for or supply of a currency will shift the equilibrium in the foreign exchange market, leading to a new exchange rate. These factors include changes in consumer tastes for goods, changes in income, changes in relative real interest rates, changes in relative inflation rates, and speculation.

INCREASED TASTES FOR FOREIGN GOODS

Because the demand for foreign currencies is derived from the demand for foreign goods, any change in the demand for foreign goods will shift the demand schedule for foreign currency in the same direction. For example, if a cuckoo clock revolution sweeps through the United States, German producers would have reason to celebrate, knowing that many U.S. buyers will turn to Germany for their cuckoo clocks. The Germans, however, will only accept payment in the form of euros, and so U.S. consumers and retailers must convert their dollars into euros before they can purchase their clocks. The increased taste for European goods in the United States would, therefore, lead to an increased demand for

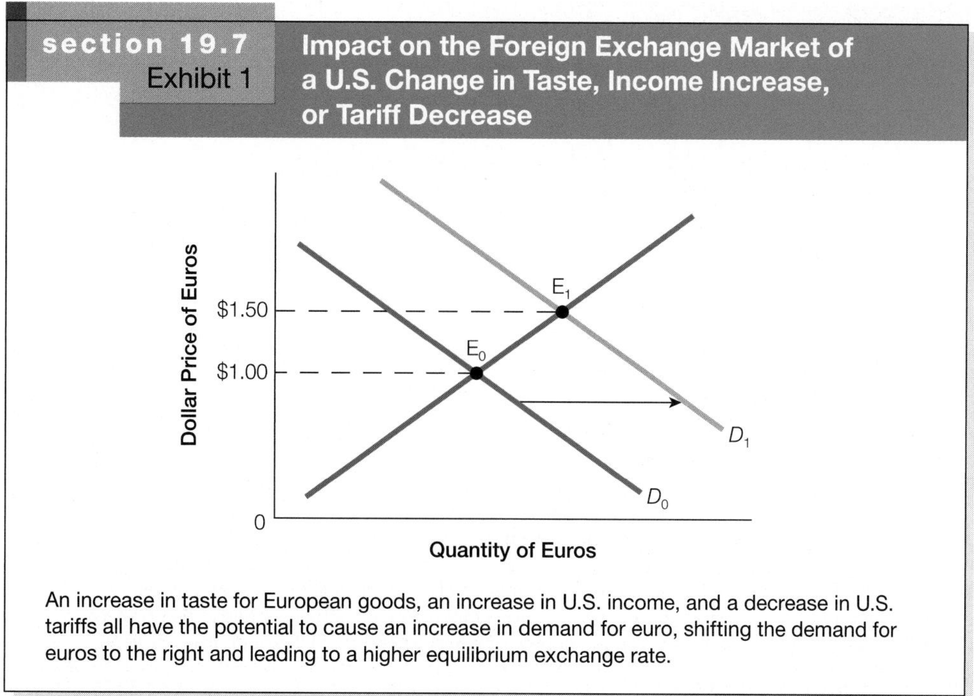

An increase in taste for European goods, an increase in U.S. income, and a decrease in U.S. tariffs all have the potential to cause an increase in demand for euro, shifting the demand for euros to the right and leading to a higher equilibrium exchange rate.

euros. As shown in Exhibit 1, this increased demand for euros shifts the demand curve to the right, resulting in a new, higher equilibrium dollar price of euros.

RELATIVE INCOME INCREASES OR REDUCTIONS IN U.S. TARIFFS

Any change in the average income of U.S. consumers will also change the equilibrium exchange rate, *ceteris paribus.* If on the whole incomes increased in the United States, Americans would buy more goods, including imported goods, so more European goods would be bought. This increased demand for European goods would lead to an increased demand for euros, resulting in a higher exchange rate for the euro. A decrease in U.S. tariffs on European goods would tend to have the same effect as an increase in incomes by making European goods more affordable. As Exhibit 1 shows, this would again lead to an increased demand for European goods and a higher short-run equilibrium exchange rate for the euro.

What impact will an increase in travel to Paris by U.S. consumers have on the dollar price of euros? In order for a consumer to buy souvenirs at the Eiffel Tower, she will need to exchange dollars for euros. This would increase the demand for euros and result in a new higher dollar price of euros.

CHANGES IN EUROPEAN INCOME, TARIFFS, OR TASTES

If European incomes rose, European tariffs on U.S. goods fell, or European tastes for American goods increased, the supply of euros in the euro foreign exchange market would increase. Any of these changes would cause Europeans to demand more U.S. goods, and therefore more U.S. dollars in order to purchase those goods. To obtain those added dollars, Europeans must exchange more of their euros, increasing the supply of euros on the euro foreign exchange market. As Exhibit 2 demonstrates, the effect of this would be a rightward shift in the euro supply curve, leading to a new equilibrium at a lower exchange rate for the euro.

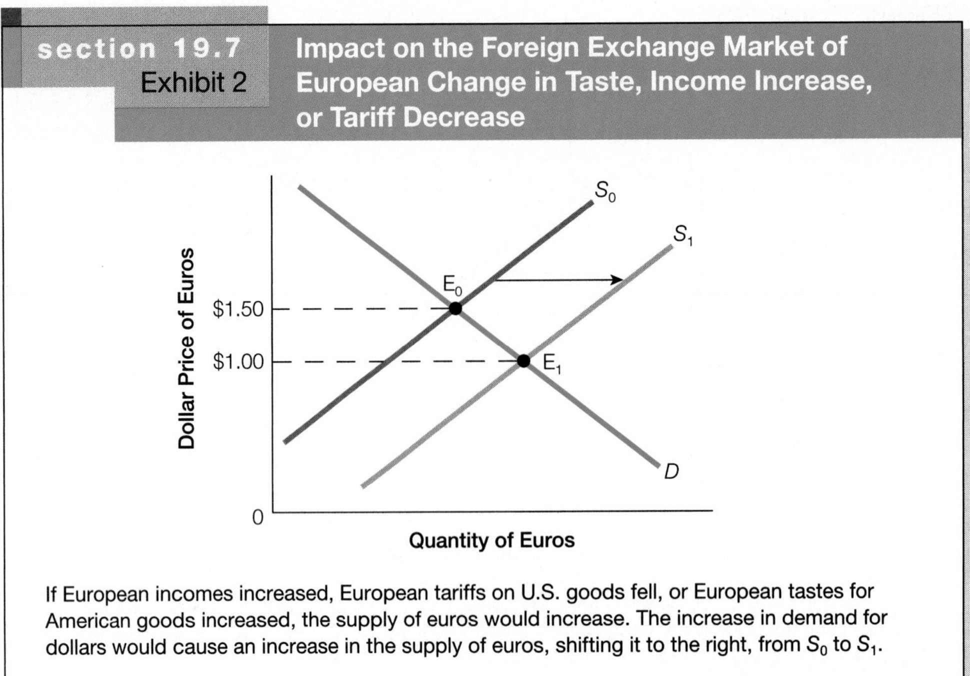

section 19.7 Exhibit 2 Impact on the Foreign Exchange Market of European Change in Taste, Income Increase, or Tariff Decrease

If European incomes increased, European tariffs on U.S. goods fell, or European tastes for American goods increased, the supply of euros would increase. The increase in demand for dollars would cause an increase in the supply of euros, shifting it to the right, from S_0 to S_1.

HOW DO CHANGES IN RELATIVE INTEREST RATES AFFECT EXCHANGE RATES?

If interest rates in the United States were to increase relative to, say, European interest rates, other things equal, the rate of return on U.S. investments would increase relative to that on European investments. European investors would thus increase their demand for U.S. investments, and therefore offer euros for sale to buy dollars to buy U.S. investments, shifting the supply curve for euros to the right, from S_0 to S_1 in Exhibit 3.

In this scenario, U.S. investors would also shift their investments away from Europe by decreasing their demand for euros relative to their demand for dollars, from D_0 to D_1 in Exhibit 3. A subsequent lower equilibrium price ($1.50) would result for the euro due to an increase in the U.S. interest rate. That is, the euro would depreciate because euros can now buy fewer units of dollars than before. In short, the higher U.S. interest rate attracted more investment to the United States and led to a relative appreciation of the dollar and a relative depreciation of the euro.

CHANGES IN THE RELATIVE INFLATION RATE

If Europe experienced an inflation rate greater than that experienced in the United States, other things equal, what would happen to the exchange rate? In this case, European products would become more expensive to U.S. consumers. Americans would decrease the quantity of European goods demanded and, therefore, decrease their demand for euros. The result would be a leftward shift of the demand curve for euros.

On the other side of the Atlantic, U.S. goods would become relatively cheaper to Europeans, leading Europeans to increase the quantity of U.S. goods demanded, and therefore, to demand more U.S. dollars. This increased demand for dollars translates into an increased supply of euros, shifting the supply curve for euros outward. Exhibit 4 shows the shifts of the supply and demand curves and the new lower equilibrium price for the euro resulting from the higher European rate.

section 19.7 Exhibit 3 **Impact of U.S. Interest Rate Increase on the Foreign Exchange Market**

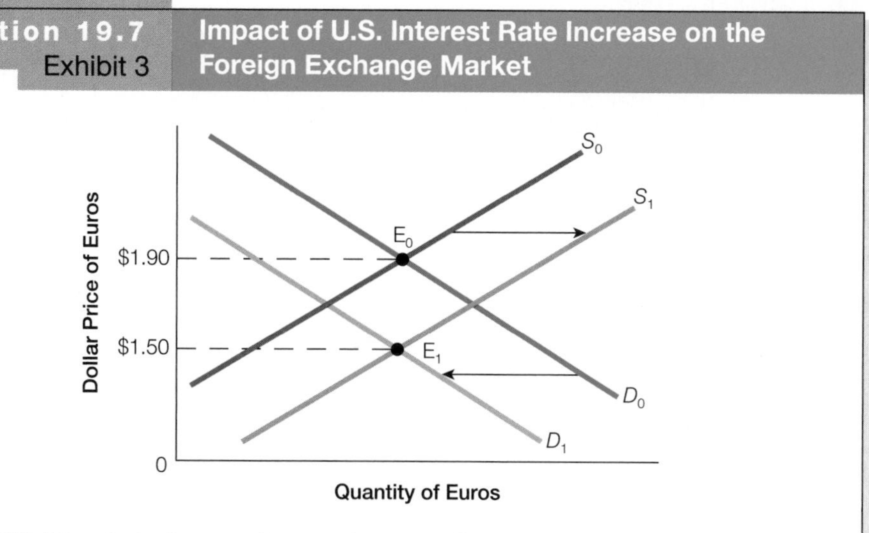

When U.S. interest rates increase, European investors will increase their supply of euros to buy dollars—the supply curve of euros increases from S_0 to S_1. In addition, U.S. investors will also shift their investments away from Europe, decreasing their demand for euros and shifting the demand curve from D_0 to D_1. This will lead to a depreciation of the euro; that is, euros can now buy fewer units of dollars.

EXPECTATIONS AND SPECULATION

Every trading day roughly a trillion dollars of currency trades hands in the foreign exchange markets. Suppose currency traders believed the United States was going to experience more rapid inflation in the future than Japan. If currency speculators believe that the value of the dollar will soon be falling because of the anticipated rise in U.S. inflation rate, those that are holding dollars will convert them to yen. This leads to an increase in the demand for yen—the yen appreciates and the dollar depreciates relative to the yen, *ceteris paribus.* In short, if speculators believe that the price of a country's currency is going to rise, they will buy more of that currency, pushing up the price and causing the country's currency to appreciate.

APPLICATION

DETERMINANTS OF EXCHANGE RATES

Q: How will each of the following events impact the foreign exchange market?
A. American travel to Europe increases
B. Japanese investors purchase U.S. stock
C. U.S. real interest rates abruptly increase relative to world interest rates
D. Other countries become less political and economically stable relative to the United States

A: A. Demand for euros increases (demand shifts right in the euro market), the dollar will depreciate and the euro will appreciate, *ceteris paribus*.

B. Demand for dollars increases (demand shifts right in the dollar market), the dollar will appreciate and the yen will depreciate, *ceteris paribus*. Alternatively, you could think of this as an increase in supply in the yen market.

C. International investors will increase their demand for dollars in the dollar market to take advantage of the higher interest rate. The dollar would appreciate relative to other foreign currencies, *ceteris paribus*.

D. More foreign investors will want to buy U.S. assets, causing an increase in demand for dollars.

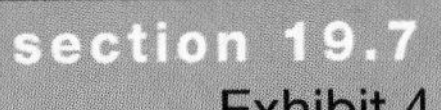

Impact of European Inflation Rate Increase on the Foreign Exchange Market

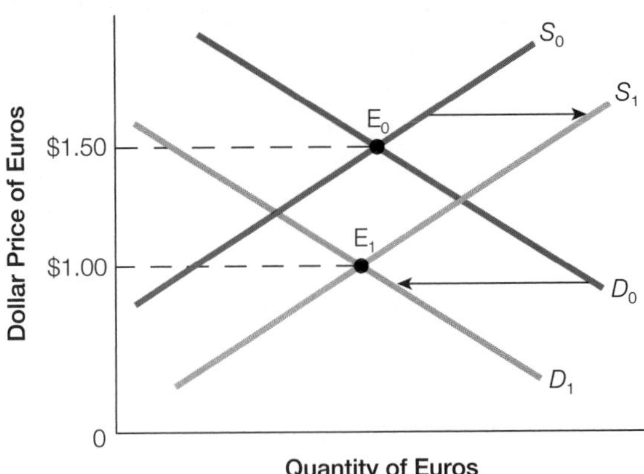

If Europe experienced a higher inflation rate than the United States, European products would become more expensive to U.S. consumers. As a result, those consumers would demand fewer euros, shifting the demand for euros to the left, from D_0 to D_1. At the same time, U.S. goods would become relatively cheaper to Europeans, who would then buy more dollars by supplying euros, shifting the euro supply curve to the right, from S_0 to S_1. The result: a new lower equilibrium price for the euro.

Section Check

1. Any force that shifts either the demand or supply curves for a foreign currency will shift the equilibrium in the foreign exchange market and lead to a new exchange rate.
2. Any changes in tastes, income levels, relative real interest rates, or relative inflation rates will cause the demand for and supply of a currency to shift.

---

1. Why will the exchange value of a foreign currency relative to U.S. dollars decline when U.S. domestic tastes change, reducing the demand for foreign-produced goods?
2. Why does the demand for foreign currencies shift in the same direction as domestic income? What happens to the exchange value of those foreign currencies in terms of dollars?
3. How would increased U.S. tariffs on imported European goods affect the exchange value of euros in terms of dollars?
4. Why do changes in tastes, incomes, or tariffs in the U.S. change the demand for euros, while similar changes in Europe change the supply of euros?
5. What would happen to the exchange value of euros in terms of U.S. dollars if incomes rose in both Europe and the U.S.?
6. Why does an increase in interest rates in Germany relative to U.S. interest rates increase the demand for euros but decrease their supply?
7. What would an increase in U.S. inflation relative to Europe do to the supply and demand for euros and to the equilibrium exchange value (price) of euros in terms of U.S. dollars?

Summary

The volume of international trade has increased substantially in the United States over the last several decades. During that time, exports and imports have grown from less than 5 percent to over 12 percent of GDP. The single most-important U.S. trading partner is Canada—it accounts for roughly one-fourth of U.S. exports and almost one-fifth of U.S. imports. Trade with Japan, Mexico, China, Germany, the United Kingdom, France, and Taiwan is also particularly important to the United States.

As economic growth occurs, regions and countries tend to specialize in what they produce best, resulting in more total output from the available scarce resources.

A nation, geographic area, or even a person can gain from trade if a good or service is produced relatively cheaper than other areas or people can produce it. That is, an area should specialize in producing and selling those items that it can produce at a lower opportunity cost than others.

Through trade and specialization in products in which it has a comparative advantage, a country can enjoy a greater array of goods and services at a lower cost.

The difference between what a consumer is willing and able to pay and what a consumer actually has to pay is called consumer surplus. The difference between what a supplier is willing and able to supply and the price a supplier receives for selling a good or service is called producer surplus.

With free trade and exports, domestic producers gain more than domestic consumers lose. With free trade and imports, domestic consumers gain more than domestic producers lose.

A tariff is a tax on imported goods. Tariffs bring about higher prices and revenues to domestic producers, and lower sales and revenues to foreign producers. Tariffs lead to higher prices and reduce consumer surplus for domestic consumers. Arguments for the use of tariffs include: tariffs help infant industries grow; tariffs can reduce domestic unemployment; new tariffs can help finance our international trade; and tariffs are necessary for national security reasons.

Like tariffs, import quotas restrict imports, lower consumer surplus, and prevent countries from fully realizing their comparative advantage.

Sometimes government tries to encourage production of a certain good by subsidizing its production with taxpayer dollars. Because subsidies stimulate exports, they are not a barrier to trade like tariffs and import quotas. However, they do distort trade patterns and cause overall inefficiencies.

The balance of payments is the record of all the international financial transactions of a nation for any given year. The balance of payments is made up of the current account, the capital account, as well as an "error term" called the statistical discrepancy. The balance of trade refers strictly to the imports and exports of (merchandise) goods with other nations. If imports of foreign goods are greater than exports, there is a balance of trade deficit. If exports are greater than imports, there is a trade surplus.

The exchange rate is the price in one country's currency of one unit of another country's currency. The exchange rate for a currency is determined by supply and demand in the foreign exchange market. If the dollar appreciates in value relative to foreign currencies, foreign goods become more inexpensive to U.S. consumers, increasing U.S. demand for foreign goods.

Any force that shifts either the demand or supply curves for a foreign currency will shift the equilibrium in the foreign exchange market and lead to a new exchange rate. Any changes in tastes, income levels, relative real interest rates, or relative inflation rates will cause the demand for and supply of a currency to shift.

Key Terms and Concepts

comparative advantage 432
consumer surplus 435
producer surplus 436
tariff 440
import quota 442
rent seeking 443
current account 446
balance of trade 447
exchange rate 449
derived demand 450

Review Questions

1. The following represents the production possibilities in two countries.

Country A		Country B	
Good X	**Good Y**	**Good X**	**Good Y**
0	32	0	24
4	24	4	18
8	16	8	12
12	8	12	6
16	0	16	0

Which country has a comparative advantage at producing Good X? How can you tell? Which country has a comparative advantage at producing Good Y?

2. Suppose the United States can produce cars at an opportunity cost of 2 computers for each car it produces. Suppose Mexico can produce cars at an opportunity cost of 8 computers for each car it produces. Indicate how both countries can gain from free trade.
3. Evaluate the following statement: "Small developing economies must first become self-sufficient before benefiting from international trade."
4. Evaluate the following statement: "The United States has an absolute advantage in growing wheat. Therefore, it must have a comparative advantage in growing wheat."
5. Explain why imposing a tariff causes a net welfare loss to the domestic economy.
6. If imposing tariffs and quotas harms consumers, why don't consumers vigorously oppose the implementation of these protectionist policies?
7. NAFTA (North American Free Trade Agreement) is an agreement between the United States, Canada, and Mexico to reduce trade barriers and promote the free flow of goods and services across borders. Many U.S. labor groups were opposed to NAFTA. Can you explain why? Can you predict how NAFTA might alter the goods and services produced in the participating countries?
8. Indicate whether each of the following represents a credit or debit on the U.S. current account.
   a. an American imports a BMW from Germany
   b. a Japanese company purchases software from an American company
   c. the United States gives $100 million in financial aid to Israel
   d. a U.S. company in Florida sells oranges to Great Britain
9. Indicate whether each of the following represent a credit or debit on the U.S. capital account.
   a. a French bank purchases $100,000 worth of U.S. Treasury notes
   b. the central bank in the United States purchases 1 million euros in the currency market
   c. a U.S. resident buys a stock on the Japanese stock market
   d. a Japanese company purchases a movie studio in California
10. How are each of the following events likely to affect the U.S. trade balance?
    a. the European price level increases relative to the U.S. price level
    b. the dollar appreciates in value relative to the currencies of its trading partners
    c. the U.S. government offers subsidies to firms that export goods
    d. the U.S. government imposes tariffs on imported goods
    e. Europe experiences a severe recession
11. How are each of the following events likely to affect the value of the dollar relative to the euro?
    a. interest rates in the European Union increase relative to the United States
    b. the European Union price level rises relative to the U.S. price level
    c. the European central bank intervenes by selling dollars on currency markets
    d. the price level in the United States falls relative to the price level in Europe
12. What happens to the supply curve for dollars in the currency market under the following conditions?
    a. Americans wish to buy more Japanese consumer electronics
    b. the United States wishes to prop up the value of the yen
13. Visit the Sexton Web site at **http://sexton.swcollege.com** and click on "Bureau of Economic Analysis" and look under the "International" section for "BOP (Balance of Payments) and related data." Locate the latest

annual figures for U.S. exports and imports. Determine whether a trade deficit or surplus exists for the United States and calculate its magnitude.

14. Visit the Sexton Web site and click on "WTO" and read the latest World Trade News. How do you think these developments will affect global trade and the United States in particular?

15. Visit the Sexton Web site and click on "Exchange Rates" and find the exchange rates at which the euro is convertible into U.S. dollars, Canadian dollars, and Brazilian reals. If the euro were to depreciate in value, what would happen to these exchange rates?

chapter 19 Study Guide

Fill in the Blanks

1. In a typical year, about ____________ percent of the world's output is traded in international markets.
2. A current account is a record of a country's current ____________ and ____________ of goods and services.
3. Because the U.S. gains claims over foreign buyers by obtaining foreign currency in exchange for the dollars needed to buy U.S. exports, all exports of U.S. goods abroad are considered a ____________ or ____________ item in the U.S. balance of payments.
4. Nations import and export ____________, such as tourism, as well as ____________ (goods).
5. The merchandise import/export relationship is often called the balance of ____________.
6. In the global economy, one country's exports are another country's ____________.
7. ____________ trade implies that both participants of an exchange of goods and services anticipate an improvement in their economic welfare.
8. The theory that explains how trade can be beneficial to both parties centers on the concept of ____________.
9. A person, a region, or a country has a comparative advantage over another person, region, or country in producing a particular good or service if it produces a good or service at a lower ____________ than others do.
10. What is important for mutually beneficial specialization and trade is ____________ advantage, not ____________ advantage.
11. The difference between the most a consumer would be willing to pay for a quantity of a good and what a consumer actually has to pay is called ____________ surplus.
12. We can better analyze the impact of trade with the tools of ____________ and ____________ surplus.
13. Once the equilibrium output is reached at the equilibrium price, the sum of ____________ and ____________ is maximized.
14. When the domestic economy has a comparative advantage in a good because it can produce it at a lower relative price than the rest of the world can, international trade ____________ the domestic market price to the world price, benefiting domestic ____________ but harming domestic ____________.
15. When the domestic economy has a comparative advantage in a good, allowing international trade redistributes income from domestic ____________ to domestic ____________, but ____________ surplus increases more than ____________ surplus decreases.
16. When a country does not produce a good relatively as well as other countries do, international trade will ____________ the domestic price to the world price, with the difference between what is domestically supplied and what is domestically demanded supplied by ____________.
17. When a country does not produce a good relatively as well as other countries do, international trade redistributes income from domestic ____________ to domestic ____________ and causes a net ____________ in domestic wealth.

18. A ____________ is a tax on imported goods.

19. Tariffs bring about ____________ prices and revenues to domestic producers, ____________ sales and revenues to foreign producers, and ____________ prices to domestic consumers.

20. With import tariffs, the domestic price of goods is ____________ than the world price.

21. If import tariffs are imposed, at the new price, the domestic quantity demanded is ____________, and the quantity supplied domestically is ____________, ____________ the quantity of imported goods.

22. Import tariffs benefit domestic ____________ and ____________, but harm domestic ____________.

23. One argument for tariffs is that tariff protection is necessary ____________ to allow a new industry to more quickly reach a scale of operation at which economies of scale and production efficiencies can be realized.

24. Tariffs lead to ____________ output and employment and reduced unemployment in domestic industries where tariffs are imposed.

25. If new tariffs lead to restrictions on imports, ____________ dollars will be flowing overseas in payment for imports, which means that foreigners will have ____________ dollars available to buy U.S. exports.

26. If a nation's own resources are depletable, tariff-imposed reliance on domestic supplies will ____________ depletion of domestic reserves.

27. An import ____________ gives producers from another country a maximum number of units of the good in question that can be imported within any given time span.

28. The case for import quotas is ____________ than the case for import tariffs.

29. Tariffs and import quotas are rather suspect and exist because of producers' lobbying efforts to gain profits from government protection, called ____________.

30. Governments sometimes try to encourage exports by ____________ producers.

31. With subsidies, a nation's taxpayers end up subsidizing the output of producers who, relative to producers in other countries, are ____________.

32. Gains from trade in terms of world output are ____________ by export subsidies.

33. Foreigners buying U.S. goods must ____________ their currencies to obtain ____________ in order to pay for exported goods.

34. The price of a unit of one foreign currency in terms of another is called the ____________.

35. A change in the euro-dollar exchange rate from $1 per euro to $2 per euro would ____________ the U.S. price of German goods, ____________ the number of German goods that would be demanded in the U.S.

36. The demand for foreign currencies is a derived demand because it derives directly from the demand for foreign ____________ or for foreign ____________.

37. The more foreigners demand U.S. products, the ____________ of their currencies they will supply in exchange for U.S. dollars.

38. The supply of and demand for a foreign currency determine the equilibrium ____________ of that currency.

39. The quantity of euros demanded by U.S. consumers will increase to buy more European goods as the price of the euro ____________.

40. As the price, or value, of the euro increases relative to the dollar, American products become relatively ____________ expensive to European buyers, which will ____________ the quantity of dollars they will demand.

41. The supply curve of a foreign currency is ____________ sloping.

42. If the dollar price of euros is higher than the equilibrium price, there will be an excess quantity of euros ____________ at that price, and competition among euro ____________ will push the price of euros ____________ toward equilibrium.

43. An increased demand for euros will result in a ____________ equilibrium price (exchange value) for euros, while a decreased demand for euros will result in a ____________ equilibrium price (exchange value) for euros.

44. Changes in a currency's exchange rate can be caused by changes in ____________ for goods, changes in ____________, changes in relative ____________ rates, changes in relative ____________ rates, and ____________.

45. An increase in tastes for European goods in the U.S. would ____________ the demand for euros, ____________ the equilibrium price (exchange value) of euros.

46. A decrease in incomes in the U.S. would ____________ the amount of European imports purchased by Americans, which would ____________ the demand for euros, resulting in a ____________ exchange rate for euros.

47. If European incomes ____________, European tariffs on U.S. goods ____________, or European tastes for American goods ____________, Europeans would demand more U.S. goods, leading them to increase their supply of euros to obtain the added dollars necessary to make those purchases.

48. If interest rates in the U.S. were to increase relative to European interest rates, other things being equal, the rate of return on U.S. investments would ____________ relative to that on European investments, ____________ Europeans' demand for U.S. investments.

49. If Europe experienced a higher inflation rate than the U.S., European products would become ____________ expensive to U.S. consumers, ____________ the quantity of European goods demanded by Americans, and therefore ____________ the demand for euros.

True or False

1. While the importance of the international sector varies enormously from place to place, the volume of international trade has increased substantially.

2. U.S. imports are considered a credit item in the balance of payment because the dollars sold to buy the necessary foreign currency add to foreign claims against U.S. buyers.

3. Our imports provide the means by which foreigners can buy our exports.

4. Nations' imports and exports of services are the largest component of the balance of payments.

5. When the U.S. runs a trade deficit in goods and services with the rest of the world, the rest of the world must be running a trade surplus in goods and services with the U.S.

6. When the U.S. runs a trade deficit in goods, it must run a trade surplus in services.
7. In the global economy, imports equal exports because one country's exports are another country's imports.
8. In voluntary trade, both participants of an exchange anticipate an improvement in their economic welfare.
9. An area should specialize in producing and selling those items in which it has an absolute advantage.
10. Differences in opportunity costs provide an incentive to gain from specialization and trade.
11. By specialization according to comparative advantage and trade, two parties can each achieve consumption possibilities that would be impossible for them without trade.
12. The difference between the least amount for which a supplier is willing to supply a quantity of a good or service and the revenues a supplier actually receives for selling it is called consumer surplus.
13. Trading at the market equilibrium price generates both consumer surplus and producer surplus.
14. Once the equilibrium output is reached at the equilibrium price, all of the mutually beneficial opportunities from trade between suppliers and demanders will have taken place.
15. The total gain to the economy from trade is the sum of consumer and producer surplus.
16. When the domestic economy has a comparative advantage in a good, allowing international trade benefits domestic consumers but harms domestic producers.
17. When the domestic economy has a comparative advantage in a good, exporting that good increases domestic wealth because, while domestic consumers lose from the free trade, those negative effects are more than offset by the positive gains captured by producers.
18. When a country does not produce a good relatively as well as other countries do, international trade benefits domestic consumers but harms domestic producers.
19. When a country does not produce a good relatively as well as other countries do, allowing international trade will increase consumer surplus less than producer surplus decreases.
20. Tariffs are usually relatively large revenue producers for governments.
21. Tariffs lead to gains to domestic producers that are more than offset by the losses to domestic consumers.
22. The history of infant industry tariffs suggests that the tariffs often linger long after the industry is mature and no longer in "need" of protection.
23. The overall domestic employment effects of a tariff imposition are likely to be positive.
24. If the imposition of a tariff leads to retaliatory tariffs by other countries, domestic employment outside the industry gaining the tariff protection would likely suffer.
25. Exporters in a country would generally be supportive of their country imposing import tariffs.

26. From a national defense standpoint, it makes more sense to use foreign supplies in peacetime, and perhaps stockpile "insurance" supplies so that large domestic supplies would be available during wars, than to impose import tariffs.

27. Like tariffs, quotas directly restrict imports, but the U.S. government does not collect any revenue as a result of the import quota, unlike with tariffs.

28. Nations have sometimes used product standards ostensibly designed to protect consumers against inferior, unsafe, dangerous, or polluting merchandise as a means to restrict foreign competition.

29. Because resources being spent on lobbying efforts could have produced something instead, the measured deadweight loss from tariffs and quotas will likely understate the true deadweight loss to society.

30. Unlike import tariffs and quotas, export subsidies tend to increase efficiency.

31. With subsidies, producers export goods not because their costs are lower than those of a foreign competitor, but because their costs have been artificially reduced by government action transferring income from taxpayers to the exporter.

32. Export subsidies lead nations to export products in which they do not have a comparative advantage.

33. U.S. consumers must first exchange U.S. dollars for a foreign seller's currency in order to pay for imported goods.

34. The exchange rate can be expressed either as the number of units of currency A per unit of currency B or its reciprocal, the number of units of currency B per unit of currency A.

35. The more foreign goods that are demanded, the more of that foreign currency will be needed to pay for those goods, which will tend to push down the exchange value of that currency relative to other currencies.

36. The supply of foreign currency is provided by foreigners who want to buy the exports of a particular nation.

37. As the price of the euro falls relative to the dollar, European products become relatively more inexpensive to U.S. consumers, who therefore buy more European goods.

38. As the value of the euro increases relative to the dollar, American products become relatively more inexpensive to European buyers and increase the quantity of dollars they will demand. Europeans will, therefore, increase the quantity of euros supplied to the U.S. by buying more U.S. products.

39. If the dollar price of euros is lower than the equilibrium price, there will be a surplus of euros, and competition among euro sellers will push the price of euros down toward equilibrium.

40. Any force that shifts either the demand for or supply of a currency will shift the equilibrium in the foreign exchange market, leading to a new exchange rate.

41. Any change in the demand for foreign goods will shift the demand curve for foreign currency in the opposite direction.

42. A decrease in tastes for European goods in the U.S. would decrease the demand for euros, decreasing the equilibrium price (exchange value) of euros.

43. An increase in incomes in the U.S. would increase the amount of European imports purchased by Americans, which would increase the demand for euros, resulting in a higher exchange rate for euros.

44. If European incomes rose, European tariffs on U.S. goods increased, or European tastes for American goods increased, the exchange rate for euros would tend to be higher.

45. A decrease in U.S. tariffs on European goods would tend to have the same effect on the exchange rate for euros as an increase in U.S. incomes.

46. If interest rates in the U.S. were to increase relative to European interest rates, the result would be a new lower exchange rate for euros, other things being equal.

47. If Europe experienced a higher inflation rate than the U.S., both the supply of euros would tend to increase and the demand for euros would tend to decrease, leading to a new lower exchange rate for euros.

48. If currency speculators believe that the United States is going to experience more rapid inflation than Japan in the future, they believe that the value of the dollar will soon be falling, which will increase the demand for yen, so the yen will appreciate relative to the dollar.

Multiple Choice

1. Assume that the opportunity cost of producing a pair of pants in the United States is 2 pounds of rice, while in China, it is 5 pounds of rice. As a result,
   a. the United States has a comparative advantage over China in the production of pants.
   b. China has a comparative advantage over the United States in the production of rice.
   c. there can be mutual gains from trade to the two countries if the United States exports rice to China in exchange for shoes.
   d. there can be mutual gains from trade to the two countries if the United States exports pants to China in exchange for rice.
   e. all of the above except c are true.

2. In Samoa the opportunity cost of producing 1 coconut is 4 pineapples, while in Guam the opportunity cost of producing 1 coconut is 5 pineapples. In this situation,
   a. if trade occurs, both countries will be able to consume beyond their original production possibilities frontiers.
   b. Guam will be better off if it exports coconuts and imports pineapples.
   c. both Samoa and Guam will be better off if Samoa produces both coconuts and pineapples.
   d. mutually beneficial trade cannot occur.

3. Mutually beneficial trade will occur whenever the exchange rate between the goods involved is set at a level where
   a. each country can export a good at a price above the opportunity cost of producing the good in the domestic market.
   b. each country can import a good at a price above the opportunity cost of producing the good in the domestic market.
   c. the exchange ratio is exactly equal to the opportunity cost of producing the good in each country.
   d. each country will specialize in the production of those goods in which it has an absolute advantage.
   e. either b or d is true.

Questions 4–6 refer to the following data: Alpha can produce either 18 tons of oranges or 9 tons of apples in a year, while Omega can produce either 16 tons of oranges or 4 tons of apples in a year.

4. The opportunity costs of producing 1 ton of apples for Alpha and Omega, respectively, are
  a. 0.25 tons of oranges and 0.5 tons of oranges.
  b. 9 tons of oranges and 4 tons of oranges.
  c. 2 tons of oranges and 4 tons of oranges.
  d. 4 tons of oranges and 2 tons of oranges.
  e. 0.5 tons of oranges and 0.25 tons of oranges.

5. Which of the following statements is true?
  a. Alpha should export to Omega, but Omega should not export to Alpha.
  b. Since Alpha has an absolute advantage in both goods, no mutual gains from trade are possible.
  c. If Alpha specializes in growing apples and Omega specializes in growing oranges, they could both gain by specialization and trade.
  d. If Alpha specializes in growing oranges and Omega specializes in growing apples, they could both gain by specialization and trade.
  e. Since Alpha has a comparative advantage in producing both goods, no mutual gains from trade are possible.

6. Which of the following exchange rates between apples and oranges would allow both Alpha and Omega to gain by specialization and exchange?
  a. 1 ton of apples for 3 tons of oranges
  b. 3 tons of apples for 3 tons of oranges
  c. 2 tons of apples for 3 tons of oranges
  d. 1 ton of oranges for 0.2 tons of apples
  e. 1 ton of oranges for 0.8 tons of apples

7. After the United States introduces a tariff in the market for widgets, the price of widgets in the United States will
  a. decrease.
  b. increase.
  c. remain the same.
  d. change in an indeterminate manner.

8. If Japan does not have a comparative advantage in producing rice, the consequences of adopting a policy of reducing or eliminating imports of rice into Japan would include the following:
  a. Japan will be able to consume a combination of rice and other goods' consumption beyond their domestic production possibilities curve.
  b. the real incomes of Japanese rice producers would rise, but the real incomes of Japanese rice consumers would fall.
  c. the real incomes of Japanese rice consumers would rise, but the real incomes of Japanese rice producers would fall.
  d. the price of rice in Japan will fall.

9. The infant industry argument for protectionism suggests that an industry must be protected in the early stages of its development so that
  a. firms will be protected from subsidized foreign competition.
  b. domestic producers can attain the economies of scale to allow them to compete in world markets.
  c. there will be adequate supplies of crucial resources in case they are needed for national defense.
  d. None of the above reflect the infant industry argument.

10. Protectionist legislation is often passed because
- **a.** employers in the affected industry lobby more effectively than the workers in that industry.
- **b.** both employers and workers in the affected industry lobby for protectionist policies.
- **c.** trade restrictions often benefit domestic consumers in the long run, though they must pay more in the short run.
- **d.** none of the above.

11. Introducing a tariff on vitamin E would
- **a.** reduce imports of vitamin E.
- **b.** increase U.S. consumption of domestically produced vitamin E.
- **c.** decrease total U.S. consumption of vitamin E.
- **d.** do all of the above.
- **e.** do none of the above.

12. A new U.S. import quota on imported steel would be likely to
- **a.** raise the cost of production to steel-using American firms.
- **b.** generate tax revenue to the government.
- **c.** decrease U.S. production of steel.
- **d.** increase the production of steel-using American firms.
- **e.** do all of the above.

13. An import quota does which of the following?
- **a.** decreases the price of the imported goods to consumers
- **b.** increases the price of the domestic goods to consumers
- **c.** redistributes income away from domestic producers of those products toward domestic producers of exports
- **d.** a and c
- **e.** b and c

14. A crucial difference between the impact of import quotas compared to that of tariffs is that
- **a.** import quotas generate revenue to the domestic government, but tariffs do not.
- **b.** import quotas generate no revenue to the domestic government, but tariffs do.
- **c.** tariffs increase the prices paid by domestic consumers, but quotas do not.
- **d.** a and c.
- **e.** b and c.

15. If the United States could produce 0.5 tons of potatoes or 1 ton of wheat per worker per year, while Ireland could produce 3 tons of potatoes or 2 tons of wheat per worker per year, the country with the comparative advantage in producing wheat is ________, and the country with the absolute advantage in producing potatoes is ________.
- **a.** the United States, the United States
- **b.** the United States, Ireland
- **c.** Ireland, the United States
- **d.** Ireland, Ireland

16. According to international trade theory, a country should
- **a.** import goods in which it has an absolute advantage.
- **b.** export goods in which it has an absolute advantage.
- **c.** import goods in which it has a comparative disadvantage.
- **d.** import goods in which it has an absolute disadvantage.
- **e.** import goods when it has either a comparative or absolute disadvantage in producing them.

17. Relative to a no-international-trade initial situation, if the United States imported wine, the U.S. domestic price of wine
  a. would rise, but domestic output would fall.
  b. would fall, but domestic output would rise.
  c. would rise, and domestic output would rise.
  d. would fall, and domestic output would fall.

18. Relative to a no-international-trade initial situation, if the United States exported wine, the U.S. domestic price of wine
  a. would rise, but domestic output would fall.
  b. would fall, but domestic output would rise.
  c. would rise, and domestic output would rise.
  d. would fall, and domestic output would fall.

19. Which of the following would be recorded as a credit in the U.S. balance of payments accounts?
  a. the purchase of a German business by a U.S. investor
  b. the import of Honda trucks by a U.S. automobile distributor
  c. European travel expenditures of an American college student
  d. the purchase of a U.S. Treasury bond by a French investment company

20. What is the difference between the balance of merchandise trade and the balance of payments?
  a. Only the value of goods imported and exported is included in the balance of merchandise trade, while the balance of payments includes the value of all payments to and from foreigners.
  b. The value of goods imported and exported is included in the balance of merchandise trade, while the balance of payments includes only capital account transactions.
  c. The value of all goods, services, and unilateral transfers is included in the balance of merchandise trade, while the balance of payments includes both current account and capital account transactions.
  d. Balance of merchandise trade and balance of payments both describe the same international exchange transactions.

21. If consumers in Europe and Asia develop strong preferences for American goods, America's current account will
  a. not be affected since purchases of American goods by foreigners are recorded in the capital account.
  b. not be affected since purchases of American goods based on mere preferences are recorded under statistical discrepancy.
  c. move toward surplus since purchases of American goods are recorded as credits on our current account.
  d. move toward deficit since purchases of American goods by foreigners are counted as debits in our current account.

22. Which of the following would supply dollars to the foreign exchange market?
  a. the sale of a U.S. automobile to a Mexican consumer
  b. the spending by British tourists in the United States
  c. the purchase of Canadian oil by a U.S. consumer
  d. the sale of a U.S. corporation to a Saudi Arabian investor

23. Which of the following will enter as a credit in the U.S. balance of payments capital account?
   a. the purchase of a Japanese automobile by a U.S. consumer
   b. the sale of Japanese electronics to an American
   c. the sale of an American baseball team to a Japanese industrialist
   d. the purchase of a Japanese electronic plant by an American industrialist

24. If the value of a nation's merchandise exports exceeds merchandise imports, then the nation is running a
   a. balance of payments deficit.
   b. balance of payments surplus.
   c. merchandise trade deficit.
   d. merchandise trade surplus.

25. When goods or services cross international borders,
   a. money must generally move in the opposite direction.
   b. payment must be made in another good, using barter.
   c. a future shipment must be made to offset the current sale/purchase.
   d. countries must ship gold to make payment.

26. The balance of payments accounts for and records information about
   a. purchases of U.S. financial assets by foreigners.
   b. purchases of foreign financial assets by Americans.
   c. the levels of imports and exports of goods and services for a country.
   d. all of the above.

27. Suppose the United States imposed a high tariff on a major imported item. Under a system of flexible rates of exchange, this would tend to
   a. cause the dollar to appreciate in value.
   b. cause the dollar to depreciate in value.
   c. increase the U.S. balance of trade deficit.
   d. increase the U.S. balance of payments deficit.
   e. do b, c, and d.

28. Under a system of flexible exchange rates, a deficit in a country's balance of payments will be corrected by
   a. depreciation in the nation's currency.
   b. appreciation in the nation's currency.
   c. a decline in the nation's domestic price level.
   d. an increase in the nation's inflation rate.

29. If high-yield investment opportunities attract capital from abroad and lead to a capital account surplus, then the
   a. nation's currency must appreciate.
   b. nation's currency must depreciate.
   c. nation must run a current account deficit under a flexible exchange rate system.
   d. nation must run a current account surplus under a flexible exchange rate system.
   e. a and c.

30. If the dollar *depreciates,* it can be said that
   a. foreign countries no longer respect the United States.
   b. other currencies appreciate.
   c. it falls in value just as it does during inflation.
   d. it takes fewer dollars to buy units of other currencies.
   e. all of the above are correct.

31. On May 16, 1999, it cost $.667 to buy one Canadian dollar. How many Canadian dollars would $1 U.S. buy?

a. $1.50
b. $1.30
c. $1.00
d. $.67

32. If the exchange rate between the dollar and the euro changes from $1 = 1 euro to $2 = 1 euro, then

a. European goods will become less expensive for Americans, and imports of European goods to the United States will rise.
b. European goods will become less expensive for Americans, and imports of European goods to the United States will fall.
c. European goods will become more expensive for Americans, and imports of European goods to the United States will rise.
d. European goods will become more expensive for Americans, and imports of European goods to the United States will fall.

33. If the price in dollars of Mexican pesos changes from $.10 per peso to $.14 per peso, the peso has

a. appreciated.
b. depreciated.
c. devalued.
d. stayed at the same exchange rate.

34. Which of the following is most likely to favor the appreciation of the American dollar?

a. a German professor on vacation in Iowa
b. an American professor on extended vacation in Paris
c. an American farmer who relies on exports
d. Disney World

35. If the dollar appreciates relative to other currencies, which of the following is true?

a. It takes more of the other currency to buy a dollar.
b. It takes less of the other currency to buy a dollar.
c. There is no charge in the currency needed to buy a dollar.
d. There is not enough information to make a determination.

36. If the United States experiences a sharp increase in exports, what will happen to demand for the U.S. dollar?

a. It will decrease.
b. It will increase.
c. It will be unchanged.
d. It will change at the same rate as supply of dollars will change.
e. There is not enough information to make a determination.

37. If fewer British tourists visit the Grand Canyon, what is the effect in the exchange market?

a. It will increase the supply of British pounds.
b. It will decrease the supply of British pounds.
c. It will increase the demand for British pounds.
d. It will decrease the demand for British pounds.

38. Suppose that the dollar rises from 100 to 125 yen. As a result,
- **a.** exports to Japan will likely increase.
- **b.** Japanese tourists will more likely visit the United States.
- **c.** U.S. businesses will be less likely to use Japanese shipping lines to transport their products.
- **d.** U.S. consumers will more likely buy Japanese-made automobiles.

39. Other things being constant, which of the following will most likely cause the dollar to appreciate on the exchange rate market?
- **a.** higher domestic interest rates
- **b.** higher interest rates abroad
- **c.** expansionary domestic monetary policy
- **d.** reduced inflation abroad

40. A depreciation in the U.S. dollar would
- **a.** discourage foreigners from making investments in the United States.
- **b.** discourage foreign consumers from buying U.S. goods.
- **c.** reduce the number of dollars it would take to buy a Swiss franc.
- **d.** encourage foreigners to buy more U.S. goods.

41. If the exchange rate between euros and dollars were 2 euros per dollar, when an American purchases a good valued at 80 euros, its cost in dollars would be
- **a.** $160.
- **b.** $80.
- **c.** $40.
- **d.** none of the above.

42. Suppose that the exchange rate between Mexican pesos and dollars is 8 pesos per dollar. If the exchange rate goes to 10 pesos per dollar, it would tend to
- **a.** increase U.S. exports to Mexico.
- **b.** decrease U.S. exports to Mexico.
- **c.** increase Mexican exports to the United States.
- **d.** decrease Mexican exports to the United States.
- **e.** do both b and c.

43. If a dollar is cheaper in terms of a foreign currency than the equilibrium exchange rate, a ________ exists at the current exchange rate that will put ________ pressure on the exchange value of a dollar.
- **a.** surplus of dollars, downward
- **b.** surplus of dollars, upward
- **c.** shortage of dollars, downward
- **d.** shortage of dollars, upward

44. In foreign exchange markets, the supply of dollars is determined
- **a.** by the level of U.S. imports and the demand for foreign assets by U.S. citizens and the U.S. government.
- **b.** solely by the level of U.S. merchandise exports.
- **c.** solely by the level of U.S. merchandise imports.
- **d.** solely by the levels of U.S. merchandise exports and merchandise imports.
- **e.** by the level of U.S. exports and the demand for U.S. assets by foreigners.

45. In foreign exchange markets, the effect of an increase in the demand for dollars on the value of the dollar is the same as that of
- **a.** an increase in the supply of foreign currencies.
- **b.** a decrease in the supply of foreign currencies.
- **c.** a decrease in the demand for dollars.
- **d.** none of the above.

46. If the demand by foreigners for U.S. government securities increased, other things being equal, it would tend to:

a. increase the exchange value of the dollar and increase U.S. merchandise exports.
b. increase the exchange value of the dollar and decrease U.S. merchandise exports.
c. decrease the exchange value of the dollar and increase U.S. merchandise exports.
d. decrease the exchange value of the dollar and decrease U.S. merchandise exports.

47. If the rate of inflation in the United States falls relative to the rate of inflation in foreign nations, U.S. net exports will tend to ________, causing the exchange value of the U.S. dollar to ________.

a. rise, rise
b. rise, fall
c. fall, rise
d. fall, fall

48. If real incomes in foreign nations were growing more rapidly than U.S. real incomes, one would expect that as a result,

a. the exchange value of the dollar would decline relative to other currencies.
b. the exchange value of the dollar would increase relative to other currencies.
c. there would likely be no effect on the exchange value of the dollar relative to other currencies.
d. there would be an indeterminate effect on the exchange value of the dollar relative to other currencies.

49. If real interest rates in the United States fell relative to real interest rates in other countries, other things being equal,

a. the exchange value of the dollar would decline relative to other currencies.
b. the exchange value of the dollar would increase relative to other currencies.
c. there would likely be no effect on the exchange value of the dollar relative to other currencies.
d. there would be an indeterminate effect on the exchange value of the dollar relative to other currencies.

50. Sweden's currency would tend to appreciate if

a. the demand for Sweden's exports increases.
b. the demand for imports by Swedes increases.
c. real interest rates in Sweden decrease relative to those of the rest of the world.
d. Sweden's inflation rate rises relative to inflation in the rest of the world.

51. A country would tend to experience currency depreciation relative to that of other countries if

a. the profitability of investments in other countries increases relative to the profitability in that country.
b. people in the foreign currency markets expect the value of the currency to fall in the near future.
c. the foreign demand for its exports decreases.
d. any of the above occurs.
e. any of the above except c occurs.

52. If the dollar depreciates relative to the yen, we would expect

a. that the Japanese trade surplus with the United States would increase.
b. that Japanese imports from the United States would decrease.
c. that Japanese exports to the United States would decrease.
d. that a and b would occur.

53. As the number of British pounds that exchange for a dollar falls on foreign currency markets
   a. the British will have an incentive to import fewer U.S. goods.
   b. the British will find it easier to export goods to the United States.
   c. the British will find U.S. goods to be more expensive in their stores.
   d. all of the above will be true.
   e. none of the above will be true.

54. If real interest rates in the United States rose and real interest rates in England fell, we would expect people to
   a. increase their demand for British pounds.
   b. borrow more from U.S. sources.
   c. buy relatively more U.S. assets.
   d. buy relatively more British assets.
   e. do both b and c.

55. If the Federal Reserve were to sell U.S. dollars on the foreign exchange market, a likely result would be
   a. a rightward shift in the dollar supply curve.
   b. at least a temporary decline in the exchange value of the U.S. dollar.
   c. at least a temporary increase in the exchange value of the U.S. dollar.
   d. a and b.
   e. a and c.

Problems

1. Using the following graph, illustrate the domestic effects of opening up the domestic market to international trade on the domestic price, the domestic quantity purchased, the domestic quantity produced, imports or exports, consumer surplus, producer surplus, and the total welfare gain from trade.

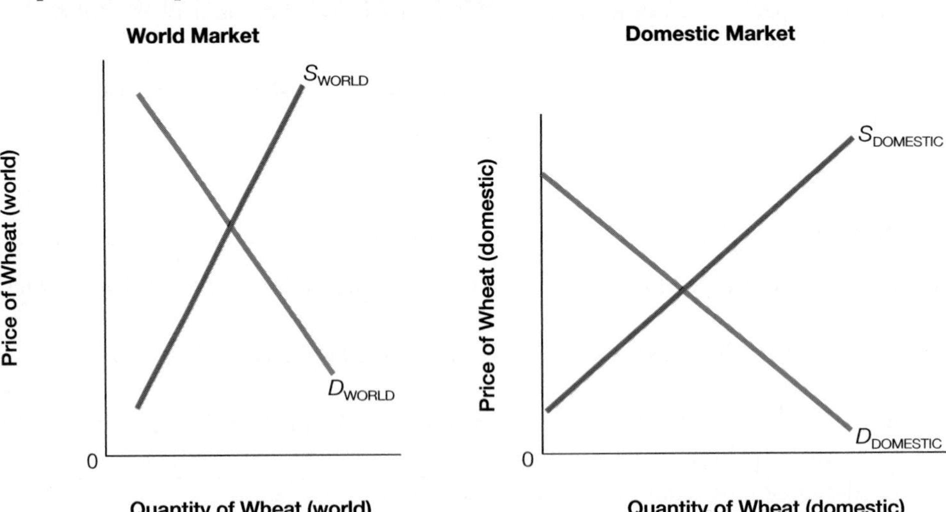

2. Use the following graph to illustrate the domestic effects of imposing a tariff on imports on the domestic price, the domestic quantity purchased, the domestic quantity produced, the level of imports, consumer surplus, producer surplus, the tariff revenue generated, and the total welfare effect from the tariff.

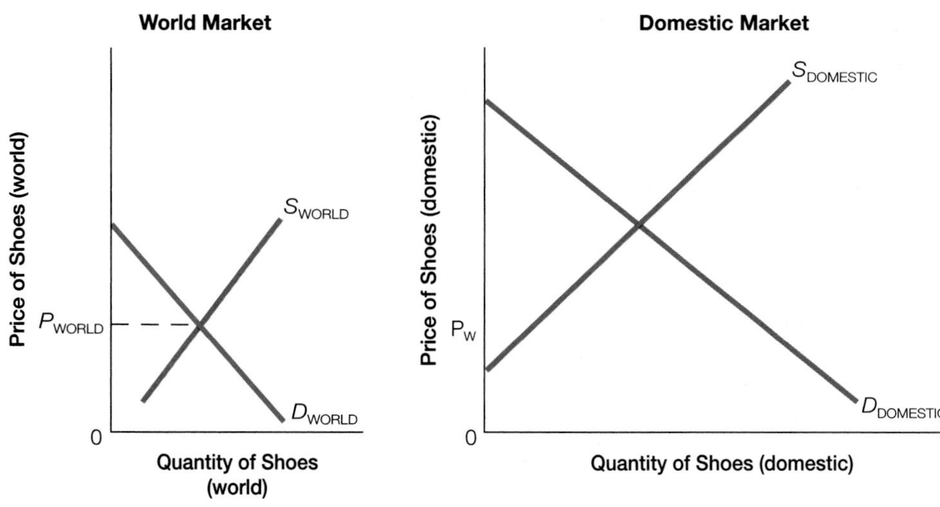

3. Assume that a product sells for $100 in the United States.

a. If the exchange rate between British pounds and U.S. dollars is $2 per pound, what would the price of the product be in the United Kingdom?

b. If the exchange rate between Mexican pesos and U.S. dollars is 125 pesos per dollar, what would the price of the product be in Mexico?

c. Which direction would the price of the $100 U.S. product change in a foreign country if Americans' tastes for foreign products increased?

d. Which direction would the price of the $100 U.S. product change in a foreign country if incomes in the foreign country fell?

e. Which direction would the price of the $100 U.S. product change in a foreign country if interest rates in the U.S. fell relative to interest rates in other countries?

4. How would each of the following affect the supply of euros, the demand for euros, and the dollar price of euros?

Change	**Supply of Euros**	**Demand for Euros**	**Dollar price of Euros**
Reduced U.S. tastes for European goods	________	________	________
Increased incomes in the U.S.	________	________	________
Increased U.S. interest rates	________	________	________
Decreased inflation in Europe	________	________	________
Reduced U.S. tariffs on imports	________	________	________
Increased European tastes for U.S. goods	________	________	________

Study Guide Answers

CHAPTER 1

Fill in the Blanks

1. limited; unlimited **2.** scarcity **3.** inputs **4.** scarcity; value **5.** trade-offs **6.** macroeconomics; microeconomics **7.** self-interest; predictable **8.** rational **9.** consequences **10.** theories; explain; predict **11.** abstract **12.** hypothesis **13.** empirical **14.** *ceteris paribus* **15.** correlation **16.** causation **17.** fallacy of composition **18.** positive **19.** normative **20.** positive

True or False

1. T **2.** F **3.** F **4.** T **5.** F **6.** F **7.** F **8.** F **9.** F **10.** F **11.** T **12.** F **13.** T **14.** T **15.** F

Multiple Choice

1. c **2.** b **3.** d **4.** d **5.** d **6.** d **7.** d **8.** d **9.** c **10.** c **11.** b **12.** d **13.** b **14.** d **15.** c **16.** d **17.** c **18.** c **19.** d **20.** c

Problems

1. **a.** This involves confusing correlation with causation.
   b. This involves confusing correlation with causation.
   c. This involves the fallacy of composition.
   d. This is a violation of the *ceteris paribus* conditions.
   e. There is no fallacy in this statement.
2. **a.** both normative and positive statements
   b. normative statements
   c. positive statements
   d. both normative and positive statements
   e. positive statements
3. **a.** microeconomics **b.** macroeconomics **c.** microeconomics
   d. macroeconomics **e.** microeconomics

CHAPTER 2

Fill in the Blanks

1. wants; resources **2.** labor; land; capital; entrepreneurship **3.** knowledge and skill; education and on-the-job training **4.** production techniques; products; profits **5.** competition **6.** wants and desires **7.** choices; wants and desires **8.** opportunity cost **9.** how much **10.** marginal; marginal; adding to; subtracting from **11.** expected marginal benefits; expected marginal costs **12.** incentives **13.** rise; fall; fall; rise **14.** specialize; lower **15.** comparative advantage **16.** skill; wasted; best **17.** language; relative availability of products; relative value; less; more **18.** voluntary; price **19.** market failure

True or False

1. T **2.** T **3.** F **4.** T **5.** T **6.** F **7.** T **8.** T **9.** F **10.** T **11.** F **12.** F **13.** T **14.** T **15.** T **16.** T **17.** T **18.** T **19.** T **20.** T

Multiple Choice

1. d **2.** b **3.** b **4.** d **5.** e **6.** e **7.** d **8.** d **9.** e **10.** b **11.** b **12.** d **13.** d **14.** b **15.** d **16.** c **17.** c **18.** d **19.** b **20.** d **21.** b **22.** b

Problems

1. **a.** \$50; \$25
   b. 3; 5; Mark would go as long as his marginal benefit was greater than the admission price.
   c. Yes; 6; Mark would buy the pass because his total benefits exceed his total cost. Once he has the pass, the marginal cost of attending one more day becomes zero, so he will go as long as his marginal benefits exceed zero.
2. **a.** \$57; \$88
   b. 43; 44; He would produce as long as the price (marginal benefit) exceeded the marginal cost.

CHAPTER 3

Fill in the Blanks

1. what; how; for whom **2.** decentralized **3.** mixed **4.** least **5.** labor intensive; capital intensive **6.** product **7.** inputs; firms; factor; input **8.** circular flow; product; factor; firms **9.** production possibilities **10.** resources; technology **11.** inside; inefficiently; potential **12.** unemployed; better **13.** efficiency; most **14.** concave; increasing **15.** opportunity cost; increases **16.** fewer; more **17.** technology; labor productivity; natural resource finds **18.** scarcity; trade-offs **19.** scarcity; choice; opportunity costs; efficiency; economic growth

True or False

1. T **2.** T **3.** T **4.** F **5.** T **6.** T **7.** F **8.** T **9.** F **10.** T **11.** F **12.** T **13.** T **14.** T **15.** T **16.** F **17.** F **18.** F

Multiple Choice

1. a **2.** c **3.** d **4.** c **5.** a **6.** d **7.** e **8.** e **9.** e **10.** c **11.** d **12.** c **13.** c **14.** e **15.** b **16.** b **17.** d **18.** e **19.** c **20.** d **21.** a **22.** c **23.** c **24.** e **25.** b

Problems

1.

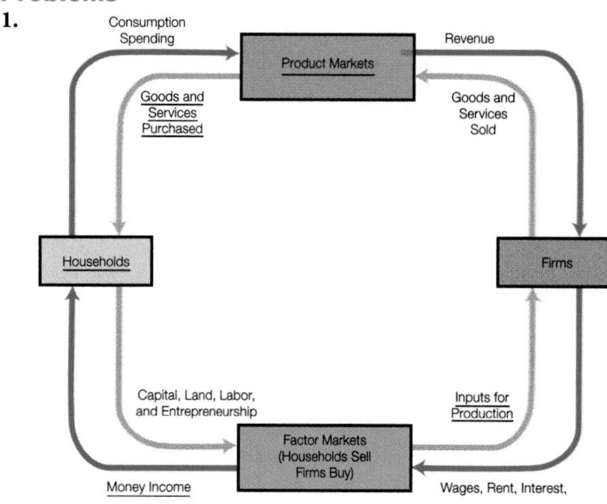

2. **a.**

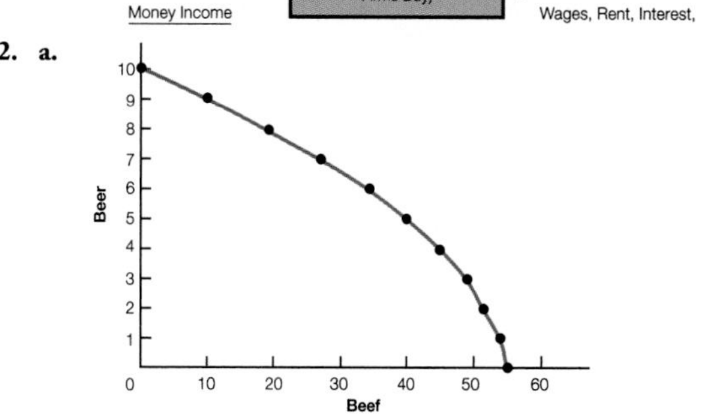

   b. 1 side of beef; 6 kegs of beer; 9 kegs of beer
   c. No; that combination is inside the production possibilities curve, which means more of one good could be produced without giving up any production of the other good.
   d. No; that combination is beyond the production possibilities curve and therefore unattainable.
3. **a.** Yes; the bowed outward shape of the production possibilities curve indicates increasing opportunity costs.
   b. Zero; because point I is inside the production possibilities curve, moving from point I to point D means that the output of food can increase with no decrease in the output of shelter.
   c. 40 units of food
   d. All of the points on the production possibilities curve are efficient because at any of those points more of one good could be produced only by sacrificing some output of the other good. However, the curve does not tell us which of those points is best from the perspective of society.

CHAPTER 4

Fill in the Blanks

1. market; exchanging **2.** trade **3.** buyers; sellers **4.** competitive **5.** quantity demanded **6.** substitution **7.** individual demand schedule **8.** market demand curve **9.** money (or absolute or nominal); relative **10.** a good's price; moving along **11.** prices of related goods; income; number; tastes; expectations **12.** rightward; leftward **13.** substitutes **14.** increase; decrease **15.** increase **16.** quantity supplied; quantity supplied **17.** profits; production; higher **18.** positive **19.** willing; able **20.** input; expectations; number; technology; regulation; taxes and subsidies; weather **21.** lower; left **22.** equilibrium; equilibrium **23.** surplus **24.** shortage **25.** surplus; more; cut back; more **26.** greater; greater **27.** higher; lower **28.** decrease **29.** increase; be indeterminate **30.** ceiling **31.** shortages **32.** decline **33.** additional **34.** unintended consequences

True or False

1. T **2.** F **3.** T **4.** T **5.** F **6.** T **7.** T **8.** T **9.** T **10.** F **11.** F **12.** T **13.** F **14.** T **15.** F **16.** T **17.** F **18.** T **19.** F **20.** F **21.** F **22.** T **23.** F **24.** T **25.** T **26.** F **27.** T **28.** T **29.** F **30.** F

Multiple Choice

1. e **2.** d **3.** d **4.** d **5.** b **6.** d **7.** b **8.** c **9.** d **10.** d **11.** c **12.** d **13.** d **14.** d **15.** c **16.** b **17.** a **18.** a **19.** c **20.** e

Problems

1. a.

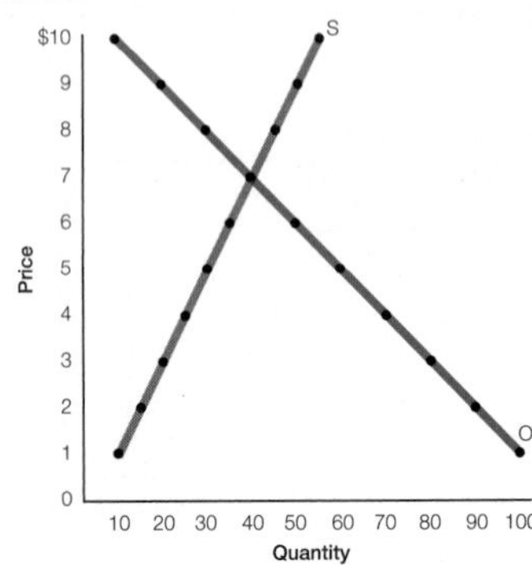

b. $7; 40 units traded

c. Surplus; at $9, above the equilibrium price, there will be a surplus of 30 units of Z (the quantity supplied at $9 [50] minus the quantity demanded at $9 [20]).

d. Shortage; at $3, below the equilibrium price, there will be a shortage of 60 units of Z (the quantity demanded at $3 [80] minus the quantity supplied at $3 [20]).

e. $8, with 45 units traded (at the new supply and demand intersection)

f. $6, with 50 units traded (at the new supply and demand intersection)

2. a. To get to point A would require a decrease in supply; to get to point B would require a decrease in supply and an increase in demand; to get to point C would require an increase in demand; to get to point D would require a decrease in supply and a decrease in demand; point E is the current equilibrium; to get to point F would require an increase in supply and an increase in demand; to get to point G would require a decrease in demand; to get to point H would require an increase in supply and a decrease in demand; to get to point I would require an increase in supply.

b. B; because it indicates a decrease in supply and an increase in demand.

c. Indeterminate; because one of the changes decreases supply and the other increases supply, we don't know what the net effect is on supply. If the effects were of the same magnitude, the result would be E; if the increase in supply were greater than the decrease in supply, the answer would be I; if the decrease in supply were greater than the increase in supply, the answer would be A.

d. C; A; A

e. G; I; G

3.

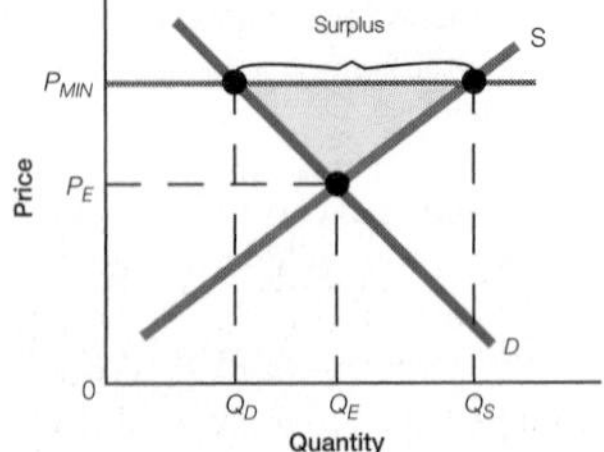

a. If the price floor is raised, the quantity supplied increases, the quantity demanded decreases, and the surplus increases; if the price floor is lowered, the quantity supplied decreases, the quantity demanded increases, and the surplus decreases.

b. The quantity supplied does not change, the quantity demanded increases, and the surplus decreases.

c. The quantity supplied increases, the quantity demanded does not change, and the surplus increases.

4.

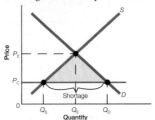

S
Price
P_E
P_C
Shortage
D
0
Q_S
Q_E
Q_D
Quantity

a. If the price ceiling is raised, the quantity supplied increases, the quantity demanded decreases, and the shortage is reduced; if the price ceiling is lowered, the quantity supplied decreases, the quantity demanded increases, and the shortage is increased.

b. The quantity supplied does not change, the quantity demanded increases, and the shortage is increased.

c. The quantity supplied increases, the quantity demanded does not change, and the shortage is decreased.

CHAPTER 5

Fill in the Blanks

1. demanded **2.** quantity demanded; price **3.** larger **4.** smaller **5.** elastic; unit elastic; inelastic **6.** close substitutes; proportion of income; time **7.** more **8.** lower **9.** greater; substitutes **10.** rise; quantity demanded **11.** fall; quantity demanded **12.** upper; elastic; inelastic **13.** supplied **14.** quantity supplied; price **15.** elastic **16.** less than **17.** more **18.** elasticity of supply and demand **19.** more **20.** rational choice; purpose **21.** total **22.** marginal **23.** increases; decline **24.** diminishing marginal utility **25.** consumer surplus **26.** demand curve; market price **27.** increase **28.** producer surplus **29.** already; output **30.** maximum; minimum **31.** consumer surplus; producer surplus **32.** as large **33.** higher; lower; gains **34.** elasticities of supply and demand

True or False

1. F **2.** T **3.** T **4.** T **5.** T **6.** T **7.** F **8.** F **9.** T **10.** F **11.** F **12.** T **13.** T **14.** F **15.** T **16.** F **17.** F **18.** T **19.** T **20.** T **21.** T **22.** T **23.** T **24.** T **25.** F **26.** F **27.** T **28.** T **29.** T **30.** T **31.** F **32.** F **33.** T

Multiple Choice

1. d **2.** b **3.** a **4.** d **5.** d **6.** b **7.** a **8.** b **9.** b **10.** b **11.** a **12.** c **13.** d **14.** c **15.** b **16.** b **17.** d **18.** d **19.** b **20.** b **21.** c **22.** d **23.** c **24.** c **25.** e **26.** b

Problems

1. The demand is relatively elastic at prices above the midpoint of a straight-line demand curve and relatively inelastic below the midpoint, so it is relatively elastic for a price change from $12 to $8 but relatively inelastic for a price change from $6 to $4.

2. Demand is inelastic, because an increase in price increases total revenue; demand is elastic, because an increase in price decreases total revenue.

3. a. 5 units of utility for the first clam; 4 units of utility for the second clam; 3 units of utility for the third clam; 2 units of utility for the fourth clam; 1 unit of utility for the fifth clam; −2 units of utility for the sixth clam.

b. No; even at a price of $0, Carrie's total utility would be reduced by consuming the sixth clam, since her marginal utility would be negative.

4. a. $30; He will produce 3 units, with total revenue of $120 and total cost of $90.

b. Producer surplus will increase from $30 to $60; he will now produce 4 units, with total revenue of $200 and total cost of $140.

5.

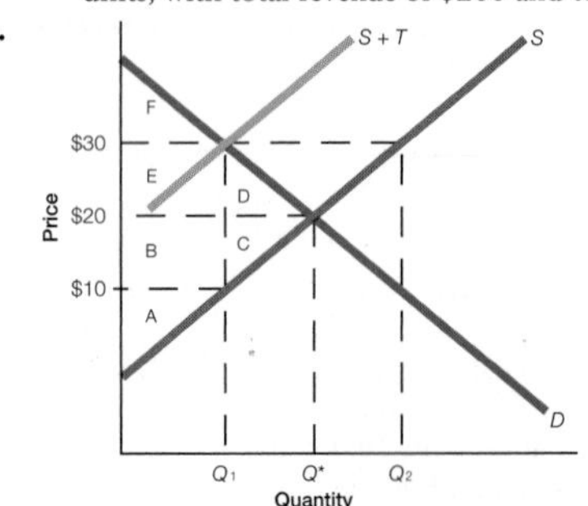

a. Consumer surplus is area F + E + D; producer surplus is area A + B + C. The area under the demand curve and above the market price represents consumer surplus; the area above the supply curve and under the market price represents producer surplus.

b. New consumer surplus is area F; new producer surplus is area A. The area under the demand curve and above the new market price (including tax), now represents consumer surplus; the area above the supply curve and below the new market price (not including tax), now represents producer surplus.

c. The deadweight loss is area C + D. The deadweight cost of the tax is the difference in the area under the demand curve and the area under the supply curve for the change in quantity exchanged which results from the tax.

d. The tax revenue is area E + B. The tax revenue raised is represented by the rectangle of which the height is the tax per unit and the length is the number of units exchanged after the tax is imposed.

CHAPTER 6

Fill in the Blanks

1. externalities **2.** negative externality; positive externality **3.** lowers; true **4.** internalize (bear) **5.** positive externalities **6.** overallocation **7.** underproduce **8.** true social **9.** nonexcludable; nonrivalous **10.** non-excludable **11.** nonrivalous **12.** free ride **13.** free-rider **14.** providing **15.** economic **16.** self-interest **17.** greater **18.** consumption-payment

True or False

1. T **2.** T **3.** F **4.** T **5.** T **6.** T **7.** T **8.** T **9.** F **10.** F **11.** T **12.** T **13.** F **14.** F **15.** F **16.** T **17.** T

Multiple Choice

1. c **2.** b **3.** a **4.** b **5.** b **6.** e **7.** b **8.** e **9.** b **10.** d **11.** a **12.** e **13.** b

Problems

1.

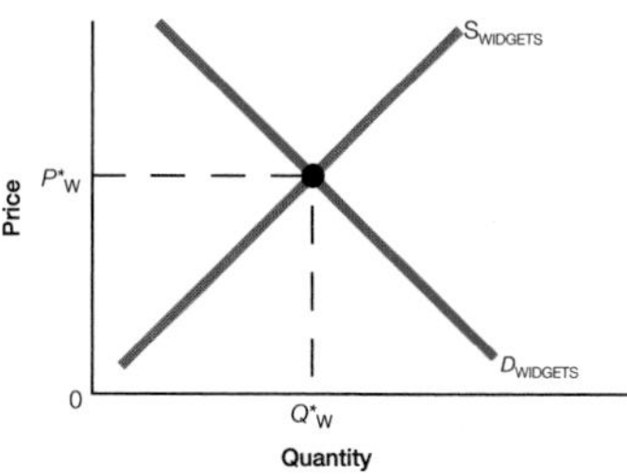

2.

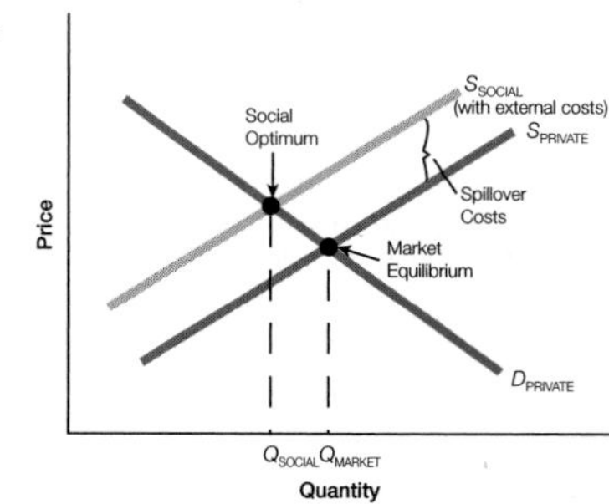

The tax equals the spillover costs indicated.

3.

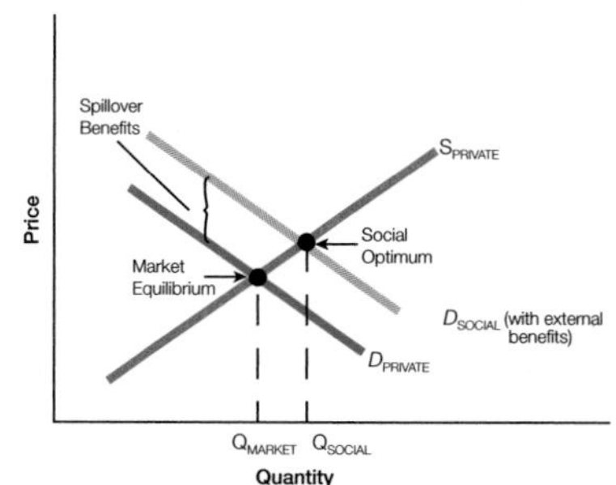

The subsidy equals the spillover benefits indicated.

CHAPTER 7

Fill in the Blanks

1. total revenues; total costs **2.** most valuable **3.** monetary **4.** opportunity **5.** maximize **6.** implicit **7.** implicit; explicit **8.** sunk **9.** short; long **10.** all **11.** variable **12.** output **13.** small **14.** diminishing marginal product **15.** fixed; variable **16.** do not vary **17.** going out of business **18.** total fixed cost **19.** variable **20.** total variable cost **21.** fixed; variable **22.** total cost; level of output **23.** total fixed cost; level of output **24.** average variable cost **25.** additional **26.** horizontal **27.** average fixed **28.** diminishing marginal **29.** less; more **30.** short; variable **31.** planning **32.** economies; constant returns; diseconomies **33.** minimum efficient **34.** input; technology **35.** diseconomies of scale

True or False

1. F **2.** F **3.** T **4.** T **5.** F **6.** T **7.** T **8.** T **9.** F **10.** T **11.** F **12.** T **13.** T **14.** T **15.** T **16.** F **17.** T **18.** T **19.** F **20.** T **21.** F **22.** T **23.** T **24.** T **25.** T **26.** F **27.** F **28.** T **29.** T **30.** T **31.** T **32.** T **33.** F **34.** T **35.** T

Multiple Choice

1. d **2.** e **3.** d **4.** a **5.** d **6.** a **7.** b **8.** d **9.** d **10.** d **11.** c **12.** d **13.** b **14.** b **15.** c **16.** c **17.** d **18.** b **19.** c **20.** c **21.** e **22.** d **23.** a **24.** e **25.** d **26.** b **27.** c **28.** c **29.** a **30.** c **31.** a **32.** d

Problems

1.

Labor (workers)	Total Product (pounds)	Marginal Product (pounds)
0	0	0
1	20	20
2	44	24
3	62	18
4	74	12
5	80	6
6	78	−2

a. Candy's Candies begins to experience diminishing marginal product with the third worker, the first one for whom marginal product begins to fall.

b. Candy's Candies experiences a negative marginal product beginning with the sixth worker.

2. a. Average Fixed Cost (*AFC*)

b. Average Variable Cost (*AVC*)

c. Average Total Cost (*ATC*)

d. Marginal Cost (*MC*)

e. Where *MC* is less than *AVC*, *AVC* is falling; when *MC* equals *AVC*, *AVC* does not change; and when *MC* exceeds *AVC*, *AVC* is rising; thus the intersection of *MC* and *AVC* is at the minimum point of *AVC*. Where *MC* is less than *ATC*, *ATC* is falling; when *MC* equals *ATC*, *ATC* does not change; and when *MC* exceeds *ATC*, *ATC* is rising; thus the intersection of *MC* and *ATC* is at the minimum point of *ATC*.

f. The point where *MC* equals *AFC* has no economic significance.

3.

Output	Total Fixed Costs	Total Variable Costs	Average Total Costs	Average Fixed Cost	Average Variable Cost	Total Cost	Marginal Cost
1	$200	$60	$ 260	$ 200	$ 60	$ 260	$ 60
2	200	100	300	100	50	150	40
3	200	120	320	66.66	40	106.66	20
4	200	128	328	50	32	82	8
5	200	180	380	40	36	76	52
6	200	252	452	33.33	42	75.33	72
7	200	316	516	28.57	45.14	73.71	64
8	200	436	636	25	54.50	79.50	120

CHAPTER 8

Fill in the Blanks

1. perfect competition; monopoly; monopolistic competition; oligopoly **2.** large; homogenous (standardized); easy **3.** price takers **4.** pure monopoly **5.** differentiated; so many **6.** a few **7.** many; small **8.** identical (homogenous) **9.** easy; large **10.** small **11.** horizontal; entire **12.** total revenues; total costs **13.** market price; quantity of units sold **14.** average revenue **15.** marginal revenue **16.** marginal revenue **17.** marginal; total cost–total revenue **18.** total revenue; total costs; marginal revenue; marginal costs **19.** average total cost; the market price **20.** economic profits; economic losses; zero economic profits

21. variable **22.** fixed costs **23.** average total costs; average variable costs **24.** marginal cost; average variable cost **25.** input prices **26.** enter the industry; expand **27.** exceeds; equals **28.** zero economic profits **29.** per-unit total costs **30.** input costs **31.** do not change **32.** rise **33.** efficient **34.** consumer surplus; producer surplus

True or False

1. T **2.** T **3.** T **4.** T **5.** F **6.** T **7.** F **8.** T **9.** F **10.** T **11.** F **12.** T **13.** T **14.** T **15.** F **16.** F **17.** T **18.** T **19.** T **20.** F **21.** F **22.** T **23.** F **24.** T **25.** F **26.** T **27.** T **28.** T **29.** T **30.** F **31.** T **32.** T

Multiple Choice

1. a **2.** e **3.** d **4.** c **5.** d **6.** b **7.** c **8.** c **9.** b **10.** d **11.** b **12.** c **13.** b **14.** a **15.** a **16.** e **17.** b **18.** d **19.** e **20.** b **21.** c **22.** d **23.** a **24.** c **25.** b **26.** a **27.** a

Problems

1. a.

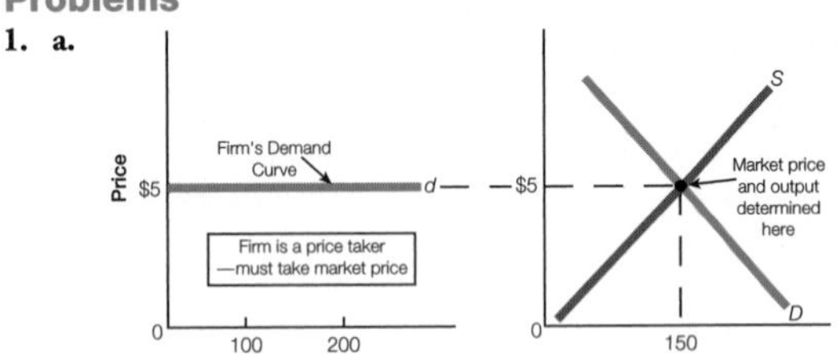

b.

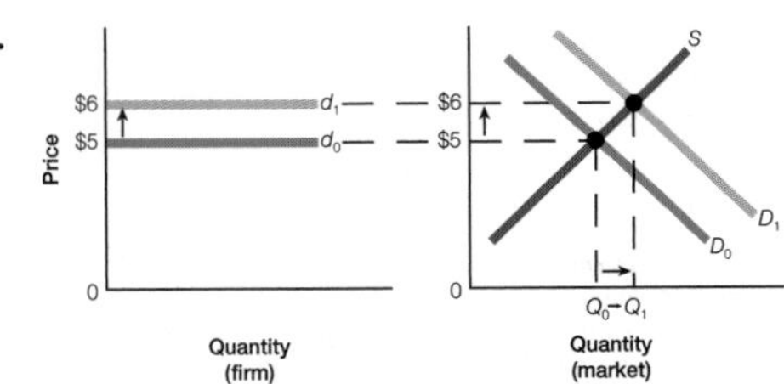

c.

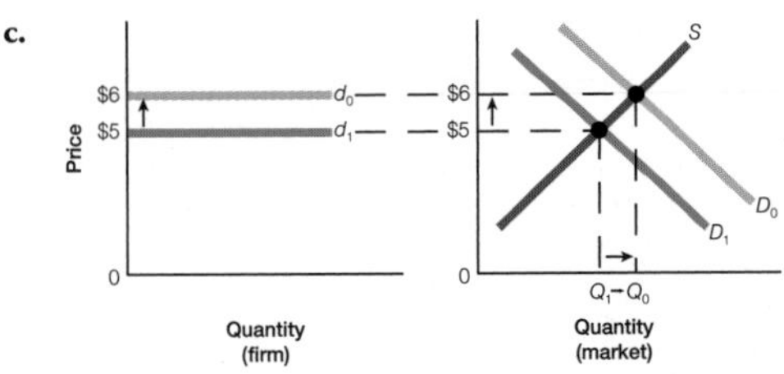

2.

Quantity	Price	Total Revenue	Marginal Revenue	Total Cost	Marginal Cost	Total Profit
6	10	60	10	30	3	30
7	10	70	10	35	5	35
8	10	80	10	42	7	38
9	10	90	10	51	9	39
10	10	100	10	62	11	38
11	10	110	10	75	13	35
12	10	120	10	90	15	30

3.

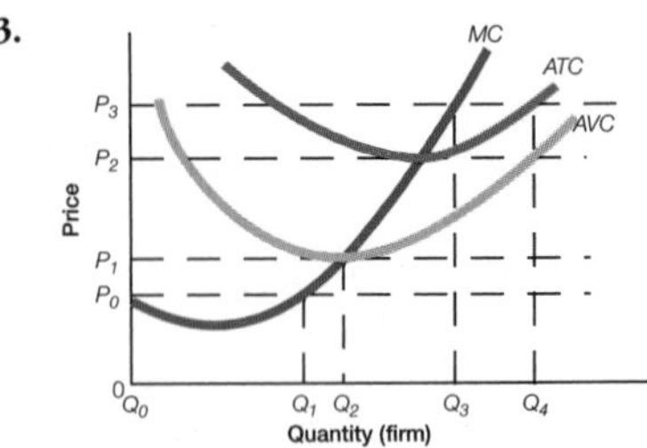

a. at P_0, zero units; at P_1, Q_2 units; at P_2, the unmarked quantity where $MC = ATC$; at P_3, Q_4 units
b. any price above P_2; P_2; any price below P_2
c. any prices below P_1
d. The firm's supply curve would be its *MC* curve above the minimum point of the *AVC* curve.

4.

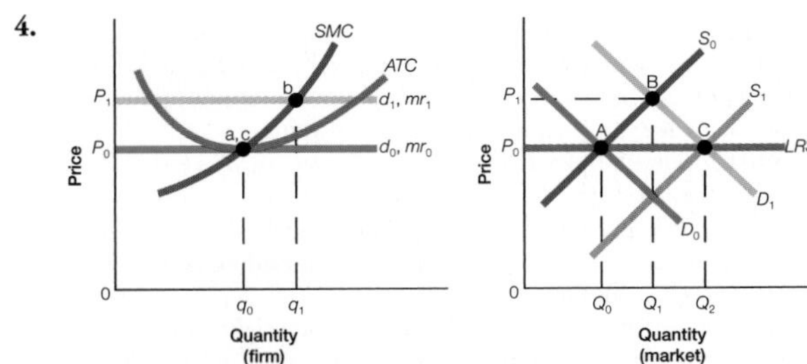

a. The answer is the movement from point a to b and from point A to B.
b. The answer is the movement from point a, returning to point c (same as point a), and from point A to point C.

CHAPTER 9

Fill in the Blanks

1. one **2.** price makers **3.** legal barriers; economies of scale; control of important inputs **4.** legal barriers to entry **5.** natural monopoly **6.** input **7.** firm **8.** rise; fall **9.** all **10.** *MR* **11.** *P* **12.** average total cost **13.** barriers to entry **14.** monopoly **15.** higher; less **16.** greater; greater **17.** technological **18.** antitrust; regulation; public **19.** antitrust **20.** high; low **21.** marginal cost; losses **22.** average cost; average total cost **23.** reduces **24.** price discrimination **25.** less; high **26.** higher; lower **27.** marginal revenue; marginal cost **28.** reselling **29.** quantity discounts **30.** consumer surplus

True or False

1. T **2.** F **3.** T **4.** T **5.** F **6.** T **7.** T **8.** T **9.** F **10.** T **11.** T **12.** T **13.** F **14.** F **15.** T **16.** F **17.** F **18.** T **19.** F **20.** T **21.** T **22.** F **23.** T **24.** T **25.** T **26.** T **27.** T

Multiple Choice

1. a **2.** e **3.** d **4.** c **5.** e **6.** b **7.** d **8.** a **9.** b **10.** c **11.** e **12.** b **13.** b **14.** d **15.** a **16.** b **17.** b **18.** b **19.** a **20.** c **21.** b **22.** e **23.** d **24.** d **25.** a **26.** a **27.** a

Problems

1.

Quantity	Price	Total Revenue	Marginal Revenue	Demand Elastic or Inelastic?
1	11	11	11	elastic
2	10	20	9	elastic
3	9	27	7	elastic
4	8	32	5	elastic
5	7	35	3	elastic
6	6	36	1	elastic
7	5	35	−1	inelastic
8	4	32	−3	inelastic
9	3	27	−5	inelastic
10	2	20	−7	inelastic
11	1	11	−9	inelastic

2.

Quantity	Price	Total Revenue	Marginal Revenue	Demand Elastic or Inelastic?	Total Cost	Marginal Cost	Profit
1	11	11	11	elastic	14	4	−3
2	10	20	9	elastic	18	4	2
3	9	27	7	elastic	22	4	5
4	8	32	5	elastic	26	4	6
5	7	35	3	elastic	30	4	5
6	6	36	1	elastic	34	4	2
7	5	35	−1	inelastic	38	4	−3
8	4	32	−3	inelastic	42	4	−10
9	3	27	−5	inelastic	46	4	−19
10	2	20	−7	inelastic	50	4	−30
11	1	11	−9	inelastic	54	4	−43

3. a.

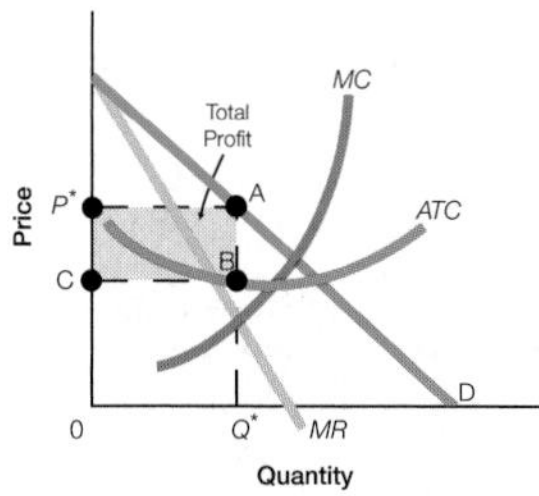

where the profit-maximizing price is P^* and the profit-maximizing quantity is Q^*

b.

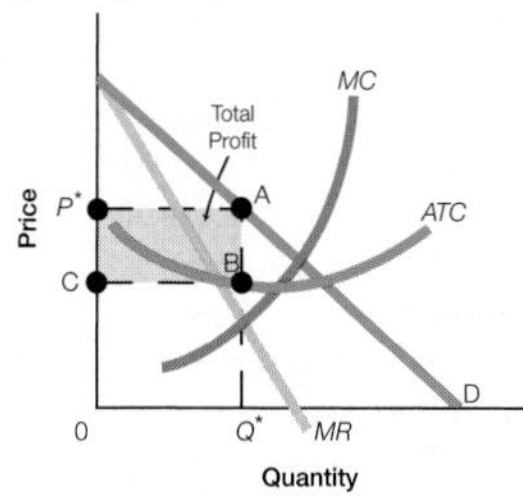

where the profit-maximizing price is P^*, the profit-maximizing quantity is Q^*, and P^* exceeds ATC at Q^*

c.

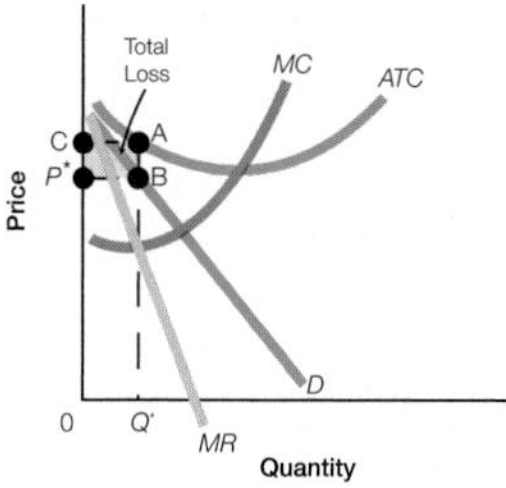

where the profit-maximizing price is P^*, the profit-maximizing quantity is Q^*, and P^* is less than ATC at Q^*

4. a.

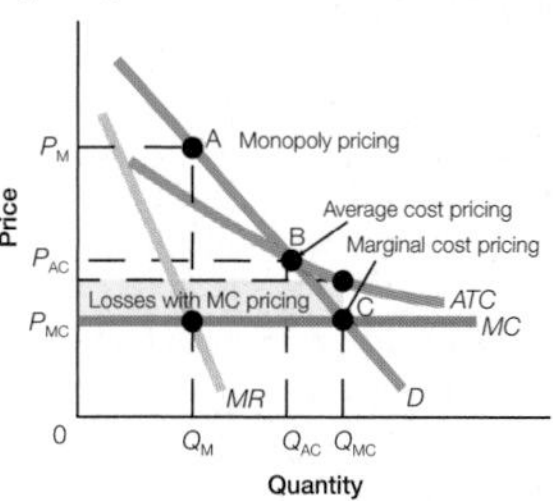

The efficient result is at point C, where demand equals marginal cost.

b.

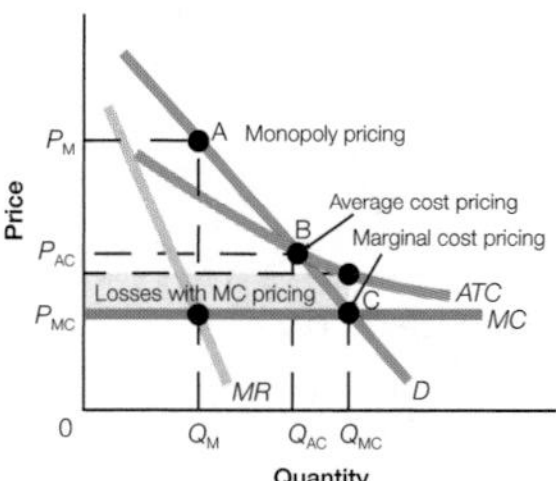

The losses with marginal cost pricing equal the shaded area in the diagram above.

c.

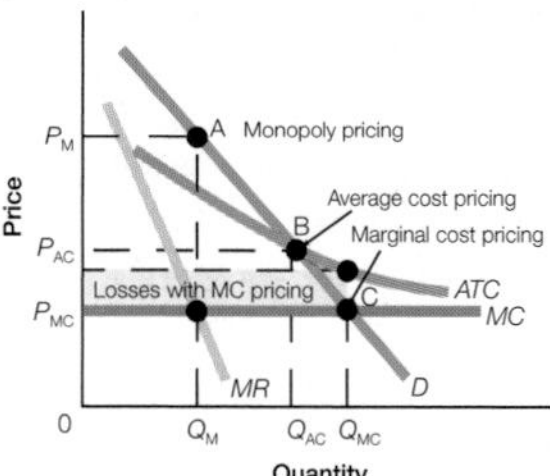

The average cost pricing solution is at point B, where economic profits are zero.

CHAPTER 10

Fill in the Blanks

1. derived; derived **2.** marginal revenue product **3.** marginal resource cost **4.** marginal revenue product; marginal resource cost **5.** variable; diminishing **6.** marginal revenue product **7.** increases; falls **8.** demanded; supplied; shortage **9.** increases; increases **10.** capital; technological; skills **11.** left **12.** right **13.** lower **14.** high; low **15.** economic rent **16.** present value **17.** exceeds **18.** age; demographic; institutional; redistributive **19.** higher; productivity; labor force **20.** age; skill; education; training; preferences **21.** job-entry **22.** productivity **23.** cost; undercut **24.** affirmative action **25.** three times **26.** more **27.** income redistribution

True or False

1. T **2.** T **3.** T **4.** F **5.** T **6.** T **7.** F **8.** T **9.** T **10.** F **11.** T **12.** T **13.** F **14.** F **15.** T **16.** F **17.** T **18.** T **19.** T **20.** F **21.** T **22.** T **23.** F **24.** T **25.** T **26.** T **27.** T **28.** F **29.** F **30.** T **31.** T **32.** T **33.** T **34.** F **35.** T **36.** T

Multiple Choice

1. e **2.** d **3.** a **4.** b **5.** c **6.** b **7.** e **8.** c **9.** e **10.** a **11.** e **12.** d **13.** d **14.** e **15.** e **16.** e **17.** b **18.** a **19.** d **20.** b **21.** e **22.** d **23.** e **24.** d **25.** a **26.** a

Problems

1.

Workers	Total Corn Output	Marginal Product of Labor
1	4,000	4,000
2	10,000	6,000
3	15,000	5,000
4	18,000	3,000
5	19,000	1,000
6	18,000	−1,000

2.

Total Workers	Total Output	Marginal Physical Product	Price	Marginal Revenue Product	Wage	Marginal Profit
1	200	200	20	4,000	2,200	1,800
2	380	180	20	3,600	2,200	1,400
3	540	160	20	3,200	2,200	1,000
4	680	140	20	2,800	2,200	600
5	800	120	20	2,400	2,200	200
6	900	100	20	2,000	2,200	−200
7	980	80	20	1,600	2,200	−600
8	1,040	60	20	1,200	2,200	−1,000

3. **a.** E **b.** C **c.** G **d.** I **e.** A **f.** B **g.** D **h.** F **i.** H

4. **a.**

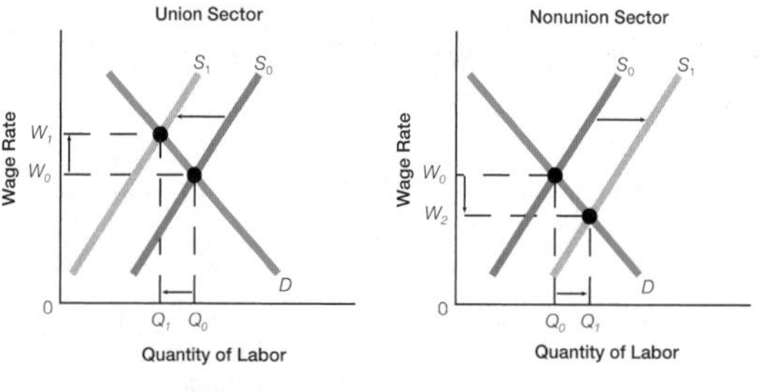

b.

Union Sector

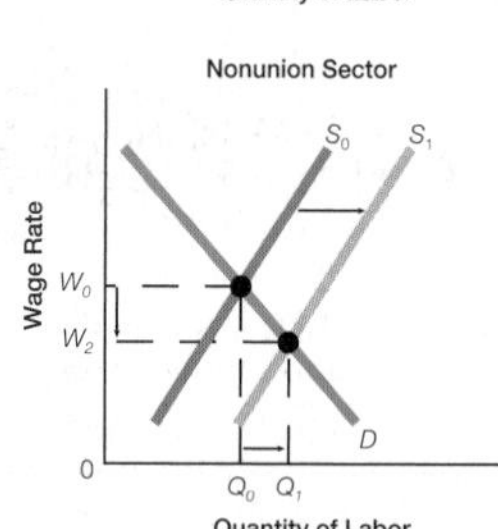

c. Union wages go up and the number of union workers hired goes down; nonunion wages go down and the number of nonunion workers hired goes up.

5. **a.** $2,673.00

b. $851.36

c. $80,000 today ($80,000 > $1,000 × 7.9038).

d. $1,000 at the end of each of 8 years from now ($1,000 times 7.0197 > $500 × 13.1661).

6. The official data may overstate the actual degree of income inequality because it fails to take into consideration differences in age, demographic factors such as the increasing number of both divorced couples and double-income families, and government redistributive activities (by ignoring the effects of taxes and in-kind subsidies).
7. **a.** Job entry discrimination occurs when a worker is denied employment on the basis of some biological feature, such as sex or race, without any regard to her productivity.
   b. Wage discrimination occurs when a worker is given employment at a wage lower than that of other workers, based on something other than productivity.
   c. Discrimination can arise as a result of information costs because past experience may suggest different likelihoods that members of particular groups will perform well. Membership in a particular group is used as a screening device to narrow down the list of job candidates, as a way to reduce information costs.
   d. In competitive industries, firms that discriminate (on some basis other than productivity) will have a cost disadvantage compared to firms that do not, allowing non-discriminating firms to undercut their prices, and potentially force discriminating firms out of business or make them change their hiring practices.
8. Economic growth could potentially reduce absolute measures of poverty by increasing real incomes. However, economic growth by itself cannot eliminate relative measures of poverty because there will always be some with lower real incomes than others.

CHAPTER 11

Fill in the Blanks

1. high; stable; high **2.** Employment Act of 1946 **3.** output **4.** unemployed; the civilian labor force **5.** employed; unemployed **6.** discouraged; labor force **7.** over **8.** losers; leavers; re; new **9.** job losers **10.** inflation **11.** mismatches **12.** high; low **13.** labor force participation **14.** short; normal **15.** greater **16.** lower **17.** structural **18.** cyclical **19.** aggregate demand **20.** structural **21.** frictional; structural **22.** natural **23.** frictional; structural **24.** technological, demographic; institutional **25.** potential **26.** greater **27.** temporarily **28.** coordinating **29.** high **30.** consumer price index **31.** erodes **32.** uncertainty **33.** raise **34.** relative **35.** menu **36.** shoe-leather **37.** nominal; inflation **38.** lower; higher **39.** leftward **40.** accurately **41.** cost-of-living **42.** short-term; long-term **43.** expansion; peak; contraction; trough **44.** rising; falling; high **45.** peak; trough **46.** below; high **47.** election **48.** forecasts **49.** leading indicators **50.** depth; duration

True or False

1. T **2.** T **3.** F **4.** T **5.** F **6.** T **7.** T **8.** T **9.** F **10.** T **11.** T **12.** F **13.** T **14.** F **15.** T **16.** T **17.** T **18.** T **19.** T **20.** F **21.** T **22.** T **23.** F **24.** T **25.** F **26.** T **27.** F **28.** T **29.** T **30.** F **31.** T **32.** T **33.** F **34.** F **35.** T **36.** T **37.** F **38.** T **39.** T **40.** T **41.** F **42.** T **43.** F **44.** T **45.** T **46.** F **47.** T **48.** T

Multiple Choice

1. d **2.** c **3.** c **4.** c **5.** e **6.** a **7.** b **8.** b **9.** b **10.** c **11.** a **12.** b **13.** e **14.** b **15.** a **16.** c **17.** b **18.** b **19.** c **20.** a **21.** b **22.** c **23.** d **24.** c **25.** e **26.** a **27.** c **28.** c **29.** d **30.** c **31.** b **32.** d **33.** b **34.** d **35.** c **36.** e **37.** a **38.** e **39.** a

Problems

1. **a.** Its labor force participation rate is 80 percent (160 million ÷ 200 million) and its unemployment rate is 12.5 percent (20 million ÷ 160 million).
   b. Its labor force participation rate would be 90 percent (180 million ÷ 200 million) and its unemployment rate would be 16.7 percent (30 million ÷ 180 million).
   c. Its labor force participation rate would be 75 percent (150 million ÷ 200 million) and its unemployment rate would be 6.7 percent (10 million ÷ 150 million).
   d. Its labor force participation rate would be 75 percent (150 million ÷ 200 million) and its unemployment rate would be 16.7 percent (30 million ÷ 150 million).
2. **a.**

job losers	**increase**
job leavers	**decrease**
reentrants	**decrease**
new entrants	**decrease**

   b. Good job prospects would tend to increase the number of job leavers by making them confident they could find better jobs; good job prospects would also attract re-entrants (for example, homemakers or retirees) and new entrants (for example, students who would leave school if offered a good enough job).
3. **a.**

retirees on fixed incomes	**hurt**
workers	**hurt (unless wages kept up with inflation)**
debtors	**help**
creditors	**hurt**
shoe-leather costs	**increase**
menu costs	**increase**

   b. Workers, debtors, and creditors would be unaffected. If retirees stayed on their fixed incomes, they would be hurt. Shoe-leather costs would be unaffected but menu costs would rise.
4. **a.** 4 percent; 7 percent
   b. Nothing; it would remain at 3 percent.

CHAPTER 12

Fill in the Blanks

1. national income **2.** GDP **3.** final; intermediate **4.** expenditure; income **5.** expenditure **6.** consumption; investment; government purchases; net exports **7.** nondurable; durable; services **8.** households **9.** vehicles **10.** more **11.** capital; produce other goods **12.** fixed; inventory **13.** increase **14.** transfer **15.** excluded **16.** income **17.** income **18.** wages; rent; interest; profits **19.** productive; factor **20.** depreciation **21.** disposable personal **22.** index **23.** consumer price index **24.** final **25.** households **26.** current; base **27.** nominal GDP; price level index **28.** real; total population **29.** reliable **30.** in the home **31.** omitted

True or False

1. T **2.** F **3.** T **4.** T **5.** T **6.** F **7.** F **8.** T **9.** F **10.** T **11.** F **12.** T **13.** T **14.** F **15.** F **16.** T **17.** T **18.** T **19.** F **20.** T **21.** T **22.** F **23.** T **24.** T **25.** F **26.** F **27.** T **28.** T **29.** T **30.** T **31.** F **32.** T **33.** F **34.** F **35.** T

Multiple Choice

1. a **2.** c **3.** d **4.** c **5.** c **6.** c **7.** b **8.** b **9.** c **10.** d **11.** b **12.** a **13.** d **14.** d **15.** c **16.** c **17.** e **18.** e **19.** e **20.** d **21.** c **22.** c **23.** c **24.** d **25.** c **26.** d **27.** b **28.** c **29.** e **30.** a **31.** e **32.** d **33.** c **34.** e **35.** e **36.** b

Problems

1. **a.** GDP is the value of all final goods and services produced within a country during a given period of time (almost always one year).
   b. To count intermediate goods as well as final goods and services would result in double counting the value of some goods and services.
   c. GDP is an attempt to measure domestic output, therefore it must exclude goods and services produced in other countries (even if those goods and services are produced by Americans in other countries).
   d. The value of used goods was included in their value when those goods were newly produced, so sales of used goods are not counted as part of GDP (although any sales commissions on such sales would be counted as newly produced services).
   e. Because such sales simply rearrange existing ownership claims, they are not counted because they are not payments for newly produced goods or services (although any sales commissions on such sales would be counted as newly produced services).
2. Consumption: $5,400
   Consumption of durable goods: $1,200
   Consumption of nondurable goods: $1,800
   Consumption of services: $2,400
   Investment: $1,400
   Fixed investment: $800
   Inventory investment: $600
   Government expenditures on goods and services: $1,600
   Government transfer payments: $500
   Exports: $500
   Imports: $650
   Net exports: −$150
   GDP: $8,250
3.

Year	GDP deflator	Nominal GDP (in billions)	Real GDP (in billions)
1997	90.9	$7,000	$7,700
1998	100	$8,000	$8,000
1999	125	$10,000	$8,000
2000	140	$14,000	$10,000
2001	150	$18,000	$12,000

4. **a.** 110 **b.** 180 **c.** 200

CHAPTER 13

Fill in the Blanks

1. short-term **2.** crucial **3.** real GDP per capita **4.** quantity; quality **5.** increases **6.** greater **7.** growth **8.** developed; less-developed **9.** labor; land; capital; technological **10.** rises; longer **11.** human **12.** capital **13.** innovation **14.** labor; land (natural resources); capital **15.** higher; greater **16.** quality; type **17.** new; improvements; innovations; doing **18.** property rights **19.** costly; stifle **20.** free trade **21.** reduction; increase **22.** fall; grows **23.** reducing; raising **24.** higher

True or False

1. T **2.** T **3.** F **4.** T **5.** T **6.** T **7.** F **8.** T **9.** T **10.** F **11.** T **12.** T **13.** F **14.** F **15.** T **16.** T **17.** T **18.** T **19.** T **20.** T **21.** T **22.** T **23.** F **24.** T

Multiple Choice

1. c **2.** d **3.** c **4.** d **5.** e **6.** e **7.** c **8.** e **9.** a **10.** d **11.** d **12.** b **13.** d **14.** b **15.** a **16.** a **17.** a **18.** d **19.** d **20.** b **21.** e **22.** d **23.** e **24.** e **25.** d **26.** c **27.** b **28.** e **29.** a **30.** c

Problems

1. a.

0.5 percent:	140 years
1 percent:	70 years
1.4 percent:	50 years
2 percent:	35 years
2.8 percent:	25 years
3.5 percent:	20 years
7 percent:	10 years

b.

1.4 percent?	$200 billion
2.8 percent?	$400 billion
7 percent?	$3,200 billion

2.

	Real GDP Growth	Real GDP Growth per Capita
An increase in population	increase	indeterminate
An increase in labor force participation	increase	increase
An increase in population and labor force participation	increase	increase
An increase in current consumption	decrease	decrease
An increase in technology	increase	increase
An increase in illiteracy	decrease	decrease
An increase in tax rates	decrease	decrease
An increase in productivity	increase	increase
An increase in tariffs on imported goods	decrease	decrease
An earlier retirement age in the country	decrease	decrease
An increase in technology and a decrease in labor force participation	indeterminate	increase
An earlier retirement age and an increase in the capital stock	indeterminate	indeterminate

CHAPTER 14

Fill in the Blanks

1. real GDP demanded **2.** consumption **3.** more **4.** more; less **5.** marginal **6.** 0.6 **7.** less **8.** open economy **9.** net exports **10.** real **11.** investment demand **12.** downward; inversely **13.** falls; rises **14.** lowering **15.** left **16.** improve; lower **17.** lower; left **18.** right **19.** lower; left **20.** upward **21.** lower **22.** less **23.** more; right **24.** investment **25.** real **26.** greater; surplus **27.** downward; inverse **28.** real wealth; interest rate; open economy **29.** rises; increase **30.** reduced; reduced; reduced **31.** more; increase **32.** rises; fewer; lower **33.** increases; increases; reduces; reduces **34.** more; less **35.** increases; increases **36.** downward **37.** rightward **38.** leftward **39.** left **40.** right; left **41.** right **42.** fewer; left

True or False

1. T **2.** F **3.** T **4.** F **5.** F **6.** T **7.** F **8.** T **9.** T **10.** F **11.** F **12.** T **13.** T **14.** T **15.** F **16.** F **17.** T **18.** T **19.** T **20.** F **21.** T **22.** F **23.** T **24.** T **25.** F **26.** F **27.** F **28.** T **29.** T **30.** T **31.** F **32.** T **33.** T **34.** T **35.** F **36.** F **37.** T **38.** T **39.** T **40.** T **41.** F **42.** T **43.** T

Multiple Choice

1. c **2.** e **3.** c **4.** a **5.** d **6.** a **7.** a **8.** a **9.** c **10.** a **11.** d **12.** a **13.** e **14.** d **15.** e **16.** c **17.** e **18.** e **19.** a **20.** c **21.** a **22.** b **23.** d **24.** b **25.** e **26.** a **27.** d **28.** c **29.** d **30.** b **31.** e **32.** d **33.** d **34.** e **35.** c **36.** d **37.** a **38.** e **39.** b **40.** d **41.** a **42.** c **43.** a **44.** b

Problems

1. a. 0.90
b. 0.80
c. 0.60
d. $300,000; 0.75
e. $120,000; 1.2

2. a. increase
b. indeterminate
c. decrease
d. increase
e. indeterminate
f. no change (change in quantity of RGDP demanded)
g. no change (change in quantity of RGDP demanded)

3. a. The quantity of investment demanded increases but the investment demand curve does not shift.
b. The investment demand curve shifts to the left.
c. The investment demand curve shifts to the right.
d. The quantity of saving supplied increases but the saving supply curve does not shift.
e. The saving supply curve shifts to the right.

4.

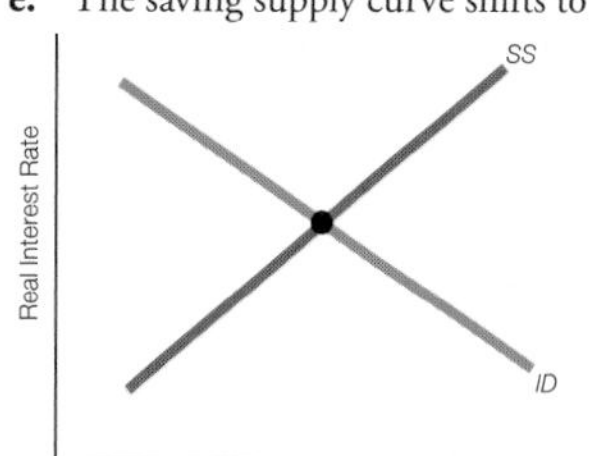

a. The investment demand (*ID*) curve would shift to the right, increasing both interest rates and the dollar amount of investment demanded.
b. The saving supply (*SS*) curve would shift to the right, decreasing interest rates and increasing the dollar amount of investment demanded.
c. The investment demand (*ID*) curve would shift to the left, decreasing both interest rates and the dollar amount of investment demanded.
d. The saving supply (*SS*) curve would shift to the right, decreasing interest rates and increasing the dollar amount of investment demanded.

5. a. decrease; decrease; decrease
b. decrease; decrease; increase; increase
c. decrease; decrease

CHAPTER 15

Fill in the Blanks

1. aggregate supply **2.** short-run; long-run **3.** output; input **4.** upward **5.** more; less **6.** profit; misperception **7.** rise; raising **8.** fall; fall; reduce **9.** relative; more **10.** all inputs **11.** outputs; inputs **12.** not affected **13.** natural rate **14.** fully **15.** long-run aggregate supply curve **16.** production costs **17.** higher; leftward **18.** right **19.** reduce; reduce **20.** rise **21.** decrease **22.** depress; increase **23.** lower; leftward **24.** reduction **25.** input; natural disasters **26.** left; not shift **27.** potential output; supply **28.** adverse **29.** potential **30.** aggregate demand; short-run aggregate supply **31.** *LRAS* **32.** shocks **33.** contractionary **34.** demand-pull **35.** increase; increase **36.** expansionary **37.** fall **38.** rise; leftward **39.** stagflation **40.** left; higher; lower; higher **41.** higher; less **42.** rightward **43.** lower; greater; lower **44.** declining **45.** at; lower **46.** long-term; minimum; efficiency; menu **47.** higher **48.** interdependence

True or False

1. T **2.** F **3.** T **4.** F **5.** T **6.** T **7.** F **8.** F **9.** F **10.** T **11.** T **12.** T **13.** T **14.** F **15.** T **16.** T **17.** F **18.** T **19.** F **20.** T **21.** F **22.** T **23.** F **24.** T **25.** T **26.** F **27.** T **28.** T **29.** F **30.** T **31.** T **32.** F **33.** T **34.** F **35.** T **36.** T **37.** T **38.** T **39.** F **40.** T **41.** F **42.** T **43.** T **44.** T **45.** T **46.** F **47.** F

Multiple Choice

1. c **2.** c **3.** b **4.** e **5.** b **6.** d **7.** d **8.** c **9.** e **10.** c **11.** b **12.** a **13.** a **14.** c **15.** d **16.** b **17.** a **18.** a **19.** a **20.** a **21.** b **22.** a **23.** a **24.** a **25.** a **26.** c **27.** d **28.** c **29.** d **30.** a **31.** d **32.** a **33.** c **34.** d **35.** c

Problems

1.

Change	Short-Run Aggregate Supply	Long-Run Aggregate Supply
An increase in aggregate demand	no change	no change
A decrease in aggregate demand	no change	no change
An increase in the stock of capital	increase (shift right)	increase (shift right)
A reduction in the size of the labor force	decrease (shift left)	decrease (shift left)
An increase in input prices (that does not reflect permanent changes in their supplies)	decrease (shift left)	no change
A decrease in input prices (that does reflect permanent changes in their supplies)	increase (shift right)	increase (shift right)
An increase in usable natural resources	increase (shift right)	increase (shift right)
A temporary adverse supply shock	decrease (shift left)	no change
Increases in the cost of government regulations	decrease (shift left)	decrease (shift left)

2. a.

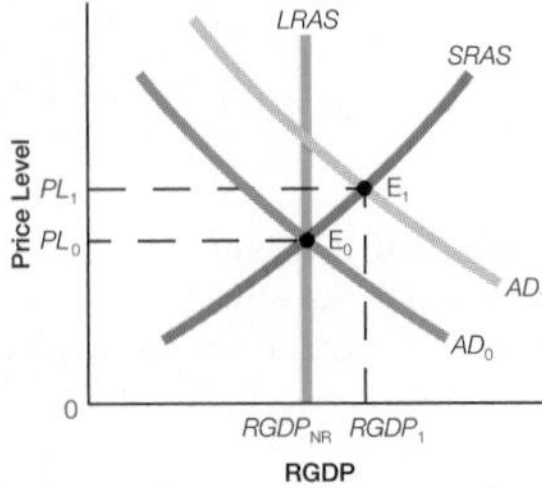

The price level increases, real output increases, employment increases, and unemployment decreases.

b.

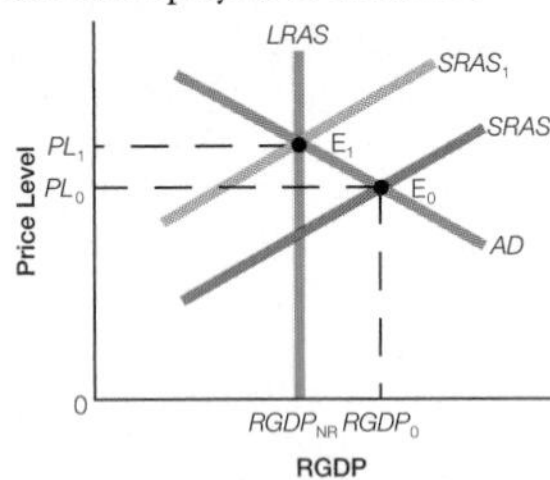

The price level ends up higher, real output ends up back where it began at potential output, employment ends up back where it began at full employment, and unemployment ends up back where it began at the natural rate of unemployment.

3. a.

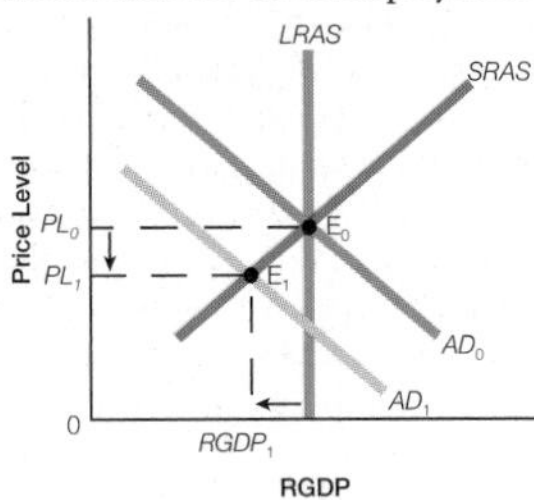

The price level falls, real output falls, employment falls, and unemployment rises.

b.

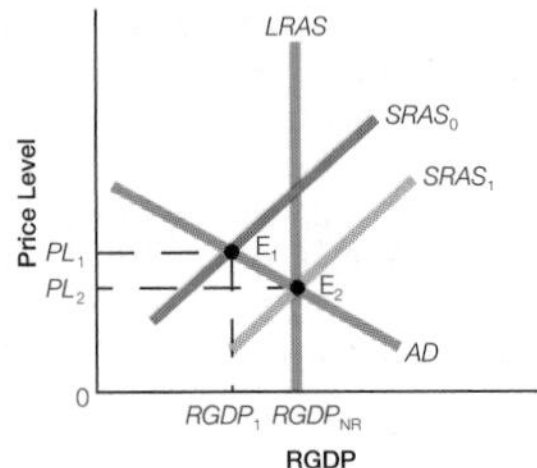

The price level ends up lower, real output ends up back where it began at potential output, employment ends up back where it began at full employment, and unemployment ends up back where it began at the natural rate of unemployment.

4. a.

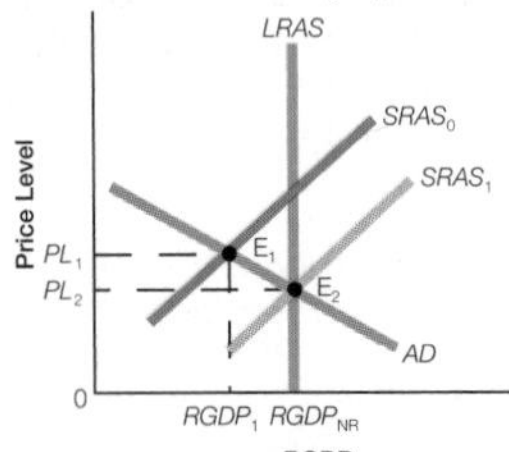

b.

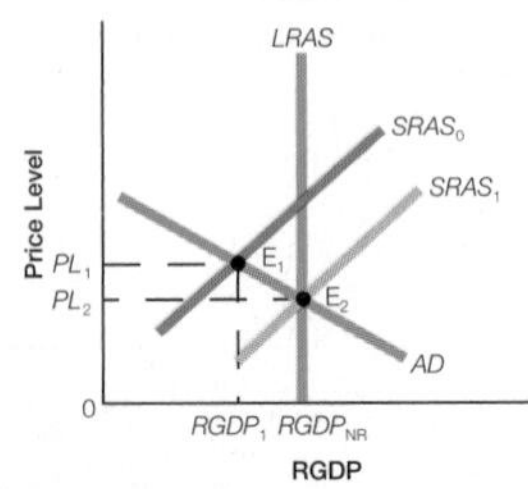

In the long run, the price level will end up lower than before, but real output and unemployment will return to their initial long-run equilibrium levels.

5. a.

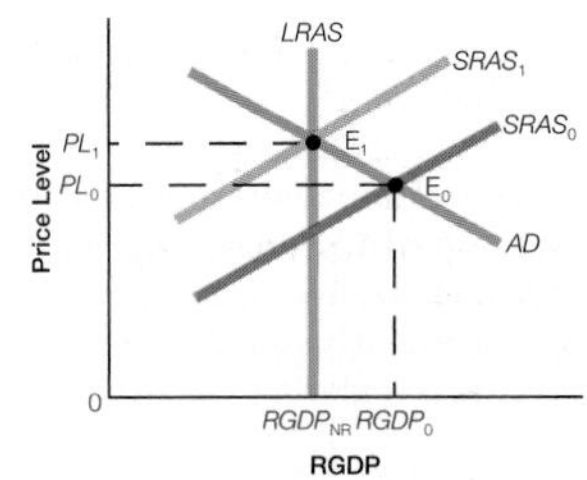

b.

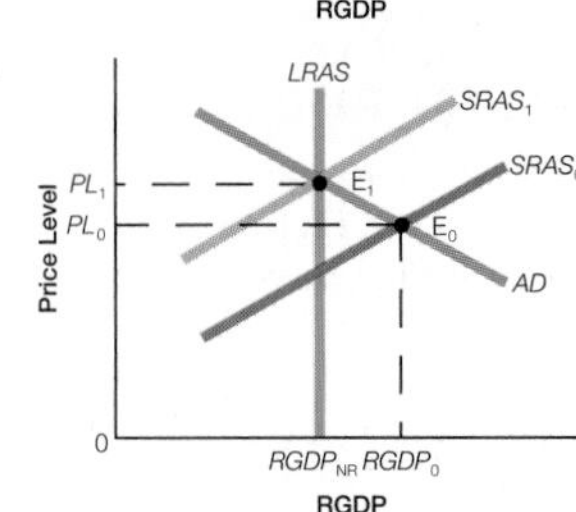

In the long run, the price level will end up higher than before, but real output and unemployment will return to their initial long-run equilibrium levels.

CHAPTER 16

Fill in the Blanks

1. fiscal policy **2.** deficit **3.** increase; increase; lower **4.** increased **5.** reduce; increase; reduce **6.** taxation; borrowing **7.** disposable; consumption **8.** multiplier **9.** incomes **10.** consumption **11.** marginal propensity to consume **12.** smaller; savings; tax **13.** multiplier **14.** larger **15.** smaller **16.** less **17.** reduce **18.** deficits **19.** increase; increase **20.** price **21.** equal to **22.** reduce; increase; decrease **23.** increase; consumption; investment **24.** lower; lower **25.** greater **26.** increases; up **27.** crowding-out **28.** increase; higher **29.** increase **30.** fall **31.** smaller **32.** time lags **33.** inflationary boom; recession **34.** automatic stabilizers **35.** tax **36.** lessened **37.** less; offsets **38.** less; less; less **39.** Laffer **40.** greater **41.** adds; lowers; increasing **42.** debt **43.** larger

True or False

1. T **2.** T **3.** F **4.** F **5.** F **6.** T **7.** F **8.** F **9.** T **10.** T **11.** F **12.** T **13.** T **14.** T **15.** F **16.** F **17.** T **18.** T **19.** F **20.** T **21.** T **22.** T **23.** T **24.** F **25.** T **26.** T **27.** T **28.** F **29.** T **30.** F **31.** T **32.** T **33.** F **34.** T **35.** F **36.** T **37.** T **38.** T **39.** T **40.** T **41.** T **42.** T **43.** F **44.** T **45.** T **46.** T **47.** T **48.** F **49.** T **50.** T **51.** T

Multiple Choice

1. a **2.** c **3.** a **4.** d **5.** d **6.** c **7.** b **8.** d **9.** d **10.** b **11.** a **12.** b **13.** a **14.** d **15.** b **16.** d **17.** c **18.** d **19.** d **20.** b **21.** d **22.** b **23.** a **24.** d **25.** d **26.** d **27.** c **28.** b **29.** c

Problems

1. a. An increase in government purchases would decrease a budget surplus.
   b. An increase in government purchases would increase aggregate demand.
   c. When the threat of a recession is developing.
2. a. An increase in taxes would decrease a budget deficit.
   b. An increase in taxes would decrease aggregate demand.
   c. When the threat of an unsustainable, inflationary boom is otherwise likely.
3. a. 1.5 b. 2 c. 4
4.

	Change in Aggregate Demand	Change in Consumption
a. 1/3	$30 billion	$10 billion
b. 1/2	$40 billion	$20 billion
c. 2/3	$60 billion	$40 billion
d. 3/4	$80 billion	$60 billion
e. 4/5	$100 billion	$80 billion

5.

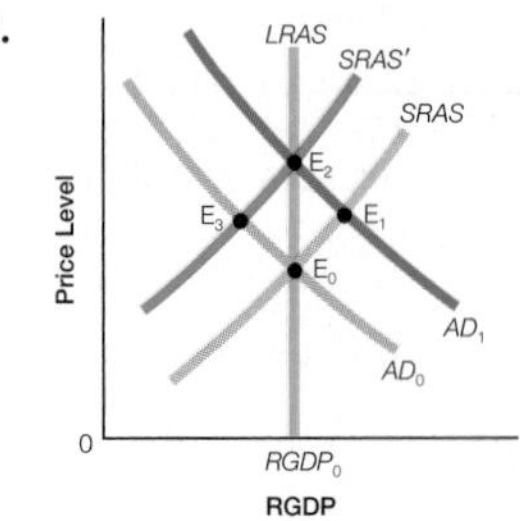

a. At point E_3.
b. The economy would end up at a long-run equilibrium at point E_2.
c. The economy would end up at a long-run equilibrium at point E_0.
d. The economy would end up at a long-run equilibrium at point E_1.
e. The economy would end up in long-run equilibrium at E_0.
f. The economy would end up in long-run equilibrium at E_2.

6. a.

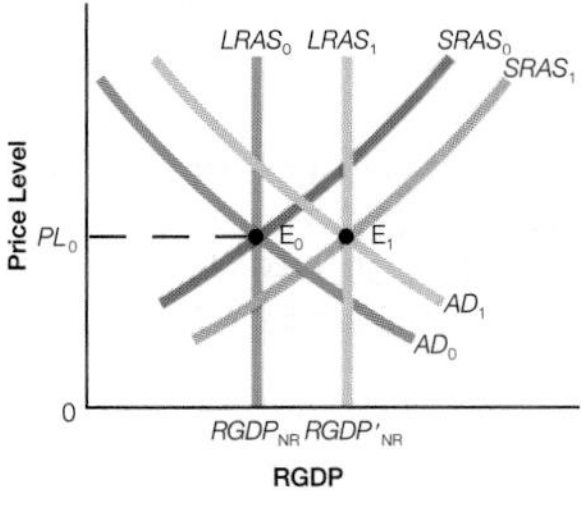

This is what happens when the supply side policy shifts aggregate demand and aggregate supply by the same amount.

b.

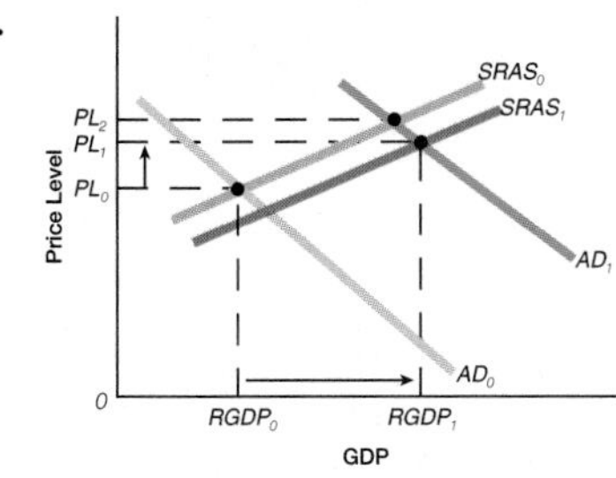

This is what happens when the supply side policy shifts aggregate demand more than aggregate supply.

CHAPTER 17

Fill in the Blanks

1. deteriorate **2.** currency **3.** fiat **4.** demand **5.** withdrawn **6.** transaction **7.** demand; other checkable **8.** transaction **9.** loans **10.** substitutes **11.** nontransaction **12.** savings; time **13.** liquid **14.** near **15.** M2 **16.** Gresham's **17.** accept **18.** private financial; government **19.** medium of exchange **20.** greater **21.** standard; store **22.** yardstick **23.** less **24.** commercial banks **25.** savings and loan associations; credit unions **26.** depositories **27.** savers; borrowers **28.** add \$1,000 **29.** higher **30.** reserve requirements **31.** fractional reserve **32.** make loans **33.** loans **34.** reserve accounts at the Federal Reserve **35.** liabilities **36.** assets **37.** deposits; the required reserve ratio **38.** non-interest-earning; interest-earning **39.** excess **40.** the money multiplier **41.** less than **42.** decline; declines **43.** fell; fell **44.** deposit insurance **45.** savings and loan

True or False

1. T **2.** T **3.** F **4.** T **5.** F **6.** T **7.** T **8.** F **9.** T **10.** T **11.** T **12.** T **13.** F **14.** F **15.** T **16.** F **17.** T **18.** F **19.** T **20.** T **21.** T **22.** T **23.** F **24.** F **25.** T **26.** F **27.** T **28.** F **29.** T **30.** T **31.** T **32.** F **33.** T **34.** T **35.** F **36.** T **37.** T **38.** T **39.** F **40.** T **41.** T **42.** T **43.** T **44.** T **45.** F **46.** T

Multiple Choice

1. b **2.** a **3.** e **4.** a **5.** d **6.** c **7.** b **8.** a **9.** d **10.** a **11.** e **12.** d **13.** d **14.** b **15.** a **16.** d **17.** c **18.** b

Problems

1.

Change	M1	M2
An increase in currency in circulation	increase	increase
A decrease in demand deposits	decrease	decrease
An increase in savings deposits	no change	increase
An increase in credit card balances	no change	no change
A conversion of savings account balances into checking account balances	increase	no change
A conversion of savings account balances into time account balances	no change	no change
A conversion of checking account balances into money market mutual funds	decrease	no change

2.

5 percent	20
10 percent	10
20 percent	5
25 percent	4
50 percent	2

3.

a.	10 percent	\$90,000
	20 percent	\$80,000
	25 percent	\$75,000
	50 percent	\$50,000
b.	10 percent	\$90,000
	20 percent	\$80,000
	25 percent	\$75,000
	50 percent	\$50,000
c.	10 percent	\$1,000,000
	20 percent	\$500,000
	25 percent	\$400,000
	50 percent	\$200,000

4.

a.	10 percent	\$10,000
	15 percent	zero (it has zero excess reserves)
	20 percent	zero (it has insufficient reserves and must call in \$5,000 in loans to meet its reserve requirement)
b.	10 percent	\$46,000
	15 percent	\$34,000
	20 percent	\$22,000

CHAPTER 18

Fill in the Blanks

1. central bank **2.** Board of Governors; Federal Open Market Committee **3.** stability; central **4.** Federal Open Market Committee **5.** money supply **6.** $M \times V$; $P \times Q$ **7.** velocity **8.** rise; rise; rise **9.** increasing; reducing; increasing **10.** monetarists **11.** less **12.** less; increases **13.** increase **14.** more **15.** open market; reserve; discount **16.** open market operations **17.** government securities; the Federal Reserve System **18.** increases **19.** excess reserves **20.** \$1,000,000 **21.** fall **22.** lowers **23.** decrease **24.** big **25.** discount **26.** more; fewer; less **27.** lower **28.** federal funds **29.** sell; raise; raise **30.** raise **31.** transactions; precautionary; asset **32.** inversely **33.** less **34.** vertical; Federal Reserve **35.** nominal **36.** right; higher **37.** lower; increase **38.** lowers; raises; reduces **39.** rise; fall **40.** increase **41.** federal funds rate **42.** decrease; increase **43.** real; nominal **44.** the nominal interest rate; the expected inflation rate **45.** reduce **46.** decrease; increase; appreciation; decrease; decrease **47.** less **48.** three; two; one; three **49.** reduce **50.** loans **51.** member; issue credit **52.** Congress; the president; the Federal Reserve System **53.** more; improve **54.** right; right; right **55.** no one **56.** neutralize **57.** higher **58.** rational expectations **59.** pessimistic **60.** flexible; quickly **61.** limited; negate **62.** little or no **63.** unanticipated; anticipated **64.** short; long **65.** not change **66.** higher; lower **67.** incorrect **68.** equal to; natural rate

True or False

1. F **2.** T **3.** F **4.** T **5.** T **6.** F **7.** T **8.** T **9.** T **10.** F **11.** T **12.** F **13.** T **14.** T **15.** T **16.** F **17.** T **18.** T **19.** T **20.** T **21.** T **22.** F **23.** T **24.** F **25.** T **26.** F **27.** F **28.** T **29.** T **30.** T **31.** F **32.** T **33.** T **34.** F **35.** T **36.** F **37.** T **38.** T **39.** T **40.** F **41.** T **42.** T **43.** T **44.** T **45.** F **46.** F **47.** T **48.** T **49.** T **50.** F **51.** T **52.** T **53.** T **54.** F **55.** T **56.** T **57.** T **58.** F **59.** T **60.** T **61.** T **62.** T **63.** T **64.** F **65.** T **66.** F **67.** F **68.** T **69.** T **70.** T

Multiple Choice

1. b **2.** d **3.** b **4.** b **5.** b **6.** a **7.** c **8.** b **9.** c **10.** a **11.** c **12.** c **13.** b **14.** e **15.** c **16.** c **17.** d **18.** b **19.** a **20.** d **21.** d **22.** a **23.** a **24.** c **25.** b **26.** c **27.** d **28.** c **29.** a **30.** a **31.** e **32.** c **33.** d **34.** d **35.** a **36.** b **37.** d **38.** a **39.** e **40.** d **41.** c **42.** d **43.** c **44.** d

Problems

1. a. MV = PQ
b. Nominal GDP would double.
c. The price level would double.
d. Nominal GDP would double.
e. Nominal GDP would remain unchanged.

2. a. decrease **b.** decrease **c.** decrease **d.** decrease **e.** indeterminate

3. a.

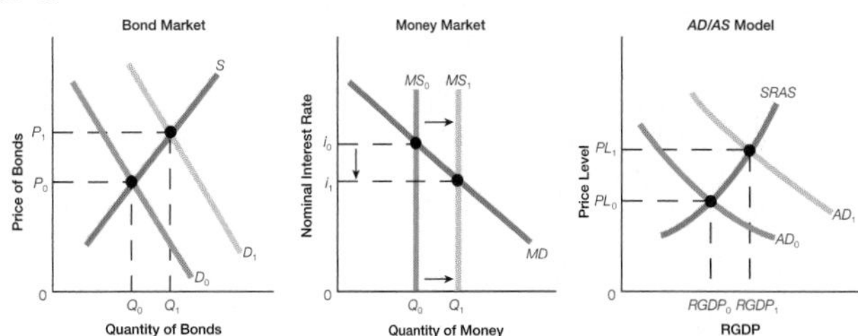

b.

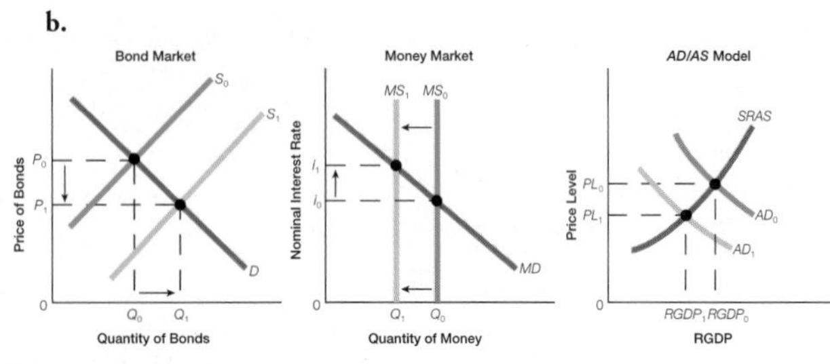

4. a.

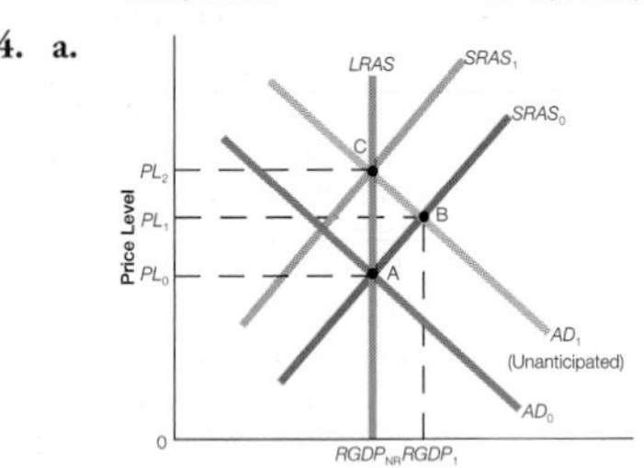

The result is indicated by the movement from point A to point B in the diagram above.

b.

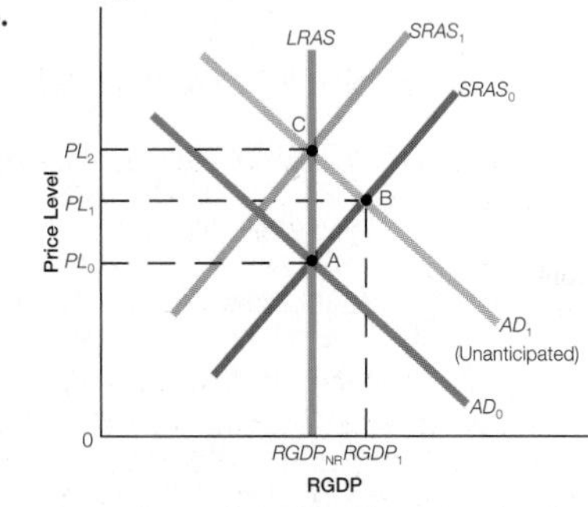

The result is indicated by the movement from point A to point C in the diagram above.

c.

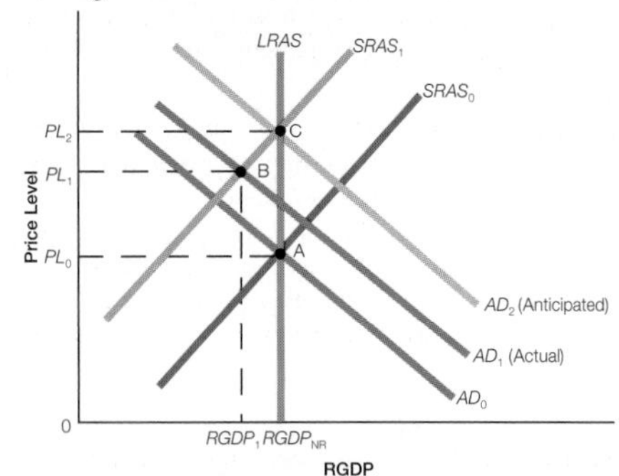

The result is indicated by the movement from point A to point B in the diagram above.

CHAPTER 19

Fill in the Blanks

1. 15 **2.** imports; exports **3.** credit; plus **4.** services; merchandise **5.** trade **6.** imports **7.** voluntary **8.** comparative advantage **9.** opportunity cost **10.** comparative; absolute **11.** consumer **12.** consumer; producer **13.** consumer surplus; producer surplus **14.** raises; producers; consumers **15.** consumers; producers; producer; consumer **16.** lower; imports **17.** producers; consumers; increase **18.** tariff **19.** higher; lower; higher **20.** greater **21.** lower; greater; reducing **22.** producers; the government; consumers **23.** temporarily **24.** increased **25.** fewer; fewer **26.** hasten **27.** quota **28.** weaker **29.** rent seeking **30.** subsidizing **31.** inefficient **32.** reduced **33.** sell; U.S. dollars **34.** exchange rate **35.** increase; reducing **36.** goods and services; capital **37.** more **38.** exchange rate **39.** falls **40.** less; increase **41.** upward **42.** supplied; sellers; down **43.** higher; lower **44.** tastes; income; real interest; inflation; speculation **45.** increase; increasing **46.** decrease; decrease; lower **47.** rose; increased; increased **48.** increase; increasing **49.** more; decreasing; decreasing

True or False

1. T **2.** F **3.** T **4.** F **5.** T **6.** F **7.** T **8.** T **9.** F **10.** T **11.** T **12.** F **13.** T **14.** T **15.** T **16.** F **17.** T **18.** T **19.** F **20.** F **21.** T **22.** T **23.** F **24.** T **25.** F **26.** T **27.** T **28.** T **29.** T **30.** F **31.** T **32.** T **33.** T **34.** T **35.** F **36.** T **37.** T **38.** T **39.** F **40.** T **41.** F **42.** T **43.** T **44.** F **45.** T **46.** T **47.** T **48.** T

Multiple Choice

1. e **2.** a **3.** a **4.** c **5.** c **6.** a **7.** b **8.** b **9.** b **10.** b **11.** d **12.** a **13.** b **14.** b **15.** d **16.** c **17.** d **18.** c **19.** d **20.** a **21.** c **22.** c **23.** c **24.** d **25.** a **26.** d **27.** a **28.** a **29.** e **30.** b **31.** a **32.** d **33.** a **34.** b **35.** a **36.** b **37.** b **38.** d **39.** a **40.** d **41.** c **42.** e **43.** d **44.** a **45.** a **46.** b **47.** a **48.** b **49.** a **50.** a **51.** d **52.** c **53.** e **54.** c **55.** d

Problems

1.

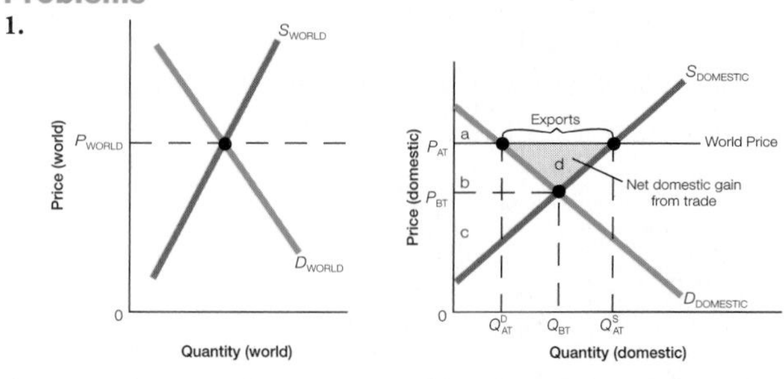

Domestic Gains and Losses from Free Trade (exports)

Area	Before Trade	After Trade	Change
Consumer Surplus (*CS*)	a + b	a	− b
Producer Surplus (*PS*)	c	b + c + d	+ (b + d)
Total Welfare from Trade (*CS* + *PS*)	a + b + c	a + b + c + d	+ d

2.

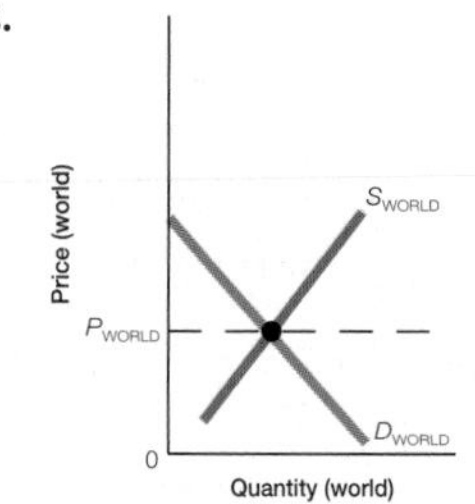

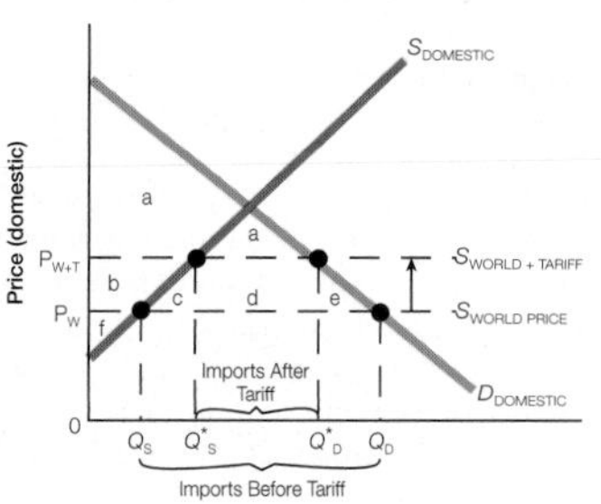

Gains and Losses from Tariffs

Area	Before Tariff	After Tariff	Change
Consumer Surplus (*CS*)	a + b + c + d + e	a	− (b + c + d + e)
Producer Surplus (*PS*)	f	b + f	+ b
Government Revenues (Tariff)	0	d	+ d
Total Welfare from Tariff (*CS* + *PS* + Tariff Revenues)	a + b + c + d + e + f	a + b + d + f	− (c + e)

3. **a.** 50 pounds

b. 12,500 pesos

c. The dollar price of the other currency would increase, making the goods cheaper in the other country.

d. The dollar price of the other currency would increase, making the goods cheaper in the other country.

e. The dollar price of the other currency would increase, making the goods cheaper in the other country.

4.

Change	Supply of Euros	Demand for Euros	Dollar price of Euros
Reduced U.S. tastes for European goods	no change	decreases	decreases
Increased incomes in the U.S.	no change	increases	increases
Increased U.S. interest rates	increases	decreases	decreases
Decreased inflation in Europe	decreases	increases	increases
Reduced U.S. tariffs on imports	no change	increases	increases
Increased European tastes for U.S. goods	increases	no change	decreases

Section Check Answers

CHAPTER 1: THE ROLE AND METHOD OF ECONOMICS

1.1 Economics: A Brief Introduction

1. Why is economics worth studying?
Perhaps the best reason to study economics is that so many of the things that concern us are at least partly economic in character. Economics helps us intelligently evaluate our options and determine the most appropriate choices in given situations. It helps develop a disciplined method of thinking about problems.

2. What is the definition of economics?
Economics is the study of the allocation of our scarce resources to satisfy our unlimited wants for goods and services.

3. Why does scarcity force us to make choices?
Scarcity means that our wants exceed our resources; such a condition forces us to make choices about how to best use those limited resources.

4. Why are choices costly?
In a world of scarcity, making a choice forces us to pick one option over another, although both options may be desirable to us. This desirable option that we do not choose is the opportunity cost of our choice.

5. Why do even "noneconomic" issues have an economic dimension?
Even apparently noneconomic issues have an economic dimension because economics concerns anything worthwhile to us (including love, friendship, charity, and so on), and the choices we make among those things we value.

1.2 Economics as a Science

1. What makes economics a social science?
Economics is a social science because it is concerned with making generalizations about human, or social, behavior.

2. What distinguishes macroeconomics from microeconomics?
Macroeconomics deals with the economy as a whole, analyzing inflation, unemployment, business cycles, economic growth, and so on. Microeconomics deals with smaller units within the economy, such as the actions of individuals, households, firms, and industries. Both, however, ultimately strive to understand human behavior.

3. Why is the market for running shoes considered a microeconomic topic?
Because a single industry is small relative to the economy as a whole, the market for running shoes (or the running shoe industry) is a microeconomic topic.

4. Why is inflation considered a macroeconomic topic?
Because inflation—a change in the overall price level—has effects on the entire economy, rather than just on a specific area or areas of the economy, it is a macroeconomic topic.

1.3 Economic Behavior

1. What do economists mean by self-interest?
By self-interest, economists mean simply that people try to improve their own situation.

2. What does rational self-interest involve?
Economists consider individuals to be acting in their own rational self-interest if they are doing their best to achieve their goals with their limited income, time, and knowledge, given their expectations of the likely future outcome (both positive and negative) of their behavior.

3. How are self-interest and selfishness different?
People are acting in self-interest when they are doing their best to achieve their goals, which may or may not be selfish. A parent working more hours to give more to their children or to a favorite charity can be self-interested, but is not selfish.

1.4 Economic Theory

1. What are economic theories?
A theory is an established explanation that accounts for known facts or phenomena. Economic theories are statements or propositions about patterns of human behavior that are expected under certain circumstances.

2. What is the purpose of a theory?
The purpose of a theory is primarily to explain and predict. Theories are necessary because the facts of a complex world do not organize themselves.

3. Why must economic theories be abstract?
Economic theories must be abstract because they cannot possibly include everything that might affect behavior. An economic theory skirts some issues to focus on the central questions it is designed to understand.

4. What is a hypothesis? How do we determine if it is tentatively accepted?
A hypothesis is a testable proposal that contains predictions about behavior in response to certain changed conditions. An economic hypothesis is a testable proposal that contains predictions about how people will react to a change in economic circumstances. It is tentatively accepted if its predictions are consistent with what actually happens. In economics, empirical analysis is performed to see if the hypothesis is supported by facts.

1.5 Problems with Scientific Thinking

1. Why do economists hold other things constant (*ceteris paribus*)?
Economists hold other things constant, or *ceteris paribus,* because they don't want outside variables to influence the relationship between the variables they are studying.

2. What is the relationship between correlation and causation?
Correlation means that two things are related; causation means that one thing caused the other thing to occur. Whereas causation implies correlation, correlation does not necessarily imply causation.

3. What misinterpretations can result from confusing correlation and causation?
Confusing correlation between variables as causation can lead to misinterpretations in which a person sees causation between two variables where there is none or where a third variable is responsible for causing both of them.

4. What is the fallacy of composition?
The fallacy of composition is the incorrect idea that if something is true for an individual, it must also be true for a group.

5. If Americans bought more gasoline in 2000, when prices averaged $1.60 per gallon, than they did in 1970, when prices averaged $0.80 per gallon, does that mean people buy more gas at higher prices? Why or why not?
No. Other things were far from constant between 1970 and 2000. The overall price level changed dramatically, as did people's incomes, the safety and convenience of automobiles, distances between home and work, and so on. Holding these and all other important determinants of gasoline purchases constant, only if people bought more gas at a higher price could we conclude that higher gas prices lead people to buy more gas.

6. If you can sometimes get a high grade on an exam without studying, does that mean that additional studying does not lead to higher grades? Explain your answer.
Sometimes a student may get a high grade on an exam without studying. However, because additional studying increases mastery of the material, it would typically increase test performance and grades. That is, although there are some unusual situations in which more studying would not raise grades, generally it does lead to higher grades.

1.6 Positive and Normative Analysis

1. What is positive analysis? Must positive analysis be testable?
Positive analysis focuses on how people do behave, rather than on how people should behave. It deals with how variable A impacts variable B. Positive analysis must be testable to determine whether evidence supports its predictions.

2. What is normative analysis? Is normative analysis testable?
Normative analysis focuses on what should be or what ought to happen; economists use this analysis to form opinions about the desirability of various actions or results. Normative analysis is not testable because there is no scientific way to establish whether one value judgment is better than another value judgment.

3. Why is the positive/normative distinction important?
It is important to distinguish between positive and normative analysis because many economic controversies revolve around policy considerations that contain both. Deciding whether a policy is good requires both positive (what will happen?) and normative (is what happens good or bad?) analysis.

4. Why are there policy disagreements among economists?
As with most disciplines, economists do disagree. However, the majority of these disagreements stem from differences in normative analysis because the evidence cannot establish whether one set of value judgments is better or more appropriate than other sets of value judgments.

5. Is the statement "UFOs land in my back yard at least twice a week" a positive statement? Why or why not?

A positive statement need not be true; it simply needs to be testable to determine whether evidence supports it. Assuming that the UFOs in question are visible or otherwise detectable, this statement is a positive one.

6. Is there any way to scientifically determine if the rich pay their fair share of taxes? Why or why not?

No. There is no scientific way to determine who qualifies as rich or what would constitute a rich person's fair share of taxes. Making decisions about such issues necessarily involves value judgments that cannot be proven right or wrong.

CHAPTER 2: THE ECONOMIC WAY OF THINKING

2.1 Scarcity

1. What qualifies something as an economic good?

An economic good, tangible or intangible, is any good or service that we value or desire. This definition includes the reduction of things we don't want—bads—as a good.

2. Does wanting more tangible and intangible goods and services make us selfish?

No. Among the goods many of us want more of is charity (helping others), so to say we all want more goods does not imply that we are selfish.

3. Why does scarcity affect everyone?

We all face scarcity because no one can have all the goods and services that he or she desires.

4. How and why does scarcity affect each of us differently?

Scarcity affects each of us differently because our desires and the resources we have available to meet those desires vary.

5. Why do you think economists often refer to training that increases the skills of workers as "adding to human capital"?

Training increases a worker's ability to produce goods, just as capital goods increase an economy's ability to produce goods. Because of this similarity in their effects on productive abilities, training is often referred to as adding to human capital.

6. What are some of the ways that students act as entrepreneurs as they seek higher grades?

There are many ways that students are entrepreneurs in seeking higher grades. They sometimes form study groups and assign different material to different members. They often share notes. They study harder for those questions they believe are more likely to be on a test. Sometimes they try to cheat or get hold of old tests. Students' efforts to find the lowest-cost ways to get higher grades include all of these and more.

7. Why might sunshine be scarce in Seattle but not in Tucson?

For a good to be scarce means that we want more of it than we can have. Residents of Tucson typically have all the sunshine they wish but may not have as much rain as they would like. For residents of Seattle, where there is much more rain than sun, the opposite might be true.

8. Why can't a country become so technologically advanced that its citizens won't have to choose?

No matter how productive a country becomes, citizens' desires will outstrip the ability to satisfy them. As we get more productive and as incomes grow, we discover new wants that we would like to satisfy. Thus our ability to produce never catches up with our wants.

2.2 Opportunity Cost

1. Would we have to make choices if we had unlimited resources?

We would not have to make choices if we had unlimited resources because we would be able to produce all the goods and services that we wanted, and having more of one thing would not mean having less of other things.

2. What is given up when we make a choice?

When we make a choice we give up the opportunity to use the same time or resources to pursue other valued alternatives.

3. What do we mean by opportunity cost?

The opportunity cost of a choice is the highest-valued foregone opportunity resulting from a decision. We can think of opportunity cost as the value of the option one would have chosen if one's most preferred option became unavailable.

4. Why is there no such thing as a free lunch?

There is no such thing as a free lunch because the production of any good uses up some of our resources, which are therefore no longer available to produce other goods we want.

5. Why was the opportunity cost of staying in college higher for Tiger Woods than for most undergraduates?

For Tiger Woods, the foregone alternative to staying in school—starting a highly paid professional golf career sooner than he could otherwise—was far more lucrative than the alternatives facing most undergraduates. Because his foregone alternative was more valuable, his opportunity cost of staying in school was higher than for most.

6. Why is the opportunity cost of time spent getting an M.B.A. typically higher for an experienced 45-year-old manager than for a 22-year-old straight out of college?

The opportunity cost for an experienced 45-year-old manager—the earnings he would have to give up during a certain time period to spend that time getting an M.B.A.—is higher than that of a 22-year-old straight out of college, whose income-earning alternatives are far less.

2.3 Marginal Thinking

1. What are marginal choices? Why does economics focus on them?

Marginal choices are choices of how much of something to do, rather than whether or not to do something. Economics focuses on marginal choices because those are the sorts of choices we most often face: Should I do a little more of this or a little more of that?

2. What is the rule of rational choice?

The rule of rational choice is that in trying to make themselves better off, people alter their behavior if the expected marginal benefits from doing so outweigh the expected marginal costs they will bear. If the expected marginal benefits of an action exceed the expected marginal costs, a person will do more of that action; if the expected marginal benefits of an action are less than the expected marginal costs, a person will do less of that action.

3. Why does rational choice involve expectations?

Because the world is in many ways uncertain, we can seldom know for sure whether the marginal benefits of an action will exceed the marginal costs. Therefore, the rule of rational choice takes into account expectations that decision makers have at the time they make their decisions; this rule recognizes that what we expect to happen is not always what does happen.

4. Why do students often stop taking lecture notes when a professor announces that the next few minutes of material will not be on any test or assignment?

The benefit for students' grades from taking notes decreases when the material discussed will not be tested or "rewarded." Because there are fewer benefits of note taking in this situation, students do less of it.

5. If you decide to speed to get to a doctor's appointment and then get in an accident because you were speeding, does your decision to speed invalidate the rule of rational choice? Why or why not?

No. The rule of rational choice is concerned with expectations at the time decisions were made. If you had thought your speeding would cause an accident, you would not have decided to speed. The fact that you got in an accident doesn't invalidate the rule of rational choice; it just means that your expectations at the time you decided to speed did not come true.

6. If pedestrians felt safer using crosswalks to cross streets, how could adding crosswalks increase the number of pedestrian accidents?

Just as safer cars can lead people to drive less safely, if pedestrians felt safer in crosswalks they might cross less safely. For example, they might take less care to look both ways. Pedestrians crossing less carefully might result in an increase in pedestrian accidents.

7. Imagine driving a car with daggers sticking out of the steering wheel and pointing directly at your chest. How safely would you drive?

Because the cost to you of an accident would be much higher in this case, you would drive more safely.

2.4 Incentives Matter

1. What is the difference between positive incentives and negative incentives?

Positive incentives either increase the benefits or decrease the costs of an action, thus encouraging it; negative incentives either decrease the benefits or increase the costs of an action, thus discouraging it.

2. According to the rule of rational choice, would you do more or less of something if its expected marginal benefits increased? Why?

You would do more of something if its expected marginal benefits increased because the expected marginal benefits would exceed the expected marginal costs for more "units" of that action.

3. According to the rule of rational choice, would you do more or less of something if its expected marginal costs increased? Why?

You would do less of something if its expected marginal costs increased because the expected marginal benefits would exceed the expected marginal costs for fewer "units" of that action.

4. How does the rule of rational choice imply that a young child is more likely to misbehave at a supermarket checkout counter than at home?

When a young child is at a supermarket checkout counter, the benefit of misbehaving—the potential payoff of pestering Mom or Dad for candy—is greater. Also, the costs of misbehaving in a supermarket are lower than they would be at home because the child's parents are less likely to punish him, or to punish him as severely, in public.

5. Why do many parents refuse to let their children have dessert before they finish their dinner?
Children often believe that the costs of eating many dinner foods exceed the benefits (i.e., "If it's green, it must be yucky."), but that is seldom true of dessert. If parents let their kids eat dessert first, children would often not eat the foods that are better for them. But by adding the benefit of getting dessert to the choice of eating dinner, parents can get their children to eat the healthier foods, too.

2.5 Specialization and Trade

1. Why do people specialize?
People specialize because by concentrating on the activities for which they are best suited, they incur lower opportunity costs. That is, people specialize in those things they can do at lower opportunity costs than other people could.
2. What do we mean by comparative advantage?
A person, region, or country has a comparative advantage when it can produce a certain good or service at a lower opportunity cost than other persons, regions, or countries could.
3. Why does the combination of specialization and trade make us better off?
Trade increases wealth by allowing a person, region, or nation to specialize in those goods and services that it produces better than others and to trade for the goods and services that others produce better than it does. Maximizing our comparative advantages in combination with trading allows us to produce, and therefore consume, more from our scarce resources than we could otherwise.
4. If you can mow your lawn in half the time it takes your housemate to do it, do you have a comparative advantage in mowing the lawn?
Your faster speed in mowing the lawn does not automatically mean that you have a comparative advantage in mowing. That can be established only relative to other tasks. The person with a comparative advantage in mowing the lawn is the one with the lowest opportunity cost, and that could be your housemate. For instance, if you could earn $12 an hour at some other task, mowing the lawn in half an hour implies an opportunity cost of $6 of foregone output. If your housemate could earn only $5 an hour at some other task, the opportunity cost to her of mowing the lawn in an hour is $5. In this case, your housemate has a comparative advantage in mowing the lawn.
5. If you have a comparative advantage in doing the dishes, and then you become far more productive than before in completing yard chores, could that eliminate your comparative advantage in doing the dishes? Why or why not?
The opportunity cost of you doing the dishes is the value of other chores you must give up to do the dishes. Therefore, an increase in your productivity doing yard chores would increase the opportunity cost of doing the dishes, and could eliminate your comparative advantage in doing the dishes.
6. Could a student who gets a C in one class but a D or worse in all other classes have a comparative advantage over someone who gets a B in that class but an A in all other classes? Explain this concept using opportunity cost.
A student who gets a C in a class is worse, in an absolute sense, at that class than a student to gets a B in it. But if the C student gets Ds in other classes, he is relatively, or comparatively, better at the C class. Similarly, if the B student gets As in other classes, he is relatively, or comparatively, worse at the B class.

2.6 Market Prices Coordinate Economic Activity

1. Why must every society choose some way to allocate its scarce resources?
Every society must choose some way to allocate its scarce resources because the collective wants of its members always far outweigh the amount that can be produced from scarce natural resources.
2. How does a market system allocate resources?
A market system allows individuals, both as producers and consumers, to indicate their desires by their actions (i.e., how much they are willing to buy or sell at various prices). The market then acts to set prices at a level that will allow buyers and sellers to coordinate their plans.
3. What do market prices communicate to society?
The prices charged by suppliers communicate to consumers the relative availability of products; the prices consumers are willing to pay communicate to producers the relative values consumers place on products. That is, market prices allow consumers and suppliers to communicate about the relative value of resources.
4. How do price controls undermine the market as a communication device?
Price controls—both price floors and price ceilings—prevent the market from communicating important information to consumers and suppliers. A price floor set above the market price prevents suppliers from communicating to consumers their willingness to sell for less. A price ceiling set below the market price prevents consumers from indicating to suppliers their willingness to pay more.
5. Why can markets sometimes fail to allocate resources efficiently?
Markets can sometimes fail to allocate resources efficiently. Such situations, called market failures, represent situations such as externalities, where costs can be imposed on some individuals without their consent (e.g., from dumping "crud" in their air or water), where information in the market may not be communicated honestly and accurately, and where firms may have market power to distort prices in their favor (against consumers' interests).

CHAPTER 3: SCARCITY, TRADE-OFFS, AND ECONOMIC GROWTH

3.1 The Three Economic Questions Every Society Faces

1. Why does scarcity force us to decide what to produce?
Because our wants exceed the amount of goods and services that can be produced from our limited resources, it must be decided which wants should have priority over others.
2. How is a command economy different from a market economy?
A command economy makes decisions about what and how much to produce centrally by members of a planning board or organization. A market economy makes those decisions as the result of decentralized decision making by individual producers and consumers, coordinated by their offers to buy and sell on markets.
3. How does consumer sovereignty determine production decisions in a market economy?
Consumer sovereignty determines production decisions in a market economy because producers make what they believe consumers will "vote" for by being willing to pay for them.
4. Do you think that what and how much an economy produces depends on who will get the goods and services produced in that economy? Why or why not?
Who will get the goods produced in an economy affects the incentives of the producers. The less a producer will benefit from increased production, the smaller are his incentives to increase his production, and the smaller will be total output in an economy.
5. Why do consumers have to "vote" for a product with their dollars for it to be a success?
In the market sector, products can be profitable only if they attract dollar votes from consumers.
6. Why must we choose among multiple ways of producing the goods and service we want?
We must choose among multiple ways of producing the goods and service we want because goods can generally be produced in several ways, using different combinations of resources. That requires a decision to be made about how to produce the goods and services we want.
7. Why might production be labor intensive in one economy but capital intensive in another?
Production will tend to be labor intensive where labor is relatively plentiful, and therefore relatively less expensive; it will tend to be capital intensive where capital is relatively plentiful, and therefore relatively less expensive. When the manner of production is different in different situations because factors of production have different relative prices, each of those methods will be more efficient where they are used.
8. If a tourist from the United States on an overseas trip notices that other countries don't produce crops "like they do back home," would he be right to conclude that farmers in the other country produce crops less efficiently than U.S. farmers?
No. The different ways of farming in different areas reflect the different relative scarcities of land, labor, and capital they face. Those factors of production that are relatively scarce in an economy are also relatively costly there as a result. Producers there economize on the use of those more costly resources by using more of relatively less scarce, and less costly, resources instead. For example, where land is very scarce, it is very intensively cultivated with relatively cheaper (less scarce) labor and capital, but where capital is very scarce, relatively cheaper (less scarce) land and labor are substituted for capital.
9. In what way does scarcity determine income?
Relative scarcity determines the market values of the scarce resources people offer to others in exchange for income.

3.2 The Circular Flow Model

1. Why does the circular flow of money move in the opposite direction from the flow of goods and services?
The circular flow of money moves in the opposite direction from the flow of goods and services because the money flows are the payments made in exchange for the goods and services.
2. What is bought and sold in factor markets?
The factors of production—capital, land, labor and entrepreneurship—are sold in factor, or input, markets.
3. What is bought and sold in product markets?
Consumer and investment goods and services and are sold in product markets.

3.3 The Production Possibilities Curve

1. What does a production possibilities curve illustrate?
The production possibilities curve illustrates the potential output combinations

of two goods in an economy operating at full capacity, given the inputs and technology available to the economy.

2. How are opportunity costs shown by the production possibilities curve?
Opportunity cost—the foregone output of one good necessary to increase output of another good—is illustrated by the slope, or tradeoff, between the two goods at a given point on the production possibilities curve.

3. Why do the opportunity costs of added production increase with output?
Opportunity costs of added production increase with output because some resources cannot be easily adapted from their current uses to alternative uses. At first, easily adaptable resources can be switched to producing more of a good. But once those easily adapted resources have been switched, producing further output requires the use of resources less well adapted to expanding that output, raising the opportunity cost of output.

4. How does the production possibilities curve illustrate increasing opportunity costs?
Increasing opportunity costs are illustrated by a bowed (concave from below) production possibilities curve. It shows that initial units of one good can be produced by giving up little of another good, but progressive increases in output will require greater and greater sacrifices of the other good.

5. Why are we concerned with unemployed or underemployed resources in a society?
We are concerned with unemployed or underemployed resources in a society because, if we could reduce the extent of unemployed or underemployed resources, people could have more scarce goods and services available for their use.

6. What do we mean by efficiency, and how is it related to underemployment of resources?
Efficiency means getting the most we can out of our scarce resources. Underemployment of resources means a society is not getting the most it can out of these resources, either because they are not fully employed or because they are not matched to the uses best suited to them.

7. How are efficiency and inefficiency illustrated with a production possibilities curve?
Efficient combinations of outputs are illustrated by points on the production possibilities curve, along which more of one good can be produced if less of some other good is also produced. Inefficient combinations of outputs are illustrated by points inside the production possibilities curve because more of both goods could then be produced with the resources available to the economy.

8. Will a country that makes being unemployed illegal be more productive than one that does not? Why or why not?
A more productive economy is one that makes the best use of those who wish to work. Making unemployment illegal (as was true in the old Soviet Union) does not eliminate underemployment, nor does it guarantee that people and other resources are employed where they are most productive (especially because it is more difficult to search for a better job when you are working than when you are not working).

9. If a 68-year-old worker in the United States chooses not to work at all, does that mean that the United States is functioning inside its production possibilities curve? Why or why not?
A person who chooses retirement rather than work must consider himself better off not working, when all the relevant considerations are taken into account. He is therefore as fully employed, given his circumstances, as he would like to be, and so there is no implication that the United States would be inside its production possibilities curve as a result. However, if such workers became more willing to work, that would shift the United States' production possibilities curve outward.

3.4 Economic Growth and the Production Possibilities Curve

1. What is the essential question behind issues of economic growth?
The essential question behind issues of economic growth is: How much are we willing to give up today to get more in the future?

2. What is the connection between sacrifices and economic growth?
The more current consumption is sacrificed in an economy, the larger the fraction of its current resources it can devote to producing investment goods, which will increase its rate of economic growth.

3. How is economic growth shown in terms of production possibilities curves?
Economic growth—the expansion of what an economy can produce—is shown as an outward shift in the production possibilities curve, with formerly unattainable output combinations now made possible.

4. Why doesn't economic growth eliminate scarcity?
Economic growth doesn't eliminate scarcity because people's wants still exceed what they are capable of producing. Thus tradeoffs among scarce goods must still be made.

5. What would happen to the production possibilities curve in an economy where a new innovation greatly increased its ability to produce shelter but did not change its ability to produce food?
This innovation would increase the amount of shelter the economy could produce, shifting out the production possibilities curve's intercept on the shelter axis, but not changing its intercept on the food axis. If shelter is on the vertical axis and food is on the horizontal axis of the production possibilities curve, such a technological change would leave the vertical intercept unchanged, but make it less steep (reflecting the reduced opportunity cost of producing additional food), shifting out the curve's intercept with the horizontal axis.

6. If people reduced their saving (thus reducing the funds available for investment), what would that do to society's production possibilities curve over time?
The less people save, the slower the capital stock of the economy will grow through new investment (because saving is the source of the funds for investment), and so the slower the production possibilities curve would shift out over time.

CHAPTER 4: SUPPLY AND DEMAND

4.1 Markets

1. Why is it difficult to define a market precisely?
Every market is different. There are an incredible variety of exchange arrangements, with different types of products, different degrees of organization, different geographical extents, and so on.

2. Why do you get your produce at a supermarket rather than directly from farmers?
Supermarkets act as middlepersons between growers of produce and consumers of produce. You hire them to do this task for you when you buy produce from them, rather than directly from growers, because they conduct those transactions at lower costs than you could (if you could do this more cheaply than supermarkets, you would buy directly rather than from supermarkets).

3. Why do the prices people pay for similar items at garage sales vary more than for similar items in a department store?
Items for sale at department stores are more standardized, easier to compare, and more heavily advertised, which makes consumers more aware of the prices at which they could get a particular good elsewhere, reducing the differences in price that can persist among department stores. Garage sale items are nonstandardized, costly to compare, and not advertised, which means people are often quite unaware of how much a given item could be purchased for elsewhere, so that price differences for similar items at different garage sales can be substantial.

4.2 Demand

1. What is an inverse relationship?
An inverse, or negative, relationship is one where one variable changes in the opposite direction from the other—if one increases, the other decreases.

2. How do lower prices change buyers' incentives?
A lower price for a good means that the opportunity cost to buyers of purchasing it is lower than before, and self-interest leads buyers to buy more of it as a result.

3. How do higher prices change buyers' incentives?
A higher price for a good means that the opportunity cost to buyers of purchasing it is higher than before, and self-interest leads buyers to buy less of it as a result.

4. What is an individual demand schedule?
An individual demand schedule reveals the different amounts of a good or service a person would be willing to buy at various possible prices in a particular time interval.

5. What difference is there between an individual demand curve and a market demand curve?
The market demand curve shows the total amounts of a good or service all the buyers as a group are willing to buy at various possible prices in a particular time interval. The market quantity demanded at a given price is just the sum of the quantities demanded by each individual buyer at that price.

6. Why does the amount of dating on campus tend to decline just before and during final exams?
The opportunity cost of dating—in this case, the value to students of the studying time foregone—is higher just before and during final exams than during most of the rest of an academic term. Because the cost is higher, students do less of it.

7. How are money prices and relative prices different?
Money prices are what are paid in dollars and cents (or other currency); relative prices are prices of goods relative to (or in terms of) the prices of other goods and services.

8. Why are economists so concerned about relative prices?
Relative prices—the prices of goods relative to other goods and services—reflect the tradeoffs people face in making choices among those goods and services in markets. Changing relative prices alter the opportunity costs of choices, changing the choices that are made.

9. The money price of most goods has risen over time. What does that mean?
Most prices have risen in money terms. The fact that most goods have risen in money prices really means that the value of money has fallen (inflation) relative to the value of goods.

10. Motel 6 began by charging $6 per night for a room back in the 1960s but now charges about $40 per night. What must have happened to the overall price level for the relative price of its motel rooms to have fallen?
If Motel 6's room prices have gone up by a factor of six since they began, their relative price is lower than before if other prices have gone up by a bigger factor over the same period, and higher than before if other prices have gone up by a smaller factor over the same period.

4.3 Shifts in the Demand Curve

1. What is the difference between a change in demand and a change in quantity demanded?
A change in demand shifts the entire demand curve, while a change in quantity demanded refers to a movement along a given demand curve.
2. If the price of zucchini increases and it causes the demand for yellow squash to rise, what do we call the relationship between zucchini and yellow squash?
Whenever an increased price of one good increases the demand for another, they are substitutes. This reflects the fact that some people consider zucchini as an alternative to yellow squash, so that as zucchini becomes more costly, some people substitute buying now relatively cheaper yellow squash instead.
3. If income rises and, as a result, demand for jet skis increases, how do we describe that good?
If income rises and, as a result, demand for jet skis increases, we call jet skis a normal good, because for most (or normal) goods, we would rather have more of them than less, so an increase in income would lead to an increase in demand for such goods.
4. How do expectations about the future influence the demand curve?
Expectations about the future influence the demand curve because buying a good in the future is an alternative to buying it now. Therefore, the higher future prices are expected to be compared to the present, the less attractive future purchases become, and the greater the current demand for that good, as people buy more now when it is expected to be cheaper, rather than later, when it is expected to be more costly.
5. Would a change in the price of ice cream cause a change in the demand for ice cream? Why or why not?
No. The demand for ice cream represents the different quantities of ice cream that would be purchased at different prices. In other words, it represents the relationship between the price of ice cream and the quantity of ice cream demanded. Changing the price of ice cream does not change this relationship, so it does not change demand.
6. Would a change in the price of ice cream likely cause a change in the demand for frozen yogurt, a substitute?
Yes. Changing the price of frozen yogurt, a substitute for ice cream, would change the quantity of ice cream demanded at a given price. This means that the whole relationship between the price and quantity of ice cream demanded has changed, which means the demand for ice cream has changed.
7. If plane travel is a normal good and bus travel is an inferior good, what will happen to the demand curves for plane and bus travel if people's incomes increase?
The demand for plane travel and all other normal goods will increase if incomes increase, while the demand for bus travel and all other inferior goods will decrease if incomes increase.

4.4 Supply

1. What are the two reasons why a supply curve is positively sloped?
A supply curve is positively sloped because (1) the benefits to sellers from selling increase as the price they receive increases and (2) the opportunity costs of supplying additional output rise with output (the law of increasing opportunity costs), so it takes a higher price to make increasing output in the self-interest of sellers.
2. What is the difference between an individual supply curve and a market supply curve?
The market supply curve shows the total amounts of a good all the sellers as a group are willing to sell at various prices in a particular time period. The market quantity supplied at a given price is just the sum of the quantities supplied by each individual seller at that price.
3. What is the difference between a change in supply and a change in quantity supplied?
A change in supply shifts the entire supply curve, while a change in quantity supplied refers to a movement along a given supply curve.
4. If a seller expects the price of a good to rise in the near future, how will that affect his current supply curve?
Selling a good in the future is an alternative to selling it now. Therefore, the higher the expected future price relative to the current price, the more attractive future sales become, and the less attractive current sales become, which will lead sellers to reduce (shift left) the current supply of that good, as they want to sell later, when the good is expected to be more valuable, rather than now.
5. Would a change in the price of wheat change the supply of wheat? Would it change the supply of corn, if wheat and corn can be grown on the same type of land?
The supply of wheat represents the different quantities of wheat that would be offered for sale at different prices. In other words, it represents the relationship between the price of wheat and the quantity of wheat supplied. Changing the price of wheat does not change this relationship, so it does not change the supply of wheat. However, a change in the price of wheat changes the relative attractiveness of raising wheat instead of corn, which changes the supply of corn.
6. If a guitar manufacturer had to increase its wages in order to keep its workers, what would happen to the supply of guitars as a result?
An increase in wages, or any other input price, would decrease (shift left) the supply of guitars, making fewer guitars available for sale at any given price, by raising the opportunity cost of producing guitars.
7. What happens to the supply of baby-sitting services in an area when many teenagers get their driver's licenses at about the same time?
When teenagers get their drivers licenses, their increased mobility expands their alternatives to baby-sitting substantially, raising the opportunity cost of baby-sitting. This decreases (shifts left) the supply of baby-sitting services.

4.5 Market Equilibrium Price and Quantity

1. How does the intersection of supply and demand indicate the equilibrium price and quantity in a market?
The intersection of supply and demand indicates the equilibrium price and quantity in a market because at higher prices, sellers would be frustrated by their inability to sell all they would like, leading sellers to compete by lowering the price they charge; at lower prices, buyers would be frustrated by their inability to buy all they would like, leading buyers to compete by increasing the price they offer to pay.
2. What can cause a change in the supply and demand equilibrium?
Changes in any of the demand curve shifters or the supply curve shifters will change the supply and demand equilibrium.
3. What must be true about the price charged for a shortage to occur?
The price charged must be less than the equilibrium price, with the result that buyers would like to buy more at that price than sellers are willing to sell.
4. What must be true about the price charged for a surplus to occur?
The price charged must be greater than the equilibrium price, with the result that sellers would like to sell more at that price than buyers are willing to buy.
5. Why do market forces tend to eliminate both shortages and surpluses?
Market forces tend to eliminate both shortages and surpluses because of the self-interest of the market participants. A seller is better off successfully selling at a lower equilibrium price than not being able to sell at a higher price (the surplus situation) and a buyer is better off successfully buying at a higher equilibrium price than not being able to buy at a lower price (the shortage situation). Therefore, we expect market forces to eliminate both shortages and surpluses.
6. If tea prices were above their equilibrium level, what force would tend to push tea prices down? If tea prices were below their equilibrium level, what force would tend to push tea prices up?
If tea prices were above their equilibrium level, sellers frustrated by their inability to sell as much tea as they would like at those prices would compete the price of tea down, as they tried to make more attractive offers to tea buyers. If tea prices were below their equilibrium level, buyers frustrated by their inability to buy as much tea as they would like at those prices would compete the price of tea up, as they tried to make more attractive offers to tea sellers.

4.6 Changes in Equilibrium Price and Quantity

1. When demand increases, does that create a shortage or surplus at the original price?
An increase in demand increases the quantity demanded at the original equilibrium price, but it does not change the quantity supplied at that price, meaning that it would create a shortage at the original equilibrium price.
2. What happens to equilibrium price and quantity as a result of a demand increase?
Frustrated buyers unable to buy all they would like at the original equilibrium price will compete the market price higher, and that higher price will induce suppliers to increase their quantity supplied. The result is a higher market price and a larger market output.
3. When supply increases, does that create a shortage or surplus at the original price?
An increase in supply increases the quantity supplied at the original equilibrium price, but it does not change the quantity demanded at that price, meaning that it would create a surplus at the original equilibrium price.

4. Assuming the market is already at equilibrium, what happens to equilibrium price and quantity as a result of a supply increase?
Frustrated sellers unable to sell all they would like at the original equilibrium price will compete the market price lower, and that lower price will induce demanders to increase their quantity demanded. The result is a lower market price and a larger market output.
5. Why do heating-oil prices tend to be higher in the winter?
The demand for heating oil is higher in cold weather winter months. The result of this higher winter heating-oil demand, for a given supply curve, is higher prices for heating oil in the winter.
6. Why are evening and weekend long-distance calls cheaper than weekday long-distance calls?
The demand for long-distance calls is greatest during weekday business hours, but far lower during other hours. Because the demand for "off-peak" long-distance calls is lower, for a given supply curve, prices during those hours are lower.
7. What would have to be true for both supply and demand to shift in the same time period?
For both supply and demand to shift in the same time period, one or more of both the supply curve shifters and the demand curve shifters would have to change in that same time period.
8. When both supply and demand shift, what added information do we need to know in order to determine in which direction the indeterminate variable changes?
When both supply and demand shift, we need to know which of the shifts is of greater magnitude, so we can know which of the opposing effects in the indeterminate variable is larger; whichever effect is larger will determine the direction of the net effect on the indeterminate variable.
9. If both buyers and sellers of grapes expect grape prices to rise in the near future, what will happen to grape prices and sales today?
If grape buyers expect grape prices to rise in the near future, it will increase their current demand to buy grapes, which would tend to increase current prices and increase the current quantity of grapes sold. If grape sellers expect grape prices to rise in the near future, it will decrease their current supply of grapes for sale, which would tend to increase current prices and decrease the current quantity of grapes sold. Because both these effects tend to increase the current price of grapes, grape prices will rise. However, the supply and demand curve shifts tend to change current sales in opposing directions, so without knowing which of these shifts was of a greater magnitude, we do not know what will happen to current grape sales. They could go up, down, or even stay the same.
10. If demand for peanut butter increases and supply decreases, what will happen to equilibrium price and quantity?
An increase in the demand for peanut butter increases the equilibrium price and quantity of peanut butter sold. A decrease in the supply of peanut butter increases the equilibrium price and quantity of peanut butter sold. The result is an increase in peanut butter prices and an indeterminate effect on the quantity of peanut butter sold.

4.7 Price Controls

1. How is rent control an example of a price ceiling?
A price ceiling is a maximum price set below the equilibrium price by the government. Rent control is an example because the controlled rents are held below the market equilibrium rent level.
2. What predictable effects result from price ceilings such as rent control?
The predictable effects resulting from price ceilings include shortages, reduced amounts of the controlled good being made available by suppliers, reductions in the quality of the controlled good, and increased discrimination among potential buyers of the good.
3. How is the minimum wage law an example of a price floor?
A price floor is a minimum price set above the equilibrium price by the government. The minimum wage law is an example because the minimum is set above the market equilibrium wage level for some low-skilled workers.
4. What predictable effects result from price floors like the minimum wage?
The predictable effects resulting from price floors include surpluses, reduced amounts of the controlled good being purchased by demanders, increases in the quality of the controlled good, and increased discrimination among potential sellers of the good.
5. What may happen to the amount of discrimination against groups such as families with children, pet owners, smokers, or students when rent control is imposed?
Rent control laws prevent prospective renters from compensating landlords through higher rents for any characteristic landlords finds less attractive, whether it is bothersome noise from children or pets, odors from smokers, increased numbers of renters per unit, or risks of nonpayment by lower-income tenants (e.g., students). As a result, it lowers the cost of discriminating against anyone with what landlords consider unattractive characteristics because there are other prospective renters without those characteristics who are willing to pay the same controlled rent.
6. Why does rent control often lead to condominium conversions?
Rent control applies to rental apartments, but not to apartments owned by their occupants. Therefore, one way to get around rent control restrictions on apartment owners' ability to receive the market value of their apartments is to convert those apartments to condominiums by selling them to tenants instead (and what was once a controlled rent becomes part of an uncontrolled mortgage payment).
7. What is the law of unintended consequences?
The law of unintended consequences is the term used to remind us that the results of actions are not always as clear as they appear, because the secondary effects of an action may cause its results to include many consequences that were not part of what was intended.
8. Why is the law of unintended consequences so important in making public policy?
It is impossible to change just one incentive to achieve a particular result through a government policy. A policy will change the incentives facing multiple individuals making multiple decisions, and changes in all those affected choices will result. Sometimes, the unintended consequences can be so substantial that they completely undermine the intended effects of a policy.

CHAPTER 5: ELASTICITIES, CONSUMER BEHAVIOR, AND WELFARE

5.1 Price Elasticity of Demand

1. What question is the price elasticity of demand designed to answer?
The price elasticity of demand is designed to answer the question: How responsive is quantity demanded to changes in the price of a good?
2. How is the price elasticity of demand calculated?
The price elasticity of demand is calculated as the percentage change in quantity demanded, divided by the percentage change in the price that caused the change in quantity demanded.
3. What is the difference between a relatively price elastic demand curve and a relatively price inelastic demand curve?
Quantity demanded changes relatively more than price along a relatively price elastic segment of a demand curve, while quantity demanded changes relatively less than price along a relatively price inelastic segment of a demand curve.
4. What is the relationship between the price elasticity of demand and the slope at a given point on a demand curve?
At a given point on a demand curve, the flatter the demand curve, the more quantity demanded changes for a given change in price, so the greater is the elasticity of demand.
5. What factors tend to make demand curves more price elastic?
Demand curves tend to become more elastic, the larger the number of close substitutes there are for the good, the larger proportion of income spent on the good, and the greater the amount of time that buyers have to respond to a change in the good's price.
6. Why would a tax on a particular brand of cigarettes be less effective at reducing smoking than a tax on all brands of cigarettes?
A tax on one brand of cigarettes would allow smokers to avoid the tax by switching brands rather than by smoking less, but a tax on all brands would raise the cost of smoking any cigarettes. A tax on all brands of cigarettes would therefore be more effective in reducing smoking.
7. Why is the price elasticity of demand for products at a 24-hour convenience store likely to be lower at 2 A.M. than at 2 P.M.?
There are fewer alternative stores open at 2 A.M. than at 2 P.M., and because there are more good substitutes, the price elasticity of demand for products at 24-hour convenience stores is greater at 2 P.M.
8. Why is the price elasticity of demand for turkeys likely to be lower, but the price elasticity of demand for turkeys at a particular store likely to be greater, at Thanksgiving than at other times of the year?
For many people, there are far fewer good substitutes for turkey at Thanksgiving than at other times, so that the demand for turkeys is more inelastic at Thanksgiving. But grocery stores looking to attract customers for their entire large Thanksgiving shopping trip also often offer and heavily advertise turkeys at far better prices than normally, which means there are more good substitutes and a more price elastic demand curve for buying a turkey at a particular store than normally.

5.2 Total Revenue and Price Elasticity of Demand

1. Why does total revenue vary inversely with price if demand is relatively price elastic?
Total revenue varies inversely with price if demand is relatively price elastic, be-

cause the quantity demanded (which equals the quantity sold) changes relatively more than price along a relatively elastic demand curve. This means that total revenue, which equals price times quantity demanded (sold) at that price, will change in the same direction as quantity demanded and in the opposite direction from the change in price.

2. Why does total revenue vary in the same direction as price, if demand is relatively price inelastic?

Total revenue varies in the same direction as price, if demand is relatively price inelastic, because the quantity demanded (which equals the quantity sold) changes relatively less than price along a relatively inelastic demand curve. This means that total revenue, which equals price times quantity demanded (sold) at that price, will change in the same direction as price and in the opposite direction from the change in quantity demanded.

3. Why is a linear demand curve more price elastic at higher price ranges and price inelastic at lower price ranges?

Along the upper half of a linear (constant slope) demand curve, total revenue increases as the price falls, indicating that demand is relatively price elastic. Along the lower half of a linear (constant slope) demand curve, total revenue decreases as the price falls, indicating that demand is relatively price inelastic.

4. If demand for some good was perfectly price inelastic, how would total revenue from its sales change as its price changed?

A perfectly price inelastic demand curve would be one where the quantity sold did not vary with the price. In such an (imaginary) case, total revenue would increase proportionately with price—a 10 percent increase in price with the same quantity sold would result in a 10 percent increase in total revenue.

5. Assume that both you and Art, your partner in a picture-framing business, want to increase your firm's total revenue. You argue that in order to achieve this goal, you should lower your prices; Art, on the other hand, thinks that you should raise your prices. What assumptions are each of you making about your firm's price elasticity of demand?

You are assuming that a lower price will increase total revenue, which implies you think the demand for your picture frames is relatively price elastic. Art is assuming that an increase in your price will increase your total revenue, which implies he thinks the demand for your picture frames is relatively price inelastic.

5.3 Price Elasticity of Supply

1. What does it mean to say the elasticity of supply for one good is greater than that for another?

For the elasticity of supply for one good to be greater than for another, the percentage increase in quantity supplied that results from a given percentage change in price will be greater for the first good than for the second.

2. Why does supply tend to be more elastic in the long run than in the short run?

Just as the cost of buyers changing their behavior is lower, the longer they have to adapt, leading to long-run demand curves being more elastic than short-run demand curves, the same is true of suppliers. The cost of producers changing their behavior is lower, the longer they have to adapt, leading to long-run supply curves being more elastic than short-run supply curves.

3. How do the relative elasticities of supply and demand determine who bears the greater burden of a tax?

When demand is more elastic than supply, the tax burden falls mainly on producers; when supply is more elastic than demand, the tax burden falls mainly on consumers.

5.4 Consumer Behavior

1. How do economists define utility?

Economists define utility as the level of satisfaction or well-being an individual receives from consumption of a good or service.

2. Why can't interpersonal utility comparisons be made?

We can't make interpersonal utility comparisons because it is impossible to measure the relative satisfaction of different people in comparable terms.

3. What is the relationship between total utility and marginal utility?

Marginal utility is the increase in total utility from increasing consumption of a good or service by one unit.

4. Why could you say that a millionaire gets less marginal utility from a second piece of pizza than from the first piece, but you couldn't say whether she got more or less marginal utility from a second piece of pizza than someone else who has a much lower level of income?

Both get less marginal utility from a second piece of pizza than from the first piece because of the law of diminishing marginal utility. However, it is impossible to measure the relative satisfaction of different people in comparable terms, even when we are comparing rich and poor people, so we cannot say who got more marginal utility from a second slice of pizza.

5. Are you likely to get as much marginal utility from your last piece of chicken at an all-you-can-eat restaurant as at a restaurant where you pay $2 per piece of chicken?

No. If you pay $2 per piece, you eat another piece only as long as it gives you more marginal utility than spending the $2 on something else. But at an all-you-can-eat restaurant, the dollar price of one more piece of chicken is zero, so you consume more chicken and get less marginal utility out of the last piece of chicken you eat.

5.5 Consumer and Producer Surplus

1. What is consumer surplus?

Consumer surplus is defined as the monetary difference between what a consumer is willing to pay for a good and what she is required to pay for it.

2. Why do the first units consumed at a given price add more consumer surplus than the last units consumed?

Because what a consumer is willing to pay for a good declines, the more of that good is consumed, the difference between what he is willing to pay and the price he must pay also declines for later units.

3. Why does a decrease in a good's price increase the consumer surplus from consumption of that good?

A decrease in a good's price increases the consumer surplus from consumption of that good by lowering the price for those goods that were bought at the higher price and by increasing consumer surplus from increased purchases at the lower price.

4. Why might the consumer surplus from purchases of diamond rings be less than the consumer surplus from purchases of far less expensive stones?

Consumer surplus is the difference between what people would have been willing to pay for the amount of the good consumed and what they must pay. Even though the marginal value of less expensive stones is lower than the marginal value of a diamond ring to buyers, the difference between the total value of the far larger number of less expensive stones purchased and what consumers had to pay may be larger than that difference for diamond rings.

5. What is producer surplus?

Producer surplus is defined as the monetary difference between what a producer is paid for a good and the producer's cost.

6. Why do the first units produced at a given price add more producer surplus than the last units produced?

Because the first (lowest cost) units can be produced at a cost that is lower than the market price, but the cost of producing additional units rises, the first units produced at a given price add more producer surplus than the last units produced.

7. Why does an increase in a good's price increase the producer surplus from production of that good?

An increase in a good's price increases the producer surplus from production of that good because it results in a higher price for the quantity already being produced and because the expansion in output in response to the higher price also increases profits.

8. Why might the producer surplus from sales of diamond rings, which are very expensive, be less than the producer surplus from sales of far less expensive stones?

Producer surplus is the difference between what a producer is paid for a good and the producer's cost. Even though the price, or marginal value, of a less expensive stone is lower than the price, or marginal value, of a diamond ring to buyers, the difference between the total that sellers receive for those stones in revenue and the producer's cost of the far larger number of less expensive stones produced may well be larger than that difference for diamond rings.

5.6 The Welfare Effects of Taxes and Price Controls

1. Could a tax be imposed without a welfare cost?

A tax would not impose a welfare cost only if the quantity exchanged did not change as a result. This would only be when supply was perfectly inelastic or in the non-existent case where the demand curve was perfectly inelastic. In all other cases, a tax would create a welfare cost by eliminating some mutually beneficial trades (and the wealth they would have created) that would otherwise have taken place.

2. How does the elasticity of demand represent the ability of buyers to "dodge" a tax?

The elasticity of demand represents the ability of buyers to "dodge" a tax, because it represents how easily buyers could shift their purchases into other goods. If it is relatively low cost to consumers to shift out of buying a particular good when a tax is imposed on it—that is, demand is relatively elastic—they can dodge much of the burden of the tax by shifting their purchases to other goods. If it is relatively high cost to consumers to shift out of buying a particular good when a tax is imposed on it—that is, demand is relatively inelastic—they cannot dodge much of the burden of the tax by shifting their purchases to other goods.

3. If both supply and demand were very elastic, how large would the effect be on the quantity exchanged, the tax revenue, and the welfare costs of a tax?

The more elastic are supply and/or demand, the larger the change in the quantity exchanged that would result from a given tax. Given that tax revenue equals the tax per unit times the number of units traded after the imposition of a tax, the smaller after-tax quantity traded would reduce the tax revenue raised, other things being equal. Because the greater change in the quantity traded wipes out more mutually beneficial trades than if demand and/or supply was more inelastic, the welfare cost in such a case would also be greater, other things being equal.

4. What impact would a larger tax have on trade in the market? What will happen to the size of the deadweight loss?

A larger tax creates a larger wedge between the price including tax paid by consumers and the price net of tax received by producers, resulting in a greater increase in prices paid by consumers and a greater decrease in price received by producers, and the laws of supply and demand imply that the quantity exchanged fall more as a result. The number of mutually beneficial trades eliminated will be greater and the consequent welfare cost will be greater as a result.

5. What would be the effect of a price floor if the government does not buy up the surplus?

Just as in the case of a tax, a price floor where the government does not buy up the surplus reduces the quantity exchanged, thus causing a welfare cost equal to the net gains from the exchanges that no longer take place. However, that floor would also redistribute income, harming buyers, increasing the incomes of those who remain able to sell successfully at the higher price, and decreasing the incomes of those who can no longer sell successfully at the higher price.

CHAPTER 6: EXTERNALITIES, PUBLIC GOODS, AND PUBLIC CHOICE

6.1 Externalities

1. Why are externalities also called spillover effects?

An externality exists whenever the benefits or costs of an activity impact individuals outside the market mechanism. That is, some of the effects spill over to those who have not voluntarily agreed to bear them or compensate others for them, unlike the voluntary exchange of the market.

2. How are externalities related to property rights?

Externalities involve goods for which there are not clearly defined property rights. For example, if you could demand, and receive, compensation for the costs that dirtier air imposes on you, you would have an effective property right to clean air, which you would give up voluntarily only if you were sufficiently compensated. But if your voluntary agreement is required, the effect is no longer an externality, but is internalized by the market mechanism.

3. How do external costs affect the price and output of a polluting activity?

Because the owner of a firm that pollutes does not have to bear the external costs of pollution, he can ignore those real costs of pollution to society. The result is that the private costs he must pay are less than the true social costs of production, so that the market output of the polluting activity is greater, and the resulting market price less, than it would be if producers did have to bear the external costs of production.

4. How can the government intervene to force producers to internalize external costs?

If the government could impose on producers a tax or fee, equal to the external costs imposed on people without their consent, producers would have to take into account those costs. The result would be that those costs were no longer external costs, but internalized by producers.

5. How does internalizing the external costs improve efficiency?

Internalizing external costs eliminates those trades where the marginal benefits to society (measured by the willingness to pay along the market demand curve) exceeded the private marginal costs, but were less than the social marginal costs (including the external costs). The resulting net gain in efficiency is that illustrated by the triangle in Exhibit 1 in this concept.

6. How do external benefits affect the output of an activity that causes them?

External benefits are benefits that spill over to others, because the party responsible need not be paid for those benefits. Therefore, some of the benefits to society of an activity will be ignored by the relevant decision makers in this case and the result will be a smaller output and a higher price for goods that generate external benefits to others.

7. How can the government intervene to force external benefits to be internalized?

Just as taxes can be used to internalize external costs imposed on others, subsidies can be used to internalize external benefits generated for others.

8. Why do most cities have more stringent noise laws for the early morning and late evening hours than for during the day?

The external costs to others from loud noises in residential areas early in the morning and late in the evening are higher, because residents are home and trying to sleep, than when many people are gone at work or already awake in the daytime. Given those higher potential external costs, most cities impose more restrictive noise laws for nighttime hours to reduce them.

6.2 Public Goods

1. How are public goods different from private goods?

Private goods are rival in consumption (two people can't both consume the same unit of a good) and exclusive (nonpayers can be prevented from consuming the good unless they pay for it). Public goods are nonrival in consumption (more than one person can consume the same good) and nonexclusive (nonpayers can't be effectively kept from consuming the good, even if they don't voluntarily pay for it).

2. Why does the free-rider problem arise in the case of public goods?

The free-rider problem arises in the case of public goods because people cannot be prevented from enjoying the benefits of public goods once they are provided. Therefore, people have an incentive to not voluntarily pay for those benefits, making it very difficult or even impossible to finance the efficient quantity of public goods through voluntary market arrangements.

3. How does the free-rider problem relate to property rights?

The free-rider problem arises in cases where property rights to goods are not easy to prescribe and enforce—cases such as externalities and public goods.

4. In what way can government provision of public goods solve the free-rider problem?

The government can overcome the free-rider problem by forcing people to pay for the provision of a public good through taxes.

5. Why is it difficult for the government to determine the proper amount of a public good to produce?

Because people do not reveal the values they place on public goods through the prices they are willing to pay in markets, unlike the case of private goods, there is no way for the government to accurately discover the magnitudes of the relevant benefits and costs, so they can take correctly take them into account.

6.3 Public Choice

1. What principles does the public choice analysis of government behavior share with the economic analysis of market behavior?

Public choice analysis of government behavior is based on the principle that the behavior of individuals in politics, just like that in the marketplace, is influenced by self-interest. That is, it applies basic economic theory to politics, looking for differences in incentives to explain people's behavior.

2. What are the differences between the public and the private sector?

Although both sectors reflect self-interested behavior, the "rules of the game" are different. For instance, the amount of information necessary to make an efficient decision is much greater in the public sector than in the private sector, and the necessary information is much more difficult to obtain when a political good is being considered, especially because those decisions affect a large number of people. Also, unlike in the private sector, public sector decisions can break the individual consumption-payment link, as some can often consume without payment and others can be forced to pay without being able to consume as a result of majority political decision-making.

3. What are the similarities between the public and the private sector?

Both sectors reflect scarcity, competition, and self-interested behavior.

CHAPTER 7: PRODUCTION AND COSTS

7.1 Profits: Total Revenues Minus Total Costs

1. What is the difference between explicit costs and implicit costs?

Explicit costs are those costs readily measured by the money spent on the resources used, such as wages. Implicit costs are those that do not represent an explicit outlay of money, but do represent opportunity costs, such as the opportunity cost of your time when you work for yourself.

2. Why are both explicit costs and implicit costs relevant in making economic decisions?

In making economic decisions, where expected marginal benefits must be weighed against expected marginal costs, all relevant costs must be included, whether they are explicit or implicit.

3. How do we measure profits?

Profit is measured as total revenue minus total cost.

4. Why is it important to look at all the opportunity costs of production?

Economic profit equals total revenue minus both explicit and implicit cost, including the opportunity cost (foregone earnings) of financial resources invested in the firm. All of your owned inputs—including your own time, equipment, structures, land, and so on—have opportunity costs which aren't revealed in explicit dollar payments. Correctly assigning implicit costs to all these owned inputs is necessary so that a correct measure of economic profits can be made. To be earning economic profits means that a firm is earning an above normal rate of return.

5. If you turn down a job offer of $45,000 per year to work for yourself, what is the opportunity cost of working for yourself?

Other things being equal, you incur a $45,000 per year implicit cost of working for yourself in this case, because that is what you give up when you choose to turn down the alternative job offer. If you turned down even better offers, your opportunity cost of working for yourself would be even higher.

7.2 Production in the Short Run

1. What is the difference between fixed and variable inputs?
Fixed inputs, such as plants and equipment, are those that cannot be changed in the short run, while variable inputs, such as hourly labor, are those that can be changed in the short run.

2. Why are all inputs variable in the long run?
All inputs are variable in the long run by definition, because the long run is defined as that time period necessary to allow all inputs to be varied.

3. What relationship does a production function represent?
A production function represents the relationship between different combinations of inputs and the maximum output of a product that can be produced with those inputs, with given technology.

4. What is diminishing marginal product? What causes it?
Diminishing marginal product means that as the amount of a variable input is increased, the amount of other inputs being held constant, a point ultimately will be reached beyond which marginal product will decline. It is caused by reductions in the amount of fixed inputs that can be combined with each unit of a variable input, as the amount of that variable input used increases.

7.3 Costs in the Short Run

1. What is the difference between fixed cost and variable cost?
Fixed costs are the expenses associated with fixed inputs (which therefore only exist in the short run), which are constant regardless of output. Variable costs are the expenses associated with variable inputs, which change as the level of output changes.

2. How are average fixed cost, average variable cost, and average total cost calculated?
For a given level of output, any average cost is calculated as the relevant total cost divided by the level of output. Average fixed cost is therefore total fixed cost divided by output; average variable cost is total variable cost divided by output; and average total cost is total cost (fixed cost plus variable cost) divided by output.

3. Why is marginal cost the relevant cost to consider when one is deciding whether to produce more or less of a product?
Marginal cost is the additional cost of increasing output one unit. That is, it is the cost relevant to the choice of whether to produce and sell one more unit of a good. For producing and selling one more unit of a product to increase profits, the addition to revenue from selling that output (marginal revenue) must exceed the addition to cost from producing it (marginal cost).

4. If the average variable cost curve were constant over some range of output, why would the average total cost be falling over that range of output?
Average total cost is the sum of average variable cost and average fixed cost. Average fixed costs fall over the entire possible range of output. Therefore, if the average variable cost curve were constant over a range of output, the average total cost curve must be falling over that range of output.

5. If your season batting average going into a game was .300 (three hits per ten at bats) and you got two hits in five at bats during the game, would your season batting average rise or fall as a result?
Your "marginal" batting average in the game was .400 (two hits per five at bats), which was higher than your previous batting average. As a consequence, because that game's marginal results were above your previous average, it raises your season batting average.

7.4 The Shape of the Short-Run Cost Curves

1. What is the primary reason that average total cost falls as output expands over low output ranges?
The primary reason average total cost falls as output expands over low output ranges is that average fixed cost declines sharply with output, at low levels of output.

2. Why does average total cost rise at some point as output expands further?
Average total cost begins to rise at some point as output expands further, because of the law of diminishing marginal product, also called the law of increasing costs. Over this range of output, adding more variable inputs does not increase output by the same proportion, so that the average cost of production increases over this range of output.

3. If marginal cost is less than average total cost, why does *ATC* fall? If *MC* is greater than *ATC*, why does the *ATC* rise?
When the marginal cost of a unit of output is less than its average total cost, including the lower cost unit will lower the average (just as getting lower marginal grades this term will decrease your GPA). When the marginal cost of a unit of output exceeds its average total cost, including the higher cost unit will raise the average (just as getting higher marginal grades this term will increase your GPA).

7.5 Cost Curves: Short Run versus Long Run

1. What are economies of scale, diseconomies of scale, and constant returns to scale?
Each of these terms refers to average, or per-unit, costs, as output expands. Economies of scale means that long-run average cost falls as output expands, diseconomies of scale means that long-run average cost rises as output expands, and constant returns to scale means that long-run average cost is constant as output expands.

2. How might cooking for a family dinner be subject to falling average total cost in the long run as the size of the family grows?
Once the appropriate larger-scale cooking technology has been adopted (i.e., in the long run, when all inputs can be varied), such as larger cooking pots, pans, and baking sheets, larger ovens, dishwashers, and so on, and more family members can be involved, each specializing in fewer tasks, that larger scale can reduce the average cost per meal served.

CHAPTER 8: COMPETITION

8.1 The Four Different Market Structures

1. Why do perfectly competitive markets involve homogeneous goods?
For there to be a large number of sellers of a particular good, so that no seller can appreciably affect the market price (i.e., sellers are price takers), the goods in question must be the same, or homogeneous.

2. Why does the absence of significant barriers to entry tend to result in a large number of suppliers?
With no significant barriers to entry, it is fairly easy for entrepreneurs to become suppliers of a product. With such easy entry, as long as an industry is profitable, it will attract new suppliers, typically resulting in large numbers of sellers.

3. Why does the fact that perfectly competitive firms are "small" relative to the market make them price takers?
Because a perfectly competitive firm sells only a small amount relative to the total market supply, even sharply reducing its output will make virtually no difference in the market quantity supplied. Therefore it will make virtually no difference in the market price. In this case, a firm is able to sell all it wants at the market equilibrium price but is unable to appreciably affect that price, therefore it takes the market equilibrium price as given—that is, it is a price taker.

4. Why is the market for used furniture unlikely to be perfectly competitive?
Perfectly competitive markets require large numbers of sellers of a homogeneous good. But used furniture by its nature cannot be standardized to the point where there can be a large number of sellers of identical used furniture pieces.

8.2 The Price-Taker's Demand Curve

1. Why would a perfectly competitive firm not try to raise or lower its price?
A perfectly competitive firm is able to sell all it wants at the market equilibrium price. Therefore, it has no incentive to lower prices (sacrificing revenues and therefore profits) in an attempt to increase sales. Because other firms are willing to sell perfect substitutes for each firm's product (because goods are homogeneous) at the market equilibrium price, trying to raise price would lead to the firm losing all its sales. Therefore, it has no incentive to try to raise its price, either.

2. Why can we represent the demand curve of a perfectly competitive firm as perfectly elastic (horizontal) at the market price?
Because a perfectly competitive firm can sell all it would like at the market equilibrium price, the demand curve it faces for its output is perfectly elastic (horizontal) at that market equilibrium price.

3. How does an individual perfectly competitive firm's demand curve change when the market price changes?
Because a perfectly competitive firm can sell all it would like at the market equilibrium price, it faces a perfectly elastic demand curve at the market equilibrium price. Therefore, anything that changes the market equilibrium price (any of the market demand curve shifters or the market supply curve shifters) will change the price at which each perfectly competitive firm's demand curve is perfectly elastic (horizontal).

4. If the marginal cost facing every producer of a product shifted up, would the position of a perfectly competitive firm's demand curve be likely to change as a result? Why or why not?
Yes. If the marginal cost curves facing each producer shifted up, there would be a decrease (leftward shift) in the industry supply curve. That would result in a higher market price that each producer takes as given, which would shift up each producer's horizontal demand curve to that new market price.

8.3 Profit Maximization

1. How is total revenue calculated?
Total revenue is equal to the price times the quantity sold. However, because the quantity sold at that price must equal the quantity demanded at that price (since to sell a product, you need a willing buyer), it can also be described as price times quantity demanded at that price.

2. How is average revenue derived from total revenue?
Average, or per-unit, revenue for a given quantity of output is just the total revenue from that quantity of sales divided by the quantity sold.
3. How is marginal revenue derived from total revenue?
Marginal revenue is the change in total revenue from the sale of one more unit of output. It can be either positive (total revenue increases with output) or negative (total revenue decreases with output).
4. Why is marginal revenue equal to price for a perfectly competitive firm?
Because a perfectly competitive seller can sell all it would like at the market equilibrium price, it can sell one more unit at that price, without having to lower its price on the other units it sells (which would require sacrificing revenues from those sales). Therefore its marginal revenue from selling one more unit equals the market equilibrium price, and its horizontal demand curve therefore is the same as its horizontal marginal revenue curve.

8.4 Short-Run Profits and Losses

1. How is the profit-maximizing output quantity determined?
The profit-maximizing output is the output where marginal revenue equals marginal cost (because profits increase for every unit of output for which marginal revenue exceeds marginal cost).
2. How do we determine total revenue and total cost for the profit maximizing output quantity?
At the profit maximizing quantity, total revenue is equal to average revenue (price) times quantity (because average revenue is total revenue divided by quantity), and total cost is equal to average cost times quantity (because average cost equals total cost divided by quantity).
3. If a profit-maximizing, perfectly competitive firm is earning a profit because total revenue exceeds total cost, why must the market price exceed average total cost?
If total revenue exceeds total cost, total revenue divided by the quantity of output, which is average revenue or price, must also exceed total cost divided by the same quantity of output, which is average total cost, for that level of output.
4. If a profit-maximizing, perfectly competitive firm is earning a loss because total revenue is less than total cost, why must the market price be less than average total cost?
If total revenue is less than total cost, total revenue divided by the quantity of output, which is average revenue or price, must also be less than total cost divided by the same quantity of output, which is average total cost, for that level of output.
5. If a profit-maximizing, perfectly competitive firm is earning zero economic profits because total revenue equals total cost, why must the market price be equal to the average total cost for that level of output?
If total revenue equals total cost, total revenue divided by the quantity of output, which is average revenue or price, must also be equal to total cost divided by the same quantity of output, which is average total cost, for that level of output.
6. Why would a profit-maximizing, perfectly competitive firm shut down rather than operate if price was less than its average variable costs?
If a firm shuts down, its losses will equal its fixed costs (because there is no revenue or variable costs). If a firm operates, and revenues exactly cover variable costs, it will also suffer losses equal to fixed costs. But if a firm cannot even cover all its variable costs with its revenues, it will lose its fixed costs plus part of its variable costs. But because those losses are greater than the losses from shutting down, a firm would choose to shut down rather than continue to operate in this situation.
7. Why would a profit-maximizing, perfectly competitive firm continue to operate for a period of time if price was greater than average variable cost but less than average total cost?
If price was greater than average variable cost but less than average total cost, a firm is earning losses, and will eventually go out of business if that situation continues. However, in the short run, as long as revenues more than cover variable costs, losses from operating will be less than the losses from shutting down (these losses equal total fixed cost), as at least part of fixed costs are covered by revenues, so a firm will continue to operate in the short run in this situation.

8.5 Long-Run Equilibrium

1. Why do firms enter profitable industries?
Profitable industries generate higher rates of return to productive assets than other industries. Therefore, firms will enter such industries in their search for more profitable uses for their assets.
2. Why does entry eliminate positive economic profits in a perfectly competitive industry?
Entry eliminates positive economic profits (above normal rates of return) in a perfectly competitive industry, because entry will continue as long as economic profits remain positive (rates of return are higher than in other industries).
3. Why do firms exit unprofitable industries?
Unprofitable industries generate lower rates of return to productive assets than other industries. Therefore, firms will exit such industries in their search for more profitable uses for their assets elsewhere.
4. Why does exit eliminate economic losses in a perfectly competitive industry?
Exit eliminates negative economic profits (below normal rates of return) in a perfectly competitive industry because exit will continue as long as economic profits remain negative (rates of return are lower than in other industries).
5. Why is a situation of zero economic profits a stable long-run equilibrium situation for a perfectly competitive industry?
A situation of zero economic profits is a stable long-run equilibrium situation for a perfectly competitive industry because in that situation, there are no profit incentives for firms either to enter or leave the industry.

8.6 Long-Run Supply

1. What must be true about input costs as industry output expands for a constant-cost industry?
Input costs remain constant as industry output expands for a constant-cost industry (which is why it is a constant-cost industry).
2. What must be true about input costs as industry output expands for an increasing-cost industry?
Input costs increase as industry output expands for an increasing-cost industry (which is why it is an increasing-cost industry).
3. What would be the long-run equilibrium result of an increase in demand in a constant-cost industry?
The long-run equilibrium result of an increase in demand in a constant-cost industry is an increase in industry output with no change in price, since output will expand as long as price exceeds the constant level of long run average cost.
4. What would be the long-run equilibrium result of an increase in demand in an increasing-cost industry?
The long-run equilibrium result of an increase in demand in an increasing-cost industry is an increase in industry output (but a smaller increase than in the constant-cost case) and a higher price. Output will expand as long as price exceeds long-run average cost, but that expansion of output increases costs by raising input prices, so that in the long run, prices just cover the resulting higher costs of production.

CHAPTER 9: MONOPOLY

9.1 Monopoly: The Price Maker

1. Why does monopoly depend on the existence of barriers to entry?
If a monopoly were unusually profitable (earning a higher than normal rate of return), entry by other firms would occur, driving its economic profits down and increasing the number of sellers, unless some barrier to entry prevented it.
2. Why is a pure monopoly a rarity?
A pure monopoly is a rarity because there are very few goods or services for which there are no close substitutes and for which there is only one producer.
3. Why does the government grant some companies like public utilities monopoly power?
In some industries, it is inherently inefficient to have more than one firm producing the good or service (i.e., that the good or service is a natural monopoly).

9.2 Demand and Marginal Revenue in Monopoly

1. Why are the market and the firm's demand curves the same for a monopoly?
The market and firm demand curves are the same for a monopoly because a monopoly is the only seller of the product under consideration. Because a monopolist is the only seller in the industry, its demand curve is the industry or market demand curve.
2. Why is a monopoly a price maker but a perfectly competitive firm a price taker?
A perfectly competitive firm is a price taker because it cannot appreciably change the quantity offered for sale on a market, and therefore it cannot change the equilibrium market price appreciably. However, because a monopoly controls the quantity offered for sale, it can alter the price by changing its output—it "makes" the price through its decision of how much to produce.
3. Why is marginal revenue less than price for a profit-maximizing monopolist?
For a monopolist, selling an additional unit requires it to reduce its price, and reducing its price reduces its revenues from units it was selling before at its previous higher price. Therefore, the monopolist's marginal revenue equals price minus this lost revenue from the reduced price on other units, and is less than price as a result.
4. Why would a monopolist never knowingly operate on the inelastic portion of its demand curve?
To maximize its profits, a monopolist will produce the output where marginal revenue equals marginal cost. But because marginal cost will be positive, this requires that marginal revenue is also positive at the profit maximizing level. Because a positive marginal revenue means that total revenue increases as quantity sold increases along a demand curve, and this only occurs if demand is relatively elastic

(elasticity of demand greater than 1), this means that a monopolist will always choose to operate on the elastic portion of its demand curve.

9.3 The Monopolist's Equilibrium

1. What is a monopolist's principle for choosing the profit-maximizing output?
A monopolist's principle for choosing the profit-maximizing output is the same as for a perfectly competitive firm: Produce all those units for which marginal revenue exceeds marginal cost, resulting in a profit-maximizing equilibrium quantity where marginal revenue equals marginal cost. The differences between a monopoly and a perfectly competitive firm arise because marginal revenue also equals price for a perfectly competitive firm, but marginal revenue is less than price for a monopolist.

2. How do you find the profit-maximizing price for a monopolist?
A monopolist produces the quantity where marginal revenue equals marginal cost. The height of its demand curve at that quantity indicates the price at which that profit-maximizing quantity can be sold.

3. For a monopolist making positive economic profits, what must be true about the relationship between price and average total cost?
Just as for a perfectly competitive firm, for a monopoly to be earning economic profits, its total revenue must exceed total cost at the profit maximizing output. But this must mean that price (average revenue) must also exceed average cost at the profit maximizing output level, for positive economic profits to be earned.

4. For a monopolist making negative economic profits, what must be true about the relationship between price and average total cost?
Just as for a perfectly competitive firm, for a monopoly to be earning negative economic profits, its total revenue must be less than its total cost at the profit maximizing output. But this must mean that price (average revenue) must also be less than average cost at the profit maximizing output level, for negative economic profits to be earned.

5. Why, unlike perfectly competitive firms, can a monopolist continue to earn positive economic profits in the long run?
Unlike perfectly competitive firms, a monopolist can continue to earn positive economic profits in the long run, because barriers to entry keep entrants, whose entry would erode those economic profits, from entering the industry.

9.4 Monopoly and Welfare Loss

1. Why does the reduced output under monopoly cause inefficiency?
The reduced output and higher prices under monopoly causes inefficiency because some units for which the marginal value (indicated by willingness to pay along the demand curve) exceeds the marginal cost are no longer exchanged (unlike in perfect competition), eliminating the net gains that such trades would have generated.

2. Does monopoly power retard innovation? Why or why not?
Monopoly has been claimed to retard innovation, but many near-monopolists are important innovators. Therefore the incentive to innovate exists in monopolistic as well as competitive market structures.

3. What does the welfare cost of monopoly represent? How is it measured?
The welfare cost of monopoly represents the net gains from trade (the difference between the marginal values of those goods indicated by the demand curve and the marginal costs of producing them) from those units of a good that would have been traded, but are no longer traded because of the output restriction of monopoly. It is measured by the area between the demand curve and the marginal cost curve for those units that are no longer traded because of the monopoly output restriction.

4. How can economies of scale lead to monopoly? How can it result in monopoly increasing rather than decreasing market output relative to the competitive market structure?
Economies of scale can lead to monopoly because output can be produced at lower costs on a larger scale than on a smaller scale, and this efficiency (cost) advantage can result in a larger firm outcompeting smaller firms. Industries with economies of scale over the entire range of industry output therefore tend toward monopoly. But if the production cost savings are greater than the price increasing effect of monopoly output restriction, the result of such a monopoly would be a lower price and a higher quantity than would be the case with a larger number of firms (i.e., a more competitive market structure).

5. Can monopoly be the result of a new innovation that leaves consumers better off than before? Why or why not?
A new innovation may result in its innovator having a monopoly on it, which would give its creator incentives to raise prices and reduce outputs like any other monopoly. But for that monopoly innovator to attract customers away from the products customers currently purchase, those customers must expect to be made better off buying it at the price charged. This means that such a monopoly has no ability to harm consumers compared to their earlier situation.

9.5 Monopoly Policy

1. What alternative ways of dealing with the monopoly problem are commonly used?
The monopoly problem (with respect to efficiency, equity, and power) is commonly dealt with through antitrust policies, regulation, and public ownership.

2. How do antitrust laws promote more price competition?
Antitrust promotes more price competition by making monopolistic practices and restrictions on price competition illegal.

3. What price and output are ideal for allocative efficiency for a regulated natural monopolist? Why is an unregulated natural monopolist unlikely to pick this solution?
The efficient price and output is where demand (marginal value) equals marginal cost, because this guarantees that every mutually beneficial trade takes place. However, with economies of scale (falling average cost curves), marginal cost is less than average cost for a natural monopolist, so that marginal cost prices would result in economic losses. An unregulated natural monopolist would not choose such a solution.

4. What is average cost pricing? How is it different from marginal cost pricing?
Average cost pricing is a regulatory approach to natural monopoly that permits the regulated natural monopolist to earn a normal rate of return on capital investment (zero economic profits). Zero economic profits requires that total revenues equal total (opportunity) costs, which requires that average revenue, or price, equals average cost. Forcing such a natural monopolist to charge prices equal to marginal cost would require a price below average cost, because marginal cost is less than average cost for a natural monopolist, implying losses to the producer, which is not sustainable over the long run.

5. What are some difficulties encountered when regulators try to implement average cost pricing on natural monopolies?
Difficulties encountered when regulators try to implement average cost pricing include difficulties in calculating costs, eroded incentives for regulated firms to keep costs down, and the risk that the regulatory agency will make decisions on a political basis rather than on an economic basis.

6. Why might a job with a regulated natural monopolist that is allowed to earn a "fair and reasonable" return have more perks (noncash forms of compensation) than a comparable job in a nonregulated firm?
A regulated natural monopolist that is allowed to earn a "fair and reasonable" rate of return has no incentive to keep costs down, because reducing costs won't allow them to earn higher profits as a result. Those potential profits the monopolist is not allowed to keep instead get converted into business expenses than benefit the management, such as lavish perks (first class air travel, hotels and meals, and so on).

9.6 Price Discrimination

1. How do we define price discrimination?
Price discrimination is defined as charging different customers different prices for the same good or service.

2. Why does price discrimination arise from the profit-maximization motive?
Price discrimination arises from the profit-maximization motive because different customers react differently to price changes (i.e., they have different elasticities of demand). Therefore, profit-maximization implies treating these different customers differently.

3. What principle will a profit-maximizing monopolist use in trying to price discriminate among different groups of customers?
A profit-maximizing monopolist will attempt to sell the output where marginal revenue equals marginal cost for each group of customers. That is, it wants to maximize profits for each group of customers separately.

4. Why will a price-discriminating monopolist charge a higher price to more inelastic demanders than to more elastic demanders?
Marginal revenue is closer to price for customers with more elastic demand curves, so prices charged those customers are lower, closer to cost, than for customers with more inelastic demand curves, whose marginal revenue is much further below price.

5. Why is preventing resale the key to successful price discrimination?
If customers who are being charged different prices for the same goods can resell the good among themselves, the lower price group will resell to the higher price group, undermining the seller's ability to charge a higher price to the groups with more inelastic demand curves.

6. Why is it generally easier to price discriminate for services than for goods?
Preventing resale is a key to successful price discrimination, and it is typically easier to prevent resale of services provided directly to customers than for goods sold to them (e.g., it is harder to resell a gall bladder surgery or plumbing repairs than to resell a computer).

CHAPTER 10: INPUT MARKETS AND THE DISTRIBUTION OF INCOME

10.1 Input Markets

1. Why is the demand for productive inputs derived from the demand for the outputs those inputs produce?
The demand for productive inputs is derived from the demand for the outputs those inputs produce because the value to a firm of the services of a productive input depends on the value of the outputs produced, and the value of the output depends on the demand for that output.
2. Why is the demand for tractors and fertilizer derived from the demand for agricultural products?
The reason farmers demand tractors and fertilizer is that they increase the output of crops they grow. But the value to farmers of the additional crops they can grow as a result is greater, the higher the price of those crops. Therefore, the greater the demand for those crops, other things being equal, the higher the price of those crops, which increases the demand for tractors and fertilizer by increasing the value to farmers of the added output they make possible.

10.2 Supply and Demand in the Labor Market

1. What is marginal revenue product?
Marginal revenue product is the additional revenue that a firm obtains from employing one more unit of an input. It is equal to the marginal product multiplied by marginal revenue.
2. Would a firm hire another worker if the marginal revenue product of labor exceeded the market wage rate? Why or why not?
A firm would hire another worker if the marginal revenue product of labor exceeded the market wage rate, because doing so would add more to its total revenue than it would add to its total costs, raising profits.
3. Why does the marginal product of labor eventually fall?
As more and more units of the variable input labor are added to a given quantity of the fixed input, land or capital, the additional output from each additional unit of labor must begin to fall at some point. This is the law of diminishing marginal product.
4. Why does diminishing marginal product mean that the marginal revenue product will eventually fall?
Because marginal revenue product equals marginal product times marginal revenue, the eventually falling marginal product means that the marginal revenue product must also eventually fall, even if the price of the output did not fall with increasing output. If the marginal revenue falls with increasing output, that will also cause marginal revenue product to fall with additional output.
5. Why is a firm hiring in a competitive labor market a price (wage) taker for a given quality of labor?
A perfectly competitive seller cannot by its output choices appreciably affect the market quantity, and thereby the market price of that output, and so it takes the output market price as given. In just the same way, a firm hiring in a competitive labor market cannot by its input (hiring) choices appreciably affect the quantity of that input employed, and therefore the market price if that input, and so it takes the input (labor) market price (wage) as given.

10.3 Labor Market Equilibrium

1. If wages were above their equilibrium level, why would they tend to fall toward the equilibrium level?
If wages were above their equilibrium level, the quantity of labor supplied at that price would exceed the quantity of labor demanded at that price. The resulting surplus of labor would lead workers frustrated by their ability to get jobs to compete the wage for those jobs down toward the equilibrium level.
2. If wages were below their equilibrium level, why would they tend to rise toward the equilibrium level?
If wages were below their equilibrium level, the quantity of labor demanded at that price would exceed the quantity of labor supplied at that price. The resulting shortage of labor would lead employers frustrated by their ability to find workers to compete the wage for those jobs up toward the equilibrium level.
3. Why do increases in technology or increases in the amounts of capital or other complementary inputs increase the demand for labor?
Increases in technology or increases in the amounts of capital or other complementary inputs increase the demand for labor by increasing the productivity of labor; as labor productivity increases, the marginal revenue product of labor (the demand for labor) increases.
4. Why do any of the demand shifters for output markets shift the demand for labor and other inputs used to produce that output in the same direction?
When any of the demand shifters for output markets change the price of that output, it changes the marginal revenue product (marginal product times price) of labor and other inputs used to produce that output in the same direction.
5. Explain why increases in immigration or population growth, increases in workers' willingness to work at a given wage, decreases in nonwage income, or increases in workplace amenities will increase the supply of labor.
Increases in immigration or population growth increases the number of potential workers; increases in willingness to work at a given wage increase hours worked; decreases in nonwage income lowers workers' incomes, increasing their willingness to work at any given wage; and an increase in workplace amenities makes working more desirable (less undesirable), also increasing workers' willingness to work at a given wage.
6. What would happen to the supply of labor if nonwage incomes increased and workplace amenities also increased over the same time period?
Higher nonwage incomes would reduce the supply of labor, but better workplace amenities would increase the supply of labor. The net effect would depend on which of these effects was of greater magnitude.
7. Why are wages in different fields not necessarily related to how important people think those jobs are?
The marginal revenue product of labor determines wages, and the marginal value that results from the forces of supply and demand does not bear any necessary relationship to how important or critical people consider that job to be in some absolute sense.
8. If the private-market wage of engineers were greater than that of sociologists, what would happen if a university tried to pay its entire faculty the same salary?
Say the university based its salaries on the average salaries elsewhere for all fields. Other things being equal, the resulting salaries would be below the equilibrium salary level for engineers, resulting in a shortage of engineering professors at that university (e.g., the would lose current engineering faculty and have a hard time hiring new engineering faculty), but above the equilibrium salary level for sociologists, resulting in a surplus of sociology professors at that university (who would seemingly never leave or retire).

10.4 Labor Unions

1. How can acting together as a group increase workers' bargaining power?
Acting together as a group gives workers increased bargaining power because it reduces competition among them for jobs.
2. Why are service industries harder to unionize than manufacturing industries?
Service industries tend to be harder to unionize than manufacturing industries because service industry jobs tend to be less standardized and service industry firms tend to be smaller.
3. How do union restrictions on membership or other barriers to entry affect the wages of members?
Union restrictions on membership or other barriers to entry reduce the quantity of labor services offered to employers, reducing the number of such jobs and increasing their wages.
4. What would increasing unionization do to the wages of those who were not in unions?
Increasing unionization would reduce the number of jobs in industries that became more unionized, increasing the supply of workers in industries that were still nonunion, and lowering the wages those jobs pay.
5. How can unions potentially increase worker productivity?
Unions can potentially increase worker productivity by providing a collective voice that workers can use to communicate their discontents more effectively, which can reduce the number of workers that quit, reducing employee training costs. They could also improve worker motivation and morale by better handling worker grievances.
6. Why does data indicating that unionization tends to lower firm profits weaken the argument that the primary effect of unionization is increased worker productivity?
If increased worker productivity was the primary effect of unionization, unionized firms should have lower costs and therefore higher profits than non-union firms. But the data seems to indicate that the opposite is true.

10.5 Land and Rent

1. If the supply of land was perfectly inelastic, how much would the price of land rise if the price of crops grown on the land doubled, other things being equal? What if the supply of land was less than perfectly inelastic?
Because the demand for land is derived from the demand for the products produced on the land, a doubling of the price of the crops raised on land would double the demand for the land. If the supply of land was perfectly inelastic, this would double the price of the land. If the supply of land was less than perfectly elastic, the higher demand would increase the quantity of land supplied, and the doubling of demand would lead the price to rise, but less than double.
2. What would happen to the economic rent earned by Madonna if her alternative earning opportunities outside singing improved? What would it do to her willingness to record and play concerts?
Because economic rent is the payment that a resource owner receives beyond what he or she would receive using the resource in its next most attractive use, an increase in Madonna's alternative earning opportunities would reduce her

economic rent from singing. However, as long as singing remains more lucrative than these alternatives, she will continue to sing, resulting in no change in her willingness to record and play concerts.

3. How does the existence of professional basketball leagues other than the NBA affect the economic rents earned by NBA players?

Because economic rent is the payment that a resource owner receives beyond what he or she would receive using the resource in its next most attractive use, other professional basketball leagues than the NBA increases players' potential incomes outside of the NBA, reducing their economic rents from playing in the NBA.

10.6 Capital and Interest

1. Why is the demand curve for capital downward sloping?

The demand curve for capital is downward sloping because the lower the interest rate, the lower the opportunity cost of borrowed funds, and the more projects that can profitably be pursued with those funds (there are more capital investment projects with higher rates of return than the opportunity cost of borrowing).

2. Why is the supply curve of capital upward sloping?

The interest rate represents the benefit savers get from saving (deferring consumption). A higher interest rate means an increase in the benefits of saving, resulting in increased saving and therefore an increase in the supply of funds available for capital investment projects.

3. If a new machine would earn a 12 percent rate of return for your firm, and you could borrow the funds to finance it at an interest rate of 15 percent per year, would you borrow the money to buy it? Why or why not?

You would not borrow the money to buy the machine, because the opportunity cost of the funds (15 percent per year) exceeds the expected returns (benefits) from investing in the machine (12 percent).

4. What happens to the present value of a stream of payments of $1,000 per year as the interest rate falls?

This change would increase the present value of the stream of payments. A lower interest rate means a given stream of payments will be discounted to present value terms at a lower rate.

10.7 Income Distribution

1. Why might patterns in the measured income distribution give an inaccurate impression?

The measured income distribution may give an inaccurate impression because it does not include all forms of income. For instance, it does not include nonmonetary income.

2. Why might measured income shares understate the degree of income inequality?

Measured income shares may understate the degree of income inequality because they do not include the nonmonetary income and privileges of the relatively well to do.

3. Why might measured income shares overstate the degree of income inequality?

Measured income shares may overstate the degree of income inequality because they don't adjust for predictable differences in incomes by age, demographic trends such as the growth of both divorce and two-earner families, taxes, in-kind income from the government (e.g., food stamps), the benefits of government programs, or movement within the income distribution over time.

4. How does the fraction of the population that is middle aged, rather than young or old, affect measurements of income inequality?

The more people are in their peak-earning, middle-age years, the higher their earnings appear relative to their lifetime incomes; the more people who are young or old, in their low-earning years, the lower their earnings appear relative to their lifetime income.

5. How does the growth of both two-earner families and divorced couples increase measured income inequality?

Combining two incomes and increasing the number of lower-income households headed by females because of divorce increases the number of families counted at both the upper and lower ends of the income distribution, which increases measured income inequality.

6. Why is it important to take account of the substantial mobility of families within the income distribution over time when evaluating the degree of income inequality in America?

The substantial income mobility within the income distribution means that someone who has a low income today will not necessarily have a low income for a long period of time; there may continue to be low-income people, but they are likely to be different people.

10.8 The Economics Of Discrimination

1. What is the difference between job-entry discrimination and wage discrimination?

Job-entry discrimination refers to a worker denied employment due to discrimination; wage discrimination refers to those who are employed, but at lower wages, due to discrimination.

2. Explain how earnings differences could reflect either discrimination or productivity differences.

Employers discriminating among workers for reasons other than productivity would result in earnings differences. But employers are also willing to pay more to more productive workers (e.g., those with more education), resulting in earnings differences. The difficulty is determining how much each accounts for differences in earnings.

3. What is the environmental explanation for differences in earnings across the sexes and races?

The environmental explanation for differences in earnings across the sexes and races is that women and minorities are not as productive because they have been prevented from gaining the necessary training and skills and because women are more likely to interrupt their careers to have and care for children.

4. How do firms' incentives to maximize profits tend to reduce the extent of discrimination?

A firm that chose not to hire an employee that has a higher marginal revenue product than his or her wage, because of some preference for discrimination, sacrifices profits as a result. Those sacrificed profits make discriminating costly, reducing its extent.

5. How can discrimination reflect imperfect information and the costs of acquiring more information about potential employees?

If an employer's past experience with a particular group has been worse than that with other groups, he or she might prefer not to hire people from that group because the probability that they will perform well is lower. But this use of past experience as a screening device for new employees only makes sense if it is costly for employers to discover the productivity of individual potential employees, rather than the average of some group, before hiring them.

6. Say you hire only purple workers. If purple workers strongly prefer to work with one another instead of with other groups, why might you prefer to hire a less-productive purple worker than a more productive non-purple worker at the same wage?

Say each of your 20 current purple workers would demand $1 more per hour to work with a non-purple worker than with another purple worker. You would then have to compare how much more productive your prospective non-purple worker was at a given wage than a purple worker, or how much less he would have to be paid for a given level of productivity, against how much more you would have to pay your other workers to work next to him. In this case, if the productivity or wage difference exceeds $20 per hour of work, the non-purple worker would be hired, but if it were less than $20 per hour of work, he would not be hired.

7. Why would subsidizing employers for hiring minority workers rather than imposing implicit quotas give employers greater incentives to expand minority job opportunities?

An implicit minority-hiring quota would raise employers' costs by making them hire workers they find less productive than those they would otherwise have hired. This reduces the profits of those firms, tending to reduce their size and number, and the number of job opportunities they offer. Subsidizing the hiring of minority workers, however, lowers the cost to employers (they would not hire them unless the subsidy more than compensated them for any reduction in productivity) of hiring minority workers, increasing their profits and expanding the number of job opportunities for minority workers.

10.9 Poverty

1. How are absolute and relative measures of poverty different?

An absolute measure of poverty is one based on whether income is sufficient to provide the basic necessities of life (food, clothing, and so on) in minimum quantities; a relative measure of poverty is based on having lower incomes relative to others (e.g., earning half the median income).

2. Why could economic growth potentially eliminate absolute measures of poverty but not relative measures of poverty?

Economic growth increases output, making it possible to bring every citizen up to some minimal absolute level of income. It does not, however, eliminate the fact that some will still have relatively lower incomes than others.

3. Some people have argued that poverty could be eliminated by rich countries. Can both absolute and relative poverty be eliminated by rich countries? Why or why not?

Absolute poverty could possibly be eliminated—providing all citizens the basic necessities of life in minimum quantities—by rich countries. However, unless a country completely equalized incomes of all its citizens, some would continue to have lower incomes than others, and such relative poverty would persist to some degree.

CHAPTER 11: INTRODUCTION TO THE MACROECONOMY

11.1 Macroeconomic Goals

1. What are the three major economic goals of most societies?

The three major economic goals of most societies are full employment (so that jobs are relatively plentiful and financial suffering from lack of income is relatively uncommon), price stability (so consumers and producers can make better decisions), and economic growth (so output, and therefore income and consumption, increases over time).

2. What is the Employment Act of 1946? Why was it significant?

The Employment Act of 1946 was a law that committed the federal government to policies designed to reduce unemployment in a manner consistent with price stability. It was significant as the first formal government acknowledgment of the primary macroeconomic goals as the goals of policy.

11.2 Employment and Unemployment

1. What happens to the unemployment rate when the number of unemployed people increases, *ceteris paribus?* When the labor force grows, *ceteris paribus?*

The unemployment rate is defined as the number of people officially unemployed divided by the labor force. Therefore, the unemployment rate rises as the number of unemployed people increases and it falls when the labor force grows, *ceteris paribus.*

2. How might the official unemployment rate understate the "true" degree of unemployment? How might it overstate it?

The official unemployment rate understates the "true" degree of unemployment by not including discouraged workers as unemployed, by counting part-time workers who cannot find full-time jobs as "fully" employed, and by counting those employed in jobs that underutilize worker skills as "fully" employed. It overstates the "true" degree of unemployment by not counting those working overtime or multiple jobs as "overemployed," by counting those employed in the underground economy as unemployed, and by including those just "going through the motions" of job search to maintain unemployment benefits or other government benefits as unemployed.

3. Why might the fraction of the unemployed who are job leavers be higher in a period of strong labor demand?

In a period of strong labor demand, people would be more confident of their ability to find other jobs, and therefore they would be more likely to leave (quit) their current jobs.

4. Suppose you live in a community of 100 people. If 80 people over 16 years old are willing and able to work, and 72 people are employed, what is the unemployment rate in that community?

The unemployment rate in this community is the number unemployed (8) divided by the labor force (80), or 10 percent.

5. What would happen to the unemployment rate if a substantial group of unemployed people started going to school full time? What would happen to the size of the labor force?

Full-time students are not considered part of the labor force, so the labor force, the number officially unemployed, and the unemployment rate would all fall if unemployed people became full-time students.

6. What happens to the unemployment rate when unemployed people become discouraged workers? Does anything happen to employment in this case?

When unemployed workers become discouraged workers, they stop seeking jobs and are no longer counted as either part of the labor force or as unemployed, reducing the unemployment rate. However, because they do not find jobs, there is no effect on employment as a result.

11.3 Different Types of Unemployment

1. Why do we want some frictional unemployment?

We want some frictional unemployment because we want human resources employed in areas of higher productivity, and some period of job search (frictional unemployment), rather than taking the first job offered, can allow workers to find more productive employment.

2. Why might a job-retraining program be a more useful policy to address structural unemployment than to address frictional unemployment?

Structural unemployment reflects people who lack the necessary skills for the jobs available, rather than a temporary period of search between jobs. A job-retraining program to develop skills to match the jobs available addresses such structural unemployment, not frictional unemployment.

3. What is the traditional government policy "cure" for cyclical unemployment?

The traditional government policy "cure" for cyclical unemployment is to adopt policies designed to increase aggregate demand for goods and services.

4. Does new technology increase unemployment?

New technology can increase unemployment among those whose skills are replaced by that technology. However, it also creates new jobs manufacturing, servicing, and repairing the new equipment, and, by lowering costs, new technology frees up more income to demand other goods and services, creating jobs in those industries.

5. What types of unemployment are present at full employment (at the natural rate of unemployment)?

At full employment (at the natural rate of unemployment), both frictional and structural unemployment, but not cyclical unemployment, are present.

6. Why might frictional unemployment be higher in a period of plentiful jobs (low unemployment)?

In a period of plentiful jobs, frictional unemployment can be higher because job opportunities are plentiful, which stimulates mobility between jobs, increasing frictional unemployment.

7. If the widespread introduction of the automobile caused a productive buggy whip maker to lose his job, would he be structurally or frictionally unemployed?

If the buggy whip maker's skills were demand in other industries, this would result in frictional unemployment, but if his skills were not in demand in other industries, this would result in structural unemployment.

8. If a fall in demand for domestic cars causes auto workers to lose their jobs in Michigan while there are plenty of jobs for lumberjacks in Montana, what kind of unemployment results?

This would be an example of structural unemployment, resulting from skills mismatched to the jobs available.

9. Why would higher unemployment compensation in a country like France lead to higher rates of unemployment?

Unemployment insurance lowers the opportunity cost to a worker from being unemployed, increasing the duration of unemployment and the unemployment rate. Higher unemployment insurance payments will decrease the opportunity cost of remaining unemployed, tending to increase the duration of unemployment and raise the unemployment rate.

11.4 Inflation

1. How does price level stability reduce the difficulties buyers and sellers have in coordinating their plans?

Price level instability increases the difficulties buyers and sellers have in coordinating their plans by reducing their certainty about what price changes mean—do they reflect changes in relative prices or changes in inflation? Eliminating this uncertainty makes the meaning of price changes clearer, allowing buyers and sellers to better coordinate their plans through the price system.

2. What will happen to the nominal interest rate if the real interest rate rises, *ceteris paribus?* What if expected inflation increases, *ceteris paribus?*

The nominal interest rate is the sum of the desired real interest rate and the expected inflation rate. If either the real interest rate or the expected rate of inflation increases, nominal interest rates will also increase.

3. Pretend you owe money to the Big River Bank. Will you gain or lose from an unanticipated decrease in inflation?

An unanticipated decrease in inflation will mean that the dollars you must pay back on your loan will be worth more than you expected, raising the real interest rate you must pay on that loan, which makes you worse off.

4. How does a variable interest rate loan "insure" the lender against unanticipated increases in inflation?

With a variable interest rate loan, an unanticipated increase in inflation does not reduce the real interest rate received by the lender, but instead increases the nominal interest rate on the loan to compensate for the increased inflation.

5. Why will neither creditors nor debtors lose from inflation if it is correctly anticipated?

Correctly anticipated inflation will be accurately reflected in the terms creditors and debtors agree to, so that neither will lose from inflation. Only unexpected inflation can redistribute wealth between debtors and creditors.

6. How can inflation make people turn to exchange by barter?

If inflation is very rapid, people lose faith in the value of their monetary unit, and this can lead to exchange by barter, because goods can then have a more predictable value than their country's money.

7. What would happen in the loanable funds market if suppliers of loanable funds expect a substantial fall in inflation, while demanders of funds expect a substantial rise in inflation?

If suppliers of loanable funds expect a substantial fall in inflation, they would demand a smaller "inflation premium" to loan money, increasing the supply of loanable funds. If demanders of funds expect a substantial rise in inflation, they will be willing to offer a greater "inflation premium" to borrow, increasing the demand for loanable funds. The increased supply of loanable funds pushes down interest rates, while the increased demand for loanable funds pushes up interest rates, so the net effect on interest rates is unknown, without further information about the relative sizes of the shifts in the curves.

11.5 Economic Fluctuations

1. Why would you expect unemployment to tend to fall during an economy's expansionary phase and to rise during a contractionary phase?

Output increases during an economy's expansion phase. To produce that increased output in the short term requires more workers, which increases employment and reduces the unemployment rate, other things being equal.

2. Why might a politician want to stimulate the economy prior to a reelection bid?
A politician may want to stimulate the economy prior to a reelection bid because there is a strong correlation between the performance of the economy and the fate of an incumbent's bid for reelection.
3. Why is the output of investment goods and durable consumer goods more sensitive to the business cycle than that of most goods?
When output is growing and business confidence is high, investment rises sharply because it appears highly profitable; when incomes and consumer confidence are high, durable goods, whose purchases are often delayed in less prosperous times, rise sharply in demand. In recessions, investment and consumer durables purchases fall sharply, as such projects no longer appear profitable, and plans are put on hold until better times.
4. Why might the unemployment rate fall after output starts recovering during the expansion phase of the business cycle?
Often unemployment remains fairly high well into the expansion phase, because it takes a period of recovery before businesses become convinced that the increasing demand for their output is going to continue, making it profitable to hire added workers.

CHAPTER 12: MEASURING ECONOMIC PERFORMANCE

12.1 National Income Accounting: Measuring Economic Performance

1. Why does GDP measure only *final* goods and services produced, rather than all goods and services produced?
If the market value of every good and service sold was included in GDP, the same output would be counted more than once in many circumstances (as when the sales price of, say bread, includes the value of the flour that was used in making the bread, and the flour, in turn, includes the value of the wheat that was used to make the flour). Only final goods and services are included in GDP to avoid such double counting.
2. Why aren't all of the expenditures on used goods in an economy included in current GDP?
Current GDP does not include expenditures on used goods because GDP is intended to measure the value of currently produced goods and services in the economy. Used goods are not currently produced, and were already counted the year they were newly produced.
3. Why do GDP statistics include real estate agents' commissions from selling existing homes and used car dealers' profits from selling used cars, but not the value of existing homes or used cars when they are sold?
Existing homes and used cars were both produced in the past, and therefore aren't counted as part of current GDP. However, the services provided this year by real estate agents and used car dealers are currently produced, so the market value of those services, measured by real estate agent commissions and the profits earned by used car dealers, are included in GDP.
4. Why are sales of previously existing inventories of hula hoops not included in the current year's GDP?
Previously existing inventories of any product are not newly produced, and are therefore not included in the current year GDP. They were already produced and counted in an earlier period.

12.2 The Expenditure Approach to Measuring GDP

1. What would happen to GDP if consumption purchases (C) and net exports ($X - M$) both rose, other things being equal?
Because GDP is the sum of consumption purchases (C), investment purchases (I), government purchases (G), and net exports ($X - M$), an increase of any of those components of GDP will increase GDP, other things being equal. Because either an increase in consumption (C) or an increase in net exports ($X - M$) increases GDP, both changes in the same time period will also increase GDP, other things being equal.
2. Why do you think economic forecasters focus so much on consumption purchases and their determinants?
Economic forecasters focus so much on consumption purchases and their determinants because consumption purchases are by far the largest component (roughly two-thirds) of GDP, so that what happens to consumption purchases is crucial to what happens to GDP.
3. Why are durable goods purchases more unstable than nondurable goods purchases?
Durable goods purchases are more unstable than nondurable goods purchases because nondurable goods are used up in a relatively short period of time, so that their purchase is hard to shift from one time period to another. Durable goods, on the other hand, provide services for several periods, so that consumer durable purchases can be significantly delayed to "make do" during economic hard times and significantly accelerated during good times.
4. Why does the investment component of GDP include purchases of new capital goods but not purchases of company stock?
New capital goods are newly produced goods, by definition, so they are included in GDP. However, sales of company stock do not involve a newly produced good or service (although the services of the broker, measured by the transaction fee, are included as a newly produced service). When someone buys shares of stock from someone else, no goods are being newly produced. Instead, already existing ownership claims on the future income of the company are simply being rearranged from one person to another.
5. If Mary received a welfare check this year, would that transfer payment be included in this year's GDP? Why or why not?
GDP includes only currently produced goods and services. But because transfer payments are not payments in exchange for newly produced goods and services, they are not included in GDP.
6. Could inventory investment or net exports ever be negative?
Yes. If end of the year inventories are smaller than beginning of the year inventories, inventory investment is negative, and if the value of exports is smaller than the value of imports, net exports are negative.

12.3 The Income Approach to Measuring GDP

1. Why should we expect the total expenditures that go into GDP to equal total income in an economy?
Every dollar of purchases that goes into GDP must be paid out to the factors of production that produced it (categorized as wages, rents, interest and profits). Therefore, total expenditures, properly measured, must equal total income, property measured.
2. Which two nonincome expense items does the income approach take into consideration?
The income approach takes indirect business taxes (because they are uses to which income is devoted, even though they are not payments for newly produced goods and services) and depreciation, or the capital consumption allowance, (because depreciation represents the amount of income that must be set aside to replace existing capital equipment as it wears out) into consideration, so that national income will equal GDP.
3. How is personal income different from national income?
Personal income, the amount of income available to spend by consumers, is not the same as national income, because owners of productive resources do not receive all of the income that they earn and they receive "unearned" transfer payments. Undistributed corporate profits and social insurance taxes, which are not received by the factors of production, must be subtracted from, and transfer payments must be added to, national income to get personal income.

12.4 Problems in Calculating an Accurate GDP

1. If we overestimated inflation over time, would our calculations of real GDP growth be over- or underestimated?
Nominal GDP is deflated by the measure of inflation being used to calculate real GDP and real GDP growth. Therefore, for a given nominal GDP growth rate, overestimating inflation over time would result in underestimating real GDP growth over time
2. Why does the consumer price index tend to overstate inflation if the quality of goods and services is rising over time?
The consumer price index does not adjust for most quality increases that take place in goods and services. Therefore, higher prices that actually reflect increased quality are counted as higher prices for a given quality, so that the consumer price index overstates increases in the cost of living.
3. Why would the growth in real GDP overstate the growth of output per person in a country with a growing population?
Real GDP growth measures what happens to output for the economy as a whole. But if the population is growing, real GDP is being split among an increasing number of people, and real GDP growth exceeds per capita real GDP growth.
4. Why doesn't the consumer price index accurately adjust for the cost-of-living effects of a tripling in the price of bananas relative to the prices of other fruits?
The consumer price index assumes that people continue to consume the same number of bananas as in the base year (survey period). Therefore the cost of the banana component of the consumer price index triples when the price of bananas triples. However, in fact, consumers will substitute other fruits that become relatively cheaper as a result of the banana price increase, so that this component of their cost of living has not actually increased as fast as banana prices.

12.5 Problems with GDP as a Measure of Economic Welfare

1. Why do GDP measures omit nonmarket transactions?
GDP measures omit nonmarket transactions because there is no accurate way to measure the values of those transactions, unlike the case for normal market transactions, where market prices can be used to measure the values involved.
2. How would the existence of a high level of nonmarket activities in one country impact real GDP comparisons between it and other countries?
Because nonmarket activities are not included in GDP, GDP would understate

the true value of total output more for a country with a relatively high level of nonmarket activities than for a country with a smaller proportion of nonmarket activities, making countries with smaller shares of nonmarket activities look larger relative to countries with larger shares of nonmarket activities.

3. If we choose to decrease our hours worked because we value the additional leisure more, would the resulting change in real GDP accurately reflect the change in our well being? Why or why not?

Decreasing hours worked would reduce real GDP, other things being equal. But if we choose to do so voluntarily, that would mean we place a higher value on the leisure time (which is not counted in GDP) than on the market output (that is counted in GDP) foregone by reducing hours worked, so the change in real GDP would not accurately reflect the change in our well being.

4. How do pollution and crime affect GDP? How do pollution- and crime-control expenditures impact GDP?

Neither pollution nor crime is included (as "bads" to be subtracted) in GDP calculations. However, market expenditures for pollution- and crime-control are included in GDP, as currently produced goods and services.

CHAPTER 13: ECONOMIC GROWTH IN THE GLOBAL ECONOMY

13.1 Economic Growth

1. Why does the production possibilities curve shift out with economic growth?

Economic growth means the ability of an economy to produce more goods and services than before. An outward shift in a country's production possibilities curve simply illustrates that fact graphically.

2. Even if "in the long run we are all dead," are you glad earlier generations of Americans worked and invested for economic growth?

The fact that earlier generations of Americans worked and invested for economic growth means that there is currently a greater stock of capital in the United States than there would have been otherwise. With more tools to work with, you are more productive, resulting in a higher income and greater consumption possibilities.

3. If long-run consequences were not important, would many students go to college or participate in internship programs without pay?

No. These are two of many examples where people sacrifice in the short run in order to benefit in the long run. Saving and research and development are other obvious examples.

4. When the Dutch "created" new land with their system of dikes, what did it do to their production possibilities curve? Why?

Building dikes in Holland increased the quantity of usable land the Dutch had to work with, and an increase in the amount of usable natural resources shifts a country's production possibilities curve out.

13.2 Determinants of Economic Growth

1. Why is no single factor capable of completely explaining economic growth patterns?

No single factor is capable of completely explaining economic growth patterns because economic growth is a complex process involving many important factors, no one of which completely dominates.

2. Why might a country with relatively scarce labor be a leader in labor-saving innovations? In what area would a country with relatively scarce land likely be an innovative leader?

A country with relatively scarce, and therefore more costly, labor would benefit more from labor-saving innovations, and so would be likely to be a leader in such innovations. Similarly, a country with relatively scarce, and therefore more costly, land would likely be a leader in innovative ways to conserve land.

3. Why could an increase in the price of oil increase real GDP growth in oil-exporting countries like Saudi Arabia and Mexico, while decreasing growth in oil-importing countries like the United States and Japan?

Because GDP measures the market value of goods and services produced, an increase in prices for what a country exports adds to its GDP. However, an increase in the price of imported oil will raise costs and reduce output in that country, other things being equal.

4. How is Hong Kong a dramatic example of why abundant natural resources are not necessary to rapid economic growth?

Hong Kong has virtually no natural resources, yet has long been among the fastest growing economies in the world, proving that abundant natural resources are not necessary to rapid economic growth.

13.3 Raising the Level of Economic Growth

1. Why does knowing what factors are correlated with economic growth not tell us what causes economic growth?

Knowing what factors are correlated with economic growth does not tell us what causes economic growth because correlation does not prove causation. A factor may cause changes in economic growth, or economic growth could cause changes in it, or changes in both the factor and economic growth may be caused by yet another variable.

2. How does increasing the capital stock lead to economic growth?

Increasing the capital stock adds to the tools workers have to work with, increasing their productivity over time, which in turn increases output over time.

3. How do higher savings rates affect long-run economic growth?

Higher savings rates provide more funds for capital investment, and greater capital investment (which often also embodies advances in technology) increases productivity and output growth.

4. Why would you expect an inverse relationship between self-sufficiency and real GDP per capita?

Because of different endowments and abilities, both people and countries have different opportunity costs of production for large numbers of goods and services (different comparative advantages). Specialization and large-scale production, combined with domestic and international trade, allows an expansion of productive and consumption possibilities by taking advantage of lower cost production, while self-sufficiency sacrifices those potential gains. Further, farmers tend to be self-employed, while non-farmers usually are not, and economic development tends to decrease the proportion of the population in agriculture.

5. If a couple was concerned about their retirement, why could that lead them to have more children if they lived in an agricultural society, but fewer children if they were in an urban society?

In an agricultural society, children can typically "earn their own keep," making them financially "profitable" investments, as well as helping to provide for their parents' retirement. In an urban society, however, children are a substantial financial liability to their parents.

6. Why is the effective use of land, labor, capital, and entrepreneurial activities dependent on the protection of property rights?

Without protected property rights, both production and exchange become far more difficult, costly, and uncertain, undermining the ability of market incentives to induce the effective use of the factors of production. Similarly, without protected property rights, the rewards to investors and those who seek new and better ways of doing things are also more uncertain, reducing the incentives to make such investments and innovations.

CHAPTER 14: AGGREGATE DEMAND

14.1 Consumption, Investment, Government Spending, and Net Exports

1. What are the major components of aggregate demand?

The major components of aggregate demand are consumption, planned investment, government purchases, and net exports.

2. If consumption is a direct function of disposable income, how does an increase in personal taxes or a decrease in transfer payments affect consumption?

Either an increase in taxes or a decrease in transfer payments decreases the disposable income of households, which reduces their demands for consumption goods.

3. Would you spend more or less on additional consumption if your marginal propensity to consume increased?

Because the definition of the marginal propensity to consume is the fraction of an increase in disposable income one would spend on additional consumption purchases, you would spend more, the higher your marginal propensity to consume.

4. What would an increase in exports do to aggregate demand, other things being equal? An increase in imports? An increase in both imports and exports, where the change in exports was greater in magnitude?

An increase in exports would increase aggregate demand, other things being equal, because net exports are part of aggregate demand. An increase in imports would decrease aggregate demand, other things being equal, by reducing net exports (demand shifts from domestic producers to foreign producers). An increase in both imports and exports will increase aggregate demand if the increase in exports exceeds the increase in imports, other things being equal, because the combination will increase net exports.

14.2 The Investment and Saving Market

1. Why does the investment demand curve slope downward?

As the real interest rate falls, additional investment projects with lower expected rates of return become profitable for firms, and the quantity of investment demanded rises.

2. What factors can shift the investment demand curve?

The investment demand curve would increase (shift to the right) if firms expect higher rates of return on their investments; if product and process innovation reduce the costs of production; if profitable new products are developed; if inventories are depleted below the levels desired by firms; if forecasts for future expected sales are strong; or if business taxes are lowered. The investment demand curve would decrease (shift to the left) in the opposite situations.

3. Why does the saving supply curve slope upward?

At a higher real interest rate, the reward for saving and supplying funds to financial markets is greater, leading to an increased quantity of saving supplied.

4. What factors can shift the saving supply curve?

The saving supply curve would increase (shift to the right) if disposable (after tax) income rose or if people expected lower future earnings. The saving supply curve would decrease (shift to the left) if disposable (after tax) income fell or if people expected higher future earnings.

5. How is the real interest rate determined?

The real interest rate is determined by the intersection of the investment demand curve and the saving supply curve, where desired investment equals desired national saving.

6. How are shortages and surpluses eliminated in the investment and saving market?

If the real interest rate was above the equilibrium real interest rate, the quantity of savings supplied would be greater than the quantity of investment demanded—there would be a surplus of savings. As savers (lenders) compete against each other to attract investment demanders (borrowers), the real interest rate will fall toward the equilibrium level. If the real interest rate was below the equilibrium real interest rate, the quantity of savings supplied would be less than the quantity of investment demanded—there would be a shortage of savings. As demanders (borrowers) compete against each other to attract savers (lenders), the real interest rate will rise toward the equilibrium level.

14.3 The Aggregate Demand Curve

1. Why is the aggregate demand curve downward sloping?

Aggregate demand shows what happens to the total quantity of all real goods and services demanded in the economy as a whole (that is the quantity of real GDP demanded) at different price levels. Aggregate demand is downward sloping because of the real wealth effect, the interest rate effect, and the open economy effect as the price level changes.

2. How does an increased price level reduce the quantities of investment goods and consumer durables demanded?

An increased price level increases the demand for money, which, in turn, increases interest rates. Higher interest rates increase the opportunity cost of financing both investment goods and consumer durables, reducing the quantities of investment goods and consumer durables demanded.

3. What is the real wealth effect, and how does it imply a downward-sloping aggregate demand curve?

A reduced price level increases the real value of people's currency holdings, and as their real wealth increases, so does the quantity of real goods and services demanded, particularly consumption goods. Therefore, the aggregate demand curve, which represents the relationship between the price level and the quantity of real goods and services demanded, slopes downward as a result.

4. What is the interest rate effect, and how does it imply a downward-sloping aggregate demand curve?

A reduced price level reduces the demand for money, which lowers interest rates, which increases the quantity of investment goods and consumer durable goods people are willing to purchase. Therefore, the aggregate demand curve, which represents the relationship between the price level and the quantity of real goods and services demanded, slopes downward as a result.

5. What is the open economy effect, and how does it imply a downward-sloping aggregate demand curve?

The open economy effect occurs because a higher domestic price level raises the prices of domestically produced goods relative to the prices of imported goods. That reduces the quantity of domestically produced goods demanded (by both citizens and foreigners), as now relatively cheaper foreign-made goods are substituted for them. The result is again a downward-sloping aggregate demand curve, as a higher price level results in a lower quantity of domestic real GDP demanded.

14.4 Shifts in the Aggregate Demand Curve

1. How is the distinction between a change in demand and a change in quantity demanded the same for aggregate demand as for the demand for a particular good?

Just as a change in the price of a particular good changes its quantity demanded, but not its demand, a change in the price level changes the quantity of real GDP demanded, but not aggregate demand. Just as a change in any of the PYNTE demand curve shifters (other factors than the price of the good itself) changes the demand for a particular good, a change in any of the $C + I + G + (X - M)$ components of aggregate demand not caused by a change in the price level changes aggregate demand.

2. What happens to aggregate demand if the demand for consumption goods increases, *ceteris paribus*?

Because consumption purchases are part of aggregate demand, an increase in the demand for consumption goods increases aggregate demand, *ceteris paribus.*

3. What happens to aggregate demand if the demand for investment goods falls, *ceteris paribus*?

Because planned investment purchases are part of aggregate demand, a falling demand for investment goods makes aggregate demand fall, *ceteris paribus.*

4. Why would an increase in the money supply tend to increase expenditures on consumption and investment, *ceteris paribus*?

An increase in the money supply would increase how many now relatively more plentiful dollars people would be willing to pay for goods in general. This would increase expenditures on consumption and investment, increasing aggregate demand, *ceteris paribus.*

CHAPTER 15: AGGREGATE SUPPLY AND MACROECONOMIC EQUILIBRIUM

15.1 The Aggregate Supply Curve

1. What relationship does the short-run aggregate supply curve represent?

The short-run aggregate supply curve represents the relationship between the total quantity of final goods and services that suppliers are willing and able to produces (the quantity of real GDP supplied) and the overall price level, before all input prices have had time to completely adjust to the price level.

2. What relationship does the long-run aggregate supply curve represent?

The long-run aggregate supply curve represents the relationship between the total quantity of final goods and services that suppliers are willing and able to produce (the quantity of real GDP supplied) and the overall price level, once all input prices have had time to completely adjust to the price level (actually, it shows there is no relationship between these two variables, once input prices have had sufficient time to completely adjust to the price level).

3. Why is focusing on producers' profit margins helpful in understanding the logic of the short-run aggregate supply curve?

Profit incentives are the key to understanding what happens to real output as the price level changes in the short run (before input prices completely adjust to the price level). When the prices of outputs rise relative to the prices of inputs (costs), as when aggregate demand increases in the short run, it increases profit margins, which increases the incentives to produce, which leads to increased real output. When the prices of outputs fall relative to the prices of inputs (costs), as when aggregate demand decreases in the short run, it decreases profit margins, which decreases the incentives to produce, which leads to decreased real output.

4. Why is the short-run aggregate supply curve upward sloping, while the long-run aggregate supply curve is vertical at the natural rate of output?

The short-run aggregate supply curve is upward sloping because in the short run, before input prices have completely adjusted to the price level, an increase in the price level increases profit margins by increasing output prices relative to input prices, which leads producers to increase real output. The long-run aggregate supply curve is vertical because in the long run, when input prices have completely adjusted to changes in the price level, input prices as well as output prices have adjusted to the price level, so that profit margins in real terms do not change as the price level changes, and therefore there is no relationship between the price level and real output in the long run. The long-run aggregate supply curve is vertical at the natural rate of real output because that is the maximum output level allowed by capital, labor, and technological inputs at full employment (that is, given the determinants of the economy's production possibilities curve), which is therefore sustainable over time.

5. What would the short-run aggregate supply curve look like if input prices always changed instantaneously as soon as output prices changed? Why?

If input prices always changed instantaneously as soon as output prices changed, the short-run aggregate supply curve would look the same as the long-run aggregate supply curve—vertical at the natural rate of real output. That is because both input and output prices would then change proportionately, so that real profit margins (the incentives facing producers), and therefore real output, would not change as the price level changes.

6. If the price of cotton increased 10 percent when cotton producers thought other prices were rising 5 percent over the same period, what would happen to the quantity of RGDP supplied in the cotton industry? What if cotton producers thought other prices were rising 20 percent over the same period?

If the price of cotton increased 10 percent when cotton producers thought other prices were rising 5 percent over the same period, the quantity of RGDP supplied in the cotton industry would increase, because with other prices (including input prices) falling relative to cotton prices, the profitability of growing cotton would be rising. If the price of cotton increased 10 percent when cotton producers thought other prices were rising 20 percent over the same period, the quantity of RGDP supplied in the cotton industry would decrease, because with other prices (including input prices) rising relative to cotton prices, the profitability of growing cotton would be falling.

15.2 Shifts in the Aggregate Supply Curve

1. Which of the aggregate supply curves will shift in response to a change in the expected price level? Why?

The short-run aggregate supply curve shifts in response to a change in the expected price level, by changing the expected production costs, and therefore the expected profitability, of producing output at any given output price level. Remember that the long-run aggregate supply curve assumes people have had enough time to completely adjust to a changing price level, so a change in the expected price level does not change expected profit margins along the long-run aggregate supply curve.

2. Why do lower input costs increase the level of RGDP supplied at any given price level?

Lower input costs increase the level of RGDP supplied at any given (output) price level by increasing the profit margin for any given level of output prices.

3. What would discovering huge new supplies of oil and natural gas do to the short-run and long-run aggregate supply curves?

Discovering huge new supplies of oil and natural gas would increase both the short-run and long-run aggregate supply curves, because those additional resources would allow more to be produced in the short run, at any given output price level, as well as on a sustainable, long-run basis (since such a discovery would shift the economy's production possibilities curve outward).

4. What would happen to short-run and long-run aggregate supply curves if the government required every firm to file explanatory paperwork each time a decision was made?

This would shift both the short-run and long-run aggregate supply curves to the left. It would permanently raise producers' costs of producing any level of output, which would reduce how much producers would produce in the short run at any given price level, as well as on a sustainable, long-run basis (since such a requirement would shift the economy's production possibilities curve inward).

5. What would happen to the short-run and long-run aggregate supply curves if the capital stock grew and available supplies of natural resources expanded over the same period of time?

Both an increase in the capital stock and increased available supplies of natural resources would shift both the short-run and long-run aggregate supply curves to the right (shifting the economy's production possibilities curve outward), increasing the both short-run and sustainable levels of real output.

6. How can a change in input prices change the short-run aggregate supply curve but not the long-run aggregate supply curve? How could it change both long-run and short-run aggregate supply?

A temporary change in input prices can change the short-run aggregate supply curve by changing profit margins in the short run. However, when input prices return to their previous levels (reflecting a return to their previous relative scarcity) in the long run, the sustainable level of real output will be no different than before. If, on the other hand, input price changes reflect a permanently changed supply of inputs (lower input prices reflecting an increased supply), a change in input prices would increase both the long-run and short-run aggregate supply curves by increasing the real output producible both currently and on an ongoing basis (permanently shifting out the economy's production possibilities curve).

7. What would happen to short- and long-run aggregate supply if unusually good weather led to bumper crops of most agricultural produce?

Because this reflects only a temporary change in output, it would increase the short-run aggregate supply curve, but not the long-run aggregate supply curve.

8. If OPEC temporarily restricted the world output of oil, what would happen to short- and long-run aggregate supply? What would happen if the output restriction were permanent?

A temporary oil output restriction would temporarily increase oil (energy input) prices, reducing the short-run aggregate supply curve (shifting it left) but not the long-run aggregate supply curve. If the oil output restriction was permanent, the oil price increase would also reduce the level of real output producible on a sustainable basis, and so would shift both short-run aggregate supply and long-run aggregate supply to the left.

15.3 Macroeconomic Equilibrium

1. What is a contractionary gap?

A contractionary gap exists when the macroeconomy is in equilibrium at less than the potential output of the economy, because aggregate demand is insufficient to fully employ all of society's resources.

2. What is an expansionary gap?

An expansionary gap exists when the macroeconomy is in equilibrium at more than the potential output of the economy, because aggregate demand is so high that the economy is operating temporarily beyond its long-run capacity.

3. What is demand-pull inflation?

Demand-pull inflation is an increased price level caused by an increase in aggregate demand.

4. What is cost-push inflation?

Cost-push inflation is output price inflation caused by an increase in input prices (that is, by supply-side forces, rather than demand-side forces). It is illustrated by a leftward or upward shift of the short-run aggregate supply curve, for given long-run aggregate supply and demand curves.

5. Starting from long-run equilibrium on the long-run aggregate supply curve, what happens to the price level, real output, and unemployment as a result of cost-push inflation?

Starting from long-run equilibrium on the long-run aggregate supply curve, cost-push inflation causes the price level to rise, real output to fall, and unemployment to rise in the short run.

6. How would a drop in consumer confidence impact the short-run macroeconomy?

A drop in consumer confidence would decrease the demand for consumer goods, other things being equal, which would reduce (shift left) the aggregate demand curve, resulting in a lower price level, lower real output, and increased unemployment in the short run for a given short-run aggregate supply curve.

7. What would happen to the price level, real output, and unemployment in the short-run if world oil prices fell sharply?

If world oil prices fell sharply, it would increase (shift right) the short-run aggregate supply curve, resulting in a lower price level, greater real output, and reduced unemployment in the short run for a given aggregate demand curve.

8. What are sticky prices and wages?

Sticky prices and wages express the idea that input prices may be very slow to adjust in the downward direction, so that the economy's adjustment mechanism may take a substantial amount of time to self-correct from a recession.

9. How does the economy self-correct?

The economy self-corrects from a short-run recession through declining wages and prices, brought on by reduced demand for labor and other inputs; the economy self-corrects from a short-run boom through increasing wages and prices, brought on by increased demand for labor and other inputs.

CHAPTER 16: FISCAL POLICY

16.1 Fiscal Policy

1. If, as part of its fiscal policy, the federal government increased its purchases of goods and services, would that be an expansionary or contractionary tactic?

An increase in government purchases of goods and services would be an expansionary tactic, increasing aggregate demand, other things being equal.

2. If the federal government decreased its purchases of goods and services, would the budget deficit increase or decrease?

If the federal government decreased its purchases of goods and services, for a given level of tax revenue, the budget deficit (the difference between government spending and government revenues) would decrease.

3. If the federal government increased taxes or decreased transfer payments, would that be an expansionary or contractionary fiscal policy?

Either an increase in taxes or a decrease in transfer payment would be a contractionary tactic, decreasing aggregate demand by decreasing people's disposable incomes and therefore reducing the demand for consumption goods.

4. If the federal government increased taxes or decreased transfer payments, would the budget deficit increase or decrease?

If the federal government increased taxes or decreased transfer payments, for a given level of government purchases, a budget deficit (the difference between government spending and government revenues) would decrease.

5. If the federal government increased government purchases and lowered taxes at the same time, would the budget deficit increase or decrease?

Increased government purchases would increase a budget deficit, other things being equal. Lowered taxes would also increase a budget deficit, other things being equal. Therefore, both changes together would increase a budget deficit.

16.2 Government: Spending and Taxation

1. What options are available for a government to finance its spending?

A government can finance its spending through taxes, borrowing, or inflation.

16.3 The Multiplier Effect

1. How does the multiplier effect work?

The multiplier effect arises because the increased purchases during each "round" of the multiplier process generates increased incomes to the owners of the resources used to produce the goods purchased, which leads them to increase consumption purchases in the next "round" of the process. The result is a final increase in total purchases, including the induced consumption purchases, that is greater than the initial increase in purchases.

2. What is the marginal propensity to consume?

The marginal propensity to consume is the proportion of an additional dollar of income that would be spent on additional consumption purchases.

3. Why is the marginal propensity to consume always less than one?

This is true because all expenditures have to ultimately be financed out of income, so that each dollar of added income cannot lead to more than a dollar of added purchases. In addition, taxes and savings also have to be financed out of income.

4. Why does the multiplier effect get larger as the marginal propensity to consume gets larger?

The larger is the marginal propensity to consume, the larger is the fraction of increased income in each "round" of the multiplier process that will go to additional consumption purchases. Because each round of the multiplier process will therefore be larger the greater the marginal propensity to consume, the multiplier will also be larger.

5. If an increase in government purchases leads to a reduction in private-sector purchases, why will the effect on the economy be less than indicated by the multiplier?

At the same time that the increased government purchases are leading to a multiple expansion of income and purchases for one set of citizens, the "crowded out" private-sector purchases are causing a multiple contraction of income and purchases for other citizens. The net effect on the economy will therefore be less than the increase in government purchases times the multiplier.

16.4 Fiscal Policy and the *AD/AS* Model

1. If the economy is in recession, what sorts of fiscal policy changes would tend to bring it out of recession?

If the economy is in recession, aggregate demand intersects short-run aggregate supply to the left of the long-run aggregate supply curve. Expansionary fiscal policy—increased government purchases, decreased taxes, and/or increased transfer payments—addresses a recession by shifting aggregate demand to the right.

2. If the economy is at a short-run equilibrium at greater than full employment, what sorts of fiscal policy changes would tend to bring the economy back to a full-employment equilibrium?

If the economy is at a short-run equilibrium at greater than full employment, aggregate demand intersects short-run aggregate supply to the right of the long-run aggregate supply curve. Contractionary fiscal policy—decreased government purchases, increased taxes, and/or decreased transfer payments—addresses a short-run equilibrium at greater than full employment by shifting aggregate demand to the left.

3. What effects would an expansionary fiscal policy have on the price level and real GDP, starting from a full employment equilibrium?

Starting from a full employment equilibrium, an expansionary fiscal policy would increase aggregate demand, increasing the price level and real GDP in the short run. However, in the long run, real GDP will return to its full employment long-run equilibrium level as input prices adjust (the short-run aggregate supply curve shifts up or left), and only the price level will end up higher.

4. What effects would a contractionary fiscal policy have on the price level and real GDP, starting from a full-employment equilibrium?

Starting from a full-employment equilibrium, a contractionary fiscal policy would decrease aggregate demand, decreasing the price level and real GDP in the short run. However, in the long run, real GDP will return to its full-employment long-run equilibrium level as input prices adjust (the short-run aggregate supply curve shifts down or right), and the price level will end up lower.

16.5 Automatic Stabilizers

1. How does the tax system act as an automatic stabilizer?

Some taxes, such as progressive income taxes and corporate profits taxes, automatically increase as the economy grows, and this increase in taxes restrains disposable income and the growth of aggregate demand below what it would have been otherwise. Similarly, they automatically decrease in recessions, and this decrease in taxes increases disposable income and acts as a partial offset to the fall in aggregate demand. The result is reduced business cycle instability.

2. Are automatic stabilizers impacted by a time lag? Why or why not?

Because automatic stabilizers respond to business cycle changes without the need for legislative or executive action, there is no appreciable lag between when business cycle conditions justify a change in them and when they do change. However, there is still a lag between when those stabilizers change and when their full effects are felt.

3. Why are transfer payments, such as unemployment compensation, effective automatic stabilizers?

Some transfer payment programs, such as unemployment compensation, act as automatic stabilizers because when business cycle conditions worsen, people can start receiving increased transfer payments as soon as they become eligible (lose their jobs, in the case of unemployment compensation). The same is true of some other welfare type programs, such as food stamps.

16.6 Possible Obstacles to Effective Fiscal Policy

1. Why does a larger government budget deficit increase the magnitude of the crowding-out effect?

A larger government budget deficit increases the demand for loanable funds, increasing the magnitude of the increase in interest rates, crowding out more private sector investment as a result.

2. Why does fiscal policy have a smaller effect on aggregate demand, the greater the crowding-out effect?

The greater the crowding-out effect, the smaller is the net effect (the increase in government purchases minus the private sector purchases crowded out) fiscal policy has on aggregate demand. For example, if each dollar of added government purchases crowds out fifty cents worth of private sector purchases, fiscal policy will have only half the effect on aggregate demand that it would if there was no crowding-out effect.

3. How do time lags impact the effectiveness of fiscal policy?

The time lag between when a policy change is desirable and when it is adopted and implemented (for data gathering, decision making, and so on), as well as the time lag between when a policy is implemented and when it has its effects, make it difficult for fiscal policy to have the desired effect at the desired time, particularly given the difficulty in forecasting the future course of the economy.

16.7 Supply-Side Fiscal Policy

1. Is supply-side economics more concerned with short-run economic stabilization or long-run economic growth?

Supply-side economics is more concerned with long-run economic growth than short-run economic stabilization. It is focused primarily on adopting policies that will increase the long-run aggregate supply curve (society's production possibilities curve) over time, by improving incentives to work, save and invest.

2. Why could you say that supply-side economics is really more about after-tax wages and after-tax returns on investment than it is about tax rates?

Because changes in after-tax wages and after-tax returns on investment are the incentives that change people's behavior, not changes in the tax rates themselves.

3. Why do government regulations have the same sorts of effects on businesses as taxes?

To the extent that government regulations impose added costs on businesses, the effects of those added costs are the same—a decrease (leftward or upward shift) in supply—as if a tax of that amount was imposed on the business.

4. Why aren't the full effects of supply-side policies seen quickly?

It will often take a substantial period of time before improved productive incentives will have their complete effects. For instance, an increase in the after-tax return on investment will increase investment, but it will take many years before the capital stock has completed its adjustment. The same is true for human capital investments in education, research and development, and so on—if a student or researcher learns more today, the full effect won't be observed immediately.

5. If taxes increase, what would you expect to happen to employment in the underground economy? Why?

The primary benefit of employment in the underground economy is the savings from not having to pay taxes (or bear some of the costs of regulations imposed on "legitimate" employment). The cost includes the risk of being caught, the difficulty of dealing on a cash-only or barter basis, and so on. As tax rates increase, the benefits of working in the underground economy increase relative to the costs, and employment in the underground economy will tend to increase, other things being equal.

16.8 The National Debt

1. What will happen to the interest rate when there is a budget deficit?

When the government borrows to finance a budget deficit, it causes the interest rate to rise, other things being equal.

2. What will happen to the interest rate when there is a budget surplus?

When there is a budget surplus, it adds to national saving and lowers the interest rate, other things being equal.

3. What are the intergenerational effects of a national debt?

Arguments can be made that the generation of the taxpayers living at the time that the debt is issued shoulders the true cost of the debt, because the debt permits the government to take command of resources that would be available for other, private uses. However, the issuance of debt does involve some intergenerational transfer of incomes. Long after federal debt is issued, a new generation of taxpayers is making interest payments to persons of the generation that bought the bonds issued to finance that debt. If public debt is created intelligently, however, the "burden" of the debt should be less than the benefits derived from the resources acquired as a result; this is particularly true when the debt allows for an expansion in real economic activity or for the development of vital infrastructure for the future.

4. What must be true for Americans to be better off as a result of an increase in the national debt?

For Americans to be better off as a result of an increase in the federal debt, the value of the investments and other spending financed by the debt must be greater than the cost of financing it.

CHAPTER 17: MONEY AND THE BANKING SYSTEM

17.1 What Is Money?

1. If everyone in an economy accepted poker chips as payment in exchange for goods and services, would poker chips be money?

Because money is anything that is generally accepted in exchange for goods or services (a medium of exchange), if everyone in an economy accepted poker chips as payment in exchange for goods and services, poker chips would be money.

2. If you were buying a pack of gum, would using currency or a demand deposit have lower transactions costs? What if you were buying a house?
If you were buying a pack of gum, or making any other such small purchase, using currency would generally have lower transactions costs than a demand deposit (checking account). However, if you were buying a house, or any other very large purchase, using a demand deposit would generally have lower transactions costs than paying with currency (it would be cheaper, easier, and safer, and it would generate a more reliable financial record).
3. What is the main advantage of transactions deposits for tax purposes? What is its main disadvantage for tax purposes?
The main advantage of transactions deposits for tax purposes is that they provide more reliable financial records for complying with record-keeping requirements for tax purposes. On the other hand, the financial records that transactions deposits generate are their main disadvantage for those who wish to hide their financial activities from tax authorities.
4. Are credit cards money?
Credit cards are not money. They are actually guaranteed loans available on demand to users, which can be triggered by consumers, which are convenient substitutes for making transactions directly with money. That is, they are substitutes for the use of money in exchange.
5. What are M1 and M2?
M1 is a narrow definition of money that focuses on money's use as a means of payment (for transactions purposes). M1 includes currency in circulation, checkable deposits, and travelers' checks. M2 is a broader definition of money that focuses on money's use as a highly liquid store of purchasing power or savings. M2 equals M1 plus other "near moneys," including savings accounts, small denomination time deposits, and money market mutual funds.
6. How have interest-earning checking accounts and overdraft protection led to the relative decline in demand deposits?
Interest-earning checking accounts provide the same ability to make transactions as non-interest earning demand deposit accounts, but are more attractive to many consumers because they earn interest. Overdraft protection means that consumers do not have to keep as much money in demand deposit accounts "just in case," to protect against overdrawing their accounts.

17.2 The Functions of Money

1. Why does the advantage of monetary exchange over barter increase as an economy becomes more complex?
As the economy becomes more complex, the number of exchanges between people in the economy grows very rapidly. This means that the transaction cost advantages of using money over barter for those exchanges also grows very rapidly as the economy becomes more complex.
2. How can uncertain and rapid rates of inflation erode money's ability to perform its functions efficiently?
Uncertain and rapid rates of inflation erode money's ability to perform its functions efficiently because money lowers transactions costs most effectively when its value is stable, and therefore more predictable. Uncertain and rapid rates of inflation reduce the stability and predictability of the value of money, reducing its usefulness as a universally understood store of value. It therefore reduces money's ability to reduce transactions costs.
3. In a world of barter, would useful financial statements, like balance sheets, be possible? Would stock markets be possible? Would it be possible to build cars?
In a world of barter, there is no common store of value to allow comparisons of all the "apples and oranges" that must be summarized in financial statements, making such statements virtually impossible. Without money to act as a common store of value, stock and other financial markets, as well as very complex (many transactions) production processes would also be virtually impossible.
4. Why do you think virtually all societies create something to function as money?
Having some good function as money lowers transactions costs, allowing increasing specialization and exchange to create increasing wealth for a society. That increase in wealth made possible by using money is why virtually all societies create something to function as money.

17.3 How Banks Create Money

1. What is happening to the number of banks now that interstate banking is allowed?
Laws against interstate banking prevented the formation of large, interstate banking organizations, resulting in a large number of American banks. However, now that interstate banking is allowed, mergers are resulting in fewer, larger, interstate banks.
2. In what way is it true that "banks make money by making money"?
Banks make money (profits) by loaning out their deposits at a higher interest rate than they pay their depositors. However, it is the extension of new loans in search of profits that creates new demand deposits, increasing the stock of money.
3. How do legal reserve deposit regulations lower bank profits?
Unlike other bank assets, legal reserves do not earn interest. Therefore, requiring a larger portion of bank assets to be held in such non-interest earning than prudent banking practice would dictate reduces bank earnings and profits.
4. Is a demand deposit an asset or a liability?
A demand deposit is an asset for its owner, but a liability of the bank at which the account is kept.
5. If the Bonnie and Clyde National Bank's only deposits were demand deposits of $20 million, and it faced a 10 percent reserve requirement, how much money would it be required to hold in reserves?
The Bonnie and Clyde National Bank would have to hold 10 percent of its $20 million, or $2 million, in demand deposits as reserves.
6. Suppose you found $10,000 while digging in your back yard and you deposited it in the bank. How would your new demand deposit account create a situation of excess reserves at your bank?
A new $10,000 deposit adds that amount to both your demand deposit account and to the reserves of your bank. But only a fraction of the added reserves are required by the addition to your demand deposit account. The rest are excess reserves, which the bank will look to convert to interest-earning loans or other assets.

17.4 The Money Multiplier

1. Why do the supply of money and the volume of bank loans both increase or decrease at the same time?
The supply of money and the volume of bank loans both increase or decrease at the same time because issuing new bank loans adds to the money supply, while calling in existing bank loans reduces the money supply.
2. Why would each bank in the money supply multiple expansion process lend out a larger fraction of any new deposit it receives, the lower the reserve requirement?
Each bank in the money supply multiple expansion process can lend up to the amount of its excess reserves. But the excess reserves created by each dollar deposited in a bank equals 1 minus the required reserve ratio. The lower this reserve requirement, the greater the excess reserves created by each new deposit, and therefore the greater the fraction any new deposit that will be loaned out in this process.
3. If a particular bank with a reserve requirement of 10 percent has $30,000 in new cash deposits, how much money could it create through making new loans?
A bank can loan up to the amount of its excess reserves. If it faces a reserve requirement of 10 percent, a new $30,000 cash deposit, would add $3,000 (10 percent of $30, 000) to its required reserves, but $30,000 to its total reserves. That deposit would therefore create $27,000 in excess reserves that the bank could lend out, and that $27,000 in increased loans would increase the money stock by an equal amount.
4. Why do banks choosing to hold excess reserves or borrowers choosing to hold some of their loans in the form of currency reduce the actual impact of the money multiplier below that indicated by the multiplier formula?
If banks choose to hold excess reserves, each bank in the money supply expansion process will lend out less, and therefore create less new money, than if they loaned out all their excess reserves. The result will be a smaller money supply than that indicated by the multiplier formula, because that formula assumes banks lend out all their excess reserves. If borrowers hold some of their loans as currency, that would reduce the amount of vault cash, which counts as a reserve, at banks. This would reduce the amount that could be loaned at each stage of the money supply creation process, and would therefore reduce the actual money multiplier below the level indicated by the multiplier formula.

17.5 The Collapse of America's Banking System, 1920–1933

1. How did the combination of increased holding of excess reserves by banks and currency by the public lead to bank failures in the 1930s?
The desire by the public for increased currency holdings, caused largely by the fear of bank failures, also forced banks to sharply increase excess reserves and reduce lending, together causing a sharp fall in the money stock. Despite substantial excess reserves, however, bank runs led to the failure of even many conservatively run banks.
2. What are the four reasons cited in the text for the collapse of the U.S. banking system in this period?
The cited reasons are (1) the large number of small banks, which were more at risk from bank runs; (2) governmental attempts to stem the distress in the banking industry that were both weak and too late; (3) the absence of deposit insurance that would have bolstered consumer confidence; and (4) fear that the economy was in a continuous downward cycle, so that there was little basis for optimism that bank loans would be safely repaid.
3. What is the FDIC, and how did its establishment increase bank stability and reassure depositors?

The Federal Deposit Insurance Corporation insures bank deposits. That guarantee of deposits eliminated the risk to depositors if their bank failed, thus eliminating the bank runs that resulted from the fear of bank insolvency. Without having to face the risk of bank runs, banks were more stable.

CHAPTER 18: THE FEDERAL RESERVE SYSTEM AND MONETARY POLICY

18.1 The Federal Reserve System

1. What are the six primary functions of a central bank?
A central bank (1) is a "banker's bank," where commercial banks maintain their own deposits; (2) provides services, such as transferring funds and checks, for commercial banks; (3) serves as the major bank for the federal government; (4) buys and sells foreign currencies and assists in transactions with other countries; (5) serves as a "lender of last resort" for banking institutions in financial distress; and (6) regulates the size of the money supply.

2. What is the FOMC and what does it do?
The Federal Open Market Committee is a committee of the Federal Reserve System, made up of the seven members of the Board of Governors, the President of the New York Federal Reserve Bank, and four other presidents of Federal Reserve Banks. It makes most of the key decisions influencing the direction and size of changes in the money stock.

3. How is the Fed tied to the executive branch? How is it insulated from executive branch pressure to influence monetary policy?
The president selects the seven members of the Board of Governors, subject to Senate approval, one every two years, for 14-year terms. He also selects the Chair of the Board of Governors for a 4-year term. However, because the President can only select one member every two years, he cannot appoint a majority of the Board of Governors for his term in office. Also, the President cannot use reappointment of his nominees or threats of firing members to pressure the Fed on monetary policy.

18.2 The Quantity Equation of Money

1. If M1 is $10 billion and M1 velocity is 4, what is the product of the price level and real output? If the price level is 2, what does real output equal?
If the money supply is $10 billion and velocity is 4 (so that $M \times V =$ $40 billion), the product of the price level and real output ($P \times Q$, or nominal output), must also $40 billion. If the price level is 2, real output would equal the $40 billion nominal output divided by the price level of 2, or $20 billion.

2. If nominal GDP is $200 billion and the money supply is $50 billion, what must velocity be?
Because $M \times V = P \times Q$, $V = P \times Q \div M$. Thus $V =$ $200 billion ÷ $50 billion, or 4, in this case.

3. If the money supply increases and velocity does not change, what will happen to nominal GDP?
If M increases and V does not change, $M \times V$ must increase. Because $M \times V = P \times Q$, and $P \times Q$ equals nominal GDP, nominal GDP must also increase as a result.

4. If velocity is unstable, does stabilizing the money supply help stabilize the economy? Why or why not?
If V is unstable, stabilizing M does not stabilize $M \times V$. Because $M \times V$ will not be stabilized, $P \times Q$, or nominal GDP, will not be stabilized either.

18.3 Implementing Monetary Policy: Tools of the Fed

1. What three main tactics could the Fed use in pursuing a contractionary monetary policy?
The Fed could conduct an open market sale of government securities (bonds), an increase in reserve requirements, or an increase in the discount rate if it wanted to pursue a contractionary monetary policy.

2. What three main tactics could the Fed use in pursuing an expansionary monetary policy?
The Fed could conduct an open market purchase of government securities (bonds), a decrease in reserve requirements, or a decrease in the discount rate if it wanted to pursue an expansionary monetary policy.

3. Would the money stock rise or fall if the Fed made an open market purchase of government bonds, *ceteris paribus?*
An open market purchase of government bonds by the Fed would increase banking reserves, thereby increasing the money stock, *ceteris paribus.*

4. If the Fed raised the discount rate from 12 to 15 percent, what effect would that have on the money supply?
Raising the discount rate makes it more costly for banks to borrow reserves directly from the Fed. To the extent that banks borrow fewer reserves directly from the Fed, this reduces total banking reserves, thereby decreasing the money stock, *ceteris paribus.*

5. What is moral suasion, and why would the Fed use this tactic?
Moral suasion is the term used to describe Federal Reserve attempts to persuade or influence banks to follow a particular course of action (e.g., be more selective in making loans) they might not otherwise take.

18.4 Money, Interest Rates, and Aggregate Demand

1. What are the determinants of the demand for money?
There are three motives for the demand for money: transactions purposes (to facilitate exchange), precautionary purposes (just in case), and asset purposes (to keep some assets in the liquid form of money). The demand for money increases (shifts to the right) if either real incomes or the price level is higher, because that will increase the nominal amount of transactions. A decrease in the interest rate will decrease the opportunity cost of holding money, increasing the quantity of money people wish to hold (moving down along the demand for money curve), but not increasing the demand for money (shifting the demand for money curve).

2. If the earnings available on other financial assets rose, would want to hold more or less money?
Because holding wealth in the form of other financial assets is the alternative to holding it in the form of money, non-money financial assets are substitutes for holding money. When the earnings (interest) available on alternative financial assets rise, the opportunity cost of holding money instead also rises, so that you would want to hold less money, other things being equal.

3. For the economy as a whole, why would individuals want to hold more money as GDP rises?
Individuals conduct a larger volume of transactions as GDP rises. Therefore, they would want to hold more money as GDP rises in order to keep the costs of those increasing transactions down.

4. Why might people who expect a major market "correction" (a fall in the value of stock holdings) wish to increase their holdings of money?
When the value of alternative financial assets is expected to fall, holding money, which will not similarly fall in value, becomes more attractive. Therefore, in the case of an expected fall in the value of stocks, bonds, or other financial assets, people would want to increase their holdings of money as a precaution.

5. How is the money market equilibrium determined?
In the money market, money demand and money supply determine the equilibrium nominal interest rate.

6. Who controls the supply of money in the money market?
The banking system, through the loan expansion process, directly determines the supply of money in the money market. However, the Fed, through the policy variables it controls (primarily open market operations, reserve requirements and the discount rate) indirectly controls the supply of money by controlling the level of reserves and the money multiplier.

7. How does an increase in income or a decrease in the interest rate affect the demand for money?
An increase in income increases (shifts right) the demand for money, as people want to hold down the transactions costs on the increasing volume of transactions taking place. A decrease in interest rates, on the other hand, increases the quantity of money demanded (moving down along the money demand curve), but does not change the demand for money.

8. What Federal Reserve Policies would shift the money supply curve to the left?
An open market sale of government securities (bonds), an increase in reserve requirements, or an increase in the discount rate would shift the money supply curve to the left.

9. Will an increase in the money supply increase or decrease the short-run equilibrium real interest rate, other things being equal?
An increase in the money supply would decrease the short-run equilibrium real interest rate, other things being equal, as the rightward shift of the money supply curve pushes the money market equilibrium down along the money demand curve.

10. Will an increase in national income increase or decrease the short-run equilibrium real interest rate, other things being equal?
An increase in national income will shift the money demand curve to the right, which would increase the short-run equilibrium real interest rate, other things being equal.

11. What is the relationship between interest rates and aggregate demand in monetary policy?
Lower interest rates will tend to stimulate aggregate demand for goods and services, other things being equal.

12. When the Fed sells bonds, what happens to the price of bonds and interest rates?
When the Fed sells bonds, it increases the supply of bonds, decreasing bond prices. The process results in reserves being removed from the banking system when the buyer's payment to the Fed payment is subtracted from his or her bank's reserve account, leading to a decrease in the money supply and an increase in the interest rate.

13. When the Fed buys bonds, what happens to the price of bonds and interest rates?

When the Fed buys bonds, it increases the demand for bonds, increasing bond prices. The process results in reserves being added to the banking system when the Fed's payment is deposited back into the banking system, leading to an increase in the money supply and a decrease in the interest rate.

14. Why is there an inverse relation between bond prices and interest rates?
There is an inverse relation between bond prices and interest rates because the process that creates more money and thus lowers interest rates is triggered by the Fed buying bonds, which bids up bond prices. Similarly, the process that reduces the money supply and thus raises interest rates is triggered by the Fed selling bonds, which bids down bond prices.

18.5 Expansionary and Contractionary Monetary Policy

1. How will an expansionary monetary policy impact real GDP and the price level at less than full employment?
An expansionary monetary policy shifts aggregate demand to the right. Starting from less than full employment, the result will be an increase in the price level, an increase in real output and a decrease in unemployment, as the economy moves up along the short-run aggregate supply curve. This increased output would be sustainable if it did not exceed the natural level of real output.

2. How will an expansionary monetary policy impact real GDP and the price level at full employment?
An expansionary monetary policy shifts aggregate demand to the right. Starting from full employment, the result in the short run will be an increase in the price level, an increase in real output and a decrease in unemployment. However, because the increase in real output is not sustainable, the long run result will be real output returning to its natural level, but prices that have risen even more, where the new aggregate demand curve intersects the long-run aggregate supply curve.

3. How will a contractionary monetary policy beyond full employment impact real GDP and the price level?
A contractionary monetary policy beyond full employment would reduce aggregate demand and would move the economy from the short-run equilibrium position beyond full employment toward the new long-run equilibrium position at full employment, preventing an inflationary boom. There is then a reduction in real GDP and the price level.

4. How will a contractionary monetary policy at full employment impact real GDP and the price level?
A contractionary monetary policy at full employment can lead to a recession in the short run. The contractionary monetary policy will shift aggregate demand to the left, leading to a reduction in real GDP and the price level.

18.6 Problems in Implementing Monetary Policy

1. Why is the lag time for adopting policy changes shorter for monetary policy than for fiscal policy?
The lag time for adopting monetary policy changes is shorter than for fiscal policy because those decisions are not slowed by the budgetary process that fiscal tax and expenditure policy changes must go through.

2. Why would a banking system that wanted to keep some excess reserves rather than lending them all out hinder the Fed's ability to increase the money stock?
A desire by the banking system to keep some excess reserves would reduce the money stock other things being equal. Therefore, such a change would at least partly offset the effects of the Fed's expansionary policy changes, which would hinder the Fed's ability to successfully use expansionary monetary policy to increase the money stock.

3. How can the activities of global and nonbank institutions weaken the Fed's influence on the money market?
The Fed has no control over global and nonbank institutions that issue credit (loan money) but are not subject to reserve requirement limitations. The Fed cannot control their behavior, and the resulting effects on economic activity, through its policy variables, like it can with U.S. commercial banks.

4. If fiscal policy was expansionary, but the Fed wanted to counteract the fiscal policy effect on aggregate demand, what could it do?
Expansionary fiscal policy would increase aggregate demand. To counteract that fiscal policy effect on aggregate demand, the Fed would want to adopt contractionary monetary policy (through an open market sale of government securities, an increase in reserve requirements, and/or an increase in the discount rate), which would tend to reduce aggregate demand, other things being equal.

5. What are the arguments for and against having monetary policy more directly controlled by the political process?
The argument for having monetary policy more directly controlled by the political process is basically that because fiscal policy is already determined by the political process, and monetary policy (which is not determined by the same political process) can offset or even neutralize the macroeconomic effects of fiscal policy, it would be better for all macroeconomic policy to be directly controlled by the political process. The argument against having monetary policy be more directly controlled by the political process is that it would be dangerous to turn over control of the nation's money stock to politicians, rather than allowing monetary policy decisions made by technically competent administrators who are focused more on price stability and are more insulated from political pressures from the public and special interest groups.

6. How is fine-tuning the economy like driving a car with an unpredictable steering lag on a winding road?
Fine-tuning the economy is like driving a car with an unpredictable steering lag on a winding road because to steer the economy successfully requires that policy makers have an accurate map of which way the economy is headed and how rapidly it is headed that way; that they know exactly how much each possible policy would affect the economy, so that they "turn the policy wheels" just the right amount; and they need to know how long it will take each possible policy before it actually "turns" the economy.

18.7 Rational Expectations

1. What is the rational expectations theory?
The rational expectations theory incorporates expectations as a central factor in the analysis of the entire economy. It is essentially the idea that people will rationally anticipate the predictable future consequences of present decisions, and change their behavior today to reflect those future consequences. For example, this would mean that people can anticipate the inflationary long-run consequences of macroeconomic policies adopted today, and that anticipation leads them to change their current behavior in a way that can quickly neutralize the intended impact of a government action.

2. Why could an unexpected change in inflation change real wages and unemployment, while an expected change in inflation could not?
An unexpected change in inflation could change real wages and unemployment precisely because it was unexpected, and people were "fooled" into changing their behavior (in the short run). An expected change in inflation would not change real wages and unemployment because no one is fooled, so no one changes their real behavior as a result.

3. Why can the results of rational expectations be described as generating the long-run results of a policy change in the short run?
The long run refers to the situation once people have had time to completely adjust their behavior to current circumstances. But under rational expectations, the long-run consequences will be anticipated and responded to today, so that people have completely adjusted their behavior to new policies in the short run. Therefore, the results of rational expectations can be described as generating the long-run results of a policy change in the short run.

4. In a world of rational expectations, why is it harder to reduce unemployment below its natural rate but potentially easier to reduce inflation rates?
Reducing unemployment below its natural rate requires that inflation is greater than expected. But under rational expectations, people are not fooled by inflationary policies (unless they are surprises), so this is hard to do. It is potentially easier to reduce inflation rates under rational expectations, though, because people will be more quickly convinced that inflation will fall when credible government policies are put in place, and it will not take an extended period of high unemployment before they adapt to the lower inflation rate that results.

5. Even if individuals could quickly anticipate the consequences of government policy changes, how could long-term contracts (e.g., 3-year labor agreements and 30-year fixed rate mortgages) and the costs of changing price lists and catalogs result in unemployment still being affected by those policy changes?
Even if individuals could quickly anticipate the consequences of government policy changes, long-term contracts can't be instantly adjusted, so the real prices and wages subject to such contracts will be at least temporarily changed by inflation "surprises," at least until such contracts can be rewritten. Similarly, price lists and catalogs will not be changed instantly when new policies are adopted, because of the cost of doing so, and those prices will not instantly adapt to new inflationary expectations. Because these prices will be "wrong" for a period after new policies are adopted, real wages and prices, and therefore unemployment, can still be affected for a period of time by policy changes.

6. Why do expected rainstorms have different effects on people than unexpected rainstorms?
Expected rainstorms don't catch you by surprise, so you prepare for them in a way that minimizes their effects (umbrellas, jackets, and so on). Unexpected rainstorms catch you by surprise, and have much greater effects, because they haven't been prepared for.

CHAPTER 19: INTERNATIONAL TRADE

19.1 The Growth in World Trade

1. Why is it important to understand the effects of international trade?
All countries are importantly affected by international trade, although the magnitude of the international trade sector varies substantially by country. Interna-

tional connections mean that any of a large number of disturbances that originate elsewhere will have important consequences for the domestic economy.

2. Why would U.S. producers and consumers be more concerned about Canadian trade restrictions than Swedish trade restrictions?

The United States and Canada are the two largest trading partners in the world. That means the effects of trade restrictions into Canada would have a far larger magnitude effect on the United States than similar restrictions imposed by Sweden (although for certain items, we have a larger magnitude trade with Sweden than with Canada, so Swedish restrictions would then be of more concern for such items).

19.2 Comparative Advantage and Gains from Trade

1. Why do people voluntarily choose to specialize and trade?

Voluntary specialization and trade among self-interested parties only takes place because all the parties involved expect that their benefits from that specialization (according to comparative advantage) and exchange will exceed their costs.

2. How could a country have an absolute advantage in producing one good or service without also having a comparative advantage in its production?

If one country was absolutely more productive at everything than another country, but it wasn't equally more productive at everything, there would still be some things it had a comparative disadvantage in. For instance, if country A was three times as productive in making X and two times as productive in making Y as country B, it would have a comparative advantage in making X (it gives up less Y for each X produced) and a comparative disadvantage in making Y (it gives up more X for each Y produced), relative to country B.

3. Why do you think the introduction of the railroad reduced self-sufficiency in the United States?

Prior to the introduction of the railroad, the high cost of transportation overwhelmed the gains from specializing according to comparative advantage in much of the United States (production cost differences were smaller than the costs of transportation). The railroads reduced transportation costs enough that specialization and exchange became beneficial for more goods and services, and self-sufficiency caused by high transportation costs declined.

4. If you can do the dishes in two-thirds the time it takes your younger sister, do you have a comparative advantage in doing the dishes compared to her?

We can't know the answer to this question without more information. It is not the time taken to do the dishes that matters in determining comparative advantage, but the opportunity cost of the time in terms of foregone value elsewhere. If your younger sister is less than two-thirds as good at other chores than you, she is relatively better at doing the dishes, and so would have a comparative advantage in doing the dishes. If she is more than two-thirds as good at other chores, she is relatively better at those chores, and so would have a comparative disadvantage in doing the dishes.

19.3 Supply and Demand in International Trade

1. How does voluntary trade generate both producer and consumer surplus?

Voluntary trade generates consumer surplus because a rational consumer will not purchase if he did not value the benefits of purchase at greater than its cost, and consumer surplus is the difference between that value and the cost they are forced to pay. Voluntary trade generates producer surplus because a rational producer will not sell additional units unless the price he received was greater than his marginal cost, and producer surplus is the difference between the revenues received and the costs producers must bear to produce the goods that generate those revenues.

2. If the world price of a good is greater than the domestic price before trade, why does that imply that the domestic economy has a comparative advantage in producing that good?

If the world price of a good is greater than the domestic price prior to trade, that implies that the domestic marginal opportunity cost of production is less than the world marginal opportunity cost of production. But this means the domestic economy has a comparative advantage in that good.

3. If the world price of a good is less than the domestic price before trade, why does that imply that the domestic economy has a comparative disadvantage in producing that good?

If the world price of a good is less than the domestic price prior to trade, that implies that the domestic marginal opportunity cost of production is greater than the world marginal opportunity cost of production. But this means the domestic economy has a comparative disadvantage in that good.

4. When a country has a comparative advantage in the production of a good, why do domestic producers gain more than domestic consumers lose from free international trade?

When a country has a comparative advantage in producing a good, the marginal benefit from exporting is the world price, which is greater than the foregone value domestically (along the domestic demand curve) for those units of domestic consumption "crowded out," and greater than the marginal cost of the expanded output. Therefore, there are net domestic gains to international trade (the gains to domestic producers exceeds the losses to domestic consumers).

5. When a country has a comparative disadvantage in a good, why do domestic consumers gain more than domestic producers lose from free international trade?

When a country has a comparative disadvantage in producing a good, the marginal cost of importing is the world price, which is less than the additional value (along the domestic demand curve) for those units of expanded domestic consumption, and less than the marginal cost of the domestic production "crowded out." Therefore, there are net domestic gains to international trade (the gains to domestic consumers exceeds the losses to domestic producers).

6. Why do U.S. exporters, such as farmers, favor free trade more than U.S. producers of domestic products who face competition from foreign imports, such as the automobile industry?

Exporters favor free trade over restrictions on what they sell in other countries because that increases the demand and therefore prices for their products, which raises their profits. Those who must compete with importers want those imports restricted rather than freely traded because that increases the demand, and therefore the prices, for their domestically produced products.

19.4 Tariffs, Import Quotas, and Subsidies

1. Why do tariffs increase domestic producer surplus, but decrease domestic consumer surplus?

Tariffs raise the price of imported goods to domestic consumers, which also results in higher prices received by domestic producers. The higher price reduces domestic consumer surplus but increases domestic producer surplus.

2. How do import tariffs increase employment in "protected" industries, but at the likely expense of a likely decrease in employment overall?

Import tariffs increase employment in "protected" industries because the barriers to lower price imports increase the demand faced by domestic producers, increasing their demand for workers. However, imports are the means by which foreigners get the dollars to buy our exports, so restricted imports will mean restricted exports (even more so if other countries retaliate with import restrictions of their own). In addition, by raising the prices domestic consumers pay for the protected products (remember that domestic consumers lose more than domestic producers gain from protectionism), consumers are made poorer in real terms, which will reduce demand for goods, and therefore the labor to make them, throughout the economy.

3. Why is the national security argument for tariffs questionable?

The national security argument for tariffs is questionable because tariffs increase current reliance on domestic supplies, which depletes the future stockpile of available reserves. With fewer domestic reserves, the country will be even more dependent on foreign supplies in the future. Buying foreign supplies and stockpiling them makes more sense as a way of reducing reliance on foreign supplies in wartime.

4. Why is the domestic argument for import quotas weaker than the case for tariffs?

Tariffs at least use the price system as the basis of trade. Tariff revenues end up in a country's treasury, where they can be used to produce benefits for country's citizens or to reduce the domestic tax burden. Import quotas, however, transfer most of those benefits to foreign producers as higher prices they receive.

5. Why would foreign producers prefer import quotas to tariffs, even if they resulted in the same reduced level of imports?

Restricting imports reduces supply, which increases the price foreign producers receive on the units they sell, benefiting them. Tariffs, on the other hand reduce the after-tariff price foreign producers receive. If both reduce foreign sales the same amount, foreign producers would clearly prefer import restrictions to tariffs.

6. Why does subsidizing exports by industries without a comparative advantage tend to harm the domestic economy, on net?

Subsidizing industries where a country has a comparative disadvantage (higher costs) must, by definition, require shifting resources from where it has a comparative advantage (lower costs) to where it has a comparative disadvantage. The value of the output produced from those resources (indirectly in the case of specialization and exchange) is lower as a result.

19.5 The Balance of Payments

1. What is the balance of payments?

The balance of payments is the record of all the international financial transactions of a nation—both those involving inflows of funds and those involving outflows of funds—over a year.

2. Why would an English purchaser of U.S. goods or services have to first exchange pounds for dollars?

Because U.S. goods and services are priced in dollars, an English consumer who wanted to buy U.S. goods would have to first buy dollars in exchange for English pounds before he could buy the U.S. goods and services with dollars.

3. How is it that our imports provide foreigners the means to buy U.S. exports?
The domestic currency Americans supply in exchange for the foreign currencies to buy imports also supplies the dollars with which foreigners can buy American exports.
4. What would have to be true in order for the United States to have a balance of trade deficit and a balance of payments surplus?
A balance of trade deficit means we imported more merchandise (goods) than we exported. A balance of payments surplus means that the sum of our goods and services exports exceeded the sum of our goods and services imports, plus funds transfers from the United States. For both to be true would require a larger surplus of services (including net investment income) and/or net fund transfer inflows than our trade deficit in merchandise (goods).
5. What would have to be true in order for the United States to have a balance of trade surplus and a current account deficit?
A balance of trade surplus means we exported more merchandise (goods) than we imported. A current account deficit means our exports of goods and services (including net investment income) were less that the sum of our imports of goods and services, plus net fund transfers. For both to happen would require that the sum of our deficit in services plus net transfers must be greater than our surplus in merchandise (goods) trading.
6. If there were no errors or omissions in the recorded balance of payments accounts, what should the statistical discrepancy equal?
If there were no errors or omissions in the recorded balance of payments accounts, the statistical discrepancy should equal zero, because properly recorded, credits and debits must be equal, because every credit creates a debit of equal value.
7. A Nigerian family visiting Chicago enjoys a Chicago Cubs baseball game at Wrigley field. How would that expense be recorded in the balance of payments accounts? Why?
This would be counted as an export of services, because it would provide Americans with foreign currency (a claim against Nigeria) in exchange for those services.

19.6 Exchange Rates

1. What is an exchange rate?
An exchange rate is the price in one country's currency of one unit of another country's currency.
2. When a U.S. dollar buys relatively more French francs, why does the cost of imports from France fall in the United States?
When a U.S. dollar buys relatively more French francs, the cost of imports from France falls in the United States because it takes fewer U.S. dollars to buy a given number of French francs in order to pay French producers. In other words, the price in U.S. dollars of French goods and services has fallen.
3. When a U.S. dollar buys relatively fewer Austrian shillings, why does the cost of U.S. exports fall in Austria?
When a U.S. dollar buys relatively fewer Austrian shillings, the cost of U.S. exports falls in Austria because it takes fewer Austrian shillings to buy a given number of U.S. dollars in order to pay American producers. In other words, the price in Austrian shillings of U.S. goods and services has fallen.
4. How does an increase in domestic demand for foreign goods and services increase the demand for those foreign currencies?
An increase in domestic demand for foreign goods and services increases the demand for those foreign currencies because the demand for foreign currencies is derived from the demand for foreign goods and services and foreign capital. The more foreign goods and services are demanded, the more of that foreign currency will be needed to pay for those goods and services.
5. As euros get cheaper relative to U.S. dollars, why does the quantity of euros demanded by Americans increase? Why doesn't the demand for euros increase as a result?
As euros get cheaper relative to U.S. dollars, European products become relatively more inexpensive to Americans, who therefore buy more European goods and services. To do so, the quantity of euros demanded by U.S. consumers will rise to buy them, as the price (exchange rate) for euros falls. The demand (as opposed to quantity demanded) of euros doesn't increase, because this represents a movement along the demand for euros caused by a change in exchange rates, rather than a change in demand for euros caused by some other factor.
6. Who competes exchange rates down when they are above their equilibrium value? Who competes exchange rates up when they are below their equilibrium value?
When exchange rates are greater than their equilibrium value, there will be a surplus of the currency and frustrated sellers of that currency will bid its price (exchange rate) down. When exchange rates are less than their equilibrium value, there will be a shortage of the currency and frustrated buyers of that currency will bid its price (exchange rate) up.

19.7 Equilibrium Changes and the Foreign Exchange Market

1. Why will the exchange value of a foreign currency relative to U.S. dollars decline when U.S. domestic tastes change, reducing the demand for foreign-produced goods?
When U.S. domestic tastes change, reducing the demand for foreign-produced goods, the reduced demand for foreign-produced goods will also reduce the demand for the foreign currencies to buy them. This reduced demand for those foreign currencies will reduce their exchange rates, relative to U.S. dollars.
2. Why does the demand for foreign currencies shift in the same direction as domestic income? What happens to the exchange value of those foreign currencies, in terms of U.S. dollars?
An increase in domestic income increases the demand for goods and services, including imported goods and services. This increases the demand for those foreign currencies to buy those additional imports, which increases their exchange rates (the exchange value of those currencies), relative to U.S. dollars.
3. How would increased U.S. tariffs on imported European goods affect the exchange value of euros in terms of dollars?
Increased U.S. tariffs on imported European goods would make them less affordable in the United States. This would lead to a reduced demand for European goods in the United States, and therefore a reduced demand for euros. This would reduce the exchange value of euros in terms of dollars.
4. Why do changes in U.S. tastes, incomes or tariffs change the demand for euros, while similar changes in Europe change the supply of euros?
Changes in U.S. tastes, incomes, or tariffs change the demand for euros because they change the American demand for European goods and services, which changes the demand for euros to buy them. Similar changes in Europe change the supply of euros because they change the European demand for U.S. goods and services, thus changing their demand for dollars with which to buy those goods and services. This requires them to exchange their supply of euros, in order to get those dollars.
5. What would happen to the exchange value of euros in terms of U.S. dollars if incomes rose in both Europe and the United States?
These changes would increase both the demand (higher incomes in the United States) and supply (higher income in Europe) of euros. The effect on the exchange value of euros would be determined by whether the supply or demand for euros shifted more (rising if demand shifted relatively more and falling if supply shifted relatively more).
6. Why does an increase in interest rates in Germany relative to U.S. interest rates increase the demand for euros, but decrease their supply?
An increase in interest rates in Germany relative to U.S. interest rates increases the rates of return on German investments relative to U.S. investments. U.S. investors therefore increase their demand for German investments, increasing the demand for euros to make those investments. This would also reduce the demand by German investors for U.S. investments, decreasing the supply of euros with which to buy the dollars to make the investments.
7. What would an increase in U.S. inflation relative to Europe do to the supply and demand for euros, and to the equilibrium exchange value (price) of euros in terms of U.S. dollars?
An increase in U.S. inflation relative to Europe would make U.S. products relatively more expensive to European customers, decreasing the U.S. goods and services demanded by European customers, and therefore the decrease the supply of euros to buy the dollars necessary for those purchases. It would also make European products relatively cheaper to American customers, increasing the European goods and services demanded by Americans, and therefore increase the demand for euros necessary for those purchases. The decreased supply and increased demand for euros results in an increasing exchange value of euros in terms of U.S. dollars.

Glossary

accounting profits total revenues minus total explicit costs
aggregate the total amount—such as the aggregate level of output
aggregate demand (*AD*) the total demand for all the final goods and services in the economy
aggregate demand curve graph that shows the inverse relationship between the price level and RGDP demanded
aggregate supply curve (*AS*) the total quantity of final goods and services suppliers are willing and able to supply at a given price level
allocative efficiency production where the price of a good equals marginal cost
automatic stabilizers changes in government transfer payments or tax collections that automatically help counter business cycle fluctuations
average cost pricing to set the price equal to average total cost
average fixed cost (*AFC*) a per-unit measure of fixed costs; fixed costs divided by output
average propensity to consume (*APC*) the fraction of total disposable income that households spend on consumption
average revenue (*AR*) total revenue divided by the number of units sold
average total cost (*ATC*) a per-unit cost of operation; total cost divided by output
average variable cost (*AVC*) a per-unit measure of variable costs; variable costs divided by output
balance of payments the record of international transactions in which a nation has engaged over a year
balance of trade the net surplus or deficit resulting from the level of exportation and importation of merchandise
balance sheet a financial record that indicates the balance between a bank's assets and its liabilities plus capital
bar graph represents data using vertical bars rising from the horizontal axis
barter direct exchange of goods and services without the use of money
boom periods of prolonged economic expansion
budget deficit government spending exceeds tax revenues for a given fiscal year
budget surplus tax revenues are greater than government expenditures for a given fiscal year
business cycles short-term fluctuations in the economy relative to the long-term trend in output
capital the equipment and structures used to produce goods and services
capital intensive production that uses a large amount of capital
causation when one event brings on another event
ceteris paribus holding all other things constant
change in demand the prices of related goods, income, number of buyers, tastes, and expectations can change the demand for a good. That is, a change in one of these factors shifts the entire demand curve
change in quantity demanded a change in a good's price leads to a change in quantity demanded, a move along a given demand curve
circular flow model of income and output an illustration of the continuous flow of goods, services, inputs and payments between firms and households
collective bargaining negotiations between representatives of employers and unions
command economies economies where the government uses central planning to coordinate most economic activities
commercial banks financial institutions organized to handle everyday financial transactions of business and household through demand deposit accounts and savings accounts, and by making short-term commercial and consumer loans
comparative advantage occurs when a person or a country can produce a good or service at a lower opportunity cost than others
competitive market A market where the many buyers and sellers have very little market power—each buyer's and seller's effect on market price is negligible
complement an increase (a decrease) in the price of one good shifts the demand curve for another good to the left (right)
constant-cost industry an industry where input prices (and cost curves) do not change as industry output changes
constant returns to scale occur in an output range where LRATC does not change as output varies
consumer price index (CPI) a measure of the trend in prices of a basket of consumable goods and services that serves to gauge inflation
consumer sovereignty consumers vote with their dollars in a market economy; this explains what is produced
consumer surplus the difference between the price a consumer is willing and able to pay for an additional unit of a good and the price the consumer actually pays; for the whole market it is the sum of all the individual consumer surpluses
consumption purchases of final goods and services
contraction when the economy is slowing down—measured from the peak to the trough
contractionary fiscal policy use of fiscal policy tools to reduce output by decreasing government purchases, increasing taxes, and/or reducing transfer payments
contractionary gap the output gap that occurs when the actual output is less than the potential output
correlation two events that usually occur together
cost-push inflation a price level increase due to a negative supply shock or increases in input prices
credit unions financial institution cooperatives made up of depositors with a common affiliation
crowding-out effect theory that government borrowing drives up the interest rate, lowering consumption by households and investment spending by firms
currency coins and/or paper created to be used to facilitate the trade of goods and services and the payment of debts
current account a record of a country's imports and exports of goods and services, net investment income, and net transfers
cyclical unemployment unemployment due to short-term cyclical fluctuations in the economy
deadweight loss the elimination of a benefit to society (consumers and producer) because of a government initiative such as a tax
deflation a decrease in the overall price level, resulting in an increase of the purchasing power of money
demand deposits balances in bank accounts that depositors can access on demand
demand-pull inflation a price level increase due to an increase in aggregate demand
depreciation annual allowances set aside to replace worn-out capital
depressions severe recessions, or contraction in output
derived demand the demand for an input derived from consumers' demand for the good or service produced with that input
diminishing marginal product as a variable input increases, with other inputs fixed, a point will be reached where the additions to output will eventually decline
discount rate interest rate that the Fed charges commercial banks for the loans it extends to them
discouraged worker an individual who has left the labor force because he/she could not find a job
diseconomies of scale occur in an output range where LRATC rises as output expands
disposable personal income the personal income available after personal taxes
double counting adding the value of a good or service twice by mistakenly counting intermediate goods and services in GDP
durable goods longer-lived consumer goods, such as automobiles
economic good a scarce good—a good that is desirable but limited
economic growth an upward trend in the real per capita output of goods and services
the economic problem scarcity forces us to choose, and choices are costly because we must give up other opportunities that we value
economic profits total revenue minus explicit and implicit costs
economic rent the payment for the use of any resource above its opportunity cost
economics the study of the allocation of our limited resources to satisfy our unlimited wants
economies of scale occur in an output range where LRATC falls as output increases
efficiency getting the most from society's scarce resources
elastic demand segment a portion of the demand curve where the percentage change of quantity demanded is greater than the percentage change in price ($E_D > 1$)
empirical analysis the use of data to test a hypothesis
Employment Act of 1946 a commitment by the federal government to hold itself accountable for short-run economic fluctuations

entrepreneurship the process of combining labor, land, and capital together to produce goods and services

equation of exchange the money supply (M) times velocity (V) of circulation equals the price level (P) times quantity of goods and services produced in a given period (Q)

equilibrium price the price at the intersection of the market supply and demand curves; at this price the quantity demanded equals the quantity supplied

equilibrium quantity the quantity at the intersection of the market supply and demand curves; at the equilibrium quantity, the quantity demanded equals the quantity supplied

excess reserves reserve levels held above that required by the Fed

exchange rate the price of one unit of a country's currency in terms of another country's currency

excise tax a sales tax on individual products such as alcohol, tobacco, and gasoline

expansion when output (real GDP) is rising significantly—the period between the trough of a recession and the next peak

expansionary fiscal policy use of fiscal policy tools to foster increased output by increasing government purchases, lowering taxes, and/or increasing transfer payments

expansionary gap the output gap that occurs when the actual output is greater than the potential output

expenditure approach calculation of GDP by adding the expenditures of market participants on final goods and services over a given period

explicit costs the opportunity costs of production that require a monetary payment

externalities a benefit or cost from consumption or production that spills over onto those that are not consuming or producing the good

factor (or input) markets the market where households sell the use of their inputs (capital, land, labor, and entrepreneurship) to firms

factor payments wages (salaries), rent, interest payments, and profits paid to the owners of productive resources

fallacy of composition the incorrect view that what is true for the individual is always true for the group

federal funds market market in which banks provide short-term loans to other banks that need cash to meet reserve requirements

fiat money a means of exchange established by government declaration

fiscal policy use of government purchases, taxes, and transfer payments to alter equilibrium output and prices

fixed costs costs that do not vary with the level of output

fixed investments all new spending on capital goods by producers

fractional reserve system a system that requires banks to hold reserves equal to some fraction of their checkable deposits

free rider deriving benefits from something not paid for

frictional unemployment unemployment from normal turnovers in the economy, such as when individuals change from one job to another

GDP deflator a price index that helps to measure the average price level of all final consumer goods and services produced

gold standard defining the dollar as equivalent to a set value of a quantity of gold, allowing direct convertibility from currency to gold

goods items we value or desire

Gresham's Law the idea that "cheap money drives out dear money"; given an alternative, people prefer to spend less valuable money

gross domestic product (GDP) the measure of economic performance based on the value of all final goods and services produced in a given period

gross national product (GNP) the difference between net income of foreigners and GDP

human capital the productive knowledge and skill people receive from education and on-the-job training

hypothesis a testable proposition

implicit costs the opportunity costs of production that do not require a monetary payment

import quota a legal limit on the imported quantity of a good that is produced abroad and can be sold in domestic markets

income approach calculation of GDP based on the summation of incomes received by the owners of resources used in the production of goods and services.

increasing-cost industry an industry where input prices rise (and cost curves rise) as industry output rises

increasing opportunity cost the opportunity cost of producing additional units of a good rises as society produces more of that good

indirect business taxes taxes, such as sales tax, that are levied on goods and services sold

individual demand curve a graphical representation that shows the inverse relationship between price and quantity demanded

individual demand schedule a schedule that shows the relationship between price and quantity demanded

individual supply curve a graphical representation that shows the positive relationship between the price and the quantity supplied

inelastic demand segment a portion of the demand curve where the percentage change in quantity demand is less than the percentage change in price ($E_D < 1$)

inflation a rise in the overall price level, which decreases the purchasing power of money

inferior good if income increases, the demand for a good decreases; if income decreases, the demand for a good increases

in-kind transfers transfers given in goods and services rather than cash

innovation applications of new knowledge that create new products or improve existing products

intangible goods goods that we cannot reach out and touch, like friendship and knowledge

interest the cost of borrowed funds

intertemporal price discrimination groups of consumers are charged different prices in different time periods

inventory investment purchases that add to the stocks of goods kept by the firm to meet consumer demand

investment the creation of capital goods to augment future production

job-entry discrimination denial of employment based upon a non-economic factor, such as race, religion, sex, or ethnicity

job leaver a person that quits his or her job

job loser an individual who has been temporarily laid off or fired

labor the physical and human effort used in the production of goods and services

labor force the number of people aged 16 and over who are available for employment

labor force participation rate the percentage of the population in the labor force

labor intensive production that uses a large amount of labor

land the natural resources used in the production of goods and services

law of demand the quantity of a good or service demanded varies inversely (negatively) with its price, *ceteris paribus*

law of diminishing marginal utility the economic principle that states that consumers will experience less satisfaction for each additional unit of good consumed

law of supply the higher (lower) the price of the good, the greater (smaller) the quantity supplied

leading economic indicators factors that economists at the Commerce Department have found that typically change before changes in economic activity

legal tender coins and paper officially declared to be acceptable for the settlement of financial debts

liquidity the ease with which one asset can be converted into another asset or into goods and services

long run a period over which all production inputs are variable

long-run aggregate supply curve the graphical relationship between RGDP and the price level when output prices and input prices can fully adjust to economic changes

M1 the narrowest definition of money; includes currency, checkable deposits, and traveler's checks

M2 a broader definition of money that includes M1 plus savings deposits, time deposits, and money market mutual funds

macroeconomics the study of the whole economy including the topics of inflation, unemployment, and economic growth

marginal cost (*MC*) the change in total costs resulting from a one-unit change in output

marginal product (*MP*) the change in total output of a good that results from a unit change in input

marginal propensity to consume (*MPC*) the additional consumption resulting from an additional dollar of disposable income

marginal resource cost (*MRC*) the amount that an extra input adds to the firm's total costs

marginal revenue (*MR*) the increase in total revenue resulting from a one-unit increase in sales

marginal revenue product (*MRP*) marginal product times the price of the product

marginal thinking focusing on the additional, or marginal, choices; marginal choices involve the effects of adding or subtracting from the current situation, the small (or large) incremental changes to a plan of action

marginal utility the amount of satisfaction that results from the consumption of the last unit of good or service

market the process of buyers and sellers exchanging goods and services

market demand curve the horizontal summation of individual demand curves

market economy an economy that allocates goods and services through the private decisions of consumers, input suppliers, and firms

market failure when the economy fails to allocate resources efficiently on its own

market supply curve a graphical representation of the amount of goods and services that suppliers are willing and able to supply at various prices

means of deferred payment the attribute of money that makes it easier to borrow and to repay loans

medium of exchange the primary function of money, which is to facilitate transactions and lower transactions costs

menu costs the cost imposed on a firm from changing listed prices

microeconomics the study of household and firm behavior and how they interact in the marketplace

minimum efficient scale the output level where economies of scale are exhausted and constant returns to scale begin

mixed economy an economy where government and the private sector determine the allocation of resources

money anything generally accepted in exchange for goods or services

money market market in which money demand and money supply determine the equilibrium interest rate

money market mutual funds interest-earning accounts provided by brokers that pool funds into investments like Treasury bills

money multiplier measures the potential amount of money that the banking system generates with each dollar of reserves

money price the price that one pays in dollars and cents, sometimes called an absolute or nominal price

monopolistic competition a market structure with many firms selling differentiated products

monopoly the single supplier of a product that has no close substitute

moral suasion the Fed uses its influence to persuade banks to follow a particular course of action

multiplier effect a chain reaction of additional income and purchases that results in total purchases that are greater than the initial increase in purchases

national income (NI) a measure of income earned by owners of the factors of production

national income accounting a uniform means of measuring economic performance

natural monopoly a firm that can produce at a lower cost than a number of smaller firms could

natural rate of unemployment the median or "typical" unemployment rate, equal to the sum of frictional and structural unemployment when they are at a maximum

near money nontransaction deposits that are not money, but can be quickly converted into money

negative externality occurs when costs spill over to an outside party that is not involved in producing or consuming the good

negative incentives incentives that either increase costs or reduce benefits resulting in a decrease in the activity or behavior

negative relationship when two variables change in opposite directions

net exports the difference between the value of exports and the value of imports

net national product (NNP) GNP minus depreciation

new entrant an individual who has not held a job before but is now seeking employment

nominal interest rate the reported interest rate that is not adjusted for inflation

nondurable goods tangible items that are consumed in a short period of time, such as food

nonexcludable once the good is produced it is prohibitively costly to exclude anyone from consuming the good

nonrivalrous occurs when everyone can consume the good simultaneously; one person's usage of it does not diminish another's ability to use it

nontransaction deposits funds that cannot be used for payment directly and must be converted into currency for general use

normal good if income increases, the demand for a good increases; if income decreases, the demand for a good decreases

normative analysis a subjective, non-testable statement—how the economy should be

oligopoly a market structure with only a few sellers offering similar or identical products

open economy a type of model that includes international trade effects

open market operations purchase and sale of government securities by the Federal Reserve System

opportunity cost the value of the best forgone alternative that was not chosen

peak is the point in time when the expansion comes to an end, when output is at the highest point in the cycle

perfect competition a market with many buyers and sellers, selling homogeneous goods, easy market entry and exit, and no firm can affect the market price

personal income (PI) the amount of income received by households before personal taxes

pie chart a circle subdivided into proportionate slices that represent various quantities that add up to 100 percent

positive analysis an objective testable statement —how the economy is

positive externality occurs when benefits spill over to an outside party that is not involved in producing or consuming the good

positive incentives incentives that either reduce costs or increase benefits resulting in an increase in the activity or behavior

positive relationship when two variables change in the same direction

potential output is the amount of real output the economy would produce if its labor and other resources were fully employed—that is, at the natural rate of unemployment

poverty line the income threshold at which an absolute level of poorness is established

poverty rate the percentage of population that falls below a determined income

present value a concept used to figure out how much future benefits are worth today

price ceiling a legally established maximum price

price controls government mandated minimum or maximum prices

price discrimination the practice of charging different consumers different prices for the same good or service

price elasticity of demand a measure of the responsiveness of quantity demanded to a change in price

price elasticity of supply the measure of the sensitivity of the quantity supplied to changes in price of a good

price floor a legally established minimum price

price index a measurement that attempts to provide a measure of the trend in prices paid for a certain bundle of goods and services over a given period

price level the average level of prices in the economy

price taker a perfectly competitive firm takes the price that it is given by the intersection of the market demand and market supply curve

private good a good with rivalrous consumption and excludability

producer goods capital goods that increase future production capabilities

producer surplus the difference between what a producer is paid for a good and the cost of producing that unit of the good; for the market, it is the sum of all the individual sellers' producer surpluses—the area above the market supply curve and below the market price

production possibilities curve the potential total output combinations of any two goods for an economy

productivity the amount of goods and services a worker can produce per hour

product markets the market where households are buyers and firms are sellers of goods and services

profit-maximizing output rule a firm should always produce at the output where $MR = MC$

profits the difference between total revenue and total cost

progressive tax the amount of an individual's tax rises as a proportion of income, as the person's income rises

public choice analysis the principles of economics applied to the political process

public good a good that has two properties: nonrivalrous in consumption and nonexcludability

real gross domestic product (RGDP) the total value of all final goods and services produced in a given time period such as a year or a quarter, adjusted for inflation

real gross domestic product per capita real output of goods and services per person

real interest rate the nominal interest rate minus the inflation rate; also called the inflation-adjusted interest rate

recession a period of significant decline in output and employment

reentrant an individual who worked before and is now reentering the labor force

regressive tax the amount of an individual's tax falls as a proportion of income, as the person's income rises

relative price the price of one good relative to other goods

rent seeking producer efforts to gain profits from government protections such as tariffs and import quotas

required reserve ratio the percentage of deposits that a bank must hold at the Federal Reserve Bank or in bank vaults

research and development (R&D) activities undertaken to create new product and processes that will lead to technological progress

reserve requirements holdings of assets at the bank or at the Federal Reserve Bank as mandated by the Fed

resources inputs used to produce goods and services

rule of rational choice individuals will pursue an activity if the expected marginal benefits are greater than the expected marginal costs

savings and loan associations financial institutions organized as cooperative associations that hold demand deposits and savings of members in the form of dividend-bearing shares and that make loans, especially home mortgage loans

scarcity exists when human wants (material and non-material) exceed available resources
secondary reserves highly liquid, interest-paying assets held by the bank
service an intangible act that people want, like treatment from a doctor or a dentist
services intangible items of value provided to consumers, such as education
shocks unexpected aggregate supply or aggregate demand changes
shoe-leather cost the cost incurred when individuals reduce their money holdings because of inflation
shortage a situation where quantity demanded exceeds quantity supplied
short run a period too brief for some production inputs to be varied
short-run aggregate supply curve the graphical relationship between RGDP and the price level when output prices can change but input prices are unable to adjust
short-run market supply curve the horizontal summation of the individal firms' supply curves in the market
short-run supply curve As a cost relation, this curve shows the marginal cost of producing any given output; as a supply curve, it shows the equilibrium output that the firm will supply at various prices in the short run
slope the ratio of rise (change in the *Y* variable) over the run (change in the *X* variable)
specializing concentrating in the production of one, or a few, goods
stagflation a situation in which lower growth and higher prices occur together
structural unemployment unemployment persisting due to lack of skills necessary for available jobs
substitute an increase (a decrease) in the price of one good causes the demand curve for another good to shift to the right (left)
substitution effect at higher prices, buyers increasingly substitute other goods for the good that now has a higher relative price
sunk costs costs that have been incurred and cannot be recovered
surplus a situation where quantity supplied exceeds quantity demanded
tariff a tax on imports
theory statements or propositions used to explain and predict behavior in the real world
theory of rational expectations belief that workers and consumers incorporate the likely consequences of government policy changes into their expectations by quickly adjusting wages and prices
time-series graph a type of line chart that plots data trends over time
total cost (*TC*) the sum of the firm's total fixed costs and total variable costs
total fixed costs (*TFC*) the sum of the firm's fixed costs
total product (*TP*) the total output of a good produced by the firm
total revenue (*TR*) the product price times the quantity sold
total utility the aggregate level of satisfaction that results from consumption of a given number of goods and services
total variable cost (*TVC*) the sum of the firm's variable costs
total welfare gains the sum of consumer and producer surplus
transaction deposits deposits that can be easily converted to currency or used to buy goods and services directly
traveler's checks transaction instruments easily convertible into currency
trough the trough is the point in time when output stops declining; it is the moment when business activity is at its lowest point in the cycle
underemployment a situation in which laborers have skills higher than necessary for a job
unemployment rate the percentage of the population aged 16 and older who are willing and able to work, but are unable to obtain a job
unintended consequences the secondary effects of an action that may occur after the initial effects
unit elastic demand demand with a price elasticity of 1; the percentage change in quantity demanded is equal to the percentage change in price
util a measure of utility equal to "one unit" of satisfaction
utility the relative measurement of satisfaction gleaned from the consumption of goods and services
variable something that is measured by a number, such as your height
variable costs costs that vary with the level of output
wage and price controls legislation used to combat inflation by limiting changes in wages and prices
wage and price inflexibility the tendency for prices and wages to only adjust slowly downward to changes in the economy
wage discrimination employment at wages lower than that of other workers based on an attribute other than productivity differences, such as race or sex
welfare effects the gains and losses associated with government intervention in markets
***X*-axis** the horizontal axis on a graph
***Y*-axis** the vertical axis on a graph

Index

Alfred Marshall (1842–1924)

Alfred Marshall was born outside of London in 1842. His father, a domineering man who was a cashier for the Bank of England, wanted nothing more than for Alfred to become a minister. But the young Marshall enjoyed math and chess, both of which were forbidden by his authoritarian father. When he was older, Marshall turned down a theological scholarship to Oxford to study at Cambridge, with the financial support of a wealthy uncle. Here he earned academic honors in mathematics. Upon graduating, Marshall set upon a period of self-discovery. He traveled to Germany to study metaphysics, later adopting the philosophy of agnosticism, and moved on to studying ethics. He found within himself a deep sorrow and disgust over the condition of society. He resolved to use his skills to lessen poverty and human suffering, and, in wanting to use his mathematics in this broader capacity, Marshall soon developed a fascination with economics.

Marshall became a fellow and lecturer in political economy at Cambridge. He had been teaching for nine years when, in 1877, he married a former student, Mary Paley. Because of the university's celibacy rules, Marshall had to give up his position at Cambridge. He moved on to teach at University College at Bristol and at Oxford. But in 1885, the rules were relaxed and Marshall returned to Cambridge as the Chair in Political Economy, a position that he held until 1908, when he resigned to devote more time to writing.

Before this point in time, economics was grouped with philosophy and the "moral sciences." Marshall fought all of his life for economics to be set apart as a field all its own. In 1903, Marshall finally succeeded in persuading Cambridge to establish a separate economics course, paving the way for the discipline as it exists today. As this event clearly demonstrates, Marshall exerted a great deal of influence on the development of economic thought in his time. Marshall popularized the heavy use of illustration, real-world examples, and current events in teaching, as well as the modern diagrammatic approach to economics. Relatively early in his career, it was being said that Marshall's former students occupied half of the economic chairs in the United Kingdom. His most famous student was John Maynard Keynes.

Marshall is most famous for refining the marginal approach. He was intrigued by the self-adjusting and self-correcting nature of economic markets, and he was also interested in time—how long did it take for markets to adjust? Marshall coined the analogy that compares the tools of supply and demand to the blades on a pair of scissors—that is, it is fruitless to talk about whether it was supply or demand that determined the market price; rather, one should consider both in unison. After all, the upper blade is not of more importance than the lower when using a pair of scissors to cut a piece of paper. Marshall was also responsible for refining some of the most important tools in economics—elasticity and consumer and producer surplus. Marshall's book *Principles of Economics* was published in 1890; immensely popular, the book went into eight editions. Much of the content in *Principles* is still at the core of microeconomics texts today.

John Maynard Keynes (1883–1946)

John Maynard Keynes was born in Cambridge, England, in 1883. Keynes' father was a political economist and logician, his mother a justice of the peace who eventually became the mayor of Cambridge.

Many would argue that Keynes was one of the most brilliant minds of the twentieth century. He was educated at Eton and Cambridge, where he studied mathematics and philosophy. Keynes had a brief, eight-week tutelage under Alfred Marshall, who tried to persuade Keynes to pursue economics. At the time Keynes wrote, "Marshall is continually pestering me to turn professional Economist . . . Do you think there is anything in it? I doubt it." Ironic, but, in fact, Keynes never did obtain a degree in economics. Upon leaving the university, Keynes began his career in the India Office of the British government. He soon became bored and, accepting a lectureship position offered by Marshall, returned to King's College, Cambridge, to teach economics, a post he held until his death in 1946.